HORSEWORDS

HORSEWORDS

The Equine Dictionary

Maria Belknap

Trafalgar Square Publishing
North Pomfret, Vermont

This second edition published in the United States of America in 2004 by
Trafalgar Square Publishing, North Pomfret, Vermont 05053

First edition published in the United States of America in 1997 by
Trafalgar Square Publishing, North Pomfret, Vermont 05053

Printed in Singapore

Design by Nancy Lawrence
Edited by Martin Diggle
Typeset by Textype, Cambridge
Colour separation by Tenon & Polert Colour Scanning Limited, Hong Kong

ISBN 1-57076-274-0

Dedication

'With all beings and all things
we shall be relatives.'

Sioux Indian precept

ACKNOWLEDGEMENTS

A book of this magnitude is born from the efforts of countless individuals from around the world, most of whom remain nameless though not forgotten. Those who left the most indelible mark on me and this work are noted below.

First and foremost, my thanks to Lee and Corry for realizing that real nurturing is about facilitating, sharing, and giving, rather than control.

Also, to Walter de la Brosse for getting me started.

To Kevin for cheering me along the homestretch.

And Caroline, for her generosity of spirit, for giving my voice an audience, and preparing the ground for my footprint.

A GUIDE TO THE USE OF THIS DICTIONARY

I The Entry Word

The words defined in this work are printed flush with the left column margin and are in bold type. They are listed in alphabetical order by letter rather than word. To facilitate word location, a guide word is located at the top of each page to indicate the first entry on that page.

II Variants

If a word has two or more accepted spellings, the most commonly used spelling is listed first, with others following in order of preferred use.

If a foreign word is pronounced the same as the entry, but spelled differently, the variant spelling is followed by a parenthetic reference to the country of origin:

> **draft** Also spelled draught (Brit); the act of pulling or drawing loads as by horses.

III Homographs

If a word has a single spelling, but two or more distinct origins or meanings, each variation is separately enumerated under the entry with the most common entry appearing first:

> **foal** (1) A young horse of either sex from the time of birth until weaning – approximately one year; from the Anglo-Saxon *foala*. (2) Also known as drop or drop a foal; said of a mare; to give birth to a foal. (3) The offspring of either a male or female parent, e.g. "He was the first foal of Doc Bar." (4) A mule (q.v.) less than two years of age.

IV Foreign Words

Foreign words assimilated into the universal equine language or which have fairly widespread usage are included in this work:

> **manège** (1) Also spelled maneige and incorrectly manege; any enclosed or open arena which is usually rectangular, but which may be square or circular, where horses are schooled or dressed (q.v.); originally of French derivation and meaning horsemanship.

V Special Entries

A. Abbreviations

Abbreviations, used in this dictionary (excluding acronyms) are in the section entitled Abbreviations Used in This Dictionary. Whenever a word used in a definition is defined elsewhere in the text, the abbreviation (q.v.) will follow the word:

> **Registered Shoeing Smith** Also known by the acronym RSS; one of three levels of training certification awarded to practicing farriers in

Britain; awarded by the Worshipful Company of Farriers (q.v.) on the basis of written, oral, and practical examinations; now known as Diploma of the Worshipful Company of Farriers (q.v.).

B. Acronyms

Common acronyms of words defined in this dictionary are listed as entries alphabetically by letter and cross-referenced to the defined entry:

> **ACHA** *see* AMERICAN CUTTING HORSE ASSOCIATION

VI Cross-references

Cross-references follow an entry and precede its definition:

> **bottle fed** Also known as hand fed; said of a foal or other young animal fed and raised by human hand when its mother is unable or is disinterested in doing so.

VII Etymologies

Any word of foreign origin or spelling is italicized when used to define an entry:

> **cabbage** Any of various cultivated varieties of the cruciferous plant, *Brassica oleracea*, especially one of the varieties with a short stem and leaves formed into a compact, edible head; in a wider sense includes such plants as cauliflower, Brussels sprouts, kale, etc.; suitable as horse feed.

Abbreviations Used in This Dictionary

AD	Anno Domini
Am	American
ant.	Antiquated
Aust	Australia
BC	Before Christ
Brit	Britain
Can	Canada
Colloq.	Colloquial
e.g.	*exampli gratia* (for example)
etc.	etcetera
Fr	France
Ger	Germany
i.e.	*id est* (that is)
kmph	kilometers per hour
mph	miles per hour
obs	obsolete
ppm	parts per million
q.v.	*quod vide* (which see, defined elsewhere in the text)
Scot	Scotland
sl	slang

A

AAAI *see* AMERICAN ALBINO ASSOCIATION, INC.

Aachen One of the world's chief show jumping (q.v.), eventing (q.v.), and dressage (q.v.) centers located in Germany; the home of Germany's International Horse Show held annually in July.

AAEP *see* AMERICAN ASSOCIATION OF EQUINE PRACTITIONERS

AAHC *see* AMERICAN ALBINO HORSE CLUB, INC.

AAOBPPH *see* AMERICAN ASSOCIATION OF OWNERS AND BREEDERS OF PERUVIAN PASO HORSES

abandoned meeting A racing term; a whole day's racing at a particular track which was not held because of adverse weather conditions or some other significant event; may occasionally be rescheduled for another date, although this is unusual.

abandoned race(s) A race, or races, cancelled after a meeting has begun (i.e. preceding races have taken place); normally a consequence of worsening weather or ground conditions rendering further racing unsafe.

abasia A trembling or quivering of the legs or an inability to walk due to a limitation or absence of muscular coordination.

Abats le Sultan An aggressive mounted game popular in Russia in which mounted participants, wearing feather-covered fencing masks and padded shirts, chase after their opponents and attempt to cut the feathers off their masks using swords or sharp daggers; the participant with the most feathers remaining on his mask at the end of the competition is considered the winner.

abaxial Situated out of, or directed away from, the axis.

Abayyan One of many pure-bred Arab (q.v.) strains.

Abbot Buggy A horse-drawn buggy designed by the Abbot-Downing Company of Concord, New Hampshire, USA, popular during the second half of the 19th century for both town and country use; hung on semi-elliptical side springs with a fairly short wheelbase; had pedal brakes and a half hood usually kept in a raised position.

abdomen Also known as belly or abdominal cavity; the hollow portion of the body between the chest and pelvis that contains most digestive, reproductive, and excretory organs, i.e., liver, kidney, and bladder.

abdominal Of or pertaining to the abdomen (q.v.).

abdominal cavity *see* ABDOMEN

abduction To draw away from the median plane of the body.

Aberdeen plait To braid (q.v.) the top portion of a draft horse's mane with colored yarn.

abort To expel the fetus or embryo from the uterus before it is viable.

abortifacient Any substance that causes abortion.

abortion *see* EQUINE ABORTION

abortion storm Simultaneous abortion in mares stabled or pastured together; may be triggered by viruses such as rhinopneumonitis (q.v.).

above the bit Also known as over the bit; said of a horse who evades correct bit contact and full control by carrying his head too high and bringing his nose significantly in front of the vertical; this posture is associated with a hollow back (q.v.) and generally impedes efficient locomotion.

abrasion A superficial wound (q.v.); any injury caused by scraping or rubbing away of the top hair layer and minimal loss of skin by friction; usually characterized by an oozing serum (q.v.), some slow ooze of blood, and a lack of damage to the subsurface.

abrupt transition A change from one gait (q.v.) to another, e.g., walk to trot, trot to canter, etc., or an alteration of the stride within a gait performed too suddenly; often caused by the rider who gives his aids too suddenly and/or without sufficient preparation.

abscess Also known as pus pocket; a collection of pusy matter in the tissue of a body organ or part, characterized by pain, heat, and swelling.

absence of the eye sockets A condition of the foal when born without orbits in the skull to accommodate the eyes; a true lethal (q.v.) condition.

absence of the turbinate bone *see* CLEFT PALATE

absolute dry matter The percentage of feed less the water content subtracted from 100 percent; used in feed analysis.

absolute ensurer *see* WHIP

absorbent Said of any substance such as surgical gauze, applied to a wound to staunch or arrest blood flow.

absorption Assimilation of fluid into the tissues.

Abu'urqub One of many pure-bred Arab (q.v.) strains.

acari *see* MITES

acariasis Infestation by mites (q.v.).

acarus A parasitic mite (q.v.) belonging to the family *Acarina*; includes mange mites, harvest mites, follicular mites, flour mites, etc.

accept the bit Said of a horse who holds the bit confidently in his mouth and responds to the contact and influence of the rider's hands on the reins without resistance or hesitation.

acceptance time The time by which a horse must be entered, registered, or nominated to participate in an event.

accessory carpal bone One of eight carpal bones comprising the knee; a disc-shaped bone located behind and to the outside of the other seven carpal bones and which forms a sharp ridge at the back of the knee.

Acchetta Pony A pony breed from Sardinia.

Accommodation A short-distance, horse-drawn, public-service stage coach first constructed in the United States about 1827; seated 12 inside with one additional seat outside adjacent to the driver; entered through side doors.

account Also known as account for or account for the fox; a hunting term; said of the hounds when they kill a fox.

account for *see* ACCOUNT

account for the fox *see* ACCOUNT

accouterments *see* ACCOUTREMENTS

accoutrements Also spelled accouterments; the tack including the saddle, bridle, and bit, worn by the horse.

accumulator bet SEE PARLAY BET

accumulator *see* PARLAY

ACE (1) *see* ACETYLPROMAZINE. (2) *see* ACEPROMAZINE

acephalia Also known as headlessness; a true lethal (q.v.) condition of the foal born without a head; the fetus is either aborted or born dead.

Acepromazine Also known by the acronym ACE; the trade name for acetylpromazine (q.v.), a commonly used tranquilizer for horses.

acetabulum Also known as hip joint; the cup-shaped depression in the pelvis created by the ilium and ischium bones which forms the pelvic component of the hip joint and receives the femur head.

acetylcholine A chemical found on the nerve endings that allows transmission of impulses from one nerve fiber to the next or to a muscle fiber.

acetylpromazine Also known by the acronym ACE; one of a group of antihistamines (q.v.), including chlorpromazine and promethazine, administered orally, intramuscularly, or intravenously, to tranquilize and sedate a horse; over-stimulation may result in the horse overcoming the calming effects of the drug; decreases blood pressure and may help to reduce the muscle spasm and pain associated with conditions such as azoturia (q.v.); intra-arterial injection results in convulsion and death.

acey ducey A racing term; a riding style in which the right stirrup leather is shorter than the left, or inside, leg which enables a jockey to maintain balance more easily on the turns; popularized by US Hall of Fame jockey Eddie Arcaro.

ACHA *see* AMERICAN CUTTING HORSE ASSOCIATION

Achean An ancient pony breed indigenous to Greece, now extinct.

Achilles tendon SEE HAMSTRING

acid A category of joint-lubricating substances including sodium hyaluronate or hyaluronate sodium; a component of normal synovial fluid that, when injected directly into an inflamed joint or into the bloodstream, improves the quality and production of synovial fluid in the horse's joints.

acid brand (1) Also known as acid mark; an identifying symbol, character, letter, or series of numbers, or any combination thereof, burned into the flesh of the horse using an acid such as hydrochloric acid (q.v.); difficult to distinguish from a hot brand (q.v.). (2) To apply a registration mark to the horse using acid.

acid detergent fiber The residue in plant material remaining after complete acid digestion of it.

acid mark *see* ACID BRAND

acidosis An abnormally high accumulation of acid in the blood and body tissues.

Acme Sporting Cart A light, Australian horse-drawn gig (q.v.) popular in the late 19th century, having a three-ring suspension system, fully upholstered driving seat, arm rests, and mud guards above both wheels.

acquired defect An imperfection, function, or condition of the horse resulting from disease or accident following birth.

acquired leukoderma The whitening of previously pigmented hair or skin due to skin trauma.

acquired marks Any permanent mark appearing on the coat or skin of the horse, e.g. saddle marks, bridle marks, collar marks, girth marks, and other harness marks, permanent bandage marks, firing and branding marks, surgical scars, and tattoo marks in which the pigment of the hair or skin is altered; may be used for identification purposes.

acridine dyes A group of coloring agents including acriflavine, aminocrine, and proflavine having microbe-inhibiting properties; used in wound powders, solutions, or emulsions for skin and wound disinfection.

across the board A racing term; to place equal bets to win, place and show, on one horse.

ACTH *see* ADRENOCORTICOTROPIC HORMONE

actin The structural protein of the muscles; important for muscle contraction and relaxation.

acting hand *see* ACTIVE HAND NO. 1

Acting Master A hunting term; one appointed temporarily to organize a hunt for one or more days, pending the appointment of a permanent Master.

actinobacillus equuli A species of bacteria responsible for foal abortion (q.v.) or death shortly after birth.

action (1) The manner and degree of movement of the horse's feet and legs. (2) A racing term; wagering activity on a horse, e.g. "The horse took a lot of action."

active hand (1) Also known as acting hand; the rider's hand on the side to which the horse is turned when neck reining (q.v.). (2) To move the hands or fingers to work the reins and activate the bit; the opposite of a quiet hand (q.v.).

active immunization An acquired immunity due to the presence of antibodies formed in response to an antigen (q.v.).

active member Said of an individual whose membership dues with an organization are paid for the current calendar year.

activity A dressage term; the energy, vigor, and liveliness as of the hind legs.

acupressure To control pain, illness, and/or injury through pressure applied to trigger points along body meridians (q.v.).

acupuncture Also known as traditional acupuncture; Chinese medicine practiced for more than 3,500 years; based on the Chinese medicine of Chi – the flow of energy comprising positive (Yang) and negative (Yin) components that travel on meridians (q.v.) throughout the body; imbalances or blockages along these meridians cause stiffness, pain, swelling, and/or sickness; to re-establish harmony between the Yin and Yang (electrical fields), acupuncture points (q.v.) are stimulated by insertion and twirling of one or more fine needles (traditional), electrical current (electro-acupuncture [q.v.]), laser beam (laserpuncture [q.v.]), burning herb moxa (moxibustion [q.v.]), the injection of fluids such as water, oil, and vitamin-B solution (aquapuncture [q.v.]), injection of air (pnemo-puncture [q.v.]), gold implants, blood-letting (hemo-acupuncture) and metal staples; used to control pain, treat internal malfunctions, anesthetize, and reduce stress.

acupuncture points Small areas, 1 inch (2.5 cm) in diameter located in the skin that have increased electrical conductivity; most are motor points located near the spots where the nerves enter the muscles, while the others are situated, for the most part, on other neurological pathways; lie along 12 meridians, paired in 2 groups of 6 (there are also 2 unpaired meridians and a band of independent trigger points not connected to any particular channel); external points are linked by the meridians to limbs, joints, sense organs, superficial tissues, and to the internal visceral organs.

acute Having a short and relatively severe course.

acute arthritis Severe, rapidly developing inflammation of a joint; may eventually dissipate or develop into chronic arthritis (q.v.).

acute laminitis A clinical type of laminitis (q.v.); inflammation of the laminae (q.v.) having a rapid onset and a brief duration; characterized by the horse's marked resistance to exercise and reluctance to stand; may result in founder (q.v.) or lead to chronic laminitis (q.v.) if left untreated.

acute mastitis Rapid onset of inflammation of the mammary gland due to bacteria-related infection; occurs occasionally in lactating mares brought on by the presence of streptococci or staphylococci organisms; symptoms may include painful swelling of the affected gland and adjacent tissue, fever, depression, stiffness at the walk, or standing with the hind legs apart; if left untreated the affected gland may abscess.

acute metritis Rapid onset of inflammation of the muscular and endometrial layers of the uterus (q.v.) caused by the introduction of contaminants following abnormal parturition (q.v.); a severe and often fatal condition; often accompanied by retention of the fetal membrane, fetid discharge, fever, depression, anorexia, laminitis, and if left untreated, sterility.

acute poison Any fast-acting agent or toxin that chemically destroys life or health within a short period of time following consumption.

acute respiratory syndrome *see* HENDRA VIRUS DISEASE

acute selenium poisoning One of three distinct forms of selenium poisoning (q.v.), the others being chronic selenium poisoning of the alkali type known as alkali disease (q.v.) and chronic selenium poisoning of the blind staggers (q.v.) type; occurs in livestock consuming, at one time, sufficient highly seleniferous plants or grains to cause severe intoxication; characterized by uncertain gait, elevated temperature, labored respiration, dilated pupils, and frothing from the nostrils; death usually occurs within a few hours; there is no known treatment.

ADA *see* ADENOSINE DEAMINASE

Adayevsky A Russian horse breed similar to, but lighter than, the Kazakh (q.v.).

added money (1) A racing term; money added to the winner's purse in addition to nomination, entry, eligibility and starting fees paid by the owners and breeders. (2) The purse put up by the event organizing committee added to the contestants' fees to make up the total prize money.

added weight Also known as overweight (Brit); a racing term; said of a horse who carries more weight than the race conditions stipulate, usually because the jockey (q.v.) exceeds the stated weight.

Addison's disease A degenerative condition caused by deficiency in the secretion of adrenocortical hormones; seen occasionally in horses, especially race horses in training.

adduction To draw towards the median plane of the body.

adductor muscles The group of muscles responsible for drawing the thigh inward.

Adeav One of two types of Kazakh (q.v.), an ancient pony breed originating in Kazakhstan; thought to have descended from the Asiatic wild horse (q.v.); the appearance has been refined by significant infusions of Don (q.v.), Akhal-Teké (q.v.), Iomud (q.v.), and Karabair blood; stands 12.1 to 13.1 hands, may have a bay, gray, palomino or chestnut coat, and has a small, light head and compact body; is less resistant to harsh conditions than the Dzhabe (q.v.), although frugal, hardy, and possessed of great stamina; used for riding.

adenoma A benign tumor originating in and affecting the glands.

adenosine deaminase Also known by the acronym ADA; one of the enzymes active in the chemistry of energy transfer.

Adequan A brand name for polysulfate glycosaminoglycan (q.v.) injected to treat some arthritic conditions.

adhesion An abnormal firm fibrous attachment between two structures as in scar tissue.

adhesive tape Also known as tape (q.v.); a cloth, paper, or synthetic strip with a sticky substance on one side and having various uses, as holding a bandage in place.

adipose Also known as fat; of or relating to body fat (q.v.); stored in the cells of adipose tissue.

adipose tissue Body tissue that can readily store and release fat as energy to the horse when normal energy sources such as glucose and the volatile fatty acids found in the bloodstream are depleted.

a distance Also known as distance; a racing term; a separation of more than 20 lengths (in the US) and 30 lengths (in Britain) between horses at the race finish, e.g. "He was beaten by a length, but it was a distance back to the third."

adjusted monitor system A cutting horse (q.v.) term; a system by which scores may be adjusted during National Cutting Horse Association (q.v.) major events held in the United States; in case of a discrepancy regarding a major penalty (q.v.), the judge monitor reviews the incident on video tape to determine if the query is valid, in which case, he will ask the judges to review the run again on video tape to assess if they want to alter their scores.

adjusted score A cutting horse term (q.v.); a competitor's score reviewed and changed under the rules of the adjusted monitor system (q.v.) used by the National Cutting Horse Association (q.v.); is posted on the scoreboard after it has been reviewed.

ad lib *see* AD LIBITUM

ad libitum Also known by the acronym ad lib; Latin; to give a horse, whether stabled or at pasture (q.v.), free access to feed.

ADMS *see* AMERICAN DONKEY AND MULE SOCIETY

Adopticon A float or show wagon drawn by a minimum of six horses first used in North America during the late 19th century for advertising purposes, street parades, and to carry a small payload.

adrenal cortex The outer cell layer of the adrenal gland (q.v.); produces hormones including those responsible for the utilization of glycogen by the muscles, provides part of the body's shock protection mechanism, and controls electrolyte balance.

adrenal gland One of two ductless, flat glands located on the front of the kidneys responsible for the secretion of hormones into the bloodstream.

adrenalin *see* ADRENALINE

adrenaline Also known as epinephrine and spelled adrenalin (Brit); a hormone secreted by the medulla of the adrenal gland (q.v.); acts primarily as a stimulant.

adrenal medulla The internal portion of the adrenal gland that produces, stores, and releases hormones including epinephrine (q.v.) and noradrenaline into the body.

adrenocorticotropic hormone Also known by the acronym ACTH; a hormone secreted by the pituitary gland responsible for controlling other hormone secretion from the adrenal glands (q.v.); contributes to the control of energy used and prevents shock through secretion of corticosteroids; production increases during times of stress.

ADT *see* AMERICAN DISCOVERY TRAIL

adult The age at which a horse stops growing; may be four, five, six, or seven years depending on the geographic region and the breed.

Advanced Level The British and Australian equivalent to Fourth Level (q.v.).

adventitial marks Also known as adventitious marks; white coat hairs resulting from destruction of the pigment cells of the underlying skin due to trauma as in acquired leukoderma (q.v.), bridle marks, collar marks, girth marks, harness marks, surgical marks, tattoo marks, etc.; must be recorded on all identification charts and breed registrations.

adventitious marks *see* ADVENTITIAL MARKS

AEI *see* AVERAGE EARNINGS INDEX

A-equi-1 Also known as Cambridge strain; one of two immunologically distinct equine influenza (q.v.) viruses endemic among horses worldwide; first isolated in 1963.

A-equi-2 Also known as Miami strain; one of two immunologically distinct equine influenza (q.v.) viruses endemic among horses throughout the world; first recognized in 1963; first appeared in Britain in 1965.

aerobe A micro-organism the existence of which requires the presence of air or free oxygen to thrive and live.

aerobic Requiring air or free oxygen to live and thrive.

aerobic bacteria Bacteria that require air or free oxygen to live and thrive.

aerobic exercise Any activity level that utilizes the horse's capacity to supply oxygen to the cells.

aerobic respiration The breakdown of energy-producing nutrients, principally glycogen, in the presence of oxygen.

aerophagia SEE WINDSUCKING

AFA *see* AMERICAN FARRIERS ASSOCIATION

afebrile Without fever (q.v.).

afferent Leading or conducting inward, as certain nerves and veins.

affiliated show Any horse show run in accordance with the rules of a larger organization, the results of which are recognized by that organization.

Affirmed An average-sized race horse standing 16 hands (1.63 m) with perfect conformation and a solid build; raced from age 2 to 4, winning in 22 of 29 starts including the prestigious American Triple Crown (q.v.) in 1978; during his career on the track won races over almost all distances between 5½ furlongs (1,100m) and 1½ miles (2,400 m); foaled in the United States in 1975 and went to stud in 1980.

African Ass Also known as African Wild Ass, Somali Wild Ass, Somali Wild Donkey, and by the scientific name *Equus africanus*; one of the world's rarest mammals; found mostly in hilly and stony deserts, and arid to semi-arid bushlands and grasslands where access to surface water is available; although the wild ass can go without water longer than other equids (q.v.), it needs water at least every second or third day; feeds mostly on grasses; most active when the weather is cooler – at dusk, dawn and during the night; adults are either solitary, or they live in a variety of temporary associations, usually lasting no more than a few months; originally widespread from the Moroccan Atlas across Saharan and possibly Sahelian Africa to Sudan and Somalia and possibly the Arabian Peninsula where it was found in regions with a brief annual rainfall of 4 to 8 inches (100–200 mm); while known to survive in the 1960s in Ethiopia and Somalia, some investigators considered those populations to be feral (q.v.); recently thought to be restricted to populations in the coastal region of the Red Sea in Djibouti, Eritrea, Ethiopia and Somalia, and possibly in Sudan; has a large black or brown patch at the base of the ears as well as at the tips, with legs the same color as the body; the progenitor of the domestic donkey (q.v.).

African horse sickness Also known as horse sickness; a highly fatal and infectious insect-borne viral disease affecting horses, donkeys, mules and other equines; caused by reovirus, a virus of the family *Reoviridae*, genus *orbivirus*; signs are variable as it occurs in four forms: African horse sickness, pulmonary form (q.v.), African horse sickness, cardiac form (q.v.), African horse sickness, mixed form (q.v.), and African horse sickness, mild form (q.v.); spread by gnats (q.v.) (Culicoides [q.v.]) and possibly other biting insects, most of which are active from twilight until dawn; recovered horses do not appear to be carriers; occurs in many parts of Africa as well as in Asia, the Middle East, and Iberian Peninsula of Europe; has not been found in the Americas or Australia; has a 3 to 5-day incubation period with 95 percent mortality; may spread quickly before diagnosed.

African horse sickness, cardiac form One of four types of African horse sickness (q.v.) characterized by distinct swelling of the head, neck, and chest as well as the area above the eyes, the eyelids, and the lips, abdominal pain, yet no loss of appetite, and small, well-defined hemorrhages in the eye membranes; has an incubation period of from 7 to 14 days and a mortality rate of about 60 percent; death results from cardiac failure.

African horse sickness, mild form Also known as horse sickness fever; one of four types of African horse sickness (q.v.) characterized by low temperatures in the morning rising to a high peak in the afternoon, accelerated pulse, slightly labored breathing, and some loss of appetite; frequently goes undetected and animals recover quickly.

African horse sickness, mixed form One of four types of African horse sickness (q.v.); a combination of the pulmonary and cardiac types with an incubation period of from 5 to 7 days; develops rapidly initially and is characterized by mild pulmonary symptoms followed by the typical swelling associated with the cardiac form.

African horse sickness, pulmonary form One of four types of African horse sickness (q.v.); characterized by an incubation period of 3 to 5 days and 95 percent mortality; symptoms include fluid-filled lungs, signs of acute respiratory difficulty appearing within three or four days, labored and rapid breathing, and elevated temperature; as the disease progresses, the head and neck extend, the ears droop, the horse coughs and sweats severely, and a yellowish fluid discharges from the nostrils; the horse's appetite may remain normal; if recovered, the horse will continue to have breathing difficulty long after other symptoms disappear.

African wild ass *see* AFRICAN ASS

afterbirth *see* AFTERBIRTH PLACENTA

afterwale The body of the harness collar (q.v.) fitted behind the hames (q.v.); consists of padding made from stout woolen cloth with straw and leather side pieces.

against the bit A dressage term; said of the horse when he presses his mouth against the bit with an unyielding neck, poll, or jaw.

against the clock *see* JUMP OFF

agalactia An absence of milk in the mare's udder after foaling.

aged *see* AGED HORSE

aged horse Also known as aged, past the mark, or past the mark of the mouth; in Thoroughbreds (q.v.), a horse 7 years or older while in most other breeds any horse 16 to 20 years old.

ageing *see* AGING

age of a horse *see* HORSE AGE

agent (1) Any substance, compound, or drug capable of producing a physical, chemical, or biological effect. (2) Also known as authorized agent; any person, other than the owner of the horse, authorized to act or conduct business on behalf of the owner; such authorization is usually given in writing.

agglutination Said of the red blood cells (q.v.); to collect or clump into groups.

agglutination antibodies Antibodies that cause red blood cells (q.v.) to collect or clump together abnormally.

agglutination test A stall-side diagnostic test (q.v.) performed to detect endotoxemia (q.v.).

aging Also spelled ageing (Brit); (1) the process of determining a horse's age by evaluating tooth eruption and wear patterns. (2) The process of growing older.

agistment Also known as gisted, stint, horse gait, gaited out, gait, or at gait; generally the prepaid use of pasture for grazing purposes, as on a weekly or monthly basis.

ah Also known as ahve or arve; a voice command used when driving agricultural horses to indicate a turn to the left.

AHC *see* AMERICAN HORSE COUNCIL

AHSA *see* AMERICAN HORSE SHOWS ASSOCIATION

ahve *see* AH

AI *see* ARTIFICIAL INSEMINATION

aids Any natural or artificial touches employed by the rider to address reflexes and communicate instruction to his horse; include natural aids (q.v.), artificial aids (q.v.), driving aids (q.v.), diagonal aids (q.v.), rein aids (q.v.), weight aids (q.v.), upper aids (q.v.), voice aids (q.v.), and lower aids (q.v.).

Aimé Felix Tschiffely *see* TSCHIFFELY, AIME FELIX

Aintree A historic British racecourse located near Liverpool in Lancashire, England; the site of the Grand National Steeplechase (q.v.), which was first run in 1839 when it was known as the Grand Liverpool Steeplechase (q.v.); the Grand National is run over approximately two circuits each 2.25 miles (3600 m) long, including a total of 30 of the racing world's most testing fences; some other, shorter, races are also run over these fences; the course also has a tighter inside track on which races are run over hurdles (q.v.) and more conventional steeplechase fences.

Aintree breast girth Also known as a racing girth, Aintree girth, Newmarket girth, Newmarket breast girth, or racing breastplate; a breastplate (q.v.) made of canvas webbing used to prevent a racing saddle from slipping backwards.

Aintree girth *see* AINTREE BREAST GIRTH

air The correct bearing of a horse in his movements (q.v.), gaits (q.v.), or paces (q.v.).

air above the ground *see* AIRS ABOVE THE GROUND

air dried feed Any feed, i.e., hay, allowed to dry naturally as in the sunlight and air.

airer saddle *see* SADDLE AIRER

aires relevés A French term; airs above the ground (q.v.).

airing Also known as workout; a racing term; said of a horse who runs a race casually as if only out for exercise; the term is generally applied to a horse who wins effortlessly because of his evident superiority, however, allowing a horse to run in this manner without making any effort to win is against the rules of racing in Britain.

airs (1) Formalized posture or movement of the horse; include low airs (q.v.) and high airs or airs above the ground (q.v.). (2) *see* AIRS ABOVE THE GROUND

airs above the ground Also known as high airs, airs, schools above the ground, movements off the ground, aires relevés, and historically as bounds; any of the various High School (q.v.) movements, collectively, performed either with the forelegs or with the fore and hind legs while the horse is above the ground; of seven types in the classical equitation of 17th-century Europe, while at the Spanish School today they have been distilled into three: levade (q.v.), courbette (q.v.), and capriole (q.v.); others include the pesade (q.v.), croupade (q.v.), ballotade (q.v.), and un pas un saut (q.v.); derived from movements performed by medieval warhorses to discourage the close proximity of foot soldiers intent on unhorsing the knight.

AIT *see* AREA INTERNATIONAL TRIAL

Akaster Turk *see* ALCOCK ARABIAN

Akhal Teké A warmblood indigenous to the former Soviet Union; descended more than 3,000 years ago from the Turkmene (q.v.); bred around the oases of the Turkmenistan desert, north of Iran; possesses outstanding speed, endurance, and is resistant to heat; stands 14.2 to 15.2 hands, is wiry with a long head and neck set on a long body and legs, has a low-set tail, and silky, sparse, and short mane and tail hair; has a flowing movement with little swing to the body; the predominant coat color is dun (q.v.) with its striking gold bloom (q.v.), although black, gray, and silver do occur; can be obstinate and bad-tempered; used for long-distance riding, racing, jumping, and dressage; the first Russian breed to have its own stud book.

a la brida A late 15th-century riding style popular around the Iberian Peninsula; the rider rode a saddle with a high pommel (q.v.) and cantle; the rider's legs were very straight and his feet pushed forward; a severe curb with a high port and cheekpieces up to 16 inches (40 cm) long was commonly used.

à la Daumont *see* DAUMONT

à la flèche A circus act in which the rider drives a horse in the lead on long reins (q.v.).

a la gineta A late 15th-century riding style practiced by the Gineta, a Moorish tribe that populated the Iberian Peninsula; similar to a la brida (q.v.), but a ring bit was used instead of the severe curb.

alazan Refers to point (q.v.) color; a Spanish term; red or dark flaxen points; sometimes used in combination with other color distinctions such as sorrel (q.v.) and chestnut (q.v.) to provide greater specificity, e.g., chestnut alazan.

albarda *see* APAREGO PACK

albata *see* GERMAN SILVER

ALBC *see* AMERICAN LIVESTOCK BREEDS CONSERVANCY

Albert Cab A horse-drawn vehicle of the Hooded Gig type popular around 1860; had a cane body hung on side springs and a small rearward platform reached by a rear step to accommodate the tiger (q.v.).

Albert Phaeton An elegant hooded Phaeton with a rearward groom's seat; hung on four elliptical springs.

albinism The state or condition of being albino (q.v.).

albino A color type; a horse having a white coat due to lack of pigmentation, pink skin, and pale, translucent eyes.

Albino (1) *see* AMERICAN WHITE HORSE. (2) *see* AMERICAN CREAM HORSE

Al Borak The mythological winged horse of the Prophet Mohammed; supposedly white in color with a human head, and possessed of incredible speed.

Alcock Arabian Also known as Pelham Arabian, Ancaster Arabian, or Akaster Turk; a gray Arabian stallion from which all gray Thoroughbreds (q.v.) are descended in direct male line; stood at service 1720 to 1725.

alcohol block To inject alcohol into the nerves of the tail of Appaloosa (q.v.), Quarter Horse (q.v.), Paint (q.v.), stock-type Pinto (q.v.), and other breed show horses to deaden or numb the nerves to achieve a quiet tail carriage; formerly achieved by nerving (q.v.); as it is now an illegal procedure for show purposes, show horses are tested for neurological response using an electrical prod.

Alderney Milk Float A horse-drawn English dairyman's float popular during the 1900s; hung on sideways-positioned, semi-elliptical springs, had a cranked axle, low-slung body work, mud flaps above the wheels, curved top or name board, and a seat positioned crosswise in the center of the body work.

Aldin, Cecil (1870–1935) A painter specializing in sporting scenes and subjects, driving and hunting specifically.

Aldridges A horse sale repository located on St. Martin's Lane, London, England until 1920 at which time it was closed; sales were mainly confined to carriage horses.

Alexandra Car A horse-drawn vehicle; an American version of the Dog Cart Phaeton (q.v.); had back-to-back seating and cut under forewheels.

Alexandra Dog Cart An English two-wheeled horse-drawn Dog Cart (q.v.) used in the late 19th century; constructed with straight rather than curved lines, a high dashboard, and high, broad mud guards; sat slightly lower to the ground than the ordinary Dog Cart; originally designed for Queen Alexandra; thought to be more suitable for women.

alfalfa (1) Also known as lucerne; a perennial legume plant of the medic family; thought to be the first cultivated forage for horses, being carried into Greece by the Persians during Xerxes' invasion in 490 BC to feed the war horses; has an average life of 4 to 16 years, is an excellent source of protein, carotene, and nitrogen, and grows in temperate and subtropical regions; will produce up to three times as much hay per acre as many of the grass hays (q.v.) and many cuttings may be made on the same field in one year; contains a fiber content of approximately 30 percent and a digestible protein content ranging from around 7.7 to 12.3 percent depending on the bloom of the alfalfa; the protein found in alfalfa contains all ten essential amino acids; may be fed green or as hay. (2) *see* ALFALFA HAY

alfalfa cubes A compressed feed composed of dried alfalfa ground less finely than that used for alfalfa pellets (q.v.) pressed into 1 to 2 inch (25–50 mm) squares; crude analysis is generally guaranteed and cube grade is usually defined on the basis of maximum fiber and minimum protein contents.

alfalfa hay Also known as alfalfa; cut and dried alfalfa; generally pressed into 50 to 100 pound (23–45 kg) bales strung with wire or rope or piled loose; may be stored for many months without sacrificing quality.

alfalfa leaf meal *see* ALFALFA MEAL

alfalfa meal Also known as alfalfa leaf meal; finely ground and heat dried alfalfa (q.v.); generally of uniform quality and composition; an excellent source of protein, minerals, and vitamins; can be made into alfalfa pellets (q.v.) immediately after drying.

alfalfa pellets A compressed feed pellet, usually cylindrically shaped, made from dehydrated alfalfa hay or dehydrated alfalfa leaf meal (q.v.); may be fed as roughage or as part of a concentrated ration; generally have a higher protein and carotene content than alfalfa (q.v.), are less dusty and are not as subject to mold, aging, and weathering.

alga The singular of algae (q.v.).

algae One of many plants of the subdivision of thallophytes found for the most part in both salt and fresh water, including pond scums, kelps, and some seaweeds.

alight *see* DISMOUNT

alignment The lining up of the horse's body parts from tail to poll (q.v.).

aliment That which nourishes; food.

alimentary Relating to food.

alimentary canal Also known as alimentary tract or alimentary system; the embryonic canal from the mouth to the anus through which food passes; evolves into the gastrointestinal tract (q.v.), esophagus, lips, etc.

alimentary system *see* ALIMENTARY CANAL

alimentary tract *see* ALIMENTARY CANAL

alkali disease Also known as bobtail disease; one of three distinct types of selenium poisoning (q.v.), the others being blind staggers (q.v.) and acute selenium poisoning (q.v.); develops in animals consuming highly seleniferous plants or grains over a period of several weeks or months; characterized by cracked hooves at the coronary band, lameness, long-bone joint stiffness due to erosion from lesions, dullness and lack of vitality, emaciation, and hair loss, usually of the mane and tail; no known methods to completely counteract selenium toxicity.

alkaloid A class of nitrogenized compounds found in living plants and containing their active principles, such as morphine, quinine, caffeine, etc.

Alken, Henry (1784–1851) A noted artist specializing in sporting scenes, driving, racing, and hunting in particular.

Alken, Henry Jr (1810–1892) A sporting artist, less regarded than his father Henry Alkden (q.v.).

a la jineta A 15th-century Spanish term; a balanced-seat riding style in which the rider's ankles hang vertically below his hips; encourages loin coiling in the horse, ensuring rider comfort and mobility.

all-age race A racing term; a horse race for two-year-old horses and older.

allantoic fluid The watery substance filling the space between the alanto-amnion and the chorio-allantois membranes surrounding the fetus in the uterus; lubricates the birth canal during birth and expulsion from the vagina precedes appearance of the foal.

Alleged A racing champion born in 1974 by Hoist the Flag out of Princess Pout; won 9 of 10 races including the arduous Prix de L'Arc de Triomphe which he won as a three-and four-year-old.

All England Jumping Course A continental-style jumping course with permanent obstacles built by Douglas Bunn in the fields of his home, Hickstead Place (q.v.), in 1960 for British horses and riders; evolved into Hickstead (q.v.) one of the greatest show jumping centers in the world.

allergen Any substance that induces an allergic reaction.

allergy Excess sensitivity producing a bodily reaction to certain substances such as food, drugs, pollen, heat, or cold which are harmless to other animals or humans.

Alley Bodger A small, low-sided, horse-drawn wagon frequently run on iron wheels; drawn by one horse and used for general purposes in the hop fields of Kent, England.

all gears Said of a driving horse when between the shafts in a Cart, in chain or sliding gears in the lead of a tandem (q.v.) to a Cart, or plough gears for plowing, cultivating, etc.

Alliance Phaeton A horse-drawn sporting version of the Park Phaeton (q.v.) popular during the 1850s and 1860s.

alligator (1) Also known as bad cow; a cutting term; a difficult-to-control cow. (2) *see* CLINCHER

all on A hunting term; said by the whippers-in (q.v.) to let the huntsman (q.v.) know all hounds are up with the pack and accounted for.

all out Said of a horse who gives maximum effort and exertion when asked by the rider.

allowance race A racing term; a non-claiming event in which published conditions drafted by the racing secretary (q.v.) stipulate jockey weight allowances according to their previous purse earnings and/or number and type of victories; a horse is allowed to carry less weight if he has won fewer times than the other competitors, or if he has earned less money; generally considered a higher class race than claiming races (q.v.), but of a lower class than stakes races (q.v.).

allowances A racing term; reductions in weight carried by competing horses due to certain race conditions: because an apprentice jockey (q.v.) is riding, to female horses competing against males or to three-year-olds competing against older horses.

all-purpose saddle Also known as utility saddle or general purpose saddle; an English saddle having a slightly deeper seat than a close contact saddle (q.v.), round cantle (q.v.), and slightly forward and padded flap; used for jumping, trail riding, and eventing.

all ready, outside and in A coaching term; said of the guard to the passengers to alert them to the eminent departure of their horse-drawn vehicle; followed by a command from the driver, "let 'em go, then," to the hostler (q.v.) and stable boys to release the horses.

all right behind A coaching phrase; said by the coachman to the passengers to alert them to departure of the vehicle.

all-round cow horse A western term; any horse capable of performing the duties required of him by a cowboy (q.v.).

all-rounder A polo term; a player sufficiently confident and knowledgeable of the game of polo (q.v.) to be able to read and interpret the game at every moment of play.

allures An archaic term; the gait (q.v.) or pace (q.v.) of the horse; of two types: natural allures (q.v.) and artificial allures (q.v.).

alopecia Local or general loss of hair, fur, or wool in the absence of other visible skin disease; may be congenital (q.v.) or associated with inflammatory skin disorders such as mange (q.v.) or ringworm (q.v.).

alpung The Austrian practice of raising young Haflinger (q.v.) stock on Alpine pastures where the thin air develops their hearts and lungs.

also eligible A racing term; a horse officially entered in a race who will not compete unless other horses are scratched creating vacancies in the field (q.v.).

also-ran A racing term; generally said of any horse failing to finish a race in first through third positions; may vary dependent upon the number of entries in the field (q.v.).

Altai A horse breed indigenous to Russia, used for riding.

alter *see* CASTRATE

Alter A Spanish-bred warmblood with similar lineage to the Andalusian (q.v.) used for riding and jumping.

Alter-Real A Portuguese horse breed; descended from Andalusian (q.v.) mares imported from the Jerez region of Spain to Portugal by the House of Braganza in 1847 where they were bred and maintained at a stud farm at Villa de Portel in Portugal's Alentejo province; the stud was later moved to Alter, from which the breed name derived; the purpose of the stud was to develop a Haute Ecole (q.v.) horse; bloodlines were seriously contaminated during the Napoleonic invasion at which time Thoroughbred (q.v.), Hanoverian (q.v.), Arab (q.v.), and Norman (q.v.) blood was introduced; government intervention enabled the consistent reintroduction of Andalusian blood in the 20th century which re-established the breed to its former type; is compact, standing 15.1 to 16.1 hands, and has a bay, brown, chestnut, and sometimes gray coat; is intelligent, quick to learn, and athletic; the action (q.v.) is elevated, but lacks extension; a good riding horse, particularly well suited to the Haute Ecole.

alum A class of double sulfates containing

aluminum and such metals as potassium, ammonium, and iron; common or potash alum is used as an astringent and styptic.

alveolar emphysema *see* CHRONIC OBSTRUCTIVE PULMONARY DISEASE

Amalgamated Society of Farriers and Blacksmiths A British organization founded in 1805 to regulate wages and employee/employer relations for farriers and blacksmiths; one of the oldest trade unions in existence.

amarinda A Spanish term; horses trained to stay with a bell mare (q.v.).

amateur *see* AMATEUR RIDER

amateur huntsman A hunting term, a gentleman, usually a Master (q.v.) who chooses to hunt his own hounds.

amateur owner A competitive division restricted to non-professional adult riders who ride horses owned by themselves or their families in hunter/jumper competitions.

amateur rider Also known as amateur or gentleman rider; one who rides a horse solely for pleasure and not for monetary award or financial gain; excludes stable hands, grooms, hunt servants, etc.

amateur whipper-in *see* HONORARY WHIPPER-IN

Amazons A race of equestrienne warriors in Greek mythology.

amble A four-beat lateral gait distinguished from the pace (q.v.) by being slower and more broken in cadence; performed in four-time without suspension; as it is not a speed gait, it is smooth, comfortable, easy to ride, and can be collected; most horses who perform the gait have a natural affinity for it.

Americaine *see* AMERICAN BUGGY

American Albino *see* AMERICAN WHITE HORSE

American Albino Association, Inc. Also known by the acronym AAAI; a United States organization founded to allay public fear about the word "albino"; superseded the American Albino Horse Club, Inc. (q.v.) in 1970 and was in turn superseded by the International American Albino Association, Inc. in 1985; began registering pure white horses, ponies, and miniature horses as "American White" (q.v.) and also accepted cream colored horses in a new division known as American Cream (q.v.).

American Albino Horse Club, Inc. Also known by the acronym AAHC; an organization founded in the United States in 1936, and incorporated in 1937 to promote and preserve the breeding records of the American Albino (q.v.), known as the American White Horse (q.v.) since 1970, reincorporated in 1970 under the American Albino Association, Inc. (q.v.) and reincorporated again in 1985 as the International American Albino Association, Inc. (q.v.).

American Association of Equine Practitioners Also known by the acronym AAEP; an association founded in the United States in 1954 to improve horse health and welfare, further the professional development of its members, and to provide resources and leadership to benefit the equine industry.

American Association of Owners and Breeders of Peruvian Paso Horses Also known by the acronym AAOBPPH; an organization founded in the United States in 1962 and incorporated as a non-profit corporation in 1967 to register pure-bred Peruvian Pasos (q.v.), promote the breed, and educate the public; the only registry recognized by the Association Nacional de Criadores and Propietarios de Caballos Peruanos de Paso, the registry in Peru.

American Bashkir Also known as American Bashkir Curly; a centuries-old pony breed originating in Bashkiria, around the southern foothills of the Urals in the former Soviet Union; reputed to have run wild in the United States in the early 1800s at which time it was quite popular with the American Indian for riding, packing and light draft; stands 13.1 to 14 hands; has a distinctive thick, curly winter coat and thick mane, tail, and forelock that enable it to survive in sub-zero temperatures; is kept outdoors where it can withstand winter temperatures of

–22 to 40°F (-30–4.4°C); the coat is usually bay, chestnut or palomino; has a short neck, low withers, elongated and sometimes hollow back, a wide and deep chest, short and strong legs, and a small foot for its size; the breed standard quotes a bone measurement of 8 inches (20 cm) below the knee and a girth measurement for stallions of 71 inches (180 cm); is docile, strong, quiet, and hardy; during a seven- to eight-month lactation period a mare can yield as much as 350 gallons (1,590 liters) of milk; the long winter coat hair is spun into cloth; due to the exceptionally hard hoof, is generally left unshod.

American Bashkir Curly *see* AMERICAN BASHKIR

American Break A horse-drawn passenger vehicle used in the Western United States during the 19th century for swift, long-distance travel; had a short wheel base, seating for six, slatted under-boot, ample luggage space, was hung front and rear on sideways-elliptical springs, and drawn by four or more horses.

American Buggy Also known as Buggy, Americaine in Western Europe, or spelled buggie; any of the family of medium-sized, light and fast, two- and four-wheeled, horse-drawn driving wagons popular in the United States from the 1830s to the 1920s; a Phaeton (q.v.) with equirotal or near equirotal wheels; similar in outward appearance to a Model T Ford; modern versions are still used by the Amish sect; drawn by a single horse.

American Cab A two-wheeled horse-drawn cab first used in New York, United States around 1832; had a driver roof seat with angled footboard, two interior seats for a total of four passengers, and rear entry; mounted on cranked axles with sideways elliptical or semi-elliptical springs.

American Cabriolet A four-wheeled, horse-drawn, low-slung carriage popular in North America during the second half of the 19th century; drawn by a pair of horses in pole gear (q.v.), hung on full sideways elliptical springs, front and rear, and protected at the rear by a half hood.

American Cream *see* AMERICAN CREAM HORSE

American Cream Horse Also known as an American Cream and incorrectly as an Albino or American Albino; an American color breed with diverse bloodlines; descended from a white foundation stallion of Morgan (q.v.) and Arab (q.v.) blood known as Old King (1906) put to Arab, Morgan, and Thoroughbred (q.v.) mares beginning in 1917; due to public demand for a registration for horses whose coats were cream-colored instead of pure white, the American Albino Association (q.v.) opened a separate stud book for creams in 1970; the result of a dilute gene, a cream bred to a cream will produce a cream 100 percent of the time; have pale cream hair varying in shades from almost white to a rich cream or any other shade that does not qualify as Palomino (q.v.), pink to pinkish-orange (pumpkin) skin pigmentation, and a mane and tail which may vary from white to russet in color; any eye color is acceptable with blue, hazel, and amber occurring most often; gray or black skin is not acceptable; is different than the American White (q.v.).

American Cutting Horse Association Also known by the acronym ACHA; an organization based in Texas, USA founded to promote cutting (q.v.) contests as a sport and encourages individuals, families, companies, and groups to become involved in breeding, training, and exhibiting cutting horses (q.v.) in the contest arena and to promote and regulate the showing of cutting horses.

American Discovery Trail Also known by the acronym ADT; the first non-motorized, coast-to-coast thoroughfare in the United States traversing 6,000 miles (9,656 km) of urban as well as rural areas from Point Reyes National Seashore in California to Henelopen State Park in Delaware; developed in the late 20th century.

American Donkey and Mule Society Also known by the acronym ADMS; a non-profit US organization established in Texas in 1967 to register and maintain the stud books for the Miniature Donkey, Donkey (q.v.), Ass (q.v.), Mule (q.v.) and Zebra hybrids.

American Farriers Association Also known by the acronym AFA; an association of farriers (q.v.) practicing in the United States organized in 1971; provides certification tests for its members since 1979, the levels of which include Certified Farrier and Certified Journeyman Farrier.

American Foxhound Club A non-profit organization originally founded in the United States in 1912 originally founded to promote the Virginia strain of American Foxhounds (q.v.); now promotes all pack hounds in North America, is the primary financial supporter of hound shows, and publishes materials and books on foxhunting (q.v.).

American Horse An all-purpose, generic riding horse developed in the Eastern United States in the early 1700s by crossing Narragansett Pacer (q.v.) mares with Thoroughbred (q.v.) stallions; larger and prettier than the Narragansett, but possessed of the same easy gaits and stamina; recognized as a breed in 1776; a precursor to the American Saddlebred (q.v.).

American Horse Council Also known by the acronym AHC; an American organization founded in 1969 to promote and protect the horse industry by communicating with Congress, federal agencies, media, public, and the horse industry itself on behalf of all horse-related interests.

American Horse Shows Association Also known by the acronym AHSA; an organization founded in the United States in 1917 to represent the United States in international equestrian affairs and to govern equestrian sport competition in the United States.

American Horse Shows Association Hunter Seat Equitation Medal A year-long horsemanship competition for junior riders culminating at the Pennsylvania National Horse Show in Harrisburg, Pennsylvania, USA each October; riders must qualify for the finals by winning a specified number of AHSA (q.v.) Medal classes throughout the year.

American Livestock Breeders Conservancy Also known by the acronym ALBC; a non-profit membership organization chartered to preserve heritage breeds of cattle, horses (Spanish Mustang [q.v.], Gotland [q.v.], etc.), goats, asses, sheep, swine, and poultry from extinction; also acts in the United States as a clearing house for information on livestock and genetic diversity.

American Mail Coach *see* CONCORD COACH

American Novice Horse Association Also known by the acronym ANHA; an organization founded in Texas, USA in 1990, to organize rodeo (q.v.) competitions for inexperienced horses including barrel racing (q.v.), pole bending, breakaway, and calf roping events; classes have career-earning limits to encourage parity of competition.

American Paint Horse Association Also known by the acronym APHA; an organization founded in the United States in 1962, following the merger of the American Paint Stock Horse and American Paint Quarter Horse Associations; dedicated to the continuance, registration, performance, and record keeping of Stock-Type Paint Horses; started the Pinto Horse Stud Book in 1963; registers foals born of registered American Paint Horses (q.v.), Quarter Horses (q.v.), or Thoroughbreds (q.v.) registered with the Jockey Club or Jockey Club-recognized organizations having a white spot on the body at least 2 inches (50 mm) long, with unpigmented skin beneath it; solid-colored horses will not be registered.

American pelham bit A single-piece or mullen mouth bit, with a slightly curved mouthpiece and cheeks (q.v.) angled backwards at the bottom; equipped to handle four reins – two snaffle and two curb.

American Quarter Horse Association Also known by the acronym AQHA; an American organization founded in 1940 to establish breed specifications and maintain a registry for the Quarter-type horse; merged with the American Quarter Racing (q.v.) and National Quarter Horse Associations (q.v.) in 1949; the world's largest breed organization.

American Quarter Racing Association Also known by the acronym AQRA; an American organization founded in the early 1940s to establish breed specifications and registry for the Quarter-type horse; merged into the American Quarter Horse Association (q.v.) in 1949.

American Rockaway *see* ROCKAWAY

American Saddlebred Also known as Kentucky Saddlehorse, Kentucky Saddlebred, Kentucky Saddler, Saddlebred, American Saddle Horse, American Saddlehorse, or Saddle Horse; a horse breed indigenous to the United States where it was developed in Kentucky by putting a Thoroughbred (q.v.) foundation sire to American Horse (q.v.), Canadian Pacer (q.v.), and Narragansett Pacer (q.v.) mares; identified as a distinct breed in the early 1800s; more than 60 percent of the horses in the first three breed registry volumes trace to the foundation sire Gaines' Denmark; today two prominent bloodlines remain: Denmark and Chief; Morgan (q.v.) blood was introduced in the 1850s; may be three- or five-gaited depending on the training; has a high-set tail achieved by nicking (q.v.), a high head set, long and arched neck, and a sloped shoulder; the gait is free and natural and has high action; stands 15 to 16 hands with an average weight of 1,000 to 1,200 pounds (454–544 kg); all coat colors are acceptable, with the most prominent being chestnut, bay, black, and brown; gray, palomino, roan, and pinto colors also occur; used for saddle, show, and harness; shown in three types of classes: light harness (q.v.), three-gaited saddler (q.v.), and the five-gaited saddler (q.v.).

American Saddlebred Horse Association Also known by the acronym ASHA; an American organization founded in 1891 to maintain the breed registry for the American Saddlebred (q.v.); was the first public association and breed registry established for an American horse breed.

American Saddle Horse *see* AMERICAN SADDLEBRED

American Saddlehorse *see* AMERICAN SADDLEBRED

American Standardbred *see* STANDARDBRED

American stage coach *see* STAGE COACH

American Stud Book The American-held registry for all Thoroughbred (q.v.) horses foaled in the United States, Puerto Rico, and Canada and of all Thoroughbreds imported into those countries from jurisdictions having a registry recognized by The Jockey Club (q.v.) and the International Stud Book Committee.

American Team Penning Championships Also known by the acronym ATPC; one of three national events established in the United States after 1980; devoted solely to the sport of team penning (q.v.).

American Triple Crown Also known as Triple Crown; a program of three classic races for three-year-olds run in the United States since 1867; consists of the 1¼ mile (2 km) Kentucky Derby (q.v.), the 1 mile, 1½ furlong (1.9 km) Preakness Stakes (q.v.) , and the 1½ mile (2.4 km) Belmont Stakes (q.v.); there is a break of two weeks between the Kentucky Derby and the Preakness and three weeks between the Preakness and Belmont Stakes; only 11 horses have won all three races constituting the American Triple Crown since its inception in 1867: (1916 [Sir Burton], 1927 [Gallant Fox], 1932 [Omaha], 1934 [War Admiral], 1938 [Whirlaway], 1940 [Count Fleet], 1943 [Assault], 1945 [Citation], 1970 [Secretariat], 1974 [Seattle Slew], and 1975 [Affirmed]); equivalent programs are run in England (English Triple Crown[q.v.]) and Canada (Canadian Triple Crown [q.v.]); American trainer Wayne Lukas has won more Triple Crown races than any other trainer in history.

American Trotter *see* STANDARDBRED

American Vaulting Association Also known by the acronym AVA; an organization established in California, USA in 1968 to promote vaulting in the United States through training of judges, creation of rules, and publishing of a bi-monthly magazine.

American White *see* AMERICAN WHITE HORSE

American White Horse Also known as Albino, American Albino, American White, and incorrectly as an American Cream; an American color breed with diverse bloodlines; descended from a white, stock-horse type of Morgan (q.v.) and Arab (q.v.) blood, known as Old King, put to Arab, Morgan, and Thoroughbred (q.v.) mares from 1917 on; physical characteristics vary considerably and may resemble the Quarter Horse (q.v.), Morgan, Thoroughbred, or Arab; has snow white coat hair, pink skin, and dark brown eyes, with black, blue and hazel also occurring; mottled skin, spotted hair or spotted skin are unacceptable, but a few, small spots on the skin of the extremities is permitted; a dominant color; white bred to color will result in white offspring 50 percent of the time, while white bred to white will produce white approximately 75 percent of the time; since 1970, two studbooks have been maintained: the American White Horse and the American Cream Horse (q.v.); due to the diversity of the bloodlines, must stand a minimum of 13.1 hands; the only pure white, non-albino horse breed in the world; the name derived from the Latin albus meaning white.

America's 500-year-old new breed *see* PASO FINO

amino acid An organic compound containing the amino group NH2 and at least one carbon group which form the basic constituents of proteins (q.v.); essential amino acid (q.v.) content determines the quality of the protein.

amino acid supplement A feed additive containing one or more of the essential amino acids (q.v.) fed to a horse to correct a deficiency.

Amish Buggy A horse-drawn American Buggy (q.v.) used by the Amish religious communities in Indiana, Pennsylvania, and Ohio, USA whose creed precludes them from using motorized transportation; popular from the 18th century through modern day; originally had a basic tray shape with a high-backed driving seat, wide enough for two passengers, leather-covered dashboard, folding hood, and brass-mounted candle lamps; now, box-shaped and enclosed on three sides with leather screens; always painted black and drawn by a single horse.

ammonia A compound of nitrogen and hydrogen; may be applied to sprains or injuries as a liniment or inhaled, when in vapor form, to stimulate respiration and the respiratory system when these are depressed.

ammoniac An exudation of an umbelliferous plant with a fetid smell used as an antispasmodic and expectorant and in some poultices (q.v.).

ammonia vapor A gas released by decomposing horse dung.

amnion *see* AMNIOTIC SAC

amniotic sac Also known as amnion or water bag; the innermost membrane surrounding the fetus (q.v.).

Ampeton A light, horse-drawn open carriage of the Landau (q.v.) type first used in London, England during the 1850s.

ampoule Also spelled ampule, a hermetically sealed glass vial or container used to hold solutions for laboratory tests or injection into the horse.

ampule *see* AMPOULE

amulet Anything worn or carried upon the person or animal, intended to act as a charm or preservative against evil, accident, or mischief, such as disease and witchcraft; originally used on camels in the desert; when used on horses, known as horse brasses (q.v.).

anabolic steroids A group of substances including tenbolone, testosterone, and nadrolone used to accelerate the recovery of weight lost due to debility or undernutrition, increase muscular development and tone, speed up tissue regeneration to help resolve bone and tissue injuries, assist in the recovery from infectious diseases, and to increase the efficiency of protein utilization; may produce male-like behavior in some mares and fillies; sudden withdrawal after prolonged administration may result in a marked loss of condition in the treated horse.

anaemia *see* ANEMIA

anaerobic exercise A period of strenuous exercise demanding muscle function without adequate oxygen.

anaesthetic *see* ANESTHETIC

anal atresia A congenital condition of foals born without an anal opening; a true lethal (q.v.) resulting in death.

analeptic A restorative; any substance that gives strength and/or stimulates the central nervous system.

analgesic Any drug which causes a temporary loss of the sense of pain without a loss of consciousness.

anaphylactic shock Also known as anaphylaxis; a shock (q.v.) condition characterized by acute, violent and often fatal systemic allergic reaction triggered by the introduction of an antigen (q.v.) to a horse who has already been exposed to and acquired sensitivity to that antigen (q.v.); may result from the injection of vaccines or drugs, exposure to food or airborne allergens, or insect bites; symptoms occur within seconds after the allergen enters the circulation and include constriction of bronchial airways and the pulmonary vascular bed which results in severe respiratory distress and death within minutes if untreated.

anaphylaxis *see* ANAPHYLACTIC SHOCK

anatomy The structure of the horse body and the relation of its parts.

Ancaster Arabian *see* ALCOCK ARABIAN

ancestry The parentage of a horse as depicted on a genealogical tree and traced through the dam (q.v.) and sire (q.v.) through several generations.

anchor pull A metal tip attached to the lower half of the hames (q.v.) fitted with an eye through which the hame clip or hame tug ring passes; the most common method of securing the traces, shoulder-pieces, or hame tugs on modern horse-drawn driving vehicles.

Ancient English Pacer Also known generically as palfrey or pad; the primary horse breed used throughout the British Isles from AD 500 to 1500; specific types were known by the location of their origin such as the Irish Hobby Horse and the Scottish Galloway (q.v.) transported by the Vikings to Iceland where they remain today as the Icelandic (q.v.); the foundation stock for the American Saddlebred (q.v.).

Andalucian *see* ANDALUSIAN

Andalusian Also spelled Andalucian and known as Royal Horse of Europe (obs), Iberian Horse, Pure Spanish Horse, Spanish Horse, Caballo Raza Pura Española or by the acronym PRE; a horse breed originating in Spain around the 8th century AD believed to have descended from the Iberian Horse (q.v.); evolved in the rugged and hilly areas of the Iberian peninsula (comprised of Spain, where they call the breed the Pure Spanish Horse [q.v.], and Portugal, where the breed is known as the Pure Blood Lusitano [q.v.]); fighting for survival over this rough terrain led to the development of a strong, arched neck, powerfully built short-coupled body, and hind legs positioned well under the rectangular and lean body; stands 15.2 to 16.2 hands, 80 percent have a gray or white coat, 15 percent are bay, and less than 5 percent are black, dun or chestnut; has small, rounded hooves, strong hock action and impulsion and a natural ability for collection; the profile is straight or sometimes convex; has small, inward-facing ears, curved neck, rounded quarters, low-set tail, a thick, long, and wavy mane and tail, an airy action, a high-stepping, impulsive trot, and a rocking canter; is a good jumper and particularly well suited to dressage and the movements of Haute Ecole (q.v.); influenced the development of most European breeds (i.e. Friesian [q.v.], Holstein [q.v.], Lippizzaner [q.v.], and Oldenburg [q.v.]) and, thanks to Columbus, most American breeds (Quarter Horse [q.v.] and Criollo [q.v.]) as well; strictly and systematically bred since 1571 with the founding of the Royal Stables in Cordoba where it is still bred and now also in Jerez and Seville.

anemia Also spelled anaemia; a deficiency in red blood cell count and/or blood hemoglobin content; commonly caused by excessive bleeding, infection, worms, dietary deficiency, and the presence of toxins in the body; symptoms include pale mucous membranes of the eyelids and a weak pulse; types include hemorrhagic anemia (q.v.), hemolytic anemia (q.v.), and nutritional anemia (q.v.).

anesthesia An artificially induced state of insensibility, especially to the sense of pain.

anesthetic Also spelled anaesthetic; of or belonging to anesthesia (q.v.); having the power to deprive of feeling or sensation; any substance that has the power to deprive of feeling or sensation; may be injected or inhaled to achieve different levels of desensitization: local anesthetic (q.v.), regional anesthetic, and general anesthetic (q.v.).

anestrus A period of sexual inactivity in the mare during which there is an absence of observable heat (q.v.) or acceptance to the stallion.

aneurine hydrochloride Synthetic thiamin (q.v.) or vitamin B_1.

A New Method and Extraordinary Invention to Dress Horses and Work them According to Nature *see* METHODE ET INVENTION NOUVELLE DE DRESSER LES CHEVAUX

Anglo-Arab A breed resulting from crossing Thoroughbred (q.v.) stallions with Arab (q.v.) mares or vice versa; originated in Britain, but is also bred elsewhere, particularly France, where it has been selectively bred for more than 150 years; in some countries, the mix may be no less than 50 percent Thoroughbred and 50 percent Arab, while in others the percentage is not stipulated; the breed registry is maintained by the Arab Horse Society in each country; generally speaking, has the soundness, endurance, and stamina of the Arab and the scope and speed of the Thoroughbred, but without its excitable temperament.

Anglo-Argentine A breed developed in South America by crossing the Thoroughbred (q.v.) with the Criollo (q.v.).

Anglo-Norman *see* NORMAN

Anglo-Persian A breed developed in Iran by crossing the Arab (q.v.) with Persian; an all-purpose riding mount.

Angular Landau *see* SHELBURNE LANDAU

ANHA *see* AMERICAN NOVICE HORSE ASSOCIATION

anhydrosis Failure of the body's sweating mechanisms; commonly occurs when both the temperature and humidity are high; symptoms include inability to sweat, increased respiratory rate, elevated body temperature, and decreased exercise tolerance; may be reversed if the horse is moved to a more temperate climate.

aniseed Also spelled anise seed; the seed of the anise, an annual umbelliferous plant, *Pimpinella anisum*, which has a licorice-like taste and aromatic smell; used in drag hunts (q.v.) as a line for the hounds to follow in the absence of a live fox.

anise seed *see* ANISEED

ankle (1) *see* FETLOCK JOINT. (2) A leg marking (q.v.); any white mark extending from the coronary band (q.v.) to just above the fetlock (q.v.).

ankle boots Also known as sesamoid boots; a light-duty brushing boot (q.v.) used to protect the fetlock joint (q.v.) including the associated ligaments and tendons above the joint; made of Kersey (q.v.), leather, or felt and held in place with buckle straps or velcro.

ankle cutter An American racing term; a horse who cuts his fetlock (q.v.) with the opposite foot while running.

ankylosing arthritis Arthritis (q.v.) characterized by severe degeneration and ulceration of the articular cartilages in conjunction with erosion and flattening of the underlying bone; degeneration results in new bone growth which fills the joint space; may be the end result of osteoarthritis (q.v.), infectious arthritis (q.v.), or severe injury such as a fracture (q.v.) or puncture wound.

ankylosis The fusion of bones in part or all of a joint due to disease, injury, or surgical procedure; results in loss of movement.

annular Shaped like a ring.

anodyne Any pain-relieving drug.

Anoplocephala manga A species of tapeworm (q.v.) varying in length from 3 to 7.5 inches (10–25 cm) and found in the small intestine and stomach; in light infestations, no signs of disease are present, while in heavy infestations, digestive disturbances and anemia (q.v.) may occur.

Anoplocephala perforliata A species of tapeworm (q.v.) varying in length from 3 to 7.5 inches (10–25 cm); found in the cecum, and in some cases, the small intestine; ulceration of the mucosa occurs quite commonly in the area of attachment; in light infestations, no signs of disease are present; in heavy infestations, digestive disturbances, unthriftiness, and anemia (q.v.) may occur.

ante-post betting A racing term; a betting option in which wagering on a race, for an agreed upon price, occurs on any day prior to the race.

ante-post price *see* FORECAST NO. 1

anterior Toward the front of the body.

anterior enteritis Acute inflammation of the small intestine resulting in signs of abdominal distress such as colic (q.v.) and diarrhea (q.v.).

anthelmintic Also known as antiparasitic; any drug or compound administered to the horse by injection (not in the United Kingdom), drenching, or oral paste to remove helminths (q.v.) and round or flat worms.

anthrax Also known as charbon or splenic fever; an acute, infectious disease caused by *Bacillus anthracis*; symptoms include elevated temperature, abnormal swelling in the throat and neck, great pain, and sudden death; rare in horses.

anti A prefix; against, as in antibacterial (q.v.).

antiarrhythmic agent Any drug used to regulate cardiac arrhythmia (q.v.).

antibacterial Any substance topically applied to destroy or inhibit the growth of bacteria.

antibiotic One of a group of substances derived from living organisms (or synthesized), administered to destroy or inhibit bacterial growth and that of other living organisms; may be administered orally, topically, or by injection depending on the drug used and the nature of the infection.

antibody Any of various substances existing in the blood or developed in immunization that counteract toxins or bacterial poisons in the system.

antibody test A laboratory test performed by technicians to measure the titer, or blood concentration, of immune activity against a known virus; in a diagnostic setting, two tests are taken several weeks apart to compare titers which rise with recent infection; a shortcoming of this test is that by the time antibody production is measurable, the disease has often run its course.

anti-brushing shoe *see* FEATHER EDGED SHOE

anti-cast roller Also known as arch-roller; a girth or surcingle fit around the girth of a stabled horse to prevent him from rolling over and/or casting (q.v.); a 3 to 4 inch (7.5–10 cm) wide girth made of leather or webbing with pads attached to the underside that fit on either side of the withers (q.v.) to prevent rubbing or pressure; bridged by an arched metal bar which sits approximately 3 inches (7.5 cm) above the withers.

anticipate Said of a horse who thinks he is aware of what is about to happen, as in what the rider or trainer will request of him, and acts accordingly, e.g. the horse may try, or succeed in trying, to make a transition before receiving the rider's aid.

anti-cribbing device *see* CRIBBING COLLAR

antifebrile Having the quality of abating fever (q.v.).

antifungal Any substance having the quality of inhibiting, controlling, or destroying a fungal infection.

antigen The molecules, primarily proteins, comprising a portion of an organism invading the body; once the body identifies an antigen, it produces antibodies (q.v.) that only attach to that antigen.

antigen drift The ability of a virus to change its form sufficiently so that it is no longer vulnerable to existing antibodies.

antigenic The nature of a substance that triggers development of an antibody when introduced into the blood or tissue.

antihistamine A class of drugs used to neutralize histamine (q.v.) production resulting from conditions including sweet itch (q.v.), laminitis (q.v.) azoturia (q.v.) and allergic skin and respiratory diseases.

anti-inflammatory Any agent, drug, or compound that reduces inflammation including redness, heat, pain, and swelling.

antimere One of two or more corresponding parts on opposite sides of the horse.

antiparasitic *see* ANTHELMINTIC

antiphlogistic *see* POULTICE

antipyretic A remedy effective in reducing fever.

anti-rearing bit *see* CHIFNEY BIT

antiseptic (1) Void of germs. (2) An agent that inhibits the growth of microorganisms such as germs.

antiserum A serum inclusive of antibodies acquired from the blood of an animal and used for injection into other animals to provide immunity against a certain disease.

anti-shadow noseband *see* SHADOWROLL NOSEBAND

anti-shying noseband *see* SHADOWROLL NOSEBAND

antisweat sheet A cloth covering for the horse's body made of a breathable, cellular cotton mesh or linen that enables the horse to cool down slowly following exercise, thus preventing chill.

antitoxin (1) A substance formed in a body, capable of counteracting a specific toxin. (2) The antibody formed in immunization with a given toxin; used to treat certain infectious diseases or to produce immunity against them.

antivenin (1) Also spelled incorrectly as antivenom; an antitoxin (q.v.) produced in the blood by repeated injections of venom, as of snakes. (2) The antitoxic serum obtained from blood treated with repeated injections of venom, as of snakes.

antivenom *see* ANTIVENIN

Antoine de Pluvinel *see* DE PLUVINEL, ANTOINE

anvil (1) A heavy iron block with a flat surface upon which a horseshoe (q.v.) is formed. (2) In human anatomy, the middle bone of the ear; the incus.

anvil blowing *see* ANVIL SHOOTING

anvil shooting (1) Also known as anvil blowing or blowing the anvil; a recreational farrier practice; to place and ignite an explosive charge between two anvils (q.v.) stacked one on top of the other to launch the top anvil into the air. (2) Also known as anvil blowing; a farrier practice; to hammer a white-hot piece of iron against a wet anvil thus producing a pistol-like sound.

aparego pack Also known as albarda or asparego; a pack saddle of Spanish origin, constructed without a tree and consisting of long stems of straw sewn into two square-shaped cloth cases joined by padded straps which pass over the back of the horse; straw-stuffed cases are placed on top of the square cases and a saddle cloth, secured by surcingles, covers the entire saddle; pack loads are distributed into two bundles and attached to the saddle; no weight is placed on the spine of the horse.

APHA *see* AMERICAN PAINT HORSE ASSOCIATION

ApHC *see* APPALOOSA HORSE CLUB, INC.

Appaloosa Also known as spotted horse or historically as Palouse Pony or Palousy; an American-bred warmblood descended from Spanish stock – some of which carried the hereditary spotting gene – introduced by the conquistadors in the 16th century and crossed with native and Quarter Horse (q.v.) type mares; breed characteristics were initially fixed by the Nez Percé Indians; was nearly eradicated in 1876 as United States troops seized tribal lands and was revived by the Appaloosa Horse Club (q.v.) in 1938 at which time it was officially recognized as a breed; six coat patterns are recognized: frost (q.v.), leopard (q.v.), varnish roan (q.v.), white blanket (q.v.), spotted blanket (q.v.), and snowflake (q.v.); a white sclera encircling the eye and at least one striped hoof on a solid-colored leg, mottled nose, lip, and genital skin are breed requirements; the mane and tail are characteristically sparse, the result of selective breeding to prevent entanglement in brush and undergrowth; originally short-coupled and of the stock type, but recent infusions of Thoroughbred (q.v.) blood have added height and more elegant lines to the breed; in Europe, and to some extent, the United States, crossed with warmbloods; possess good stamina, speed, and agility; the name derives from a corruption of the word Palouse, a river area located in northeastern Oregon where the Nez Percé Indians selectively bred this horse throughout the 18th and 19th centuries; the highly-valued horses of this area were soon known as Palouse ponies, which led to the singular a Palouse Pony, and ultimately Appaloosa.

Appaloosa Horse Club, Inc. Also known by the acronym ApHC; an organization founded in Moscow, Idaho, USA in 1938 to preserve, improve, promote, and enhance the Appaloosa (q.v.); the third largest breed registry in the world; original registration requirements included a classic blanket (q.v.) or leopard coat pattern (q.v.), mottled (q.v.) skin, white sclera (q.v.), and at least one striped hoof with a solid-colored leg.

appeal To address another person or authority for a decision regarding a score, time, penalty, disqualification, suspension, and the like received in a competition or from an association.

appendageal system An outgrowth of the epidermis (q.v.), with which it is contiguous; consists of hair follicles and sebaceous and aprocrine glands.

Appleby Fair A Gypsy fair held annually in June since about 1300 in Appleby, North Westmorland England; Gypsies convene to sell their horse stock to interested buyers.

appointment card Also known as card or fixture card; a hunting term; an invitation sent out to interested hunters by the hunt Secretary to inform them of the date, time, and place of meets occurring in the subsequent month.

appointments Saddlery and harness worn by a horse at work or show.

apprentice (1) One bound, often by a legal document, to learn a profession, as in an apprentice jockey (q.v.), apprentice trainer, etc. (2) A coaching whip similar to the cat o' nine tails.

apprentice allowance A racing term; a reduction in the weight carried by a horse ridden by an apprentice jockey (q.v.) when competing against jockeys; the amount of the allowance, as well as the conditions relating to such, varies from area to area; in US usually 10 pounds (4.5 kg) until the jockey has five wins, 7 pounds (3 kg) until the 35th win, or 5 pounds (2.25 kg) for one calendar year from the 35th win; is not granted apprentice jockeys (q.v.) when competing in stakes races (q.v.).

apprentice jockey Also known as apprentice, jockey apprentice, bug, or bug boy; a racing term; a rider, usually young, serving an apprenticeship to a jockey (q.v.) in the US and, in Britain, to a trainer; so called because of the "bug" or asterisk appearing next to the jockey's name in the official racing program; a rider who has not ridden a specified amount of winners within a specific time period; receives weight allowances on all their mounts (subject to race conditions) based on the number of winners they have ridden; in the US this allowance amounts to a 10 pound (4.5 kg) weight reduction until the 5th winner, 7 pounds (3 kg) until the 35th winner, and 5 pounds (2.25 kg) for one calendar year following the date of the 5th winner.

apprentice, the Slang; a severe whip formerly used by drivers of heavy coaches.

approach The act of drawing near to an object or point, as in a horse to a jump.

appui Also spelled appuy; a historical French dressage term; the feeling of contact between the horse and rider achieved through the reins as the horse accepts the bit on the bars of his mouth; is ideally firm, yet light.

appuy *see* APPUI

appuyer A French dressage term; two-track (q.v.).

appuyer en renvers A French dressage term; haunches-out (q.v.).

appuyer en travers A French dressage term; haunches-in (q.v.).

appuyer épaule en dedans A French dressage term; shoulder-in (q.v.).

appuyer épaule en dehors A French dressage term; shoulder-out (q.v.).

apricot dun Refers to coat color; the lightest shade of red dun (q.v.); the body hair is light red tending to a yellow shade with a pale red, brown, or flaxen mane and tail.

apron (1) A racing term; the paved area located between the grandstand and the racing surface. (2) Also known as skirt; a heavy skirt worn by a side-saddler (q.v.) to cover her legs, boots, and the side-saddle horns when mounted. (3) A cloth, rubber or leather covering used by drivers of horse drawn vehicles to keep them warm, dry, and clean.

apron face A face marking (q.v.); a wide, white blaze extending from the forehead to the muzzle and wrapping around and including both upper and lower lips.

AQHA (1) *see* AMERICAN QUARTER HORSE ASSOCIATION. (2) *see* AUSTRALIAN QUARTER HORSE ASSOCIATION

AQRA *see* AMERICAN QUARTER RACING ASSOCIATION

aquapuncture A type of acupuncture (q.v.); stimulation of precise body points along body meridians (q.v.) by injection of fluid such as water, oil, vitamin B, or herbal and homeopathic solutions into trigger points; the solution continues to stimulate the points for an additional 10 to 15 minutes after removal of the needles; used to control pain, treat physical issues, anesthetize, and/or reduce stress.

Arab Also known as Arabian Horse, Arabian, drinker of the wind (colloq.), and son of the desert (colloq.); one of the oldest and purest horse breeds having been clearly depicted on the walls of limestone caves with other animals of the hunt between 25,000 and 40,000 years ago; the first and most rigorous breeders of the Arab were the Bedouins; first written documentation of the breed dates back 3,000 years; the breed became even more cherished when the Islamic prophet Mohammed made the Arab a cornerstone in his Holy Wars – he improved his army by elevating the horse to a sacred level, promising his followers that if they bred and cared for fine cavalry horses they would be blessed; as the Moslem religion grew, the Arab was introduced into North Africa, Spain, and France; of three main types: Assil (q.v.), pure-bred Arab (q.v.), and the Arab breed (q.v.); used for riding and light draft; has excellent endurance and speed, a straight or distinctively dished profile, small ears, fine bone structure, and stands 14 to 15 hands; has only 17 thoracic vertebrae instead of 18 and 5 lumbar vertebrae instead of 6; may have a gray, bay, chestnut, black or, more rarely, roan coat.

Araba A Turkish horse-drawn wagon popular in the 18th and 19th centuries having a canopy top and crosswise seating; drawn by a pair of horses or oxen, driven by harem women, and guided by dismounted servants.

Arab breed One of three basic types of Arabian horse; includes the blood of horses with uncertain origins, or whose pedigree reflects the influence of the Berber, Persian, Syrian, Egyptian Arab, and other related breeds.

arabesque A vaulting position; the vaulter (q.v.) stands on the back of a moving horse on one leg with the other leg, usually straight, stretched out behind.

Arab Horse Society A British organization founded in 1918 to promote the breeding and encourage the re-introduction of Arab (q.v.) blood into English light-horse breeds; maintains registries for Arabs, Anglo-Arabs (q.v.), and part-bred Arabs (q.v.).

Arabian *see* ARAB

Arabian Horse *see* ARAB

Arabian Race A part-bred Arab (q.v.) bred at the Bablona stud, located in Hungary after 1816; the progeny of pure-bred Arab stallions crossed with mares of oriental appearance who carried strains of Spanish, Hungarian, and Thoroughbred (q.v.) blood; the foundation of the Shagya Arabian (q.v.).

arc A barrel racing term; the bend achieved by the horse when turning around a barrel, which correctly extends from his nose, through the poll, shoulder, and into the loin.

Arcera An ancient Roman four-wheeled, horse-drawn, covered carriage used by the sick or infirm; alleged to be the oldest Roman vehicle on record; drawn by either horses or oxen; superseded by the litter (q.v.).

arched back *see* ROUNDED BACK

arch pelham A bit having a single-piece mouthpiece that curves characteristically in the center to accommodate the tongue; has cheeks and is used with two sets of reins, a curb chain, and sometimes a lip strap.

arch roller *see* ANTI-CAST ROLLER

Ardennais Also known as "the cart horse of the north" or French Ardennais; a heavy-draft breed from the Ardennes region of France from which the name derived; originated approximately 2,000 years ago at which time it was smaller and less massive; in the early 19th century crossed with Arab (q.v.), Thoroughbred (q.v.), Percheron (q.v.), and Boulonnais to increase size and draft capability; is gentle, docile, and calm yet energetic, is tough, has a compact, yet large frame, stands 15 to 16 hands, and weighs 1,540 to 2,200 pounds (699–998 kg); may have a bay, roan, red roan, gray, palomino, or chestnut coat although brown and light chestnut coats are tolerated and black excluded; has a heavy head, a straight or snub profile, small ears, large eyes, a short neck and back, heavily muscled quarters and shoulders, short, feathered legs with a broad hoof, and an enormous bone structure; the stud book was established in 1929; used for heavy draft, farm work, and raised for human consumption.

Ardennais du Nord *see* TRAIT DU NORD

Ardennes *see* BELGIAN ARDENNES

Area International Trial Also known by the acronym AIT; a show jumping competition sponsored by the British Show Jumping Association (q.v.).

arena The specific area of any work-out, competition, or contest – physical, mental, or figurative; Latin meaning sand as used in an arena; from ancient Rome where the ground of the amphitheaters, upon which gladiators fought or wild animals were turned on human victims, was covered with sand to soak up spilled blood.

arena director A rodeo term; one responsible for conducting rodeos (q.v.) according to PRCA (q.v.) rules.

arena footing The surface material used in an arena (q.v.); may consist of grass, sand, wood products, rubber, leather, stone, or some combination thereof.

arena polo Also known as indoor polo; a polo game (q.v.) played in an enclosed arena approximately 300 by 150 feet (91 by 46 m) in size and having goalposts set at either end, 10 feet (3 m) apart; considerably smaller than a polo field (q.v.); the game follows the same basic rules and principles of field polo, although the strategies are different, and teams consist of only three members.

Argentine Criollo *see* CRIOLLO

Argentine Polo Pony Also known as Argentine Pony; a polo pony (q.v.) developed in Argentina by putting imported Thoroughbred (q.v.) stallions to native Criollo (q.v.) mares; is tough, distinctly Thoroughbred in appearance, but shorter strided and possessing better bone, stronger joints and sturdier hooves; stands about 15.1 hands.

Argentine Pony *see* ARGENTINE POLO PONY

Argentine snaffle A snaffle bit (q.v.) having a jointed snaffle mouthpiece and hinged shanks; used with a curb chain.

arginine An essential amino acid (q.v.), vital in the composition of proteins.

Ariègeois *see* MERENS

Arkle One of the finest steeplechasers (q.v.) of all time; a big, heavy bay with an incredible spring, he dominated steeplechasing (q.v.) for 3 seasons until a fractured pedal bone ended his career; ran 35 races; over fences, he was beaten only 4 times.

Arkwright bit Also known as Lowther bit or Lowther riding bit; a curb bit (q.v.) in which the curb rein hangs directly from the cheekpiece without a neck.

Arlington Cab A horse-drawn vehicle of the Hansom Cab (q.v.) type invented by Mr. Knight of Dorchester, England; the apron or half-door was replaced by tall curving doors with sliding glass; the doors extended from the roof footboard and formed a half-circle; the doors slid around to the side of the vehicle body in grooves; the doors could be either driver or passenger operated.

armchair ride (1) A racing term; an easily won victory that did not require the jockey (q.v.) to urge the horse forward. (2) A hunting term; a horse who is easy to hunt.

aromatherapy The use of essential oils (q.v.) to treat and heal emotional and physical ailments through the sense of smell.

arrhythmia Also known as cardiac arrhythmia or heartbeat irregularity; a fairly common disturbance of the heart rate and rhythm; may be treated with antiarrhythmic agents and may disappear or be less pronounced following exercise.

arterial bleeding Loss of blood from an artery (q.v.); bleeding is profuse, brisk, and bright red; pulsations may be visible and tissues surrounding the wound may swell rapidly.

arterial fibrillation A gross irregularity of heart rhythm with a variation in heart sound intensity and pulse due to rapid and ineffective contractions of the chambers of the heart; may occur in the absence of underlying cardiac disease or in conjunction with other cardiac disease such as mitral insufficiency; occurs most commonly in draft and other large horses; may be definitively diagnosed by the electrocardiogram (q.v.).

arteritis *see* EQUINE VIRAL ARTERITIS

artery One of a system of cylindrical vessels or tubes that convey the blood from the heart to all parts of the body, to be brought back to the heart by the veins.

arthritis Generally, inflammation of a joint (q.v.); specifically a complicated condition that may involve the bones, articular cartilages, joint capsule, and associated ligaments of a joint(s); includes serous arthritis (q.v.), osteoarthritis (q.v.), infectious arthritis (q.v.), and ankylosing arthritis (q.v.).

arthritis of the fetlock joint *see* OSSELETS

arthritis of the hock *see* HOCK SPAVIN

Arthrobotrys oligospora A species of predatory fungus found in many parts of the world used to control small strongyle (q.v.) populations by trapping and penetrating them, then absorbing their contents; research is underway to develop an oral product containing the fungal predator which, when administered to livestock, will be excreted in the feces (q.v.) along with the strongyle eggs or larvae, enabling them to attack the parasites before they can migrate onto surrounding soil or grass where they would be ingested during grazing; considered an effective alternative to chemical anthelmintics (q.v.).

arthroscope A narrow tube containing a fiber optic instrument connected to a video camera that is inserted into a joint via a small incision to enable viewing inside a joint or through which to conduct microscopic surgery.

arthroscopic surgery Also known as arthroscopy; microsurgery, generally in or around a joint, performed using an arthroscope (q.v.); less invasive than conventional surgery techniques, resulting in a swifter recovery.

arthroscopy *see* ARTHROSCOPIC SURGERY

articular cartilage Also known as joint cartilage or commonly as gristle; one of six types of cartilage (q.v.) found in the body structure of the horse; is firmly attached to and covers the ends of the bones where they meet in a joint (q.v.), protects the underlying bone, and transmits forces to the underlying subchondral bone; has limited powers of regeneration, and damage to it cannot be completely repaired.

articular fracture A break in a bone that extends into a joint.

articular windgall *see* ARTICULAR WINDPUFF

articular windpuff Also known as articular windgall; a soft, painless, fluid-filled swelling which develops between the cannon bone and the suspensory ligament (q.v.) due to excessive accumulation of synovial fluid; often occurs in conjunction with a tendinous windpuff (q.v.); may be caused by intense training followed by a period of rest, excessive exercise on hard surfaces, and the cumulative effects of imbalances produced by poor conformation or improperly trimmed hooves.

articulating ringbone A ringbone (q.v.) condition; bony growth has attached to the joints between the long and short pastern or the short pastern and the pedal bone; lameness usually results and there is no effective cure.

articulation (1) Limb joints; where two or more bones meet forming a joint. (2) The act or manner of moving a body part.

artificial aid Any means other than natural aids (q.v.) by which the rider communicates instruction to the horse including the use of spurs (q.v.), whip (q.v.), martingale (q.v.), and/or other gadgets.

artificial airs *see* ARTIFICIAL ALLURES

artificial allures Also known as artificial airs; any trained gait or pace of the horse, other than the walk, trot, and canter, i.e. the high and low airs (q.v.).

artificial breeding To generate progeny (q.v.) by means other than natural cover (q.v.); includes artificial insemination (q.v.) or embryo transfer (q.v.); not approved by some associations such as the Jockey Club (q.v.).

artificial coloring Any change of color to the coat, mane, tail, or forelock that does not result from natural processes, e.g. dyeing.

artificial drag A hunting term; a man-laid scent trail used in a drag hunt (q.v.); left by dragging, on foot or horseback, a scent-soaked cloth, sponge, etc. in a pattern mimicking a run of a fox; the scent liquid is generally strong-smelling and similar to the fox's scent, but not derived from the fox.

artificial insemination Also known as capsule or by the acronym AI; an unnatural method of impregnating the mare for the purpose of producing off-spring; semen collected from the stallion, using nonsurgical methods, is generally frozen and transported to the mare where it is deposited in the body of her uterus during estrus (q.v.) using a plastic insemination pipette; utilized when the stallion (q.v.) serves mares in widely spread locations, to protect a valuable stallion from injury during breeding, to increase the number of mares a given stallion can service, and to impregnate mares whose anatomical conformation precludes natural cover (q.v.); banned by some breed associations such as the Tennessee Walking Horse Breeder & Exhibitors Association, United States Trotting Association, the American Saddle Horse Association and the Jockey Club (q.v.).

artificial scent A hunting term; a manufactured scent similar to that of a fox or other prey laid in a drag hunt; may be produced from aniseed (q.v.), fox feces, solid litter from tame fox's kennel, or fox or mink secretions.

artificial vagina A device used to collect semen from stallions for artificial insemination (q.v.) or laboratory purposes; generally a rubber sheath, surrounded by warm water, encased in a metal cylinder into which the horse's penis is inserted and in which the semen is collected.

artist A coachman, deft in his handling of the whip and reins.

Art of Horsemanship, The A treatise on horse training and handling written by Xenophon (427–354 BC).

artzel A face marking; any form of white marking on the horse's forehead.

arve *see* AH

arytenoid cartilage Triangular-shaped cartilage (q.v.) located in the upper part of the entrance to the larynx (q.v.), the opening and closing of which it controls.

ascorbic acid *see* VITAMIN C

ascending oxer *see* STEP OXER

Art of Horsemanship, The A treatise on horse training and handling written by Xenophon (q.v.).

Ascot Landau A horse-drawn English vehicle of the Landau (q.v.) type used for the British Royal Family's traditional drive down the course at Royal Ascot.

aseptic Free from germs that cause disease.

ASH *see* AUSTRALIAN STOCK HORSE

ASHA *see* AMERICAN SADDLEBRED HORSE ASSOCIATION

as hounds ran Also known as the hounds ran; a hunting term; the distance covered by the hounds in a run (q.v.), measuring each turn from field to field, as opposed to the distance measured in a straight line from start to finish.

Asian Wild Horse *see* ASIATIC WILD ASS

Asiatic Wild Ass Also known as Onager; a wild ass (q.v.) of the genus *Equus*; of two subspecies: *Equus hemionus* and *Equus kiang*; has a rust-colored coat with a light dorsal stripe; travels in herds throughout Iran, Afghanistan, and northern India; has no domestic descendants.

Asiatic Wild Horse Also known as Asian Wild Horse, Mongolian Wild Horse or by the scientific name *Equus przewalski* 'Poliakov'; an ancient pony breed first discovered in 1881 by Colonel Poliakov in the Daqin Shan Mountains bordering the Gobi desert in Mongolia; although now extinct in the wild, a few animals remain in captivity; efforts are underway to re-establish the breed in the wild; historically used as mounts for the Huns and Chinese; stands 12 to 14 hands, has a palomino or yellow dun coat with dark legs, mane, and tail, mealy markings on the muzzle and zebra markings (q.v.); has a large, heavy head, broad forehead, long ears, small, almond-shaped eyes, short, bristly mane and tail, long back and short legs; is strong and hardy.

asil Also spelled asl; an Arabic word; a pure-bred Arab (q.v.) as out of an Arab mare served by a pure-bred Arab stallion.

Asinus isabellinus The scientific name for the Isabella quagga (q.v.).

ask the question Also known as question; to push a horse to his physical limits as in a race or gallop.

asl *see* ASIL

asparego *see* APAREGO PACK

asphyxia Interrupted breathing causing a lack of oxygen or excess of carbon dioxide in the body.

ass Also known as burro (particularly west of the Mississippi River, USA), donkey (particularly east of the Mississippi, USA), Rocky Mountain Canary, Colorado Mocking Bird, jackstock, or by the scientific term *Equus asinus* from which the current name derives; a quadruped of the horse family historically used as a beast of burden; descended from the African wild ass and includes the African wild ass, domestic donkey (q.v.), and onagers (q.v.); of four size classifications: miniature donkey (up to 36 inches [91 cm]), standard donkey (36 to 48 inches [91–122 cm]), large standard donkey (48 to 56 inches [122–142 cm]), and mammoth jackstock (54 inches [137 cm] and up for jennets and 56 inches [142 cm] and taller for jacks); used for breeding mules (q.v.), driving, packing, show, sheep protection, post-weaning foal companionship, and halter-breaking young calves and horses; an easy keeper and long lived, often living 30 to 40 years.

Assateague Also known as Assateague Pony; a pony originating on the island of Assateague off the Atlantic coast of the United States; adjacent to the Chincoteague Islands on which originated the Chincoteague Pony (q.v.), to which it is identical.

Assateague Pony *see* ASSATEAGUE

Assil Also known as Kocklani, Koklani, Kohuail, Koheil, Khamsa, or Kamsat (by the various different tribes that bred it); the true Bedouin Arab; can be classified into three sub-breeds: the Kuhailan (q.v.), the Siglavy (q.v.), and the Muniqi (q.v.).

Associate Farriers Company of London Also known by the acronym AFCL; a recognition of advanced farrier skill awarded by the Worshipful Company of Farriers (q.v.), London, England; superseded by the Associate of the Worshipful Company of Farriers (q.v.).

Associate of the Worshipful Company of Farriers Also known by the acronym AWCF; a certification of advanced farrier skill awarded by the Worshipful Company of Farriers (q.v.), London, England; to qualify, recipients must have previously obtained and held, for a minimum period of two years, a Diploma of the Worshipful Company of Farriers (q.v.) and passed written, oral, and practical examinations.

Assyrians The first military power to utilize troops of cavalry and war chariots in battle.

asterisk A figure resembling a star, thus *, used in printing and writing such as in-breeding publications, to denote an imported horse when placed in front of a horse's name, or when placed in front of a jockey's name, or beside the weight a horse is to carry, denotes an apprentice jockey (q.v.).

asternum A structure or piece of tissue in the region of, but not attached to, the sternum (q.v.).

as the hounds ran *see* AS HOUNDS RAN

Astley, Philip The father of the modern circus (q.v.); in 1769, 1,500 years after the last known Roman circus, he left the British Army and began to give trick riding exhibitions in London, England; his program included clowns, rope artists, acrobatics, High School (q.v.) acts, trick riding, and ballet on horseback; having determined it was easier to maintain balance on a horse if cantering in a circle rather than in 'en linge' (q.v.), he seated his audience in the round; the circus ring became standardized at 42 feet (13 m) in diameter, a size large enough to allow a horse to go fast, yet small enough to keep him under control.

astride Said of the rider; seated with one leg on each side of the horse.

astringent Any liquid substance used to constrict or tighten the tissues.

Asturcon *see* GALICIAN

Asturian *see* GALICIAN

ataxia Also known as wobbles, wobbler disease, or wobbler syndrome; loss of coordination of the muscles, especially of the extremities and broad posture, characterized by wandering or broad staggering movements; sometimes affecting, or the result of, nerve function.

at bay A hunting term; said of the quarry (q.v.), especially a stag, when it has turned to face hounds, which are held off by the huntsman (q.v.).

ATCP *see* AMERICAN TEAM PENNING CHAMPIONSHIPS

at fault Also known as to be at fault or fault; a hunting term; said of the hounds when checked (q.v.) or held.

at gait *see* AGISTMENT

at grass (1) *see* PASTURE NO. 1. (2) A horse spelled or resting from his usual routine as due to injury, age, or retirement.

atheroma Degenerative change in the inner and middle coats of the arteries.

atlas The first vertebra of the vertebral column (q.v.), which unites the neck with the bones at the back of the head in the cervical region and enables the head to move up and down.

at loss A hunting term; said of the hounds (q.v.) when they are unable to follow the line of the fox (q.v.).

at pasture Also known as out to pasture; said of a horse maintained in a fenced area on ground covered with native or cultivated grasses and grass-legume mixes.

at rest Said of a horse temporarily relieved of or not performing his normal routine or work.

Atropa belladonna *see* DEADLY NIGHTSHADE

atrophy The wasting away of the body, an organ, or body part, as caused by inadequate nutrition, injury, or inactivity; generally used to describe muscles.

at stud *see* STAND AT STUD

at the end of the halter Said of a horse sold with no guarantee other than title.

at walk *see* WALK NO. 2

auction Public sale of property such as horses, tack, and/or real estate to the highest bidder; payment is generally required at the "fall of the hammer" or declaration of sale delivered by the auctioneer (q.v.) unless other arrangements have been made.

auctioneer One whose business it is to sell things by auction (q.v.).

Australian Bow Wagon A horse-drawn farm wagon originally used in Victoria, Australia in the 1870s; drawn by a single heavy horse in shafts or by a tandem pair; had low, single-plank sides, a short wheel base, curved sideboards protecting both the front and rear wheels, and an unsprung axle.

Australian cheeker bridle *see* AUSTRALIAN NOSEBAND

Australian loose-ring cheek snaffle Also known as Fulmer snaffle; a bit consisting of a single jointed mouthpiece with long cheeks (q.v.) on either side and loose-rings attached to the long cheeks; may be used with or without bit keepers (q.v.) to alter pressure.

Australian noseband Also known as Australian cheeker bridle; a piece of tack; a noseband (q.v.) that attaches to the bridle headpiece, runs down the middle of the horse's face, splitting in two on the bridge of the nose and attaching inside the bit rings; lifts the bit in the mouth and prevents the horse from getting his tongue over it and applies pressure on the horse's face; used on pullers or horses who have a tendency to put their tongues over the bit.

Australian Pony A pony breed native to Australia which descended from Welsh Mountain ponies (q.v.) and Welsh ponies (q.v.) brought to Australia in 1803; by 1920 established as a fixed type; stands 12 to 14 hands, generally has a gray coat although any color is permitted by the breed society except piebald (q.v.) and skewbald (q.v.), has a light head, arched neck, full mane, high withers, short and straight back, a full girth, and short legs with good bone; is strong and well-balanced; used for riding; the stud book, maintained by the Australian Pony Stud Book Society (q.v.), was established in 1929.

Australian Pony Stud Book Society An Australian organization established in 1929 to oversee breeding and registration of, and maintain the Stud Book for, the Australian Pony (q.v.).

Australian Road Wagon A horse-drawn driving wagon, similar to the phaeton (q.v.), used on the rougher roads of the Australian outback; had a large umbrella basket and rearward boot (q.v.), narrow perch, pedal brake that operated on the rear wheels, and was hung on crosswise elliptical springs front and back.

Australian simplex safety iron A safety stirrup designed to ensure the escape of the foot in the event of a fall; has a forward curve on the outer side of the iron that allows the rider to readily kick free of the stirrup should trouble arise.

Australian Spring Dray A horse-drawn, two-wheeled heavy cart historically used in Australian cities to recover dead and/or injured horses; could be tipped in a rearward direction, had an ample, slatted ramp on which to load the horse or carcass, plank or panel sides, a low cross bench in the front from which the dray was driven and was hung on sideways semi-elliptical springs.

Australian Stock Horse Also known by the acronym ASH; originally horses of Waler (q.v.) origin; a warmblood descending from Arab (q.v.), Thoroughbred (q.v.), and Anglo-Arab (q.v.) stock put to native Australian mares; since the beginning of the 20th century outside contributions have been limited to Anglo-Arab blood; stands 14.2 to 16 hands, may have a coat of any solid color, has well-muscled legs, solid hooves, strong joints, good endurance, and ability to carry weight; appearance varies greatly; used in competitive sports including polo, on cattle stations, and as a cavalry mount; the Australian Stock Horse Society (q.v.) maintains the stud book which was established in 1971.

Australian Stock Horse Society An organization founded in New South Wales, Australia in the 1960s to promote and standardize breed characteristics of the Australian Stock Horse (q.v.), formerly known as Walers (q.v.), and to maintain the stud book.

Australian Veterinary Association Also known by the acronym AVA; the professional body representing veterinarians in Australia.

Australian Waler *see* WALER

Authorisation Spécial A pink card issued by the National Equestrian Federation (q.v.) to a rider that permits him to participate in international dressage, show jumping, or combined training events.

authorized agent *see* AGENT NO. 2

automatic timer Also known as electronic eye; an electronic apparatus used to record the times of equine competitions such as show jumping and rodeo; two timers are used, one placed at the start and the other at the course finish; the horse breaks an electronic beam on passing the starting and finishing points, which triggers and stops the timer.

autonomic nervous system That part of the nervous system which innervates the blood vessels, heart, viscera, smooth muscles and glands and regulates involuntary actions.

autopsy *see* POST-MORTEM EXAMINATION

Auto-top Buggy A horse-drawn, tray-bodied American buggy (q.v.) with a folding top similar to that of the Model T Ford, popular in the United States during the 1900s.

Autumn Double A racing term; an event consisting of two races, the Cesarewitch Stakes and the Cambridgeshire Stakes, held annually each autumn in Newmarket, England.

autumn hunting *see* CUB HUNTING

auxiliary reins Any rein (q.v.) used in conjunction with the normal reins, as when training or schooling a horse; include side reins (q.v.), draw reins (q.v.), etc.

auxiliary starting gate A racing term; a second starting gate (q.v.) placed alongside of the primary gate when the number of entrants exceeds the capacity of the primary starting gate.

Auxois A horse breed indigenous to 6th-century France at which time it descended from the old Burgundian horse; received infusions of Percheron (q.v.) and Boulonnais (q.v.) blood in the 19th century and, more recently, Ardennais (q.v.) and the Trait du Nord (q.v.); is quiet, good natured, willing, very strong, and possessed of great endurance; stands 15.1 to 16 hands and weighs 1,650 to 2,425 pounds (748–1,100 kg); may have a bay or roan coat, although chestnut and red roan do occur; the head is light and the legs slender in proportion to the heavy body; the breed is strictly controlled according to type and coat color; the Stud Book has been maintained since 1913 by the Syndicat du Cheval de Trait Ardennais de l'Auxois; used for heavy draft and farm work; branded on the left neck with the letters TX.

AVA (1) *see* AMERICAN VAULTING ASSOCIATION. (2) *see* AUSTRALIAN VETERINARY ASSOCIATION

Avelignese An ancient coldblood pony originating in Avelengo, Italy, from which the name derived; traces to the Middle Ages, sharing heritage with the Haflinger (q.v.) through the foundation sire Folie out of a native mare and sired by the Arab stallion El Bedavi XXII; bred in the mountain areas of northern, central, and southern Italy; generally has a chestnut or golden coat with a flaxen mane and tail; a blaze is common and white on the legs is minimal; has a light head with a slightly concave profile, broad forehead, muscular neck, short back and legs, muscular croup, hard hoof, and stands to 14 hands; is frugal, hardy, docile, quiet, trustworthy, and resistant to fatigue; bear a brand featuring the edelweiss with the letters HI in the center (Haflinger Italy) while the Haflinger has the same brand centered with an H (Haflinger); used for medium-heavy draft, riding, packing, and farm work.

aveola A small cavity, cell, or pit on the surface of an organ, i.e., the lungs.

average The mean sum of a score, e.g. the sum of all scores divided by the number of competitors.

Average-Earnings Index Also known by the acronym AEI; a racing term; a breeding statistic that compares racing earnings of a stallion or mare's foals to those of all other foals racing at that time; 1.00 is considered average.

Avermectins A group of chemical compounds, derived from a fungus discovered in Japan in 1975, effective in very low doses against nematode and external parasites; Ivermectin (q.v.) is the most commonly used.

Avondale *see* GOVERNESS CART

avulsion The pulling or tearing away of a part of a structure as in an avulsion fracture.

avulsion of the hoof wall at the heel Also known as heel crack or heel avulsion; a disruption in the horny wall at the heel; may begin as a small separation at the heel and gradually progress until the hoof wall at the quarter becomes separated from the underlying dermal laminae (q.v.); most commonly the result of trauma; lameness ranges from mild to severe.

AWCF *see* ASSOCIATE OF THE WORSHIPFUL COMPANY OF FARRIERS

axle Also known as axle tree (because the axle was originally made of wood); the metal axis upon which the wheels of a vehicle turn; consists of two axle arms (q.v.) connected by the axle bed (q.v.).

axle arm One of two arms on which the vehicle wheel rotates.

axle bed (1) The strip of metal connecting the two axle arms in a vehicle. (2) The center transverse member of the bottom of the carriage of a four-wheeled horse-drawn vehicle; the counter part of the transom; it takes the perch bolt in the center and is bolted to the futchells (q.v.) and wheel stays if used.

axle tree *see* AXLE

axle-tree maker Also known as fireman; one responsible for forging and shaping the iron used in the making of axles (q.v.) for horse-drawn vehicles.

axial Situated in, around, or along the axis of the body.

axis (1) An imaginary line through the center of the body of the horse around which all or part of the body is symmetrically arranged. (2) The second bone in the backbone or vertebral column of the horse; permits head rotation and connects to the atlas (q.v.).

away from you A hunting term; said by a member of the field to indicate there is a ditch on the far side of a fence.

Aylesbury Wagon A box-type, horse-drawn English farm or road wagon with high spindle sides and a relatively short wheel base; drawn by a single horse.

Ayrshire Harvest Cart A low-sided cart used in the western Lowlands of Scotland; had an unsprung or dead axle and semi-permanent end ladders.

Azaline A tub-bodied horse-drawn vehicle of the Buggy (q.v.) type popular in Pennsylvania, USA; had parallel sides.

azotemia An excess of nitrogen-containing compounds in the blood.

azoturia *see* EQUINE MYOGLOBINURIA

azulejo *see* GREY OVERO

Azteca A relatively new breed developed in Mexico by crossing Andalusian (q.v.) stallions with Quarter Horse (q.v.) mares or vice versa, or by crossing Andalusian stallions with improved Criollo (q.v.) mares; must have a minimum of ⅜ and a maximum of ⅝ Spanish or Quarter Horse blood, while blood from horses not registered as Criollo (q.v.) may not exceed ¼; breed selection began in 1972; a hardy, fast, and agile horse used for leisure riding, competitive sports, light draft, and farm work; females must stand at least 14.3 hands and males 15 hands; all solid coat colors are acceptable.

B

babble A hunting term; the speaking of a hound other than when on the line of a fox (q.v.).

babbler A hunting term; a hound who, when on the hunt, speaks (q.v.) for reasons other than being on the line of a fox (q.v.), e.g. from excitement, when unsure of the scent, or when trailing the lead hound by a good distance.

Babieca The Andalusian (q.v.) mount of Spain's national hero Ruy Diaz; died in the 11th century at the age of 40 and was buried at the monastery of San Pedro de Cardena, where a monument stands in his honor.

babesiosis *see* EQUINE PIROPLASMOSIS

Babolna The Hungarian state stud, famous for its Arab (q.v.) breeding program.

baby A racing term; a two-year-old horse.

Baby Huey *see* SEATTLE SLEW

baby race An American racing term; a 2-, 3-, or 4-furlong (402, 604, or 805 m) race for two-year-olds, held early in the year.

babysitter (1) A made, gentle horse used by a trainer to give lessons to novice riders. (2) An easy-to-control cow or horse.

baby teeth *see* DECIDUOUS TEETH

back (1) *see* REIN BACK. (2) A racing term; to place a bet on a horse. (3) That portion of the horse's body between the withers (q.v.) and the loins (q.v.). (4) *see* NUMBER FOUR POSITION. (5) Also known as backing; to accustom the unbroken horse to the saddle and weight of the rider. (6) An English term; to mount a horse for the first time after breaking (q.v.) and sit upon his back. (7) Also known as backing; a harness term; to make a horse put his weight into the shafts (q.v.).

back at the knee *see* BACKWARD DEVIATION OF THE CARPAL JOINTS

backband The leather strap that passes over the back of the horse to which the tugs are buckled in harness tack, threaded through a slot in the saddle; normally made of leather with four rows of double stitching; strength is essential as it may have to support the weight of the vehicle through the tugs (q.v.) and shafts.

back blood A hereditary trait found in a family of horses which may influence the conformation of succeeding generations.

backbone *see* VERTEBRAL COLUMN

back-breeding Also known as back-crossing; to mate a heterozygote (q.v.) offspring with either of its parental homozygotes (q.v.); characteristics usually show 1:1, thus if a pure black stallion is mated to all homozygous chestnut mares, black foals (heterozygotes) will result; if the resulting black fillies are bred back to their black sire, their progeny will be one pure black to every one impure black; can be employed as a means of test-mating or test-crossing to determine whether a horse will consistently produce the same type or will produce offspring of two different types.

back cinch *see* FLANK CINCH

back cross The progeny resulting from mating a heterozygote (q.v.) offspring with either of its parental homozygotes (q.v.).

back-crossing *see* BACK-BREEDING

Back Door Cab A horse-drawn vehicle of the Wagonette-Brougham (q.v.) type popular in the late 19th century; entered from the rear, hung on sideways-elliptical springs front and rear, and used for both public and private transportation purposes.

Backdoor Omnibus *see* BOULNOIS CAB

backed *see* BACKHANDER

back 'em off A cutting term; said of the rider; to back (q.v.) the horse away from the cow because he is either stepping into the cow, or is ahead of it.

backer (1) A racing term; one who places a bet on a horse. (2) One who rides a horse for the first time.

back fence A cutting term; the designated area of the fence located directly behind the herd; in competition, the horse is penalized three points each time the cow being worked stops or turns within 3 feet (91 cm) of this fence.

backgammon board *see* GAMMON BOARD

backhand cut A polo term; any stroke of the ball hit backwards at an angle away from the horse.

backhander Also known as backed, backhand shot, and back shot; a polo stroke in which the player hits the ball in the direction opposite to that traveled by the horse; may be a backhand cut (q.v.), tail shot (q.v.), or cut away shot (q.v.).

backhand shot *see* BACKHANDER

backing (1) *see* BACK NO. 5. (2) *see* BACK NO. 7

back jockey The top skirt (q.v.) of a western saddle.

back line (1) A polo term; a line drawn perpendicular to each side of the goal area on either end of a polo field (q.v.) which marks the longitudinal terminus of the playing field; a ball passing beyond this line is considered out of play. (2) *see* TOP LINE

back not round Said of a horse who hollows or flattens his back, instead of dropping his haunches and swinging well under his body with his hind legs.

back of the knee *see* BACKWARD DEVIATION OF THE CARPAL JOINTS

backover saddle fall To kick out of the stirrups and roll backwards off the croup (q.v.) of a running or galloping horse; a maneuver performed by trick riders or movie stunt people.

back pad A non-rigid protective pad used to protect the back of the horse and to provide secure footing for the vaulter (q.v.) when standing on the horse's back; may not extend more than 28 inches (71 cm) from the back edge of the vaulting roller (q.v.), nor exceed 36 inches (91 cm) width or ⅘ inch (2 cm) thickness, except directly under the roller where any thickness is allowed.

back racking The removal of feces (q.v.) from the horse's rectum by hand.

back shot *see* BACKHANDER

backside *see* BACKSTRETCH

back strap (1) A single or double leather strap that holds the crupper dock (q.v.) in position around the dock (q.v.) of the horse's tail; passed through a dee on the back of the pad in a harness crupper and to the saddle on a saddle crupper to which it may be buckled or stitched; prevents the saddle or harness pad from shifting onto the horse's withers (q.v.). (2) The strip of leather that runs from the top of the counter (q.v.) down the back seam of a riding boot to protect the stitching from wear and to create a more finished look.

backstretch (1) Also known as backside; a racing term; the straight part of the track on the far side (q.v.) between the turns. (2) Also known as backside; a racing term; that area of the track consisting of the stable area, dormitories, track kitchen, chapel, and recreation area for stable employees.

back up (1) A racing term; said of a horse who slows down noticeably when being raced. (2) *see* COLD BACK. (3) *see* REIN BACK

backward deviation of the carpal joints Also known as palmar deviation of the carpal joints, calf knees, sheep knees, back at the knee, back of the knee, and incorrectly, as tied-in below the knee; a conformation defect in which the horse's forelegs bend slightly back at the knees giving a concave or cupped appearance; the opposite of buck knee (q.v.).

backwards shoe Also known as reverse shoe, open toe egg-bar, or Napoleon shoe; a conventional horseshoe attached to the hoof in reverse position; the heels of the shoe support the toe of the hoof while the toe of the shoe supports the heels of the hoof; generally requires extra nail holes.

bacteria Any of the disease-producing microscopic organisms of the class *Schizomycetes*, having round, spiral, or rod-shaped bodies, which occur in soil, water, organic matter, and animal tissues.

bactericidal Any substance used to destroy the growth of bacteria (q.v.).

bacteriostatic Any substance used to prevent the multiplication of some bacteria (q.v.) and some other disease-causing agents, but not destroy them.

bacterin A suspension of killed or attenuated bacteria (q.v.) injected into a living body to stimulate development of immunity to the same kind of bacteria.

bacterium The singular of bacteria (q.v.).

bad actor A difficult and uncomfortable horse to ride.

bad cow *see* ALLIGATOR

bad doer A horse who lacks appetite, usually because of illness, pain, fatigue, nervousness, and/or loneliness.

Baden-Baden An international racing venue; the location of the Iffezheim race-course.

Badge of Honor An award presented by the FEI (q.v.) to riders competing in Prix des Nations (q.v.) events.

badge horse *see* BADGER

badger Also known as badge horse; a racing term; an inexpensive horse used by the owner to qualify him for track privileges.

badger-pied Refers to hound coat color; having a fawn- or cream-colored head, legs, body, and stern with the ears and back shading into black with lighter tips to the ears.

bad hands Said of a rider whose hands are heavy, rough, and insensitive on the rein and therefore on the mouth of the horse through the bit; the opposite of good hands (q.v.).

badikins A swingle tree (q.v.) when used with a farm horse.

Badminton (1) Also known as Badminton House; the location of the first three-day event horse trials held in Great Britain; first sponsored by the then Duke of Beaufort in 1949, it has been held annually since as the Badminton Horse Trials (q.v.). (2) The home of the Duke of Beaufort's Foxhounds, a line of foxhunting hounds dating to 1720.

Badminton Horse Trials Also known as Badminton Three Day Horse Trials; a three-day horse trial (q.v.) event held annually since 1949 at Badminton House near the village of Badminton, England.

Badminton House *see* BADMINTON

Badminton Three Day Horse Trials *see* BADMINTON HORSE TRIALS

bad traveler A horse who does not travel nor haul well, being anxious.

bag fox Also known as bagman or dropped fox; a hunting term; a fox caught and held in captivity until needed for a hunt (q.v.), at which time it is turned loose at a specified location in advance of the oncoming hounds (q.v.); prohibited by many foxhunting associations including the Master of Foxhounds Association in Britain.

Baggage Cart A two-wheeled, horse-drawn vehicle used to transport military stores; usually hooded with low, wickerwork sides and solid or disc-type wheels; sometimes drawn by a pair of horses in double shafts or pole gear (q.v.), but more commonly drawn by a single horse; used from the late Middle Ages through the mid-17th century.

Baggage Wagon A larger, four-wheeled version of the Baggage Cart (q.v.) drawn by two or more horses in pole gear (q.v.).

bagging A breaking (q.v.) technique similar to sacking out (q.v.), in which the horse is restrained on either side by side-lines attached to the halter on one end and affixed to two sturdy posts or walls on the other; a bag is waved about his head and body to encourage him to kick, which when he does so, causes him to fall.

bagman (1) *see* BAG FOX. (2) A commercial traveler or salesman; (obs).

Bagman's Gig A two-wheeled horse-drawn vehicle of the Gig (q.v.) type; seated two, was drawn by a single horse, and equipped with a spacious luggage boot (q.v.) used for transporting commercial samples.

bag of marbles Said of a horse who has multiple bone fractures (q.v.) in a small area.

Bahama grass *see* BERMUDA GRASS

Baiga Any Russian horse race 9 to 18 miles (15–30 km) long when held cross-country and open to unlimited numbers of riders or 9 to 12 miles (15–20 km) long when conducted on a racetrack, in which case there is a limit of 20 riders.

baited An obsolete coaching term; said of a horse when stabled and fed.

balance (1) Said of the horse when his weight and the weight of the rider are distributed equally over the foot of each leg; a balanced horse will move freely and correctly. (2) Said of the horse's foot, when viewed from the front or rear, if the medial axis of the leg, pastern and foot are in a straight line, and when viewed from the side if the medial axis of the pastern coincides with the axis of the foot which is parallel to the hoof wall at the toe.

balanced seat Said of the rider having a secure, upright posture independent of the reins who thus does not interfere with the movements or equilibrium of the horse.

balance not maintained Said of the horse when his weight, and that of the rider, are not equally distributed over the foot of each leg, resulting in poorly executed movements or gaits.

balance rein A training tool utilized to teach bridleless riding to a horse using such methods as TTEAM (q.v.); a round, ½ inch (13 mm) rope or strap placed around the base of the horse's neck which, in conjunction with a bridle, acts much like a rein; an upward motion of the rein can encourage the horse to shift his weight off his forehand and move into self-carriage thus enabling him to achieve roundness and lengthening of the neck.

balancing strap A leather strap attached to the center of the off-side cantle of the side-saddle (q.v.) which runs on top of the girth; sometimes used as a stabilizing hand hold for the side-saddler (q.v.).

bald (1) Without hair. (2) Said of a bald faced (q.v.) horse.

bald face Also known as white face; a face marking (q.v.) consisting of a wide, white blaze covering most of the face including the forehead, the area around the eyes, the nostrils, and most of the upper lip, or a portion thereof, often extending into the cheeks.

balding gag bit A bit (q.v.) consisting of a jointed mouthpiece (q.v.) with large, loose-ring cheek gags used with a single rein; prevents the effect of the gag until considerable pressure is applied; commonly used on polo ponies.

balding gag bridle A headstall used in conjunction with a balding gag bit (q.v.).

balding girth A leather girth (q.v.) consisting of a single piece of leather split into three sections below the buckle attachment, which are plaited under the belly; reduces the girth width in the area of the forearm and the potential for chaffing or galling (q.v.) the horse; the center section is generally reinforced by additional leather.

baldy A white-faced cow.

bale (1) To form into a bundle or bale, as in hay (q.v.). (2) Compressed hay formed into a square-shaped bundle and bound with wire or twine. (3) A partition suspended horizontally from the ceiling at trace height to separate horses tied parallel to each other in an enclosed area, thus creating open, individual stalls; usually a thick piece of wood about 7 feet long by 1 foot 6 inches wide (213 × 46 cm).

Balearic An ancient pony breed found on the island of Majorca off the coast of Spain; may have a bay or brown coat, is generally Roman-nosed, and has a fine head; used for draft and driving.

Bali A Balinese pony breed believed to have descended from the Ancient Asiatic Pony; has an upright mane and is generally bay with a black mane and tail, eel stripes on the legs, a black dorsal stripe, and dark points; is strong, frugal, quite docile and very quiet, has low withers and a short, straight back, and stands 12 to 13 hands; used for riding and packing.

Balios Also spelled Balius; in mythology, one of two immortal horses, the other being Xanthos (q.v.) that Poseidon gave to Peleus as a wedding present; was the offspring of Zephyrus, the west wind (or Zeus), and the Harpy Podarge; pulled Achilles' chariot during the Trojan War.

Balius *see* BALIOS

balk Also spelled baulk and known as jib; a vice; the refusal of a horse to pass or jump a certain point or object, ultimately stopping and refusing to move forward; may back away from the object.

balky horse A horse who stops and refuses to move.

ball *see* MEDICINE BALL

ball a horse Also known as balling; to administer gelatin-encapsulated medicine to a horse using a balling gun (q.v.), balling iron, or by hand.

ball and bucket race A mounted event in which competitors make repeated trips from one end of an arena to the other carrying one ball at a time and placing that ball in a bucket; the winner is the one who moves all the balls from one end of the field to the other in the shortest amount of time.

ball and socket joint A joint (q.v.); the point of junction of two moveable bones in which the end of one bone rests in a socket or cup of another, as in the hip joint.

ballet on horseback *see* DRESSAGE

balling (1) Said of snow when it forms into a compact ice-like lump in the space within a horseshoe (q.v.) in horses ridden in the snow; may be prevented by applying grease to soles of the hoof or using a balling pad (q.v.). (2) *see* BALL A HORSE

balling gun An out-dated tubular device made of wood, leather, steel, or brass used to administer a ball (q.v.) to a horse.

balling pad A rubber pad fitted between the horseshoe (q.v.) and hoof to prevent snow from packing into the area.

balloon bit A hack curb bit (q.v.) with a fancy cheek (q.v.) in the shape of a balloon.

ballotade An air above the ground (q.v.) in which the horse half rears, then jumps forward, drawing his hind legs up below his quarters (all four feet are at the same height), before landing on all four feet; the horse shows his heels as though he is about to kick, but does not throw them out.

balloted out Said of a horse excluded by a draw when the number of horses entered for a competitive event exceeds the time available to run the event; in especially well-supported forms of competition, such as eventing [q.v.], some organizing bodies operate a scheme whereby competitors can indicate the degree of priority they place on participation in particular events (being allowed a limited number of "priority" events); in such cases, the balloting system is first applied to those for whom that particular event is not a main priority; may also occur in racing if the number of declared entries exceeds the safety limit for a particular race; in some races, especially handicaps, the balloting process is confined to the lower-weighted entries.

balls *see* TESTES

Baluchi A pony breed indigenous to Baluchistan, in Punjab, India; stands 15.2 hands (155 cm) and has a bay, chestnut or gray coat.

Bampton Fair A fair held in Devon, England annually each October, since 1258; noted for the sale of Exmoor Ponies (q.v.) occuring there.

Banamine The trade name for a non-steroidal, anti-inflammatory (q.v.) drug known as flunixin meglumine used to control inflammation and pain associated with colic (q.v.) and muscle injury.

Banbury bit (1) *see* BANBURY CURB. (2) *see* BANBURY POLO PELHAM

Banbury curb Also known as Banbury bit; a bit with cheeks (q.v.) which revolve independently around the hour-glass-shaped mouthpiece; the shape of the bit prevents the horse from taking hold of it with his teeth, while the independently moving cheeks discourage one-sidedness (q.v.).

Banbury polo pelham Also known as Banbury bit; a pelham bit (q.v.) having a straight mouthpiece with an hour-glass shaped center; the mouthpiece slots into the cheeks, which allows the cheeks to move independently of each other.

band *see* HERD

bandage (1) A leg wrapping used to provide support or protection against injury to the horse's lower leg; types include standing bandage (q.v.), exercise bandage (q.v.), stable bandage (q.v.), and stocking bandage (q.v.). (2) A strip of cloth or gauze used in dressing and binding wounds, restraining hemorrhages, etc.; includes pressure bandage (q.v.) and spider-web bandage (q.v.). (3) To dress a wound; to apply a bandage to.

bandage bow Also known as compression bow; a bowed tendon (q.v.); enlarged, swollen, and/or torn or broken tendon fibers and/or tendon sheaths caused by too tight or uneven wrapping of the legs; results in loss of circulation to the tissue, swelling, reduced nutrition to and removal of waste products from the tissue, and reduced tendon viability (ability to contract and expand); soft tissue fibers are pushed towards the cannon bone and tear; has the appearance of a bow-string drawn back from the wood of the bow.

bandana Also spelled bandanna; a large, colorfully printed kerchief popularized by the cowboys of the American West.

bandanna *see* BANDANA

Bandy A native horse-drawn cart used in India; had a small platform rigged between two disc wheels supported by an unsprung or dead axle and sometimes hooded by a canopy of rough matting; drawn either by a pair of large ponies or a yoke (q.v.) of small oxen.

bandy legs *see* LATERAL DEVIATION OF THE CARPAL JOINTS

bandy-legged (1) Also known as bow-legged; said of a horse displaying lateral deviation of the carpal joints (q.v.). (2) Said of a rider having legs set wide apart at the knees and close at the ankles; results in greater comfort when riding a horse; the term may have been coined in the 17th century by a comparison of the legs to a curved stick called a "bandy" used in the game of hockey.

banged *see* BANG TAIL

bangtail (1) Slang; a race horse (q.v.). (2) *see* BANG TAIL

bang tail Also known as square tail, banged, or spelled bangtail; said of the horse's tail when tied short or cut off square below the points of the hocks; in Australia, a tail which has been squarely cut below the last bone of the tail.

bang up (1) Also known as banging up; to tie up the tail of draft or harness horses so that the tail hair does not catch in the harness (q.v.) and reins (q.v.). (2) An obsolete coaching term; said of a horse-drawn vehicle when elaborately appointed purely for leisure driving.

bank Any natural or artificial jumping obstacle consisting of a constructed mound of dirt with a platform or flat top, a slope on the take-off side, and a steep downside; usually covered with grass.

bank and ditch A jumping obstacle consisting of a constructed mound of dirt with a platform or flat top and a ditch located at the base of the mound on the take-off side; usually covered with grass; in natural settings the ditch may not necessarily be on the take-off side; also, especially in Ireland, banks may have ditches on both sides.

banker (1) A horse who jumps on and off a bank (q.v.) rather than over it. (2) A British term; a horse who attempts to negotiate an obstacle that is not a bank as though it were, e.g. a hedge as though it were a solid bank. (3) A British racing term; a horse believed certain to win a race.

banker bet A British racing term; a bet placed on a horse thought to be a certain winner.

bar (1) Also known as bars of the mouth; the portion of the lower jaw of a horse between the incisors (q.v.) and molars, on which the bit mouthpiece lies. (2) Also known as saddle bars or bars of the saddle; metal projections located under the saddle flap and built into the sweat flap, to which the stirrup leathers (q.v.) are attached; open towards the rear of the saddle. (3) Also known as bar of the hoof; the continuation of the wall of the hoof which turns inward at the heel and runs parallel to the frog; an important portion of the weight-bearing surface of the foot. (4) *see* SWINGLE TREE

Barb Formerly known as Barbary Horse; an ancient oriental breed originating along the Barbary coast region of North Africa which is now Morocco, Algeria, Tunisia, and Libya; introduced into Europe in the 7th century where it had considerable influence on other breeds such as the Andalusian (q.v.); nearly died out as a pure-bred in the mid-19th century; is currently raised as a pure-bred among the nomadic populations of North Africa, while elsewhere the breed has been crossed with the English Thoroughbred (q.v.) or Arab (q.v.) as in the Libyan Barb or Libyan; is athletic and unusually resistant to changes in climate, fatigue, and disease; develops late and does not reach maturity until its 6th year; the coat may be brown, black, bay, dark chestnut, or gray; stands 14 to 15 hands and has a long head, sloping quarters, and rather low-set tail; is extremely fast over short distances and possesses great stamina over longer ones; is an easy keeper; used for riding.

Barbary Horse *see* BARB

barbed wire Also known as wire, devil's rope or devil's hatband; thin strands of wire twisted together, having sharp-pointed barbs projecting at even and short intervals, stranded between fence posts to contain livestock; until 1868 all fencing wire used in the United States was smooth, without barbs of any kind.

barbed wire boom The period between 1868 and 1888 during which more than 700 barbed wire (q.v.) designs were patented in the United States.

Barbican, The A horse repository located in London, England specializing in the sale of commercial horses, notably those used to pull funeral carriages; closed about 1920.

bar bit A bit with a straight or slightly curved and solid mouthpiece.

Barco-de-tierra The Spanish equivalent of an American Landship (q.v.); a rough-made horse-drawn earth-boat or wagon used by the Spanish settlers on the South American Pampas; had wickerwork sides, high wheels with numerous spokes, and was drawn by pairs or larger teams of horses or oxen.

bardella A heavy stock saddle (q.v.) with hooded stirrups, used by the Italian butteri (q.v.).

Bardi Horse *see* BARDIGIANO

Bardigiano Also known as Bardi Horse; an ancient mountain pony originating in the northern Appenine region of Bardi, Italy; is almost identical to the Haflinger (q.v.) and resembles the Dale (q.v.) and Mèrens; stands 13.1 to 14.1 hands (males under 13.2 hands cannot be registered); the coat may be bay, brown, or black, while chestnut and light bay are not allowed by the breed registry; limited white markings on the legs and a small star are allowed; has a small head, broad forehead, full fetlock, small ears, a substantial neck with a good arch, wide withers, medium back, short loins, deep girth, wide chest, and well-formed legs with clean joints; is strong, hardy, docile, and quick moving; used for riding, light draft, and farm work

bardot A French term; a hinny (q.v.).

bards Any of various pieces of defensive armor historically worn by the horse to protect the breast and flanks from wounds in combat and, occasionally, for ornamental purposes.

bareback *see* BAREBACK RIDING

bareback riding Also known as bareback or Indian style; to ride a horse without the aid of a saddle or blanket.

barefoot Also known as unshod or smooth; said of a horse without horseshoes (q.v.).

Bareme A French term; any of three rules tables established by the Fédération Equestre Internationale (q.v.) by which show jumping competitions are judged; Table A covers jumping only, and Table C, speed.

Barenger, James (1780–1831) A noted British equestrian artist.

barge (1) An American horse-drawn vehicle used to transport large numbers of passengers and luggage; had a long, covered body with open sides, curtains, and inward-facing bench seats, was entered from the rear, and drawn by four horses driven from a low front seat. (2) A roomy, usually flat-bottomed boat used chiefly for the transport of goods on inland waterways; traditionally propelled by towing, as by a horse.

barge horse Any horse used to pull a barge along a canal as was common in England and North America until the late 19th century; horses were either ridden or led along towpaths located parallel to the waterways, or walked freely if fitted with a nosebag to prevent browsing en route.

bark An American hunting term; the cry of a hound or fox.

barker Also known as dummy foal, wanderer, convulsive foal, or barker foal; a foal afflicted with neonatal maladjustment syndrome (q.v.), in which the foal may "bark"; lethal in 50 percent of cases.

Barker Brougham A small, four-wheeled, horse-drawn carriage of the Brougham (q.v.) type drawn by a single horse in shafts; seated two forward-facing passengers, was low-slung, fully paneled with an upholstered and fully enclosed body, and had elegant and generous curves.

barker foal *see* BARKER

Barker Quarter Landau A horse-drawn vehicle of the Landau (q.v.) type used in the mid-19th century; had a dropped center or well for the passengers' feet and curved rather than square corners.

barley (1) Also known as barley grain; a grain from the cereal plant of the same name and of the species *Hordeum*; the most widely grown grain crop in the world today and the fourth most commonly grown crop in the United States; comparable to oats with a protein content of 12 percent and a fiber content ranging from 5 to 6 percent; high in niacin, low in fiber, and considered a heavy feed; easier to overfeed than oats or corn and may upset the digestive system; more easily digested and its nutrient better utilized if fed in a crushed, crimped, rolled, or ground form. (2) *see* BARLEY GRASS

barley grain *see* BARLEY

barley grass A cereal plant of the species *Hordeum*; the most widely grown grain crop in the world today; produces barley grain (q.v.) fed as a supplement to horses.

barley hay Cut and dried grass hay (q.v.) made from barley (q.v.) grain grass; contains approximately 5 percent digestible protein and 27 percent fiber.

Barlow, Francis (1626–1704) A noted sporting artist.

bar mouth A generic term; any straight-mouth snaffle bit (q.v.).

barn (1) A covered building in which hay and grain are stored and domestic animals housed. (2) *see* TRAINING BARN

barn crazy (1) Said of a horse who resents being retained in an enclosed area such as a barn, preferring movement and open space as provided by a pasture, paddock, or an in-and-out stall (q.v.). (2) *see* BARN SOUR

barn sour Also known as barn crazy or herd bound; the reluctance of a horse, cow, etc. to leave the herd, a particular equine buddy, or a physical location that represents security as would be afforded by a herd (the barn or the pasture which represents the herd's focal point – food, water, and social interaction) because of the anxiety produced by separation; a primal safety instinct.

baroque movement The manner in which a horse moves as characterized by high, round and elastic strides with much suspension; so called because it was characteristic of the manège horses of the 17th century; today such movement is typical of Andalusians (q.v.) and Lipizzans (q.v.).

Barouche An ancient four-wheeled horse-drawn vehicle of the coach family; had full undergear and lower panels, but no upper panels, a half-hood which covered the rear seat only, and a box seat for the driver raised well above the bodywork; passengers normally faced in the direction of travel, although some vehicles had folding seats on which others might be seated vis-à-vis (q.v.); generally a town vehicle used for summer driving drawn by a pair of horses in pole gear (q.v.); derived from the Latin birotus meaning two-wheeled.

Barouche Landau *see* LANDAU BAROUCHE

Barouche Sociable *see* SOCIABLE BAROUCHE

Barouchet A smaller, lighter version of the Barouche (q.v.) drawn by a single horse.

barrage *see* JUMP OFF

Barraud, Henry (1811–1874) A British equestrian artist of French descent; collaborated with his brother William Barraud (q.v.) to create portraiture of Hunts, huntsmen, and well-known Masters of Hounds including the famous work of John Warde (q.v.) on his horse Blue Ruin.

Barraud, William (1810–1850) A British equestrian artist of French descent; collaborated with his brother Henry Barraud (q.v.) to create portraiture pictures of Hunts, huntsmen, and well-known Masters of Hounds including the famous work of John Warde (q.v.) on his horse Blue Ruin.

barrel (1) The part of the horse's body between the forearms (q.v.) and loins (q.v.). (2) An empty metal or wooden 44 gallon (200 liter) vessel, approximately cylindrical, used as a turning point in a barrel race (q.v.). (3) *see* VAULTING BARREL

barrel horse Any horse used as a mount by a barrel racer (q.v.) to compete in a barrel race (q.v.); generally exhibits great speed, power, and agility; Quarter Horses (q.v.) or Quarter Horse crosses are commonly used.

barrel race A timed western riding competition in which the rider must circle three barrels set in a clover-leaf pattern; the distance between the barrels may vary; the winner is the rider who successfully rides around all three barrels and crosses the finish line without toppling a barrel, in the fastest time.

barrel racer One who barrel races (q.v.).

barrel turn A cutting horse term; an undesirable turn of the cutting horse executed on the forehand rather than the haunches.

Barrel Top Wagon Also known as Bow Top Wagon, Leeds Wagon, Lincolnshire Wagon, Midland Wagon, Yorkshire Wagon, or Bell Wagon; a horse-drawn vehicle of the Gypsy Wagon (q.v.) type; was light, unlikely to overturn, and inconspicuous; has low side walls surmounted by a bowed wooden roofing frame which supported a green canvas sheet to keep rain out.

barren Also known as barren mare or, in Scotland, eild; said of a mare who is sterile (q.v.), infertile (q.v.), or not in foal.

barren mare *see* BARREN

barrier (1) Also known as tape; a string, elastic band, or electronic beam that serves as a temporary barricade across the start- or finish-line of a race or other competition as in timed rodeo events. (2) *see* STARTING GATE

barrier draw A racing term; the position a horse assumes in the starting gate (q.v.) at the start of a race.

bar pressure Pressure on the indenture gap in the lower jaw as applied by the bit.

bars The plural of bar (q.v.).

bar shoe Any horseshoe (q.v.) that is not interrupted by an opening between the heels; the most frequently used of all therapeutic horseshoes; used to apply pressure to, or relieve pressure from, one part of the foot; are fitted so that 1/16 to 1/8 inch of daylight can be seen between the heels of the shoe and the heels of the hoof wall when the bar is resting on the frog; so called because an extra length of steel, a bar, attaches the heels of the shoe; of several types including the curved bar shoe (q.v.), heart-bar shoe (q.v.), mushroom bar shoe (q.v.), egg-bar shoe (q.v.), tongue bar shoe (q.v.), jumped-in bar shoe (q.v.), and whip-across bar shoe (q.v.).

bars of the hoof *see* BAR NO. 3

bars of the mouth *see* BAR NO. 1

bars of the saddle *see* BAR NO. 2

barstock Also known as stock; the metal from which hand- or ready-made horseshoes are forged.

Barthais Also known as Barthais Pony; a French-bred pony indigenous to the plains of Challosse near the Adour River; a taller and heavier version of the Landais (q.v.) from which it was originally considered a separate breed.

Barthais Pony *see* BARTHAIS

basal Relating to, or being essential for, the maintenance of the fundamental vital activities of an organism.

basal cell Any one of the innermost cells of the deeper epidermis of the skin.

basal crack A sand crack (q.v.) beginning at the ground surface of the hoof which splits towards the coronet (q.v.).

basal metabolic rate The rate at which heat is given off by a horse at complete rest.

bascule The convex rounded outline of a horse jumping in correct style over an obstacle of significant height

baseball Also known as wheeling; a racing term; a daily-double play in which the bettor (q.v.) couples a horse in one race with all horses in another.

base color Refers to coat color; the dominant color of the horse as determined from the body, neck and head area.

base narrow Refers to conformation; said of the horse when the distance between the center lines of the hooves at their placement on the ground is less than the distance between the center lines of the limbs at their origin in the chest as viewed from the front, or the center lines of the limbs in the thigh region when viewed from behind; may be accompanied by toe-in (q.v.) or toe-out (q.v.) conformation.

base wide Refers to conformation; said of the horse when the distance between the center lines of the hooves on the ground is greater than the distance between the center line of the limbs at their origin in the chest when viewed from the front, or the center lines of the limbs in the thigh region when viewed from behind.

Bashkir Also known as Bashkir Curly or Bashkirsky; a centuries-old pony breed originating in Bashkiria, around the southern foothills of the Urals in the former Soviet Union; of two distinct types: the Mountain Bashkir (q.v.) and the Steppe Bashkir (q.v.); stands 13.1 to 14 hands, has a distinctive thick, usually bay, chestnut, or palomino coat which becomes curly in the winter and a thick mane, tail, and forelock; is kept outdoors where it can withstand winter temperatures of −22 to −40°F (−30 to −40°C) and locate food under heavy snow; has a short and thick neck, low withers, elongated and sometimes hollow back, a wide and deep chest, short and strong legs, and a small foot for its size; the breed standard quotes a bone measurement of 8 inches (20 cm) below the knee and a girth measurement for stallions of 71 inches (180 cm); is docile, strong, quiet, and hardy; used for packing, light draft, riding, and to provide meat, milk and clothing (the long winter coat hair being spun into cloth); in a seven- to eight-month lactation period a mare can yield as much as 350 gallons (1,590 liters) of milk; due to the exceptionally hard hoof, it is generally left unshod; when bred in the United States, known as the American Bashkir Curly (q.v.).

Bashkir Curly *see* BASHKIR

Bashkirsky *see* BASHKIR

basic gaits The horse's natural forms of locomotion characterized by a distinctive rhythmic movement of the feet and legs; include the walk (q.v.), trot (q.v.) and canter (q.v.).

basic seat A compulsory exercise performed in vaulting (q.v.) competitions in which the vaulter (q.v.) sits in the deepest part of the horse's back with both arms stretched outwards from the sides of his body with the finger tips held at eye level and the shoulders, hips, and heels on the same vertical line.

Basil Nightingale *see* NIGHTINGALE, BASIL

Basket Phaeton Also known as Lady's Basket Phaeton, beach carriage or, in America, wagon; a horse-drawn vehicle of the Phaeton (q.v.) type designed during the 1860s for park driving in fashionable districts; had an optional rumble seat and basketwork sides of a curved or rounded profile; British versions had sideways-elliptical springs, while the American type had crosswise elliptical springs.

Basque Also known as Basque Pony, Basque Pottok, Pottok (meaning small horse in Basque), and spelled Pottock; a semi-wild pony breed indigenous to the mountainous Basque regions of Spain and Southwest France; thought to have descended from the prehistoric horse of the Solutrè; improved by crosses to Welsh Section B (q.v.) stallions and Arabs (q.v.); the coat is generally brown or black, although bay, chestnut, piebald, and skewbald do occur; has a well-proportioned head, but long ears, an overhanging upper lip covered with whiskers, a short neck, long back, full, but shaggy mane and tail and small hooves; the hind legs are commonly cow-hocked (q.v.); of three types the Standard (q.v.), Piebald (q.v.), and Double (q.v.) standing 11 to 14.2 hands; less refined than the Landais (q.v.); is very hardy and tough; used for riding, light draft, farming, and jumping.

Basque Pony *see* BASQUE

Basque Pottok *see* BASQUE

basse école Exercises by which students learn to mount a horse; the basse in 19th century riding schools was an incline.

Basseri An Iranian horse breed; contributed to the development of the Plateau Persian (q.v.).

basset *see* BASSET HOUND

basset hound Also known as basset; a dog with short, crooked legs and a long body; used for hunting.

bastard strangles A condition occurring when the swollen glands typical of strangles (q.v.) burst, releasing the bacteria which caused the infection into the bloodstream, infecting other body organs such as the spleen, kidneys, lungs, liver, and brain, in which case, death may result.

Bastard Coach *see* CHARABANC

Basterna A Roman horse litter (q.v.) with poles attached to a horse in front and a horse behind, as in the form of a sedan chair.

bastos *see* SKIRT NO. 1

Basuto Also known as Basuto Pony; a pony breed originating in Basutoland (now Lesotho) South Africa; derived from the Cape Horse (q.v.) crossed with native stock and, after 1822, English Thoroughbred (q.v.), Persian, and Arab (q.v.) blood; a hardy and courageous breed with tremendous endurance capable of covering 60 to 80 miles (97–129 km) per day carrying more than 200 pounds (91 kg); used extensively as a troop mount in the Boer War and is now used for polo and flat racing as well as general riding; may have a bay, brown, gray, or chestnut coat, stands 14 to 14.1 hands, is thickset, having a long, muscular neck, prominent withers, long back, low-set tail, and slender, strong legs; is reliable, hard-working and tolerant.

Basuto Pony *see* BASUTO

bat (1) Also known as cosh; a whip (q.v.) generally less than 24 inches (61 cm) in length and having a flattened end. (2) A racing term; slang; to strike a horse with a whip to encourage increased speed or to gain attention.

Batak Also known as Batak Pony or Deli Pony; a pony breed originating on the island of Sumatra, Indonesia; descended from Arab (q.v.) stallions put to selected native mares; stands 12 to 13 hands and may have a coat of any color although brown is most common; is gentle, lively, and frugal; used for riding; has a light head, arched, well-shaped neck, short back, and sturdy legs.

Batak Pony *see* BATAK

bathing machine A box-like horse-drawn dressing room mounted on large, straight or dished wheels drawn by a single horse attached to the vehicle by chain trees; ridden rather than driven into the sea water; when the axle trees were level with the water, the horse was unhitched and steps let down from the front of the vehicle into the water for the bathers to descend; to remove the machine from the water, the unhitched horse was harnessed to the rear of the vehicle and the front steps retracted; the sides of the bodywork were often striped in primary colors; the prototype was first used in Weymouth, England, by George III when seabathing became popular for both fashion and health.

Battenburg Phaeton A four-wheeled horse-drawn vehicle of the Dog Cart (q.v.) type; had an outward-curving body with splashboards over the wheels; was hung on four elliptical springs, seated four passengers back-to-back, and was pulled by either a single horse or a pair.

battery Also known as machine or joint; a racing term; an illegal electrical device used by a jockey to encourage the horse to run faster.

Battlesden Car *see* BATTLESDEN CART

Battlesden Cart Also known as Battlesden Car; a small, two-wheeled, horse-drawn pleasure vehicle, popular in England during the second half of the 19th century; pulled by a large pony or cob; similar in design to a two-wheeled Dogcart (q.v.), but with a much lower body and hung on elliptical springs with shafts interior to the body and splashboards which formed a semi-circle over the wheels.

Battle Wagon Slang; a toughly constructed, horse-drawn vehicle designed to withstand the rigors of a Combined Driving cross-country course; (sl).

batwing chaps Also known as batwings; a type of chaps (q.v.); a full-length leather covering of the legs held together and onto the body by means of a belted waistband; wraps around the leg, closing on the outside of the leg by means of buckles or zippers; are wide and flared at the bottom to cover the foot and stirrup; worn by Western enthusiasts, specifically cutters (q.v.) to camouflage the action of the leg and spur in cutting horse (q.v.) competitions.

batwings *see* BATWING CHAPS

Baudet de Poitou Also known as Poitou Ass or Poitou Donkey; a rare donkey breed developed in the province of Poitue, France from which the name derived; stands 14 to 15 hands and is characterized by a huge head and ears and a thick, long, shaggy, dark brown or black coat without cross or strip, which commonly hangs in long cords or shaggy shanks; prized as a mule-breeding jack; a true draft animal, does not make good riding stock; jacks are kept exclusively for breeding, and the jennets are covered in late February or March following their second birthday.

Baulk *see* BALK

Bay (1) Refers to coat color; any shade of red with black points ranging from almost yellow to yellow mixed with black; may be confused with brown; variations include red bay, mahogany bay, blood bay (q.v.), and sandy bay (q.v.). (2) A hunting term; the noise made by a hound (q.v.) when on the scent.

bay-brown Refers to coat color; a variation of bay (q.v.); a brown coat with a bay muzzle (q.v.), black limbs (q.v.), mane, and tail.

bay roan Also known as red roan; refers to coat color; a variation of roan (q.v.); any shade of red coat mixed with white hairs and dark to black points with no white hairs.

bayo *see* DUN

bayo cayote Refers to coat color; a dun (q.v.) horse with a black dorsal stripe (q.v.).

BD *see* BRITISH DRESSAGE

BDS *see* BRITISH DRIVING SOCIETY

Beach Carriage *see* BASKET PHAETON

Beach Phaeton An American four-wheeled, horse-drawn vehicle of the Phaeton (q.v.) type; generally used for summer excursions at seaside resorts; easy to enter due to the low open sides; hung on sideways-elliptical springs front and rear and drawn by a pair of cobs or large ponies in pole gear (q.v.).

Beach Wagon A horse-drawn American pleasure wagon used for holiday excursions, especially around the coastal regions of New England; from 1860 through the early 1900s had a simple tray-like construction, double rows of forward-facing seats, a canopy top, open sides, and was hung on sideways-elliptical springs; drawn by a single horse.

beagle One of a breed of small hounds having a smooth coat, short legs, and drooping ears, used to hunt hares and other small game on foot; provide early hunting experience for many Masters (q.v.).

beagling A hunting term; to hunt hare on foot using beagles (q.v.) to flush and follow the prey; beagles are followed by the huntsman (q.v.) assisted by numerous whippers-in (q.v.), and followed by the field (q.v.).

beak Also known as horn or bick; the round, tapered, and relatively pointed end of a farrier's anvil (q.v.).

beaked shoe *see* EXTENDED-TOE SHOE

beam A hunting term; the distance between the main antlers of a stag (q.v.).

bean (1) A mass of smegma (q.v.) collected in the cavity in the head of the penis, surrounding the end of the urethra; sometimes obstructs or prevents passage of urine by pressing on or stopping up the urethra. (2) Any of several kinds of smooth, edible, kidney-shaped seeds of any leguminous plant of the genus *Phaseolus* including the kidney bean, string bean, lima bean, etc.; sometimes fed to horses at hard work in combination with corn to reduce the heat value of the feed. (3) *see* CUP NO. 1

beaning Also known as wedging; to temporarily disguise unsoundness in a horse using any number of methods, such as wedging a stone in the shoe of the sound foot to cause a temporary pain, so that, being tender in both front feet, the horse appears to go sound.

bean-shooter A horse who throws his front feet vigorously forward at the trot, with little or no flexion, effective "landing" before the feet touch the ground; an undesirable trait.

bear foot *see* CLUB FOOT

bear in Also known as bearing in or lug in; a racing term; said of a horse who runs with his body turned to the inside rail rather than straight, often deviating from a straight course; may be due to weariness, infirmity, inexperience, or overuse of the whip or reins by the jockey.

bearing The general balance (q.v.) and carriage of the horse.

bearing in *see* BEAR IN

bearing out *see* BEAR OUT

bearing rein (1) *see* CHECK REIN. (2) *see* INDIRECT REIN

bearing rein drop *see* GAG RUNNER

bearing rein post A circular hook inserted perpendicular to the harness backband through which the bearing rein (q.v.) passes to the driver's hands.

bearing strap Also known as trace bearer, trace carrier, quarter strap, or tug strap; a narrow leather strap used to keep the harness traces level and to support cart horse breeching (q.v.); the strap is passed over the loins and through a slot in the crupper back strap; fitted with loops through which the traces pass; always used on a tandem leader when long traces are employed and occasionally on team and pair harness.

bearing surface (1) The points in the

horse's mouth upon which the bit acts through applied pressure. (2) The ground-side surface of the hoof upon which the horse's weight is borne.

bear out Also known as bearing out or lug out; a racing term; a horse who runs with his body turned away from the inside rail, especially on the turns and who often deviates from a straight course; may be due to weariness, infirmity, inexperience, or overuse of the whip or reins by the rider.

Bear Step Katouche A special award presented to specific class winners at the National Appaloosa Show each year in the United States; hand-crafted from solid silver and turquoise by Shatka Bear Step and donated by him to the Appaloosa Horse Club (q.v.).

bear-skin cape Historically, a cape worn by coachmen (q.v.) of elite town carriages during cold weather; made out of bear hide with the hair still attached.

beast Any four-footed animal as distinguished from birds, fishes, insects, and man; used by some to refer to a horse.

beat (1) To flog a horse with a whip. (2) A racing term; an unfortunate defeat, as when a horse is passed in the last stride of a race. (3) Exhausted; tired. (4) A footfall within a gait; a hoof or pair of hooves virtually simultaneously striking the ground; the walk has four beats, the trot two and the canter three.

Beaufort, 8th Duke of Also known as Blue Duke; designed the Beaufort Phaeton (q.v.) and reigned as the President of the Coaching Club from July 12, 1871 through 1897.

Beaufort Phaeton Also known as Hunting Phaeton; a horse-drawn vehicle; a large version of the Mail Phaeton (q.v.) accommodating six instead of four passengers and having an extra middle seat; used mainly in hunting country to transport viewers to hunt meets and to exercise coach and carriage horses; designed by the Duke of Beaufort for whom it was named.

Beberbeck A German horse breed descended from Arab (q.v.) and Thoroughbred (q.v.) stallions put to local mares bred at the Beberbeck Stud near Kassel, Germany from the 1700s through 1930 at which time the Stud was closed; still bred today, but in greatly reduced numbers; resembles a heavy Thoroughbred; stands about 16 hands, generally has a bay or chestnut coat, and is used for riding and light draft.

bed *see* BEDDING

bedding Also known as litter and bed; the material placed on the floor of a stall, stable, or trailer as a bed for horses; used to provide cushion against a hard floor and lessen leg problems, insulate against the cold, absorb urine, and make removal of feces (q.v.) easier; different materials are used depending on availability and cost factors, including straw (q.v.), rice hulls, wood shavings (q.v.), sawdust (q.v.), paper (q.v.), bracken, and sand.

bed down To lay bedding (q.v.) in a stall (q.v.), stable (q.v.), or loose box (q.v.).

Bedford Cart A two-wheeled, general-purpose horse-drawn English farm cart with fixed sideboards above high wheels and an unsprung or dead axle popular in the 19th century with farmers or dealers for carrying goods; passengers sat dos-à-dos (q.v.) with two facing forward and two backward; the rear passengers placed their feet against a tailboard let down on chains to form a foot rest; had a square-shaped body hung on two semi-elliptical springs with shafts interior to the bodywork; made in various sizes and capacities; drawn by a single horse.

Bedford cord A very hard wearing fabric used as a cushion and valance cover on horse-drawn vehicles such as dogcarts (q.v.) and gigs (q.v.) and for driving aprons and breeches (q.v.).

Bedouin Arab *see* ASSIL

beef A racing term; a protest filed by one jockey, usually about another.

beefy hocks Said of the horse's hocks (q.v.) when thick and meaty.

Beetewk A heavy-draft breed originating on the banks of Beetewk river in the former Soviet Union; bred by Peter the Great who put Dutch stallions to local mares, and the progeny to Orlov Trotting (q.v.) stallions; is docile, obedient, and has high spirits, good action, great strength behind, and is capable of pulling up to approximately 3 tons (3 tonnes).

beet pulp *see* SUGAR-BEET PULP

BEF *see* BRITISH EQUESTRIAN FEDERATION

behind the bit Also known as behind the bridle, overbent, or below the bit; an evasion whereby the horse refuses to take proper bit contact and draws his chin into his chest, his nose thereby coming behind the perpendicular; may be an act of actual disobedience, but is more commonly a response to an over-severe or badly fitting bit, or to the rider's unyielding or over-restrictive hands.

behind the bridle *see* BEHIND THE BIT

behind the movement Said of a mounted rider whose body is behind the imaginary vertical drawn perpendicular to the back of the horse; may result in too much weight placed on the loins of the horse thus impeding the action of the hind legs and movement of the horse's back.

behind the vertical Said of the horse's head when his muzzle (q.v.) is behind an imaginary line drawn perpendicular to the ground; the opposite side of the vertical line from in front of the vertical (q.v.).

belch To expel gas from the stomach suddenly through the mouth; uncommon in horses and a sign of a more serious condition.

Belgian Ardennais *see* BELGIAN ARDENNES

Belgian Ardennes Also known as Ardennes or Belgian Ardennais; a coldblood once considered an offshoot of the Belgian Brabant (q.v.), but now classified as a division of the French Ardennais (q.v.) with which it shares the same features; originally from the Ardennes plateau in France from which the name derived; thought to have descended from the heavy draft horses used by Julius Caesar put to Arab (q.v.) in the 18th century; breed characteristics were firmly established in the 19th century; is hardy and frugal having tremendous endurance, stands about 15.3 hands, is compact and heavily built with a wide, deep chest, a big, broad head, short, heavily feathered, massive legs, and a well-crested neck; predominant coat colors are bay, roan, and chestnut; has a gentle temperament; used for heavy draft and agricultural work and is particularly well suited to work in hilly country; the stud book is maintained by the Societé Royale pour le Cheval de Trait Ardennais.

Belgian Brabant *see* BRABANT

Belgian Draft *see* BRABANT

Belgian Draft horse *see* BRABANT

Belgian Heavy Draft *see* BRABANT

Belgian Road Cart A light, two-wheeled, horse-drawn driving and exercise cart popular in Belgium during the 1900s; hung on a three-spring system with pivoting shackles; noted for its low bodywork and wide gauge track which made it safe for road work with inexperienced horses.

bell (1) A signal sounded to initiate a performance, to identify when a competitor goes off course (q.v.), when the starter opens the starting gate at a race track, or to mark the close of betting at a race track. (2) A hollow metallic device that, when struck, gives forth a ringing sound; attached to the harness for decoration, to coaches for safety, etc. (3) *see* BUGLE. (4) To trim an animal's tail hair into a distinctive bell-shaped pattern; commonly used on mules; the pattern is used for identification, as to show where a horse or mule should be in a pack string.

Bellas Formas A Paso Fino (q.v.) show class in which horses are judged 60 percent on conformation, 30 percent on quality and naturalness of gait, and 10 percent on appearance, grooming, and manners; the horse is generally shown with two handlers using Bellas Formas lines (q.v.); Spanish meaning "beautiful lines".

Bellas Formas lines Two long lines approximately 20 to 30 feet (6–9 m) long, attached to either side of a halter by which handlers show the Paso Fino (q.v.) horse in Bellas Formas (q.v.) classes; the handlers stand to either side and to the rear of the horse.

bell boots *see* OVER-REACH BOOTS

Bellerophon The Prince of Corinth in Greek mythology who tamed the winged horse, Pegasus (q.v.) and rode him to destroy the dragon-like monster, the Chimera; success encouraged him to attempt to fly Pegasus to Olympia to live with the gods; Zeus, angered by his mortal ambition, sent a gadfly to bite Pegasus, which spooked the horse and unseated Bellerophon who fell to the earth crippled and blinded.

bell mare Also known in South America as madrina; originally, in America, any mare with a specially toned bell strapped around her neck, used to lead a mule train (it is generally accepted that a mule train will pull harder and faster if led by a mare); in the rest of the world and in America today, any mare with a bell around her neck who other horses will follow when in pasture or range, hobbled or free.

bell terret *see* FLY TERRET

Bell Wagon *see* BARREL TOP WAGON

belly *see* ABDOMEN

belly band (1) A wide double leather strap that passes under the belly of the horse just to the rear of the fore flank to keep the harness tugs (q.v.) in place and to prevent the collar (q.v.) from choking the horse. (2) *see* GIRTH NO. 1

belly clip Also known as neck clip; to shave or cut the body hair of the horse from under the belly upwards between the forelegs, and up along the lower line of the neck to the jaw.

belly strap A leather strap with a buckle on each end attached to a dee (q.v.) on the lower side of each harness trace (q.v.) between the pad and the trace carrier and passed through a loop on the rear of the girth; used to prevent the traces from slipping over the back of the horse if he turns towards the shaft horse (q.v.).

Belmont Stakes One of three classic races for three-year-old horses comprising the Triple Crown (q.v.) instituted in the United States between 1865 and 1875; a 1½ mile (2.4 km) race first run in 1867 at Jerome Park; moved to Belmont Park located in New York in 1905 where it has been run annually every June since; named for August Belmont, the leading owner and breeder of race horses in the 1860s.

below the bit *see* BEHIND THE BIT

Belvoir tan Refers to foxhound coat color; dark rich mahogany and black coloring with no white unless in the form of a collar; descended from a black and tan hound named Senator, currently mounted and on display at Belvoir Castle, Great Britain.

bench A hunting term; a slatted, wooden bench raised approximately 1 foot (30 cm) off the ground upon which kenneled hounds sleep; in the winter they are bedded with straw.

bench knees *see* LATERAL DEVIATION OF THE METACARPAL BONES

bend (1) A racing term; any turn in the race track (q.v.). (2) The flexion of the horse from nose to tail; may be to the left or right; is more of a rider sensation than a physical actuality.

bending line A jumping term; an imaginary curved line from one obstacle to another where such obstacles are not placed in a straight line; a rider follows this line when jumping.

bending race Also known as a pole race; a mounted competition in which competitors weave, one at a time, in and out of a number of vertically placed poles set in a straight line; the winner is the competitor who completes the course in the fastest time without knocking down any poles.

bending tackle A type of tack used to alter the carriage (q.v.), e.g., raise the head, of the horse by encouraging flexion of the neck and jaw.

Benjamin Also known as upper Benjamin; a coaching term; an overcoat worn by coachmen made of boxcloth (q.v.).

Benjamin Marshall *see* MARSHALL, BENJAMIN

benign Any illness or medical condition which is neither malignant (q.v.) nor likely to recur; has a good chance of responding to treatment.

Benna A crude horse-drawn farm cart used in Ancient Rome having a wooden plank floor and rope sides woven with straw or grass; drawn by either a pair of oxen or horses.

Bennett, James Gordon Considered the father of American polo (q.v.); introduced the game in the United States in 1876 by assembling players, knowledge, equipment, and Texas horses to play in the first loosely structured matches; the first game was played indoors at Dickle's Riding Academy located in New York, USA.

Benno von Achenback *see* VON ACHENBACH, BENNO

Bentinck bit A curb bit (q.v.) with a gate-port mouth.

Bent-panel Cart A light, horse-drawn, two-wheeled dogcart (q.v.) with outwardly curved sides, a shallow foot well, and false side slats or louvers; favored by lady drivers on account of the protection from mud and splashes it provided; drawn by a small horse or large pony in curved shafts.

Bent-sided Dog Cart A horse-drawn vehicle of the Dog Cart (q.v.) type; similar to a Battenburg Phaeton (q.v.) except that the side panels were steamed and bent in such a manner as to create splashboards.

Beradi The progeny (q.v.) of a Persian Arab (q.v.) mare and a non-Arab stallion.

Berber A Barb (q.v.) from Barbary, Africa.

Beresford Cabriolet A horse-drawn vehicle of the Gig (q.v.) type; had a folding hood and seated two to four passengers; the low body was cab-fronted and was hung on cee and elliptical springs.

Berkley bit A pelham bit (q.v.) with auxiliary rings attached to the top ring on the cheeks; usually mullen mouthed (q.v.); similar to a rugby pelham.

Berlin (1) Also known as Berlin Coach and spelled Berline; a horse-drawn coach or chariot developed in the mid-17th century and so named because its first public appearance was made in the streets of Berlin, Germany; had a Berlin suspension (q.v.) and two parallel braces in a longitudinal plane outside the main bodywork; on some models, the braces could be tightened, raised, or lowered by means of an attached windlass; not popular in Britain or the United States until the mid-18th century; usually drawn by a pair of horses in pole gear. (2) *see* BERLIN SUSPENSION

Berlin Coach *see* BERLIN

Berline *see* BERLIN

Berline suspension *see* BERLIN SUSPENSION

Berlingot *see* VIS-Á-VIS

Berlin Rockaway A light, horse-drawn passenger vehicle popular in North America having full-sized panels and glazed upper quarters; not a true Berlin (q.v.) as it was hung on leaf springs rather than braces.

Berlin suspension Also spelled Berline suspension; the undergear on which a Berlin was supported.

Bermuda grass Also known as Bahama grass, devil grass, scutch grass, or couch grass; a trailing and stoloniferous grass, *Cynodon dactylon*, native to southern Europe and grown in other warm climates, particularly India, the Southern United States, and the Caribbean islands, for pasture, lawns, etc.

Bermuda hay Cut and dried hay (q.v.) made from Bermuda grass (q.v.); common to the southern and coastal regions of the United States; may be cut four to five times per year from the same stem of grass; similar in nutritional content to early bloom Timothy (q.v.) and has a protein content higher than that of cereal grass hays such as oat or barley (q.v.).

bestride To ride astride, as on a horse.

bet (1) Also known as stake, stakes, stake money, wager, play, or box; a betting term; a sum of money laid or pledged on the result of any uncertain event such as a horse race. (2) A betting term; also known as stake, lay, wager, or betting; to pledge a sum of money on the outcome of an uncertain event, e.g. a horse race; includes post betting (q.v.) and ante-post betting (q.v.).

beta-carotene A derivative of vitamin A (q.v.).

bet declared off Also known as declared off; a racing term; any wager announced as no longer valid or canceled by the race stewards (q.v.); as due to the scratch of an entry at the gate.

better (1) Having good qualities in a greater degree than another. (2) To make better; to improve. (3) A state of improvement. (4) *see* BETTOR

betting The act of placing a bet (q.v.).

betting board A betting term; a board upon which bookmakers (q.v.) display the odds of horses competing in a given race.

betting book Also known as book; a betting term; a bookmaker's tally, as maintained in a ledger, of the amounts of each bet placed and the odds necessary to ensure profit.

betting favorite *see* FAVORITE

betting ring (1) The area at a racetrack where authorized bookmakers (q.v.) conduct their business. (2) An organized, generally illegal, group of bookmakers (q.v.).

betting shop A betting term; a licensed, on- or off-track, bookmaker's (q.v.) office which takes bets (q.v.) on events such as horse races.

betting ticket *see* TICKET NO. 2

bettor Also known as punter or player and spelled better; one who places a wager or bet (q.v.).

between hand and leg *see* ON THE AIDS

between the flags (1) The area between the red and white flags (q.v.) on a jumping obstacle or course through which a mounted rider must pass when in competition. (2) An antiquated British term; *see* POINT-TO-POINT

BEVA *see* BRITISH EQUINE VETERINARY ASSOCIATION

Beverly Car A square-sided version of the governess cart (q.v.), finished with clear varnish over natural wood rather than painted in solid colors.

Beyer number A racing term; a handicapping tool in which a numerical value is assigned to each race run by a horse based on his final time and the track condition; enables one to objectively compare different horses running on different racetracks; popularized by Andrew Beyer from which the name derives.

Bhotia *see* BHUTIA

BHS *see* BRITISH HORSE SOCIETY

BHSAI *see* BRITISH HORSE SOCIETY ASSISTANT INSTRUCTOR

BHSI *see* BRITISH HORSE SOCIETY INSTRUCTOR

Bhutia Also spelled Bhotia; a pony breed originating in the Himalayan mountains of northern India; is similar in genetic makeup to the native Tibetan and Spiti (q.v.) pony breeds; stands 13 to 13.1 hands, has a gray coat, short neck, shaggy mane, straight shoulder, short, strong legs, is frugal, and has good endurance; used for riding and packing; divided into three subgroups: the Tattu (q.v.), Chyanta (q.v.), and the Tanghan (q.v.).

Bian Also known as Bianconi Car or Biancononi Car; a horse-drawn, four-wheeled, public passenger vehicle of the Irish Jaunting Car (q.v.) type introduced in the early 19th century; used primarily for long-distance journeys in Southern Ireland in districts not served by stage coaches prior to the advent of railways; seated six passengers dos-à-dos down the sides of the vehicle, facing outwards; had knee flaps to protect the passengers' lower legs and was drawn by a either a unicorn (q.v.) or pair (q.v.); introduced by Irishman Charles Bianconi.

Bianconi, Charles (1786–1875) An Italian, commonly known as Bian; responsible for creating the first public transport system in Ireland and developing the Bian (q.v.).

Bianconi Car *see* BIAN

Biancononi Car *see* BIAN

bib A stout piece of leather strapped to the throat latch of the halter (q.v.) which prevents a horse from reaching and biting at its blanket (q.v.).

bib martingale Also known as web martingale; a running martingale (q.v.) in which the area between the split auxiliary reins is covered or filled with baghide or similar material; used on excitable and young horses to prevent them from entangling their legs and other equipment in the martingale.

bick *see* BEAK

bid A price offered to purchase a horse, tack, or real estate at an auction (q.v.).

bidder One who offers a bid at an auction (q.v.), as for a horse.

Bidet Breton Also known as Bidet d'Allure; one of four types of Breton (q.v.) defined according to size, the others being the Postier Breton (q.v.), Corlay (q.v.), and Heavy Draught Breton (q.v.); a horse breed believed to have originated in Brittany, France more than 4,000 years ago where it descended from native steppe horses from the Breton Mountains crossed with Oriental stallions and mares; highly prized as a military mount during the Middle Ages because of its alluring, comfortable gait, said to be between a brisk trot and an amble (q.v.); stood about 14 hands.

Bidet d'Allure *see* BIDET BRETON

bienséance A 17th-century French term; to have mores and manners; to adhere to the Classical Rules, as the rules proposed by Aristotle, which included the banning of violence at such events as mounted duels, on stage.

Biga A Grecian horse-drawn cart pulled by two horses abreast.

big apple An American racing term; any major racing circuit.

big head *see* OSTEODYSTROPHIA FIBROSA

big head disease *see* OSTEODYSTROPHIA FIBROSA

big hitch Four, six, eight, or more horses connected to a vehicle for the purpose of pulling it.

big knee *see* CARPITIS

big leg *see* STOCK UP

Bigourdan A horse breed descended from the Iberian Horse improved with Arab (q.v.) and Thoroughbred (q.v.) blood; basically, a tall Tarbenian (q.v.).

big race A racing term; the primary race of any race day.

Big Red Either of three chestnut Thoroughbred (q.v.) racing champions: Man O'War (q.v.), Phar Lap (q.v.), or Secretariat (q.v.).

bight of reins That portion of the reins (q.v.) passing between the rider's thumb and finger and out on top of the hand to the bit (q.v.); in English style, the reins pass out of the bottom of the hand to the bit.

big Q A racing term; a betting option in which the bettor (q.v.) selects two quinellas (q.v.) in two nominated races.

bike *see* SULKY

Bike Wagon A light, American, horse-drawn vehicle; had a tray-shaped body 22 inches (56 cm) wide and 56 inches (142 cm) long, hung on two elliptical springs and a perch; the wheels were mounted on bicycle axles and the dash was leather covered; the forward-facing seat had rallied sides, was well upholstered, and accommodated the driver and one passenger.

bilateral Pertaining to or affecting both sides.

Bilgoraj Konik A breed of Konik (q.v.) believed to be a direct descendant of the wild horse.

biliary fever *see* EQUINE PIROPLAMOSIS

Bill Daly A racing term; a famous American 19th century race horse trainer who promoted the racing style of taking the lead as soon as possible out of the gate, setting the pace, and remaining in the lead to the finish (q.v.); such jockeys are said to be "on the Bill Daly" (q.v.).

billet *see* STUD FASTENING

billets Fox manure.

binder A hunting term; the top horizontal branch of a cut and laid fence (q.v.) or jump, e.g. a small sapling woven between the stakes or a rail placed on top of a wire fence; used to make the jump safer for the horse.

biological control Also known as biological fly control; a method of suppressing and/or controlling fly (q.v.) populations in and around the stable using commercially available natural enemies of targeted flies, e.g. wasps.

biological fly control *see* BIOLOGICAL CONTROL

biopsy (1) The process of removing tissue from living patients for diagnostic examination. (2) A sample obtained by biopsy.

biomechanics (1) The study of the body movements and of the forces acting on the musculoskeletal system. (2) The manner in which the muscles move to produce and sustain various forms of action; in the horse, mainly locomotion.

biotin Also known as vitamin H; an intestinally synthesized, B-complex vitamin necessary for proper skin, hair, and hoof wall health.

biothane Plastic-covered nylon from which some tack such as bridles and martingales (q.v.) is made; popular with eventers and those who compete in ride and tie (q.v.) competitions.

Birdcatcher spots Refers to coat color; random, small white spots scattered over any base color; named after the Thoroughbred (q.v.) stallion, Birdcatcher, who had them; unrelated to any other pattern and the genetics that cause them are unknown; usually frowned upon in breeds that favor dark, solid colors.

birdsville disease A frequently fatal disease of horses occurring in central and northern Australia caused by ingestion of the poisonous plant *Indigophera enneaphylla*; early signs include incoordination, drowsiness, an abnormal gait with the forelegs which are raised high, and some lack of control of the hind limbs including dragging; affected horses are prone to stand rather than move about; recovery is rare.

bird-eyed Said of a horse who shies at imaginary objects; (obs).

Birotum A small, horse-drawn gig or chariot used in Ancient Rome, particularly during the period AD 313 to 337; used for both public hire and private use, drawn by a single horse, and generally had a rearward luggage rack.

birth bag *see* AMNIONIC SAC

bishop (1) Any old, horse-drawn vehicle refurbished to appear new and up-to-date. (2) *see* BISHOPING

bishoping Also known as bishop or tampering; the dishonest practice of artificially altering the teeth of older horses to represent them as young horses; where black marks on the incisors have disappeared with age, they are reproduced by drilling and staining or burning holes in the tooth surface; easily detected by evaluating tooth table shape and evaluation of enamel rings.

bit A device normally made of metal or rubber attached to the bridle, and placed into the horse's mouth to control head position, pace, and direction; manipulated by the rider through the reins; consists of the cheekpieces (q.v.) and the mouthpiece (q.v.).

bit burr Also known as burr; a round piece of leather, plastic, or rubber 2 to 3 inches (5–7.5 cm) in diameter faced with bristles on one side, slit from one outside edge to the center, and fitted around the bit mouthpiece just inside the cheekpiece (q.v.); the bristled side lies against the corner of the horse's mouth, which it irritates; prevents the horse from leaning to, and assists in turning from, the side; generally used on only one side of the bit.

bitch (1) *see* BITCH HOUND. (2) *see* BITCH FOX

bitch fox *see* VIXEN

bitch hound Also known as bitch; a female hound (q.v.).

bitch pack A hunting term; a pack of hounds composed entirely of bitch hounds (q.v.).

bit cover A tubular piece of rubber fitted over the bit mouthpiece; used to enlarge the bit.

bite (1) To cut, break, penetrate, or seize with the teeth; a vice. (2) The horse's teeth, collectively.

bit guard Also known as bit shield, cheek leather, cheek guard, or in England, as lozenge; a round piece of leather or rubber 2 to 3 inches (5–7.5 cm) in diameter, slit from the outside edge to the center, where there is a hole large enough to fit the bit mouthpiece; prevents the bit from catching on the horse's lips.

biting Said of a horse who bites (q.v.).

biting louse Also known as *Damalinia equi*; a louse (q.v.); an external, biting and sucking parasite which feasts on the dander and hair of the horse; less than 1⁄10 inch in length and visible to the naked eye as a small or light-gray object; may be detected by inspecting the mane, root of the tail, inside the thighs, or on the underside of the saddle blanket following exercise; are not transmitted to people.

bit keys *see* KEYS

bitless bridle Any bridle without a bit where control is achieved through pressure on the nose and the curb groove instead of the mouth; the hackamore (q.v.) is the most common.

bit roller *see* ROLLER NO. 2

bit shield *see* BIT GUARD

bitted *see* BITTED UP

bitted up Also known as bitted; said of a horse when the bridle and bit are in position on his head and in his mouth.

bitting rig Tack used to artificially achieve a head set in the horse; consists of a surcingle, back strap, crupper (q.v.), over-check (q.v.), side reins (q.v.), bridle (q.v.), or any combination thereof.

black Refers to coat color; coat hair and points must be black with no obvious hairs of other colors including brown on the muzzle or flanks; may have white markings on the face and/or legs; may fade to a rusty color in the sun; rare in most breeds except the Percheron (q.v.), Fell pony (q.v.), North American Spanish horse, and Friesian (q.v.); variations include jet black (q.v.) and smoky black (q.v.).

Black and Tan American slang; a four-wheeled, black and tan colored, horse-drawn cab of the Growler (q.v.) type used in the United States from the 1880s on for cheap service; considered disreputable in more fashionable areas.

Black Beauty Perhaps the best known fictitious story about the life of a horse, published in 1877 and written by Mrs. Anna Sewell.

Black Bess The high quality mare, perhaps fictitious, owned by British highwayman and common thief, Dick Turpin; Turpin is said to have ridden Black Bess in his famous ride from London to York as recounted in Harrison Ainsworth's novel *Rookwood*.

Black Brigade (1) Black horses, usually Flemish (q.v.) stallions, used in the late 19th century to pull hearses; usually stood about 16 hands. (2) Gelded black stallions used in London, England to transport coal.

black-brown Refers to coat color; a black body with the muzzle, and sometimes the flanks, a brown or tan.

black bullfinch A jumping obstacle; one of two types of bullfinch (q.v.); an excessively thick, live hedge which is jumped through, not over.

black cell tumor *see* MELANOMA

black fly Any of several small, black-bodied flies of the genus *Simulium*; a swarming daytime feeder that delivers painful bites, feeding on blood from relatively hairless body areas such as inside the ears, the genitals, and along the belly line and chest; bites may result in severe allergic reactions and small hemorrhages.

black-letter work *see* BULLET WORK

Black Maria A four-wheeled, box-like police or prison van drawn by two horses in pole gear (q.v.) and driven from a high seat at roof level; entered from the rear, had a slatted clerestory for ventilation, generally no windows, and was hung on sideways elliptical springs front and rear; used in Britain and North America from the 1830s through the 1920s; named for Queen Victoria whose nickname was Maria.

black marks Refers to coat color; small areas of black hairs among white or other colored coat appearing anywhere on the body.

Black Mass The Quadrille (q.v.) of the Cadre Noir (q.v.) in which French traditional classical equitation is preserved.

Black Masters Funeral service owners who, prior to the advent of the automobile, used gelded black stallions known as the Black Brigade (q.v.) to draw funeral carriages.

black points Refers to coat color; the tail, ear rims, mane, tail, and lower legs of the horse when black.

black saddler A saddle maker specializing in cart and carriage harnesses.

blacksmith Also known as smithy; one who forges all types of items out of hot metal; often confused with farrier (q.v.).

blackthorn A thorny European shrub, the wood of which is used to make whips owing to its elastic quality.

black tobiano *see* PIEBALD

black type A racing term; a type of print often used in sale catalogues to distinguish race horses who have won or been placed in at least one stakes race (q.v.).

black water *see* EQUINE MYOGLOBINURIA

bladder A distendible sac with muscular and membranous walls which serves as a receptacle for the urine secreted by the kidneys.

Blagden Also known as Chubbarie and spelled Blagdon; a breed of spotted horse previously bred at the Royal Stud in Britain; now thought to be extinct.

Blagdon *see* BLAGDEN

Blair bridle *see* MECHANICAL HACKAMORE

blank (1) Also known as draw blank; a hunting term; said of a fox den, earth, or hiding place which does not contain a fox. (2) *see* BLANK DAY

blank day Also known as blank; a hunting term; any day in which the hounds (q.v.) fail to find a fox.

blanket (1) Also known as blanket pattern; refers to a coat color pattern; a symmetrical pattern of white on the haunches of a non-white horse; common to many breeds of horses, but most notably the Appaloosa (q.v.) and the Pony of the Americas (q.v.); may vary in size from a pattern covering the croup and hips of the horse, to one which covers most of the body; of three types: solid with sharply defined edges, roan with edges blending into the colored coat, and flecked (q.v.) where the edges blend into the body color with flecks of white hairs. (2) *see* HORSE BLANKET. (3) *see* SADDLE BLANKET. (4) To put a horse blanket (q.v.) on a horse.

blanket clip To shave or cut the body hair of the horse from the neck and belly; useful for horses pastured during the day and stabled at night.

blanketed Said of a horse wearing a horse blanket (q.v.).

blanket finish A racing term; an extremely close race finish in which the horses are so closely grouped they could be, figuratively, covered with one blanket.

blanket pattern *see* BLANKET

blanket riding To ride a horse without the aid of a saddle, using instead a saddle blanket (q.v.) held in position with a surcingle (q.v.); now replaced by a bareback pad (q.v.).

blaze A face marking (q.v.) consisting of a band of white which covers most of the forehead between the eyes, the entire width of the nasal bone, and the area between, but not including, the nostrils.

Blazers, The Also known as Galway Blazers; a famous foxhound pack from County Galway, Eire founded in the early 19th century.

blazing scent *see* BURNING SCENT

bleed (1) To draw blood from a horse using a syringe. (2) To lose blood.

bleeder (1) A horse who bleeds from the nostrils, as during a workout or race; a condition resulting from rupture of the capillaries surrounding the alveoli in the lungs known as exercise-induced pulmonary hemorrhage (q.v.); 75 percent of race horses may have blood in their upper airways after racing. (2) Any horse from which blood is drawn under controlled conditions for use in the production of serums and vaccines.

blemish A minor conformation fault, mark, or scar which is not inherited and is considered unattractive, but does not affect the horse's soundness or performance in any way; includes, but is not limited to, capped hock (q.v.), corneal scars (q.v.), dermal inclusion cysts (q.v.), and rope burns (q.v.).

blind (1) Also known as blind of an eye; void of the sense of sight; may be congenital or acquired, temporary or permanent and caused by injury, disease as to the retina, optic nerve or brain, or dietary deficiency in which case it is known as moon blindness (q.v.); the sudden onset of blindness in one or both eyes has been reported as a result of optic nerve atrophy associated with trauma and night blindness (q.v.) as a result of intense sunlight glare; a blind horse will rely more heavily on sound as a sense and will move with a hesitant gait; horses blind in one eye only may be prevented from competing in certain events for safety reasons; horses blind in both eyes may still be useful in competition when driven in harness. (2) One of two blinkers (q.v.). (3) *see* BLIND COUNTRY

blind boil A painful suppurating inflammatory sore forming a central core, caused by microbic infection which does not break or erupt the skin's surface.

blind bucker A horse who bucks without discrimination or any sense of direction; will often collide with objects in his path.

blind country Also known as blind; a hunting term; said of the country when the growth of weeds and brush obscures the obstacles and terrain ahead making it difficult for riders to gage the jumps and footing.

blinder A horse who performs beyond expectations.

blinders *see* BLINKERS

blind halter A driving bridle; (sl).

blindness The condition of being blind (q.v.).

blind obstacle Any obstacle (q.v.) to be jumped by the horse for which the landing side is not visible at take-off.

blind of an eye *see* BLIND NO. 1

blinds *see* BLINKERS

blind spavin Arthritis (q.v.) of the lower joints of the hock where the bone has degenerated without visible bone growth; the horse will go lame without showing outward signs of spavin (q.v.).

blind splint An inflammatory process of the interosseous ligament in the leg; difficult to detect because swelling occurs on the inner side of the splint, between the small metacarpal bone and suspensory ligament.

blind staggers One of three distinct types of selenium poisoning (q.v.), the others being alkali disease (q.v.) and acute selenium poisoning (q.v.); develops in animals consuming highly seleniferous plants or grains over a period of weeks or months; manifests in three stages: i) tendency to wander or wander into objects due to impaired vision; ii) wandering increases, the forelegs become weak, vision impairment progresses, and appetite diminishes; iii) paralyzed tongue, subnormal temperature, and death following respiratory failure; no specific antidote.

blind switch A racing term; said of a jockey who finds his mount pocketed (q.v.) behind other horses and who must decide whether to hope for an opening or to drop back and go around the pack.

blinker One of two blinkers (q.v.).

blinker plate The metal plate which is covered with leather to make blinkers (q.v.); keeps the leather in a concave shape to avoid rubbing of the eye; made in a variety of shapes including round, square, hatchet, and dee.

blinkers Also known as blinders, blinds, or winkers; racing and harness equipment consisting of leather-covered metal plates attached to the cheek-pieces of the bridle or hood; used to restrict the horse's vision to the sides and rear in either or both eyes; in harness or driving available in round, hatchet, dee, or square shapes; often decorated with a metal ornamentation.

blinker stays Also known as winker stays; a small strap which connects the left and right blinkers together at the center of the crownpiece by means of a buckle; allows adjustment of blinker width.

blister (1) A collection of watery matter or serum which causes the skin to rise and separate from the lower tissues. (2) Also known as vesicant or resciant; a liquid or paste counter-irritant (q.v.) applied to the skin of the leg to cause blistering and inflammation; used to increase blood supply and flow, and therefore to promote healing. (3) Also known as blistering; to apply a counter-irritant to the skin to cause blistering and inflammation, to treat chronic or subacute inflammation of joints, tendons and bones by encouraging blood flow to the area to hasten the healing process.

blister beetle A small poisonous insect ½ to ¾ inch (12–19 mm) long; found throughout the continental United States and the agricultural areas of Canada generally during late summer; has a wide host range including alfalfa (q.v.), sweet clover, lucerne (q.v.), soybean, potato, tomato, melon, cotton, and eggplant; contains a potent irritant and vesicant, cantharidin (q.v.), which when ingested by the horse causes blister beetle poisoning (q.v.).

blister beetle poisoning Poisoning most often observed in horses, although sheep and cattle are also affected; caused by ingestion of blister beetles (q.v.) which swarm in alfalfa (q.v.) (and other crops) prior to baling and are thus bound into the bales; beetles contain cantharidin, a potent irritant and vesicant (q.v.), which produces ulceration of the oral, esophageal, and gastric mucosa, cystitis, and nephritis; clinical manifestations include colic, salivation, shock, frequent urination, and occasionally, synchronous diaphragmatic flutter (q.v.); there is no specific treatment although administration of fluids and mineral oil is often useful.

blistering *see* BLISTER NO. 3

bloat *see* COLIC

block (1) *see* NERVE BLOCK. (2) A small chunk of wood, ½ to 3 inches (1.3–7.6 cm) wide, fit between the axle and the spring to adjust the vehicle height to that of the horse(s) pulling it.

blocked heels Said of the horse's heels or heel bulbs when nerve sensitivity is deadened by injection of a short-term acting anesthesia to the area as for diagnostic purposes.

blocking-up A coaching term; to adjust the height of a horse-drawn vehicle to fit the horse(s) pulling it, using blocks (q.v.).

blocks (1) Large, square heel calks on manufactured race horse shoes. (2) More than one block (q.v.).

blond sorrel ruano Refers to coat color; a variation of sorrel (q.v.); a light sandy-red coat with pale areas around the eyes and on the muzzle, flanks, and the inside of the legs, with pale lower legs; a common color of the American Belgian Draft Horse (q.v.).

blood (1) The fluid that circulates in the arteries and veins of the horse and conveys oxygen, hormones and food to the tissues and organs and returns waste products to the liver and kidneys whence it is excreted; assists in the control of body temperature; is red in color and consists of 60 percent pale yellow plasma and 40 percent red and white blood cells; red blood cells (q.v.) transport oxygen and white blood cells act as a defense mechanism against infection; accounts for approximately ⅛ of the horse's total body weight. (2) *see* BLOODED NO. 1

blood bay Refers to coat color; a dark shade of bay (q.v.) in which the coat is a dark purplish red with little or no black hairs mixed in but with black points.

blood blister *see* HEMATOMA

blood cell A basic, structural unit of the blood.

blood count A determination of the number and proportion of red and white cells in a specific volume of blood.

blooded (1) Also known as blood; a hunting term; said of a young hound given its first taste of blood from the kill. (2) A hunting term; said of a hunter who, having never before been present when a fox was killed, has the blood of the kill applied by the Master of the Hunt (q.v.) to the forehead or cheeks; a generally obsolete ceremony dating from the days of the Druids. (3) Of good blood or breed, as Thoroughbred (q.v.) horses.

blood heat The normal temperature of horse's blood, 98 to 100 °F (36–37.7 °C).

blood horse (1) A pedigree horse. (2) *see* THOROUGHBRED

bloodhound One of a breed of medium to large, powerful dogs with a very acute sense of smell, used for tracking game.

bloodhounding A variation of drag hunting (q.v.) originating in Britain in the 1970s; the quarry, a small group of runners (7 or less), usually from a local athletic club, is given approximately 20 minutes start before being pursued by a pack of bloodhounds (q.v.) that follow their scent; the mounted field follow the hounds; each run continues until either the runners are caught (and licked) by the hounds, or the predetermined Ôline' is completed; each line is usually in the region of 2 miles (3.2 km) long, across natural country with a variety of obstacles; typically four or so lines will be run in the course of the hunt, with approximately a 20-minute break between each.

blood-letting The act of letting blood or bleeding a horse, as by opening a vein, as a remedial measure.

bloodline The lineage of a horse; the pedigree (q.v.).

blood marks Refers to coat color; patches of red colored hairs growing into a gray coat; can become progressively larger, ultimately resulting in a uniformly red coat; an extremely rare occurrence.

blood plasma The clear, almost colorless fluid of the blood when separated from blood corpuscles by centrifuge.

blood poisoning *see* SEPTICEMIA

blood pressure The pressure exerted by the blood against the inner walls of the blood vessels, varying in different parts of the body, with exertion, excitement, strength of the heart, age, or health.

blood spavin Displacement of the main vein of the hind leg appearing on the inside of the upper part of the hock above a bog spavin (q.v.); the resulting soft lump can be emptied by manipulation, but frequently refills; is rarely treated.

blood sport Any pastime, as foxhunting (q.v.), in which killing is involved.

blood stock *see* BLOODSTOCK NO 3

bloodstock (1) The stock or bloodlines used to perpetuate a breed. (2) Horses of any breed, characteristic, etc., by which that breed or type is perpetuated; the bloodlines used to continue a breed. (3) Also spelled blood stock; Thoroughbreds (q.v.), particularly race and stud horses.

bloodstock agent One who represents or advises a Thoroughbred (q.v.) buyer or seller at a public auction or private sale, generally on a commission basis.

bloodstock sale A sale or auction of Thoroughbred (q.v.) horses, particularly those used, or whose bloodlines are used, in racing.

blood test Analysis of a blood sample to obtain information on blood cells present, enzyme activity, and electrolyte balance;

includes packed cell volume (PCV), total plasma protein (TPP), glucose concentrations, and hormone and enzyme assays.

blood tit *see* BLOOD WEED

blood-typing A method of examining the blood factors unique to each horse, much like fingerprinting, to determine the true identity and parentage; required of all newborn foals before they can be registered, raced, or used for breeding purposes; is 96 percent accurate; now being replaced by DNA testing (q.v.) which is 99 to 100 percent accurate.

blood 'un *see* THOROUGHBRED

blood urea nitrogen Also known by the acronym BUN; the urea nitrogen level in the blood; an indicator of the kidney's ability to excrete urea from the body.

blood weed Also known as blood tit; an antiquated term; a lightly built Thoroughbred (q.v.) lacking substance and/or bone.

bloodworm *see* LARGE STRONGYLE

bloom The shine or luster on the horse's coat as achieved by grooming or from added dietary fat in the form of oil.

blow (1) Also known as blow wind and blowing; said of the horse; to exhale with heavy, loud, and accelerated breathing following strenuous exercise in an effort to return to normal respiration. (2) Said of the horse who exhales air forcefully from the nostrils; a sign of suspicion, unfamiliarity, etc. (3) To allow a horse to catch his breath following a period of exertion.

blow a stirrup Also known as lose a stirrup; said of the rider whose foot slips out of the stirrup iron (q.v.).

blow away Also known as gone away or blowing away; a hunting term; said of the huntsman; to send the hounds after the fox with a signal from the hunting horn (q.v.).

blower An antiquated racing term; telephone service between a bookmaker (q.v.) and his connection at the racetrack.

blow fly Any of the various two-winged, filth-breeding flies, family Calliphoridae, which deposit their eggs or larvae on flesh, meat, or in wounds.

blow him Also known as cook him; said of a rider or trainer who overtrains a young horse causing him to tire, sour, or burn out emotionally from stress.

blow his nose A racing term; to give a horse a short gallop prior to a race to clear his wind in preparation for a horse race.

blow home Also known as blow hounds home; a hunting term; a series of long, connected notes blown on the hunting horn (q.v.) indicating the hunt (q.v.) is over.

blow hounds home *see* BLOW HOME

blowing *see* BLOW NO. 1

blowing away *see* BLOW AWAY

blowing out (1) A hunting term; said of the huntsman (q.v.) when he calls the hounds out of an empty covert or one in which they lost the fox. (2) A racing term; the act or process of running a blow out (q.v.).

blowing the anvil *see* ANVIL SHOOTING NO. 1

blow off a cow A cutting term; said of a horse who makes a bigger move than necessary to stay with the cow or when tricked by the cow, overanticipates its movements, and moves in the opposite direction.

blow out A racing term; a brief workout, usually three furlongs (q.v.) or a half mile in length occurring one or two days prior to a race; designed to sharpen or maintain the condition of the horse.

blow up (1) A dressage term; said of a horse who breaks gait, misbehaves, or panics. (2) Said of a horse who bucks (q.v.). 3) Said of a horse who inhales and holds his breath whilst the girth is being tightened.

blow wind *see* BLOW NO. 1

Blue Duke *see* BEAUFORT, 8TH DUKE OF

blue dun *see* GRULLO

blue eye *see* WALL EYE

bluegrass One of several, fine-leafed grasses of the *Poa* genus of temperate and arctic forage grasses, as bluestem (q.v.) or Kentucky bluegrass (q.v.), highly valued for pasturage and hay.

blue grass country An area located in Kentucky, USA, where the grass is so rich in phosphates and lime, which produce strong bones, that it is ideal for breeding horses.

blue nose *see* PHOTOSENSITIZATION

blue riband *see* BLUE RIBBON

blue ribbon Also known as blue riband; a piece of blue ribbon signifying the highest award, as for first prize or place.

blue roan (1) Refers to coat color; any roan (q.v.) horse with a bluish tinge to the coat color.

bluestem Also known as bluestem grass; any of the various tufted grasses, genus *Andropogon*, grown in the United States for hay and forage.

bluestem grass *see* BLUESTEM

bluestem grass hay Cut and dried hay made from bluestem grass (q.v.) common to the central United States; is highly palatable and contains a digestible protein content of approximately 3 percent and a fiber content of approximately 34 percent which is slightly higher than Timothy (q.v.) and Bermuda grass (q.v.) hays.

blue stone *see* COPPER SULFATE

blue vitriol *see* COPPER SULFATE

bluff A head covering or wrap having covered leather eye sockets; put over the head of a bad-tempered or excitable horse to keep it quiet and calm.

Boadicea (d. AD 62) Also spelled Boudicca; a British queen thought to have maintained the first racing stud (q.v.).

Board *see* TOTALIZATOR BOARD

board fence Also known as plank jump; a jumping obstacle consisting of long, narrow, flat and often painted board supported by the standards (q.v.).

boards Also known as side boards or polo boards; a polo term; 9 by 11 inch (23 × 28 cm) wooden boards which define the side lines (q.v.) of the polo field (q.v.) in England, the United States and Argentina; use is optional and today chalk is more commonly used.

boat race *see* FIXED RACE

bobbery pack A hunting term; a mixed pack of hounds (q.v.) or dogs used for hunting; the practice and term are believed to have originated in India.

bobble A racing term; said of a horse who takes a bad step out of the starting gate; generally due to the track surface giving way under foot; may cause the horse to duck his head, stumble, or nearly fall to his knees.

bobbing Said of the horse's head when it rises and falls with each stride; as in a lame horse or one evading the bit.

bobby back *see* SWAY BACK

bobby backed *see* SWAY BACKED

bob tail *see* DOCK TAIL

bob tailed (1) *see* DOCK TAILED. (2) A hunting term; said of a fox with little or no tail.

bobtail disease *see* ALKALI DISEASE

bocado (1) *see* MOUTHPIECE. (2) A bit popular in South America, consisting of a strip of leather passed under the tongue and tied under the chin.

body (1) Also known as torso; the main part of the horse as distinguished from the head and limbs. (2) *see* INTERIEUR

body brush A grooming tool consisting of tightly packed, soft, natural or synthetic bristles or hair set in an attached handle of wood or plastic, used to remove dust, dirt, and sweat from the horse's coat.

Body Break *see* SHOOTING BREAK

body clip *see* FULL CLIP

body horse The middle horse of a lead team pulling a horse-drawn vehicle.

bodymaker *see* JOINER

body protection *see* FLAK JACKET

body roller *see* ROLLER NO. 1

bodyside A driving term; the part of the collar (q.v.) which lays against the horse's shoulders.

body team A driving term; the pair of horses positioned between the wheelers (q.v.) and the swing team (q.v.) in an eight-horse hitch.

body wash *see* BRACE NO. 1

bogey (1) A jumper, hunter and eventing term; a problem fence. (2) An American term; said of muddy ground.

bog rider A cowboy (q.v.) whose responsibility it is to rescue cattle mired in the mud.

bog spavin Also known as tarsal hydrarthrosis; overproduction of synovial fluid in the joint capsule of the hock resulting in a soft liquid- or tissue-filled swelling; generally occurs on the inside and upper front of the hock joint; rarely interferes with the usefulness of the horse and may not cause lameness, although it does create an unsightly blemish; may be caused by faulty conformation, strains, sprains resulting from rapid turning and quick stops, deficient nutrition or insufficient systemic levels of vitamins A and D, calcium and phosphorous; has a tendency to recur; rest is essential.

boil A painful suppurating inflammatory sore forming a central core, caused by microbic infection; may break or erupt the skin.

boil over (1) An American term; said of a horse; to start bucking (q.v.). (2) An American racing term; said of a horse who wins a race by a decisive margin when not expected to do so.

Bokara Also known as Bokara Pony and spelled Bokhara; a pony descended from the Persian horse (q.v.) from Turkestan.

Bokara Pony *see* BOKARA

Bokhara *see* BOKARA

bold eye The eye of the horse when large, expressive, and prominent.

bold-face type A racing term; a darker type style used to highlight a horse's name in a sales catalogue; when in bold letters, the horse has won at least one sweepstakes (q.v.), while bold and lower case letters, denote a second or third placing in at least one sweepstakes race.

bold front Said of the horse whose well-muscled neck is set squarely onto the forequarters resulting in a proud head carriage.

bolet *see* BOLUS

bollard *see* ROLLER BOLT

bolster The timber frame running parallel to the axles, front and rear, on a horse-drawn vehicle; connected the vehicle body to the axles by means of leather thorough-braces (q.v.) or similar fittings.

Bolster Wagon A primitive, horse-drawn, four-wheeled buggy developed in the United States in 1814; lacked rearward springs, but had side bar suspension and crosswise bolsters (q.v.) to support an overhanging load.

bolt (1) *see* BOLTING. (2) Also known as run away or take off; said of a horse who breaks out of control or tries to run away, generally running dangerously fast, without concern for his safety or that of the rider; may be a vice or caused by momentary fright. (3) *see* BOLT A FOX

bolt a fox Also known as bolt; a hunting term; said of the hounds to remove or force a fox out of a drain, hole, or other protection.

bolter (1) A horse who eats too fast. (2) A horse who breaks out of control or runs away, refusing to respond to the control of the bit, to turn, to slow down, or to stop; may be due to bad teeth, a poorly fitting bit, a hard mouth (q.v.), fear, etc.

bolt hook The bearing rein hook located on top of the driving saddle; curved and shaped like a half-ring.

bolting (1) Also known as bolting food or bolt; a vice; said of a horse who eats its food too quickly; may be due to boredom, bad teeth, insufficient feed, or lack of roughage and may result in digestive problems including colic (q.v.) and choking (q.v.); may be prevented by placing large stones in the manger, feeding smaller amounts more frequently throughout the day, and increasing roughage. (2) Said of a horse that bolts (q.v.).

bolting food *see* BOLTING NO. 1

bolus Also known as bolet; any mass of food swallowed by the horse.

bomb calorimeter A device used to determine gross energy value of feed, i.e. calories; a known quantity of food is incinerated in the device which is then placed into a defined volume of water; the number of degrees the water is raised is used to calculate the feed's calorie content.

bombproof Any safe, reliable, and quiet horse, as used by a green rider.

Bonaventia An American term; a Jenny Lind (q.v.).

bone (1) The measurement describing the circumference around the cannon bone halfway between the knee and fetlock joint; used to determine conformation of a horse or hound, e.g., to have good bone; the ability of the bone to carry weight. (2) The hard, porous material which forms the skeleton of the horse and from which all soft tissues are suspended or to which they are joined; contains most of the minerals in the horse's body, especially calcium (q.v.) and phosphorus (q.v.); strength is directly related to collagen composition, not mineral mass; classified into five categories depending on shape: compact, flat, long, roofing, and irregular. (3) *see* BONING

bone chip A loose bone fragment resulting from injury to a bone that does not result in fracture (q.v.).

bone in the ground A hunting term; the state of the ground during or immediately following a frost in which the ground is hard under a soft surface.

bone meal Crushed or finely ground bones fed as a calcium-phosphorus feed supplement.

bone shaker Antiquated slang; any cheap, hired, horse-drawn carriage.

bone spavin Also known as jack, jack spavin, or arthritis of the hock; an outgrowth of bone tissue on the inside and front of the bone surface of the hind legs below the hock joint at the point where the hock tapers into the cannon bone; deposition of new bone may cause lameness, yet bony enlargements do not invariably accompany the condition; caused by faulty confirmation, local stress or trauma, malnutrition, or mineral imbalance; the affected horse may drag the toe, display shortened forward hoof flight and limited hock action; a very common form of lameness in horses.

boning Also known as bone; the antiquated practice of polishing black, Bordeaux leather riding boots using a bone, preferably a deer shank bone, in conjunction with paste or liquid blackening; the shank is rubbed over the surface of a cleaned and polished boot prior to rubbing with a chamois.

bonnet (1) A face marking (q.v.); a white head with pigmented ears and a pigmented area around the eyes. (2) *see* SHILL

bon veneur A French hunting term; a good huntsman (q.v.) or Hunt Master (q.v.).

bony growth *see* EXOSTOSIS

Booby Hut A horse-drawn vehicle; a sleigh popular in Boston, USA; had a closed body entered through a half-glass, full-length door and step, two windows on either side of the rear seat, and was driven from a high box; suspended on thoroughbraces (q.v.).

boodge *see* SWORD CASE

booge *see* SWORD CASE

book (1) A racing term; a jockey's schedule of riding assignments. (2) *see* BETTING BOOK.

(3) The group of mares sent to a stallion in one given year; if he covers the maximum number of mares allowed by his manager (about 40 for race horses), he is said to have a full book (q.v.). (4) *see* THE BOOK

bookie *see* BOOKMAKER

bookmaker Also known as bookie (sl); a professional betting person who accepts wagers.

booster An additional dose of a vaccine administered to either enhance or continue protection against a particular disease.

boot (1) A protective and/or supportive covering for the legs or feet of the horse made of leather, plastic, rubber, or other synthetic materials. (2) *see* RIDING BOOT. (3) To clip the long hair of the fetlock and lower leg. (4) Also known as trunk; a receptacle on a coach or carriage used to contain luggage; differentiated as front boot (q.v.) and rear boot (q.v.). (5) A racing term; said of a jockey who kicks his horse, as when coming in on the home stretch. (6) *see* HALF STOCKING

boots and saddles A racing term; a bugle call sounded when jockeys (q.v.) mount and enter the racetrack (q.v.) for the post parade; formerly a bugle call to cavalrymen; from the French cavalry command "bout selle" meaning to put saddle, which became "boot and saddle" in England and "boots and saddles" in the United States.

boot home a winner A racing term; to ride a winning horse in a race.

boot hook A J-shaped metal hook used, generally in pairs, to pull on riding boots; has a wooden, bone, plastic, or ivory handle attached perpendicular to the long, straight side of the hook; the curved part of the hook is inserted into the boot mule ear (q.v.) of which there are two per boot.

boot jack Also known as jack; a contrivance, usually made of wood, used to assist in removing a boot from the foot of the rider; of many shapes and sizes; in one design, the rider stands on the rear portion of the jack with one foot, wedges the heel of the other boot into a "V" on the other end, and pulls up on the leg; the boot remains in the jack.

boot tread (1) The step attached to the front boot (q.v.) of a horse-drawn coach, used by travelers to get into the box (q.v.). (2) The, usually textured, sole of a riding boot (q.v.).

boot tree A wooden or plastic form put into the leg, and in some cases foot, of a tall boot, to preserve its shape when not worn.

borer A horse who constantly pulls on the bit by thrusting his head forward and downward.

boring Said of a horse in action when he pulls on the bit by thrusting his head forward and downward.

bosal Also known as bosal noseband; a semi-oval, braided, rawhide, leather, or rope noseband which terminates in a heel knot (q.v.) tied under the jaw; used with a bosal hackamore (q.v.); rests at a 45 degree angle between the bridge of the nose and the chin of the horse; control is achieved by pressure applied to the bridge of the nose by the bosal and the tender area behind and under the jaw by the heel knot when the reins are raised by the rider; available in various sizes and diameters.

bosal noseband *see* BOSAL NOSEBAND

Bosnian Also known as Bosnian Pony; an ancient pony breed originating in Bosnia-Herzegovina; descended from the Tarpan (q.v.), stands 12.1 to 14 hands and may have a bay, brown, black, gray, chestnut, or palomino coat; has refined features overall, yet a rather heavy head and short neck, deep and wide chest, and short, muscled legs; is docile, steady, and hardy; used for riding, packing, light farm work and light draft; breeding stallions are government controlled, while mares are in private ownership; resembles the Hucul (q.v.).

Bosnian Pony *see* BOSNIAN

bosomy Said of a horse with an over-wide chest (q.v.).

boss *see* ROSETTE NO. 1

botfly *see* HORSE BOTFLY

bot larvae *see* HORSE BOT

bot *see* HORSE BOT

both legs out of the same hole Said of a horse with a very narrow chest whose forelegs are thus set too close together.

both sides of the road Also known as two sweats; a phrase used into the early 20th century; to work a coach team twice in the same day.

bots More than one bot (q.v.).

bottle fed Also known as hand fed; said of a foal or other young animal fed and raised by human hand when its mother is unable or is disinterested in doing so.

bottom (1) A racing term; the foundation of a race track surface. (2) A racing term; equine stamina, strength, and resolution. (3) A racing term; a horse assigned an outside post position and listed last in the race program. (4) An obsolete English hunting term; a fence with a big, deep, and jumpable ditch. (5) An obsolete English hunting term; an unjumpable ditch or brook running at the bottom of a deep gully or ravine; obs.

bottom bar The lowest slot or ring into which a rein (q.v.) can be buckled or secured on a curb bit (q.v.).

bottom line The last entry or line on a pedigree form; contains distaff (q.v.) information.

botulism Also known as forage poisoning or shaker foal syndrome; an intoxication, not an infection, resulting from the ingestion of the toxin *Clostridium botulinum*, a spore-forming anaerobic (q.v.) bacterium found in food; reproduces in decaying plant or animal matter and persists in most farm soils, animal intestines, and feces; the bacteria live for years in a benign spore form, waiting for warmer, wetter conditions and a protein source to feed on; toxins bind to nerve endings rendering them useless and paralysis ensues; as little as one milligram can kill a horse with 98 percent of the cases fatal; of the five known types: types B and C are most common in horses; type B progresses slowly and is easily diagnosed while type C does not impair eating until just prior to death and is often confused with tying up (q.v.), equine encephalomyelitis (q.v.), or plant poisoning; is particularly destructive of foals; symptoms in foals include impaired nursing, inability to swallow, decreased eyelid and tail tone, dilated pupils, and progressive muscular weakness and tremors leading to collapse and an inability to rise; symptoms in adults include motor weakness to total paralysis of the entire voluntary and much of the involuntary musculature, muscle tremors over the flanks after exertion, drool, a weak and unsteady gait, falling and an inability to rise, and ultimately death from respiratory paralysis; an antitoxin is available.

Boudicca *see* BOADICEA

Bourbannais One of a group of French half-bred horses.

Boulnois Cab Also known as Backdoor Omnibus, Duobus, Minibus, or Sice of an Omnibus; a four-wheeled, closed, horse-drawn carriage with a small, elongated body resembling a small Omnibus (q.v.); developed by Mr. Boulnois in 1830; seated two passengers vis-à-vis (q.v.); driven from a seat on the front of the roof and drawn by a single horse, hung on sideways elliptical springs front and rear and entered by a step and door from the rear; used privately and for hire; because it was easy for passengers to slip from the cab undetected upon arriving at the destination, thus leaving the fare unpaid, the life of this cab was short.

Boulonnais A coldblood breed originating in Northern France; descended from the ancient North European heavy horse crossed with eastern horses sometime in the 1st century AD; Arab (q.v.) blood was introduced during the time of the Crusades and in the 14th century the breed was crossed with Andalusian (q.v.) and Mecklenburg (q.v.); in the 17th century, it was named Boulonnais at which time two types emerged: (1) the smaller Mareyeur (q.v.) and (2) the larger horse standing 15.3 to 16.2 hands which is still bred and used for draft; has a distinctive head with a straight profile and particularly large eye, a thick, but graceful neck, prominent withers, silky skin with visible veining, a compact body, broad and straight back, short, strong limbs with wide joints, thick cannons and a lack of feathering, and a characteristic double-muscling of the croup; the mane and tail are full and the tail is set high; the predominant coat color is gray, usually dappled, although chestnut and bay occur occasionally; has straight, relatively long, swift, and energetic action; the Stud Book dates from 1886.

Boulster Wagon A four-wheeled, horse-drawn vehicle; a large version of the Bolster Wagon (q.v.) frequently used in public service; had two or three rows of crosswise seating, a hard-standing top, open sides, roller blinds, side curtains, and a driving apron across the forward seating; drawn by one or two horses harnessed in pole gear (q.v.); the bodywork was raised on bolsters (q.v.), but all seats were sprung individually.

bounce (1) Said of the mounted rider who is out of balance and/or rhythm with the horse; the rider does not sit quietly on the horse's back. (2) A racing term; said of a jockey who disengorges himself of food following a meal to maintain race weight.

bounce fence A jumping obstacle consisting of two fences without a stride between them; the horse touches down between the two elements and takes off without taking a stride.

boundary rider An Australian term; a ranch worker whose responsibility it is to ride the property perimeter or range fence line on large cattle and sheep stations to look for and repair holes in the fence.

Bounder *see* OXFORD CART

bounds *see* AIRS ABOVE THE GROUND

Bourbonnais *see* CHAROLLAIS

Bourdalou Also known as coach pot or, convenience, or carriage convenience; a chamber pot carried in a closed carriage for use by ladies in transit; commonly transported in a small box.

bout selle A French cavalry command; to put saddle.

bovine Of the ox kind; a cow.

bowed Said of a horse who has had, or is currently suffering from, a bowed tendon (q.v.).

bowed tendon Also known as tendon bow; any true physiological damage to the tendon or tendon sheath, specifically tearing or breaking of one or more of the tendonous fibers; usually occurs in the superficial flexor tendon of the front leg, although bows of the hind legs do occur; may be precipitated by fatigue, deep going, uneven terrain, improper shoeing, obesity, excessively tight-fitting running bandages or boots, work on slippery surfaces, long, weak pasterns, sudden changes in stress loads, low heel angles, and long toes; symptoms may include diffuse swelling over the tendon area, heat, and pain; lameness may or may not be present; hemorrhage and inflammation cause swelling and development of adhesions between the tendon and tendon sheath; a chronic bow is characterized by a firm, prominent swelling; of three classifications depending on the location: high bow (q.v.), low bow (q.v.), and middle bow (q.v.); as much as one year's rest may be required for a bowed tendon to heal completely.

bow hocks A conformation defect in which the hock joints are turned away from the body.

bowing A barrel racing term; said of a horse who, when rounding a barrel, strides out too quickly before gaining position for the next barrel; results in a wide, gradual turn which leaves the horse out of position for the next turn and results in a slower time.

bow legs *see* LATERAL DEVIATION OF THE CARPAL JOINTS

bow-legged *see* BANDY-LEGGED

bowline knot One of the few knots tied in a rope in which the loop does not get smaller when pulled.

bowling *see* THROW-IN

Bow Top Wagon *see* BARREL TOP WAGON

box (1) Also referred to as the box; an eventing term; an enclosed collecting area where competitors and their mounts spend the 10-minute compulsory halt before beginning Phase D of the Speed and Endurance test and where the second compulsory veterinary inspection occurs. (2) A competitive calf-roping term; the area along the side of the chute where the horse and rider wait until the start of a calf-roping run. (3) Also known as coachman's seat; the seat from which the coachman drives a horse-drawn vehicle. (4) A British term; a stall (q.v.). (5) *see* TRAILER NO. 2. (6) *see* BET NO. 1. (7) *see* BOX SEAT. (8) A wagering term; any combination bet whereby all possible numeric combinations are made.

boxcloth A fabric historically used for gaiters and outdoor wear, especially that used in coach driving.

boxed A horseshoe (q.v.) in which the outer edge of the hoof-facing side is rounded or beveled.

boxed in A racing term; said of a horse trapped behind, or to the side of, other horses in the field (q.v.).

boxed trifecta *see* TRIFECTA BOX

box foot *see* CLUB FOOT

boxing (1) A racing term; a technique in which the bettor (q.v.) selects three key horses in a trifecta (q.v.) and backs (q.v.) them in all possible combinations; an expensive option, that may yield high monetary rewards. (2) An English term; to transport a horse in a trailer van, truck, or rail car. (3) A dressage term; exaggerated or artificial action of the forelegs; a term usually applied to the trot.

box loop Also known as full safe, pipe, or pipe loop; a large, box-shaped leather keeper used on harness to hold the point of straps on the bridle cheek-pieces, hame and shaft tugs, crupper, and breeching; much wider than standard keepers (q.v.).

box seat Also known as box; a cushioned passenger's seat in a horse-drawn vehicle located adjacent to the coachman's seat (q.v.); a seat of honor.

box spur A spur (q.v.), consisting of a long, straight shank terminating in a thin square.

box stall *see* STALL NO. 1

box trifecta *see* TRIFECTA BOX

Box Wagon Also known as Show Wagon or Hackney Show Wagon (q.v.); a light, four-wheeled, pneumatic-tired wagon used for showing Hackney horses and ponies; has a shallow, box-shaped body hung on a perch undercarriage with two transverse-elliptical springs and a single, stick-backed driving seat; the shafts curve downwards towards the front axle.

boxwalker *see* STALL WALKER

boxy foot *see* CLUB FOOT

boxy hoof *see* CLUB FOOT

boy Racing slang; a jockey (q.v.).

BPHS *see* BRITISH PERCHERON HORSE SOCIETY

Brabancon *see* BRABANT

Brabant Also known as Brabançon, Belgian Brabant, Belgian Draft, Belgian Draft horse, Belgian Heavy Draft, race de trait Belge, or Flanders horse; an ancient horse breed descended from the Ardennais (q.v.) and the product of centuries of selective breeding; principally bred in Brabant, Belgium from which the name derived; by 1890 there were three main groupings based on bloodlines rather than conformation: Orange I, Bayard, and Jean I; a massive horse standing 16 to 17 hands and weighing up to 2,200 pounds (998 kg); has a thick back, short and extremely strong limbs with feathering (q.v.), huge and powerful quarters, a short, thick neck, and a small head in comparison to the body size; coat colors vary from line to line with bays, duns, and grays occurring, but red-roans with black points, sorrels and chestnuts predominating; is docile and obedient, strong, willing, matures early, long lived and has a slow but vigorous action; the stud book dates back to 1885; used for slow heavy pulling and farm work; instrumental in the development of the Shire (q.v.), Great Horse (q.v.), Clydesdale (q.v.), Suffolk Punch (q.v.), Irish Draft (q.v.), and American Belgian.

brace (1) Also known as body wash or tightener; any solution, liniment, or lotion containing menthol, wormwood, aromatics, alcohol, or other counter-irritant applied to the horse's body and/or legs to create mild topical stimulation and increase circulation. (2) A hunting term; two foxes (or game); one fox equals half a brace so, for example, five foxes equal two and a half brace. (3) A pair or couple of geldings (q.v.). (4) A sewn leather strip from which the bodies of some horse-drawn vehicles were hung on the chassis; used to check excessive motion in the vehicle body. (5) Also known as the brace; a polo term; the stance from which a polo player takes a stroke (q.v.) on the ball. (6) To make straight and firm, as in the rider's back when communicating direction to the horse.

brace bandage *see* EXERCISE BANDAGE

brachygnathism *see* OVER-SHOT JAW

bradoon *see* BRIDOON

bradoon hanger *see* GAG RUNNER

bradycardia Slowness in the beating of the heart, with corresponding slowness of the pulse-rate.

braid *see* PLAIT

brain fever *see* EQUINE ENCEPHALOMYELITIS

brain staggers *see* EQUINE ENCEPHALOMYELITIS

Brake *see* BREAK

brake Also known as coach retarder; a mechanical device used to decelerate or stop the motion of a wheel or vehicle by means of friction.

brake lever A long-handled metal bar used to apply the brakes on a horse-drawn vehicle either through forward or reverse pressure applied to the lever.

bran Also known as broad bran; the outer coating of wheat, rye, or other grain kernel which is separated from the flour in milling; contains less digestible energy, but more protein, fiber, and phosphorus than whole grain; highly laxative when fed as a mash (q.v.); may inhibit calcium absorption.

branch (1) An offshoot or subdivision of blood vessels, nerves, air tubes, lymphatics and so on. (2) The horseshoe surface from toe to heel on each side of the foot. (3) *see* BRANCHE. (4) An arm-like part diverging from the main stem, as in a stag's antler.

branche Also spelled branch; *see* CHEEK NO. 1

brand (1) Also known as ranch brand, ownership brand, or vanity brand; any mark or simple, easy, recognizable pattern on the hide or tissue of a horse made by burning with a hot iron or acid, freezing or tattooing to designate ownership; designs and/or numbers must be registered and issued to the owner, and may only be placed on the body on an area of the animal designated by the registration; duplicate brands may exist as many brands are only valid in the state or country or to the individual or ranch to which registered. (2) Also known as punch; the process of applying a brand (q.v.) to a horse.

Brandenburg Also known as Brandenburger; a multi-purpose warmblood developed in the 15th century at the Prussian Neustadt Stud; was heavy enough to serve as an all-purpose farming horse, yet light enough for use as a carriage horse; after World War II, the breed was re-established as an all-around sport horse using Hanoverian (q.v.), Trakehner (q.v.), and English Thoroughbred (q.v.) stallions; has a lively temperament, medium-sized head, well-set neck of medium length, a straight and strong back, long croup and is well-muscled; is generally bay and stands 15 to 16 hands.

Brandenburger *see* BRANDENBURG

brander (1) One who marks with a brand (q.v.). (2) *see* BRANDING IRON

branding iron Also known as brander or iron; an iron rod attached perpendicularly to a simple, easy, recognizable steel or iron pattern at one end used to apply a brand (q.v.) to the horse's hide.

bran disease *see* OSTEODYSTROPHIA FIBROSA

bran mash A mixture of bran (q.v.), usually wheat, and hot water mixed to a wet, but not sloppy consistency; used as a laxative, poultice, and, when mixed with sweeteners, to administer medications such as bute (q.v.) to a horse; salt may be added to improve palatability.

bray (1) The characteristic cry of the donkey (q.v.). (2) A loud or discordant noise resembling a donkey's bray.

braze To join metal surfaces using brass, bronze, or copper as a filler material, as in farriery (q.v.).

Break Also spelled Brake; a 19th century, open, heavy, four-wheeled, horse-drawn passenger vehicle with an elevated driving seat used for sporting and general purposes; drawn by a pair of horses in pole gear (q.v.) or a team; had a longitudinal seat which could be removed when luggage was carried; types include the Shooting Brake (q.v.), Skeleton Brake (q.v.), and Wagonette Brake (q.v.); the name derived from its original purpose which was to train and break young horses to drive, although it was also used for exercising.

break (1) Also known as break in; to train a young horse to accept a rider, obey commands, and accept direction and control. (2) *see* FRACTURE. (3) Also known as break stride; said of the horse; to change the gait at the command of the rider, as in "To break into a gallop"; in Britain, to fall out of one gait into another. (4) To turn and run, as in "The cow is going to break for the gate"; to run away. (5) A racing term; to leave the gate at the start of a race.

breakage A racing term; the difference between true mutuel odds and the lesser, rounded amounts (to the nearest $0.10) given to the winning bettor(s); the difference is usually divided between the track and the state and, in some cases, breeding or other funds, in varying proportions.

break covert A hunting term; said of a fox who leaves or escapes his hiding place.

break down (1) Said of a horse; to lose soundness or ability to perform due to an incapacitating illness or injury representing a physical disorder. (2) To lacerate the suspensory ligament or fracture a sesamoid bone, so that the back of the fetlock drops to the ground.

break in *see* BREAK NO. 1

Break-in Cart *see* BREAKING CART

breaking bit Also known as mouthing bit; a straight bar bit to which keys (q.v.) are attached in the center, used on a horse who has not previously had a bit in his mouth.

Breaking Cart Also known as Break-in Cart, Single Shaft Cart, Long-shafted Cart, or Single Break; a low, two-wheeled, training or exercise vehicle used to break single horses to draft; usually built to trainer specifications; has an elevated driving seat, an open, skeletal body, long shafts equipped with tug attachments to prevent breeching, and sometimes a rear drop extension to protect the driver in the event the horse falls over backward; a smaller version of the Skeleton Break (q.v.).

breaking cavesson *see* LUNGEING CAVESSON

breaking head collar *see* LUNGEING CAVESSON

breaking out Also known as break out; said of a horse who begins to sweat again after having been cooled out following exercise; may also occur due to illness, lack of fitness, excitement, stress and/or electrolyte imbalance.

breaking roller *see* TRAINING ROLLER

breaking tackle A generic term; any tack used to break (q.v.) a horse; may include lungeing cavesson (q.v.), side reins (q.v.), driving and lungeing reins (q.v.), bridle (q.v.), and crupper (q.v.).

break in the air A racing term; said of a horse who leaps into the air at the start of a race rather than moving forward.

break maiden Also known as earn a diploma; a racing term; said of a horse or rider who wins the first race of his career.

break out *see* BREAKING OUT

breakover Said of the foot; the act of the hoof rolling forward, lifting from the ground heel to toe.

breakover point The center point of the hoof over which the hoof naturally rolls at each lift off; determined by the conformation of the coffin bone and the leg joints above it

break stride *see* BREAK NO. 3

break the barrier A rodeo term; said of a horse and rider who pass through the barrier (q.v.) before it is released; results in a 10-second penalty.

break the start (1) An American racing term; said of a horse, to leave the starting gate as when racing. (2) A British racing term; said of a horse, to create a false start in a race, e.g., to break out of the gate (q.v.) before it is opened at the start of a flat race, or to break the starting tape in a National Hunt race.

break to harness To train a horse to drive.

break up A hunting term; said of the hounds (q.v.) when they tear at the carcass of the hunted fox.

break water A generic term; the expulsion of allantoic fluid during the first stages of giving birth.

breast Also known as brisket; that part of the horse's body below and in front of the insertion of the neck into the shoulder; the lowest portion of the breast.

breast band *see* BREAST COLLAR

breast bone Also known as sternum; the bone in the center of the chest to which the lower ends of the ribs are attached.

breast collar Also known as breast band or Dutch collar when used for driving; a wide leather strap fitted around the front of the shoulders just below the juncture of the neck, held in place by a narrow wither strap; easily adjusted to fit various horses of similar size, but with different shaped necks; used in conjunction with driving, Western, and some English saddles to prevent the saddle from slipping backward.

breast girth *see* BREASTPLATE

breast high A hunting term; said of the quarry's scent (q.v.) when it rises from the ground to the level of the hounds' noses so they are able to hunt at full speed.

breast piece *see* BREASTPLATE

breast plate *see* BREASTPLATE

breastplate Also known as breast piece or breast strap, incorrectly as breast girth and spelled incorrectly breast plate; a wide leather strap that encircles the horse's chest, attaching on both sides to the saddle dees, directly to the girth on either side, or to the girth between the forelegs; depending on the type, may be used in conjunction with a neck strap; used to prevent the saddle from slipping backward when dictated by conformation or terrain or for ornamental and show purposes.

breast strap *see* BREAST PLATE

breather A slowing of pace or speed to allow a horse to rest, conserve, or renew his strength for a short spell during exercise such as a race.

breathing bridoon A narrow, straight snaffle (q.v.) having a number of holes drilled through the mouthpiece (q.v.); thought to be effective with wind-suckers (q.v.).

bred (1) *see* COVERED. (2) Said of a horse from a specific geographic area, as in Kentucky-bred.

bred horse *see* THOROUGHBRED

breech birth Also known as breech delivery; birth of a foal in which the foal's hindquarters (q.v.), instead of the front legs and nose, are presented first in the birth canal.

breech delivery *see* BREECH BIRTH

breeches Also spelled britches; previously, trousers reaching to or just below the knees and often tapered to fit closely; now, any sleek, snugly fitting riding pant made of natural and/or synthetic fabric that closes tightly at the ankle; generally worn with a top or knee-high boot (q.v.).

breeching Also known as britchin' when used on farm horses; a broad leather band fitted around the haunches of the horse and attached either to the driving harness and shafts or directly to the saddle; supports the weight of brakeless, two wheeled horse-drawn vehicles when pulling up or descending hills, or backing; and to prevent riding and pack saddles from slipping forward.

breeching body A driving term; that part of the breeching (q.v.) which rests against the body of the horse.

breeching dee A metal staple screwed onto the shafts through which the breeching straps (q.v.) pass before being buckled.

breeching strap A strap which passes through the ring on the quarter-strap of the breeching, goes around the shaft and through the breeching dee (q.v.) before being buckled.

breed (1) The progeny or race from a particular stock or line of horses that, as a result of selective breeding, have certain distinguishable characteristics which are passed on through successive generations; generally resulting from known parents, the pedigree of which can be traced back a minimum of three generations; pedigrees are recorded in a stud book. (2) *see* COVER

breed class Any horse show class held for a specific horse breed.

breeder (1) One responsible for the selection of a sire (q.v.) to which a dam (q.v.) is mated; one who breeds horses. (2) One who owns a stud or stud farm where mares are sent for breeding. (3) The owner of a dam at the time of service unless the dam was under lease at the time of breeding. (4) *see* BROODMARE

Breeders' Cup American Thoroughbred racing's year-end championship; consists of seven races: the Breeders' Cup Sprint (q.v.), Breeders' Cup Juvenile Fillies (q.v.), Breeders' Cup Distaff (q.v.), Breeders' Cup Mile (q.v.), Breeders' Cup Juvenile (q.v.), Breeders' Cup Turf (q.v.), and the Breeders' Cup Classic (q.v.) conducted on one day at a different racetrack each year; purses and awards total $10 million; the $250,000 Breeders' Cup Steeplechase (q.v.) was formerly (dropped in 1994) part of the Breeders' Cup, but was not conducted on the same day or necessarily the same track.

Breeders' Cup Classic A 1¼ mile (2 km) race for three-year-old horses and older first run in 1984; one of seven Thoroughbred, year-end, championship races run on Breeder's Cup Day (q.v.) in the United States.

Breeders' Cup Day The single day per year on which the seven Breeders' Cup (q.v.) races are conducted in the United States.

Breeders' Cup Distaff A 1⅛ mile (1.8 km) race for mares and fillies, three years old and older, first run in 1984; one of seven, Thoroughbred, year-end championship races run on Breeder's Cup Day (q.v.) in the United States.

Breeders' Cup Juvenile A 1¹⁄₁₆ mile (1.7 km) race for two-year-old horses first run in 1984; one of seven Thoroughbred, year-end championship races run on Breeder's Cup Day (q.v.) in the United States.

Breeders' Cup Juvenile Fillies A 1¹⁄₁₆ mile (1.7 km) race for two-year-old fillies first run in 1984; one of seven Thoroughbred, year-end, championship races run on Breeder's Cup Day in the United States.

Breeders' Cup Mile A 1 mile (1.6 km) turf race for three year-old horses and older first run in 1984; one of seven Thoroughbred, year-end, championship races run on Breeder's Cup Day in the United States.

Breeders' Cup Sprint A 6 furlong (1.2 km) race for three-year-old horses and older first run in 1984; one of seven Thoroughbred, year-end, championship races run on Breeder's Cup Day (q.v.) in the United States.

Breeders' Cup Steeplechase A 2⅝ mile (4.2 km) jump-race event for three-year-old and older Thoroughbreds; conducted over a turf course; a year-end Breeders' Cup (q.v.) event first run in 1986 and dropped, due to financial deficits, from the annual slate of racing events in 1994; was not conducted on Breeders' Cup Day (q.v.) nor necessarily on the same track.

Breeders' Cup Turf A 1½ mile (2.4 km) turf race for three-year-old horses and older first run in 1984; one of seven

Thoroughbred, year-end, championship races run on Breeder's Cup Day in the United States.

breeding (1) The act of reproducing the species (2) The quality of the bloodline achieved through careful and controlled selection of the dam (q.v.) and sire (q.v.).

breeding boots Also known as covering boots; padded felt boots, heavily reinforced with leather, strapped onto the mare's hind feet during natural cover (q.v.) to protect the stallion from her potentially damaging kicks.

breeding certificate Written verification of the name of the breeding stallion and the mare covered, the dates the covering took place, or in the case of pasture breeding, the period the mare was exposed to the stallion, signed by the stallion owner.

breeding contract A binding agreement between the owners of the stallion and mare stating the amount of the payment due for breeding services and the contractual obligations of each party.

breeding fund A state fund established on a state-by-state basis in the United States to provide cash bonuses to horses bred within the state in which a fund is established.

breeding hobbles Also known as serving hobbles or mating hobbles; straps that encircle and secure the mare's hocks that prevent her from kicking the stallion during natural cover (q.v.); in another version, a rope is connected to a collar around the mare's neck, passed between her forelegs and attached to the hind pasterns.

breeding season The period during which males and females of a species demonstrate receptivity to mating.

breeding soundness evaluation of the mare An examination of a mare's breeding potential based on her history and a reproductive examination including estrus detection, visual examination of the perineum, rectal examination, examination by vaginal speculum, endometrial culture, endometrial biopsy and cytology.

breeding soundness evaluation of the stallion An examination of the stallion's breeding potential based on his history and a reproductive examination including evaluation of his sex organs and semen.

breed registry An official book of a breeding association in which mares, after passing certain tests, are entered and officially permitted to be used for breeding.

breed type Also known as type; the ideal or standard of perfection for any breed (q.v.) as detailed in the appropriate stud book or in registration papers.

breeze (1) Also known as breezing; a racing term; to exercise the horse at a controlled and relaxed speed. (2) A racing term; a rider hired to exercise or breeze race horses. (3) To ask a horse for increased speed.

breeze in A racing term; said of a horse who wins a race easily.

breezing *see* BREEZE NO. 1

Breton A coldblood breed believed to have originated in the province of Brittany in northwest France more than 4,000 years ago; descended from native steppe horses crossed with Oriental stallions and mares; when heavier draft capabilities were necessary, was crossed with Ardennais (q.v.), Percheron (q.v.), and Boulonnais (q.v.) blood and, in the 19th century Norfolk Trotter (q.v.) and Hackney (q.v.); of three size types: heavy draught, draught post, and mountain draught and three distinct morphological types: the Draught Breton (q.v.), the Postier Breton (q.v.), and the Corlay (q.v.); one of the smallest heavyweight breeds, the coat is generally chestnut or chestnut roan with a flaxen mane and tail; bay, gray, roan, and red roan also occur while black is not a breed color; has a square yet well-proportioned head with a heavy jaw, broad forehead, short ears, broad nose with flared nostrils, a short, broad, muscular and arched neck, and straight back, broad loins, a wide double croup and short and powerful legs with heavy joints; the tail is commonly docked; stands 15 to 16 hands and weighs 1,540 to 1,980 pounds (699–899 kg); registered foals are branded on the left side of the neck with a cross surmounting a splayed, upturned V; has been used to improve other heavy draft breeds as well as heavy draft and farm work; is docile, energetic, lively, and has great endurance.

Brett A horse-drawn vehicle; a transatlantic version of the European Britzka (q.v.); had a shallow body hung on two elliptical springs in front and two elliptic and two cee springs behind, one forward-facing and one rear-facing passenger seat, and a folding hood which covered the forward seat; seated four passengers; drawn by two or more horses in pole gear (q.v.).

brewers dried grains Also known as brewers grains, spent grains, and erroneously as distillers grains; the dried extracted residue of barley malt, alone or in mixture with other cereal grains or grain products; high in protein and fiber and containing a digestible energy content equal to or higher than that of oats; may contain pulverized, dried, or spent hops; generally fed dry although may be fed wet if obtained fresh from the breweries and fed immediately.

brewers grains *see* BREWERS DRIED GRAINS

brewer's horse Heavy horses, most commonly Shires (q.v.), but sometimes other heavy breeds, used to pull brewer's drays (delivery vehicles); this form of delivery is now largely superseded by mechanical vehicles, but many breweries, especially in Britain, retain drays and dray horses (q.v.) for showing and promotional purposes and, in some cases, for local deliveries.

brewers yeast A yeast, *Saccharomyces*, suitable for use as a ferment in the making of malt liquors; filtered from beer following the fermentation process; a good source of B-complex vitamins.

Brewster America's oldest carriage-building firm; established in the early 19th century by James Brewster

Breyerfest The largest show in the world for Breyer horses (q.v.) held every July in Lexington, Kentucky, USA; a four-day event for enthusiasts sponsored by Breyer Molding Company; includes performance horse, breed, and costume classes for models in original finish and remade, as well as lectures and vendors.

Breyer Horse Plastic or porcelain model horses noted for their realistic appearance; often modeled after live horses; manufactured since 1954 by Breyer Molding Company; are sold as toys, collected by hobbyists, and shown at model horse shows, the largest being Breyerfest (q.v.).

Breyer Molding Company A United States manufacturing company that, since 1954, has manufactured Breyer Horses (q.v.).

brick wall A solid jumping obstacle consisting of brick or faux brick blocks; a wall (q.v.).

bride hunt of the Mongols *see* KHIS-KOUHOU

bridesmaid A horse/rider combination regularly placing second in a competition.

bridge jumper A racing term; a bettor (q.v.) who specializes in placing large show bets on short-priced horses.

bridging the reins A method of holding the reins (q.v.); the right rein is run through the rider's right hand to the left and the left rein run through the left hand to the right; the reins overlap or "bridge" between the rider's hands with the rider holding both right and left reins in each hand.

bridle (1) Tack, usually made of leather, or synthetic materials, placed on the horse's head and fitted over the ears to control the horse with or without a bit; consists of the headstall (q.v.), and reins (q.v.), and usually though not always, a bit (q.v.). (2) To put a bridle on a horse.

bridle cheekpiece *see* CHEEKPIECE NO. 2

bridled Said of a horse fitted with a bridle (q.v.).

bridle gate Also known as hunting gate and hand gate; a hunting term; any small fence gate wide enough to accommodate the passage of a horse and rider.

bridle hand A 16th and 17th century term; the left hand; the reins were held in the left hand, to free the right to hold a weapon.

bridle head *see* HEADSTALL

bridle hook A fixture suspended from the

ceiling or a cross bar, used to hold bridles prior to cleaning; consists of four or more J-shaped hooks sharing a common center stem.

bridle lame *see* REIN LAME

bridleless cutting A cutting term; to demonstrate the cow sense (q.v.) of a horse by cutting a cow(s) without the use of a bridle; weight, leg, and spur aids may be used.

bridle lip strap *see* LIP STRAP

bridle mark An adventitial mark (q.v.); white coat hairs in the head area resulting from destruction of the pigment cells of underlying skin due to an ill-fitting or dirty bridle.

bridle path (1) Also known as bridle trail or bridleway (Brit.); a natural-surfaced path or road used for riding horseback, walking, and, in some cases the driving of cattle; vehicular traffic, and in some countries and instances bicycles, are prohibited. (2) That part of the horse's head near the poll (q.v.) and just behind it, across which the crownpiece of the bridle passes; the mane is commonly clipped in this area.

bridles well *see* GOES WELL INTO THE BRIDLE

bridle teeth *see* CANINE TEETH

bridle trail *see* BRIDLE PATH NO. 1

bridle wise Said of a horse trained to obey the aids of the bridle and bit.

bridling An English term used in the 18th through the 20th centuries; to render the head and neck light and flexible by teaching the horse to bend his neck at the poll and to relax his lower jaw; the lightness of the head and neck reacts on the shoulders and through them on the entire forehand.

bridoon Also known as bridoon bit or flying trench and spelled bradoon; a light, jointed, usually narrow-gage, snaffle bit used in conjunction with a curb bit (q.v.) in a double bridle (q.v.); controlled by reins other than those attached to the curb; may be plain, twisted, eggbutt, or have a ring in the center.

bridoon bit *see* BRIDOON

bridoon rein The rein attached to the bridoon bit (q.v.).

bright (1) Quick-witted or intelligent. (2) A cutting horse term; alert, as in, "The horse is bright on the cow."

bright on the cow A cutting term; said of the horse when alert or focused on the cow.

brindle Refers to hound coat color; tawny with streaked or spotted darker markings.

Brinekind noseband Also known as Jobey or Bucephalus; a leather cavesson-type noseband (q.v.) used in conjunction with a curb bit on strong pullers; exerts pressure around the nose when the curb rein is used; has a padded strap attached to the noseband which divides into two smaller straps which pass around and strap behind the jaw and hook into the curb hooks on opposite sides; made to measure for each horse.

brisket *see* BREAST

Brisker *see* BRITZKA

Briskie *see* BRITZKA

britches *see* BREECHES

britchin' *see* BREECHING

Britchka *see* BRITZKA

British Dressage Also known by the acronym BD; an organization founded in Britain to improve the standard of riding, training of horses and horsemanship in Great Britain by promoting, fostering and regulating dressage and to manage the representation of Great Britain in international dressage competitions and advise the British Equestrian Federation on all dressage matters.

British Driving Society, The Also known by the acronym BDS; an association founded in Great Britain 1957 to perpetuate interest in, and encourage and assist those involved with, driving horses and ponies.

British Equestrian Federation Also known

by the acronym BEF; an organization established in 1972 as the senior coordinating body for the British Horse Society (q.v.) and the British Show Jumping Association (q.v.).

British Equine Veterinary Association Also known by the acronym BEVA; the governing body representing most veterinarians licensed in Great Britain.

British Field Sports Society An organization founded in 1930 in Great Britain to encourage interest in all equestrian field sports; subsumed into the Countryside Alliance in March 1997; headquartered in London, England.

British Horseracing Board The governing authority for horseracing in Great Britain; founded in 1993 to take over from the English Jockey Club (q.v.) as racing's governing authority.

British Horse Society Also known by the acronym BHS; a British organization founded in 1947 by merger of the National Horse Association of Great Britain (q.v.) and the Institute of the Horse and Pony Club, Ltd. (q.v.); headquartered in Stoneleigh, Warwickshire, England, to promote the interests of horse and pony breeding and to encourage the use and protection of horses and ponies and to promote and facilitate the acquisition and distribution of the knowledge of the various arts and sciences connected with the horse and pony and the use and management thereof throughout Britain.

British Horse Society Assistant Instructor Also known by the acronym BHSAI; an assistant riding instructor (q.v.) certified by the British Horse Society (q.v.).

British Horse Society Instructor Also known by the acronym BHSI; a riding instructor (q.v.) certified by the British Horse Society (q.v.).

British Percheron Horse Society, The Also known by the acronym BPHS; a British organization founded in 1919 to establish and maintain the purity of the Percheron (q.v.) in Great Britain.

British Racehorse, The An illustrated journal devoted to the bloodstock (q.v.) industry in Great Britain and Ireland; established in 1949 by a resolution of The Thoroughbred Breeders' Association (q.v.).

British Riding Clubs A network of regional riding clubs throughout Britain offering local, regional, and national competitions in most disciplines; affiliated with the British Horse Society (q.v.).

British Show Hack and Cob Association A British organization founded in 1938 to further interest in riding hacks and cobs (q.v.).

British Show Jumping Association A British organization founded in 1923 to regulate all show jumping activities conducted there.

British Show Pony Society A British organization founded in 1949 to regulate showing of children's riding ponies.

British Spotted Horse A British-bred horse type rather than a breed; of mixed lineage, carries the spotting gene common in such breeds as the Appaloosa (q.v.) and Knabstup (q.v.); bred for coat pattern rather than conformation.

British Spotted Horse Society A British organization founded in 1947 to promote the interests of the riding-type British Spotted Horse (q.v.).

British Thoroughbred *see* THOROUGHBRED

Britschka *see* BRITZKA

Brittany Pack Horse *see* SOMMIER

brittle feet *see* BRITTLE HOOVES

brittle hooves Also known as brittle feet; abnormally dry hooves which are prone to breaking due to a dry condition of the horn; associated with dry air and lack of moisture in the soil.

Britzka Also known as Britchka, Britzska, Britzschka, Britschka, Brisker, or Briskie; originally an open, four-wheeled, horse-drawn traveling wagon popular in Poland and Eastern Europe; developed into a traveling carriage in Austria in 1818; later versions had a rearward platform with a rumble seat large enough to accommodate three carriage servants and a straight rather than a curved bottom line; the interior could be converted to a sleeping compartment for one or two persons lying at full length; generally hung on cee-springs; drawn by four or six horses and driven by a coachman (q.v.), although it was later postillion (q.v.) controlled.

Britzschka *see* BRITZKA

Britzska *see* BRITZKA

broad bran *see* BRAN

Broad-wheeled Wagon Also known as Flying Wagon (18th Century), Stage Wagon, or Snail of the King's Highway (Brit); a slow-moving (3 to 4 mph [4.8–6.4 kmph]), canvas-covered, wide-wheeled, cumbersome goods and passenger wagon popular in Britain among those unable to afford Mail or Stage Coach (q.v.) travel; pulled by 4, 6, or 8 horses driven by a waggoner (q.v.), either mounted or on foot, and armed with a long whip; first used in the 16th century; owing to the tremendous road damage caused by the narrow-rimmed wheels, a law was passed in 1753 which established a minimum wheel width of 9 inches (22.9 cm); failure to comply with this measurement resulted in a stiff penalty.

brockamore *see* MECHANICAL HACKAMORE

brocket Also known as knobbler or knobber; a two-year-old male deer.

broke Tamed and trained, as in a horse.

broken amble *see* RACK

broken canter *see* DISUNITED CANTER

broken crest Also known as fallen neck or lop neck; said of the horse's neck when so heavy, it breaks over and falls to one side.

broken down Said of a horse in less than perfect physical condition due to injury, trauma, or overuse.

broken kneed Said of a horse whose knees are scarred by injury; does not signify bone fracture.

broken knees The horse's knees when scarred, indicating that he has fallen or been injured; does not signify bone fracture.

broken neckline A dressage term; the position of the neck when there is excessive longitudinal flexion approximately ⅓ of the way down the neck, so that the poll is no longer the highest part of the skeleton and the topline of the neck no longer forms an even, smooth, arc.

broken wind *see* CHRONIC OBSTRUCTIVE PULMONARY DISEASE

brokk One of five natural gaits of the Icelandic (q.v.); a trot (q.v.) used when traversing rough country.

bromegrass hay Cut and dried grass hay generally made from the smooth variety of bromegrass; hardy and grown in the Central Plains of the United States; frequently mixed with legumes (q.v.) for improved palatability, yield, and quality; contains a digestible protein content ranging from approximately 6.2 percent to 9.8 percent and a crude fiber content ranging from 34.2 to 38.5 percent.

bronc *see* BRONCO

bronc buster Also known as buster, bronco buster, bronc twister, bronc peeler, or bronc snapper; one who breaks or trains broncos (q.v.).

bronc busting The handling and breaking of broncs (q.v.) so that they may be ridden.

bronc chaps Chaps (q.v.), generally brightly colored, loosely fitted and secured only to mid thigh to allow the lower leg portion to move freely; enhances the spurring action of the rider and the bucking action of the horse.

bronchioles Small, tubular air passages in the lungs.

bronchitis A respiratory condition characterized by inflammation of the bronchial tubes and forced expiration.

broncho *see* BRONCO

bronchoconstriction A narrowing of the smaller airways of the lungs triggered by the release of histamines (q.v.).

bronchodilator Any substance that, when inhaled, causes the air passages of the lungs to widen.

bronchospasm Abnormal involuntary contraction of the muscles surrounding the bronchioles (q.v.).

bronco Also known as bronc or bronk and spelled broncho; an unbroken or imperfectly broken wild horse; Spanish for rough and rude.

bronco buster *see* BRONC BUSTER

bronc peeler *see* BRONC BUSTER

bronc rider One who rides wild, unbroken horses, as in a rodeo event.

bronc riding Also known as buck jumping; a rodeo event in which a competitor rides a bareback bronco fitted with a wide leather band strapped circumferentially around his body just behind the shoulder from which a leather handhold protrudes and onto which the rider secures his grip.

bronc saddle A saddle used in breaking horses.

bronc snapper *see* BRONC BUSTER

bronc twister *see* BRONC BUSTER

bronk *see* BRONCO

broodmare Also known as breeder; a mare who has previously foaled and is expected to continue to have foals; kept primarily for breeding purposes.

broodmare sire *see* DAM'S SIRE

broomstock *see* BROOMTAIL NO. 2

broomtail (1) *see* SWITCH TAIL. (2) Also known as broomstock; any small horse, such as some mustangs (q.v.), not considered worth the effort to break (q.v.).

Brotherhood of Working Farriers Association Also known by the acronym BWFA; an organization of farriers founded in the United States in 1989.

brothers Also known as full brothers or own brothers; a relationship of male horses by the same sire (q.v.) and out of the same dam (q.v.).

brothers in blood Said of male horses by the same sire out of full sisters, or by full brothers out of the same dam.

Brougham Also known as Fly, Fly-by-night, and from the mid-19th century on, as a small Station Cab; a small, four-wheeled, horse-drawn town carriage first built around 1839; inspired if not actually designed by Lord Brougham, a statesman of the early 19th century, for whom it was named; seated two forward-facing passengers, was low-slung, fully paneled and had an upholstered and fully enclosed body fitted with windows, popular well into the 1920s; of two main types: Peter's Brougham (q.v.) and Barker Brougham (q.v.).

Brougham Cab A two-wheeled, single-horse vehicle, which was a cross between a Bougham (q.v.) and a Hansom Cab (q.v.); had a fully enclosed, Hansom-type body which could be entered from either side by curving, full-length, half-glass doors; the shafts terminated in the front of the vehicle to which they were connected by iron brackets; the driver sat on a high seat at the rear of the vehicle which he reached by two back steps.

bowband Also known, in driving terms, as front; that part of the bridle that lies flat across the forehead below the ears and above the eyes of the horse, attaches to the headstall (q.v.) by the cheekpieces (q.v.) and passes through loops on either side of the browband on both sides; prevents the headstall (q.v.) from slipping backwards on the neck.

brown Refers to coat color; having the color of coffee or chocolate, a combination of red, black, and yellow without red tones and having dark or black points; variations include dark brown (q.v.), medium brown, light brown (q.v.), and seal brown (q.v.).

brown saddler A saddle maker specializing in saddles, bridles, etc., as opposed to a black saddler (q.v.).

Bruce Lowe System *see* BRUCE LOWE FIGURE SYSTEM

Bruce Lowe Figure System Also known as Bruce Lowe System or Lowe Figure System; a method of identifying racing Thoroughbred (q.v.) families; each family is identified by number according to the female ancestor from which it descended; all Thoroughbred progeny were traced back to 43 foundation mares (q.v.) and were allotted numbers according to the number of times their descendants won classic (q.v.) races; developed by Australian Bruce Lowe in the early 20th century.

bruise (1) To injure by a blow or pressure without laceration. (2) Discoloration due to bruising.

bruised sole A contusion of the foot, without laceration, resulting from stones, irregular ground, or other trauma such as poor shoeing which can predispose a horse to bruising; may or may not be associated with lameness.

Brumby A wild horse indigenous to Australia descended from domestic horses turned loose on the ranges during the mid-19th century following the gold rush; is hardy and unrefined, stands approximately 15 hands, and has a rather heavy head, short back, sturdy legs, and a coat of any color; in the 1960s, due to organized culling of the wild herds, was brought close to extinction; the name derived from the aboriginal word baroomby meaning wild.

Brumby runner An Australian bush horseman who chases, captures, and tames Brumbies (q.v.).

Brunswick An American four-wheeled horse-drawn vehicle similar to a Surrey (q.v.); had a fringed awning over the two forward-facing seats; the body was hung on two elliptic springs and a perch.

brush (1) To run a horse at top speed over a short distance. (2) A hunting term; the tail of a fox. (3) A hand-held instrument consisting of natural or synthetic bristles or hair set in an attached handle of wood, plastic, or leather used for removing dirt or dust, polishing or smoothing, or applying cream, paint, or conditioner. (4) A hunter jumper term; said of a horse when jumping who lightly touches a rail or plank, but does not drop it. (5) A racing term; said of two horses that slightly touch or collide while running. (6) A harness racing term; the brief peak(s) of speed reached by a horse in a race or training mile.

brush box An artificial jumping obstacle consisting of brushwood or other suitable hedging material grown in a planter box.

brush boots *see* BRUSHING BOOTS

brush fence A jumping obstacle (q.v.), either natural or artificial, consisting of brushwood or some other suitable hedging material.

brushing Also known as cutting; said of a horse in motion when one limb lightly strikes another, as in interfering (q.v.).

brushing boots Also known as brush boots or splint boots; a protective covering of the horse's legs made of felt, leather or synthetic materials used to protect the fetlock joint and cannon bone against brushing (q.v.) or knocks from the shoe or hoof of another leg when the horse is in action.

brushing ring boot *see* FETLOCK RING BOOT

bubble (1) A cutting term; the imaginary area or space surrounding a cow or herd of cattle in which they feel secure; size is determined by how far a cutter can penetrate the herd before it reacts to his presence; the fresher the cattle the larger the bubble; the direction and speed of a cow's movements can be influenced by the position of the cutter's horse near the edge of the bubble. (2) The horse's personal space over which he feels dominant

Bucephalus (1) Alexander the Great's famous war horse; could not be broken or ridden by anyone but Alexander; died in 326 BC and was buried by the Jhelum River, India in the city of Bucephala (Jalapur) which Alexander built to honor his horse. (2) *see* BRINEKIND NOSEBAND

buck (1) Action of the horse; a series of acrobatic jumps in which the horse springs with a quick leap, dropping his head and arching his back and simultaneously kicking with his hind legs and landing on stiffened forelegs; may be a deliberate attempt to unseat the rider in which case it considered a vice. (2) The lower part of the body of a horse-drawn vehicle. (3) Also known as stag or staggart (obs) in parts of Europe and Great Britain; a male deer (more than four years of age), antelope, rabbit, or hare. (4) *see* BUCKED

buckaroo Also known as vaquero and spelled buckeroo; a cowboy; a bronco (q.v.) buster; a herder of cattle.

Buckboard A four-wheeled, open-passenger, horse-drawn vehicle popular in the United States from 1826 through the 1900s in which a long, flexible board or frame was fastened to the axle without the use of springs, had one or two rows of crosswise seating, was drawn by a single horse or pair, and was generally driven by a coachman from a box (q.v.).

Buckboard Phaeton An American two-passenger hooded vehicle; had a tray-shaped body and wheels of equal height.

bucked Also known as buck; said of a horse suffering from bucked shins (q.v.), e.g. "The young Thoroughbred bucked."

bucked knees *see* FORWARD DEVIATION OF THE CARPAL JOINTS

bucked shins Also known as shinbuck or sore shins; a temporary, usually bilateral, unsoundness involving the horse's forelimbs resulting from skeletal immaturity and concussion; associated with the stretching or tearing of the overlying periosteum (q.v.) of the large metacarpal (cannon bone) or, less frequently, the small metatarsal bone and characterized by a warm, painful swelling over the front of the bones, initial lameness, and a shortened stride; bone abnormality is not common although saucer fractures (q.v.) are sometimes seen; confined almost chiefly to young Thoroughbreds (q.v.) in training or racing, although it is possible for older horses to buck (q.v.); occurs more commonly in the United States than other countries, probably due to different training and racing conditions.

buckeroo *see* BUCKAROO

bucket (1) A cylindrical container for scooping up or holding liquids or solids. (2) To ride hard, as a horse.

Bucket Seat Gig A horse-drawn vehicle of the Gig (q.v.) type; had two independent forward-facing seats, placed side-by-side and resembling modern car seats.

buck eye An antiquated term; a prominent eye.

buckhound A hound used by hunters to pursue deer or other small game; similar to the staghound but smaller.

bucking Said of a horse who performs more than one buck (q.v.) in a row, usually until either the rider is unseated or the horse tires; may be considered a vice.

buck itself out Said of a horse who has stopped bucking due to exhaustion or because he cannot unseat the rider.

buck jumping (1) The act of a bucking (q.v.) horse whereby he arches his back, lowers his head, and jumps into the air off of all four legs at once; repeated with great rapidity. (2) *see* BRONC RIDING

buck-kneed Said of a horse displaying forward deviation of the carpal joints (q.v.).

buckle (1) A clasp consisting of a rectangular or curved rim with a tongue and catch; used to fasten together two loose ends. (2) To fasten or join together with a buckle.

buckle guard Also known as buckle safe; any piece of shaped leather incorporated into the tack between a buckle and the horse to prevent the buckle from rubbing on the horse's hide.

buckle safe *see* BUCKLE GUARD

buck line A line attached to the draw chain used in multiple draft hitches (q.v.) to keep a horse from getting ahead of his mate.

buckskin (1) Refers to coat color; a type of dun (q.v.) having a grayish-brown yellow coat, black points, and a head of a similar, but darker color than the body; wither and dorsal stripes (q.v.) and stripes over the knees and hocks may occur; variations include zebra dun (q.v.), dusty buckskin (q.v.), smutty buckskin (q.v.), and silver buckskin (q.v.). (2) The skin of a buck or deer; normally a yellow or grayish color historically used in the American West for clothing.

budget A leather storage box attached to the fore-carriage of a horse-drawn vehicle when used for out-of-town travel.

Budenny *see* BUDYONNY

Budonny *see* BUDYONNY

Budyonny Also known as Budonny, Budenny, or Budyonovsky; a Russian warmblood developed at the Rostov military stud in the 1930s by Marshal Budyonny who intended to create a military mount by putting Thoroughbred (q.v.) stallions to Don (q.v.) mares with the best of the resulting progeny interbred; an officially recognized breed since 1948; has excellent conformation, a strong, close-coupled body which is deep through the girth, strong and has generously boned legs, an elegant head, long neck, and stands 15.1 to 16 hands; 80 percent of the breed have a chestnut coat with a rich golden sheen, although bays and grays also occur; is calm, sensible, and has great stamina; rigorously tested over long distances and on the track; excels at steeplechasing and, due to its jumping ability, performs well as an all-round sport and riding horse.

Budyonovsky *see* BUDYONNY

buffalo fly A fly species, *Haematobia irritans exigua*, the primary pest of cattle, water buffalo, and, occasionally, horses; distributed throughout northern Australia and New Guinea, and is found in parts of southern, southeastern, and eastern Asia, and Oceania, but does not extend into New Zealand; leaves bite wounds on the shoulders and withers, yet during hot weather moves to shaded body areas; may provide a sight for screwworm (q.v.) infestation; afflicted animals suffer blood loss and irritation; flies are easily controlled by insecticides.

buffer *see* CLINCH CUTTER

bug *see* APPRENTICE JOCKEY

bug boy *see* APPRENTICE JOCKEY

Buggie (1) *see* BUGGY. (2) *see* AMERICAN BUGGY

Buggy (1) Also spelled Buggie and known as Hooded Gig; a light, English-type, horse-drawn vehicle of the Gig (q.v.) type having curved shafts and a folding head (q.v.); drawn by a single horse; popularized in the early 19th century; from the Hindu baygi-gi, meaning to move (2) *see* AMERICAN BUGGY

bugle (1) Also known as bell; the sound a stag (q.v.) makes during mating season. (2) Also known as pole-bar, neck bugle, or yoke; the cross-bar used to support the pole when a pair (q.v.) is put to a two-wheeled vehicle.

build The body structure of the horse.

Builder's Cart A strong, two-wheeled, horse-drawn cart; had an oak frame, elm sides, and ash shafts; used to transport builder's materials.

Built-up Brake A horse-drawn vehicle of the Drag (q.v.) type; the body was hung on a perch and telegraph springs (q.v.) and had a boot (q.v.) which ran the full length of the body from footboard to rumble.

built uphill *see* UPHILL

bulbs *see* HEEL BULBS

bull (1) *see* STALLION. (2) An uncastrated male cow.

bulla A large blister (q.v.).

bull dog (1) Refers to conformation type; a small horse having huge, muscled quarters, a short back and an over-muscled front end between the shoulders; used to describe conformation in such breeds as Quarter Horses (q.v.) and Pintos (q.v.). (2) Harness racing slang; a stayer (q.v.). (3) *see* BULL DOG QUARTER HORSE

bulldog bite *see* UNDER-SHOT JAW

bulldogger (1) A horse used for steer wrestling (q.v.). (2) *see* STEER WRESTLER

bulldogging *see* STEER WRESTLING

bull dog Quarter Horse Also known as bull dog; a Quarter Horse (q.v.) conformation type; a small horse having huge, muscled quarters, a short back, and an over-muscled front end between the shoulders which is more massive than a standard Quarter Horse.

bullet *see* PULL NO. 5

bullet work Also known as black-letter work; a racing term; the best workout time clocked by a horse for a particular distance on a given day at a track; from the printer's "bullet" that precedes the time of the workout in the daily listings.

bullfinch A jumping obstacle; a thick, overgrown live hedge which, due to the height, must be jumped through, not over; of two types: black bullfinch (q.v.) and hairy bullfinch (q.v.).

bull neck Said of the horse's neck when short, thick, and difficult to flex.

bulling *see* GRUNTING

bull nose foot *see* DUBBED

bull pen (1) Also known as round pen; an enclosed area at least 30 feet (9 m), but generally 100 to 200 feet (30 60 m) in diameter, with high, solid walls more than 6 to 8 feet (1.8–2.6 m) or more high, in which a horse is worked or trained. (2) An auction ring. (3) Also known as bull ring; an American racing term; a small racetrack usually less than 1 mile (1.6 km) in length with sharp turns.

bull rider One who rides bulls in a bull riding (q.v.) competition.

bull riding A standard rodeo event, in which the contestant rides a bull equipped only with a rope wrapped around its body behind the shoulder and over the withers (q.v.); the rider may hold onto this rope with only one hand, the other hand held up in "high salute" until the ride is completed.

bullring *see* BULL PEN NO. 3

bump A polo term; a movement in which one player rides into, or bumps, another to spoil his shot on the ball; the angle of the collision should not exceed 45 degrees, although the faster the horse of the player performing the bump is traveling, the smaller this angle should be.

bumper (1) A racing term; an amateur rider. (2) A racing term; a race for amateur riders. (3) A British racing term; a flat race for horses who are intended for careers racing over fences; often ridden by novice or amateur riders.

bump the bit A cutting term; said of the rider; to inadvertently pull back with one or both reins just enough to make the horse feel and react to the bit; may be caused by holding the reins unevenly or too tightly.

BUN *see* BLOOD UREA NITROGEN

Burford saddle Previously known as Morocco saddle; a military saddle used in the first half of the 17th century.

Burghley A stately home in England near Stamford in Lincolnshire, which is the home of the Burghley Horse Trials (q.v.).

Burghley Horse Trials A major autumn three-day event held annually in Burghley, Britain since 1961.

Burmah Buggy A two-wheel, horse-drawn light Gig (q.v.) or hooded buggy of the English type; hung on sideways, semi-elliptical springs; widely used in Burma and India during the second half of the 19th century; drawn by a single horse or pony.

Burmese Also known as Shan or Shan Pony; a riding and pack pony bred by the hill tribes in Shan State in eastern Burma; similar to the Manipuri (q.v.) but taller, slower, and not as quick off the mark; is small and rather plain looking, stands about 13 hands (1.32 m), has a brown, bay, black, chestnut, or grey coat, small, light head with a straight profile, and almond-shaped eyes; the back is straight and fairly long, the croup sloping, the girth deep, the shoulder not sloping, slender and strong legs and a small foot with strong horn; active, but not always reliable.

burner A small piece of rawhide or leather laced onto the lariat (q.v.) honda (q.v.); prevents the honda from wearing out.

burning scent Also known as screaming scent, red hot scent, or blazing scent; a hunting term; said of the scent of the quarry (q.v.) when so strong that the hounds are able to pursue the line without hesitation.

burr (1) *see* BIT BURR. (2) A small round iron plate positioned inside the fellow (q.v.), upon which the point of the iron is riveted after being driven through the tire.

burra *see* JACKEROO

burro (1) A Spanish term; an ass (q.v.). (2) *see* ASS

bursa A sac or sac-like cavity containing synovial fluid (q.v.) situated over bony prominences or between tendons, which acts as a pad or cushion.

bursatti *see* CUTANEOUS HABRONEMIASIS

bursitis Inflammation of a bursa (q.v.) characterized by rapid swelling due to an accumulation of synovial fluid, local heat, and pain; may be location-specific as in capped hocks (q.v.), capped elbow (q.v.), shoe-boil, or navicular bursitis.

burst A hunting term; said of the hounds (q.v.); a fast, quick run on a fox.

Burton Wagon Also known as Showman's Wagon; a horse-drawn vehicle, the largest of the Gypsy Wagons (q.v.), weighing approximately 1½ tons (1.36 tonnes); the front wheels were smaller than the rear, with all four resting under the boldly painted body; gargoyles frequently adorned the four corners of the roof and rain was directed through their mouths; had planked sides and hay or luggage rack in the rear; the interior was fitted with a folding double bed, cupboards, and a mantle; drawn by a strong single horse.

bury A jumping term; said of a rider who rides his horse too close to the fence to jump it from the proper distance.

bus (1) A contraction of Omnibus (q.v.). (2) Slang; any large, horse-drawn passenger vehicle.

bush track Also known as flapping track (Brit.); a racing term; an unofficial race meeting.

Business Buggy An American four-wheeled, hooded Buggy with rattan sides and space behind the forward-facing seats for carrying samples.

buster *see* BRONC BUSTER

Butazolidin A brand name for phenylbutazone (q.v.).

Butazone A brand name for phenylbutazone (q.v.).

butcher boots Black hunt boots (q.v.) without tops.

bute *see* PHENYLBUTAZONE

butt cap The metal cap or end of the hand-held portion of a whip.

Butterfly Slang; any short-distance, horse-drawn, public transportation Coach (q.v.).

butterfly bars *see* JUMPED-IN BARS

butteri Mounted cattlemen from the Maremma regions of Tuscany and Latium, Italy, who commonly used the Maremmana (q.v.) for light draft and riding.

butteris An ancient farrier tool used for trimming hooves; a long, sharp chisel pushed by means of the farrier's shoulder; although still used in some parts of the world, it has not been in use in the United States since the 1930s.

buttermilk horse *see* PALOMINO

buttermilk roan *see* SABINO

buttocks *see* HINDQUARTERS

button stick A coaching term; a flat strip of slotted metal or wood slid under the buttons of a livery coat to protect the cloth when the buttons are polished.

buttress foot *see* PYRAMIDAL DISEASE

Buxton bit A heavy harness curb (q.v.) bit having curved cheeks with two slots for the reins, one halfway down the cheek and one at the bottom; the lower ends of the cheeks are connected by a narrow bar to prevent the lead reins from becoming caught under the bit; mouthpiece size varies considerably.

buy-back Also known as charge-back; a racing term; said of a horse put through public auction who did not reach the reserve (q.v.) set by the consignor and was, therefore, retained.

buy sight unseen To purchase a horse on the basis of verbal or written description rather than visual evaluation.

buzkashi Also known as goat-lifting, goat-dragging, or dragging the goat; the wild and ruthless national sport of Afghanistan; a rudimentary and rugged type of polo or mounted rugby; of two types: the more primitive and essential form of the game known as tudabarai (q.v.) and the 20th Century version, qarajai (q.v.); although played in widely divergent fashions, the object is to gain control of a decapitated calf carcass or stuffed goat skin; historically, the skin of a freshly killed goat was stuffed with sand, sewn up, and left to soak in water overnight and may ultimately weigh as much as 66 to 88 pounds (30–40 kg); may be played by several teams consisting of 25 or more players, with some matches involving more than 1,000 players; each rider or chapandazan (q.v.), carries a short, wooden-handled whip with which they may strike an opponent, but not his mount; the playing field is not limited in size and obstacles such as hills and rocks are looked upon with favor; two single goalposts are positioned approximately ½ mile (800 m) apart about which are drawn circles of about 50 yards (46 m) in diameter; the game is started by an umpire who throws the goat skin (now, often a goat-skin ball) into the middle of the pack; umpires decide which team wins; a contraction of *buz* meaning goat, and *kashidan* meaning to pull; its origins are uncertain, although an early form was likely developed soon after the domestication of the horse by Central Asian tribes.

buzzer A battery-powered vibrator or other electric-shock device used to frighten a horse into running faster or jumping; is illegal on the track or in the show ring, but is often used as a training device.

BVMS *see* BACHELOR OF VETERINARY MEDICINE & SURGERY

BVSc *see* BACHELOR OF VETERINARY SCIENCE

BWFA *see* BROTHERHOOD OF WORKING FARRIERS ASSOCIATION

by Also known as sired by; a foal is said to be 'by' the sire and 'out' of the dam.

bye day A hunting term; an extra hunt meeting held by a Hunt (q.v.) during the Christmas holiday or to make up for hunt days lost due to bad weather.

Byerley Turk An Arab (q.v.) stallion, one of the three founding sires of the English Thoroughbred (q.v.), originally captured from the Turks at the siege of Budapest and brought back to England by Captain Byerley for whom it was named; was never raced; all Thoroughbreds (q.v.) in the world today trace their ancestry in direct male line to this horse, the Godolphin Arab (q.v.), or Darley Arabian (q.v.).

by the rack A betting term; said of a bettor, to purchase every possible daily-double (q.v.) or other combination ticket.

C

CAA *see* CARRIAGE ASSOCIATION OF AMERICA

Cab A horse-drawn, two-wheeled coach brought to London, England from Italy, via Paris, during the early 19th century; frequently used for public hire; the first rival of the Hackney coaches; from the 1820s on, developed in many two- and four-wheeled versions; by the 1860s, the primary types included the four-wheeled Growler (q.v.), driven from a box seat, and the two-wheeled Hansom Cab (q.v.) driven from a rearward skeleton seat situated at roof level; later types were fitted with taximeters, for recording distances and fares, from which the name taxi derives; derived from Cabriolet, meaning two-wheeled coach.

caballada A Spanish term; a band of horses.

caballero A Spanish term; a cowboy (q.v.).

caballo A Spanish term; a horse (q.v.).

Caballo Chileno *see* CHILENO

Caballo de Paso Fino *see* PASO FINO

Caballo Peruano de Paso *see* PERUVIAN PASO

Caballo Pura Raza Española Also known by the acronym PRE; *see* ANDALUSIAN

caballos cuñeros A bullfighting term; the horse ridden by a picador (q.v.); generally cold-blooded draft horses of no particular breed, although a number are Heavy Draft Bretons (q.v.); usually weigh no less than 1,435 pounds (650 kilos) so as not to be knocked off of their feet when battered by the bull; are blindfolded so as not to shy from the charging bull and wear a type of padded armor which covers the body to about mid-cannon; serve as a "wedge" between the picador and the bull thus enabling the picador to jab with the pic (q.v.); from the Spanish *cuña*, meaning wedge.

cabbage Any of various cultivated varieties of the cruciferous plant, *Brassica oleracea*, especially one of the varieties with a short stem and leaves formed into a compact, edible head; in a wider sense includes such plants as the cauliflower, Brussels sprouts, kale, etc.; suitable as horse feed.

Cab-fronted Gig *see* MORGAN CART

cable link Also known as cable-link snaffle; a snaffle bit (q.v.) with a rough-link chain mouthpiece.

cable-link snaffle *see* CABLE LINK

cabman One who drove a horse-drawn Cab (q.v.) for hire; employed by a cab master (q.v.).

cab master One who owned public transportation Cabs (q.v.) and horses which they either hired out to cab men (q.v.) or worked themselves.

Cab Phaeton Also known as Mi-lord; a horse-drawn vehicle invented in London, England in 1835; the body was hung on four elliptical springs, was pulled by a single horse driven from a low seat located in front of the passenger's seat; later, somewhat modified versions became known as the Victoria (q.v.).

Cabriole *see* CABRIOLET

Cabriolet Also known as Cabriole; a two-wheeled, open, boxless, horse-drawn carriage with a shell-shaped body mounted high above road level, with flexible shafts, a folding hood, and either whip or cee-spring suspension originating in the 1700s; in 19th-century England, it was used by the wealthy class; usually drawn by a powerful coach horse of a hunter type, and driven by the owner with a short youth or mature short man, standing on a rearward platform; from the French version of the Italian *capriolo* meaning kid or young goat as related to the skipping or swaying movements of the vehicle.

Cabriolet Phaeton A four-wheeled horse-drawn vehicle popular in the 1800s; suspended on four elliptical springs and driven from a high box behind which was low seating for four passengers vis-à-vis (q.v.).

Cachar Polo Club A polo club founded in Cachar, India in 1859; considered the oldest polo club in existence.

cactus cloth A coarsely woven cloth used to rub out sweat marks from the horse's coat and to stimulate blood flow.

cad (1) English slang; a conductor of London's early horse buses; noted for their rough demeanor. (2) A 19th-century term; a man who worked in stables which supplied post horses (q.v.); looked after the horses, washed the Post Chaises (q.v.), called the post boys (q.v.) at night when a chaise was needed for hire, lit the lamps, and occasionally rode the post chaise.

cade An English term; a bottle-raised foal.

cadence Also known as expression; the quality of the horse's pace demonstrating rhythm, impulsion and elasticity; from the Latin *cado* to fall.

cadenettes Curls that form in the long ear hair of the Poitou ass (q.v.).

Cadre Noir A select group of horsemen of the French Cavalry School at Saumur (q.v.) who practice High school (q.v.) riding in accordance with the French tradition of classical equitation (q.v.); became the instructor's corps for the school at Saumur; the name means black frame which was derived from the distinctive uniform these horsemen wear: a black three-pointed hat, black high-neck tunic, and white or black breeches.

CAF I *see* CERTIFIED APPRENTICE FARRIER, LEVEL ONE

CAF II *see* CERTIFIED APPRENTICE FARRIER, LEVEL TWO

Café-au-Lait (1) *see* PALOMINO. (2) *see* ISABELLA

cala One of nine scored events in a charreada (q.v.); an individual reining competition for charros (q.v.).

Calabrese A warmblood indigenous to the district of Calabria, Italy; originally of Arab (q.v.) derivation, it was later crossed with Andalusian (q.v.) and presently Thoroughbred (q.v.) blood; Oriental blood is periodically reintroduced to perpetuate breed characteristics; stands 16 to 16.2 hands, has a brown, black, bay, chestnut, or gray coat, a well-formed, although slightly convex head, prominent withers, slanted croup, short loins, and is short-coupled; used for riding.

Calash *see* CALECHE

calcification The deposition of calcium salts in degenerating muscle tissue.

calcium A soft, metallic, white element which, in conjunction with phosphorus (q.v.), comprises 75 percent of the minerals in the horse's body and approximately 90 percent of the minerals in the skeleton; is required for bone mineralization including bone formation, growth, maintenance, and repair; required for normal muscular activity, blood clotting, release of hormones, and enzyme activation; the dietary requirement is much greater during early growth of the foal than for maintenance of the mature horse, is appreciably higher in the final stages of pregnancy and during lactation, and is up to 50 percent higher for aged horses than for the maintenance of younger horses; work does not increase calcium requirements as a proportion of the diet; an improper calcium-phosphorus ratio (q.v.) may result in serious diseases or physical problems such as osteomalacia, osteoporosis, osteofibrosis, crooked or enlarged joints or weakening of the bones, shifting lameness, especially connected with the hocks, and rickets; first added routinely to commercial horse feeds manufactured in the United States in the mid 1930s; excess levels can interfere with absorption of trace minerals such as zinc (q.v.), while excessive zinc, iron (q.v.), and/or manganese (q.v.) can disrupt calcium and phosphorus absorption.

calcium blood level The amount of the mineral calcium (q.v.) carried in the blood.

calcium carbonate A colorless, crystal or gray powder occurring naturally in chalk, calcite, limestone, and marble; used as an antacid and protectant in the treatment of diarrhea.

calcium-phosphorus ratio The amount of calcium (q.v.) compared to phosphorus (q.v.) in the horse's diet; the average optimal feed ratio is 1.1 up to 1.5 to 1; if the ratio is higher than 1.5 to 1, phosphorus is either added to feed or pastures.

calculator A racing term; a clerk responsible for computing pari-mutuel (q.v.) odds.

calcutta A gambling option utilized for some Western and/or English performance events; each exhibitor is given a number which is auctioned off to the highest bidding spectator; the bet pays places 1st to 6th and in some cases through 10th place; the amount of the payoff is contingent on the type of event and/or if there is any added money (q.v.).

Calèche (1) Also known as Canadian Calèche or Marche Donc (sl) and spelled Calash or Kalesch (Ger); a two-wheeled, vehicle of the Chaise or Gig (q.v.) type drawn by a single horse; generally hooded, driven from a narrow seat above the dashboard, and hung on side and cee-springs. (2) Also known as French Calèche; a horse-drawn vehicle; a development of the four-wheeled Barouche (q.v.) or German Wagon, but with extra seating and improved suspension; one of the first vehicles to be equipped with springs.

Calesa A two-wheeled, horse-drawn passenger cart or heavy gig used in the Philippines from the mid-1800s through the 1940s; hung on semi-elliptical springs, drawn by a single horse, and driven by a coachman seated on the rear of the vehicle.

calesh The folding top on a horse-drawn carriage (q.v.).

Calesso A two-wheeled, horse-drawn, hooded gig, popular in Italy from the late 1700s through the early 1900s; drawn by one horse in shafts and a second horse harnessed alongside, but outside the shaft.

calf (1) A stag (q.v.), hind (q.v.), or cow in its first year. (2) *see* GASKIN

calf horse Any horse from which a rider ropes a calf.

calf-knees *see* BACKWARD DEVIATION OF THE CARPAL JOINTS

calf roper One who ropes a calf using a lariat (q.v.) as in competition.

calf-roping: (1) A standard rodeo event in which a mounted rider rides after a calf that has been given a 10 to 30 foot (3–9 m) start, attempts to lasso it using a lariat (q.v.), if the calf is lassoed, ties the lasso off on the saddle horn to prevent the calf from moving forward, dismounts quickly, and ties the calf's three legs together with a piggin' string (q.v.). (2) Said of a cowboy (q.v.) or ranch hand who ropes a cow using a lariat (q.v.).

calico paint *see* SABINO

California A four-wheeled, horse-drawn vehicle introduced in California USA in the 1800s to carry coal; the coal box was hung on wooden springs and thorough-braces (q.v.).

California Mud Wagon *see* CONCORD MUD WAGON

calk Also known as calkin, caulkin, sticker, cork, mud sticker, or blocked heel and spelled caulk or cawk; a cleat or grip formed on the heels and sometimes the toes of horseshoes to increase traction, alter movement, or adjust stance; used as early as the 10th century, now largely replaced by studs (q.v.).

calkin *see* CALK

calking An injury such as a nick, cut, or bruise to the coronary band (q.v.) caused by the horseshoe; most common in horses whose shoes have calks (q.v.) or in rough-shod (q.v.) horses.

calking boots *see* STABLE BOOTS

calk shoe Any horseshoe to which calks (q.v.) have been added to improve traction, alter movement, or adjust stance.

call (1) A racing term; the stage of a race at which the running positions are recorded, e.g., quarter-mile call. (2) A racing term; to describe a race to the audience.

calling A polo term; said of the team captain (q.v.) or any team member who voices instructions to the player in control of the ball, e.g., turn back, back-hander (q.v.), mine, etc.

calling the odds *see* CALL OVER

call of the card *see* CALL OVER

call over Also known as call of the card and calling the odds; a racing term; to name the horses in a race and give the latest betting odds on each.

calorie The amount of heat required to raise the temperature of one gram of water one degree centigrade; now used by the National Research Council as a method of describing food energy values.

Calorie Also known as kilocalorie; the equivalent of one thousand calories (q.v.).

Camargue Also known as Camargue Pony, Camargue Horse, or White Horse of the Sea; a breed indigenous to the salt-marsh delta of the Rhône in the Camargue area of Southern France; thought to have descended from the prehistoric horse of Solutré, the origins of which date to around 20,000 BC; in the 19th century, received infusions of Arab (q.v.), Thoroughbred (q.v.), Anglo-Arab (q.v.), and Postier-Breton (q.v.) blood, which did not result in significant modifications to type to the breed as a whole; lives in the wild and is used by the Gardiens (q.v.); at risk of extinction in the mid 20th century; has had its own breed registry since 1967; develops slowly and is not full-grown until it is 5 to 7 years old, stands 13.1 to 14.2 hands, rarely exceeding 15 hands, and usually has a white or light gray coat, although bay and brown occur very rarely; foals are born black, dark gray or brown, but their coat lightens with age; has a large head, with pronounced jaws, short, broad ears, a short neck which is thick at the base, straight back, and long loins; noted for its depth of girth; the mane is full and shaggy; is firey, independent, and courageous; the action is peculiar to the breed, having an active, high-stepping, and long-striding walk, a jarring and rarely used trot, and a free gallop and canter; branded on the left hind hip; used for riding and packing.

Camargue Pony *see* CAMARGUE

Camargue Horse *see* CAMARGUE

Cambridge mouth A bit in which the mouthpiece (q.v.) is slightly ported and roughed on only one side.

Cambridge strain *see* A-EQUI-1

camera patrol A racing term; equipment used to film a race while in progress.

Campagne riding A dressage-based riding style introduced in the 18th century by the cavalry who needed a horse that could be ridden in face-to-face single combat and formation who was agile and safe cross-country whilst utilizing as little energy as possible.

Campagne school Elementary training of the riding horse involving ordinary collection; the horse becomes equally balanced over all four legs with his neck rolled so that his nose is approximately on a horizontal line with his hips and his nose and forehead slightly in front of the vertical; the poll is the highest point.

camp drafting An Australian rodeo contest in which a rider separates a bull from the herd and drives it at a gallop around a course marked with straight poles.

camped (1) Said of a horse when either the fore or hind limbs attach to the horse's body either too far forward or rearward; a conformation defect. (2) A dressage term; said of the horse standing in the halt when his hind legs are too far behind the vertical.

camped in front A conformation defect in which the entire forelimb, from the body to the ground, is too far forward when viewed from the side; may also be present in such conditions as laminitis (q.v.) and bilateral navicular disease (q.v.).

camped behind A conformation defect in which the entire hind limb is placed too far backward when viewed from the side; a perpendicular line dropped from the hip joint would hit at the toe instead of halfway between the toe and heel; often associated with upright pasterns behind.

camphor A whitish, translucent, volatile, and aromatic crystalline substance obtained chiefly from the tree *Cinnamomum camphora*, the camphor tree; used as an irritant, stimulant, and a pain reliever when applied to areas of inflammation, sprains, etc.; is a mild blister (q.v.) and a rubefacient (q.v.).

Campolino One of three types of Criollo (q.v.) found in Brazil, the other two being the Criollo of Rio Grande do Sul (q.v.) and the Mangalarga (q.v.); descended from Andalusian stock brought to South America by the conquistadors in the 16th century; similar to the Mangalarga but with a heavier frame and more bone; stands 14.3 to 15.4 hands and is used for riding and light farm work.

Camp Wagon *see* CHUCK WAGON

canadette The highly prized characteristic coat of the Baudet de Poitou (q.v.); is notably long and shaggy without a cross or stripe, always dark brown or black, and often hangs in long cords or shaggy hanks.

Canadian bars *see* WHIP-ACROSS BARS

Canadian Calèche *see* CALECHE NO. 1

Canadian Cutting Horse The Canadian equivalent of the American Quarter Horse (q.v.) from which it descended and closely resembles in both physical appearance and temperament; a warmblood standing between 15.2 and 16.1 hands; is intelligent, fast, and agile; any coat color is acceptable.

Canadian Driving Society A Canadian organization founded in Ontario to promote and encourage individuals to drive horses, mules, donkeys, and ponies for competition, recreation, pleasure, and work activities.

Canadian Pacer An easy-gaited horse breed indigenous to Canada during the period 1800 to 1840; believed to have been Narragansett Pacers (q.v.), some perhaps having crosses to French stock; Tom Hal, Copperbottom, and Davy Crockett were three of the original 17 foundation sires of the American Saddlebred (q.v.).

Canadian Triple Crown A program of three classic races for three-year-olds; consist of the Queen's Plate, Prince of Wales Stakes, and Breeders' Stakes; equivalent races are run in America (American Triple Crown [q.v.]) and England (English Triple Crown [q.v.]).

Caned Whiskey A light, one-horse chaise popular in the late 18th and early 19th centuries; hung on shallow, sideways platform springs, was seldom headed, frequently lacked a dashboard, seated either one or two passengers, and had a canework covered body; so named because it could whisk over the ground at great speed.

canine (1) The singular of canines. (2) Of or like a dog; pertaining to or characteristic of dogs.

canines (1) *see* CANINE TEETH. (2) More than one dog.

canine teeth Also known as canines, bridle teeth, or tushes; small, pointed teeth (q.v.) located one on each side, top and bottom, in the interdental space between the third incisor and second premolar of the horse's mouth; four appear in the male horse at age five or those horses cut (q.v.) after puberty, with two to four appearing in five-year-old males who were cut before the onset of puberty; two small vestigial lower canines may appear on mares.

canker A chronic softening of the horn-producing tissues of the foot, involving the frog and the sole in one or all four feet, although most commonly the hind feet; primarily a disease of heavy draft horses, although it is found in light horses as well; is frequently well advanced before detection; the frog may appear to be intact, but has a ragged, oiled appearance; the horn tissue of the frog loosens easily, revealing the swollen, foul-smelling corium; the disease may extend to the sole and to the hoof wall which is what differentiates it from thrush (q.v.); treatment must be radical and intensive.

cannon (1) *see* CHEEK NO. 1. (2) *see* CANNON BONE

cannon bone Also known as cannon, shin, large metacarpal bone, or large metacarpal; the principal bone of the foreleg located between the knee and the pastern joint; the only bone in the body of the horse which has attained its full length at birth and will not grow during the life of the horse; the circumference just below the knee is often used as a measurement of bone (q.v.); the corresponding bone in the hind leg is known as the shank (q.v.).

Canoe Landau Also known as Sefton Landau; a Landau (q.v.) with a rounded-bottom profile when viewed from the side.

canola meal A meal by-product derived from varieties of rapeseed (q.v.) containing less than three milligrams of glucosinotate per gram of seed.

canteen A small vessel or flask, as of tin, used by soldiers and others for carrying water and other liquids for drinking; from the Spanish cantina (q.v.).

canter A rocking, three-beat gait in which the horse's hooves strike the ground in the following order: one hind foot, the other hind foot and its diagonally opposite forefoot together, the remaining forefoot, followed by a moment of suspension when all four legs are in the air before the sequence repeats; the horse is said to be on a left or right lead depending on which forefoot strikes the ground as the single foot at the end of the three-beat sequence, thus a horse on a left lead will perform the sequence: right hind, left hind and right fore together, left fore; include the broken canter (q.v.), collected canter (q.v.), cross canter (q.v.), counter-canter (q.v.), disunited canter (q.v.), extended canter (q.v.), false canter (q.v.), flat canter (q.v.), medium canter (q.v.), and working canter (q.v.).

canter change of leg *see* FLYING CHANGE

canter left Said of a horse working at the canter (q.v.) when he leads with his left leg or near foreleg (q.v.).

canter right Said of a horse working at the canter (q.v.) when he leads with his right or off side foreleg (q.v.).

cantharadin A potent irritant and vesicant (q.v.) found in blister beetles (q.v.).

cantharadin poisoning Poisoning (q.v.) as a result of ingestion of hay containing beetles, *Epicanta vittata*, which contain cantharadin; death may result.

cantharides Plural of cantharis (q.v.).

cantharidism A morbid state caused by the use of cantharides (q.v.).

cantharidize To treat with cantharides (q.v.).

cantharis Also known as Spanish fly; a substance obtained from dried and crushed bodies and wings of blister beetles (q.v.) of the genus *Cantharis vesicatoria,* or *Lytta vesicatoria,* and in some cases the Chinese blister fly *Mylabris phalerata*; used in medicine, especially externally to blister (q.v.) and formerly as a stimulant; has an irritant action on the genital and urinary organs by which it is eliminated from the body.

cantina A Spanish term popularized in the American southwest from which the term canteen (q.v.) derived; a pouch or bag hung on a saddle used to carry water

cantle The protuberant afterpart or rear bow of the saddle located behind and above the seat.

cantle-boarding A rodeo term; said of a bronc rider (q.v.) who spurs his horse so far back that his spurs (q.v.) strike the cantle (q.v.) of the saddle.

Canute's Forest Law A law proclaimed in England in 1016 to protect and improve New Forest Pony (q.v.) stock.

cap (1) Also known as cap fee or capping fee; a hunting term; the fee payable by a visitor, who is not a member of a Hunt (q.v.), to participate in a day of hunting; historically visitors paid in silver dropped into the hunt cap (q.v.) of the hunt Secretary (q.v.). (2) A driving term; that part of the harness extending upward in front of the top hame strap (q.v.). (3) *see* HUNT CAP

caparison (1) Ornamental covering for a horse. (2) Decorative trappings and harness. (3) A large rectangular cloth placed under the saddle.

cap case A large trunk attached to the rear body of a horse-drawn traveling coach.

cap curb *see* JODHPUR CURB

cape (1) A driving term; a waterproof garment worn over the coachman's coat which covered the top of the apron and box cushion. (2) A driving term; the flap of leather attached to the top of the harness collar (q.v.) which covers the seam; in dress harness, is adorned with a crest, while in working harness, it bears the number of the horse.

Cape Cart Also known as Cape Wagon; a large, two-wheeled, horse-drawn country cart used in South Africa; seated three passengers and a driver; hung on thoroughbraces and protected by a falling hood; driven to a pair of swift horses in curricle gear with a center pole; developed by Dutch settlers in Cape Province during the early 19th century and later exported to New Zealand and Australia; the rear part could be converted to a sleeping compartment; frequently used for military transport during the Boer War.

Cape Horse A South African horse breed descended from Barb (q.v.) and Arab (q.v.) horses imported by the Dutch East India Company in 1653; Thoroughbred (q.v.) and English Roadster blood was later added; its numbers have declined greatly in recent years; served as foundation stock for the Basuto Pony (q.v.).

Capel A thick-set farm horse used in medieval times.

capel Also known as capulet; a swelling on the point of the hock (q.v.) or point of the elbow (q.v.).

Cape Wagon *see* CAPE CART

cap fee *see* CAP NO. 1

capillaries More than one capillary (q.v.).

capillary One of a network of minute blood vessels between the termination of the arteries and the beginnings of the veins; from the Latin *capillus* meaning hair.

capillary refill time Also known by the acronym CRT; the amount of time required for blood profusion to return to a gum area following application of pressure; normal refill time is one to two seconds; a slower time may indicate low blood pressure, shock, or dehydration.

capped elbow Also known as shoe boil; a fluid-filled inflammation of the elbow joint bursa; may result from repeated concussion (as from the stirrup iron), rubbing (as due to bedding on hard floors), impact-related injury (kicks, falls, contact with horseshoe heels, etc.); a blemish (q.v.) which may or may not interfere with performance.

capped hock A fluid-filled inflammation of the bursa overlying the point of the hock; may result from repeated concussion, rubbing (as due to bedding on hard floors), impact-related injury (kicks, falls, contact with horseshoe heels, etc.); a blemish (q.v.) which may or may not interfere with performance.

capped knee *see* CARPITIS

capping fee *see* CAP NO. 1

Caprilli, Federico (1868–1907) An Italian cavalry officer considered to be the father of the forward seat (q.v.) jumping technique which he introduced in 1907; published the Principi di Equitazione di Campagna in 1907.

capriole A classical air above the ground (q.v.); the highest and most complete leap of the high airs (q.v.) in which the horse half rears with his hocks drawn under his body, then jumps forward and high into the air; at the height of the horizontal jump, the horse kicks out strongly with his hind legs, the soles of his feet turned upwards; when the movement is completed, the horse lands, collected, on four legs; originated in medieval times, where, by using such leaps and kicks of the horse, the rider in combat could rid himself of his adversaries.

capsular ligament The outer covering of a joint capsule in the ball and socket, shoulder, and hip joints.

capture myopathy *see* TYING UP

capulet *see* CAPEL

Car (1) A four-wheeled, horse-drawn vehicle first used in the territory of Gaul, in the ancient Roman province of Gallia; the term derived from the Latin *carrus* meaning, four-wheeled vehicle. (2) A generic term; any superior two-wheeled, horse-drawn vehicle such as a Governess Car (q.v.); used in Britain in the early 19th century.

Caravan (1) A horse-drawn house-on-wheels used by gypsies, showmen, and other nomadic people from the mid-19th century through the 1930s; evolved from a tent fixed to a cart which was used for business during the day and for sleeping at night; of many different types. (2) A medieval passenger wagon popular in the 13th and 14th centuries; unsprung, drawn by three horses in tandem (q.v.), and controlled by a postillion (q.v.) on the shaft horse.

carbohydrates chemical compounds consisting of hydrogen, oxygen, and water; the major source of energy and heat in the horse's diet; include starches, sugars, and fiber; most are consumed in the form of green plants which constitute a major class of animal food.

card (1) *see* RACE CARD. (2) *see* APPOINTMENT CARD. (3) *see* TICKET NO. 2

cardiac Pertaining to the heart.

cardiac arrhythmia *see* ARRHYTHMIA

cardiac muscle An involuntary, striated muscle (q.v.) that controls the rhythmic contraction of the heart.

cardiac shock Circulatory collapse characterized by a progressive diminishing circulating blood volume relative to the capacity of the vascular system, leading to acute failure of blood perfusion to the vital organs; caused by damage to the heart pump.

cardiovascular Pertaining to the heart and blood vessels.

care dog *see* CUR DOG

career (1) A historic battle term; the demarcation of the line a rider must take when making a charge or a tilt against an opponent; from the French *carrière*. (2) A dressage term; the line taken to enter or depart the manège.

Caretta (1) A horse-drawn country cart popular in Sicily and southern Italy from about AD 476 through the mid-20th century; drawn by a single horse or pony in straight shafts (q.v.); had a richly carved body and framework with side panels painted with scenes from legends, biblical stories, and so on. (2) An early four-wheeled, horse-drawn coach or carriage used in Italy for ceremonial purposes; frequently lined with scented leather and expensive fabric; records pertaining to the use of this vehicle date to 1273.

car fit Said of a horse who experiences severe fright while being shipped, e.g. in a truck, trailer, van, train, or plane.

caries Also known as tooth decay; a bacterial infection of the tooth (q.v.) recognizable by strong, foul-smelling breath; is rarely a problem in horses unless trauma related.

Cariole (1) A two-wheeled, horse-drawn gig with a narrow body and unsprung or dead axle; used in the country districts of Norway throughout the 19th century; driven from a low rearward platform that doubled as a luggage grid; drawn by a single horse or large pony harnessed between exceptionally long shafts; seated one passenger. (2) A horse-drawn Canadian sleigh with a curved dash built to accommodate two passengers on a rear seat; driven from a small, low seat located in front of the passenger's seat.

carnation A flower; any of the numerous varieties of the clover-pink *Dianthus caryophillus* having fragrant flowers of many colors; yellow carnations are worn in the lapels of British Driving Society (q.v.) members at their meets.

Caroche An open, dead axle, horse-drawn carriage generally used for ceremonial purposes in France during the late 15th and early 16th centuries; drawn by six or more horses, was box shaped, had luxurious internal appointments, and ran on equirotal (q.v.) wheels.

carousel Also spelled carrousel; an orchestrated ride to music performed by a group of riders who execute figures on horseback; designed to resemble formal dances such as the quadrille (q.v.) or the lancers; usually performed in fancy attire; first presented in 1828 at the French Cavalry School at Saumur (q.v.), where it is still officially performed by the Cadre Noir (q.v.); also presented at the Spanish Riding School in Vienna (q.v.).

carpal joint *see* CARPUS

Carpathian Pony *see* HUCUL

Carpentum (1) Either a two- or four-wheeled, horse-drawn passenger vehicle used in Ancient Rome from the first century AD; a luxury vehicle, hung on side braces of toughened leather; entered from the rear; drawn by a pair of horses harnessed in curricle gear; named after Camenta, a worthy matron and mother of Evander, one of the founders of Rome. (2) A low-slung, elegant, and headed carriage with a fixed or standing top designed about 1840.

carpitis Also known as popped knee, sore knee, big knee, capped knee, or swing leg; acute or chronic inflammation of the joint capsules and associated structures of the knee (q.v.) resulting from torn knee ligaments or fractures of any of eight carpal bones; common to immature Thoroughbreds (q.v.) or horses in hard training, especially when unfit.

carpus Also known as knee or carpal joint; the gliding joint (q.v.) of the horse's front leg; connects the foreleg (q.v.) to the lower leg (q.v.), and consists of eight carpal bones (radial, intermediate, and ulnar) joined by ligaments (q.v.).

carpus varus *see* LATERAL DEVIATION OF THE CARPAL JOINTS

carpus vulgus *see* MEDIAL DEVIATION OF THE CARPAL JOINTS

Carrera de sortijas A mounted gaucho game popular in Argentina; a form of tilting (q.v.) at the ring; two gauchos, starting side by side simultaneously, gallop towards two finger-sized rings suspended parallel and so high that riders must stand in the stirrups and stretch out their arms to reach the rings; riders use pencil-sized pieces of wood to pick up the rings; the rider who successfully picks up the ring and crosses the finish line first is the winner.

Carrette (1) A four-wheeled horse-drawn bus or short stage coach used in many Australian towns and cities between 1895 and 1920; driven from a raised seat at the fore-end protected by an extended roof canopy; had longitudinal, inward-facing seating and was drawn by two horses in pole gear (q.v.). (2) A low-slung horse-drawn omnibus hung on sideways-elliptical springs and having cranked axles; drawn by two horses in pole gear; mainly used in Chicago, USA from the early 1890s into the early 20th century.

Carretto An ornately designed and painted horse-drawn cart popular in Sicily; the body and wheels were carved and harness embellished with decorative stone and plumage.

carriage (1) Also known as carriage parts, chassis, undercarriage, running gear, or gear; the supporting underworks of a horse-drawn vehicle consisting of the wheels, springs, axles, forecarriage sections, fifth wheel, perch, splinter bar, and futchells. (2) The manner in which a horse carries himself with or without a rider; evaluated in terms of attitude, manner, and style when standing or moving; requirements differ according to breed and use specifications.

Carriage An open or semi-open, horse-drawn passenger vehicle of superior quality; generally run on four wheels, although some two-wheeled types such as the Curricle (q.v.) and Cabriolet (q.v.) existed; from the Latin *carrus* meaning car and the old French *carier* meaning wagon or cart.

Carriage Association of America Also known by the acronym CAA; the oldest and largest international organization devoted to preservation of horse-drawn vehicles; founded in New Jersey, USA in 1960; dedicated to proper preservation, restoration, and care of carriages and sleighs and also encourages the fine art of driving them; is active in more than 25 countries worldwide.

Carriage Builders and Harness Makers Art Journal A fully illustrated periodical published in Britain during the 1800s; contained articles and advertising related to carriage and harness products, inventions, and ideas.

carriage convenience *see* BOURDALOU

carriage head *see* CARRIAGE HOOD

carriage horse Any relatively light, elegant horse suitable for pulling a private or Hackney carriage (q.v.).

carriage hood Also known as carriage head, head, hood, or top; the fabric top of a carriage whether in a raised or lowered position.

carriage parts *see* CARRIAGE NO. 1

carriage stepping block Also known as carriage stone; an iron, wood, stone, or brick block used by passengers to 'mount' a carriage; manufactured in a variety of designs usually incorporating two to three steps; usually had a post with a ring to which the horse could be tied to align the carriage when the horse was tethered.

carriage stone *see* CARRIAGE STEPPING BLOCK

Carri-Coche Also known as Cart Coach; a horse-drawn vehicle popular in Buenos Aires, Argentina; for town work, commonly pulled by one or two postillion driven horses; occasionally pulled by three horses abreast; the body had sliding glass windows and was entered by steps through a door in the rear; hung on two straight shafts and two wheels by two braces of untanned hide twisted into cords.

carries the scent *see* CARRY THE SCENT

Carrinho A small, neat, single-horse-drawn cart used mainly for agricultural purposes in Portugal; usually dead axle.

Carromata A two-wheeled pony cart with a standing or fixed top used in the Philippines during the mid-19th century; drawn by a single pony.

Carrosse à cinq sols *see* OMNIBUS

carrot A biennial plant, *Dacus carota*, of the parsley family, with fern-like leaves and a long, orange-red root fed as a supplement; high in beta carotene which is converted into vitamin A (q.v.) in the digestive tract.

carrousel *see* CAROUSEL

carry (1) A hunting term; said of the ground when it holds the scent of the fox picked up from contact with the pads of the foot. (2) Said of a tent-pegger (q.v.) when he successfully places the lance tip through the eye of the tent peg in the mounted sport of tent-pegging (q.v.).

carry a good head Also known as carry a wide head; a hunting term; said of the hounds, when running a fox, who spread out, fan-like, to catch every turn and twist in the line of the fox (q.v.).

carry a line Also known as work a line; a hunting term; to follow the line of the fox (q.v.).

carry a wide head *see* CARRY A GOOD HEAD

carry both ends *see* WEAR ITSELF WELL

carry scent *see* CARRY THE SCENT

carry the ball A polo term; said of a player who retains possession and control of the ball while moving down the field towards the goal (q.v.).

carry the bar A driving term; a horse whose bar (q.v.) is an inch or two in front of its partner's.

carry the horn A hunting term; to hunt (q.v.) hounds.

carry the line *see* CARRY THE SCENT

carry the scent Also known as carries the scent, carry scent, or carry the line; a hunting term; said of a hound (q.v.) when he actually follows the line of a fox (q.v.) when the pack is running.

carry the target A racing term; said of a horse who runs in last position the entire race.

Cart (1) A generic term; any two-wheeled, horse-drawn vehicle designed for speed and flexibility over rough terrain. (2) A country or sporting vehicle drawn by a cob or pony; less expensive and ornate than coaches (q.v.) or carriages (q.v.), and generally owner driven; many named for the territory in which they were used, e.g. the Essex Cart, while others were named for the purpose for which they were constructed, e.g. the Governess Cart (q.v.), or for the builder, e.g. Morgan Cart (q.v.).

Cart Coach *see* CARRI-COCHE

carted Said of a rider whose mount has run away with him.

carter One who drives a working team of horses.

cart gear *see* FILL GEAR

cart horse Generally, a heavy, cold-blooded (q.v.) draft horse.

cart horse of the north, the *see* ARDENNAIS

Carthusian A horse breed indigenous to Spain; considered a type of Andalusian (q.v.), originated at studs founded by Carthusian monks in Seville and other parts of Andalusia, who from 1476, devoted themselves to the selective breeding of Andalusian horses; has good conformation, elegant action and is strong and athletic; stands approximately 15.2 hands and the coat is usually gray, although chestnut and black also occur; most descended from the stallion Esclavo; used for riding and light draft.

cartilage Also known as soft bone; tissue composing most of the skeleton in embryos and young vertebrates, then converted, for the most part, into bone in mature higher vertebrates; is insensitive, has no blood supply, and is dependent upon synovial fluid for nutrition; in the mature horse, cartilage is soft and pliable and absorbs shock to the skeleton; bone may convert back to cartilage due to mineral imbalance as in big head disease (q.v.), this however, is reversible; of three types: elastic cartilage (q.v.), hyaline cartilage (q.v.), and fibro cartilage (q.v.).

carting *see* CARTY

carting bred Said of a medium to heavy boned horse of mixed breeding whose body type is well suited to light draft.

carty Also known as carting; a horse of mixed breeding, but generally containing some cold blood (q.v.).

Caslick's operation Commonly referred to as suturing; the process of occluding part of the mare's vagina with stitches to prevent air and contaminants from entering her reproductive track when not being used for breeding.

Caspian An ancient pony breed originating in what is now Iran around 3,000 BC; thought to be a progenitor of the Arab (q.v.); believed extinct in the 10th century, but in 1965 a number of specimens were found in the Elburz Mountains and on the shores of the Caspian Sea; stands 9.2 to 11.2 hands although breed requirements specify the height between 10.2 and 12 hands; the coat may be chestnut, bay, or gray with white head and leg markings the exception; has a small head, short ears, large eyes, flared nostrils, a slightly arched neck with a full mane and tail, short back, and sturdy, well-built legs; is strong, quiet, and docile, has good endurance, and is a natural jumper; used for riding.

cast (1) Also known as cast horse; said of a horse when he becomes lodged on the ground between a vertical surface and his withers (q.v.); occurs when a horse falls, rolls, or lies down in too small a space or too close to a fence, wall, or manger and is unable to get up without assistance; the more strenuously he struggles to right himself, the more prone he is to injury. (2) Said of a horse; to throw a horseshoe. (3) A plaster bandage used to set broken bones or torn ligaments. (4) A hunting term; any effort made by the hounds, whether on their own initiative or at the direction of the huntsman (q.v.), to recover the scent of the fox at a check (q.v.). (5) An inferior or unsuitable horse. (6) Also known as casting a horse; to throw a horse onto the ground using ropes or hobbles (q.v.) or other means to break, clip, shoe, administer medical treatments, etc. (7) *see* CAST THE HOUNDS. (8) *see* THROW OFF

cast horse (1) Also known as a principal horse; any horse used by a principal actor when shooting a movie; a horse who has a primary role in a film as opposed to a horse used in the background. (2) *see* CAST NO. 1

casting a horse *see* CAST NO. 6

casting coat *see* SHEDDING OUT

cast the hounds Also known as cast; a hunting term; said of the huntsman (q.v.) who, when the hounds (q.v.) following the line of a fox (q.v.) have lost the scent, moves the pack in the direction in which he thinks a fox has moved in an attempt to recover the lost line.

castors *see* CHESTNUTS

castrate Also known as cut, mark, geld (from the Scandinavian meaning barren), alter, or emasculate; to remove the testicles of a male horse to render him sterile, more docile, and facilitate control in the presence of mares; may be performed at any age, although generally not prior to one year; may be performed at any time of the year, although it is most commonly carried out in the spring or autumn because of the absence of flies; commonly performed using an emasculator (q.v.).

cataract Optification of the eye lens due to genetics, illness such as diabetes, or trauma such as ultraviolet radiation; may lead to impaired vision or blindness.

cataplasm (1) To anoint or to spread as a plaster. (2) A treatment or plaster used to reduce inflammation and pain; mud or clay is one of the basic ingredients; when applied to the entire circumference of the leg provides the support normally associated with bandages or wrapping.

catch To find a mare in season (q.v.) when she is turned out to pasture (q.v.).

catch-as-catch-can A calf-roping term; said of a roper (q.v.) allowed to rope a calf in any fashion he chooses so long as he turns the rope loose when throwing the loop, and so long as the rope holds the calf until the roper reaches it.

catch colt An orphaned colt (q.v.); obs.

catch-driver A harness racing term; a driver not directly employed by a stable who is hired for his skill; receives a flat fee plus a percentage of winnings (generally 5 percent) for each race.

catch hold Said of a horse who suddenly takes hold of the bit and begins to pull.

catchhold A hunting term; said of a huntsman (q.v.) when he moves the hound pack to a point where he thinks the fox (q.v.) has moved or where it was last seen.

catching a double thong Also known as catching a whip or folding a whip; a driving term; to double up a long thong (q.v.) onto the whip when the extra length is not necessary; when doubled, the thong length would preferably be about 2 feet 6 inches (0.8 m), the rest of the thong being wound around the stick and the handle; long driving whips are customarily used when driving a tandem (q.v.), unicorn (q.v.), or team (q.v.).

catching a whip *see* CATCHING A DOUBLE THONG

catch pigeons (1) A racing term; sprinting racehorses. (2) A British racing term; a horse in training who is working well.

catch rope A roping term; the lariat holding a roped animal.

catch up *see* ROUND UP

catch weight An American racing term; the optional weight carried by a horse competing in a race when the conditions of a race do not specify a weight.

catechu An astringent used to soothe intestinal inflammation associated with enteritis (q.v.) or diarrhea (q.v.); usually combined with chalk (q.v.) and kaolin and administered by stomach tube.

caterpillar *see* LARVA

cat foot A hunting term; said of a hound having a round foot with short toes and high, well-developed knuckles; characteristic of English hounds.

cat hairs The long, untidy hairs which grow in a horse's coat following a second clipping; appear early in the new year.

cat-hammed Said of a horse having weak hocks (q.v.) and long, relatively thin thighs and legs.

cathartic *see* PURGATIVE

Catol A two-wheeled, horse-drawn Norwegian Dogcart (q.v.); seats two passengers sitting one behind the other.

cattle (1) Domesticated four-legged bovine animals, including cows, bulls, and steers. (2) *see* HORSES

cattle blocking A mounted South American rodeo game held in a round arena surrounded by a wooden partition; the gaucho, riding a horse trained to maneuver a steer in position up against a wooden partition, uses the horse's chest, legs, etc. to block the steer against the partition; points are awarded according to which part of the horse's body is used to block the steer.

cattle drive To move a walking herd of cattle from one location to another accompanied by mounted riders.

cattleman One engaged in rearing or tending cattle.

cattlemen's carnivals *see* RODEO

cattle settler A cutting term; a mounted rider who quiets a herd of cattle (q.v.) so that when another rider penetrates the herd they do not scatter; achieved by riding back and forth in front of the cattle, allowing them to become familiar with the horse.

caudal Situated near or directed toward the hindquarters or tail of the horse.

caught one Also known as one heeled; a roping term; said of the roper; to lasso (q.v.) only one of two hind feet of a steer (q.v.) when roping.

caul *see* PLACENTA

caulk *see* CALK

caulkin *see* CALK

caulks *see* CALK

caustic A group of substances including copper sulfate (q.v.), phenol, antimony trichloride, and silver nitrate, used to destroy excess granulation tissue and minor superficial tumors in the horse; cause cell death and precipitation of protein (q.v.) to form a scab.

cavaletti *see* CAVALLETTI

cavalletti Also spelled cavaletti; a series of small wooden jumps, generally 4 inches (10 cm) wide x 10 feet (3 m) long, used in the basic training of a riding horse; invented by Federico Caprilli (q.v.) for his 'system natural'; used to encourage the horse to adjust his stride, improve his balance, and loosen and strengthen his muscles; although the plural of cavalletto, corruption of the language has led English-speaking equestrians to use cavalletti for both singular and plural forms; from the Italian meaning little horses.

cavallo An Italian term; a horse (q.v.).

Cavalo de Pura Raca Lusitano Also known by the acronym PSL; *see* LUSITANO

cavalry Mounted soldiers collectively; that part of a military force whose troops serve on horseback (q.v.).

cavalry hold A method of holding the reins (q.v.) when mounted; the rider holds all four reins of a double bridle (q.v.) in either the right or left hand, thus freeing the other hand to carry a weapon.

cavalryman Also known as horseman; a soldier who serves on horseback.

cavalry remount Any horse ridden by a mounted soldier.

cavalry twill A type of fabric used for cavalry uniforms after 1914; was first made in khaki in western England for regiments serving in the First World War.

cavelletto An Italian term; the singular form of cavalletti (q.v.).

Cavendish, William, Duke of Newcastle (1592–1676) A celebrated 17th-century cavalryman and horse trainer noted for his sympathetic treatment of the horse; established the famous riding school at Antwerp, Belgium and published there a number of books on horsemanship including, but not limited to, *Methode et Invention Nouvelle de Dresser les Chevaux* and *A New Method and Extraordinary Invention to Dress Horses and Work With Them According to Nature.*

cavesson *see* CAVESSON NOSEBAND

cavesson noseband Also known as cavesson; tack separate from, but used in conjunction with, a bridle; a leather noseband customarily used with the English snaffle bridle, which encourages the horse to keep his mouth closed; consists of a slip head with a nosepiece that lays across the bridge of the nose and buckles under the jaw approximately 2 inches (5 cm) below the cheek bones, but above the bit; from the French *caveçon* meaning to curb or restrain.

cavvy An American buckaroo term used mainly in the Great Basin and northwest of America; a ranch outfit's saddle horses.

cawk *see* CALK

CCIO *see* CONCOURS COMPLET INTERNATIONAL OFFICIEL (OFFICIAL INTERNATIONAL THREE-DAY EVENT)

CDIO *see* CONCOURS DE DRESSAGE INTERNATIONAL OFFICIEL (OFFICIAL INTERNATIONAL DRESSAGE TOURNAMENT)

Cecil Aldin *see* ALDIN, CECIL

cee-spring A driving term; a metal, c-shaped spring used in vehicle suspension; first introduced in 1790 as an improvement to the whip-spring.

Celle Stud A breeding facility located near Hanover, Germany, where it is believed to have existed for more than two centuries.

CEM *see* CONTAGIOUS EQUINE METRITIS

centaurs Ancient mythical Greek beings dwelling in the mountains of Thessalay who were imagined as men with the bodies of horses and half bestial natures; according to fable, they were the offspring of the God Ixion and a cloud.

center line A dressage term; the line, usually imaginary, down the center of the long aspect of the dressage arena from the "A" to the "C" marker; used as a reference for performance of many movements.

center of gravity An imaginary point or axis around which the mass of a body or limb is balanced.

central incisors Also known as centrals or first incisors; 4 of 12 incisor teeth (q.v.) in the horse consisting of the two front middle teeth, upper and lower; present at birth as milk teeth (q.v.) and later replaced by permanent teeth (q.v.).

Central Mountain Horse *see* CORLAY

centrals *see* CENTRAL INCISORS

cereal grass hay Also known as seed hay; a cut and dried grass hay (q.v.) made from common cereal grain grasses such as oat, barley, wheat, and rye with oat hay (q.v.) being the most commonly fed; has a lower calcium content than other hays; it is therefore important to monitor the calcium-phosphorus ratio (q.v.) of the horse when feeding without supplements; generally cut when green to ensure palatability; varieties include barley hay (q.v.), Timothy (q.v.), Bermuda (q.v.), bluestem grass (q.v.), bromegrass hay (q.v.), wheat grass hay (q.v.), Sudan grass hay (q.v.), and prairie hay (q.v.).

cerebellar hypoplasia A genetically based disease in which a foal is born with an inadequately formed brain motor control center; the foal will be stiff-legged and uncoordinated.

certificate of registration A legal document attesting to the horse's physical description, age, pedigree, breeder, and owner; generally issued by the appropriate breed and/or performance associations.

certificate of veterinary inspection Also known by the acronym CVI; a certificate prepared by a veterinarian that certifies a horse is free of communicable diseases and is vaccinated against specific diseases; required when a horse is transported across state or country lines; in the United States (Arkansas, Delaware, Florida, Georgia, Ohio, and Rhode Island) and Canada, temperature readings are also required.

Certified Apprentice Farrier, Level One Also known by the acronym CAF I; a certification awarded to student and novice farriers by the Brotherhood of Working Farriers Association (q.v.) on the basis of a practical examination.

Certified Apprentice Farrier, Level Two Also known by the acronym CAF II; a certification awarded to graduates and professional farriers just starting practice by the Brotherhood of Working Farriers Association (q.v.) on the basis of written and practical examinations.

Certified Farrier Also known by the acronym CF; a certification of knowledge and skill awarded to farriers practicing in the United States by the American Farriers' Association (q.v.) on the basis of written and practical examinations.

Certified Journeyman Farrier Also known by the acronym CJF; a certification awarded to a farrier by the American Farriers Association on the basis of written and practical examinations.

Certified Journeyman Farrier, Level One Also known by the acronym CJF I; a certification awarded to farriers with more than one year of practical experience by the Brotherhood of Working Farriers Association (q.v.) on the basis of written and practical examinations.

Certified Journeyman Farrier, Level Two Also known by the acronym CJF II; a certification awarded to farriers with more than three years of practical experience by the Brotherhood of Working Farriers Association on the basis of written and practical examinations.

Certified Master Farrier Also known by the acronym CMF; the highest level of achievement and certification awarded to a farrier by the Brotherhood of Working Farriers Association (q.v.).

certified pedigree option Also known by the acronym CPO; a registration option offered by the Appaloosa Horse Club (q.v.) since 1982 for non-characteristic horses, that is those not showing typical Appaloosa characteristics, e.g., a blanket (q.v.); must have at least one ApHC-registered parent; can be used in Appaloosa (q.v.) breeding programs when mated with colored horses (q.v.) and can compete in ApHC-sanctioned events.

cervix The narrow or neck portion of an organ; generally the outer end of the uterus.

CF *see* CERTIFIED FARRIER

chafe Said of the skin when rubbed to the point of irritation, but not to gall (q.v.).

chaff (1) Also known as chop; any mixture of hay (q.v.), such as meadow hay, green-cut oat hay, or straw, cut into small lengths and used as a feed stuff; often blended with molasses to increase nutritive value and palatability. (2) Also known as cravings; the residue from corn after removal of the kernel from the cob.

chain horse Also known as chain team; a driving term; the center or swing pair in a team of six horses; so called because the center pair are frequently separated by a chain instead of a pole.

chain-mouth snaffle A bit (q.v.) consisting of a flat, or cable-link chain mouth attached to two cheek rings (q.v.).

chain shanks *see* CROSS TIES

chain team *see* CHAIN HORSE

Chair-back Gig A horse-drawn vehicle of the Gig (q.v.) type popular during the late 18th century; had a rounded Cabriolet-type body fitted with a chair or stick-back seat; originally hung on leather braces swung on cee- or shallow whip springs, with semi-elliptical springs used in later models.

chair seat Said of the English rider seated too far back in the saddle, with the stirrups too short, and thus the thigh too horizontal.

Chaise Also referred to in 19th-century North America as Shay; a horse-drawn vehicle widely used in Western Europe and the North American Colonies in the late 18th and early 19th centuries; drawn by a single horse or cob in curved shafts; generally mounted on thoroughbraces, cee-springs, a combination of both, or balanced on resilient shafts without further suspension; seated at least one passenger alongside the driver; the driver's seat was protected by a falling hood.

chalán *see* LLANERO

chalk *see* CHALK HORSE

chalk board A racing term; a board or slate upon which the betting odds of horses competing in a given race are identified by bookmakers (q.v.).

chalk horse Also known as chalk; a racing

term; the betting favorite or most heavily played horse in a race; from the days when bookmakers identified the odds of each horse in chalk written on chalk boards.

chalk jockey An antiquated racing term; a jockey who has not ridden in a sufficient number of races to warrant his name being placed on the number board (q.v.), it is therefore written in chalk.

chalk player A racing term; one who prefers to place bets (q.v.) on favored horses.

challenge (1) A racing term; said of a horse vying for the lead. (2) *see* CHALLENGE A LINE

challenge a fox *see* CHALLENGE A LINE

challenge a line Also known as challenge a fox or challenge; a hunting term; said of a hound who speaks to the line of a fox (q.v.) before the rest of the pack, or when a hound speaks to support another hound who opens on a fox (q.v.).

Challon, Henry Bernard (1770–1849) Appointed painter of animals to Kings George IV and William IV; some of his race horse portraits and hunting scenes were engraved in mezzotint.

chambon Also known as chambon martingale; a lungeing aid used to encourage the horse to lower his head and upper neck while simultaneously raising the base of his neck to achieve a rounded top line (q.v.) and improved engagement of the hocks under the body; consists of a martingale (q.v.) attached to the girth (q.v.) between the legs, the branches of which (usually of cord) pass through rings on either side of a poll pad and attach to the bit (q.v.) rings; the action is on the poll (q.v.); although it must not be used to ride in, it can be used to lunge (q.v.) a horse over jumps.

chambon martingale *see* CHAMBON

chambrière A 16th and 17th-century term; a lunge whip (q.v.) used to school a horse in the pillars (q.v.).

chamfrain *see* CHAMFRON NO. 1

chamfron (1) Also known as chamfrain and spelled chanfron; a headstall (q.v.) used in medieval armor to protect the horse's head when in battle. (2) To fasten a rein or bridle on a horse.

champ Said of a horse who chews or plays with the bit while it is in his mouth.

Championnat Hippique International Also known by the acronym CHI; *see* ROYAL INTERNATIONAL HORSE SHOW (CHI)

Championnat Hippique International Officiel Also known by the acronym CHIO; *see* ROYAL INTERNATIONAL HORSE SHOW (CHIO)

Championnat Hippique National Also known by the acronym CHN; a nationally authorized horse show.

chanfron *see* CHAMFRON NO. 1

changar A type of polo (q.v.) played in Persia more than 2,500 years ago; from the Persian word meaning mallet.

change An antiquated coaching term; a location along a route traveled by horse-drawn public transportation vehicles where tired or spent team horses could be swapped out for rest horses (q.v.).

change hands A 16th and 17th-century French term; the action (q.v.) of the horse's legs when changing leads (q.v.).

change in the air *see* FLYING CHANGE

change lead *see* CHANGE OF LEAD

change of hand *see* CHANGE OF REIN

change of lead Also known as change lead or lead change; said of a horse; to change the leading leg (q.v.) at a gallop or canter.

change of leg *see* FLYING CHANGE

change of leg in the air *see* FLYING CHANGE

change of leg through the trot *see* SIMPLE CHANGE

change of ponies A polo term; to exchange a horse used in one chukker (q.v.) for a fresh horse; required after each chukker or at any point during a chukker if a horse is injured; an interval of 3 minutes is permitted to change horses, while if a change is due to injury, the clock is stopped.

change of rein Also known as change of hand; said of the rider; to change direction of travel from left to right or vice versa when riding.

change rhythm To increase or decrease the rate of the horse's steps within a gait (q.v.).

channel Also known as saddle channel or saddle chamber; the open portion of the saddle between the two panels and beneath the seat which runs from the pommel (q.v.) to the cantle (q.v.) parallel to the vertebral column of the horse's back.

chapandazan An Afghanistani rider; a participant in the wild and ruthless game of Buzkashi (q.v.).

chaparajos *see* CHAPS

chaparreras *see* CHAPS

chape The white tip of the fox's tail.

chaperos *see* CHAPS

Chapman Horse *see* CLEVELAND BAY

Chapman, John Secretary of the Two-Wheeled Carriage Company; aware of the shortcomings of J. A. Hansom's early cabs, designed an improved cab and sold the patent to the Hansom Company who ultimately named the vehicle the Hansom Cab (q.v.).

chappararos *see* CHAPS

chaps Also known as chaperos, chappararos, chaparajos, or chaparreras and spelled shaps; leather leggings which cover the rider's leg from the ankle, midcalf, or knee to the hip where they are held in place by means of a buckled belt; the legging wraps to outside of the rider's leg where it is closed by means of zippers, snaps, or ties; originally worn by cowboys to protect their legs from the elements, temperature, and abrasion; in addition to the historical uses, now worn to improve grip in the saddle, prevent chaffing, and as show attire; from the Spanish chaparreras; types include chinks (q.v.) and shotgun chaps.

Char-à-banc *see* CHARABANC

Charabanc Also known as Charabanc Break or Bastard Coach (sl) and spelled Char-à-banc; a four-wheeled, open, horse-drawn benched carriage of French origins introduced in the 1830s; had two or more rows of crosswise seating for passengers seated vis-à-vis (q.v.); driven to either a two- or four-in-hand team by a coachman from a high box; usually open, but sometimes fitted with a canopy head or a cover mounted on standards; frequently used as a mobile grandstand at race meetings and other sporting events; some were fitted with front and rear slatted under boots (q.v.) to carry sporting dogs; literally translated from French to mean "car with a bench."

Charabanc Break *see* CHARABANC

Char à Côté A horse-drawn vehicle of Swiss origins designed for travel on narrow mountain roads; was long and narrow and hooded; accommodated three passengers seated side-by-side facing the left-hand side of the road; luggage was stored on a board by the rear wheels; the driver sat directly behind the horse's hind legs, with his feet nearly dragging the ground.

charbon *see* ANTHRAX

Chare A horse-dawn vehicle thought to be the predecessor to the Chariot (q.v.).

charge-back *see* BUY-BACK

charger A cavalry (q.v.) mount, generally used by an officer.

Chariot From the French *char* meaning wheeled vehicle or the Latin *carrus* for car or wagon; (1) A two-wheeled, horse-drawn hunting or war vehicle thought to have originated in China or the Middle East around 2,000 BC; drawn either by a single horse or several horses abreast, in which case the center horse was positioned between shafts while the outer horses were only connected by traces (q.v.); was high in the front, had sturdy wheels, a low center of gravity, and was entered from the rear; used for racing, some types of military training, and ceremonial purposes. (2) A four-wheeled coupé or cut-down coach which usually seated two forward-facing passengers; popular from the late 17th through the late 19th centuries; eventually replaced by the Brougham (q.v.); drawn by two horses in pole gear (q.v.); originally hung on cee-springs, but later on sideways-elliptical springs, had an underperch, high box seat with an elaborate hammercloth, and a dummy board on which the servants or footmen rode.

chariot racing An ancient Greek sport in which two-wheeled, horse-drawn, open-backed vehicles were raced on a straight or oval course; a popular spectator sport for more than 1,500 years, became an Olympic sport in 408 BC.

Charles Bianconi *see* BIANCONI, CHARLES

Charles B. Newhouse *see* NEWHOUSE, CHARLES B.

Charles Cooper Henderson *see* HENDERSON, CHARLES COOPER

Charley *see* FOX

Charlie *see* FOX

Charlier shoe Also known as periplantar shoe; an obsolete type of horseshoe (q.v.); the shoe was placed in a groove cut into the hoof wall, thus allowing the frog, in theory, to be in constant contact with the ground; invented by a Frenchman of the same name.

Charolais *see* CHAROLLAIS

Charollais Also spelled Charolais and Charrolais and known as a Charollais Half-Bred; descended from Anglo-Normans (q.v.); stands 15 to 16.2 hands, may be of any solid color, and is renowned for its soundness; together with two similar breeds, the Bourbonnais and the Nivernais, are collectively known as Demi-Sang Charollais (q.v.).

Charollais Half-Bred *see* CHAROLLAIS

charreada Also known as charro rodeo; a Mexican style rodeo (q.v.) consisting of nine scored events including the cala (q.v.), coleaderos (q.v.), jinete de novillos (q.v.), terna en el ruedo (q.v.), paso de la muerte (q.v.), piales en el lienzo (q.v.), and the mangana (q.v.) in which special attention is paid to specific customs of costumes and mannerisms; dates back to post-revolutionary Mexico in the early 20th century when it was a fiesta conducted to pay homage to the traditions of Mexican horsemanship including skilled riding and roping; some events are now outlawed in parts of the United States.

charro A Mexican cowboy (q.v.).

Charrolais *see* CHAROLLAIS

charro rodeo *see* CHARREADA

chart *see* RESULT CHART

chase (1) *see* STEEPLECHASE. (2) A hunting term; the pursuit of deer, foxes or coyotes by a pack of hounds.

chaser (1) A coachmaker's employee responsible for embossing custom decorative designs on metal carriage parts; arms and crests on door handles and axle tree ends were common. (2) *see* STEEPLECHASER NO. 1

'chaser *see* STEEPLECHASER NO. 1

Chatelaine A small pony-drawn Gig (q.v.) frequently driven by ladies in the southern states of North America during the mid-19th century.

chatter Also known as shower, shower the ground, shower down on one, chatter the ground, or dancing; a cutting term; said of the horse who, in anticipation of the movement of the cow, patters his front feet in small, vertical steps.

chatter of the bars The sound the dee (q.v.) of the main bar creates when in contact with the pole hook (q.v.) on a horse-drawn vehicle in motion.

chatter the ground *see* CHATTER

chaugán An ancient Persian mounted game resembling lawn tennis developed around 525 BC, from which polo (q.v.) derived.

chaunter *see* SHILL

cheap John American slang; a farrier (q.v.)

who attempts to build his/her clientele by charging rates for his services below those customarily charged in the area.

check (1) A hunting term; said of the hounds when they lose the scent of the fox and stop pursuit; the field (q.v.) will wait while the hounds search for the line or are cast (q.v.) by the huntsman (q.v.). (2) *see* CHECK REIN. (3) A quick take and give of the outside rein by the rider to slow the forward impulsion (q.v.) of the horse.

checkerboard team *see* CROSS TEAM

check point Any location where a veterinarian evaluates the physical condition of a horse competed in physically demanding events such as long-distance rides (q.v.), combined training (q.v.), three-day events (q.v.), and horse trials (q.v.).

check rein Also known as bearing rein, check, overcheck, overdraw, overhead check, or Kemble Jackson, and spelled checkrein; a fixed rein commonly used on trotting and pacing harness horses; runs from each side of the bit, comes together on the bridge of the nose, and passes between the eyes, over the poll, to the backband of the harness or to the saddle; maintains the horse's head and neck in an upward-extended position while racing.

checkrein *see* CHECK REIN

cheek (1) Also known as cheekpiece, branch, cannon, sidepiece, or on western bits, shank; the vertical portion of the bit outside of the mouth including the purchase (q.v.) and shank (q.v.); generally attached at right angles to the mouthpiece and connects to the reins; prevents the bit from slipping through the horse's mouth; of two types: full-cheek (q.v.) and half-cheek (q.v.). (2) *see* CHEEKPIECE NO. 2. (3) Either side of the face of the horse below the eye and above the lower jawbone. (4) Also known as riser; a coaching term; the frame upon which the seat of a horse-drawn vehicle such as a Drag (q.v.) is constructed.

cheek guard *see* BIT GUARD

cheek leather *see* BIT GUARD

cheekpiece (1) *see* CHEEK NO. 1. (2) Also known as bridle cheekpiece; that portion of the bridle which lies flat against the cheek (q.v.) of the horse, attaches to the bit on the lower end and buckles to the crownpiece (q.v.) on the upper; is adjustable to obtain the correct position of the bit in the mouth.

cheek teeth *see* MOLARS

cheer A hunting term; the call of the huntsman (q.v.) to encourage the hounds.

Chef d'Equipe The manager of a national equestrian team responsible for making all arrangements for team competition abroad.

chef-de-race A racing term; a list of superior Thoroughbred (q.v.) sires used in the Dosage (q.v.) formula.

chelloschisis *see* CLEFT LIP

cherry bay *see* RED BAY

cherry rollers *see* ROLLERS NO. 2

Cheshire martingale A standing martingale (q.v.) consisting of an auxiliary, adjustable strap attached on one end to the girth which passes between the forelegs, splits into two branches and attaches on the other to the bridoon rings of a double bridle (q.v.); the split ends have chains and spring hooks attacked; may be fitted with a neck strap (q.v.) to keep it in place.

chesnut *see* CHESTNUT NO. 1

chest Also known as thorax or thoracic cavity; the cavity of the body of the horse formed by the spine, ribs, and breast bone between the shoulders and below the windpipe which contains the lungs and heart.

Chester A city located in England; considered the earliest home of modern English horse racing where it commenced in 1540.

chestnut (1) Also spelled chesnut; refers to coat color; a medium red coat color with points of the same color; determining the difference between sorrel (q.v.) and chestnut depends largely on the breed under consideration; the differences between sorrel (q.v.), chestnut, and liver chestnut are very subtle with some horses changing color during their lifetimes; in Thoroughbred (q.v.), Arab (q.v.), Morgan, (q.v.) and Suffolk (q.v.) breeds, all reds are designated as chestnut (some breed associations insist on the spelling 'chesnut'); draft horses may be classified as either chestnut or sorrel depending upon the depth of the red; color variations include chocolate chestnut (q.v.), liver chestnut (q.v.), chestnut tostado (q.v.), chestnut alazán (q.v.), and chestnut ruano (q.v.). (2) *see* CHESTNUTS

chestnut alazán Refers to coat color; of the chestnut (q.v.) color group; a medium red coat color with red or dark flaxen points.

chestnut imprinting The process of identifying a horse on the basis of the pattern of his chestnuts (q.v.); similar to fingerprints in that no two patterns are alike.

chestnut ruano Refers to coat color; of the chestnut (q.v.) color group; a medium red coat color with light flaxen points.

chestnuts Also known as horse chestnuts, horse eyes, night eyes, or castors; horny growths or calluses located on the inside of the horse's legs, above the knees on the forelegs and below the hocks on the hind; differently patterned from horse to horse, as fingerprints, and may be used to identify a horse through a process known as chestnut imprinting (q.v.); vestigial (q.v.) toes.

chestnut tostado Refers to coat color; of the color group chestnut (q.v.); a medium red coat color with brown points.

Cheval de Arièges *see* MERENS

Cheval de Selle Français The general heading under which French half-bred horses are grouped.

Cheval du Poitou *see* MULASSIER

chewing the bit A dressage term; said of the horse when he gently and softly mouths the bit showing jaw mobility and relaxation; causes salivation for a 'wet mouth.'

chew wood Said of a horse who eats or chews on wood surfaces as out of boredom or dietary deficiency.

CHF *see* CONGESTIVE HEART FAILURE

CHI *see* CHAMPIONNAT HIPPIQUE INTERNATIONAL

chicken coop A hunting term; a two-sided panel (q.v.) with a peaked roof placed over the top wire of a wire fence to make it safe for horses to jump; so called because it resembles a chicken hutch roof; the most popular type of panel.

Chien de Gascoigne *see* GASCOIGNE, CHIEN DE

Chifney bit Also known as anti-rearing bit; a circular bit developed in the late 1700s by Samuel Chifney for whom it is named; may have a reversed half-circle mouth in which case it is used to prevent rearing.

Chik Kee *see* LEGEND OF THE EIGHT HORSES

Chileno Also known as Caballo Chileno; a Criollo (q.v.) horse bred in Chile; similar in appearance and temperament to the Argentine Criollo from which it descends, but is more sturdy and resistatnt to disease.

chime A hunting term; said of the hounds; to give tongue (q.v.) in unison when on the scent of the quarry.

China eye *see* WALL EYE

China Pony A collective term; any pony breed indigenous to China.

Chincoteague Also known as Chincoteague Pony; a pony breed indigenous to the Chincoteague Islands located off of the eastern coast of Virginia and Maryland, USA; believed to have descended from Moorish ponies sometime in the 1600s; improved by the introduction of Shetland (q.v.) blood; all coat colors occur although piebald (q.v.) and skewbald (q.v.) are most common; breed appearance and conformation have degenerated over the years; stands about 12 hands, has a long head and neck, slightly pronounced withers, straight back, and solid legs; is rebellious, stubborn, hardy and resistant to harsh weather conditions; used for light draft and riding; wild herds spend most of the year on the uninhabited island of Assateague; every last Thursday and Friday of July a group of the ponies are swum across the channel to the island of Chincoteague where they are sold in a public auction; those ponies not swum across the channel remain known as the Assateague (q.v.).

Chincoteague Pony *see* CHINCOTEAGUE

Chinese Also known as Chinese Pony; a pony breed indigenous to China which descended from the Asiatic Wild Horse (q.v.); similar to other breeds found throughout the Far East and is therefore more of a type than a true breed; breeding has never been controlled; frequently yellow dun (q.v.) although other colors do occur; primitive markings (q.v.), specifically zebra markings (q.v.) on the legs and the eel stripe (q.v.) are common; stands 12 to 13 hands, has a small head, with a straight profile, shaggy forelock, mane, and tail, slanted eyes and small ears, short neck, and straight back; is quite hardy, strong, sure-footed, and quite rebellious; is fast over short distances and used for riding, packing, and some farm work.

Chinese Pony *see* CHINESE

chin groove *see* CURB GROOVE

chinked back *see* JINKED BACK

chinked neck *see* JINKED NECK

chinks Short, knee or midcalf-length, fringed chaps (q.v.).

CHIO *see* CHAMPIONNAT HIPPIQUE INTERNATIONAL OFFICIEL

chip Said of a horse who, when jumping an obstacle, adds an unnecessary stride; a stutter step that may signify discomfort, lack of confidence, or loss of balance.

chiropractic A system of healing based on the theory that disease results from a lack of normal nerve function; treatments consist of scientific manipulation, specifically adjustment of body structures (spinal column) and physical therapy when necessary.

chloral hydrate A infrequently used drug, now largely replaced by modern sedatives and analgesics, used as a general anesthetic and administered intravenously (q.v.).

chlorhexidrine An antiseptic agent found in powders, creams, and pre-operative skin preparations.

chloride A compound of chlorine (q.v.) (an element or radical); an electrolyte responsible, in conjunction with sodium, for maintaining osmotic pressure (q.v.), acid-balance metabolism, and kidney function.

chlorine A gaseous element used in such applications as bleach, disinfectant, and in water purification.

chlorpromazine One of a group of antihistamines administered to the horse to tranquilize, sedate, or calm depending on the dose administered.

CHN *see* CHAMPIONNAT HIPPIQUE NATIONAL

chocolate chestnut Refers to coat color; a variation of chestnut (q.v.); the coat color is uniformly dark- to medium-brown chocolate with brown points.

choke To stop or restrict the breath of, as due to a partially or completely blocked esophagus (q.v.); may be caused by rapid inhalation of improperly chewed food or consumption of non-food items such as wood, fabric, etc.; symptoms include repeated gulping efforts to swallow, oozing alarming amounts of saliva mixed with food from the nose, distress, straining for breath, arching the neck, and trying to cough; veterinary treatment may be necessary to dislodge the impaction; less dangerous than choking (q.v.).

choked down *see* CHOKING UP

choking Said of a horse with an obstruction in his windpipe; usually arises from inflammatory disease, allergic reaction, trauma, such as a kick to the throat, or a lodged foreign object; signs include an audible snoring sound as the horse strains to get air into his lungs and frantic behavior; a modified Heimlich maneuver, a swift powerful kick just behind the ribs, may dislodge an object, this method will not work in cases of disease, allergy, or trauma; in most cases, an immediate tracheotomy must be performed to allow air to enter below the obstruction; extremely rare; a desperate situation that often ends in death; more dangerous than choke (q.v.).

choking down *see* CHOKING UP

choking up Also known as choked down, choking down, soft palate disease, dorsal displacement of the soft palate, or tongue swallowing; thought to be related to a disruption in the anatomical relationship between the larynx and the soft palate (the larynx fits into a small hole in the soft palate, forming an air- and food-tight seal); when the seal between the larynx and soft palate is broken, as in a race horse, the normally nasally breathing horse breathes through his mouth causing air to pass above and below the soft palate, producing a gurgling noise and severe airway obstruction; the situation corrects itself when the horse swallows and the soft palate and larynx return to their normal positions; occurs most commonly in race horses, but also seen in eventers and hunters; in some cases, may be prevented by the use of a drop noseband (q.v.), tongue strap (q.v.), or a milder bit; in horses where no primary cause can be identified, surgery is usually advocated.

Chola The sturdiest of three types of Peruvian-bred Criollo (q.v.) or Salterno (q.v.) horses, the other two being the Costeño (q.v.) and the Morochuco (q.v.); descended from Spanish stock brought to South America by the conquistadors in the 16th century.

choline An intestinally synthesized B-complex vitamin important in the metabolism of fat and for maintaining cell structure; deficiency is unreported in horses.

chondroprotective Any animal-derived protein identical to the cartilage and joint-fluid components found in the connective tissue, particularly the fascia, throughout the horse's body; used to reduce athletic pain mechanically and physiologically by encouraging more normal joint function; may be injected or ingested; the proteins migrate to the joints via the bloodstream, unless injected directly into the joint where they reduce inflammation and destructive enzymes; in most cases they stop and/or heal existing cartilage damage; from chondro, relating to the cartilage (q.v.).

chondroitin sulfate Also known by the acronym CS; a popular nutraceutical (q.v.) containing glutamic acid, proline, glycine, and glucuronic acid used to facilitate production of natural lubricants essential to healthy joint function; helps maintain cartilage (q.v.) elasticity, reduces inflammation, and improves joint flexibility; extracted from bovine trachea, animal cartilage, and the Australian Perna canalculus mussel; inhibits cartilage-destructive enzymes, has similar benefits to, but is slower acting than, glucosamine (q.v.).

chop (1) *see* CHAFF. (2) A mixture of corn or roots with bran. (3) A hunting term; said of the hounds when they kill a fox before it has been hunted or had a chance to run. (4) The exchange of two horses between two parties usually accompanied by a payment on one side.

chop bedding Chopped straw, waste hay, fodder, or corn cobs when used to bed a stall.

chopped fox A hunting term; a fox killed in his covert (q.v.) before having the opportunity to make a run (q.v.).

chopping (1) An antiquated driving/coaching term; to hit a horse with the whip (q.v.) on the thigh rather than between the collar (q.v.) and the pad. (2) A driving term; to signal a team to turn by pulling either set of reins to the desired side.

Chorioptes A mites (q.v.); one species, *Chorioptes equi*, is known with numerous varieties; infestation causes chorioptic mange (q.v.).

Chorioptes equi The species of Chorioptes (q.v.) responsible for chorioptic mange (q.v.).

chorioptic mange Also known as leg mange, itchy heel, itchy leg, foot mange, or symbiotic mange; mange (q.v.) caused by infestation of the parasitic mite *Chorioptes equi*; usually confined to the legs or root of the tail and characterized by great itching, stomping, rubbing of one leg against the other, skin thickening, papules, scabs, and skin lesions; lesions are primarily found on the lower part of the hind legs, although in severe cases they may spread to the flanks, shoulders, and neck; severe itching, scales, crusts, thickening of the skin, and in neglected cases, a moist condition in the fetlock region; symptoms subside in the summer, but reappear with cold weather; an affected horse will stamp his feet and rub his lower legs in an attempt to relieve the pain.

chromogen A molecule capable of changing color when adjusted by the appropriate enzyme.

chronic Long-lasting or recurring frequently over a long period of time.

chronic arthritis A slowly developing, low-grade inflammation of the joint usually resulting in some degree of permanent damage.

chronic laminitis A persistent and long-term inflammation of the laminae (q.v.) characterized by changes in the shape of the foot; the hoof will grow rapidly, especially at the heel, resulting in long, dished feet with many laminitic rings (q.v.) which are close at the toe and divergent at the heel; as the condition progresses, the sole becomes thickened and either flattened or convex, and the pedal bone (q.v.) begins to rotate, and is forced downward to press on the horny sole; in severe cases the pedal bone may penetrate the sole just in front of the point of the frog and the hoof may slough.

chronic metritis Inflammation of the mammary gland due to bacteria-related infection; may originate as a sequel to acute metritis (q.v.), yet is more commonly due to injury or infection insufficiently severe to produce an acute attack; symptoms may include unthriftiness post-foaling, temperature fluctuating a degree or two above normal, a dirty, sticky, grey, pus-like vaginal discharge which causes irritation and frequent clitoral erections; the mucous membrane of the vagina appears inflamed and swollen; in other cases, the pus collects in the uterine cavity and is only discharged in large amounts every few days or weeks.

chronic obstructive pulmonary disease Also known as obstructive pulmonary disease, heaves, broken wind, alveolar emphysema, equine asthma or by the acronym COPD; a chronic allergic airway disease due to developing hypersensitivity to allergens such as organic dust, pollen, and fungal spores found in moldy or dusty hay and stables with poor ventilation; allergens cause constriction of the muscles in the walls of the small airways, swelling of the airway lining, and excess mucus production, all of which contribute to narrowing of the airways and require increased effort to breathe, especially exhale; the horse attempts to compensate for restricted air flow by coughing to clear the mucus from its breathing passages; symptoms include coughing, wheezing, reduced exercise capacity, labored breathing, and a slight increase in respiratory rate and expiratory effort; the most common cause of chronic coughing in horses; seen most frequently in confined horses aged five or older; is not curable but is manageable by placing the horse in a minimal-dust environment.

chronic poison Any toxin, e.g. plant, for which the degree of physiological damage is a function of quantity consumed; poisoning may result over a period of days or weeks and may be fatal.

Chubbarie *see* BLAGDEN

Chuck Wagon Also known as Camp Wagon, Round-up Wagon, or Food Wagon; a four-wheeled horse-drawn vehicle pulled by two or more horses in pole gear (q.v.) used as a mobile kitchen on farms and ranches in the Western states of North America; usually dead axle, with a fully sprung driving seat and a covered canvas top stretched over hoops attached to the frame.

chukka *see* CHUKKER

chukker Also known as period and spelled chukka; one of six periods in a polo game (q.v.) consisting of 7 minutes of regular play with up to 30 seconds of overtime; if during the 30-second overtime period the ball goes out of play for any reason, e.g. a foul, the chukker will be ended by the umpire; play is stopped at the end of each period to allow players to change their mounts which are usually only played for two periods, with at least one chukker of rest between those played; from the Hindi language meaning a circle.

chute (1) A racing term; an extension of either the homestretch (q.v.) or the backstretch (q.v.) of a race track; gives competing horses the opportunity to run a long straight stretch from the starting gate to the first turn or the last turn prior to the finish, rather than starting or ending on a turn. (2) A rodeo term; a stall in which rodeo horses and bulls are saddled, bridled, and mounted and from which they are released and/or ridden into the arena, as for competition.

Chyanta A subgroup of the Bhotia (q.v.) pony breed; originated in the Himalayan mountains of northern India; stands about 12.2 hands, has a gray coat, short neck, shaggy mane, straight shoulder, and short, strong legs; is frugal and has good endurance; used mainly for riding.

CI *see* COMPARABLE INDEX

CID *see* COMBINED IMMUNODEFICIENCY

cimarron A South American term; a wild horse.

cinch (1) A 3 to 4 inch (7.5–10 cm) wide strap that holds the Western saddle in place on the back of the horse and prevents it from slipping sideways and to some extent forward or rearward; connects the two sides of the saddle underneath the horse's belly just behind the front legs/shoulder; may be made of leather, cotton, wool, or synthetic materials; the equivalent of the girth (q.v.) on an English saddle. (2) Also known as cinch up; to fasten or tighten the girth (q.v.) of a Western saddle. (3) *see* FLANK CINCH

cinch bound Also known as girth shy, cinchy, or girthy; said of a horse who objects to tightening of the cinch (q.v.) or girth (q.v.) by inhaling and/or holding his breath, crow-hopping (q.v.), or bucking.

cinch up *see* CINCH NO. 2

cinchy *see* CINCH BOUND

circle curb hook *see* MELTON

circuit A geographical grouping of tracks or horse shows which are coordinated to run in sequence within a given season.

circus A grand scale entertainment, generally performed in round rings in one or more large tents since 1769; performance rings or stages are surrounded by tiered spectator seating; may feature acts performed by humans, animals, or both; unlike the Roman circus (q.v.), the spectacle does not end fatally for man or beast; Philip Astley is considered the father of the modern circus.

Cisium A two-wheeled, horse-drawn Roman gig driven by fashionable men at high speeds; had high, light, and flat wheels for speed, slatted sides for lightness, and decoration; drawn by a single horse or less frequently by two or three abreast; derived from the Latin *cito* meaning quick or speedy.

cisplatin A heavy-metal derivative of platinum used in chemotherapy (q.v.).

citrus pulp The peel and residue of citrus fruit resulting from juice production; contains an acid detergent fiber almost as high as that found in hay (q.v.) which is more efficiently digested than hay fiber, a digestible energy content equivalent to that of oats (q.v.), and a crude protein content of about 7 percent which is not efficiently digested.

CJF *see* CERTIFIED JOURNEYMAN FARRIER

CJF I *see* CERTIFIED JOURNEYMAN FARRIER, LEVEL ONE

CJF II *see* CERTIFIED JOURNEYMAN FARRIER, LEVEL TWO

CL *see* CORPUS LUTEUM

claim A racing term; the money paid by a horse buyer to the owner of that horse when claiming (q.v.) him following a claiming race (q.v.).

claimer Also known as claiming horse; a racing term; a horse who runs in a claiming race (q.v.).

claiming Also known as halter; a racing term; the process by which a licensed person may buy a horse entered in a designated race for a predetermined price; the new owner assumes title to the claimed horse (q.v.) once it leaves the starting gate (q.v.), although the original owner is entitled to any winnings; specific rules and arrangements for claiming may vary from country to country.

claiming box A racing term; a small storage box in which claims (q.v.) are placed before the start of a claiming race (q.v.); specific rules and arrangements may vary from country to country.

claiming horse *see* CLAIMER

claiming race A racing term; an event in which all entered horses are eligible for purchase at a set price by any owner of another starter (q.v.) in the same race, his agent, or those who have received a claim certificate from the stewards; claims must be made before the race; are generally of a lower class than allowance races (q.v.); the lower the claiming price, the lower the class of the horse; specific rules and arrangements may vary from country to country.

Clarence A horse-drawn farm coach first used in England in the 1840s; hung on either cee or elliptical springs without an underperch, seated four passengers inside vis-à-vis (q.v.), was drawn by a single horse, and coachman driven from a low box; use declined in the 1880s, with many being converted to cabs; an enlarged version of the Brougham (q.v.); named for the Duke of Clarence.

Clarence Cab Also known as Growler (on account of the noise the vehicle made during movement); a single-horse-drawn vehicle popular in the late 1800s which seated four passengers inside vis-à-vis (q.v.), was hung on either cee or elliptical springs without an underperch and coachman driven from a low box; an enlarged version of the Brougham (q.v.).

Clarence patent loops Harness keepers (q.v.) made of nickel or brass instead of leather.

Clarence Rockaway A horse-drawn vehicle similar in design to the Rockaway (q.v.) and Clarence (q.v.); had a covered body, a low box seat built into the front of the vehicle; hung on elliptic springs.

Clarence Surrey A more formal version of the Clarence (q.v.), outfitted with a hammer cloth box and a rear platform for footmen.

clarity A dressage term; marked distinction between the footfalls of a gait.

Clasher Squire Osbaldenston's horse raced against Clinker (q.v.) in 1829.

class A racing term; a horse possessing good pedigree, stamina, speed, conformation, endurance, and heart.

Classic Also known as Classic races; any of five primary English flat races for nominated three-year-old horses; the1,000 Guineas and the Epsom Oaks are for fillies only, while the 2,000 Guineas, Derby, and the St. Leger are open to entire colts and fillies and constitute the English Triple Crown; the United States equivalents are the Kentucky Derby (q.v.), the Preakness Stakes (q.v.), the Belmont Stakes (q.v.), and the Coaching Club American Oaks.

classic Also known as classic distance; a racing term; a specific distance; the American classic distance is 1¼ miles (2 km), while the European classic distance is 1½ miles (2.4 km); that said, of the 5 English Classic races, 2 are run over 1 mile (1.61 km), 2 over 1½ miles (2.4 km) and 1 over 1¾ miles and half a furlong 2.92 (2.81 km).

classical airs A dressage term; any of the movements of the High school (q.v.) or haute école (q.v.) consisting of movements on the ground (q.v.) and airs above the ground (q.v.).

classical equitation Also known as classical school; a riding style developed in the baroque riding halls of Europe during the Renaissance.

classical school *see* CLASSICAL EQUITATION

classic distance *see* CLASSIC

classic fino The most collected of the three distinct forward speeds of the lateral, four-beat gait of the Paso Fino (q.v.); footfall is exceedingly rapid with short steps; performed on a fino board (q.v.).

Classic races *see* CLASSIC

claybank Also known as claybank dun; refers to coat color; a variation of dun; (q.v.) most commonly, a yellow dun (q.v.), in which the coat hairs are mixed with red and the points red.

claybank dun *see* CLAYBANK

clay bed A bed of thick, wet clay in which horses affected with laminitis (q.v.) were historically stood for treatment.

clean (1) Without defect, blemishes or unsoundness. (2) *see* CLEAR ROUND NO. 1. (3) *see* CLEAR ROUND NO. 2. (4) Free from dirt or filth.

clean bred A horse of any breeding whose pedigree contains only pure blood (q.v.).

clean ground A hunting term; ground which has not been stained or soiled by the scent of a fox other than the one being hunted, or by the scent of other animals.

clean leg (1) Said of the leg of the horse which has little or no feathering (q.v.) around the fetlock (q.v.). (2) Said of a horse's leg when free of blemishes or signs of prior injury.

clean round (1) see CLEAR ROUND NO. 1. (2) see CLEAR ROUND NO. 2.

clear *see* JUMP CLEAN

clear round (1) Also known as clean round or clean; a show jumping or cross-country term; said of a horse/rider combination that completes an event or round without incurring jumping or time faults; when more than one horse per competition has a clear round, a jump-off (q.v.) results. (2) Also known as clean round or clean; a British jumping term; said of a horse/rider combination that completes an event or round without incurring jumping faults.

cleat *see* TOE GRAB

cleft (1) Also known as crosscrack; an interruption of the continuity of the hoof wall occurring at right angles to the direction of the horn tubes; may result from injury to the coronet (q.v.); most commonly caused by tread wounds from the opposite foot, abscesses, or over-reaching. (2) Partially split, divided halfway, having deep fissures, as in a lip or hoof.

cleft lip Also known as harelip and formally as chelloschisis; disruption of the continuity of the lip due to a disturbance of the process making up the jaws and face during embryonic development; cleft of the lower lip is rare and usually occurs at midline; cleft of the upper lip is usually associated with cleft palate (q.v.) and may be complete or partial.

cleft palate Also known as absence of the turbinate bone; disruption of the continuity of the roof of the mouth due to incomplete fusion of the embryonic processes of the upper jaw; previously thought to be solely hereditary, but recent evidence indicates that ingestion of toxic agents, use of steroids, and some viral infections during pregnancy are also causes; may involve the palate alone, or may extend from the lip, through the alveolar bones of the upper jaw; evidenced by milk dripping from the nostrils of the foal when nursing, or respiratory infection; in some cases may be surgically treated, otherwise euthanasia is recommended; considered a partial lethal (q.v.).

clench (1) *see* CLINCH NO. 1. (2) *see* CLINCH NO. 2

clench block *see* CLINCH BLOCK

clench cutter *see* CLINCH CUTTER

clencher *see* CLINCHER

clerk of the course A racing term; a mounted (unmounted in the United Kingdom), licensed race official responsible to the race stewards (q.v.) for general race arrangements including conduct of the horses to the starting gate, return of the horses to the saddling enclosure following the race, and the control and safety of riderless horses.

clerk of the scales A racing term; one responsible for weighing the jockeys and their tack prior to, and following, a race.

Cleveland Bay Also known as Chapman Horse and previously as Yorkshire

Packhorse; a horse breed originating in the Middle Ages in the Cleveland district of Yorkshire, England where it was used as a packhorse by traveling merchants known as "chapmen," hence the common name; during the 18th century infused with Thoroughbred (q.v.) and Arab (q.v.) blood at which time it became a prized coach horse; the coat may be brown or bay with a small star and a few white or gray hairs around the coronet or heels with no other white markings accepted; stands 16 to 16.2 hands and is docile, strong, and clean-legged; used for eventing, combined training, hunting, and driving.

Cleveland Bay Horse Society of Great Britain A British organization founded in 1884 to promote interest in the Cleveland Bay (q.v.).

click (1) *see* FORGE NO. 1. (2) *see* CLUCK

clicketing A hunting term; said of a female fox when in season (q.v.).

client (1) One who turns to another for professional services such as training, hauling, grooming, etc. (2) A racing term; one who purchases betting information from a tipster.

climb A racing term; a fault in a horse's stride in which the horse exhibits unusually high foreleg motion which results in an inefficient stride; often occurs when the horse is tired or flustered.

clinch (1) Also spelled clench; the visible point of the nail left projecting from the wall of the hoof which the farrier (q.v.) bends over and hammers in and downward into the hoof wall to secure the horseshoe to the foot. (2) To nip off the portion of the horseshoe nail (q.v.) which protrudes from the hoof wall, leaving sufficient length to turn down using a clencher (q.v.) to form a clinch (q.v.).

clinch block Also spelled clench block; a farrier's tool; a small rectangular or square-shaped piece of metal which the farrier (q.v.) holds against the wall of the hoof below the point of the protruding horseshoe nail; after the nail has been driven into the hoof wall, the clench block is held against the base of the point of the nail, while the head of the nail is struck.

clinch cutter Also known as buffer and spelled clench cutter; a farrier's tool consisting of two metal heads, a blade and a point, connected by a span of metal; the blade is approximately 1 inch (25 mm) wide and is used to cut or raise the clinches while the point is used to push nails and broken stubs out of the hoof.

clincher Also spelled clencher and known as clinching tong; a large, pritchel-tipped tool used by a farrier (q.v.) to pull the protruding tip of the horseshoe nail down against the hoof wall.

clinching tong *see* CLINCHER

clinker A top-class horse.

Clinker A 16.1, bay hunter (q.v.) Thoroughbred (q.v.) gelding owned by Captain Ross and ridden by Dick Christian in the famous 1829 horse race staged in Britain against Squire Osbaldenston's horse Clasher (q.v.).

clip (1) To shave or cut the body hair of the horse, as in winter growth before it has shed or to trim whiskers, bridle path (q.v.), etc.; clip patterns include blanket clip (q.v.), full clip (q.v.), hunter clip (q.v.), body clip (q.v.), and trace clip (q.v.). (2) A thin, V-shaped or round extension of the horseshoe used to hold the shoe onto the hoof in situations where nails alone are insufficient; the metal of the shoe is pulled up in a trianglular shape along the outside of the hoof wall and pressed into the hoof; of two types: toe clips (q.v.) and quarter clips (q.v.). (3) Said of the horse; to strike and cut the leg or foot with the opposing or rear foot or horseshoe attached thereon. (4) *see* U BOLT

clipped oats The edible grain of oat (q.v.) grass which has been processed to remove the pointed ends of the hulls, a process that lowers fiber content.

clipped out right *see* FULL CLIP

clipper One who removes body, mane, tail, and face hair from the horse using devices such as clippers (q.v.).

clippers A battery or electrically operated mechanical device used to cut body, mane, tail, and face hair from the horse; available with interchangeable blades.

clock (1) *see* TIME CLOCK. (2) To record the time elapsed, as in a horse race.

clocker A racing term; one who times workouts and races, generally for betting information.

clop To produce a sharp, hollow sound, as if by a horse's hooves.

close (1) A racing term; the final odds on a horse as in 2 to 1 at close. (2) A racing term; said of a horse who is gaining ground on the leader.

Close Basket *see* RALLI CAR

close breeding *see* INBREEDING

close contact saddle Also known as forward seat saddle, hunt seat saddle, hunting saddle, or Italian saddle; an English saddle with a relatively flat seat, square cantle (q.v.), rounded and padded flap, and small knee rolls used for jumping.

close-coupled *see* SHORT-COUPLED

closed carriage Any horse-drawn vehicle with a falling hood and permanently or semi-permanently raised sides.

closed fracture Said of a broken bone which is not exposed through the skin.

closed halt A dressage term; the posture of the horse at the halt; the horse is secure in balance and attitude and his hind legs are sufficiently under his body so that the weight of the rider and horse is distributed evenly over all four legs.

closed top Also known as Victoria top; a driving term; a falling hood on a horse-drawn vehicle.

close fast A racing term; said of a horse who gains quickly on the leader (q.v.).

close nail *see* NAIL BIND

closer A racing term; a horse who generally runs best in the latter part of a race, coming from off the pace.

clothes *see* HORSE BLANKET

clothes basket *see* RALLI CAR

clover hay A legume hay (q.v.) made from cut and dried clover of the subgroup trifolium; generally grown and dried in mixtures with other legumes such as alfalfa (q.v.) or grasses such as Timothy (q.v.), as clover is low-growing and tends to mat when dried; red, white, crimson, alsike, and ladino varieties are most commonly fed to horses; contains approximately the same digestible protein and total nutrients as found in alfalfa hay (q.v.).

club foot Also known as box foot, boxy foot, boxy hoof, donkey foot, donkey hoof, or bear foot; the horse's hoof when abnormally upright; may vary in severity; the heels may be closed instead of open or there may be slight tendon contraction causing a concave deformation of the hoof wall at the toe; prevents the frog from contacting the ground and functioning as an anti-concussive and non-slip device; when unilateral (q.v.), may be due to injury while a bilateral (q.v.) condition may be inherited or due to nutritional deficiency.

clubhouse turn An American racing term; the turn of the race track to the right of the grandstand, generally beginning on the homestretch (q.v.); so called because the clubhouse is usually to the right of the general stands.

club the reins A driving term; said of the driver who takes all of the reins into one hand.

cluck Also known as click; a sound made by the rider or driver with the tongue usually as a signal to the horse to increase speed.

Clydesdale A popular heavy-draft breed which originated at the beginning of the 18th century in Scotland's Clyde valley from which the name derived; descended from hardy native breeds put to Flemish and Friesian (q.v.) stallions; stands 16 to 17 hands and weighs approximately 1,540 to 2,000 pounds (699–907 kg); generally has a brown, bay, or black coat, with chestnut and roan occurring less frequently; white markings on the face and legs are quite common as is prominent feathering (q.v.) on all four legs which often extends over the wall of the hoof; the hind legs are frequently cow-hocked (q.v.); is calm, sociable, strong and hardy; the stud book was established in 1878;

historically used for hauling coal, farm work, and carriage while the modern horse is used for heavy draft, farm, and some carriage work.

Clydesdale Horse Society of Great Britain and Ireland An organization established in 1877 to maintain and perpetuate the quality and purity of the Clydesdale (q.v.).

CMF *see* CERTIFIED MASTER FARRIER

Coach Any enclosed, four-wheeled, horse-drawn passenger vehicle, used either in private or public service; usually drawn by a team (q.v.), but sometimes by a pair and driven by a coachman or postillion (q.v.); introduced during the late Middle Ages in the town of Krocs (pronounced croach) Hungary, from which the corruption of the name survived; used in continuous service in a variety of types through the 1920s including the Stage Coach (q.v.), Concord Coach (q.v.), Drag Coach (q.v.), Mail Coach (q.v.), State Coach (q.v.), and Park Coach (q.v.).

coach dog *see* DALMATIAN

coach horn Also known as yard of tin, three feet of tin, horn, or coaching horn; a straight funnel-ended horn, commonly made of brass or copper used by coachmen and/or coach guards to clear the road and announce the approach of a horse-drawn vehicle by means of a series of short notes or snatches of tunes; in pre-railway days were seldom more than 36 inches (91 cm) in length, while modern ones measure 52 inches (132 cm) or more.

coach horse Any horse such as a Hackney (q.v.), Friesian (q.v.), Cleveland Bay (q.v.) or Percheron (q.v.), used to draw a coach (q.v.).

Coaching Club An English organization established in 1870 to organize and conduct coaching events; the constituency consisted of owners of private four-in-hand coaches (q.v.) which met regularly through 1939 for organized drives, usually starting from the Magazine in Hyde Park, London.

coaching crop Also known as coaching whip, driving whip, or tandem whip; a wood, fiberglass, bone, plastic, metal, or leather rod having a leather or cord thong attached on one end, used as an aid by coachmen to drive harness and coach horses.

coaching horn *see* COACH HORN

coaching marathon A long-distance race for four-horse Coaches first organized by the Royal International Horse Show (q.v.) in 1909 in England; Coaches depart from a specified location at staggered intervals, the drive ending in the show ring within a specific amount of time without a change of coachman; points are awarded for turnout (q.v.) and condition of the horses on arrival in the show ring, not for speed.

coaching revival That period beginning in 1860 when a renewed interest in coaching evolved; this followed the end to coaching initiated by railway travel.

coaching whip *see* COACHING CROP

coachman Also known as dragsman; a man employed to drive one or more horses pulling a Coach (q.v.) or Carriage (q.v.).

coachmans' coat A single-breasted, front-buttoned coat, with two pairs of buttons at the rear worn by a coachman (q.v.); the coat tails were stitched about 5 inches below the top buttons to prevent them from flying apart; had pocket flaps on false pockets just above the hips; is slightly longer than a groom's coat.

coachman's elbow The salute given by a coachman (q.v.), who, rather than raising his hat, raises his whip hand to face level, with the whip held aslant to his body thus raising the elbow, a position from which the name derived.

coachman's seat *see* BOX NO. 3

coach pot *see* BOURDALOU

coach retarder *see* BRAKE

coarse Said of a horse lacking refinement and quality.

coarseness around the jowl Said of a horse having an accumulation of flesh at the jowl which restricts head flexion.

coarse punched A nail hole in a horseshoe located towards the inner edge of the horseshoe web (q.v.).

coat (1) The hair (q.v.) covering the body of the horse or hound. (2) A warm outer garment covering at least the upper part of the human body.

coating *see* COVERT CLOTH

coat pattern Refers to coat color; any of the white hair patterns occurring in the horse's coat; of three types: individual white hairs, asymmetrical patches of white, and symmetrical patches of white; horses are described first by the appropriate color designation followed by the pattern of white present, e.g., black patterned leopard; such patterns include, but are not limited to, tobiano (q.v.), overo (q.v.), sabino (q.v.), splashed white (q.v.), piebald (q.v.), skewbald (q.v.), rabicano (q.v.), frosty (q.v.), blanket (q.v.), leopard spotting (q.v.), varnish marks (q.v.), snowflake (q.v.), and mottled (q.v.).

coat up *see* HAIR UP

cob Originally known as rouncy and spelled runcy; a type not a breed; a small, heavy-boned, short-coupled, and muscular horse or pony usually standing under 15.3 hands, having great depth of girth, and a short neck, legs, and cannon bones; most are a combination of two or more breeds; is capable of carrying up to 200 pounds (91 kg); originally used as a hack for heavy riders.

cobalamin *see* VITAMIN B_{12}

cobalt A mineral component of vitamin B12 (q.v.) required for the synthesis thereof; the dietary requirements for a mature horse are extremely low and are usually met by a normal diet.

cobby Said of a close-coupled (q.v.) and stoutly built horse, as a cob (q.v.).

coccygeal bones Also known as coccygeal vertebrae or tail bones; those bones numbering 15 to 21, which are a direct extension of the spinal column and constitute the tail.

coccygeal vertebrae *see* COCCYGEAL BONES

cockade A brooch or fastening used on three-cornered hats introduced into England and Germany in the second half of the 18th century; now an oval- or fan-shaped rosette (q.v.) used as a badge of office; fastened to the side of a liveried servant's top hat when in formal dress.

cocked ankles An American term; bent forward or cocked fetlocks, a condition usually found in the hind feet and commonly attributable to improper hoof trimming; results in short toes, long heels, and in some cases, lameness.

cock eye Also known as woodcock eye and spelled cockeye; an oval-shaped metal eye ring attached to the end of lead trace (q.v.) by which the trace is secured to the lead bar hook in harness tack; when viewed in profile is said to resemble a cock's eye.

cockeye *see* COCK EYE

cock fence A jumping obstacle; a natural hedge or thorn fence trimmed to a low level.

cock horse A driving term; an extra horse, usually of a flashy color, used in the lead of a team (q.v.) to help pull a heavily loaded stage uphill; always ridden by a cock horse boy (q.v.).

cock horse boy Generally, a young, lightweight boy trained to ride a cock horse (q.v.).

Cocking Cart Also known as Suicide Gig; a two-wheeled, horse-drawn English vehicle popular in the late 18th century for travel to sport events such as cock fights from which the name derived; mounted on high wheels and had a slatted underboot for carrying fighting cocks or dogs; seated two in the front and had a high rearward seat for a groom; generally drawn by a tandem (q.v.); a later version, popular in the 1890s and 1900s for pleasure driving, could be drawn by three horses abreast.

cocktail (1) The common name for a half-bred English hunter (q.v.). (2) Also spelled Cock Tail; a racing term; a horse of racing quality, but not a Thoroughbred (q.v.); only one parent may be registered in the General Stud Book (q.v.). (3) *see* DOCK TAIL

Cock Tail *see* COCKTAIL NO. 2

cock-throttled A horse whose head and neck are badly set on, the line of the gullet (q.v.) being convex and similar to that of a cockerel.

cocoa shells The thin covering of the cocoa bean; contain approximately 15 percent protein, 17 percent fiber, 10 percent ash and 0.5 to 2 percent theobromine, which when used in small amounts may increase cardiac output, urine excretion, appetite, and may function as a smooth muscle relaxant; high intake may cause a loss of appetite, diarrhea, and death.

codeine A white, crystalline, slightly bitter alkaloid opiate used as an analgesic, constipant, sedative, and hypnotic; administered orally or mixed with honey or molasses into a paste to be applied to the tongue.

co-favorite A racing term; one or more horses sharing favouritsm and given identical odds (q.v.).

coffee-housing A hunting term; said of mounted riders who chat with each other rather than attending to the activity of the hunt (q.v.).

Coffin Cab A two-wheeled, horse-drawn, coffin-shaped vehicle of the Hackney (q.v.) type used in London, England in the first half of the 18th century prior to the Hansom Cab (q.v.); carried two passengers and was drawn by a single horse.

coffin bone *see* THIRD PASTERN

coffin head The horse's head when coarse, ugly faced, and lacking jaw prominence.

Coggins test A blood test used to detect the presence of antibodies for the equine infectious anemia (q.v.) virus.

cold (1) A racing term; said of a horse unfit to win a race due to his physical condition or jockey intervention. (2) *see* STALE LINE

cold back Also known as back up; said of a horse showing initial resistance to fitting the saddle and tightening the girth; a condition generally alleviated by fitting the saddle loosely and walking the horse for some time before mounting.

cold blood Also know as occidental horse (obs); a generic term; any heavy-boned, even-tempered Northern European horse breed descended from the northern forest type horse, e.g. the tundra and steppe horses; not actually cold blooded, but originally from the colder climates; does not have any Arab blood; includes such breeds as the Shire (q.v.), Suffolk (q.v.), Percheron (q.v.), and Clydesdale (q.v.).

cold blooded Said of a cold blood (q.v.) horse.

cold brand *see* FREEZE BRAND

cold fit *see* COLD SHOE NO. 2

cold jawed Said of a horse having a tough mouth, one resistant to the effects of the bit.

cold hose To run a stream of cold water on or over an injury as to reduce inflammation.

cold line *see* STALE LINE

cold scent *see* STALE LINE

cold shoe (1) *see* READY-MADE SHOE. (2) Also known as cold fit or cold shoeing; to shoe a horse with ready-made (q.v.) horseshoes, i.e. factory-shaped to fit the hoof, without the benefit of the forge (q.v.); a much faster shoeing process than hot shoeing (q.v.), although perhaps less precise.

cold shoeing *see* COLD SHOE NO. 2

cold shoer Any farrier who shoes horses without the benefit of a forge (q.v.) to shape the horseshoe (q.v.) to the hoof.

cold trailing A cutting horse term; said of a horse in a working position who lags well behind the movement of the cow.

coleaderos One of nine scored events in a charreada (q.v.) in which a charro (q.v.) tails a wild bull.

colic Also known as gripes, stomach staggers, spasms of the gastrointestinal tract, or incorrectly as bloat and enteric fever; abdominal pain of any origin; caused by digestive disorders which may result from improper chewing, systemic disease, circulatory disturbances, digestive system infection, neuromuscular disturbances, twisting of the intestine, fatty tumors, gastric dilation due to grain overload, toxicity, bots, water deprivation, nutritional factors such as feed high in fiber or poor in quality, sudden changes in feed, and feed too high in energy; associated pain is caused either by obstruction of the ingesta (q.v.), resulting in increased gas production that stretches the intestines, or by spasms in the alimentary canal; symptoms include lack of appetite, pawing, kicking at the abdomen, getting up and down, rolling, restlessness, flank watching and/or biting, elevated skin temperature, sweating (due to pain), increased and/or thready pulse, abnormal mucosa color, gut sounds, feces or the lack thereof, and body postures such as dog-sitting or a sawhorse stance; Arabs (q.v.) are 2.5 times more prone to colic than Thoroughbreds (q.v.); types include torsion colic (q.v.), sand colic (q.v.), impaction colic (q.v.), intussception colic (q.v.), and false colic (q.v.).

colic in foals A digestive tract disorder of foals characterized by acute abdominal pain; most commonly caused by intussception (q.v.) which only responds to immediate surgery; colic (q.v.) occurring within the first 48 hours of life is caused chiefly by impaction of the large intestine due to meconium retention; may also be caused by a ruptured bladder or *atresia coli.*

colitis-X A sporadic disease of unknown origin occasionally affecting several horses within a group; all ages other than foals are affected, but it occurs most commonly in two- to five-year-olds; may be associated with endotoxic shock (q.v.); many affected horses have a history of stress or upper respiratory infection one to three weeks prior to onset; symptoms include copious, watery, mucoid and occasionally blood-stained diarrhea, depression, mild abdominal discomfort, rapid onset of hypovolemic shock, and elevated heart rate as the disease progresses; death may occur within three hours of onset, or in less acute cases, within 24 to 48 hours.

collagen granuloma A condition in which rotten collagen fibers in the skin's structure are buried between layers of healthy tissue, forming hard bumps; are slow growing and commonly appear on the back and sides of the horse where they may be rubbed raw by tack and/or blankets; may be surgically cored to allow expulsion of the dead fibers.

collapse Said of a horse when he loses the desired posture or body line.

collar (1) *see* HARNESS COLLAR. (2) *see* WHIP COLLAR

collar buttons Refers to coat color; a few concentrated spots of black hair on the neck just below where it joins the body; common to donkeys.

collar mark An adventitial mark (q.v.); white coat hairs in the neck and shoulder area; result from destruction of the pigment cells of underlying skin by a poorly fitting collar.

collar of a whip *see* WHIP COLLAR

collar work A driving term; any work uphill, pulling heavy loads, or that which requires the horse to strain against the collar (q.v.).

collect (1) To put a horse into an optimal state of balance using seat and leg aids in conjunction with quietly restraining hands; impulsion generated in the hindquarters is contained by the rider's hands; the horse's strides are active and shortened rather than long; his outline is characterized by lowered haunches, hocks engaged well beneath the body, a convexly rounded top line (q.v.), rounded and flexed neck, a softly flexed poll and a relaxed jaw. (2) Said of a bettor (q.v.); to win a wager on a horse, event, etc.

collected Said of a horse moved forward from behind and ridden into the bit with his neck flexed, jaw relaxed, hocks well under the body, back up, and his weight over the haunches.

collected canter A gait variant in which the horse is ridden at the canter (q.v.) into the bit with his neck flexed and arched, jaw relaxed, hindquarters engaged and active, forehand light, and shoulders supple and free; the stride is shorter than at other canter variations, but lighter and more mobile.

collected trot A gait variant in which the horse is ridden at the trot (q.v.) into the bit with his neck flexed and arched, jaw relaxed, hocks well under the body with energetic impulsion, and the weight over the haunches; the horse is moved forward from behind; the steps are shorter, but lighter and more mobile than at other trot variations.

collected walk A pace in which the horse is ridden at the walk (q.v.) into the bit with his neck flexed, jaw relaxed, hocks well under the body with good action, and the weight over the haunches; the horse is moved forward from behind; the movement is vigorous with each step placed in regular sequence; the stride is shortened and shows greater activity than at the medium walk (q.v.).

collecting ring The enclosed area on a show ground where competitors are assembled prior to competition.

collection Also known as self-carriage; a learned weight-bearing posture of the horse; the increased and energetic engagement of the hind legs, elevation of the back, and lightening the forehand resulting in improved balance; the degree of collection desired varies greatly from sport to sport.

Collier *see* PIT PONY

Collier's Horse *see* KNOCKER

colon impaction Also known as constipation; difficult, painful, or infrequent passage of feces resulting from inactivity, debility, senility, obstruction due to a foreign body, dehydration, or poor feeding.

Colorado Mocking Bird *see* ASS

Colorado Ranger A horse type evolved from the Appaloosa (q.v.) to which it is similarly colored; found in the Colorado region of the United States.

color breed To develop desired coat colors by means of selective breeding.

colored (1) Also known as colored horse; said of an Appaloosa (q.v.) showing any coat color combination approved by the Appaloosa Horse Club (q.v.). (2) Also known as colored horse; any horse showing more than one coat color.

colored horse (1) *see* COLORED NO. 1. (2) *see* COLORED NO. 2

colors (1) Also known as silks, racing silks, or racing colors; a racing term; a uniquely patterned jockey jacket and cap selected by the owner of the mount and worn by the jockey (q.v.) during a race, a practice introduced in Newmarket, England in 1767; the distinctive patterns and colors are registered annually with The Jockey Club (q.v.) and with the appropriate state racing authority by the owner; made of silk, nylon, or light wool (Britain); known as silks because they were originally made only of that material; at some smaller tracks, colors designate post positions (q.v.), e.g., yellow for post position one, blue for two, etc. (2) A hunting term; distinctively colored hunt coat collars (q.v.) worn by the hunt staff and such members of the field as have been invited to wear them by the Hunt Master (q.v.).

colostrum Also known as first milk; the thick, extra-rich milk secreted by the mare's mammary glands upon birth of a foal; contains globulins and proteins that provide the foal with temporary (two to three months) immunity against infectious disease until such time as the foal's system begins producing sufficient antibodies.

colt A young, uncastrated male horse less than three years of age or, in Thoroughbreds (q.v.), less than four years.

colt bit *see* TATTERSALL BIT

colt foal The male sex of a foal (q.v.).

coltsfoot Also known as horsefoot or horsehoof; a perennial composite herb having small, yellow flowers and large heart-shaped leaves; used medicinally.

coma A state of prolonged unconsciousness, usually due to disease or injury, from which it is difficult or impossible to rouse the horse.

comb (1) A toothed instrument of bone, rubber, plastic, or metal used for arranging, cleansing, or adjusting the hair, as the mane. (2) To dress, as the hair, with or as with a comb.

combination (1) Also known as combination obstacle; any obstacle (q.v.) consisting of two or more separate jumps or elements of any type which are numbered and judged as one unit which usually have a single or double non-jumping stride between each portion; under FEI (q.v.) rules, the maximum distance between any two of the fences may not exceed 39 feet 4 inches (11.98 m), as measured from the inside element of the two fences at ground level. (2) Also known as combination bet; racing term; any across-the-board (q.v.) bet for which a single mutuel ticket is issued.

combination bet *see* COMBINATION NO. 2

combination horse Also known as ride and drive horse (Brit.); any horse used for both riding and driving.

combination fence *see* COMBINATION NO. 1

combination obstacle *see* COMBINATION NO. 1

combined immunodeficiency Also known by the acronym CID; a genetically based fatal disease resulting in a failure of the immune system.

combined driving trial A driving competition consisting of four phases: Competition A, Section One (q.v.), presentation, Competition A, Section Two, dressage test, Competition B (q.v.), the marathon phase, and Competition C (q.v.), the obstacle course; the competitor with the lowest overall penalty score wins.

combined test An eventing (q.v.) term; a special combined training event conducted in one day which consists of dressage and show jumping phases.

combined training *see* HORSE TRIALS

come back to A racing term; said of a horse who slows down after taking the lead in the start of a horse race allowing the other horses in the field to close the gap.

come in front of the vertical Said of the horse who moves his head forward from a position perpendicular to the ground.

comes again *see* SECOND WIND

Comet An exceptionally fast horse-drawn Coach (q.v.) which ran daily on the London to Brighton road, England.

come to a halt To cease forward movement of the horse from any pace or gait.

coming Said of a horse approaching one year of age, as in "The bay was coming three years of age".

command Gogue One of two types of de Gogue (q.v.); a training device consisting of an arrangement of straps, fastened on one end to the girth or chest ring, which split and run through rings on either side of a poll pad, down through the bit rings on the same side, and attach to the reins, other than the snaffle rein, on the other; assist the action of the bit by restricting the position of the horse's head and neck through action on the poll (q.v.); may be controlled by the rider.

commingle A racing term; to combine the mutuel pools from off-track sites with the host track.

comminuted fracture A break in a bone consisting of more than two fragments.

commission bet Any wager in which a percentage of the resulting winnings is paid to the party who placed the bet on behalf of the first.

commit A cutting horse term; said of a horse/rider team who demonstrates its intention to work a specific cow by looking at and stepping towards it.

committed A cutting term; said of a horse in competition when he has visibly cut a cow from the herd and is obligated to work it.

common Said of a horse of coarse appearance; generally the progeny of non-pedigree or generic bloodstock.

common alum Also known as potash alum; a type of alum (q.v.) used in medicine as an astringent and styptic.

common bay *see* BAY

common blood Non-pedigree or purebred, as in the breeding of a horse.

common bone Said of bone of inferior quality; lacks density, is coarse-grained, and has a large central core.

common-bred Said of a horse bred from mixed, non-pedigree or generic stock.

common riding *see* HAYWICK COMMON RIDING

common salt *see* SODIUM CHLORIDE

Commons, Open Spaces, and Footpaths Preservation Society An English organization founded in 1865 to create, protect, and maintain public footpaths, bridlepaths, and other highways.

Comparable Index Also known by the acronym CI; an Average-Earnings Index (q.v.) for stallions; establishes statistics for all the progeny of mares to whom a stallion was bred when the mares were bred to other stallions, e.g. a stallion with an AEI of 2.00 might have a CI of 1.00 which means that those same mares produced foals who earned a 1.00 AEI when bred to other stallions; a stallion can improve the mare's rating or the converse.

competition An athletic contest between riders, horses, and/or horse and rider combinations.

Competition A Section One A driving term; usually the first phase of a four-phase combined driving trial (q.v.); a total of 50 marks can be gained based on presentation, with 10 potential points each for: the driver and grooms or social passengers acting as grooms, the horse or horses, the vehicle, the harness, and the overall impression; a score of 10 is deemed excellent and 1 very bad.

Competition A Section Two A driving term; usually the second phase of a four-phase combined driving trial (q.v.); a dressage test in which the driver maneuvers a horse-drawn vehicle around markers (q.v.) to demonstrate that the horse(s) is obedient, calm, supple, and has correct paces; full use of the arena and smooth transitions are important in achieving a good score; 11 movements are required.

Competition B Also known as marathon phase; a driving term; usually the third of four phases of a combined driving trial (q.v.) the objective being to test the fitness and stamina of the horse or horses and to test the judgment of pace and horsemastership of the competitors; usually occurs on one or two days following Competitions A Sections One and Two; consists of sections A–E, with section E involving the negotiation of obstacles.

Competition C Also known as obstacle course; a driving term; the final phase of a four-phase combined driving trial (q.v.); the objective being to test the fitness, obedience, and suppleness of the horse following Competition B; drivers navigate a course consisting of up to 20 obstacles such as cones, on top of which rubber balls are balanced, laid out in a smooth pattern in a dressage arena; faults are incurred when either cones or balls are toppled; competitors with the lowest score going into this phase go first.

competition studs Low-volume metal heads screwed into the ground-side surface of a specially prepared horseshoe (q.v.) to increase traction on slippery surfaces such as grass or mud; available in a variety of shapes and sizes to suit different conditions and needs; are not designed for use on roads and should be removed after use as they distort foot balance; when removed from the shoe, oiled cotton or a similar substance is inserted into the holes to prevent them from being clogged.

competitive trail ride *see* ENDURANCE RIDE

complete feed A ration, usually commercially prepared, containing all essential food elements except water and perhaps salt.

complete fracture A break in the bone that extends through both bone surfaces.

complete test *see* THREE-DAY EVENT

complementary lameness Lameness in a previously sound limb due to pain in another limb; pain causes uneven weight distribution on one or more of the other limbs.

compound feed Any ration containing a mixture of ingredients, e.g. pelleted feed and grain, to which various supplements such as minerals and vitamins have been added.

compound fracture Also known as open fracture; a bone break in which the broken bone penetrates the skin and is exposed; the risk of infection is very high.

compression bow *see* BANDAGE BOW

compulsory exercises A vaulting term; a group of movements in a vaulting competition consisting of the vault on, simple dismount, basic seat, flare (q.v.), stand (q.v.), mill (q.v.), scissors (q.v.), and flank (q.v.); are the basis of all freestyle compositions.

compulsory halt The 10-minute break between the speed and endurance phases in a three-day event (q.v.).

computerized tomography Also known as CT scanning; a diagnostic technique; a large scanning instrument revolves around a body part in a 180-degree arc, while a pencil-thin electromagnetic beam records images in slices of the structure; the resulting images are used to pinpoint abscesses, tumors, cysts, etc. that escape detection by traditional X-rays (q.v.).

concave face *see* DISH FACE

concentrated feed Food stuff containing high nutritional value, e.g. oats, corn, barley, or feed pellets.

conchal sinus *see* DENTIGEROUS CYST

concho A metal disc, often made of silver, set on a leather rosette on a Western saddle used to secure thongs, or for decoration.

Concord *see* CONCORD COACH

Concord Coach Also known as American Mail Coach, Concord Wagon, and, in the 1820s, as Concord; the most popular horse-drawn Coach or Stage used in North America with versions later used in Australia, New Zealand, and South Africa; oval shaped, hung on leather thoroughbraces, and had double benches for passengers seated vis-à-vis (q.v.); mail and valuables were carried in a fore-boot while ordinary luggage was strapped to the roof or contained within the rear boot, the latter having a sloping top; drawn by teams of from four to eight horses depending on the terrain and vehicle size; driven from a box seat which the driver generally shared with a guard; on some 16 seaters, there was a separate guard's seat in the rear, perched on a skeleton framework; built to withstand extremely rugged road conditions; developed by Downing and Company of Concord, New Hampshire, USA, for which the vehicle was named.

Condord Mud Wagon Also known as Poor Man's Concord or California Mud Wagon; an American-made wagon similar to the Concord Coach (q.v.), yet using more simple joinery.

Concord Wagon *see* CONCORD COACH

Concours Complete *see* THREE-DAY EVENT

Concours Complete d'Equitation *see* THREE-DAY EVENT

Concours Voltige d'Amitie Also known by the acronym CVA; an international vaulting (q.v.) event open to competitors from the host country and up to four foreign nations.

Concours Conde Frederick the Great's favorite horse; was originally from England, fleabitten gray (q.v.), and lived 42 years.

condition The state of health and fitness of the horse.

Condition Book A racing term; a publication produced by the track racing secretary which identifies the purses, terms of eligibility, and weight formulas for each race to be run over a period of about two weeks at a specific track; used by horsemen to determine in what race to enter a horse based on eligibility.

conditioner (1) *see* TRAINER. (2) A racing term; a workout or race used to encourage fitness in the horse. (3) A liquid or cream applied to the mane and tail of the horse to moisturize and prevent tangling.

condition race Also known as terms race; a racing term; any race other than a handicap race (q.v.) for which specific entry conditions exist, e.g. for horses that have not won a race of $10,000.

conditions A racing term; the specifics of a race such as purse size, eligibility for entry, and weight formulas or concessions.

condition scoring A method of rating the relative thinness or fatness of a horse on a scale of one to nine developed at Texas A&M University, USA; provides a framework for visual weight assessment; not an objective method of calculation.

condylar fracture A break in the distal (q.v.), knobby end of a long bone such as the cannon bone, which serves to form an articulation with another bone.

Conestoga Wagon A large, tough, horse-drawn, covered farm and freight wagon popular in the United States during the 1750s; had a canvas top supported by 8 to 13 sloping tilts, a floor and bodywork of wooden planking curved slightly downwards to the fore-carriage, front boards and tail gates inclined outwards at both the front and rear, with a significant amount of overhang beyond the axle trees, and a driving seat pulled out from the front of the wagon on the near side; drawn by teams of six or more horses or oxen depending on the weight of the load pulled; much larger than the Prairie Schooner (q.v.).

confidential An antiquated British term; a horse suitable for a novice or elderly rider.

confinement *see* PARTURITION

conformation The shape or body structure of a horse, with particular attention paid to proportion and skeletal angulation.

congenital (1) Acquired during the development of the fetus in the uterus and not through heredity. (2) Existing at or dating from birth.

congenital abnormality *see* CONGENITAL TRAIT

congenital defect *see* CONGENITAL TRAIT

congenital deformity *see* CONGENITAL TRAIT

congenital mark Any mark on the coat of the horse inclusive of the limbs, body and head, present from birth, but not as a result of heredity; may be used for identification purposes, e.g., wall eye (q.v.), hair whorl (q.v.), different tail and mane color, etc.

congenital trait Also known as congenital abnormality, congenital deformity, or congenital defect; any structural or functional defect acquired during the development of the fetus in the uterus; may or may not have clearly established causes, although environmental, nutritional or genetic factors may contribute; not necessarily hereditary.

congestive heart failure Also known by the acronym CHF; cessation of the horse's heart function; occurs when a horse's heart muscle is so severely damaged or overworked that it loses its strength and can no longer pump blood efficiently; symptoms include flared nostrils, a swollen chest and belly, weak or erratic pulse, and an increased heart rate while at rest; the blood pools around the heart and in the lung area, eventually leaking through the tissues, collecting under the skin, causing the horse's underline to appear swollen; diagnostics include X-rays (q.v.), echocardiography (q.v.), and electrocardiography (q.v.); although rare, may strike horses of any age.

Connaught Buggy A low, hooded, horse-drawn vehicle of the Gig (q.v.) type hung on side- and cee-springs; named after the Duchess of Connaught who ordered one for her personal driving in India.

connections *see* STABLE CONNECTIONS

Connemara Also known as Connemara Pony or, generically, as native pony; the only horse breed indigenous to Ireland; an ancient pony breed which benefited from crosses with Barbs (q.v.) and Spanish Horses (q.v.), infusions of Arab (q.v.) blood, and more recently the English Thoroughbred (q.v.); is hardy, docile, intelligent, sound, and generally raised in the wild; stands 13 to 14.2 hands, has a small head with a generally straight profile, a long, well-formed neck, high withers (q.v.), full mane and tail, sturdy and well-muscled legs often measuring 7 to 8 inches (18–20 cm) at the cannon, and a slightly sloping croup; coat colors include gray, dun, black, bay, brown, and occasionally roan or chestnut; piebalds and skewbalds are not accepted by the breed society; historically used for farming and packing, but now used for riding and jumping; the Stud Book was established in 1924.

Connemara Breeders' Society *see* CONNEMARA PONY BREEDERS' SOCIETY, THE

Connemara Pony *see* CONNEMARA

Connemara Pony Breeders' Society Also known as the Connemara Breeders' Society; an organization founded in Eire in 1923 to encourage the breeding of the Connemara (q.v.), to develop and maintain them as a pure breed, and to maintain the Stud Book.

Conquistadors The 16th-century Spanish conquerors of Mexico widely credited with the reintroduction of horses to the western hemisphere.

consignor One who offers a horse for sale through an auction.

consolation double A racing term; a payoff to holders of daily double (q.v.) tickets which pair a scratched horse from the second race with a winning horse from the first.

constipation *see* COLON IMPACTION

Con Sullivan *see* SULLIVAN, CON

contact The connection between the rider's hands and the horse's mouth achieved through the reins.

Continental Chaise A horse-drawn vehicle of the Gig (q.v.) type popular in the mid-18th century; had a small, ornately carved and gilded body with painted side panels; hung on leather braces (q.v.); the carved dash had an exaggerated curve.

continental martingale A martingale (q.v.); an auxiliary rein or strap used to assist the action of the bit by restricting the position of the horse's head and neck; consists of an arrangement of straps, fastened to the girth at one end which pass through the bridle on either side of the poll (q.v.), and down to the bit rings on the other; encourages a low head set through applied pressure on the poll and bridge of the nose.

contract rider A racing term; a jockey (q.v.) obligated by contract to provide his services first to the contract holder/owner of the mount (q.v.) before riding for another.

contracted feet *see* CONTRACTED HEELS

contracted heels Also known as contracted feet; a narrowing of the horse's heels (q.v.) and frog (q.v.) due to a lack of frog pressure; more common in the fore than the hind feet of light horses; may be caused by improper shoeing or trimming of the feet; symptoms include a shortened stride and heat around the quarters (q.v.) and heels; a narrow foot is not necessarily a contracted one.

contusion A blunt injury that does not break the skin, but which damages the deep tissues and/or bone; characterized by swelling, heat, and tenderness.

convenience (1) *see* BOURDALOU. (2) A coaching term; a manner of springing horse-drawn vehicles popularized in 1691. (3) *see* CONVENIENCY

conveniency Also known as convenience; a roof-top basket in which passengers traveled on the tops of some Coaches (q.v.); popular around 1767.

convulsive foal *see* BARKER

cooked (1) Said of a young horse overtrained to the point of souring; as due to stress and other associated emotional strain. (2) A British racing term; said of an exhausted horse.

cook him *see* BLOW HIM

cool down *see* COOL OUT

cooler (1) A lightweight, frequently vented wool, acrylic, cotton, or other fabric horse blanket draped over the neck and back of a horse to promote lowering body temperature slowly after a workout, race, show, etc. (2) A racing term; a horse restrained by the rider to prevent him from running well.

cool out Also known as cooling out or cool down; to restore a horse, overheated by exercise, to normal body temperature following a workout, as by walking him quietly.

cooling out *see* COOL OUT

coon foot Said of the horse's hoof when the pastern slopes more than the dorsal surface of the hoof.

coon-footed Said of a horse having a foot in which the pastern slopes more than the dorsal surface of the hoof wall, the axis being broken at the coronary band (q.v.); occurs in either the fore or hind feet.

coon hound A dog bred to hunt raccoon; usually keen scented and medium bodied, i.e. blue-tick hound.

Cooper, J.C. An English coachbuilder credited by some with having designed the Victoria (q.v.) in the late 1860s.

Copaicut Also spelled Copicutt; a four-wheeled, horse-drawn passenger wagon or phaeton (q.v.) widely used in North American colonies during the late 18th century; outfitted with two parallel, forward-facing cross seats, the rear seat was hung on thoroughbraces rather than springs; the rear portion of the vehicle slanted outwards; drawn by a single horse.

copal A slightly yellow, transparent resin imported from South America in the 1800s used for preparing a hard-wearing coach varnish.

COPD *see* CHRONIC OBSTRUCTIVE PULMONARY DISEASE

cope Also known as cope forward; a hunting term; a cheer of the whippers-in (q.v.) meaning to ride forward as in "cope forward".

cope forward *see* COPE

Copenhagen The Duke of Wellington's horse ridden in the battle of Waterloo; a grandson of Eclipse (q.v.).

coper *see* HORSE DEALER

Copicutt *see* COPAICUT

Coppa Delle Nazione *see* NATIONS CUP

copper A reddish-brown, malleable, ductile, metallic element that is required in trace amounts in the diet of the horse for bone, cartilage, and elastin formation, utilization of iron, and formation of the pigments of the hair; dietary requirements are estimated at between 5 to 8 ppm; deficiency is rare and excess copper can be toxic; when used in bit construction, causes the horse's mouth to salivate and thus remain soft.

copper sulfate Also known as blue stone or blue vitriol; a compound occurring in large, transparent, deep-blue triclinic crystals used as an astringent (q.v.) and caustic (q.v.) agent in the reduction of granulation tissue (q.v.) when applied either as a paste or dry crystal, or as an anti-fungal treatment for ringworm (q.v.).

coprophagy To eat manure; a vice in mature horses and a normal developmental stage in foals.

cording The cruel, and now illegal, practice of tying a stiff cord around the horse's tongue and attaching the ends to either side of the bit cheekpieces so that a slight jerk on the reins cuts the tongue with the cord; it was believed that the sudden pain would cause the horse to step higher.

cording-up *see* TYING-UP SYNDROME

cordobán Cordovan (q.v.) leather.

cordovan (1) Made of cordovan leather. (2) A soft, fine-grained, colored leather manufactured from split horse, pig, and goat hides. (3) Of or belonging to Córdoba, Spain. (4) Also known as shelly cordovan or shell cordovan; leather tanned from the inner layer of horse hide from the haunches; distinguished by its non-porous, dense, and long-wearing qualities. (5) A variable color, generally a dark grayish red.

Corinthian British slang popular in the

1800s; any aristocratic, wealthy amateur sportsman, who liked to drive well-horsed coaches, Curricles (q.v.) and High Flyer Phaetons (q.v.).

Corinthian whip A driving whip fashionable in England between 1811 and 1820.

corium Also known as cutis or true skin; the sensitive vascular layer of the skin beneath the epidermis (q.v.)

cork (1) *see* BLOCKED HEEL NO. 2. (2) *see* CALK

Corlay Also known as Central Mountain Breton; a cold blood believed to have descended from native steppe horses in Brittany, France more than 4,000 years ago; the smallest of three distinct morphological types of Breton (q.v.) derived from crosses with Arab (q.v.) and Thoroughbred (q.v.) blood; stands 14.3 to 15.1 hands; considered the "real" descendent of the ancient Breton (q.v.); has the same general features as the Draught Breton, but is smaller and has a more dished face; used for riding and light, fast draft work; is very rare, and possibly extinct.

corn (1) Also known as maize; a low fiber (2 to 2½ percent), high carbohydrate, low-protein (about 10 percent digestible protein which is deficient in several amino acids, notably lysine), high starch (65 to 75 percent), high fat (4 percent) and high energy grain second only to oats (q.v.) as a horse feed; ranges in color from white to yellow; contains a higher level of vitamin A (q.v.) than other feed grains and is a good source of vitamin E (q.v.), thiamin, niacin, and riboflavin; may be fed whole, cracked, or on the ear. (2) British slang; any cereal feed. (3) A specific type of bruising occurring in the sole of the foot at the angle between the hoof wall and the bar; most common in the forefeet on the inner quarter and is usually associated with poor shoeing. (4) Refers to coat color pattern; small, dark spots appearing in the coat which are unrelated to scarring; the number of dark spots generally increases with age; provides further detail to the roan (q.v.) classification by identifying the color of the spots, e.g. a blue roan with corn spots would be known as a blue corn; the term originated in the American West as the color pattern resembles the arrangement of dark kernels on an Indian ear of corn.

corneal scar A mark appearing on the cornea of the eye after a wound has healed; when fresh, surrounded by a bluish, misty cloud; tends to dissipate over a period of months or years and may turn brown with age.

corner incisors Also known as corners or third incisors; 4 of the horse's 12 incisor teeth (q.v.) located on either side of the laterals (q.v.) top and bottom; appear about 10 months after birth.

corner man A cutting term; a mounted rider responsible for keeping a herd of cattle in the center of a pen and flowing around the cutter (q.v.) while he selects a cow, and to prevent the selected cow from returning to the herd.

corners *see* CORNER INCISORS

Cornet's Chase The principal event of the Haywick Common Riding (q.v.) held annually the first full week of June in Scotland; the event re-enacts the capture of a standard from the men of Haywick in 1514; the townspeople chase a bachelor and the standard-bearer up the steep slope of Vertish Hill.

Corning Buggy Also known as Corning Wagon; an American horse-drawn vehicle similar in design to the Coal Box Buggy; hung on side bars or elliptic springs; designed by Erastus Corning in 1875.

Corning Wagon *see* CORNING BUGGY

coronary (1) Related to the vascular system of the heart. (2) Related to the coronet (q.v.).

coronary band Also known as coronet or coronet band; the part of the leg at the distal (q.v.) end of the pastern where the hair stops and hoof growth begins between the perioplic ring (q.v.) and the sensitive laminae (q.v.); consists of fibro-fatty tissue beneath a vascular fleshy covering from which the hoof wall emanates; lies in the coronary groove located on the upper border of the hoof wall; similar to the quick in the human nail.

coronary bone *see* SHORT PASTERN BONE

coronary contraction of the foot Also known as local contraction of the foot; a narrowing of the heels at the horn immediately below the coronary cushion; an arbitrary subdivision of contracted heels (q.v.).

coronary crack A sand crack (q.v.) emanating from the coronary band (q.v.) and traveling downward.

coronary sinus *see* QUITTOR

Coronation Coach *see* STATE COACH

coronet (1) *see* CORONARY BAND. (2) A leg marking (q.v.); a narrow band of white extending from the coronary band (q.v.) upward approximately one inch; extends circumferentially around the foot and includes the heel.

coronet band *see* CORONARY BAND

coronoid process *see* LOWER JAW

corpora nigra An irregular, awning-like projection of the eye's iris, located over the upper edge of the pupil; shields the retina from excessive light.

corpus luteum Also known as yellow body and by the acronym CL; a mass of endocrine (q.v.) cells formed in the ruptured ovarian follicle after departure of the unfertilized egg; secretes progesterone, the hormone that maintains pregnancy.

corral (1) A round enclosure used to turn out, break, or hold horses and other animals. (2) To confine, as in a corral; to seize or capture.

corrected score Any score awarded in a competition (q.v.) that is changed by the officials due to objection, calculation error, or posting error.

corrective shoe (1) Any horseshoe (q.v.) that compensates for a defect in the stance or gait of a horse. (2) *see* THERAPEUTIC SHOE

corrective shoeing To put horseshoes on a horse to change his balance or way of traveling as to modify gait and conformation faults.

correctness A dressage term; the straightness of the limb action, e.g., faults would be winging (q.v.), paddling (q.v.); may be evaluated directly or indirectly in the latter case, in which it is evaluated to the degree to which purity (q.v.) is affected.

corrida de toros A classic Spanish bullfight performed by the bullfighter and picador (q.v.).

corse dei Berberi The famous Berber horse race conducted in Rome in 1400 of which Pope Paul II was the patron.

cortex *see* DIAPHYSIS

corticosteroids Analogs of the hormone cortisol primarily produced by the adrenal glands (q.v.) which function as anti-inflammatory hormones and influence metabolism, healing, allergic reactions, kidney function, and the body's electrolyte balance; the anti-inflammatory effects cannot be realized without side effects that influence tissue healing, hormonal balance, and so on; may be used intravenously (q.v.), intramuscularly (q.v.), intra-articularly (q.v.), locally, or topically (q.v.); may be natural or synthetically produced for injection.

cortisol Also known as hydrocortisone; a hormone produced in the adrenal gland (q.v.) which affects the metabolism of fat and water, muscle tone, nerve stimulation, and inflammation.

cortisone A colorless crystalline steriod hormone produced in the adrenal cortex prepared from the adrenal glands of certain domesticated animals or made synthetically; acts chiefly on carbohydrate metabolism, and used to treat inflammation; administered either orally or intramuscularly.

Corvina A horse-drawn Gallic war chariot with scythe-hubbed wheels first used in Britain and Gaul during the time of the Roman conquests; entered from the rear rather than the front and drawn by a pair of fast horses harnessed with side traces and a neck yoke.

Cosequin A patented combination of glucosamine (q.v.), purified chondroitin sulfate (q.v.) and manganese ascorbate used to optimize skeletal joint function, reduce inflammation, and to rebuild cartilage and its major components.

cosh *see* BAT

Cossack hang strap Also known as foot loop; an optional stirrup (q.v.) connected by leathers to a vaulting saddle.

costal arch The arch of the chest cavity formed by the last nine ribs and the costal cartilage (q.v.) that connects them.

costal cartilage Cartilage (q.v.) that joins the ribs to the sternum to create the costal arch (q.v.); remains as cartilage for the life of the horse.

Costeño One of three types of Peruvian-bred Criollo (q.v.) or Salterno (q.v.) horses, the other two being the Morochuco (q.v.) and the Chola (q.v.); descended from Spanish stock brought to South America by the Conquistadors in the 16th century; has a distinctive high-stepping gait known as the paso lano (q.v.).

Cosy Car A pony-size, low, hooded horse-drawn vehicle of the Gig (q.v.) type; seated two.

cottage windows Horse-drawn stage coach windows when divided into four small panes.

cotton eye Said of the horse's eye when showing a lot of white around the iris.

cottonseed meal Also called cottonseed oil meal; a high protein, high energy concentrate produced from the residue of the cotton seed after oil extraction; total protein varies from 30 to 40 percent and the fat from 2 to 6 percent in an inverse relationship to the protein; higher in fiber, but lower in lysine than soybean meal; supplementation should not exceed 15 to 16 percent of the total ration due to the presence of gossypol, a chemical substance which may be toxic.

cottonseed oil meal *see* COTTONSEED MEAL

couch grass *see* BERMUDA GRASS

cough Expulsion of air from the horse's lungs marked by sudden loud noise; may result from inflammation or irritation to the lower or upper airways including the pharynx, larynx, or trachea.

couldn't beat a fat man A racing term; said of a slow horse.

counter (1) The strip which covers the rear seam on the leg of a riding boot. (2) *see* HEEL NO. 3

counter-canter Also known as galop faux, false canter, or counter lead; a dressage movement; the horse leads with his outside leg (q.v.) on a circle or bend instead of the inside leg (q.v.) or natural lead; used as a suppling, balancing, strengthening, and straightening exercise.

counter half-pass A dressage term; a half-pass (q.v.) movement performed through X; the horse moves with one bend from the long-side corner to X where the bend is reversed and the horse moves to the opposite corner on the same long side; flexion must change uniformly throughout the entire length of the horse's body.

counter-irritant An agent that when applied produces a localized irritation to counteract irritation or relieve pain or inflammation elsewhere.

counter lead *see* COUNTER-CANTER

country (1) A hunting term; the area over which a pack of hounds may hunt as authorized by the governing associations. (2) A rural district as opposed to cities or towns.

Countryside Alliance An organization founded in London, England in March 1997 from an amalgamation of three groups: the British Field Sports Society (q.v.), Countryside Movement, and the Countryside Business Group; originally founded to oppose an anticipated ban on hunting with dogs, this membership campaign organization also promotes the interests of rural people, including their rural livelihoods and communities, all field sports (hunting, angling, and shooting), wildlife management, jobs, landscapes and freedoms; it represents these interests in the media, Parliament, schools, and throughout the United Kingdom.

coup *see* COUP STICK

Coupe *see* COUPÉ

Coupé Also spelled Coupe; a closed, four-wheeled, horse-drawn town Carriage with a truncated, closed body designed for greater compactness and improved appearance; entered by side doors, seated four, was drawn by a single horse or pair, and driven by a coachman from a box located in front of the box window; hung on elliptical springs under the coachman's seat in which the wheels turned; from the French word for cut.

coupé A class of accommodation offered on Diligence (q.v.) horse-drawn vehicles in 19th and 20th-century Europe; accommodated three forward-facing passengers on enclosed seats located behind the wheelers (q.v.); had limited leg space due to seat proximity to the horses.

Coupé Dorsay *see* DORSAY

couple (1) A hunting term; two hounds; the number of hounds in a pack is counted in couples and couples and a half, e.g. four and half couples equals nine hounds; one hound is known as one hound rather than one half a couple. (2) To fasten, link, or join together in a pair or pairs as in hounds by means of leather collars connected by a short chain, or one horse to another by means of a harness. (3) *see* HITCH NO. 2

coupled (1) Also known as coupled entry or entry; an American racing term; said of two or more horses belonging to the same owner or trained by the same person who run as an entry (q.v.) and comprise a single betting unit; a bet on one horse of an entry is a bet on both; in the program the horses would be listed, regardless of post position, as 1, 1A, and so on. (2) A hunting term; said of two hounds joined together by means of leather collars connected by a short chain.

coupled entry *see* COUPLED

couples (1) A hunting term; hound collars joined by a metal distance link; this link is generally carried on the dee-ring (q.v.) of the whippers-in's saddle. (2) A driving term; the two buckle or snap-hook ends of a lead rein.

coupling (1) The length and muscle development of the loin area of the horse between the last rib and the point of the hip which connects the hindquarters to the forehand. (2) A driving term; an adjustment of the coupling reins (q.v.).

coupling buckle The buckle on the coupling rein (q.v.) which joins it to the draft rein (q.v.) in pair and team harnesses.

coupling rein The shorter piece of a pair rein buckled to the bit on one end and to the draft rein (q.v.) on the other; used in pair and tandem team driving.

coupling up A driving term; to fasten the coupling reins (q.v.) to the draft reins (q.v.) in pair and team driving.

coup stick Also known as coup; a light pole between 5 and 6 feet (1.5–1.8 m) long to which the feathers or scalps taken by an American Indian were attached; believed that the more coups on a stick, the greater the warrior; historically attached to the lodge pole of the teepee, or carried by the mounted warriors as proof of bravery; replicas of the coup sticks are often carried in Appaloosa (q.v.) Indian Costume classes in horse shows; from the American Indian coup (pronounced coo) meaning a trophy of the scalp or feathers.

courbette Also known as curvet; a classical air above the ground (q.v.) in which the horse rears to an angle of 45 degrees (30 degrees in a more advanced courbette), and when reaching a height of more than 8 feet (2.4 m), leaps forward several times on his hind legs while maintaining bent forelegs; usually performed on a straight line, but in the past, also executed bearing right and left.

course (1) *see* TRACK NO. 1. (2) A show jumping or cross-country circuit consisting of a number of obstacles typically jumped in a particular order or within a pre-set "time allowed" to avoid time penalties and within the "time limit" (often twice the time allowed) to avoid elimination; the exception to this being certain jumping competitions known variously as Gambler's Stakes (q.v.), Take Your own Line, High Score, etc. (3) A hunting term; said of hounds who hunt by sight rather than scent, as in to look for or "course" the quarry. (4) To follow.

course builder One responsible for building show jumping or cross-country courses.

course de brague A mounted military exercise or sport performed in 16th and 17th-century Europe; the rider, mounted on a galloping horse, used a hand-held lance to hook a ring(s) suspended from a post at head height and carry it off.

course designer One responsible for designing show jumping or cross-country courses constructed by the course builder (q.v.).

coursing The sport of hunting hares with greyhounds.

court A hunting term; (obs); the paved yard attached to a hound kennel.

Court Hansom Also known as French Four-wheeled Hansom; a Hansom Cab (q.v.) built on four wheels; the driver's seat was placed behind the roof and the front wheels in front of the dash.

cover (1) Also known as mate, breed, serve, service, cover a mare, or stint (obs); said of a stallion when he copulates with a mare. (2) The width of the horseshoe. (3) A hunting term; any natural area that provides protection for animals from disturbances such as the elements. (4) *see* COVERT

cover a mare *see* COVER

covered Also known as serviced, bred, stocked, or stinted (obs); said of mare inseminated by a stallion.

covered school An enclosed building used for riding and or schooling horses.

covered up A racing term; said of a horse competing in a race who has other horses in front of him by deliberate design of the rider or driver.

Covered Wagon *see* PRAIRIE SCHOONER

covering boots *see* BREEDING BOOTS

covert Also known as draw or cover; a British hunting term; a thicket or small wooded or bushy area less than 100 acres (40 hectares) in size in which foxes (q.v.) may hide or lie.

covert coat A lightweight, shower-proof, thigh-length top coat historically made of fine lightweight, Venetian twill and worn by men who hacked to the covert (q.v.) side.

covert cloth Also known as coating or covert coating; a top quality twilled cloth woven with a whipcord weave of cotton, wool, or worsted; used for raincoats, overcoats, and covert coats; warp threads of worsted twist produce a flecked-looking fabric.

covert coating *see* COVERT CLOTH

covert hack A smooth-riding horse capable of negotiating small jumps, used to ride to a hunt meeting (q.v.), but not used in the hunt.

cow (1) The female of the bovine (q.v.) species. (2) Generically, a male or female bovine.

cowboy (1) Also known as cow poke, cow hand, or cow puncher; one who looks after cattle on a ranch and who, historically, performed this work on horseback. (2) A man possessing the skill of a cowboy, as those associated with the rodeo.

cowboy boots Any ankle-, knee- or calf-high boot worn by a Western enthusiast when riding or working horses or other livestock; manufactured in leather or synthetic materials; leather boots, knee or calf-high boots are frequently tooled (q.v.).

cowboy polo A mounted game played by two teams of five players; the players move a small white ball down the field and through goalposts located at either end of a rectangular arena using a long mallet carried in the right hand; the game features longer mallets and is played at a much slower pace than high-goal polo (q.v.); the goals can be no more than 250 yards (229 m) apart and the width of the field cannot exceed 200 yards (183 m); consists of 6, 7½ minute chukkers (q.v.) or periods.

cowboy shoe (1) A short-heeled horseshoe available in the same sizes as hot shoes (q.v.), developed for use when a forge is not practical; both front and hind shoes have the same web width and weight where formerly, the front shoes would be wider and heavier; nail holes are roughly punched, require opening with a pritchel (q.v.), and are spaced far apart and close to the outside edge; heels are square-cut and unfinished; secure nailing requires dubbing (q.v.); used by the military, ranchers, packers, and outfitters; a difficult shoe to fit and frequently results in a poor shoeing. (2) Also known as cowboy shoeing; to shoe a horse by adjusting the hoof size to fit the horseshoe; the shape of the shoe is only opened or closed at the heel; once the shoe is nailed on, the foot is trimmed to fit the shoe and rasped down to match its shape.

cowboy shoeing *see* COWBOY SHOE NO. 2

cowboy shod Also known as rough shod; said of a horse shod (q.v.) without consideration for hoof shape, the hoof being shaped to fit the shoe.

cowgirl (1) A woman who looks after cattle on a ranch and does this work on horseback. (2) A woman possessing the skill of a cowgirl, as those associated with the rodeo (q.v.).

cow-gulleted saddle *see* CUT BACK NO. 2

cow hand *see* COWBOY NO. 1

cowhide The hide or skin of a cow, may or may not be made into leather; 95 percent of all saddlery is made from cowhide.

cow-hocked Said of a horse whose limbs are base-narrow (q.v.) to the hock and base-wide from the hock to the feet.

cow hocks *see* MEDIAL DEVIATION OF THE HOCK JOINTS

cow horn A hunting term; an American hunting horn (q.v.) used exclusively when hunting with American foxhounds.

cow horse Also known as cow pony or range horse; a horse ridden by a cowboy when working cattle; commonly Quarter Horses (q.v.) or Quarter Horse crosses less than 16 hands tall.

cowing A cutting horse term; said of a horse when focused on a cow.

cow kick A strike with the hoof made when the horse strikes forward and to the outside with one of his hind legs; enables a horse to strike a rider or handler standing beside him.

cowlick A hair pattern on the head of the horse; a tuft of hair which grows in a wayward direction and turns upward as if licked by a cow; may be used for identification purposes.

cow man A Western American term; an owner of cattle; a rancher; a cowboy (q.v.).

cow-mouthed saddle *see* CUT BACK NO. 2

cow poke *see* COWBOY NO. 1

cow pony *see* COW HORSE

cow puncher (1) Historically, one whose responsibility it was to punch or brand (q.v.) cattle. (2) *see* COWBOY NO. 1

cow sense *see* COW SMART

cow-side leg A cutting term; the rider's leg parallel to the cow being worked.

cow smart Also known as cowy, cow sense, good cow sense, or to have a lot of cow; a cutting term; said of a horse possessed of the innate ability, desire, and mental aptitude to read and anticipate the movements of a cow.

cow with a lot of feel A cutting term; said of a cow who works and turns well against a horse.

cow works A Western term; all aspects of working cattle from branding (q.v.) to gathering (q.v.).

cowy *see* COW SMART

coyote dun Refers to coat color; a yellow coat with black hairs mixed in, black points, and primitive marks (q.v.); the equivalent of dark buckskin (q.v.).

CPO *see* CERTIFIED PEDIGREE OPTION

crab (1) *see* POLE HOOK. (2) To give unfavorable criticism of a horse as to reduce his value. (3) An unfavorable feature of a horse, e.g. blemish, fault, or unsoundness.

crabber One who gives an unfavorable criticism of a horse, often for a fee.

crab bit A type of bit used in harness racing; prongs, upwardly curving towards the horse's nose, are attached to the cheekpieces (q.v.); applied rein pressure encourages the horse to tip his head up; prevents the horse from bearing down on the bit and thus, pulling on the reins.

crack To fracture without breaking, as in a bone, i.e., a hairline crack, or the hoof, i.e., sand crack (q.v.), toe crack (q.v.), or quarter crack (q.v.).

cracked heels *see* SCRATCHES

cracked hoof A vertical split in the hoof wall; may extend from the coronary band (q.v.) down, or from the base of the hoof upwards; may result from injury, concussion, improper shoeing, or environmental or stabling conditions and can be remedied with corrective shoeing (q.v.); identified on the basis of location on the hoof, e.g. quarter crack (q.v.) and toe crack (q.v.).

cracking the nostrils *see* HIGH-BLOWING

cradle A light frame made of wood or aluminum dowels fastened at intervals by leather straps to form a wide "necklace" which is fitted around the horse's neck from the throat to the shoulder; used to prevent the horse from biting or licking wounds, blankets, etc.

cramped action Said of a horse who does not move freely.

Crane-neck Chariot An elegant horse-drawn carriage popular in the 1700s; had double-bow cranes which supported the coach box in the front and the coachman's cushion in the rear, an intricately decorated body embellished with crests, and was hung on braces from whip springs; designed and built by William Felton.

Crane-neck Flyer *see* HIGH FLYER PHAETON

cranial Of or pertaining to the skull or cranium.

crash skull (1) *see* RACING HELMET. (2) *see* HELMET NO. 1

Craven Cart A horse-drawn, two-wheeled, general-purpose vehicle similar in design to the Ralli Car (q.v.); the back let down to accommodate two rearward-facing passengers; the forward-facing seat accommodated one passenger and the driver; parts of the side panels, under the curving mudguards, were caned.

cravings *see* CHAFF NO. 2

crawler An obsolete driving term; a cabman who loitered to pick up fares rather than returning to a cabstand as was customary; considered a nuisance by other cabbies and a finable offense by the police.

creamy dun *see* GOLDEN DUN

crease A groove cut into the ground-side surface of a horseshoe which fills with dirt to create mild traction.

creasing (1) Also known incorrectly as fullering; the act or process of cutting a crease (q.v.) into the ground-side surface of a horseshoe. (2) The decorative pattern of triangles and diamonds pressed onto the outer surface of a box loop (q.v.).

creep feeder A manger (q.v.) from which a foal, but not dam, can feed; available in many designs.

creeping splint One of four types of splints (q.v.); slowly multiply end-to-end, like a string of pearls, from the top to the mid-point of the splint bone, filling the splint groove; may result from inadequate rest following an interosseous splint (q.v.).

cremello Refers to coat color; a nearly white, cream-colored coat and points with blue eyes.

crescent brass One of four primary historic patterns of horse brasses (q.v.); the pattern of the crescent moon, one of the images of the pagan gods struck into brass or other metal and placed on the harness or other tack of the horse to ward off the Evil Eye; worshippers of water used a crescent pointing down, since water always descends.

crest The upper aspect of the horse's neck (q.v.).

crest panel A tiny narrow panel located immediately below the window on which the owner's crest or monogram or the name and address of the coach proprietor is painted; on Stage and Road Coaches, the names of the towns where the journeys started and finished were also inscribed there.

crested whorl A hair pattern; a whorl (q.v.); a change in direction of the flow of the hair in which two opposing sweeps of hair meet from diametrically opposite directions along a line and rise up to form a crest.

crew hole *see* DART HOLE

crib (1) The act of cribbing (q.v.). (2) *see* MANGER

cribber (1) Also known as crib-biter; a horse who cribs (q.v.). (2) *see* WIND-SUCKER

cribbing (1) see wind-sucking. 2) Also known as crib biting, stump sucking, or wood chewing; a vice; the act of chewing wood, i.e. as of a door, stable wall, gate, manger, etc.; inhalation of air through the mouth often occurs in the process resulting in wind-sucking (q.v.); generally due to boredom, or, in some cases, dietary deficiency; wood surfaces can be coated with distasteful substances to deter chewing.

cribbing collar Also known as anti-cribbing device or cribbing device; a collar, generally metal reinforced, fitted around the horse's throatlatch/neck to restrict wind-sucking (q.v.); the collar digs into the horse's neck when he flexes it while wind-sucking.

crib-biting *see* CRIBBING NO. 2

crib-biting device *see* ANTI-CRIBBING DEVICE

cricket *see* ROLLER NO. 2

cricket bit Any ported Western bit having a roller inserted into the port.

cricoid cartilage One of six types of cartilage (q.v.) in the horse's body; forms rings.

crinet Medieval armor used to protect the neck and throat of the horse.

Criollo Also known as Argentine Criollo; an Argentinean horse breed descended from Spanish stock (Arab, Barb, and Andalusian) brought to South America in the 16th century by the Conquistadors; is sturdy, compact, and very muscular, with a short, broad head, straight profile, wide-set eyes, short legs with plenty of bone, strong joints, and hard feet; is willing, tough, agile, and possesses great endurance; all coat colors are acceptable; stands 14 to 15 hands; the historical mount of the gauchos; when crossed with Thoroughbred (q.v.) blood became the base for the Argentine polo pony (q.v.); the stud book was established in 1918; other South American countries produce their own versions of the breed, all of which have the same origins as the Argentine Criollo, but which possess different names and slightly different characteristics according to their environment; these include the Chileno (q.v.), Guajira (q.v.), Llanero (q.v.), Salterno (q.v.), Mangalarga (q.v.), Campolino (q.v.), and Criollo of Rio Grande do Sul (q.v.).

Criollo of Rio Grande do Sul One of three types of Brazilian-bred Criollo (q.v.) horses, the other two being the Mangalarga (q.v.) and the Campolino (q.v.); of the same origins as the Criollo, but possessing slightly different characteristics attributable to local environmental conditions; descended from Spanish stock brought to South America by the Conquistadors in the 16th century; has a Barb-like appearance.

Crioulo A Brazilian-bred Criollo (q.v.) cross; obtained by crossing Altér Reals (q.v.) with Brazilian Criollos: Mangalarga (q.v.), the Criollo of Rio Grande do Sul (q.v.), and the Campolino Criollos (q.v.); has a high-set tail, long neck, is frugal and tough, and used for riding and herding.

crockery eye *see* WALL EYE

crooked halt A dressage term; said of a horse who stopped with his quarters (q.v.) to left or right of his forehand so that he is not straight.

crookedness (1) Said of the horse; lacking parallelism in the line of travel, e.g., haunches left or right of center. (2) Misalignment of the horse's body parts from tail to poll, e.g., popped shoulder or twisted neck. (3) Lack of directness in the line of travel, e.g., weaving (q.v.).

crop (1) A short, stiff, straight-stock whip with a loop at one end; commonly used by jockeys, hunters, and jumpers. (2) A group of foals sired during a single stallion's season at stud. (3) A group of horses born within the same year. (4) To cut short, as in the horse's tail.

crop-eared Said of a horse whose ears, or the tips thereof, are missing as having been cut or frozen off.

crop-out Also known as crop-out Quarter Horse, any foal produced by two registered Quarter Horses (q.v.) who has more white on it than the American Quarter Horse Association (q.v.) color rule allows; cannot qualify for registry with the American Quarter Horse Association, but will qualify for the American Paint Horse Association (q.v.) registry; crop-out Thoroughbreds (q.v.) also occur, but the Jockey Club does not have a registry color requirement.

crop-out Quarter Horse *see* CROP-OUT

crop-out Thoroughbred *see* CROP-OUT

cropper (1) A racing term; a spill of the horse and rider; usually occurring in jump-type races. (2) A British term; to fall heavily, as in a horse, rider or both.

cross (1) *see* SHOULDER CROSS. (2) To pass from side to side.

cross-breeding Also known as outcrossing or crossing; the mating of two registered pure-bred horses of two different breeds.

crossbred Said of a horse produced by mating a sire (q.v.) and dam (q.v.) of different breeds.

cross canter *see* DISUNITED CANTER

crosscrack *see* CLEFT

cross-country (1) Any sport or event conducted across fields and open country without following roads or highways. (2) A timed component of the endurance phase of a combined training (q.v.) event or horse trial (q.v.); riders negotiate obstacles constructed of natural materials (timber, stone, etc.) or occurring naturally in open country.

cross-country course A jumping course established in open country with natural surroundings in which the obstacles are generally constructed from timber, stone, water, etc.

cross-country ride To ride on horseback a distance over natural terrain.

cross firing Said of a horse in motion when the diagonal fore and hind feet contact on the inside i.e. the inside of the hind foot hitting the inside quarter of the diagonal forefoot (q.v.); common in pacers (q.v.)

cross hook A polo term; a defensive move; a player reaches over the top of his opponent's mount with his mallet (q.v.) in an attempt to intercept the striking mallet before it contacts the ball.

crossing (1) Also known as crossing the line; a polo term; a principal infringement in the game of polo occurring when a defensive player crosses the imaginary trajectory of the ball in front of the oncoming offensive player in control of it. (2) *see* CROSS-BREEDING

crossing feet *see* ROPE WALKING

crossing the line *see* CROSSING

crossing traces *see* CROSS TRACES

cross matched *see* CROSS TEAM

cross noseband *see* GRAKLE NOSEBAND

cross over noseband *see* GRAKLE NOSEBAND

cross team Also known as checkerboard team or cross matched; a driving term; a team of four horses of two different colors; the horses of similar colors are usually positioned diagonal to each other, i.e. the near leader and the off wheeler are of the same color.

cross the stirrups Said of a mounted rider; to take the right stirrup (the leather and iron), cross it over the withers of the horse, and lay it on the left shoulder and vice versa with the left stirrup; encourages the rider to develop a balanced seat without aid of the stirrups; improves the rider's seat and is a test in some hunt seat equitation classes in the United States.

cross tie To secure the head of a horse by means of two straps both attached at one end to the side of the horse's halter and at the other end to a fixed object.

cross ties Also known as pillar reins, rack chains, or head collar chain shanks; 1 or 2, 2 to 3 foot (61–91 cm) long strap (leather, chain, elastic, etc.) fitted with hooks or clips at one end and attached to walls, posts, or other secure objects on the other between which the horse is tied, as when grooming or tacking up.

cross traces Also known as crossing traces; a driving term; the practice of hooking the inside traces (q.v.) of one of the lead horses to the inside hook of his partner's bar to better distribute the draft (q.v.) from an unequally matched team.

crotch seat An incorrect position of the mounted English rider in the saddle; the lower back is typically arched partially shifting the balance from the seat bones to the forward aspect of the pubic arch; is mechanically weak, inefficient, and incorrect.

croup (1) Also known as rump, crupper, or crupper line; the upper line of a horse's quarters, from the root of the tail to the loins. (2) An acute obstruction of the voice box.

croupade A High school (q.v.) air above the ground (q.v.); the horse rears from a standstill and performs a single vertical jump with the fore and hind legs drawn up towards his belly; the leap is higher than that in the courbette (q.v.).

crouper mount A technique used by trick and circus riders, movie stunt people, etc., to get on the back of the horse without using the stirrups; the rider runs towards a standing horse from behind, leaps towards the croup (q.v.) placing one hand on each haunch, and lands seated in the saddle.

croup high Pertains to conformation (q.v.); said of the horse when the point of the croup (q.v.) is higher than the point of the withers (q.v.); fairly common in young horses whose skeletal structure does not always grow at a uniform rate, in which case the condition may correct itself; in the mature horse, this type of conformation puts the horse on the forehand, thus limiting full engagement of the hindquarters (q.v.); may also be a function of incorrect training, whereby the horse is habitually allowed to go onto his forehand to such an extent that his forehand appears relatively lower than his croup.

crowd A racing term; said of a jockey who rides too close to another horse, forcing his jockey to check (q.v.) or change course.

crow hopping Said of the horse; to make a short, mild jump in any direction.

crowned An antiquated term; a horse with broken knees (q.v.) from which a portion of hair has worn away.

crownpiece Also known as headpiece; that part of the bridle (q.v.) that connects to the cheekpieces (q.v.) and crosses over the poll (q.v.) behind the horse's ears.

CRT *see* CAPILLARY REFILL TIME

Cruciferae A family of plants including cabbage (q.v.), cauliflower, Brussels sprouts, broccoli, kale, and others; from crucifer, so called because family members bear flowers having a cross-like, four-petaled corolla; infrequently fed to horses due to the goitrogenic (q.v.) compounds they contain which impair iodine (q.v.) production.

crude fat The material extracted from moisture-free feeds by ether process; consists of fats and oils and small amounts of waxes, resins, and coloring matter.

crude fiber The part of the feed which comes from the cellulose and lignin part of plants, both of which are poorly digested by the horse.

crupper (1) *see* HARNESS CRUPPER. (2) *see* SADDLE CRUPPER. (3) *see* CROUP NO. 1

crupper dock Also known as dockpiece; a padded leather loop fitted under the dock (q.v.) of the horse's tail on one end, and stitched or buckled to the back strap on the other; prevents the harness pad or the riding saddle from slipping forward; commonly filled with linseed which exudes a certain amount of natural oil and thus prevents friction.

crupper line *see* CROUP NO. 1

crupper strap A leather strap which connects to the riding saddle or harness pad on one end and buckles to the crupper dock (q.v.) on the other; as a unit, in conjunction with the crupper dock, constitutes the harness crupper (q.v.) or riding crupper (q.v.) and prevents the saddle or harness pad from slipping forward.

crust of the hoof *see* HOOF WALL

crust of the wall *see* HOOF WALL

cry (1) *see* SPEAK. (2) Also known as voice, music, or tongue; a hunting term; the sound the hound makes when in pursuit of a fox; varies with the quality of the scent.

cryogenic That method of physics dealing with very low temperatures at which gases such as nitrogen liquefy; cryogenics are used in many applications including branding (q.v.) and preserving organic material.

cryogenic brand *see* FREEZE BRAND

cryosurgery Selective destruction of tissue by freezing, usually with liquid nitrogen.

Crystal Cab An American, four-wheeled horse-drawn vehicle of the Cab (q.v.) type popular in New York City, USA during the 1870s and 1880s; characterized by large glass windows or lights instead of opaque side panels.

cryptorchid *see* RIG

cryptorchidism A genetic developmental defect in which one or both testicles are retained above the scrotum.

CS *see* CHONDROITIN SULFATES

Csikos Cowboys or herdsman whose primary responsibility it is to tend to herds of horses grazed on the Hungarian plains.

CSIO *see* CONCOURS DE SAUT INTERNATIONAL OFFICIEL (INTERNATIONAL SHOW JUMPING TOURNAMENT)

CT scanning *see* COMPUTERIZED TOMOGRAPHY

cub A young fox from birth, usually March through November 1, although it may be born any time between Christmas and May; the average litter size is five.

Cuban Carriage Also known as Volante; a two-wheeled, horse-drawn vehicle popular in Cuba; the wheels are located at the end of the shafts, behind the Gig-shaped body; hung on cee-springs.

cubbing *see* CUB HUNTING

cubbing season *see* CUB HUNTING SEASON

cubes Also known as hay cubes or nuts; a compressed feed generally composed of grass or legume hay which is often shaped into 1 to 2 inch (25–50 mm) squares; other feeds, minerals, and vitamins are sometimes added; the hay used is ground less finely than that in pellets; cube analysis is often guaranteed and the grade is generally identified (cube grade depends on the maximum fiber and minimum protein contents); cubing eliminates the dust associated with most hays.

cub hunting Also known as cubbing or more recently as autumn hunting (Brit); a hunting term; to hunt foxes prior to the beginning of the regular hunting season (between the end of July and the end of September in the United States and the end of harvest until the end of October in the United Kingdom) to teach young, unentered (q.v.) hounds (q.v.) to hunt, and persuade fox cubs (nearly full-grown) to leave their coverts (q.v.); historically conducted to reduce fox overpopulation; a cap (q.v.) is usually not taken.

cub hunting season Also known as cubbing season; a hunting term; the period preceding the beginning of the formal fox hunting season during which time nearly full-grown fox cubs are located and encouraged to run.

culicoides A tiny, swarming insect which feeds overnight on the blood of its hosts by the thousands; has a relatively painless bite, although saliva may cause seasonally hyperallergic reactions in susceptible horses.

culicoides hypersensitivity *see* SWEET ITCH

cull (1) An unwanted horse disposed of by the owner. (2) To separate from, as in "The horse was culled from the herd."

culture (1) The cultivation of micro-organisms, as bacteria, in an artificial medium for scientific study or medical use. (2) The product or growth resulting from cultivation.

cup (1) Also known as mark or bean; the outer visible section of the internal enamel/grinding surface of the teeth, specifically the incisor teeth (q.v.); cup depth and appearance changes as the horse ages – originally oval, the cup becomes more oval, then flat, round, triangular, and finally disappears at about 12 years; effective in determining horse age. (2) A trophy awarded to winning horse owners as in stakes races (q.v.). (3) The flat or dished metal support inserted into a standard and used to support a rail to be jumped.

cup horse A racing term; a horse who performs best in races longer than 1⅛ miles (1.8 km); in Britain, any flat-race horse suited to major staying races, i.e. distances of 2 miles (3.28 km) and greater.

Cup of Nations *see* NATIONS CUP

cuppy Said of wet or moist ground into which the horse's feet could sink during competition; the surface breaks up and shows hoof prints.

cuppy track The racetrack surface when moist or wet into which the horse's hooves sink.

curb (1) A thickening or bowing of the plantar tarsal ligament, approximately 4 inches (10 cm) below the point of the hock (q.v.), due to strain; not necessarily accompanied by lameness. (2) *see* CURB BIT

curb bit Also known as curb; a bit consisting of two metal cheekpieces and a ported mouthpiece which brings pressure to bear on the bars of the mouth using leverage instead of direct pressure; the reins are attached to rings on the cheek pieces; used in conjunction with a curb strap (q.v.) or curb chain (q.v.).

curb chain A small metal, metal and elastic, leather, plastic, or nylon chain attached by hooks (in English) or by buckles or a strap (in Western) to the cheeks of a curb or pelham bit; passed under the lower jaw and twisted clockwise until it lies flat in the chin groove (q.v.); increased pressure on the lower rein increases the leverage and tightens the curb chain; when used with Western bits must be a minimum of ½ inch (13 mm) wide.

curb groove Also known as chin groove; a furrow in the underside of the lower jaw just above the lower lip where the curb chain rests when put into action.

curb hook A metal hook attached to the top rings on the cheeks (q.v.) of a curb or pelham bit (q.v.) to which the curb chain (q.v.) is attached; the hook portion faces away from the horse's cheek; made in pairs and vary in length from ½ to 2½ inches (13–64 mm); the Melton (q.v.) is the most popular.

curb rein One of two reins attached to the lower rings of the cheeks (q.v.) of a curb bit (q.v.).

curby hocks *see* EXCESSIVE ANGULATION OF THE HOCK JOINTS

cur dog Previously known as care dog; a hunting term; any dog other than a foxhound (q.v.) responsible for the care of a herd of sheep and for coursing (q.v.) a fox.

curl A roping term; the upward coiling of a thrown rope as it encircles the neck of the calf, horse, etc.; a good curl indicates that the loop has been well thrown.

Curragh Also known as Curragh Racecourse; the headquarters of flat racing in Ireland hosting all five Classic Races (q.v.) and up to 13 other high quality racedays; owned and managed by the Irish Turf Club, founded in Kildare in the 1760s; the course area dates to the 3rd century when chariot races where held there; from *Cuireach*, the Gaelic word for racecourse.

Curragh Racecourse *see* CURRAGH

current odds *see* FORECAST NO. 1

Curre-type A hunting term; a foxhound (q.v.), generally English-bred, having at least one strain of Welsh foxhound blood in its pedigree; developed by the late Sir Edward Curre.

Curricle (1) A horse-drawn two-wheeled carriage of Italian origin popular in Britain during the late 18th and early 19th centuries; either open or headed (q.v.), but usually had a falling hood, seated two, side-by-side, with a liveried groom positioned on a rearward or rumble seat, was hung on cee-springs, and was drawn by a pair of horses harnessed by means of traces and a center pole; the main hauling power was through the traces; said to correct the effects of sway or uneven motion; difficult to drive as the horses had to move together at the same pace and stride; replaced by the Cabriolet (q.v.); the name derived from the Latin, *curriculum*, meaning light chariot. (2) To put a pair of horses to a two-wheeled vehicle by means of a curricle bar (q.v.).

curricle bar A harness term; a steel bar placed above and horizontal to the backs of a pair (q.v.) and attached to their saddle pads; used in conjunction with a supporting strap and a curricle harness to support the pole of a Curricle (q.v.) vehicle.

curry To rub the horse's coat hair with a hard or pliable curry comb (q.v.) until dirt is loosened and can be brushed off with a body brush (q.v.); stimulates circulation and helps to build muscle tone by massaging the large muscle masses.

curry comb A hand-held instrument or comb set with very short teeth on one side; used to scrape dirt and debris from a brush (metal curry comb [q.v.]) or to clean and comb a horse (rubber curry comb [q.v.]).

Curtain Rockaway A version of the Rockaway (q.v.) fitted with leather curtains.

curved bar shoe A bar shoe (q.v.) in which the bar connecting the two heels of the shoe is curved above or below the ground surface; used to apply or to relieve frog pressure, especially when the frog is small and atrophied or large and protruding; when the bar is curved toward the frog may be used to treat contraction, and when curved away from the frog, may be used to treat thrush, corns, or sheared heels.

curvet A historical English term used by riding masters in the 16th and 17th centuries; a skirmish movement of attack similar to the present-day levade (q.v.); the horse rears onto deeply flexed haunches at an angle of no more than 30 degrees; marking time with the forelegs, he takes a series of small leaps forward or to the left or right; the name derived from the French courbette (q.v.), a movement to which it bears no resemblance.

curtal Also spelled curtall; an antiquated 16th and 17th-century term; a horse whose tail is cut short and whose ears are sometimes cropped.

curtall *see* CURTAL

cushion A racing term; the loose top surface of a track.

cut (1) *see* CASTRATE. (2) To make an incision in the tissue. (3) Also known as cut out; a cutting term; to select a cow and separate it from the herd. (4) A cutting term; the location of cows cut (q.v.) from the herd.

cut and laid A hunting term; a fence constructed from a natural hedge; hedge branches are partially cut through and woven horizontally between a series of vertically positioned stakes.

cut and set tail *see* SET TAIL

cut and slash A hunting term; said of the hounds when they range too far from the field when attempting to locate a fox (q.v.).

cutaneous habronemiasis Also known as summer sores, bursatti, jacksores, or draschiasis; a skin disease caused by a parasite of the genus *Habronema* (q.v.); larvae of this worm are deposited by infected flies on open wounds where they migrate and feed, extending the wound and preventing healing; may also feed on genitalia or moist eye membranes, in the latter case the condition is known as ocular habronemiasis (q.v.); larvae cause large, perhaps multiple, weepy and painful granular lesions, which appear in warm weather, heal spontaneously in winter and reappear in spring; these larvae do not complete their development to adult stage.

cutaneous streptothricosis *see* DERMATOPHILUS

cut a voluntary Hunting slang; said of the rider who chooses to fall off his horse rather than go down with it.

cut away *see* CUT SHOT

cut away coat *see* SHAD BELLY

cut away shot *see* CUT SHOT

cut back (1) *see* CUTBACK SADDLE. (2) Formerly known as a cow-mouthed saddle or cow-gulleted saddle; any English-type saddle (q.v.) in which the pommel is cut away so it sits more easily on a high-withered horse.

cutback saddle Also known as cut back or saddle seat saddle; a long, flat saddle resting low on the horse's back; designed to place the rider's weight over the loins of the horse; used on Saddlebred (q.v.), Tennessee Walking Horse (q.v.), and certain classes of the Arab (q.v.) and Morgan (q.v.) show divisions.

cut corners Also known as cutting corners; a dressage term; said of the dressage rider who fails to ride the horse into the corners of the dressage arena.

cut down A racing term; said of a horse injured in a race by the horseshoe of another horse or by striking himself with his own shoe.

cut for shape A cutting term; said of a mounted rider; to drive cattle into the center of an arena or other area, wait for them to move around the horse in an attempt to return to the herd, and to cut and work one of the remaining cows.

cutis *see* CORIUM

cut out *see* CUT NO. 3

cut out under the knees A conformation fault; when viewed from the side, the front surface of the horse's cannon bone just below the knee has a cut or dished out appearance.

cut shot Also known as cut away or cut away shot; a polo term; any fore- or backhand stroke of the ball hit at an angle away from the horse.

Cutter (1) A small horse- or pony-drawn sleigh; had a very high, S-shaped front or dash which prevented snow thrown up by the horse's hooves from covering the driver and passengers; joined to the runners by tall and narrow iron struts; of two primary types: the Albany Cutter (q.v.) with rounded sides and the Portland Cutter (q.v.). (2) A light, four-wheeled passenger vehicle drawn by a single horse.

cutter (1) A cutting term; one who separates a cow or cows from a herd as for doctoring, branding, or to hold until ropers arrive; frequently performed for sport. (2) A hunting term; a hound (q.v.) who, rather than hunt with the pack, runs ahead hoping to locate the scent of the fox (q.v.) and thus become the leader.

cutter's cross A cutting term; a two-handed grip on the reins used by the rider when training a cutting horse (q.v.); the reins are held in the opposing hands, i.e. left rein to right hand and vice versa.

cutter's slump A cutting term; the posture a cutter (q.v.) assumes when working cattle; the rider sits deep in the saddle with a relaxed, slightly convexly curved back and forward-slumped shoulders.

cutting (1) A contest between a cow and a horse; the cutter (q.v.) slowly and deliberately guides his horse into a herd so as not to disturb the cows, and selects one calf to separate from the herd; once a cow is cleared from the herd, the rider positions himself and his horse between the cow and the herd; when the cow tries to return to the security of the herd, the cutter's horse meets it and sends it back to the cuts (q.v.); evolved on cattle ranches where riders would sort groups of cattle or single out individual cows for doctoring, branding (q.v.), sale, and the like; performed as a competition in the United States since 1898. (2) *see* BRUSHING

cutting corners *see* CUT CORNERS

cutting horse Also known as cutting pony; a cow horse; any horse used to work cattle selected from the herd; the ability is predominantly instinctive, the talent being developed not trained; Quarter Horses (q.v.) or Quarter Horse crosses are commonly used.

cutting horse competition An organized event in which the talent and ability of the horse and rider to cut cows from a herd during a 2½ minute ride are demonstrated; the first advertised cutting competition took place in Huskell, Texas, USA in 1898; organized as a sport in the United States in 1946 with the formation of the National Cutting Horse Association (q.v.).

cutting pony *see* CUTTING HORSE

cutting saddle A Western-type saddle with a relatively flat seat, a long, narrow horn that allows the rider to brace and pull with the movements of the horse, and a low cantle; is lightweight and has fenders that permit easy backward and forward motion of the legs and a feel for the horse under the leather; generally has a back cinch (q.v.).

Cut-under Buggy An American horse-drawn vehicle popular in the 18th and 19th centuries; had an arched body under which the front wheels turned, a folding hood, was hung on two elliptic springs, one under the dash and the other behind the rear boot, and seated two forward-facing passengers.

CVA *see* CONCOURS VOLTIGE D'AMITIE

CVI (1) An international vaulting event with no limit to the number of foreign nations participating. (2) *see* CERTIFICATE OF VETERINARY INSPECTION

cyano-cobalamin The water-soluble vitamin B_{12} which contains cobalt.

D

D *see* DEE-RING

dagger pencil Also known as a sword pencil; a type of striping brush with which decorative lines were painted on horse-drawn vehicles; had hairs cut to a point fixed to a tiny wooden handle.

daiku *see* POLO

daily double Also known as double; a racing term; a betting option in which the bettor (q.v.) attempts to select the winning horses in two consecutive nominated races, usually the first and second, buying a single ticket on the double choice; to win this bet, both selected horses must win their respective races.

daily energy requirement The daily amount of calories required by a horse to maintain weight; individual metabolic rate, air temperature, performance demands, pregnancy, lactation, and growth must be considered when establishing this base requirement.

Daily Racing Form Also known as The Form; a racing term; a daily newspaper containing news, past performance data, and handicapping information on race horses; used by bettors (q.v.) and odds makers (q.v.).

daily triple *see* PICK THREE

daisy-cutter Said of a horse who, when moving at the trot, appears to skirt the surface of the ground; such horses are predisposed to stumbling.

Dales Also known as Dales Pony or generically as native pony (q.v.); a pony breed originating along the eastern slopes of the Pennine range, England, from the High Peak in Derbyshire to the Cheviot Hills near the Scottish Border; a close, but heavier and larger, relative of the Fell pony (q.v.); descended from the Celtic pony, crossed with Norfolk Cobs (q.v.) for speed in the 18th century, Norfolk and Yorkshires for additional speed in the 19th century, and Clydesdale (q.v.) stallions in the late 19th and early 20th centuries to create a vanner (q.v.); stands up to 14.2 hands and has a black, brown, sometime a bay or gray and occasionally a roan coat; white markings may include a star and/or snip on the head and white from the fetlock (q.v.) on the hind leg only; the cannons should display 8 to 9½ inches (20.3 – 24.1 cm) of flat bone and well-defined tendons; the feet are large and round; is short-coupled (q.v.), deep through the chest, has well-sprung ribs, a strong, ample neck, slightly in-curving ears, and a long forelock coming straight down the face; is tremendously strong, has a remarkable weight-carrying capacity, is calm and sensitive, and a good keeper; historically used underground in Britain's ore and coal mines, as a general farm animal, and for packing; currently used under harness in competitive driving and as an all-purpose riding mount.

Dales Pony *see* DALES

Dales Pony Improvement Society A British organization founded in 1916 to encourage and improve the Dales (q.v.) breed standard and to maintain the breed registry; reorganized as the Dales Pony Society (q.v.) in 1964.

Dales Pony Society A British organization which superseded the Dales Pony Improvement Society (q.v.) in 1964 at which time the word "improvement" was dropped from the name and a grading-up registry was established to improve the breed.

dally Also known as go to the horn; a roping term; the quick turn or loop of one end of the lariat (q.v.) around the saddle horn (q.v.) to secure the rope after roping an animal; executed by the roper (q.v.).

Dalmatian Also known as coach dog; a large, 50 to 90 pound (23–41 kg), short-haired white dog with black or brown spots historically used to accompany horse-drawn vehicles and protect cargo from theft; trained to run between the wheels of the vehicle, immediately behind the horse's heels.

Dalric cuff A German-made, glue-on (q.v.) horseshoe (q.v.); consists of a plastic rim and 1½ inch (38 mm) plastic cuff that extends upward from the rim at an angle consistent with the hoof angle; a forged shoe is riveted to the ground-side surface of the plastic rim; the cuff and shoe combination is glued to the hoof using an epoxy or space-age glue; commonly used in massive hoof reconstructions.

dam The female parent of a horse; a foal is said to be "out of" the dam; listed on the bottom side of the pedigree.

dam's sire Also known as broodmare sire; the sire (q.v.) of a broodmare; used in reference to the maternal grandsire of a foal.

Damage Fund A hunting term; a small cap (q.v.) assessed by some hunts (q.v.) on a per-meet basis, to all present, including foot followers, to compensate landowners and others for damage to their property incurred during the hunt.

Damalinia equi *see* BITING LOUSE

dancing *see* CHATTER

dancing competition A mounted sport performed on the islands of Sumba and Sumbawa, Indonesia in which Sumba (q.v.) and Sumbawa (q.v.) ponies, ridden bareback in bitless bridles by young boys, are lunged by a trainer who directs their movements; bells are attached to the ponies' knees and the ponies dance in time to the beat of a tom-tom drum; are judged on elegance and lightness of the performance.

Dandi A litter (q.v.) used in India and the Middle East; suspended from a single pole and carried between two men or pack animals.

Dandy A horse-drawn railway carriage used in Cumberland, England between 1861 and 1914.

dandy brush Also known as whisk; a wooden-backed brush (q.v.) with natural or synthetic bristles used to remove heavy dirt or mud from the coat and legs of a horse.

dangler A type of fly terret (q.v.).

Danish Horse (1) *see* DANISH WARMBLOOD. (2) *see* FREDERIKSBORG

Danish Sport Horse *see* DANISH WARMBLOOD

Danish Spotted Horse *see* KNABSTRUP

Danish Warmblood Previously known as the Danish Sport Horse or Danish Horse; a Danish warmblood developed by crossing locally bred Fredriksborg (q.v.)/ Thoroughbred (q.v.) mares with pedigree Anglo-Norman (q.v.), Thoroughbred, Trakehner (q.v.), and Polish stallions; stands 16.1 to 16.2 hands and is most commonly bay, although all coat colors do occur; is naturally well balanced and excels in dressage and show jumping.

Danubian A Bulgarian warmblood developed during the early 20th century around the Danube Plain from which the name derived; descended from Nonius (q.v.) stallions crossed with Gidran (q.v.) mares; stands approximately 15.2 hands, has a black or chestnut coat, compact body, strong neck, powerful quarters, deep body, and relatively slender legs; used for light draft and riding, particularly jumping.

dapple Refers to coat color pattern; a coat with small spots, patches, dots, or circular markings which contrast in color or shade with the body color; may be present on horses of any color, although most visible in silver dapples (q.v.) and grays.

dapple gray Refers to coat color; a gray coat interspersed with white hairs; a progressive color, in that horses are born black and turn gray with age.

Darashomi *see* DARASHOURI

Darashouri Also known as Darashomi or Slurazi; one of two types of Persian Arab (q.v.) indigenous to Iran, specifically the Fars region of southern Iran; is elegant, strong, spirited, energetic, and athletic, stands 14.1 to 15.1 hands, and has a bay, chestnut, gray, or rarely black, coat; used for riding.

Darby, The *see* EPSOM DERBY

Daresbury Phaeton A horse-drawn driving carriage designed for modern cross-country competitions; has a traditional wood-finished body, hollow steel under-gear, shock-absorbers, hydraulic disc brakes and a spare wheel; drawn either by a pair of horses or a four-in-hand team (q.v.).

dark A racing term; said of a race track or a day on which there is no racing.

dark bay *see* MAHOGANY BAY

dark brown Refers to coat color; a shade of brown (q.v.), very close to black, smoky black, or faded black (q.v.).

dark buckskin *see* SMUTTY BUCKSKIN

dark grullo *see* SMUTTY GRULLO

dark horse A racing term; an underrated horse or one about whom little is known; so named because his abilities were "kept in the dark."

dark muzzle Refers to coat color; said of a horse having a dark nose, as in donkeys (q.v.).

Darley Arab *see* DARLEY ARABIAN

Darley Arabian Also known as Darley Arab; one of three foundation sires of the English Thoroughbred (q.v.); a pure-bred kehilan Arab (q.v.) of the Managhi (q.v.) strain imported into England in 1705 by Mr. Richard Darley for whom he was named; foaled in 1700, stood about 15 hands, and was a bay with a blaze and three white socks (q.v.); became the most famous of the Eastern sires having sired Bulle Rocke, the first Thoroughbred (q.v.) brought to the United States; all Thoroughbreds (q.v.) in the world today trace their ancestry in direct male line to the Godolphin Arab (q.v.), Byerley Turk (q.v.), and Darley Arabian.

dart hole Also known as crew hole (Brit); the holes at the end of the traces (q.v.) through which the trace hook passes.

Dartmoor *see* DARTMOOR PONY

Dartmoor Pony Also known as Dartmoor or generically as a native pony (q.v.); an ancient pony breed originating in Dartmoor, a rugged mountain area in Devon, England; one of nine breeds native to the British Isles; influenced in the 19th century by the introduction of Welsh pony (q.v.), Cob (q.v.), Exmoor pony (q.v.), Arabian (q.v.), small Thoroughbred (q.v.) and Shetland pony (q.v.) blood; Shetland blood was introduced in an attempt to produce a pony for use in Britain's coal mines; this later introduction threatened breed purity and between 1941 and 1943, it nearly fell to extinction with only two males and twelve females registered; since 1899 a strict breed registry has been maintained; registry guidelines prohibit entries standing more than 12.2 hands; most commonly bay, brown, black, and gray, while chestnut is rarer; piebald and skewbald coloring is not permitted and extensive white markings are discouraged; has a relatively small head, a well-proportioned neck with a full mane, good back, and slender legs with short cannons; is hardy, a good keeper, and is noted for its lack of knee lift having a low and long action; an ideal mount for children due to its temperament and action; used for all types of riding.

Dartmoor Pony Society A British organization established to promote and encourage the breeding of pure-bred Dartmoor Ponies (q.v.); has maintained a strict breed registry since 1899.

dash (1) An archaic racing term; a horse race decided in a single trial. (2) A racing term; a sprint race. (3) *see* DASHBOARD

dashboard Also known as dash; that part of a horse-drawn vehicle located in front of the driver's and passengers' legs which protects them from dirt thrown up by the hooves of the horse; made of wood or leather sewn onto an iron frame.

daughter of the horseleech A 16th-century term; (obs); any rapacious insatiable person, or bloodsucker who clings to another robbing him of ideas, money, or other resources; the daughters of such people would, presumably, be more grasping.

Daumont Also known as à la Daumont; a method of turning out a team pulling a horse-drawn vehicle popular in the 18th century; the horses are put to a vehicle such as a Landau (q.v.) or Barouche (q.v.) from which the driving seat has been removed; the nearside horses are ridden by postillions (q.v.) in full livery who also control the offside horses; posting harness is used; first developed and named for Duc D'Aumont.

day rug *see* SHEET

day sheet *see* SHEET

DE *see* DIGESTIBLE ENERGY

dead heat A racing term; said of two or more horses arriving at the finish line simultaneously.

dead meat An antiquated racing term; said of a horse entered in a race whose owner(s) have no intention of allowing him to win.

deadly nightshade Also known as *Atropa belladonna*; a highly toxic, low-growing plant with spreading green stems and narrow, pointed leaves about 4 inches (10 cm) long which produce white, star-shaped flowers and round, dark fruit approximately ¼ inch (6 mm) in diameter; has an unpleasant taste and odor, but horses will sometimes nibble at it out of boredom or hunger; the toxin acts like an addictive drug, once "hooked" the horse will seek it out, eventually ingesting enough to cause chronic poisoning (q.v.); poisoning affects each horse at a different rate and may often cause an adverse reaction days or weeks following exposure.

dead-sided Said of a horse whose sides are numb to the action of the leg, spur, or whip aids.

dead track A racing term; said of the track surface that lacks resilience.

dead weight *see* LEAD NO. 3

deafness Loss of hearing; profound deafness in both ears is relatively easy to diagnose, while partial or unilateral deafness is difficult to diagnose; may be congenital or acquired.

deal (1) A board or plank as made of fir or pine, usually longer than 6 feet (1.8 m), wider than 7 inches (17.8 cm) and thicker than 3 inches (7.6 cm) used as carriage flooring. (2) A British term; any inferior softwood.

Dealer's Break *see* SKELETON BREAK

dealer's whip A steel-lined, long whip used by horse dealers.

Decemjugis A Roman chariot driven to ten horses abreast.

deciduous teeth Also known as temporary teeth, milk teeth or baby teeth; any tooth present at birth, appearing shortly thereafter, or gradually appearing until the horse is approximately nine months old; in-wear (q.v.) within approximately six months following eruption; include the first, second, and third incisors (q.v.) and premolars (q.v.) on each side and occasionally the canine teeth (q.v.); remain until replaced by the permanent teeth (q.v.) compared to which they are usually smaller, whiter, relatively shorter, and have constricted necks and flat roots.

declare off *see* SUSPEND NO. 2

declared off (1) *see* RACE DECLARED OFF. (2) *see* BET DECLARED OFF

declaration Also known as declaration of runners; a racing term; a written statement provided by a horse owner, trainer, or a designate of either, prior to a race or competition, which declares that a specific horse will participate.

declaration of runners *see* DECLARATION

declaration to win A racing term; a public announcement made by the owner of more than one entrant in a horse race, that he will try to win with one mount but not the other(s); against the rules of racing in Britain.

declared (1) An American racing term; a horse withdrawn from a stakes race in advance of scratch time. (2) Also known as declared a runner; a European racing term; said of a horse confirmed to start in a race.

declared a runner *see* DECLARED NO. 2

dee *see* DEE-RING

dee-cheek snaffle *see* DEE-RING SNAFFLE

deep (1) A racing term; said of a recently harrowed racing surface to which top soil has been added to increase the holding quality of the footing. (2) Internal, close to the center of gravity of the horse. (3) A hunting term; said of soft or heavy footing.

deep crack *see* PENETRATING CRACK

deep cut A cutting term; a maneuver performed by the horse and rider when selecting a cow to work; a cut or movement far enough into a herd of cattle that leaves the horse completely surrounded by cows; in competition, one deep cut for each 2½ minute ride is required.

deep flexor tendon A tendon (q.v.) located in the back of the foreleg between the knee and the foot and between the hock and the foot in the hind leg; functions in conjunction with the superficial flexor tendon (q.v.) to flex the pastern (q.v.) and knee in the fore and to extend the hock (q.v.) in the hind leg.

deep going Said of wet ground made heavy by rain, in which the hooves of the horse sink deeply.

deep in the girth Also known as deep through the girth; said of a horse who has well-sprung ribs (q.v.) and a good chest capacity as measured circumferentially behind the elbows and over the withers.

deep laceration An injury that penetrates all layers of the skin and in some cases to the level of the muscle or fascia, tendons, or even bone; the edges of the wound will gape apart.

deep-litter method A manner of bedding a stall in which fresh bedding is added daily on top of the existing bedding; the stall is completely mucked out every few months.

deep stretch A racing term; a race position very close to the finish line.

deep through the girth *see* DEEP IN THE GIRTH

deer fly A blood-sucking fly of the genus *Chrysops*, considered a large solitary daytime feeder which is most voracious early and late in the day; along with the horse fly (q.v.); considered the most significant pest in North America; about the size of a house fly (q.v.) with patterned wings; painful bites cause localized swelling.

dee-ring Also known as D, D-ring, or dee; a metal, D-shaped fitting found on saddles, other tack, and harnesses.

dee-ring bit Any bit having dee-shaped cheekpieces (q.v.); as in a dee-ring snaffle (q.v.).

dee-ring snaffle Also known as racing snaffle, dee-shaped snaffle, dee-cheek snaffle, D-ring snaffle, or Meyer's D cheek; a bit having a single-jointed mouthpiece with slightly tapered and curved arms that join to the flat side of the D-shaped cheekpieces; commonly used on race horses and young stock; the D shape prevents the bit from slipping into or through the horse's mouth.

deer neck *see* SWAN NECK

dees More than one dee (q.v.).

dee-shaped snaffle *see* DEE-RING SNAFFLE

defect Any trait or condition, usually undesirable, which effects the present or future performance or appearance of a horse.

definitive host Also known as principal host; the animal haboring sexually mature parasites.

de Foix, Gaston The French author of *Le Livre de la Chasse* published in 1387, which became the textbook on hunting in France; translated into English during the same period as The Master of Game.

degenerative joint disease Also know by the acronym DJD; *see* OSTEOARTHROSIS

de Gogue *see* DE GOUGE MARTINGALE

de Gouge martingale Also known as Gogue, Gouge martingale, de Gouge, or headset; schooling tack; an auxiliary rein or strap used to assist the action of the bit by restricting the position of the horse's head and neck; of two types: (a) independent Gogue consisting of an arrangement of straps fastened to the chest ring or girth on one end, which pass over the poll (q.v.) pad on either side of the temples, and connect to the bit rings on the other and (b) command Gogue consisting of an arrangement of straps fastened on one end to the girth or chest ring, which pass through rings on either side of a poll pad, to the bit rings, and attach to a rein other than the snaffle rein on the other; the action is on the poll (q.v.) and may be controlled by the rider; encourages a low head set.

de la Guérinière, François Robichon (1688–1751) Also known as 'The Father of Classical Equitation', his influence changed the course of classical equitation (q.v.) and his teachings formed the basis for modern equitation; largely due to his work, two veins of classical equitation developed in Europe, one based on the French Schools of Versailles and Saumur (q.v.), and the other in the Spanish Riding School of Vienna (q.v.); developed a system of suppling and gymnastic exercises designed to cultivate and extend the horse's natural movements, invented the shoulder-in (q.v.), made improvements on two- and four-track (q.v.) work, made extensive use of lateral work, and designed the modern saddle, still used today in the Spanish Riding School, in which the size of the pommel (q.v.) and cantle (q.v.) were reduced and knee and thigh rolls were incorporated; authored the classic book on equitation, *Ecole de Cavalerie*, published in 1733.

delayed lethal An inherited lethal (q.v.); any disease or condition genetically transmitted to the foal that generally results in foal death sometime following birth.

delay in uterine clearance *see* PERSISTENT MATING-INDUCED ENDOMETRITIS

Deli Pony *see* BATAK

delivery document A document given to the buyer or buyer's agent upon settlement of a sale of a horse which authorizes the buyer to take possession of the horse from the consignor at a sale or auction (q.v.).

Demi-Daumont Said of a coach team, when a pair, instead of the entire team is turned out Daumont (q.v.).

Demi-Landau *see* LANDAULETTE

Demi-Mail Phaeton Also known as a Semi-Mail Phaeton; a horse-drawn vehicle favored by gentlemen for town and country use in the 19th century; had a body similar to the Mail Phaeton (q.v.) with a hooded front seat and a groom's seat in the rear, allowing room between the two for luggage; had no perch, but was built with elliptical springs in front and mail springs behind.

demi-pique *see* DEMI-PIQUED SADDLE

demi-piqued saddle Also known as demi-pique; a heavy saddle with half a saddle horn used by 18th-century cavalry and travelers.

demi-pirouette *see* HALF-PIROUETTE

demi-passade A classical movement performed by the horse whereby he traverses back and forth over a specified short straight track at a fast pace, making a quick reversal and return.

Demi-Sang Charollais A group of breeds consisting of the Charollais (q.v.), Bourbannais (q.v.), and Nivernais.

Demi-Sang de Centre A regional subgroup of the general heading Cheval de Selle Français of half-bred horses bred in France; include the Limousin (q.v.) and Charollais (q.v.).

Demi-Spider Phaeton A horse-drawn vehicle of the Spider Phaeton (q.v.) type having a hooded front seat for the driver and a passenger and a railed rear seat for the groom; the lower outline was straight from the footboard (q.v.) to well behind the groom's seat; hung on four elliptical springs; there was no boot (q.v.) along the body.

demi-volte A dressage term; one half of a 6-, 8-, or 10-meter circle executed on two-tracks (q.v.); when the half circle is complete, the horse returns to the track in a straight rather than a curved line.

Democrat Wagon An American horse-drawn, square-box wagon with a fixed top; used to convey passengers and luggage.

demodectic mange A skin disease caused by the infestation of the parasitic mite *Demodex folliculorum*, which lives in the hair follicles and sebaceous glands of the skin; characterized by pustular blisters, ulcers, and scabs principally around the eyes and on the forehead with lesions spreading from the face to the shoulders and ultimately the entire body; seldom diagnosed in horses and less contagious than sarcoptic mange (q.v.).

den *see* FOX DEN

den dog An American hunting term; a hound who, when a fox goes to ground (q.v.), remains at the den (q.v.) and gives tongue (q.v.).

denerve *see* NERVE

Dennett *see* DENNETT GIG

Dennett Gig Also known as Dennett; a horse-drawn Gig (q.v.) introduced in England in the early 19th century; resembled the Stanhope Gig (q.v.), yet had a unique form of suspension: a crosswise set of springs and two lengthwise springs, joined by D-links; each set of springs was rumored to be named after one of three Dennett sisters, renowned on the London stage for their beauty, wit, and nimble dancing.

dental pulp The soft interior core of the tooth (q.v.) containing nerves and blood vessels.

dental star Also known as tooth star or star; the closed distal end of the pulp cavity in the incisor teeth (q.v.); first appears as a thin line across the chewing surface when the horse is about eight years old; the filling of this cavity is of a lighter color than the tooth body; by about 15 years of age this mark is distinct and round, appearing on the center of the table surface of the teeth; an accurate indicator of age of the horse.

dental table The masticatory surface of the tooth.

dentigerous cyst Also known as an ear fistula or conchal sinus; an infrequently occurring tumor with a center consisting of a different material than surrounding tissue, e.g., hair or tooth tissue; evidenced by a draining tract located at the edge of the ear, or by a soft, painless swelling in front of the base of the ear; as long as it remains open, it will drain a sticky, saliva-like liquid; if sealed, will swell to considerable size; may be surgically removed.

deoxyribonucleic acid Also known by the acronym DNA; a protein compound found in chromosomes which determines individual hereditary characteristics; consists of a long chain molecule comprising many repeated and varied combinations of four nucleotides: subdivisions of the molecule are believed to be the genes.

depilation Removal or loss of hair.

de Pluvinel, Antoine (1555–1620) A horseman, trainer, and author of *The Maneige Royal* (1623) and *L'Instruction du Roy, En l'Exercice de Monter à cheval* (1625); promoted the humane treatment of the horse with his method of "gentling" rather than "breaking."

Depot Wagon Also known as Station Wagon; a horse-drawn American family carriage popular from the 1850s to the early 1900s; drawn either by one or two horses, depending on size; fitted with two or three rows of crosswise, forward-facing seats, the last of which was removable to create luggage space; similar to a Rockaway (q.v.), except that the undercarriage was straight rather than curved.

depressant Any substance that slows the activity of the circulatory, respiratory, or central nervous systems.

depth The distance between the withers (q.v.) and the girth (q.v.).

derby (1) A cutting term; any competition for four-year-old horses. (2) A racing term; a stakes race for three-year-old horses, e.g. Kentucky Derby (q.v.) or Epsom Derby (q.v.).

Derby (1) *see* EPSOM DERBY. (2) *see* KENTUCKY DERBY

Derby Bank at Hickstead One of the most notorious obstacles in show jumping; a bank (q.v.) that drops a full 10 feet (3 m) on the downside.

Derby Stakes *see* EPSOM DERBY

derma Also known as dermis; the sensitive, blood-vessel-supplied layer beneath the epidermis (q.v.) containing the sweat and sebaceous glands; supports, nourishes, and to some degree regulates, the epidermis (q.v.) and appendages.

dermal inclusion cyst Small cystic bumps which sometimes appear along the center line of the horse's back; caused by the inward growth of hairs; the top half of each bump may be surgically severed to allow the hair to grow to the surface.

dermatitis Inflammation of the skin.

dermatophilus Also known as dermatophilus infection, cutaneous streptothricosis or mud fever (obs); skin infection caused by *Dermatophilus congolensis*, a gram-positive bacterium with some fungus-like characteristics; results in chronic dermatitis (q.v.), in which the hairs stand erect and matted in tufts; follows prolonged wetting of an animal, tick infestation, insect bites, vegetative wounds, etc.; examples in horses include greasy heel (q.v.) and rain scald (q.v.).

dermatophilus congolensis A gram-positive bacterium having some fungal-like characteristics, e.g. the production of branching filaments; causes dermatophilus (q.v.).

dermatophilus infection *see* DERMATOPHILUS

dermatophytosis *see* RINGWORM

dermis *see* DERMA

de-rotation A condition of the foot in which the outer surface of the hoof wall at the toe and the face of third phalanx are greater near the coronet (q.v.) than near the ground; may be due to dubbing (q.v.).

demitis Inflammation of the ligament, as resulting from tearing of the ligament fibrils.

descent The horse's parentage as proved by the genealogical tree over a period of several generations.

descente de main et des jambes A French term; to yield with the hand and legs, while the horse maintains the same flexion, cadence, and rhythm in the movement executed.

D-shaped blinker A blinker (q.v.) shaped like an inverted 'D'.

destrier (1) An archaic term; a French war-horse especially as used in medieval tournaments. (2) The side on which the squire led his master's horse; the right; from the Middle French *destre* meaning right and the Latin *dextra* meaning right side.

destroy *see* EUTHANIZE

developer *see* RUBBER BAND

devil grass *see* BERMUDA GRASS

devil's hatband *see* BARBED WIRE

devil's rope *see* BARBED WIRE

Devonshire slipper stirrup iron A metal, slipper-shaped, closed-toe stirrup (q.v.), which supports and protects the rider's foot; hung and swings freely on a bar horizontally attached to the stirrup leathers.

deworm To administer anthelmintics (q.v.) to a horse to trigger elimination of internal parasites; available in paste and injectable forms.

dexter Any of several driving bits.

dh *see* DEAD HEAT

DI *see* DOSAGE INDEX

diagnostic ultrasound The use of high frequency sound waves, above the range of the human ear, to image internal structures as to determine injury, illness, etc.

diagonal The forefoot and its diagonally opposite hind foot which move in unison at the trot; normally referenced by the leading forefoot (q.v.), e.g. the "left diagonal" consists of the left fore and right hind.

diagonal aid An aid (q.v.) applied in conjunction with other complementary aids, to the side of the horse opposite from the side most obviously influenced by the combination of aids, e.g. right leg pressure applied behind the girth is a diagonal aid when used in initiating a left canter (q.v.).

diamond bars *see* JUMPED-IN BARS

diaphragm The partition or membrane separating the chest cavity from the abdominal cavity.

diaphragmatic hernia Also known as rupture; protrusion of abdominal contents through the diaphragm.

diaphysis Also known as cortex; the shaft of a long bone including both the bone and marrow layers.

diarrhea An ailment characterized by abnormally frequent and fluid evacuation of the bowels.

dickey Also spelled dicky and known as driving seat in the early 20th century; 19th century slang; the rear seat of a horse-drawn vehicle, commonly used by a servant.

dicky *see* DICKEY

Dicky Coach (1) A horse-drawn coach or carriage in which the box seat (q.v.) was separated, or appeared to be separated, from the main bodywork. (2) Slang; any horse-drawn passenger vehicle with a rear or rumble seat.

Dick Turpin *see* TURPIN, DICK

die in the herd A cutting horse term; said of the rider who, when in competition, rides his horse into a herd of cattle to select another cow, but fails to do so before the buzzer sounds to end the run (q.v.).

diestrus Also spelt dioestrus; the period in the mare's breeding cycle during which she will not accept the stallion; sometimes divided into two separate periods: proestrus (q.v.), the period just prior to the occurrence of estrus (q.v.), and metestrus (q.v.).

dietary essential amino acids Also known as essential amino acids or by the acronym DEAAs; any of the ten amino acids (q.v.) which make up natural proteins (q.v.) without which normal metabolic function cannot occur; are essential for the growth, maintenance, and repair of the body tissues of the horse and must be supplied by the horse's ration as they are not internally synthesized.

Digby *see* GOVERNESS CART

digestible energy Also known by the acronym DE; the total energy produced from carbohydrates, fats, and proteins, less the energy remaining in the feces and by-products formed during digestion; the value most commonly used to describe the energy content of animal feeds in the United States.

digestive system Also known as digestive tract; the system consisting of the mouth (lips, teeth, tongue, and salivary glands), the esophagus, the true stomach, the small intestine, liver, pancreas, the large intestine, rectum, and anus; the primary functions are motility, evacuation, digestion, and absorption (to convert food and drink into a form absorbable by the body tissues).

digestive tract *see* DIGESTIVE SYSTEM

digit The portion of the horse's leg below the fetlock including the coffin and long and short pastern bones.

digital cushion *see* PLANTAR CUSHION

Diligence A heavy, lumbering, horse-drawn stage coach used throughout Europe during the 19th and early 20th centuries; provided long-distance transportation with different classes of accommodation at different fares determined by location of the seats within the vehicle: (a) coupé, (b) roof, (c) intérieur (q.v.), and (d) rear; pulled by a four-horse team or, more commonly, a team of five with three horses harnessed abreast in the lead.

dimethyl sulfoxide Also known by the acronym DMSO; an organic chemical derived from wood pulp which is rapidly absorbed into the system through the skin; utilized as a carrier to help transport other substances through the skin and has anti-inflammatory (q.v.), antibacterial (q.v.), and analgesic (q.v.) properties; is administered topically to treat acute lameness, pruritis (q.v.), lacerations, and other traumas to the musculoskeletal system, to reduce pain, and intravenously as a free-radical scavenger, anti-inflammatory agent, and to treat pneumonia; has an unpleasant odor and taste.

dinks Chaps (q.v.) that extend only to the knee; frequently fringed.

dioestrus *see* DIESTRUS

dip (1) A Western roping term; the downward angle of the lariat (q.v.) achieved during the swing. (2) The hollow of the back as in a sway-backed horse.

dip back *see* SWAY BACK

dip backed *see* SWAY BACKED

Diphron A Greek war chariot with a high front shield, entered from the rear and drawn by two or more horses harnessed abreast.

diploma A racing term; the first win of a horse's career.

Diploma of the Worshipful Company of Farriers Also known as dip WFC, by the acronym DWCF and previously as Registered Shoeing Smith; one of three levels of training certification awarded to practicing farriers in England by the Worshipful Company of Farriers of London (q.v.) on the basis of written, oral, and practical examinations.

dip WFC *see* DIPLOMA OF THE WORSHIPFUL COMPANY OF FARRIERS

direct flexion The longitudinal flexion (q.v.) of the horse at the poll and in the jaw.

direct rein Also known as plow rein, opening rein, open rein, or guiding rein; to use the rein (q.v.) on the side to which a turn is desired to draw the horse, specifically the nose and head, in the direction of the desired turn with the body following.

Dioropha A horse-drawn vehicle of British design first unveiled in 1851; built on the lines of a Barouche (q.v.), but had a detachable roof; the roof was removed by means of ropes and pulleys; if the roof was not used, a hood covered the rear seat; had sliding windows.

dirt track A racing term; a racetrack (q.v.) with a surface consisting of sand and soil.

dirty mare Said of a mare who experiences problems conceiving; applies to as many as 85 percent of broodmares who experience conception problems; may be due to different categories of complications, namely: mares with acute infections, mares with long-standing, severe infections, and mares unable to clear their uteri of breeding by-products

discord lupus A type of lupus (q.v.); an immune-mediated disorder rarely seen in horses, characterized by inflammation of the facial skin.

dish (1) A breaking away of the horny wall of the hoof. (2) Any indentation appearing on the hoof wall. (3) *see* DISHING

dish profile *see* DISH FACE

dish face Also known as dish profile, concave face, or stag face; said of the face of the horse when concave below the forehead as formed by a depression of the nasal bones; common to Arabs (q.v.) and sometimes seen in some other breeds.

dishing Also known as winging or paddling; outward deviation of the foot during flight; the foot breaks over the outside toe and lands on the outside wall; is naturally occurring in laterally gaited horses such as the Andalusian (q.v.) and Peruvian Paso (q.v.) and common in high-going, pigeon-toed (q.v.), and narrow-based horses.

dislocated knee cap *see* SLIPPED STIFLE

dislocated patella *see* SLIPPED STIFLE

dismount Also known as light or alight; to get off a horse.

disobedient Said of a horse who ignores the training or evades aids of the rider and does not perform the requested movement.

displaced fracture A break in a bone in which the bone fragments have moved out of alignment; depending on the degree of displacement, the pieces generally require realignment for satisfactory healing to occur.

disqualified Said of a horse or rider excluded from competition due to rule infringement.

disqualify (1) To be asked to withdraw from competition due to a serious fault of either the rider or horse. (2) Also known by the acronym dq; a racing term; to lower the actual finishing place of a horse following completion of a race by official action as due to interference with another horse in the field, carrying incorrect weight, or competing under the influence of an illegal substance, etc.

distaff Also known as female tail or distaff side; the female lineage of a pedigree.

distaffer A female horse.

distaff race A racing term; any race in which only mares or fillies can be entered.

distaff side *see* DISTAFF

distal Furthest away from the center of the horse's body or center of gravity, as in "The injury was distal (below) to the knee."

distal phalange *see* THIRD PASTERN

distal phalanx *see* THIRD PASTERN

distal profusion The total circulation of blood through all tissues.

distal pulse The rhythmic beating or throbbing of the arteries in the foot caused by heart contractions which force blood to move through the vessel; taken at the lateral rear of the fetlock.

distal sesamoid *see* NAVICULAR BONE

distal sesamoid ligament Also known as distal sesamoidean ligament; strong, fibrous bands of tissue consisting of fibro-elastic (yellow) and fibrous (white) types which serve to connect the sesamoid bones to the long and short pastern bones; strengthen and limit joint range.

distal sesamoidean ligament *see* DISTAL SESAMOID LIGAMENT

distance (1) *see* A DISTANCE. (2) *see* DISTANCE, THE

distanced An American racing term; said of a horse so far behind the rest of the field (q.v.) that he is unable to regain a position of contention.

distance of ground *see* ROUTE

Distance, The (1) Also known as distance; a racing term; the 240-yard (220 m) straightaway on a racecourse before the finish (q.v.). (2) A British racing term; the final furlong (220 yards/201 m) on a racecourse.

distemper *see* STRANGLES

distillers dried grains *see* DISTILLERS GRAINS

distillers grains Also known as distillers dried grains; the substance resulting from grain or a grain mixture following removal of ethyl alcohol from the yeast fermentation of grain; corn and rye grains are most commonly used; contain approximately 25 percent protein, 13 percent crude fiber, and a high digestible energy content; very palatable to horses.

disunited Said of the horse's gait when the normal stride sequence is disrupted, as in disunited canter (q.v.) or disunited gallop (q.v.); may be due to rider imbalance, poor training or condition, etc.

disunited canter Also known as cross canter or broken canter; said of a cantering horse whose sequence of footfall is incorrect e.g., taking one lead with the forelegs and the opposite lead with the hind; may be due to a lack of balance, back stiffness, etc.

disunited gallop Also known as false gallop; said of a galloping (q.v.) horse who takes one lead with the fore and the opposite lead with his hind legs; the sequence of hoof beats is: off hind, near hind, near fore, off fore (leading leg) or near hind, off hind, off fore, near fore (leading leg); uncomfortable to ride and may lead to lower-leg injuries.

ditch A natural jumping obstacle; a depression with or without water.

diuretic Any substance used to increase the production of urine.

dividend Also known as pay off; a racing term; the sum paid to a bettor (q.v.) following a successful bet on the totalizator (q.v.).

division A racing term; a horse race divided into two different races by the track officials because the number of entries exceeds available space.

divot A piece of sod torn up by the horse's hooves in a polo match, race, hunt, etc.

divot stomping Also known as earth stomping, stomping divots, or stomping earth; the tradition of replacing the mounds of earth torn up by the horse's hooves on the polo field, racetrack, and in some hunted areas, etc. by pushing them down with one's foot or heel, as to maintain field condition.

Dixon, Henry Hall (1822–1870) An English author who penned, under the pseudonym The Druid, such equestrian works as the *Post and Paddock* (1856), *Silk and Scarlet* (1858), *Scott and Seabright* (1862), *Field and Fern* (1865), and *Saddle and Sirloin* (1870).

DJD *see* DEGENERATIVE JOINT DISEASE

DMSO *see* DIMETHYL SULFOXIDE

DNA *see* DEOXYRIBONUCLEIC ACID

DNA testing A biotechnical identification procedure; adopted by some horse registries such as The Jockey Club (q.v.) to verify parentage of a horse; is 99 percent accurate and, in many cases, has replaced blood-typing which is only 96 percent accurate; DNA strands of an offspring are compared to those of suspected parents; when matches between the strands of the offspring and parents appear in loci in a regular and consistent manner, a match is considered approved.

dobbin A British term; a workhorse used in agricultural service.

dock (1) Also known as flag; to amputate the horse's tail bone to a length of about 6 inches (15 cm) with a docking knife or scissors and cauterize the cut end with a docking iron (q.v.); commonly practiced on certain classes of horses, such as harness horses and cobs, through 1948 to yield a neater appearance and to prevent the reins from becoming caught under the tail; illegal in most countries since 1949 and restricted in England by the Docking and Nicking Act (q.v.). (2) The solid portion or bone of the tail including both hair-covered and bare sides.

dock and set To remove part of the dock (q.v.) of the tail, cut the tendons, and set the tail so that when healed, it is carried high.

docked *see* DOCKED TAIL

docked tail Also known as docked; said of the tail of the horse when part of the dock (q.v.) has been amputated.

dock tailed Also known as bob tailed; said of a horse with a short or docked (q.v.) tail.

docker Coaching slang; a whip (q.v.) used by poor class drivers.

Docking and Nicking Act A law passed in Great Britain in 1948 making it illegal to dock (q.v.) or nick (q.v.) the tail of the horse to improve his appearance for show purposes.

docking iron A metal iron which, when heated was used to cauterize the amputated dock (q.v.).

dockpiece *see* CRUPPER DOCK

dock tail Also known as cocktail or bob tail; a horse having a tail cut or bobbed to a length of about 6 inches (15.2 cm).

doctor To administer first aid.

Doctor's Wagon A light, four-wheeled American horse-drawn vehicle having a hooded single seat with a small seat behind; the seat sides were caned and the body hung on two transverse elliptical springs from a perch undercarriage.

doer *see* GOOD DOER

dog (1) A racing term; any obstacle (commonly rubber traffic cones) placed adjacent to the inner rail on the race track during workout periods to close off a portion of the track when muddy; prevents horses from running there or tearing up the surface during workouts. (2) A cheap horse or one who simply fails to perform; a sluggish horse. (3) A British racing term; said of a horse who does not attempt to win a race, as due to temperament. (4) Also known as hound; a domesticated quadruped of various species, the so-called *Canis familiaris*. (5) Also known as hound; to follow or track with dogs.

Dog Cart *see* DOGCART

Dogcart Also known as Gig and spelled Dog Cart; an open, horse-drawn, English sporting cart used for general purposes and to carry gun dogs who were contained in a slatted compartment beneath the driver's seat; both two- and four-wheeled types existed, the latter being known more correctly as a Dogcart Phaeton (q.v.); the two-wheeled version was drawn by one or two horses, while the four-wheeled was always drawn by a pair; both derived from the 18th-century Shooting Gig (q.v.); seated four passengers, including the driver, back-to-back (q.v.); one passenger and the driver faced forward and two passengers faced backward; hung on sideways elliptical springs.

Dogcart Phaeton Also known as Road Phaeton, Dog Phaeton, Four-wheeled Dogcart or Double Dogcart; a horse-drawn vehicle similar in use and design to a Dogcart (q.v.), but having four wheels instead of two; seated four with carriage for dogs located beneath the seats; drawn by a single pair or a team of small ponies; now quite popular for FEI (q.v.) events and private use.

dog fall A steer wrestling term; said of a steer (q.v.) thrown by the cowboy so that all four feet and the head face different directions; an illegal throw; to obtain a time, the cowboy must turn the steer over or let it stand and re-throw it legally.

dog fox A male fox (q.v.).

dogger An American term; one who purchases asses, mules, horses, and/or hybrids live, on the hoof, at auctions with the sole intent of slaughtering them for pet food.

dog hound A male hound (q.v.).

dog-leg stick *see* DOG-LEGGED WHIP

dog-legged whip Also known as dog-leg stick; a driving whip in which the stock is attached at a right angle to the shaft.

Dog Phaeton *see* DOGCART PHAETON

Dølechest *see* DØLE GUDBRANDSAL

Døle Gudbrandsdal Also known as Gudbrandsdal, Døler Pony, Dolehest or Norwegian; an ancient pony breed originating in Norway's Gudbrandsdal Valley from which the name derived; similar to the English Fell Pony (q.v.) and the British Dales Pony (q.v.), probably having shared similar ancestors in the Friesian (q.v.); infusions of English Thoroughbred (q.v.) in the 19th century and that of heavy draft resulted in a breed of mixed origins; has a natural trotting ability which is most developed in a lighter version of the breed known as the Døle Trotter (q.v.); stands 14.2 to 15.2 hands and weighs 1,190 to 1,390 pounds (540–631 kg); the coat is generally bay, brown or black, with palomino and gray occurring rarely; has a heavy and rather square head, full forelock, mane, and tail, short back, broad chest, short legs with heavy feathering from the cannons to the coronet (q.v.), and broad feet; originally used for general farm work and hauling timber; now used for heavy draft, farming, and, due to its exceptional trotting ability, trotter racing; contributed to the development of the North Swedish Horse (q.v.).

Døler Pony *see* DØLE GUDBRANDSDAL

Døle Trotter Also known as Norwegian Trotter; a light-boned version of the Døle Gudbrandsdal (q.v.) from which it is bred using a greater input of blood from other trotter breeds; the stud book was established in 1941; registered in breed records with a T preceding the registration number.

dolls A racing term; portable wooden barricades set on some racecourses to keep the horses on track.

domador A South American term; a horse trainer (q.v.).

dominant gene *see* GENE DOMINANT

Don Also known as Donsky; a Soviet-bred warmblood descended from Turkmene (q.v.) and Karabakh (q.v.) stallions bred to native steppes mares during the 18th and 19th centuries; into the early 20th century, improved with Orlov (q.v.), Thoroughbred (q.v.), and Strelet Arab blood; the largest of the native breeds and the historical mount of the Don Cossacks from which the name derived; stands 15.1 to 15.3 hands, has a chestnut, light bay, or brown coat with a golden sheen, deep body, long straight neck, back and shoulder, and long legs, has a tendency towards calf-knees (q.v.); is hardy, frugal, energetic, and known for its great stamina; used for riding, long-distance racing, and light harness.

done Said of an exhausted horse.

donkey An ass (q.v.), derived from the English dun (the usual color) and the suffix "ky" meaning small, thus "little dun animal".

donkey foot *see* CLUB FOOT

donkey hoof *see* CLUB FOOT

donkey stripe *see* DORSAL STRIPE

Donsky *see* DON

doorman A British term; a farrier assistant responsible for hoof trimming, nailing on the shoes, and clenching the nails.

dope (1) Any substance illegally given to a horse to alter his behavior or ability to perform; sometimes used on the race track to either increase or decrease the horse's speed and in other equestrian sports to modify behavior; an illegal practice that carries heavy penalties in all equestrian sports. (2) Also known as nobble; to administer any illegal substance to a horse. (3) A racing term; slang; information or data, as in the previous performance, of a racehorse.

doped fox Also known as touched up fox; a hunting term; said of a fox whose scent has been synthetically enhanced to ensure the hounds have a sufficiently strong scent to follow; generally placed at the entrance/exit of the fox den where the fox is certain to encounter it; a practice not sanctioned by the Master of Foxhounds Association.

dope out a race A racing term; said of one who reads or solicits information pertaining to the past performances of specific horses competing in a race.

dope test *see* DRUG TEST

doping Also known as nobbling; the process of giving dope (q.v.) to a horse; to dope (q.v.).

Doris Clare Zinkeisen (B 1918) *see* ZINKEISEN, DORIS CLARE

Dormeuse Also known as Dormeuse Chariot; a closed, long distance, horse-drawn traveling Chariot widely used in France and other Western European countries from the 1820s; had a forward extension of the body into which the passengers' feet could be extended when sleeping, a mattress located in the boot, the seat cushions that made up the bed; hung on cee- or sideways-elliptical springs, had a hooded rumble for servants, and a sword case built into the back of the body; entered by half-glass doors from either side; drawn by four horses in pole gear (q.v.) and often postillion (q.v.) driven; developed in parallel with the Britzska (q.v.).

Dormeuse Chariot *see* DORMEUSE

dorsal (1) Relating to or situated near or on the back. (2) Situated away from or directed away from the axis.

dorsal deviation of the carpal joints *see* FORWARD DEVIATION OF THE CARPAL JOINTS

dorsal displacement of the soft palate *see* CHOKING UP

dorsal stripe Also known as list, ray, eel stripe, donkey stripe, or stripe; a black, brown, red, or gold primitive mark (q.v.) running from the withers, down the middle of the back, into the tail; can occur on any coat color.

D'orsay Also known as Coupé Dorsay; a light, horse-drawn carriage of the Brougham (q.v.) type having a high-slung body set on curved springs attached to the front and back of the frame.

dos-à-dos A French term; back-to-back passenger seating in a horse-drawn carriage.

dosage Also known as dosage system; a racing term; a system that identifies a horse's athletic ability patterns based on a list of prepotent sires; each of the sires is placed into one of five categories: brilliant, intermediate, classic, solid, and professional, which quantify speed and stamina; each generation of sires is worth 16 points.

dosage index Also known by the acronym DI; a racing term; a mathematical reduction of the dosage profile (q.v.) to a number reflecting a horse's potential for speed and stamina; the higher the number, the more likely a horse is suited to sprinting; the average DI is approximately 40.

dosage profile A list of dosage points given prepotent sires in each of five categories: brilliant, intermediate, classic, solid, and professional; used to develop the dosage index (q.v.).

dosage system *see* DOSAGE

double (1) Also known as double fence, doubles, or double combination; a jumping obstacle consisting of two consecutive elements (q.v.) with one or two non-jumping strides between them; in competition, numbered and judged as a single obstacle, the two elements being designated as A and B. (2) Also known as double bank; a hunting term; usually a bank, but sometimes another natural obstacle, with a ditch on both the take-off and landing sides (3) Also known as "double the horn"; a hunting term; a series of short, quick, staccato notes blown on a hunting horn (q.v.) indicating that a fox has been found or crossed a ride. (4) Also known as doubles betting; a racing term; said of a bettor (q.v.) who selects two horses to win in two different races; if the first horse wins, the winnings and the original stake are re-invested on the second horse; both horses must win for the bettor to collect. (5) *see* DAILY DOUBLE

Double One of three types of Basque (q.v.) pony, a semi-wild, exceptionally hardy pony indigenous to the Basque region of France standing 12.2 to 14.2 hands.

double back (1) Said of the horse's back (q.v.) when the spine is arched and higher than the muscles on either side. (2) Also known as runs his foil; a hunting term; said of a fox (q.v.) that runs back along its own line to confuse the hounds (q.v.).

double bank *see* DOUBLE NO. 2

double bridle Also known as full bridle, show bridle, or Weymouth bridle; the most sophisticated of bridles; a bridle (q.v.) equipped with both curb (q.v.) and bridoon (q.v.) bits attached to two sets of cheekpieces and two sets of reins; the bridoon, fitted in the mouth above the curb, acts to raise the head by applying pressure on the corners of the lips; the curb acts on a number of points in the mouth and on the head to lower the latter and retract the nose, the degree of pressure imposed being governed by cheek length above and below the mouthpiece; the longer the cheek above the mouthpiece, the greater the poll pressure (which induces downward action); the longer the cheek, the greater the overall leverage achieved; poll pressure is transmitted by the forward movement of the curb eye, through the bridle cheek and thus to the headpiece; this is achieved when the curb rests at an angle of about 45 degrees in the mouth and thus causes the bit eye to move forward and downward; mouth pressure depends on the shape of the mouthpiece; may be either slide-cheek or fixed cheek, the former being more severe as it yields about an extra ½ inch (1.27 cm) of leverage when the bit is put into play; compulsory in advanced and FEI (q.v.) dressage tests; originated sometime in the 1780s or 1790s.

double combination *see* DOUBLE NO. 1

double cryptorchid Any horse with improper, bilateral testicular descent; a rig (q.v.); generally an inherited genetic feature classified as a partial lethal (q.v.).

Double Dogcart *see* DOGCART PHAETON

double fence *see* DOUBLE NO. 1

double gaited Said of a horse who can either trot or pace with good speed.

double handful A racing term; a double wrap of the reins around the jockey's hands; used to control the pull of horse.

double harness A driving term; harness for a pair of horses.

double horse A motion picture term; any horse(s) used to replace the principal horse (q.v.) in action shots or when performing stunts or tricks; only used if the principal horse (q.v.) cannot perform the stunt or if it is too dangerous for him to perform.

Double Klepper *see* TORIC

double muscling Said of a horse having pronounced muscling over the croup; common in heavy-horse breeds.

double note A fox hunting term; a sharp staccato note blown on the horn to indicate the beginning of the hunt.

double of oxers *see* DOUBLE OXER

double oxer Also known as double of oxers (Brit); a jumping obstacle consisting of two oxers (q.v.) positioned with one or two strides between them typically constructed with an ascending aspect and can, therefore, only be sensibly jumped from one side; basically an in-and-out (q.v.).

double-ring snaffle *see* WILSON SNAFFLE

doubles *see* DOUBLE NO. 1

doubles betting *see* DOUBLE NO. 4

double the horn *see* DOUBLE NO. 3

double thong A driving term; said of the thong (q.v.) of a four-horse whip when caught on the crop.

double volte A dressage term used at the Spanish Riding School (q.v.); a 6-meter circle ridden twice.

douga Also spelled duga; an arched, wooden yoke used on Russian carriages, troikas, and sleighs fixed to the shafts and passed high over the horses' necks; used to separate the shafts and, in some cases, acts as a bearing rein; frequently adorned with bells.

doughnut *see* SAUSAGE BOOT

doughnut boots *see* SAUSAGE BOOT

dourine A venereal disease of horses transmitted during coitus; recognized on the Mediterranean coast of Africa, southern Africa, the Middle East, and South America; symptoms include swelling of the external genitalia and urethral discharge in the stallion and vaginal discharge in the mare, progressive emancipation, and mortality in 50 to 70 percent of the cases if left untreated.

down in front Said of a horse whose conformation is such that his forehand is, when viewed horizontally, lower than the hindquarters.

Downs *see* EPSOM DOWNS

down wind To be in a position where the wind blows from an object or place towards you carrying a scent or sound; when downwind from your quarry (q.v.), it cannot smell you.

dq *see* DISQUALIFIED

D-ring snaffle *see* DEE-RING SNAFFLE

draft (1) A hunting term; to cull a hound from the pack or to acquire one from another pack. (2) A hunting term; hounds not needed by the Hunt (q.v.) which are sold or given away. (3) *see* DRAFT HORSE. (4) A hunting term; to select the hounds for a particular day of hunting. (5) Also spelled draught (Brit); the act of pulling or drawing loads as by horses. (6) Also spelled draught (Brit); a team of horses for pulling a load.

Draft Breton *see* DRAUGHT BRETON

draft horse Also known as draft and spelled draught horse; any medium- or heavy-breed horse used to pull a vehicle.

drafted hound A hunting term; said of a hound removed from the pack or on loan from another Hunt (q.v.).

draft pack A hunting term; any pack of

hounds purchased from another Hunt (q.v.), the hounds having been culled from the original pack.

drafty Having the heavy characteristics of a draft horse (q.v.).

drag (1) A hunting term; the line taken by a fox to his earth. (2) A hunting term; a trail of scent, frequently artificial, left by dragging on horseback or on foot an object soaked in any of a number of types of strong-smelling liquid similar to the scent of a fox; generally laid between one and three hours before a drag hunt (q.v.); must be of sufficient length to require at least one check (q.v.). (3) An American term; a horse who regularly lags behind the others. (4) Any awkward heavy horse-drawn vehicle.

Drag Also known as Park Coach, Private Drag, Private Coach, or Four-in-Hand Coach; a four-wheeled, horse-drawn vehicle similar to, but more elegant than, the Road Coach (q.v.); used for private or park driving, sporting purposes, and as a mobile grandstand at the races, polo matches, and other sporting events; generally painted with family colors and driven by amateurs; the box seat held the coachman and one passenger to his left; had two roof seats built to carry four passengers and a rumble seat for two grooms; the interior compartment was rarely used, although trimmed with cloth, leather, or whipcord (q.v.); drawn by four horses and either postillion (q.v.) or coachman (q.v.) driven.

dragging the goat *see* BUZKASHI

drag horse (1) A hunting term; the horse used by the dragman (q.v.) when laying the artificial scent (q.v.) used in a drag hunt (q.v.). (2) A driving term; a horse used in a team to pull a Drag (q.v.); should match other horses used in the team in both stride and color without flashy white markings; the wheelers can be slightly taller than the leaders.

drag hound A hunting term; a hound (q.v.) trained to follow drag (q.v.) scent.

drag hunt A hunting term; a hunt (q.v.) conducted on horseback in which the hounds follow an artificial scent (q.v.) or trail laid by dragging a bag of suitable scented material across the ground to closely simulate the run of a wild fox; common in areas where foxes are scarce; is generally faster than a live hunt (q.v.).

dragman A hunting term; one responsible for laying the artificial scent (q.v.) used in a drag hunt (q.v.); may be performed mounted or on foot; lays the scent over a stretch of country (q.v.) in such a way as to simulate the run of a wild fox.

drag prop *see* DRAG STICK

drag shoe Also known as skid, skid pan, slipper, skid-shoe, vehicle skid, or wagon-lock; a driving term; a tire-shaped iron shoe or plate placed under each wheel of a heavily-laden, horse-drawn vehicle before descending a steep hill; attached to the vehicle by means of a skid chain (q.v.) whether in use or not and used as a brake.

drag shoe chain A link chain by which the drag shoe (q.v.) is attached to a horse-drawn vehicle.

dragsman *see* COACHMAN

drag staff *see* DRAG STICK

drag stick Also known as drag prop or drag staff; a round stick or piece of wood about 3 inches (7.5 cm) thick, tipped with a sharp iron spike approximately 4 inches (10 cm) long fitted to the rear axles of most horse-drawn vehicles between the center of the axle and the rear offside wheel; used as a brake to take the weight off the horse and prevent the vehicle from running backwards, when not in use or parked on an incline; when not used may be hung on the rear axle.

Drag Wagon A heavy American horse-drawn vehicle used to haul logs; pulled by a pair or team; had a strong platform constructed on an axle between a pair of wheels; one of the timber was placed on the support, while the other dragged along the ground

Draschia megastoma *see* LARGE-MOUTHED STOMACH WORM

draschiasis *see* CUTANEOUS HABRONEMIASIS

draught (1) *see* DRAFT NO. 5. (2) *see* DRAFT NO. 6

Draught Breton Also known as Fast Heavy Draft Breton, Fast Heavy Draught Breton, Heavy Draught Breton, Draft Breton, Heavy Draft Breton, or previously as Grand Breton; one of three distinct morphological types of Breton (q.v.) believed to have evolved more than 4,000 years ago in Brittany, France; descended from native Brittany stock crossed with Ardennais (q.v.) and Percheron (q.v.) blood in the 19th century; is selectively bred and must pass performance tests in harness to qualify for inclusion in the stud book which it has shared with the Postier Breton (q.v.) since 1909; is slightly smaller and less elegant than the Postier Breton and resembles the Suffolk Punch (q.v.); renowned for its great strength relative to its size; the coat is generally chestnut, but bay, gray, roan, and red roan also occur – black is not a breed color; has a well-proportioned head with a heavy jaw, broad forehead, short ears, and flared nostrils, a short, broad, and muscular neck, short and straight back, broad loins, sloping croup, and short, powerful legs with heavy joints; the tail is generally docked; stands 15.2 to 16.2 hands and weighs 1,540 to 1,980 pounds (699–898 kg); registered foals are branded on the left side of the neck with a cross surmounting a splayed, upturned V.

draught horse *see* DRAFT HORSE

draught reins The primary reins (q.v.) used in pair and team driving controlled by the coachman; attach to the outside of the bit of each horse and buckle to the coupling reins (q.v.) which connect to the inside of the bit of the partner horse.

draw (1) *see* DRAW A COVERT. (2) The horse's position in the working order that determines in which order he will work or compete against other horses, as in "What is your draw?" (3) A hunting term; the sequence in which a huntsman (q.v.) draws his coverts (q.v.) during a day of hunt (q.v.). (4) A driving term; said of a horse(s); to pull a vehicle. (5) *see* COVERT

draw a covert Also known as draw; a hunting term; said of a huntsman (q.v.) and hounds (q.v.) when they thoroughly search a covert (q.v.) for a fox (q.v.).

draw a hound A hunting term; said of a huntsman (q.v.) or whipper-in (q.v.) when he moves the hounds (q.v.) from the kennel lodging rooms to the feeding rooms.

draw blank *see* BLANK NO. 1

draw cattle A cutting term; the ability of a cutting horse to mesmerize a cow without threatening or frightening it, and to make it approach him.

draw off *see* DRAW A HOUND

draw reins Two leather or synthetic straps or ropes attached to the girth, saddle, or harness used as a training aid to encourage the horse to lower and/or set his head; run through the bit rings to the hands of the rider or driver.

draw yard A hunting term; the yard or other area where the hounds are collected and retained prior to being drawn off by the huntsman (q.v.) to their respective kennels.

dray To convey by means of a dray.

Dray (1) Also known as Transfer Dray in North America or Flat in Scotland and northern England; a heavy, low, strong, four-wheeled, horse-drawn freight vehicle first introduced during the 17th century; lacked fixed sides and, generally, springs; some had a raised seat for the driver while others were controlled from the ground; used primarily as a brewery delivery vehicle; usually drawn by a team of draft horses (q.v.). (2) A tall, Australian, two-wheeled, heavy-duty, horse-drawn cart used on farms for general purposes.

dray horse Any heavy-breed horse used to pull a Dray (q.v.)

Dr. Bristol *see* DR. BRISTOL BIT

Dr. Bristol bit Also known as trotting man's bit or Dr. Bristol; a snaffle bit (q.v.) with a double-jointed mouthpiece; the jointed arms are connected by a small, flat, angled plate or flat link; each end of the mouthpiece is attached to a ring to which the reins are connected; is more severe than a French snaffle (q.v.).

drench (1) Any medicine suspended in water, thin gruel, or oil and administered as a drink to a horse. (2) To administer liquid medicine to a horse through his mouth.

dress (1) A 16th-century term still in use today; to place or set in position, put into alignment, or prepare according to certain principles; from the French *dresser* (q.v.). (2) To apply bandages or medications. (3) Also known as finish; a farrier's term; when shoeing, to clean and remove the outer hoof coating using complete strokes of a rasp.

dressage (1) Also known as ballet on horseback; a term popular after the turn of the 19th century; the harmonious development of the physique and ability of the horse to make him calm, supple, confident, attentive, and keen, thus achieving perfect understanding with his rider; loosely, any form of ring or school riding; derived from the French dresser (q.v.), to place or put into position; an Olympic sport since 1912. (2) One of three phases of a three-day event; conducted on the first day of competition; a set program consisting of about 20 different movements of medium difficulty performed at the walk, trot, and canter in a dressage arena (q.v.); marks are awarded by a panel of three judges who assess accuracy and fluency of the performance, balance, rhythm, impulsion, and suppleness in the horse as well as the rider's seat and aid application.

dressage arena The flat, smooth, rectangular area in which dressage tests (q.v.) or maneuvers are performed; in international competitions, measures 60 by 20 meters (65.6 × 21.8 yd), while a smaller arena, used in lesser competitions, measures 40 by 20 meters (43.7 × 21.8 yd); surface types include grass, sand, stone chips, woodchips, plastic, and a variety of composites.

dressage competition Any organized event in which riders and horses perform dressage tests (q.v.); open to professional or amateur riders, or both, on horses and ponies of all different breeds, subject to rule requirements concerning age and height; each horse and rider performs a test individually in front of one to five judges; each judge scores the test movement-by-movement, on a scale of zero to ten; the horse/rider with the highest percentage score places first in the class.

dressage competition, dress code The approved attire for a dressage rider in competition, as based on tradition: white or light-colored breeches, tall, black boots, white shirt with choker, stocktie (q.v.) or necktie, dark blue or black jacket, and a black velvet hunt cap (q.v.), derby, or top hat (q.v.); top hat and dark tailcoat is only worn for tests above Fourth Level (q.v.).

dressage competition, tack The type of equipment used on a horse competing in a dressage competition; may include an English saddle (q.v.), plain snaffle bit (q.v.), or a double bridle (q.v.) (optional at fourth and Fifth Levels and mandatory at FEI levels; restraining equipment such as martingales (q.v.), tie-downs (q.v.), draw reins (q.v.), etc. are forbidden.

dressage de academique A French term; advanced dressage work performed in the manège (q.v.) that leads to the haute école (q.v.).

dressage de manège A French term; general schooling of the horse in the ring (q.v.) or manège (q.v.).

dressage des obstacles A French term; schooling the horse over fences.

dressage level A degree which reflects the usual progression of a horse's training established for the purpose of competition; as a horse becomes stronger and more flexible, the performance requirements at each level become gradually more difficult; there are between two and four tests at each level; in competition, a rider usually rides a test one level below the horse's current training stage; consist of: Training Level (q.v.), First Level (q.v.), Second Level (q.v.), Third Level (q.v.), Fourth Level (q.v.), Fifth Level (q.v.), and the FEI Levels (q.v.): Prix St. Georges (q.v.), Intermediare I, Intermediare II, and Grand Prix (q.v.); in Australia and Britain consist of: Preliminary Level (q.v.), Novice Level (q.v.), Elementary Level (q.v.), Medium Level (q.v.), Advanced Level (q.v.), and FEI Levels.

dressage markers Plastic, metal, or wooden, free-standing markers upon which the alphabetical letters used to mark specific points around the perimeter of a dressage arena are printed; the rider performs movements defined by these markers; in the small arena, eight markers A, K, E, H, C, M, B, and F are used clockwise around the edge of the arena starting with A at the center line and D, X, and G mark the center line; in the large arena, four additional markers, R, S, V, and P are used around the perimeter.

dressage test A series of dressage movements performed at specific locations and in a defined order within the dressage arena (q.v.) during competitions within a specified amount of time; are of varying standards and consist of progressively more difficult movements at each level of performance; test scores are based on the total points attained, with each individual movement scored on a basis of 0 (failure to perform) to 10 (excellent).

dressage whip A whip (q.v.) used by dressage riders to control, correct, or punish a horse; consists of a lacquered wood, thread, fiberglass, bone, plastic, metal, or leather shaft attached to leather hand grip generally made of leather; in competition, measures 32 inches (81 cm) long while a 30 to 42 inch (76–107 cm) whip is commonly used for schooling.

dressed Said of a horse trained to carry out full collection with his hocks well engaged under him, poll raised, and head carried in the vertical.

dresser A French term; to prepare, train, or school a horse; to put into place.

dresseur A French term; an expert horseman or horsemaster whose living is dependent upon the Classical Art of riding.

dressing (1) The act of one who, or that which, dresses. (2) That with which something is dressed, as bandages for a wound.

dress leather An animal hide tanned into leather, smoothed and leveled, softened with oil, and, frequently, dyed.

drift (1) A cutting term; said of a horse who slowly loses his position relative to the herd (q.v.) of cattle. (2) A change from one pace to another in which there is no distinct difference between the speed or pace, e.g. canter (q.v.) to trot (q.v.).

D-ring *see* DEE-RING

D-ring snaffle *see* DEE-RING SNAFFLE

drinker of the wind *see* ARAB

drive (1) Said of the rider; to push a ridden horse forward into the bit using the influence of the seat and back. (2) To force or push a herd of cattle forward in a controlled and calm manner, generally from a mounted position. (3) A racing term; all-out exertion of the horse when tired, such as on the homestretch (q.v.). (4) A hunting term; the urge of the hounds (q.v.) to follow quickly the line of a fox (q.v.) so as not to lose the scent. (5) *see* LONG LINE. (6) Also known as tool; a coaching term; to operate a horse-drawn Wagon.

driver (1) A driving term; one who directs the speed and movements of the horse(s) from a vehicle hitched to the horse(s). (2) A driving term; one with less talent than a coachman (q.v.).

driving (1) A racing term; said of a horse running under extreme pressure from the jockey. (2) Said of one who maneuvers a horse-drawn vehicle.

driving aids Any combination of natural and/or artificial aids (q.v.) used by the rider or ground trainer to move the horse forward into the bit.

driving blinkers Also known as harness blinkers; a type of blinkers (q.v.); typically made from leather and of four shapes: D, round, hatchet, and square, often ornamented on the outside.

driving hammer Also known as shoeing hammer; a farrier's tool consisting of a solid, metal head set crosswise on a handle used to drive horseshoe (q.v.) nails and to turn over or wring off the tips of the nails after they have been driven into the hoof wall when attaching a horseshoe.

driving lines *see* LONG LINES

driving seat (1) *see* DICKEY. (2) A coaching term; the seat upon which the coachman sits and from where he drives the horse(s).

driving whip *see* COACHING CROP

driving with a full hand A driving term; a method of holding two sets of reins in one hand; each rein passes between different fingers; occasionally used in tandem driving.

Droischa *see* DROSKY

Droitska *see* DROITZSCHKA

Droitzschka Also known as Russian Droschki and in England as the English Droitzschka (q.v.) and spelled Droitska; a horse-drawn German pleasure or passenger vehicle adapted from the Drosky (q.v.); a four-passenger vehicle which carried two passengers seated on a crosswise seat positioned just a few inches above the rear axle, and two seated outside on an enlarged box seat shared with the driver; had a low center of gravity, a half-hood, was hung on sideways elliptical or semi-elliptical springs, and was drawn by either one or two horses.

drooping quarters The horse's quarters (q.v.) when sloped sharply downward and lack roundness.

drop (1) Also known as face drop, face piece, forehead piece, or forehead drop; a driving term; the decorative part of the harness which lies on the horse's forehead; generally oval shaped with a pointed tip and made of patent leather emblazoned with the owner's crest or monogram; worn in show and drag harnesses. (2) *see* FOAL NO. 2. (3) Said of a male horse; to relax the genital muscles and allow the penis to fall from the sheath (q.v.). (4) *see* DROP FENCE

drop a foal *see* FOAL NO. 2

drop backed *see* SWAY-BACKED

drop down (1) A racing term; said of a horse running against lower class horses than he had previously been competed against. (2) *see* DROP ON A COW

drop fence A jumping obstacle in which the landing side of the fence is lower than the take-off side.

drop noseband Also known as dropped noseband; a noseband (q.v.) in which the front nosepiece passes across the bottom of the nasal bone and the rear nosepiece passes below the bit, fastening in the chin groove (q.v.); prevents the horse from opening his mouth or shifting his jaws to escape the action of the bit; frequently used in conjunction with a snaffle bit; originated in the German cavalry.

drop on a cow Also known as drop down; a cutting horse term; said of a horse who lowers or drops down low onto the extended forehand prior to and when working a cow; the horse appears to crouch, its haunches raised significantly higher than the forehand.

drop-out Quarter Horse *see* CROP-OUT

dropped back *see* SWAY BACK

dropped crease shoe *see* FEATHER-EDGED SHOE

dropped elbow *see* RADIAL PARALYSIS

dropped fox *see* BAG FOX

dropped noseband *see* DROP NOSEBAND

dropped sole Also known as pumiced foot or prolapsed sole; a condition of the hoof in which the sole dropped to, or beyond, the level of the bearing surface of the hoof wall; the sole is flat and has no concavity; in extreme cases it may be convex; a sequel to chronic laminitis (q.v.) characterized by heavy rings in the hoof wall.

dropped spur *see* PRINCE OF WALES SPUR

droppings *see* FECES

drop the stirrups Also known as quit the stirrups (Brit); said of the rider; to remove one's feet from the stirrup irons (q.v.) and continue riding without them to develop balance, a secure leg position, and improved seat; the stirrups may be left hanging or crossed over the horse's withers.

Droschki *see* DROSKY

Droshky *see* DROSKY

Drosky Also known as Droischa or Russian Cab and spelled Droshky and Droschki; a four-wheeled, horse-drawn passenger carriage; originally seated two passengers on an upholstered cross-plank, which was eventually changed to a well-padded bench near road level protected by a half-hood; drawn by three horses abreast, decorated with silver bells; the center horse, positioned between shafts and under a wooden arch, did most of the pulling at a trot while the outer horses cantered with outward-turned heads for show.

drover One who drives herds of cattle or sheep to market on horseback (in the United Kingdom on foot); most common in the period prior to the advent of railroads and improved highways.

drug test Also known as dope test; the use of blood, urine, and saliva tests to determine whether illegal substances were administered to a horse to alter performance or mask injury.

dry lot To isolate or confine a horse in a corral or other enclosed area denuded of vegetation and to hand-feed a regulated amount so as to control weight or treat a medical condition.

dry matter The portion of feed not made up of water.

dry single A jumping obstacle; a constructed mound of dirt with a platform or flat top.

dry work A cutting term; to train, work, or show a cutting horse without using cattle, the emphasis being on reining; the opposite of wet work (q.v.).

dual forecast *see* EXACTA BOX

dub (1) Also known as dump (Brit.); to fit the hoof (q.v.) to the horseshoe (q.v.) instead of the shoe to the hoof; accomplished by rasping down the outside hoof wall. (2) Also known as dump; to dress back the toe of the hoof to treat such conditions as founder (q.v.), toe flare, etc.

Dubai World Cup The world's richest horse race; a 1¼ mile (2 km) race run at Dubai's (United Arab Emirates) al Sheba Racecourse.

dubbed Also known as dumped, dumped toe, dubbed toe, dubbed foot, or bull nose foot; said of the hoof when the dorsal (q.v.) surface has been ground off due to excessive rasping to fit the foot to a horseshoe, as a result of lameness which may cause the horse to drag its foot, or to treat such conditions as founder.

dubbed foot *see* DUBBED

dubbed toe *see* DUBBED

Duc A horse-drawn formal park or show vehicle lacking boot (q.v.) or luggage space; a cross between a Pony Phaeton and a Victoria (q.v.); driven by the sole occupant, but frequently accompanied by a gentleman outrider (q.v.) or liveried groom; usually hung on sideways elliptical springs, although a few early types were mounted on cee-springs.

Duckett's dot An imaginary point about ⅜ inch (10 mm) behind the apex of the frog at the center of the toe arc on a properly trimmed hoof.

dude Also known as greenhorn or tenderfoot; an American term; one inexperienced in the rigors of ranching, a person from the city, or an Easterner who spends a vacation on a ranch; a stranger.

dude ranch A ranch, generally cattle, in the United States which offers accommodations and riding facilities to dudes (q.v.).

duga *see* DOUGA

Duke of Newcastle *see* CAVENDISH, WILLIAM, DUKE OF NEWCASTLE

Du Lee *see* LEGEND OF THE EIGHT HORSES

Dulmen A primitive pony breed originating in the Merfelder Bruch region of North Reine Westphalia; recorded as early as 1316; currently numbers about 100 animals; the stallions of similar breeds are being reintroduced to prevent extinction.

dumb jockey A bitting device used to train young horses to elevate the front end; consists of a wooden pole attached perpendicularly to a surcingle (q.v.) supported by a line to a tail crupper (q.v.); the wooden pole is fitted with rings through which the reins pass to the bit and back to the sides of the surcingle; pressure on the backbone causes hollowing of the back and the reins hold the head up and in a collected position; frequently used in the training of Saddlebreds (q.v.).

dumb jockeying Said of the horse; hollowing of the back and carrying the weight on the haunches, pushing out the chest, and elevating the front end.

dumb rabies *see* PARALYTIC RABIES

dummy *see* ROPING DUMMY

dummy calf *see* ROPING DUMMY

dummy foal *see* BARKER

dump (1) Said of a horse who unseats his rider. (2) *see* DUB NOS. 1 AND 2

Dump Cart *see* TIP CART

dumped (1) Said of a rider unseated by action of the horse. (2) *see* DUBBED

dumped toe *see* DUBBED

dumping To shorten the toe of the hoof by rasping (q.v.).

dumpling A carriage term; a large and comfortable box cushion found on some horse-drawn coaches (q.v.).

dun Also known as bayo or gateado; refers to coat color; a generic term; all lighter-colored horses which may or may not have black points (q.v.); more specifically, yellow horses with black points which include all shades of yellow mixed with other colors to create variations from pale, creamy gold, to a dirty tan; commonly have amber (hazel) eyes, although some have gray eyes; horses with non-black points include red and yellow duns; variations include dusty dun (q.v.), grullo (q.v.), claybank (q.v.), coyote dun (q.v.), golden dun (q.v.), silver dun (q.v.), zebra dun (q.v.), lilac dun (q.v.), red dun (q.v.), and yellow dun (q.v.).

dun-factor horse Any horse displaying a dun (q.v.) coat and, frequently, primitive marks (q.v.).

Duncan gag Also known as Duncombe gag or Nelson gag; a gag bit (q.v.) consisting of a plain or twisted gag mouth with small upward cheeks (q.v.) fitted with two holes through which the gag reins (q.v.) pass.

Duncombe gag *see* DUNCAN GAG

dung *see* FECES

dung eating *see* FECES EATING

Duobus *see* BOULNOIS CAB

Duquesa A horse-drawn carriage of the Victoria (q.v.) type; usually drawn by a pair of horses in pole gear (q.v.), was protected by a half hood, seated two in the box seat, and frequently had a rearward or rumble seat for carriage servants; used in Spanish cities as a ladies' carriage; the Spanish word for duchess.

durchlassigkeit *see* THOROUGHNESS

dusty buckskin *see* DUSTY DUN

dusty dun Also known as dusty buckskin; refers to coat color; a type of dun (q.v.) or zebra dun (q.v.) with a brownish cast to the yellow coat, black points (q.v.), and a head of a similar color to the body; the color appears similar to olive grullo without the dark head.

Dutch A racing term; to take advantage of booking percentages by eliminating heavily bet noncontenders, and betting on other horses in exact amounts necessary to yield profit regardless of which horse wins.

Dutch collar *see* BREAST COLLAR

Dutch Draught Also known as Dutch Horse; a Dutch horse breed developed around 1914 to work sand and clay agricultural lands; derived from New Zealand-type mares crossed with Brabant (q.v.) stallions and later with Belgian Ardennes (q.v.); is massively built and heavy-boned, stands up to 16.3 hands, has strong, muscular, well-feathered legs with broad joints, and solid hooves; is quite active, has a kind disposition, and great stamina; usually chestnut, bay, or gray; used for draft and farm work.

Dutch Horse *see* DUTCH DRAUGHT

Dutchman's team To hitch the larger horse of a two-horse team on the near side (q.v.), a position customarily held by the smaller horse.

Dutch triple Also known as gans; a four-beat gait similar to the rack (q.v.).

Dutch Warmblood A Dutch horse breed developed by crossing the Gelderland (q.v.) and Groningen (q.v.) with English Thoroughbred (q.v.) and other French and German warmbloods; is quiet and willing, stands about 16.2 hands, has a brown, black, chestnut, or gray coat, supple and flowing action, and is used for light draft, carriage, and riding, particularly jumping and dressage; the Stud Book was established in 1958.

dutfin Any bridle used on a farm horse; (sl).

DVM The acronym for Doctor of Veterinary Medicine; a veterinarian (q.v.).

DWCF *see* DIPLOMA OF THE WORSHIPFUL COMPANY OF FARRIERS

dwell (1) A racing term; said of a horse slow to break from the gate. (2) Also known as dwelling; a hunting term; said of a hound who, instead of pressing forward on the line of a fox (q.v.), runs to the rear of the pack and gives tongue (q.v.).

dwelling (1) A pause or suspension in the movement of the horse's foot whereby the stride appears to be completed before the foot reaches the ground; common in trick horses. (2) *see* DWELL NO. 2

dynamic exercises A vaulting term; compulsory exercises performed by a vaulter (q.v.) in competition; consist of the mill (q.v.), flank (q.v.), scissors (q.v.), and all freestyle movements not required to be held for a specific number of strides; require the vaulter, using the rhythm of the horse, to change position to face backwards and sideways.

dysplasia of the growth plate *see* PHYSITIS

Dystrophia ungulae *see* SEEDY TOE

Dzhabe Also spelled Dzhabye; one of two types of Kazakh (q.v.), an ancient pony breed originating in Kazakhstan; thought to have descended from the Asiatic Wild Horse (q.v.) refined by significant infusions of Don (q.v.) blood; stands 12.1 to 13.1 hands, generally has a bay or liver chestnut coat, although brown, bay, and mouse dun also occur, a coarse head, and thick neck; is frugal and possessed of great stamina and legendary hardiness; very resistant to both cold and fatigue; used for riding.

Dziggetai A species of wild ass (q.v.) inhabiting the elevated steppes of the Tartary, a region of eastern Asia controlled by the Tartars in the 13th and 14th centuries.

E

each way A racing term; two bets placed together, a win bet and a place bet, on any race with five or more runners; if you back a horse each way, it does not need to win for you to collect money; depending on the number of runners in a race and the type of race, the horse may come in second, third, or fourth for you to collect; if the horse wins, you basically win twice: for the win and for the place.

ear down A method of restraining a horse through twisting or biting the ear.

ear fistula *see* DENTIGEROUS CYST

Earl of Derby, Edward, 17th (1865–1948) One of the greatest patrons of the British racing turf, and a successful owner and breeder of race horses having won 20 classics (q.v.); founded and named the Epsom Derby (q.v.).

early foot A racing term; said of a horse who exhibits good speed at the beginning of a race.

early to trot A dressage term; premature transition to the trot before a marker (q.v.); may result from the horse's anticipation of a change of pace or gait before receiving the rider's aid to do so.

early to walk A dressage term; premature transition to the walk before a marker (q.v.); may result from the horse anticipating a change of pace or gait before receiving the rider's aid.

ear mange Chorioptic mange (q.v.) occurring in or around the ears.

ear mark To cut a notch in a horse's ear to identify him when turned out to graze on common land.

earmuff solid cloth covering placed over the horse's ears to limit or eliminate distracting sounds.

earn a diploma *see* BREAK MAIDEN

earn your tops A hunting term; said of a hunter who has ridden with a Hunt (q.v.) for sufficiently long to earn the right to wear a top boot (q.v.) (men earn cordovan or brown tops while women earn black patent leather); a status symbol; the amount of time one must ride with a specific Hunt to qualify varies between Hunts.

ear stripping To stroke the ear of the cold or tired horse, from the base to the tip, to induce circulation and provide comfort.

earth *see* FOX DEN

Earth Cart A solidly built horse-drawn vehicle; had a iron-reinforced oak frame and loose, removable side boards; used to haul builder's materials.

earth stomping *see* DIVOT STOMPING

earthstopper A hunting term; one employed to block the entrance to the fox's earth (q.v.) the night preceding the day of a hunt when a fox is out and to prevent his return.

earth stopping Also known as stopping earth; a hunting term; to block the earth (q.v.) of a fox the night preceding the day of a hunt to prevent its return; generally performed by the terrier man; commonly conducted in Great Britain, but not in the United States, to control fox populations.

ease *see* EASE UP

ease up Also known as ease; to gradually reduce the speed of the horse.

easily A racing term; said of a horse; to run or win without opposition or urging by the jockey.

East Bulgarian A Bulgarian warmblood developed during the late 19th century by crossing Thoroughbred (q.v.), English Half-bred (q.v.), Arab (q.v.), and Anglo-Arab (q.v.) horses; one of three primary horse breeds indigenous to Bulgaria; is elegant, well-built, stands 15 to 16 hands, has a chestnut or black coat, small head, straight profile, deep girth and long, straight back; is energetic, hardy, fast, and versatile; used for riding, agriculture, and competitive sports from dressage to cross-country.

Eastern equine encephalomyelitis Also known by the acronym EEE; one of three alphaviruses associated with equine encephalitis (q.v.); occurs in the eastern United States and Canada; wild birds serve as the principal reservoirs of the virus; epidemics tend to occur in mid- to late summer; clinical signs occur about 5 days after infection and most deaths occur 2 to 3 days later; signs include fever, impaired vision, irregular gait, wandering, reduced reflexes, circling, incoordination, yawning, teeth grinding, drowsiness, pendulous lower lip, inability to swallow, photophobia, head-pressing, inability to rise, paralysis, occasional convulsions, and death; those with mild cases recover within a few weeks, but may suffer from residual brain damage; mortality is 50 to 90 percent.

Eastern horse That group of horses consisting of the Arab (q.v.), Barb (q.v.), Turk (q.v.), and Syrian breeds.

East Friesian Also spelled East Frisian; a German warmblood descended from Friesian (q.v.) stock crossed with Spanish, Neapolitan (q.v.), Cleveland Bay (q.v.), Anglo-Arab (q.v.), Norman (q.v.), Thoroughbred (q.v.), Oldenburg (q.v.), and, after 1940, Arab (q.v.) blood from stallions standing at the Marbach and Balbolna studs in Hungary; recent introduction of Hanoverian (q.v.) blood has produced an all-round sporting horse; developed in parallel to the Oldenburg through the 1940s; stands 15.2 to 16.1 hands, has a brown, bay, black, gray, or chestnut coat, a well-proportioned head, prominent features, a long and straight back, and strong legs with broad joints; used for riding and light draft.

East Frisian *see* EAST FRIESIAN

East Prussian Horse *see* TRAKEHNER

easy boot A tough, lightweight, urethane, hoof-shaped boot worn on a bare (q.v.) or shod hoof to provide protection and traction; covers the hoof from the ground-side surface to the coronet (q.v.) and is held in place by means of levered cables.

easy gait Any smooth, lateral gait such as the rack (q.v.), running walk (q.v.), fox trot (q.v.), or stepping pace.

easy keeper Also known as a good keeper; said of a horse who is not prone to digestive problems and easily maintains his weight and healthy appearance from an average or less than average ration.

écart A racing term; the degree of deviation from the standard number of dosage strains; an expression used in the Vuillier Dosage System.

ECG *see* ELECTROCARDIOGRAM

echini Also known as hedgehog; a spiked roller (q.v.) used on the mouthpiece of a Grecian bit.

echocardiography The use of ultrasound to evaluate the heart muscle to diagnose congestive heart failure (q.v.).

Eclipse One of history's greatest Thoroughbred (q.v.) sires; foaled in England in 1764; was never beaten in a race and sired 335 champion horses; his blood appears in approximately 90 percent of all Thoroughbred pedigrees.

Eclipse Award A racing term; recognition given in the United States since 1971 to the North American divisional racing champions as selected by vote of the Daily Racing Forum (q.v.), Thoroughbred Racing Associations, and the National Turf Writers Association.

Eclipse Stakes A racing term; a 1¼ mile (2 km) race held on a Saturday every July at Sandown Park, England.

Ecole de Cavalerie A book published in 1733 by François Robichon de la Guérinière (q.v.) in which he describes his training methods including suppling exercises such as the shoulder-in (q.v.), which he invented.

écuyer A French term most commonly used during the 16th and 17th centuries; historically, a recognized, often noble born, master of equitation who served at court; royal blood is no longer a requisite of title; capitalized when used in a title.

Edelweiss Pony *see* HAFLINGER

edema Also spelled oedema; swelling due to excessive accumulation of fluid in connective tissue or a serous cavity.

edematous Relating to a condition of edema (q.v.).

edge splint One of four varieties of splints (q.v.); affects the back rim of the cannon bone; generally due to a tear in the tissues linking the splint and the accessory carpal bone at the back of the knee; feels gravelly along the backside of the splint bone; usually causes lameness after high-speed work.

EDM *see* EQUINE DEGENERATIVE MYELOENCEPHALOPATHY

educating *see* SCHOOL NO. 2

Edward, 17th Earl of Derby *see* EARL OF DERBY, EDWARD THE 17th

Edwin Landseer *see* LANDSEER, SIR EDWIN

EEE *see* EASTERN EQUINE ENCEPHALOMYELITIS

eel stripe *see* DORSAL STRIPE

EFA *see* EQUESTRIAN FEDERATION OF AUSTRALIA

EGE *see* EQUINE GRANULOCYTIC EHRLICHIOSIS

egg-bar shoe A bar shoe (q.v.); a therapeutic horseshoe in which the heels or shoe branches are joined to form an arch bar under the heels; yields more heel support than a conventional shoe and prevents possible interference with the opposing limb; used on horses with low, sloping heels, or those suffering from founder (q.v.) or navicular disease (q.v.); so called because the shoe is egg shaped.

eggbutt A barrel-shaped joint hinge used to join the bit (q.v.) mouthpiece (q.v.) to the cheek (q.v.).

eggbutt snaffle The most commonly used single-jointed snaffle bit (q.v.); has slightly tapered arms that widen from the joint to the cheekpieces where they attach to barrel shaped, fixed rings; has less movement than a loose-ring bit snaffle (q.v.).

egg-link pelham A pelham bit (q.v.) having a double-jointed mouthpiece with an oval, or egg-shaped, center link.

eglentine High-quality stainless steel used in the manufacture of stirrup irons (q.v.), bits (q.v.), spurs (q.v.), and some bridles (q.v.).

EHRF *see* EQUINE HEALTH RESEARCH FUND

EHV 1 *see* EQUINE HERPESVIRUS 1

EHV 2 *see* EQUINE HERPESVIRUS 2

EHV 3 *see* EQUINE HERPESVIRUS 3

EI *see* EPITHELIOGENESIS

EIA *see* EQUINE INFECTIOUS ANEMIA

EIAV *see* EQUINE INFECTIOUS ANEMIA VIRUS

eighth *see* FURLONG

8th Duke of Beaufort *see* BEAUFORT, 8TH DUKE OF

eight-horse hitch A driving term; a heavy horse hitch consisting of eight horses; the wheelers (q.v.) are separated by the wagon pole, the body and swing teams are separated by a swing pole, and the leaders have no pole between them; driven with eight reins, four held in each hand; each rein corresponds to one horse.

eighth pole A racing term; a colored post located on the inside rail (q.v.) of a racetrack (q.v.) exactly one furlong (q.v.) from the finish.

eighths A driving term; the fourth pair of mules from the front of the wagon in a 20-mule team.

eight nail A farrier's term; to fasten a horseshoe (q.v.) to the hoof using 8 nails, 4 per side.

eild A Scottish term; a barren mare (q.v.).

Einsiedler Also known as Swiss Halfbred or Swiss Anglo-Norman; a Swiss horse breed developed around 1064; throughout the 20th century French blood was systematically introduced and, in the 1960s, Anglo-Norman; is docile, stands

15.2 to 16.2 hands, has a straight back, slightly sloping croup, prominent withers, a slightly convex or straight head, and strong, and well-jointed legs; any solid coat color is acceptable, but chestnut and bay are most common; a good all-round riding and driving horse; the name derived from the stud of its origin, Kloster Einsiedel, and the town of Einsiedel.

EIPH *see* EXERCISE-INDUCED PULMONARY HEMORRHAGE

EKG *see* ELECTROCARDIOGRAM

Ekka *see* EKKA CART

Ekka Cart Also known as Ekka; a two-wheeled, horse-drawn driving cart popular in India and the Far East; carries one, is driven without traces, the draft comes through the shafts to the pad which is prevented from slipping rearwards by a breast collar onto which some of the pulling power is transferred; either driven by an occupant or led by a servant; usually hooded or screened.

elastic cartilage A type of cartilage (q.v.) found in the horse's ears, neck, windpipe, and voice box; is tough, pliable and provides support to membranes and muscles.

Elberfeld Horses A group of horses used by William von Osten of Berlin to prove his theories on equine intelligence; included the Russian stallion Kluge Hans (q.v.) and two Arab (q.v.) stallions; von Osten appeared to train Klug Hans to calculate by pawing the ground with his hoof, to read, and to differentiate colors, up to the general standard of knowledge of a 14-year-old child; von Osten's studies gained enormous publicity, but in 1904, the German psychologist, Oskar Pfungst, demonstrated that the stallion answered to unconscious signs from von Osten; at the outbreak of World War I, the horses were disbanded.

elbow The upper joint of the foreleg (q.v.).

elbow boots Sheepskin or felt lined open boots worn on the elbows of the forelegs to protect them from injury; used on horses having high-stepping foreleg action.

elbow hitting Limb contact in which the horse hits his elbow with the shoe of the same hind limb; common in those horses shod with weighted shoes.

El Caballo de Paso Fino *see* PASO FINO

El Caballo Tigre The Spanish name for the Tiger Horse (q.v.).

Electioneer One of four sons of Hambletonian 10 from which more than 90 percent of all modern Standardbreds (q.v.) can trace descent.

electro-acupuncture A type of acupuncture (q.v.); stimulation of precise points along body meridians (q.v.) using a mild electric current to control pain, treat internal malfunctions, anesthetize, or reduce stress; administered through the skin via fine needles or moist sponges surrounding the area; more intense than traditional needling.

electrocardiogram Also known by the acronyms ECG and EKG; a graphic tracing of the electrical impulses produced by the heart muscle; does not detect valvular malfunctions, shunts, flow rates, or pressure changes, but can detect abnormal heartbeat patterns.

electrocardiograph An instrument used to record electric potentials associated with the electric currents that traverse the heart.

electrocardiography Study of the heart through graphic records of the electrical impulses produced by the heart.

electrolytes Simple, water-soluble inorganic compounds essential for many of the chemical processes of the body; include sodium chloride, sodium acetate, sodium bicarbonate, potassium chloride, and lactate; excreted from the body in sweat (q.v.) with broken down proteins, waste products and oxidants.

electronic eye *see* AUTOMATIC TIMER

electronic identification A method of horse identification adopted in some countries including the United States as a regulatory tool to thwart horse theft; ownership and breed information is encased in a transponder sealed in a glass pellet scarcely larger than a grain of wild rice which is implanted into the nuchal ligament running along the crest of the horse's neck; the microchip contained therein is encoded with a unique identification number of nine or ten digits that can be read when a scanner is passed along the neck; is permanent, unalterable, foolproof, and inexpensive; administration, registration, detection, and placement of the chip on the horse's body are not standardized and different microchip systems exist worldwide, each having its own detection system; cannot be removed, so some horses may have more than one chip.

Elementary Level The British and Australian equivalent of Second Level (q.v.).

elements A jumping term; the individual obstacles that, together, constitute a combination jump (q.v.), e.g. the three individual jumps in a treble.

Elephant and Castle Also known as The Elephant; a horse repository located in London, England, where every Monday until the late 1960s, large numbers of horses, ponies, donkeys, harness, saddlery, and horse-drawn vehicles were auctioned.

elephant polo *see* PACHYDERM POLO

elevated body temperature see HYPERTHERMIA

elevation (1) Said of the horse; raising of the head and neck (including the base of the neck) freely from the withers, in conjunction with flexion of the poll and jaw (2) A dressage term; the height to which the legs are raised in the piaffe (q.v.) and passage (q.v.).

elf's foot *see* FLIPPER FOOT

eligible Said of a horse or rider qualified to compete according to established conditions for the breed or sport.

elimination (1) Said of a rider; excluded from participation in further competition due to infractions incurred or the state of the mount's health. (2) To discharge waste as in feces or urine.

ELISA *see* ENZYME-LINKED IMMUNOSORBENT ASSAY

elk lip A loose and overhanging upper lip.

Elliott, Obadiah In 1802 invented a method of building horse-drawn carriages without a perch; this method led to the introduction and use of elliptic springs in 1804, which revolutionized carriage building.

elliptic spring A type of spring introduced in 1804 for use on horse-drawn vehicles; consists of two side-springs, one in a upwards curve and the other in a downwards curve which, together, formed an oval; the body of the vehicle was typically joined to the upper spring and the axle to the lower; revolutionized carriage building; invented by Obadiah Elliott (q.v.).

El Morzillo The black horse belonging to Hernando Cortèz, conqueror of Mexico, in the 16th century; died during Cortèz's expedition to Guatemala in 1524 at which time he was deified by the natives in the form of a large stone statue which was ultimately destroyed by the Spanish Franciscan missionaries in 1697.

emasculate *see* CASTRATE

emasculator A stainless steel tool commonly used to remove the testicles from a horse.

emergency grip Said of a rider who clamps both legs tightly into the pommels of a side-saddle (q.v.) for security as when jumping.

embouchure A 16th and 17th century French term; a mouthpiece (q.v.).

embryo The egg from conception through approximately 40 days.

embryo transfer Removal and transfer of an inseminated embryo from a donor mare implanted in a recipient mare; limited application in horses due to registration restrictions of most breed associations.

EMND *see* EQUINE MOTOR NEURON DISEASE

EMP *see* EQUINE MORBILLIVIRUS PNEUMONIA

empty A racing term; said of the horse lacking the energy necessary to complete a drive to the finish (q.v.).

empty horse A vaulting term; said of the vaulting horse following concurrent dismounts of all vaulters; considered a fault in any freestyle program.

EMV *see* EQUINE MORBILLIVIRUS

encephalin A morphine-like neurotransmitter secreted by the brain.

encephalitis *see* EQUINE ENCEPHALITIS

encephalomyelitis Inflammation of both the brain and spinal cord; of three primary types in horses: Eastern equine encephalomyelitis (q.v.), Western equine encephalomyelitis, and Venezuelan equine encephalomyelitis (q.v.).

end line A polo term; one of two short ends of a polo field (q.v.) measuring 160 yards (146 m) in length; in conjunction with the side lines (q.v.), define the playing area of the polo field; the ball is considered out of bounds if it passes outside of this line.

endocrine (1) Of or pertaining to any of the ductless or endocrine glands (q.v.). (2) The internal secretions of a gland.

endocrine gland Any of the ductless glands such as the thyroid or adrenal, the secretions of which pass directly into the bloodstream from the gland cells.

endectocide An antibiotic product administered to a horse to kill round and flat worms, mange mites, and insect parasites including horsefly bot larvae found in the stomach; include such products as Ivermectin (q.v.).

endometrial Of or pertaining to the endometrium (q.v.).

endometritis A bacterial infection of the mucous membrane lining of the uterus; the leading cause of sterility in mares.

endometrium The mucous membrane lining of the uterus (q.v.).

endorphins Morphine-like proteins produced in nerve tissue to suppress pain and regulate emotional state; acupuncture (q.v.) is believed to trigger their release into the bloodstream.

endoscope A flexible medical instrument inserted through an incision in the skin or a body passage; enables a veterinarian (q.v.) to view the interior of a body cavity; many are constructed with metal tubes fitted with magnifying lenses, an eyepiece, and a light bulb; the fiber-optic endoscope (q.v.) is one version of this instrument.

endosteum A fine vascular membrane lining the internal cavities of the long bones within which lies the bone marrow.

endotoxemia The presence of endotoxins (q.v.) in the blood; may cause shock.

endotoxic shock A sustained inadequacy of blood profusion in the tissue resulting from systemic toxicity caused by an endotoxin (q.v.) from certain bacteria.

endotoxin A toxin of a micro-organism; separates from the cell body on its disintegration.

endurance The horse's ability to sustain prolonged stressful effort or activity, e.g. a racehorse's endurance.

edurance race Any competition conducted over natural terrain in which the speed and physical capability of participating horses is tested; the distances may vary from 25 to 100 miles (40–160 km) in length.

endurance ride Also known as competitive trail ride or long distance ride; a speed and endurance race over varying distances, topography, elevation, and footing; ride length depends on the season with shorter rides run earlier in the year and longer more difficult and strenuous events later in the year; may vary from 25 to 100 miles (40–160 km) in length and may be conducted over a period of one, two, or three days; competing horses are subject to veterinary inspections before, during, and after each event and may be withdrawn by the veterinarian at any time if deemed necessary to protect the horse; the greatest race of this type, the Great American Horse Race (q.v.) was run in 1976 from New York to California and covered a distance of about 6,000 miles.

enema Introduction of soapy water, oil, or other liquid directly into the rectum of the horse for medicinal purposes by means of a pump or special apparatus.

energizer A component of an electric fence; delivers an electrical current ranging from less than 1,000 volts to more than 10,000 volts with 4,000 to 7,000 volts most effective; may emit voltage in a steady current or in pulses lasting as little as 1/10,000 of a second and sequenced about one second apart.

energy A measure of heat; the actual or potential ability to do work as enabled by carbohydrates (q.v.), fats, and proteins in the horse's diet with carbohydrates being the body's primary source of energy; use is displayed through physical activity, growth, milk production, or repair of body tissues; energy deficiency may result in weight loss, insufficient lactation, reduced performance, or slowed growth while excess energy can cause such ailments such as weight gain, founder (q.v.), and colic (q.v.); deficiency may be caused by inadequate or poor quality feed, parasite loads, and dental problems; of four types: digestible energy (q.v.), gross energy (q.v.), metabolizable energy value (q.v.), and net energy value (q.v.).

energy cascade A scale of feed energy value; each step represents a lower energy value than the one preceding it; includes: gross energy (q.v.), digestible energy (q.v.), metabolizable energy (q.v.), and net energy (q.v.).

engage Said of a horse who rounds his back and brings his hind legs well under his body.

engaged (1) *see* ENGAGE. (2) A racing term; a horse entered in a race.

engagement (1) A racing term; a Stakes (q.v.) nomination. (2) A riding commitment.

engage the hindquarters Said of the horse when he carries more of his weight (and the rider's) on his hind legs; requires a great degree of impulsion; the horse steps further under his body with his hind legs while remaining light on the aids.

engaging the hindquarters Said of the horse when optimally balanced and collected (q.v.).

English Buggy A hooded Gig (q.v.).

English Black *see* GREAT HORSE, THE

English Connemara Pony Society *see* ENGLISH CONNEMARA SOCIETY

English Connemara Society Also known as English Connemara Pony Society; an English organization founded in 1947 to encourage the breeding and utilization of improved types of Connemara Ponies (q.v.) in England.

English Droitzschka A heavy, low-bodied, four-wheeled, horse-drawn vehicle of the Droizschka (q.v.) type; had a passenger seat situated over the rear axle and a body low at the center to accommodate the travelers' legs, in front of which was the arch in the wagon body in which the front wheels turned; was reinforced with iron plates, drawn by two ponies, or a single horse, and was driven from a two-person box seat; being low to the ground and unlikely to overturn, it was suitable for use by the elderly.

English Great Horse *see* GREAT HORSE

English hunting iron *see* HUNTING IRON

English Jockey Club, The A British association of individuals and horse owners established in 1750 to promote and control racing in England; in 1993 handed over many of its responsibilities to The British Horseracing Board (q.v.); it retained responsibility for those areas including disciplinary matters, racecourse medical and veterinary arrangements, licensing, security, and conduct of a race day.

English rein *see* GERMAN MARTINGALE

English saddle Also known as pancake; a saddle with long side bars, reinforced cantle and pommel, no horn, and a leather seat supported by webbing and stretched between the saddle bow and cantle.

English stirrup Any stirrup (q.v.) suspended from the leathers (q.v.) on an English-type saddle; may be made of stainless steel, iron, nickel alloy, or chrome-plated iron.

English Thoroughbred *see* THOROUGHBRED

English Triple Crown Also known as Triple Crown; three races for three-year-old Thoroughbreds (q.v.) run in England consisting of the 2,000 Guineas (q.v.), Epsom Derby (q.v.), and St. Leger Stakes; winning all three races in a single year is considered the greatest accomplishment of a Thoroughbred; since 1850, 15 horses have won all three races constituting the English Triple Crown: 1850 (West Australian), 1862 (Gladiateur), 1863 (Lord Lyon), 1883 (Ormonde), 1888 (Common), 1890 (Isinglass), 1894 (Galtee More), 1896 (Flying Fox), 1897 (Diamond Jubilee), 1900 (Rock Sand), 1912 (Pommern), 1914 (Gay Crusader), 1915 Gainsborough), 1932 (Bahram), and 1967 (Nijinsky); a filly has never won; equivalent programs are run in America (American Triple Crown [q.v.]) and Canada (Canadian Triple Crown [q.v.]).

English trot *see* POST NO. 4

enlarged Also known as carted (Brit); an obsolete hunting term; said of a deer transported to and released at a stag hunt (q.v.) where it was pursued by mounted riders and stag hounds.

en ligne A vaulting term; to be on or in a line; a vaulting style practiced in France and the United States in which the horse gallops free in a straight line while the vaulters perform six compulsory figures and four of their own choice upon his back; dates from the 18th century; use an en ligne vaulting saddle (q.v.) rather than a vaulting roller (q.v.).

ensilage A method of storing and preserving green fodder in silos or pits covered with plastic; the stored substance, silage (q.v.), is tightly pressed and undergoes slight fermentation in anaerobic conditions.

enter (1) Also known as enter a hound; a hunting term; to train a young hound (q.v.) to hunt fox (q.v.). (2) To nominate a horse to participate in a competition; usually on an entry form.

enter a hound *see* ENTER NO. 1

entered (1) Also known as an entered hound; a hunting term; said of a hound (q.v.) upon completing his first cub hunting (q.v.) season, usually at one and one half years of age. (2) Trained to hunt, as in a hound.

entered hound *see* ENTERED

enteric fever A fever of the intestines; a loosely applied term for diarrhea (q.v.) and colic (q.v.).

enteritis Inflammation of the intestinal or bowel lining; may be triggered by bacteria, chemical or vegetable poisons, or moldy or damaged food containing harmful fungi.

enterolith Also known as intestinal stone or stone; a mineral formation created in the large intestine which resembles a stone commonly found in the soil or river bottom; frequently begins with the presence of a small foreign object accidentally ingested with the food, after which dietary minerals begin to crystallize in layers around the object; generally made up of magnesium, ammonium, and phosphates which are found in high levels in alfalfa; horses more than 12 to 14 years are most commonly affected; most frequently treated with surgical removal although alteration of the acidity of the digestive tract may prevent the crystallization process that leads to enteroliths (q.v.).

enter the lists To enter into the enclosures or palisades in which 16th-century tilting (q.v.) exercises were conducted.

entire *see* STALLION

entry (1) A hunting term; a young unentered (q.v.) hound. (2) A horse intended to participate in a competition. (3) *see* COUPLED

entry fee The amount of money a contestant or nominator pays to enter a horse in a event, competition, or race.

environmental trait Any structural or functional defect acquired by a horse after birth and during growth.

enzyme assay A blood test performed to measure blood enzyme levels.

enzyme-linked immunosorbent assay Also known by the acronym ELISA; a stall-side diagnostic tool (q.v.) which serves as the basis for the majority of stall-side kits; uses a self-checking system in which a known sample (a control) is tested at the same time as the actual sample under evaluation; when properly run is a very precise and specific method of testing; test results are conveyed in color.

eohippus Also known as dawn horse or by the scientific name *hyracotherium*; believed to be the earliest ancestor of the horse in equine evolution; existed about 55 to 50 million years ago.

epidemic Common to or affecting a whole population or great number in a community at the same time, as in a contagious disease.

epidermis The outer, non-vascular, non-sensitive layer of the skin, covering the true skin or cutis (q.v.); lacks blood vessel supply; produces keratin and melanin.

epidural anesthesia A pain-killing procedure in which anesthetic (q.v.) is injected into the space around the spinal cord.

epiglottis A triangular-shaped cartilage (q.v.) located at the base of the airway above the soft palate and in front of the arytenoid cartilage which covers the airway during swallowing.

epinephrine *see* ADRENALINE

epiphyseal cartilage One of six types of cartilage found in the body structure of the horse; develops at the upper and lower aspects of the long leg bones from the epiphyseal plates (q.v.).

epiphyseal fracture A crack along the line of the epiphyseal cartilage; results in the epiphysis of a bone separating from the shaft; occur in young horses before bone ossification.

epiphyseal plates Also known as physeal plates; the upper and lower aspects of long leg bones, including the growth plate (q.v.), at which lengthening of the bone occurs; the lengthening process involves generation of new cartilage cells which are converted into bone; an increase in cell production or failure of timely change of cartilage to bone may be associated with physitis (q.v.).

epiphysis The spongy extremity of a bone which is attached to the shaft for the purpose of forming a joint with the similar process of the adjacent bone; covered by cartilage; developed from a separate center of ossification, which in the young horse is connected to the shaft of the bone by a plate of cartilage that disappears in the adult, being replaced by bone.

epiphysitis *see* PHYSITIS

epispastics Any substance which produces blistering (q.v.) on the skin.

epistaxis Also known as nosebleed or nasal hemorrhage; bleeding from the nose as caused by blood vessel rupture anywhere in the respiratory tract or guttural pouch; a sign, not a disease; most commonly triggered by vessel rupture in the lungs, gutteral pouch, or nasal cavity, in that order; when precipitated by exercise (as in race-related stress) is, almost always, the result of pulmonary hemorrhage.

epitheliogenesis imperfecta Also known by the acronym EI; an inherited condition in which there is a gap in the epithelium (q.v.) which readily bleeds and heals with scar tissue; foals are frequently born prematurely or die shortly thereafter due to septicemia (q.v.).

epithelium The layer or layers of cells of which the skin and mucous membranes are formed.

EPM *see* EQUINE PROTOZOAL MYELOENCEPHALITIS

Epona The Celtic goddess, protector of horses and cavalry.

Epsom Derby Also known as The Derby, Derby Stakes, or The Darby (Colloq.); a horse race traditionally held on the first Wednesday of June and most recently the first Saturday since 1780 at the Epsom Downs (q.v.) course located just south of London, England; run on a U-shaped, 1½ mile (2.4 km), left-handed racecourse consisting of hills and turns; named for and by the 12th Earl of Derby; considered the most demanding test of jockeys (q.v.) and three-year-old horses in the world.

Epsom Downs Also known as The Downs

or Downs; an undulating, U-shaped, 1½ mile (2.4 km) left-handed racecourse consisting of hills and turns; located 15 miles (24 km) south of London, England; considered the most demanding test of flat-race jockeys and horses in the world; the site of the Epsom Derby (q.v.).

Epsom hill *see* TATTENHAM HILL

Epsom Oaks Also known as Oaks or The Oaks; a racing term; one of 5 English classic races; a 1½ (2.4 km) mile stakes race for three-year-old fillies run annually since 1779 at the Epsom Downs (q.v.) course just south of London, England; conducted at the same meeting as the Epsom Derby (q.v.).

epsom salts Hydrated magnesium sulfate used as a laxative, purgative, and general cathartic.

equerry A prince or noble person responsible for the care and handling of horses.

equestrian (1) One who rides horseback. (2) Of or pertaining to horsemen or horsemanship.

Equestrian Federation of Australia Also known by the acronym EFA; an organization responsible for overseeing and controlling most amateur horse sports in Australia; directly affiliated with the FEI (q.v.).

equestrian nail A nail-and-screws device used to stabilize a fractured bone; a ⅝ to ¾ inch (16–18 mm) long nail inserted into the bone-marrow canal to bridge two broken long bone components; is stabilized by four screws, two at each end and inserted perpendicular to the bone; a state-of-the-art procedure that does not injure as much soft tissue or impede the bone's surface blood supply as much as traditional plate-and-screws stabilization (q.v.) technique.

equestrienne A female equestrian (q.v.).

Equibase Company A United States partnership between The Jockey Club (q.v.) and the Thoroughbred Racing Association (q.v.) to establish and maintain an industry-owned, central database of racing records.

Equidae The family of mammals consisting of the genus *Equus* (q.v.).

equine (1) A horse, including all members of the family Equidae (q.v.) consisting of horses, zebras, and asses. (2) Of, or pertaining to, the horse.

equine abortion Expulsion of the fetus (q.v.) before 300 gestation days, at which time the fetus cannot survive because of immaturity.

equine arteritis *see* EQUINE VIRAL ARTERITIS

equine ascarid *see* LARGE ROUNDWORM

equine asthma *see* CHRONIC OBSTRUCTIVE PULMONARY DISEASE

equine biliary fever *see* EQUINE PIROPLASMOSIS

equine coital exantha A benign viral venereal disease of horses affecting both sexes; is primarily spread at coitus; although rare in unmated horses, passive transfer by gynecological manipulation is possible; immunity is short-lived; previously thought to be caused by equine herpesvirus 3 (q.v.), it is now believed to be caused by a mixed viral infection; characterized by multiple, circular, red nodules up to 1½ inch (2 mm) in diameter appearing on the vulval mucosa and skin and on the perineal skin 4 to 8 days after mating; lesions progress to vesicles and pustules that rupture forming shallow ulcers; healing occurs within in 3 weeks leaving white scars.

equine contagious metritis Also known by the acronym CEM; a highly contagious bacterial venereal disease; resides in infected stallions in the prepuce and on the surface of the penis and is transmitted during coitus; mares develop a profuse, sticky discharge two to six days following service; the conception rate is low, but after the infection subsides, fertility is regained in ensuing estrual periods; may be passed to foals at birth, who then retain the infection until they reach breeding age.

equine contraception A population-control measure; ovulating mares are injected with a vaccine containing the *zona pellucida* protein extracted from pig ovaries; the protein prompts the mare to produce antibodies that attack her own ova (q.v.), rendering her infertile for that ovulatory cycle; a single, three-year vaccine is under development; developed to limit wild horse populations.

equine degenerative myeloencephalopathy Also known by the acronym EDM; a genetically based disease of the spinal cord and brain stem causing weakness and incoordination.

equine dysautonomia *see* GRASS SICKNESS

equine encephalitis Also known as encephalitis, sleeping sickness, brain fever, or brain staggers; a viral, epidemic disease which may be carried by birds, mosquitoes, or other blood-sucking insects, which results in inflammation of the brain and spinal cord; symptoms include high fever, drowsiness, lack of coordination, teeth grinding, partial loss of vision, inability to swallow food, and possible paralysis; generally fatal, but vaccinations are available to immunize horses against attack; affects horses, but chickens, pheasants, etc., act as a reservoir of infection; can be transmitted to man; the alphaviruses most closely associated include Eastern equine encephalomyelitis (q.v.), Western equine encephalomyelitis (q.v.), and Venezuelan equine encephalomyelitis (q.v.).

equine granulocytic ehrlichiosis Also known by the acronym EGE; an ailment transmitted by the Western black leg tick characterized by flu-like signs including headache, fever, chills, shaking, and nausea; can lead to fatal organ damage; cannot be passed from horses to people or vice versa.

equine grass sickness *see* GRASS SICKNESS

Equine Health Research Fund Also known by the acronym EHRF; an United States organization established in 1985 by the American Horse Shows Association (q.v.) to raise funds to support ongoing research in the fields of equine health and equine sports medicine for all breeds and disciplines of show horses; studies funded range from pharmacology to lameness.

equine herpesvirus Also known as herpesvirus or by the acronym EHV; a highly adaptable virus of three strains: equine herpesvirus 1 (q.v.), equine herpesvirus 2 (q.v.) and equine herpesvirus 3 (q.v.); responsible for a number of diseases including equine viral arteritis (q.v.) and equine coital exanthema (q.v.).

equine herpesvirus 1 Also known by the acronym EHV 1; a strain of equine herpesvirus (q.v.); causes equine viral rhinopneumonitis (q.v.); produces acute respiratory catarrh, nasal discharge, cough, mild fever, and in mares, abortion or abortion storms (q.v.).

equine herpesvirus 2 Also known by the acronym EHV 2; a strain of herpesvirus (q.v.) found ubiquitously on the respiratory mucosa, conjunctiva; it is believed to be the cause of equine keratoconjunctivitis.

equine herpesvirus 3 Also known by the acronym EHV 3; a strain of equine herpesvirus (q.v.); causes equine coital exanthema (q.v.).

equine infectious anemia Also known as swamp fever or by the acronym EIA; a highly contagious and potentially fatal, blood-borne viral disease; there is no vaccine or treatment; the responsible virus, equine infectious anemia virus (EIAV), is most frequently transmitted between horses living in close proximity by large biting insects such as horse flies (q.v.) and deer flies (q.v.); presents itself in three degrees of infectiousness: *acute* – the most damaging and difficult to diagnose because the signs appear rapidly and often only an elevated body temperature is noted; $\frac{1}{5}^{th}$ teaspoon of blood from a horse with acute EIA contains enough virus to infect 1 million horses; horses die within two to three weeks; *chronic* – if the horse survives the first acute bout he may develop a recurring clinical disease characterized by fever (a sudden rise to 105 °F or, rarely as high as 108 °F, then drop to normal until the next onset), petechial hemorrhages (minute blood-colored spots appear on the mucous membranes), depression, weight loss, dependent edema (on the legs and under the chest and other underbody surfaces), and anemia; $\frac{1}{5}^{th}$ of a teaspoon of blood from a chronic case during a feverish episode contains enough virus to infect 10,000 horses, *inapparent* – most horses are inapparent carriers showing no overt clinical abnormalities due to infection; survive as reservoirs of infection for extended periods; have significantly lower EIAV (q.v.) blood levels than horses with active clinical signs; only one horse fly (q.v.) out of six million is likely to pick up and transmit EIAV from a horse with inapparent infection level; often difficult to differentiate from other fever-producing diseases such as anthrax (q.v.), influenza (q.v.), and equine encephalitis (q.v.); the first retrovirus-induced disease for which a diagnostic test was approved.

equine infectious anemia virus Also known by the acronym EIAV; the virus causing equine infectious anemia (q.v.); categorized as a retrovirus, it contains genetic RNA material, which it uses to produce DNA; the DNA is then incorporated into the genetic makeup of the infected cells; most frequently transmitted between horses living in close proximity by large biting insects such as horse flies (q.v.) and deer flies (q.v.); insect transmission is dependent on insect number and habit, horse population density, the amount of blood transferred between horses, and the level of virus in the blood of the infected horse from which the initial blood meal was obtained; all infected horses are thought to remain lifetime carriers.

equine influenza Also known as influenza, stable cough, the cough, or Newmarket cough; an acute, highly contagious, respiratory disease characterized by respiratory inflammation and cough, fever (often as high as 106 °F), muscle soreness, and in less mild cases, loss of appetite; caused by one of two virus strains: A-equi-1 (q.v.) or A-equi-2 (q.v.).

equine intestinal threadworm *see* STRONGYLOIDES WESTERI

equine leptospirosis Also known as leptospirosis; a contagious, essentially water-borne disease of horses due to infection with various leptrospiral organisms; infections may be asymptomatic or may result in a variety of disease conditions including fever (103 ° to 105 °F) for two to three days, dullness, anorexia, hemoglobinuria (q.v.), abortion (several weeks after the fever), and death; generally transmitted from skin or mucous membrane contact with urine, and to a lesser extent by intake of urine-contaminated feed or water.

equine lupus A rare immune-mediated disorder manifesting in two types: localized known as discord lupus (q.v.) and systemic lupus erythematosus (q.v.).

equine malaria *see* EQUINE PIROPLASMOSIS

equine monocytic erhlichiosis *see* POTOMAC HORSE FEVER

equine morbillivirus Also known by the acronym EMV; *see* HENDRA VIRUS DISEASE

equine morbillivirus pneumonia Also known by the acronym EMP; *see* HENDRA VIRUS DISEASE

equine motor neuron disease Also known by the acronym EMND; a nervous system disease manifesting in the neurons of the brain and spinal cord which slowly destroys their ability to contract skeletal muscles, characterized by weight loss, trembling and quivering muscles when standing, profuse sweating, and lying down; vitamin E (q.v.) deficiency is thought to make horses more susceptible to the factors, as yet unidentified, that trigger it; similar to Lou Gehrig's disease in people.

equine myoglobinuria Also known as equine rhabdomylosis, azoturia, exertional myopathy, exertion myopathy, exertion myopathy syndrome, paralytic myoglobinuria, Monday-morning disease, Monday-morning sickness, myosistis, over-straining sickness, black water, or incorrectly as tying up disease; a disease affecting the horse's skeletal and cardiac muscles, occurring within minutes to an hour or more following the onset of physical exertion after a period of rest and, generally, unrestricted feed; seems to relate more to excess total energy consumption than carbohydrate content of the feed as previously believed; suggested that the cause is an accumulation of glycogen in muscle, liberating excessive lactic acid during exercise; characterized by muscle cramping and fasciculations leaving the muscles firm and painful to the touch, profuse sweat, a tucked-up appearance, a stiff, stilted gait, and a reluctance to move; there is a tendency to knuckle-over at the fetlocks; urine may be red wine or coffee-colored; in severe cases, the temperature is generally elevated, yet seldom reaches 104 °F; in severe cases, recumbency and death may result; occurs most commonly in stabled horses rather than pastured, and horses older than 4 years; is different from tying up (q.v.); draft horses not worked on Sunday, but given full feed were commonly afflicted with this disease when put to work on Monday, hence the common name of Monday-morning sickness.

equine piroplasmosis Also known as piroplasmosis, babesiosis, equine biliary fever, equine malaria, Texas fever, horse tick fever, tick fever, biliary fever, or tristeza (in Latin America); a contagious, tick-borne protozoal disease of the bloodstream caused by *Babesia caballi* or *Babesia equi*; infections may be preacute, acute, chronic, or not apparent; symptoms may include fever, listlessness, red urine, jaundice, loss of appetite, constipation and diarrhea; death may result if left untreated; is a particularly significant disease problem in the tropics and southeastern United States.

equine protozoal myeloencephalitis Also known by the acronym EPM; a debilitating neurological disease caused by a single-cell, microscopic parasite protozoan, *Sarcoytis neurona*, infecting horse feed and water; protozoa may find their way into the spinal cord where inflammation and eventually nerve-cell damage result in vague lameness, incoordination, and weakness; ataxia (q.v.) is a warning sign; associated ataxia is usually unilateral; the horse will show signs that he does not have an accurate feeling of where his feet are; therapy response is highly variable; without prompt treatment progressive incapacitation may necessitate euthanasia.

equine purpura An acute, frequently fatal, non-contagious, apparently allergenic disease affecting the horse; characteristically occurs as a consequence of strangles (q.v.), 1 to 3 weeks following the initial infection; symptoms include a sudden onset of subcutaneous edema in the area of the head, eyes, lips, belly, and legs, the appearance of small red spots caused by hemorrhage in the mucous membranes, diarrhea, colic (q.v.), or in severe cases, anemia; lasts approximately 1 to 2 weeks followed by recovery in about 50 percent of the cases; relapses are common as are secondary bacterial infections; death may be rapid due to suffocation or anemia and toxemia of secondary infection in drawn-out cases.

equine recurrent uveitis *see* PERIODIC OPHTHALMIA

equine respiratory syndrome *see* HENDRA VIRUS DISEAS

equine rhabdomyolysis *see* EQUINE MYOGLOBINURIA

equine ulcerative lymphangitis Also known as ulcerative lymphangitis; a slightly contagious skin condition which develops in the lower pectoral and ventral abdominal regions; characterized by diffuse or local swelling, pitting edema, and lameness of the adjacent limb; abscesses have a thick, fibrous capsule and may enlarge up to 8 inches (20 cm) before rupturing; most common in warm climates.

equine variola *see* HORSE-POX

equine verminous arteritis Also known as verminous arteritis; swelling of the cranial mesenteric artery due to arterial wall thickening and fibrosis caused by the effects of migrating strongyle worm larvae (*Strongylus vulgaris*); symptoms often appear during or shortly following work and include the sudden onset of abdominal pain, fever, nostril flaring, a pulse rate of 70 to 80, and head turning towards the right flank; following recovery, abdominal pain may return at frequent intervals over weeks or months, the horse may show resistance to backing, turning in a small circle, or jumping.

equine vesicular stomatitis A localized inflammation of the soft tissues of the mouth characterized by blisters or other lesions which are generally confined to the upper surface of the tongue, but which may involve the inner surface of the lips, angles of the mouth, and gums; secondary lesions may appear on the feet.

equine viral arteritis Also known as viral arteritis, arteritis, equine arteritis, the acronym EVA, and colloquially as pink-eye; an acute, highly contagious viral disease characterized by fever, conjunctivitis, edema of the lungs, legs, and other body parts, nasal discharge and congestion, loss of appetite, and in mares, abortion – more than 50 percent of afflicted mares abort; damages the arteries, especially the smaller ones; spread through body fluids of infected animals, e.g. respiratory secretion, semen, and urine for approximately three weeks following infection; can be carried by asymptomatic horses; mortality is low and a vaccine is available.

equine viral rhinopneumonitis Also know as rhinopneumonitis or by the acronym EVR; a contagious viral infection caused by equine herpesvirus 1 (q.v.); transmitted by direct and indirect contact with virus-laden nasal discharge, aborted fetuses, or placenta; signs include 102 to 107 °F (39–42 °C) fever, congestion, serous discharge from nasal mucosa and conjunctiva, cough, malaise, and sometimes constipation followed by diarrhea; in some outbreaks central nervous symptoms may appear including ataxia (q.v.) and incoordination; pregnant mares may abort individually or in abortion storms (q.v.).

equipage The horse-drawn carriage and its attendants.

equirotal Wheels of equal size as used on horse-drawn coaches or carriages.

equitation The act or art of riding on horseback.

equitation class Any English riding competition in which the rider, not the horse, is judged; the rider must demonstrate good seat and hands and sufficient management of the horse to perform the prescribed tests, either over fences or on the flat, in a smooth, controlled and accurate manner; riders are classified according to their age and previous winnings in equitation classes.

equivalent odds A racing term; odds which mutuel price horses would pay for each $1 bet.

Equus A Latin term; horse; the genus of the family *Equidae*, the technical classification for all domesticated horses and some of their closely related feral and wild counterparts including the ass (q.v.) and zebra.

Equus africanus The scientific name for the African Ass (q.v.).

Equus asinus The scientific name for the ass (q.v.).

Equus burchellii quagga The scientific name for the Quagga (q.v.).

Equus caballus The scientific name for the horse (q.v.).

Equus ferus The scientific name for the wild horse.

Equus ferus ferus The scientific name for the Tarpan (q.v.).

Equus ferus przewalski The scientific name for Przewalski's Horse (q.v.)

Equus hemionus The scientific name for a subspecies of the Asiatic Wild Ass (q.v.).

Equus kiang The scientific name for a subspecies of the Asiatic Wild Ass (q.v.).

Equus hemionus kiang The scientific name for the Kiang (q.v.).

Equus ibericus The scientific name for the Iberian horse (q.v.).

Equus lambei The scientific term for the Ice Age horse (q.v.).

Equus przewalski "Poliakov" *see* ASIATIC WILD HORSE

Equus quagga *see* QUAGGA

Eridge Car *see* ERIDGE CART

Eridge Cart (1) Also known as Eridge Car; a low-slung, but well upholstered, four-wheeled vehicle of the Dogcart (q.v.) type; the front wheels were placed well ahead of the body to allow for easy turning in confined spaces and the hand brake only worked on the rear wheels; the fore-carriage appeared to be detached from the rest of the vehicle, yet was attached by strong, slender side irons of a skeletal structure; introduced in limited numbers during the late 19th century; hung on full-elliptical side springs throughout with an undercarriage similar to that of a Pony Phaeton (q.v.); seated two forward and two rearward facing passengers; drawn by a single horse or large pony and usually owner driven. (2) A low-slung, two-wheeled vehicle for two.

ergot (1) The small, horny growth on the back of the fetlock joint; a vestige of the second and fourth digits found in extinct ancestors of the horse; made of material similar to that of the hoof, it grows from the surface of the skin downward; may be nonexistent in some horses and several inches long in others. (2) The spurs of a horse's hooves. (3) A compound of the fungus *Claviceps purpuria* which grows under warm, moist conditions; affects the seeds of small grains and grasses such as fescue, but principally rye; consumption by horses may cause ergot poisoning (q.v.).

ergot poisoning An abnormal condition of the horse produced by consumption of any of the small grains and several grasses such as fescue (q.v.), with rye being particularly susceptible, attacked by the fungus *Claviceps purpuria*; results in a hard, dark-colored fungal growth two to four times the length of the kernel; produces a compound called ergot which stimulates the smooth muscles and may cause the blood supply to the tail, limbs, and ears to be so reduced that dry gangrene develops causing the extremities to drop off; may also cause abortion in pregnant mares.

ermine marks A leg marking (q.v.); dark black or brown spots occurring near the coronary band (q.v.) in any of the white leg marking patterns; generally accompanied by a dark stripe through the hoof wall at the location of the spot.

erythrocyte *see* RED BLOOD CELL

escutcheon The division of hair beginning below the point of the hip and extending towards the flanks.

esophagus Also known as the gullet and spelled oesophagus; the muscular passage by which food and liquid are taken into the stomach; extends from the pharynx to the stomach.

Esseda A lightly constructed, horse-drawn chariot used, especially in war, by the ancient Britons, the Gauls, the Belage, and later, by the Romans for purposes of convenience and luxury; entered from the fore rather than the aft; purposely constructed as noisy as possible, probably by the creaking and clanging of the wheels, to evoke havoc in the enemy; drawn by a pair of horses or large ponies in pole gear (q.v.) with neck yokes.

essential amino acid *see* DIETARY ESSENTIAL AMINO ACID

essential oil Commercially available volatile oil extracted from plants by means of steam distillation and containing a mixture of active constituents; highly aromatic; used in aromatherapy (q.v.).

Essex Cart A two-wheeled, horse-drawn sporting vehicle drawn by a cob or pony; usually owner driven.

Estonian Klepper *see* TORIC

estrous Of or pertaining to estrus (q.v.).

estrous cycle Also spelled oestrus cycle; the complete cyclic series of physical, biological and chemical changes in the mare which lead to ovulation and the shedding of the egg from the ovary; consist of estrus (q.v.), metestrus, diestrus, and proestrus; averages 21 days, but may vary from 17 to 26 days.

estrum *see* ESTRUS

estrus Also spelled oestrus and known as estrum, heat, season, and receptivity; the period of highest sexual excitability in the mare during which conception is possible; signs include squatting, urinating, clitoral eversion, tail swishing, and squealing; generally occurs from early spring through autumn in intervals lasting between 17 and 26 days; in spring and summer, the intervals may last as long as a few hours to 5 or 7 days depending on the mare's age, whether she is maiden (q.v.) or not, seasonal conditions, feed, and exercise level; discontinues in the pregnant mare until about 9 days post foaling.

ethology The scientific study of the function and evolution of animal behavior.

euthanasia Painless killing, as to euthanize (q.v.).

euthanize Also known as put down, put to sleep, and destroy; to humanely kill a horse or hound due to age, illness, or injury, e.g. by injecting a specific chemical into the bloodstream.

EVA *see* EQUINE VIRAL ARTERITIS

evade Said of the horse; to avoid the rider's or lunger's commands or aids (q.v.) using learned methods. (2) A dressage term; avoidance of the difficulty, correctness, or purpose of the movement, often without active resistance or disobedience, e.g., tilting of the head, opening the mouth, broken neckline, etc.

evener A driving term; a bar located between the drawbar and single bar (q.v.) used to equalize the pulling power of three, four, five, or six horses harnessed abreast in single trees (q.v.).

evening pink *see* EVENING PINK COAT

evening pink coat Also known as evening pink; the formal red hunt coat worn by members of a Hunt (q.v.) at Hunt Balls (q.v.) or dinners.

evening stable An English racing term; the evening feeding time (q.v.).

evenly A racing term; said of a horse who neither gains nor loses position during a race, e.g. "The horse runs evenly".

even money Also known as evens or even money bet; a racing term; a wager in which the betting odds are one to one; the person making the bet stands to win the same amount as wagered if the horse places as anticipated.

even money bet *see* EVEN MONEY

evens *see* EVEN MONEY

event (1) A combined training (q.v.) competition. (2) Each of the items in a program consisting of various contests.

eventer A horse or equestrian (q.v.) possessing the training, versatility, and stamina to compete in horse trials (q.v.).

eventing *see* HORSE TRIALS

EVR *see* EQUINE VIRAL RHINOPNEUMONITIS

ewe neck Said of the horse's neck when the top line is concave and the lower line is longer, more heavily muscled, and outwardly bulging than the top line; head carriage is elevated making control more difficult.

exacta Also known as perfecta, exactor (Can) or straight forecast (Brit); a racing term; a betting option in which the bettor (q.v.) selects the first two horses under the wire (q.v.) in the exact order in a single race.

exacta box Also known as quinella, one two, or dual forecast (Brit); a racing term; a betting option in which the bettor (q.v.) selects the first and second place horses in either order in any single race.

exactor *see* EXACTA

ex aequo A Latin term; equally, as when two or more horses gain the same number of points in a competition.

excessive angulation of the hock joints Also known as sickle hocks, curby hocks, or sabre hocks; forward deviation of the lower leg from the hock to the hoof, giving the impression of a sickle when viewed from the side; results in a weight transfer from the front of the hoof to the back; an inherited condition considered a conformation fault in riding horses; may cause curb (q.v.), spavin (q.v.), and navicular (q.v.) related issues.

excrement *see* FECES

excused A racing term; a horse permitted by race authorities to withdraw (q.v.) from a race after the official scratch time.

exercise bandage Also known as brace bandage or track bandage; a bandage (q.v.) approximately 3 inches (7.5 cm) wide and 6 to 7 feet (1.8–2.1 m) long; made of cotton flex or elasticized material; used to support and protect the horse's legs while he is at work or exercise; covers the leg between the knee or hock (q.v.) and fetlock (q.v.); if applied too tightly, may result in bandage bow (q.v.).

exercise boy A racing term; originally, boys or young men who rode race horses in workout sessions; as women have now entered the field the more generic "exercise rider" (q.v.) is used.

exercise-induced pulmonary hemorrhage Also known as lung hemorrhage, exercise related epistaxis, or by the acronym EIPH; the occurrence of hemorrhage (q.v.) in the lungs as a consequence of mechanical stress caused by soaring capillary blood pressure in the lungs during or following moderate to strenuous exercise; evidenced by bilateral epistaxis (q.v.); occurs in many horses with normal lungs and is not breed-specific although it is common in race horses and other high-performance equine athletes; a horse suffering from this syndrome is known as a bleeder (q.v.).

exercise related epistaxis *see* EXERCISE-INDUCED PULMONARY HEMORRHAGE

exercise related myopathy *see* EQUINE MYOGLOBINURIA

exercise rider One responsible for riding race horses in workout sessions.

exercise sheet *see* QUARTER SHEET

exertional myopathy *see* EQUINE MYOGLOBINURIA

exertional rhabdomyolysis *see* EQUINE MYOGLOBINURIA

exertion myopathy *see* EQUINE MYOGLOBINURIA

exertion myopathy syndrome *see* EQUINE MYOGLOBINURIA

exhibitor An owner, lessee, contestant, handler, trainer, and/or rider involved in the showing of horses.

Exmoor Pony Also known generically as native pony; one of nine mountain and moorland pony breeds originating in Britain of which it is thought to be the oldest; found in Exmoor in south-western England from which the name derived; believed to have descended from the prehistoric wild horse used by the Celts; has a heavy mane, well-proportioned head and neck, wide-set, toad eyes (q.v.), long and slightly hollow back, slightly sloping shoulder and croup, deep chest, and sturdy, well-muscled legs; generally has a bay-brown or dun coat and may have mealy coloring on the muzzle and underbelly which extends to the inside of the forearms and legs; white markings are not permitted by the breed registry; stands 11.2 to 12.3 hands, is sturdy, hardy, and possessed of good speed; when well trained and competently ridden, can make an excellent child's pony.

Exmoor Pony Society, The An English organization founded in 1921 to improve and encourage the breeding of Exmoor Ponies (q.v.) of the moorland type; ponies are entered in the National Pony Stud book.

exostoses More than one exostosis (q.v.).

exostosis Also known as bony growth; any abnormal growth or deposit of bone projecting outward from the bone surface; may result from injury, conformation fault, or heredity and may cause mechanical interference; most common forms include: splints (q.v.), ringbone (q.v.), bone spavin (q.v.) and some sidebones (q.v.).

exotic wager A racing term; any bet (q.v.) other than win (q.v.), place (q.v.), or show (q.v.).

expansion (1) The practice of fitting the posterior half of the horseshoe larger than the hoof to allow the heel to spread. (2) The act of expanding or the state of being expanded; to spread out.

Experimental Free Handicap Also known as Free Handicap; a racing term; a year-end projection of the best two-year-old race horses of the season in North America, as selected by a panel under guidance from The Jockey Club (q.v.); selection is based on performances in unrestricted races with separate lists created for male and female horses.

expert whip A skilled driver.

expression (1) A cutting term; the alertness of a horse in front of a cow. (2) *see* CADENCE

extend (1) A racing term; to push a horse to his limits in a race. (2) To lengthen a gait.

extended canter A lengthened gait in which the cantering horse covers as much ground as possible without losing rhythm, lightness, or calmness; achieved by great impulsion from the hindquarters.

extended gait A lengthening of the stride at any gait, as in extended canter (q.v.), extended trot (q.v.), or extended walk (q.v.).

extended heel Also known as extension; the outside heel of the horseshoe when more than ½ inch (6.5 mm) beyond the heel of the hoof; usually fitted parallel to the foot center-line and in line with the direction of travel.

extended-toe shoe Also known as beaked shoe; a horseshoe in which the shoe is fitted well forward of the natural toe of the foot exposing the bottom of the hoof wall at the toe; alternately, a projection may be welded onto the center of the horseshoe toe to slow foot breakover and prevent it from knuckling over; used on the feet of club-footed horses or horses with contracted tendons.

extended trot A lengthened gait in which the trotting horse covers as much ground as possible without losing the rhythm of his steps as achieved by impulsion from the hindquarters; the horse remains on the bit, but lowers and extends his neck.

extended walk A lengthened gait in which the horse remains on the bit, but covers as much ground as possible at the walk without losing the regularity of his steps; the hind feet touch the ground in front of the marks of the forefeet.

extension (1) Maximum extension of the stride in any gait without loss of balance or rhythm. (2) *see* EXTENDED HEEL

extensor process disease *see* PYRAMIDAL DISEASE

extensor tendon The tendon (q.v.) that extends the knee or ankle joint, pastern, foot, and elbow.

extravagant action Said of the horse; to have high knee and hock movement, as in the Hackney Pony (q.v.) and certain other breeds.

exudate The fluid or cell discharge from a sore or wound characterized by dry, crusty, scab-like sores.

eye (1) The organ of sight. (2) The uppermost ring on the cheekpiece (q.v.) of a bit to which the bridle cheekpiece (q.v.) is attached.

eye appeal A cutting term; the ability of a horse to earn extra points in a cutting horse competition due to an attractive working style that sets him apart from other horses.

eye for a country A hunting term; said of a huntsman who knows the location of all roads, trails, and jumpable areas in the country hunted and is capable of anticipating the line a fox (q.v.) will take.

F

FAA *see* FACTEUR D'ANGLO-ARAB

face drop *see* DROP NO. 1

face fly A swarming daytime feeder, *Musca autumnalis* similar in appearance to a common house fly (q.v.); occurs throughout southern Canada and most of the United States (except Florida, Texas, and New Mexico); was introduced into Nova Scotia from Europe where it was well established in 1950/51; females feed in large numbers around the eyes and muzzle on facial secretions such as tear fluid, nasal mucus, and saliva to obtain protein for egg development; they also feed on other sources such as blood from wounds and milk on foal's faces; possess small, rough spines on their mouthparts which cause irritation and mechanical damage, as to the eye tissue; the complete life cycle from egg to adult requires 12 to 20 days; control is difficult.

face marking Any white mark appearing on the horse's face or head; describes the extent of white including star (q.v.), star, stripe, and snip (q.v.), star and stripe (q.v.), snip (q.v.), snip lower lip (q.v.), strip (q.v.), stripe (q.v.), stripe and snip (q.v.), blaze (q.v.), bald face (q.v.), apron face (q.v.), paper face (q.v.), race (q.v.) and white muzzle (q.v.).

face piece *see* DROP NO. 1

facet syndrome pain Pain resulting from stretching of the joint capsule secondary to increased stress on the synovial joints; the associated muscles may respond by contracting to form a muscular splint of the area.

Facteur d'Anglo-Arab Also known by the acronym FAA; a French Anglo-Arab (q.v.) with less than 25 percent Arab (q.v.) blood as required by the stud book registry.

factory-made horseshoe *see* MACHINE-MADE SHOE

fade A racing term; said of a horse who tires and drops out of contention in a race.

fade back A cutting term; a cue given by the rider to the horse to back off, yet remain hooked (q.v.) to the cow being worked.

fadge *see* HOUNDPACE

faeces *see* FECES

failing scent A hunting term; said of the scent (q.v.) of a fox (q.v.) when it gradually becomes more faint.

failure of passive transfer Also known by the acronym FPT; the reduced ability of a newborn foal to fight off infectious disease; results from failure to receive protective antibodies from the mare's colostrum (q.v.).

faint Said of the fox's scent when weak and difficult to follow.

fair catch Also known as legal catch; said if the header's lariat falls around the horns, head, or neck of a steer or calf.

Fairville Cart An Australian, horse-drawn Gig hung on a three spring or Dennett suspension system with detachable shafts.

Falabella A miniature horse breed developed by the Falabella family, Buenos Aires, Argentina; derived from a Shetland Pony (q.v.) deliberately down-bred with crosses of the smallest horses and thereafter through close in-breeding; the smallest horse in the world; although is not suitable for riding, is a popular pet and used for light harness; most colors occur with the Appaloosa (q.v.) coat being highly sought after; stands under 34 inches (86 cm), has an ample mane and tail, small head and ears, large eyes, high withers, short back, and slender legs; is quiet, intelligent, very strong for its size, and possessed of a graceful action; cow-hocks (q.v.) are common.

fall (1) Said of a horse in competition when his shoulder and flank or quarters on the same side touch the ground or an obstacle and the ground. (2) Said of a rider in competition who has separated from his horse, who has not fallen, in such a way that he must remount or vault into the saddle. (3) To drop or come down suddenly from a seated, standing, or erect postion.

fall and drag A stunt performed on horseback; a rider performs a backwards roll off the hip of a moving horse on cue and drags behind the horse with the aid of a cable which runs from the rider's harness down one pant leg to a quick-release system connected to a second length of cable attached to the saddle D-ring (q.v.).

fallen back *see* HOLLOW BACK NO. 1

fallen neck *see* BROKEN CREST

fall in Also known as lean in; said of an unbalanced or stiff horse who, at any gait, falls off a true circle by dropping his shoulder in and throwing his weight onto it; the haunches will generally fall outside of the true circle.

falling out A dressage term; said of a horse whose outside shoulder falls off a true circle on a corner, circle, or in the shoulder-in by dropping his shoulder and throwing his weight onto it, or that the horse has left the original line to the outside.

falling top *see* FOLDING HOOD

fall into the trot A dressage term; said of an unbalanced cantering horse who, either when given the aid to trot, or simply through further loss of balance, pitches into a running trot on the forehand.

fallopian tube *see* OVIDUCT

false belly band A leather or synthetic band fitted over the belly band (q.v.) on pair and team harness horses; prevents the hame tug buckle from moving up and down when the horses are in action; buckles on one side to the hame tug buckle and on the other to the hame tug point.

false canter *see* COUNTER-CANTER

false collar A flat leather pad shaped to fit under the harness collar (q.v.) to protect the shoulders of an unfit or soft horse, one new to harness work, or one whom the collar does not fit from abrasion.

false extension Also known as goose-stepping or toe flipping; the trot (q.v.) when the horse's forelegs are hyper-extended to the extent that the horse's toes flip out in an extended manner often contacting the ground behind a vertical line to which they were extended whilst above the ground; generally a sign of tension, constraint, stiffness, or insufficient engagement and propulsion from the hindquarters.

false favorite A racing term; a horse competing in a race who is favored for no reason sustainable by his form relative to the field (q.v.)

false gallop *see* DISUNITED GALLOP

false leg Also known as false leg or leg guard; a coaching term; an iron leg guard worn by the postillion (q.v.) on the outside of his right leg to protect it from being injured by the pole (q.v.).

false nostril An anatomical peculiarity of the horse's nostril; the top edge of the nostril forming a blind pocket which sometimes flaps when the horse canters resulting in a noise known as high-blowing (q.v.).

false martingale A strap connecting the harness collar (q.v.) to the girth (q.v.); used on pair or team wheelers to hold the collar down and the hames (q.v.) onto the collar.

false ribs Of the horse's 18 ribs, those numbering 9 to 18 as counted from the chest, which are not attached to the sternum.

false rig A completely castrated horse who demonstrates masculine behavior such as attempting to round up mares, attraction to a mare in heat (q.v.), full erection, and occasionally, ejaculation.

false quarter A horizontal crack in the hoof wall caused by disease or injury which affects the growth of the hoof wall from the coronary band (q.v.) and results in permanent hoof wall weakness; generally does not result in lameness provided the soft internal tissue of the foot is not exposed and corrective shoeing is used.

false sole *see* RETAINED SOLE

false start A racing term; said of a race when the regulation start is interrupted as due to mechanical failure of one or more of the gate stall doors or when one or more horses begin a race before receiving formal authorization to do so.

falter A racing term; said of a horse who tires badly.

family (1) A specific group of related objects or living things with a common or associated characteristic, function, or origin, as in the family Equidae to which the horse belongs. (2) The lineage of a horse as traced though either the male or female, depending on the breed of horse.

fancied A racing term; said of a horse favored to win a race.

fancy Said of a horse with a refined appearance.

fancy curb Any single-rein curb bit (q.v.) with elaborately designed cheeks (q.v.).

fancy matched A team of harness horses of distinctly different markings and coloring.

fanning (1) A rodeo term; said of a bronc rider (q.v.); to wave one's cowboy hat in the air and slap one's mount with it to encourage a heartier buck. (2) An old coaching term; light use of the whip (q.v.).

fantail *see* FAN TAIL

fan tail Also spelled fantail; the tail of a docked horse (q.v.) when cut shorter on the sides, tapering to a longer tip.

Fantasia A mounted Moroccan sport performed using mostly gray and black horses of Berber (q.v.) descent; a mock attack performed by two opposing, weapon-bearing bands, enacted in a thrilling manner.

farcy *see* GLANDERS

farm pony *see* WELSH PONY OF COB TYPE

farrier Also known as horseshoer or incorrectly as blacksmith or smithy; one specializing in shoeing horses; formerly one who cared for all aspects of a horse's health; it is believed the word derived from the Low Latin word *ferraius*, meaning a worker in iron and from the old French *ferrer*, to shoe a horse.

Farriers (Registration) Act A British law passed in 1975 prohibiting horseshoeing by unqualified persons; provides for the training and examining of farriers by the Worshipful Company of Farriers (q.v.) of London.

Farriers and Blacksmiths, Amalgamated Society of *see* AMALGAMATED SOCIETY OF FARRIERS AND BLACKSMITHS

farriery (1) The art of shoeing horses. (2) The place where a farrier (q.v.) works.

far side (1) Also known as off side; the right side of the horse when viewed from behind; the opposite of near side (q.v.). (2) A racing term; that portion of a racetrack on the side opposite the viewing boxes, stands, and clubhouse between the bends.

far turn A racing term; the bend of the track (q.v.) off the backstretch (q.v.).

fasciola hepatica *see* LIVER FLUKE

fascioliasis Also known as fluke disease; liver fluke (q.v.) infestation.

fast (1) Swift; rapid. (2) *see* FIRM NO. 2

fast cheek *see* FIXED CHEEK

fast gait Refers to any gait that is not a slow or middle gait (q.v.).

Fast Heavy Draft Breton *see* DRAUGHT BRETON

Fast Heavy Draught Breton *see* DRAUGHT BRETON

fast martingale *see* STANDING MARTINGALE

fast mouth Said of the bit mouthpiece (q.v.) when fixed solidly to the bit cheekpiece (q.v.); does not move in any direction: up, down, or sideways.

fast track A racing term; a dry, hard dirt racing surface on which horses clock better times than on other tracks; the equivalent of a firm track on grass.

fat *see* ADIPOSE

Father of Classical Equitation, The *see* DE LA GUÉRINIÈRE, FRANÇOIS ROBICHON

Father of Foxhunting, The *see* WARDE, JOHN

fats Also known as lipids; soft, solid organic compounds composed of carbon, hydrogen, and oxygen; a useful, and far more concentrated source of energy for the horse than carbohydrates (q.v.) or protein (q.v.); aids in the absorption of some nutrients including the fat-soluble vitamins A, D, E, and K, and is essential for tissue function; supplies unsaturated essential fatty acids including linoleic, linolenic, and arachidonic; can be of vegetable or animal origin.

fat-soluble vitamin Any vitamin that dissolves in fat or oil; can be stored in the body for later use.

fault (1) A weak point in the conformation of a horse. (2) A scoring unit used to record a knockdown, refusal, or other offense committed by a competitor and/or his mount in an event such as show jumping, eventing, etc.; the number of penalties assessed varies by type of competition and the severity of the infraction. (3) *see* AT FAULT

favor a leg (1) Said of a horse with an injured leg who declines to place his full weight on it; a clear indication of lameness. (2) Said of a horse who always leads with the same front leg at the canter or gallop irrespective of the direction traveled.

favorite A racing term; the horse considered likely to win a specific race who has the shortest odds placed against him.

feather (1) Also known as feathering; a hunting term; said of a hound when he waves or moves his hindquarters and tail side-to-side while moving along the presumed line of the fox (q.v.) with his nose to the ground; indicates that the scent is faint and that the hound is uncertain whether he is on the scent of a fox; the hound will not speak (q.v.). (2) Also known as feathering; the long hairs growing from the region of the fetlock, ergot, and pastern on the lower legs of some breeds such as the Clydesdale; may extend along the entire lower leg and over the foot and hoof wall. (3) A racing term; extremely lightweight, as in the jockey (q.v.).

feathered whorl A hair pattern; a type of whorl (q.v.); a change in direction of the flow of the hair in which two sweeps of hair meet along a line, with the direction of flow of each sweep at an angle to the other so that together they form a feathered pattern.

feather edging A driving term; to drive a horse-drawn vehicle extremely close to anything.

feather-edged shoe Also known as anti-brushing shoe, interfering shoe, speedy-cutting shoe, dropped crease shoe, or knocked-down shoe; a corrective horseshoe used on horses and ponies who brush (q.v.); the inner branch is feathered and fitted close in under the hoof wall to reduce the risk of the foot striking the opposite leg; being slightly higher on the inside, this type of shoe causes the horse to move slightly wider than normal, which also helps to prevent brushing; there are no nail holes on the inner branch of the horseshoe, thus the shoe is only nailed on the outside.

feathering (1) *see* FEATHER NO. 1. (2) *see* FEATHER NO. 2

feather in the eye Also known as speck in the eye; any mark across the horse's eyeball that does not touch the pupil; may be a congenital blemish or one caused by injury.

febrile Feverish; having an elevated body temperature.

fecal exam A laboratory test in which technicians quantify the horse's parasite burden by taking microscopic counts of worm eggs in manure samples.

feces Also spelled faeces and known as manure, dung, droppings, excrement, or horse shit; the solid dark brown to green or yellowish discharge from the intestines of the horse; a full-grown horse will defecate eight to nine times a day, averaging a total of 40 pounds (18 kg) of manure; feces from a healthy horse will be formed in well-shaped balls.

feces eating Also known as dung eating or coprophagy; a vice (q.v.); said of a horse who consumes excrement.

Fédération Equestre Internationale Also known by the acronym FEI and as International Equestrian Federation; the international governing body for officially recognized equestrian competitions including the Olympic Games; founded in 1921 by Commandant G. Hector of France; headquartered in Brussels; affiliation required for any nation wishing to participate in official international competitions.

Fédération Equestre International, Dressage Bureau The international governing division responsible for dressage; lays down and maintains up-to-date rules covering standards of performance, the rules and guidelines for judges and competition organizers, judges qualifications, and all other factors that directly affect the sport of dressage; each national federation maintains its own dressage bureau to control national affairs, through which contact is maintained worldwide on matters of principle and method.

Federico Caprilli *see* CAPRILLI, FEDERICO

Federico Grisone *see* GRISONE, FEDERICO

fee (1) The cost of nominating or entering a horse in a race or other event. (2) The amount paid to a professional rider for competing a horse(s) in a race or other event. (3) *see* STUD FEE

feed (1) To give food to; to supply with nourishment. (2) *see* FORAGE

feed bag *see* NOSEBAG

feed bucket A cylindrical, hand-held container used to transport feed to a horse or from which a horse may eat; not to be confused with a manger (q.v.).

feeder (1) One whose responsibility it is to feed horses or other livestock. (2) *see* MANGER

feeding time Also known in Britain as foddering time (obs) or fothering time (obs); the time at which a horse is fed.

feed stuff Also known as food stuff; any nutritive substance fed to livestock; food.

feet (1) More than one foot (q.v.). (2) The base of an anvil (q.v.).

FEI *see* FÉDÉRATION EQUESTRE INTERNATIONALE

FEI Level Also known as International Level; advanced dressage competitions consisting of tests at four levels: Prix St Georges (q.v.), Intermediare I, Intermediare II, and Grand Prix; distinguished from lower-level dressage competitions by the inclusion of flying changes (q.v.) and pirouettes (q.v.), and at the Grand Prix Level, some of the haute école airs (q.v.); tests are standardized worldwide under the jurisdiction of the FEI (q.v.).

FEI World Cup An annual show jumping competition governed by the FEI (q.v.) in which the world's top riders compete to determine the reigning world champion; held in a different location every year.

Fell Also known as Fell Pony and generically as a native pony (q.v.); a light draft and riding pony originating in Cumbria, Britain; the name derives from the Fells, the wild and hilly moorlands of Westmorland and Cumberland on the western slopes of the Pennines; descended from *Equus celticus* (q.v.), Friesian (q.v.) horses brought to Great Britain by the Roman legionaries, and the Galloway (q.v.); genetically related to the Dales Pony (q.v.) compared to which it has a better riding shoulder; stands 13 to 14 hands, is generally black, brown, bay or gray and devoid of white markings, although a white star is acceptable; has a small, quality head, large nostrils, and small ears, luxuriant mane and tail, prominent withers, a long back, short croup, long, sloping shoulder, sturdy legs with a minimum 8 inches (20 cm) of bone, considerable feathering (q.v.), and bluish, round hooves; is extremely strong, frugal, a good trotter, and good-natured, but lively; used for centuries in the Pennine lead mines, to transport goods and people from the mines to the ports, and for farming; now used under harness in competitive driving and for riding.

felloe *see* FELLOW

fellow (1) Also spelled felloe or fellowe or known as felly; that portion of the carriage wheel rim that holds the spokes in place and rests inside the iron tire. (2) One belonging to one of several learned societies.

fellowe *see* FELLOW NO. 1

Fellow of the Worshipful Company of Farriers Also known by the acronym FWCF; the highest certification level awarded by the Worshipful Company of Farriers of London (q.v.) to farriers practicing in Britain; recipients must have achieved the level of Associate of the Worshipful Company of Farriers (q.v.) a minimum of one year prior to application, completed a written thesis 21 days prior to certification, and also oral and practical examinations.

Fell Pony *see* FELL

Fell Pony Society A British organization founded in 1927 to promote the breeding and registration of pure-bred Fell Ponies (q.v.) in the National Pony Stud Book; to qualify for registration as a pure-bred, both the dam (q.v.) and sire (q.v.) must be registered, the cannon bone must have a minimum circumference of 8 inches (20 cm), and white coloring is limited to stars and minimal white on the legs.

felly *see* FELLOW NO. 1

Felton, William An 18th century coach-builder and author of the first book on the subject (published in 1794) entitled "*A Treatise on Carriages*".

female tail *see* DISTAFF

femur Also known as the thigh bone; the primary bone (q.v.) in the horse's thigh; extends from the hip joint (q.v.) to the stifle (q.v.).

fence (1) Any obstacle over which a horse and rider jump; of four basic types: vertical (q.v.), spread (q.v.), water (q.v.), and combination (q.v.); may be natural or man made. (2) *see* RAIL NO. 2. (3) Also known as to fence; to jump over an obstacle.

fencing man *see* TERRIER MAN

fender (1) Also known as sudadero or Western stirrup leather; one of two wide pieces of leather attached on either side of the saddle under the Western saddle seat to which the stirrups (q.v.) are attached. (2) *see* SPLASHBOARD

Fenners bit Also known as parallel bit; a pelham bit (q.v.) with two mouthpieces (q.v.) joined by a rubber band at the center of the mouth; the upper mouthpiece slides up and down while the lower one slides backwards into the mouth of the horse.

feral Any animal living in a self-sustained population following a history of domestication.

Ferneley, John (1782–1860) A renowned equestrian artist with specific interest in foxhunting scenes.

ferrule A hunting term; the shaft of a hunting horn (q.v.).

fertile The ability of the stallion to produce sperm and the mare to produce ovum (q.v.) so that if mating occurs offspring may result.

fertility (1) The state of being fertile; the ability to produce offspring. (2) Also known as fertility rate; the ability of a stallion (q.v.) to produce offspring as measured by the number and frequency with which mares are covered; the state of being fertile (q.v.); varies significantly from stallion to stallion and from the same stallion at different times.

fertility rate *see* FERTILITY

fertilize *see* IMPREGNATE

fetgangur One of five natural gaits of the Icelandic (q.v.); used by a horse under pack.

fetlock (1) Technically, the tuft of hair

located externally behind the fetlock joint (q.v.) of both the fore and hind legs. (2) *see* FETLOCK JOINT. (3) A leg marking (q.v.); white extending from the coronary band (q.v.) up to and including some of the fetlock joint (q.v.) bulge.

fetlock boots A protective leg covering made of felt, leather, and/or synthetic materials used to protect the hind fetlock joint from strikes and blows; generally worn in pairs.

fetlock joint Also known as fetlock, ankle, or metacarpalphalangeal joint; the point of junction of the cannon bone (q.v.) and long pastern including the sesamoid bones; present in both the fore and hind legs.

fetlock ring *see* FETLOCK RING BOOT

fetlock ring boot Also known as brushing ring boot, fetlock ring, or ring boot; a hollow rubber ring fitted over the fetlock of the foreleg and held in place by means of adjustable straps to protect the fetlock joint from strikes and blows.

fetus The developing embryo from 41 days after fertilization until birth.

fever in the feet *see* LAMINITIS

fever rings *see* HOOF RINGS

few spotted leopard Refers to coat color pattern; one of three types of leopard spotting (q.v.); a predominantly white horse with a few colored spots and areas of colored skin.

FHOD *see* FLEXIBLE HYDROACTIVE OCCLUSIVE DRESSING

Fiacre A horse-drawn French Hackney (q.v.) Coach used for ambulance and cab service introduced in the mid-17th century; named after St. Fiacre, an early patron of hospitals and the suffering poor; early versions seated six and were drawn by a pair of horses while later they seated four and sometimes two passengers, and were drawn by a single horse in shafts. (2) *see* FIAKR

fiador A narrow cotton rope used in conjunction with a hackamore (q.v.) to keep the bosal (q.v.) from dropping below the chin; attached to either side of the browband (q.v.), passes under the throat, and connects to the end of the bosal; functions similar to a throat latch (q.v.).

Fiakr Also spelled Fiacre; a horse-drawn, public cab or carriage used predominantly in Austria, Bohemia, and other parts of Central Europe; closely resembled the Fiacre (q.v.).

fiber Also known as roughage and spelled fibre; matter composed of plant filaments; provides bulk to the horse's diet, required to aid and stimulate the digestive process; the primary component of feces (q.v.).

fiber optics The use of light-conducting flexible fiber bundles to deliver light to and from internal spaces.

fiber-optic endoscope Also known as fiber-optic scope; a flexible medical instrument slid through an incision in the body to enable a veterinarian to view the interior of a body cavity; constructed of a flexible tube containing light-conducting fiber bundles which reflect an image into an eyepiece.

fiber-optic scope *see* FIBER-OPTIC ENDOSCOPE

fiber shoe *see* ROPE SHOE

fibre *see* FIBER

fibrin A white insoluble fibrous protein formed from fibrinogen by the action of thrombin especially in the clotting of blood.

fibrinogen The blood protein component responsible for blood clotting.

fibro cartilage A type of cartilage (q.v.) found in the nose and some supporting joints of the horse; is relatively stiff and brittle.

fibrosus Also spelled fibrous; the singular form of fibrosis (q.v.).

fibrosis An accumulation of fibrous tissue in organs where it is not normally found.

fibrous *see* FIBROSUS

fibula The long, slender bone of the hind leg attached to the upper and lower ends of the tibia (q.v.); situated below the stifle joint and extending to the hock (q.v.).

fiddle Slang; a whip (q.v.).

fiddle head A large, coarse, and ugly-shaped head, as of a horse.

fiddling *see* GINGERING

field (1) A racing term; the entire group of horses entered in a race. (2) *see* PARIMUTUEL FIELD. (3) A betting term; all bets placed other than those placed on the favorite (q.v.). (4) Also known as hunt field or followers; a hunting term; the mounted followers, other than the hunt staff (q.v.); usually led by a Field Master. (5) Any section of land suitable for tillage or pasture. (6) *see* PADDOCK NO. 1

field boarder A horse maintained in a pasture for a fee.

field boots Tall black or brown leather riding boots laced at the ankle and over the instep; lacing enables the wearer to walk with comfort; less formal than a dress boot (q.v.).

Field Cart A two-wheeled horse-drawn country cart similar in design to a Dogcart (q.v.); had back-to-back seating for four; the shafts ran outside the square body which was hung on two side-springs and one cross-spring.

field horse An American racing term; two or more starters running as a single betting unit (entry), when there are more starters in a race than positions on the totalizator board.

Field Master Also known as Master of the pack; a hunting term; one designated to lead and control the field (q.v.), keeping them apprised of the movement of the fox and when the hounds (q.v.) are drawing (q.v.) or hunting (q.v.).

field trials A hunting term; a competitive event for foxhounds bred to hunt as individuals rather than as a pack; Walker, Trigg, and July foxhound (q.v.) strains are commonly used; in the United States, are regulated by the National Foxhunters Association.

Fifth Level A dressage competition level actually composed of four tests, each representing an alternative to the FEI Level (q.v.) tests (Prix St. Georges [q.v.], Intermediare I [q.v.], Intermediare II [q.v.], and Grand Prix [q.v.]).

fifth wheel A circular piece of iron attached to the front underside of a four-wheeled, horse-drawn carriage; forms a bearing for the front axle and the under-carriage assembly.

figging *see* GINGERING

figure (1) A racing term; said of a horse; to have a winning chance. (2) A racing term; the handicapper's (q.v.) rating number that identifies the winning chance of a horse. (3) A dressage term; a geometrical component of a dressage test such as a circle, change of rein (q.v.), figure eight (q.v.), etc.; erroneously used interchangeably with "movement".

figure eight (1) Also known as figure of eight (Brit); a dressage movement in which the horse and rider consecutively scribe two circles of the same diameter, the first on one rein and the second on the other rein; direction is changed immediately on completion of the first circle, the shape of an 8 thus being described; the circles touch, but do not overlap. (2) *see* GRAKLE NOSEBAND. (2) *see* FIGURE EIGHT BANDAGE

figure eight bandage Also known as figure eight or figure eight wrap; refers to the manner in which a bandage is wrapped on the leg rather than a type of bandage; the leg is encircled by the wrap once or twice below the hock or knee; next, the wrap is angled up across the front of the joint, then downward crossing the joint from the inside to the outside to form an X; this criss-cross is repeated several times with stabilizing loops both above and below the joint made as necessary.

figure eight noseband *see* GRAKLE NOSEBAND

figure eight wrap *see* FIGURE EIGHT BANDAGE

figure of eight *see* FIGURE EIGHT

file *see* FLOAT

filled leg *see* FILLET STRING

fillet strap *see* FILLET STRING

fillet string Also known as rug fillet, fillet strap, or tail string; the string, strap, or braid of fabric passed under the horse's tail which connects the two rear flaps of a horse blanket (q.v.) or sheet (q.v.) to hold it in place and prevent it from slipping.

fill gear Also known as cart gear or thiller gear; single harness used on a farm horse between the shafts when carting.

Fillis, James (1843–1913) An influential British riding master, well known authority on horses, and author of *Breaking and Riding* and other instructional works; lived most of his life in France, although in 1898 he was appointed riding master to the School of Cavalry for Officers in St. Petersburg, Russia where he remained until 1910.

Fillis method A method of holding the reins of a double bridle (q.v.) developed by James Fillis (q.v.); the curb reins pass around the little fingers while the snaffle reins pass from above over the index finger of each hand; allows for effective use of the snaffle reins.

filly A young female horse under three years of age and in Thoroughbreds (q.v.) under four years of age; from the Anglo-Saxon *fola* meaning young horse, the feminine of which is filly.

film patrol A racing term; the crew that records a horse race on film or tape.

filterable virus Any virus that can survive a special laboratory filtering procedure and remain infectious.

find (1) A hunting term; said of a hound (q.v.) who discovers the line of a fox (q.v.) or coyote and gives tongue (q.v.). (2) *see* UNKENNEL

fine punched A farriery term; said of a horseshoe with a nail hole located relatively close to the outer edge of the web (q.v.).

finish (1) A racing term; the sequence in which race horses cross the finish line (q.v.). (2) see FINISH LINE. (3) The final push to the finish line. (4) *see* DRESS No 3. (5) *see* FLASH NOSEBAND

finish fast A racing term; said of a horse who gains on the leader on the last stretch of a race.

finishing post Also known as winning post; a racing term; the end of a racecourse that is the finish line (q.v.).

finish line Also known as finish, finish wire, or wire; an electronic beam or overhead wire spanning the width of a racetrack which marks the end of the racecourse; the first qualified horse to cross the beam or run under the wire is the race winner.

finish wire *see* FINISH LINE

finish work A farrier term; the rasping action performed by a farrier when cleaning the exterior hoof wall using a hoof rasp.

Finnish Also known as Finnish Horse; a coldblood historically bred in two types: (a) the heavy, or Finnish Draught (q.v.) and (b) the light-heavy, known as the Finnish Universal (q.v.); descended from native ponies crossed with a mixture of many warm and coldblood types imported to Finland; stands 14.3 to 15.2 hands, is strong with good bone, docile, good-natured, and hard working; has good staying power and usually has a chestnut coat with white markings, although brown, bay, or black coats are also common; a good all-round horse, used for driving, timber hauling, riding, and trotting; the only official Finnish breed.

Finnish Draught One of two types of Finnish (q.v.); a coldblood used for heavy pulling; heavier than the Finnish Universal (q.v.).

Finnish Horse *see* FINNISH

Finnish Universal One of two types of Finnish (q.v.); a coldblood used for riding, light draft, trotting, racing, and farming; lighter than the Finnish Draught (q.v.).

Fino board Also known as pista, sounding board, or Fino strip; a 30 foot (9 m) long, approximately 2 to 3 foot (61–91 cm) wide wooden board upon which the Classic

Fino (q.v.) gait of the Paso Fino (q.v.) is demonstrated; in the Classic Fino Division, the horse is required to traverse the length of the board to demonstrate its even, unbroken, and rapid footfall.

Fino strip *see* FINO BOARD

fire (1) *see* FIRING. (2) A racing term; a burst of speed by a horse competing in a race.

fire brand *see* HOT BRAND

fireman (1) A farrier (q.v.) who uses a forge (q.v.) to shape horseshoes (q.v.). (2) *see* AXLE-TREE MAKER

firing Also known as fire; to apply or insert an extremely hot needle, pin, or iron to a blemish (q.v.) or unsound area to hasten and strengthen the reparative process by increasing blood supply; treatment may be graduated from a slight puncturing of the skin to a bone-deep penetration; of two types: line firing (q.v.) and pin firing (q.v.).

firm track A racing term; a firm, resilient turf strip on which horses run faster than other surfaces; the equivalent of a fast track (q.v.).

first flight A hunting term; those members of the field (q.v.) who travel closest to the hound (q.v.) pack.

first incisors *see* CENTRAL INCISORS

first jockey A racing term; the principal person hired by an owner or trainer to ride his horses in competition.

first leg A racing term; the first half of a double (q.v.).

First Level Also known as Novice Level in Britain and Australia; a lower-level dressage competition level in which horses perform a test requiring a greater level of balance and suppleness than Training Level (q.v.) (Preliminary in Britain); the horse must demonstrate that he has developed impulsion (q.v.) and a greater ability to balance and carry himself; includes gait transitions, smaller circles (15 and 10 meters), lengthening of stride, and leg-yielding.

first lock The first part of the mane located just behind the poll and ears, where the bridle path (q.v.) is cut.

first milk *see* COLOSTRUM

first over Also known as first overland; a harness racing term; said of a horse racing on the outside of the track (q.v.) without another horse directly in front of him.

first overland *see* FIRST OVER

first phalanx *see* LONG PASTERN

first premolars *see* WOLF TEETH

first season hound A hunting term; a hound (q.v.) hunted for the first time.

first show *see* FORECAST NO. 1

first turn A racing term; the first bend in the track beyond the starting point.

first whipper-in One of two principal assistants to the huntsman (q.v.) from whom instructions are received; assists in control of the hounds (q.v.), maintenance of the kennels including collection of flesh (q.v.), assisting with hunt staff horses, and when out hunting, turns the hounds to the huntsman.

Fischer von Erlach, Josef Emanual An architect who, between 1729 and 1735, designed and oversaw the building of the Winter Riding Hall, the present home of the Imperial Spanish Riding School (q.v.).

fish eye *see* WALL EYE

fishmeal An animal source of high energy supplemental protein made from several different kinds of fish; an excellent source of amino acids (q.v.), calcium (q.v.), phosphorus (q.v.), and selenium (q.v.); seldom fed to horses because of cost and lack of palatability.

fissure fracture A longitudinal crack through only one side of a bone.

fistula An abnormal channel from a natural body cavity or duct in the skin to the exterior or internal surface; a drainage tract.

fistulous withers A primarily infectious inflammatory disorder of the bursae of the withers caused by the organisms *Brucella abortus* or *Actinomyces bovis*, or trauma from cuts, abrasions, bites, or badly fitting tack, or worm infestation; symptoms include initial swelling, followed by the development of a fistula (q.v.) between the infected bursa and a weeping lesion on the skin; inflammation leads to considerable thickening of the bursa wall; may result in lameness; best treated if diagnosed early; a pommel pad (q.v.) is effective in alleviating trauma related to a poor-fitting saddle.

fit Said of a horse in good physical condition.

five-eighths pole A racing term; a marker pole located on the inside rail (q.v.) exactly five furlongs from the finish line.

five-gaited Said of horse capable of performing two artificial gaits, the slow gait or four-beat stepping pace (q.v.) and the rack (q.v.) in addition to the walk, trot, and canter; depending on the training, pacers and gaited horses may be three- or five-gaited.

five-gaited horse Any horse possessing five gait variations including the slow or four-beat stepping pace (q.v.), and the rack (q.v.) in addition to the walk (q.v.), trot (q.v.), and canter (q.v.); typical of American Saddle (q.v.) and Tennessee Walking Horses (q.v.).

five-gaiter saddler One of three types of horse show classes for the American Saddlebred (q.v.) in which demonstration of the walk, trot, canter, slow gait (q.v.), and rack (q.v.) are required; the other two classes being light harness (q.v.) and three-gaited saddler (q.v.).

five springs A method of springing horse-drawn vehicles consisting of two side-springs, two elbow springs, and one cross-spring; the weight of the vehicle is transferred to the axle via the elbow-springs and cross-springs through the side-springs.

five-ten *see* PICK SIX

fixed cheek Also known as fast cheek; a curb bit (q.v.) where the mouthpiece (q.v.) is fixed solidly to the cheeks (q.v.) and does not move in any direction, up, down, or sideways.

fixed head *see* HUNTING HEAD

fixed race Also known as boat race; any horse race in which the winner has been determined in advance of running the race; a practice not supported by The Jockey Club (q.v.) or other racing associations, but which occasionally occurs.

fixture card *see* APPOINTMENT CARD

Fjord Also known as Fjord Pony, Westlands Pony, or Vestlandhest (Norway); an ancient pony breed originating in Norway; has retained the primitive characteristics of its forebears such as a dun coat, black and silver mane, eel stripe (q.v.), and zebra markings (q.v.) on the legs; stands 13 to 14.1 hands, has a small head, short neck, upright mane, compact body, sloping croup, full tail, and sturdy legs with light feathering; is frugal, stubborn and tireless; used for riding, packing, light draft, and farm work; historically used by the Vikings as a war-time mount.

Fjord Hucul Pony Also spelled Fjord Huzule Pony; a recently developed pony breed developed by crossing Norwegian Fjord ponies with Hucul ponies from the Carpathian Mountains.

Fjord Pony *see* FJORD

flag (1) A piece of cloth of varying size, shape, design, and color, usually attached at one edge to a staff or cord, and used as a sign, standard, symbol, or signal. (2) To place a flag on something or use it to signal. (3) *see* FLARE. (4) A hunting term; the floor of a hound's kennel. (5) *see* DOCK NO. 1

flag down A racing term; to signal an exercise rider that the horse he is riding is working too hard.

flagman A rodeo official responsible for signaling the end of elapsed time in timed events or competitions.

flake (1) Also known as section; a segment of a bale of hay usually equal to one feeding portion, that being approximately 3 pounds (1.4 k). (2) A British term; a single grain, as of corn.

flak jacket Also known as body protection; a protective vest worn by jockeys (q.v.) and eventers (q.v.) while competing to protect the kidneys, ribs, and back.

Flanders Horse *see* BRABANT

flank (1) The part of the horse behind the ribs and below the loins which extends down to the belly. (2) A vaulting term; a compulsory movement (q.v.) performed in vaulting (q.v.) competitions; the vaulter, (q.v.), seated on the horse's back, swings both legs straight forward, then backwards into an extended handstand position, then flexes the hips and rotates them, legs together, to the inside, where the vaulter slides into a sitting position on one buttock; from this position, the vaulter swings his legs backward and again into a handstand, pushes off the grips on the vaulting roller (q.v.) and lands behind and to the outside of the horse. (3) A Western term; to bring a cow or other animal to the ground as for doctoring, branding, etc.

flank cinch Also known as hind cinch or back cinch; the second girth (q.v.) used on Western saddles; usually hangs loose approximately 1 to 2 inches (25–50 cm) beneath the belly of the horse, lies approximately 12 inches (30 cm) behind the front girth (q.v.), and is never drawn tight; used to keep the back of the saddle in place on the back of the horse.

flanker A Western term; one who bring a cow or other animal to the ground as for doctoring or branding.

flanking A calf roping term; said of the roper; to take the catch rope (q.v.) in one hand, reach across the back of a calf or other animal with the opposite hand to pick it up and lay it on its side in preparation for tying its feet.

flank strap A leather strap or rope tightened around the flank area of a horse or bull to encourage him to buck; commonly used in rodeo competitions.

flap (1) Also known as saddle flap; the leather panel laid over the sweat flap, girth straps, and buckle guard of an English saddle upon which the rider rests his leg. (2) *see* SWEAT FLAP

flapper A racing term; a horse who runs in an unauthorized race event.

flapping Also known as flapping meeting; a racing term; an unofficial race meeting not governed by Jockey Club (q.v.) race rules.

flapping meeting *see* FLAPPING

flapping track *see* BUSH TRACK

flaps *see* SKIRT NO. 1

flare (1) Also known as flag; a compulsory exercise performed in vaulting competitions; the vaulter (q.v.) kneels on the back of the horse on one knee, while the other leg and opposite arm are outstretched, back and forward respectively; the hand and raised foot must be at the same height with the side of the foot facing upwards; the vaulter's spine is arched. (2) Outward distortion of the hoof wall; may be medial, lateral, or at the toe; caused by unequal weightbearing on the wall due to neglect or upper limb deviation.

flared foot The horse's hoof when the hoof wall is outwardly distorted; may be lateral, medial, or at the toe; caused by unequal weight bearing on the wall due to neglect or upper limb deviation.

flash (1) A racing term; the change of odds information on the tote board (q.v.). (2) *see* FLASH NOSEBAND. (3) *see* STRIPE

Flash noseband Also known as finish or flash; a hybrid noseband (q.v.) that combines a standard cavesson (q.v.) with another loop attached to the front of the cavesson nosepiece; this loop passes in front of the bit, lies in the chin groove, and is buckled on the left side just below the bit; the cavesson exerts some downward pressure on the upper jaw while the dropped loop exerts closing pressure on the lower jaw; used to prevent the horse from opening his mouth.

flask *see* HUNTING FLASK

flat (1) Also known as flat work; to school or exercise a horse without incorporating cavalletti (q.v.) or jumps. (2) An American racing term; the area around the winning post (q.v.) on the opposite side of the course to the grandstand and official enclosure. (3) A racing term; said of a racing surface, other than a jump course. (4) *see* DRAY. (5) *see* FLAT RACE

flat and laid on Said of the reins when made with two layers of leather; a narrow strip about ½ inch (1.27 cm) wide is laid down the center of 1-inch (2.54 cm) reins and secured by two rows of stitching.

flat bone Said of the cannon bone (q.v.) which appears wide and flat when viewed from the side; the reverse of round bone (q.v.); does not mean that the bone is actually flat; a complimentary term.

flat canter Said of a horse lacking sufficient suspension between canter strides.

flat catcher Said of a horse who looks outwardly sound and of good build, but upon closer examination, has defects.

flat foot A foot lacking normal concavity in the sole; is usually acutely angled and flaring with a long toe and low heels; the horse in motion will often land on his heels to avoid sole bruising; present in some draft breeds; may be inherited and is much more common in the fore than hind feet.

flat footed (1) Said of a horse who does not place his foot squarely or evenly on the ground striking first with the toe rather than the heel; commonly caused by a low hoof wall and associated with a large, soft frog; horses raised on soft ground are particularly prone to this. (2) Said of a horse lacking normal concavity in the sole.

flat foot walk A natural, inherited, loose, four-beat gait, slower than the running walk (q.v.) in which each foot strikes the ground separately at regular intervals: left fore, right rear, right fore, left rear; the hind hooves may overstep the print of the fore by as much as 18 inches (46 cm); characterized by a bobbing or nodding of the head, flopping of the ears, and a clicking of the teeth in rhythm with the movement of the legs; the center of balance is somewhat behind the movement so that the horse appears to squat.

flat pace A smooth, lateral gait in which both legs on the same side leave and strike the ground simultaneously.

flat plates A type of horseshoe (q.v.) typically used on horses racing on turf courses to prevent destruction of the racing surface, or on young horses to avoid leg strain.

flat race Also known as flat or racing on the flat; a racing term; a horse race conducted on flat ground without obstacles such as hedges, hurdles, or fences.

flat-sided Also known as slat-sided or slab-sided; said of a horse whose ribs are neither rounded nor well-sprung (q.v.), resulting in the impression of a straight instead of a curved side; a conformation fault.

flat saddle An English saddle; one without a high pommel or cantle as used for hunting (q.v.), jumping (q.v.), and dressage (q.v.).

flatten out A racing term; said of an exhausted horse who drops his head below the level of the withers (q.v.).

flatulence Also known as gas or wind; the expulsion of gases generated in the alimentary canal from the rectum; gas production generally results from indigestion.

flat work *see* FLAT

flatworm *see* TAPEWORM

flax Any plant of the genus *Linum*; a slender, erect, annual plant with blue flowers, cultivated for its fiber and seeds.

flaxen Refers to mane and tail color; pale, yellowish, and light-colored.

flaxey An American term; said of a horse having a blonde-colored or flaxen mane or tail.

flaxseed *see* LINSEED

fleabitten (1) Refers to coat color; any light-colored horse, e.g., white or gray, whose coat is covered with small, brown marks. (2) A mangy-looking horse.

fleabitten gray Refers to coat color; a horse with a gray (q.v.) coat into which small flecks of color are mixed as in brown or white.

fleaseed Also known as psyllium seed; the seed of the fleawort (q.v.); when crushed and consumed, absorbs large amounts of moisture and becomes slippery and gelatinous in the intestinal tract; used as a mild laxative and preventive for sand colic (q.v.).

fleawort Also known as psyllium; an Old World plantain, *Plantago psyllium*, having seeds that swell and become gelatinous when moist and are used as a mild laxative.

flèche, à la *see* A LA FLÈCHE

flecked Refers to coat color; randomly distributed irregular collections of white hairs throughout the coat.

flecked blanket One of three blanket types common to non-white horses of many breeds, most notably the Appaloosa (q.v.) and Pony of the Americas (q.v.); the edges of blanket blend into the body color with flecks of white hairs.

flecked roan *see* SABINO

Flehmen *see* FLEHMEN POSTURE

Flehmen posture Also known as Flehmen; the horse's body posture when stimulated by certain odors, pain, or sexual arousal; the head and neck are outstretched and the upper lip curls upward, which concentrates the airflow over the vomeronasal organ.

Flehmen response The reaction of the horse to certain odors, pain, or sexual arousal characterized by the Flehmen posture (q.v.).

flesh (1) A hunting term; meat upon which hounds (q.v.) are fed. (2) The amount of weight on a horse, hound, cow, etc., e.g. "That horse had too much flesh". (3) *see* ROUGH OUT

flesh hovel An antiquated hunting term; a room where carcasses were skinned and boned and the meat hung until fed to the hounds (q.v.).

flesh marks Refers to coat color; patches of skin lacking pigment or which differ in color from the rest of the body.

flexible Said of a horse capable of moving the muscles to cause the full bending of a joint between the bones to allow a supple (q.v.), fluid motion; generally refers to movement of the neck, spine, and/or legs.

flexible hydroactive occlusive dressing Also known by the acronym FHOD; a generic wound cover made of a polymer that becomes a gel upon contact with wound fluids; is impermeable and blocks out contaminants and irritants to create a second skin; promotes rapid healing of difficult wounds; originally developed for human application.

flexing hocks Significant hock bend or flexion; is characteristic of, but not peculiar to, the Hackney Pony (q.v.) and essential in execution of the levade (q.v.)

flexion The act of bending of the joints; especially the bending of the horse's head at the poll (q.v.) and the rounding of the neck in response to the aids (q.v.); occurs in two planes: longitudinal (from back-to-front), and lateral (sideways).

flexor tendon A tendon (q.v.) that when stimulated enables joint flexion.

flews A hunting term; the overhanging lips of the upper jaw of a foxhound.

flier (1) A vaulting term; a vaulter performing an exercise who is supported by other vaulters and does not contact the horse. (2) A horse at full gallop (e.g. in a steeplechase) who takes off a long way from a jump, using sheer speed in lieu of precision and timing to clear it.

flies The plural of fly (q.v.).

flight (1) A vaulting term; the movement of a vaulter (q.v.) through the air when performing an exercise; starts as soon as the body is in the air and ends when some part of the body comes in contact with the ground or horse. (2) A jumping term; said of the horse's passage through the air whilst jumping an obstacle. (3) The act of fleeing; a hasty or precipitated departure.

flipper foot Also known as elf's foot; said of the hoof when the toe is extremely overgrown and flared.

float (1) Also known as tooth file, floating, rasp, tooth rasp, file teeth, or file; to file off the sharp edges and points that develop on the outside edges of the upper molars (q.v.) and the inside edges of the lower molars using a rasp. (2) *see* HORSE-

BOX NO. 1. (3) A racing term; to drag a flat plate or wooden implement over the surface of a wet track to help drain standing water.

Float (1) A horse-drawn American goods wagon or dray widely used during the second half of the 19th century; either sprung or dead axle with a sprung seat; drawn by a single horse. (2) An English horse-drawn, two-wheeled, low-loading vehicle, with a forward-facing seat, used for both agricultural and retail delivery purposes such as for milk delivery; generally mounted on cranked axles and entered from the rear.

floating *see* FLOAT NO. 1

floating leaders A driving term; said of lead horses in a team (q.v.) who do not move freely forward.

flog a dead horse To revive a feeling of interest that has died or to engage in a fruitless undertaking; it being as difficult to stir up interest in a mute issue as to try to get a dead horse to pull a load by flogging it; the phrase in French translates more literally, *chercher a ressusciter un mort*, to seek to resuscitate a corpse.

Floyd Hansom A horse-drawn vehicle of the Hansom Cab (q.v.) type built for private use; appeared in 1885, had back and side windows, a glazed hood which let down from the roof to protect the passengers from bad weather, a luxurious interior appointed with ivory fittings, mirrors, parcel and umbrella racks, watch case and a bell with which to signal the driver.

fluke Any of several trematode flatworms parasitic in sheep, man, and snails; two subtypes may affect horses: *Gastrodiscus aegyptiacus* (q.v.) and *Fasciola hepatica* (q.v.).

fluke disease *see* FASCIOLIASIS

fluorine An element in the chlorine family; although no minimum dietary requirements have been established, it has been determined that small quantities are important for bone and tooth development, while excess fluorine, fifty parts/million or more in the horse's ration, is highly toxic and can result in severe skeletal damage including thickened bones, enlarged fetlock joints, and worn down teeth.

flute bit A bit in which the front side of the straight-bar mouthpiece (q.v.) is perforated with holes; used on wind-suckers (q.v.).

flutters Rapid and ineffective contractions of the heart chambers.

fly (1) Any of a large group of insects with two transparent wings including the horse fly (q.v.), black fly (q.v.), face fly (q.v.), horn fly (q.v.), stable fly (q.v.), housefly (q.v.), deer fly (q.v.), culicoides (q.v.), and mosquito. (2) *see* BROUGHAM

fly bonnet Also known as fly cap; a single-piece crocheted hood that covers the ears and forehead of the horse and ties under the throat; the forehead piece swings freely with the horses movement and in so doing protects the horse from flies and gnats.

Fly-by-night *see* BROUGHAM

fly cap *see* FLY BONNET

flyers *see* FLY TERRETS

fly fence *see* FLYING FENCE

fly fringe Connected vertical strips of leather or other material connected to the browband (q.v.) of some bridles or harness headstalls for decorative or protective purposes, e.g. to keep flies out of the horse's eyes.

flying angel A vaulting term; a freestyle exercise in which the flier (q.v.) is supported (by another vaulter) at the shoulders in a horizontal position with arms and legs outstretched.

flying change Also known as flying lead change, flying change of leg, change in the air, change of leg in the air, or canter change of leg; an advanced movement in which the cantering horse makes a complete, clean change of leading leg during the moment of suspension following the third beat of the canter stride; may be executed in a series such as at every fourth, third, second, or first stride; the horse should remain calm and straight with lively impulsion and a consistent rhythm and balance.

flying change of leg *see* FLYING CHANGE

flying lead change *see* FLYING CHANGE

Flying Coach Any horse-drawn, high-speed, six passenger Coach (q.v.) which traveled during the 17th and 18th centuries between Manchester and London, England (barring accidents) in four days (ordinary coaches of the period traveled half as fast) clocking between 4 and 4½ miles per hour (6.4–7.2 kmph).

flying fence Also known as fly fence (Brit); a jumping obstacle; a natural or man-made bank that does not have to be jumped on or off or any fence that can be cleared (q.v.) at a gallop (q.v.).

flying mount *see* RUNNING QUICK MOUNT

flying pace One of five natural gaits of the Icelandic (q.v.); a two-beat lateral gait in which the pairs of legs on the same side move together and touch down together, with a clear moment of suspension; a fast gait used for racing over short distances in which the horse may reach a speed of 30 mph (48 kmph).

flying trench *see* BRIDOON

Flying Wagon (1) *see* LONG WAGON. (2) *see* BROAD WHEELED WAGON

fly link A single ring located in the center of a curb chain (q.v.), set at a different angle than the other rings, through which the lip strap (q.v.) passes.

fly mask A covering for the face of the horse worn for protection from flies and gnats; generally made of fine-gauged mesh; fitted over the ears just behind the poll, connects under the throat, and covers the face of the horse from the ears to just above the muzzle.

fly net A band of strings attached to the bridle browband (q.v.); the strings fall over the forehead and eyes of the horse, their movement prevents flies and gnats from landing on and annoying the horse.

fly sheet Also known as skim sheet; a thin linen, cotton, or synthetic covering for the body of the horse buckled across the chest (q.v.) and under the belly (q.v.); is breathable and used in the summer months to protect the horse from flies.

fly terrets Also known as flyers, hoddlers, bell terrets, or swingers; a form of terret (q.v.); small rings or loops attached to the bridle or head collar browband (q.v.) used on heavy harness horses; used for decoration and to frighten flies in summer; of three types: swingers, danglers, and hodders.

fly wisk A switch consisting of a horse-hair thong attached to a wooden or leather handle used by the rider to remove flies from the horse; the horse hair is often gray.

foal (1) A young horse of either sex from the time of birth until weaning -- approximately one year; from the Anglo-Saxon *fola*. (2) Also known as drop or drop a foal; said of a mare; to give birth to a foal. (3) The offspring of either a male or female parent, e.g., "He was the first foal of Doc Bar." (4) A mule (q.v.) less than two years old.

foal heat Also known as nine-day heat; the estrus period (q.v.), occurring approximately 9 to 11 days after foaling, during which the mare shows signs of heat (q.v.).

foal heat scours Diarrhea (q.v.) that commonly occurs in the mare seven to nine days after foaling.

foal share A breeding term; a contractual arrangement between two parties: the stallion owner puts up one stallion season (q.v.) and the mare owner puts up the mare; the two parties share in the resulting live foal.

foaling *see* PARTURITION

foaling stall Any loose box with ample lighting and air in which the mare can foal.

fodder (1) *see* FORAGE. (2) *see* FEED

foddering time *see* FEEDING TIME

foetus *see* FETUS

foil Also known as stain or foil the ground; a hunting term; to obliterate or disturb the quarry's scent as by crossing over it; a quarry may foil its own scent.

foiled Also known as stained; a hunting term; said of the scent of the quarry when obliterated by sheep, horses, cattle, etc. which cross its line.

foiled line Also known as stained line; a hunting term; said of the line of the fox (q.v.) when obliterated by the scent of sheep, horses, cattle, etc.

foil the ground *see* FOIL

folacin Also known as folate and formerly folic acid; an intestinally synthesized B-complex vitamin necessary for cell metabolism and normal blood formation; although deficiency in horses is quite rare, anemia related deficiency may occur.

folate *see* FOLACIN

folding a whip *see* CATCHING A DOUBLE THONG

folding head *see* FOLDING HOOD

folding hood Also known as folding head or falling top; a convertible or folding leather top found on a horse-drawn vehicle.

folic acid *see* FOLACIN

follicle (1) A small sac or cavity in the ovary (q.v.) containing a developing egg surrounded by a covering of cells; may be found in various stages of development and/or degeneration in the active, mature ovary at any time during the natural breeding season; contains the ovum (q.v.) which may be fertilized by the stallion's sperm. (2) A small anatomical cavity or deep, narrow-mouthed depression, as in a hair follicle.

follicle stimulating hormone A hormone formed in the anterior lobe of the pituitary gland that stimulates growth of ovum-containing follicles (q.v.) in the ovary (q.v.) and activates sperm-forming cells.

follicular stage The period during the estrous cycle (q.v.), including proestrus (q.v.) and estrus (q.v.), during which follicles (q.v.) are formed and the mare becomes receptive to the stallion.

followers *see* FIELD NO. 4

fomentation The application of hot, moist substances to the body by some vehicle such as wool or flannel to ease pain; should not be hotter than the hand can bear.

Fontana safety rail An American racing term; an aluminum rail used on racetracks since 1981, designed to help reduce injuries to horse and rider; has more of an offset or slant than former constructions to provide greater clearance between the rail and the vertical posts and a protective cover to keep the horse and rider from striking the posts.

food stuff *see* FEED STUFF

Food Wagon *see* CHUCK WAGON

foot (1) *see* HOOF. (2) A racing term; speed.

footboard A driving term; the part of a horse-drawn vehicle on which the driver and passengers rest their feet; commonly attached to the wagon at an angle of 33 degrees to the horizontal.

footboard lamp A driving term; a small lamp attached to the footboard (q.v.) of a horse-drawn coach (q.v.) to illuminate the pole head (q.v.).

footfall The sequence of steps at any gait (q.v.).

footing The condition of the surface of a track, arena, course, or field; may be good, bad, wet, etc., e.g., The footing was wet and dangerous.

foot-lock *see* FEATHER

foot loop *see* COSSACK HANG STRAP

foot mange Chorioptic mange (q.v.) occurring on the foot.

foot polo A polo term; a training exercise performed by a walking polo player to work eye to ball to hand coordination; to practice polo strokes and movement of the ball down the field while walking.

foot rest A driving term; a movable foot-rest used on two-wheeled horse-drawn vehicles; generally made of rubber-covered wood shaped so that the feet rest at a 90 degree angle to the legs.

foot stool (1) Also known as shoeing block; a wood or metal block upon which a farrier (q.v.) rests the horse's foot when crimping nails used to set the horseshoe to the hoof or to perform other processes. (2) A driving term; shallow wooden boxes placed above the front and rear boots (q.v.) of a horse-drawn carriage upon which roof-seat passengers rested their feet.

forage (1) Also known as fodder or feed; the food fed to, or consumed by, herbivores, e.g. horses; consists of the entire plant, stalk, leaves, and grain in a fresh, dried, or ensilaged state; of two types: grasses such as Timothy (q.v.), orchard grass, fescue, Bermuda grass (q.v.), etc. and legumes including alfalfa (q.v.), clover (q.v.), lespedza (q.v.), etc.; an excellent source of energy and other nutrients. (2) To wander in search of food.

forage poisoning *see* BOTULISM

forbidden substance Also known as illegal substance; any stimulant, depressant, tranquilizer, or local anesthetic which might affect the performance of the horse and, in some cases, the rider, the use of which is not allowed under various competition rules, both during competition and for such a period which may influence competition performance; in some disciplines, random tests for such substances are performed and a positive result usually leads to disqualification.

forearm That portion of the foreleg (q.v.) between the elbow and the knee; contains two bones, the radius and ulna.

forebody Also known as front end; the forward half of a horse-drawn vehicle.

forecarriage That section of a four-wheeled, horse-drawn carriage consisting of the undercarriage of the front wheels including the front axle, the lower half of the wheel plate, axle bed, sway bar, futchells (q.v.), splinter bar, and associated smaller parts.

forecast (1) Also known as ante-post price (Brit), first show (Brit), or current odds (Brit); a betting term; the bookmakers' odds on each horse running in a race as based on past performance. (2) A betting term; an estimation of the likely odds of horses in a race, before the actual book has been made. (3) A betting term; a wager in which two horses will finish first and second; a "straight forecast" selects the horses in correct order, a "dual forecast" in either order.

forefoot Also known as front foot or forehoof; either of the front feet of the horse.

forefooted A roping (q.v.) term; said of a horse, steer, or other animal roped by the front feet.

foregirth A flat strap approximately 2 inches (5 cm) wide, made of nylon or other material having two leather-covered metal projections with rearward facing hooked tops; is put on the horse in advance of the saddle, buckling behind the shoulder, slightly in front of the saddle girth; the hooks prevent the saddle from slipping forward onto the withers of a horse who is down in front (q.v.) or when riding downhill; available in different shapes and sizes.

forehand Also known as front or incorrectly as forequarters; the part of the horse including the head, neck, shoulders and forelegs (q.v.) in front of the horse's center of gravity.

forehead That part of the face above the eyes and between the temples.

forehead drop *see* DROP NO. 1

forehead piece *see* DROP NO. 1

forehoof *see* FOREFOOT

foreign body Any substance or particle present in the body of the horse that is not part of the tissues or bones, e.g. nails, glass, wood splinters, and gravel.

foreleg Also known as front leg; either of the horse's two front limbs.

forelimb Either of the front legs of the horse including the forearm (q.v.) and foreleg (q.v.).

forelock Also known as foretop; the part of the mane that extends between the ears and falls onto the forehead.

forequarters (1) That portion of the horse's body consisting of the withers (q.v.), shoulders (q.v.), and front legs (q.v.). (2) *see* FOREHAND

Forest *see* NEW FOREST PONY

Forester's pace The long, low canter (q.v.) of the New Forest Pony (q.v.).

Forest Pony *see* GOTLAND

foretop *see* FORELOCK

forewale A driving term; the foremost rim of a collar (q.v.); generally made of leather and stuffed with straw until firm.

forfeit (1) *see* SCRATCH. (2) A racing term; a sum of money consisting of part or all of the entry fee for a race, that is not refundable to the owner or nominator of a horse if the horse is withdrawn from competition. (3) To sacrifice an entrance fee by scratching a horse from a race after the field (q.v.) has been set.

forfeit list A racing term; a list of horses maintained by the racing authorities who are ineligible to compete until the conditions of the forfeiture are resolved.

forge (1) Also known as click; limb contact in which the hind foot hits the sole of the forefoot on the same side; recognized by the clicking noise that occurs when one shoe strikes the other; indicates the horse is generally unbalanced, moving too much on the forehand, which delays the foreleg break-over; occurs in tired, green, or immature horses, those with a short back and long legs, or when shod incorrectly. (2) Also known as shoeing forge; a furnace in which a horseshoe or other metal is heated and wrought. (3) To shape or form a horseshoe or other metal object by heating and hammering. (4) To move with a sudden increase of speed and power, as in a horse on the homestretch.

forhoss Also known as forhust; (obs); the leader in a team when driven at length.

forhust *see* FORHOSS

fork (1) Also known as saddle fork or swell fork; the open portion of the under-side of the saddle (q.v.) that rests upon or above the horse's withers (q.v.). (2) Also known as stable fork or pitchfork; a tool having a long, approximately 4 foot (1.2 m) handle attached to the head with two or more prongs; used for holding or lifting as in mucking out (q.v.) stalls or pitching hay. (3) To ride astride a horse.

Forked Slipe A primitive horse-drawn Irish Slide Car constructed from the forked branches of a tree or large bush boarded across the center; attached to the harness of a draft animal by chains or leather traces.

form (1) A racing term; the past performance of a race horse (q.v.). (2) A hunting term; an indentation or hollow in the ground in which a hare will lie.

formal season A hunting term; that part of the hunt season beginning with the opening meet, around the first of November; hunt staff and members of the field (q.v.) are required to wear formal hunting clothes during this period.

form player A racing term; a bettor (q.v.) who selects horses upon which to bet based on their past-performance records.

form sheet A racing term; a list of horses competing in a race and their past racing performances.

Form, The *see* DAILY RACING FORM

forrard Also known as forrard on; a hunting term; a huntsman's cheer to the hounds to encourage chase of the quarry.

forrard on *see* FORRARD

Fort Riley seat *see* FORWARD SEAT

40 horse hitch *see* SCHLITZ 40-HORSE HITCH

Forty Horse Hitch *see* SCHLITZ 40-HORSE HITCH

forty thieves An antiquated term; gypsies and hawkers found at horse fairs.

forward (1) *see* NUMBER ONE POSITION. (2) A dressage term; toward the direction ahead or in front of the horse, or moving or lending toward that direction.

forward deviation of the carpal joints Also known as dorsal deviation of the carpal joints, bucked knees, knee sprung, goat knees, over in the knees, or over at the knee; a conformation defect; said of a horse whose knees have a forward bend or curve and project too far forward in front of the vertical line of the leg.

forward seat Also known as Fort Riley seat and Italian seat; the position of the mounted rider; the rider takes more weight in the stirrups, eases weight from the seat, and bends slightly forward at the hips to position weight over the horse's shoulders and neck; enables the rider to stay over the center of gravity more easily when jumping; re-introduced by Federico Caprilli (q.v.) in 1890, as pictorial evidence indicates the style existed during the time of Xenophon (q.v.) approximately 400 BC.

forward seat saddle *see* CLOSE CONTACT SADDLE

fothering time A corruption of foddering-time (q.v.).

foul To commit an act, e.g. a dangerous act, that is contrary to the rules of the game played; in the game of polo (q.v.) may be called due to charging, intimidation, foul hooking (q.v.), or crossing the line of the ball.

foul hooking A polo term; a principal infringement in the game of polo in which a player hooks (q.v.) an opponent's mallet at a level higher than the horse's withers.

foundation mare Also known as taproot mare; one of the original, primary mares used to establish the characteristics of a breed.

foundation pedigree option Also known by the acronym FPO; a registration option offered by the Appaloosa Horse Club (q.v.) since 1994 for non-characteristic Appaloosa (q.v.) horses; to qualify, at least half a horse's ancestors, four generations back, must also be registered Appaloosas (q.v.).

foundation sire One of the original, primary stallions used to establish the characteristics of a particular breed for ensuing generations.

founder A chronic condition sequel to laminitis (q.v.) with some degree of pedal bone rotation; internal deformity of the foot results from pedal bone rotation caused by simultaneous detachment from the hoof wall and the constant pull of the deep flexor tendon on the pedal bone; pedal bone rotation may progress to perforation of the sole just in front of the frog; may be triggered by a number of external conditions such as excess protein or water intake as in grain founder (q.v.), grass founder (q.v.), postparturient founder (q.v.), road founder (q.v.), water founder (q.v.), and hypothyroidism (q.v.).

founder rings *see* HOOF RINGS

founder stance The standing position sometimes assumed by a horse afflicted with acute laminitis; a horse places his hind and forefeet well forward of their usual positions; the hind feet bear an inordinate amount of the horse's body weight while the forefeet only bear weight at the heels.

four at length A driving term; a team of four farm horses put to (q.v.), one in front of the other; controlled by two men, one who walked on the offside of the forhoss (q.v.) and the other on the offside of the lash-horse (q.v.), by means of whips placed over the necks of the horses; neither harness nor verbal commands were used.

four-beat stepping pace *see* SLOW GAIT NO. 1

Fourgon A four-wheeled, horse-drawn luggage van or wagon used in the late 19th and early 20th centuries to carry luggage and servants to a destination in advance of a traveling carriage; well sprung and fitted with a hooded row of crosswise seats for personal servants.

4-H *see* FOUR-H CLUB

4-H Club *see* FOUR-H CLUB

Four-H Club Also known as 4-H or 4-H Club; a rural youth organization founded in the United States by the Department of Agriculture offering instruction in agriculture and home economics.

Four Horsemen Also known as Four Horsemen of the Apocalypse; the riders of the four horses described in the apocalyptic vision in Rev. 6: 2–8, which represents the four plagues of humankind: war, famine, pestilence, and death; the figure representing death rides a white horse, war a red horse, famine a black horse, and plague a pale horse.

Four Horsemen of the Apocalypse *see* FOUR HORSEMEN

four-in-hand (1) A vehicle drawn by a hitch of four horses consisting of two pairs with one pair harnessed in front of the other, and one driver. (2) Also known as a four-in-hand team; a four-horse team consisting of two wheelers (q.v.) and two leaders (q.v.).

Four-in-hand Coach *see* DRAG NO. 5

Four-in-Hand Driving Club A horse-drawn vehicle driving club established in Great Britain in 1856; club members, who at its inception numbered 30, met twice annually for drive-to dinners; the only driving club in Great Britain until 1870, at which time the Coaching Club (q.v.) was formed.

four-in-hand team *see* FOUR-IN-HAND NO. 2

four-point trim A hoof trimming technique; the heels are trimmed back to the widest point of the frog, the toe is beveled upward, and the quarters rasped down until they no longer bear weight on a firm surface; the weight of the horse is therefore only borne on four points: one on each side of the toe and each heel.

Fourth Level Also known as Advanced Level in Britain and Australia; a dressage competition test in which a horse is required to show a high degree of suppleness, balance, impulsion, and lightness while remaining reliably on the bit (q.v.), straight, and cadenced; new movements include flying changes of lead every third and fourth strides, and half-pass (q.v.) and half-pirouette (q.v.) at the canter.

four-time (1) Describes a gait in which the correct sequence of footfall in one complete stride consists of four regular hoofbeats, e.g. the walk. (2) Describes a faulty form of canter in which the footfalls of the diagonal pair of legs do not occur simultaneously, thus the three-time beat of the correct gait becomes an irregular four beats; associated with lack of impulsion and/or lack of balance. (3) A version of the tempi changes (q.v.); a movement in canter whereby four strides on one lead are followed by a flying change (q.v.) and four strides on the other lead, in a sequence.

Four-wheeled Dogcart *see* DOGCART PHAETON

Four-Wheeler A four-wheeled, one-horse-drawn cab used in London, England.

fox Also known as Charley or Charlie; any of a group of wild carnivorous mammals, genus *Vulpes*, of the dog family, having bushy tails, commonly reddish-brown or gray fur, and weighing 8 to 12 pounds (3.6–5.4 kg); especially noted for their cunning and speed; hunted on horseback for more than 300 years.

fox den Also known as den, fox earth or earth; a hole or series of holes having underground chambers in which foxes (q.v.) live and raise their cubs.

fox dog *see* FOXHOUND

fox earth *see* FOX DEN

foxhound Also known as fox dog; one of the various breeds of fleet, keen-scented, keen-sighted hounds bred and trained to hunt foxes.

Foxhound Kennel Stud Book, The A breeding record of foxhounds (q.v.) first compiled in 1841 in Britain; the first volume contained a list of the King of England's buckhounds and 46 packs of foxhounds; subsequent volumes have been issued at frequent intervals; registers two strains of foxhounds under the heading American Hounds: (1) the Penn-MaryDel (q.v.) and (2) Rappahonnock River Valley strains.

fox hunt *see* FOX HUNTING

foxhunter Any handy horse possessed of good stamina and jumping ability ridden by a hunter (q.v.) when following hounds in their pursuit of the fox.

Foxhunter An international show jumper

(q.v.) foaled in 1940 by the Thoroughbred (q.v.) sire Erehwemos and out of Catcall who descended from a pure-bred (q.v.) Clydesdale (q.v.) mare; represented Great Britain, tallied 78 international wins, and was retired in 1956.

fox hunting Also known as hunting or fox hunt; to hunt for live fox or coyote from horseback or on foot, with a pack of hounds; due to the scarcity of wild fox in many regions today, foxes released from captivity, coyotes, and fox scent are used as quarry; a traditional sport in Britain where it gained the height of its popularity in the 18th century.

fox hunting club *see* HUNT

fox kennel A hunting term; a fox den located above the level of the surrounding ground.

fox sense A hunting term; the innate ability of a hound to locate a bedded fox and to recover its line after a check (q.v.).

fox terrier A small, smooth- or wire-haired dog of the terrier family formerly used to hunt and dig for small burrowing animals such as foxes (q.v.) and rabbits (q.v.) and engage the quarry underground or drive it out; from the French, *terrier,* meaning "of the earth", or "earth dog".

fox trot (1) A slow, short, unevenly spaced, four-beat gait with distinct over-striding of the hind hooves; the horse walks actively from the front shoulder trotting behind, the hind hooves stepping onto the track of the fore and then sliding forward; the left hind foot strikes the ground followed quickly by the diagonal or right forefoot, followed by a slight pause and then the right hind; accompanied by a rhythmic movement of the head; the sliding action minimizes the concussive effect of the trot; the horse can maintain this gait for long distances at a regular 5 to 10 miles (8–16 km) per hour. (2) A social dance, in duple or quadruple time, characterized by various combinations of short, quick steps.

FPO *see* FOUNDATION PEDIGREE OPTION

FPT *see* FAILURE OF PASSIVE TRANSFER

fractions A racing term; race times taken at quarter-mile intervals in races and work-outs.

fractional time A racing term; the running time taken at various points between the start and finish of a horse race.

fracture Also known as break; to become separated into parts as a bone; of twelve types: comminuted fracture (q.v.), compound fracture (q.v.), condylar fracture (q.v.), fissure fracture (q.v.), metacarpal fracture (q.v.), oblique fracture (q.v.), saucer fracture (q.v.), sesamoid fracture (q.v.), slab fracture (q.v.), spiral fracture (q.v.), simple fracture (q.v.), or stress fracture (q.v.).

frame The size of the horse in relation to other horses of the same breed or used for the same purpose, as in large framed.

Franches-Montagnes A small draft warmblood originating in the Jura region of Switzerland by putting imported Anglo-Norman (q.v.) stallions to native, Bernese Jura mares; English half-bred hunter and Ardennes (q.v.) blood was introduced in early days of the breed; since that time, the breed has remained relatively pure; is early developing, steady, sure-footed, active, calm, powerfully built, cob-type with a rather heavy head, a full forelock falling over a broad forehead, small ears, a muscular, arched neck, short back, and slightly sloping croup; may be bay or chestnut; used for light draft, farm work, and riding.

Francis Barlow *see* BARLOW, FRANCIS

Francis Galton *see* GALTON FRANCIS

François Robichon de la Guérinière *see* DE LA GUÉRINIÈRE, FRANCOIS ROBICHON

Frederiksborg Also known as Danish Horse and spelled Frideriksborg; a horse breed developed in 1562 at the Royal Stud in Frederiksborg, Denmark by King Frederik II, by crossing Neapolitan (q.v.) and Andalusians (q.v.) after contributing to the development of the Lipizzaner (q.v.) and the Orlov Trotter (q.v.), it fell into a period of decline until 1939, at which time it was further developed with the addition of Friesian (q.v.), Oldenburg (q.v.), and later, Thoroughbred (q.v.) and Arab (q.v.) blood; stands 15.1 to 16.1 hands, has a chestnut coat , good temperament, small foot, full and fairly deep chest, strong shoulder, straight back, and well-proportioned, although slightly convex, head; used as a military charger, school horse in the great European riding schools, under light harness, carriage, and riding.

free action Said of a horse who has good impulsion from behind, is balanced, and moves the front feet well out in front of his body.

freedom A dressage term; the amplitude of the range of motion of the horse's fore and hind limbs.

free dressage Said of a horse; to perform tricks without a rider as in a circus (q.v.).

free handicap (1) A racing term; a race in which no nominating fees are required. (2) *see* EXPERIMENTAL FREE HANDICAP

free jump *see* JUMP FREE

freelance A racing term; said of a jockey who is not under contract to a stable or owner.

freemartin A filly twin of a colt.

free radical An atom lacking one or more electrons; attempts to replace the missing electron(s) by scavenging the body and robbing electrons from healthy cells; this process creates a damaging free radical chain reaction in the body that erodes the cell membranes and can alter the manner cells encode genetic information in the DNA (q.v.).

Free Roaming Wild Horse and Burro Act Legislation passed in the United States in 1971 to protect wild horses and burros from harassment, death, and capture; subsequent amendments prohibit tracking by helicopter.

Freestyle *see* KÜR EXERCISE

freestyle exercise *see* KÜR EXERCISE

freestyle reining Reining maneuvers conducted to music in a format designed by each competitor; a sanctioned National Reining Horse Association (q.v.) class since 1992.

free walk A relaxed walk (q.v.) in which the horse is allowed to lower his head, stretch out his neck, and relax his back; may be ridden on loose or long reins.

freeze brand (1) Also known as freeze mark, cold brand, or cryogenic brand; an identifying symbol, character, letter, or series of numbers, or any combination thereof, burned into the flesh of the horse using a bevel-edge "iron" made of brass, copper, steel, or iron super-cooled in liquid nitrogen to 320 °F below zero; the length of time the iron is applied to the hide to achieve the mark depends on the type of metal it is made of, the strength of the brander, the age, sex and breed of the horse, the time of year, and the strength of the horse's hide; on dark-colored horses, the iron is applied to the hide sufficiently long to freeze the hair and skin, without killing the hair follicle, within the mark, the hair will grow in white; the ideal mark has a bald center surrounded by white hair; on roans (q.v.), grays (q.v.), whites (q.v.), palominos (q.v.), buckskins (q.v.), and Appaloosas (q.v.) prone to roaning, the iron is left on long enough to kill the hair follicle, leaving a pink, hairless mark; AHSA (q.v.) rules state that a horse shall not be discounted for a freeze brand, although the color-added rule may be exercised by some judges. (2) To apply an identifying symbol, character, letter, or series of numbers, or any combination thereof to the hide of the horse using an iron super-cooled to 320 °F below zero in liquid nitrogen.

freeze brand iron A bevel-edged iron made of brass, copper, steel, or iron used to freeze brand (q.v.) a horse.

freeze mark *see* FREEZE BRAND

Freiberger A relatively new warmblood breed developed at the Avenches Stud in Switzerland based on the Franches-Montagnes (q.v.) improved with heavy infusions of Shagya Arabian (q.v.) and Norman blood; a riding horse standing 15.2 to 16 hands with an Arabian-type head, good shoulders and quarters, short back, deep girth, and strong legs with plenty of bone; is active, intelligent, and possessed of great stamina.

French Anglo-Arab A French-bred Anglo-

Arab (q.v.); a horse breed developed in 1843 by veterinarian E. Gaynot at the Le Pin and Pompadour stud farms, located in France; developed from a nucleus of broodmares of Oriental origin interbred with local horse populations to produce the Tarbenian and Limousin (q.v.) breeds with the addition of other Arab (q.v.) and Thoroughbred (q.v.) blood; a solidly built horse standing 15.2 to 16.3 hands with good conformation, and powerful hindquarters; must have at least 25 percent Arab (q.v.) blood and lack other horse breed pedigrees other than Arab, Anglo-Arab, or Thoroughbred for at least the last six generations; a solid-colored coat dominates in bay, brown, black, and chestnut; used for riding, racing, and other competitions.

French Ardennaise *see* ARDENNAISE

French bridoon A snaffle bit (q.v.) having a double-branched mouthpiece, the branches of which are connected in the middle with a small, flat plate approximately ¾ inch (19mm) long; acts in the same way as a French snaffle (q.v.), but has a lighter and thinner mouthpiece.

French brushing boot A light-duty brushing boot (q.v.); is shorter than an ankle boot (q.v.) and only protects the fetlock joint.

French Calèche *see* CALECHE NO. 2

French Cavalry School at Saumur Previously known as the French School, School of Saumur, or the School of Mounted Troop Instruction; one of two riding schools established in France in the early 18th century to teach the French school of classical equitation (q.v.) which was combined with other forms of competitive sport; influenced by François Robichon de la Guérinière (q.v.); favors Thoroughbred (q.v.) and Anglo-Arab (q.v.) horses; the home of the Cadre Noir (q.v.).

French chasing boot A heavy-duty brushing boot (q.v.) somewhat taller than an ankle boot (q.v.), which protects the fetlock joint and part of the lower cannon bone.

French clip *see* STUD FASTENING

French Four-Wheeled Hansom *see* COURT HANSOM

French noseband *see* SHADOW ROLL NOSEBAND

French Phaeton A horse-drawn carriage of the Phaeton (q.v.) type; hung on front and rear sideways-elliptical springs, seated two on the driving seat, with two rearward cross seats in a semi-open compartment, and was entered through side doors; had slatted compartments for gun dogs under both the passenger and driving seats; drawn by a single horse in shafts or a pair in pole gear (q.v.).

French Saddle Horse *see* SELLE FRANÇAIS

French Saddle Pony Also known as Selle Français although that name usually pertains to the Selle Français (q.v.) horse; a pony breed newly developed in France through the selective crossing of native mares with Arab (q.v.), Connemara (q.v.), New Forest (q.v.) and Welsh (q.v.) stallions; stands 12.1 to 14.2 hands; all colors are permitted; has a small head, long neck, straight back, a wide, deep chest, and strong legs with well-formed joints; is quiet, yet energetic; used for jumping, dressage, and under harness.

French School *see* FRENCH CAVALRY SCHOOL AT SAUMUR

French snaffle A snaffle bit (q.v.) having a double-branched mouthpiece; the branches are connected by a small, flat plate approximately ¾ inch (19mm) long; acts in the way same as a French bridoon (q.v.), but has a heavier and thicker mouthpiece; less severe than a Dr. Bristol (q.v.).

French Tilbury Tug *see* TILBURY TUG

French tie *see* MUD TIE

French Trotter Also known as Norman Trotter; a French breed developed in 1836 by putting Thoroughbred (q.v.), half-bred English Hunters, and Norfolk Trotters (q.v.) to Norman (q.v.) mares; two Thoroughbreds had particular influence on the breed, Young Rattler and The Heir of Linne; 90 percent of modern Trotters trace back to five descendants of these two stallions: Conquerant, Lavater, Normand,

Phaeton, and Fuschia; a tall, light-framed horse, with a fine head, prominent withers, strong back, and sloping hindquarters: lacks uniformity in conformation; stands 15.1 to 16.2 hands, with a bay, black, chestnut, dark chestnut, or occasionally gray coat; an athletic and fast horse used for trotting, riding, and cross-breeding.

fresh (1) Said of a horse who is feeling good, spirited, slightly excitable, and perhaps a little strong, as on early mornings, cool days, or when not having been worked. (2) *see* FRESH CATTLE

fresh cattle Also known as fresh or unsettled; a cutting term; cattle that have not previously been used in cutting events or competitions.

fresh-catched coachman An obsolete driving term; a newly trained driver.

freshener A racing term; to lay off an overworked horse to restore his energy.

fresh fox A hunting term; any fox, other than the one originally pursued by the hounds (q.v.) at the beginning of the hunt; the hounds may switch to the line of a fresh fox of their own accord.

fresh line A hunting term; any new scent left by a fox or other prey.

Frideriksborg *see* FREDERIKSBORG

Friendship Stakes A stakes race (q.v.) held in the United States for two-year-old, Accredited Texas-Bred Thoroughbred horses; sponsored by the Texas Thoroughbred Breeder's Association.

Friesian Also known as Harddraver meaning "good trotter" in Dutch and spelled Frisian; one of the oldest breeds in Europe indigenous to the Netherlands; has a compact and strong build, a short, but well-arched neck, straight and short back, broad chest and loins, full and long mane and tail hair, feathered legs, large, strong feet, an exclusively black coat, very rarely presenting white markings on the forehead, and stands approximately 15 hands; the leg action is characteristically high; used for carriage driving, farming, and dressage.

Friesian Chaise Also known as Sjees; a two-wheeled, horse-drawn vehicle of the Gig (q.v.) type pulled by two Friesian (q.v.) horses harnessed on either side of a pole; traditionally, the traces and reins were made of white rope and the harness decorated with white trimmings.

Frisian *see* FRIESIAN

frock coat A knee-length coat worn by members of the Hunt (q.v.); staff members will wear square-skirted frock coats while members of the field will wear round-skirted ones.

frog (1) The V-shaped, elastic-like portion of the rear underside of the hoof between the bars which acts as a buffer to absorb impact and prevent slipping; expands laterally when bearing the weight of the horse. (2) A driving term; the single loop which connects the reins when using the Hungarian driving style.

frog cleft The natural depression located in the center of the widest part of the frog (q.v.).

from the horse's mouth From the original source.

front (1) *see* BROWBAND. (2) *see* FOREHAND

front boot A storage compartment located between the driving seat and the front axle of most horse-drawn coaches.

front end *see* FOREBODY

front foot *see* FOREFOOT

front leg *see* FORELEG

front runner A racing term; a horse who prefers to run in the front of the field (q.v.).

frost Refers to coat color pattern; white specks of hair on a dark body; one of six symmetrical Appaloosa (q.v.) coat color patterns recognized by the Appaloosa Horse Club (q.v.).

frost nail A special horseshoe nail designed to provide temporary, hard-surface traction.

frosty Also known as skunk tail; refers to coat color; white hairs at the base of the tail, in the mane, down the back, over the pelvic bones, and on other bony points such as the hocks.

frozen track A racing term; a frozen running surface.

frush *see* THRUSH

full (1) *see* STALLION. (2) *see* FULL MOUTH NO.1

fullblood *see* HOTBLOOD

full book Said of a stallion (q.v.) when bred to the maximum number of mares allowed by his manager in any given year.

full bridle *see* DOUBLE BRIDLE

full brothers *see* BROTHERS

full cheek The vertical portion of the bit exterior to the mouth and extending above and below the mouthpiece (q.v.) to which the bridle cheekpieces (q.v.) and reins are attached.

full-cheek snaffle A bit; a straight or jointed mouthpiece fitted on either end with fixed rings to which arms are attached above and below the mouthpiece on the mouth-side of the bit; the rings prevent the bit from running through the mouth of a horse if he runs sideways or refuses to turn; when attached to the cheekpiece of the bridle is considered a leverage bit, acts on the sides of the mouth, the lips, and the corners of the mouth; commonly used on jumpers.

full clip Also known as body clip or clipped right out; to remove the entire coat of the horse including the head and leg hair; the mane may be clipped or left full; used mainly on horses shown or worked through the winter and spring.

full collar An adjustable, oval-shaped piece of harness equipment placed over the head of the horse and fitted around the neck and against the shoulders to support the hames (q.v.) to which the traces are attached.

full cry A hunting term; said of the pack when every hound cries on the line of a fox (q.v.).

fullered shoe A horseshoe (q.v.) having a narrow groove cut into the ground-side surface; the groove fills with dirt and thus provides traction and prevents suction.

fullering (1) To cut a groove into the ground side of barstock (q.v.) before it is shaped into a horseshoe to provide traction for the shoe and a seat for the nail heads. (2) A blacksmithing term; to spread metal by forcing a wedge or similar edge tool into it. (3) *see* CREASING. (4) A two-phase process in which horseshoe stock is worked prior to the nail groove being cut so that the web is the same width before and after fullering.

full halt A complete stop of the horse achieved by the total halting of the rider's hands and bracing of the back.

full hand A driving term; a method of holding the four reins of a team, all four reins are held in the left hand, the near lead rein passes over the index finger, the off lead rein over the second finger, the near wheel rein over the third finger, and the off wheel rein over the little finger.

full horse *see* STALLION

full mouth (1) Also known as made mouth, made or full; the horse's mouth at five years of age, when all of the teeth (40 in the male and 36 in the female) have grown in. (2) A horse six years old or older.

full pass Also known as full travers, traverse, sidepass or side step; an advanced dressage movement performed on two tracks (q.v.); the horse moves laterally without noticeable forward movement; executed from a standstill; the horse's outside legs step over those of the inside, the hoofmarks of the fore and hind legs marking two parallel lines; introduced for military purposes to allow the riders to correct their position between one another when in formation.

full pastern *see* PASTERN

full port Also known as high port; the portion of a curb bit (q.v.) that curves upward in the center of the mouthpiece ½ to 1¼ inches (13–32 mm); can be extremely severe; presses against the roof of the mouth while the mouthpiece on either side acts on the bars.

full safe *see* BOX KEEPER

full sisters *see* SISTERS

full stocking A leg marking (q.v.); consists of white which extends from the coronet (q.v.) to the bottom of the knee on the foreleg and to the bottom of the hock on the hind; not accepted by some horse registries such as the American Quarter Horse Association (q.v.).

full travers *see* FULL PASS

fully headed Said of any fully enclosed horse-drawn carriage.

fully mouthed Said of a horse having a full set of permanent teeth (q.v.), 36 in female horses (female horses do not have canines) or 40 in the male; usually occurs by approximately five years of age.

Fulmer snaffle *see* AUSTRALIAN LOOSE-RING CHEEK SNAFFLE

funeral horse *see* BLACK BRIGADE

funk Said of a temperamental horse who gets onto his toes, breaks into a sweat, or shows other signs of nervousness.

Furioso Also known as Furioso-North Star; a warmblood descended from two English stallions, Furioso and North Star, imported to the Mezöhegyes Stud, Hungary around 1840; both were put to Norman (q.v.) mares but, initially, the two lines were kept separate; in 1885, the Furioso and North Star lines were crossed to create the Furioso strain; stands 16 to 16.2 hands, has a brown, bay, or black coat with white markings the exception, a muscular body, straight back, sloping hindquarters, and low-set tail; exceptionally versatile, it is a good all-round riding horse and goes equally well under harness.

Furioso-North Star *see* FURIOSO

furious driving Reckless coach racing; a chargeable offense in 19th-century England, as for coach drivers of heavy wagons drawn by four and five horses, and wagoneers.

furious rabies Rabies (q.v.) infection in which the excitative phase is predominant, the affected horse will demonstrate the classical mad-dog syndrome in which the horse becomes irrational and viciously aggressive; the facial expression is anxious and alert, the pupils dilated, all fear and caution of natural enemies lost, paralysis absent, the horse may appear extremely agitated as evidenced by rolling as with colic (q.v.) or biting or striking viciously and self-inflicted wounds may result.

furlong Also known as eighth (sl), panel, and historically as furrow long (deemed to be the length of a ploughed field); a racing term; a distance of ⅛ mile, 220 yards or 660 feet (0.20 km).

furniture Also known as mountings or horse furniture; a late 19th- and early 20th-century term for the metal buckles or mountings used on harnesses or saddlery as made from a variety of metals including solid nickel, solid brass, steel, or any metal plated with silver or brass; all the buckles used in a harness should be made of the same metal and design, and match that of the vehicle fittings and lamps.

furosemide A medication used in the treatment of bleeders (q.v.); acts as a diuretic (q.v.) and reduces pressure on the capillaries; commonly known by the trade name Lasix.

furrow long The length of a plowed field; became the unit of measure in horse race distances – a distance of ⅛ mile (0.20 km).

futchell A driving term; longitudinal pieces of wood that support the splinter bar, pole (q.v.), or shaft (q.v.) at one end and attach to the axle-tree bed and to the sway bar (q.v.) on the other.

futchell stay An iron plate used to strengthen a wooden futchell (q.v.) on a horse-drawn carriage.

futurity (1) A racing term; a stakes race for two-year-old horses nominated for the race before birth. (2) A cutting event for three- and four-year-old cutting horses.

fuzztail *see* MUSTANG

fuzztail running To herd and catch wild horses or mustangs (q.v.).

FWCF *see* FELLOW OF WORSHIPFUL COMPANY OF FARRIERS

G

gad (1) *see* SPUR. (2) A racing term; a jockey's whip.

gadfly *see* HORSE BOTFLY

GAG *see* GLYCOSAMINOGLYCAN

gag (1) *see* GAG BIT. (2) *see* GAG CHEEK

gag bit Also known as gag; any snaffle bit (q.v.) equipped with full or half rings into which holes or slots are cut in the top and bottom and through which rolled leather or cord cheekpieces pass; the cheekpieces are attached to gag reins (q.v.) below the bit; when the rider draws down or back on the rein, the bit slides upward along the cheekpieces, putting pressure on the poll and corners of the mouth rather than the bars; a strong bit effective for hard-to-control horses; include half-Balding gag bit (q.v.) and others.

gag bridle A bridle (q.v.) used in conjunction with a gag bit (q.v.); acts primarily to raise the head by lifting up the bit against the corners of the horse's mouth; action achieved by the bridle cheeks, usually rolled leather or cord, which pass through two aligned holes at the top and bottom of the bit ring before attaching to the rein; it is customary to fix a second rein to the bit so that it lies above the gag rein, this enables use of the gag rein only when necessary.

gag cheek Also known as gag or gag cheekpiece; that portion of a gag bit attached on either side to the bit mouth-piece and through which the cheekpieces (q.v.) pass.

gag cheekpiece *see* GAG CHEEK

gag rein Any rein used in conjunction with a gag bit (q.v.) and gag bridle (q.v.); attached to the bit cheekpieces (q.v.).

gag runner Also known as bradoon hanger or bearing rein drop; a small leather strap with a dee-ring on one end, buckled to each side of the crown piece on the other, and through which the bearing rein passes before connecting to the pad.

gags The two cheekpieces (q.v.) of a gag bit (q.v.).

gained gaits Any of the horse's paces developed by systematic riding training; include the school gaits, cross-over steps, etc.

gait (1) A specific, repeated mode of locomotion characterized by a distinctive rhythmic and timed movement of the feet and legs; may be natural, i.e. typical to most breeds and types, as in the walk, trot, canter and gallop or acquired through breeding and/or training, as in the amble (q.v.), rack (q.v.), etc.; include the basic gaits (q.v.) and gained gaits (q.v.). (2) An obsolete British term; agistment (q.v.).

gaited *see* GAITED HORSE

gaited horse Also known as gaited; any horse having three natural gaits: walk, trot, canter, or walk, jog, and lope, and at least one acquired gait or one inherent to the breed such as the stepping pace (q.v.), rack (q.v.), or single-foot; common to such breeds as Tennessee Walker (q.v.), Fox Trotter (q.v.), Paso Fino (q.v.), and Peruvian Paso (q.v.).

gaited out *see* AGISTMENT

Galiceño A pony breed originating in the 15th century in the Spanish region of Galicia from which the name derived; descended from the Portuguese Garrano (q.v.) transported to Mexico in the 16th century by the Conquistadors; stands 12 to 13.2 hands, usually has a bay, black, or chestnut coat with piebald (q.v.), skewbald (q.v.), and albino (q.v.) color patterns not accepted; has an average head, short and muscular neck, pronounced withers, short back, narrow chest, relatively straight shoulder, strong, long legs, and a small foot; is docile, intelligent, versatile, courageous, a naturally good jumper, and possessed of speed and endurance; since 1959, popularity has spread throughout the United States where it is a favored harness and children's riding and jumping pony.

Galician *see* GALICIAN PONY

Galician Pony Also known as Asturcon or Asturian in Asturia; an ancient pony breed originating in the Spanish regions of Galicia, from which the name derived, and Asturia, particularly the Asturian mountains, located in Spain; is very hardy, docile, frugal, and adept at locating forage; has a brown or black coat which becomes notably longer, thicker, and lighter colored in winter; except for a star, white markings are not permitted; has a heavy head, small ears, long neck, a thin, flowing mane, low-set tail, and tough, short legs; used for riding and light draft; recent efforts have saved the breed from extinction.

gall (1) A sore and/or swelling on the hide of the horse caused by friction as by ill-fitting or dirty tack. (2) To put a sore and/or swelling on a horse, e.g. "To gall a horse."

gallop (1) Also known true gallop or, in coaching terms, as springing; the fastest of the natural gaits; a four-beat action, in which the sequence of footfall is one hind foot, the other hind foot, the forefoot lateral to the first-impacting hind foot, the forefoot lateral to the second impacting hind foot, followed by a moment of suspension; the stride is more extended and the moment of suspension longer than in the canter (q.v.); the fastest of the gaits. (2) *see* RUN NO. 3

gallop for wind To gallop (q.v.) a horse in circles to ascertain whether he is sound in the wind (q.v.).

galloping ground of western coaches An antiquated British term; a straight stretch of road between the English towns of Hounslow and Staines along which coachmen would let their teams stretch out.

galloping sheet *see* QUARTER SHEET

gallop up To ask a horse to gallop (q.v.) by means of the rider's aids.

Galloway (1) An ancient British Pacer bred between Nithsdale and the Mull of Galloway, Scotland, extinct since the 19th century; the favored mount of the border raiders and Scottish drovers; stood between 13 and 14 hands, was hardy, sure-footed, possessed great stamina and strength, and was fast under saddle and harness; had a brown, black, or bay coat and was renowned for its hard blue hooves; thought to have been part of the running horse stock which contributed to sires of the 17th and 18th centuries from which descended the English Thoroughbred (q.v.); contributed to the gene pool of the Fell Pony (q.v.). (2) A specific height class in riding and in-hand show classes; of two types: small Galloway for animals standing 14 to 14.2 hands and large Galloway for animals 14.2 to 15 hands.

galon (1) A Mexican term; a heavy or draft horse. (2) A contraction of get along, pronounced g'long; a voice command to urge working horses into their harness collars.

galop depart A dressage term; said of a horse when he transitions from a stop, halt, or walk into a canter.

galop faux *see* COUNTER-CANTER

galop juste *see* TRUE CANTER

Galton, Francis (1822–1911) A geneticist who developed the theory of genetic inheritance known as Galton's Law (q.v.).

Galton's Law The theory of genetic inheritance developed by Francis Galton (q.v.); inheritance is determined ¼ by the sire (q.v.), ¼ by the dam (q.v.), 1/16 by each of the grandparents, 1/64 by each of the great grandparents, and so on with each ancestor contributing just ¼ as much to the total inheritance as the generation closer to the individual; incorrectly assumes that individual heredity is completely determined by the heredity of the ancestors; the relationship between ancestor and descendant is halved with each additional generation intervening between them; often used as a stamina index by Thoroughbred (q.v.) breeders.

Galvayne's groove Also known as Galvayne's mark; a longitudinal, dark-colored groove in the upper third incisors (q.v.); appears when the horse is about 10; begins at the gum line of the upper corner incisor at about 10 years, moving halfway down the tooth by 15 years, covering the entire length of the tooth by 20 years, seen in the bottom half of the tooth at 25 years, and disappearing at about 30 years; is less reliable than other indicators for estimating age in the young horse, but is quite valuable in placing the age of the older horse.

Galvayne's mark *see* GALVAYNE'S GROOVE

Galvayne, Sydney A renowned British horse breaker and trainer active in the late 19th century; his technique involved using the strength of the horse against itself.

Galway Blazers *see* BLAZERS, THE

Gambler's Choice *see* GAMBLER'S STAKES

Gambler's Stakes Also known as Gambler's Choice; a timed jumping competition in which each fence is awarded a point value based on the difficulty of the jump; each competitor is free to select the jumps and the course he or she will ride to accumulate the most points; normally a fence cannot be rejumped more than once in the course; the rider obtaining the most points within the time allowed wins.

game (1) Also known as wild game; wild animals, including birds and fish, hunted or taken for sport or profit. (2) Lame, as in a leg. (3) A betting term; (obs); to squander in gambling; as to game away a fortune on race horses. (4) A diversion in the form of chance, skill, endurance, or a combination of these, pursued according to certain rules.

gamete A mature sex cell.

gammon board Also known as backgammon board; a coaching term; the six roof-top seats on a horse-drawn coach, the hind-roof seat in particular; named for Mr. Gammon, who in 1788, initiated an Act of British Parliament which, for safety reasons, limited the number of roof-seat passengers.

gammy legged Also known as gummy legged; said of a horse whose legs, when stocked up (q.v.) due to strain or hard work, do not reveal the tendons below the knee and hock.

gans *see* DUTCH TRIPLE

ganted up *see* TUCKED UP

gap (1) A racing term; an opening in the outside rail where horses enter and leave the race track (q.v.). (2) A racing term; a narrow opening between runners through which a horse can be urged.

Garden-seat Bus A horse-drawn bus used in London, England prior to replacement by the automobile; passengers were seated outside on double, forward-facing seats with a central gangway; succeeded the Knifeboard Bus (q.v.).

garden spot A harness racing term; a horse racing in second position on the rail (q.v.).

Garden, The *see* NATIONAL HORSE SHOW

Gardiens Southern French herdsmen who ride the Camargue Pony (q.v.) and are responsible for herding the famous black bulls of the region.

Garrano Also known as Minho; a pony breed originating in the Portuguese regions of Minho and Tras os Montes, located along the boarder with Spain; an ancient breed dating to the Paleolithic era, it has remained virtually unaltered in appearance for thousands of years; received selected infusions of Arab (q.v.) blood, although Arab characteristics are noticeably absent; influential in the development of the Andalusian (q.v.) and, in the 16th century, the Galiceño (q.v.); is lightly built, strong, hardy, sure-footed, and stands 10 to 12 hands; almost always chestnut in color and has a luxuriant mane and tail; used for packing, light agricultural work, riding, and trotting races.

Garrison finish A racing term; a victory from a come-from-behind horse; named for Snapper Garrison who commonly finished in such a fashion.

Garron Also known as Mainland Pony; one of two distinct morphological types of Highland Pony (q.v.) standing up to 14.2 hands.

garry *see* GHARRY

garter Also known as jodhpur strap; a narrow, buckled, leather strap historically used to hold the breeches constant in the boot by passing through small loops sewn onto the breeches at the front and rear.

between the second and third buttons, and through a small loop attached to the top rear seam of a field or dress riding boot; now used as an appointment of taste; buckled on the outside of the leg.

gas *see* FLATULENCE

Gascoigne, Chien de A breed of blue-mottled hound; believed to be the oldest strain of hunting hound indigenous to France.

gaskin Also known as second thigh or calf; that part of the hind leg above the point of the hock (q.v.).

Gaston de Foix *see* DE FOIX, GASTON

Gastrodiscus aegyptiacus A fluke (q.v.) found in the large intestines of horses, pigs, and warthogs; infection is most common in the dry season because snails, the intermediate host, congregate around permanent water where the most palatable grazing also occurs; symptoms include bloody diarrhea and rapid weight loss.

gastrointestinal Relating to or affecting the stomach and intestines.

gastrointestinal tract Also known as GI tract; the tract consisting of the stomach and intestines.

Gastrophilus haemorrhoidalis One of three types of botfly (q.v.), the other two being *Gastrophilus intestinalis* (q.v.) and *Gastrophilus nasalis* (q.v.); a small fly with a yellow and black banded body (nose botfly) which lays its yellow and black eggs on the head hairs of the horse in the late summer and autumn in temperate climates and during spring, summer, and autumn in warmer climates; has a life cycle similar to *Gastrophilus intestinalis* (q.v.), but the eggs hatch spontaneously and then enter the horse's mouth where they spend approximately one month followed by eight months in the stomach; found occasionally in all countries, but is most common in Russia and parts of Asia.

Gastrophilus intestinalis One of three types of botfly (q.v.), the other two being *Gastrophilus haemorrhoidalis* (q.v.) and *Gastrophilus nasalis* (q.v.); the most common of the bots (q.v.), it is found in most horses; a small fly with a yellow and dark banded body, the female of which attaches her eggs to the hairs on the forelegs, shoulders, neck, and mane of the horse in the late summer and autumn in temperate climates and during spring, summer, and autumn in warmer climates; first-stage larvae are stimulated to hatch by moisture, warmth, and friction of the horse's tongue and lips when biting itself; the hatched larvae burrow into the soft tissues of the tongue and gums around the molar teeth where they remain for about one month before they are swallowed; the second- and third-stage larvae then attach to the stomach wall where they spend approximately nine months before they are passed in the feces where they develop for one month to the adult stage.

Gastrophilus nasalis One of three types of botfly (q.v.), the other two being *Gastrophilus intestinalis* (q.v.) and *Gastrophilus haemorrhoidalis* (q.v.); a small yellow fly with a yellow and dark banded body (throat or chin botfly), the female of which attaches her eggs to the hairs on the head and face of the horse in the late summer and autumn in temperate climates and during spring, summer, and autumn in warmer climates; has a life cycle similar to *Gastrophilus intestinalis* (q.v.), but the eggs hatch spontaneously and then enter the horse's nasal cavity where they spend approximately one month followed by eight months in the stomach.

gate (1) A single vertical jumping obstacle (q.v.) consisting of spaced, horizontal slats supported by standards (q.v.). (2) *see* STARTING GATE. (3) To eliminate a horse from a show competition for refusal in an over fence class, going off course, or improper or dangerous behavior of either the horse or exhibitor or both based on the rules and opinion of the judge e.g. "That horse was gated".

gateado *see* DUN

gate card A racing term; a card issued by the starter which verifies that a horse is correctly schooled in starting gate procedures; required of all competing horses.

gather *see* ROUND UP

Gato One of two Criollo (q.v.) horses ridden by Aimé Tschiffely (q.v.) in his famous two and a half year, 10,000 mile (16,000 km) ride from Buenos Aires, Argentina to Washington DC, USA; died at the age of 36.

Gaucho A cowboy/cowhand (q.v.) from the pampas regions of Argentina, Uruguay, and the Rio Grande do Sul State in southern Brazil; thought by many to be the world's finest roughriders (q.v.); posses their own dress, tradition, and culinary traditions.

gay A horse who carries his head and tail well and has a free and airy walk (obs).

Gayoe *see* GAYOL

Gayol Also spelled Gayoe; a pony breed native to the Gayol Hills of Northern Sumatra, Indonesia from which the breed name derived; is less lively, heavier and has shorter and thicker legs than the Batak (q.v.).

gear (1) The equipment and accessories used in harness driving, excluding the vehicle, and in polo, excluding the bridle and saddle. (2) *see* CARRIAGE

gee Also known as heck; a voice command used on agricultural horses to indicate a turn to the right.

gee up *see* GET-UP

geld *see* CASTRATE

Gelderland Also known as Gelderlander; a horse breed developed in the Gelderland Province of the Netherlands by crossing native mares with Andalusian (q.v.), Neapolitan, Norman (q.v.), and Norfolk Roadster (q.v.) stallions; Anglo-Norman (q.v.), Oldenburg (q.v.), and Hackney (q.v.) blood was introduced in the 19th century and English Thoroughbred (q.v.) in the 20th century; is elegant, stands 15.2 to 16 hands, has a chestnut, bay, black, or gray coat, commonly has white markings, a long and rather flat head, crested neck, high-set tail, short-coupled body, and a high-stepping trot; used for light draft, driving, riding for leisure, and jumping.

Gelderlander *see* GELDERLAND

gelding A castrated (q.v.) male horse who cannot sire offspring; from the Scandinavian *geld* meaning barren.

gelding donkey Also known as John; a castrated ass (q.v.), one incapable of siring offspring.

Gemmi Cart A two-wheeled, horse-drawn vehicle used in Switzerland to transport passengers over the Gemmi Pass from which the name derived; passengers traveled facing the rear on a narrow single seat fitted between the wheels; had a wind-on brake attached to the near side (q.v.) shaft (q.v.).

gene The element or unit of a chromosome which carries and transfers an inherited characteristic from parent to offspring, and determines the development of some particular character or trait in the offspring.

gene dominant Also known as dominant gene; that member of an allelic (alternative forms of) pair of genes which asserts its effects over the other dissimilar member (recessive) of a gene pair.

gene lethal A gene (q.v.) resulting in a condition that may lead to death at or shortly after birth, or a foal with a condition which will affect health or use in the long term.

general anesthesia An artificially produced, body-wide state of insensibility, especially to the sense of pain, achieved by putting the patient into a state of conscious sleep as with drugs.

general anesthetic Any substance that has the power to deprive feeling or sensation to the body by putting the patient into a conscious sleep.

general purpose saddle *see* ALL-PURPOSE SADDLE

General Service Wagon Also known by the acronym GS Wagon; an open, horse-drawn vehicle with a container back and a single seat for the driver used to convey goods; pulled by a pair or team on a long rein; either coachman or postillion (q.v.)

driven; resembled an open lorry.

General Stud Book Also known by the acronym GSB; *see* STUD BOOK

gene recessive Also known as recessive gene; that member of an allelic (alternative forms of) pair of genes which does not assert effect over the other dissimilar member (dominant) of a gene pair.

generous Said of a horse who gives his best when performing in a race or other competition.

gennet *see* JENNET

genetic progress The process of obtaining desired traits by means of selective breeding.

genetics The science of heredity and the evolutionary similarities and differences of related organisms, as produced by the interaction of the genes; the inherited features and characteristics of an organism or group or type of organisms.

genotype selection Breeding stock selection based on genetic makeup rather than appearance.

genotyping Verification of parentage by DNA testing (q.v.) nasal mucous, hair, blood, etc.; considered superior to blood-typing (q.v.).

gentlemen, I leave you here An antiquated British coaching phrase; a signal from the mail coachman to his passengers to provide a monetary tip.

gentleman jockey An antiquated racing term; an amateur rider, generally in a steeplechase (q.v.).

gentleman rider *see* AMATEUR RIDER

genu *see* STIFLE

George IV *see* PARK PHAETON

George IV Phaeton *see* PARK PHAETON

George Wilkes One of four sons of Hambletonian 10 from which more than 90 percent of all modern Standardbreds (q.v.) can trace descent.

Géricault, Jean Luis André Théodore (1791–1824) One of the most powerful and noted equestrian artists of all time; noted artist of equestrian scenes; noted for the influence his work had on other sporting painters of the era rather than the work itself; killed in a fall from a horse.

German Coldblood *see* RHINELAND HEAVY DRAFT

German martingale Also known as English rein or Market Harborough; a martingale (q.v.) consisting of two leather straps attached to a girth (q.v.) ring which pass between the forelegs, one strap runs from girth through the left bit ring and fastens to the left rein while the other passes through the right bit ring and connects to the right rein; downward pressure on the mouth occurs when the horse raises his head.

German posting A method of controlling a four-horse hitch using a single postillion (q.v.); the near leader (q.v.) was rein controlled, while the off leader was not; speed of the team was maintained by the postillion using voice commands and a long whip.

German silver Also known as albata or white brass; a usually white alloy of copper, zinc, and nickel, used for making some ornamental tack and bits.

German Wagon A horse-drawn vehicle introduced in Great Britain in the 1760s; a German version of the Barouche (q.v.); had full undergear and lower panels, but no upper panels, a half-hood which covered the rear seat only, and a raised box seat for the driver located well above the body work.

germinal In the earliest stage of development.

germ plasm Germ cells and their precursors which bear hereditary characteristics.

gestation *see* GESTATION PERIOD

gestation period Also known as gestation; the term of the pregnancy from the time of conception to birth (approximately 335 days or 11 months); the term for colts is generally a few days longer than for fillies.

get Also known as progeny or offspring; the offspring of a stallion, i.e. a foal is the get of a stallion and the produce (q.v.) of a mare; may refer to one or more progeny (q.v.).

get a bite *see* GET HANGED

getaway day A racing term; the last day of a race meeting (q.v.).

get down A cutting horse term; the action of the horse lowering himself down to the level of the cow being worked.

get hanged Also known as get a bite; a driving term; said of the lash or thong of a team whip when it becomes caught in the harness (q.v.) or on the bars (q.v.).

get into A racing term; said of a jockey, to whip a horse.

get into the ground Also known as getting down into the ground; a cutting and reining term; said of a horse who executes a good sliding stop (q.v.), setting deep onto his haunches.

get onto your belly Said of the jockey nearing the race finish; to flatten the body forward as low along the withers as possible to facilitate the kick to the finish.

getting down into the ground *see* GET INTO THE GROUND

get to the heads A hunting term; said of the whipper-in (q.v.), who, in an attempt to stop rioting (q.v.) hounds (q.v.), runs ahead and turns them rather than giving chase.

getty up *see* GET-UP

get under Also known as get underneath; a jumping term; said of a horse who takes off too near to the jump.

get underneath *see* GET UNDER

get-up Also known as getty up, gee up, or giddap; a voice command to go or move forward and, when repeated, to increase speed.

get wood on it A polo term; to make contact with the polo ball using the mallet (q.v.).

Gharry Also spelled Garry: (1) An open, four-wheeled carriage drawn by a single horse and driven from an elevated seat; frequently used as a cab or sight-seeing vehicle in parts of India and the Middle East. (2) A large, fully headed or enclosed, oblong public carriage used by natives throughout India; driven from a roof seat; usually dead axle and designed without windows.

giddap *see* GET-UP

Gidran *see* GIDRAN ARABIAN

Gidran Arabian Also known as Gidran or Hungarian Anglo-Arab; a horse breed developed in Hungary in 1816; the present-day breed results from crossings with Thoroughbred (q.v.) and Arab (q.v.); now of two types: Middle European and Southern and Eastern European; the Middle European Gidran (q.v.) is more stout than the Southern and is often used in harness; the Southern and Eastern European Gidran (q.v.) is lighter and is an all-purpose competition horse; stands 16.1 to 17 hands, has Arab characteristics, and usually has a chestnut coat, although bay and black do occur; used for riding, light draft and is particularly suited to jumping; its name derived from the stallion Gidran, an Arab (q.v.) of the Siglavy strain.

Gig (1) Historically, a two-wheeled passenger vehicle used in country districts, but later adapted for town driving; usually owner-driven and noted for the ease with which it could be turned in a confined space; all types were open in the front, enclosed at the back, and had ample luggage space below the cross-seat; drawn by a single horse or pair; varieties include Bagman's Gig (q.v.), Chairback Gig (q.v.), Dennett Gig (q.v.). Whiskey Gig (q.v.), Liverpool Gig (q.v.), Rib Back Gig (q.v.), Stanhope Gig (q.v.), Skeleton Gig (q.v.), and Seven Spring Gig (q.v.). (2) *see* SULKY NO. 1. (3) *see* DOGCART

gimp Slang; a lame or limping horse.

gimpy Slang; said of a lame (q.v.) or limping horse.

gingering Also known as fiddling or figging; insertion of ginger or another irritant such as cayenne pepper into the horse's anus to stimulate high tail carriage; specifically used on Saddlebreds (q.v.), Morgans (q.v.), and Arabs (q.v.), although it is illegal in the latter breed; the irritation of the ginger causes the horse to lift its tail; considered cruel.

gin horse A horse used for draft work and around mills.

ginney *see* GROOM NO. 2

girl *see* GROOM NO. 2

girth (1) Also known as belly band; a 3 to 4 inch (7.5–10 cm) wide strap that holds the English saddle in place on the back of the horse and prevents it from slipping sideways and to some extent forward; connects the two sides of the saddle underneath the horse's belly just behind the front legs/shoulder; may be made of leather, cotton, wool, or synthetic materials; the equivalent of the cinch (q.v.) on a Western saddle. (2) *see* HEART GIRTH

girthed Said of a saddle or other tack held in place by a girth (q.v.).

girth gall A gall (q.v.) that develops in the belly area behind the elbow of the horse where the girth (q.v.) generally passes; caused by dirty, stiff, or badly fitting girths, as those too tight or too loose; similar to a blister; horses with thin, sensitive skin are most prone.

girth mark An adventitial mark (q.v.); permanent white coat hairs in the girth area; results from destruction of the pigment cells of underlying skin by a poorly fitted girth or one that rubs.

girth measurement *see* HEART GIRTH

girth place The place on the horse's belly just behind the forelegs, marked by a depression in the underline, where the girth (q.v.) is fitted.

girth safes Flat, single layered pieces of leather, 3 to 4 inches (7.5–10cm) wide with horizontal slots cut into them and through which the girth straps (q.v.) pass; used to protect the saddle flap from being rubbed by the girth buckles and to smooth out the buckle bulge under the rider's legs.

girth shy *see* CINCH BOUND

girth straps Narrow leather straps attached vertically to the English saddle tree on both sides to which the girth buckles are attached when saddling the horse; there are usually three straps on each side of the saddle, although lightweight saddles may have only one.

girth up To tighten the girth (q.v.) on a horse.

girth weight tape A measuring tape calibrated in pounds or kilograms rather than inches or centimetres which is placed around the girth (q.v.) of the horse to measure his weight; the margin of error may be as much as 5 percent.

girthy *see* CINCH BOUND

gisted *see* AGISTMENT

GI tract *see* GASTROINTESTINAL TRACT

give a leg up *see* LEG UP NO. 1

give and take of the reins Said of the rider; to relax and tighten the grip of the fingers on the reins to remove and re-apply bit pressure on the bars of the horse's mouth to encourage him to accept the bit (q.v.).

give an iron shot A cutting term; said of the rider; to give the horse a short, quick spur jab.

give tongue Also known as throw tongue or throw his tongue; a hunting term; said of a hound (q.v.) when he bays or barks on the line of (q.v.) the quarry.

give with the hands Said of the rider; to relax the grip of the fingers on the reins and thus release bit pressure on the bars of the horse's mouth.

glanders Also known as farcy; a contagious and usually fatal disease caused by *Pseudomonas mallei*; characterized by eye and nasal discharge and ulcerating nodules occurring most commonly in the upper respiratory tract, lungs, and on the skin; one of the world's oldest diseases, it has been largely eliminated from horse populations today; may be transmitted to man.

Glass Coach A horse-drawn vehicle of the Coach (q.v.) type introduced in the 17th century, so named because of the glass panels above the elbow line.

glass eye *see* WALL EYE

gleet *see* NASAL GLEET

Glover, Webb, & Liversidge Ltd. A horse-drawn coach-building firm established in 1720 in London, England.

glucosamine As a condroprotectant is a building block of cartilage; effective as a raw material to aid the equine body in cartilage production and as a stimulus for cartilage component synthesis; believed to significantly reduce joint pain, tenderness, and swelling; a precursor to glycosamino-glycons (q.v.).

glucosamine HCI A type of glucosamine (q.v.); aids the body's production of joint lubricants and compounds necessary to maintain healthy cartilage (q.v.) and joint function.

glucosamine sulfate A type of glucosamine (q.v.) more bio-available and readily absorbed than glucosamin HCI (q.v.); aids in the body's production of joint lubricants and compounds necessary for maintenance and repair of connective tissue, healthy articular cartilage, and joint function.

glucose One of the simple sugars formed by hydrolysis of complete carbohydrates; the form in which carbohydrates (q.v.) are assimilated in the body.

glucose concentration The amount of sugar in the blood.

glucose concentration test A procedure performed to measure blood sugar (glucose q.v.) levels.

glue-on shoe A therapeutic shoe (q.v.) generally used on horses with reconstructed hooves, shelly feet, and fractured coffin bones; commonly made of plastic, has clip-like plastic extensions on the inside and outside rims, and a thin aluminum plate set inside the rim; attached to the hoof with epoxy or other adhesive.

gluteal The scientific term for the region of the buttocks, and to structures associated, such as gluteal arteries, muscles, nerves, etc.

gluteal muscles Any of three large muscles of the rump that extend the hip and push the body forward; consist of the gluteus superficialis, gluteus medius, and gluteus profundus

glycosaminoglycon Also known by the acronym GAG; one of the substances found in cartilage (q.v.) and in the viscous synovial fluid surrounding joints; there are nine in total of which three are chondroitin sulfates (q.v.); it is believed that ingested chondroitin sulfates will migrate to the joints where they inhibit destructive enzymes and contribute to cartilage repair.

goad *see* STICK NO. 1

goal (1) *see* GOAL BOX. (2) The act of scoring points by placing a ball in a designated area, space, or object. (3) A polo term; the value of a player to the team, not the number of goals a player is expected to score; a player may be ranked as a high-, medium-, intermediate-, or low-goal player. (4) *see* POLO GOAL

goal box Also known as goal; a polo term; the area, space, or object into which polo players attempt to hit the ball in an effort to score.

goal handicap *see* POLO HANDICAP

goal post One of two vertical poles located on the short ends of a playing field which define the goal box (q.v.); in polo, set 8 yards (7 m) apart and stand a minimum of 10 feet (3 m) high; there is no cross piece connecting the posts which are made to collapse on impact; a goal is considered to be scored if the ball passes between the posts or what would constitute the upward prolongation of such.

goal rating *see* POLO HANDICAP

goat-dragging *see* BUZKASHI

goat knees *see* FORWARD DEVIATION OF THE CARPAL JOINTS

goat-lifting *see* BUZKASHI

goat snatching The national game of Uzbekistan; a mounted team sport in which a rider, traveling at a gallop and carrying a goat, tries to evade the attempts of other riders to take the goat away from him; played on the Karabair (q.v.), the breed indigenous to the area.

Go Cart An American horse-drawn vehicle of the Cabriolet (q.v.) type having two wheels and a cranked axle.

Godolphin Arab *see* GODOLPHIN ARABIAN

Godolophin Arabian Also known as Godolphin Barb or Goldolphin Arab; one of three Arab (q.v.) foundation sires of the English Thoroughbred (q.v.) to which all Thoroughbreds (q.v.) in the world today trace their ancestry in direct male line; a kehilan (q.v.) Arab imported to England in 1728 by Mr. Edward Coke; upon Mr. Coke's death, was bought by the Earl of Godolphin for whom he was named; stood just under 15 hands, had a bay coat, and lop ears; died in 1753.

Godolphin Barb *see* GODOLPHIN ARABIAN

goes well Said of a horse having a lively, high-stepping action.

goes well into the bridle Also known as bridles well; said of a horse who accepts the bit without pulling or evasion.

Gogue *see* DE GOGUE MARTINGALE

Gogue martingale *see* DE GOGUE MARTINGALE

going Said of the condition of a track or other surface over which a horse is expected to travel, e.g. "The going was good."

going amiss A racing term; said of a mare in training who comes into season at the time she is due to race.

going away A racing term; said of a horse who wins a race while increasing the lead.

going big A Standardbred harness racing term; said of a driver who goes as fast as possible at the beginning of the race.

going short Also known as short; said of a horse having a short, uncertain gait (q.v.); may indicate lameness or a tendency to such.

going under the wire A racing term; (obs); said of a horse who wins a race; so called because the finish line was originally marked by a wire spanning the track.

go into the cow A cutting term; said of a horse who, when prompted by the rider, steps forward up to the cow.

goiter Also spelled goitre (Brit); a morbid enlargement of the thyroid gland, forming a protuberance on the side or front part of the neck; may be fatal if not treated and is transmittable to unborn foals *in vivo* (q.v.); caused by dietary iodine excess or deficiency.

goitre *see* GOITER

goitrogenic Tending to produce goiter (q.v.).

go large A dressage term; said of the rider, to proceed around the arena on the rail as after performing smaller circles.

golden age of coaching The period between 1815 and 1840 during which horse-drawn mail and stage coaches reached the height of popularity.

golden age of fox hunting A hunting term; the period between 1820 and 1890 regarded as the premier fox hunting period during which time the great estates in Britain were still intact, motorways and cars were nonexistent, and there were no fumes, fertilizers, etc. to confuse the scent.

golden age of racing A racing term; the 40-year period following the American Civil War during which horse racing in America came of age.

Golden Dorado *see* PALOMINO

golden dun Also known as creamy dun; refers to coat color; a type of dun (q.v.) having yellow coat hairs mixed with white.

golden horse *see* PALOMINO

Golden horse of the Queen *see* PALOMINO

golden horse of the West *see* PALOMINO

Golden Horse Society, The (1) A British organization founded in 1947 to maintain the Palomino (q.v.) breed registry and promote interest in the breed. (2) An organization founded in Waitakere City, New Zealand to maintain the register of all dilutes and stallions who may throw color including Palomino (q.v.), Dun (q.v.), Buckskin (q.v.), Cremello (q.v.), and Perlino (q.v.).

Golden One *see* PALOMINO

Gold State Coach A custom-made, horse-drawn vehicle of the coach (q.v.) type built in 1953 for the coronation procession of Queen Elizabeth II of England.

gonad The male or female reproductive gland that produces gametes, sperm, or ovum (q.v.); a testis (q.v.) or ovary (q.v.).

Gondola of London *see* HANSOM CAB

gone away *see* BLOW AWAY

gone in the wind Said of a horse who has difficulty breathing normally as caused by whistling (q.v.), roaring (q.v.), or broken wind (q.v.) etc.

gone to ground Also known as go to ground; a hunting term; said of a fox or other prey who has taken refuge from the chase in the ground, drain, or other shelter.

gonitis Inflammation of the stifle joint; may be precipitated by: persistent upward fixation of the patella (q.v.), injuries to the medial or lateral collateral ligaments of the joint or the cruciate ligaments of the menisci, erosions of the articular cartilage, bacterial infection of the joint due to puncture wounds (q.v.), etc.; signs are variable depending on the cause and extent of the physiological changes and may include supporting- and swinging-leg lameness, shortened forward leg flight, a flexed fetlock in which only the hoof toe touches the ground when resting, or the horse carries his leg in a flexed position.

Gooch Wagon An elegant, lightweight, under-cut, single-horse-drawn vehicle of the Spider Phaeton (q.v.) type; had a small rumble seat in the rear for a groom, and four wire wheels; designed by and named for Mr. Vivian Gooch.

good bone Said of a horse; to have good bone structure which is indicative of weight-bearing ability and ruggedness; varies from breed to breed.

good bottom A racing term; a wet or dry track that is firm under the cushion (q.v.).

good cow A cutting horse term; a cow who acknowledges the horse when cut from the herd, but does not panic and bolt.

good cow sense *see* COW SMART

good curl A roping term; a well-thrown lariat (q.v.) or rope.

good doer Also known as doer; said of a horse who readily eats his ration (q.v.) and is not a picky eater; may be prone to overeating.

good front *see* GOOD REIN

good hack A horse who is quiet to ride, alert, and sound in the wind (q.v.).

good hands Said of a rider whose hands are both light and sensitive on the rein and therefore on the horse's mouth.

good head A hunting term; said of hounds who hunt fast on a wide front.

good in the dirt A jumping term; said of a horse who jumps and/or performs well on muddy or wet ground.

good keeper *see* EASY KEEPER

good mouth (1) Said of a horse having a soft and sensitive mouth who is responsive to the action of the bit. (2) A horse 6 to 10 years old.

good nick A horse in good physical condition.

good night A hunting term; a salutation extended from the hunters to the Master (q.v.) at the end of a hunting day, however early that may be.

good nose Said of hay (q.v.) that smells

sweet; a quality determining factor.

good outlook *see* GOOD REIN

good rein Also known as good front or good outlook; said of a horse who is well muscled in the front end and has a balanced neck on his body.

good roof Also known as good top (obs); said of a horse having a good top line (q.v.).

good top *see* GOOD ROOF

good track A racing term; a race track that is almost a fast track (q.v.) or a turf track that is slightly softer than a firm track (q.v.).

go off feed Said of a horse who is not eating normally, as due to illness, stress, etc.

go on A racing term; said of a horse who wins a better class of race than previously run.

goose-rumped Also known jumping rumped; said of a horse having a short, steep croup (q.v.) that narrows at the point of the buttocks; caused by an elevation of the backbone or a lack of muscle over the top of the hindquarters.

goose stepping *see* FALSE EXTENSION

go-round (1) *see* ROUND. (2) A Western term; one of a series of rodeo events.

Gorst Gig A horse-drawn, hooded vehicle of the Gig (q.v.) type having a boot (q.v.) under the seat; hung on sideways-elliptical springs.

go short Said of a lame horse or one with restricted forward movement which shortens the stride.

Gotland Also known as Swedish Gotland, Forest Pony, Skogsruss, or incorrectly Skogruss; one of the world's oldest and smallest horse breeds, having existed for more than 10,000 years on the Swedish island of Gotland located in the Baltic Sea from which the name derived; descended from the Tarpan (q.v.); historically served as a cavalry mount for the Goths, the Swedish Vikings, and the Swedish warrior kings; highly prized for its speed, maneuverability, endurance, and easy-keeper (q.v.) qualities; facing the extinction of the breed in the 1880s due to loss of habitat, the Swedish government placed it under strict government protection and allowed the limited introduction of Oriental blood to ensure a strong genetic base; again, due to poaching resulting from World War I food shortages, was nearly hunted to extinction; although still considered a rare breed, world-wide numbers are on the increase; weighs an average of 600 to 650 pounds (272–295 kg), stands 12 to 14 hands, and has a sturdy build somewhat more stocky than a Hackney (q.v.) and larger than a Shetland (q.v.); is long-lived, healthy, very resilient, loves water and has an intelligent, lively, and gentle temperament; all solid coat colors occur with black, bay, buckskin, and sorrel most common; most have a dorsal stripe (q.v.) and very few white markings such as a star (q.v.) or coronet (q.v.), but never spots or patches; has a broad forehead, sometimes a dished profile, wide-set eyes, muscular and crested neck, strong back, rounded croup, and a full mane and tail with light fetlock feathering (q.v.); used by both adults and children for pleasure riding, driving, and jumping; are bloodtyped and registered in the United States with the Gotland Horse Registry, administered by the American Livestock Breeds Conservancy (q.v.).

go to ground *see* GONE TO GROUND

go to the horn *see* DALLY

gouch-eared Said of a horse having ragged or cropped ears as due to frostbite or accident.

gouge Said of the rider; to make a quick, hard jab with a spur.

Governess Car *see* GOVERNESS CART

Governess Cart Also known as Avondale (Am), Digby (Northumberland, Brit) Jingle (Somerset, Brit), Governess Car, Tub Cart, or Tub Car; a small, two-wheeled, pony- or donkey-drawn vehicle with a round or tub shape introduced around 1880; entered through an outward-opening rear door, had sideways seating that followed the interior perimeter of a foot well, two midway driving positions, one on each side of the vehicle, with scooped-out wall portions to provide the driver room to twist his body for better control of the reins, and stained and grained bodywork; some were designed with cane basketwork and hoods; mounted on cranked axles hung with sideways-elliptical springs; designed to carry a governess and the children in her charge; often had considerable sideways motion.

grab a quarter *see* OVER-REACH

grabbing slack *see* PULLING SLACK

grabbin' the apple *see* PULLING LEATHER

Grackle *see* GRAKLE NOSEBAND

Grackle noseband *see* GRAKLE NOSEBAND

grade (1) *see* GRADE HORSE. (2) A show jumping term; a level of competition in which the weakest competition occurs at the lowest grade. (3) A dressage term; a level of competition ranging from training level (q.v.) at the novice end of performance ability to Grand Prix on the highest.

Grade I A racing term; the highest of three levels of premiere sweepstakes races (q.v.) held in the United States each carrying a minimum purse of $50,000 (US); consists of all top races such as the Kentucky Derby (q.v.); always designated by a Roman numeral.

Grade II A racing term; the middle of three levels of premiere sweepstakes races (q.v.) held in the United States, each carrying a minimum purse of $50,000 (US); consists of all middle-caliber races based on the quality of the horses competing and as designated by a panel of racing industry experts; always designated by a Roman numeral.

Grade III A racing term; the lowest of three levels of premiere sweepstakes races (q.v.) held in the United States, each carrying a minimum purse of $50,000 (US); consists of all third best races as based on the quality of the horses competing and as designated by a panel of racing industry experts; always designated by a Roman numeral.

grade horse (1) Also known as grade; a horse who does not carry enough blood of any specific breed to meet breed registration requirements, but who shows some, although not all, specific breed characteristics; "grade" may be suffixed to the name of any breed, e.g., grade Hackney (q.v.). (2) A horse having one registered or pure blood (q.v.) parent and the other parent of mixed or unknown breeding.

graded race Also known incorrectly as group race (q.v.) or pattern race; a racing term; a premiere stakes race held in a country as designated by a panel of racing industry experts; of a higher class than non-graded stakes, carry a minimum purse of $50,000, and eligibility cannot be restricted in any way other than by sex or age; in the United States, constitute 15 percent of all stakes races and are divided into grades designated by Roman numerals: Grade I (q.v.), Grade II (q.v.), and Grade III (q.v.) as based on the quality of the competing horses; established at the request of European authorities in 1973 to classify select races in North America.

grade up Also known as grading up; a breeding system in which a superior-quality, registered stallion is bred to a lesser-quality, unregistered mare or registered mare of another breed to improve the breed by producing horses similar in type and conformation to the stallion; some stud books (q.v.) will accept horses produced from a grading up program of the 4th generation.

grading up *see* GRADE UP

Graditz A Thoroughbred stud founded in Germany in 1686.

graduate (1) A racing term; a horse or jockey who wins his first race. (2) A racing term; a horse who has moved up into allowance, stakes, or handicap racing.

graduated-side iron *see* HUNTING IRON

grain A single fruit or seed of a food plant or cereal grass such as wheat, oats, barley, and corn.

grain founder Also known as grain overloading; founder (q.v.) caused by ingestion of excessive amounts of carbohydrate from grain; results in inflammation of the sensitive laminae (q.v.) of the hoof.

Grainger martingale An adjustable, auxiliary strap used to prevent the horse from throwing his head up; attached to the girth as a single strap that passes between the horse's legs and splits into two branches that buckle to either side of a secondary noseband positioned below the cavesson noseband (q.v.); may be fitted with a neck strap to keep it in place; more severe than a standing martingale (q.v.).

grain overloading *see* GRAIN FOUNDER

grain sorghum *see* SORGHUM

Grakle noseband Also known as figure eight, figure-eight noseband, cross noseband, Mexican noseband, and commonly though incorrectly spelled Grackle noseband; a noseband named for the 1931 Grand National winner Grakle; a noseband having its own headstall and consisting of two straps which cross over the bridge of the nose diagonally at a point nearer the eyes than the nostrils; one strap passes in front of the bit and buckles in the curb groove, while the other passes above and behind the bit buckling behind the jaw approximately 2 inches (5 cm) below the check bones; the center part at the cross-over point rests on the nose bone rather than on the cartilage below it; used to still jaw movement in strong horses; prevents the horse from crossing his jaws and/or opening his mouth; cannot be used in dressage competitions, but may be used in jumping or the dressage phase of eventing competitions.

gram-negative bacteria Families of bacteria that do not stain blue in laboratory examination; used to help identify specific bacterial causes of infection.

Grand Breton *see* DRAUGHT BRETON

Grand Circuit A program of harness racing on the major tracks common around the turn of the 19th century.

Grand dam Also known as second dam; the mother of a horse's dam unless otherwise specified, as in paternal grandam (q.v.).

Grand Liverpool Steeplechase *see* GRAND NATIONAL STEEPLECHASE

Grand National, The *see* GRAND NATIONAL STEEPLECHASE

Grand National Steeplechase Also known as The Grand National, The National, The Liverpool Steeplechase (obs), or Grand Liverpool Steeplechase (obs); a handicap steeplechase (q.v.) conducted over 4 miles, 856 yard (7.22 km) at Aintree (q.v.) racecourse located in Liverpool, England since 1839; the race has 30 fences and a water jump 15 feet (4.5 m) wide.

Grand Pardubice A grueling steeplechase (q.v.) held annually in Czechoslovakia on the second Sunday in October since 1874; a 4½ mile (7.2 km) course over ploughed fields with 31 fences, the most difficult of which is the 16 foot 5 inch (5 m) wide Taixis, a ditch fronted by a natural fence 5 feet (1.5 m) high and 5 feet (1.5 m) wide.

Grand Prix (1) A race for first class horses. (2) A dressage term; the highest level of dressage competition in which the horse must demonstrate pirouettes (q.v.) at the canter, flying changes each third, second, or every stride, piaffe (q.v.), and passage (q.v.).

grandsire Also known as second sire; the father of a horse's sire unless otherwise specified, as in maternal grandsire (q.v.).

granulated tissue Small, rounded tissue masses composed of capillaries and connective tissue cells which grow outward from the body to fill a wound opening.

grapes Characteristic fungal growth developing as a result of scratches (q.v.).

grass Any plant of the family Gramineae characterized by jointed stems, sheathing leaves, and flower spikelets upon which grazing animals pasture; when harvested and dried, is fed as grass hay (q.v.).

grass belly *see* HAY BELLY

grass burner *see* GRASS CUTTER

grass clippings The vegetative material resulting from grass mowing operations; may be fed immediately after cutting without possible risk of colic or colic-like symptoms; crude protein levels may vary widely, with levels of 25 to 30 percent not uncommon.

grass cutter Also known as grass burner; a polo term; said of a polo ball hit with such force by the polo player (q.v.) that it travels at a higher speed than the average shot, thus grazing the surface of the grass field.

grass founder Founder (q.v.) caused by ingestion of excessive amounts of protein found in lush pastures; results in inflammation of the sensitive laminae of the hoof; occurs most often in horses turned out to pasture following a prolonged period of feed on cured grasses, as during the winter.

grass hay Cut and dried grasses (q.v.) and grains (q.v.); are high in fiber, but have relatively low nutritional content and are generally lower in protein than legume hays (q.v.), the digestible protein content being less than 5 percent; may be fed freely with little likelihood of overfeeding, colic (q.v.), or founder (q.v.) resulting; commonly mixed with legume hays to create a hay of moderate protein content.

grass pen A hunting term; a kennel area where bitches in season (q.v.) are confined.

grass sickness Also known as grass tetany, equine grass sickness, or equine dysautonomia; an 85 to 90 percent fatal condition of unknown origins involving a progressive degeneration of the nerves that control gut function; results in a drastic slowdown of the digestive system; victims waste away and eventually die of dehydration or malnutrition; characterized by colic-like symptoms including abdominal pain, distention, and in severe cases, rupture, loss of the ability to swallow, drooling, depression, restlessness, elevated pulse rate, patchy sweating, involuntary movement of the fine muscles over the shoulders and flanks, and food discharge from the nostrils; occurs at any age after weaning and at any time throughout the year, but the peak incidence is in spring in two- to seven-year-old horses; generally associated with horses kept solely at grass, although the condition has been reported in housed stock; death occurs within 24 hours (preacute), four days (acute), and 21 days (subacute), while chronic cases may continue for weeks or months; confirmation of grass sickness currently can be made only through a postmortem examination of the nerve cells, although a new technique is under development that uses a surgical biopsy of the small intestine to check for nerve cell damage; no diagnostic test is available; reported in Europe, Australia, Japan, England, Scotland, and the United States.

grass slip A racing term; written authorization granted by race track authorities to a jockey, trainer, or owner to exercise a horse on a turf course.

grass tetany *see* GRASS SICKNESS

grass yard A British hunting term; a wire-enclosed paddock where hounds and puppies may be left to exercise and to air themselves.

gravel A lay term; the supposed migration of a piece of gravel from the white line (q.v.) towards the coronet band (q.v.) of the foot; bacterial invasion of the sensitive structures of the foot results in pus and gas which create intense pain; gas and pus vent at the top of the coronary band with lameness occurring before drainage.

gray (1) Also spelled grey; refers to coat color; a pattern of white hairs mixed with colored body and point hairs; gray horses are born colored, i.e. not white or gray, and become progressively more white with each shedding; the mane and tail may either remain dark or go white before the coat grays; dappling (q.v.) is common and the skin is always pigmented; graying tends to mask white patterns on the horse as he ages. (2) Also known as graying; refers to coat color; said of the coat; to change from any color to gray.

gray fox Also known as *Urocyon cineroargenteus*, a carnivorous mammal of the dog family having a pointed muzzle, erect ears, long bushy tail, and gray coat, which is noted for its cunning and alertness; native to the United States and Canada where it is the primary quarry of foxhounds; usually runs in circles.

graying *see* GRAY NO. 2

gray overo Also known as azulejo (q.v.) in Argentina; refers to coat color; a gray (q.v.)

horse with large ragged patches of white.

Grayson-Jockey Club Research Foundation An American charitable organization founded in 1989 by the merger of the Grayson Foundation and The Jockey Club Research Foundation; devoted to equine medical research.

gray ticked Refers to coat color; sparsely distributed white hairs throughout the coat on any part of the body.

grazing bit A curb bit (q.v.) having backward-slanted cheek shanks; designed to enable the horse to graze with the bit in his mouth.

grease heel *see* SCRATCHES

greased heel *see* SCRATCHES

greasy heel *see* SCRATCHES

Great American Horse Race The longest endurance ride (q.v.) recorded; conducted in the United States from New York to California, over a period of three months, and a distance greater than 6,000 miles.

great coat Also known as postboy's coat or postboy waistcoat; a heavy overcoat slit to the waist worn by the postillion (q.v.) to protect him from rain and cold; the tails which hung down on either side of the saddle were pulled forward, to cover the thighs, and were tucked under the knee.

Great Horse Also known as English Great Horse or the English Black; England's medieval war horse developed in the early 10th century and used well into the middle of the 15th century; was strong enough to carry a knight in full armor bearing heavy weapons, and agile enough to move about in combat; also used for jousting (q.v.); contributed to development of the most powerful draft breeds in northern Europe.

green (1) *see* GREEN HORSE. (2) *see* GREEN RIDER. (3) A trotter or pacer not previously raced against the clock. (4) A hunter (q.v.) in his first or second year of showing over obstacles 3 feet 6 inches (1.1 m) or higher.

green broke A recently broken horse who is inexperienced and requires further training.

green horn *see* DUDE

green horse Also known as green; a broken, but not fully trained horse.

green hunter Any horse bred, and/or appropriate to follow hounds (q.v.) in the sport of hunting (q.v.) who still requires training.

green meat Basic horse feed consisting of hay, grass, and straw.

green prospect Any young, unbroken horse purchased for his show potential.

green rider Also known as green; an inexperienced rider.

grey *see* GRAY

greyhound gutted Said of a horse having a tightly drawn-in stomach as caused by undernourishment and too little feed bulk.

grid A jumping term; a series of obstacles (q.v.) laid out in a straight line and in such a manner that they are intended to be ridden as an entity; normally used to develop the horse's gymnastic athleticism.

grid-iron port An oval-shaped metal tongue piece having circular ends that may be clipped around the bit mouthpiece (q.v.), on either side of the existing port (q.v.), to extend its length and action; lies along the tongue in the direction of the throat; has a metal cross in the arch to prevent the tongue from catching on it; prevents the horse from getting its tongue over the bit.

Griffen Also spelled Griffin; a Mongolian pony breed used in China for polo (q.v.); is tough, handy, agile, and possessed of good speed.

Griffin *see* GRIFFEN

grinders *see* MOLARS

grinding teeth A vice; said of a horse who rubs or grates his teeth together, as due to boredom, excitement, anger, resistance to the bit, or tension.

grip Said of the rider; to hold the saddle tightly between the knees or lower legs.

gripes *see* COLIC

Grisone, Federico A 16th-century Italian nobleman; established a riding school in Naples and was one of the first to promote the use of combined aids and the leg rather than the spur (q.v.).

grissel *see* ROUNT

grizzle *see* ROUNT

groin Also known as lisk; the fold or hollow on either side of the body where the thigh meets the abdomen.

Groningen Also known as Groningen Horse; a Dutch warmblood (q.v.) developed by crossing Friesians (q.v.) and Oldenburgs (q.v.); stands 15.2 to 16 hands, has a great depth of girth, powerful quarters and shoulders, short legs, and a black, dark brown, or bay coat; is an easy keeper; nearly disappeared following World War II and is still quite rare; bred for light draft and riding.

Groningen Horse *see* GRONINGEN

groom (1) Also known as strap or swipe; to curry or care for, as in horses; the act of brushing and cleaning a horse in preparation for or following exercise or work. (2) Also known as lad (Brit), girl, servant (obs), or in racing circles, as guinea and spelled ginney (because winning British owners of raced stock would tip the groom a guinea); one responsible for the care of horses.

grooming kit Collectively, the brushes, combs, and other equipment used to groom (q.v.) a horse.

grooming stable rubber *see* STABLE RUBBER

groom's coat A coaching term; a single-breasted coat customarily worn by the groom (q.v.); had buttons down the front, three pairs of buttons down the rear, and no pockets.

grooving The act or process of cutting or burning a horizontal groove across the fibers of the hoof wall to alter the way in which stress, as in a crack, is transferred up the hoof wall.

Grosbos An equine training venue located near Paris, France.

gross energy The caloric content of feed defined in terms of the energy potential it contains; established by incinerating a known quantity of feed in a bomb calorimeter placed inside a defined quantity of water; the number of degrees the water temperature is raised is used to calculate the caloric content of the feed; does not establish how well the calories will be used.

gross feeder Said of a hound or horse who overeats.

Grosvenor Dogcart A horse-drawn vehicle of the Dogcart (q.v.) type; had back-to-back seats for four, dashboard lamps, a built-in apron, and was hung on sideways-elliptic springs.

ground (1) *see* GROUND TIE. (2) A coaching term; the area traveled by a coachman, e.g. "The coachman's ground was the forty miles between London and Sawbridgeworth."

grounded A racing term; said of a jockey (q.v.) suspended from competition by racing authorities for rule infractions.

grounding The process of touching down on the ground after being raised in stride, as the hoof.

ground line A jumping term; an actual pole or rail or an imaginary line drawn at the base of a fence from which the take-off (q.v.) spot is judged.

ground man One who, from a position on the ground, aids a mounted rider by setting fences, cavalletti (q.v.), and grid lines, raising and lowering rails (q.v.), and providing instruction on riding style or technique.

ground money A rodeo term; the entry fee and purse money split equally among all contestants in an event when no individual winner is determined.

ground pole Also known as ground rail, guard rail, or take-off rail; a round pole approximately 10 to 12 feet (3–3.6 m) long and 4 to 6 inches (10–15 cm) in diameter laid on the ground in front of a jump to assist the horse and/or rider in gauging the jump take-off (q.v.); also used in constructing jumping grids and gymnastics; such poles offer no height options and are unstable if the horse mis-steps and starts them rolling beneath his feet.

ground rail *see* GROUND POLE

ground shy Said of a horse with an abnormal fear of objects found on the ground.

ground tie Also known as ground; to let the reins drop to the ground after dismounting to cue the trained horse to remain standing where he is.

group race (1) Also known as pattern race; a racing term; a method established in 1971 by racing organizations in Britain, France, Germany, and Italy to classify select stakes races run in Europe; are divided into grades designated by Arabic numerals 1, 2, or 3; capitalized when used in a race title as in Group 1 Epsom Derby; equivalent to a graded race (q.v.) in North America. (2) *see* GRADED RACE

Growler *see* CLARENCE CAB

growth cartilage *see* GROWTH-PLATE

growth plate Also known as growth cartilage; a layer of cartilage (q.v.) between the diaphysis and epiphysis (q.v.) of a long bone.

growth rings *see* HOOF RINGS

grub *see* LARVA

grulla The feminine of grullo (q.v.).

grullo Also known as slate-grullo, grulla, or mouse dun or blue dun by English riders or when describing European breeds; refers to coat color; slate-colored, having a slate- or tan-colored body with only slight variations of shade and a dark head; commonly has wither and dorsal stripes (q.v.), stripes over the knees and hocks, and black skin; the Spanish word for a crane of the same color; an ancestral color of the Tarpan (q.v.); in strong sunlight may fade to an olive grullo (q.v.).

grunting Also known as bulling or grunt to the stick; said of a horse who, when threatened, frightened, (as historically by the anticipated blow of a stick to the belly), or following excessive work, emits a grunting noise; was deemed to be a potential sign of wind unsoundness; if the horse emitted no noise, he was presumed to be sound of wind (q.v.).

grunt to the stick *see* GRUNTING

GSB *see* GENERAL STUD BOOK

GS Wagon *see* GENERAL SERVICE WAGON

Guaga A small, four-wheeled, horse-drawn public carriage used in Cuban towns and cities throughout the 19th century; entered from the rear and drawn by four ponies abreast.

Guajira A Colombian-bred Criollo (q.v.); descended from Spanish stock brought to South America by the Conquistadors in the 16th century; the name derived from the region of the same name.

guard rail *see* GROUND POLE

Gudbrandsdal *see* DØLE GUDBRANDSDAL

Guérinière, François Robichon de la *see* DE LA GUÉRINIÈRE, FRANÇOIS ROBICHON

Guerney A horse-drawn vehicle of the Cab (q.v.) type popular in the United States around the turn of the 19th century; patented by A. J. Guerney.

guide terrets Small, upright metal rings fastened onto the pads used on the team wheelers (q.v.), through which the reins of the leaders (q.v.) pass.

guiding rein *see* DIRECT REIN

guinea *see* GROOM NO. 2

guinea hunter English slang; one paid to liaise between the seller and buyer of a horse(s) for payment; historically gypsies.

gullet *see* ESOPHAGUS

gullet plate (1) An arch-shaped iron fork attached to the front of the saddle tree (q.v.) to provide strength to the saddle. (2) The metal, generally aluminum, part of some types of cribbing (q.v.) straps; fits on either side of the esophagus on the underside of the neck; used to prevent cribbing.

gumbo A racing term; heavy mud, as on the racetrack.

gummy legged *see* GAMMY LEGGED

Gustav Rau *see* RAU, GUSTAV

Gustavus A famous English trotter purported to have traveled 20 miles (32.18 km) in 1 hour and 14 minutes; owned by Mr. Burke and worked in the late 1830s and early 1840s.

gutteral pouch One of two sacs connected to the eustachian tube (q.v.) located between the ear and throat of the horse and open to the throat; thought to function as a pressure regulator in the airway.

gymkhana Mounted competitive games which improve agility, sharpen reactions, and develop rider and horse physical fitness; evolved from mounted exercises performed by Indian soldiers during the British colonial period; a British word derived from a combination of the word gymnastics and the Hindustani *gend-khana* meaning sports ground.

gyp A female foxhound (q.v.); used instead of bitch (q.v.) which in some circles is considered indelicate.

gyp horse A regional British term; a horse having one parent a light breed and the other a heavy breed.

Gypsy Wagon An enclosed, horse-drawn, four-wheeled Wagon (q.v.) used by gypsies as a road home.

H

habit (1) Historically, the clothing worn by a woman riding side-saddle; consisted of a jacket and matching long skirt or shaped panel worn over the breeches and boots. (2) Also known as riding gear and riding habit; a generic term; the clothing, including the boots, belts, etc., worn by an English rider, male or female.

habitat The natural locality in which a plant or animal is found.

habituation A training technique; a decrease in responsiveness of the horse upon repeated exposure to a stimulus.

Habronema Also known as stomach worm; generally refers to parasitic worms of the species *Habronema* (*Habronema muscae*, *Habronema microstoma*, and *Draschia megastoma*) found in the stomach and *Trichostrongylus axei* found in the small intestine and stomach; adult worms vary in size from ¼ to 1 inch (6–25 mm); the lavae pass in the feces and are ingested by fly maggots that develop in manure; stomach worm larvae develop within the maggots and become infective at about the time the adult fly emerges from its pupa; the larvae are then deposited as flies feed on a horse's lips, nostrils, and fleshy wounds; the horse becomes infected internally if he licks and swallows these larvae, which will mature in the stomach; horses can also become infected by ingesting infected feed or water; larvae deposited on wounds do not complete their development to adult stage, but remain in the wound area causing cutaneous habronemiasis (q.v.); *Draschia megastoma* occurs in tumor-like swelling on the stomach wall while other species are free-moving in the stomach mucosa.

Habronemiasis Infection of horses with worms of the genus *Habronema* (q.v.), the cause of "summer sores" (q.v.) and a usually mild chronic gastritis.

hack (1) Also known as riding out; to exercise a horse lightly. (2) Any refined riding horse used for riding at an ordinary gait over roads, trails, etc.; is a recognized type, not an established breed; not to be confused with Hackney (q.v.); a contraction of Hackney from the period when carriage horses were used for riding; classifications include covert hack (q.v.), road hack (q.v.), and park hack (q.v.); from the French *haquenée*, meaning work-worn. (3) *see* SHOW NO. 3

Hack *see* HACKNEY COACH

hackamore (1) Also known as jaquima from which the word was Anglicized, or incorrectly as hackamore bit; a bitless bridle (q.v.) consisting of a leather headstall (q.v.) attached to a semi-oval plaited leather or rawhide bosal (q.v.) knotted under the chin of the horse to which a hair or cotton rope mecate (q.v.) is attached; a cotton fiador (q.v.) serving as a throat latch (q.v.); may attach to the headstall and mecate which acts as a throat latch (q.v.); the bosal generally sits at a 45 degree angle from the bridge of the nose to the chin; control is achieved through pressure applied to the bridge of the nose and the poll. (2) *see* MECHANICAL HACKAMORE

hackamore bit (1) *see* HACKAMORE. (2) *see* MECHANICAL HACKAMORE

hack classes Any competition for hacks (q.v.) held at a major horse show; may be divided into weight classes on the basis that a 10 stone (62.5 kg) hack should be able to provide a comfortable ride all day for a person of that weight; size classes include: (a) Show, Ladies: a horse larger than 14.2 hands but not exceeding 15.3 hands and capable of carrying a lady riding side-saddle, (b) Show, Large: a horse between 15 and 15.3 hands to be ridden astride; and, (c) Show, Small: a horse standing between 14.2 and 15 hands to be ridden astride.

hackles Erectile hairs along the neck and back of a hound commonly raised in excitement and/or anger.

hackles up Said of a hound (q.v.) when the erectile hairs along the neck and back stand upright as due to anger, excitement, and/or fear; a hound in pursuit of a fox (q.v.) will have his hackles up when close to the fox and running for blood.

Hackney Also known as Hackney Horse; a compact trotting horse breed developed in Great Britain; descended from Norfolk Trotters (q.v.) crossed with native and Arab (q.v.) horses; formerly any active riding horse used for road work, now used chiefly for driving; characterized by its high-stepping trot and far-reaching action; stands between 14.0 and 15.2 hands, is solid colored with some white, and generally has a flat shoulder; the stud book (q.v.) was established in 1883.

Hackney Coach Also known as Hack; a four-wheeled, springless, six-passenger public service vehicle drawn by a pair of horses in pole gear (q.v.) with the near side horse sometimes postillion (q.v.) driven; used in London, Paris, and other European cities throughout the 17th and 18th centuries; frequently the discarded coaches of the wealthy patched-up for additional years of service; smaller versions were drawn by a single horse.

Hackney Horse *see* HACKNEY

Hackney Horse Society, The A British organization founded in 1883 to publish a Stud Book, improve the Hackney (q.v.), and to promote and encourage breeding of Hackney (q.v.) harness horses, cobs, and ponies.

Hackney Pony A pony breed originating in early 19th century Great Britain; developed by crossing the Hackney (q.v.) with Fell (q.v.) and Welsh Ponies (q.v.) and selected trotters and roadsters; the coat may be brown, black, gray or roan with white markings permitted; stands 12.1 to 14 hands (q.v.), has a light head, arched neck, pronounced withers, a long and rounded croup, slender, yet strong legs, and somewhat straight-hocked hind legs; is fiery, energetic, and fast; registered in the Hackney stud book; until the beginning of the 20th century used by tradesmen to pull delivery vehicles, now used predominantly for show.

Hackney Show Wagon *see* BOX WAGON

Hackney stand Any location where Hackney Coaches (q.v.) assembled, waiting to be hired; the first recorded stand was established in London, England in 1634.

hack on A hunting term; to ride one's horse to a meet of hounds or to the next draw during a day's hunt.

hack out To ride a horse for pleasure in the field or on a trail or road as opposed to working in a manège (q.v.) or arena (q.v.).

Hack Show, Ladies *see* HACK CLASSES

Hack Show, Large *see* HACK CLASSES

Hack Show, Small *see* HACK CLASSES

haematinic *see* HEMATINIC

haematocrit (1) *see* HEMATOCRIT NO 1. (2) *see* HEMATOCRIT NO. 2

haematoma *see* HEMATOMA

Haematopinas asini *see* SUCKING LOUSE

haemoglobin *see* HEMOGLOBIN

haemoglobinemia *see* HEMOGLOBINEMIA

haemoglobinuria *see* HEMOGLOBINURIA

haemolysis *see* HEMOLYSIS

haemolytic anemia *see* HEMOLYTIC ANEMIA

haemolytic jaundice A jaundice (q.v.) condition caused by the dissolution of red blood cells and the liberation of the cell contents; occurs when destruction of red cells, which rupture continuously throughout the lifespan of any individual, is increased to such an extent that the bone marrow cannot adequately produce replacement cells and the liver is unable to clear the blood of the large quantities of bile pigment; may also be caused by bacteria, virus, or parasites which occur in such conditions as equine infectious anemia (q.v.), equine leptospirosis (q.v.), and equine piroplasmosis (q.v.), respectively.

haemorrhage *see* HEMORRHAGE

haemorrhagic anemia *see* HEMORRHAGIC ANEMIA

Hafflinger *see* HAFLINGER

Haflig *see* HAFLINGER

Haflinger Also spelled Hafflinger and known as Haflig or Edelweiss Pony; a coldblood (q.v.) pony breed originating in the Southern Austrian Tyrol, around the mountain village of Hafling from which the name derived; the base stock descended from the now extinct Alpine Heavy Horse crossed with Noriker (q.v.), Hucul (q.v.), Bosnian and Korik (q.v.); all modern pure-bred Halflingers can be traced to the Arab stallion El Bedavi XXII; the breed is a fixed type with an unmistakable appearance: is always chestnut or palomino with a flaxen mane and tail, stands up to 14 hands, has a broad head, large eyes, open nostrils, small ears, long back, muscular loins and quarters, tough hooves, and short legs, a free action, and a long-strided walk; is frugal, sure-footed, tough, hardy, sound, and kind; young stock raised on Alpine pastures to develop their hearts and lungs and are not worked until four years of age; often lives and remains active well into its 40s; used for packing and draft; branded with Austria's native flower, the Edelweiss, with the letter H in the center; the Italian-bred version of this breed is known as the Avelignese (q.v.).

ha-ha A drop fence (q.v.) with a ditch or an obstacle such as a wall concealed in a purpose-built hollow; the horse jumps down and into the hollow, takes one or more strides, negotiates the ditch or other obstacle and immediately jumps back out the other side.

HAHS *see* HOOVED ANIMAL HUMANE SOCIETY

hair A fine filament which originates in the hair follicles and grows from the skin of the horse; performs a thermoregulatory function, protecting the horse from extreme changes in air temperature.

haircloth *see* HORSEHAIR NO. 2

hair color Refers to coat color; any of five primary colors: brown, black, bay, chestnut, or white, variations of which include dun (buckskin), gray, palomino, pinto (calico or paint), and roan.

hairies More than one hairy (q.v.).

hair up Also known as coat up; said of a horse; to grow a winter coat, e.g. "The horse did not hair up much."

hairy (1) *see* HAIRY BULLFINCH. (2) Slang; any heavy-breed horse such as the Shire (q.v.); so called because of the heavy leg feathering (q.v.).

hairy bullfinch Also known as hairy; a jumping obstacle; a live, thin and straggly hedge jumped through rather than over.

Half-Balding gag bit A bit with a jointed mouthpiece (q.v.) and large, loose-ring half-cheek gags (q.v.) used with a single rein; prevents the effect of the gag until considerable pressure is applied.

halfblood *see* WARMBLOOD

half-bred Also known as part-bred; said of any horse which is not definitively Thoroughbred (q.v.), draft, or pony which is of mixed or crossed parentage.

half-breed (1) A horse out of different blood strains, as in out of different races or breeds. (2) A horse sired by a Thoroughbred, but not out of a Thoroughbred (q.v.) mare; is not eligible for entry into the General Stud Book (q.v.), but may be registered in the Half-Bred stud book.

half-breed bit Any curb bit (q.v.) with a high port and a cricket (q.v.); popular in the southwest United States.

half-brother A relationship of two male offspring out of the same dam (q.v.), but by different sires (q.v.); does not apply to horses who only share the same sire.

half-cannon *see* SOCK

half-chaps *see* LEGGINGS

half-cheek The vertical portion of the bit exterior to the mouth; extend below the bit mouthpiece (q.v.) to which the cheek-pieces (q.v.) attach above and the reins below.

half-cheek snaffle A snaffle bit (q.v.) consisting of a straight or jointed mouth-piece fitted at either end with fixed rings which attach to straight- or spoon-shaped (wider and slightly curved toward the horse's jaw at the top) arms; the cheeks (q.v.) may extend either above the mouth-piece as in an upper-cheek snaffle (q.v.) or below as in a lower-cheek snaffle (q.v.); the cheeks prevent the bit from running through the mouth of a horse if he runs sideways or refuses to turn.

half-halt The imperceptible, almost simultaneous, coordinated action of the seat, legs, and hands of the rider performed to increase the attention and balance of the horse before the execution of any movement or transition to lesser or higher gait or pace; does not completely halt the movement of the horse, but has a collecting effect.

half-mile pole A racing term; a vertical pole located on the infield rail 4 furlongs from the finish.

half-miler (1) A racing term; a track ½ mile (804 m) long. (2) A racing term; a horse who prefers running on a ½ mile (804 m) track.

half-moon bit *see* MULLEN MOUTH BIT

half-moon mouth *see* MULLEN MOUTH BIT

half-pass A lateral dressage movement performed free of the track, in which the horse bends uniformly on two tracks throughout his body in the direction in which he is moving; the horse moves on an angle (in some cases as much as 45 degrees) from his median line; the horse's shoulders move slightly in advance of the hindquarters (q.v.), the outside legs crossing in front of the inside legs; there is only slight lateral flexion; principally a traverse (q.v.) executed in a semi-lateral direction.

half-pass counter change *see* COUNTER HALF-PASS

half-pastern Also known as sock (Brit); a leg marking (q.v.); white on the foot of the horse which extends from the coronary band (q.v.) halfway up the pastern (q.v.).

half-pirouette Also known as demi-pirouette; one half of a pirouette (q.v.); the horse turns 180 degrees pivoting on his inside hind leg and scribing a half circle with his forelegs.

half-schooled Said of a horse who has had some training and willingly obeys the basic aids (q.v.).

half-sister A relationship of two female offspring out of the same dam, but by different sires; does not apply to horses that only share the same sire.

half stocking Also known as boot; a leg marking (q.v.); white on the horse's leg extending from the coronary band (q.v.) to the lower half of the cannon bone just above the fetlock joint (q.v.).

half-struck Also known as set back; said of a horse-drawn carriage folding hood when positioned halfway between being fully open and completely closed.

half-volte Also known as demi-volte; a dressage movement; one half of a 6-meter circle.

half-volte and change A dressage movement; the horse moves off the track (q.v.), haunches-in (q.v.) and scribes one half of a 6-meter circle, returning to the track at a 45 degree angle traveling in the opposite direction; other volte (q.v.) movements include the renvers volte (q.v.), renvers half-volte (q.v.), and half-volte (q.v.).

half-volte reversed *see* RENVERS HALF-VOLTE

halloo *see* VIEW HALLOO

halt To bring a horse to a stop, preferably balanced and square.

halt early A dressage term; said of a horse who stops before the marker (q.v.).

halt late A dressage term; said of a horse who stops after the marker (q.v.).

halter (1) Also known as a head collar; a bitless leather, nylon, or natural fiber headstall (q.v.) with or without a detachable rope, strap, or chain by which a horse is led or tied. (2) Racing slang; to claim (q.v.) a horse. (3) To put a halter on the head of a horse.

halter break To train a horse to allow a halter to be put on and to respond to being led by a rope, strap, or chain attached to the halter.

halter broke Said of a horse trained to wear a head stall and lead.

halter man A racing term; an owner or trainer who specializes in buying horses from claiming races (q.v.).

halter puller A horse who pulls back on the halter rope when tied; a vice.

halter pulling Said of the horse who pulls against the halter rope when tied; a vice.

halter rope *see* LEAD LINE

Hambletonian 10 An in-bred descendant of Messenger foaled in 1849; sired 1300 foals in 27 years; the founding sire of the Standardbred (q.v.), more than 90 percent of all modern Standardbreds can trace their lineage to four of Hambletonian 10's sons: George Wilkes, Dictator, Happy Medium, and Electioneer.

hame A curved wood or brass-plated steel piece fitted around the exterior edge of a harness collar (q.v.) worn by the horse; two hames are used on each collar; may be made in one or two sections; a terret (q.v.) through which the rein passes is fixed to the top half of each hame; transfers the draft to the collar and supports the harness tugs (q.v.), trace chains, and hame straps (q.v.).

hame chain A small-linked chain used to connect the bottom ends of the hames (q.v.).

hame draught *see* PULL NO. 5

hame rein A short rein buckled to the bit and looped over the hame horn; used on heavy-horse harness to prevent the horse from lowering his head excessively.

hames The plural of hame (q.v.).

hames collar *see* HARNESS COLLAR

hames horns *see* HORN OF THE HAMES

hame strap A leather harness strap used to hold the tops and/or the bottoms of the hames (q.v.) together; passes through the hame eyes and connects to the collar (q.v.).

hame top eye The slot at the top of the hame (q.v.) through which the hame strap (q.v.) passes before being buckled.

ham-fisted *see* MUTTON-FISTED

hammer cloth Also spelled hammercloth; heavy woven cloth used to cover the coachman's seat in state and dress horse-drawn vehicles; often trimmed with gold braid.

hammercloth *see* HAMMER CLOTH

hammer head Said of a coarse-headed horse.

Hammock Wagon A horse-drawn vehicle popular in 11th century England; the body resembled a hammock and was hung from large hooks imbedded in posts supported by the axles between the four wheels.

hamschackle To restrain a horse using a rope or strap connecting the head to one of the forelegs.

hamstring (1) Also known as Achilles tendon; the fibrous cord joining the gaskin muscles to the point of the hock (q.v.). (2) Also known as hock; to cut the hamstring or hamstrings of the horse; to cut, cripple, or render powerless.

hamstrung Said of a horse disabled by injury to the Achilles tendon above the location of the hock (q.v.).

hand Also known by the acronyms hh and Hh; a linear measurement of a horse's height equaling 4 inches (10.16 cm); calculated from the ground to the highest point of the withers; smaller increments are expressed in inches rather than decimal points or fractions; thus, a horse 65 inches tall would be 16.1 hands, i.e. 16 hands plus 1 inch; derived from the time when the height of horses was measured by the number of spans of a man's hand, each span estimated at 4 inches (10.16 cm).

hand breeding Also known as hand mating or service in-hand; mating of a stallion and mare orchestrated by a handler; includes teasing (q.v.), washing, the act of coitus, and the return of the mare and stallion to their respective living quarters.

hand canter A semi-extended canter (q.v.) between a promenade canter (q.v.) and a gallop.

hand fed *see* BOTTLE FED

hand-forged horseshoe *see* HOT SHOE NO. 2

hand gallop A controlled, balanced gait (q.v.) in which the horse travels at about 18 mph (29 kmph).

hand gate *see* BRIDLE GATE

hand holder A braided loop occasionally attached to the interiors of closed horse-drawn carriages as a hand rest for travelers.

hand horse A coaching term; the far side horse (q.v.) when two horses are postillion (q.v.) controlled.

handicap (1) A burden of additional weight, or a disadvantage of distance or time, imposed on those entrants deemed superior to equalize the chances of all competitors in a race or contest. (2) A racing term; to allot different weights to the horses in a race, based on their past performance, with the intention of equalizing the chances of all; this process is carried out by a designated official, usually the racing secretary (USA) or official handicapper (UK). (3) *see* HANDICAP RACE. (4) *see* POLO HANDICAP

handicapper (1) A racing term; one, generally the racing secretary (official race handicapper in Britain), responsible for assigning the weights to be carried by each horse running in a handicap race (q.v.). (2) A US racing term; one who places bets on horses based on a thorough study of their past performances.

handicap race Also known as handicap; a racing term; a race in which competing horses carry weight assigned by the racing secretary (official handicapper in Britain) to equalize the winning chances of all entrants; the superior horse, as determined by the racing secretary's assessment of his past performance, carries the highest weight, while lesser competitors, as based on perceived ability, carry less.

Handicap Triple Crown A United States racing term; a mythical award given a horse who wins all three classic handicaps – the Brooklyn, Suburban, and Metropolitan – in one season.

handily A racing term; said of a horse who works or races with moderate effort and little or no urging.

handiness The extent to which a horse is nimble, light-footed, and agile.

handle (1) A racing term; the total amount bet on a race, in a day, meeting, or season. (2) *see* HANDPIECE. (3) To touch or feel using the hands; to work or train as a horse.

handled Said of a young horse who has been touched, brushed, haltered, and led prior to breaking.

handler One responsible for the handling (q.v.) of a horse.

handling The initial phase of training a young horse; includes imprinting (q.v.), haltering, grooming, and basic socialization.

handmade horseshoe *see* HOT SHOE NO. 2

hand mating *see* HAND BREEDING

hand-piece A carriage term; that part of the rein held in the hand.

handpiece Also known as handle; that portion of the whip (q.v.) between the cap and collar (q.v.) where it is held by the user.

hand ride A racing term; said of a rider who urges a horse toward a longer, faster, more rhythmic stride without use of a whip by rolling his hands forward on the horse's neck and lifting his head at the beginning of each stride.

hand rub To massage or rub the legs of the horse to improve circulation and prevent and/or reduce swelling.

hands (1) The extremity of the arm consisting of the palm, four fingers, and thumb; a rider may have good hands (q.v.) or bad hands. (2) The plural of hand (q.v.), e.g. "How many hands is that horse?"

hand sale To finalize the sale of a horse on the basis of a hand shake; the outstretched hand of the person making the sale is struck by the person making the offer (obs).

handy Said of a nimble, light-footed, and agile horse.

hang Also known as hang fire (Brit); a racing term; said of a horse running a race who is unable to produce a finishing kick and is therefore unable to improve his position on the homestretch (q.v.).

hang fire *see* HANG

hanging on An obsolete coaching term; said of one of a pair of horses who hangs away from the other.

hang the knees Said of a jumping horse who fails to fold his knees and tuck his legs into his body when jumping.

hang up your bars An obsolete coaching term; said of one who retires from coaching as a profession.

Hanover *see* HANOVERIAN

Hanoverian Also known as Hanover; a warmblood (q.v.) developed in the Hanover and Lower Saxony districts of West Germany in the 17th century through the breeding of imported Spanish, Neapolitan, and Oriental stallions to local mares; at this time the breed was only suited to draft and farm work; English Thoroughbred (q.v.) blood was introduced around 1714, and in 1735 George II, Elector of Hanover, established a stud in the small town of Celle where the breed was further improved and lightened; by the end of the 19th century input of English blood was stopped to avoid further change to the breed, and after 1924, Trakehner (q.v.) and Arab (q.v.) blood was introduced to produce a riding competition horse; breed development and breeding is strictly controlled by a performance and licensing system; the modern horse stands 16 to 17.2 hands, is quiet, courageous, athletic and powerful, has impressive action (q.v.), yet little knee action, and a long stride; the coat is generally chestnut, brown, black, or gray and white markings are frequent; has a well-proportioned head, long neck, pronounced withers, a long back, strong, well-muscled legs, and a tough hoof; used for show jumping, hunting, dressage, eventing, and harness; the Westphalian (q.v.) is the Hanoverian bred under another regional title.

Hanoverian Cream (1) *see* PALOMINO. (2) *see* ISABELLA

Hans Kluge A Russian stallion, one of a number of horses collectively known as the Elberfeld Horses (q.v.), used by William von Osten (q.v.), a Berliner, to prove his theories on equine intelligence; von Osten appeared to train the stallion to calculate by pawing the ground with his hoof, read, and differentiate colors, up to the general standard of knowledge of a 4-year-old child; von Osten's studies gained enormous publicity, but in 1904, German psychologist, Oskar Pfungst, demonstrated that the stallion answered to unconscious signs from von Osten; at the outbreak of World War I, the horses were disbanded.

Hansom *see* HANSOM CAB

Hansom Cab Originally known as Hansom Safety Cab and subsequently as Hansom, the Gondola of London, or Two-wheeler; a two-wheeled, horse-drawn vehicle patented in 1834 by John Chapman (q.v.) who later sold the patent to Joseph Hansom of the J.A. Hansom Cab Company for which it was named; had a closed, low-slung body, high wheels, a rearward driving seat positioned high above the back of the vehicle, and a curved dashboard at the rear of the shafts bringing the hindquarters of the horse fairly close to the vehicle for increased control; seated two forward-facing passengers on a single cross-seat, their legs protected by knee flaps; entered from the front by a folding door with a sliding glass window; not very popular in the United States; some three-wheeled versions were manufactured; from the 1890s most had solid rubber tires and were hung on semi-elliptical side springs while others were fitted with solid silver accessories and interior mirrors; seldom used by unescorted women; drawn by a single horse.

Hansom Safety Cab *see* HANSOM CAB

Hanoverian Cream (1) *see* PALOMINO. (2) *see* ISABELLA

Happy Medium One of four sons of Hambletonian 10 from which more than 90 percent of all modern Standardbreds (q.v.) can trace descent.

hard boot An American racing term; one from Kentucky whose horse training methods are of the old school; so called for their typically, mud-caked boots.

harbourer An old English stag hunting (q.v.) term; one selected by the Hunt Master to identify the stag (q.v.) to be hunted; generally a local gamekeeper or farrier familiar with the ground hunted

hard and fast A calf roping term; said of a roper (q.v.); to take a double half-hitch of the lariat (q.v.) on the saddle horn (q.v.) to secure it when dismounting to tie off (q.v.) a cow or calf.

Harddraver *see* FRIESIAN

hardel An obsolete hunting term; to couple (q.v.) hounds (q.v.).

hard horse Said of a horse resistant to illness and unsoundness.

hard keeper Said of horse prone to digestive disturbances, who does not maintain his weight nor a healthy appearance from a normal diet; is difficult to fatten and train as any dietary change, including the quality of the feed, may result in weight loss or digestive problems.

hard-mouthed Said of a horse whose bars of the mouth have become callused and desensitized to the action of the bit because of continued bit pressure; most commonly caused by bad hands (q.v.).

hard palate The anterior bony arch of the roof of the mouth (q.v.) which, in conjunction with the soft palate (q.v.), separates the nasal and oral cavities.

hard-pressed A hunting term; said of a fox when the distance between it and the pursuing hounds narrows.

hard track A racing term; a turf track lacking resilience.

hare (1) A hunting term; to hunt rabbits or hare. (2) Also known as puss; a small mammal of the genus *Lepus* in the family Leporidea having long ears, a divided upper lip, short tail, and long hind legs adapted for leaping.

hare foot A hunting term; said of a hound's foot when long and narrow, resembling that of hare, fox, or coyote.

harelip *see* CLEFT LIP

hare-pied Refers to hound coat color; a cream- or fawn-colored head, legs, body, and stern with the ears and back shading into brown; the ears have light tips.

hark A hunting term; to listen.

Harma A hunting or war chariot used by the Ancient Persians; drawn by teams of two, three, or four horses harnessed abreast; entered from the rear.

harmony The balanced interrelationship of the horse and rider or the body parts to one another.

harness (1) Also known as harness tack; the combination of leather pieces and metals used to connect a horse to a wagon, carriage, cart, etc.; generally consists of a bridle (q.v.), collar (q.v.), hames (q.v.), tugs (q.v.) or traces (q.v.), back band (q.v.), belly band (q.v.), and breeching (q.v.). (2) To put a harness on a horse(s). (3) *see* HITCH NO. 2

harness blinkers *see* DRIVING BLINKERS

harness collar Also known as neck collar, hames collar, or collar; a thick, padded, oval ring fitted around the neck and against the shoulders to support the hames (q.v.) to which the traces (q.v.) are attached, and by which a vehicle is pulled; consists of the forewale (q.v.) and afterwale (q.v.); good fit is essential; available in different sizes, shapes, and weights depending on the horse and the use.

harness crupper Also known as crupper; a back strap used to prevent the pad from slipping forward; attached on one end to a dee located on the back of harness pad and to the crupper dock (q.v.) on the other.

harness loops *see* KEEPERS

harness martingale A leather strap used to prevent the collar (q.v.) from riding up on the horse's neck; attached on one end to the girth (q.v.) and to the lowest end of the collar (q.v.) on the other; similar to the standing martingale (q.v.) used on the saddle horse.

Harness Race Cart An American Sulky (q.v.) of the Gig (q.v.) type having small wheels and a safer, more permanent seat than an ordinary sulky; used when driving long-gaited horses for racing and other sport purposes.

Harness Race Sulky A modern, two-wheeled Racing Sulky (q.v.) with shafts curved in a continuous, bow-like formation from the underframe direction; mounted on wire-spoked wheels with pneumatic tires; the skeleton seat is 27 inches (69 cm) from ground level; quite popular in the United States and Australia.

harness rack An open rack made of iron, plastic-covered iron, or wood on which harness tack (q.v.) is hung when not in use; accommodates the collar (q.v.), pad, crupper (q.v.), bridle (q.v.), and reins (q.v.).

harness racing Also known as pacing or Standardbred racing; a sport in which Standardbreds (q.v.), trotters (q.v.) and pacers (q.v.), race a distance of 1 mile (1.6 km); contested on two gaits, the trot (q.v.) and the pace (q.v.); a third gait, running, often manifests itself, but a horse who runs must return to his natural gait or face disqualification; competing horses are driven by drivers seated in two-wheeled carts pulled behind the horse; speeds average 25 to 30 mph (32–48 km/h); competing horses may not be younger than two nor older than 15 years of age; generally considered a native American sport which commenced in 1806, although it actually traces back more than 3,000 years.

harness tack *see* HARNESS NO. 1

harness tackle *see* HARNESS NO. 1

harras An enclosure or establishment in which stallions and mares are retained for breeding.

harrier A hunting term; a light-bodied hound traditionally bred to hunt hare (q.v.) from horseback; measures 18 to 21 inches (46-53 cm) at the shoulder; smaller than a foxhound (q.v.); in Britain many harrier packs hunt mainly or only foxes.

harrier pack A hunting term; a pack of hounds measuring 18 to 21 inches (46–53 cm) at the shoulder, entered (q.v.) to hare (q.v.).

harrow (1) A long-handled tool having a metal-toothed head attached perpendicular to the shaft used to rake and loosen the upper race track or arena surface. (2) To rake and loosen the soil using a hand harrow or a tractor pulling a harrow attachment.

Harry Highover's pelham A curb bit (q.v.) popular at the turn of the 19th century; had a two-inch port (q.v.) attached to a bridoon (q.v.) mouthpiece.

hat (1) Any of various head coverings for men and women usually consisting of a crown, sides, and continuous brim. (2) *see* HELMET

hatchet blinkers A driving or harness blinker (q.v.); hatchet-shaped, leather-covered metal plates attached to the cheek-pieces of the bridle or to a hood (q.v.), used to restrict the horse's vision to the sides and rear in either or both eyes.

hat rack An emaciated horse.

hat trick A racing term; said of a jockey who wins three races on a single program.

haunch Also known as hip; one half of the pelvis including the hip joint (q.v.), the upper part of the thigh, and all their fleshy covering parts.

haunches That portion of the horse consisting of the buttocks and hips (q.v.).

haunches-in *see* TRAVERS

haunches-out *see* RENVERS

haute école Also known as High School; the classical school or method of advanced equitation in which the horse is trained to a very high level of performance in dressage (q.v.) including the high airs (q.v.) and low airs (q.v.).

haute école airs FEI Level dressage movements consisting of piaffe (q.v.) and passage (q.v.).

have a handful A coaching term; to take the reins of a team.

have a leg Said of a horse having unsoundness or swelling in one or more legs.

have a lot of cow *see* COW SMART

have one in the boot A racing term; said of a jockey who rides a horse upon which the owner or trainer has made bets including those made on behalf of the jockey.

having a handful A coaching term; said of the driver who has picked up the reins of a team (q.v.).

having manners Said of a horse who is willing and obedient to the desires of his rider.

haw (1) A coaching term; a voice signal given by the driver of a horse-drawn vehicle to instruct the team to turn to the left. (2) *see* NICTATING MEMBRANE

hay Cut and dried grasses, legumes, and cereal crops; a primary source of roughage in the diet of non-pastured horses; high in fiber, calcium, and protein and a primary source of vitamin D if sun-cured; of two varieties: grass hay which includes cereal grass hays (q.v.) and legume hay (q.v.); generally pressed into 50 to 100 pound (23–45 kg) bales strung with wire or rope, or loose stacked; may be stored for many months without sacrificing quality; include Timothy hay (q.v.), Bermuda hay (q.v.), bluestem grass hay (q.v.), bromegrass hay (q.v.), wheat grass hay (q.v.), sudangrass hay (q.v.), Johnsongrass hay (q.v.), orchard grass hay (q.v.), prairie hay, and grass hay (q.v.).

hay bale Any bound bundle of grass or legume hay (q.v.); generally rectangularly shaped, bound with twine or wire, and weighing, depending on the hay's moisture content, 50 to 100 pounds (23–45 kg); large operations are now turning to larger bales, in excess of one ton, in which the hay is rolled and bound in a shape similar to a jelly roll.

hay belly Also called grass belly; said of a horse having a distended belly due to excessive feeding of bulky rations such as hay (q.v.), straw (q.v.), or grass (q.v.).

hayburner Also known as oatburner; a racing term; said of a horse who does not win enough to pay his feed bill.

haycock *see* HAYSTACK

hay cubes *see* CUBES

haylage Vacuum-packed hay sealed immediately following cutting and drying; little nutritional value is lost in this process; frequently fed to horses with dust allergies or a tendency to cough.

hayloft An area located above the first floor in a barn or stable, where hay and other items may be stored.

haynet A string, rope, or corded net containing loose hay (q.v.) or alfalfa (q.v.); hung to enable the horse to eat without the hay touching the ground; a common method of feeding horses in transit.

hay rack Also known as rack; a framework, grating, or stand situated above ground level that holds fodder (q.v.) for horses or cattle.

haystack Also known as haycock; a conical pile of loose hay (q.v.) or bales stacked outdoors.

hay tea A beverage for sick horses made by infusing hay in hot water and allowing it to steep.

Haywick Common Riding Also known as common riding; a Scottish ceremony conducted on horseback during the first full week in June and extending over several days; consists of many individual events, the principal one known as the Cornet's Chase (q.v.); the date of origin is unknown.

haze Said of a cowboy (q.v.); to keep a steer or calf running in a straight line parallel to a wrestler (q.v.) or roper (q.v.).

hazer A cowboy (q.v.) who rides on the side of the steer or calf opposite to the wrestler or roper to keep it running in a relatively straight line and prevent it from running away from the wrestler's or roper's horse.

Hb *see* HEMOGLOBIN

HCG *see* HUMAN CHORIONIC GONADOTROPIN

HCT *see* HEMATOCRIT

head (1) The upper part of the horse's body attached by the neck to the body; the head and neck comprise close to 20 percent of the horse's body weight. (2) A racing term; a measurement of the margin between horses competing in a race; the length of the horse's head, e.g. "The horse won by a head". (3) *see* CARRIAGE HEAD. (5) *see* HEADSTALL

head a cow Also known as heading; a cutting term; to position a ridden horse in front of a cow to force it to change direction or stop.

head a fox A hunting term; to turn back a fox; generally performed by the hounds (q.v.), although sometimes performed by the field (q.v.).

head bumper Also known as poll guard; a felt or shearling-lined leather cap which provides extra protection to the sensitive poll region of the horse's head during shipping; extends from the top of the neck just behind the poll to just above the eyes, with holes cut for the ears; attaches at the temples to the halter (q.v.).

head cap *see* HOOD

head carriage The position and manner in which the horse carries his head and neck; natural head carriage is dependent upon the individual's conformation and certain types of carriage are more or less characteristic of different breeds.

head collar *see* HALTER

head collar chain shanks *see* CROSS TIES

headed (1) A racing term; said of a racing horse who loses said race at the finish by a head (q.v.). (2) A hunting term; said of a fox having been turned from his original line (q.v.). (3) Said of a horse-drawn vehicle with a top.

header (1) A team calf roping term; one who is most talented at, and whose responsibility it is in competition, to rope the horns, head, or neck of the calf; works in conjunction with a heeler (q.v.). (2) *see* HEAD HORSE

head fly Also known as plantation fly; a non-biting muscid, *Hydrotaea irritans*, found in large numbers in northern European countries, especially Denmark and Britain; a secretion feeder attracted to the mouth, nose, ears, eyes, and wounds; produces one generation every year; most active from early June until late September and is common in the vicinity of thickets or woodland in which it shelters between feeding periods.

head horse Also known as header; a stout, strong, fast mount from which a roper (q.v.) ropes the head of a steer; trained to accelerate and make a sharp turn to the left once the steer is roped.

heading *see* HEAD A COW

headland A hunting term; the edge of a field.

head lap *see* HOOD

headlessness *see* ACEPHALIA

head of the saddle *see* POMMEL

head of the stretch A racing term; the beginning of the straight run to the finish (q.v.) on a racetrack.

headpiece (1) *see* HEADSTALL. (2) *see* CROWN PIECE

head plate A metal ornament, frequently silver, used to adorn some types of horse-drawn carriages; sometimes embossed with crests or other decoration.

headset (1) *see* DE GOUGE MARTINGALE. (2) The position and carriage (horizontal and vertical) of the horse's head on the neck, relative to the ground.

head shaking Said of the horse who shakes his head side-to-side, up-and-down, snorting, sneezing, and rubbing the nose on objects or on the ground while moving; it is believed that sunlight and exercise may trigger a response of the central nervous system, a tingling sensation or inappropriate stimulation of the sensory branches of the trigeminal nerve in the muzzle, which causes the horse to shake his head; the pain felt by the horse is referred to as neuropathic and may be persistent or intermittent; manifest in all breeds and disciplines; thought that horses exposed to Equine herpesvirus (q.v.) are at increased risk.

headstall Also known as headpiece, bridle head, or head; the part of the bridle or hackamore (q.v.) placed on the horse's head for the purpose of holding a bit, bosal (q.v.), or similar device in the horse's mouth or on his nose, and to which the reins are attached.

heads up (1) A hunting term; said of the hounds who, having lost the scent, raise their heads to search for it. (2) Also known as head up; a call of caution; an announcement to pay attention; may be communicated from one rider to another or to a person on the ground, as when in close proximity.

heads up, sterns down A hunting term; said of hounds (q.v.) running a fox (q.v.) at top speed with the scent at breast height (q.v.) in which case their heads will be held high and their hindquarters low.

head terret A coaching term; a fixed upright metal ring attached to that portion of the crownpiece (q.v.) between the ears of the wheeler's bridle through which the leader's reins pass; now generally attached to the bridle cheekpiece at brow level.

head to the wall *see* TRAVERS

head up (1) Said of a horse who momentarily evades the action of the bit by raising his head. (2) *see* HEADS UP NO. 3

health certificate A document issued by a licensed veterinarian (q.v.) to evidence that a horse has been examined and is sound and free from any contagious condition at the time of examination; such a horse is said to vet clean (q.v.).

Hearse A four-wheeled, horse-drawn carriage in which coffins were transported pulled by horses called the Black Brigade (q.v.); frequently glass sided and painted black, except those which carried children, which were white.

heart (1) The hollow muscular organ which circulates blood received from the veins throughout the body by means of rhythmic contractions and dilations; consists of 4 cavities and can weigh between 8 and 16 pounds (3.62–7.25 kg) in the average horse. (2) Said of a horse who has great courage and willingness as in, "Sea Biscuit won the race because of his heart."

heart-bar shoe A therapeutic horseshoe (q.v.) of the bar shoe (q.v.) type used to treat some cases of navicular by relieving pressure on the center of the frog, and founder by applying pressure slightly behind the point of the frog to prevent further coffin bone rotation; the shoe branches (q.v.) are left long and welded into an arc behind and join at the center of the heels to create a heart shape.

heartbeat irregularity *see* ARRHYTHMIA

heart brass One of four primary historic patterns of horse brass (q.v.); the heart pattern was struck into brass or other metal and attached to the horse harness or elsewhere to ward off the evil eye.

heart girth Also known as girth, girth measurement, or heart room; the distance around the horse's body measured behind the elbows and over the withers; may be used to calculate the horse's weight using the following equation: heart girth (in inches) x length (in inches from the point of the shoulder to the point of the hip)/241.3.

heart room *see* HEART GIRTH

heat (1) *see* ESTRUS. (2) *see* ROUND

heat bumps Hives (q.v.) triggered by elevated body or ambient air temperature.

heat cramps Spasm or cramping of the leg muscles due to electrolyte and fluid imbalance.

heat exhaustion Inability of the horse's body to maintain the normal cooling mechanism because of overheating; may be triggered by high environmental temperature, poor ventilation, high humidity, and/or overexertion in warm weather; symptoms include weakness, staggering, rapid breathing, elevated body temperature, heavy sweating and rapid heart rate.

heat prostration A nonspecific term; prostration (q.v.) due to heat.

heatstroke Also known as sunstroke; failure of the heat regulatory mechanism at the central nervous system level caused by a severe response to overheating; the regulatory mechanism shuts down and the body quits trying to cool itself; may be triggered by elevated environmental temperature, poor ventilation, high humidity, and/or overexertion in warm weather; is more severe than, but not necessarily precipitated by, heat exhaustion (q.v.); symptoms include hot body temperature, dehydration, dry skin, rapid breathing and/or respiratory failure; may result in neurological collapse, shock (q.v.) gradual physiological failure, and ultimately, if untreated, death.

heave line A ridge of abdominal muscles extending from the middle of the flank diagonally forward and down the rib cage (q.v.) to the point of the elbow; caused by pronounced contraction of the abdomen and digestive tract against the diaphragm when expelling air from the lungs.

heaves *see* CHRONIC OBSTRUCTIVE PULMONARY DISEASE

heavy boned Said of a horse having a large and heavy bone structure.

Heavy Draught Breton *see* DRAUGHT BRETON

heavy fronted Said of a horse having a very broad chest; undesirable in riding horses, yet desirable in draft horses.

heavy headed A racing term; said of a horse who fights the reins, responds slowly to guidance, and/or prefers to run with his head low.

heavy horse Any horse possessing characteristics of the large draft breeds such as the Clydesdale (q.v.), Shire (q.v.), Suffolk Punch (q.v.), or Percheron (q.v.).

heavy top Said of a horse having a thick, coarse neck and shoulders which appear out of proportion with the rest of his body.

heavy track (1) A racing term; a racing surface that is drier than mud, and often slower. (2) A racing term; the wettest possible condition of a turf track.

heavy transport collar A collar (q.v.) used on horses in heavy army work; ranged in size from 23 to 27 inches (58–69 cm) and were substantially larger and wider than those used on draft horses.

Hecca A two-wheeled, horse-drawn passenger cart popular in India; had a movable or canopy top and little or no metal work in the construction; the shafts met at a point above the horse's withers giving the vehicle a pronounced rearward inclination; the driver sat cross-legged on a small platform of the fore-part.

heck *see* GEE

Hedijn Any progeny (q.v.) of a Persian Arab (q.v.) stallion and non-Arab mare.

hedgehog *see* ECHINI

Heecul *see* HUCUL

heel (1) A leg marking (q.v.); a white spot (q.v.) or mark located across, or on one side of, the heel. (2) One of two bulb-like areas located on the rear, underside portion of the hoof (q.v.); consists of hoof wall and frog tissue; provides shock absorption to the leg. (3) Also known as running heel, heel way, hunting the heel line, or counter; a hunting term; said of hounds (q.v.) who run the line (q.v.) of a fox (q.v.) in the opposite direction to which the fox is traveling.

heel avulsion *see* AVULSION OF THE HOOF WALL AT THE HEEL

heel boot Also known as shin or ankle boot; a heavy-duty brushing boot (q.v.) that protects the point of the fetlock and a portion of the lower cannon bone against brushing (q.v.).

heel bulbs Also known as bulbs; two

rounded sections of the horse's foot located on either side of the back of the hoof above the coronary band (q.v.).

heel calk A calk (q.v.) located on the heel of the horseshoe; provides braking traction as the hoof lands, but no grip at breakover (q.v.).

heel catch A roping term; said of a thrown rope that holds a steer from behind the shoulder and back, around the flank, or on one or both of the heels, but not by the tail only.

heel crack (1) A vertical crack in the hoof wall at the heel, starting at the bearing surface, extending a variable distance up the hoof wall, or originating at the coronary band (q.v.), and extending downward; may occur in either the fore or hind feet; more severe than toe crack (q.v.) as the sensitive laminae (q.v.) are usually involved. (2) *see* AVULSION OF THE HOOF WALL AT THE HEEL

heeler (1) A team roping term; one most talented at, and whose responsibility it is in competition, to rope the hind legs of a calf or steer; works in conjunction with a header (q.v.). (2) *see* HEEL HORSE

heel horse Also known as heeler; a stout, strong, fast mount from which a heeler (q.v.) ropes the hind legs of a calf or steer in team roping.

heel knot The knot of the bosal (q.v.) located under the chin, to which the reins and lead rope are usually attached in a hackamore (q.v.) bridle.

heel nerve (1) *see* PALMAR DIGITAL NEURECTOMY. (2) *see* PALMAR DIGITAL NERVE

heel way *see* HEEL NO. 3

heel white A leg marking; both heels on the leg are white.

heifer A young female cow.

height The tallness of the horse as measured perpendicularly from the bottom of the hoof, excluding the shoe to the highest point of the withers; defined in hands (q.v.).

held Said of a covered mare who becomes pregnant after mating, as in "The mare held to the service."

hell bent for leather Also known as hell for leather or ride hell for leather; an American term popular in the early 1800s; to press a horse to extreme speed; to move at a reckless speed regardless of the consequences, namely hell, fire, and damnation; may have derived from all of a lather, as in the condition of a horse following such a ride.

hell cart 17th-century slang; any horse-drawn passenger vehicle that splashed pedestrians with mud or forced them into the gutter when it passed.

hell for leather *see* HELL BENT FOR LEATHER

helmet (1) Also known as hat, cap, or crash skull; a lightweight protective headgear fitted with anti-concussive pads and a chin strap worn to reduce or prevent head injuries. (2) *see* RACING HELMET. (3) *see* HUNT CAP

helminth A large class of parasitic worms which include various forms of roundworms (q.v.) (nematodes), tapeworms (cestodes) and flukes (trematodes).

helminthiasis An unhealthy condition of the body resulting from worms.

helminthic (1) Any agent that causes worms to be expelled. (2) Pertaining to worms.

hematinic Also spelled haematinic; any agent that improves the blood quality by increasing hemoglobin and erythrocyte (q.v.) levels.

hematocrit (1) Also spelled haematocrit; a centrifugal device used to determine the percentage of red blood cells in a given volume of whole blood. (2) Also spelled haematocrit and known by the acronym HCT or as packed cell volume; the ratio of red blood cells to total blood volume, expressed as a percentage; may reveal dehydration, anemia, or other disorders.

hematoma Also known as blood blister and spelled haematoma; an abnormal collection of blood in an organ, space, or body tissue due to a break in the wall of a blood vessel; generally caused by impact-related injuries.

hem gears The harness worn by a farm horse in the lead of a tandem (q.v.).

hemoglobin Also known by the acronym Hb and spelled haemoglobin; the oxygen-carrying protein pigment of red blood cells.

hemoglobinemia Also spelled haemoglobinemia; excessive hemoglobin (q.v.) levels in the blood plasma; a symptom of hemolytic anemia (q.v.).

hemoglobinuria Also spelled haemoglobinuria; the presence of free hemoglobin (q.v.) in the urine of the horse; a type of hemolytic anemia (q.v.); may result from poisoning, presence of a blood parasite, viral infection, antigen/antibody reaction, or severe stress.

hemolysis Also spelled haemolysis; a breakdown of red blood cells.

hemolytic anemia Also spelled haemolytic anemia; an abnormal blood condition characterized by a deficiency of erythrocytes (q.v.) due to poison, blood parasites, viral infection, or by an antigen/antibody reaction; symptoms include pale mucous membranes, jaundice (q.v.), lowered PCV (q.v.) and hemoglobin levels, hemoglobinuria (q.v.), hemoglobinemia (q.v.), and elevated temperature.

hemorrhage Also spelled haemorrhage; blood loss.

hemorrhagic anemia Also spelled haemorrhagic anemia; an abnormal condition of the blood characterized by a deficiency of hemoglobin and/or erythrocytes (q.v.); caused by an actual decrease in the blood volume due to acute blood loss from trauma, parasites, or internal hemorrhage from ulcer, abscess, etc.; symptoms include pale mucous membranes, rapid pulse, evidence of bleeding, cold limbs, weakness, and depression.

hemp A tall annual herb, *Cannibis sativa*; hashish and marijuana are derived from the female plant, while the tough fiber of the male plant is used to make fabric and rope; historically used to make halters while individual fibers were used by saddlers for sewing.

Henderson, Charles Cooper A 19th-century British artist renowned for his coaching scenes.

Hendra virus Previously known as equine morbillivirus, EMV, or by the acronym HV; a respiratory virus of the family *Paramyxoviridae* first isolated in Hendra, Australia in 1994 from which the name derived; responsible for Hendra virus disease (q.v.); symptoms include shallow breathing and respiratory distress, lethargy, nervous disorders, staggers, and head butting; afflicted horses ultimately die of cardiac arrest.

Hendra virus disease Also known as equine morbillivirus pneumonia, EMP, equine respiratory syndrome, acute respiratory syndrome, or by the acronym HVD; caused by the lethal virus, Hendra virus (q.v.) of the family *Paramyxoviridae* first isolated in Hendra, Australia in 1994; transmission requires direct contact with respiratory secretions of infected animals; fruit bats are believed to be the natural 'host'; characterized by fever to 105 °F (41 °C), respiratory distress, increased respiratory and heart rates, head butting, blood-tinged foamy discharge from the nose and mouth as the virus attacks the blood vessels and causes pulmonary edema; afflicted horses ultimately die of cardiac arrest (q.v.); a zootropic (q.v.) disease; no known cases have been reported outside Australia.

hengest A historical term common from AD 476 to 1450; a horse, generally a gelding.

Henry Alken *see* ALKEN, HENRY

Henry Alken Jr. *see* ALKEN, HENRY JR

Henry Barrad *see* BARRAD, HENRY

Henry Bernard Challon *see* CHALLON, HENRY BERNARD

hepatic jaundice Jaundice (q.v.) occurring secondary to disease of the liver.

herb Any plant or portion thereof put into culinary or medicinal use.

herbalism Also known as herbology; the

practice of treating physical ailments and conditions with natural agents and physical means.

herbalist Also known as herbal practitioner; one studied and practiced in the art of herbalism (q.v.).

herbal medicine *see* HERBALISM

herbal practitioner *see* HERBALIST

herbal treatment Herbs taken orally or applied topically in poultices, oils, or tinctures to treat physical and emotional conditions.

herbology *see* HERBALISM

herd (1) Also known as band; a group of animals of one kind kept together under human control, as cows or horses. (2) A group of wild animals. (3) A racing term; to alter the course of the horse so as to prevent another from improving his position. (4) To keep together, to assemble or move animals together; to lead, gather, and drive as if in a herd.

herd bound *see* BARN SOUR

herder One who herds (q.v.) domestic animals.

herd help A cutting term; riders who assist the cutter (q.v.) by holding the herd together and preventing a separated cow from returning to the band; in competition, consists of two volunteer herd holders (q.v.) and two turnback riders (q.v.).

herd holder A cutting term; one of two riders positioned close to the fence, one on either side of a contained herd of cattle, whose responsibility it is to help contain the herd when the cutter (q.v.) is driving cattle or working a cow.

herd-side leg A cutting term; the rider's leg parallel to the herd (q.v.).

herdsman A manager, breeder, or tender of livestock.

hereditary defect Any undesirable physical condition, disability or characteristic passed from parents to the progeny (q.v.).

hereditary multiple exostoses A hereditary condition resulting in the growth of numerous bony protrusions from the normal contour of affected long bones as well as the ribs and pelvis; in some cases may severely restrict movement while in other horses severe lameness rarely results.

hereditary trait Any characteristic, feature, or ability passed from the genetic make-up of either or both parents to the offspring.

heredity Also known as inheritance; the transmission of characteristics of parents to offspring through chromosomes which bear their genes.

heritability The extent to which a characteristic, feature, or ability is generally passed from the genetic make-up of either or both parents to the offspring.

Hermosillo bit A hand-made Mexican curb (q.v.) having loose curved cheekpieces (q.v.) and a port provided with a cricket (q.v.); usually inlaid with a distinctive silver design on the shanks or cheekpieces (q.v.).

hernia Also known as rupture; the protrusion of any internal tissue through the wall of its containing cavity; most occur in the abdominal cavity and may be any one of several types: umbilical hernia (q.v.), inguinal hernia (q.v.), direct or indirect (scrotal) hernia (q.v.), and ventral hernia (q.v.); are classified as either: (a) reducible, characterized by a noninflammatory, painless, soft, elastic, compressible swelling that may vary from time to time where the protruding organ can be pushed back into the correct body cavity, (b) irreducible where the protruding organ has become attached to other body parts and because it is enlarged cannot be pushed back into the cavity, or (c) strangulated where the blood supply to the protruding section of the organ has been cut off requiring immediate surgical removal before infection or gangrene results.

herniae The plural of hernia (q.v.).

herpesvirus *see* EQUINE HERPESVIRUS

herring-gutted Also known as single-gutted; said of a horse whose body is flat sided, running upward sharply from the girth, and lacking depth of the flank.

heterozygote A horse who does not breed true to type because either the dam or sire contributes at least one pair of genes with different characteristics.

Heythrop Hounds Also known as The Heythrop; a pack of foxhounds (q.v.) (although originally harriers) used to hunt the Heythrop County located in the Cotswolds, Great Britain; the Master and hunt servants of this pack still wear green livery because they were servants of the Duke of Beaufort whose livery colors were green.

hh An acronym for hands high (q.v.).

Hh An acronym for hands high (q.v.).

hickory *see* SPIDER WHEEL

Hickstead One of the greatest show jumping centers in the world; located in Sussex, England, since 1960 it has been home to the Hickstead Derby meeting and has subsequently hosted four major meetings each year and also lesser meetings and some dressage competitions; built on the grounds of Hickstead Place (q.v.).

Hickstead Place The home of Douglas Bunn who, in 1960, started the All England Jumping Course there to provide a continental-style jumping facility with permanent obstacles for British horses and riders; since 1961, the site of many internationally recognized horse shows.

hidden ride A riding technique in which the rider slips from the horse's back to his side and rides along in a prone position, supporting his weight by the mane, reins, and/or a neck grip; developed by the Roman cavalry to reduce the size of the target to the enemy.

hidebound (1) Said of a horse, cow, etc. whose skin is tight over the body, having lost the fatty tissue normally underlying the skin, due to dehydration (q.v.), parasites, or disease. (2) One whose mind is firmly fixed, inelastic, cramped, and of set opinion.

high airs *see* AIRS ABOVE THE GROUND

high-blowing Also known as cracking the nostrils; a distinct sound sometimes made by a galloping horse caused by excessive flapping of the false nostril (q.v.); disappears as speed is increased and is not an unsoundness.

high bow One of three classifications of bowed tendon (q.v.) identified on the basis of location, the other two being middle bow (q.v.) and low bow (q.v.); any true physiological damage to the tendon or tendon sheath, most commonly of the superficial flexor tendon of the foreleg; specifically, tearing or breaking of one or more of the tendinous fibers of the tendon just below the knee; may be precipitated by fatigue, deep going (q.v.), uneven terrain, improper shoeing, obesity, excessively tight-fitting running bandages or boots, work on slippery surfaces, long, weak pasterns, sudden changes in stress loads, low heel angles, or long toes; symptoms may include diffuse swelling over the tendon area, heat, and pain; lameness may or may not be present.

Highflier Phaeton *see* HIGH FLYER PHAETON

High Flyer *see* HIGH FLYER PHAETON

High Flyer Phaeton Also known as High Flyer or Crane-neck Phaeton and spelled Highflier Phaeton; a four-wheeled, horse-drawn driving Phaeton (q.v.) popular in the late 18th century; had extremely large wheels, those in the front being more than 5 feet (1.5 m) in diameter, while the rear wheels may have exceeded 6 feet (1.8 m), a leather hood, and a long rear platform for two servants; the curricle-shaped body was hung from whip springs behind and elbow springs in front; drawn either by a single horse or pair, although a few might be driven four-in-hand or to a team of six – in the latter case, the near-side leader was postillion (q.v.) ridden.

high ground *see* UPPER GROUND

high hook A polo term; a defensive move; to intercept the swing of an opponent's mallet above the level of the horse's withers using one's own mallet.

Highlander Any Thoroughbred (q.v.) horse

descended from the Godolphin Barb (q.v.); imported to the United States in the 1820s where they contributed to the early development of the American Saddlebred (q.v.).

Highland *see* HIGHLAND PONY

Highland Pony Also known as Highland and generically as a native pony (q.v.); an ancient pony breed originating in the Scottish Highlands and the Scottish islands following the Ice Age; its ancestry is similar to the Fell (q.v.) and Dale (q.v.); Percheron (q.v.) blood was introduced in the 16th century, followed by Spanish and Arab (q.v.) blood in the 17th; of two varieties: (1) the Western Isles Highland Pony (q.v.) standing 12.2 to 13.2 hands and (2) the Mainland Pony (q.v.) also known as a Garron that stands up to a height of 14.2 hands; has primitive markings (q.v.) including an eel stripe (q.v.) and zebra marks (q.v.) on the legs; the coat may be gray, palomino, mouse, dun, bay, brown, black, or liver chestnut with a silver mane and tail; has a well-proportioned head, a long, muscular neck, full mane and tail, well-muscled legs with feathering on the lower parts; used for riding, packing, light draft, and farm work; is free from heredity disease, long-lived, docile, affectionate, and hardy.

Highland Pony Society A British organization founded in 1923 to promote the general interests of the breeders and owners of Highland Ponies (q.v.); registers ponies in the National Pony Stud Book.

high leader The nearside leader of a 20-mule team; driven by voice commands in conjunction with a single jerk line (q.v.) which runs through the harness rings on all near-side mules to the leader.

high line *see* TIE LINE

high lows *see* PADDOCK BOOTS

high port *see* FULL PORT

high ringbone Formation of new bone in the joint linking the long and short pastern bones.

high roller Said of a horse who leaps high into the air when bucking (q.v.).

High School *see* HAUTE ÉCOLE

High School horse Also known as school horse (q.v.); any horse trained in the haute école (q.v.) or classical airs (q.v.).

high school movement Any advanced action, gait, and or figure performed or executed by a horse trained in dressage (q.v.); includes the piaffe (q.v.), passage (q.v.), pesade (q.v.), levade (q.v.), pirouette (q.v.), courbette (q.v.), croupade (q.v.), ballotade (q.v.), and capriole (q.v.).

high weight Also known as top weight; a racing term; the top weight carried by a horse in a race.

hill topper A hunting term; mounted riders who follow hounds (q.v.) at a distance behind the rest of the field (q.v.), mostly on lanes and roads, through gates, and without jumping; generally beginners or those on green horses (q.v.).

hind A hunting term; a female red deer.

hind boot Also known as rumble; a coaching term; a straw-lined basket located over the rear axle in which passengers traveled; in the early 19th century, replaced by a wooden box to which a lid and seat were eventually added.

hind cinch *see* FLANK CINCH

hind foot Either of the horse's back feet.

hind footboard A coaching term; a leather-covered, narrow platform, attached to the rear of a town carriage, on which the servant stood.

hind hunting A hunting term; to hunt female red deer from horseback; generally begins in early November, continuing until mid-March.

hind leg Also known as hind limb or rear leg; the hind limb, specifically the portion of the horse's leg (q.v.) between the hock (q.v.) and coronary band (q.v.).

hind limb *see* HIND LEG

hindquarters Also known as quarters or buttocks; the rear or hind end of a horse including the croup (q.v.) to a point a few inches below the root of the tail, rump (q.v.), haunches (q.v.), gaskin (q.v.), and rear legs.

hindquarters-in *see* TRAVERS

hindquarters-out *see* RENVERS

hind standard A coaching term; ornate framing located on either side of the hind footboard (q.v.) of some horse-drawn town chariots and coaches (q.v.); made of a combination of carved wooden pillars and ornamental iron; used for decoration to balance the profile of the carriage, and to serve as mounting handles for the servants climbing onto the footboard.

hind sticker A racing term; a horseshoe (q.v.) having a cleat on the outside rather than the inside edge.

hinge joint The point of junction between two moveable bones where the joint (q.v.) may be extended, as in the knee joint.

hinny Also known as bardot or jennet; the hybrid progeny of a horse or pony stallion and a donkey mare; male and female progeny look more like a horse with the body of an ass, having a light head, short ears, and a full tail (the head and tail of a hybrid inherit the characteristics of the sire); often difficult to differentiate from a mule (q.v.); bred more rarely than mules because the dam throws offspring that mature smaller and because asses do not conceive as readily to stallions as they do to jacks (q.v.); males are generally castrated.

hip *see* HAUNCH

hip bone *see* ILIUM

hip brand Any identifying mark, symbol, number, or combination thereof, applied to the hip of a horse using a flame-heated, red-hot iron in hot branding (q.v.), cryogenics when freeze branding (q.v.), or acid.

hip down Said of a horse having a healed fracture (q.v.) of the point of the hip (q.v.); the healed point of the hip may appear lower than customary.

hip joint *see* ACETABULUM

hip number An identification number sprayed onto the hip of horses presented at Thoroughbred (q.v.) sales.

hipogryph *see* HIPPOGRIFF

Hipparchikos Also spelled Hopparchikos; a treatise on Xenophon's (q.v.) duties as a cavalry commander and the training of cavalry mounts; the earliest known written work on the subject of cavalry training written in 365 BC.

Hipparion An early Pliocene mammal with three toes; in the theory of evolution it is believed to be one of the earliest ancestors of the horse.

Hippike The treatise on horsemanship written by Xenophon (q.v.) in 365 BC in which he describes the fundamental principles of horse training still recognized today; a different work than *Hipparchikos* (q.v.).

Hippocrene Also known as horsewell; the mythical fountain or stream that sprung from Mount Helicon following a swift blow of Pegasus' (q.v.) hoof.

hippologist One specializing in hippology (q.v.).

hippology The study of the horse.

hippodrome (1) In ancient Greece and Rome, a course for horse and chariot races. (2) Any arena (q.v.) or structure in which equestrian or other events were conducted.

Hippodrome de Vincennes The leading French trotting raceway; a 1½ mile (4.2 km) track recognized as the supreme test for both harness and saddle trotters; begins downhill, then levels out until the last 1,000 yards (900 m), which have a severe uphill gradient.

hippogriff Also spelled hipogryph; a mythological animal having the body and hind parts of horse and the wings, claws, and head of a griffin.

hipposandal Thought to be the oldest horseshoe (q.v.), consisted of a metal sole tied to the horse's hoof with leather straps; developed by the Romans sometime between the 1st and 4th centuries AD.

hip strap *see* BEARING STRAP

hireling A hunting term; a horse rented for a day or season of hunting (q.v.).

hirsutism Abnormal hair growth.

Hispano Also known as Spanish Anglo-Arab, Spanish Arab, or Hispano Arabian; a Spanish horse breed descended from Arab Spanish mares put to English Thoroughbred (q.v.) stallions; is quiet, but energetic, agile, intelligent, and has great courage and spirit; has more pronounced Arab characteristics than Anglo-Arab (q.v.), stands 14.3 to 16 hands, and usually has a bay, chestnut, or gray coat; is versatile, being well suited to many types of equestrian events including jumping, dressage, and to test the fighting spirit and stamina of young bulls bred for bull-fighting.

Hispano Arabian *see* HISPANO

histamine A substance produced by the body in response to an allergy or infection which causes pruritis (q.v.), urticaria (q.v.), and bronchoconstriction (q.v.); neutralized by antihistamines (q.v.).

hitch (1) To tie a horse to an object, e.g. "Hitch the horses to a rail." (2) Also known as couple, hitch up, put to, hook up, hitch to, or harness; to harness or yoke and secure one or more horses to a coach or carriage as for pulling. (3) The connection between the horse(s) and the horse-drawn vehicle. (4) The connection between the horse trailer and the vehicle pulling it. (5) A gait defect noted in the hind legs; the horse appears to skip at the trot; results from uneven stride length between the hind legs. (6) A generic term; the horses used to pull a horse-drawn vehicle, e.g. "The draw chain is used in multiple draft hitches."

hitch and hop Slang; said of the action of a Hackney (q.v.) when he momentarily breaks his trotting stride to a half-canter, hesitates as he puts in a short stride, and continues with an elevated cadence and pace.

Hitchcock gag A fast-action gag bit (q.v.); consists of a single- or double-jointed loose-ring mouthpiece with a smaller, second ring attached at right angles to the bit cheekpiece; a rounded leather or cord gag rein runs from the rider's hands, through holes in the secondary ring, up to and through a pulley attached to the bridle cheekpiece, and back down to the bit.

hitching (1) Said of a horse afflicted with a hind-leg gait defect resulting from uneven hind-leg stride length; the horse appears to skip at the trot. (2) *see* HITCH NO. 3. (3) *see* HITCH NO. 4

hitching bar *see* HITCHING RACK

hitching post Also known as horse post; a fixed and sometimes elaborate vertical standard to which a horse or team (q.v.) can be tied to prevent straying.

hitching rack Also known as hitching rail or hitching bar; a fixed horizontal rail supported by two or more vertical posts to which a horse or team can be tied to prevent straying.

hitching rail *see* HITCHING RACK

hitch up *see* HITCH NO. 2

hitch to *see* HITCH NO. 2

hit off the line A hunting term; said of the hounds (q.v.) when they return to the line of a fox (q.v.), particularly after having lost the scent.

hit the hay To go to bed; to sleep.

hit the line A hunting term; said of the hounds when they pick up the scent of the quarry and begin to give tongue (q.v.).

Hittie Handbook for the Treatment of the Horse The earliest known treatise on the care and use of the horse for battle and chariot racing; inscribed on six clay tablets around 1360 BC.

hives Also known as urticaria; a skin ailment characterized by multiple, small, round, elevated eruptions which are flat topped, and approximately 0.5 mm in diameter; may be produced by toxic irritating products of plants (i.e. nettle rash [q.v.]), insect stings or bites, the inhalation or ingestion of allergens, food sensitivity (i.e. protein bumps [q.v.] or sweet feed bumps [q.v.]), change of diet, bedding, intestinal parasites, or an allergic reaction to foreign proteins including serums, vaccines, antibiotics (particularly penicillin), and bacterins; welts may appear within a few minutes or hours following exposure; can develop anywhere on the body, but occur mainly on the neck, back, flanks, eyelids, and legs; in advanced cases, may occur on the mucous membranes of the mouth, nose, conjunctiva, rectum, and vagina.

hobble (1) To bind a horse's forelegs together to restrain movement as with hobbles (q.v.). (2) One half of a set of hobbles (q.v.).

hobbles Leather, rope, chain, or other material straps which encircle the horse's pasterns (q.v.) or fetlock joints (q.v.) of the forelegs to restrict but not prevent movement; are connected by a short strap or chain which ties the forelegs together; designed to allow the horse sufficient leg movement to graze, but not flee.

hobble strap Any strap component of hobbles (q.v.).

hobby (1) A generic term used since the 12th century; any strong, active, rather small riding horse standing less than 14 hands; a slightly different breed than the Irish Hobby (q.v.). (2) *see* HOBBY HORSE NO. 3

hobby horse (1) A figure of a horse fastened about a performer's waist in a morris-dance or pantomime. (2) A dancer wearing a hobby horse (q.v.). (3) Also known as stick horse or hobby; a long stick having an wooden or fabric horse's head at one end which a child straddles in mimicry of sitting on a horse, but which is propelled by the child walking or running. (4) *see* ROCKING HORSE

Hobday *see* LARYNGEAL VENTRICULOTOMY

Hobday'd Also spelled Hobdayed (Brit); said of a horse on whom a laryngeal ventriculotomy (q.v.) has been performed to correct roaring (q.v.).

Hobdayed *see* HOBDAY'D

Hobday, Sir Frederick (1870–1939) A distinguished veterinary surgeon who practiced in London, England during the late 19th and early 20th centuries; wrote several surgical books and developed the surgical procedure for relief of roaring (q.v.) known as laryngeal ventriculotomy (q.v.).

hock (1) Also known as tarsus; the large joint (q.v.) or region of the horse's hind limb which connects the tibia and fibula to the cannon bone; when raised from the ground, appears as if bent backward. (2) *see* HAMSTRING

hock boot A protective covering of the hock (q.v.) used to provide support; may be constructed of leather or synthetic materials; closed behind the hock, open and strapped in the front.

hockey on horseback *see* POLO

hock flexion test *see* SPAVIN TEST

hock spavin Chronic, progressive, irreversible arthritis of the hock as due to bone spavin (q.v.).

hocks well let down Said of a horse's hocks (q.v.) when relatively low to the ground; a preferred conformation characteristic, indicating short cannon bones.

hoddlers *see* FLY TERRETS

hog To remove the entire mane with clippers.

hog back (1) *see* ROACH BACK. (2) Also known as hog's back; any show or cross-country, single-element jumping obstacle consisting of three rails; the first and last rails are set at the same height with the middle rail positioned higher than the other two.

hog-backed *see* ROACH BACKED

hogged back *see* ROACH BACK

hog mouth *see* UNDER SHOT JAW

hogged mane Said of the horse's mane when completely removed by shaving or cutting.

hog's back *see* HOG BACK

hog tie To bind or tie a minimum of three legs of a horse or other animal together to prevent him from standing or moving.

hog tied Said of a horse or other quadruped whose legs (a minimum of three) are bound to prevent standing or moving.

hoick *see* YOIKS

hoick holloa A hunting cheer voiced to draw the attention of the huntsman or hounds to a fox.

hoicks *see* YOIKS

hold (1) *see* HOLD HOUNDS ROUND. (2) A hunting term; a covert (q.v.) in which a fox rests. (3) A cutting term, to contain a herd of cattle in preparation for working.

holder A frequently tasseled or ornamented braid or webbing strap attached by staples to the back of a horse-drawn carriage onto which servants riding on the footboard (q.v.) would hold.

hold hard A hunting term; a warning of the huntsman (q.v.) to the field (q.v.) to stop or take care not to override the hounds (q.v.).

hold hounds round Also known as hold; a hunting term; said of the huntsman when he makes a cast (q.v.)

holding A racing term; said of a soft or heavy track.

holding scent A hunting term; said of the fox's scent (q.v.) when good enough to enable the hounds (q.v.) to follow his line.

holding up Also known as hold up; a hunting term; to turn a young fox back into his covert (q.v.) when he attempts to run into the open.

hold up *see* HOLDING UP

hold your horses To take it easy, be patient, control one's temper, or slow down; an admonition tracing back to the American country fairs of the 19th century where racing was a favorite pastime; harness races were especially difficult to initiate because the horses, sensing the eagerness of the drivers, were constantly breaking from the line and had to be called back; the restraint of the horses was figuratively transferred to refer to human restiveness and the restraint thereof.

holloa A hunting term; a cry of the hunter, commonly the whipper-in (q.v.), to indicate that he has sighted a fox.

hollow back (1) Also known as sagging back or fallen back; a dressage term; a fault in which the horse drops his back resulting in a concave top line (q.v.) as opposed to a convex one; may result when the horse fails to move from behind and/or evades bit action by raising his head. (2) *see* SWAY BACK

hollow backed *see* SWAY BACKED

hollow wall *see* SEEDY TOE

holly Trees or shrubs of the genus *Ilex,* a wood from which some whip (q.v.) shafts are made.

Holstein Also known as Hosteiner or Holsteiner; a German-bred warmblood developed in the early 14th century as a war horse; infusions of Oriental, Spanish, and Neapolitan blood made the horse lighter, while Thoroughbred (q.v.) and Cleveland Bay (q.v.) blood refined the conformation and improved the gallop, and Yorkshire Coach Horse blood gave the breed its high, wide action and excellent temperament; in the 19th century used exclusively as a harness horse; since 1945, Thoroughbred blood has been used to produce a lighter competition horse with greater speed and scope; stands 16 to 17 hands and generally has a bay, brown, black, chestnut, or gray coat; historically used under harness, yet now used for dressage, show jumping, and eventing; heavier built than the Hanoverian (q.v.).

Holsteiner *see* HOLSTEIN

Holyhead Mail, The A 19th-century British mail coach which regularly completed its 260-mile (418 km) route in less than 20 hours, stopping 27 times to change horses.

homebred (1) A racing term; a horse foaled in the state where he races. (2) Said of a horse bred by his owner.

home ground *see* UPPER GROUND

homeopathic aggravation *see* HOMEOPATHIC HEALING EVENT

homeopathic healing event Also known as homeopatic aggravation; a condition resulting in the first few weeks of homeopathic (q.v.) treatment, in which patients experience an intensification of their physical symptoms or emotional status or a return of previous symptoms; an indication that the body is responding to the homeopathic remedy (q.v.) and is working to eliminate the disease process that is at the root of all the symptoms.

homeopathic preparation *see* HOMEOPATHIC REMEDY

homeopathic remedy Also known as homeopathic remedy or homeopathic preparation; a medicament prepared from various plant, mineral, and animal sources using a process of serial dilution; more than 2,000 such formulations exist; frequently described by the use of the old Latin name of the drug, substance, or composition employed, followed by a designation of the dilution: X or D for decimal dilution, c or cH for centesimal dilution, and O for mother tinctures (q.v.).

homeopathic treatment To treat a horse using homeopathy (q.v.).

homeopathy Also spelled homoeopathy (Brit); a highly systematic, scientific method of therapy based on the principle of stimulating the organism's own healing process to accomplish cure; the horse is evaluated as a whole being, mental, emotional, and physical, and the prescribed remedy (q.v.) is based on the unique patterns found on all three levels; this means the horse is given the remedy that will stimulate the particular organism to heal itself at that particular moment recognizing that each organism possesses its own mechanisms for healing including chemical and physiological processes and many more subtle ones that are yet to be understood; the dynamic healing energy in the organism which is known as the vital force (q.v.) is stimulated by the homeopathic remedy; the system was devised and verified by Samuel Hahnemann, a German physician, nearly 200 years ago; offers a safe, effective and natural way of healing by activating the body's own natural defenses and releasing the inner power of self-healing.

home straight *see* HOMESTRETCH

homestretch Also known as home straight or stretch; a racing term; the straight part of the racetrack (q.v.) between the final turn and the finish.

homoeopathy *see* HOMEOPATHY

homozygote A plant or animal which breeds true to type and will never throw (q.v.) individuals of another type, having inherited a pair of genes identical with respect to characteristic.

honda A Western term; a small eye or loop in the end of the lariat (q.v.) through which the balance of the rope is passed to form a larger loop.

honest Said of a kind and reliable horse.

honest hound A hunting term; said of a dependable and trustworthy hound (q.v.).

honey bay *see* SANDY BAY

honey roan Refers to coat color; a roan (q.v.) pattern on a light sorrel alazán (q.v.) or blond sorrel.

honor (1) A cutting term; a cow who acknowledges and looks at the horse and rider. (2) A hunting term; said of the pack (q.v.) when it runs to an individual hound who has located the line of a fox (q.v.) and has given tongue (q.v.).

honor a line A hunting term; said of a hound when it gives tongue (q.v.) on a scent.

honorary huntsman A hunting term; the Master or an amateur when hunting.

honorary whipper-in Also known as an amateur whipper-in; a whipper-in (q.v.) who, unlike a professional whipper-in (q.v.), does not receive payment for services.

hood (1) Also known as head cap or head lap; a fabric covering for the head, ears, and/or part of the neck when used in cold or wet weather for protection and just the head when blinkers (q.v.) are used on competition horses such as race horses. (2) *see* CARRIAGE HOOD

Hooded Gig *see* BUGGY NO. 1

hooded port A bit port (q.v.) covered with copper.

hooey A calf roping term; the half-hitch put into the piggin string (q.v.) by the cowboy when tying off the feet of the calf; completes the tie (q.v.).

hoof (1) Also known as horse hoof or foot; the horny covering of the distal end of the horse's leg including the third phalanx, navicular bone, tendons, ligaments, digital cushion, sensitive laminae (q.v.), and pedal joint; absorbs and reduces shock to the leg resulting from foot impact with the ground averages 40 to 45 percent moisture. (2) The entire foot of the horse. (3) *see* HOOF IT

hoof alignment The balance of the hoof from front to back.

hoof angle Also known as toe angle; the degree of slope at which the dorsal line of the hoof intersects with the plane of its ground-side surface.

hoofbeat The sound of a hoof (q.v.) striking the ground or other hard surface.

hoofbound Said of a horse having a dry and contracted hoof that results in pain and lameness.

hoof dressing Any substance or compound, cream, oil, gel, liquid, or paste, applied to the hoof, wall and sole, to address, i.e., maintain, hoof hydration (q.v.).

hoofer (1) One who travels on foot. (2) A professional dancer.

hoof gauge A farrier's tool used to determine hoof angle (q.v.).

hoof head The area where the hoof joins the leg at the coronary region.

hoof horn The horny, tough, insensitive parts of the hoof, such as the hoof wall.

hoof hydration The moisture content of external hoof structures; directly related to the hoof's mechanical properties; if the wall suffers from either dehydration or over-hydration it becomes susceptible to developing cracks and splits.

hoof it Also known as hoof; to walk, e.g. "Having lost his horse, the cowboy had to hoof it down the road."

hoof knife A wood-handled, 2½ to 3 inch (6–7.5 cm) long knife with a slightly curved, wide blade and upturned end used to pare away the dead sole from the hoof, remove ragged parts from the frog, to relieve pressure on corns and cracks, and remove foreign bodies from the foot; available in right- and left-handed styles.

hoofless Lacking hooves (q.v.).

hoof-like Resembling a hoof (q.v.), especially having a horny texture as a hoof.

hoof nippers A pritchel-type farrier's tool having long handles and a wide cutting tip; used to remove the surplus growth of the hoof wall; available in a variety of sizes.

hoof oil Any of a variety of lubricants applied to the hoof to moisturize and maintain pliability.

hoof pick A hooked metal or plastic hand-held tool used to remove dirt, stones, and other debris from the ground-side surface of the horse's hoof.

hoof print An impression or hollow made by a hoof (q.v.).

hoof rasp Also known as rasp; a long-handled, coarse file having separate, point-like teeth used to level the bearing surface of the hoof after trimming.

hoof rings Also known as growth rings, founder rings, laminitic rings, or fever rings; any horizontal distortion of the exterior hoof wall, which is visible the entire circumference of the hoof; reflects the dynamic ability of the hoof to adapt to internal or external forces; may be caused by any local injury, abrupt change in the quantity, quality, and/or type of nutrition, other metabolic insults such as a change in environment or season, or body-wide illness that compromises circulation to part or all of the foot; generally appear on all four feet.

hoof sealant Also known as sealant; any number of artificial varnishes applied to the exterior hoof wall which limit moisture loss from the hoof surface.

hoof tester A long, thin-handled instrument with a large, pincher-type tip, used to apply leveraged pressure to the walls and sole of the hoof to detect bruises or punctures, or to diagnose foot bone diseases or injuries.

hoof wall Also known as horn, wall, wall of the hoof, crust of the hoof, or crust of the wall; the horny portion of the hoof visible when the horse is standing with his feet flat on the ground; consists of the toe, quarters (q.v.), and the heel.

hook (1) A small curve appearing on the exterior surface of the upper corner incisor teeth of the seven-year-old horse; generally disappears when the horse is 9, return when he is 11, and is often present until the horse is 17 or 18; an unreliable means of estimating the age of a horse, but may be used to strengthen an estimate; is generally removed by floating. (2) Also known as hooking; a polo term; a defensive move performed to spoil an opponent's shot on the ball; the defensive player places his mallet in front of his opponent's before it contacts the ball; of two types: cross hook (q.v.) and high hook (q.v.). (3) A cutting term; said of a cutting horse who seizes the attention of the cow being worked.

hooked A cutting horse term; a horse whose total attention is focused on the cow he is working.

hook fastening *see* STUD FASTENING

hooking *see* HOOK NO. 2

hook up *see* HITCH NO. 2

hoola hoop Coaching slang; metal hoops fixed to the outer sides of the vehicle wheels to increase vehicle width to attain standard vehicle measurements for competition purposes.

hoop tire Also spelled hoop tyre; the tire of an iron-shod, horse-drawn vehicle wheel; specifically, the hoop of hot iron placed onto the wooden wheel; as the tire cooled, it shrank and held the felloes (q.v.) and spokes together.

hoop tyre *see* HOOP TIRE

Hoor Progeny (q.v.) of two Persian Arabs (q.v.).

hooved Having hooves.

Hooved Animal Humane Society Also known by the acronym HAHS; an organization founded in 1971 in the United States to investigate animal cruelty and neglect, perform animal rescue, and to promote education and legislation benefiting the humane treatment of hooved animals.

hooves The plural of hoof (q.v.).

hop A racing term; to illegally drug a horse.

Hopparchikos *see* HIPPARCHIKOS

hopped A racing term; said of an illegally drugged horse.

hopping bobs A 19th-century American children's game played in the winter; children would wait for a horse-drawn bob sled to approach; as it passed, the children would hop onto the rear sled runner and ride it until dislodged or discovered by the driver.

hopples Originally known as Indiana pants; leather straps used to restrain and/or retrain the movement of the legs on trotting and pacing horses so that they maintain their desired gaits, e.g. to keep pacers from trotting and trotters from pacing; consist of a pair of leather straps with semicircular loops hung on hopple hangers from a crupper (q.v.) and neck straps; the straps are placed on the gaskin and forearm, connecting the fore and hind legs of the same side in pacers, and the diagonal fore and hind legs in trotters; developed in 1885 by railroad conductor John Browning.

hormone A secretion of the endocrine gland distributed through the bloodstream or in bodily fluids; affects the action of tissues, glands, and organs other than the endocrine gland, e.g. growth, digestion, and reproduction; synthetic or man-made hormones are often used to overcome deficiencies.

hormone assay A blood test performed to assess hormone levels in the blood.

horn (1) *see* HUNT HORN. (2) *see* HOOF WALL. (3) *see* COACH HORN. (4) *see* SADDLE HORN. (5) *see* BEAK. (6) *see* HORN NECK

horn basket Also known as horn case; a leather case or basket in which the guard's horn was stored; historically strapped to the right rear of a horse-drawn coach where it was in reach of the head groom.

horn case *see* HORN BASKET

horn fly A blood-sucking fly (q.v.) most common in Europe, North Africa, Asia Minor, and the Americas in the waning days of summer and early fall; feeds almost exclusively on the head, neck, and belly of horses and cattle; a swarming daytime feeder similar in appearance to a stable fly (q.v.), although more slender and about half the size; they burrow into the skin, where they may take as many as 24 blood meals per day.

horn neck Also known as horn; the vertical shaft upon which the saddle horn of a Western saddle sits on one end and which inserts perpendicular to the pommel (q.v.) on the other.

horns of the hames Also known as hames horns; the upper part of the hames (q.v.) over which the hame rein is secured.

horny laminae *see* INSENSITIVE LAMINAE

horny sole The layer of hard horn (q.v.) approximately ⅜ inch (9.5 mm) thick secreted by the sensitive sole; composed of variable-length horn tubules, is concave on the ground surface, and attaches to the frog towards the rear of the hoof; protects the sensitive inner part of the foot from impact and assists in providing support.

horse (1) Also known as prad (q.v.), hoss (sl), jaraman (Aust), or *Equus caballus*; a large, solid-hooved, herbivorous, grazing mammal, domesticated by man since prehistoric times and used as a beast of draft and burden and for carrying a rider; distinguished from the other existing members of the genus *Equus* and family *Equidae* by the long hair of the mane and tail, the usual presence of a callosity on the inside of the hind leg below the hock, and other less constant characteristics; evolved more than one million years ago. (2) To ride horseback. (3) To give a person a horse to ride. (4) To control by brute force. (5) Said of a mare; to be in season (q.v.). (6) Large or coarse of kind. (7) Hauled or powered by a horse, e.g., horse barge. (8) A male horse; a stallion (q.v.). (9) A racing term; a stallion four years or older.

horse age Also known as age of a horse; the amount of time a horse has lived; may be determined by registration papers, breeder's certificate, tooth eruption and wear patterns, or the feel of the ribs, jaw and tail; for registration purposes, computed from the first of January, regardless of the actual date on which the horse was foaled; one horse year is said to be equivalent to 5 to 7 human years.

horse-and-buggy (1) Of or relating to the era before the advent of the automobile and other socially revolutionizing major inventions. (2) Clinging to outworn attitudes or ideas, e.g. "The horse-and-buggy city planners."

Horse and Hound A weekly periodical first published in 1884; includes stories and information on racing, hunting, and showing.

horse apples Horse droppings or manure (q.v.).

horseback (1) To ride astride a horse. (2) Given thorough consideration as in "a horseback opinion."

horsebacker A person on horseback (q.v.).

horse bee *see* HORSE BOT

horse blanket Also known as blanket, clothes, horse clothes, or rug; a covering worn by the horse to provide warmth, refuge from biting insects, protection from the weather, and to keep the coat clean; available in a variety of designs, weights and materials as dictated by the use for which it is intended; generally wool or synthetic lined; held in place by a roller or strapping including a rug fillet (q.v.).

horse block *see* MOUNTING BLOCK

horse boat A boat for conveying horses and cattle.

horse bot Also known as horse bee, bot larvae, or bot; the larval stage of the horse botfly (q.v.); occurs in the horse's stomach where it may live for months; most horses are affected.

horse botfly Also known as botfly or gadfly; any of several botflies (q.v.) chiefly attacking horses; a fly with a yellow and dark banded body which lays tiny yellow eggs on the leg, shoulder, nose, and throat hair of horses during the summer months whence they are ingested and passed into the digestive tract where they hatch into larvae and feed on the stomach lining; of three types: *Gastrophilus intestinalis* (q.v.) (the most common), *Gastrophilu nasalis* (q.v.) (throat or chin botfly, abundant, but not found in colder climates), and *Gastrophius haemorrhoidalis* (q.v.) (nose botfly, found occasionally in most countries, but is common in Russia and parts of Asia).

horse-box (1) Also known as box or in Australia as float or horse float; a truck equipped to carry and transport horses; the horse compartment is positioned over the vehicle axles rather than pulled behind the vehicle. (2) A square-shaped, well-sprung vehicle used to transport horses; usually headed, with a crosswise driver's seat located at roof level with an angled footboard; drawn by a single horse or pair; horses were loaded by means of a rear ramp which formed the tailboard; obs. (3) *see* TRAILER NO. 2

horseboy *see* HOSTLER

horse brass Historically, a protective amulet (q.v.) worn by people and attached to the harnesses of draft horses and oxen to distract and ward off evil spirits; these shiny, hammered brass, nickel plate, or other metal amulets were thought to repel the evil eye with their images of the pagan gods; it was believed that the evil eye was most powerful when the potential victim was triumphant, therefore horses were decked out with protective amulets at all festivals and important events; there are approximately 3,000 different known patterns, but all are of four basic patterns: sun circle or sunflash brass (q.v.), crescent brass (q.v.), heart brass (q.v.), and horseshoe brass (q.v.); today used solely for decoration and show; in the late 19th and early 20th centuries were often struck for special events and to denote specific trades, e.g. an anchor for dock teams.

horse breaker *see* TRAINER NO. 1

horsebrush Any of several plants of the genus *Tetradymia*, family Compositae, occurring on the rangelands in the western United States which are a major cause of bighead disease (q.v.), particularly in sheep.

horsecar (1) Also known as streetcar; an American term; a horse-drawn vehicle operated over a street tramway or light railway, frequently on a channel rail; invented in 1831. (2) A vehicle equipped to transport horses.

horse cassia An East Indian cassia plant of the genus *Cassia marginata*, having long pods containing a black, cathartic pulp used as a horse medicine.

horse cavalry Cavalry troops mounted on horseback as distinct from mechanized cavalry.

horse chestnut (1) A large Asian tree, *Aesculus hippocastanum* of the family Hippocastanaceae, the horse-chestnut family, that has palmate leaves and erect conical clusters of showy flowers; is widely cultivated as an ornamental and shade tree. (2) *see* CHESTNUTS

horse clothes *see* HORSE BLANKET

horse-coper *see* HORSE DEALER

horsecorser A dealer in horses, particularly a tricky one; (obs).

horsecourser *see* HORSECORSER

horsecouper *see* HORSE DEALER

horse dance (1) A dance performed by many North American Indians in which a rearing horse is imitated. (2) A dance executed on either a live horse or hobby horse (q.v.).

horse dealer Also known as horse trader or in Britain as a coper, horse-coper, or horsecouper; one who buys, sells, and/or trades horses and ponies for profit or commission; previously one who used shrewd or underhanded methods to influence the sale, trade, or purchase of a horse.

horse devil Also known as tumbleweed; a wild indigo, *Baptisia lanceolata*, common to the southern United States that when dried and withered is rolled around by the wind, sometimes frightening horses.

horse doctor *see* VETERINARIAN

horse drawing A competition in which the pulling power of draft horses is tested.

horse-drawn vehicle Also known as vehicle; almost any cart, sled or carriage; from the Latin *vehiculum,* meaning carriage.

horse drench (1) A liquid dose of horse medicine. (2) A device for administering medicine to a horse.

horse eyes (1) *see* CHESTNUTS. (2) More than one eye (q.v.) of the horse.

horseface Any person having a long and homely face.

horse fall A movie industry term; a fall performed on cue by a stunt horse (q.v.), i.e. in battle scenes, cavalry charges, and race horse accidents.

horsefeathers Slang; nonsense.

horseflesh (1) Also known as horse meat; the flesh of the horse especially when slaughtered for food. (2) A generic term; horses, especially those used for driving, racing, or riding.

horse float *see* HORSE-BOX NO. 2

horsefly (1) Any large, stocky, swift-flying, two-winged insect of the family Tabanidae, genus *Tabanus,* having in the female a piercing, blade-like proboscis with which the blood is sucked, inflicting painful bites which result in swelling; range in size from less than ⅓ to 1¼ inches (8.5–32 mm) long and have clear wings; as much as two drops of blood may be extracted with each bite; along with the deer fly (q.v.), considered the most important pest in North America; the life cycle can last from one to two years depending upon the species and location in which it is found; the larvae are aquatic or semi-aquatic; males of the family feed on flowers and vegetable juices; difficult to control with fly-control compounds. (2) Any of several flies that annoy the horse.

horse foot *see* HOOF

horsefoot *see* COLTSFOOT

horse gait *see* AGISTMENT

horse genetian Any number of weedy plants of the honeysuckle family, with opposite leaves, inconspicuous flowers, and leathery fruit.

horse gram A leguminious tropical plant, *Polichos biflorus*, the pod of which is used in southern India as food for horses and cattle.

Horse Guard The building opposite Whitehall, London, housing this guard and certain departments of the war office.

Horse Guards A handpicked group of cavalry riders, especially the English Household Cavalry, from which guards for the sovereign are selected.

horse hair *see* HORSEHAIR

horsehair Also spelled horse hair: (1) The hair of the horse, particularly of the mane and tail. (2) Also known as haircloth; stiff, woven fabric made of horsehair. (3) Made, covered, or stuffed with horsehair; the tail hair, twisted and baked in the oven to make it springy, is generally used for stuffing.

horse head The head of the horse.

horsehide (1) The hide of the horse. (2) Leather made from a horsehide. (3) The ball used in the game of baseball.

horse hinny A male hinny (q.v.).

horse hoe A horse-drawn surface cultivator.

horse hoof *see* HOOF

horsehoof *see* COLTSFOOT

horse identification Any of several methods used to permanently mark a horse including hot brands (q.v.), acid brands (q.v.), freeze brands (q.v.), tattoos (q.v.), and microchips (q.v.) to prove ownership.

horse identifier An American racing term; one responsible for checking the lip tattoo of each horse as he enters the paddock (q.v.) prior to a race; responsible for verifying that the horses entered in a given race are the actual ones racing.

horse in-hand *see* LUNGE

horse jockey (1) *see* JOCKEY. (2) One who deals in horses; (obs).

horsekeeper One who has charge of horses.

horse knacker *see* KNACKER

horseknop Knapweed, *Centaurea nigra*, especially the black flower head of the plant.

horse latitudes Either of two belts or regions in the area of 30 degrees N and 30 degrees S latitude characterized by barometric high pressure, calms, and light, baffling winds.

horse laugh A loud and boisterous laugh.

horseleech (1) An aquatic sucking worm, of great size and sucking capability, with which veterinary surgeons historically used to remedy common diseases of the horse; the worm was used to suck the bad blood from the horse. (2) A veterinarian (q.v.) or farrier; (obs). (3) An importunate beggar.

horseleechery Veterinary (q.v.) practice; (obs).

horseless Having no horse, especially not requiring one; self-propelled as an automobile, i.e. horseless carriage (q.v.).

horseless carriage An automobile, especially earlier models.

horse-like Resembling a horse.

horse litter *see* LITTER NO. 3

horse louse *see* LOUSE

horseman (1) A man on horseback. (2) One skilled in riding horses. (3) One who raises, manages, trains or tends to horses. (4) *see* CAVALRYMAN.

Horseman's Benevolent and Protection Association A trade association of race horse owners and trainers.

horsemanship The art of riding on horseback; equestrian skill.

Horseman's Sunday Service A religious service originating in 1949 in Britain and held annually at Tattenham Corner, Epsom Downs (q.v.) to bless all horses, ponies, and donkeys, whether ridden or driven; now held at other locations throughout the world.

horsemen More than one horseman (q.v.).

Horse Marines *see* TELL THAT TO THE HORSE MARINES

horsemastership A generic term; the care, maintenance, and use of a horse in all pleasure and commercial activities.

horse meat *see* HORSEFLESH

horsemen More than one horseman(q.v.).

horse mule Also known as john mule or jack; a male mule (q.v.); generally gelded, since stallions, although sterile, are sexually active.

horse nail *see* HORSESHOE NAIL

Horse of the Year Award A year-end competition for zone finalists in Pony Club Mounted Games (q.v.); the overall winner collects the Prince Philip Cup.

horse opera A novel, story, motion picture, or broadcast dealing with life in the western United States, especially during the latter half of the 19th century, and usually having cowboys as the principal characters.

horse parlor *see* HORSE ROOM

horse pistol A large pistol formerly carried by horsemen (q.v.).

horseplay (1) Rough or rowdy play or practical jokes. (2) To engage in horseplay.

horseplayer One who habitually bets on horse races.

horseplaying Betting on horse races.

horse pond A place where horses are watered.

horse post (1) *see* HITCHING POST. (2) A mail carrier who makes his deliveries on horseback. (3) Mail service performed by a horse post.

horsepower The power that a horse exerts in pulling; technically speaking, the rate at which work is accomplished when a resistance (weight) of 33,000 pounds is moved one foot in one minute, or 550 pounds is moved one foot in one second; a term conceived in the 18th century by Scottish engineer James Watt to explain the work rate of his new machinery, steam engines; calculated as the average rate of power of dray horses used in London breweries multiplied by 1.5, e.g. to be 10 horsepower an engine had to have the power of 15 muscular dray horses.

horsepower hour The work performed or energy consumed by working at the rate of one horsepower hour for one hour; equal to 1,980,000 foot-pounds.

horse-pox Also known as equine variola; a viral disease of horses related to cowpox and marked by a vesiculopustular eruption of the skin, especially on the pasterns, and may be confused with greasy heel (q.v.); pain may involve the lips, mouth, nostrils, or vulva; loss of appetite and salivation may occur; recovery may take two to four weeks; the horse becomes debilitated and young ones may die.

horserace *see* RACE

horse race *see* RACE

horse racer (1) One who keeps horses for racing purposes. (2) *see* JOCKEY

horse racing Also known as sport of kings; a racing term; the racing of horses for sport.

horse rake A large rake or harrow pulled by a horse.

horse riding *see* RIDING

horse room Also known as horse parlor; a bookmaker's (q.v.) establishment where information on race horses and races are provided and where bets on them are placed.

horse rough An attachment to the ground-side surface of a horseshoe used to prevent slipping on icy roads; superseded by calks (q.v.) and studs (q.v.).

horse run A contrivance used to pull a loaded car, wheelbarrow, etc., up a runway from an excavation by horsepower (q.v.).

horses Also known as cattle (slang); more than one horse (q.v.).

Horses and Ponies Protection Association A British organization founded in 1937 to protect native pony breeds at fairs, sales, and in transit and to improve conditions for and encourage more strict supervision of, slaughter horses.

horse's ass A stupid or incompetent person; considered vulgar.

horse sense Practical good sense; common sense.

horse shit (1) *see* FECES. (2) Nonsense, bunk; considered vulgar.

horseshoe (1) Also known as shoe; a metal, U-shaped plate which follows the outline of the horse's foot to which it is attached to provide protection from rough surfaces; prior to AD 70, consisted of broom slippers, while in the 1st through 4th centuries AD, consisted of a metal plate fitted to the hoof with leather strapping (Roman hipposandal [q.v.]); nailed types were first used in the 9th century and became widely known sometime after AD 400; during the Dark Ages and Medieval times, the horseshoe was crescent-shaped and resembled a snake which was thought to be divine and keep witches away. (2) 18th-century slang; the female genitals. (3) A form of quoits played by tossing horseshoes at a stake driven into the ground, the object being to encircle the stake or come as close to it as possible; in regulation play, stakes are driven 40 feet (12.19 m) apart. (4) *see* SHOE. (5) Shaped like a horseshoe. (6) A horseshoe crab.

horseshoe brass Shiny, hammered brass, nickel plate, or other metal amulet struck with a horseshoe pattern and attached to the harness and other tack to ward off the evil eye and bring good luck; the heels of the horseshoe generally pointed up, although brasses for towns or districts near the sea always had the heels pointing down to protect against the dangers of water; other patterns include sunflash brass (q.v.), crescent brass (q.v.), and heart brass (q.v.).

horseshoeing *see* SHOE

horseshoe nail Also known as horse nail or nail; a thin, pointed, soft steel nail with a heavy flaring head used to fix a horseshoe (q.v.) to the hoof; generally four-sided, with a tapered shaft, and a tip beveled on the inside; a pattern or trademark is stamped on the inside face of the head to make it possible to determine the inside from the outside of the nail.

horseshoe pad Also known as pad or shoe pad; a leather, plastic, or rubber lining cut in the shape of the ground-side surface of the hoof which is placed between the horseshoe and hoof to provide protection and padding to the sole.

horseshoer *see* FARRIER

horseshoe vetch Also known as horse vetch; a plant, genus *Hippocrepis*; so named because of the shape of the seed pods.

horse show Also known as show; a meeting at which competitions are held to test or display the qualities and capabilities of horses and their riders, drivers, or handlers; may take place on one or over multiple days; prizes are awarded depending on performance or the judge's selection.

horse sickness *see* AFRICAN HORSE SICKNESS

horse sickness fever *see* AFRICAN HORSE SICKNESS, MILD FORM

horse sponge A coarse bath sponge, *Spongia equina*, of the Mediterranean.

horse standard *see* MEASURING STICK

horse stinger An obsolete British term; a dragonfly, although these insects do not actually sting horses.

horse sugar The sweetleaf tree, *Symplocos tinctoria,* of the southwestern United States, its sweetish leaves used as a fodder for cattle and as a source of yellow dye.

horse tail (1) *see* TAIL NO. 1. (2) The horse's tail as a former Turkish ensign denoting the rank of Pasha. (3) Any of a number of related rush-like, flowerless plants of the genus, *Equisetum,* with hollow, jointed stems and scale-like leaves. (4) A fossil bivalve; a hippurite.

horse tailing To take charge of a herd of horses, as in drovers (q.v.) when herding horses over long distances.

horse tamer *see* TRAINER NO. 1

horse thistle A thistle of the genus *Cirsium.*

horse tick Any tick that feeds on a horse.

horse tick fever *see* EQUINE PIROPLASMOSIS

horse trade (1) A commercial negotiation conducted to buy and sell a horse(s). (2) Any negotiation accompanied by shrewd bargaining and reciprocal concessions.

horse trader *see* HORSE DEALER

horse trading The act; practice; or instance of making a horse trade (q.v.).

horse trailer *see* TRAILER NO. 2

horse trainer *see* TRAINER NO. 1

horse tree A leafless Australian tree of the genus *Casuarina.*

horse trials Also known as militaire (obs), military trials (obs), eventing, or combined training (US); an equestrian event which originated in the army cavalry schools of continental Europe as a military training exercise to test the stamina and versatility of the military mounts; consists of three phases: show jumping, endurance, and dressage conducted over a period of one, two, or three days by the same horse/rider team; in three- (q.v.) and two-day events (q.v.), the endurance competition is made up of Phase A, short roads and tracks, Phase B, steeplechase, Phase C, long roads and tracks, and Phase D, cross-country; the three-day event first appeared in the Olympic Games in 1912.

horse tripping Any Mexican competitive event as performed at charreadas (q.v.) in which a horse is herded, lassoed (q.v.), and toppled to the ground; include piales en el lienzo (q.v.) and the mangana (q.v.); now illegal in a number of states within the United States.

horse vetch *see* HORSESHOE VETCH

horse walker *see* HOT WALKER NO. 1

horseweed Any of a group of strong-smelling, weedy plants of the mint family, having clusters of small, yellow flowers.

horsewell *see* HIPPOCRENE

horsewhip (1) *see* WHIP NO. 1. (2) To flog with, or as if with, a whip made to be used on a horse.

horse whisperers Also known as whisperers; a school of horse trainers known for their horse training and calming technique which involved breathing into their nostrils; the most famous was John Rarey, who, in the mid-19th century, demonstrated the technique around the world.

horse whispering A method of horse training involving gentling and calming rather than force; evolved in the United States during the 19th century, the practitioners thereof being called horse whisperers (q.v.).

horse with the fine walk *see* PASO FINO

horsewoman (1) A woman on horseback. (2) A woman knowledgeable in riding and maintaining horses; a woman possessed of good horse sense.

horsewomen More than one horsewoman (q.v.).

horsewood A West Indian tree, *Calliandra comosa,* having showy, deep-red flowers.

horseworm Botfly (q.v.) larva.

horse wrangler *see* WRANGLER

horsey (1) *see* HORSY. (2) Characteristic of horsemen (q.v.) and horsewomen (q.v.). (3) Relating to or resembling a horse.

horsily In a horsey manner.

horsiness The quality or state of being horsey (q.v.).

horsing (1) Said of a mare in heat (q.v.) who demonstrates signs of estrus (q.v.). (2) To engage in horseplay (q.v.).

horsing stone *see* MOUNTING BLOCK

horsy Also spelled horsey; associated with the nature or quality of horses; engrossed with horses, as with their breeding or racing.

hoss *see* HORSE NO. 1

Hosteiner *see* HOLSTEIN

hostler Also known as horseboy and spelled ostler (Brit); a man in charge of the stabling of horses and other stock at an inn.

hot (1) Also known as hot horse; said of a horse whose body temperature has risen above normal levels due to exercise or illness. (2) A racing term; a stable or jockey on a winning streak or expected to win. (3) Said of an easily excitable horse.

hotblood Also known as fullblood; a fine-boned, high-spirited horse, generally of Arab (q.v.) or Thoroughbred (q.v.) extraction; so called because of the temperament exhibited and because the original stock came from the hot regions of the Middle East and North Africa.

hot-blooded (1) Said of a horse of Eastern or Oriental blood. (2) Said of a horse possessed of a fiery, high-strung, or excitable temperament.

hot brand (1) Also known as fire brand or hot iron brand; an identifying mark, symbol, number or any combination thereof, applied to the hide of a horse using a flame-heated, red-hot metal iron; generally found on the hip and for some breed registrations on the shoulder or neck; does not hold up in a court of law as proof of ownership as is easily altered; now used predominantly to identify breed registration; identified on the basis of location, i.e. hip brand (q.v.). (2) To apply an identifying mark, symbol, or number to the hide of a horse using a shaped, flame-heated, red hot iron; the hot iron burns the hide sufficiently to create scar tissue in the shape of the mark, symbol, or number.

hot fit Also known as hot set; to hold a hot shoe against the prepared bottom of the hoof until sufficiently scorched to identify high spots on the horn which must be removed to make the surface of the hoof level; also used to seat clips; generally performed when hot shoeing (q.v.).

hot horse *see* HOT

hot iron brand *see* HOT BRAND

hot nail A horseshoe nail when driven too close to the white line resulting in a condition known as nail bind (q.v.).

hot quit A cutting term; said of the cutter (q.v.) who lifts his hand or pulls off (q.v.) a cow in competition while the cow is still facing him and is actively trying to return to the herd; a three-point penalty; a cutter may only quit a cow when that cow is obviously turned away from his horse or when he comes to a dead stop in the arena.

hot set *see* HOT FIT

hot shaping To modify the shape of a horseshoe to fit the hoof after heating it in a forge (q.v.).

hot shod Said of a horse shod using horseshoes shaped and fitted to the hoof using a forge (q.v.).

hot shoe (1) A long-heeled machine-made horseshoe. (2) Also known as handmade horseshoe or hand-forged horseshoe; any horseshoe manually made or shaped as in a forge (q.v.). (3) To shoe a horse with horseshoes shaped and fitted to the hoof using the heat of a forge (q.v.); often accompanied by hot fitting (q.v.).

hot shoer A farrier (q.v.) who, using a forge, hot fits (q.v.) horseshoes to a horse.

hot shot An electrical charge administered to a horse by a rider to shock it into bucking more strongly, to improve scores, or encourage him to jump when he might otherwise refuse; illegal in competition.

hot up Said of a horse who becomes easily excited.

hot walk To walk a horse to cool him down following a workout.

hot walker (1) Also known as horse walker (Brit); one employed to walk horses to cool them out. (2) An electronic, variable-speed walking machine to which one or more horses are tied as for exercise or to cool down (q.v.) following exercise; consists of multiple, overhead arms branching out from a center platform or engine; only one horse is attached per arm; horses move in a circle around the center platform; direction is generally reversible.

hound (1) Any of various dog breeds trained to hunt by scent or sight, e.g. scent hounds (q.v.) or sight hounds (q.v.). (2) To pester, nag, or bother. (3) *see* DOG NO. 4. (4) *see* DOG NO. 5

hound couples A hunting term; a harness used to connect two dogs together; consists of two dog collars connected by a chain and swivel.

hound gait *see* JOG NO. 1

hound gloves A hunting term; gloves made of horse hair worn by a handler to massage hounds (q.v.).

hound hunt (1) A hunting term; a fox hunt in which the hounds pursue the fox with little scent and no sightings. (2) A hunting term; a hunt in which mounted followers do little but stand and watch because the hounds, working hard in a confined area, do not cause the fox to run in a manner in which it can be pursued on horseback.

hound jog *see* JOG NO. 1

houndpace *see* JOG NO. 1

hounds (1) More than one hound (q.v.). (2) *see* WINGS NO. 2

Hounds Please A hunting term; a verbal warning to the field (q.v.) to be aware of the hounds (q.v.) and to move the horses out of the way.

hounds will meet *see* MEET NO. 2

hound trot *see* JOG NO. 1

housefly Also known as *Musca domestica*; a two-winged, swarming, non-biting, daytime-feeding insect; a fly.

housen A large leather flap, located behind the hames (q.v.), on a heavy horse collar; holds the bearing rein down; folded back to protect the area behind it in poor weather.

housing *see* SHABRAQUE

hovel An American term; any three-sided shed located in a field or meadow used to shelter horses turned out to pasture; typically of poor quality.

hovering trot *see* PASSAGE-LIKE TROT

hub Also known as nave or wheel hub; the thick center piece of a wheel into which the spokes attach and the axle is inserted.

huaso A Chilean cowboy/cowhand (q.v.).

Hucul Also known as Carpathian Pony and spelled Huzul, Huzule, and Heecul; a pony breed native to the Carpathian region of Poland where it descended from the Tarpan (q.v.) with later infusions of Arab (q.v.) blood; ranged wild for thousands of years; has been formally bred in Great Britain and Poland since the 19th century; stands 12 to 13 hands and all coat colors occur with dun (q.v.) and bay (q.v.) most common; has a short head and a low-set tail, is very hardy, frugal, calm, sure-footed, and has good endurance; used for pack and draft.

huick *see* YOICKS

hull *see* SADDLE

hulled peanut meal A high protein, high-energy concentrate produced from the residue of peanuts hulled before oil extraction and processing; contains 40 percent more protein and energy than unhulled peanut meal (q.v.).

human chorionic gonadotropin Also known by the acronym HCG; a hormone found in the urine of women during the first 50 days of pregnancy; sometimes used to stimulate ovulation in mares.

humerus The bone of the foreleg between the shoulder joint and elbow joint; has a rounded head which, with the corresponding depression of the scapula, forms the ball-and-socket shoulder joint.

hummel *see* NOTT STAG

humor *see* HUMOUR

humour Also spelled humor; a historical British and 18th-century American term; any edematous swelling of the leg; now known as stock up (q.v.).

hung (1) Also known as hung fire (Brit), a racing term; said of a horse who does not advance his race position when encouraged to do so by the jockey. (2) A British racing term; said of a horse in a race who veered off a straight course, due to tiredness, loss of balance, unsoundness, etc.

Hungarian Arabian *see* SHAGYA ARABIAN

Hungarian Shagya *see* SHAGYA ARABIAN

hunt *see* HUNT A COW

Hunt (1) Also known as Hunt club or fox hunting club; a hunting term; an organization or group of hunters (q.v.) having complied with the standards of, and been recognized and registered by, the governing association of the area – in the United States, this being the Masters of Foxhounds Association of America; is always capitalized. (2) Also known as Hunt country; a hunting term; a geographical area delineated by a mixture of historical precedent, and in the case of dispute, arbitrated by the Master of Foxhounds Association (q.v.), hunted by a specific pack of foxhounds; is always capitalized.

hunt a cow Also known as hunt; a cutting term; said of a horse who follows the movement of a cow with his eyes.

hunt ball A hunting term; a black tie gala generally held during the hunt season or in conjunction with some formal event to raise money and involve the community in the Hunt (q.v.).

hunt boots Also known as jockeys; tall black riding boots worn by participants in a Hunt (q.v.); may have mahogany, flesh, or patent leather (q.v.) tops.

hunt button A hunting term; a brass, silver, or black button engraved with a design, monogram, or distinctive lettering representative of a particular Hunt (q.v.); staff and members of the field invited to do so by the Master of the Hunt are authorized to wear the buttons with an appropriately colored hunt collar, both in the hunting field and with hunt evening dress; award of buttons is purely subjective; a brass or silver button is worn on a pink coat (q.v.) and a black bone button with a white design is worn on the black coat.

hunt cap Also known as helmet, cap, hunting helmet, or hunting cap; a hard-shell helmet (q.v.) historically covered with black velvet and worn only by Masters (q.v.), ex-Masters, Field Masters, Hunt Secretaries, hunters, and children when on the hunt; adopted by women for hunting and riding in the 1940s; now, any black helmet worn by English riders in competition and practice in hunting, eventing, jumping, and dressage.

Hunt club *see* HUNT

hunt coat A coat (generally wool) worn by members of the Hunt (q.v.) when hunting; men wear scarlet or black coats, while gray, black, and dark blue are acceptable for women.

hunt collar A fawn- or cream-colored fabric jacket collar presented to members of the Hunt (q.v.) when awarded hunt buttons (q.v.).

hunt colors The coat color worn by Hunt staff, e.g., a green coat typically denotes harriers (q.v.) while yellow coats are worn by the Berkeley Hunt (q.v.) in Great Britain.

Hunt Committee A hunting term; the annually elected Board of Directors of a Hunt (q.v.); hold title to all Hunt property including land, buildings, hounds (q.v.), horses, tack (q.v.), staff clothes, and miscellaneous equipment; has two primary responsibilities: (1) appointment of a Master (q.v.) or Joint Masters (q.v.) for a fixed term of office and (2) collection of funds to finance the Hunt.

Hunt country *see* HUNT NO. 2

hunter (1) Any horse bred, trained, and/or appropriate to follow hounds (q.v.) in the sport of hunting (q.v.); possesses stamina and jumping ability and is generally Thoroughbred (q.v.) or Thoroughbred cross; a type not a breed. (2) *see* HUNT FOLLOWER. (3) *see* SHOW HUNTER

hunter clip To remove the horse's coat leaving the hair on the legs up to the height of the elbows and thighs and a saddle patch (q.v.) on the back unclipped; the coat is left on the legs to protect the horse against cold, mud, and cracked heels, and the saddle patch saves a sore back under the saddle.

hunter pace An American sport developed and first conducted by the Blue Ridge Hunt in Virginia, USA in March 1954; two-person teams compete over lengthy courses in pursuit of an undisclosed goal within a predetermined ideal time; courses are 4 to 10 miles (6.4–16 km) long, include a number of obstacles ranging in height from 2½ to 3½ feet (76–107 cm), and at least one, 3- to 10-minute rest stop; teams set off from the starting area at 3- to 5-minute intervals; competitors are timed out when they leave the start and in at the finish; placings are determined by how closely a team's time matches the predetermined course time; time is meant to reflect the pace of an actual hunt over the same course.

hunter's bumps Also known as sacroiliac desmitis; acute and severe strain of the sacroiliac ligaments; occurs when the tuber sacral is pushed upward and forward because of torn ligament attachments; symptoms include pain in the pelvic area, hind limb lameness, shortened stride, quarters asymmetry, and, in some cases, a reluctance to jump; seen most commonly in hunters and jumpers.

hunter seat *see* HUNT SEAT

Hunters Improvement and National Light Horse Breeding Society A British organization founded in 1885 to improve and promote the breeding of hunters (q.v.) and other horses used for riding and driving.

hunter trials A hunting term; a competitive event for horses and ponies held by most Hunts (q.v.) and associated organizing bodies; horses are ridden over a course of obstacles, preferably natural, made to look like those encountered in a natural hunt field, within a specified amount of time.

Hunter-Type Pinto One of four Pinto (q.v.) conformation types developed with specific breed goals and standards in mind; of predominantly Thoroughbred (q.v.) conformation and breeding, although a running-style Quarter Horse may also be found in this classification; may be medium to tall and display refinement, quality, substance, and balance required for under saddle and jumping classes.

hunt field *see* FIELD NO. 4

hunt flask Also known as flask; a hunting term; a small, flattened container, usually metal, used to carry liquor while hunting; may be carried on the person, in a leather holster, or in a sandwich case, either being attached by short leather straps to the saddle dees (q.v.).

hunt follower Also known as hunter; a hunting term; one who rides in a hunt (q.v.).

hunt horn Also known as horn or hunting horn; a cylindrical instrument, usually 9 to 10 inches (23–25 cm) long and made of copper with a silver, nickel or German silver mouthpiece, ferrule, and bands; carries only one note, D or A, the quality of which is affected by the length and diameter of the tube; carried by the Master, Huntsman (q.v.), or whippers-in (q.v.) and used to signal to the hounds (q.v.) and the field (q.v.).

hunting (1) Also known as running; the sport of following, chasing, or searching, whether mounted or on foot, fox, stag, hare, or drag line behind a pack of hounds; to be held separately from shooting (q.v.). (2) *see* FOX HUNTING

hunting bow A black gossamer ribbon tied in a bow which adorns the back of the hunt cap (q.v.); the tails or feathers of the bow are worn pointing upward by the Hunt Master (q.v.), while all others wear the tails pointing downward.

hunting box A hunting term; a small house occupied primarily during the hunting season.

hunting cap *see* HUNT CAP

hunting gate *see* BRIDLE GATE

hunting head Also known as fixed head, near head, near horn, near pommel, top pommel, or second pommel; the higher of the two padded pommels (q.v.) or horns on the side-saddle (q.v.); sits above the leaping head (q.v.) and supports the rider's right leg.

hunting helmet *see* HUNT CAP

hunting horn (1) *see* HUNT HORN. (2) *see* LEAPING HEAD

hunting iron Also known as plain hunting iron, standard hunting iron, swaged-side stirrup iron, English hunting iron, or graduated-side iron; the most common English-style stirrup (q.v.) having symmetrically tapered and slightly rounded sides and a perpendicular eye (q.v.) located at the top and center of the arch through which the leathers (q.v.) run; usually made of stainless steel, although may be constructed of nickel alloys or chrome-plated iron, depending on the desired function.

Hunting Phaeton *see* BEAUFORT PHAETON

hunting saddle *see* CLOSE CONTACT SADDLE

hunting season Also known as season; a hunting term; the period during which time organized hunts (q.v.) are conducted; in most countries, when both cub-hunting (q.v.) and formal seasons are considered, runs from late August through late March.

hunting stock (1) *see* STOCK TIE. (2) Hounds or horses used in the pursuit of quarry (q.v.).

hunting the circle A reining term; said of the rider in competition who follows a prior competitor's pattern, rather than creating his own; may also be said of the horse who follows a previously ridden track.

hunting the heel line *see* HEEL NO. 3

hunt livery A hunting term; the distinctive coat, collar, and buttons of a particular Hunt (q.v.) worn by the staff and/or members of that Hunt.

Hunt Master *see* MASTER

hunt race *see* POINT-TO-POINT

hunt seat Also known as hunter seat (Brit); the traditional position of the rider in the English saddle derived from cavalry methods and orientated toward riding on the flat and jumping; historically the rider sat back into the saddle with feet and legs pushed forward, the main concern being rider safety over obstacles and rough ground; the modern rider has adopted a lighter, more forward and balanced position with the upper body.

hunt seat saddle *see* CLOSE CONTACT SADDLE

Hunt Secretary A hunting term; one responsible for maintaining the notes, files and records of the Hunt (q.v.), collecting cap (q.v.) money, and maintaining relationships with owners of the land over which the hunt is conducted.

hunt servant (1) A hunting term; any salaried employee of a Hunt (q.v.), i.e., the huntsman (q.v.), kennel huntsman, or whippers-in (q.v.). (2) *see* PAD GROOM

huntsman A hunting term; one in charge of the hounds (q.v.) during the hunt (q.v.), unless the Master is hunting his hounds as an amateur huntsman in which case the responsibility is assumed by the Master or his appointee; supported by assistance from the whippers-in (q.v.); normally lives in residence at the hunt kennels (q.v.).

hunt staff A hunting term; the Master or Joint Master(s) (q.v.), huntsman (q.v.), and whipper-in (q.v.) responsible for the management of the hounds (q.v.) and conduct of the hunt; some authorities, as in Britain, do not include the Master.

Hunt subscription A hunting term; the annual fee paid by each member of a Hunt (q.v.) for the right to participate in all hunts identified on the appointment card (q.v.); varies according to the number of days normally hunted each week and the individual Hunt, and is generally paid in advance every May 1st.

hunt terrier A small, short-legged terrier such as a Jack Russell Terrier, used by a Hunt (q.v.) to spook foxes from earths, drains, or other hiding places inaccessible to the hounds (q.v.).

hunt tie *see* STOCK TIE

Hunt Treasurer A hunting term; one of the Hunt officers (q.v.) responsible for maintaining the Hunt's financial records/accounts.

hurdle Any one of a series of wattle fences over which a horse must jump in hurdle racing (q.v.); constructed of brush in the United States.

hurdle race A race conducted on horseback in such countries as England, France, New Zealand, and Australia in which participants race over a course having four to six, and sometimes more, low hurdles in the first mile, with an additional jump generally added approximately every quarter mile thereafter.

Hurlingham Polo Club The first polo club (q.v.) established in the western world: London England, in 1873.

hurry Said of a horse in any gait who takes short, rapid steps or strides which make inefficient use of his energy and represent an undesirably quick rhythm for that gait.

Huzul *see* HUCUL

Huzule *see* HUCUL

HV *see* HENDRA VIRUS

HVD *see* HENDRA VIRUS DISEASE

hyaline cartilage One of three types of cartilage (q.v.) found in fetuses, newborns, elk antlers, etc.; can ossify into bone.

hyaluronate sodium *see* ACID

hyaluronic acid The thick, lubricating fluid within a joint.

hybrid The offspring of two animals of different species or races; in the horse world, the offspring of any two species of the genus *Equus* which includes the ass, horse, zebra, and onager; all these species will mate with each other, the resulting progeny being a hybrid; is generally normal in all respects except that it may be infertile due to the different chromosome numbers of the different species; e.g. the mule (q.v.) is a hybrid of a horse and ass.

hydrochloric acid An aqueous solution of hydrogen chloride, HCI, a strong, fuming, highly corrosive acid used in industry, research, medicine, and to brand (q.v.).

hydrocortisone *see* CORTISOL

hyperimmune plasma A blood product exposed to an antigen (q.v.) to stimulate immunity above those levels required for protection; used to create harvestable antibody levels.

Hyperion An English Thoroughbred who won the Epsom Derby in 1933 and eventually became one of the greatest sires in Europe.

hyperkalemic periodic paralysis Also known by the acronym HYPP; a genetically transmitted muscular disorder characterized in some horses by muscle tremors, sweating, respiratory difficulty, weakness, and recumbency; affected horses have a defect in the channel that regulates the amount of sodium entering the muscle cell with an excess of sodium causing the muscle fibers to depolarize and the muscles to twitch involuntarily; serum blood levels are generally, but not always, elevated during attacks; the sodium channel defect is due to a genetic mutation inherited from one or both parents; began as a point mutation in a single horse which has been linked to, but not absolutely proven to have come from, the Quarter Horse halter sire Impressive (q.v.); a serious issue for Quarter Horse (q.v.), Paint (q.v.), and Appaloosa (q.v.) owners.

hyperlipemia A recently identified disease affecting plump donkeys, ponies, and particularly mares in foal, although rare in horses as a whole; characterized by an excess of fat molecules, primarily triglicerides, in the blood; obesity, stress, pregnancy, gastrointestinal problems (usually from parasitism), malnutrition, a lack of appetite, or an insensitivity to insulin interfere with the amount of carbohydrate fuel in the blood; the body responds by flooding the bloodstream with fat, which the liver and kidneys are unable to process and therefore shut down; symptoms include a loss of appetite, lethargy, and depression followed by a reluctance to move, lack of coordination, weakness, mild and intermittent colic (q.v.), diarrhea, head pressing, circling, convulsions, and death; is fatal in 65 percent of all cases within six to ten days; treatment is difficult.

hypermobility Increased motion in a motor unit (q.v.); results in stress to the ligamentous components and associated structures due to the pathologically increased range of motion; may indicate facet syndrome pain (q.v.).

hyperparathyoidism A significant increase in parathyroid hormone activity; may result in the loss of calcium from the bones.

hypersensitivity Overreaction to any substance such as shampoo, equipment cleaning solutions, plant secretions, etc. that contact the skin; characterized by tenderness, heat, weeping sores, and pitting edema; symptoms will generally subside within one to three days following removal of the irritant.

hyperthermia Also known as elevated body temperature or raised body temperature; elevated body temperature above the normal range as caused by disease, overexertion, or high environmental temperature or humidity; exhibited in heat exhaustion (q.v.) and heatstroke (q.v.).

hyperthyroidism A treatable condition caused by abnormally high secretions of the hormones triodothyronine (T_3) and thyroxin (T_4) from the thyroid gland (q.v.); characterized by increased metabolic rate, thirst, weight loss, vomiting, diarrhea, increased feces volume and appetite, enlargement of the thyroid gland, heart murmurs, and congestive heart failure; protrusion of the eyeballs may occur.

hypomobility Joint fixation or lack of motor unit (q.v.) motion causing a joint or vertebra to lose function over all joint surfaces; evidenced by decreased range of motion in the affected area evidenced as a disruption of spinal movement including lateral bending and the inability to flex at the poll; when occurring in one motor unit usually results in hypermobility (q.v.) in adjacent motor units as the body attempts to maintain a normal level of vertebral function; unresolved fixations result in local muscle atrophy from disuse or from decreased nerve supply to the muscles.

hypomagnesemia A disease caused by inadequate levels of magnesium (q.v.) in the diet or absorption thereof; symptoms include muscle incoordination and nervousness.

hypothalamus An organ in the brain responsible for the regulation of body processes through the production of hormones or by direct control of the nerve cells.

hypothermia A state of abnormally low body temperature triggered by viral infection, internal bleeding or substantial external bleeding, and/or low environmental temperatures; symptoms include chills, disorientation, pale (loss of circulation) or muddy gums (circulation static), and energy loss.

hypothyroidism A treatable hormonal condition caused by abnormally low secretions of triodothyronine (T_3) and thyroxin (T_4) from the thyroid gland (q.v.); characterized by decreased metabolic rate, weight gain, hair loss, lethargy, and development of a crested neck.

hypovolemic shock Circulatory collapse characterized by a progressively diminishing circulating blood volume relative to the capacity of the vascular system, leading to acute failure of perfusion of vital organs; caused by decreased blood volume through either blood loss or dehydration; symptoms include increased capillary refill time (q.v.), pale mucous membranes, ataxia (q.v.), low pulse pressure, irregular respiratory rate, and low body temperature.

HYPP *see* HYPERKALEMIC PERIODIC PARALYSIS

hyracotherium A lower Eocene mammal the size of a fox, having four toes; thought to be an ancestor of the horse.

I

IAAA *see* AMERICAN ALBINO HORSE ASSOCIATION, INC.

IAD *see* INFLAMMATORY AIRWAY DISEASE

IAHA *see* INTERNATIONAL ARABIAN HORSE ASSOCIATION

Iberian *see* IBERIAN HORSE

Iberian Horse (1) Also known as Iberian or by the scientific name *Equus ibericus*; an ancient horse breed that contributed to the development of the Barb (q.v.). (2) *see* ANDALUSIAN. (3) *see* LUSITANO

ice Also known as icing; to anesthetize and/or reduce swelling and inflammation in the feet or legs of a horse by standing or packing them in ice; commonly practiced on the racetrack (q.v.).

Ice Age horse Also known by the scientific name *Equus lambei*; a horse species that roamed the Eurasian tundra steppes until about 8,000 BC, at which time it became extinct; stood about 14 hands, had a coat consisting of short, blackish-brown hair above the hoof that became chestnut further up the leg, a long, flaxen mane and dorsal stripe (q.v.); the jaw and tooth structure were markedly different than that of *Equus caballus* (q.v.).

Icelandic Also known as Icelandic Horse or Icelandic Pony; a pony breed descended from ancient English Pacers taken to Iceland by the Norsemen between AD 860 and 935; in AD 930, laws were passed that prevented the importation of horse stock, thus keeping the breed pure for more than 1,000 years; in general, most horses are 5-gaited and have been selectively bred since 1879 to maintain the quality of these gaits which include the fetgangur (q.v.), brokk (q.v.), stökk (q.v.), skied (q.v.), and tølt (q.v.) and, in some cases, the flying pace (q.v.); is small, stocky, has a deep girth, short back and legs, large head set onto a short, thick neck, an abundance of mane and tail hair, and feathering on the heels; stands up to 13.2 hands; is extremely intelligent, docile, hardy, and sure-footed, has great endurance and is noted for its homing instinct; although usually gray or dun, there are 15 recognized coat color combinations; often kept in semi-feral conditions; used for mining, farming, transportation, racing (since 1874) and as a food source for the Icelanders who depend upon it as a staple of their diet.

Icelandic Horse *see* ICELANDIC

Icelandic Pony *see* ICELANDIC

ice skid A drag shoe (q.v.) used to hold a horse-drawn carriage/coach on an icy slope; a 2 to 4 inch (5–10 cm) long iron link with protruding teeth placed under a tire of a hind wheel and attached by a floating ring to the axle.

ICF *see* INTERN CLASSIFICATION FARRIER

ichthamol An ointment made from a coal-tar base used to treat bacterial infections including abscesses.

icing *see* ICE

ICSI *see* INTRACYTOPLASMIC SPERM INJECTION

icterus *see* JAUNDICE

Ideal Pinto Driving Class A Pinto (q.v.) performance event; horses pull two- or four-wheeled vehicles and are judged 50 percent on performance and manners, 25 percent on conformation, and 25 percent on color.

identical twin *see* MONOVULAR TWIN

ileocolonic aganglionosis Also known as lethal white syndrome; a genetically based, fatal disease in which the foal is born without part of his intestine and will develop colic (q.v.) soon after birth.

ilium Also known as shaft or hip bone; the bone of the ilia or flank which extends up and above the base of the pelvis and sacrum, the internal angles of which form part of the croup and point of the hip (q.v.).

illegal substance *see* FORBIDDEN SUBSTANCE

IM *see* INTRAMUSCULAR

immune stimulant Any natural or synthetic substance which provokes the body's immune and inflammatory responses to defend against illness and/or injury.

immune system A body-wide group of tissues including, but not limited to, the lymph system, spleen, bone marrow, and intestinal tissues, which are responsible for identifying and combating foreign substances.

Immunomodulation An ill-defined chronic soft-tissue soreness that does not respond to nonsteroidal anti-inflammatory drugs such as bute (q.v.) and which may result from a defective immune response.

impact The contact or striking of one object against another, as in the hoof to the ground.

impaction An obstructive lodging of food or food matter in the intestines.

imperial Also known as lunch box; a box positioned between the roof seats of a drag (q.v.), traveling coach, or chariot in which lunch for the passengers was stored.

Imperial Mercury An unusual, 16 passenger, horse-drawn vehicle divided into 4 compartments by doors and glass; patented in 1780 by Crispus Claggett.

Imperial Spanish Riding School of Vienna Also known as Spanish School, Spanish Riding School, Spanish Riding School of Vienna, or Imperial Riding School of Vienna; a riding school founded in Vienna, Austria in 1572 to instruct nobility in classical equitation; originally, a wooden arena located adjacent to the Imperial Palace; the present location, the Winter Riding Hall, was built in 1735; so called because of the high percentage of Spanish and/or Andalusian (q.v.) horses used there; now, Lipizzaner (q.v.) stallions are used exclusively to ensure preservation and development of the natural gaits of the breed which are specifically suited to the steps and movements of dressage (q.v.), including the airs above the ground (q.v.): the levade (q.v.), courbette (q.v.), and the capriole (q.v.); only male riders are admitted and training may last from four to eight years; considered the home of classical riding.

Imperial Riding School of Vienna *see* IMPERIAL SPANISH RIDING SCHOOL OF VIENNA

import To introduce a horse to one country from another; all registered imported horses are identified by either an asterisk in front of the name (e.g., *Flarisco [Ger]), or by the abbreviation Imp. in front of the name, and the country of export (e.g. Imp. Flarisco [Ger]).

impost A racing term; the weight assigned to or carried by a horse in a race; consists of the jockey, saddle, boots, pants, and silks, and, if necessary, lead pads inserted into the saddle.

impregnate Also known as fertilize; to make pregnant by means of artificial (q.v.) or natural insemination.

Impressive The Quarter Horse halter sire responsible for passing the genetic defect hyperkalemic periodic paralysis (q.v.) on to his descendants.

imprinting The initial act of socializing the foal performed by a knowledgeable handler shortly after initial contact of the foal with the mare following birth; includes the constant handling of the foal's body, lifting his feet, inserting a gloved finger in the anus, and another into both nostrils until resistance to this type of activity is nullified.

Improved Maremmana A modern Maremmana (q.v.) breed crossed with Thoroughbred (q.v.) to increase stature and refine appearance; the cross resulted in a loss of hardiness and the exceptional stamina which characterized the breed.

improver A European term; a farrier (q.v.) whose professional status is between that of an apprentice and journeyman (q.v.).

impulsion The horse's desire to move forward, fueled by the energy generated by the hindquarters (q.v.); this energy can be channeled to produce a range of different forms of active, vigorous movement from high collection to extension.

inactive A dressage term; said of the horse when his hind legs appear to move lazily and do not step forward under his body.

in and out (1) A jumping obstacle consisting of two or three jump elements in which the individual elements are separated by one or two strides. (2) Also known as in and out stall; any stabling circumstance in which a horse has access to both a covered and, generally, protected stall and to a paddock or run.

in-and-outer Also known as runs hot and cold; a racing term; a horse who runs inconsistently.

In-and-out stall *see* IN AND OUT

inattentive Said of a horse who does not listen to the rider's aids; often due to distraction.

in-blood A hunting term; said of hounds (q.v.) having made a recent kill.

in-bred Said of the progeny (q.v.) of a closely related dam and sire.

in-breeding Also known as close breeding; mating of closely related horses such as mother-to-son, sister-to-brother, and father-to-daughter; seldom practiced in horse-breeding operations because of the high risk of producing offspring with poor dispositions and faults.

incarceration Displacement and entrapment of a segment of bowel, as by a hernia (q.v.) or mesenteric tear.

incisor teeth Also known as incisors or pincers; the horse's 12 front (6 upper and 6 lower) teeth; consist of 4 central incisors (q.v.), 4 lateral incisors (q.v.), and 4 corner incisors (q.v.); used for cutting rather than grinding; the central incisors begin to erupt at 2½ years followed by the lateral and corner incisors at one year intervals thereafter.

Incisors *see* INCISOR TEETH

Incitatus Also known as Porcellus meaning little pig; Emperor Caligula Gaius Caesar's racing stallion; besides a stall of marble, a manger of ivory, purple blankets and a collar of precious stones, Caesar even gave Incitatus a house and made him a citizen of Rome; his name means swift and speeding.

incomplete fracture A fracture (q.v.) which does not extend completely through the bone.

independent Gogue A type of de Gouge martingale (q.v.); schooling tack used to assist bit action by restricting the position of the horse's head and neck; consists of an arrangement of straps fastened to the chest ring or girth on one end which split and run through the poll (q.v.) pad on either side of the temples, and to the bit rings on the other.

independent seat Said of a rider whose balance and body position on the horse are maintained without relying on the reins or stirrups for support.

index A racing term; a number that identifies a specific results chart; when printed in racing papers, directs the player to a chart of a horse's most recent race and the statistics thereof.

Indian broke A horse trained to allow mounting from the off side.

Indian martingale (q.v.) An auxiliary rein or strap used to assist the action of the bit by restricting the position of the horse's head and neck; consists of a strap fastened to the girth at one end which forms a noseband on the other; the noseband contricts progressively tighter the higher the horse raises his head.

Indian pony (1) *see* PINTO. (2) Any horse ridden or owned by a native American Indian.

Indian style (1) Also known as swing up; a method of mounting a horse in which the rider stands at the shoulder of the horse facing the haunches, grabs hold of the horse's mane with both the left and right hands, and swings up on the back of the horse with the right leg leading. (2) *see* BAREBACK RIDING

Indiana pants *see* HOPPLES

indirect rein Also known as bearing rein or opposite rein; to use the rein to apply pressure to the neck of the horse on the side opposite to which a turn is required, e.g. to signal the horse to turn to the right, the rider applies pressure to the left side of the neck using the left rein.

indoor polo *see* ARENA POLO

in estrus Also known as in season, in heat, or in use; said of a mare in estrus (q.v.).

infectious arthritis Arthritis (q.v.) involving inflammation of the joint capsule caused by the introduction of infectious organisms into the joint through a wound or via the blood or lymph systems; the joint capsule appears distended and hot to the touch; infection destroys the joint cartilages and underlying bone and causes new bone growth which ultimately results in ankylosing arthritis (q.v.) or osteoarthritis (q.v.).

inferior check ligament The direct continuation of the posterior ligament of the knee which provides support to the deep flexor tendon (q.v.); located below the knee.

infertile Unable to conceive.

infield A racing term; the area encompassed by the inside rail of a race track.

infield rail *see* INSIDE RAIL

inflammatory airway disease Also known by the acronym IAD; an irritative airway disease thought to be associated with persistent viral infection or the chronic pulmonary stress and inhalation of particulate matter associated with training and racing; normally strikes two- and three-year-old performance horses; symptoms include a slight nasal discharge and occasional light coughing early in exercise.

influenza *see* EQUINE INFLUENZA

in foal Said of pregnant mare.

in front of the vertical The horse's head carriage when his muzzle (q.v.) is forward of an imaginary line drawn perpendicular to the ground; the opposite side of the vertical line from behind the vertical (q.v.)

in full cry A hunting term; said of a pack of hounds in strong pursuit of a quarry (q.v.) and giving tongue (q.v.).

infundibulum The funnel-like depression in the biting surface of the incisor teeth (q.v.) which becomes the cup.

infusion The introduction of fluid other than blood, e.g. a mare's uterus is sometimes infused with a sterile saline solution post-foaling to clean it out.

ingesta Food or drink consumed by the horse.

inguinal Pertaining to the groin area located between the leg and pelvis.

inguinal hernia A hernia (q.v.) occurring in the groin area; a condition where tissue descends into the inguinal canal leading to the scrotum in the male horse but does not enter it; surgical correction almost invariably leads to simultaneous castration.

in hand (1) A racing term; said of a horse running under moderate control, at less than top speed. (2) To lead or work a horse from the ground. (3) *see* IN-HAND CLASS

in-hand class Also known as in hand; any show class in which livestock is led, usually in a show bridle or halter, unsaddled and without harness, in and around the show ring through various gaits and patterns; horses are judged on conformation, condition, and/or movement.

in-hand line A cotton or synthetic rope or piece of webbing 6 feet (1.8 m) long and approximately 1 inch (2.5 cm) wide, attached to the bridle by a hook and snap or buckle; used in dressage when training a horse in such movements as piaffe (q.v.) and passage (q.v.) from the ground; the horse is worked in a straight line or in a fixed position, not on a circle.

in heat *see* ESTRUS

inheritance *see* HEREDITY

inherited lethal Any condition or disease genetically transmitted to the foal which may affect lifespan or future productivity; genetic abnormalities are classified as either lethal or non-lethal; a lethal factor leads to death of the affected animal while a non-lethal inherited weakness may only make the horse less fit for purpose; lethals may be of three types: delayed lethal (q.v.), partial lethal (q.v.), or true lethal (q.v.).

in light A racing term; said of a horse running in a handicap race who, on the basis of past performance or the expectation that he is improving, appears to be leniently weighted.

Innervation Distribution of nerves to a part of the body.

inositol A B-complex vitamin produced by intestinal synthesis; necessary for proper metabolism and which may function as a coenzyme, although the exact function and horse's daily dietary requirements have not been determined; deficiency is unlikely to occur.

inquiry (1) An official investigation into a competition to determine whether a rule infraction occurred; initiated by an objection (q.v.) lodged by an official or competitor. (2) A racing term; a sign flashed on the tote board (q.v.) to indicate there is an inquiry on a specific race.

in rut Said of a deer or stag during rut (q.v.).

in season *see* ESTRUS

insecticide Any substance or preparation used to kill insects and to suppress and/or control insect populations in and around the stable.

inseminate To introduce semen, as into a mare, either by natural action of the stallion or artificial means.

insemination The act of inseminating.

insensitive laminae Also known as horny laminae; the layer located just under the hoof wall which attaches the hoof wall to the coffin bone; does not contain blood vessels.

in shape (1) A racing term; said of a horse who is ready to win. (2) Said of a well-conditioned horse.

inside (1) The side of the horse on the inside of the movement, e.g. when on a circle right the inside is the right side of the horse; some authorities, when referring to counter-canter, use the terms 'inside' and 'outside' with reference to the horse's bend, rather than the direction of travel; in such specific cases, these terms will have the opposite meaning from the usual definition. (2) Also known as inside position; a racing term; the racing position closest to the rail (q.v.). (3) A racing term; anything or anyone located to the left side of a horse during a race; only applies to left-hand tracks.

Inside Car A horse-drawn vehicle popular in Ireland; not unlike a Governess Car (q.v.) in construction; the driver sat upon an exposed seat in the front of the vehicle.

inside leg The mounted rider's leg on the inside of the movement, e.g. in a circle to the right, the rider's right leg would be the inside leg.

inside position *see* INSIDE NO. 2

inside rail Also known as infield rail, running rail or fence; a racing term; the inside rail or fence separating the racing strip (q.v.) from the infield (q.v.).

inspection Visual examination of the horse to evaluate quality and/or condition for registration, breeding, health (veterinary inspection [q.v.]), sale, etc.

inspector One authorized or designated by an individual or organization to visually inspect a horse to gather data both in report and pictorial form; may be authorized to tattoo any horse which has passed breed registry inspection.

Institut du Cheval An organization founded in Pompadour, France to register French-bred horses and maintain complete computerized files on such horses including ancestry, offspring, and track performance records.

Institute of the Horse A British organization founded in 1925; in 1928 started a sub-branch scheme in different parts of England to encourage riding; this scheme, the forerunner to the Pony Club (q.v.), was inaugurated as a junior branch and became the Pony Club in 1929; that same year, the Institute of the Horse and the Pony Club became jointly known as the Institute of the Horse and Pony Club, Ltd (q.v.).

Institute of the Horse and Pony Club, Ltd. A British organization founded in 1929 through merger of the Institute of the Horse (q.v.) and its junior branch, the Pony Club (q.v.); merged with the National Horse Association (q.v.) in 1947 together they became known as the British Horse Society (q.v.).

insufficient immobility A dressage term; said of a horse who has not come to a complete halt; may include a leg shift, altered head position, or not holding the halt long enough.

insufficient lengthening A dressage term; any increase in stride length within a gait in which the horse does not demonstrate enough difference between the two gait variants e.g. collection to working, working to medium, etc.

insulin A hormone secreted by the pancreas; controls blood-sugar levels and the utilization of sugar by the body.

intercostal Situated between the ribs (q.v.) as in cartilage (q.v.) or muscle (q.v.).

interdigitate (1) To interlock, as the fingers of both hands or the insensitive and sensitive laminae (q.v.) within the hoof. (2) Collision between legs.

interfere A racing term; said of a horse who impedes another horse during a race.

interfering A gait fault causing the horse to strike any part of the inside of one limb with the foot or shoe of the opposite foot; injury may be at any spot from the coronary band to the carpus, is more common to the forelimbs, and is most common to the fetlock (q.v.) and second metacarpal (q.v.); temporary causes include fatigue and faulty trimming or shoeing while a permanent condition is due to faulty confirmation.

interfering shoe *see* FEATHER-EDGED SHOE

intérieur Also known as body; a class of accommodation offered on Diligence (q.v.) horse-drawn vehicles during the 19th and 20th centuries in Europe; accommodated six or eight passengers seated vis-à-vis (q.v.) between the rear (q.v.) and coupé (q.v.).

Intermediare I Also known as Intermediate I, an upper-level dressage competition; between Prix St. Georges (q.v.) and Intermediare II.

Intermediare II Also known as Intermediate II, an upper-level dressage competition; between Intermediare I and Grand Prix (q.v.).

Intermediate An American jumping term; a second-level jumper (q.v.) between Preliminary (q.v.) and Open.

Intermediate I The British and Australian equivalent to Intermediare I (q.v.).

Intermediate II The British and Australian equivalent to Intermediare II (q.v.).

intern Also spelled interne; an advanced student gaining practical experience under supervision of one more experienced.

International American Albino Association, Inc. Also known by the acronym IAAA; an organization that superseded the American Albino Association, Inc. (q.v.) in 1985; maintains breed registries for the American Cream (q.v.), and American White (q.v.), and acts as the National Recording Club (q.v.) for horses, ponies and miniature horses.

International Arabian Horse Association Also known by the acronym IAHA; an American organization founded in 1950 to register Anglo-Arab (q.v.) and Half-Arab Horses, regulate competition and exhibition of Arab Horses, and establish show and judging criteria for Arab (q.v.), Half-Arab, and Anglo-Arabian horses, at events across the United States and Canada; acquired the official stud book for Half-Arabian and Anglo-Arabian horses from the American Remount Association in 1951.

International Equestrian Federation *see* FEDERATION EQUESTRE INTERNATIONALE

International Federation of Pony Breeders, The A British organization founded in 1951 to develop international markets for different pony breeds and to serve as a liaison between breeders and buyers.

International Horse Show *see* ROYAL INTERNATIONAL HORSE SHOW

International Level *see* FEI LEVEL

International Society for the Protection of Mustangs and Burros Also known by the acronym ISPMB; an American organization founded in 1965 by a woman known as Mustang Annie to register and campaign for the protection of wild horses and burros in North America.

International Test A dressage term; any of four standard advanced-level dressage tests devised by the FEI (q.v.) and conducted at the FEI Level (q.v.); include Prix St. Georges (q.v.), Intermediare I (q.v.), Intermediare II (q.v.), and Grand Prix (q.v.); revised about every four years to prevent horses from becoming too narrowly routined; always completed within 8 to 12 minutes.

International Union of Journeymen Horseshoers of the United States and Canada Also known by the acronym IUJH, as Platers Union, or formerly as Journeyman Horseshoers National Union; an association of farriers (q.v.) organized in Philadelphia, USA in 1874, membership being based on a comprehensive forging and practical horseshoeing tests; evolved from draft horseshoers to include racetrack horseshoers; superseded by the Journeyman Horseshoers National Union in 1893.

International Veterinary Acupuncture Society Also known by the acronym IVAS; an international association of veterinarians using acupuncture (q.v.) to treat horses; organized in the United States in 1974; trains and certifies veterinarians worldwide in the use of acupuncture.

Intern Classification Farrier Also known by the acronym ICF; a level of ability of student and novice farriers awarded by the American Farriers Association (q.v.) on the basis of written examination; is not a certification.

interne *see* INTERN

interosseous splint A splint (q.v.) occurring between the cannon and splint bones at the mid-splint bone area; characterized by a bump over the area; not usually accompanied by lameness.

interphalangeal arthritis *see* RINGBONE

interrupted stripe A face marking; any long, narrow, white marking on the horse's face that runs in a relatively straight line from the forehead, at eye level to, or almost to, an imaginary line which connects the top of the nostrils; is no wider than the width of the nasal bone.

intersesamoidian Refers to any structure present between the sesamoid bones (q.v.), e.g. ligaments (q.v.).

interstitial Within the spaces between the tissues.

intestinal stone *see* ENTEROLITH

intertrack wager A racing term; a bet placed at one racetrack on a horse(s) running in a horse race at another track.

intertrack wagering A racing term; to place a wager at one racetrack on a horse(s) running in a horse race at another track.

in the book Said of a horse accepted for, or entered in, the General Stud Book (q.v.) for the breed.

in the bridle *see* ON THE BIT

in the can An American racing term; said of a horse who does not finish in the money (q.v.).

in the cheek Said of the reins (q.v.) when attached to the mouthpiece (q.v.) rings of a bit such as a Liverpool (q.v.).

in the hand *see* ON THE BIT

in the huntsman's pocket hunting term; said of members of the field (q.v.) who ride too close to the huntsman (q.v.) and interfere with his hunting the hounds (q.v.).

in the money (1) Also known as run in the money; a racing term; technically, said of any horse competing in a race who finishes in one of the top four positions; the bettor (q.v.) is only paid a dividend if the horse places in first, second, or third position. (2) Also known as run in the money; said of a horse whose finishing position results in a payoff for either the owner or bettor.

in the plate Said of a rider seated on the saddle on a horse.

in the soup A historical hunting term; said of a rider having fallen from the horse into water.

in the white Said of a horse-drawn carriage following construction, but before painting and trimming.

in tough A racing term; said of a horse racing against a field (q.v.) he is unlikely to beat.

intra-articular Within the joint (q.v.) space.

intracytoplasmic sperm injection Also known by the acronym ICSI; to take a sperm sample and inject it into the egg which is then implanted in a mare.

intradermal Administered directly into the skin, as in an injection.

intradermal injection To inject a liquid substance directly into the skin.

intrahecal Into a sheath; intraspinal.

intramedullary Within the marrow cavity of long bones, as in intramedullary pins used in the treatment of fractures.

intramuscular Also known by the acronym IM; administered directly into muscle tissue, as in an injection.

intramuscular injection To inject a substance directly into the muscle tissue.

intra-peritoneal injection Any injection (q.v.) made directly into the abdominal cavity.

Intratracheal Into the windpipe as to administer anesthesia (q.v.).

intravenous Also known by the acronym IV; administered directly into the bloodstream through a vein, as in an injection.

intravenous injection To inject a substance directly into a vein or artery as with a needle.

intussusception The telescoping of one section of the intestines by an adjoining section.

in use *see* IN ESTRUS

in velvet Said of a stag (q.v.) between April and July or August, during which the antlers are covered by velvet (q.v.).

invitational Any competitive event in which participating horses and riders must be invited to attend and participate.

in vitro fertilization Also known by the acronym IVF; a laboratory method of fertilizing an ovum (q.v.); the ovum, surgically removed from the mare, is fertilized in a test tube with sperm from a donor male, then returned to the uterus of the original female donor or a surrogate mother to complete the gestation period; effective in humans and most other animal species, but historically difficult to implement in horses.

in vivo Within the living animal.

involuntary muscle Any muscle (q.v.) not controlled by will, as that which operate in such involuntary movements as breathing and digestion.

involution The process by which an organ returns to its former size and cellular state, as in the return of the uterus and mammary glands to normal state following pregnancy or lactation.

in wear Said of horse's teeth (q.v.) when newly erupted and having grown out from the gums sufficiently to be used in normal chewing.

in whelp A hunting term; the state of a bitch (q.v.) when carrying young.

iodine (1) A mineral component of the hormone thyroxin (q.v.), produced in the thyroid gland; essential for reproduction and normal physiological processes, influences the metabolic rate and oxygen consumption, increases the uptake and utilization of glucose by the cells, and increases protein synthesis; dietary requirements for the horse have not been established, although estimates indicate rations containing 0.1 parts per million are satisfactory for the mature horse, a level generally achieved in the normal diet; deficiency may result in an enlarged thyroid gland (goiter [q.v.]), high foal death rate, or poor growth; levels in excess of 40 milligrams per day may be toxic. (2) A non-metallic halogen element obtained usually as heavy, shiny, blackish crystals and used especially in medicine, photography, and analysis. (3) A tincture of iodine used especially as a topical antiseptic.

iodine deficiency Lack of sufficient levels of systemic/tissue iodine as required for normal body function; may result in goiter (q.v.).

Iomud Also known as Jomud or Yomud; a Russian warmblood developed by the Iomud Turkoman tribe from the ancient Turkmene (q.v.); previously popular as a cavalry mount and today excels at long distance races; similar to the Akhal-Teké (q.v.) in its stamina, but is not as fast and is smaller and more highly strung; has Arab (q.v.) characteristics, standing about 15 hands with a compact, sinewy body, and long legs; generally has a gray coat although bays and chestnuts do occur; is exceptionally resistant to heat and able to survive without water for long periods; is particularly well-suited to cross-country racing due to its stamina, speed, and natural jumping ability; used for riding and racing.

iris The pigmented, muscular eye structure located behind the cornea; dilates and contracts the pupil to regulate the amount of light reaching the retina.

Irish Car *see* JAUNTING CAR

Irish Cob An Irish horse; a type rather than a breed bred since the 18th century; developed by crossing Connemara (q.v.), Irish Draft (q.v.), and English Thoroughbred (q.v.); breed characteristics are not stable and it often exceeds the height limits for cobs (q.v.); stands 15 to 15.3 hands, has a short neck and back, powerful, but short legs, and may have a bay, brown, black, gray, or chestnut coat; used for riding and light draft.

Irish Draft *see* IRISH DRAUGHT

Irish Draught Also known as Irish Draft; an all-purpose Irish breed; of uncertain origin, although it is thought to have resulted from upsizing of the Connemara (q.v.) with Clydesdale (q.v.) crosses during the 19th century; stands 15 to 17 hands, has sound, strong legs with little hair on the fetlocks, a strong, yet heavy-looking shoulder, free and straight natural action, and a brown, bay, chestnut, or gray coat; the stud book was established in 1917; a natural jumper and when put to Thoroughbred (q.v.) stallions results in top Irish Hunters (q.v.).

Irish Half-bred *see* IRISH HUNTER

Irish hobby A 16th and 17th century Irish term; any equine sport including racing.

Irish Hunter Also known as Irish Half-bred; an Irish riding horse of substance, with clean, sound limbs and good bone; developed as the horse of the hunt; it is a 'type', not being of any particular breed, but usually a combination of Thoroughbred (q.v.) with something else, usually the Irish Draught (q.v.); stands 15 to 17.1 hands, has a slightly convex head profile, a short back, slightly sloping croup, and any solid coat color, including gray; although considered a half-breed, the name is capitalized and listed with other breeds due to constancy of the physical characteristics; bred for hunting, show jumping, and eventing.

Irish Jaunting Car *see* JAUNTING CAR

Irish martingale Also known as Irish rings or spectacles; an auxiliary rein used to prevent the reins from entangling or being thrown over the head of a raucous or nervous horse or when jumping; consists of two metal rings connected by a short leather strap through which the bridle reins run and connect to the bit rings; positioned between the chest and chin of the horse.

Irish rings *see* IRISH MARTINGALE

Irish Slide Car A wheel-less, horse-drawn cart popular in Ireland through the early 20th century; had two poles which formed the shafts to the rear of which a large, laundry basket was fixed and a load transported; the ends of the poles dragged along the ground on one end and were attached to the collar (q.v.) by means of rope traces on the other; pulled by a single horse.

Irish Sport Horse A relatively new horse breed developed in Ireland by crossing Irish Draught (q.v.) with Thoroughbred (q.v.); has great bone due to the limestone in the grass upon which they are raised; bone density is passed on at least through two generations in horses bred outside of Ireland; the breed registry is maintained by the Irish Horse Board in Dublin, Eire.

iron (1) An essential mineral in the horse's nutrition; a constituent of hemoglobin contained in red blood cells which is responsible for transporting oxygen body-wide; also contained in some enzymes responsible for utilization of food components; deficiency causes anemia; the dietary requirement is low, estimated at approximately 40 parts per million. (2) A metallic element, silver-white and malleable, widely found in combination and used in the form of steel as for bits. (3) *see* STIRRUP NO. 1. (4) *see* BRANDING IRON

Iron Cart A waterproof, two-wheeled, box-shaped, horse-drawn cart used to transport water and/or liquid manure for agricultural purposes; constructed of bolted and cemented cast iron plates; had an outlet hose, valve, and pump with which to spread the contents.

iron gray Refers to coat color; a dark gray (q.v.) horse with little dappling.

iron horse A locomotive.

iron shot A cutting term; a quick jab, as with a spur.

irregular Said of the horse when one or more steps or strides differ in rhythm, being shorter or longer than the others; may or may not be due to unsoundness.

irregular pacing walk A walk (q.v.) in which both legs on the same side move forward almost simultaneously, the natural four-beat gait of the walk almost becoming two beats; results from tension and stiffness and is considered a fault.

isabella Also known as Café-au-Lait in France, Hanoverian Cream in England and spelled Y'sabella; refers to coat color; a very light, cream-colored shade of palomino (q.v.); have nonblue eyes and white, flaxen, or ivory mane and tail; in Europe, refers to all palominos (q.v.); in the United States, registries restrict isabella-colored horses.

Isabella quagga Also known by the scientific name *Asinus isabellinus*; an extinct wild ass of a pale yellow color; roamed in large herds throughout Africa until the late 19th century.

Ischaemia *see* ISCHEMIA

ischemia Also spelled ischaemia; a temporary or permanent, localized body tissue anemia (q.v.) due to blocked blood supply.

isolation barn A facility where sick horses are stabled separate from healthy ones.

ISPMB *see* INTERNATIONAL SOCIETY FOR THE PROTECTION OF MUSTANGS AND BURROS

Italian Heavy Draft A medium-sized coldblood draft horse originating in 1860 at which time it was developed at the Deposito Cavalli Stalloni stud farm in Ferrara, Italy; descended from the Breton (q.v.) crossed with Ardennes (q.v.) and Percheron (q.v.); historically bred for farm work, but due to mechanization is increasingly bred for human consumption.

Italian jumping style *see* FORWARD SEAT

Italian saddle *see* CLOSE CONTACT SADDLE

Italian seat *see* FORWARD SEAT

itchy heel *see* CHORIOPTIC MANGE

itchy leg *see* CHORIOPTIC MANGE

IUJH *see* INTERNATIONAL UNION OF JOURNEYMAN HORSESHOERS OF THE UNITED STATES AND CANADA

ITW *see* INTERTRACK WAGERING

IV *see* INTRAVENOUS

IVAS *see* INTERNATIONAL VETERINARY ACUPUNCTURE SOCIETY

Ivermectin The most active of the avermectins (q.v.); is a potent anthelmintic, effective at very low dose administered orally to horses in a paste formulation to control roundworms and horse bots (q.v.).

IVF *see* IN VITRO FERTILIZATION

J

jab (1) To poke or prod as with a spur. (2) *see* JOBBING THE MOUTH

jaca A Spanish term; a nag or pony.

jack (1) Also known as jackass or stallion donkey; a male donkey (q.v.) or ass (q.v.). (2) *see* BONE SPAVIN. (3) *see* HORSE MULE. (4) *see* BOOT JACK

jackass *see* JACK NO. 1

Jack Cart A primitive, flat, horse-drawn cart made in horse, cob, and pony sizes used in the hilly regions of southwest of England; had hoop-raves above the wheels and no sideplanks or spindles.

jackeroo Also known as roo or burra; an Australian term; a young person, male or female, in apprenticeship to learn how to work with livestock, principally horses, sheep, and cattle on large stations; the apprenticeship generally lasts a period of four years.

jack-knifing Also known as straight bucking; said of a bronc (q.v.) when he bucks by clicking his fore and hind legs together beneath his body when in mid-air, or when he crosses them so that their positions are reversed.

jackpot Prize money consisting of all entry fees collected for a particular event and to which no purse money is added.

Jackson Wagon A horse-drawn wagon made in Jackson, Mississippi, USA.

jack sores *see* CUTANEOUS HABRONEMIASIS

jack spavin *see* BONE SPAVIN

jackstock More than one American mammoth jack (q.v.) or jennet (q.v.).

jade Also known as jadey; a worthless, uncontrollable, or worn-out horse; from the Icelandic jalda meaning mare and the Scottish yaud, meaning an old mare.

jadey *see* JADE

Jaf One of two breeds derived from the Persian Arab (q.v.) indigenous to Kurdistan; is more highly regarded than the Darashouri (q.v.), being accustomed to harsh desert conditions; is spirited but gentle, hardy, tough, wiry, possessed of great stamina, and particularly noted for its tough, hard hooves; has Arab (q.v.) characteristics, stands about 15 hands, and generally has a bay, chestnut, or gray coat.

jagger (1) A peddler's pack horse (q.v.). (2) *see* JAGGER WAY

Jagger Wagon A square-boxed, unsprung horse-drawn buggy used in New York, USA; hung on bolsters.

jagger way Also known as jaggin way or jagger; an obsolete term; a path traveled by pack ponies and horses carrying coal or lead ore.

jaggin An obsolete British term; any small pack load carried by a pack pony or horse.

jaggin way *see* JAGGER WAY

jail An American racing term; said of the first month a claimed horse is in a new barn when racing law requires it to run at a 25 percent higher claiming price or remain idle as in, "The horse is in/out of jail."

jaivey *see* JARVEY

jam Also known as traffic jam; a racing term; a bunching up of horses on the racetrack when they are racing.

James Barenger *see* BARENGER, JAMES

James Gordon Bennett *see* BENNETT, JAMES GORDON

James Pollard *see* POLLARD, JAMES

James Selby *see* SELBY, JAMES

James Todhunter Sloan *see* SLOAN, JAMES TODHUNTER

jammed heel Said of the heel of the horse's foot when pushed up into the foot, as by an incorrectly fitted horseshoe; the heel bulb and coronary band are correspondingly distorted.

janet A female mule (q.v.).

japan A coating put on leather to give it the shiny surface known as patent leather (q.v.).

Japanese encephalitis Also known by the acronym JE; the most important flavivirus that causes equine encephalitis; principally mosquito-transmitted; recognized throughout the Far East; mortality in horses is less than 5 percent.

japanned leather *see* PATENT LEATHER

japanner One employed to glaze and work leather specifically to patent and enamel it for use in carriages and harness.

japanning The process of applying japan (q.v.) to leather.

jaquima *see* HACKAMORE NO. 1

jar Extra sharp horseshoe calks (q.v.).

jaraman The Australian aboriginal word for horse (q.v.).

jarvey Also known as jaivey; an Irish term; the driver of a Hackney Carriage (q.v.) or Jaunting Car (q.v.).

jaundice Also known as icterus; a symptom, not a disease; a yellowness of the skin, sclera of the eye and mucous membranes of the mouth, vagina, and eyelids due to the accumulation of bile pigment which is normally excreted by the liver into the intestines; if the liver is incapable of clearing the bloodstream of the pigment, its concentration increases until it finally spills into the tissues to stain not only the skin, but muscles, brain, and other organs; of three types: hemolytic jaundice (q.v.), obstructive jaundice (q.v.), and that caused by liver damage.

Jaunting Car Also known as Irish Car, Irish Jaunting, Jaunty Car, Side Car, or Outside Car; a, traditional Irish, horse-drawn, two-wheeled public transportation vehicle first used in Dublin in 1813; evolved from the Trottle Car; hung on shallow, sideways, semi-elliptical springs, the driver's seat was positioned above the outward-curving shafts, higher than passenger seating, had two parallel passenger seats running front to rear which shared a common backrest, and footboards; some versions had a parcel storage area located between the driver's and passenger's seats; drawn by a single horse.

Jaunty Car *see* JAUNTING CAR

Java An Indonesian pony breed indigenous to the island of Java; influenced by Arab (q.v.) blood, is similar in conformation to the Timor (q.v.), but is slightly taller and stronger; is docile, willing, strong and hardy, stands approximately 12 hands, and may have a coat of any color; has a heavy head, short, thick and muscular neck, a straight, long back, and long, well-muscled legs; used to pull sados (q.v.).

jaw Consists of the upper and lower jawbones of which there are two; these bones are firmly united to the other face bones; the upper and lower jaw have a number of deep sockets which contain the teeth.

jawbone A bone of the jaw (q.v.), especially the lower jaw or mandible.

JBM *see* JUST BEAT MAIDEN

J.C. Cooper *see* COOPER, J.C.

JE *see* JAPANESE ENCEPHALITIS

jennet (1) Also known as she ass, jenny, mare donkey in Britain, and spelled gennet; a female ass (q.v.). (2) *see* HINNY

Jennet A small Spanish horse bred in Granada, Spain by the Berbers from the upland regions of Andalusia thought to have descended from the Andalusian (q.v.); very popular in the Middle Ages.

jennet jack A male of the ass (q.v.) species bred to females of the ass (q.v.) species to produce stock.

jenny *see* JENNET

Jenny A small open carriage, either two- or four-wheeled, drawn by a small pony or donkey; usually hung sideways on semi-elliptical springs.

Jenny Lind A horse-drawn, light, four-wheeled American buggy named for the Swedish opera singer of the same name, by whom it was frequently driven when in the United States; had a forward-facing seat protected by a canopy placed in the center of the box-shaped body which was only 2 feet 6 inches (76 cm) wide; hung on transverse springs and a perch.

jerk (1) To lead a string of pack animals from horseback. (2) A Western roping term; the abrupt stop of the roped calf by the horse.

jerking slack *see* PULLING SLACK

jerk line (1) A western American term; a team of horses, ranging in number from six to 20, strung out two abreast. (2) Also known as jerk-line string; a driving term; a single rein fastened to the brake handle of a wagon or coach that runs through the driver's hand, passes through rings on the harness of all nearside horses or mules to the bit of the nearside lead horse; the driver directs the team to turn to the right with jerks on the rein, and a turn to the left by a steady pull on the same rein. (3) A roping term; a long, soft rope which is attached to the bridle bit, passed through a ring or pulley attached to the swell of the saddle, and tucked into the roper's belt which when the roper dismounts the horse and runs to the calf, is pulled loose from the roper's belt and signals the horse to step backwards to keep the rope taut.

jerk-line string *see* JERK LINE NO. 2

Jerky A small, low, one-horse, four-wheeled, topless American Buggy (q.v.); when fitted with a hood (q.v.), known as a Surrey (q.v.).

Jersey Van A brightly painted horse-drawn vehicle used for carting produce from the farms to the ship yards; had longitudinal seating on both sides, was hung on a combination of Telegraph springs and semi-elliptic springs; pulled by one or a pair of ornately harnessed horses driven from a transverse seat at the front.

jet black Refers to coat color; a pure black (q.v.) body with same-colored points, even when viewed in strong sunlight.

JHNU *see* JOURNEYMAN HORSESHOERS NATIONAL UNION

jib *see* BALK

jibbah an Arab (q.v.) conformation point; the bulge between the ears and down across the first third of the nasal bone formed by the frontal and parietal bones of the forehead; is most pronounced in foals up to the second year, modifying with maturity, and is rounder and more pronounced in mares.

jibbing *see* BALKING

Jic A very severe driving bit, the mouthpiece of which protrudes through the cheek-pieces and terminates in small rings exterior to the mouth to which the driving lines are attached.

jig An irregular, four-beat jog trot performed by some horses in lieu of walking (q.v.); is generally the behavioral by-product of discomfort, anticipation, or insecurity.

jiggle (1) *see* JOG. (2) Said of the rider; to shake the reins in short, visually imperceptible movements to encourage the horse to pick up, release pressure on, or stretch into the bit.

jilleroo A female jackeroo (q.v.).

jineteada A South American rodeo; usually includes two competitions, one for amateurs and one for professional riders, and such events as bronco riding.

Jingle (1) Any horse-drawn cart having long shafts. (2) An Irish, public-hire vehicle, pulled by a single horse. (3) *see* GOVERNESS CART

jinked back Also known as chinked back; said of the horse's back when one of the vertebral bony processes of the spine hooks or catches over another; may result in pinched nerves and atypical movement; realignment may be achieved with chiropractic (q.v.) treatment or massage.

jinked neck Also known as chinked neck; said of the horse's neck when one of the vertebral bony processes in the neck hooks over another; may result in pinched nerves and atypical movement; realignment may be achieved with chiropractic (q.v.) treatment, massage, etc.

Jinker A headed or open, horse-drawn driving cart produced in both horse and pony sizes popular in the towns and cities of Victoria, Australia.

jinking A condition of the vertebral column caused by injury or, in some cases, normal movement, in which one of the vertebral bony processes hooks over another; symptoms include malalignment of the vertebral column and atypical or unusual movement; may be located in the neck or back where the condition is known as jinked neck (q.v.) or jinked back (q.v.), respectively.

job *see* JOBBING THE MOUTH

jobbing the mouth Also known as job or jab; said of the rider; to intentionally or involuntarily jerk the bit in the mouth of the horse through the reins.

Jobey *see* BRINEKIND NOSEBAND

job horse *see* RENTAL HORSE

job master An obsolete term; one who offers horses, vehicles, and/or harness for hire for riding or driving by the season, month, etc.

jockey (1) Also known as horsejockey, horse racer, or boy (sl) and spelled jockie; an amateur or professional who rides a racehorse as in competition; a flat jockey generally weighs between 94 and 116 pounds (43–53 kg), while jump jockeys may weigh more; from "jack," a general term for any unidentified peasant, and the Scottish jock, a groom, the juvenile of which is jockie; by the 17th century, jockie widely applied to young horse dealers from which the first hired riders were drawn for racing. (2) An obsolete term; an unreliable person, or one with a poor reputation who deals in horses. (3) *see* JOCKEY FOR POSITION. (4) A thin sheet of metal molded to the shape of the front and rear tops of riding boots; used to guide the boot over the lower edge of the breeches when putting them on. (5) A British term; grease or dirt patches on the underside of a saddle; this term is now falling into disuse.

jockey agent A racing term; a professional who negotiates riding contracts, and other aspects of a jockey's business; may charge a fee of 20 percent or more on the rider's earnings.

jockey apprentice *see* APPRENTICE JOCKEY

Jockey Club, The (1) An American association of individuals and horse owners organized to promote and control horse racing and formulate rules for it; incorporated in New York, USA in 1894, maintains the American stud book and registry, and approves all registered Thoroughbred (q.v.) names; limited to approximately 75 members; bodies of the same name and, traditionally, with similar roles, exist in Britain, France and Hong Kong. (2) An area of a race track reserved for club members consisting of box seats, a restaurant, and lounges.

jockey fee A racing term; a sum paid to a jockey for riding a horse in a sanctioned horse race.

jockey for position Also known as jockey; a racing term; said of a jockey who attempts to maneuver his mount into a favorable race position.

jockeys (1) *see* HUNT BOOTS. (2) More than one jockey (q.v.).

Jockeys' Guild An association of race riders established in the United States.

jockey's race A racing term; a horse race in which, because of the characteristics of the horses involved, or because several are thought to be equally capacitated, the outcome is largely determined by strategic planning of the riders.

jockeys' room Also known as jocks' room or weighing room (Brit); a racing term; a room at a race track where competing jockeys store their tack, prepare for, and/or unwind from, a race.

jockey stick A driving term; a stick fastened to the hame (q.v.) of the near horse (q.v.) and the bit of the off horse (q.v.) used to prevent the horses from crowding each other; controlled by a single rein.

jockie *see* JOCKEY NO. 1

jock's room *see* JOCKEY'S ROOM

jodhpur boots *see* PADDOCK BOOTS

jodhpur breeches *see* JODHPURS

jodhpur curb Also known as cap curb; a bit consisting of two metal cheekpieces and a mouthpiece with a large center link; eliminates pressure on bars of the mouth using leverage instead of direct pressure; the reins are attached to rings on the cheek pieces (q.v.); used in conjunction with a curb strap (q.v.) or curb chain (q.v.).

jodhpurs (1) Also known as jodhpur breeches; a traditional riding pant cut to flare at the thigh and fit tight over the lower leg to the ankle; with the advent of stretch fabrics, have taken on a sleek, slim fit; worn with jodhpur boots (q.v.) or in some cases shoes; always considered informal; developed by British officers stationed in Jodhpur, India from which the name derived. (2) *see* OVERALLS NO. 1

jodhpur strap *see* GARTER

jog (1) Also known as hound trot, hound gait, houndpace, hound jog, jiggle, or jog trot; a hunting term; a slow trot between a walk and trot with a shortened stride length; the rider remains seated and does not post; usually performed on a loose rein; originally, the pace, about 6 mph (9.5 kmph), that hounds traveled on the road when in route to or returning from a hunt. (2) A racing term; a slow warm-up exercise in which the horse is exercised for several miles on the track, but traveling in the opposite direction to that in which races are run.

Jog Cart Also known as Jogging Cart; a low-slung, horse-drawn exercise cart used for training and exercising trotting horses; is longer and heavier than a Racing Sulky (q.v.) and has one seat for one or two passengers, and a slatted floor.

Jogging Cart *see* JOG CART

jog trot *see* JOG NO. 1

John *see* GELDING DONKEY

John Chapman *see* CHAPMAN, JOHN

john mule *see* HORSE MULE

John Rarey One of the most famous horse whisperers of the 19th century; demonstrated the technique of horse whispering (q.v.) around the world.

Johnsongrass A tall, perennial grass, *Sorghum halepense*, used for horse and cattle feed.

Johnsongrass hay A cut and dried grass hay made from Johnsongrass (q.v.); related to the sorghums (q.v.), is commonly grown in the southern United States, and is generally cut at the early-bloom stage to yield 2 to 3 cuttings; contains approximately 3 percent digestible protein.

John Rarey *see* RAREY, JOHN

John Warde *see* WARDE, JOHN

joiner Also known as bodymaker; one employed by a carriage maker to build horse-drawn vehicles.

joint (1) The point of junction of two moveable bones; named in accordance with location, e.g. the tibia and cannon bones join in the hock joint; of two types: hinge joint (q.v.) and ball and socket joint (q.v.). (2) *see* BATTERY

joint capsule The sac-like membrane enclosing the joint space and which secretes synovial fluid (q.v.).

joint cartilage *see* ARTICULAR CARTILAGE

jointed bit Any bit in which the mouthpiece (q.v.) connects or links in one or more places, i.e. a single joint as in a single-joint snaffle or a double joint as in a Dr. Bristol (q.v.); the action applies nutcracker pressure to the tongue.

jointed snaffle Also known as plain jointed snaffle; any snaffle bit (q.v.) having a jointed rather than a straight mouthpiece; the mouthpiece consists of two arms which taper down and interlock in the center of the bit; has a nutcracker action on the tongue and lips; varies in severity considerably depending on mouthpiece size, arm shape, and joint looseness; the greater the curve of the arms and the tighter the joint, the less sharp the nutcracker action on the tongue.

joint evil *see* JOINT ILL

joint fluid *see* SYNOVIAL FLUID

joint ill Also known as joint evil, navel ill or navel infection; a serious and often fatal disease of foals up to six months of age in which foals may be born dead or die shortly after birth; caused by the bacterium *Actinobacillus equuli* which enters the umbilical opening shortly after birth; symptoms include a breakdown of the joint surfaces resulting in painful joint swelling, particularly in the legs, fever, anemia, and an elevated white blood cell count.

Joint-Master A hunting term; one appointed by the Hunt Committee to share the responsibilities of the Master (q.v.); responsibilities are generally defined in writing and vary from Hunt to Hunt.

joint oil *see* SYNOVIAL FLUID

Join-Up A training technique pioneered by Monty Roberts (USA) in which yearlings, difficult horses, etc. are started or retrained using an 'advance and retreat' method of developing trust and communication; a psychological process of making the horse believe you and he are on the same team, part of the same herd, etc.; in this process, one advances on the horse, who then retreats; the process is then reversed with one withdrawing and the other advancing.

Jomud *see* IOMUD

Josef Emanual Fischer von Erlach *see* FISCHER VON ERLACH, JOSEF EMANUAL

jostle A racing term; said of a jockey (q.v.) or horse competing in a race; to make physical contact with or bump another horse during a race.

jostling stone *see* MOUNTING BLOCK

journeyman (1) *see* JOURNEYMAN RIDER. (2) *see* JOURNEYMAN FARRIER

journeyman farrier Also known as journeyman; a farrier who, having completed an apprenticeship, is free to sell his labor to a farrier shop; due to the mobile nature of most farriers today, the traditional journeyman farrier is rare.

Journeyman Horseshoers National Union Also known by the acronym JHNU; an association of draft horse farriers (q.v.) organized in Philadelphia, United States in 1874; in 1893, the name was changed to International Union of Journeyman Horseshoers of the United States and Canada (q.v.).

journeyman rider Also known as journeyman; a American racing term; an apprentice jockey (q.v.) after having ridden a 40th winner or reached the anniversary of one's first win.

Joust A combat between two mounted knights clad in armor and bearing lances.

jowl That portion of the head contained within the branches of the jaw bone.

Jucker Any light, elegant horse used in Hungary to pull an owner-driven carriage.

Jucker Carriage A Hungarian light, four-wheeled, horse-drawn, owner-driven vehicle.

Judge Monitor An auxiliary judge used at all National Cutting Horse Association events held in the United States, whose responsibility it is to review any run (q.v.) on video tape for which there is a discrepancy between the judges concerning a major penalty.

jughead (1) A stupid horse. (2) A horse having a large and ugly head.

jugular vein One of two large veins located on either side of the horse's windpipe (q.v.) in the underside of the neck which transport blood from the head and neck to the chest.

Jules Charles Pellier *see* PELLIER, JULES CHARLES

jump Said of a horse who springs clear of the ground or other support by means of a sudden muscular effort.

jump blind Said of a horse; to or jump through an untrimmed hedge, or over an overgrown ditch or obstacle or course when the landing side (q.v.) is not visible from the take-off point.

jump clean Also known as clear jump clear; a jumping term; to jump an obstacle or course without touching or dropping a rail.

jump clear *see* JUMP CLEAN

jumped A historical American cowboy term; said of a herd of wild horses which, when warned by a neigh from the stallion, gallop off.

jumped-in bars A therapeutic horseshoe of the bar shoe (q.v.) type; consists of a bar welded between the heels of an open keg or calk shoe (q.v.) or other projections on both heels; so called because the bar is placed (using a forge) or jumped-in between the heels of an existing shoe; the bar may be created in a variety of patterns and named accordingly, e.g. butterfly bars, diamond bars, etc.

jumper (1) Any horse breed or type trained to compete over jumps; in competition, must be able to negotiate obstacles ranging in height from 3 feet 6 inches to 5 feet (1–1.5 m) or more with spreads (q.v.) of up to 6 feet (1.8 m), depending on the division in which they compete. (2) A racing term; a horse who runs in steeplechases or hurdle races. (3) One who rides a horse over jumping obstacles.

jumper's bump An obvious enlargement at the point of the croup erroneously thought to increase a horse's power when jumping; considered a conformation fault.

jump flat Said of a horse who jumps over an obstacle with a flat back and head held high.

jump free Also known as free jump, jump free, or jump loose; said of a horse who jumps over obstacles in an enclosed arena without a rider, instead being controlled from the ground by voice commands or long lines (q.v.).

jump jockey A racing term; a jockey (q.v.) who specializes in hurdle (q.v.) or steeplechase (q.v.) races.

jumping chute Also known as jumping lane, Weedon lane, or Weedon; a narrow chute, commonly the width of a jump, designed with high walls on either side, through which a horse may be ridden or free jumped over one or a series of obstacles; generally used to train horses to jump.

jumping derby A jumping event in which the horse jumps natural or natural-looking fences over a longer course than in most show jumping (q.v.), as in the Hickstead and Hamburg Derbies.

jumping lane *see* JUMPING CHUTE

jumping on the lunge To jump a horse (generally riderless) over obstacles guided by a lunge line (q.v.) attached to the side ring of a lungeing cavesson (q.v.); the horse is encouraged to jump through the use of rein, voice, and whip aids.

jumping order Also known as starting order; a jumping term; the sequence in which a horse is placed to participate in a competition, e.g. first, second, fifth, twelfth, etc.; determined in advance of an event by drawing; gives each rider an equal chance of attaining a favorable position – riders near the end of the starting order have the advantage of seeing how the first riders complete the course (q.v.).

jumping rumped *see* GOOSE-RUMPED

jumping powder *see* STIRRUP CUP

jumping saddle Also known as jump seat saddle; a variation of a close contact saddle having a deeper seat and slightly more pronounced knee blocks (q.v.).

jump into the canter Said of a horse who, when in transition from the trot to the canter, strides as if about to jump; the front legs are higher off the ground than the hind and the head and neck are usually raised.

jump off Also known as barrage or against the clock; a show jumping term; a round (q.v.) in which all those riders who have previously completed the course without faults, compete over a final, timed, and shortened course to decide the winner; the competitor with the least number of jumping faults in the fastest time is the winner; in some forms of competition, the first jump off might not be timed and, instead, conducted over a higher, shortened course, with a timed jump off to follow if there is still inequality.

Jump Seat Carriage Any American horse-drawn vehicle having one or more adjustable folding seats which can be hidden when not used; can quickly convert a two-passenger vehicle into a four-seat carriage.

jump seat saddle *see* JUMPING SADDLE

Jump Seat Wagon Also known as Shift Seat Wagon; a four-wheeled, horse-drawn American vehicle of the Wagon (q.v.) type; had two canopy-covered, forward-facing seats, which could be converted into a single seat vehicle by folding the front seat down and jumping the rear seat forward; the body was 10 inches (25 cm) wider than that of a Jenny Lind (q.v.).

jump standard *see* STANDARD

jump stand *see* STANDARD

Junky A two-wheeled, horse-drawn vehicle used in some parts of Australia.

junior An American Horse Shows Association (q.v.) distinction of competitors determined by age; any rider 8 years old or younger, who competes in an equestrian event; other Associations may have different definitions of the term.

Just Beat Maiden Also known by the acronym JBM; a racing term; a horse who has only won a maiden race (q.v.) and no other and who is given a small chance against more experienced runners he meets in open competitions.

Justin Morgan A small, 14 hand bay (q.v.) foaled in the United States in 1790; the foundation sire of the Morgan (q.v.) who was sired by a Thoroughbred (q.v.) and out of a mare of mixed Arab (q.v.) Welsh Cob (q.v.), Harddraver (q.v.) and Fjord (q.v.) blood; named after his second owner, Justin Morgan; all Morgans trace to his three sons: Sherman, Woodbury, and Bullrush; the Morgan played an important role in the evolution of American breeds such as the Standardbred (q.v.), Saddlebred (q.v.), and the Tennessee Walking Horse (q.v.).

Jutland An ancient medium to heavy coldblood developed on Jutland Island, Denmark where it has existed for thousands of years, and from which the name derived; used in the Middle Ages for jousting (q.v.) and carrying heavily armored knights into battle; the modern breed was strongly influenced by Suffolk Punch (q.v.), specifically Oppenhein LXII in 1860, Cleveland Bay (q.v.), and more recently, Ardennes (q.v.) blood; bears a marked resemblance to the Schleswig (q.v.); has a heavy, common head, great depth of chest and girth, short and heavily feathered legs, and stands 15.2 to 16 hands; a chestnut coat with flaxen mane and tail is most common, although roan, bay, and black coats also occur; has tremendous endurance and is strong, docile, and gentle; numbers are on the decline due to mechanization; used for heavy draft and farm work.

jute The glossy fiber of either of two East Indian tiliaceous plants, genus *Corchorus olitorius* and *Corchorus capsularis* used in the manufacture of coarse cloths such as burlap and twine as used in some horse blankets and sheets.

jute rug Any covering made of jute (q.v.) strapped or tied onto the horse's body to protect him from cold and/or moisture.

juvenile A two-year-old horse.

K

Kabachi A Russian equestrian sport similar to tiling (q.v.); the rider, while galloping, throws his spear with the intent of placing it through a small hoop placed atop a post 3.2 yards (3 m) tall.

Kabarda *see* KABARDIN

Kabardin Also known as Kabarda; a Soviet-bred warmblood originating in the Caucasian mountains in the 15th century; descended from indigenous mountain stock crossed with Arab (q.v.), Turkmene (q.v.), and Karabakh (q.v.) blood; is well suited to steep, mountainous terrain and is gifted with a well-developed sense of direction and long life span; is sure-footed, agile, strong, and possessed of great endurance; a popular sport horse used for riding and packing as well as the improvement of other breeds such as the Tersky (q.v.); has strong Oriental features, stands 14.1 to 15.1 hands, and usually has a bay, brown, or black coat with gray occurring infrequently; has a long neck, strong legs, and excellent feet, but the quarters tend to be rather weak and sickle hocks (q.v.) are prevalent; the ears have a distinctive inward turn.

Kadir Cup A mounted pig-sticking competition held annually at the Meerut Tent Club, India where it was first conducted in 1874; breaks in the annual competition occurred in 1879 and 1890 for the Afghan war and from 1915 through 1918 for World War I; the name derived from the rough terrain surrounding the Ganges-Kadir country which historically teemed with wild boar.

Kaimanawa A feral horse breed found in New Zealand; due to years of isolation, now recognized as genetically different from other horse breeds; there are two strains of the breed, northern and southern, which do not mix; the northern strain is isolated to the Kaimanawa mountains of the central North Island, from which the name derived; both strains stand 13 to 14 hands, are intelligent, sure-footed and willing; protected by the Kaimanawa Wild Horse Preservation Society.

Kalesch *see* CALECHE

Kamsat *see* ASSIL

Karabair An ancient warmblood indigenous to the Central Asian mountains, specifically those in Uzbekistan; although the exact origins of the breed are unknown, its Oriental appearance suggests Mongolian and Arab (q.v.) descent; bred in three different sizes standing 14.2 to 15 hands; is very resistant to cold and fatigue, extremely sure-footed, agile, and fast, resembles a stocky Arab (q.v.), and generally has a gray, bay, or chestnut coat; used for light draft, driving, packing, riding, and mounted sports such as goat snatching (q.v.).

Karabakh A Soviet-bred warmblood originating in the mountains of Karabakh separating northwest Iran from Azerbaijan; of Oriental origins influenced by Arab (q.v.), Persian (q.v.), and Turkmene (q.v.) blood; stands 14 to 14.1 hands and generally has a golden dun coat, but chestnut, bay, and gray do occur; is tough and sure-footed, has a small, fine head having the typical Arab dished profile, low-set tail, and good feet; is calm, energetic, strong, enduring, and has good action; used for riding, equestrian games, racing, and limited harness work; numbers appear to be reducing.

Karacabey A warmblood developed at the beginning of the 20th century at the Karacabey Stud, Turkey; descended from local mares crossed with Nonius (q.v.) stallions; is tough, versatile, has good conformation, stands 15.1 to 16.1 hands and may have a coat of any solid color; previously used by the Turkish cavalry and is well suited to saddle and light draft work; the only Turkish breed to display uniformity of type and consistent transmission of characteristics.

Karrozin A four-wheeled, horse-drawn passenger carriage drawn by a single horse or large pony used in Malta; seated four passengers vis-à-vis (q.v.), under a high canopy or roof, and was hung on four sideways-elliptical springs with high clearance above road level.

kasen A Japanese term; sweet itch (q.v.).

Kathi *see* KATHIAWARI

Kathiawari Also known as Kathi; a pony breed indigenous to the western Coast of India, in the former princely state of Kathiawari; descended from small (about 13 hands), frugal native ponies crossed with Arabs (q.v.); a tough, hardy, tenacious, and unpredictable breed which thrives on little feed; stands approximately 14 to 15 hands, is very light and narrowly framed, having a weak neck and quarters, low-set tail, sickle hocks (q.v.), and ears that curve distinctively inwards, almost touching at the tips; all coat colors occur including skewbald (q.v.) and piebald (q.v.); used for riding, packing, farming, light draft, and the best ones, racing; virtually identical to the Marwari (q.v.).

kave Also known as port or porting; the pawing, scraping, or stomping action of the horse with his front legs, especially in stall bedding.

Kazakh An ancient pony breed originating in Kazakhstan; thought to have descended from the Asiatic Wild Horse (q.v.) refined by significant infusions of Don (q.v.) blood; stands 12.1 to 13.1 hands and has good hard limbs and feet; is bred in two distinct types: the Dzhab (q.v.) and the Adaev (q.v.); is willing, quiet, frugal, strong, and possessed of great stamina and legendary hardiness; the young are often fattened for human consumption and the mares produce milk for the same purpose.

keep *see* PASTURE

keep a horse at grass To maintain a horse in a pasture (q.v.) where he feeds exclusively off pasture grass; a minimum of 1 acre (4,047 sq m) per horse, but preferably 3 acres (1.2 hectares), is necessary.

keeper Also known as runner, harness loop, or space loop; any fixed or sliding leather loop used on saddlery, particularly bridles, through which the ends of the straps pass to keep them in place.

keep the horse to the track Said to the rider; to make one's horse follow a previously made path.

keg shoe *see* MACHINE-MADE SHOE

Kehilan An Arabic term; any pure-bred Arab (q.v.).

Keiger Horse *see* KEIGER MUSTANG

Keiger Mustang Also known as Keiger Horse; a dun-factor wild horse first discovered in the Steens Mountains of Southern Oregon, USA, in 1978 at which time it was identified by the US Bureau of Land Management as a distinct type; although commonly believed to have descended from the Spanish horses brought to North America by the Conquistadors, it is now believed that the strain may be much older; stands 14 to 15.2 hands, is short-backed, has durable legs, strong hooves, a willing disposition, and is extremely sure-footed; zebra and dorsal striping is common with fawn-colored inner ears and ear coat hair that is darker on the upper one third than the lower two thirds; protected by the Wild Horse and Burro Act (q.v.) and the Keiger Mesteño Association (q.v.); the name derived from the Keiger Gorge, located in the Steens Mountains, Oregan.

Keiger Mesteño Association An organization founded in Burns Oregon, USA in 1987 to protect and preserve the Keiger Mustang (q.v.) from dilution by other breeds and extinction.

kelpie Also spelled kelpy; a malevolent water spirit of Scottish legend, usually shaped like a young horse, who lurks in lakes and rivers and rejoices in or causes drownings of those who attempt to ride him.

kelpy *see* kelpie

kelshie (1) Also spelled kelsie; a woven basket hung on either side of a klibber (q.v.) used to carry peat in the Shetland Islands north of Scotland. (2) *see* KLIBBER

kelsie (1) *see* KLIBBER. (2) *see* KELSHIE

Kemble Jackson *see* CHECK REIN

kendrick girth A 1½ inch (38 mm), double-folded strap used to hold an English saddle in place, preventing it from slipping sideways and to some extent forward on the back of the horse; connects the two sides of the saddle beneath the horse's belly just behind the forelegs/shoulder; may be constructed of leather, cotton, wool, or synthetic materials.

kennel (1) Also known as kumel; a hunting term; a fox bed located above, rather than in, the ground. (2) The buildings and/or yards where hounds (q.v.) are maintained, i.e. bred or boarded.

kennel coat A hunting term; an ankle-length white cotton or linen coat worn by hunt staff (q.v.) or hound handlers to keep the hunting or day clothes of the wearer clean when in the kennel (q.v.).

kennel huntsman A hunting term; one employed by the Hunt (q.v.) to oversee the care and maintenance of the hounds (q.v.); is generally assisted by an amateur huntsman (q.v.) who actually manages the hounds and acts as a first whipper-in (q.v.) on hunt days.

kennel man A hunting term; one who works in the hunt kennels under the supervision of a huntsman (q.v.) or kennel huntsman (q.v.).

Kentucky bluegrass One of the blue grasses, *Poa pratensis*, growing in tufts and having bluish-green stems; especially the grass of Kentucky, USA, which due to the limestone soil and water is rich in phosphates and lime, two minerals which contribute to strong bones in horses.

Kentucky Derby Also known as Derby; a 1¼ mile (2 km) race for three-year-old horses established in 1875 at Churchill Downs, Louisville, Kentucky, USA and run annually since; in 1896 the distance was reduced from 1½ to 1¼ miles (2.4–2 km); one of three classic races (q.v.) comprising the Triple Crown (q.v.), the other two being the Belmont Stakes (q.v.) and the Preakness Stakes (q.v.); the last of the three races to be established.

Kentucky Saddlebred *see* AMERICAN SADDLEBRED

Kentucky Saddler *see* AMERICAN SADDLEBRED

kept-up Said of horse maintained in a stable rather than a pasture (q.v.) during the summer.

keratoma A rare horn tumor developing in the deep aspect of the hoof wall; lameness may or may not be present.

Kerry Pony A robust and hardy pony breed, from Kerry County, Ireland from which the name derived; used for riding and driving during the 19th century.

Kersey A coarse and ribbed woolen or woolen and cotton cloth historically used for ankle boots (q.v.) and trousers.

Kersey protection boots Any ankle boot (q.v.) when made of Kersey (q.v.).

key bugle A copper wind instrument similar to a cornet in appearance, but having keys instead of valves, historically used by Stage Coach (q.v.) guards.

key horse A racing term; a single horse used in multiple combinations in an exotic wager (q.v.).

keys Also known as bit keys or players; shaped metal pieces attached to the mouthpiece of some bits such as breaking bits (q.v.) to encourage the horse to accept the bit; the horse will play with the keys using his tongue.

Khamsa *see* ASSIL

Khis-Kouhou Also known as bride hunt of the Mongols; a popular Russian equestrian sport; young men ride after the girls and attempt to kiss them; the girls retaliate fiercely with their whips.

kiang Also spelled kyang; a wild ass (q.v.), *Equus hemionus kiang*, inhabiting Tibet and Mongolia; may have a dorsal stripe (q.v.), but no shoulder or leg stripes; stands 12.2 to 14 hands, has a variably colored coat, ears longer than those of horses, but shorter than those of the true ass, and long, narrow hooves with long heels; in the natural state is generally found in valleys 12,000 to 15,000 feet (3,660–4,570 m) above sea level.

Kibitka A roughly made, horse-drawn posting wagon used in Russia and other parts of Europe beginning in the late 15th century; had a wooden framework held together by strands of rope which supported hay-filled cushions or bundles of straw for passenger seating; sometimes protected by a canvas sheet secured over tilts or bows; pulled by teams of various numbers.

kick (1) Said of the horse; to strike out with either of the hind legs in defense, or out of meanness, anger, fear, etc.; may be considered a vice; in hunting, the tail of a horse who kicks is tagged with a red ribbon. (2) To win as in a wager, competition, or bet (q.v.).

kicking Also known as shelling (sl); a coaching term; tipping of the guards by the passengers.

kicking strap A wide leather strap used to keep the quarters (q.v.) down if a draft horse is prone to kicking; attaches on one end to the left shaft (q.v.), passes over the loins of the horse, through a loop on the crupper (q.v.), and connects to the right shaft on the other.

kick over the traces (1) A driving term; said of a Cart or Coach driver; to release control of the traces (q.v.) to avert an accident such as when a horse gets a leg over a trace. (2) Said of a horse when he kicks his leg so high as to entangle in the traces (q.v.).

kidney link A jointed, kidney-shaped metal link which takes the place of a bottom hame strap or hame chain in some pair and team harnesses; sometimes opens at the center top, so that it may pass through the bottom hame eyes.

kidney link ring A metal ring attached to the lower side of the harness kidney link to which the pole strap or pole chain is fastened in pair and team harness.

kill (1) To deprive of life in any manner; cause the death of; slaughter; to destroy. (2) Also known as worry; a mainly American hunting term; raw horsemeat or other meat fed to the hounds as a reward following the hunt; either individually fed to each hound or buried in a natural hole, drain pipe, etc. to allow the pack to seek it out; a development from the old British practice of encouraging hounds to tear or 'worry' the carcass of the dead fox.

kilocalorie *see* CALORIE

Kimberley horse disease Also known as walkabout disease; a seasonally occurring disease of horses in the Kimberley district of Western Australia; most common in the wet season – January to April; horses of all ages and breeds are susceptible; caused by consumption of Whitewood (*Atalaya hemiglauca*); characterized by anorexia, dullness, wasting, irritability, biting other horses, yawning (q.v.), and gnawing at wooden posts; muscular spasms lead to a phase of mad, uncontrolled and directionless galloping; gallops become more frequent and less violent, gradually leading to a walking stage in which the horse demonstrates a slow, staggered gait and low, stiff head carriage.

kimberwick *see* KIMBLEWICK

kimblewick Also known as Spanish snaffle or Spanish jumping bit and spelled kimberwick; a pelham (q.v.) bit requiring one instead of two reins (q.v.), having a straight, low-ported mouthpiece (q.v.), and short cheeks (q.v.) with dee-rings (q.v.) topped with a square eye running the full length of the cheeks; when the rider's hands are held in a standard position, the bit acts as a snaffle (q.v.), but when lowered, or when used in conjunction with a martingale (q.v.), the resulting action is similar to that of a curb (q.v.); of five types: the true kimblewick, Uxeter kimblewick (q.v.), Whitmore kimblewick (q.v.), mullen-mouth true kimblewick, and single-jointed true kimblewick (q.v.).

kinesiopathy The functional pathology of movement that can manifest as hypomobility (q.v.) or hypermobility (q.v.) of the motor unit (q.v.).

Kineton noseband Also known as Puckle noseband or lever noseband; a severe noseband (q.v.) used on hard-pulling, soft-mouthed, horses; consists of a headstall and nosepiece joined by semi-circular metal loops which fit around the cheeks of the bit; the nosepiece is generally adjustable on both sides; when fitted correctly, the metal pieces touch, but do not apply pressure to, the bit unless aided by rein action; use of the reins applies pressure to both the bridge of the nose and the bit causing the horse to lower his head so bit action can be implemented; named for the village of Kineton in which the inventor Puckle lived.

king bolt *see* PERCH BOLT

King George V Cup An annual show jumping competition for individuals conducted under FEI (q.v.) rules at the Royal International Horse Show in England.

King of Aintree *see* RED RUM

kinked tail Said of the tail of the horse when, as due to injury, a twist or bend in the tail bone develops; may be corrected by rebreaking and splinting.

Kinsey splint A splint used to stabilize fractured bones while preserving the health of the arteries preventing preoperative circulation trouble; invented in 1980 to replace the air cast.

Kiplingcotes Race Also known as Yorkshire Derby; the oldest known horse race in the world; run on a 4-mile (6.4 km) course over old tracks and roads in the Yorkshire Wolds, England on the third Thursday of every March; founded by a group of foxhunters in 1619.

Kirgiz *see* NOVOKIRGHIZ

Kirghiz *see* NOVOKIRGHIZ

Kirgis *see* NOVOKIRGHIZ

kiss the eighth pole A racing term; said of a horse who finishes far behind the field.

kitchen A racing term; a horseman's restaurant located in the backstretch (q.v.) area.

Kladrub *see* KLADRUBER

Kladruber Also known as Kladrub; a Czechoslovakian warmblood developed in 1572 at the Royal Stud in Kladruby using Andalusian (q.v.) stallions; Neapolitan blood was periodically used and, in the 1920s, Shagya Arabian (q.v.); breeding is strictly controlled; historically used as a carriage horse and stood at an average height of 18 hands; recent breeding has resulted in a more active horse standing 16.2 to 17 hands which is still used for harness work, but also for riding, particularly dressage; is black or gray in color and is similar in appearance to the Andalusian from which it derived.

Klepper A native pony breed believed to have descended from native Latvian and Estonian mares crossed with Norfolk Roadster (q.v.); stands 13 to 15 hands, possess great strength and endurance, and has a good trot; instrumental in development of the Toric (q.v.).

klibber Also known as kelshie or kelsie; a wooden saddle specifically designed for use on Shetland Ponies (q.v.).

Kluge Hans *see* HANS, KLUGE

Knabstrup Also known as Danish Spotted Horse or Knabstruper; a Danish horse breed which traces back to a spotted mare called Flaebehoppen, who in 1808 was put to a Frederiksborg (q.v.) stallion and founded a line of spotted, lighter-built horses argued by some to be a type rather than a true breed; stands about 15.3 hands, with spotted Appaloosa (q.v.) patterns on a roan body; used predominantly for circus; the current breeding accent is on coat pattern rather than conformation.

Knabstruper *see* KNABSTRUP

knacker Also known as horse knacker; a British term; one who buys and slaughters old and/or worn out horses for pet food rather than human consumption.

knackery Also known as knacker's yard; a British term; a horse slaughter yard.

knacker's yard *see* KNACKERY

knee The name, incorrectly applied, to the carpus (q.v.) of the horse; this joint actually corresponds to the human wrist.

knee block *see* KNEE ROLL

knee boot A coaching term; the apron sometimes attached to the dashboard of a horse-drawn vehicle; is generally stored rolled and unrolled and pulled up over the passenger's or driver's legs in poor weather.

knee boots *see* KNEE CAPS NO. 1.

knee caps (1) Also known as knee boots, knee protectors, or knee pads; a protective covering for the horse's knees providing support and/or protection while eventing, jumping, breeding, or shipping; may be made of felt, neoprene, or leather. (2) *see* KNEE GUARDS. (3) *see* PATELLA

knee guards Also known as knee caps; a padded full-front, leather covering for the polo player's knee; used to protect the knee from bruises and abrasions resulting from impact with other riders, horses, and mallets (q.v.); buckles behind the knee.

knee-narrow conformation *see* MEDIAL DEVIATION OF THE CARPUS JOINTS

knee pad *see* KNEE CAPS NO. 1

knee protectors *see* KNEE CAPS NO. 1

knee roll Also known as knee block; a pad of varying length or thickness attached to the underside of the saddle-flap (q.v.) at about knee level; provides the rider with improved grip and security in the saddle.

knees and hocks to the ground Also known as well to the ground or near to the ground; a British term; said of a horse having short cannon bones (q.v.).

knees narrow *see* MEDIAL DEVIATION OF THE CARPUS JOINTS

knee splint One of four types of splints (q.v.); affects the nerve-packed joint capsule between the tops of the splint and cannon bones; the most serious of the splints, usually appearing as a small, but supersensitive bump coupled with marked lameness.

knee sprung *see* FORWARD DEVIATION OF THE CARPAL JOINTS

knees wide *see* LATERAL DEVIATION OF THE CARPAL JOINTS

knifeboard A coaching term; a roof-top seat on some coaches run in London, England; accommodated three passengers; made the coach top-heavy and was, therefore, not favored.

Knifeboard Bus A horse-drawn bus used in London, England in the middle 19th century; had outside, roof-top passenger seating back-to-back on long benches reached by steps located at the rear of the bus; superceded by the Garden-seat Bus (q.v.).

knobber *see* BROCKET

knobbler *see* BROCKET

knocked-down shoe *see* FEATHER-EDGED SHOE

knocker Also known as Collier's horse; a horse trader's term; a horse with cow hocks (q.v.) and/or sickle hocks (q.v.).

knock in A polo term; to initiate play by hitting the polo ball onto the field from the back or sidelines; different than throw-in (q.v.).

knock knees *see* MEDIAL DEVIATION OF THE CARPAL JOINTS

knot head A disparaging term; a problem horse, one who is unintelligent, or potentially a threat to himself or his rider.

knots *see* SIDEBONES

knuckling at the fetlock *see* KNUCKLING OVER

knuckling of fetlock *see* KNUCKLING OVER

knuckling over Also known as overshot fetlock, knuckling of fetlock, knuckling over at the fetlock, or knuckling at the fetlock; a condition in which the fetlock joints, fore and hind, are slightly flexed forward, instead of remaining extended, in the resting horse or collapse forward when it in action; commonly due to a) thickening and contraction of the tendons or ligaments behind the cannon bone or as due to age or injury or b) chronic foot lameness, such as ringbone (q.v.), navicular, etc; in newly born foals, the condition generally disappears as the foal gains control of his muscles and the joints they activate.

knuckling over at the fetlock *see* KNUCKLING OVER

Kocklani *see* ASSIL

Koheil *see* ASSIL

Kohuail *see* ASSIL

Konik A Polish pony breed; descended from the Tarpan (q.v.), which it closely resembles, refined by infusions of Arab (q.v.) blood; is hardy, willing, frugal, has great endurance and power for its size, is long lived, extremely resistant to hunger and cold, stands 12 to 13.3 hands, may have a dun, palomino (with occasional zebra markings [q.v.] on the legs), or bay coat, has a slightly heavy head, long mane and tail, and a short, straight back; bred selectively at two state studs in Popielno and Jezewice; is similar to the Hucul (q.v.); several native breeds are referred to generically as Konik meaning small horse, with each breed having its own name, e.g. the Bilgoraj Konik (q.v.) and Mierzyn (q.v.).

Kornokoff iron *see* OFFSET STIRRUP

Kossiak A breeding herd of Russian Steppe Horses (q.v.).

KryoKinetics Associates, Inc. A United States company which developed a method of permanently identifying horses using an unalterable freeze marking (q.v.) system known as the international Alpha System; developed in the 1960s at Washington State University, the system uses a series of six to eight (always eight in the United States and in most European countries) angles and alpha-symbols to identify the breed, state or country of registration, year of birth, and breed registration or state number; all wild burros (q.v.) and horses (q.v.) under the protection of the United States government who are given up for adoption, are registered using this technique; many breed associations including the Thoroughbred (q.v.), Arab (q.v.), Saddlebred (q.v.), Standardbred (q.v.), Morgan (q.v.), Quarter Horse (q.v.), etc., also endorse use of this system.

Kuhailan *see* ASSIL

kumel *see* KENNEL NO. 1

kumiss Fermented mare's or camel's milk used as a drink by the Tartar nomads of Asia.

kür exercises Also known as freestyle exercise; a vaulting term; any optional exercise performed by the vaulter (q.v.), of which there are more than 250 types.

kür program A vaulting term; an event consisting of kür exercises (q.v.).

Kustanair Also known as Russian Steppe Horse; an ancient oriental breed from Kazakhstan; now evolved into two distinct types: one which is light and elegant, having been crossed with Thoroughbred (q.v.), and the other more solid, resulting from Orlov (q.v.) and Don (q.v.) crosses; stands 14 to 15.1 hands, has a solid-colored coat, long, well-muscled legs, and a light head; used for riding and light draft.

Ku Wong *see* LEGEND OF THE EIGHT HORSES

kyang *see* KIANG

L

labor birth *see* PARTURITION

labored A dressage term; the horse's gait or movement when executed with tremendous effort.

lace An ornate braid used in the interiors of some horse-drawn vehicles as a hand-hold for travelers.

laced reins Leather reins (q.v.) the outer edges of which are laced with ⅛ inch (3 mm) wide leather strands; are easy to grip particularly when wet.

lacing *see* ROPE WALKING

laceration Any injury that penetrates the skin; includes superficial laceration (q.v.) and deep laceration (q.v.).

lacking impulsion Said of a horse who lacks sufficient energy to move forward at a regular gait or pace.

lacking collection Said of a horse who performs a movement with insufficient collecting.

lacking rhythm Said of a horse whose gait, pace, or movement is irregular and uneven.

lactate To secrete milk from the mammary glands.

lactating mare Any mare producing milk; generally has a foal at foot.

lactation (1) The secretion of milk; a mare may produce 30 gallons (13.6 liters) per day. (2) The period during which the mare produces milk.

lactational anestrus The period of sexual inactivity in the nursing mare during which there is an absence of observable heat (q.v.) or acceptance of the stallion.

lactic acid A by-product of the breakdown of stored carbohydrates; occurs in excess when there is insufficient oxygen supply to the cells, especially muscle cells as during strenuous exercise; an increase in lactic acid may result in muscle fatigue, inflammation, pain, and, in severe cases, azoturia (q.v.).

lactic acidosis A condition resulting from excess lactic acid (q.v.) circulating in the bloodstream; a common result of overexertion and the source of stiffness following exercise.

lad *see* GROOM NO. 2

Lady Suffolk Sulky An American, two-wheeled, metal-framed, horse-drawn exercise cart; named after the famous trotting mare Lady Suffolk.

Lady's Basket Phaeton *see* BASKET PHAETON

Lady's Chaise A low, two-wheeled, hooded, horse-drawn vehicle of the Chaise (q.v.) type; had forward-facing seats and easy access thus being suitable for a lady; originated in France.

Lady's Phaeton *see* PARK PHAETON

large standard donkey A donkey (q.v.) standing 48 to 56 inches (1.2–1.4 m) tall.

lame Said of the horse when his ability to perform is in some way impaired due to disease or injury of the bone, tendon, ligament, muscle, or other tissues or structures in one or more of the limbs; impairment may change gait or stance and may be accompanied by pain.

lame hand Also known as spoon; an obsolete driving term; a poor coachman.

lameness *see* LAME

lamina The singular of laminae (q.v.).

laminae Hoof membrane layers; contain from 500 to 600 (depending on the size of the hoof) fine, leaf-like projections and tubules which originate on the inside of the hoof wall at the coronary cushion and extend to the lower edge of the pedal bone (q.v.); bind the hoof wall to the pedal bone; of two types: (a) sensitive laminae (q.v.) which contain blood vessels and cover the external surface of the pedal bone and the lateral cartilages, interlocking with the insensitive laminae (q.v.) and (b) insensitive laminae which originate in the hoof wall and do not contain a blood supply.

laminitic condition *see* LAMINITIS

laminitic rings *see* HOOF RINGS

laminitis Also known as fever in the feet and laminitic condition; a painful inflammation of the sensitive laminae (q.v.) precipitated by any number of factors including (a) excessive ingestion of grain, lush pasture, and/or cold water, (b) allergic reaction to the proteins in highly concentrated foods, (c) retained placenta at parturition, (d) overuse on hard surfaces, (e) standing for long periods during transport or recovery from injury, or (f) obesity; characterized by heat and pain at the coronary band, a pounding digital pulse, muscular trembling, accumulation of blood in the laminae, increased systolic pressure, sweating, and uniform tenderness in the feet; may occur in the forefeet, all four feet, or very occasionally, only the hind feet; broadly classified as acute laminitis (q.v.), subacute laminitis (q.v.), or chronic laminitis (q.v.), and may result in founder (q.v.).

lampas Also known as lampers or palatitis; a condition, not a disease, in which the hard palate (q.v.) becomes inflamed; occurs in young horses during eruption of the permanent incisors (q.v.) and in horses of any age as a result of stomatis (q.v.); is self-limiting and requires no treatment.

lampers *see* LAMPAS

lancer bit A plain-cheek curb bit (q.v.) with two vertical slots in the lower end of the cheekpieces (q.v.); may be used with one or two reins.

Landais A pony breed indigenous to the Landes region of southeastern France; thought to have derived from the Tarpan (q.v.) crossed with Arab (q.v.) as early as AD 732, and Welsh (q.v.) blood, after 1970; stands 11.1 to 13 hands and may have a brown, black, bay, or chestnut coat; has a small head, short, pointed ears, straight profile, a long neck that is thick at the base, short back, hard hooves, and a thick and silky mane and tail; is independent, hardy, an easy keeper, and resistant to harsh weather conditions; used for riding and light draft.

Landau Also known as Sociable Landau; a four-wheeled, open or semi-open horse-drawn carriage designed and first used in the late 16th century in Landau, Bavaria from which the name derived; usually had two half-hoods made of harness leather which, when necessary, could be brought together to form an enclosed compartment; had opposite cross seats for four passengers seated vis-à-vis (q.v.); evolved into two primary types: (a) square roofed with angular bodywork and (b) more elegant rounded or canoe-shaped; both were hung on cee springs, but later on sideways elliptical and semi-elliptical springs or a combination of both; usually drawn by a pair of horses in pole gear (q.v.), although a few smaller types were pulled by a single horse in shafts; most were driven from a box seat, with the larger versions postillion (q.v.) controlled; varieties include the Landau Barouche (q.v.) and the Landaulette (q.v.).

Landau Barouche Also known as Barouche Landau; a horse-drawn vehicle of the Barouche (q.v.) type; popular particularly in England from the 18th through the early 19th century on; had a higher than average box seat (q.v.), a rumble seat for two grooms, and was generally amateur driven to a four-in-hand team.

Landau Grand Daumont A postillion-driven Landau (q.v.) with outriders; named for the French nobleman, Duc d'Aumont.

Landaulette Also known as Demi-Landau; a coupé version of the Landau (q.v.); a four-wheeled, horse-drawn carriage seating two forward-facing passengers with the rear protected by a falling hood (q.v.); drawn by either a single horse in shafts or a pair in pole gear (q.v.); hung on sideways-elliptical and semi-elliptical springs; named for the city of Landau, Bavaria where the Landau was first used.

Landau Sleigh An American Sleigh with a Landau-shaped body; passengers entered through small doors between two front-facing seats; driven from a high front box.

Landau Wagonette A four-wheel horse-drawn vehicle of the Wagonette (q.v.) type; had a leather hood which opened longitudinally to lie back towards the sides of the road; ultimately became known as a Lonsdale Wagonette.

landing (1) A vaulting term; that part of the exercise following the vaulter's (q.v.) dismount from the horse to land standing on the ground. (2) A jumping term; the contact made by a horse with the ground on the far side of an obstacle (q.v.).

landing side The far side of any obstacle (q.v.) onto which a horse lands after clearing the obstacle.

lane creeper *see* NEW FOREST PONY

Landship *see* BARCO-DE-TIERRA

Landseer, Sir Edwin (1802–1873) A popular Victorian artist specializing in animal, including horse, portraits.

lap-and-tap (1) A Western roping competition; a race run without using a starting gate. (2) A steer wrestling and calf roping term; a timed competition in which a mounted rider rides after a calf that has not been given a head start, attempts to lasso it using a lariat (q.v.), then ties the lasso off on the saddle horn to prevent the calf from moving forward (if the calf is lassoed), dismounts quickly, and ties the calf's three legs together with a piggin' string (q.v.).

lapped on A harness racing term; said of a horse whose nose is at least opposite the hindquarters of the horse ahead of it at the finish.

lapping traces *see* LAP TRACES

lap traces Also known as lapping traces; a driving/coaching term; to cross the traces (q.v.) of a four-in-hand team to keep the leaders together and to keep the inside traces away from the horse's sides to reduce friction; the trace of one leader crossing over to the other and returning to its own bar.

large colon The section of the large intestine located between the cecum and small colon where, together with the cecum, digestion and absorption occur; in the horse, measures 8 to 18 inches (20–46 cm) in diameter and 10 to 12 feet (3–3.6 m) long.

large metacarpal *see* CANNON BONE

large metacarpal bone *see* CANNON BONE

large-mouthed stomach worm Also known as *Draschia megastoma*; a species of roundworm (q.v.) parasitic to the horse worldwide; adult worms are whitish, 10 to 13 mm (approx. fi inch) long and have an indirect life cycle, with either the housefly or the stable fly necessary for the transmission of the stomach worm to the horse; larvae of the worm are passed in the feces and are ingested by the fly maggots that develop in manure, stomach worm larvae develop within the maggots and become infective at about the time the adult fly emerges from its pupa; the infective larvae are deposited as the flies feed on the horse's lips, nostrils and/or flesh wounds; the horse become infected internally if he licks and swallows these larvae, which then mature in the stomach; horses may also become infected by ingesting contaminated feed or water; larvae deposited on wounds do not complete their development to adult stage, instead remaining in the wound area where they cause cutaneous habronemiasis (q.v.); adult worms are of little significance, but the larvae that infect the tissues around the eyes and in wound areas may cause annoyance and disfigurement; the larvae also provoke formation of tumor-like growths in the stomach wall, which may rupture and block passage of food from the stomach or cause gastritis, thirst, colic, and pica.

large roundworm Also known as equine ascarid or *Parascaris equorum*; the largest and most common of the roundworms (q.v.) parasitic to the horse; a stout, whitish worm, the female may reach 20 inches (50 cm) in length; heavy infestations may result in pica, colic (q.v.) or unthriftiness or, in significant cases, partial intestinal blockage; the larvae, which migrate to the horse's lungs after hatching in the stomach, may cause catarrhal bronchitis or bronchial-pneumonia; immunity to the worms generally develops at about 18 months; infective eggs may survive for years in contaminated soil.

large strongyle Also known as bloodworm, redworm, palisade worm, or sclerostome; a class of parasitic roundworm affecting all ages of horse; of three different species: *Strongylus vulgaris*, up to 1 inch (25 mm), *Strongylus edentatus*, up to 1¾ inches (45 mm), and *Strongylus equinus*, up to 2 inches (50 mm); the most destructive of all equine internal parasites; have a six-month life cycle; the eggs, laid in the large intestine, are passed in the feces; the infective larvae live on the grass, then, when ingested, travel to the large intestine where they burrow into the gut wall and migrate through the body where they may be found in the liver, peri-renal tissues, flanks, pancreas, and cranial artery; can permanently damage intestinal blood vessels and walls resulting in lameness, verminous colic (q.v.), hemorrhage, and/or death; eggs may live outside the horse on pasture for a considerable time and are resistant to low temperatures; mixed infections of large and small strongyles are the rule.

lariat Also known as lasso, reata (Sp), or rope; a long, coiled, rawhide, hemp (common through the 1970s), horsehair, or polyethylene rope with a honda (q.v.) on one end; used for catching horses, cattle or other animals; from a contraction of the Spanish *el lazo* which became lasso and *la reata* from *reatar* (to bind again) which became riata and ultimately lariat; available in left- and right-hand types.

lariat neck ring Also known as neck ring; a relatively rigid circle of rope placed around the base of the horse's neck used by the rider to turn a trained horse without the aid of a bit or reins.

lark A hunting term; said of members of the field who jump fences unnecessarily, as when the hounds (q.v.) are not running or on the return from the hunt.

larva Dependent on the type of insect may also be known as worm, grub, or caterpillar; the stage which follows the egg in the life cycle of an insect.

larvae More than one larva (q.v.).

laryngeal Relating to or used on the voice box.

laryngeal hemiplegia Also known as roaring or whistling; a disease of the larynx (q.v.) caused by partial or total paralysis of the nerves enervating the muscles which elevate the arytenoid cartilages and open and close the larynx; affected horses make an abnormal inspiratory noise, typically a whistle or roar when exercising; in 90 percent of the cases, the left side of the larynx remains paralyzed; may be surgically corrected with a laryngoplasty (q.v.).

laryngeal ventriculotomy Also known as ventricle stripping or Hobday; a surgical operation performed on the larynx to alleviate roaring (q.v.); the mucosal lining of the afflicted laryngeal saccule, usually the left, is stripped and allowed to heal as an open wound, a process that takes about 3 to 5 weeks; the horse must be stalled for 2 to 2½ months during recovery; if surgery is performed soon after the horse is diagnosed as a roarer (q.v.), chances of recovery are approximately 70 percent; named for the veterinary surgeon who originated the operation, Sir Frederick Hobday (q.v.).

laryngoplasty Also known as tie-back surgery; a surgical procedure performed on the larynx (q.v.) to correct laryngeal hemiplegia (q.v.) in which a permanent suture is inserted through the arytenoid cartilage (q.v.) to hold it out of the airway and allow the horse to breath freely.

larynx Also known as voice box; the organ found in the upper respiratory tract at the back of the lower jawbone; fits in a small hole in the soft palate to form an airtight, food-tight seal; functions to keep unwanted substances out of the airway and to produce voice; equivalent to the human Adam's apple.

laserpuncture A type of acupuncture (q.v.); stimulation of precise body points along the horse's body meridians (q.v.) using a low-intensity laser beam to control pain, treat internal malfunctions, anesthetize, and reduce stress; 100 percent noninvasive.

lash (1) Also known as point of the whip, whiplash; a silk or braided horse-hair attachment to the whip thong (q.v.) which is in turn connected to the crop (q.v.). (2) To strike out.

lash horse Also known as lash hoss; the trailing horse in a team when driven at length.

lash hoss *see* LASH HORSE

Lasix A drug used to lower blood pressure in horses and treat bleeders (q.v.).

lasso (1) *see* LARIAT. (2) *see* ROPE NO. 3

late Said of the horse; execution after the aids or late execution as a consequence of aids given late by the rider; usually applied to flying changes and transitions.

late behind Also known as late change; said of a horse performing a flying change (q.v.); at the moment of suspension in the canter, the horse changes the lead correctly with the foreleg, the hind leg changing a full or half stride later.

late change *see* LATE BEHIND

late double A racing term; a second daily double (q.v.) offered during the later part of a race program.

lateral (1) Outside, away from the center line of the body, at the side; as in flexion, bend, or suppleness. (2) A dressage term; impurity in the walk or canter, as in a non-straight movement.

lateral aids Any natural aid (q.v.) or artificial aid (q.v.) used in combination on the same side of the horse, i.e. right rein used in conjunction with the right leg.

lateral deviation of the carpal joints Also known as bow legs, carpus varus, bandy legs, or knees wide; a congenital condition of the legs and knees; the feet are closely set and the knees turned out; may be accompanied by a base-narrow (q.v.), toe-in conformation; the term bandy legs (q.v.) may have been coined in the 17th century by a comparison of the legs to a curved stick called a bandy used in the game of hockey.

lateral deviation of the metacarpal bones Also known as offset knees or bench knees; a congenital condition of the cannon bone which is offset to the lateral side and does not follow a straight line from the radius; medial splints (q.v.) are a common result.

lateral flexion The extent and uniformity with which a horse bends his body from head to tail, left or right; a function of muscle suppleness and development.

lateral gait A gait in which the horse's feet on the same side make contact with the ground simultaneously, or nearly simultaneously.

lateral incisors Also known as laterals or second incisors; 4 of the horse's 12 incisor teeth (q.v.) located left and right, top and bottom, on either side of the central incisors (q.v.); appear between 4 to 6 weeks after birth.

lateral movements *see* LATERAL WORK

laterals *see* LATERAL INCISORS

lateral work Also known as lateral movements, work on two-tracks, or side steps; any movement in which the sequence of steps in the walk, trot, or canter remains unchanged, the hind feet do not follow in the path of the forefeet, and the horse moves forward and sideways; the legs involved in the movement cross over in front of those that are on the ground.

lateral wedge shoe A horseshoe thicker on one branch than the other; used to alter the mediolateral foot balance.

lather Also known as soap or proteinaceous sweat; a white, frothy substance composed of fluids containing salts (potassium and sodium) electrolytes, water, and broken-down protein structures emitted from the horse's pores in the process of perspiration; occurs in horses in poor condition and stressed (physically or emotionally) or horse in good condition and heavily stressed.

lathered up Also known as soaping; said of a horse who discharges lather (q.v.).

latigo Either of two leather straps (4 to 5 feet [1.2–1.5 m] long on the near side and 1 to 1½ feet [30–46 cm] long on the off side) attached to the Western saddle rigging to which the cinch is connected by means of a buckle or threading.

Latvian Also known as Latvian Harness Horse; a warmblood descended from the ancient forest horse of northern Europe; the modern breed dates from the 17th century when warmbloods, including the Oldenburg (q.v.), were crossed with native Latvian stock; to add substance, coldblood crosses were also made to such breeds as the Finnish Draught (q.v.) and the Ardennes (q.v.); firmly established as a breed in 1952; an all-purpose draft horse used for harness and under saddle; is strong, has good endurance, a docile and calm attitude, short legs with good bone and some feathering, and stands 15.1 to 16 hands; the coat is generally bay, brown, or chestnut.

Latvian Harness Horse *see* LATVIAN

Latvian Heavy Draft The name by which the Lithuanian Heavy Draft (q.v.) is known when bred in Latvia.

lavage Therapeutic flushing with a large volume of fluid.

lavender roan *see* LILAC ROAN

law (1) A hunting term; said of the huntsman who holds the hounds (q.v.) for a short while before putting them onto the line of the fox (q.v.) to give the fox a sporting chance. (2) A hunting term; in coursing, the start given to the hare before the greyhounds are released.

Lawrence Wagon An American horse-drawn Buggy (q.v.) named for the designer James Lawrence.

lawn clippings Also known as turf grass clippings; the cut remnants of fresh grass (q.v.); may cause colic (q.v.) and, as such, are not generally used as horse feed unless absolutely necessary.

lawn meet A hunting term; any meet of a Hunt (q.v.) held at a private estate or house by invitation of the owner.

Lawton Buggy A horse-drawn vehicle; a Lawton Gig (q.v.) when fitted with a hood.

Lawton Gig A horse-drawn vehicle; a superior type of Liverpool Gig (q.v.) manufactured by the English firm of Lawton during the second half of the 19th century.

lay (1) Also known as lie (Brit); A racing term; said of a jockey who deliberately occupies a running position while waiting to make a strategic move, e.g., "To lay third off the pace." (2) *see* BET NO. 2. (3) The part of the breast collar (q.v.) sewn on top of the breast piece padding to the tug buckle on either side; the pole strap and neck piece tug dees are attached to the lay.

lay off A racing term; to reduce or eliminate one's liability for a bet (q.v.).

lay-up To pull a horse from training to allow it to recuperate from injury or illness, or to rest.

lazy back The back rest of a seat in a horse-drawn vehicle if it can be folded down.

lazy walk A four-beat gait executed in four-time in which the horse drags his toes and lacks engagement, balance, and forward swing of the striding leg.

lead (1) To guide or conduct a horse from one place to another by showing the way; the rider may show the way either on foot or from a mounted position on another horse. (2) *see* LEADING LEG. (3) Also known as dead weight or weight; a racing term; blocks, normally lead, placed in pockets in a lead pad (q.v.) to make up the difference between the actual weight of the jockey and saddle (q.v.) and the weight the horse has been assigned to carry in a race. (4) *see* LEAD LINE

lead bag *see* LEAD PAD

lead bar A coaching term; also known as single bar or splintree; one of two bars hooked on either end to the main bar to which a pair of leaders is attached when put to in front of a pair of wheelers.

lead change *see* CHANGE OF LEAD

leader Also known as lead horse; a driven horse who leads one or more horses to pull a vehicle.

leaders The head team consisting of a pair

of horses harnessed in front of a four-, six-, or eight-horse hitch pulling a vehicle.

lead harness A combination of leather straps by which the lead horses (q.v.) are connected to a vehicle; generally consists of a bridle (q.v.), collar (q.v.), hames (q.v.), tugs or traces (q.v.), back band (q.v.), belly band (q.v.), and breeching (q.v.).

lead horse (1) *see* LEADER. (2) The highest-ranking stallion or mare in a herd.

lead hounds A hunting term; hounds (q.v.) who run in front of the pack when running a fox (q.v.).

leading leg Also known as lead; either of the front legs leading the gait, striking the ground in front, and independent of, the other three at the canter (q.v.) or gallop (q.v.); will either be a right lead (q.v.) or left lead (q.v.).

leading rein A single, long rein (q.v.) by which the bridled horse is guided by a handler walking alongside; attached to either of the bit (q.v.) rings (generally the left) by a quick-release attachment.

leading sire A stallion (q.v.) possessed of premiere qualities including temperament, physical ability, conformation, color, bloodline, etc.

leading stud A breeding facility which produces outstanding stallions.

lead line Also known as lead rope, lead, or halter rope; a leather or webbing strap, chain, or rope, or any combination thereof, attached to the halter and used to lead the horse.

lead pad Also known as lead bag or weight cloth; a racing term; a saddle pad equipped with small pockets designed to carry thin slabs of lead (q.v.); the lead is used to make up the weight difference between a jockey and the saddle and the weight the horse is assigned to carry.

lead pony *see* PONY NO. 3

lead rope *see* LEAD LINE

leak A cutting term; the action of a horse during or after a turn that causes him to move forward towards the cow he is cutting instead of staying back; often results in the horse losing the working advantage (q.v.).

leaky roof circuit A racing term; a geographical grouping of minor racetracks.

lean head Said of the horse's head when the muscles, veins, and bony projections are clearly visible.

lean in *see* FALL IN

lean on the bit Said of an off-balance horse who attempts to balance himself by leaning against the bit for support through the reins and the rider's hands.

leaping head Also known as lower pommel, leaping pommel, or hunting horn; the lower of two padded pommels or horns on the side-saddle (q.v.); used as an emergency grip to prevent the side-saddler's left knee from rising up; is detachable, being screwed into a socket on the side-saddle tree, may be adjusted to fit the size of the rider's leg, and curves outwards over the rider's left thigh; replaced the top pommel which made it difficult and unsafe to jump fences; invented in 1830 by Jules Pellier (q.v.) at which time it revolutionized side-saddle riding and entirely altered the concept of cross-country riding.

leaping pommel *see* LEAPING HEAD

leash *see* LEASH OF FOXES

leash of foxes Also known as leash; a hunting term; three foxes (q.v.).

leather (1) The skin of animals, especially that of cattle, dressed and prepared for use by tanning or similar processes; the best hides for tack come from slow-maturing cattle such as Aberdeen Angus; the slower the growth, the more the hide's substance has a chance to develop and the greater the resulting hide strength. (2) *see* WHIP NO. 1

leathers (1) Also known as stirrup leathers, stirrup straps, or straps; adjustable straps by which the stirrup irons (q.v.) are attached to the English saddle (q.v.) at the bars; historically, made of leather hence the name, but may now be purchased in a variety of synthetic materials and in a variety of lengths and widths. (2) A type of riding breeches (q.v.) made of leather.

leave it A polo term; a call from one team member to another meaning do not touch the ball.

Ledge Wagon A four-wheeled horse-drawn vehicle of the Gypsy Wagon (q.v.) type; had a ledge extending over the top of the wheels which formed a longitudinal seat on either side of the interior.

Leeds Wagon *see* BARREL TOP WAGON

leery An antiquated term; a horse lacking energy and heart when working, the cause being attitudinal, not physical.

left diagonal In trot, the horse's left foreleg and right hind leg moving in unison as a pair.

left half-pass A lateral dressage (q.v.) movement performed free of the track, in which the horse bends uniformly from head to tail in movement to the left; the horse moves forward and to the left on two-tracks (q.v.) with his shoulders slightly in advance of the hindquarters (q.v.); the right legs cross in front of the left.

left-hand course A racing term; a racetrack (q.v.) on which the horses run counter clockwise.

left lead Said of the horse when his left fore and hind legs lead at the canter or gallop.

left rein (1) To move to the left. (2) The rein attached to the near-side bit ring. (3) To use the left rein to communicate direction to the horse.

leg (1) The portion of the horse's fore or hind limb below the knee or hock. (2) Any portion of a tall riding boot between the ankle and the knee; may be lined, unlined, or partially lined and is sometimes cuffed.

leg aids Also known as lower aids; the rider's legs when employed to communicate with the horse, e.g. to produce forward movement and to shift or hold the haunches.

legal catch *see* FAIR CATCH

legal hook A polo term; any hook (q.v.) of an opponent's shot conducted below the level of the withers of an opponent's horse.

leg barring *see* ZEBRA STRIPES

leg brace (1) *see* SURGICAL LEG BRACE. (2) Any brace (q.v.) applied to the horse's legs.

leg 'em up *see* LEG UP NO. 4

Legend of the Eight Horses A 9th-century BC Chinese legend; the Emperor of the Chow Dynasty, full of wanderlust, wanted to travel the world; to do so he collected eight horses: Wah Lau, Luk Yee, Chik Kee, Pak O, Ku Wong, Yu Lung, Du Lee, and Sam Chee, capable of traveling 30,000 li (Chinese miles) in one day; while traveling he climbed the Kun Lun mountains where he encountered a goddess, Si Wong Mu; during his extended visit with her, the Baron of Chu attempted to seize the Emperor's throne; had it not been for the stamina of his eight horses, he would have been unable to rush home to suppress the efforts of the Baron and save his throne.

legging A roping term; said of a roper; to lift a calf's front leg to tip him onto his side in preparation for the tie (q.v.); an alternative move to flanking (q.v.).

leggings Also known as half-chaps or Richmonds (obs); a covering of the rider's legs from below the knee to the ankle worn to protect the leg from abrasion or dirt and to create better grip in the saddle; made of smooth or rough-out leather (q.v.), canvas, or synthetic material, close on the outside of the rider's leg by means of velcro, snaps, zippers, lacing, buckles, or any combination thereof; held down by a strap passing underneath the arch just in front of the boot or shoe heel; worn with paddock boots (q.v.) or shoes.

leg guard *see* FALSE LEG

leg lock A racing term; said of a jockey who hooks an opponent's leg with his leg to slow or impair the performance of the opponent's horse; an illegal maneuver.

leg mange *see* CHORIOPTIC MANGE

leg marking Any white mark on the horse's leg defined by the pattern, pattern location, and the limb marked; the skin under these marks is unpigmented; may be used as a means of identification; includes white spot (q.v.), heel (q.v.), coronet (q.v.), pastern (q.v.), half pastern (q.v.), fetlock (q.v.), sock (q.v.), stocking (q.v.), half stocking (q.v.), and ermine (q.v.) marks.

legs out of the same hole Said of a horse having a very narrow chest; generally such horses will stand base-wide (q.v.).

legume Any species of plant of the legume family, Leguminosae, that bear pod-like fruits which split along two seams, as a pea pod; plants of this family are used for fodder and fertilizer.

legume hay A cut and dried hay made from legumes such as alfalfa (q.v.) and clover (q.v.); a good source of vitamins A, B, and D, and higher in calcium (q.v.), phosphorus (q.v.), nitrogen, and protein (q.v.), but lower in fiber and also richer, generally higher yielding, and more laxative than grass hays (q.v.); contain a higher nitrogen content because the roots of these plants are covered with bacteria known as rhizobia which converts gaseous nitrogen to fixed nitrogen.

leg up (1) Also known as give a leg up; to help a rider to mount a horse by lifting him into the saddle by the following steps: a) the helper stands at the horse's left shoulder facing the haunches; b) the rider faces the saddles standing on his right foot, his left leg bent at the knee; c) the helper supports the left leg with both hands; d) the rider pushes off of his right leg and the helper lifts upward on the rider's left leg simultaneously; e) the rider swings his right leg over the saddle, where he lands in a seated position. (2) A racing term; to increase the speed and stamina of a horse with work. (3) A racing term; a jockey's riding assignment. (4) Also known as leg 'em up; to bring a horse back to fitness following a period of inactivity.

leg-yield A lateral movement performed on two tracks, forward and sideways, in which the horse moves away from the rider's leg applying pressure, e.g. if the rider applies pressure with his off-side (q.v.) leg just behind the girth (q.v.), the horse will move to the near side (q.v.).

Leicester Car A two-wheeled country cart with a forward-facing driver's seat which accommodated two; had two inward-facing seats at the back reached by a rear door and step.

Le Livre de la Chasse A 14th century book by French author Gaston de Foix (q.v.); became the textbook on hunting in France.

Le Manelge Royal A 17th century treatise on horse training written by Antoine de Pluvinel (q.v.) in which he delineated his training method of "gentling" rather than "breaking" horses.

length A racing term; a horizontal unit of measure, 8 or 9 feet (2.4–2.7 m), roughly the distance from the horse's nose to his tail; a unit of measure by which margins between the winning horse and other competing horses are calculated as in fractions or numbers of lengths.

lengthening insufficient A dressage term; said of a horse who does not demonstrate sufficient difference between two paces, e.g., collected to working trot, working trot to extended, etc.

leopard A horse with leopard spotting (q.v.).

leopard marking *see* LEOPARD SPOTTING

leopard spotting Also known as leopard marking; refers to coat color pattern; a white or colored body with an extensive blanket (q.v.), having colored spots on the white which extend over the entire body; spots can vary from a few to several centimeters in diameter; the leopard gene is dominant and rarely skips a generation; of three types: patterned leopard (q.v.), unpatterned leopard (q.v.), and few spotted leopard (q.v.); one of six symmetrical Appaloosa (q.v.) coat color patterns recognized by the Appaloosa Horse Club (q.v.).

lepping *see* SHOW JUMPING

lepping contest *see* SHOW JUMPING

leptospirosis *see* EQUINE LEPTOSPIROSIS

lespedeza Any one of several herbs or shrubs of the genus *Lespedeza*, in the legume family, cultivated as forage or as a soil binder.

lespedeza hay A legume hay (q.v.) made from cut and dried lespedeza (q.v.); contains a digestible protein content ranging from 11.7 percent in a pre-bloom second cut, to 7.5 percent in a full-bloom second cut; drought resistant and grows well in poor soil.

lethal dominant white A dominant gene that produces a white foal with blue or hazel eyes; homozygous foals die in utero and all white horses with the dominant white gene are heterozygotes; when such horses are mated, 25 percent of the embryos will be homozygous.

lethal white syndrome *see* ILEOCOLONIC AGANGLIONOSIS

leucocyte *see* WHITE BLOOD CELL

leukocyte *see* WHITE BLOOD CELL

leucoderma *see* LEUKODERMA

leukoderma Also spelled leucoderma; an acquired, permanent whitening of previously pigmented skin or hair as a result of trauma, as due to poorly fitting tack or bits, cryogenic surgery, etc.; the resulting destruction of pigment cells is permanent and adventitial marks (q.v.) result.

leu-in A hunting term; to put the hounds into a covert (q.v.).

levade A classical air (q.v.); a movement in which the horse's forehand is elevated on deeply bent hind legs, the hocks lowered to 8 to 10 inches (20–25 cm) above the ground; the longer the levade is held, the more difficult it is to perform; the base for the courbette (q.v.).

leve Also spelled levée; a 16th- and 17th-century term; to raise, as in the lance which the knight used when tilting (q.v.).

levée *see* LEVE

level *see* LEVEL PACK

level crossing *see* RAILWAY CROSSING

level mover Said of a horse who moves evenly and in a balanced manner with legs swinging freely and toes pointed forward.

level pack Also known as level; a hunting term; said of a pack of hounds matched in color, size, conformation, and working ability.

lever noseband *see* KINETON NOSEBAND

Lexington One of the greatest American-bred stallions of the 19th century; a champion sire on no fewer than 16 occasions; stigmatized in Britain by being pronounced ineligible for inclusion in the General Stud Book (q.v.)

LHLT *see* LOW HEEL, LONG TOE

liberty Said of a horse who moves freely.

Liberty horse A circus horse who, in a group and without a rider, carries out movements on command.

lie *see* LAY NO. 1

lice (1) More than one louse (q.v.). (2) Also spelled lise or list; a 16th and 17th century French term; the walls or other barriers which enclosed a space established for tilting (q.v.).

lift (1) *see* LIFT HOUNDS. (2) A dressage term; the height to which the horse raises hind legs in the piaffe (q.v.) or passage (q.v.).

lift hounds Also known as lift; a hunting term; said of the huntsman (q.v.) when he takes the hounds (q.v.) off the line of the hunted fox (q.v.) and moves them forward to a location where he believes the fox has run.

ligament A strong band of tissue consisting of fibro-elastic and fibrous types which connect one bone to another, provide support, strengthen the joints, and limit joint range.

light *see* DISMOUNT

light brown Refers to coat color; a shade of brown (q.v.) less red than bay (q.v.) with which it is easily confused.

light harness One of three types of horse show classes for the American Saddlebred (q.v.) in which demonstration of the walk and animated park trot are required.

light horse Any horse, other than a heavy horse or pony, used or suitable for hacking (q.v.) or hunting (q.v.).

light in-hand Said of a bridled horse whose neck and back muscles are relaxed and who accepts the bit.

lightness (1) Said of the horse; the buoyancy of the horse on his feet: lightness of the forehand as a consequence of the horse engaging, and carrying more weight on, his hindquarters. (2) Said of the rider; the degree to which the grip on the reins is relaxed or firm.

light of bone Said of a horse lacking sufficient bone circumference to support his body weight and that of the rider without strain.

light seat The position of the mounted English rider when posting to the trot; the weight is on the thighs rather than on the seat bones.

lilac dun Refers to coat color; a rare variation of dun (q.v.); a lilac or dove-colored body with chocolate points; the skin is light brown or pink and the eyes amber.

lilac roan Also known as lavender roan; refers to coat color; a roan (q.v.) pattern with white hairs uniformly mixed into the coat of a dark or liver chestnut (q.v.); the points and head are dark or liver chestnut with no white hairs.

limb The leg and the structures above it which join it to the trunk of the horse, e.g. forelimb (q.v.) and hind limb (q.v.).

limb mark *see* LIMB MARKING

limb marking Also known as limb mark; any perceptible change in the predominant color of the horse's coat occurring on the leg below the knee or hock; include coronet (q.v.), ermine marks (q.v.), sock (q.v.), stocking (q.v.), or pastern (q.v.).

limited-age event A cutting horse (q.v.) event restricted to horses between the ages of three and six.

limited partnership An agreement of two or more individuals who cooperatively purchase a horse to race, show, or for breeding purposes, the costs and profits of which are distributed according to the agreed terms.

Limousin Also known as Limousin Half-Bred; a heavyweight, half-bred horse indigenous to the Limousin area of France from which the name derived; descended from native mares crossed with Thoroughbred (q.v.), Arab (q.v.), Anglo-Arab (q.v.), and Anglo-Norman (q.v.) stallions; is large boned, stands 16 to 17 hands, and generally has a chestnut or bay coat; of the group Cheval de Selle Français (q.v.) and the regional group Demi-Sang du Centre, as is the Charollais (q.v.).

Limousin Half-Bred *see* LIMOUSIN

linchpin Also spelled lynch pin; a metal or wooden pin passed through a hole in the end of the axle arm beyond the wheel hub to hold the wheel onto the arm.

Lincolnshire Cart A strong, two-wheeled, tipping, horse-drawn farm cart; had an oak frame and removable paneled sides; the wheels were iron-shod and about 3½ inches (8.9 cm) wide.

Lincolnshire Wagon *see* BARREL TOP WAGON

lindell Also known as side pull; a soft latigo leather headstall with a stiff lariat nosepiece to which the reins are attached; used to start young horses or encourage mature horses who overbend to relax and lengthen; may be used in conjunction with a snaffle bit and as a transition to a neck ring (q.v.).

line (1) The ancestors of a horse on the male side by which a blood relationship between horses is defined. (2) The profile of a horse. (3) The direction of travel. (4) *see* LINE OF THE FOX

linear whorl A hair pattern; a whorl (q.v.); a change in direction of hair flow in which two opposing sweeps of hair meet from diametrically opposite directions along a line.

line-back Refers to coat color pattern; said of a horse having a dark dorsal stripe (q.v.) which continues and darkens into the tail; may be black, brown, red, or gold; a primitive mark (q.v.).

line-breeding Mating of horses of common ancestry, several generations removed; presents the same dangers inherent to inbreeding programs, but slightly less intensified.

line drive *see* LONG LINE NO. 1

line firing To insert hot needles and/or pins in a series of vertical lines in a blemish or unsound area (as the legs), as a treatment to hasten and strengthen the reparative process by increasing blood supply.

line gaited Said of a horse who trots with each hind foot following directly in line with its lateral forehoof (q.v.).

line of the ball A polo term; an imaginary line, behind or in front of, a travelling ball; a concept governing traffic on the polo field during play.

line of the fox Also known as line; a hunting term; the scent trail of an animal.

lines (1) *see* LONG LINES NO. 2. (2) *see* REINS NO. 2

linseed Also known as flaxseed; the small, flat and shiny seed of flax (q.v.); has a high protein and fat content; usually fed as a hot or cold mash, jelly, or tea; must be soaked and then boiled to split the seeds as unsoaked seeds are highly poisonous.

linseed meal Also known as linseed oil meal; a high-protein, high-energy concentrate produced from the residue of the linseed (q.v.) following oil extraction; contains 30 to 32 percent protein and from 1 to 5 percent fat; lower in protein quality than soybean meal because it is low in several amino acids and has a low-palatability factor; credited with producing a nice finish on the hair coat.

linseed mash A wet mash made with linseed meal (q.v.) or linseed (q.v.) combined with bran (q.v.) and water used as a feed supplement or poultice; must be fed within 24 hours to avoid spoiling.

linseed oil The oil obtained by pressing the linseed (q.v.); is not used as an equine supplement.

linseed oil meal *see* LINSEED MEAL

L'Instruction du Roy, En l'Exercice de Monter à Cheval A book written in 1625 by Antoine de Pluvinel (q.v.) on the subject of training riding horses.

Lippizzan *see* LIPIZZANER

Lipizzana *see* LIPIZZANER

Lipizzaner Also known as Lippizzan or Lipizzana; an Austrian-bred warmblood named for the village of Lipizza, previously part of northwest Yugoslavia, where Archduke Charles II founded the Imperial Austrian Stud and the breed in 1580; descended from Andalusian (q.v.) stock put to a nucleus of native Karst horses; succeeding generations were crossed with Neapolitan (q.v.), Arab (q.v.), Kladruber (q.v.), and Frederiksborg (q.v.); a sturdy, late developing horse standing 14.2 to 16 hands; born with a dark, black-brown, brown, or mousy-gray coat which gradually lightens to gray or white between the ages of six and ten; has a large head, small ears, crested neck, compact body, and full mane and tail; action is high rather than low and long; used extensively at the Imperial Spanish Riding School of Vienna (q.v.), and is well suited to the airs above the ground (q.v.), pleasure riding, carriage, and light farm work.

lip marking Any colored marking on the lip of the horse.

lips the bars Said of a horse who plays with the bit shanks with his lips when bitted (q.v.).

lip strap Also known as bridle lip strap or curb strap; a narrow leather or nylon strap which holds the curb chain in position and softens the impact of the curb chain on the soft chin groove tissue; buckles onto the bit shanks.

lip tattoo A registration tattoo (q.v.) placed on the inside lip of a horse, as in American race horses.

lise *see* LICE NO. 2

lisk *see* GROIN

list (1) *see* DORSAL STRIPE. (2) *see* LICE NO. 2

listed race A racing term; a sweepstakes (q.v.) race of lower quality than group or graded races (q.v.).

Lithuanian Heavy Draft A Lithuanian coldblood originating in the late 1890s; descended from the local Zhmud (q.v.) put to the Finnish Horse (q.v.) and Swedish Ardennes (q.v.); registration and breeding have been strictly controlled since 1963 with all breeding stallions undergoing rigorous performance tests; is massively built and medium-sized with short, lightly feathered legs and good bone; the neck is quite short, thick, muscular and arched, and the mane full; sickle hocks (q.v.) are common, but the action is free, fast, and attractive; has a quiet temperament, stands 15 to 16 hands, is quite strong, and has enormous powers of traction; the coat is typically chestnut with black, roan, bay, and gray also occurring; used for heavy draft; known as a Latvian Heavy Draft (q.v.) when bred in Latvia.

litter (1) A group of young born to the same mother at the same time, e.g. a litter of puppies or cubs. (2) *see* BEDDING. (3) Also known as horse litter; a wheel-less carriage on shafts supported between either horses or mules in tandem (q.v.) or on the backs of human bearers who support a single passenger in a seated or reclined position; later versions were box-shaped with a semi-open or headed top.

live foal guarantee A provision in a breeding contract which guarantees the owner of the covered mare a live, standing, nursing foal as a result of a purchased covering; generally gives the owner of the mare the right to return to the same stallion in the following season in the event that the mare fails to produce a live foal as a result of the initial covering.

live hunt A hunting term; any hunt in which the hounds pursue the trail or scent left by a live animal; the opposite of a drag hunt (q.v.).

liver (1) A large, reddish-brown glandular organ positioned in the upper right-hand side of the abdominal cavity; divided by fissures into several lobes, secretes bile, and performs various metabolic functions such as controlling erratic swings in blood sugar, fluid, protein, and electrolyte levels and the accumulation of body toxins; when it malfunctions, the body becomes poisoned by its own metabolic toxins and diminishes the appetite and thirst mechanisms. (2) *see* LIVER CHESTNUT

liver chestnut Also known as liver; refers to coat color; one of the darkest chestnut (q.v.) or red shades; the coat consists of a mixture of red and black hairs with similar-colored points.

liver chestnut alazán Refers to coat color; one of the darkest of the red shades; the coat consists of a mixture of red and black hairs with red or dark flaxen points.

liver chestnut tostado Refers to coat color; one of the darkest of the red shades; the coat consists of a mixture of red and black hairs with leg hairs that become progressively lighter towards the hoof.

liver chestnut ruano Refers to coat color; a dark red shade; the coat consists of a mixture of red and black hairs with light flaxen points.

liver fluke Also known as *Fasciola hepatica*; a trematode flatworm parasitic in man, sheep, snails and occasionally horses; roughly leaf-shaped, although considerable variations exist, and about 1 inch (25 mm) long; generally found in the bile ducts of the liver, but is also found in other organs; the amphibious mud snail is the intermediate host; horses become infected when they graze in poorly drained or marshy pastures in common with infected sheep or cattle; may cause abdominal pain, anemia, hepatitis, and poor performance.

Liverpool A jumping obstacle consisting of a small, shallow water hole over which a bar (q.v.) supported by two standards (q.v.) is suspended; the rail and water hole are jumped and scored as a single element.

Liverpool bit A circular-cheeked driving bit with a straight bar mouthpiece smooth on one side and corrugated on the other; has a sliding pivot action; the part of the shank below the mouthpiece is flat and has two rein slots; above the top rein slot is a circle bisected by a perpendicular bar to which the mouthpiece is attached by sliding action.

Liverpool Gig A fully enclosed, square-sided, elegant yet sturdy, horse-drawn vehicle of the Gig (q.v.) type; had no rearward access to the luggage space, but did have a large buck (q.v.) under the cross seat; first made and used in the mid-19th century England, although its use later spread throughout Great Britain.

Liverpool horse Any horse capable of jumping the Grand National course at Aintree (q.v.).

Liverpool Steeplechase, The *see* GRAND NATIONAL STEEPLECHASE

live weight A racing term; the weight of a jockey excluding his tack, as contrasted with dead weight (q.v.).

livery (1) A horse boarded at a facility other than the owner's, for which a fee is paid. (2) The care and feeding of a horse for a set fee. (3) A hunting term; clothing worn by professional members of the Hunt (q.v.). (4) The clothing or 'uniform' worn by coachmen and associated servants employed by titled people, estate owners, etc. (5) *see* STABLE NO. 2

Livery Company Also known as Livery Guild; one of several trade associations in London, England, that sprang from the medieval guilds; concerned with the standards and traditions of work within respective guilds as well as the welfare of the members; now predominantly associated with equestrian-related trades such as saddle and harness makers, farriers, coachbuilders, etc.

Livery Guild *see* LIVERY COMPANY

livery man (1) A British term; one entitled to wear livery (q.v.), especially a freeman of the City of London. (2) Any owner or employee of a livery stable (q.v.).

livery stable (1) A stable where horses and carriages are tended or kept. (2) *see* STABLE NO. 2

livestock Also known as stock; domesticated animals, such as cattle and horses, bred or maintained on a farm for use and/or commercial profit.

Llanero (1) A Venezuelan-bred Criollo (q.v.); a warmblood descended from Spanish stock brought to South America by the Spanish Conquistadors in the 16th century; has a lighter and less solidly built frame than the Argentine Criollo (q.v.), a head similar to a Barb (q.v.) with a rather convex profile, stands approximately 14 hands, and may have a dun, yellow with a dark mane and tail, white, yellow cream, or pinto (q.v.) coat; used for ranch work and riding. (2) Also known as chalán; a cowboy or cowhand from either Venezuela or Columbia.

loaded shoulder Said of the horse's shoulder when excessively thick due to either muscle or fat.

loafer A racing term; a horse who is unwilling to race well without hard urging by the jockey.

loafing hound A hunting term; a hound who leaves the work of hunting to the rest of the pack.

lob A racing term; a cooler (q.v.).

lobbing and sobbing Said of a horse so exhausted following hard work that he is not in full control of his actions or coordination.

lobo dun Refers to coat color; a grullo (q.v.) of the dun (q.v.) color group; the body hair is slate-colored and mixed with black resulting in a darker coat color especially along the top line (q.v.).

local anesthesia An artificially produced, localized insensibility, especially to the sense of pain.

local anesthetic Any substance that deprives feeling or sensation to a specific body area; generally administered by injection.

local contraction of the foot *see* CORONARY CONTRACTION OF THE FOOT

lock (1) Also known as sure thing; a racing term; a guaranteed win, e.g. "That horse has a lock on the race." (2) The amount of turn possible in the forecarriage and front wheels of a horse-drawn vehicle, e.g., "The coach had a quarter distance lock."

lockjaw *see* TETANUS

lock the stable door after the horse is stolen To take belated precautions; dated to the Romans as quoted from Plautus' Asinaria "*Ne post tempus proedoe proesidium parem*" (After the time of plunder one provides protection); English use is found in John Gower's Confessio amatis (1390): "For whan the grete Stiede [steed] is stole, thenne he [Negligence] taketh hiede, and maketh the door fast."

loco (1) To poison with loco weed (q.v.) (2) Crazy.

loco disease *see* LOCOISM

locoism Also known as loco disease; a disease of horses, cattle, and sheep caused by loco weed (q.v.) poisoning; characterized by loss of sense, and ultimately, death.

loco weed Any of various plants of the legume family, genera *Astragalus* and *Oxtropis*, found in the southwestern United States that, when ingested by horses or cattle, produces locoism (q.v.).

lodging rooms A hunting term; the rooms in a hunt kennel (q.v.) where the hounds (q.v.) sleep and are kept.

loft An area in some barns, usually a second floor, where hay is stored.

loin The body part(s) on either side of the vertebral column between the false ribs and the hip bone.

loin cloth *see* QUARTER SHEET

loin rug *see* QUARTER SHEET

loins More than one loin (q.v.).

Lokai A warmblood of mixed ancestry which originated in southern Tadzhikistan on the western side of the Pamir mountain range; for many centuries local stock was crossed with Karabair (q.v.), Arab (q.v.), and Iomud blood by the Lokai people, from which the name derived; from the 16th century, stock was improved with crosses to Akhal-Teké (q.v.), Karabair, and Arab blood; stands 14 to 14.2 hands, has a long neck, short back, sloping croup, notably tough hooves, and a chestnut coat with golden highlights, although bay, or gray and rarely black or dun also occur; used for riding, packing, and mounted competitive sports.

lolls the cricket A Western term; said of the horse when he plays with the bit roller (q.v.) with his tongue.

London Cart Horse Parade Society An English organization founded in London in 1890 to improve the general condition and treatment of cart horses.

London color A light shade of brown-tanned leather, from which saddlery is made.

London International *see* ROYAL INTERNATIONAL HORSE SHOW

London tan A slightly darker shade of brown tanned leather than London color (q.v.); used to make saddlery.

London Van Horse Parade Society A British organization founded in 1904 to improve the general condition and treatment of van and light draft horses used for commercial purposes.

Lone Region That area of the United States encompassing the Great Basin: southeastern Oregon, southwest Idaho, and north and northeastern Nevada.

long *see* LONG ON A COW

long and low A dressage term; carriage in which the horse lowers and stretches out his head and neck, reaching forward and downward into a longer rein; this is the carriage called for when "letting the horse gradually take the reins out the hands" is required in a test.

Long Car A horse-drawn vehicle popular in Ireland; coachman-driven from a center seat, had outward facing, longitudinally placed passenger seating.

long-coupled Said of a horse who has more distance between the last rib and the point of the hip than average or preferred.

Long distance ride *see* ENDURANCE RIDE

longe *see* LUNGE

longeing cavesson *see* LUNGEING CAVESSON

longeing whip *see* LUNGE WHIP

longe line *see* LUNGE LINE

longer *see* LUNGER

longe rein *see* LUNGE LINE

longe whip *see* LUNGE WHIP

long in the tooth Said of an old horse.

longitudinal flexion The flexion of the horse's joints in a longitudinal plane, e.g., from front to back.

long line Also known as long rein, line drive, or drive; to drive or move a horse while moving behind or to the side of the horse on foot and using long lines (q.v.) to introduce hand aids, supple the horse, improve impulsion, and teach advanced moves such as piaffe (q.v.); the long lines are attached to either side of the bit or cavesson (q.v.).

long lines Also known as long reins, lines, driving lines, or reins; 39 to 46 foot x 1 inch (12–14 m × 25 mm) long reins used to long line (q.v.) a horse; may be made of leather, natural fiber, or synthetic material with approximately 5 feet (1.5 m) of halyard ending in snap hooks or buckles on one end; with one rein is attached to each bit ring or to either side of the cavesson; the total length allows the long liner (q.v.) the ability to maintain a distance of 6½ to 7½ yards (6–6.4 m) from the horse and to scribe circles 16.4 to 22 yards (15–20 m) in diameter.

long liner One who drives a horse between two long lines (q.v.).

long on a cow Also known as long; a cutting term; said of a horse who moves ahead of the cow being worked instead of remaining across from its shoulder or head; may result in the cow gaining the working advantage (q.v.) and cutting back to the herd.

long pastern Also known as P1, PI, first phalanx, os suffranginis, or long pastern bone; the top one of three bones comprising the lower part of the horse's leg and part of the foot.

long pastern bone *see* LONG PASTERN

long rein *see* LONG LINE

long reins *see* LONG LINES

longset A method of hitching six horses to pull a vehicle uphill; the two leaders are driven by the postillion (q.v.) and the remaining four by the coachman.

Long-Shafted Cart *see* BREAKING CART

longshot A racing term; an entry not well regarded by bettors (q.v.); may result in the possibility of longer odds and higher payoffs.

long side One of two long sides of a rectangular arena or manège (q.v.).

Long Wagon Also known as Flying Wagon, Stage Wagon, Whirlicote, or Medieval Long Wagon; a horse-drawn, dead-axle traveling carriage used throughout Britain and Europe in the 13th and 14th centuries; was headed with rich embroidery work and had inner seats slung on the hammock principle; drawn by teams of six or more postillion-controlled horses.

Lonsdale Wagonette A luxurious horse-drawn vehicle of the Wagonette (q.v.) type; had a low-hung, rounded body, and falling hood; introduced in 1893 by the fifth Earl of Lonsdale after whom it was named; previously known as Landau Wagonette.

look A cutting term; the expression of the horse when facing a cow.

looker An antiquated British term; one who, for a reward or fee, watches horses or cattle grazing on unfarmed marsh land surrounded by dykes to ensure their well-being.

look for a hole in the fence A racing term; said of a horse who would rather run back to the barn than continue running in a race; a quitter.

look of eagles A racing term; said of a good horse with a proud look in his eyes, as though he knows he is good.

loop on two-tracks A dressage term; said of a horse when returning to the track (as after completing a half-circle or loop up one side of the arena), who moves sideways in a half-pass (q.v.) or leg-yield (q.v.) instead of the hind legs following the fore.

loops not equal A dressage term; said of parts of a serpentine (q.v.) scribed in the arena by the horse under saddle that are not equal in size or shape; only used when the rider performs movements of three or more loops.

loose box *see* STALL

loose jump *see* JUMP FREE

loose mount Said of a horse who continues to race or jump a course after losing his rider.

loose rein (1) Reins that have been dropped by the rider to yield extra length to allow slack and eliminate contact between the rider's/driver's hands and the bit. (2) A cutting term; said of the rider in competition; to drop the reins to allow the horse to work an isolated cow; points are deducted from the score if the reins are used to guide the horse during this part of the contest.

loose-ring A cheekpiece (q.v.); a variably sized ring passed through a hole in the end of the bit mouthpiece in a manner that allows movement of the mouthpiece on the bit cheekpieces.

loose-ring snaffle A snaffle bit (q.v.) having ring cheeks which pass through the ends of the mouthpiece so as to allow movement of the mouthpiece.

loose seat The position assumed by the English rider in the saddle; the thighs and knees are relaxed, neither tense or gripping; the rider stays in the saddle by balance rather than grip.

lope A smooth, slow, three-beat gait; the Western equivalent of the canter (q.v.), compared to which it is less collected.

lop ears Said of the horse's ears when they flop over or hang down in a pendulous fashion; does not affect hearing and may be surgically corrected; a conformation defect.

lop neck *see* BROKEN CREST

loriner One who makes the metal parts of saddle and harness tack such as bits (q.v.), curb chains (q.v.), and stirrup irons (q.v.).

Loriners Company, The A livery company (q.v.) organized in England sometime around 1245 to represent loriners (q.v.).

Lorrie *see* LORRY

Lorry Also known as Lurry and spelled Lorrie; any open, horse-drawn dray, truck, or trolley used for general hauling and delivery; common in the country districts of Northern England; frequently unsprung with equirotal or near equirotal wheels, and drawn by a single horse in shafts, or more frequently by teams of chain horses which could pull up to 8 tons; driven from the fore-end of the platform in a standing position.

Los Caballos de Paso Fino *see* PASO FINO

lose a cow A cutting term; said of a cutter when the cow being worked returns to the herd before he has had the opportunity to quit it; in cutting horse competitions, a five-point penalty.

losing flesh Said of a horse losing weight, as due to parasite infestation, bad teeth, insufficient feed or water, etc.

lose the working advantage A cutting term; said of the horse when he loses the attention of the cow being worked; the cow controls the actions of the horse instead of the horse holding and controlling the movements of the cow.

lost a horseshoe 18th century German slang; said of a seduced girl (Sie hat ein Hufeisen verloren).

lost shoes An obsolete British term; said of an exhausted horse.

lot of horse in a little room A British term; a short-coupled (q.v.), short, compact horse having good bone.

lots of color Refers to coat color; said of an Appaloosa (q.v.) who shows a lot of white.

louse Also known as horse louse; an external, biting and sucking parasite; demonstrates a high degree of host specificity and two different species may infest the horse: the biting louse (q.v.) and the sucking louse (q.v.); although less than 1⁄10 inch (2.5 mm) in length, are visible to the naked eye as small or light-gray objects; may be detected by inspecting the mane, root of the tail, inside of the thighs, or on the underside of the saddle blanket following exercise; is not communicable to humans.

low airs Normalized posture or movements of the horse performed near the ground; include the passage (q.v.), piaffe (q.v.), gallopade, change of hands (q.v.), volte (q.v.), demi-volte (q.v.), passade (q.v.), pirouette (q.v.), and terre à terre (q.v.).

low bow One of three classifications of bowed tendon (q.v.) identified on the basis of location; any true physiological damage to the tendon or tendon sheath, most commonly to the superficial flexor tendon of the foreleg; specifically, tearing or breaking of one or more fibers of the lower third of the tendon; may be precipitated by fatigue, deep going, uneven terrain, improper shoeing, obesity, excessively tight-fitting running bandages or boots, work on slippery surfaces, long, weak pasterns (q.v.), sudden changes in stress loads, low heel angles, and long toes; symptoms may include diffuse swelling over the tendon area, heat, and pain; lameness may or may not be present.

Lowe Figure System *see* BRUCE LOWE FIGURE SYSTEM

lower aids *see* LEG AIDS

lower-cheek snaffle A half-cheek snaffle bit (q.v.) consisting of a straight or jointed mouthpiece (q.v.) fitted at either end with fixed rings and a straight- or spoon-shaped (wider and slightly curved toward the horse's jaw at the top) arm attached to the rings below the mouthpiece on the mouth-side of the bit; used on driving horses to prevent the bit from running through the horse's mouth if he runs sideways or refuses to turn; acts on the corners and sides of the mouth and the lips.

lower ground A 19th century coaching term; the last part of the road or journey.

lower jaw Also known as coronoid process or mandible; one of two jawbones in the horse's mouth; composed of a single bone firmly attached to other face bones.

lower pommel *see* LEAPING HEAD

low heel, long toe Also known by the acronym LHLT; a hoof condition in which the heels are excessively low due to trimming, wear, or underrun growth and the toe often long, as in a flare; may precipitate navicular disease (q.v.).

low ringbone A type of ringbone (q.v.); a bony growth developing inside the hoof in the joint connecting the short pastern (q.v.) and pedal bone (q.v.); not to be confused with sidebone (q.v.) which is a different condition.

low scenting hounds A hunting term; said of hounds (q.v.) who follow the line of the fox (q.v.) with their noses to the ground; are especially useful when the scent is light.

Lowther bit *see* ARKWRIGHT BIT

Lowther riding bit *see* ARKWRIGHT BIT

low wither Said of a horse whose withers (q.v.) are lower than his croup.

lozenge *see* BIT GUARD

lucerne *see* ALFALFA

lug (1) *see* LUGGER. (2) A racing term; said of a tiring horse who bears in or out, failing to maintain a straight course.

lugger Also known as lug; a horse who leans on the bit when ridden or driven.

lug in *see* BEAR IN

lug out *see* BEAR OUT

Luk Yee *see* LEGEND OF THE EIGHT HORSES

lumbar muscles The muscles of the loins

adjoining the lumbar vertebrae.

lunch box *see* IMPERIAL

lung Also known as pipe; either of two sac-like respiratory organs located in each thoracic cavity (q.v.).

lunge Also known as roping, horse in-hand, and spelled longe; to exercise or train the horse on a single long line (q.v.) attached to the bridle, lungeing cavesson (q.v.) or halter (q.v.) in a circle around the trainer on the flat or over jumps.

lungeing cavesson Also known as breaking cavesson, breaking head collar, or training cavesson and spelled longeing cavesson; a specially designed halter or head collar with an adjustable throat latch (q.v.), noseband (q.v.), and headpiece to which long lines (q.v.) or a lunge line (q.v.) may be attached; generally has three ring attachments on the noseband, one at each side and one on the center front, and two on the brow band, one on each side; used to train a horse from the ground, a long line (q.v.) may be attached to the center ring to permit lungeing either to left or right without changing gear; the side and brow rings may be used in conjunction with two long reins (q.v.) to drive or long line (q.v.) the horse.

lunge circle The track scribed by the horse as he is worked around the lunger (q.v.); in vaulting (q.v.) this circle must be at least 42 feet (13 m) in diameter.

lunge line Also known as lunge rein, and spelled longe line; a cotton or synthetic rope or piece of webbing 20 to 30 feet (6–9 m) long and approximately 1 inch (25 mm) wide, attached to the halter, bridle, or lungeing cavesson (q.v.) by a hook and snap or buckle; used to train or exercise the horse from the ground; customarily the horse is worked in a circle.

lunger Also spelled longer; one who lunges (q.v.) a horse.

lunge rein *see* LUNGE LINE

lunge whip Also spelled longe whip or longeing whip; a whip (q.v.) approximately 4 feet (1.2 m) long, with a lash at least 4.4 yards (4 m) long, and a short handle which enables the lunger (q.v.) to reach the horse as much as 6½ yards (6 m) away while working him in a circle.

lung hemorrhage *see* EXERCISE-INDUCED PULMONARY HEMORRHAGE

lungworm An internal parasite, *Dictyocaulus arnfieldi*, which lives in the air passages of the lungs (q.v.); the male worm may reach approximately 1 inch (25 mm) and the female 2 inches (50 mm) in length; has a complete life cycle in the horse; may be found in many countries throughout the world, particularly those with temperate climates; may cause bronchitis, pneumonia, or both.

lungworm infection An infection of the lower respiratory track caused by the internal parasite, *Dictyocaulus arnfieldi*; symptoms include coughing, increased respiratory rate, bronchitis or pneumonia or both; the clinical signs of infection in foals and donkeys, the latter being prone to carry large populations, are few, while in older horses, unthriftiness is common; it is advisable to treat horses pasturing with donkeys for this parasite.

Lurry *see* LORRY

Lusitano Also known as Iberian Horse, Pure Blood Lusitano, Cavalo de Pura Raca Lusitano or by the acronym PSL; a Portuguese breed believed to share bloodstock origins with the Andalusian (q.v.) in the Iberian Horse (q.v.); evolved in the rugged and hilly areas of the Iberian peninsula (comprised of Spain, where they call the breed the Pure Spanish Horse [q.v.] or Andalusian [q.v.], and Portugal, where the breed is known as the Pure Blood Lusitano); fighting for survival over this rough terrain led to the development of a strong, thick, arched, well-set-on neck, powerfully built, short-coupled and lean body with substantial depth of girth; the hooves are small and rounded and the legs positioned well under the body; the hock action and impulsion are strong; has a natural ability for collection; stands 15.2 to 16.2 hands, 80 percent have a gray or white coat, 15 percent are bay, and less than 5 percent are black, dun or chestnut; the profile is straight or sometimes convex; is intelligent, frugal, agile, and docile; has a fine, small head, inward-facing ears;

historically used for military purposes and as a carriage horse, while today it is used for light farming, light draft, riding, and in the bullfighting ring by the rejoneadores (q.v.); numbers appear to be declining.

lynch pin *see* LINCHPIN

lymph The yellow, nutritive liquid exuded from the blood vessels into the tissue spaces and drained back into the veins via the lymph vessels; important in fighting infection and maintaining the body's fluid balance.

lymphatic Relating to the lymph (q.v.).

lymphangitis Also known as lymphangitis of horses; an inflammation of the lymph vessels and nodes primarily affecting one or, in some cases, both of the pelvic limbs; develops following infection of streptococcus (q.v.), and less frequently by staphylococcus or corynebacterium bacteria; lack of exercise may be a contributing factor; the onset of symptoms is abrupt and pain is severe; symptoms include fever, anorexia, increased pulse and respiration rates, a hot, spreading, painful swelling that may involve the entire limb, swollen lymph ducts, and the exudation of fluid at areas including the hock and the medial aspect of the thigh; severe lameness accompanies the swelling; recurrent attacks are not uncommon; observed more frequently in horses in good condition; treatment with penicillin-based antibiotics is usually successful.

lymphangitis of horses *see* LYMPHANGITIS

Lynwood Palmer *see* PALMER, LYNWOOD

M

Macardy *see* MECATE

machine *see* BATTERY

machine made Said of a horseshoe machined or made and formed in a factory.

machine-made shoe Also known as keg shoe or factory-made shoe; any factory-made, preformed horseshoe; available in a variety of sizes.

Mackintosh (1) Originally, a cloth coat made waterproof by means of India rubber; currently, any similar garment made of modern fabric. (2) Cloth made waterproof by means of an India rubber coating.

macs A British term; originally, riding breeches made of Mackintosh (q.v.); sometimes worn by jockeys when racing in wet weather; currently, any similar garment made of modern fabrics.

mad-dog syndrome The classic irrational and aggressive behavior demonstrated by a horse in which the excitative rabies (q.v.) phase is predominant.

made (1) Said of a fully educated and trained horse. (2) *see* FULL MOUTH NO. 1

made field hunter Any fully trained horse bred, and/or appropriate to follow hounds (q.v.) in the sport of hunting (q.v.); the type is largely influenced by the country over which he will be used.

made pack A hunting term; said of the pack of hounds (q.v.) when the young entries (q.v.) and the older entered (q.v.) hounds have begun to work as a team.

made mouth *see* FULL MOUTH NO. 1

mad woman An obsolete coaching term; an empty stage coach.

madrina *see* BELL MARE

Magenis snaffle Also, yet incorrectly, spelled McGuinness; a bit (q.v.) with a straight or jointed mouthpiece with slits into which revolving rollers are fitted; attached to the ring cheeks on either side and used with one set of reins; acts on the tongue, the bars (in the straight snaffle), the sides of the mouth (in the jointed snaffle), the lips, and corners of the mouth.

magnesium An essential mineral required by horses in small amounts for proper bone and tooth development; the requirement for growing horses is estimated to be 0.1 percent of the diet and for mature horses 0.9 percent; most feeds contain adequate dietary amounts; deficiency may result in hypomagnesemia (q.v.).

magnesium sulfate *see* EPSOM SALTS

magnetic therapy A non-invasive physical therapy technique utilizing magnetic fields to treat soft tissue and bony injuries; a magnetic field or series of magnetic signals or pulses (pulse magnetic field therapy [q.v.]) are applied to the body, sending weak electrical signals to cells that influence their interaction with ions and regulate their function; the magnetic field triggers blood vessel dilation and stimulates tissues to increase circulation, reduce inflammation, and expedite healing.

magpie Also known as magpie hop; a dressage term; said of the horse when his hind feet come down together as in the canter pirouette and flying changes.

magpie hop *see* MAGPIE

mahogany bay Also known as dark bay; refers to coat color; a variation of bay (q.v.); a red coat mixed either with black hairs or red hairs with black tips; black is more abundant along the top line and particularly around the croup and withers; may be confused with seal brown.

maiden (1) Also known as maiden mare or primigravida; a mare who has never been covered, produced a foal, or a mare in foal who has not yet delivered. (2) Also known as maiden horse; a racing term; a horse of either sex, who has not won a race of any distance on a recognized racetrack (q.v.). (3) *see* MAIDEN RACE. (4) A show horse who has not previously won an event. (5) A jockey who has not won a race of any distance on a recognized racetrack.

maiden allowance A racing term; authorization for a maiden (q.v.) horse to carry reduced weight in a race other than a maiden race (q.v.).

maiden class Any horse show class for maiden (q.v.) horses exclusively.

maiden horse *see* MAIDEN NO. 2

maiden mare *see* MAIDEN NO. 1

maiden race Also known as maiden; a racing term; any race for horses of either sex who have not previously won a race of any distance on a recognized track; competing horses must be maidens when race entries are placed, but not necessarily at the time of the race.

Mail Cart A light, two-wheeled, horse-drawn cart used to collect and deliver mail; manufactured in horse, pony, and cob sizes, but sometimes drawn by a donkey; hung on sideways-elliptical springs.

Mail Coach A horse-drawn public coach used in England during the 18th and early 19th centuries to carry both the Royal Mail and passengers, the latter as a secondary consideration only; introduced to replace mounted postboys (q.v.); originally ran between London, Bath, and Bristol, but was later extended as a system to other parts of England; originally hung on elbow springs and braces and carried inside passengers only, with the guard and driver sharing a box seat; eventually suspended by a combination of crosswise and sideways semi-elliptical springs connected by D links known as telegraph springs (q.v.); by 1829, 94 mail coaches were in operation; the number of each coach was painted on the rear of the vehicle and the Royal Coat of Arms painted on the body panels; drawn by four-horse teams which worked in stages of 7 to 10 miles (11–16 km) between inns and posting houses traveling at an average speed of approximately 11 mph (18 kmph).

Mail Phaeton A massive, horse-drawn vehicle of the Phaeton (q.v.) type popular in the 1820s; resembled a mail or stage coach without an enclosed passenger compartment; frequently used for exercising coach horses, leisure driving, and mail delivery; drawn by two or more horses harnessed in pole gear (q.v.) using chain rather than leather traces; had mail hubs and axles, a strong underperch, and was hung on sideways, semi-elliptical or telegraph springs (q.v.); the high front seat was hooded while the rear groom's seat was contained in an open compartment entered through side doors by means of iron steps.

mail spring *see* TELEGRAPH SPRING

main bar The largest of three bars hanging from the swingle tree (q.v.) of a horse-drawn vehicle, to which the traces are connected.

Mainland Pony *see* GARRON

maize *see* CORN

major penalty A cutting term; any three- or five-point penalty infraction.

make a check A racing term; said of a horse who places first through fifth, e.g. "Sisters Aliby made a check."

make and break To break (q.v.) a young horse.

make a run A racing term; said of a horse who increases his speed and moves up in the field.

Malapolski A recently developed Polish warmblood bred mostly in southern Poland; descended from Oriental stock crossed with Thoroughbred (q.v.), Furioso (q.v.), and Gidran Arabian (q.v.); characteristics vary by region, but are similar to those of the Wielkopolski (q.v.); stands 15.3 to 16.2 hands, has a solid-colored coat of any color, and a calm, well-balanced temperament; used for riding and light draft and jumping.

male tail *see* TAIL NO. 2

malignant histiocytoma A slowly spreading, giant cell tumor of the soft parts.

mallenders An antiquated term; a condition of the skin involving an eruption on the back of the knee joint of the foreleg, characterized by a scurfy thickening of the skin, watery discharge, and loss of hair; may be caused by injury or infection.

mallet *see* POLO MALLET

Malvern Dogcart A two-wheeled horse-drawn vehicle of the Dogcart (q.v.) type; hung on two side springs with shafts under the body; the floor and sides appear triangular; the top of the body, the splash-boards and seat rails were rounded.

Malvern Phaeton *see* SPORTING PHAETON

mameluke bit Also known as turkey bit or turkey curb; a curb bit (q.v.) having a ported mouth in the center of which is attached a large ring.

mammoth jack stock A donkey (q.v.) or jennet (q.v.) standing 54 inches (1.37 m) or taller or a jack (q.v.) 56 inches (1.4 m) or taller.

manada A South American term; a herd of wild mares led by a mustang (q.v.); often number in excess of 50 mares to 1 stallion.

Managhi *see* MUNIQI

Mancha One of two Criollo (q.v.) horses ridden by Aimé Tschiffely (q.v.) in his famous 2½-year, 10,000-mile (16,000 km) ride from Buenos Aires, Argentina to Washington DC, USA; died at the age of 40.

manchero A Spanish term; one who travels on horseback, his primary consideration being the safety, well-being, and schooling of his horse.

Manchester Market Cart A strong, two-wheeled horse-drawn vehicle popular in 19th-century Britain; used as a trade cart or to transport servants, carting luggage, or game; had back-to-back seating for four and paneled sides railed to the top.

Manchester team *see* TRANDEM

mandible *see* LOWER JAW

mane The hair growing along the neck of the horse between the poll and withers (q.v.).

mane and tail comb A hand-held metal- or plastic-toothed instrument used to untangle or remove debris from the mane and tail.

mane drag *see* PULLING COMB

manège (1) Also spelled maneige and incorrectly menege; any enclosed or open arena which is usually rectangular, but which may be square or circular, where horses are schooled or dressed (q.v.); originally of French derivation and meaning horsemanship. (2) Historically, the exercises performed in the manège; the training of the horse in the low and high airs (q.v.), including lateral and vertical suppling exercises.

manège figures *see* SCHOOL FIGURES

maneige *see* MANEGE

Maneige Royal, The The classic book on equitation written by Antoine de Pluvinel (q.v.) in 1623 in which he explains the "principal rules pertaining to his method of bringing horses to the perfect obedience of man" by means of a return to the gentler ways of Xenophon (q.v.); harmony of horse and rider through moderation, harmony, order, and 'bienséance' (q.v.) was stressed; a representation of the Classical Humanism of the 17th century.

Mangalarga One of three types of Brazilian-bred Criollo (q.v.), the other two being the Criollo of Rio Grande Do Sul (q.v.) and the Campolino (q.v.); a warmblood descended from Spanish stock brought to South America by the Conquistadors in the 16th century crossed with Andalusian (q.v.), Altér-Real (q.v.), and Argentine Criollo (q.v.); has a distinctive gait between a trot and canter known as the marcha (q.v.).

mangana A Mexican rodeo event in which targeted mares retained in a circular arena are hazed (q.v.) and herded by mounted or walking charros (q.v.) around the perimeter of the ring, the objective being to snare the mare's front legs and bring her down to a shoulder roll; of two types: the mangana a pie (q.v.) and the mangana a caballo (q.v.); one of nine scored events in a charreada (q.v.); now illegal in many states in the USA.

mangana a caballo A Mexican rodeo event; one of nine scored events in a charreada (q.v.) in which targeted mares retained in a circular arena are hazed (q.v.) and herded by mounted charros (q.v.) around the perimeter of the ring, while the mounted competitor prepares to throw his rope from horseback; the objective being to snare the mare's front legs and bring her down to a shoulder roll; now illegal in many parts of the United States.

mangana a pie A Mexican rodeo event; one of nine scored events in a charreada (q.v.) in which targeted mares retained in a circular arena are hazed (q.v.) and herded by walking charros (q.v.) around the perimeter of the ring, while the competitor prepares to throw his rope from a standing position on the ground; the objective being to snare the mare's front legs and bring her down to a shoulder roll; now illegal in many parts of the United States.

manganese A mineral utilized by enzymes in the formation of cartilage; although no exact dietary requirements have been established, the horse requires trace dietary amounts; deficiency is uncommon, yet symptoms include shortened or crooked limbs, deafness due to improper development of the bones of the inner ear, and the birth of deformed foals.

mange A contagious skin disease caused by infestation of parasitic mites (q.v.); may be spread by contact with diseased animals or their attendants or from contaminated objects or stalls; transmission occurs when larvae, nymphs, or fertilized females are transferred to a susceptible host; causes incessant and increasing itching of the affected skin; of four types: sarcoptic mange (q.v.), chorioptic mange (q.v.), demodectic mange (q.v.), and psoroptic mange (q.v.).

manger Also known as crib or feeder; a container designed to hold food from which a horse may feed at will; may be free-standing or built into or attached to the wall of a stall, barn, etc.

manier (1) A 17th-century French term; to school or handle a horse. (2) A 17th-century French term; to put a horse into the low and high airs (q.v.).

Manipur *see* MANIPURI

Manipuri Also known as Manipur; an ancient pony breed indigenous to India where it descended from the Asiatic Wild Horse (q.v.) and Arab (q.v.); stands 11 to 13 hands, has a light, well-proportioned head, almond-shaped eyes, full mane and tail, and sturdy legs; is strong, fast, energetic, and hardy; may have a bay, brown, gray, or chestnut coat; used for riding.

Man o'War Also known as Big Red; a chestnut Thoroughbred (q.v.) believed by many to be the finest American-bred race horse of all time; foaled in the United States in 1917, retired from racing in 1921, retired from stud in 1943, and died in 1947 at the age of 30; won 20 of 21 starts.

manure *see* FECES

manure spray An insecticide (q.v.) sprayed over stored manure to control fly populations in and around stabling facilities by killing fly larvae; only used when manure cannot be removed from the premises on a weekly basis; sprayed manure may be toxic to certain crops, mammals, and birds.

marathon An American flat-racing term; any horse race longer than 1¼ miles (2 km).

marathon phase *see* COMPETITION B

marcha Also known as marchador; the distinctive gait of the Mangalarga (q.v.), between a trot and canter.

marchador *see* MARCHA

Marche Donc (1) *see* CALECHE NO. 1. (2) A driver's cry to a horse to increase pace, i.e., 'Marche' followed by 'Marche Donc', meaning 'Walk' and 'Go on walk.'

marching A dressage term; said of the horse when his steps in the walk are purposeful.

Marchioness Emily Mary Salisbury *see* SALISBURY, MARCHIONESS EMILY MARY

mare (1) Any female horse more than four years of age, at which point she is considered sexually mature; in Thoroughbreds (q.v.), any horse five years or older; an Anglo-Saxon word derived from mearth, meaning horse, the feminine of mearth being mere, pronounced mare. (2) Any female horse who has borne a foal.

mare donkey *see* JENNET

mare hinny A female hinny (q.v.).

Maremmana An Italian horse breed used as a light draft or farm horse and as a mount for the Italian police and the butteri (q.v.) of the Maremma region of Tuscany and Latium, from which the name derived; is solidly built, adaptable to every type of terrain, able to withstand bad weather conditions, very hardy, and an economical feeder; stands 15 to 15.3 hands, and any solid coat color is acceptable with bay, brown, chestnut, and black occurring most often; currently crossed with Thoroughbred (q.v.) to improve stature and refine the appearance, but at the expense of the hardiness and exceptional stamina that characterized the breed; historically bred in the wild.

mare mule Also known as a molly mule; a female mule (q.v.).

Marengo Napoleon's gray Arab stallion, a favorite charger, whom he rode during his Austrian and Italian campaigns and at the battle of Waterloo in 1815; his skeleton is preserved and on display at the Royal United Service Institution, London, England.

mare's month A racing term; the month of September which, in theory, is the month mares who did not run well during the summer improve their performance.

mare's nest A discovery or accomplishment found to be bogus or worthless.

Mareyeur One of two sub-types of the Boulonnais (q.v.); is smaller and stands less than 16 hands; the name means horse of the tide, as the breed was originally used to transport fish from Boulogne to Paris, France; nearly extinct.

mark (1) *see* CUP NO. 1. (2) *see* CASTRATE. (3) *see* MARKING

marked to ground Also known as mark the fox to the ground; a hunting term; said of the hounds (q.v.) when they run a fox (q.v.) so that it takes refuge in an earth (q.v.) which they identify by giving tongue (q.v.) and digging.

Market Harborough *see* GERMAN MARTINGALE

marking Also known as mark or body marking; any change from the predominant coat color of the horse's body exclusive of the head or limbs.

mark the fox to the ground *see* MARKED TO GROUND

Marocco A performing horse active in Europe during the late 16th and early 17th centuries who, on command from his owner Thomas Bankes, would rap out the numbers on a appearing rolled dice with his hoof, lie down, sit up, rear, and dance; having attributed his powers to black magic, the Italians ordered Marocco and his owner to be burned at the stake; although Bankes returned safely to England, the fate of his horse remains a mystery.

Marshall, Benjamin (1767–1835) An acclaimed artist whose subjects included hunters, race horses, hacks, and sporting groups.

martingale Any auxiliary rein or strap used to assist the action of the bit by restricting the position of the horse's head and neck; consists of a strap, or arrangement of straps, fastened to the girth at one end, passed through the forelegs, and depending on the type, attached on the other end to the reins, noseband, or directly to the bit; include the German martingale (q.v.), running martingale (q.v.), standing martingale (q.v.), Cheshire martingale (q.v.), continental martingale (q.v.), chambon (q.v.), grainger martingale (q.v.), harness martingale, Indian martingale (q.v.), purgi martingale (q.v.), de Gouge martingale (q.v.) and Irish Martingale (q.v.), although the last is not a true martingale.

martingale pulley A pulley or wheel used in conjunction with a running martingale (q.v.) to allow the split auxiliary rein to move freely as the horse moves his head; eliminates any pressure to the outside of the bit which may result; the martingale is attached between the forelegs to the girth (q.v.) at one end, splits into two branches one of which connects to each bit ring; the two split reins are joined together by a cord which moves around the pulley.

Marwari Any pony breed indigenous to the state of Jodhpur, India; descended from small (about 13 hands), frugal native ponies crossed with Arabs (q.v.); is tough, hardy, tenacious, unpredictable, thrives on little feed, stands approximately 14 to 15 hands, and may have a coat of any color including skewbald (q.v.) and piebald (q.v.); is very light and narrowly framed, and has a weak neck and quarters, low-set tail, sickle hocks, and ears that curve distinctively inwards, almost touching at the tips; used for riding, packing, farming, light draft, and the best ones, racing; virtually identical to the Kathiawari (q.v.).

Maryland Hunt Cup One of the oldest and most celebrated steeplechases (q.v.) in the United States; run annually since 1896 in Glyardson, Maryland, USA over a permanent course built in natural hunt country; the fences are constructed of solid timber up to 5 feet 6 inches (1.7 m) tall.

mascot A companion for a pastured horse, the most common of which include ponies, dogs, goats, cats, and chickens.

mash Steamed or cooked grains or the outer shells of the grain which, when cooled, are fed to the horse; used as a laxative, poultice, and, when mixed with sweeteners, to administer medications; bran mash (q.v.) is the most common.

mask A hunting term; the head of a fox.

massage The act or art of treating the body by rubbing or kneading to stimulate circulation and healing and/or increase suppleness.

Master Also known as Master of Foxhounds, Hunt Master, The Master, and by the acronym MFH; a hunting term; one appointed by the hunt committee (q.v.) to, either solely or with joint Masters, organize and manage all aspects of the hunt including the hiring and firing of professional members of the hunt staff such as the huntsman (q.v.), kennel huntsman (q.v.), and whippers-in (q.v.) and appointment of honorary whippers-in, the Field Master (q.v.), and the Hunt Secretary; the term of appointment is determined by the Hunt Committee; normally provided with a sum of money by the committee collected from followers, subscriptions, capping fees (q.v.), and Hunt social functions; required to make any shortfall of funds necessary to hunt the country (q.v.); may also hunt hounds as an amateur huntsman there are still some private packs (notably in Britain) where the Master is self-appointed and therefore not beholden to the committee in the usual way.

master (1) To become adept at or expert in some activity. (2) One skillful or experienced enough to train others and to independently pursue his own trade.

Master of Foxhounds *see* MASTER

Master of Game, The *see* DE FOIX, GASTON

Master of Hounds Also known by the acronym MH; one responsible for managing hounds used in the hunt including stag hounds (q.v.), drag hounds (q.v.), harriers (q.v.), beagles (q.v.) or bassett (q.v.) hounds.

Master of the Foxhounds Association of America An organization founded in 1907 to promote the sport of fox, coyote and drag hunting (q.v.) in the United States and Canada, improve foxhound (q.v.) breeds, register and annually recognize Hunts (q.v.) which have met its standards, and assign and record the boundaries of the individual Hunt counties (q.v.) in North America.

Master of the Game, The The English translation of *Le Livre de la Chasse*, Gaston de Foix's (q.v.) tome on the subject of hunting (q.v.); first published in 1387.

Master of the Pack *see* FIELD MASTER

Mastership A hunting term; the period of time during which a Master (q.v.) presides over a specific Hunt (q.v.).

mastitis Inflammation of the mammary

gland; almost always due to bacteria-related infection.

Masuren A Polish warmblood breed based on horses left behind at the Trakehnen Stud at the end of World War II (1945); breed to the standards of the Trakehner breed; bred in the Masury district, chiefly Liski, from which the name derived; used for riding and light draft.

match (1) Also known as match race; a racing term; historically a race between two horses, the terms of which are agreed upon in advance by the owners of the horses and for which there is no prize; nowadays, the term is sometimes applied to any race in which there are only two runners. (2) *see* POLO MATCH. (3) *see* MATCHED

matched Also known as match; said of horses of similar size, color, conformation, breed, etc., e.g. a matched pair.

matched betting A racing term; standard betting (q.v.) without a bookmaker (q.v.) as on the internet; anyone can offer odds on a race, including the bettor; a similar system, generally known as "the betting exchanges" operates in Britain.

match race *see* MATCH

mate *see* COVER

maternal grandsire The sire of a horse's dam (q.v.).

mating fee *see* STUD FEE

mating hobbles *see* BREEDING HOBBLES

mating posture The position assumed by the mare in preparation to receive the stallion during covering; her forelegs are positioned in front of the vertical, her back is slightly arched, and her hind legs slightly spread and extended behind the vertical.

matron A mare who has produced a foal.

mature horse A horse of either sex who has reached five years of age, at which time his mouth is said to be made (q.v.).

maturity A racing term; a horse race for four-year-old horses entered to compete before their birth.

maxim of Guthrie The propensity for any animal to respond to a stimulus in the same manner in which it responded to the same stimulus when last used; the primary consideration in training.

McCarty *see* MECATE

McGuinness *see* MAGENIS SNAFFLE

ME *see* METABOLIZABLE ENERGY VALUE

meal (1) A cooked porridge or pudding (q.v.) of corn or oats, generally mixed with meat, fed to foxhounds. (2) The edible part of any grain, and of certain leguminous plants, coarsely ground and unsifted, such as cornmeal, oatmeal, peanut meal, soybean meal, and the like.

mealy bay *see* SANDY BAY

mealy nose Said of the horse's nose when oatmeal colored.

measuring stick Also known as horse standard; a straight, generally rigid stick, calibrated in inches, centimeters, and hands (q.v.) fitted at right angles with a sliding arm by which the height of the horse is determined; the stick is placed parallel to the forelegs while the arm is slid downward along the stick shaft until it rests upon the withers (q.v.) where the measurement is read; both the shaft and right-angle arm generally contain a spirit level (q.v.).

measuring tape A long cloth, metal, or paper tape marked in inches or centimeters and hands used to measure the height of the horse.

meat for manners *see* MEAT FOR WORK

meat for work Also known as meat for manners; an antiquated term; the free keep of a horse in exchange for the use of the horse for work.

meat and bone meal A high energy supplemental protein made from mammalian tissues, exclusive of hair, hoof, horn, hide trimmings, manure, and stomach contents; although a good source of protein (q.v.), calcium (q.v.), and phosphorus (q.v.), it is not commonly added to rations as it appears to be unpalatable to horses.

mecate Also known as McCarty or Macardy; a rope rein, often made of braided horsehair, attached to the heel knot of a bosal (q.v.); used as a combination lead rope (q.v.) and rein (q.v.).

mechanical hackamore Also known as hackamore, brockamore, hackamore bit, or in Europe as Blair bridle; a bitless bridle; consists of a headstall, noseband (generally a half noseband which does not connect under the jaw), two long metal shanks, connected one to each side of the half noseband, and left and right reins attached to the respective shanks; control is achieved through pressure applied to the bridge of the nose and, when used in conjunction with any type of curb chain or strap, on the bridge of the nose (q.v.) and the chin groove (q.v.).

Mecklenburg A German warmblood once prized as a carriage horse; although smaller than the Hanoverian (q.v.), has many similar characteristics; after 1945, the breed was revived in East Germany where stallions were controlled by the state and mares generally belonged to individual breeders; is strong and courageous, stands 15.3 to 16 hands, may have a brown, bay, chestnut, or black coat; used as a riding and cavalry mount.

meconium The blackish contents of the intestines of the newborn foal, its first feces; the mare's first milk contains a purgative which causes the foal to discharge this feces shortly after birth.

medial Relating to the middle or inner portion of a body or to any position close to the axis (q.v.).

medial deviation of the carpal joints Also known as knock knees, carpus vulgus, knee-narrow conformation, or knees narrow; a conformation abnormality in which the horse's knees deviate towards each other, breaking the vertical line from the shoulder to the hoof; results in increased strain on the medial collateral ligaments.

medial deviation of the hock joints Also known as cow hocks or tarsus valgus; a conformation abnormality in which the hocks (q.v.) are too close, point toward one another, and the feet are separated at the toe; when viewed laterally, the horse may also appear sickle-hocked (q.v.).

medial patellar desmotomy A simple surgical procedure performed on stifled (q.v.) horses; the medial patellar ligament is cut at its base to prevent the patella from locking over the trochlea; the horse can return to work with about five days; the only adverse effect of this procedure is that the horse can no longer completely relax or sleep standing up.

medication list An American racing term; a list maintained by the track veterinarian and published by the track and Daily Racing Forum (q.v.) which identifies those horses competing under the influence of legally prescribed medications.

medicine Any substance used to treat disease or relieve pain.

medicine ball Also known as medicine pill, physic ball, or ball; a medicinal compound encapsulated in gelatin and administered into the horse's mouth by hand or using a balling gun (q.v.), or balling iron; a somewhat antiquated method of administering medicine and drugs to horses.

medicine pill *see* MEDICINE BALL

medicine hat Refers to coat color pattern; an arrangement of colored areas on a predominantly white horse, specifically a colored spot that covers both ears and the poll; colored patches on the chest, flank, and base of the tail are also common.

Medieval Long Wagon *see* LONG WAGON

mediolateral balance The distribution of the horse's weight over the medial and lateral halves of the hoof.

Medium Breton *see* POSTIER-BRETON

medium canter A gait variant between the working and extended canter (q.v.); the horse moves forward on the bit with free, balanced, and moderately extended strides with impulsion (q.v.) from the hindquarters; the the whole movement is balanced and unconstrained; the head may come slightly in front of the vertical (q.v.).

Medium Level The British and Australian equivalent to Third Level (q.v.).

medium trot A gait variant between the working and extended trots (q.v.), which is more round than the latter; the horse moves forward on the bit with free, balanced, and moderately extended strides with impulsion from the hindquarters; the whole movement balanced and unconstrained; the head may come slightly in front of the vertical.

medium walk A free, regular, and unconstrained walk (q.v.) of moderate extension; the horse walks energetically, but calmly, with even steps, the hind feet touching the ground in front of the imprints of the forefeet; while the horse is on the bit, the head may come slightly in front of the vertical.

meet (1) Also known as meeting; a racing term; a race meeting. (2) Also known as hounds will meet; a hunting term; the location where the hunt servants (q.v.), hounds (q.v.), and field (q.v.) assemble before the hunt (q.v.); a contraction of hounds will meet from the days when several neighboring landowners would bring their own hounds to the meet where they would be combined and hunted as one pack. (3) Also known as meeting; a hunting term; the hunt itself.

meeting *see* MEET

megrim *see* STAGGERS

melanoma Also known as black cell tumor; a tumor of the pigment-producing skin cells appearing in hairless areas around the muzzle or ears, under the tail, or in the anus or perineal area, the fresh or cut surface of which is characteristically jet black; the hard, dome-shaped, hairless, small bumps appear benign at the onset, but may turn malignant and spread rapidly without warning; malignant melanomas are usually larger and softer than benign growths; single, rapidly growing melanomas on young horses are generally malignant from the onset; occur in 80 percent of gray horses beyond the age of 15.

Melbourne Cup One of the most prestigious Australian horse races; a handicap race (q.v.) run over a distance of 2 miles (3.2 km).

Melton (1) Also known as circle curb hook; a circular curb hook (q.v.) to which the curb chain (q.v.) is attached; consists of a hook fitted inside a ring; the hook portion faces away from the horse's cheek. (2) Also known as Melton cloth; a smooth, strong, tightly woven wool having a short nap, used for overcoats and other outdoor garments; popularized in the town of Melton Mowbray, England, for which it is named.

Melton cloth *see* MELTON NO. 2

Melton Mowbray The geographic center for hunt meets of the Belvoir, Cottesmore, and Quorn Hounds, located in Leicestershire, England.

melts into the ground A reining term; said of a horse who digs into and slides low to the ground when performing a sliding stop (q.v.).

membrana nictans *see* NICTITATING MEMBRANE

menege *see* MANEGE

Mèrens Also known as Ariègeois, cheval de Ariègeois, or cheval de Mèrens; an ancient horse breed originating some 30,000 years ago in the Pyrenean mountain chain dividing France from Spain; originally named for the Ariège river which flows through the region; is very similar to the Fell (q.v.) and a near duplicate of the Dale (q.v.); has a solid black coat with reddish highlights appearing in winter; white markings are rare, although white hairs on the flanks do occur; stands 13 to 14.1 hands, has a relatively coarse head framed by a heavy mane and forelock, small ears, a short neck which is thick at the base, a long back, well-muscled croup, long, full tail, and short legs; cow hocks (q.v.) are common; is sure-footed, an easy keeper, and well adapted to mountainous terrain and long harsh winters, but is intolerant of heat; used for farm work, riding, and packing.

Merlins *see* WELSH PONY

meridians A grid of 12 paired and 2

unpaired energetic pathways through the body; connect internal organs with external features, such as joints and sense organs; each meridian bears an organ name, e.g., heart meridian, bladder meridian, etc.; traditional Chinese medicine such as acupuncture (q.v.) and acupressure (q.v.) utilizes trigger points along these meridians.

mesair (1) *see* MEZAIR NO. 1. (2) *see* MEZAIR NO. 2

mesenteric artery A vessel supplying blood to the intestines; passes through the tissues connecting the intestines to the back abdominal wall.

mesentery A fold of the abdominal lining from which the intestine and associated organs are suspended from the backbone.

Messenger An English Thoroughbred (q.v.) imported to the United States in 1788 to which more than 90 percent of all Standardbreds (q.v.) trace their descent; thought to have played an equal if not more important role in development of the Standardbred breed than Hambletonian 10 (q.v.).

metabolizable energy *see* METABOLIZABLE ENERGY VALUE

metabolizable energy value Also known by the acronym ME or metabolizable energy; the digestible energy (q.v.) of feed consumed by the horse less the energy lost to gas and urine, but not to body heat production; measured in calories; only useful for describing the amount of energy available in a feed for metabolic processes at the tissue level.

metacarpal (1) Of or pertaining to the metacarpus (q.v.). (2) *see* METACARPAL BONE

metacarpal bone Also known as metacarpal; either of the splint bones (small metacarpal [q.v.]) or the cannon bone (large metacarpal [q.v.]) of the foreleg.

metacarpal fracture A break in any of the metacarpal bones (q.v.) in the foreleg.

metacarpalphalangeal joint *see* FETLOCK JOINT

metacarpus The part of the foreleg between the knee and fetlock, including the cannon and splint bones.

metal curry comb A metal, hand-held instrument or comb set with very short teeth on one side used to scrape dirt and debris from a brush.

metal horse *see* VAULTING BARREL

metaphysis The part of the bone beyond the growth plate (q.v.) including the zone of trabeculae projecting from the growth plate.

metatarsal Belonging to the metatarsus (q.v.); a bone of the metatarsus.

metatarsal bone Either the cannon bone or splint bones of the hind leg.

metatarsus The part of the hind limb, especially the bony structure, between the tarsus (q.v.) and the fetlock, including the cannon and splint bones.

Methode et Invention Nouvelle de Dresser les Chevaux Also known as *A New Method and Extraordinary Invention to Dress Horses and Work Them According to Nature*; a treatise on horse training written by William Cavendish, Duke of Newcastle (q.v.).

methylsulfonylmethane Also known by the acronym MSM; a supplemental source of bio-available sulfur used in production of connective tissue, enzymes, hormones, and immunoglobins; an oral crystalline dietary derivative of DMSO (q.v.) with the same anti-inflammatory (q.v.) properties, but without the unpleasant odor; patented in 1986.

Métis Trotter A Russian warmblood developed in the early 20th century and officially recognized as a breed in 1949; descended from Orlov (q.v.) crossed with imported American Standardbreds (q.v.); has a flowing, far-reaching action and is slightly knock-kneed (q.v.) with cow-hocked (q.v.) hind limbs, which result in dishing (q.v.); much faster than the Orlov, but less so than American and European trotters; stands 15.1 to 15.3 hands and usually has a gray, black, or chestnut coat.

metoestrus The period in the estrous cycle (q.v.) following ovulation and during which the corpus luteum (q.v.) develops.

Metropolitan Drinking Fountain and Cattle Trough Association An English organization founded in 1865 to build and maintain drinking fountains for people and water troughs for stock; now defunct, although some of the appliances still exist.

metritis Inflammation of the muscular and endometrial (q.v.) uterine (q.v.) layers caused by the introduction of contaminants during parturition (q.v.); may be acute or chronic, localized or involving more than one uterine tissue; of two forms: acute metritis (q.v.) and chronic metritis.

mewing Said of a stag (q.v.) when shedding his antlers.

mews A British term; stables or coach houses, usually with living quarters, situated around a court, alley, or back lane; from the French *muer*, meaning a place where molting falcons were confined; in 1537, the royal stable at Charing Cross was built on a site where the royal hawks were kept and thus the name derived.

Mexican noseband *see* GRAKLE NOSEBAND

Meyer's D cheek *see* DEE-RING SNAFFLE

mezair (1) Also spelled mesair; a dressage term; a High School movement (q.v.) in which the horse conducts a series of successive levades (q.v.), between which the forefeet touch the ground simultaneously and the horse moves forward a short step. (2) Also spelled mesair; a dressage term; one half a courbette (q.v.).

MFH *see* MASTER OF FOXHOUNDS

MH *see* MASTER OF HOUNDS

Miami strain *see* A-EQUI-2

microchip *see* ELECTRONIC IDENTIFICATION

middle bow One of three classifications of bowed tendon (q.v.) identified on the basis of location, the others being low bow (q.v.) and high bow (q.v.); any true physiological damage to the middle third of the tendon or tendon sheath, most commonly of the superficial flexor tendon of the foreleg; specifically, tearing or breaking of one or more of the tendon fibers; may be precipitated by fatigue, deep going (q.v.), uneven terrain, improper shoeing, obesity, excessively tight fitting running bandages or boots, work on slippery surfaces, long, weak pasterns, sudden changes in stress loads, low heel angles, or long toes; symptoms may include diffuse swelling over the tendon area, heat, and pain; lameness may or may not be present.

middle distance A flat-racing term; in America, a horse race longer than 7 furlongs (1.4 km), but less than 1⅛ miles (1.8 km); in Britain, a horse race of approximately 10 to 12 furlongs (2–2.4 km).

middle distancer One of three morphological Thoroughbred (q.v.) types; has a sloping croup and shoulder and a rather short back; a Thoroughbred best suited to running middle distances (q.v.).

Middle European Gidran One of two types of Gidran Arabian (q.v.); a Hungarian breed developed in 1816 from an Arab (q.v.) of the Siglavy strain crossed with Thoroughbred (q.v.); is heavier than the Southern and Eastern European Gidran (q.v.), and is thus used predominantly in harness.

middle gait Refers to any gait of the horse that is not slow or fast as in a trot (q.v.), running walk (q.v.), foxtrot (q.v.), rack (q.v.), fino (q.v.) tølt (q.v.).

middle ground A coaching term; that part of the coaching journey between the upper ground (q.v.) and lower ground.

middlings *see* WEATINGS

Midland Wagon *see* BARREL TOP WAGON

midsection That portion of the horse's body between the forehand (q.v.) and the hindquarters (q.v.), i.e. from the withers to the front portion of the flanks (q.v.).

Mierzyn One of several Polish pony breeds; essentially a medium-sized Konik (q.v.); is an easy keeper (q.v.), resistant to cold and hunger, and possessed of amazing power and endurance for its size; stands about 14 hands.

mildew Any of numerous minute parasitic fungi producing a whitish coating or discoloration on plants and grains.

mile pole A racing term; a colored post located on the infield rail (q.v.) exactly 1 mile (1.6 km) from the finish line (q.v.).

militaire *see* HORSE TRIALS

military boots White canvas, non-supporting, decorative boots worn on the horse's lower legs when in formal or ceremonial dress, as for parades.

military trials *see* HORSE TRIALS

milk protein An animal source of high energy supplemental protein derived from several products such as dried skim milk, dried buttermilk, dried whole milk, dried whey, and casein; contains an excellent combination of amino acids, plus vitamins, and a good balance of calcium and phosphorus.

milk teeth *see* DECIDUOUS TEETH

mill Also known as round the world; a vaulting (q.v.) term; a compulsory exercise (q.v.) in which the vaulter (q.v.) performs a complete circle above the horizontal line of the withers by swinging one leg at a time over the horse's back or neck; in competition, the vaulter must move each leg every four canter strides.

miller's disease *see* OSTEODYSTROPHIA FIBROSA

miller's offal *see* WEATINGS

milling A 19th-century coaching term; said of a horse when kicking.

milo *see* SORGHUM

Mi-lord *see* CAB PHAETON

Milton Wagonette A horse-drawn vehicle of the Wagonette (q.v.) type popular in the late 19th century; convertible to a Stanhope Phaeton by moving one longitudinal seat into a transverse position across the rear of the vehicle; hung on four elliptic springs.

mineral Any inorganic compound, containing no animal or vegetable matter, some of which are necessary for proper body growth and function; constitute components and building materials of body tissues and catalytic compounds that help trigger reactions within the body; excess intake may be as harmful as deficiency; the exact equine requirements are still undetermined, but there are at least 16 minerals which are considered essential because they normally occur in the body tissues; the essential minerals are sodium (q.v.), choline (q.v.), phosphorus (q.v.), calcium (q.v.), potassium (q.v.), magnesium (q.v.), manganese (q.v.), iodine (q.v.), copper (q.v.), iron (q.v.), zinc (q.v.), chlorine (q.v.), cobalt (q.v.), sulfur (q.v.), fluorine (q.v.), and selenium (q.v.).

Minho *see* GARRANO

Miniature Donkey A donkey (q.v.) standing 28 to 36 inches (71–91 cm) tall which descended from the Miniature Mediterranean Donkey (q.v.); native to, but now thought to be nearly extinct in, Sicily and Sardinia; extensively bred in the United States; weighs 250 to 450 pounds (113–204 kg), has a life expectancy of 30 to 35 years, body hair that ranges from flat to curly, to long and shaggy and in texture from smooth to wiry, is thrifty, an easy keeper, and adaptable to any climate or altitude; most will show a shoulder cross (q.v.).

Miniature Landau A horse-drawn vehicle of the Landau (q.v.) type; is small, easy to enter, suitable for invalids and the elderly, and generally drawn by a pair of ponies.

Miniature Mediterranean Donkey A donkey breed native to the Mediterranean islands of Sicily and Sardinia; of two subtypes: Sicilian (q.v.) or Sardinian (q.v.); nearly extinct in the land of their origin, but are extensively bred in the United States as Miniature Donkeys (q.v.).

Miniature Sardinian Donkey *see* SARDINIAN

Miniature Sicilian Donkey *see* SICILIAN NO. 2

Minibus *see* BOULNOIS CAB

minor penalty A cutting term; a one-point penalty infraction.

minus pool A racing term; racetrack (q.v.) money added to the pool (q.v.) to cover insufficient funds in pari-mutuel betting (q.v.) as when so much money is bet on a horse (usually to show), that the pool is insufficient (after deduction of state tax and commission) to pay winning ticket holders the legal minimum odds of 1 to 10.

mise en main A French dressage term; to flex the horse's jaw; literally, "put in-hand."

misfit Said of a horse not representative of his breed and/or is unsuitable for the purpose for which he is being used.

miss (1) A polo term; said of a polo player who takes a stroke on the ball and fails to contact the ball with the mallet. (2) A cutting term; said of the horse; to overrun a cow; results in a loss of working position (q.v.) and, in competition, a one-point penalty; a horse will often have a miss prior to losing a cow. (3) A roping term; to fail to lasso the calf, steer, or other animal with a thrown rope.

Missouri Fox Trotter Also known as Missouri Fox Trotting Horse; a warmblood established around 1820 in the Ozark Mountains of Arkansas and Missouri, USA; descended from Spanish Barb (q.v.) stock put to Morgans (q.v.) and Thoroughbreds (q.v.) followed by infusions of Saddlebred (q.v.) and Tennessee Walking Horse (q.v.); is plain, compact, sure-footed, and moves in a smooth, broken, four-beat gait known as the fox trot (q.v.); walks from the shoulder in front and trots behind, the hind hooves stepping onto the track of the fore hooves and sliding forward; this sliding action minimizes the concussive effect and produces a very smooth ride which the horse can maintain for long distances at an average speed of 5 to 10 mph (8–16 kmph); the canter is halfway between the fast, long-rein lope (q.v.) of the cow pony (q.v.) and the high, slow gait of Walkers and Saddlebreds; the breed society prohibits the use of artificial aids to achieve leg height; has a strong, compact body, intelligent head, tapered muzzle, long neck, low-set tail, and stands 14 to 16 hands; all coat colors occur including skewbald (q.v.), piebald (q.v.), chestnut, bay, black, gray, and occasionally roan; usually ridden in Western tack; the stud book was established in 1948.

Missouri Fox Trotting Horse *see* MISSOURI FOX TROTTER

mistaught Also known as mistetched; said of an improperly or badly broken horse who, as a result of such training, possesses a vice or vices.

mistetched *see* MISTAUGHT

mitbah The angle at which the neck of an Arab (q.v.) attaches to the head; at the crest, the neck angles gently towards the head, creating an arched neck set.

mites Also known as acari; any of several species of small external parasites, infestation by which may cause mange (q.v.).

mixed gait (1) Said of a harness racing horse who is capable of competing at both the trot and pace (q.v.). (2) Said of a horse who fails to stick to any one true gait at a time.

mixed lameness Lameness evident both when the horse's limb is in motion and when supporting weight.

mixed markings More than one type of marking (q.v.) on the horse, e.g. dorsal stripe (q.v.), coronet (q.v.), sock (q.v.), stripe (q.v.), etc.

mixed meeting A racing term; a meeting where both flat and steeplechase or hurdle races are conducted on the same day.

mixed pack A hunting term; a group of hounds consisting of both bitches (q.v.) and dog hounds (q.v.).

mixed sale A horse sale in which only one breed, such as Thoroughbred (q.v.), is offered; consists of different classifications within the breed: mares, yearlings, horses in training, etc.

mixed stable A racing term; a stable where both flat and National Hunt horses are kept.

mob (1) An Australian term; a herd of cattle. (2) *see* MOB A FOX

mob a fox Also known as mob; a hunting term; said of the hounds when they surround a fox without giving it a chance to run.

mocha A soft, suede leather saddle made from sheep or goatskin used by pony express riders (q.v.) due to its exceptional light weight.

model horse Any authentic, small-scale reproduction of a horse, generally made in plastic, e.g. a Breyer Horse (q.v.); used as a toy and collected by hobbyists.

modern Also known as modern type; a large, well-developed Stock-Type Pinto (q.v.).

modern type *see* MODERN

modesty boards A coaching term; wooden boards fixed horizontally to the top of horse-drawn vehicle with roof-top seating; prevented pedestrians from glimpsing the ankles of lady passengers seated there; the boards were subsequently used for advertising.

Mohammed's Ten Horses Ten horses who, according to legend, formed the foundation stock of the Prophet Strain (q.v.); it is believed that in the days of Mohammed only horses with superior intelligence and obedience were used for war purposes, such horses were trained to follow the bugle; when the Prophet Mohammed required horses he selected a herd from which he would make his selection; the herd was fenced off from the river until their thirst became excessive at which time he ordered the fence removed; when the horses rushed to the river to quench their thirst, a bugle was sounded, and only ten of the horses obediently responded to the bugle call; those ten horses comprised the foundation of the Prophet Strain.

mohawk *see* MOHAWK ATTACHMENT

mohawk attachment Also known as mohawk; a straight bar fitted with rubber ball washers that attaches by means of two up-turned hooks to the eyes of the pelham bit (q.v.) cheeks; anchored above and in the center to the pelham mouthpiece by means of a rubber ring; increases the size of the bit bearing surface on the tongue and bars of the mouth.

Moifaa A New Zealand race horse who, in 1904 at the age of 8 while en route from New Zealand to England, was lost at sea in a storm; he washed ashore on an island where he roamed for two weeks before being rescued; sent on to England, he was entered in the Grand National Steeplechase against 25 other horses, a race he won by eight lengths in 9 minutes, 59 seconds.

molars Also known as grinders, cheek teeth, or molar teeth; 12 permanent grinding teeth, 3 on each side of each jaw top and bottom, located behind the premolars (q.v.); the first of the permanent teeth (q.v.) to erupt; do not replace deciduous teeth (q.v.); first appear between 6 and 12 months while the second and third molars appear at 1 to 1½ year intervals thereafter; the normal chewing action on the molars produces sloping instead of horizontal surfaces; because of the sloping wear on these teeth, the outside edge of the upper molars and the inside edge of the lower molars develop sharp points which may catch on the tongue and cheek membranes and cause painful ulcers to form; removal of these sharp points requires floating (q.v.).

molar teeth *see* MOLARS

molasses A by-product of sucrose refined from sugar cane, sugar-beets, dried citrus pulp (q.v.), or from grain starch, the fermentation of which produces yeast, an excellent source of B vitamins; supplies little or no protein or phosphorus; may be fed dried or wet although wet is preferred; often added to rations to improve taste and decrease dust; molasses from cane sugar is an excellent source of energy and contains significant amounts of calcium.

molly mule *see* MARE MULE

moment of suspension The precise moment when all four of the horse's feet leave the ground, whether on the flat or jumping.

Monday morning complaint *see* STOCK UP

Monday-morning disease *see* EQUINE MYOGLOBINURIA

Monday morning evil *see* STOCK UP

Monday morning leg *see* STOCK UP

Monday-morning sickness *see* EQUINE MYOGLOBINURIA

money rider A racing term; a jockey who excels in high-stakes races.

Mongolian Also known as Mongolian Pony; an ancient pony breed originating in Mongolia; has had great influence on all Asiatic breeds due to its widespread use by the Mongols as a war mount; is found in a number of different types which evolved according to greatly differing environmental factors; stands 12 to 14 hands, may have a brown, black, mouse dun, or palomino coat, has a heavy head, short ears, thick forelock, mane, and tail, short withers, strong back, and sturdy, well-boned legs; is hardy, frugal, and active; used for riding, packing, light draft, and farm work.

Mongolian Pony *see* MONGOLIAN

Mongolian Wild Horse *see* ASIATIC WILD HORSE

monkey A British racing term; a bet of £500.

monkey crouch Also known as monkey-on-a-stick; a racing term; a riding position popularized by jockey Tod Sloan; the jockey rides with short stirrups and his body bent forward over the withers of the horse.

monkey-on-a-stick *see* MONKEY CROUCH

Monte Foreman bit A bit having extra rings attached to the headstall which prevents the curb chain or lip strap from pinching the corners of the horse's mouth; designed by horseman Monte Foreman.

monorchid A male horse when one of the testes fails to descend normally into the scrotum.

monovular twin Also known as identical twin; one of two young brought forth at birth resulting from the fertilization of one egg which splits in two; the young will be identical; extremely rare in horses.

moon blindness *see* PERIODIC OPHTHALMIA

mope A coaching term; to place shields over the horse's eyes to prevent him from seeing forward, a technique used to control or subdue unruly horses.

moped Said of a horse whose eyes were shielded to prevent him from seeing forward.

Moray Car A two-wheeled, horse-drawn vehicle popular with ladies in the 19th century; had back-to-back seating for four and a tail board which let down on chains; the shafts ran outside the body which was hung low on two side-springs.

Morgan An American warmblood descended from a cross of Thoroughbred (q.v.), Arab (q.v.), Welsh Cob (q.v.), Harddraver (q.v.), and Fjord (q.v.) blood; stands 14.1 to 15 hands, may have a bay, chestnut, or black coat with white markings, a short, broad back, strong shoulders, short, strong legs, well-crested neck of medium length, and a full mane and tail; the gaits are comfortable, long, and elastic; is versatile, tough, and even-tempered; used for hunting, dressage, park classes, Western and pleasure riding, driving, and trail riding; contributed to development of the Standardbred (q.v.), Saddlebred (q.v.), and Tennessee Walking Horse (q.v.).

Morgan Cart Also known as Cab-fronted Gig; a horse-drawn vehicle developed in the 1890s; had a low entrance and dashboard which often curved to the rear end of the shafts, thus resembling the fore-end of a Hansom cab (q.v.); some later types were hooded; named for its designer and builder.

morning glory Also known as morning horse; a racing term; a horse who clocks good times in the morning workouts or training gallops, but fails to live up to the same potential when raced.

morning horse *see* MORNING GLORY

morning line A racing term; the forecast of probable odds for each horse in a given race as calculated by an experienced track handicapper (q.v.); usually printed in the program and posted on the totalizator (q.v.) prior to betting.

morning stable An English racing term; the morning feeding time (q.v.).

Morocco saddle *see* BURFORD SADDLE

Morochuco One of three types of Peruvian Salterno (q.v.) horses bred in the Andes, the other two being the Costeño (q.v.) and the Chola (q.v.); descended from Spanish stock brought to South America by the Conquistadors in the 16th century; occasionally has a protruding forehead and small ears.

morral *see* NOSEBAG

mort A hunting term; a horn signal or yell signifying the death of the fox or other hunted prey following the hunt.

Mosenthall Cart A horse-drawn country cart; seated two forward-facing and one rearward facing passengers seated back-to-back; was rectangular shaped, the tail board let down to form a footboard for the back-seat passengers, the shafts ran inside the body which was cane paneled and hung on two side- and one cross-spring.

mosquito Any of various dipterous insects of the family *Culicidae*; a tiny, swarming, dusk, dawn, and overnight feeder, being the most common of the bloodsucking insects; more than 3,000 species exist worldwide with about 150 in the United States; most species avoid bright sunlight; males do not bite while females do; females have a long proboscis which they use to puncture the skin and suck blood from their hosts; the bites are annoying, but leave no lasting traces unless exposure is extreme; however, may be dangerous transmitters of disease.

mother tinctures The concentrated form of a medicament used in homeopathic remedies (q.v.).

motor nerve Any of the whitish fibers extending from the brain and spinal cord and spreading throughout the body which enervate muscles and when stimulated cause muscle function.

motor unit Two adjacent vertebrae (q.v.) and their associated structures.

mottled Refers to a coat color pattern; small white spots appearing on the muzzle, genitalia, and around the eyes of some horses, most commonly those with symmetrical patterns of white.

mottled skin Also known as parti-colored skin; a speckled pattern of pigmented skin consisting of small, round, dark spots characteristic to the Appaloosa (q.v.); appears in the anus region, on the udder and sheath, and on the muzzle; differs from mottled (q.v.) which is a coat color pattern.

mount (1) To get on a horse in preparation to ride. (2) The act of the stallion straddling the mare to copulate. (3) Also known as riding mount; a riding horse. (4) An American term; a number of cow ponies used by one man.

Mountain Bashkir Also known as Mountain Bashkir Curly; one of two distinct types of Bashkir (q.v.), a centuries-old pony breed originating in Bashkiria, around the southern foothills of the Urals in the former Soviet Union; due to the introduction of Don (q.v.) and Budonny (q.v.) blood, is smaller and lighter than the Steppe Bashkir (q.v.); stands 13.1 to 14 hands, has a distinctive thick, curly winter coat and thick mane, tail, and forelock that enables it to survive in sub-zero temperatures; is kept outdoors where it can withstand winter temperatures of −22 to 40 °F (−30–44 °C); the coat is usually bay, chestnut or palomino; has a short and long neck, low withers, elongated and sometimes hollow back, a wide, deep chest, short, strong legs, and a small foot for its size; the breed standard quotes a bone measurement of 8 inches (20 cm) below the knee and a girth measurement for stallions of 71 inches (1.8 m); is docile, strong, quiet, and hardy; used for packing, light draft, riding, and to provide meat, milk and clothing for human consumption and use; in a 7- to 8-month lactation period a mare can yield as much as 350 gallons (1,590 liters) of milk; the long winter coat hair is spun into cloth; due to the exceptionally hard hoof, is generally left unshod.

Mountain Bashkir Curly *see* MOUNTAIN BASHKIR

Mounties *see* ROYAL CANADIAN MOUNTED POLICE

mounting block Also known as horsing stone (obs) jostling stone (obs), horse block, or pillion post; any stepped block or platform approximately 2 to 2½ feet (61–76 cm) high on which a rider stands to facilitate mounting a horse.

mountings *see* SEE FURNITURE

Mounting Wagon A four-passenger, American, horse-drawn vehicle used in the Rocky Mountains during the 19th century; was hung on two side springs and one elliptic spring.

mount money A rodeo term; the money paid to a rodeo competitor who rides, ropes, and/or bulldogs in an exhibition, but not in a competition.

Mounty One Royal Canadian Mounted Policeman (q.v.).

mouse dun *see* GRULLO

moustache *see* MUSTACHE

mouth (1) The opening through which man or animals intake food and liquid; the cavity containing the teeth (q.v.), bars (q.v.), tongue, etc. (2) *see* MOUTHPIECE

mouth a horse *see* MOUTHING NO. 1

mouthing (1) Also known as mouth a horse; to determine the age of the horse by examining the teeth (q.v.) for wear and eruption. (2) Said of a bitted horse who chews or plays with the bit. (3) To accustom a young, unfamiliar horse to the bit.

mouthing bit *see* BREAKING BIT

mouthpiece Also known as mouth, embouchure (obs), or bocado; that portion of the bit (q.v.) which rests on the tongue and bars (q.v.) of the horse's mouth and which attaches to the bridle cheekpieces (q.v.).

mouthy (1) A hunting term; said of a hound who babbles (q.v.). (2) Said of a horse who is active with his mouth, e.g. licking, biting, nibbling, etc.

mouthy hound A hound who babbles (q.v.).

moved at halt A dressage term; said of a horse when he has made a satisfactory halt and then moved his head, stepped back, rested a leg, or shifted his quarters slightly.

movement The act of moving; the course, process, or result of change position.

movements off the ground *see* AIRS ABOVE THE GROUND

movements on the ground A dressage term; any of the classical airs (q.v.) performed by the horse on the ground; consist of simple and flying changes (q.v.), turns on the forehand (q.v.) and haunches, lateral work (q.v.), shoulder-in (q.v.), shoulder-out (q.v.), travers (q.v.), renvers (q.v.), passage (q.v.), pirouette (q.v.), piaffe (q.v.), levade (q.v.) and pesade (q.v.).

move off To move the horse forward from a standing position.

move off the leg Said of a horse who moves away from the rider's leg pressure; may be a forward or lateral movement.

move up (1) A racing term; to gain ground. (2) A racing term; said of a horse who runs in a higher-class race than previously entered.

moxibustion A type of acupuncture (q.v.); the stimulation of precise points along body meridians (q.v.) by burning a herb known as moxa, and more commonly mugwort, over those points; delivers penetrating heat with amazing effectiveness; frequently used to alleviate pain and muscular problems.

MSM *see* METHYLSULFONYLMETHANE

Mtidaudaschweba A professional, long-distance race conducted in the Caucasus mountains, Russia; the course covers 3 to 4 miles (5–7 km) and the competitors, who ride bareback, are mostly herdsmen and workers on stud farms.

muck *see* MUCK OUT

muck out Also known as mucking out, muck, or skepping (derived from skep, a box on wheels used to haul away soiled bedding); the process of removing droppings and soiled bedding from a stall and replacing it with fresh bedding.

mucking out *see* MUCK OUT

mucosa *see* MUCOUS MEMBRANE

mucous (1) Pertaining to or resembling mucus (q.v.). (2) To secrete or contain mucus (q.v.).

mucous membrane Also known as mucosa; a membrane rich in mucous glands, specifically, one that lines body passages and cavities which communicate directly, or indirectly, with the exterior; produces mucus (q.v.) which moisturizes and protects the lining.

mucus The viscid, slippery secretion produced by mucous membranes (q.v.); usually rich in mucins; moisturizes and protects the lining of all body passages and cavities.

mudder Also known as mud runner, webfoot, or mudlark; a racing term; a horse who runs well on a wet, muddy, or sloppy track.

muddy dun Refers to coat color; the darkest of the red dun (q.v.) shades; the body hair is a light brownish red or brownish yellow, the points (q.v.) chocolate brown, and the head usually brown; resembles grullo (q.v.) except that brown and light brownish red replace the black and slate.

muddy track A racing term; said of a wet racetrack which does not contain standing water.

mud fever *see* DERMATOPHILUS

mudguard *see* SPLASHBOARD

mudlark *see* MUDDER

mud runner *see* MUDDER

mud sticker *see* CALK

mud tie Also known as French tie; to fold and tie up the horse's tail to prevent it from entangling in the harness or collecting brush and other debris; commonly used on draft horses.

mugger A western term; a cowboy who holds a horse or cow so his partner can saddle and mount the horse or work with the cow.

mug's horse An easily ridden horse who appears hot (q.v.) and difficult.

Muhamed One of the famous Elberfeld horses (q.v.); blindfolded by a sack, Muhamed could calculate cube roots after only four months of training; he could also add subtract, multiply, and divide; to signal a math answer such as 54, he would tap his left foot five times, his right four times.

Mulassier Also known as Poitevin, Trait du Mulassier, Trait Mulassier Poitevin, Trait Poitevin, or Cheval du Poitou; a nearly extinct, heavy-draft breed from the Poitiers region of France from which the name derived; descended from local mares crossed with Norwegian, Danish, and Dutch horses brought there for swamp reclamation works ordered by Henri IV in 1599; now principally used to produce the Mule Poitevine (q.v.); has a long neck with a thick mane, powerful legs with huge feet and coarse, abundant feathering; often dun, bay, black, or gray in color; usually referred to in old texts as "coarse", "plain" or "unremarkable"; is lethargic, well balanced, and strong with good endurance; stands 15 to 17 hands and weighs 1,540 to 1,980 pounds (699–898 kg); the genealogical registry dates back to 1884; used for heavy draft, farming, and mule production.

mule The progeny of a jack (q.v.) and a mare (q.v.) or a male horse with a female donkey; a horse has 64 chromosomes and a donkey 62, the union of which produces a sterile hybrid – a mule with 63 chromosomes; mules may be either male or female but because of the odd number of chromosomes they cannot usually reproduce, however a small percentage of female mules may produce foals; looks generally like a donkey head (heavy head, long ears) on the body of a horse (fine-boned legs with small hooves), the horse also contributing horse-like tail, size, speed and strength; generally more robust than a hinny (q.v.); the female of the species is known as a mare mule (q.v.) and the male as a horse mule (q.v.); unlike other equines, the mule is able to see all four of his feet at one time and because of this the species is renowned for surefootedness.

mule ears (1) The ears of a mule. (2) Also known as rat tails; two leather or fabric loops or 'ears' stitched one each to the left and right sides of the inside lining of a tall riding boot; used by the rider to pull on the boot; may be used with or without boot hooks (q.v.).

mule feet The horse's hooves when long, narrow, high heeled, and thin between the toe and quarters.

mule footed Said of a horse having a long, narrow hoof with high heels, and a narrow hoof wall between the toe and quarters.

mule heels A horseshoe (q.v.) with both heels extended beyond the posterior limit of the hoof.

Mule Poitevine Also known as Poitou Mule; an exceptionally large mule standing more than 16 hands, having short, stout legs, wide hooves, a heavy head, and the characteristic cadanette (q.v.) coat which is generally dark brown, black or dun; born from the cross of a Baudet du Poitou (q.v.) with a Mulassier (q.v.) mare; developed in the province of Poitue France from which the name derived.

mule shoeing contest A timed competition in which farriers (q.v.) trim mules' feet and preshape horseshoes; judged principally on speed with farriers often taking less than five minutes to trim and shoe all four feet; a common component of Mule Days competitions held in the United States.

muley cattle A Western term; said of hornless cattle.

mullen mouth *see* MULLEN MOUTH BIT

mullen mouth bit Also known as half moon bit, half moon mouth, mulling mouth, or mullen mouth; a snaffle bit (q.v.) with a straight-bar mouthpiece slightly bent or curved to accommodate the shape of the tongue; acts on the lips, tongue, and bars (q.v.); appropriate for horses with a low palate and/or those who do not like tongue pressure; also a good transition bit when changing from a snaffle (q.v.) to the double bridle (q.v.); the mouthpiece may be rubber coated.

mullen mouthed Any bit with a mullen mouth (q.v.).

mulling mouth *see* MULLEN MOUTH BIT

multi-jointed snaffle A snaffle bit (q.v.) in which the mouthpiece has more than one joint, as in a Dr. Bristol (q.v.); is more severe than a regular snaffle; applies more pressure to the tongue than the roof of the mouth.

Munighi *see* MUNIQI

Muniqi Also known as Munighi and Managhi; one of three distinct sub-breeds of the Assil (q.v.); tends to be more elegant in appearance and has longer limbs, a longer neck and back, and straight profile compared to the Siglavy (q.v.) and Kuhailan (q.v.).

Murakosi *see* MURAKOZ

Murakoz Also known as Murakosi or Murakozer; a coldblood developed in the 20th-century town of Murakoz, Hungary from which the name derived; descended from native Mur-Insulan mares crossed with Percheron (q.v.), Belgian Ardennes (q.v.), and Noriker (q.v.) stallions; in the 1920s one fifth of all horses in Hungary were Murakoz; stands about 16 hands, usually has a chestnut coat with a flaxen mane and tail, although bay, brown, and black coat colors do occur, a strong frame, small withers, hollowed back, round hindquarters, and some feathering (q.v.); is swift-moving and good tempered; used for draft and agricultural work.

Murakozer *see* MURAKOZ

Murch's Cab Also known as Murch's Chariot; a four-wheeled horse-drawn vehicle of the cab type, designed by C. Murch of Cincinnati, Ohio, USA, about 1880; carried six passengers, had an ample roof-top luggage rack, and footboard; entered through the rear via folding steps; large and heavy with a short wheelbase, it was able to turn in its own length; drawn by a medium-heavy horse; popular until about 1900.

Murch's Chariot *see* MURCH'S CAB

Murgese Also spelt Murghese; an Italian warmblood descended from Arab (q.v.) and Barb (q.v.) crosses more than 200 years ago; selective breeding of the modern breed began in 1926; the name derived from the famous horse breeding region of Murge near Puglia, Italy; reared in the wild to produce a hardy nature; stands 14 to 16 hands, has a prominently jawed head, broad neck, full mane, pronounced withers, straight and occasionally hollow back, large leg joints, and a docile, but lively nature; the coat is usually chestnut, although brown, black, and gray with a black head occur; used for riding, particularly cross-country, farm work, and light draft.

Murghese *see* MURGESE

Murrieta Gig A horse-drawn hooded vehicle similar to a Curricle (q.v.); was hung on two transverse springs, situated parallel to the axle, which were attached to two side-springs bolted to the axle.

Musca domestica The scientific name for the housefly (q.v.).

muscle Tissue consisting of elongated fibers, generally in the form of sheets or bundles, that contract on stimulation and produce bodily motion; of three types: striped muscle (q.v.), smooth muscle (q.v.), and cardiac muscle (q.v.).

muscle atrophy A reversible diminution in muscle (q.v.) volume due to a decrease in the size of individual muscle cells; occurs when a muscle is not subjected to sustained periods of tension.

musculoskeletal Relating to, or involving both the musculature and skeleton, including the bones, muscles, ligaments, tendons, and joints of the body.

musculoskeletal system The structure of the horse including musculature and skeletal components.

mushroom bar shoe A bar shoe (q.v.) in which the shoe is bent in at the quarters and frog (q.v.) with the edges welded together; hole(s) are generally punched in the stem to rivet pads or leather wedges to the bar; used to apply pressure to the frog and relieve pressure from the heels, especially in horses with sore heels or corns (q.v.).

music *see* CRY NO. 2

mustache Also spelled moustache; hair growing near the horse's mouth.

Mustang Also known as fuzztail or incorrectly as wild horse; a small, warmblooded, wild horse of western North America and Mexico descended from European-bred horses including the Andalusian (q.v.) introduced by the Spanish Conquistadors in the 16th century; served as the foundation stock for a large number of the American breeds; stands 13.2 to 15 hands, is sturdy, tough, has a lightweight frame, good bone, notably tough feet, a common, heavy head, may have a coat of any color, and is highly adaptable; at the beginning of the 20th century numbers exceeded two million, herds are now reduced to less than 30,000; the name derived from the Spanish mesteña, meaning wild and untamed, as in a horse; protected by the Free Roaming Wild Horse and Burro Act (q.v.) of 1971.

muster An Australian term; a cattle round-up.

mute (1) A hunting term; said of the hounds (q.v.) when they hunt the line of a fox (q.v.) without giving tongue (q.v.). (2) *see* PACK

mutton-fisted Also known as ham-fisted; said of a heavy-handed, but not necessarily rough, rider.

mutton-withered A horse having a low wither (q.v.) and a heavily muscled shoulder.

mutual field *see* PARI-MUTUEL FIELD

mutel clerk Also known as teller; a racing term; one responsible for accepting bets placed at the racetrack.

mutuel pool *see* PARIMUTUEL POOL

muzzle (1) The lower end of the horse's nose including the nostrils, lips, and chin. (2) A protective covering for the nose which may be made of leather, netting, or synthetic fabrics; used to prevent the horse from biting, eating such things as dung, fencing, or bedding, or tearing at wound coverings, wraps, and blankets; held in position by a single strap which rests on the bridle path (q.v.) behind the ears. (3) To put a muzzle on a horse.

muzzle in a pint pot An antiquated term; said of a horse, such as an Arab (q.v.) with a muzzle so refined and small it would fit in a pint-sized pot.

myoglobinuria The presence of muscle pigment in urine as due to azoturia (q.v.)

myopathy Non-inflammatory muscle degeneration, as occurs in muscular dystrophy.

myositis *see* EQUINE MYOGLOBINURIA

N

nag Also known as yaboo (obs); a saddle horse; any aged, slow, worthless horse.

nagging The process of training and schooling a horse for hunting or riding.

nagsman An English term; a man who made his living breaking and schooling horses used for road hacking and hunting.

nail (1) *see* QUICK. (2) *see* HORSESHOE NAIL. (3) To attach a horseshoe to the horse's hoof by means of nails.

nail cutter Also known as nail nipper; a long-handled, pritchel-type tool made of metal used to cut off clinched, turned-over, and wrung-off nails to an equal length.

nail bind Also known as close nail or shod too close; to place a horseshoe nail too close to the white line (q.v.) when fitting a horseshoe to the hoof; results in pressure on the sensitive laminae (q.v.) causing pain, shortened stride, or temporary lameness; generally less serious than quick (q.v.).

nail into the quarter A farrier's term; when nailing a horseshoe to (q.v.) the hoof using 6 nails, the toe nail is pointed toward the quarter, the quarter nail is directed upward and the heel nail is pointed toward the quarter; helps limit the chance of quicking (q.v.).

nail nipper *see* NAIL CUTTER

nail prick *see* QUICK

nail quick *see* QUICK

name A racing term; to enter a horse in a race.

Nangqen Horse An exotic horse breed indigenous to that part of western China which was once part of greater Tibet; a small, dun-factor (q.v.) horse with a black mane, small head, thin neck, enlarged lungs, and strong bones; written record of the breed dates as early as AD 366.

nap (1) Said of a horse who fails to obey the aids as evidenced by reluctance to leave his companions, the stable, etc.; may develop into rearing, bucking, etc. as an act of defiance. (2) A racing term; a good betting tip. (3) A British betting term; a professional tipster's very best pick of the day – the horse he thinks is sure to win.

nape *see* POLL

Napoleon shoe *see* BACKWARDS SHOE

napping A vice; said of the horse, to demonstrate resistance or refuse aids.

nappy Said of a horse who refuses to obey the aids (q.v.), e.g. to refuse to leave the stall when led.

NARHA *see* NORTH AMERICAN RIDING FOR THE HANDICAPPED ASSOCIATION

Narragansett Pacer A fast pacing horse descending from Norfolk Trotters (q.v.), Galloway (q.v.) and Hobby Horses (q.v.) brought to North America in 1625 by English colonists; developed by commercial breeders in Rhode Island and Virginia and named for the Narragansett Bay of Rhode Island, USA; became a major commercial product in the 1650s at which time hundreds were sold to the Canadians and Spanish plantation owners in the West Indies; due to losses from export and cross-breeding, had disappeared from the United States by 1820; when Narragansett mares were put to Thoroughbred (q.v.) stallions in the early 18th century, the American Horse (q.v.) was created from which the American Saddlebred (q.v.) ultimately evolved; also contributed to the gene pool of the Morgan (q.v.), Paso Fino (q.v.), and Standardbred Pacer (q.v.).

narrow behind Said of the horse whose croup, quarters, and thighs lack muscle; may also be a consequence of conformation.

nasal gleet Also known as gleet; a colored nasal discharge.

nasal hemorrhage *see* EPISTAXIS

NASFHA *see* NORTH AMERICAN SELLE FRANÇAIS HORSE ASSOCIATION, INC.

nasogastric tube A long tube capable of reaching from the horse's nose to the stomach; used to administer veterinary treatments.

natal Of, or pertaining to, birth.

National Cutting Horse Association Also known by the acronym NCHA; an organization founded in 1946 in Fort Worth, Texas, USA, to develop a standard format for cutting horse (q.v.) contests, including rules for judging.

National Equestrian Federation The national governing body of equestrian events and activities in any country; affiliated with the FEI (q.v.).

National Horse Association of Great Britain A British organization founded in 1922 to further the welfare of the horse and pony and interests of horse and pony owners and breeders; subsumed into the British Horse Society (q.v.) in 1947.

National Horse Show Also known as The National or The Garden; a premier horse show first organized in the United States in 1883; held annually in Madison Square Garden, New York, USA.

National Master Farriers and Blacksmiths Association A British organization founded in 1905 to promote the welfare of farriers (q.v.) and blacksmiths (q.v.).

National Pony Society A British organization founded in 1893 to encourage the breeding, registration and improvement of British riding ponies and Mountain and Moorland ponies and to foster the welfare of ponies in general.

National Quarter Horse Association An American organization founded in the early 1940s to establish breed specifications and a registry for the Quarter-type horse; merged into the American Quarter Horse Association (q.v.) in 1949.

National Recording Club Auxiliary Also known by the acronym NRC; an auxiliary registry of the American White (q.v.) and American Cream (q.v.) registries for off-colored foals of American White or American Cream Horses, or any grade horse, which carries white or cream genes who can be used for future breeding of whites or creams; horses brought into the breed for good cross-over may also be registered.

National Reining Horse Association Also known by the acronym NRHA; a nonprofit organization founded in Ohio, USA in 1966 to organize, promote, and establish purses for shows, develop rules for showing and judging, create a forum and guidelines for breeders and trainers, and to promote the use of the reining horse (q.v.); open to all breeds.

National Road Transportation Federation An amalgamation of local associations organized in Great Britain; membership was originally restricted to operators of horse-drawn vehicles.

national sire A state-owned stud horse (q.v.).

national stud A state-owned stud farm (q.v.).

National Trotting Association of Great Britain A British organization founded in 1952 to promote trotter (q.v.) racing.

National Veterinary Medical Association of Great Britain and Ireland A British organization founded in 1881 to promote and oversee the interest and practice of veterinary medicine in Great Britain and Ireland.

Nations Cup Also known as Prix des Nations, Cup of Nations, or Coppa Delle Nazione; an international show jumping event open to four riders from each participating country, each riding one horse; open to female competitors since 1953.

native pony (1) Any pony indigenous to a particular country. (2) Any pony breed indigenous to Great Britain, including the Welsh Pony (q.v.), Shetland Pony (q.v.), Dartmoor (q.v.), New Forest Pony (q.v.), Highland Pony (q.v.), Exmoor (q.v.), Fel (q.v.), Dales (q.v.), and Connemara (q.v

NATRC *see* NORTH AMERICAN TRAIL RIDE CONFERENCE

natural aids Any means by which the rider uses his own physical attributes to communicate instruction to the horse; include legs, hands, and the influence of the body, seat, and voice; differ from artificial aids (q.v.).

natural allures Any untaught gait or pace of a horse, e.g. walk, trot, and canter.

natural cover Impregnation of the mare by a stallion under natural rather than orchestrated conditions; the most commonly used method of breeding; differs from artificial insemination (q.v.) or embryo transfer (q.v.).

natural fence Any naturally occurring jumping obstacle as opposed to one constructed specifically for the purpose of equestrian sport; include fallen logs, stone walls, gates, hedges, etc.

natural insemination To inseminate (q.v.) as by natural cover (q.v.).

natural paint marking Refers to coat color; a predominant hair color with at least one contrasting area of solid white hair with some underlying pink, or unpigmented skin present in the prescribed zone (q.v.) on the horse at the time of birth; on a predominantly white horse, at least one contrasting area of colored hair with some underlying dark pigmented skin must be present in the prescribed zone on the horse at the time of birth; in both cases, the marking must exceed a 2 inch (5 cm) diameter and occur in the prescribed zone.

naturopathy A method of treating and healing emotional and physical conditions using natural agents and physical means.

natural slant The natural, slightly curved, bow of the horse's body; the horse does not naturally move straight.

nave *see* HUB

navel ill *see* JOINT ILL

navel infection *see* JOINT ILL

navicular (1) *see* NAVICULAR BONE. (2) *see* NAVICULAR DISEASE

navicular bone Also known as navicular or distal sesamoid; the small, flat, boat-shaped bone located behind the coffin joint in the hoof; regulates the angle at which the deep flexor tendon attaches to the coffin bone (q.v.).

navicular bursitis *see* NAVICULAR DISEASE

navicular disease Also known as podotrochlitis, navicular, or navicular bursitis; a chronic degenerative condition of the navicular bone which may involve the flexor surface of the bone and the overlying deep digital flexor tendon; essentially unknown in donkeys and ponies; the exact cause is unknown; the condition is both chronic and degenerative although it may be managed in some horses through corrective shoeing and in some cases nerving (q.v.) of the affected limb; symptoms include stumbling, shortened stride, and a characteristic pointing of the toe of the forefoot when the horse is resting, whereby the pressure of the deep flexor tendon on the painful area is relieved; if both forefeet are affected, the horse points alternately.

NCHA *see* NATIONAL CUTTING HORSE ASSOCIATION

Neapolitan An ancient, extinct warmblood similar to the Andalusian (q.v.).

Neapolitan School A classical riding school founded in Naples, Italy in 1532 by Federico Grisone (q.v.) who is considered the first of the classical masters.

near horn *see* HUNTING HEAD

near head *see* HUNTING HEAD

near horse Also known as near leader; a driving term; the horse on the left of a tandem (q.v.).

near leader *see* NEAR HORSE

near pommel *see* HUNTING HEAD

nearside Also known as nigh side; the left side of the horse when viewed from the horse's tail and on the right side when viewed from the head; the term evolved from two situations: (a) in the days when horsemen wore swords, the sword hung to the left side, therefore the rider mounted from the left to avoid interference with the blade and (b) in England, traffic keeps to the left; therefore, the coachman stood on the left side of the horse to be on the side of the road and out of traffic.

nearside backhand shot A polo term; the swing of the polo mallet (q.v.) from right to left over the neck of the horse to strike the ball in a backward direction, e.g. opposite to the direction of travel.

nearside forehand shot A polo term; the swing of the polo mallet (q.v.) from right to left across the neck of the horse to strike the ball in a forward direction, e.g. in the direction of travel.

nearside horse The left-hand horse in a pair used to pull a horse-drawn vehicle.

nearside rein A coaching term; the left rein; does not have a buckle at the hand end.

near to the ground *see* KNEES AND HOCKS TO THE GROUND

neck (1) That portion of the horse's body connecting the head to the shoulders; conformation types include ewe neck (q.v.), bull neck (q.v.), and swan neck (q.v.). (2) A racing term; a measure of distance; approximately ¼ of a length (q.v.); accepted as the length of the horse's neck including the head.

neck bugle *see* BUGLE

neck clip *see* BELLY CLIP

neck collar *see* HARNESS COLLAR

neck rein To guide or direct the horse using rein contact against the neck rather than bit action, e.g. to turn the horse to the right, or offside, pressure with the nearside rein is applied to the neck with the supporting hand (q.v.); commonly used in Western riding.

neck reining To neck rein (q.v.) a horse.

neck ring *see* LARIAT NECK RING

neck rope A Western roping term; a rope that encircles the neck of the horse halfway between the poll and withers, through which the tail of the catch rope (q.v.) is passed and tied to the saddle horn (q.v.); keeps the trained horse straight on the calf and prevents him from turning away from the calf while the roper is flanking or tying.

neck shot Also known as under the neck shot; a polo term; the polo player strikes the polo ball (q.v.) by reaching under his horse's neck from either side.

neck strap A narrow, adjustable leather strap fitted around the base of the horse's neck, through which the martingale (q.v.) passes, and by which it is held in place.

neck stretcher An adjustable elastic cord used to encourage the horse to lower his head and stretch his neck; attached between the horse's forelegs to the girth (q.v.), passes from the girth through the left bit ring, over the poll, through the right bit ring, and connects back to the girth; adjusts to apply pressure to the horse's poll when he is above the bit (q.v.).

negative reinforcement Negative reward used to modify behavior; a punishment.

neigh *see* WHINNY

neighboring A Western term; to help one's neighbor with cow works (q.v.).

Nelson gag *see* DUNCAN GAG

nematodes *see* ROUNDWORMS

neonatal maladjustment syndrome Also known by the acronym NMS; a condition of foals characterized by gross behavioral disturbances; foals appear normal at birth with signs developing within 12 hours of birth; signs include loss of affinity for the mare and sucking reflex, apparent blindness, aimless wandering, and emission of a barking noise; mortality is approximately 50 percent.

neonate A foal (q.v.) less than three or f days old.

nerve (1) Any of the cord-like connecting the body organs w central nervous system and part nervous system with each other, and carrying impulses to and from the brain or a nerve center to convey sensation and originate motion. (2) Also known as denerve, nerving, unnerve, or neurectomy; to surgically cut a nerve (q.v.) or nerve group to eliminate normal nerve response to the targeted area; performed for pain-reduction purposes, as in a palmar digital neurectomy (q.v.) and for cosmetic purposes in show horses (the tail nerve is cut to achieve a quiet tail); is not always an effective way to treat pain and may result in neuroma (q.v.) development. (3) A hunting term; said of a hunter; to display courage in the hunting field.

nerve block Also known as block; to anesthetize a nerve (q.v.) to eliminate feeling to the area it supplies, as for diagnostic purposes.

nerves A hunting term; said of a hunter; to display fear in the hunt field.

nerving *see* NERVE

net energy value Also known as net energy; the energy of feed actually utilized by the horse to maintain life or which is incorporated into the tissue; the energy remaining after subtracting waste energy from the total energy content of a specific food; measured in a calorimeter and is described in calories for a specific amount of feed; differs from digestible energy (q.v.).

nettle bumps Also known as nettle rash; hives (q.v.) triggered by exposure to the leaves of the stinging nettle.

nettle rash *see* NETTLE BUMPS

neurectomy *see* NERVE

neuroendocrine Pertaining to the interaction between the nervous and endocrine systems (q.v.).

euroma A benign tumor appearing on the erve sheath due to repeated trauma on e severed stumps of cut nerves.

opathy Nerve pathology or nerve ference due to hypermobility (q.v.); ccur directly or indirectly in the spine; types: facilitation and inhibition.

neurotransmitters Chemical messenger in the nervous system responsible for conveying electrical impulses across the space between the cells.

Newcastle, William Cavendish, Duke of *see* CAVENDISH, WILLIAM, DUKE OF NEWCASTLE

New Forest *see* NEW FOREST PONY

New Forest Hunt Club A British group founded in 1789 to organize and monitor hunting of the New Forest region in Great Britain.

New Forest Pony Also known as Forest, New Forest, native pony (q.v.), or commonly as lane creeper (so called because it leaves the forest for the villages in winter in search of food and shelter, devouring gardens and decorative shrubbery); a pony breed originating in the heavily wooded New Forest region of southern England; domesticated as early as 1079 by William the Conqueror; efforts to improve the breed began as early as 1016 with the passing of Canute's Forest Law (q.v.), followed by the introduction of Welsh (q.v.) mares in 1208, Thoroughbred (q.v.), Arab (q.v.) and Barb (q.v.) stallions in the 18th and 19th centuries, and subsequently other pony breeds including Welsh (q.v.), Fell (q.v.), Dale (q.v.), Dartmoor (q.v.), Exmoor (q.v.), and Highland (q.v.); presently, mares are crossed with standard-size horses to produce stock suited to light draft, polo (q.v.), and other equestrian sports; all coat colors except piebald (q.v.), skewbald (q.v.), and blue-eyed creams occur with bays and browns predominating; usually stud-bred; stands 12 to 14 hands, has a long and sloping shoulder, long and low action, and is intelligent and easily trained; the stud book is maintained by the New Forest Pony Breeding and Cattle Society (q.v.).

New Forest Pony Breeding and Cattle Society A British organization founded in 1938 following the amalgamation of earlier societies to promote development of the New Forest Pony (q.v.) and to maintain the breed registry; the stud book (q.v.) was opened in 1960.

Newhouse, Charles B. (1805–1877) A British artist known for his coaching and road scenes.

New Kirgiz *see* NOVOKIRGHIZ

Newmarket The English racing center established in the mid-17th century; renowned for the racehorses bred and trained there; the location of the National Stud and numerous other Thoroughbred (q.v.) studs, the former headquarters of the Jockey Club (q.v.) which was formed there by racings' elite in 1750, and two primary racecourses, the now defunct Round and Summer Courses where the 1,000 and 2,000 Guineas, and the Cesarewitch and Cambridgeshire handicap races were run; there are still two effectively distinct courses: the July Course and the Rowley Mile, the latter being 2 miles 2 furlongs long with only one bend; more than 200 races per year are run in Newmarket.

Newmarket boots A tall riding boot, the foot and sole of which are made of leather, while the leg is made of a waterproof canvas.

Newmarket breast girth *see* AINTREE GIRTH

Newmarket cough *see* EQUINE INFLUENZA

Newmarket girth *see* AINTREE GIRTH

Newmarket Plate *see* NEWMARKET TOWN PLATE.

Newmarket Town Plate Also known as Newmarket Plate or Town Plate; the first horserace run on the Newmarket (q.v.) round course in 1664; founded by Charles II.

Newport Pagnell A two-wheeled, horse-drawn country cart; had a paneled body with turned spindles at the top, back-to-back seating for four, and was hung on two side-springs.

New Zealand Cobb Coach A horse-drawn vehicle of the Concord Coach (q.v.) type used for long-distance passenger transport and mail delivery in New Zealand until the late 19th century; seated 14 passengers.

New Zealand Driving Society Also known by the acronym NZDS; a New Zealand organization founded in 1983 to liaise between the driving clubs and to stimulate interest in driving horses and ponies and vehicle restoration.

New Zealand Horse Society Also known by the acronym NZHS; a New Zealand organization founded to organize and oversee amateur equine sports.

New Zealand rug An extremely durable, traditionally waterproof, partially lined, canvas rug (q.v.) used to cover and protect a turned out horse from the weather.

niacin A B-complex vitamin; important for normal metabolism; a component of two coenzymes: nicotinamide adenine dimecleotide and nicotinamide adenine dinucleotide; deficiency is uncommon in horses as normal dietary levels are synthesized in adequate quantities by bacterial flora of the cecum and colon and in the tissues from the amino acid, tryptophan.

nibble Mutual grooming as by small bites, particularly on the shoulder or withers.

nibbles *see* TREATS

nick (1) Also known as prick or nicking; to surgically sever the small tendons and muscles under the tail of the horse to achieve a more elevated tail set (q.v.) or carriage; a crupper (q.v.) is used to set the tail; performed almost exclusively on American Saddlebreds (q.v.). (2) An exceptional horse, the product of two different bloodlines.

nicker Also known as whicker; a low-pitched, vibrating sound emitted by the horse to denote pleasurable anticipation.

nicking (1) *see* NICK NO 1. (2) A breeding term; the mating of two different bloodlines to produce certain desired results, e.g. greater speed, improved bone, better size, etc.

nictitating membrane Also known as third eyelid, haw, or *membrana nictans*; a thin sheath of tissue underlying the upper and lower eyelids; one of three eyelids found in the horse, dog, and certain other animals.

Nigerian A pony breed indigenous to Nigeria where it probably descended from the Barb (q.v.); has more the appearance of a horse and stands at the upper size limit of the pony category; has a mark sloping croup, weak and poorly developed hindquarters, a rather flat head with a straight profile, small, pricked ears, a short neck, and pronounced withers; the back is straight, the girth deep and has strong, slender, medium-length legs; is strong, willing, and docile; used for riding, packing, and light draft.

nigh side *see* NEAR SIDE

night blindness Also known as nyctalopia; a condition that sometimes affects horses and mules in countries or areas where sunlight glare is very intense during the day; at night, such animals are unable to see and will readily stumble on easily discernible objects.

nightcap A racing term; the last horse race listed in a racing program.

night eyes *see* CHESTNUTS

Nightingale, Basil (1880–1910) A noted painter of hunting portraits and scenes and of race horses.

night latch A safety strap attached to a Western saddle which the rider holds on to in order to stay on a contrary horse; passes under the saddle horn (q.v.) and ties to the outside around either the left or right swell (q.v.).

night roller A roller (q.v.) when used to hold a night rug (q.v.) in place.

nisakinetum A Russian equestrian sport in which spear-bearing participants mounted on galloping horses attempt to knock balls from atop several wooden posts arranged in a line.

nit The egg of a louse (q.v.) or other parasitic insect; a louse in the immature stage; generally white or yellow in color, about the size of a pin head and sometimes found in the horse's hair.

Nivernais *see* CHAROLLAIS

NMS *see* NEONATAL MALADJUSTMENT SYNDROME

obble *see* DOPE NO. 2

bbling *see* DOPING

noble science A hunting term; the art and science of hunting a pack of foxhounds (q.v.).

nod (1) Said of a horse who lowers and raises his head with each stride; may denote lameness (the horse drops his head when he bears weight on the good leg and jerks his head upward when it is placed on the bad) or failure to accept the bit. (2) An American racing term; to give a jockey permission to dismount following a race. (3) A racing term; said of a horse who lowers and extends his head, his nose reaching the finish ahead of a close competitor.

noisy A hunting term; said of mouthy (q.v.) hounds.

Nom de Course A racing term; the stable name, or a name adopted by an owner or group of owners for racing purposes.

nominate To propose, offer, or pay a fee to make a horse eligible to compete in an event.

nomination Also known as noms; the act of nominating; the state of being nominated.

nomination fees An amount of money paid to make a horse eligible to compete in an event; are part of the prize money.

nominator A racing term; one who owns a horse at the time he is nominated to compete in a stakes race.

noms *see* NOMINATION

non-articular fracture A break in a bone which does not involve a joint.

non-articulating ringbone A ringbone (q.v.) condition where the bony growth has not attached to the joints between the long and short pastern or the short pastern and the pedal bone; may not result in lameness.

non-characteristic registration A registration category for horses who do not represent recognizable characteristics of a specific breed; both the dam and the sire must be registered by a common registry for color-type breeds such as the Appaloosa (q.v.), Pinto (q.v.), and Paint (q.v.).

noncontender A racing term; said of a horse running in a race who is not expected to win.

nondescript horse A movie industry term; a plain-looking horse used by extras or for background action in a film.

nondisplaced fracture A break in a bone in which the bone fragments remain in alignment.

non-essential protein Any of 14 of the 24 known amino acids (q.v.) produced in the horse's gastro-intestinal tract from the 10 essential amino acids (q.v.) and other food components; unnecessary for growth, maintenance, or repair of body tissues.

non-hand-fed mare Said of a New Forest Pony (q.v.) mare who has never been off the forest except to participate in an annual New Forest Pony show.

non-leading leg *see* TRAILING LEG

Nonius A warmblood breed developed at the Mezöhegyes stud, Hungary, in the early 19th century; descended from the French stallion Nonius (sired by an English half-bred and out of a Norman [q.v.] mare) put to Andalusian (q.v.), Arab (q.v.), Kladruber (q.v.), Norman, and English half-bred mares; the smaller type stands 14.2 to 15.2 hands, while the larger stands 15.2 to 16.2 hands; has a bay, black, or brown coat, elegant head, long neck, and strong back; is strong, hardy, and of docile, but lively temperament; used for harness and riding.

non-pro The contraction of nonprofessional (q.v.).

non-professional Also known as non-pro; said of a rider who does not accept payment for work or prize money in any equestrian event, including monies for the training of the horse or rider, competing of the horse, or buying and selling of horses; the opposite of a professional (q.v.).

non-progressive color pattern Refers to coat color pattern; coat color remains the same from birth through old age; the opposite of progressive color pattern (q.v.).

non-steroidal anti-inflammatory drug Also known by the acronym NSAID; any drug which intercepts the chemicals that trigger and maintain inflammation by blocking prostaglandin activity and the blood-clotting effects of thromboxane; reduces the perception of pain without impeding healing.

non-sweater Said of a horse whose sweating mechanisms fail, a condition known as anhydrosis (q.v.).

Norfolk Cart A two-wheeled, horse-drawn vehicle of the Dogcart (q.v.) type developed and used in the English county of Norfolk beginning in the mid-19th century; frequently slat-sided with a grained and varnished finish; hung on sideways semi-elliptical springs (q.v.) with either curved or straight shafts; carried four dos-a-dos (q.v.).

Norfolk Roadster *see* NORFOLK TROTTER

Norfolk Trotter Also known as Norfolk Roadster or Roadster; an extinct pony breed native to Norfolk, England from which the name derived; its bloodlines are rooted in Yorkshire and Arab (q.v.) stallions; was a short-legged, strong trotter, possessed of exceptional speed, fortitude, and endurance; served as foundation stock for most trotting breeds, as well as many riding horses; the closest surviving relation is the Hackney (q.v.).

Noric Horse *see* NORIKER

Noriker Also known as Pinzgauer, Pinzgauer Noriker, Oberlander, Noric Horse, or South German Coldblood; a Roman horse breed developed in the province of Noricum which corresponds roughly to present Austria; thought to have descended from tough Haflinger Ponies (q.v.) crossed with Neapolitan, Burgundian, and Andalusian (q.v.) blood in the 16th century; a sure-footed, heavy draft horse standing 15.1 to 16.1 hands; the coat is generally bay, chestnut, or spotted, while dapple (q.v.) and gray are rare; has a slightly heavy head with a straight or slightly convex profile, a short neck, flowing, wavy mane, broad withers a long, slightly-hollow back, and wel muscled legs with broad joints ar feathering (q.v.); used for heavy draft a farm work and is well-suited for work in the mountains; stallion selection is carefully controlled with weight pulling, walking, and trotting trials mandatory before a horse can stand at stud.

normal shoeing *see* PHYSIOLOGICAL SHOEING

norman A hoof shape pattern in which the hoof is generally round with the widest part of the hoof located midway between the toe and heels.

Norman Also known as Anglo-Norman, Norman Horse, or French Saddle Horse; an ancient horse breed originating more than 1,000 years ago at which time it was used as a heavy draft war horse; descended from a mix of German, Arab (q.v.), and Barb (q.v.) blood which produced a sturdy saddle horse which was crossed with English Thoroughbred (q.v.) and Norfolk Trotter (q.v.) in the 18th and 19th centuries; more recent introductions of Thoroughbred blood have resulted in a hunter-type horse known as the Selle Français (q.v.) whose stud book is a continuation of that for the Norman; stands about 16 hands and usually has a bay or chestnut coat; used for riding and jumping.

Norman Horse *see* NORMAN

Norman Percheron Association An American organization founded in 1876 to maintain the stud book and promote breeding and use of Percheron (q.v.) horses; the first pure-breed stock association formed in the United States; in 1877 the name was changed to the Percheron Association.

Norman Trotter *see* FRENCH TROTTER

North American Riding for the Handicapped Association Also known by the acronym NARHA; an American organization founded in 1981 to organize equine events, facilities, and programs for handicapped individuals.

North American Selle Français Horse Association, Inc. Also known by the acronym NASFHA; an American organization formed in the 1990s to promote and register Selle Français (q.v.), Anglo-Arab (q.v.), and other French breed horses in the United States under official agreement with the French Ministry of Agriculture, National Stud Farms Division, and the Institut du Cheval (q.v.); all registered horses are automatically entered in the appropriate French stud book and issued a French passport and identification documents.

North American Trail Ride Conference Also known by the acronym NATRC; an American organization founded in 1961 to sanction competitive trail rides; horse and rider are judged separately -- the riders are evaluated on horsemanship skills, safe riding practices, and a safe camp environment while the horses are judged on soundness, manners, conditioning, and way of going; such events are not races, although there is a specific time limit for event completion; horses must be at least four years old to compete.

Northern Dales Pony Society, The A British organization founded in 1957 to improve and encourage breeding and use of the pure-bred Dales Pony (q.v.).

Northern Hackney Horse Club A British organization founded in 1945 to further interest in Hackney (q.v.) horses, cobs, and ponies.

North-Hestur *see* NORTH SWEDISH TROTTER

Northlands A relatively rare Norwegian pony breed descended from the Asiatic Wild Horse (q.v.) and the Tarpan (q.v.); since the 1920s, selection criteria for breeding stock has been loosely standardized; is strong, frugal, of good temperament and energetic, stands about 13 hands, may have a chestnut, bay, brown, or gray coat, has a well-proportioned head, short neck, long back, rounded croup, sturdy, well-muscled legs, and full forelock, mane and tail; used for riding and light draft.

North Swedish *see* NORTH SWEDISH HORSE

North Swedish Horse Also known as North Swedish; an active, heavy, medium-sized Swedish cold blood; descended from an amalgam of breeds based on ancient Scandinavian stock; most closely related to the Døle Gudbrandsal (q.v.); is powerful, has a large head, short neck, long, deep body, short, strong legs with plenty of bone, a special aptitude for trotting, lively striding action, is an easy keeper, long lived, and is notably resistant to disease; possesses a kind temperament, and tremendous pulling power; stands 15.1 to 15.3 hands and commonly has a dun, brown, chestnut, or black coat; used for heavy draft and farm work; the breeding program is systematic and includes hauling tests and regular veterinary inspections.

North Swedish Trotter Also known as North-Hestur; the same breed, but a lighter version of the North Swedish Horse (q.v.); bred by careful selection to develop its natural trotting ability; has a long and active stride and is a popular harness race horse.

Norwegian *see* DØLE GUDBRANDSDAL

Norwegian Trotter *see* DØLE TROTTER

nose (1) That portion of the horse's head including the muzzle (q.v.) and mouth. (2) Also known as short head (Brit.); a racing term; the narrowest possible winning margin in a race being less than a head (q.v.) as, "The horse won by a nose" (q.v.). (3) A hunting term; the ability of the hound (q.v.) to follow and remain on the line (q.v.) of a fox (q.v.) regardless of whether the scent (q.v.) is breast high (q.v.) or faint.

nosebag Also known as feed bag or morral; a bag made of hemp, webbing, canvas or other suitably strong material to which an adjustable strap attaches; fits over the horse's muzzle and is held in place on the horse's head by means of the strap passed behind the horse's ears; used to provide feed to horses away from the stable and to reduce waste, as when tethered, harnessed, etc.

noseband A piece of tack, separate from, but used in conjunction with, a bridle; consists of a nosepiece which applies pressure to the bridge of the nose in the front and buckles under the horse's jaw; the nosepiece, in front and under, is joined by a sliphead similar to a bridle headpiece; used for a variety of purposes and consists of many types including the Australian noseband (q.v.), Brinekind noseband (q.v.), drop noseband (q.v.), cavesson noseband (q.v.), Grakle noseband (q.v.), Kineton noseband (q.v.), shadow roll noseband (q.v.), bosal (q.v.), and Flash noseband (q.v.).

nosebleed *see* EPISTAXIS

nose bridle *see* BITLESS BRIDLE

not a boy's horse Said of a strong and/or difficult horse; requiring a strong and experienced rider.

not accepting hand A dressage term; said of a horse who resists action on the bit when contact is taken; manifest in many ways including tongue hanging out, leaning on the bit, head tossing, etc.

not between leg and hand A dressage term; said of a horse who is not sufficiently under control of the leg and hand aids of the rider.

not enough angle A dressage term; said of the shoulder-in movement when the rider has not asked the horse to bring his forehand sufficiently off the track.

not enough collection Said of a horse failing to demonstrate sufficient hindquarter engagement; results in steps that are too long and in movement on the forehand (q.v.).

not enough difference A dressage term; said when variations required within a gait are not sufficiently evident, e.g. there is little discernible change when a horse is asked to move from working to medium trot.

not enough extension Said of a horse who does not show sufficient stride lengthening.

not enough from behind A dressage term; said of the horse when his hind legs do not come sufficiently under him.

no time (1) Also known by the acronym NT; a rodeo term; said of a rider; to fail to qualify in a timed cattle event by exceeding the time allowed; signaled by the flagman (q.v.) waving his flag. (2) A team sorting (q.v.) term; called if any calf crosses the foul line out of numerical order or passe across the foul line and then retreats to th original side.

not lowering enough A dressage term; said of the horse as when on a long or free rein; the horse fails to stretch into the bit and lower his head to take up the slack created by the ride lengthening the rein.

Nottingham Cart Also known as Nottingham Cottage Cart; a light, two-wheeled, horse-drawn vehicle of the Dogcart (q.v.) type; had hood-protected rear seats and was frequently flat-sided; popular from the mid-19th century in Nottingham, England, from which the name derived.

Nottingham Cottage Cart *see* NOTTINGHAM CART

nott stag Also known as hummel (Scot); a British term; a stag (q.v.) that does not grow antlers.

novice An inexperienced horse or rider; a beginner.

Novice Level The British and Australian equivalent of First Level (q.v.).

Novokirghiz Also known as Kirghiz, Kirgiz, New Kirgiz, or Kirgis; a Russian warm-blood indigenous to the mountains of Soviet Central Asia and China; descended from old Kirghiz (q.v.) stock bred by nomadic tribesmen, the modern breed was developed between 1930 and 1940 through introduction of Thoroughbred (q.v.) and Don (q.v.), and later half-bred Anglo-Don, blood; is ideally suited to working at high altitudes, sure-footed and tough, has a longish back, straight shoulder, short, strong legs with good bone, and strong feet; stands 14.1 to 15.1 hands and may have a coat of any solid color although bay occurs most often; is good tempered and active; used for riding, harness, and packing.

NRC *see* NATIONAL RECORDING CLUB

NRHA *see* NATIONAL REINING HORSE ASSOCIATION

NSAID *see* NON-STEROIDAL ANTI-INFLAMMATORY DRUG

NT *see* NO TIME

umb A cutting term; a cow that is not hreatened or challenged by a horse and shows little desire to return to the herd.

number A hunting term; the number appearing after the name of a hound (q.v.) in a show catalogue; refers to the year in which a hound (q.v.) was entered (q.v.), which is usually one year after the hound was born.

number ball Also known as pill; a racing term; a small, numbered ball selected in a blind draw from a number box (q.v.) to determine post positions (q.v.) of the horses.

number board A racing term; an electronic board upon which post positions (q.v.) are identified after the number balls (q.v.) are drawn; includes the name of the horse and jockey for a given race, as well as any pertinent information such as if a horse will be wearing blinkers (q.v.).

number box A racing term; a box containing number balls (q.v.).

number cloth Also known as saddle cloth; a racing term; a square, white linen cloth cut slightly larger than the saddle which bears the number corresponding to the horse's program number; given to the jockey at the time of weighing out, is included in the jockey's weight, and is placed under the saddle so that the number is visible; the jockey may opt to wear an armband bearing the same number.

number four A polo term; the player in the number four position (q.v.).

number four position Also known as back; a polo term; one of four positions on a polo team (q.v.) the responsibility of whose it is to protect the goal (q.v.) and guard the number one position (q.v.) on the opponent's team.

number 1 *see* PROP, THE

number one (1) A polo term; the player assuming the number one position (q.v.). (2) *see* NUMBER ONE POSITION

number one position Also known as forward; a polo term; one of four positions on a polo team (q.v.); the most forward offensive player.

number three A polo term; the player assuming the number three position (q.v.).

number three position Also known as quarterback; a polo term; one of four positions on a polo team (q.v.); is usually the team captain or quarterback; along with the number two position (q.v.), is the highest rated and the most experienced player on the team; the pivotal player between offense and defense.

number two A polo term; the player assuming the number two position (q.v.).

number two position A polo term; one of four positions on a polo team (q.v.) usually played by the highest rated and the most experienced player on the team; responsible for pushing both offensive and defensive play; is played as aggressively as the number one position (q.v.), yet deeper and harder.

numnah Also incorrectly known as saddle cloth; a saddle-shaped pad (q.v.) cut slightly larger than the saddle, placed between the saddle and the back of the horse to absorb sweat and provide protection; may be made of felt, sheepskin, or cloth-covered foam or rubber.

nursery handicap A racing term; a race for two-year-old horses usually run after September 1.

nutcracker A horse who grinds his teeth.

nutcracker springs (1) A coaching term; four elliptic springs, collectively, when used together on one horse-drawn vehicle. (2) A coaching term; two elbow springs when used one above the other and joined to each other at one end and to the horse-drawn vehicle body and undercarriage on the other.

nutraceutical Any food supplement reputed to have health benefits such as reducing or relieving symptoms including, but not limited to, inflammation; a word coined in 1989 by The Foundation for Innovation in Medicine to describe feed; little is known about how the active ingredients in these products – chondroitin sulfates (q.v.), methylsulfonylmethane (q.v.), yucca (q.v.), etc. – work although it is thought they may scavenge free radicals, change joint fluid viscosity, affect circulation, boost or otherwise alter metabolic pathways, and/or provide dietary supplements whose functions are yet unknown.

nutritional anemia A type of anemia (q.v.); an abnormal condition of the blood characterized by a deficiency in the production of red blood cells; may be caused by a deficiency in protein (q.v.), minerals (q.v.), and/or vitamins in the horse's diet.

nutritional hyperparathyroidism *see* OSTEODYSTROPHIA FIBROSA

nutritional muscular dystrophy *see* WHITE MUSCLE DISEASE

nuts (1) *see* CUBES. (2) *see* TESTES

NZDS *see* NEW ZEALAND DRIVING SOCIETY

NZHS *see* NEW ZEALAND HORSE SOCIETY

O

Oaks *see* EPSOM OAKS

oakum A farrier term; medicated hemp used for hoof packing; usually used in conjunction with a horseshoe pad (q.v.).

oatburner *see* HAYBURNER

oat grass Any wild species of oat; any of certain oat-like grains.

oat hay A cut and dried grass hay (q.v.) made from oat grass after harvesting the grain; first- and second-cuts average 4.3 percent digestible protein and 33 percent fiber.

oats (1) A cereal grass, *Avena sativa*, cultivated for its edible grain used as a feed for animals. (2) The edible grain of the cereal grass, *Avena sativa*; higher in fiber content than corn (q.v.), barley (q.v.), or rye (q.v.) and higher in protein content than corn; contains between 12 and 13 percent protein and 11 to 12 percent fiber as calculated by weight with weight being an important factor in judging quality – the higher the weight per bushel, the greater the proportion of kernel to husk; the average weight per bushel is 32 pounds (14.5 kg); best fed by weight and not by volume; may be fed whole or processed, i.e., clipped (q.v.), rolled, crushed, or crimped to improve digestible energy content; processing results in some loss of nutritional quality and may result in grain fermentation and/or deterioration.

Obadiah Elliott *see* ELLIOTT, OBADIAH

obedience Said of the horse; the act or habit of obeying; submission.

Obel Lameness Grades A system of rating degrees of lameness resulting from laminitis (q.v.); developed by Niles Obel in 1948.

Obel Grade I A degree of lameness resulting from laminitis (q.v.) as defined by the Obel Lameness Grades (q.v.); the horse frequently shifts weight between the feet, demonstrates no discernible lameness at the walk, but bilateral lameness at the trot.

Obel Grade II A degree of lameness resulting from laminitis (q.v.) as defined by the Obel Lameness Grades (q.v.); the horse will not resist having a leg lifted or walking, but does show lameness at the walk.

Obel Grade III A degree of lameness resulting from laminitis (q.v.) as defined by the Obel Lameness Grades (q.v.); the horse will resist having a leg lifted and is resistant to walk.

Obel Grade IV A degree of lameness resulting from laminitis (q.v.) as defined by the Obel Lameness Grades (q.v.); the horse will walk only if forced to do so.

Oberlander *see* NORIKER

obesity The condition of being fat; overweight.

objection Also known as protest; a complaint submitted to an event organizing body against another competitor or about an official call or rule infringement.

objection flag A racing term; a red flag raised on the number board (q.v.) following completion of a race indicating that an objection (q.v.) has been filed.

objection overruled To rule or decide against an objection (q.v.); in racing denoted by the raising of a white flag on the number board (q.v.) to replace the objection flag (q.v.).

objection sustained To rule in favor of an objection (q.v.); in racing denoted by the raising of a green flag on the number board (q.v.) to replace the objection flag (q.v.).

oblique fracture A break of a bone at an angle.

oblique shoulder *see* SLOPING SHOULDER

obstacle course *see* COMPETITION C

obstructive pulmonary disease *see* CHRONIC OBSTRUCTIVE PULMONARY DISEASE

obstructive jaundice A jaundice (q.v.) condition caused by obstructed bile flow from the liver to the duodenum; causes increased pressure in the bile duct which causes a backflow of bile pigment into the blood with the concentration of pigment increasing until deposited in the tissues and signs of jaundice (q.v.) appear, e.g. yellowing of the eyeballs, skin, and urine; may be caused by inflammation of the duodenum, bot larvae entering the bile duct, tumors, roundworm (q.v.) migration through the liver, or certain types of impaction of the large or small intestines.

occidental horse Any cold blood (q.v.) horse; (obs).

occipital crest *see* POLL

occult spavin Arthritis (q.v.) of the lower aspect of the hock (q.v.) caused by development of a growth between the two bones of the hock (q.v.) just below the joint on the inner side; difficult to detect because of the lack of visible signs.

ocular habronemiasis A cutaneous habronemiasis (q.v.) of the eye cause by a parasite of the genus *Habronema* (q.v.); larvae of this worm are deposited by infected flies in the eye mucosa where they cause eye watering, sometimes sensitivity to sunlight, wart-like lesions on the nicitating membrane of the skin around the eye and rarely a mass of granulation tissues involving the entire conjuctiva.

odd board *see* TOTALIZATOR BOARD

odd colored Refers to coat color; a coat consisting of large, irregular patches of more than two colors which may merge into each other at the patch edges.

odds A racing term; a betting quote on a horse running in a race; determined, in the first instance, by a combination of mathematical probability and the bookmaker's own opinion, subsequently modified in response to the amount of money bet on the horse as compared to the money bet on other horses.

odds man A racing term; an employee responsible for calculating the changing betting odds and numbers and amounts of bets staked in any given horse race; employed at tracks where totalizators (q.v.) are not used.

odds-on A racing term; betting odds (q.v.) of less than even money (q.v.).

oedema *see* EDEMA

oesophagus *see* ESOPHAGUS

oestrus *see* ESTRUS

oestrus cycle *see* ESTROUS CYCLE

off (1) Also known as the off; a racing term; the race start time. (2) A racing term; the difference between the track record and the final race time. (3) Said of a lame horse, e.g. "He's off in the right front." (4) A racing term; the slowness of a horse as expressed in a time or lengths comparison (q.v.) between what it should run, or what other horses have run, e.g. "He is off his best time." (5) Said of a horse who has passed a certain year of his age, e.g. in his fifth year, the horse is said to be five off. (6) A racing term; to begin a race, e.g. "They're off."

offals *see* WEATINGS

off-course bet *see* OFF-TRACK BET

off horse Also known as off leader; a driving term; the horse on the right of a tandem (q.v.).

office, the A British jumping term; said of the rider; to communicate to the horse through aids to take off at a jump.

official (1) A racing term; a notice displayed when the results of a race are confirmed. (2) An individual invested with authority at an equine event.

off his feed Said of a horse who is not eating normal quantities of food as due to illness, injury, fatigue, etc.

off leader *see* OFF HORSE

offset knees *see* LATERAL DEVIATION OF THE METACARPAL BONES

offset stirrup Also known as Kornokoff iron; a modified hunting iron (q.v.); has an off-center eyelet positioned toward the outside of the stirrup and forward-sloping sides; the foot tread is inclined upward and canted to encourage correct leg position, forcing the heels down and the toes in.

offside (1) *see* FAR SIDE. (2) Said of a horse/player in illegal territory, or ahead of the ball, as in mounted games such as polo (q.v.).

offside backhand A polo term; the rearward swing of the polo mallet (q.v.) by a mounted polo player (q.v.) from the horse's nose towards his tail on the right side; the player hits the polo ball (q.v.) in the direction opposite to that traveled.

offside forehand A polo term; the forward swing of the polo mallet (q.v.) by a mounted polo player (q.v.) from the rear of his horse toward the nose on the right side; the player hits the polo ball (q.v.) in the direction of travel.

offside horse The right-hand horse in a pair used to pull a horse-drawn vehicle.

off the bit Said of a horse who fails to carry himself easily, is unbalanced, does not move from behind, and resists the aids (q.v.); may be due to the horse being behind the bit (q.v.) or above the bit (q.v.).

off the board (1) A racing term; said of a horse who fails to finish in the money (q.v.). (2) A racing term; a horse so lightly supported that his odds exceed 99 to 1.

off the pace A racing term; said of a horse who trails the early leaders.

off the top A racing term; the practice of deducting a fixed sum or percentage from the mutuel pool (q.v.) before paying off winning ticket holders.

off-track (1) *see* OFF-TRACK BETTING. (2) A racing term; said of a racing surface that is not fast.

off-track bet Also known as off-course bet; any wager made at a site other than the racetrack where the race(s) bet on is being run.

off-track betting Also known as off-track or by the acronym OTB; a racing term; betting conducted at legalized betting venues other than the racetrack; may be operated by the tracks, management companies specializing in parimutuel (q.v.) wagering, or by independent corporations authorized by individual states; money wagered is usually combined with on-track betting pools.

off-track betting site A racing term; a legal location where bets, other than those placed at the track at which the race is run, are placed.

ogee A coaching term; a horse-drawn vehicle when the body lines are curved.

old scent *see* STALE LINE

oil (1) Any of a large class of substances typically unctuous, viscous, combustible, liquid at ordinary temperatures, and soluble in ether or alcohol, but not in water; used for food, moistening, lubricating, etc.; those used for food are generally derived from oilseed grains. (2) To moisten, smear, lubricate, or condition with oil, as in leather or hooves. (3) To administer mineral oil to a horse through a nasogastric tube (q.v.) to relieve gas or help the horse pass an intestinal blockage.

oil cake A mass of seeds or pulp remaining after the extraction of oil from cottonseed, linseed (q.v.), or coconut fruits; used as a feed for livestock and as a fertilizer.

oiled Said of a horse given mineral oil through a nasogastric tube (q.v.) to relieve gas or to help the horse pass an intestinal blockage.

oilseed Also known as oilseed grains; any seed grown as a source of oil (q.v.), such as linseed (q.v.), cottonseed, and soybean.

oilseed grains *see* OILSEED

oilseed meals The edible part of any oilseed (q.v.) grain remnant following extraction of the oil; include cottonseed meal (q.v.), linseed meal (q.v.), and soybean meal (q.v.); fed in conjunction with grain to offset protein deficiencies and balance rations; the fat and protein content varies slightly depending on the extraction method used.

Oldenburg The heaviest of the German

warmbloods; derived from the Friesian (q.v.) during the 17th century for use as a strong carriage horse; over the years, Spanish, Neapolitan, Norman and Cleveland Bay (q.v.) blood was introduced, later, due to reduced requirements for carriage horses, Anglo-Arab, Thoroughbred and Hanoverian blood was introduced to develop an all-purpose riding and competition horse; stands 16.2 to 17.2 hands, has a bay, brown, black or gray coat, rarely chestnut, relatively short legs for its size, a high-set tail, broad croup (q.v.), pronounced withers, straight back and a wide and deep-set chest.

old heavy *see* STAGE COACH

old scent *see* STALE LINE

Oleander A Thoroughbred stallion foaled in 1924; one of Germany's greatest racing stallions.

olive dun *see* OLIVE GRULLO

olive grullo Also known as olive dun; refers to coat color; a grullo (q.v.) of the color group dun (q.v.); the coat hair is a yellowish grullo color, the points black, and the head dark; sometimes included in the buckskin (q.v.) group.

Omnibi *see* OMNIBUS

Omnibus Also known as Carrosse à cinq sols (Fr, obs), Omnibi (sl), Omnis (sl), or Bus; a horse-drawn, four-wheeled, single or double-decked public service bus originally developed by French philosopher Blaise Pascal in 1662 and operated as Carrosse à cinq sols until about 1663 or 1664; reintroduced again in Paris in 1829; drawn by a pair of horses or three horses abreast; used predominantly in the inner suburbs and city centers; earlier types were entered from the rear, with either longitudinal or crosswise seating for six with luggage generally carried on a railed roof.

Omnis *see* OMNIBUS

Onager *see* ASIATIC WILD ASS

on a loose rein Said of a horse ridden or driven with the reins so long as to permit slack and eliminate contact between the rider's/driver's hands and the bit.

on-course bet *see* TRACK BET

one-day event A three-phase eventing (q.v.) competition consisting of dressage (q.v.), show jumping (q.v.), and cross-country phases conducted over a period of one day with all three phases performed by the same rider/horse team; in some cases, if the number of entries is high, the cross-country phase may be conducted on a second day.

on-edge Said of a nervous horse.

one for the road *see* STIRRUP CUP NO. 2

one heeled *see* CAUGHT ONE

100 Mile Western States Ride *see* TEVIS CUP RIDE

one run A racing term; said of a horse who expends all his energy in a single burst of speed, usually on the stretch (q.v.).

one-sided (1) Said of a horse who bends more easily to one side than the other, as due to unbalanced muscle development, injury, etc. (2) Also known as one-sided mouth; said of the horse when only responsive to the action of the bit on either the left or right side.

one-sided mouth *see* ONE-SIDED NO. 2.

one-sidedness The state of being one-sided (q.v.).

One Thousand Guineas A 1–mile (1.6 km) horse race for three-year-old fillies first run in England in 1809 at the Newmarket (q.v.) meet.

one two *see* EXACTA BOX

on foot A hunting term; said of a fox (q.v.) when the hounds (q.v.) have located his line (q.v.) in a covert (q.v.) and he begins to move.

on his toes Said of a fidgety horse who is eager to move forward.

on-site diagnostic test *see* STALL-SIDE DIAGNOSTIC TEST

on terms (1) A hunting term; said of hounds able to continue hunting because the scent remains strong. (2) A British racing term; said of a horse or horses who have a chance of catching the leader.

on the aids Also known as between leg and hand; said of a horse framed between the rider's hands and legs, who is fully responsive to the rider's actions including natural and artificial aids (q.v.).

on the Bill Daly Said of a jockey who, in a race, uses the riding style promoted by Bill Daly (q.v.), i.e. to take the lead as soon as possible out of the gate, set the pace, and remain in the lead to the finish (q.v.); commonly used prior to the turn of the 20th century.

on the bit (1) Also known as in the bridle or in the hand; said of a horse who takes a light, gentle contact on the bit and is responsive to any slight change in the pressure applied to the bit through the reins; the horse carries himself easily, is well balanced, moves from behind, and does not resist application of the aids (q.v.). (2) A racing term; said of a horse eager to run.

on the board A racing term; a horse who finishes a race placed – usually implies in one of the first three positions.

on the chin strap A racing term; said of a horse who wins by a wide margin.

on the flags A hunting term; exhibiting of hounds (q.v.) at the kennel for visitor viewing; so called because the hound kennels were historically floored with flagstone and when exhibited, the hounds were paraded on this flooring.

on the forehand Also known as too low or on the hand; said of a horse who places a disproportionate amount of his weight on his shoulders and front legs, with little engagement of the hindquarters; the horse's forehand will be lower than it should be and the horse will be unbalanced, the gaits short, and he will frequently lean on the bit (q.v.) using the rider's hands for support.

on the ground A racing term; a jockey suspended from competition.

on the hand (1) *see* ON THE FOREHAND. (2) Said of the horse when allowed to lean on the bit, using the rider's hands as support.

on the leg Also known as showing too much daylight; said of a horse having disproportionately long legs.

on the lock A coaching term; said of the wheels of a horse-drawn vehicle when turned as far as possible without hitting the vehicle's body.

on the muscle (1) Said of a fit horse. (2) Said of a strong horse who pulls against the bit.

on the nose A racing term; to back a horse to win a race.

on the rail (1) A racing term; said of a horse who runs close to the inside rail (q.v.). (2) A racing term; said of the bookies set up alongside the track rail; (Brit).

on the right rein (1) To move to the right as in a horse under saddle. (2) A dressage term; said of a horse when the right rein is the inside rein.

on top A racing term; said of a horse running in the lead.

on-track bet *see* TRACK BET

on two tracks A dressage term; the horse's movement when the forelegs follow a different track than that of the hind, as in lateral movements (q.v.); an inexact term which often does not correctly convey what is happening, e.g. in the shoulder-in the horse's four legs actually follow three tracks.

oozing A slow leak or trickling of fluid such as blood or serum (q.v.) from a wound.

open (1) Also known as open event; any competition in which any rider, professional, or non-professional, is eligible to perform. (2) Also known as open on a fox; a hunting term; said of the hounds (q.v.) when they first speak (q.v.) on the line of a fox (q.v.). (3) A hunting term; a fox's earth that is not stopped.

Open A jumping term; an advanced

jumping division in which competitors are not restricted from entering by previous winnings.

open bridle A bridle (q.v.) without blinds or blinkers (q.v.) covering the eyes.

open ditch (1) A jumping obstacle consisting of a short slant rail, followed by a shallow ditch that, under most competition rules, is not more than 6 feet (1.8 m) wide, and a brush fence or hedge. (2) A hunting term; any natural or manmade ditch in the ground without necessarily a guard rail or defining dimensions.

open event *see* OPEN NO. 1

open fracture *see* COMPOUND FRACTURE

open-front shelter Any covered horse shelter open on one or two sides; generally, the opening faces away from the prevailing wind.

open-hocked Said of a horse who is wide at the hocks and narrow between the hooves.

open knee An immature knee; the knee of the one- to three-year-old horse when the distal end of the radius growth plate is still cartilaginous.

Open Lot Wagon A four-wheeled horse-drawn vehicle of the Gypsy Wagon (q.v.) type; had a bowed canvas top and an open-frame front fitted with canvas curtains.

opening meet A hunting term; the first meet (q.v.) of the formal hunting season.

open mare Also known as yeld; a broodmare who was not covered during the previous breeding season.

open on a fox *see* OPEN NO. 2

open race A racing term; a horse race with lenient terms of eligibility in which a wide variety of horses are allowed to enter and compete.

open rein *see* DIRECT REIN

open toe egg-bar shoe *see* BACKWARDS SHOE

open top collar Any harness collar (q.v.) that can be spread open at the top to facilitate slipping it over the horse's head; once in place, it is closed and held together with a housing strap before the hames (q.v.) are put on; used on a horse with a wide head and narrow neck; may lose rigidity with use and is liable to produce shoulder sores and/or pinching.

open tug That part of the harness used on a single horse through which the shafts (q.v.) pass; a stout, oval-shaped leather band which buckles at the top to the backband (q.v.) and passes through the top of the saddle.

Opera Bus Also known as Station Bus or Private Omnibus; a small, single-decker, privately owned, horse-drawn bus used for theater-going; first used in the 1870s; had longitudinal seating reached through a rearward opening door, folding steps, and was drawn by a single horse in shafts.

opposite rein *see* INDIRECT REIN

opthalmia Inflammation of the eye and associated membranes characterized by pain and discharge.

optic nerve The nerve (q.v.) that transmits electrical impulses from the light-sensitive retina of the eye to the brain.

optimum take-off zone A jumping term; the ideal area in which a horse must take off to clear a jump; varies according to the height and type of jump to be cleared as well as the horse's stride and jumping ability.

optimum time *see* TIME ALLOWED

optional claimer A racing term; a race for horses to be claimed (q.v.) for a fixed price, at a price within a limited range, or for horses who previously ran at such a price, but which are not entered to be claimed.

optional fence (1) A jumping term; a fence that is not flagged for inclusion in the course, but which competitors may jump to save time or give them an improved line; if a competitor fails at such a jump, the penalty is only that of time wasted. (2) Any jumping obstacle consisting of tw upright fences positioned side-by-si facing the rider; the rider has the option to jump either the left or right fence; the fences may be of different types and/or difficulty and may present different distances to the next fence.

orange dun Refers to coat color; a light red dun (q.v.) coat with red or light red points.

orchard grass hay A cut and dried grass hay (q.v.) made from orchard grass; contains a digestible protein content of approximately 4.2 percent; generally cut at the early-bloom stage to insure palatability and satisfactory nutritional levels.

ordinary hack *see* ROAD HACK

ordinary walk *see* WALK

original *see* RIG

Orloff Trotter *see* ORLOV TROTTER

Orlov *see* ORLOV TROTTER

Orlov-Rostopchin *see* RUSSIAN SADDLE HORSE

Orlov Trotter Also known as Russian Trotter, Orlov, and spelled Orloff Trotter; a Russian-bred warmblood developed in the 1780s from an Arab (q.v.) stallion put to Danish and Dutch mares; considered one of the world's best trotting breeds and is the most widely known and commonly used breed in Russia; named after Count Alexis Orlov who founded the Krenov Stud in 1778 where the breed was developed; through a process of strict selection and introduction of Danish, Dutch, English, Russian, Polish and Arab mares, together with important contributions from Thoroughbred (q.v.) stallions, a breed of distinctive characteristics was developed; the stud book was founded in 1865 and was originally open to any horse who could run 914 yards (0.8 km) in less than 2 minutes; now, the registry is only open to those horses with both the dam and sire listed in the Stud Book; the coat is most commonly gray, although black and bay also occur, stands 15.1 to 17 hands, has a light, powerful build, elegant conformation, long back, and a long, swan neck; is docile, but energetic; used for trotting races, harness, and riding.

orra horse The progeny of a Highland (q.v.) mare and a draft horse.

orthopedic Pertaining to the skeletal system.

osmosis The tendency, when two solutions of differing concentrations are separated by a semi-permeable membrane, for the solution of higher density to pass through the membrane until the two solutions are equalized in pressure.

os pedis ***see*** THIRD PASTERN

osselets Also known as arthritis of the fetlock joint and spelled osslets; a bony growth occurring on the fetlock or ankle joint; results from inflammation of the enveloping membrane of the bone caused by injury such as a wound, bruise, sprain, etc., and the repeated strain and trauma of hard training in young horses; symptoms include a short choppy gait, pain with ankle flexion and a soft, warm, sensitive, swelling of the front and sometimes the side of the fetlock joint.

ossification Bone formation in the connective tissue of chronically traumatized or inflamed muscles.

osslets *see* OSSELETS

os suffraginis *see* LONG PASTERN

osteoarthritis *see* OSTEOARTHROSIS

osteoarthrosis Also known as osteoarthritis or degenerative joint disease; inflammation and progressive degeneration of one or more joints due to ageing or mechanical factors; characterized by a progressive loss of articular cartilage, and bone; occurs most frequently in the joints below the radius of the foreleg and femur in the hind; most commonly seen in older horses and may be a associated with repeated trauma, conformation faults, blood disease, traumatic joint injury, subchondral bone defects, and excessive intra-articular corticosteroid injections.

osteodystrophia fibrosa Also known as miller's disease, bran disease, big head, big head disease, or nutritional hyperparathyroidism; a generalized bone disease primarily caused by calcium deficiency with phosphorus excess resulting from diet or parathyroid problems; signs include symmetric enlargement of the mandible and facial bones, loosening of the teeth, and in advanced cases, flattening of the ribs with fractures and detachment of the ligaments if the horse is worked; horses of both sexes and all ages are susceptible, with lactating mares, foals and mules more at risk; is relatively uncommon, but if left untreated, may result in death.

osteomyelitis Bone infection caused by microorganisms which may gain access through broken tissue resulting from comminuted or compound fractures (q.v.)

osteoporosis Demineralization of the bones; may cause fracture (q.v.); uncommon in horses.

ostler *see* HOSTLER

OTB *see* OFF-TRACK BETTING

Our Dumb Friends League An English organization founded in 1897 to promote animal welfare; now defunct.

outcrossing *see* CROSS-BREEDING

outfit (1) A ranch (q.v.) including all the equipment and employees. (2) A Western term; the personal equipment of a cowboy.

outlaw *see* ROGUE

outlier A hunting term; a fox (q.v.) found in the open rather than a covert (q.v.).

outline The profile or silhouette of the horse, showing carriage or posture.

out of Said of a horse's maternal parentage, e.g. "The foal was out of the mare Ziva."

out of blood Also known as short of blood; a hunting term; said of hounds who have not killed hunted prey for some time.

out-of-bounds A polo term; said of a ball that crosses the side or end lines, or goes over the sideboards thus requiring stop of play (q.v.); necessitates a throw-in (q.v.) by the umpire.

out of position A cutting term; said of a horse who is unable to respond quickly enough to the movements of the cow being worked to maintain control over it and loses the working advantage (q.v.).

out of the money A racing term; said of a horse who, technically, finishes in any position other than first, second, or third.

outraves A coaching term; extension rails that protruded outward from the top of the sides, and sometimes the front and rear, of some commercial and farm carts to facilitate carrying a top load; held in position by iron supports.

outrider A racing term; a mounted employee who escorts horses competing in a race to the post (q.v.).

outrigger A coaching term; the extension beyond the shafts to which an outspanner (q.v.) is harnessed by means of a swingle tree (q.v.), as when harnessing in a troika (q.v.).

outside (1) The side of the horse on the outside of the movement, e.g. when riding a horse on a right circle the outside is the left side of the horse. (2) A dressage term; the side away from the center of the arena.

Outside Car *see* JAUNTING CAR

outside leg The rider's leg nearer the arena perimeter or on the outside of a circle or turn; in certain movements such as counter-canter (q.v.), the rider's 'outside leg' may sometimes be defined with reference to the lateral bend of the horse taking precedence over the geographical or geometrical location, e.g. when going right around the arena in counter-canter, the rider's left leg, that closer to the outside of the arena, would be considered the outside leg in normal terminology, yet because in this instance the horse will be somewhat incurved to the left, the rider's right leg may be described as the outside leg.

outside mare A mare not owned by the facility which boards or breeds her.

outsider (1) A racing term; a race horse (q.v.) given long odds by the odds maker because his chances of winning are slim. (2) *see* OUTSIDE PASSENGER

outside passenger Also known as outsider

a coaching term; one who traveled on an outside, roof-top seat on horse-drawn vehicle, generally for a lesser fee.

outside seat *see* ROOF SEAT

outspanner A coaching term; one of two horses put to the outside in a troika (q.v.), or a horse put to on an outrigger (q.v.) alongside the shaft horse.

out to pasture (1) *see* RETIRED. (2) *see* AT PASTURE

out to walk *see* WALK NO. 2

ova More than one ovum (q.v.).

ovary One of two female reproductive glands in which ova (q.v.) and sex hormones are produced; connected to the uterus by the oviducts (q.v.).

overalls (1) Also known as jodhpurs; tight dress riding pants with a stirrup through which the foot passes; worn with a silk hat and tail coat (q.v.) in hack classes. (2) Loose, stout trousers, usually with a part extending over the chest and supported by shoulder straps.

over and under A Western term; to use the long ends of the split reins of a Western bridle to slap the belly of the horse as a reprimand or to encourage movement, the ends being whipped from side to side, or from over to under the horse.

over at the knees *see* FORWARD DEVIATION OF THE CARPAL JOINTS

overbent *see* BEHIND THE BIT

overbite *see* OVER-SHOT JAW

over-carted Said of a horse or pony pulling a vehicle too large, but not necessarily too heavy, for its size.

overcheck *see* CHECK REIN

over collected Said of a horse moving in an enforced and incorrect form of collection, typically overbent (q.v.), with a an artificially shortened neck, tight back, and imperfect hindquarter engagement.

overdraw *see* CHECK REIN

overface (1) Also known as overfacing; to encourage a horse to jump a fence that is either too large or too difficult for him to jump. (2) To provide a horse with excessive quantities of feed.

overfaced Said of a horse asked to jump an obstacle that is clearly beyond his capabilities.

overfacing *see* OVERFACE NO. 1

overflexed A dressage term; said of the horse when he is behind the vertical as due to excessive longitudinal flexion in the poll and/or upper joints of the neck.

overgirth *see* SURCINGLE

overhead check *see* CHECK REIN

over-horsed Said of the rider when his horse is too much to handle, whether that be due to size, speed, training, etc.

over in the knees *see* FORWARD DEVIATION OF THE CARPAL JOINTS

overland Also known as scenic route; a racing term; a horse who runs wide on the turns, thus losing ground.

overlay A racing term; said of a horse posting higher odds than expected when based on past performance.

overmark *see* OVERTRAIN

overnight *see* OVERNIGHT RACE

overnight race Also known as overnight; a racing term; any race in which the entries close 72 hours (exclusive of Sundays) or less before the post time (q.v.) for the first race on the day the race is to be run.

overnights A racing term; a printout available from the racing secretary's office the day prior to that on which a race is to be run which identifies entries in the next day's races.

overo Refers to coat color pattern; a basic solid base coat with large, asymmetrical patterns of horizontally arranged white patches where the definition between the white and colored areas is ragged; white body patches occur in the middle of the sides of the body, neck, and occasionally the belly, rarely extending to the top line (q.v.); the white is irregular, rather scattered or splashy, and is often referred to as calico; head markings are distinctive, with bald face (q.v.), apron face (q.v.), or bonnet face (q.v.) common; the eyes are frequently, but not always, blue and one or more legs may be colored; a bald face (q.v.) and a small white spot on the side of the horse is the minimum extent; small spots frequently have a butterfly shape; may be predominantly dark or white, but rarely all white; the tail is usually one color.

over-reach Also known as grab a quarter; minor limb contact to the heel bulb (q.v.) and adjoining area of the foot caused by the toe of the hind foot when it catches the forefoot on the same side; the hind foot advances more quickly than in forging; may occur as a consequence of jumping or galloping, particularly on muddy, slippery, or wet ground; the heel can be protected with over-reach boots (q.v.).

over-reach boots Also known as bell boots, racking boots, or over-reaching boots; a bell-shaped protective hoof and coronary band covering made of leather, rubber, and/or synthetic materials used to protect the heels of the forelegs from injury by the toe of the hind shoe or hoof.

over-reaching boots *see* OVER-REACH BOOTS

over-ride (1) A hunting term; said of the rider; to ride too close to the hounds (q.v.). (2) A cutting term; to push a horse into the cow and not wait for him to react instinctively. (3) To ride a horse at an excessive speed for too long a time without regard for his physical condition.

over-run Also known as over run the line; a hunting term; said of the hounds when they run past the line of the fox (q.v.) because the scent has been diverted by a change of course or foil (q.v.).

over run the line *see* OVER-RUN

overshot fetlock *see* KNUCKLING OVER

over-shot jaw Also known as brachygnathism, overbite, parrot mouth, parrot jaw, or over-shot mouth; a congenital malformation of the mouth in which the upper jaw is longer than the bottom jaw and the teeth in the top jaw overshoot or protrude beyond the lower teeth; thought to be inherited; may cause the horse to have difficulty eating.

over-shot mouth *see* OVER-SHOT JAW

over-step *see* OVERTRACK

over-straining disease *see* EQUINE MYOGLOBINURIA

overstride *see* OVERTRACK

over the bit *see* ABOVE THE BIT

over the bridge A horse dealer's term; a horse with a weak back.

over the odds A racing term; said of a backer when he or she obtains a longer price than that offered at the start of the race.

over the sticks Said of a horse; to jump over an obstacle.

overtrack Also known as overstep or overstride; a dressage term; said of the horse whose movement is straight and whose hind feet overlap the impressions of the fore.

overtrain Also known as train off (Brit) and overmark; to work or train a horse so hard that his peak performance is surpassed and, in fact, begins to deteriorate.

over-turned A dressage term; said of the horse when he turns more than 180 degrees in a half-pirouette (q.v.) or more than 360 degrees in a full pirouette (q.v.).

overweight (1) A racing term; said of a jockey who exceeds the weight assigned his mount; in American, a jockey may be a maximum of 5 pounds (2.3 kg) overweight, a situation that is either posted on an information board or announced over the public address system prior to the race. (2) A racing term; extra pounds carried by a horse, in excess of officially assigned weight, because the jockey is too heavy.

oviduct Also known as fallopian tube; one of two ducts, left and right, connecting th ovary (q.v.) to the uterine horn (q.v.).

ovulation Release of the ovum (q.v.) from the ovary.

ovum An egg; the female reproductive cell produced in the ovary (q.v.).

owlhead (1) A horse who is impossible to train. (2) A horse who looks around a lot.

owl headed Said of a horse who looks around a lot.

own brothers *see* BROTHERS

owner One named on the certificate of registration or bill of sale for a horse; one to whom a horse belongs.

ownership brand *see* BRAND NO. 1

owns *see* OWN THE LINE OF A FOX

own sisters *see* SISTERS

own the line *see* OWN THE LINE OF A FOX

own the line of a fox Also known as owns or own the line; a hunting term; said of a hound (q.v.) who has given tongue (q.v.) on the line of a fox (q.v.).

OX A suffix to the name of any pure-bred Arab.

oxbow stirrup A stirrup (q.v.) with a round bottom, and slightly curved sides made of metal, plastic, leather, or other material; connected to a Western saddle by stirrup leathers (q.v.); used to support the rider's foot.

oxer Also known as post and rails or ox fence; a parallel fence utilizing two sets of standards and any combination of poles, angles, or spreads which is jumped as a single unit; of two types : square oxer (q.v.) and step oxer (q.v.); the term evolved in England where the trails in and out of town were originally lined with posts and rails set wide enough apart to allow passage of oxen without difficulty; hunters traveling through these towns would jump the posts and rails at an angle perpendicular to the trails used by the oxen.

ox fence *see* OXER

Oxford Cart *see* OXFORD DOGCART

Oxford Dogcart Also known as Bounder or Oxford Cart; a light, fast, horse-drawn vehicle of the Dogcart (q.v.) type suspended on a pair of very high wheels with red-painted spokes, hung on semi-elliptical springs, and seating four, dos-a-dos (q.v.); named after the city of its origins; frequently driven by sporting undergraduates attending Oxford University.

Oxyuris equi Also known as pinworm or seatworm; a nematode worm, found mainly in the large intestine; the largest known pinworm, the female being 3 to 5.9 inches (7.5–15 cm) long; male worms are smaller and fewer in number; the females pass toward the rectum where they lay their eggs (ejected as a green or yellowish mass) on the perineum around the anus; the eggs, flattened on one side, become embryonated in a few hours; adult worms cause perineal irritation during egg laying; infestation is characterized by rubbing of the tail and anus, which may result in broken hairs and bare patches around the tail and buttocks.

oyster feet Said of the horse's hooves when rather flat, white, and displaying horizontal rings; occurs as a result of laminitis (q.v.).

P

P1 *see* LONG PASTERN

PI *see* LONG PASTERN

P2 *see* SHORT PASTERN

PII *see* SHORT PASTERN

P3 *see* THIRD PASTERN

PIII *see* THIRD PASTERN

pace (1) A two-beat lateral gait with suspension performed in two-time in which the hind and foreleg (q.v.) on the same side move forward simultaneously; is smooth and fast, ranging from 12 to more than 30 mph (19–48 kmph); results in more rotation of the spine from side-to-side and less lateral bending than the trot (q.v.); an inborn affinity. (2) A racing term; the speed of the leaders at each stage of a race. (3) Also known as passe; a herd of asses (q.v.). (4) A dressage term; the variation within the gait, e.g., collected, working, lengthened, medium and extended; the variation in meters per minute occurs ideally because of the change in stride length with no change in tempo.

pacemaker (1) *see* PACE SETTER. (2) *see* RABBIT

pace not true Said of a horse who does not perform a pace (q.v.) or gait in the correct time, e.g., a walk should be performed in four-time, trot in two-time, and canter three-time.

pacer Also known as wiggler, sidewheeler, or sandshifter; any horse bred and naturally gaited to pace (q.v.).

pace setter Also known as pacemaker; a racing term; a horse who takes the lead and sets the pace/speed for the other horses in the field (q.v.).

pachyderm polo Also known as elephant polo; a mounted game consisting of two 10 minute chukkers (q.v.) with a 15-minute half-time, played on elephants ranging from 20 to 40 years old, although some younger, and faster, elephants are used; small elephants are played in the offensive positions and each elephant is ridden by two individuals, a mahout and the polo player; developed in 1982 by Jim Edwards and James Manclark in southern Nepal; has similar rules to equine polo (q.v.), with a few exceptions: (a) one player from each team must remain on his side of the midfield at all times, (b) only two players from each team may be within the boundaries of an arc marked around the goal, (c) riding off (q.v.) and hooking (q.v.) are not permitted, (d) played on a 120 by 70 yard (110 × 64 m) field, and (e) mallets (q.v.) are 98 to 110 inches (2.5–2.8 m) long depending on elephant size and are made of a bamboo upper and cane lower shaft; the sport is officially recognized by the Nepal Sports Council and the Nepal Olympics Association; at the beginning of each season, the teams in the World Elephant Polo Tournament are divided into two leagues determined by a handicapping committee; each team plays the other teams in its league with finalists competing for the championship on the last day of the tournament.

pacing *see* HARNESS RACING

pack (1) Also known as pack of hounds or previously as mute; a hunting term; a group of hounds (q.v.) who cooperatively hunt a fox (q.v.), coyote (q.v.), stag (q.v.), etc. (2) A bundle, parcel, or bale for transport on the back of a animal.

pack animal Any animal used to carry burdens for conveyance to another location.

packed cell volume *see* HEMATOCRIT

packer One who works packing goods and supplies onto the backs of livestock (horses, mules, donkeys, burros, llamas, etc.) and who is responsible for transporting such goods to another location.

pack horse Also known as somer or sumpter; a horse used to carry burdens for conveyance to another location.

Packington Blind Horse The foundation sire of the Shire (q.v.) who stood at stud 1755 through 1770; had a black coat and white feathering (q.v.).

pack of hounds *see* PACK

pack pony A pony used to carry burdens for conveyance to another location.

pack saddle A saddle designed to carry burdens for conveyance by pack animals (q.v.).

pack string Also known as string; a number of livestock carrying burdens for conveyance to another location tied together and following one behind the other; so called, because the animals string behind the packer (q.v.).

pad (1) *see* SADDLE PAD. (2) The foot of a fox or hound. (3) That part of the harness tack bridging the horse's back. (4) *see* HORSESHOE PAD. (5) *see* ANCIENT ENGLISH PACER. (6) *see* SADDLE NO. 4. (7) The central part of a carriage step. (8) *see* STIRRUP PAD

pad cloth A decorative patent leather (q.v.) or cloth pad placed under the harness saddle, or pad, to provide extra padding or lining; cut in the same shape as the harness pad.

paddling *see* DISHING

paddock (1) Also known as field; an enclosed, fenced area used for grazing or exercising horses. (2) Also known as racecourse paddock or walk ring; a racing term; an oval enclosure located near the race track where horses are walked and riders mount before the start of the post parade.

paddock boots Also known as high lows or jodhpur boots; low boots no taller than 1 to 2 inches (2.5–5 cm) above the ankle bone made of leather or synthetic materials and available in laced, zipper, and pull-on styles.

paddock judge (1) A racing term; one responsible for all activity in the paddock (q.v.) and saddling areas. (2) A British term; anyone skilled at assessing a horse's chance in a race based on an appraisal in the paddock.

paddock sheet *see* SUMMER SHEET

pad groom Also known as second-horse man or hunt servant; a special groom responsible for riding a lady's hunter to a hunt meeting and returning with the covert hack (q.v.) or to ride the fresh hunter to a check (q.v.) in the hunt and return with the tired horse.

pad horse *see* ROAD HACK

pad saddle An outer covering fitted over a side-saddle (q.v.) having stirrups (q.v.) on either side; allows the rider to sit astride the horse saddled with a side-saddle (q.v.).

pad scent *see* STALE LINE

pad tree A wooden or metal frame to which harness pads are attached.

Pahlavan An Iranian warmblood descended from Plateau Persian (q.v.) crossed with Arab (q.v.) and Thoroughbred (q.v.); stands 15.2 to 16 hands, may have a coat of any solid color, and is strong and elegant; used for riding.

paint (1) Refers to coat color; an asymmetrical pattern of white patches on any base color; the patches are generally well defined and there are no white hairs mixed into the colored areas; several specific patterns occur, namely tobiano (q.v.), overo (q.v.), sabino (q.v.), and splashed white (q.v.). (2) A spotted cow. (3) A counter-irritant used to increase blood circulation to the leg area and promote healing; a mild blister (q.v.).

Paint *see* PAINT HORSE

Paint Horse Also known as Paint; an American-bred, stock-type warmblood whose breeding is based upon bloodlines of registered American Paint Horses, Quarter Horses (q.v.), or Jockey Club (q.v.) recognized registered Thoroughbreds (q.v.) who meet minimum color requirements; must have a definite natural paint marking (q.v.), white leg markings extending above the knees and/or hocks, glass, blue, or wall eyes (q.v.), an apron (q.v.) or bald face (q.v.), white on the lower jaw or lower lip, a blue zone around a natural paint marking, a two-color mane with one color being natural white, dark spots, or freckles in the white hair on the face or legs, white areas completely surrounded by a contrasting color in the non-visible zone, excluding the head and a contrasting area of another color in the non-visible zone including the head; the spectrum of colors ranges from almost total color with minimal white markings to almost total white with minimal dark markings; overo (q.v.), tobiano (q.v.), and tovero (q.v.) coat patterns occur with piebald (q.v.), skewbald (q.v.), or medicine hat (q.v.) coloring; most can be double registered as Pintos (q.v.) and as either Stock- or Hunter-type horses, but not every Pinto is a Paint.

pair (1) Two horses hitched and driven abreast. (2) Two horses ridden side by side, or competing in an event as one entry, as in pair classes. (3) Two things similar in form and situated close to one another.

pair jumping A show jumping event in which two riders ride a course, and jump all obstacles, side by side.

pairs More than one pair (q.v.).

Pak O *see* LEGEND OF THE EIGHT HORSES

palate Also known as roof of the mouth; that part of the mouth that separates the nasal and oral cavities; consists of the hard palate (q.v.) and soft palate (q.v.).

palatitis *see* LAMPAS

palfrey *see* ANCIENT ENGLISH PACER

palisade worm *see* LARGE STRONGYLE

palmar Also known as volar; relating to the rear or lower surface of the foreleg below the knee, including the knee, fetlock, pastern, and hoof.

palmar deviation of the carpal joints *see* BACKWARD DEVIATION OF THE CARPAL JOINTS

palmar digital nerve Also known as heel nerve; the primary nerve (q.v.) innervating the forefeet; often cut to relieve forefoot pain associated with navicular disease (q.v.).

palmar digital neurectomy Also known as heel nerve; to cut a portion of the palmar digital nerve in the forefeet to relieve pain related to navicular disease (q.v.); to nerve (q.v.) the palmar digital nerve (q.v.).

Palmer, Lynwood (1868–1941) A British equestrian artist and leading authority on horsemanship, driving, and shoeing.

palmar process The rearmost portion of either side of the third pastern (q.v.).

palomino Refers to coat color; a horse having a golden coat which may vary from pale yellow to dark cream, white, or flaxen (q.v.), with an ivory mane and tail; white markings are only permitted on the face and the lower legs; found in many horse and pony breeds, except purebred Thoroughbreds (q.v.) or Arabs (q.v.).

Palomino Also known as Palomino horse, golden horse, buttermilk horse, golden horse of the West, Café-au-Lait (Fr), Golden One, Golden Dorado, Hanoverian Cream (Brit), or previously as Isabella, Y'sabella, and Golden Horse of the Queen; a color type developed in the 15th century by Queen Isabella of Spain for her personal use; of Arab (q.v.) and Barb (q.v.) descent; believed to have been brought to America by the Spaniards; the name is believed to have derived from Juan de Palomino who received a horse of this color type from the explorer Cortez or from the Spanish 'paloma' meaning dove; selectively bred in the US since the mid-1930s; progeny must have one registered Palomino parent and the other of Quarter Horse (q.v.), Arab, or Thoroughbred (q.v.) blood; cannot show draft, pony, or Paint (q.v.) breeding; the eyes should be dark or hazel and both of the same color although blue eyes have recently been allowed; white markings are permitted on the face and are limited to a blaze (q.v.), snip (q.v.), or star (q.v.) and on the legs below the knees or hocks; the coat must be golden, but may vary from pale yellow to dark cream, with a white, flaxen (q.v.), or ivory mane and tail containing no more than 15 percent dark (black, sorrel, chestnut) or off-colored hair; the skin must be dark colored without pink spots; zebra marks (q.v.), dorsal striping (q.v.), and/or white hairs interspersed within the coat associated wi gray, roan, or rabicano patterns are unacceptable; stands 14 to 17 hands; physical characteristics vary and does not breed true to type; used for riding, parades, stock work, and driving.

Palomino Horse *see* PALOMINO

Palomino Horse Association, Inc. Also known by the acronym PHA; an American organization founded in California in 1932, with full field work commencing in 1935; organized to perpetuate and improve the Palomino (q.v.) through recording bloodlines and issuing registration certificates to qualifying horses.

Palomino Horse Breeders of America, Incorporated Also known by the acronym PHBA; an American organization established in 1941 to collect, record, preserve blood purity and improve breeding of Palominos (q.v.); primarily a color registry with pedigree a secondary requirement.

Palominos More than one Palomino (q.v.).

Palouse Pony *see* APPALOOSA

Palousy *see* APPALOOSA

palpate To examine using the sense of touch.

pancake *see* ENGLISH SADDLE

pancreas A large lobulated gland of vertebrates that secretes digestive enzymes and the hormone insulin and glucagons.

panel (1) Racing slang; one furlong (q.v.). (2) A hunting term; two thin, flat pieces of wood, generally oak, 16 feet (4.8 m) long or less, placed horizontally onto triangular frames on either end and positioned at right angles over the top of barb wire fences; the height of the panels may vary from 3 to 3½ feet (91 cm–1.07 m) with a spread at the bottom (on the ground) from 5 to 5½ feet (1.5–1.7 m); used to enable hounds and hunters to cross fence lines safely. (3) Also known as saddle panel; the padded part of the English saddle (q.v.) between the saddle tree and the back of the horse; there is one panel on each side of the horse's spine, separated by a channel (q.v.); distributes the rider's weight evenly over the horse's back; made in various sizes and shapes and stuffed with different materials including felt and horse hair. (4) *see* SWEAT FLAP

Panel Cart A two-wheeled, horse-drawn country cart similar in design to a Dogcart (q.v.); had back-to-back passenger seating, paneled vehicle sides surmounted by an iron rail which formed mounting handles for the passengers at the front and back and supported the splash boards on the sides; was hung on two side-springs.

pangaré Refers to coat color pattern; the area over the muzzle, eye, and on the inside of the legs and flanks when a lighter shade than the body color; coloring effect does not change the descriptive name, that is, a blond sorrel is also a pangaré; Spanish for mealy muzzle.

pannier A pack consisting of two bags or cases for carriage by an animal.

pantothenic acid A B-complex vitamin; bacterial synthesis in the intestinal tract is thought to be sufficient to meet the daily dietary requirement of approximately 15 PPM; a component of coenzyme A, which is integral to the metabolism of fat, carbohydrates, and some amino acids; deficiency is uncommon in horses fed good quality hay or pasture.

Papach-oinu A 10-minute Russian equestrian sport conducted on a playing field; each rider attempts to snatch as many hats as possible off the heads of other riders without losing his own.

paper Also known as shredded paper; a substance manufactured from rag, wood, or other vegetable fiber reduced to a pulp, shredded, and used as bedding (q.v.) material; is absorbent, dust free, and the carbon content in the ink reduces odors; may be pelleted to improve manageability.

paper face A face marking (q.v.); said of a horse with a completely white head; different than a bonnet (q.v.).

parabola The figurative arc made by a horse from the point of take-off to the point of landing when jumping an obstacle.

Parascaris equorum A common large

roundworm affecting the horse and generally found in the small intestine; the female may reach 19.7 inches (50 cm) long; pica, colic (q.v.), and unthriftiness may result from heavy infestations; the larvae, which migrate to the lungs after hatching in the stomach, may cause catarrhal bronchitis or broncho-pneumonia.

parallel *see* PARALLEL BARS

parallel bars Also known as parallel; a jumping obstacle consisting of two sets of posts and rails of the same height jumped as a single element.

paralytic myoglobinuria *see* EQUINE MYOGLOBINURIA

paralytic rabies Also known as dumb rabies; a rabies (q.v.) condition characterized by early paralysis of the throat and masseter muscles, profuse salivation, inability to swallow, a lack of aggression or viciousness, paralysis progressing rapidly to all body parts, coma, and death within a few hours.

Paranoplocephala mamillana A species of tapeworm (q.v.) varying in length from 3 to 6 inches (7.6–15 cm) and found in the small intestine and the stomach; in light infestations, no signs of disease are present, while in heavy infestations digestive disturbances may occur.

Parascaris equorum *see* LARGE ROUNDWORM

parasite A plant or animal living in or on a living organism, often injuring the host.

parasitoid (1) Any predator that feeds on flies (q.v.). (2) tiny, non-stinging members of the wasp family which lay their eggs in fly pupae, the juveniles of which consume the pupae before they are able to develop wings and fly; used in biological control (q.v.).

parasympathetic nervous system That section of the autonomic nervous system (q.v.) consisting of nerves (q.v.) originating in the sacral and cranial regions of the body; responsible for slowing the heart beat, contracting the pupils, dilating the blood vessels, and, generally, any body function in contrast to the sympathetic nervous system (q.v.).

parcel carter *see* VANNER

Parcel Van A four-wheeled, horse-drawn delivery van; had a forward-facing driving seat protected by the roof, oval side windows in the front, removable roof and mahogany-paneled sides, and was hung on four elliptic springs; was easily converted into an open vehicle.

parcours A show jumping or driving course.

pariani *see* ALL-PURPOSE SADDLE

parier mutual *see* PARIMUTUEL

parietal bones Those bones comprising the top of the horse's skull.

parimutuel Previously known as parier mutual or Paris mutuals; a racing term; a system of horserace betting developed in 1865 by Frenchman Pierre Oller in which all the money bet (less a small percentage for track management and taxes) is divided up among those holding winning and placing tickets in proportion to the amount bet; the French equivalent of the English tote or totalizator (q.v.); Oller called this system "parier mutuel" meaning "mutual stake" or "betting among ourselves"; as the system was adopted in England it became known as "Paris mutuals," and soon thereafter "pari-mutuels"; in many countries, this system is the only legal form of government-controlled, on-course betting on races.

parimutuel field Also known as mutuel field or field; a racing term; two or more lightly regarded horses grouped as a single parimutuel (q.v.) betting entry when the number of starters exceeds the number of betting units on the totalizator (q.v.).

parimutuel pool Also known as mutuel pool, pool, or stake money; a racing term; the total amount bet in any race by all bettors (q.v.) to win (q.v.), place (q.v.), or show (q.v.) or the amount bet on a daily double (q.v.), exacta (q.v.), quinella (q.v.), etc.

Parisian A four-wheeled, horse-drawn open carriage popular in the late 19th century; had an angular skeleton body hung on four elliptic springs, and was entered by steps attached to the middle of the body on each side; driven from a rear, forward-facing, stick-back (q.v.) seat; passengers sat on a railed seat facing the driver while the groom rode on a railed seat behind the driver.

Paris mutuals *see* PARIMUTUEL

Park Coach *see* DRAG NO. 3

park course A British term; any steeplechase course in Britain other than Aintree (q.v.).

parked out A harness racing term; said of a trotter (q.v.) or pacer (q.v.) when the positions of his rivals prevent him from reaching the inside rail, thus forcing him to the outside where he must cover more ground; such a horse rarely wins a race.

park hack A hack that comes as close as possible to having perfect conformation, gaits, manners, and behavior when compared with other hacks.

Park Phaeton Also known as Lady's Phaeton, George IV, George IV Phaeton, or Peter's Phaeton; a light, elegant, open, horse-drawn vehicle of the Phaeton (q.v.) type adapted for park driving; frequently had a rumble seat and a falling hood; drawn by a single horse in shafts or a pair in pole gear (q.v.).

park trot A balanced, showy trot (q.v.) having collection and high action; the forelegs are raised until the forearm is horizontal, if not higher; the hind legs are active and flexed as much as the forelegs.

parlay Also known as accumulator, accumulator bet, or parlay bet; a racing term; a multi-race bet in which the winnings earned on the first race are subsequently wagered on each succeeding race; if one bet in the sequence is lost, the whole bet fails.

parlay bet *see* PARLAY

parallel bars *see* SQUARE OXER

parallel bit *see* FENNERS BIT

parrot jaw *see* OVER-SHOT JAW

parrot mouth *see* OVER-SHOT JAW

Part A racing term; a word used by the International Cataloguing Standards Committee to separate races held in different countries for sales cataloguing purposes; races held in Part I countries (q.v.) are accepted for graded races (q.v.) and black type (q.v.) purposes; races held in Part II countries (q.v.) are accepted for black-type purposes only, without group or grade designations; races held in Part III countries (q.v.) are not accepted for cataloguing purposes.

part-bred *see* HALF-BRED

Part-Bred Arab Any Arab (q.v.) having at least 25 percent and as much as 50 percent Arab blood, the balance being blood of any breed other than Thoroughbred (q.v.).

part color Refers to coat color; any coat consisting of more than one color, e.g. piebald (q.v.), skewbald (q.v.), or spotted (q.v.).

part-colored skin *see* MOTTLED SKIN

Parthian shot To shoot an arrow backwards from the back of a galloping horse, as in pretend retreat; said of the Parthians – considered the most expert horsemen of the ancient world – who, during the middle of the 3rd century BC, won many victories using this technique.

partial lethal An inherited lethal (q.v.) condition; any disease or condition genetically transmitted to the foal which only becomes lethal under certain circumstances, but which may result in restricted use or shortened life span; may include heart defects, reproductive disorders, cataracts, and umbilical and scrotal hernias.

Part I countries A racing term; a grouping of countries established by the International Cataloguing Standards Committe to separate horse races; consist of Argentina, Australia, Brazil, Canada, Chile, France, Germany, Great Britain, Ireland, Italy, New Zealand, Peru, South Africa, United States, and Hong Kong (the International Cup only), and Japan (the Japan Cup only); there are three different groupings.

Part II countries A racing term; a grouping of counties consisting of Belgium, Hong

Kong (except the Hong Kong International Cup), India, Japan (except the Japan Cup), Malaysia, Mexico, Panama, Puerto Rico, Scandinavia, Singapore, Spain, Uruguay, and Venezuela established by the International Cataloguing Standards Committee to separate horse races for cataloguing purposes; there are three different groupings.

Part III countries A racing term; those countries not included in Part I countries (q.v.) or Part II countries (q.v.); the designation is established by the International Cataloguing Standards Committee to separate horse races held in different countries for cataloguing purposes.

parturition Also known as foaling, labor birth, or confinement; the process of giving birth including labor and delivery; a few days before foaling, softening of the bones and waxing (q.v.), the night of foaling, the mare will look for a spot to foal, milk begins to run, and uterine contractions begin pushing the two front legs and foal's nose to the vaginal opening, the water breaks and the foal is forced out of the vaginal canal, and the foal is fully delivered, but the umbilical cord remains intact.

part wheel A racing term; to use a key horse(s) (q.v.) in different, but not all possible, exotic betting combinations.

pas de deux A dressage term; a freestyle dressage program ridden by two riders.

paso A natural, four-beat, lateral gait unique to the Peruvian Paso (q.v.) in which the forelegs arc, or dish, to the outside as the horse strides forward with the fore and hind legs moving simultaneously; the hind legs take very long, straight strides with the quarters held low and the hocks well under the body; can produce a top speed of 11 to 15 mph (18–24 kmph); the three gait divisions include: the paso corto (q.v.), paso fino (q.v.), and paso largo (q.v.); unlike the lateral limb movements of other gaited breeds; from the Spanish *paso*, meaning step.

Paso (1) *see* PERUVIAN PASO. (2) *see* PASO FINO

paso corto (1) One of three distinct forward speeds of the Paso Fino (q.v.); a natural evenly spaced, easy-traveling four-beat lateral gait with moderate forward speed and extension; collection varies with class requirements; must be performed at a definite change of speed from the Paso Largo (q.v.). (2) One of three divisions of the paso (q.v.) gait unique to the Peruvian Paso (q.v.); the normal easy traveling gait in which the forelegs arc out to the side with each stride.

paso de la muerte One of nine scored events in a charreada (q.v.) in which a charro (q.v.) leaps from the back of his mount to that of a bareback mare galloping alongside his mount.

paso fino Also known as Paso Fino gait; the slow, collected, and elevated display gait unique to the Peruvian Paso (q.v.) in which the forelegs arc out to the side with each stride; one of three divisions of the paso (q.v.).

Paso Fino Also known as America's 500 year old new breed, Paso Fino Horse, El Caballo de Paso Fino, Paso, or horse with the fine walk; a warmblood descended from Barb (q.v.), Andalusian (q.v.), and Spanish jennet crosses; brought to the Dominican Republic by Columbus in the 15th century; used as remount stock for the Conquistadors in the early 16th century; selectively developed in Colombia, the Dominican Republic, Puerto Rico and Venezuela before introduction to the United States; is not related to the Peruvian Paso (q.v.); has a naturally occurring, lateral, four-beat gait performed at three speeds with varying degrees of collection: classic fino (q.v.), paso corto (q.v.), and paso largo (q.v.); the gait is unique to the breed and requires strong hock action; footfall is up and down and performed in the same sequence as a natural equine walk, i.e. left rear, left fore, right rear, right fore; the breed is never shown at the trot; stands 13 to 15.2 hands with 13.3 to 14.2 most common; full size is frequently not reached until five years of age; all coat colors occur, with bay, chestnut, gray and black most common; white markings may be present.

Paso Fino gait *see* PASO FINO

Paso Fino Horse *see* PASO FINO

Paso Fino Horse Association, Inc. An American organization founded to promote, protect, and improve the Paso Fino (q.v.); superseded the Paso Fino Owners and Breeders Association (q.v.) in 1973.

Paso Fino Owners and Breeders Association An American organization founded in 1972 to promote, protect, and improve the Paso Fino (q.v.) breed; superseded by the Paso Fino Horse Association, Inc.(q.v.) in 1973.

paso lano The distinctive high-stepping gait of the Costeño (q.v.).

paso largo (1) One of three distinct forward speeds of the Paso Fino (q.v.); an evenly spaced four-beat lateral gait with rapid forward motion obtained by quickened footfall and some lengthening of the stride; performed at a definite change of speed from the paso corto (q.v.); although speeds of 15 to 20 mph (24–32 kmph) are not uncommon, forward speed varies between horses. (2) One of three divisions of the paso (q.v.) gait unique to the Peruvian Paso (q.v.); an extended, fast gait in which the horse may achieve speeds up to 16 mph (26 kmph); the normal easy traveling gait in which the forelegs arc to the outside with each forward stride.

paspalum A prolific and common grass of temperate and subtropical climates; an excellent feed in early growth stages, which diminishes in food value when seeding; ergot poisoning (q.v.) may result if the mature seed heads are consumed.

pass *see* TWO-TRACK

passade A movement performed on two-tracks (q.v.) in which the horse, traveling on a straight line, makes a small demi-volte (q.v.) and changes leads (q.v.).

passage Also known as redopp or Spanish step; a shortened, very elevated, cadenced, and collected trot (q.v.) with accentuated flexion of the knees and hocks and an extended moment of suspension as each pair of diagonal legs is raised; the hindquarters (q.v.) are more engaged than at other trots; a low air (q.v.) High School movement (q.v.) taught under saddle from the Italian *passagiare* meaning to walk or promenade.

passage-like trot Also known as passagey trot or hovering trot; a dressage term; a trot in which the phase of support of one diagonal pair of legs is prolonged while there is hesitation in the forward travel of the other diagonal pair of legs; the resulting movement appears floating or hovering.

passagey trot *see* PASSAGE-LIKE TROT

passe *see* PACE NO. 3

passing gaited Said of a horse whose hind feet trot wider than the fore.

passive immunity Resistance to disease or infection provided by antibodies (q.v.) produced in an immune animal and transferred to one who was not previously immune, e.g. the immunity provided to a foal by the mare through the colostrum (q.v.) in her milk.

passive transfer Movement of existing antibodies (q.v.) from one animal to another, as by means of injection.

paste Any drug, e.g. a sedative or anthelmintic, incorporated into a semi-liquid or paste, contained in a tube, and administered into the horse's mouth by means of a plunger built in to the tube.

pasteboard track A racing term; an exceptionally fast racing surface; is generally thin, hard, and results in faster track times than other surfaces.

pastern (1) The portion of the leg between the fetlock joint and the coronary band (q.v.) of the hoof. (2) *see* PASTERN BONES. (3) Also known as white pastern or full pastern; a leg marking (q.v.) consisting of white extending from just below the fetlock (q.v.) to the coronary band.

pastern bones Three bones which, collectively, comprise the horse's lower leg that provide structural support between the fetlock and hoof; the top bone is known as the long pastern, first phalanx, or os suffraginis, the middle bone is the short pastern (q.v.), and the lower bone the third pastern (q.v.).

pastern joint The joint (q.v.) between the long and short pastern bones (q.v.).

pastern white A leg marking; white covers the entire pastern.

past the mark *see* AGED HORSE

past the mark of the mouth *see* AGED HORSE

pasture (1) Also known as keep; ground covered with native or cultivated grasses and grass-legume mixes upon which animals graze. (2) To maintain a horse in a fenced area on ground covered with native or cultivated grasses and grass-legume mixes, e.g. "Will you pasture your horse this winter?"

pastured Said of a horse at pasture (q.v.).

patch Refers to coat color; a well-defined irregular area of coat hair differing in color from the body.

patella Also known as knee cap; the bone that lies at the front of the stifle joint in the tendon of the large extensor muscles of the joint, just in front of and above the true femorotibial joint; is roughly pyramid shaped with the apex pointing downwards; patellar dislocation constitutes the condition known as slipped stifle.

patent A racing term; a betting option in which the bettor places bets on three different horses running in three different races; in total seven bets are placed: three singles, three doubles, and a treble (q.v.).

patent leather Also known as japanned leather; a high-gloss leather made from specially treated, tanned, varnished hides.

patent infundibulum A painful infection of the incisor cup which ultimately leaves the tooth with an open center.

patent safety A hunting term; said of a hunter (q.v.), to carry the rider safely.

paternal grandam The mother of a horse's sire.

pathological shoe *see* THERAPEUTIC SHOE

pathological shoeing *see* THERAPEUTIC SHOEING

pathology The science dealing with the nature of diseases, their causes, symptoms, and effects on the organism.

Pato An Argentinean mounted sport originating around 1610 and banned in its original form in 1822; two teams of mounted riders numbering from a few dozen to more than several hundred would try to catch a live duck sewn into a piece of leather and then ride carrying the duck to the house of a beloved where it would be thrown down in front of the door; the game often lasted for many hours; since 1937, played with fixed rules in which two four-man teams play on a field measuring 90 by 200 meters using a leather ball weighing 2.75 pounds (1250 grams), with four leather hand grips, which, as in basketball, has to be thrown into the opponent's basket; play usually consists of six seven-minute periods, with one five-minute break between each period; each team member has two horses which he rides alternately.

Pato-lorrarine A French mounted sport similar to Pato (q.v.); players carry long-handled sticks with netted baskets on the far end with which they attempt to pick up a ball from the ground, carry and deposit it in one of two nets suspended from poles located at either end of the playing field.

patrol judge A racing term; any of a number of officials who monitor the progress of a horserace from different locations around the track.

pattern shoe (1) Also known as rest shoe; a bar shoe (q.v.) with high heels connected at the base by a solid bar that raises the heel of the foot to prevent it from sinking into the ground; used to treat damaged flexor tendons; functions as an extreme wedge shoe. (2) *see* STIFLE SHOE

patterned leopard Refers to coat color pattern; a distinct type of leopard spotting (q.v.) in which the spots flow out of the flank and over the horse's entire body.

pattern race (1) *see* GROUP RACE. (2) *see* GRADED RACE

pay off *see* DIVIDEND

pay for a dead horse Also known as work for a dead horse; to perform work for which payment has already been made.

PCV *see* PACKED CELL VOLUME

peacock A horse possessed of style, color, and presence who thus attracts attention.

peacock neck Said of a horse having a very high neck carriage, the head being flexed strongly at the poll.

Peacock safety iron A commonly used children's stirrup (q.v.); designed to release the foot in the event of a fall; a standard hunting iron design in which the outer metal side is replaced with a thick rubber band hooked to the top and bottom of the iron; in an emergency, the rubber band disconnects from the iron, thus releasing the foot.

peanut meal A high protein, high energy concentrate produced from the residue of peanuts after oil extraction; although the protein content is equivalent to that of soybean meal (q.v.), it is more expensive and has only half the lysine content; has a short shelf life and may go rancid or become moldy within six to eight weeks; available as hulled peanut meal (q.v.) or unhulled peanut meal (q.v.).

peanut skin The outer, protective layer of a peanut; although a good source of nitrogen, it is of limited nutritional value and palatability to most horses due to the high tannin content.

pea A variable annual leguminous vine, *Pisum sativum*, cultivated for its round, smooth, or wrinkled edible protein-rich seeds which have a high energy content and are fed split, crushed, or micronized.

peck *see* PECK AT A JUMP

peck at a jump Also known as peck; said of a horse who stumbles before or, more commonly after, an obstacle, to the extent that he stretches his neck out in an attempt to rebalance and nearly falls on landing.

pecking order A hierarchy within an animal group that establishes who is dominant.

pedal *see* STIRRUP

pedal bone *see* THIRD PASTERN

pediculosis Lice (q.v.) infestation.

pedigree A record of the ancestry of an animal; lineage; generally recorded in a stud book with the male pedigree identified on the top line (q.v.), the female on the bottom line (q.v.).

pedigree breeding To breed horses selected on the basis of individual merit and ancestry.

pee (1) *see* URINATE. (2) *see* URINE

peel Also known as peeling; a cutting term; said of a cow to split away from the rider to return to the herd as the rider drives through it.

peeling *see* PEEL

Pegasus The mythical winged horse, made from the body of Medusa, who caused the stream Hippocrene (q.v.) to spring from Mount Helicon with a single blow of his hoof; after he created the stream, he was captured and ridden off by Bellerophon who used a golden bridle; later, Pegasus threw Bellerophon (q.v.) and flew into outer space where he became the northern constellation bearing his name; a Greek word meaning strong.

pegs *see* STUDS

Pegu Pony A small, hardy Indian pony.

Pelethronius The former King of Lapithae, Thessaly, said to have invented bridles and saddles.

Pelham *see* PELHAM BIT

Pelham Arabian *see* ALCOCK ARABIAN

Pelham bit Also known as pelham; a single mouthpiece bit with cheeks combining snaffle (q.v.) and a curb (q.v.) actions in one bit; designed to be used with either one or two sets of reins, a curb chain, and sometimes a lip strap; the snaffle reins are always heavier than the curb reins; the snaffle action acts on the lips, bars, and tongue to guide the horse and lift his head while the curb action acts on the poll (q.v.) for control and to achieve the head set; if the mouthpiece has a port (q.v.), the curb action will also act on the roof of the horse's mouth; differs from a curb bit in that it has a dee-cheek on either end of the bit to which the snaffle reins are attached; well suited for use on horses and ponies of cobb type who have trouble fitting the curb/bridoon combination of a double bridle; of many types, most notably the kimblewick.

Pelham bridle Any bridle fitted with a pelham bit (q.v.); accommodates two sets of reins and, normally, a noseband.

pelleting The process by which moistened supplements and processed roughages are heated and forced through dies that create uniformly shaped nuggets which are used as feed.

pellets Compressed, usually cylindrically shaped, commercial feed available in four basic types: (a) pelleted single ingredient such as alfalfa, (b) pelleted grain mixture, (c) pelleted supplement containing high levels of protein, minerals, and vitamins, and (d) pelleted ration containing roughage and grain in a mixture that meets all of the horse's nutritional requirements; reduces feed storage requirements, decreases the cost of transportation due to reduced bulk, reduces feed-related dust, may greatly reduce the appearance of hay belly (q.v.), prevents the horse from sorting out feed, and reduces the possibility of over- or underfeeding supplements.

Pellier, Jules Charles A Parisian riding master active in the 1830s who invented the leaping head (q.v.) which revolutionized side-saddle (q.v.) riding.

pelt The skin of an animal with the hair or wool attached.

pelvic Of, relating to, or located in or near the pelvis (q.v.).

pelvic girdle The bony, cartilaginous arch supporting the hind limbs.

pelvic limb Either of the two hind limbs.

pelvis A basin-shaped structure in the skeleton of the horse formed by the pelvic girdle (q.v.) and adjoining bones of the spine which rests on the femurs.

penalty (1) A handicap or punishment assessed for committing an offense. (2) *see* POLO PENALTY

Penalty 1 A penalty (q.v.) assessed for committing an offense in a polo match; an automatic goal for the fouled team; the ends of the field do not change following penalty award.

Penalty 2 A penalty (q.v.) assessed for committing an offense in a polo match; a free hit from the center of the 30-yard line, nearest the fouling team's goal, or if preferred by the team captain, from the point the foul occurred, to an undefended goal; the fouling team is positioned behind its end line (q.v.)

Penalty 3 A penalty (q.v.) assessed for committing an offense in a polo match; a free hit from the center of the 40-yard line to an undefended goal.

Penalty 4 A penalty (q.v.) assessed for committing an offense in a polo match; a free hit from the center of the 60-yard line to a defended goal for the fouled team; no member of the fouling team shall be closer than 30 yards to the ball when the umpire says "play".

Penalty 5 A penalty assessed for committing an offense in a polo match; a free hit on the goal for the fouled team from the point of the infraction or from midfield.

Penalty 6 Also known as safety; a penalty (q.v.) assessed for committing an offense in a polo match when a defending player hits the ball across his own backline; results in a free hit from a point on the 60-yard line opposite where the ball crossed the line for the fouled team; both teams are free to position themselves anywhere on the field, except that no member of the fouling team shall be closer than 30 yards to the ball when hit.

Penalty 7 A penalty (q.v.) assessed for committing an offense in a polo match; removal of a player from the fouling team whose handicap is nearest above that of the player disabled by the foul; the removed player is selected by the captain of the fouled team.

Penalty 8 A penalty (q.v.) assessed for committing an offense in a polo match; a mount of the fouling team is ordered off the field.

Penalty 9 A penalty (q.v.) assessed for committing an offense in a polo match; forfeiture of the match.

Penalty 10 A penalty (q.v.) assessed for committing an offense in a polo match; the Umpire may exclude a player for part or all of the remaining periods of the game.

penalty goal A polo penalty awarded when a player commits a dangerous or deliberate foul in the vicinity of his team's goal box to prevent an opponent's score; the team fouled is given a goal and the ball is thrown in 10 yards in front of the fouled team's goal; the teams do not switch ends.

penalty point Any point(s) deducted from a competitor's score for assessed infractions.

penalty zone The rectangular area surrounding a cross-country obstacle in horse trials (q.v.); under US rules extends 33 feet (10 m) before the jump, and 66 feet (20 m) after the jump and to a width of 33 feet (10 m) on each side of the boundary flags marking the obstacle limits; only faults occurring within the penalty zone are marked against the competitor.

pendulous lip Said of the horse's lip when it hangs low and lifeless.

Peneia One of three remaining pony breeds indigenous to Greece, bred in the district of Eleia in the Peloponnese; more refined than the Skyros (q.v.) or Pindos (q.v.) which may indicate Arab (q.v.) influence; stands 10.1 to 14 hands, may have a bay, black, chestnut, or gray coat, is an easy keeper, frugal, hardy, and quiet; used for riding, light farm work, and packing

penetrating crack Also known as deep crack; any fissure or crack in the hoof that exposes the sensitive laminae or results in lameness.

penis The male copulatory organ formed primarily of erectile tissue which also serves as the male organ of urination.

penning (1) The annual roundup of wild horses to remove yearling colts and old stallions. (2) *see* TEAM PENNING

Penn-Marydel Foxhounds, Inc. An American organization incorporated in 1934 to promote and preserve the strain of foxhounds (q.v.) bred and hunted for generations in the southeast sections of Pennsylvania, Maryland, and Delaware; the name of the strain and association derived from a contraction of these three states.

People's Horse *see* SEATTLE SLEW

perch (1) Also known as reach; the main timber in the undercarriage of a horse-drawn carriage; runs from the front of the vehicle to the rear and curves slightly downward. (2) Said of the rider; to ride in the English saddle with the weight borne on the pubis rather than the seat bones; the result of an arched back.

perch bolt Also known as king bolt; a pin connecting the perch (q.v.) to the fore axle and transom and thus to the horse-drawn vehicle upon which the front wheel assembly and undercarriage of a four-wheeled, horse-drawn vehicle rotates.

Percheron A coldblood breed originating in the Le Perche region of Normandy, France, from which the name derived; descended from ancient indigenous heavy-draft breeds crossed with Norman (q.v.) and Oriental blood sometime around the 8th century AD; is well-proportioned, heavy, stands 15.2 to 17.2 hands, and most commonly has a gray, typically dappled, coat although black and roan occur rarely; has a full mane and tail, fine head, straight profile, slightly arched neck, short legs with broad joints and no feather (q.v.), powerful hindquarters, and hard, blue-horn hooves; has great freedom and grace of movement; is quiet and docile, but energetic; the French-kept stud book, maintained by the Société Hippique Percheronne (q.v.), dates to 1883; since 1911 the stud book has been restricted exclusively to horses from registered parents; is used for draft and farm work and has recently been crossed with Thoroughbred (q.v.) and Thoroughbred-type horses to produce hunter, jumper, and dressage mounts.

Percheron Association An American organization founded in 1876 as the Norman Percheron Association (q.v.) and renamed to its present name in 1877; chartered to maintain the stud book and promote breeding and use of the Percheron Horse (q.v.).

Percheron Horse Association of America An American organization that superseded the Percheron Society of America (q.v.) in 1934; chartered to promote and preserve the Percheron (q.v.) breed and maintain a national stud book.

Percheron Society of America An American organization founded in 1905 to establish registration standards for the Percheron (q.v.); continued until 1934, at which time it was subsumed by the Percheron Horse Association of America (q.v.).

perfecta *see* EXACTA

Performance Thoroughbred Registry Also known by the acronym PTR; an American registry established in 1994 by the Jockey Club (q.v.) to recognize Thoroughbreds (q.v.) and Thoroughbred crosses which compete off the racetrack and to document the performance and pedigree records of non-racing Thoroughbreds and mixes.

period *see* CHUKKER

periodic ophthalmia Also known as moon blindness or equine recurrent uveitis; inflammation of the uveal tract (especially of the iris and ciliary body) characterized by tearing, half-closed lids, resistance to eye examination, eyes sunken into the sockets; the iris gradually loses its luster and appears a dull yellow color, the cornea becomes blurred, and the fluid in the rear portion of the eye becomes thick and turbid-looking; may involve one or both eyes; the period of inflammation may last up to 10 days, after which the eye(s) gradually return to normal, although in some cases total blindness may result and/or lesions of the retina; common in Europe, the United States, and Asia; one of the most common inflammatory conditions affecting the eyes of horses, donkeys, mules, or ponies; the condition disappears and returns in cycles that are often completed within a one-month period thus the name; many causes have been proposed, including vitamin A (q.v.) deficiency, but few verified.

periople A thin, varnish-like tissue produced by the horn-producing cell layer of the perioplic ring (q.v.); generally extends about ¾ to 1 inch (19–25 mm) down the wall from the coronary band (q.v.), except at the heel where it blends in with the frog; protects the sensitive coronary band at the junction of the skin and hoof and has the same consistency as the horny frog; the underside flakes off and is carried down as the hoof wall grows out to produce hoof varnish.

perioplic band *see* PERIOPLIC RING

perioplic ring Also known as perioplic band; a narrow ring located just above the coronary band (q.v.) and next to the hair line which secretes the periople (q.v.); composed of papillae like those of the coronary band, but smaller in size.

periosteum A thin, tough, fibrous membrane which covers the entire length of the bone; overlays cells capable of becoming bone-forming cells and attaches tendons and ligaments to the bone.

periostitis Inflammation of the periosteum (q.v.) resulting from a direct blow to the periosteum (q.v.) or a lifting of the periosteum away from the underlying bone; the bone-forming cells respond by creating new bone; when the inflammation subsides, a bony lump generally remains; commonly occurs in the small and large metatarsal and metacarpal bones.

periplantar shoe *see* CHARLIER SHOE

peristalsis A series of wave-like contractions of the smooth muscles of the gut, which move the organ contents through the body to be processed.

peritonitis Inflammation of the membrane lining of the abdominal walls and covering the abdominal organs; difficult to diagnose.

perlino Refers to coat color; a nearly white or cream-colored coat having slightly red or blue points; the horse will have blue eyes.

permanent premolars *see* WOLF TEETH

permanent teeth Any of the teeth that supplant the deciduous teeth (q.v.); include the first, second, and third molars (q.v.), wolf teeth (q.v.), first, second, and permanent third incisors (q.v.), and the second, third, fourth, and permanent second premolars (q.v.); fully formed when the horse is about five years old.

permanent white A registry classification for the American White (q.v.); a white horse produced from a dam and sire of registered stock of any breed; proof of reproducibility of color is not a requirement.

Persian *see* PERSIAN ARAB

Persian Arab Also known as Persian; an Arab (q.v.) bred and raised in Iran; a strong, athletic horse standing 14.1 to 15.1 hands and having a bay, chestnut, or gray, rarely black, coat; more robust than other Arab strains, but has a similar head and body lines; protected from the introduction of other than Persian Arab blood and as such, a stud book separate from other strains is maintained; two breed types are derived from the Persian Arab, the Jaf (q.v.) from Kurdistan and the Darashouri (q.v.) from the Fars region.

Persian Horse *see* PLATEAU PERSIAN

perspire *see* SWEAT

Peruvian Paso Also known as Caballo Peruano de Paso, Paso or Peruvian Stepping Horse; a Peruvian warmblood originating in the mid-16th century; descended from Spanish stock put to Barb (q.v.), Friesian (q.v.), jennet (q.v.), and Andalusian (q.v.) mares; to systematically develop its characteristic gait, the paso, the breed has been very selectively bred without introduction of outside blood for several centuries; the only naturally gaited breed in the world that can guarantee its gait to 100 percent of its offspring; the gaits are not induced or aided by training or devices and include the paso (q.v.), paso corto (q.v.), paso fino (q.v.), and paso largo (q.v.); the action of the breed is known as termino (q.v.); shown without shoes and with a short, natural hoof; can reach speeds up to 16 mph (26 kmph), stands 14.1 to 15.1 hands, and may have a coat of any solid color, as well as gray, and roan with bay and chestnut coats most common; has great stamina, a naturally low-set tail, a well-sprung and very deep rib cage, medium head, short to medium-length back, and a fairly short, well-muscled neck; is not related to the Paso Fino (q.v.).

Peruvian Stepping Horse *see* PERUVIAN PASO

pesade A High School (q.v.) movement performed in place; the horse raises his forelegs off the ground and folds them at a sharp angle while lowering his hocks under his center of gravity (q.v.); the body is maintained at an angle of 45 degrees for several seconds, the hind legs being set firmly on the ground; is usually higher and straighter than the levade (q.v.).

petechial fever *see* PURPURA HEMORRHAGICA

petechial hemorrhage *see* PURPURA HEMORRHAGICA

Peter's Brougham A horse-drawn carriage of the Brougham (q.v.) type designed with angular lines.

Peter's Phaeton *see* PARK PHAETON

PHA *see* PALOMINO HORSE ASSOCIATION

Phaeton A comfortable, swift, light, four-wheeled, horse-drawn buggy used in 18th century Western Europe for exercising and driving purposes; at first characterized by large wheels, a driver's seat protected by a falling hood, high bodywork, and seated one or two passengers; drawn by a single horse, pairs, or teams of four and six and hung on cee or elbow springs; later models were both smaller and more substantial, adapted for pony draft, with rearward, crosswise seating and improved suspension; many versions evolved including the Basket Phaeton (q.v.), Pill Box Phaeton (q.v.), High-flyer Phaeton (q.v.), Park Phaeton (q.v.), Mail Phaeton (q.v.), Stanhope Phaeton (q.v.), and Spider Phaeton (q.v.); the name derived from Phaeton, who drove the sun chariot in classical mythology.

phalange *see* PHALANX

phalangeal bone *see* PHALANX

phalanges More than one phalanx (q.v.).

phalanx Also known familiarly as phalange or phalangeal bone; any of the three primary digital bones of the foot; in order towards the foot, include: long pastern (q.v.), short pastern (q.v.), and third pastern (q.v.).

Phar Lap Also known familiarly as Big Red or Bobby Boy; a chestnut gelding considered one of Australia's greatest race horses; foaled in New Zealand in 1927 and died in 1932, probably of poisoning; stood 17 hands, weighed 1,250 pounds (567 kg), and had massive hind legs, the hind feet of which overstepped the marks of the fore by more than 12 inches (30.48 cm); started 51 times for 37 wins, 3 seconds, and 2 thirds.

PHBA *see* PALOMINO HORSE BREEDERS OF AMERICA, INCORPORATED

phenylbutazolidan *see* PHENYLBUTAZONE

phenylbutazone Also known as phenylbutazolidan, Butazolidin, Butazone, or bute; a non-steroidal, anti-inflammatory, analgesic drug (q.v.) used to reduce pain and inflammation in the treatment of traumatic or inflammatory musculoskeletal disorders and lameness; may cause gastrointestinal irritation; horses are not permitted to participate in most types of competition if the substance is present in their system.

PHF *see* POTOMAC HORSE FEVER

phill horse *see* SHAFT HORSE

phosphorus A solid, non-chemical element, the second most important mineral in the horse's body; in conjunction with calcium (q.v.), is required for bone mineralization including bone formation, growth, maintenance, and repair and comprises 75 percent of the minerals in the horse's body and approximately 90 percent of the skeletal minerals; high levels inhibit calcium availability.

photo finish A racing term; said of a race so close it is necessary to review film shot by a narrow-field-of-vision camera located at the finish line to determine the winner; first used to record a photo finish in 1890 at Sheepshead Bay, USA.

photophobia Abnormal sensitivity to sunlight.

photosensitization Also known as blue nose; sun sensitivity of the horse caused by a systemic chemical reaction; a more painful and chronic problem than sunburn (q.v.); excessive amounts of a chemical found in most legumes (q.v.), especially clovers and some weeds, are converted to photosensitive chemicals in the liver, which then circulate through the bloodstream and, when exposed to sunlight through unpigmented white skin, react and destroy the tissue; affected areas turn purple prior to the skin sloughing off, after which painful and persistent scabs and scars develop.

photosynthesis Synthesis of chemical compounds with the aid of radiant energy and especially light; specifically, formation of carbohydrates from carbon dioxide and a source of hydrogen (as water) in the chlorophyll-containing tissues of plants exposed to light.

physeal plate *see* EPIPHYSEAL PLATE

physeal dysplasia *see* PHYSITIS

physes Plural of physis (q.v.).

physic Any medicine that causes a horse to purge his gastrointestinal contents.

physic ball *see* MEDICINE BALL

physiology The science of animal organisms, their organs, and their function, i.e. the function of the body.

physiological shoeing Also known as normal shoeing; to balance the hooves and attach horseshoes (q.v.) taking into account the normal foot movements.

physis The parts of a bone involved in its increase in length, i.e. growth plate (q.v.).

physitis Also known as epiphysitis, physeal dysplasia, or dysplasia of the growth plate; pain associated with abnormal activity in the growth plates (q.v.) of certain long bones in rapidly growing young horses; commonly involves the distal (q.v.) ends of the radius, tibia, third metacarpal/ metatarsal bones, or the proximal aspect of the first phalanx; is most common in yearlings; characterized by slight swelling and heat around the growth plate, boxy looking affected joints, and in some cases, lameness; may be due to malnutrition, conformational defect, faulty hoof growth, fetal malpositioning, compression of the growth plate, or toxicosis (q.v.).

piaffe The most collected of all dressage (q.v.) movements and a key foundation of all High School movements (q.v.); a ground movement in which the horse performs a highly cadenced trot (q.v.) in place; the trot has no forward movement and has moments of suspension between each diagonal step; the forelegs are light and elevated higher than the hind feet.

piales *see* PIALES EN EL LIENZO

piales en el lienzo Also known as piales; a Mexican rodeo event; specifically, a type of horse tripping (q.v.); one of nine scored events in a charreada (q.v.) in which a mare is goaded out of a pen into a long, wide chute leading to a circular arena; before she reaches the end of the chute, a mounted charro (q.v.) gallops up behind and lassos (q.v.) her hind legs; the charro then takes a wrap of the lariat around the saddle horn and attempts to stop the mare within a specified distance after she leaves the chute; points are awarded based upon the difficulty of the throw; now illegal in some states in the United States.

Piano Box Buggy An horse-drawn, four-wheeled, square-shaped vehicle introduced in 1855 in New York, USA.

pic A wooden-handled lance used by a picador (q.v.) in a corrida de toros (q.v.); is approximately 17 feet (5 m) long having a sharp point and a 4 inch (10 cm) crusetta attached at right angles to the distal end; the point is about the size of a little finger and 3 inches (7.5 cm) long; the crusetta prevents the point from penetrating the shoulder muscles of the bull too deeply.

pica Depraved appetite.

picador A participant in a corrida de toros (q.v.); responsible for poking the heavy shoulder muscles of the bull with a pic (q.v.) to weaken them sufficiently to cause the bull to lower its head and, therefore, be fought more easily; mounted on a heavily padded horse called caballo cuñero (q.v.).

pick (1) An American racing term; a multi-race bet in which the bettor (q.v.) selects winners of all included races; the most common wagers of this type are pick three (q.v.), pick six (q.v.), and pick nine (q.v.); other countries have bets to which the same criteria are applied, but the name varies from country to country, e.g. 'Tote jackpot' in Britain. (2) To select, to choose, e.g. a perfect mount.

pick-axe *see* PICK-AXE TEAM

pick-axe team Also known as pick-axe; a team of horses consisting of three leaders and two wheelers (q.v.) or two leaders and one wheeler used to pull a horse-drawn vehicle.

pick nine A racing term; a wager in which the bettor (q.v.) attempts to select the winners of nine consecutive races.

pick six Also known as pic six or five-ten; a racing term; a wager in which the bettor (q.v.) attempts to select the winners of six consecutive races; if no bettor selects all six winners, a small percentage of the pool may be distributed to those who picked five winners out of the six with the balance of the pool carried over to the following day's pick six.

pick three Also known as daily triple; a racing term; a wager in which the bettor (q.v.) attempts to select the winners of three consecutive races.

pick up (1) Also known as pick up hounds; a hunting term; to obtain the attention and regain control of the hounds (q.v.). (2) To obtain the use of a horse(s) for use in competitions, as in "To pick up a ride." (3) To increase speed.

pick up a lead Said of the horse; to initiate movement with either the right or left foreleg as appropriate.

pick up his face A Western term; said of a rider, to ask the horse for increased collection and more contact with the bit.

pick up hounds *see* PICK UP NO. 1

pickup man A rodeo term; a mounted arena official who assists bareback and saddle bronc (q.v.) competitors in dismounting from their horses when the required ride time ends.

picnic races Race meetings held in the Australian Outback; amateur riders and their mounts compete for small prizes on primitive bushland racetracks (q.v.)

pic six *see* PICK SIX

piebald Refers to coat color; a black horse with tobiano (q.v.), overo (q.v.), sabino (q.v.), or splashed asymmetric patterns of white; the lines between the black and white are well-defined.

Piebald One of three types of the semi-wild Basque (q.v.) indigenous to the Basque region of France; stands 11 to 13 hands and is very hardy.

pied Refers to hound (q.v.) coat color; an asymmetric pattern of color on a cream or fawn-colored body, head, legs, and stern; characteristic of English-bred hounds; differs from badger-pied (q.v.) and hare-pied (q.v.).

pigeon-toed Also known as pin toes, toed in, or toe in; a congenital condition in which the toes of one or both of the horse's forefeet are turned towards each other when viewed from the front; usually accompanied by base-narrow (q.v.) condition; generally causes the horse to plait (q.v.) when moving.

pig-eyed Said of a horse having small, deep-set, narrow, squinty eyes with thick lids.

piggin' string *see* PIGGING STRING

pigging string Also known as piggin' string or pigging strap; a roping term; a length of twisted, narrow-gauge nylon or cotton with a loop woven in one end, used by calf ropers to tie the feet of the calf; available in different strengths and lengths.

pigging strap *see* PIGGING STRING

pig-mouthed Also known as swine chopped; a hunting term; a hound with an undershot (q.v.) lower jaw.

pigskin The skin of the pig or hog or leather made from it; used in the manufacture of some saddles.

pig sticking The sport of hunting wild boar from horseback using a spear; developed by British officers stationed in India in the early 19th century.

pigtail The small rope by which horses strung in a pack string (q.v.) are connected to one another; fastened to the rear end of the saddle of the horse or mule in front and to the halter of the animal following, and so on.

pike *see* TURNPIKE GATE

piker An obsolete driving term; one who contrived to bypass a toll-gate without paying when driving a horse-drawn vehicle.

Pilentum An open, four-wheeled, horse-drawn vehicle operated in the 1830s; had a low-slung body hung on four elliptic springs; was entered on either side by a small door; carried four to six passengers depending on vehicle size and was drawn by a single horse or pair of coachman-driven horses.

pill (1) A small, usually globular or rounded, mass of medical substance designed to be swallowed. (2) *see* NUMBER BALL

pillar reins *see* CROSS TIES

pillars Heavy posts set wide enough apart to accommodate the breadth of an average horse, between which the horse is tied; used for centuries to increase balance and rhythm and to teach levade (q.v.) and other airs above the ground (q.v.), a practice used more commonly in Europe than in Britain or the United States.

pillars of the stud book The three Arab (q.v.) sires to which all Thoroughbreds' lineage can be traced: Byerley Turk (q.v.), Godolphin Arabian (q.v.), and Darley Arabian (q.v.).

Pill Box Slang; a small, horse-drawn vehicle of the Phaeton (q.v.) or Chariot (q.v.) type used by a doctor on his daily rounds during the 18th century; drawn by a single horse in shafts.

Pill Box Phaeton A horse-drawn vehicle of the Phaeton (q.v.) type; a larger and sturdier version of the pill box (q.v.), having room for one passenger; commonly used in the Atlantic coast states of North America during the 18th century to transport and sell pills and potions.

pillion (1) Also known as pillion saddle; a cushion or pad placed behind the saddle on a horse upon which another rider sits, especially a woman. (2) To ride on a pillion.

pillion post A mounting block (q.v.); so called because it was used by ladies who rode on pillions (q.v.).

pillion saddle *see* PILLION NO. 1

pincers *see* INCISORS

pilot (1) A hunting term; to lead or guide one in the hunt field. (2) A British hunting term; said of the fox who is, in a sense, the ultimate leader of the hunt.

pinched back (1) A racing term; said of a jockey caught in a jam of horses who is forced to fall back during the horse race. (2) Said of the horse's back when the nerves or muscles are cramped as due to a poorly fitting saddle, lack of padding beneath the saddle, injury, etc.

pinchers *see* PULL OFF

Pindos One of three remaining ancient native Greek pony breeds, the others being the Skyros (q.v.) and Peneia (q.v.); evolved from native mares put to Oriental stallions; bred in the mountain regions of Thessaly and Epirus; stands 12 to 13 hands, generally has a dark gray coat although bay, black, and brown also occur, is strong, hardy, possessed of exceptional stamina for its size, and is very frugal; used for light farm work, packing, and riding.

pin firing Also known as point firing; to insert extremely hot pointed pins and/or needles into a blemished (q.v.) or unsound area to stimulate circulation and tissue growth; treatment may be graduated from a slight puncturing of the skin to bone-deep penetration; when applied in line pattern, is known as line firing (q.v.).

pinhooker (1) A racing term; one who buys a racehorse(s) with the intention of reselling him at a profit. (2) A British racing term; one who buys unraced young-stock with the intention of reselling at a profit.

pin horse Also known as body horse or pin-hoss; the middle horse of three horses driven abreast or the horse in front of the shaft horse (q.v.) when farm horses were driven four-at-length.

pin-hoss *see* PIN HORSE

pink *see* PINK COAT

pink coat Also known as scarlet coat or pink; a hunting term; the traditional scarlet or red hunt coat worn by huntsmen (q.v.) and competitors participating in upper-level events.

pinkeye *see* EQUINE VIRAL ARTERITIS

pinned ribbons A coaching term; driving reins when buckled at the ends.

pinto (1) Refers to coat color; an asymmetrical pattern of well-defined white patches on any base color; no white hairs are mixed into the colored areas; several specific patterns occur: tobiano (q.v.), overo (q.v.), sabino (q.v.), splashed white (q.v.), with overo and tobiano most common. (2) *see* PINTO

Pinto Also known as Indian pony; an American-bred, color-type warmblood selectively bred and recognized as a distinct breed; descended from Barb (q.v.) stock brought to America by Spanish Conquistadors in the 16th century and crossed with native Mustangs (q.v.); of two patterns: tobiano (q.v.) which occurs most commonly and overo (q.v.); according to legend, considered by the American Indian to have magical powers, possessed of natural camouflage, and especially capable in war; height varies, but registered horse must stand more than 14 hands, ponies 8½ to 14 hands, and miniatures under 8½ hands or 34 inches (86 cm); coat coloring is either piebald (q.v.) or skewbald (q.v.); has a sparse mane and tail, the result of selective breeding to prevent entanglement in the undergrowth, pink skin, blue eyes, and white or multi-colored hoof markings; four conformation types are accepted: Stock-Type Pinto (q.v.), Hunter-Type Pinto (q.v.), Pleasure-Type Pinto (q.v.), and Saddle-Type Pinto (q.v.); breed characteristics apart from the coat color are poorly defined; an Appaloosa (q.v.) or a horse with Appaloosa ancestry cannot be a Pinto; recognized as a breed in 1963; used for riding and light draft; a Spanish word meaning painted.

Pinto Horse Association of America, Inc. Also known by the acronym PtHA; an American organization founded in 1947 and officially incorporated in 1956 to maintain color registries for Pinto (q.v.) horses, ponies, and miniature horses, to improve conformation and breeding, and to increase public interest in the breed; the stud book was started by the American Paint Horse Association (q.v.) in 1963; recognizes four conformation types: Stock-Type Pinto (q.v.), Hunter-Type Pinto (q.v.), Pleasure-Type Pinto (q.v.), and Saddle-Type Pinto (q.v.); to qualify for entry in the registry, a horse must have at least one registered parent, with the other parent either Quarter Horse (q.v.) or English Thoroughbred (q.v.); the registry maintains both Breeding Stock and Color Divisions.

Pinto Horse Breeding Stock Division A division of the PtHA (q.v.) registry chartered with maintaining bloodline records of solid-colored horses with color in their pedigrees or horses lacking sufficient body markings to quality for registration in the PtHA Color Divisions.

pin toes *see* PIGEON-TOED

pinworm *see* OXYRURIS EQUI

Pinzgauer *see* NORIKER

Pinzgauer Noriker *see* NORIKER

pipe (1) A hunting term; a branch or hole of a fox's den. (2) *see* LUNG. (3) *see* BOX LOOP

pipe loop *see* BOX LOOP

pipe collar A harness collar (q.v.) reshaped with a cut out to accommodate the windpipe; used on horses prone to choking.

pipe-opener A sharp, short gallop (q.v.) to stimulate the circulatory system and clear the lungs of the horse before extended or fast work.

pipe stall An open enclosure constructed of horizontal, spaced, round rails, generally made of metal pipe, used to contain a horse; pipe stalls vary in size and may have a covered manger.

proplasmosis *see* EQUINE PIROPLASMOSIS

pirouette A High School (q.v.) dressage movement in which the horse scribes a circle almost in place; the horse's forehand inscribes a full circle, the radius of which is hardly more than the horse's body length, while the hind legs inscribe a very small circle, about the diameter of a dinner plate, the horse pivoting around his inside hind leg, which marks time to the rhythm of the movement; ridden in collected walk (q.v.), collected canter (q.v.), or piaffe (q.v.); lightness of the forehand is essential.

pirouette on the center *see* TURN ON CENTER

pirouette sur le center *see* TURN ON CENTER

pirouette sur les haunches *see* TURN ON THE HAUNCHES

piss (1) *see* URINATE. (2) *see* URINE

pista *see* FINO BOARD

pitch fork *see* FORK NO. 2

pit pony Also known as pitter or collier; a British term; the common name for ponies (Shetland [q.v.], Welsh [q.v.], Fell [q.v.], Dartmoor [q.v.], Exmoor [q.v.], Icelandic [q.v.], etc.) used in coal mines to retrieve and haul coal to the surface; used in this capacity for the last three centuries; lived in stables as much as 4 miles (6.4 km) underground during the work week and were turned out to pasture on the weekends; the last four pit ponies were put into retirement in February 1994.

Pit Ponies' Protection Society A British

organization founded in 1927 to improve the conditions under which pit ponies (q.v.) or other animals were worked underground; now defunct.

pitter *see* PIT PONY

pivot (1) Also known as pivot on the hindquarters; a Western term; a half-turn on the haunches performed at either the canter (q.v.) or gallop (q.v.); the horse swings his forelegs around his inner hind leg. (2) *see* TURN ON THE FOREHAND. (3) *see* TURN ON THE HAUNCHES

pivoted Said of a horse who fails to pick up one of his hind legs when performing a walk pirouette (q.v.).

pivoting A dressage term used in reference to pirouettes (q.v.) and or turns on the haunches or forehand; said of the horse when he avoids picking up a foot in the proper rhythm, turning around a grounded or stuck foot.

pivot on the hindquarters *see* PIVOT NO. 1

place (1) An American racing term; said of a horse, to finish a race in second position. (2) *see* PLACE BET. (3) A position won in a competition, e.g. "Sundancer won first place."

place bet Also known as place; an American racing term; any wager placed on a horse to finish a race in first or second position.

placed A racing term; said of a horse to finish second or third in a race; not to be confused with place.

placenta Also known as afterbirth or caul; the fetal membranes which develop in the uterus (q.v.) in early pregnancy, which connect the unborn fetus to the lining of the mare's uterus by the umbilical cord, nourishes the fetus, and removes waste products from it; formed within the first 15 days of fetal life by the fusion of two embryonic membranes, the chorion and the allantois; within 90 days of fertilization, attaches to the uterine wall; is passed by the mare at foaling.

placentation Development of the placenta (q.v.) and attachment of the fetus (q.v.) to the uterus during pregnancy.

place pool An American racing term; the sum of money wagered in a horse race for second place finishers.

placing judge An American racing term; a race official who posts the order in which horses finish in a race.

plain horseshoe A machine-made (q.v.) or hand forged horseshoe (q.v.) without calks (q.v.) or special features other than creasing of the nail holes.

plain hunting iron *see* HUNTING IRON

plain jointed snaffle *see* JOINTED SNAFFLE

plait (1) To braid; to interweave, as in the locks or strands of the mane or leather. (2) A braid.

plaited reins A rein (q.v.) in which the handpiece and/or the entire length of rein is made of braided or plaited leather; offers improved grip over a smooth rein (q.v.).

plaiting (1) *see* ROPE WALKING. (2) *see* PLAIT

plank A component of a jumping obstacle; a flat, wide piece of wood, painted or natural, supported by standards (q.v.), over which a horse jumps.

plank jump *see* BOARD FENCE

plantar Pertaining to the sole of the hoof or the back of the hind limb from the hock (q.v.) to the hoof.

plantar cushion Also known as digital cushion; a mass of fibro-fatty tissue, filling the space behind the coffin bone and separating it from the frog, which forms the bulb of the heel; functions as a shock absorber for the foot.

Plantation Walker *see* TENNESSEE WALKING HORSE

Plantation Walking Horse *see* TENNESSEE WALKING HORSE

plaster *see* POULTICE

plate (1) A shallow circular vessel, from which food may be served; used as a prize for winning an equestrian event; generally made of silver or silver plate; usually less valuable than a cup. (2) Refers to horseshoes (q.v.) used on racehorses; available in a variety of types including flat plates (q.v.), racing plates (q.v.) and training plates (q.v.). (3) To apply a silver or gold veneer to a less precious metal.

plate-and-screws stabilization A technique used to stabilize a fractured leg bone; a metal plate is placed the length of the bone over the break and attached both above and below the break with screws inserted into the stable portion of the bone; in some cases now replaced by the equestrian nail (q.v.).

Plateau Persian Any Arab-type horse indigenous to the plateau regions of Iran; an amalgamation of breeds including the Jaf (q.v.), Darashouri (q.v.), Arab (q.v.), Shiragazi (q.v.), Quashquai (q.v.), Basseri (q.v.), Yamoote, and Bakhtiari; stands about 15 hands, generally has a gray, bay, or chestnut coat, good action, is strong, and sure-footed.

plater (1) A farrier specializing in shoeing race horses, specifically flat track (q.v.) or Thoroughbred (q.v.) and Quarter Horse (q.v.) running horses. (2) Also known as selling plater; a racing term; a horse who runs in cheap claiming races (q.v.); so called because of the silver plates formerly awarded to winners of such races.

plate spread *see* SPREAD NO. 4

Platers Union *see* INTERNATIONAL UNION OF JOURNEYMAN HORSESHOERS OF THE UNITED STATES AND CANADA

platform boot A luggage compartment located above the front axle on some horse-drawn carriages; replaced the coachman's seat; such vehicles were generally postillion-driven.

platform spring *see* TELEGRAPH SPRING

play *see* BET

player *see* BETTOR

players *see* KEYS

pleasure class A horse show class in which horses or mules are judged on the basis of gait execution at the walk, trot, canter, and backing.

Pleasure-Type Pinto One of four Pinto (q.v.) conformation types developed with specific breed goals and standards in mind; of predominantly Arab (q.v.) or Morgan (q.v.) breeding and build displaying conformation qualities suited to a variety of both English and Western events; of medium size, has a comparatively horizontal croup, a naturally high tail carriage, and a well-muscled thigh and gaskin.

pleurisy Also known as pleuritis; inflammation of the membrane lining the chest and covering the lungs; characterized by fever, painful and difficult breathing, and fluids in the chest cavity.

pleuritis *see* PLEURISY

pleuropneumonia A debilitating and possibly deadly inflammation of the lungs which causes or is closely followed by pleurisy (q.v.).

Pleven A warmblood developed in the late 19th century in Pleven, Bulgaria, from which the name derived; descended from Russian Anglo-Arab (q.v.) stallions crossed with pure-bred Arabs (q.v.) or local half-bred mares; until breed characteristics were fixed, around 1938, only Arab (q.v.) and Gidran (q.v.) stallions were used, after which Thoroughbred (q.v.) blood was selectively introduced; stands about 15.2 hands, has a chestnut coat, and Arab-like features; a good all-round horse equally suited to light agricultural work, riding, and competitive sports; a natural jumper.

plough (1) *see* PLOW. (2) *see* PLOUGHLAND

ploughland Also known as plough; a hunting term; the fields over which a hunt is conducted.

plow (1) Also spelled plough; to make furrows or turn up the soil. (2) To work with a plow. (3) An agricultural implement for cutting furrows in and turning up the soil.

plow handles *see* PUMP HANDLES

plow rein *see* DIRECT REIN

plug (1) A horse of common breeding and poor conformation. (2) A slow moving and tired horse.

plugging a collar The process of stuffing a harness collar (q.v.) with wetted straw until the neck lining is appropriate for the horse it is to fit.

PMU *see* PREGNANT MARE URINE

PMU farm Any facility where mares are maintained for the purpose of urine (q.v.) production and collection from which estrogen is extracted; during the period October through March, the time of highest estrogen levels in the urine of pregnant mares, mares are hooked up around the clock to a harness attached to a funnel that collects the urine from the urethra and carries it down a tube depositing it into a one-gallon container; when estrogen levels decrease in the mare's urine prior to foal (q.v.) birth , around April, the mare is put to pasture (q.v.) at the same facility; following birth she is re-impregnated while pastured with her foal and on October 1 is returned to the collection line; water intake is often restricted to raise urine estrogen concentrations.

pnemo-puncture A type of acupuncture (q.v.); stimulation of precise body points along body meridians (q.v.) of the horse achieved by injection of air into those points; used to control pain, treat internal issues, anesthetize, and reduce stress.

poached A hunting term; said of the footing around a jump when cuppy (q.v.), muddy, or cut-up.

pocket (1) A barrel racing (q.v.) term; the turning area between the horse and the barrel; size varies between horses. (2) *see* IN THE HUNTSMAN'S POCKET

pocketed A racing term; said of a horse competing in a race who is surrounded by other horses and unable to increase his speed until an opening presents itself.

podotrochlitis *see* NAVICULAR DISEASE

point (1) *see* POINT TEAM. (2) A hunting term; the location to which the whippers-in (q.v.) are sent to watch for a fox (q.v.) breaking a covert (q.v.). (3) Also known as point of a run; a hunting term; the distance, as the crow flies, between the two most widely separated points traveled by the hounds (q.v.) while running a fox. (4) Any external area on the horse's body, e.g. hock, nose, flank, etc. (5) *see* POINT A COW. (6) The pointed end of any strap.

point a cow Also known as point; a cutting term; said of the cutting horse (q.v.) when he focuses on the cow being worked with his ears forward.

pointers The pair of mules in front of the wheelers (q.v.) in a 20-mule team.

point firing *see* PIN FIRING

pointing (1) Said of a resting horse who stands with one foreleg placed further forward than the other; the horse assumes this position to relieve the weight and therefore pressure on the pointed foot; usually indicates that there is something wrong with the forward leg, although the horse may alternate the pointed leg if both forefeet are affected; a sign of navicular disease (q.v.). (2) Refers to the action in any gait, but generally the trot, when the horse places the toes of his forefeet on the ground before the heels; normally the horse would strike the ground with the entire flat surface of the foot (toe and heel together); may relieve heel pressure common in navicular disease. (3) A perceptible extension of the stride with little flexion in the leg; a condition common in Thoroughbreds (q.v.), Standardbred (q.v.), and long-strided horses bred and trained for speed.

pointing your leaders *see* POINT THE LEADERS

point of a run *see* POINT NO. 3

point of call A racing term; the position of a horse running in a race as noted at different locations on the racetrack (q.v.) and posted on a chart; the point at which the racing position is noted varies with the distance of each race.

point of the croup *see* POINT OF THE HIP

point of the hip Also known incorrectly as point of the croup; the bony prominence located approximately 4 inches (10 cm) behind the last rib and formed by the internal angles of the ischium (q.v.).

point of the shoulder The bony prominence formed by the scapula and humerus (q.v.) of the forearm.

point of the whip *see* LASH NO. 1

points (1) Also known as points of the horse; the tail, ear rims, mane, tail, and lower legs of the horse; grouped on the basis of color, i.e. black points or nonblack points. (2) Ready-knitted tips for a whip (q.v.). (3) The beginning and ending of a cross-country (q.v.), point-to-point (q.v.), or steeplechase (q.v.).

points of the horse *see* POINTS NO. 1

point team Also known as point; the team (q.v.) of horses positioned behind the leaders (q.v.) in an eight-horse hitch (q.v.).

point the leaders Also known as pointing your leaders; said of the coachman (q.v.) when he indicates to the lead horses of a team by looping or pointing the rein(s) that a change of direction to the right or left is about to occur.

point-to-point Also known as hunt race; an amateur mounted competition in which competitors historically raced from one place, or point, to another over open fields and paddocks rather than on a race course, the average distance being 3½ miles (5.6 km); since the early 20th century, most are run on courses that essentially mimic minor steeplechase tracks, the standard distance of which is 3 miles (4.8 km), with a few races of 2½ miles (4 km) (usually for younger horses), and a few 4 miles (6.4 km) or more; generally restricted to horses who have been regularly hunted with a recognized pack of hounds and for which the owner has obtained and registered a Master of Hounds' certificate; first held in Great Britain several centuries ago.

poison (1) Any agent that chemically destroys health or life upon contact or absorption by an organism; may be slow-acting, occurring over a period of days or weeks, or fast acting. (2) To destroy by means of poison. (3) To put poison on or into.

Poitevin *see* MULASSIER

Poitevine *see* POITEVIN

Poitue Ass *see* BAUDET DE POITOU

Poitou Donkey *see* BAUDET DU POITOU

Poitou Mule *see* MULE POITEVINE

polarization stress analysis A technique used to determine whether or not cryogenic (q.v.) alteration of a brand or area of hair has occurred.

pole (1) *see* RAIL NO. 1. (2) A racing term; a marker placed at measured distances around the track which indicate the distance to the finish, e.g. the quarter pole is located ¼ mile (400 m) from the finish. (3) Also known as coach pole; a piece of wood attached to and projecting from the undercarriage of a horse-drawn vehicle on either side of which horses are harnessed and by which the vehicle is pulled; the end of the pole fits between the futchells (q.v.) and is secured by a pole pin (q.v.); on the pole end, there is a metal mounting with a ring on either side to which the pole straps (q.v.) or pole chains (q.v.) attach. (4) A training aid used on pacers (q.v.) and trotters (q.v.); a pointed pole, generally made of wood, placed on the side opposite that to which the horse pulls; buckled to the saddle pad, pointed end forward, and extends through a ring on the headpiece, protruding a few inches beyond the horse's nose.

pole-bar *see* BUGLE

pole chains Short steel chains attached to the pole (q.v.) of a horse-drawn vehicle by which the horses hold the vehicle when descending or ascending a hill; attached to the pole head either by a hook or a chain passed through its own ring on one end and to the kidney link of the hames collar on the other; at the turn of the 19th century owner-driven vehicles employed pole chains while coachmen-driven vehicles used pole straps (q.v.).

pole-end horses *see* SWING PAIR

pole gear The parts of the harness collectively, used to attach the horses to the pole (q.v.) of the vehicle they pull; consist of: pole, pole chains (q.v.), pole head (q.v.), pole straps (q.v.), pole pin (q.v.) and pole hook (q.v.).

pole head A moveable steel fitting on the pole (q.v.) of a horse-drawn coach and some other vehicles to which the pole chains (q.v.), pole straps (q.v.), or pole pieces (q.v.) attached.

pole hook Also known as crab or swan neck (sl); a hook on the end of the coach pole (q.v.) from which the main and lead bars hang in a team harness.

pole race *see* BENDING RACE

pole pieces *see* POLE STRAPS

pole pin A steel pin securing the pole (q.v.) between the futchells (q.v.) on a horse-drawn vehicle.

pole straps Also known as pole pieces; a short piece of leather attached to the pole (q.v.) of a horse-drawn vehicle by which the horses hold the vehicle when descending or ascending a hill; put through a ring on the pole head and through its own keeper to hold it in position with the buckle on the outside and the strap on the pole side; at the turn of the 19th century owner-driven vehicles employed pole chains (q.v.) while coachmen-driven vehicles used pole straps.

poling Also known as poling-up or pole-piecing; to attach the pole chains (q.v.) or pole pieces (q.v.) to the hames collar.

polish (1) To make smooth and glossy, usually by friction. (2) The shine of the horse's coat when clean and groomed. (3) A substance used to impart a gloss.

Polish Warmblood *see* WIELKOPOLSKI

poll Also known as nape or occipital crest; the highest point of the horse's head, just between the ears.

pollard *see* WEATINGS

Pollard, James (1772–1867) A noted English artist of hunting and sporting scenes, particularly coaching and driving subjects.

poll evil An inflammatory disorder of the bursae of the poll (q.v.); is primarily infectious in origin, caused by the organism *Brucella abortus* or *Actinomyces bovis*, but may also be caused by worm infestation or trauma from cuts, abrasions, bites, or badly fitting tack such as halters, headstalls, and bridles; symptoms include initial swelling, followed by the development of a fistula (q.v.) between the infected bursa, a weeping lesion on the skin, and sensitivity about the head and poll.

poll guard *see* HEAD BUMPER

polo Also known as hockey on horseback (obs), chaugán (obs), daiku (obs), or pulu (obs); a mounted ball game originating in Persia around 521 to 486 BC played by 2 teams of 4 mounted players, on a field a maximum of 300 by 200 yards (274 × 183 m) in size where the goals can be no more than 250 yards (228 m) apart; consists of 6, 7½ minute chukkers (q.v.) or periods during which mounted players attempt to move a polo ball down the field and through the goalposts by means of a polo mallet (q.v.); also played on bicycles, elephants (pachyderm polo [q.v.]), and camels; arena polo (q.v.) has also gained popularity in recent years.

polo ball A white sphere, 3¼ inches (8 cm) in diameter and weighing 5½ ounces (156 g) used by polo players to play polo (q.v.); originally made of bamboo root, most are now made of either a lightweight wood or plastic.

polo boards *see* BOARDS

polo boots Any knee-high, unlaced brown leather boot worn by a polo player (q.v.); typically zip up the front from the top of the foot to the knee.

Polo Cart *see* POLO GIG

polo club An organization of polo teams and players defined on the basis of region or association; simple polo clubs were established in Manipuri Indian villages during the mid 19th century; the first polo club in the Western world was officially established in London in 1873 and was controlled by the Hurlingham Polo Club (q.v.).

polocrosse A mounted game originating in Australia; a horseback version of lacrosse in which riders scoop up a polo ball in a small net attached to the distal end of a long stick, throw or carry it down the field to score by putting the ball between the goalposts.

polo field Also known as polo ground or polo pitch; a 10-acre (4 hectares) grass field, 300 by 200 yards (274 × 183 m) wide, unless boards (q.v.) are used to keep the ball in play in which case it is only 160 yards (146 m) wide, upon which the game of polo is played; has two sets of goalposts (q.v.), each set being positioned 8 yards (7 m) apart and about 10 feet high, on each long end of the field, and penalty lines marked in white chalk at 30, 40, and 60 yards (27, 36.5, and 55 m) from each back line (q.v.); the center line is similarly marked; the object is to score goals by maneuvering a polo ball (q.v.) down the field and hitting it between the goalposts.

polo game *see* POLO MATCH

Polo Gig Also known as Polo Cart; a horse-drawn Sporting Gig (q.v.) popular in the late 19th century; used to exercise or drive a polo pony to a match; had crude disc brakes and a wickerwork basket to hold polo mallets (q.v.).

polo ground *see* POLO FIELD

polo handicap Also known as goal rating, polo rating, goal handicap, or handicap; a rating awarded each polo player, male or female, on the basis of general mastery of the fundamentals of the polo game, horsemanship, sense of strategy and conduct, and pony quality; expressed in number of goals, e.g. a "10 goal player"; ratings range from C (minus 2 goals) to 10, with 10 being the best rating; the system was instituted in 1888; player handicaps are revised annually by the USPA (q.v.) or appropriate national body; about ⅔ of the rated players carry a rating of 2 goals or less while ratings of 5 goals and above generally belong to professional players; team handicaps (q.v.) are also awarded; the Americans introduced this handicapping system in 1891.

poloist *see* POLO PLAYER

polo mallet Also known as mallet, polo stick, or stick; a shaft made from a bamboo cane with a hand grip and leather loop on one end and a hard wooden head made from bamboo root or a hard wood such as maple attached at a right angle to the shaft on the other; the shaft is more narrow and flexible towards the mallet head; varies in length from 48 to 52 inches (1.2–1.3 m); used by polo players to strike and move the ball down the field to the goal; the ball is struck broadside of the mallet head, not on the narrow ends; for safety reasons, the mallet is always held in the right hand.

polo match Also known as polo game and match; a mounted game played by 2 teams of 4 players lasting approximately 1½ hours and divided into 6, 7½ minute chukkers (q.v.); when played on the flat, reflects the score as goals are made, and when played by the handicap, the sum total rating of the players on the team is subtracted from that of the opposing team, any difference being awarded to the lower rated side in goals on the scoreboard, i.e., a 26-goal team will give 2 goals to a 24-goal team.

polo mount *see* POLO PONY

polo penalty Also known as penalty; a handicap imposed for infringement of polo rules; there are 10 penalties: Penalty 1 (q.v.), Penalty 2 (q.v.), Penalty 3 (q.v.), Penalty 4 (q.v.), Penalty 5 (q.v.), Penalty 6 (q.v.), Penalty 7 (q.v.), Penalty 8 (q.v.), Penalty 9 (q.v.), and Penalty 10 (q.v.), 6 of which are awarded as free hits toward the goal from a set distance and 4 as non-stroke penalties; generally assessed to prevent play which may be considered dangerous to either the horse or rider; the severity of the foul committed and the position on the field where it occurred, determines the penalty awarded.

polo pitch *see* POLO FIELD

polo player Also known as poloist; one who plays polo (q.v.).

polo pony Also known as polo mount; any horse ridden by a polo player (q.v.) to play polo (q.v.); commonly of Thoroughbred (q.v.) blood although the tougher Argentine Polo Ponies (q.v.) with their better bone and in-bred talent for the sport dominate the game; generally stands 15 to 15.3 hands, is distinctly Thoroughbred in appearance, has speed, stamina, courage, good balance, and a bold, lively temperament; the mane is usually roached (q.v.) to prevent interference with the mallet (q.v.) and the tail tied; referred to as ponies due to the height limit imposed on them until early this century; each player uses an average of 6 horses per match and rides a different one in each chukker (q.v.); no pony may play more than two chukkers per match; credited with being 75 to 80 percent of the player's game.

polo positions Any one of four positions played by players on a polo team; consist of number one position (q.v.), number two position (q.v.), number three position (q.v.), and number four position (q.v.).

polo rating *see* POLO HANDICAP

polo spur A blunt spur (q.v.) the shank of which is flattened on the horse-side.

polo stick *see* POLO MALLET

polo stroke A polo term; to strike the polo ball with the mallet (q.v.); there are four principal strokes: offside forehand (q.v.), offside backhand (q.v.), nearside forehand (q.v.), and nearside backhand (q.v.) and eight subsidiary strokes: neck shots (q.v.), nearside and offside, under the tail shots (q.v.) nearside and offside, forehand cuts (q.v.), offside and nearside, backhand cuts (q.v.), offside and nearside.

polo team A polo term; one of two opposing sides in a polo game; consists of four players each; each team is designated by a different shirt color; players wear jerseys numbered 1 to 4 which correspond to their assigned positions; the number one position, the forward, is an offensive player; the number two and number three positions are usually the highest rated and the most experienced, with number two position responsible to push the play both on offense and defense and the number three position being the quarterback or field captain; the number four position, the back, is primarily responsible for protecting the goal; in defense each player is assigned a man to cover: number 1 usually covers the opposing number 4 and number 2 the opposing number 3.

polo widow A polo term; the wife of a dedicated polo player (q.v.).

polycythemia A blood disease caused by overproduction of red blood cells; thickens and slows blood flow causing delays in oxygen and energy delivery to the muscles and other tissues; results in stamina loss; occurs spontaneously in certain Standardbred (q.v.) families; manifested almost exclusively in stallions and is aggravated by intense training; the concentration of red cells in an exercising polycythemic horse's blood can run over 80 percent, well above the normal range of 55 to 60 percent.

polycythemic Said of a horse suffering from polcythemia (q.v.).

polysulfated glycosaminoglycan Also known by the acronym PSGAG; a glycosaminoglycan (q.v.), a category of joint-lubricating substances chemically similar to the components of cartilage; when injected intramuscularly or directly into a joint, stimulate synovial-fluid production and quality.

POM *see* POST-OPERATIVE MYOPATHY

pommel (1) Also known as saddle head or head of the saddle; the protuberant part of the front and top of the saddle formed by the saddle bow (q.v.). (2) The knob or ball on the hilt of a sword or dagger.

pommel blanket *see* POMMEL PAD

pommel pad Also known as wither pad or pommel blanket; a small, oval sheepskin, wool, etc. pad positioned under the pommel (q.v.) to protect the withers (q.v.) from chafing; used on horses with prominent withers.

Ponsonby Gig An elegant, low, cab-fronted, horse-drawn vehicle of the Gig (q.v.) type; had a hooded body and was hung on a combination of three-quarter and cee-springs.

pony (1) A horse of either sex who, at maturity, does not exceed 58 inches (14.2 hands) in height (except for Arabs (q.v.) or Falabellas (q.v.) which are always considered horses); in some countries the height limit is set at 14 hands; from the Latin *pullus*, meaning foal and *pullanus*, meaning colt which in old French became *poulain* and *poulenet* (pronounced pool-ney) and in 18th-century Scotland the word was subsequently modified to *powney* (pronounced poo-ney) where it became strongly associated with the small Scottish horses found in the Shetlands; pooney was ultimately shortened to the present-day spelling of pony. (2) Also known as ride and lead (Brit); to lead a horse while mounted on another. (3) Also known as lead pony; an American racing term; a quiet horse used to lead young or unpredictable racehorses to and from the training track or to the post. (4) In gambling, the sum of $50.00 (£25.00 in Britain).

Pony Break A light, Australian, horse-drawn vehicle used for exercise purposes; drawn by four or more small ponies.

Pony Club An British organization started as a sub-branch of the Institute of the Horse (q.v.) to interest young people in sport and riding and, at the same time, to offer the opportunity for instruction in horse care and safety and riding skills; in 1929 was inaugurated into the Institute of the Horse as a junior branch at which time the two organizations became the Institute of the Horse and Pony Club Ltd. (q.v.); with clubs in 40 countries, is the largest association of riders worldwide.

Pony Club Mounted Games Also known as Prince Philip Mounted Games; a mounted games competition which emerged as a Pony Club (q.v.) activity in Great Britain in 1957 to provide Pony Club members with an opportunity to hone their equestrian skills through various skill-based competitions such as gymkhanas (q.v.) even if they didn't necessarily have "show ponies"; limited to riders under the age of 15 mounted on ponies at least 4 years old; zone finalists compete in the Horse of the Year Show held every October where they compete for the Prince Philip Cup.

pony express A postal system operated between St. Joseph, Missouri and Sacramento, California, USA from 1860 to 1861 in which mail was carried by predominately young, generally orphaned, relay riders mounted on swift ponies; a total of 420 horses and 80 riders covered the 1,900 mile distance in an average of 10 days stopping at 190 stations; the cost of letter delivery (from Missouri to California) was $5.00; in its 19-month history, there was only 1 human death; the system was replaced by the telegraph.

pony express mount (1) A method of mounting a horse; to run alongside a galloping (q.v.) horse and, using the saddle horn, swing into the saddle without the aid of the stirrup; so called because it was readily used by pony express riders (q.v.) to mount their horses quickly; now used by trick riders and movie stunt people. (2) Any horse ridden by a pony express rider (q.v.) for the purpose of mail delivery.

pony express rider One who rode as a relay mail delivery person in the United States from 1860 until 1861.

pony goal A polo term; a goal scored when the polo ball (q.v.) is deflected across the goal line by the feet or legs of a polo pony (q.v.).

Pony of the Americas An American pony breed developed in 1956; has conformation between a Quarter Horse (q.v.) and Arab (q.v.) and the coat color pattern of an Appaloosa (q.v.), stands 11.1 to 13.1 hands, has a nice head, prominent withers, short and straight back, well-muscled croup and loins, wide and deep chest, strong legs, and a hard, vertically striped hoof; all Appaloosa coat patterns are acceptable including snowflake (q.v.), leopard (q.v.), frost (q.v.), marble, spotted blanket (q.v.), and white blanket (q.v.); is versatile, docile, and fast; an all-purpose pony and children's mount used for trotting, jumping, flat racing, distance riding, and trekking.

pony roach *see* ROACHED MANE

pony speed test An Australian horse race in which ponies ridden by light boys are raced around a ¼ mile (400 m) circuit at show grounds.

pony tail (1) A human, long-hair style in which the hair is pulled to the back of the head, gathered with a rubber band or clip, thus resembling a pony's tail. (2) The tail of a pony.

pool *see* PARIMUTUEL POOL

poor doer Also known as poor keeper; a

horse having a picky appetite who goes off his feed easily; may be undernourished; generally influenced by psychological causes.

poor keeper *see* POOR DOER

Poor Man's Concord *see* CONCORD MUD WAGON

pop a splint Said of a horse, to develop a splint (q.v.).

pop-eyed Said of a horse with prominent or bulging eyes.

popped knee *see* CARPITIS

popped sesamoid *see* SESAMOIDITIS

Porcellus *see* INCITATUS

port (1) The portion of the bit mouthpiece that curves upward in the center of the mouthpiece under which the tongue fits; the shape governs the degree of pressure exerted on the bars (q.v.); a deep, wide port allows more room for the tongue and puts more direct pressure on the bars through the mouthpiece; if high, acts on the roof of the mouth. (2) *see* KAVE

port de bras A vaulting term; a warm-up exercise performed by vaulters (q.v.) to stretch the hamstring and quadriceps muscles and spine; the straight arms are raised up, above the head, forward towards the ground, and then backward as high as possible, passing on either side of the hips; the body bends only at the waist.

ported Said of a curb bit when designed with a port (q.v.).

porting *see* KAVE

Portland Cutter A small horse-drawn sleigh having straight or nearly straight lines and a very high S-shaped front or dash to prevent snow, thrown by the horse's hooves, from covering the driver and passengers; the oldest type of Cutter (q.v.) in the USA; first used in 1816.

Portland Wagon A large, hooded, horse-drawn vehicle first released in 1894; driven to a pair and used to drive to a covert (q.v.).

position (1) To flex or bend the horse to either the left or right. (2) A situation, place, or location especially with reference to other objects as a horse in position to an obstacle.

positive reinforcement Positive reward given for and to encourage desired behavior.

positive identification system Any system used to identify a horse using methods such as photographs, tattooing (q.v.), brands (q.v.), identifying scars, and face, leg, and coat markings.

post (1) A racing term; the starting and ending positions on a racetrack. (2) A racing term; to record a win, e.g. "He posted 12 wins in 13 starts." (3) *see* POST POSITION. (4) Also known as rising trot, take the bump, trotting light, English trot, or trot English; the movement of the rider rising from and returning to the saddle with the rhythm of the trot.

post and rails *see* OXER

post betting A racing term; betting (q.v.) in which wagering does not begin until the numbers of all competing horses are posted.

post boy *see* POSTILLION

postboy *see* POSTILLION

Postboy *see* POST CHAISE

postboy waistcoat *see* GREAT COAT

postboy's coat *see* GREAT COAT

Post Chaise Also known as Yellow Bounder or Postboy; a four-wheeled, two-door, closed, horse-drawn traveling carriage or Chariot used for public hire between inns and post houses where fresh horses and drivers could also be engaged; driven either to pairs in pole gear or four-in-hand (q.v.) teams guided by a postillion (q.v.) riding the near-side horse (q.v.); outfitted with a large luggage rack between the front and rear wheels, a smaller luggage space on the roof, a sword case for dress or ceremonial swords attached to the rear-ward part of the bodywork, no driver's box seat, and was hung on either whip or cee springs; a system of cross-country travel using this vehicle was introduced in England in 1743.

post entry Nomination of a horse to participate in a competition, usually on an entry form, on the day immediately prior to the event.

posterior Situated behind or towards the rear.

posterior digital nerve One of two nerves (q.v.) that run behind and slightly to each side of the center of the pastern (q.v.); provide sensation to the back half of the foot and the sole.

post horse A horse led or ridden by a postillion (q.v.) which pulled hired carriages over specified distances, usually about 10 miles (16.1 km), depending on the nature of the country, after which it was either worked back pulling a vehicle traveling in the opposite direction or ridden back by a postillion (q.v.).

Postier *see* POSTIER BRETON

Postier Breton Also known as Medium Breton or Postier; a coldblood originating in Brittany, France; one of three distinct morphological types of Breton (q.v.) which descended during the Middle Ages from the Roussin (q.v.) crossed with Percheron (q.v.), Ardennes (q.v.), and Boulonnais (q.v.) blood and, in the 19th century, Norfolk Trotter (q.v.) and Hackney (q.v.) blood; is heavier and larger than the Bidet Breton (q.v.) and has shared the same stud book with the Draught Breton (q.v.) since 1909; is selectively bred and must pass performance tests in harness to qualify for inclusion in the book; the coat is generally chestnut, but bay, gray, roan, and red roan also occur – black is not a breed color; has a well-proportioned head, heavy jaw, broad forehead, short ears, flared nostrils, a short, broad, muscular neck, short and straight back, sloping croup, and short, powerful legs with heavy joints; the tail is customarily docked; stands 15 to 16 hands and weighs 1,540 to 1,980 pounds (699–898 kg); registered foals are branded on the left side of the neck with a cross surmounting a splayed, upturned V.

postilion *see* POSTILLION

postillion Also spelled postilion and known as post boy or postboy; one who drives a team of horses from a saddle or near leader (q.v.) when four or more horses are used to draw (q.v.) a carriage (q.v.), or one who rides the near horse when only one pair is used with a driver in the box (q.v.).

posting (1) *see* POST NO. 2. (2) A method of travel of the wealthy using hired vehicles of various types including the Post Chaise (q.v.), which afforded a level of privacy unavailable in Stage Coaches (q.v.); pulled by a post horse (q.v.).

posting house An inn where postillions (q.v.) and post horses (q.v.) could be hired.

post master The owner of a post horse(s) (q.v.); (obs).

post mortem (1) Subsequent to death, as in an examination of the body. (2) *see* POST-MORTEM EXAMINATION

post-mortem examination Also known as autopsy or post mortem; examination of the body made after death.

post parade A racing term; movement of horses from the paddock to the starting gate (q.v.) in front of the stands prior to a race.

postparturient founder Inflammation of the sensitive laminae (q.v.) of the mare's hoof caused by retention of the placental membranes in the uterus following foaling.

post position Also known as post; a racing term; the position of the horse in the starting gate (q.v.); determined from the inner rail (q.v.) of the course outward, i.e. position number 1 is nearest the rail; may be drawn by ballot or selected by the handicapper using a number ball (q.v.) at the close of entries the day prior to the race.

post race An American racing term; a flat race in which one may enter, for a flat fee, two or more horses and may compete one or all of them.

post time A racing term; the time at which all horses are required to be at the starting gate (q.v.) and ready to start a race.

potash alum *see* COMMON ALUM

potassium An essential electrolyte (q.v.) responsible for maintaining proper acid-alkali balance and osmotic pressure within the cells and works in conjunction with sodium to control nerve and muscle commands; foals require up to 1 percent potassium in a purified diet, while mature horses only require about 0.4 percent; dietary requirements are satisfied by a diet containing at least 35 percent roughage; potassium loss can result from high fluid excretion following strenuous exercise, exercise in high heat, or in cases of serious intestinal disturbances such as diarrhea or kidney failure; deficiency impairs transmission of nerve impulses which may trigger muscular paralysis or heart arrhythmia.

Pot Cart, Four-Wheeled Also known as Potter's Cart (obs); a four-wheeled, horse-drawn cart used to convey goods and for lodging as necessary; had a rounded frame draped with roofing canvas; originally driven by gypsies who used it to carry and sell inexpensive pottery.

Pot Cart, Two-Wheeled A two-wheeled, horse-drawn cart with a canvas roof and curtains; had a window in the match board wall at the rear through which light entered.

potenza *see* PUISSANCE

Potomac horse fever Also known as equine monocytic erhlichiosis or by the acronym PHF; an often fatal disease resulting from infection by *Ehrlichia risticii*, a member of the same family of organisms responsible for Rocky Mountain tick fever (q.v.); a higher risk is found in pastured horses as they are more likely to be exposed to the PHF causative agent: insect predation throughout the dawn, daylight, dusk, and night-time feeding cycles; despite evidence linking insects to infection, the specific vector responsible for the unpredictable transmission of the disease remains unknown; named after the Potomac River Valley in the United States where the disease was first recognized in 1979; symptoms include fever, diarrhea, mild to severe colic (q.v.), and laminitis (q.v.).

Potter's Cart *see* POT CART, FOUR-WHEELED

Pottock *see* BASQUE

Pottok *see* BASQUE

poultice Also known as plaster or antiphlogistic; any soft, pasty dressing composed of meal, clay, or other mollifying substance, to be applied to a sore or inflamed body part to soothe pain, draw out inflammation, promote healing, and, in some cases, to hasten formation of an abscess; may include ingredients such as camphor, mint, or eucalyptus.

poultice boot A boot constructed of plastic, leather, canvas, etc., filled with a poultice or into which a poulticed hoof is put to treat hoof-related ailments.

poulticed To have been treated with a poultice (q.v.).

poulticing An ancient and versatile treatment method designed to cleanse wounds, relax tissues, alter temperature, and draw out swelling, infection, and local soreness through application of a poultice (q.v.).

powder A racing term; slight physical contact between horses during a horse race (q.v.).

Powrys Cob An ancient Welsh pony breed which evolved in the 12th century from Welsh Mountain Ponies (q.v.) put to imported Spanish and Barb (q.v.) stock; used as a remount of the English armies; the base stock for the modern Welsh Cob (q.v.).

prad A Victorian term; a horse (q.v.).

prairie hay A cut and dried grass hay (q.v.) made from a mixture of wild native grasses the quality of which varies widely depending on the variety of grasses included; good hay may contain a digestible protein content of as much as 4.2 percent if cut early; popular in the western United States.

Prairie Schooner Also known as Ship-of-the-Plains or Covered Wagon; a horse-drawn American emigrant wagon of light or medium weight and dimensions which first came into popularity during the gold rush period of the 1820s; headed by a canvas top supported on bow-shaped hoops; either sprung or dead axle, could carry up to three tons (3 tonnes), had lever brakes which acted on both rear wheels, and was drawn by either two or four horses in pole gear; not to be confused with the much larger Conestoga Wagon (q.v.).

PRE *see* ANDALUSIAN

Preakness *see* PREAKNESS STAKES

Preakness Stakes Also known as Preakness; a 1 mile, 1½ furlong (2.89 km) race for 3–year-old horses run annually in May since 1873 on the Pimlico course in Baltimore, Maryland, USA; one of three American classic races comprising the Triple Crown (q.v.).

preferred An American racing term; said of a horse given priority entry for a specific race; is usually a previous winner or a horse bred or foaled in the area.

preferred list An American racing term; a list of horses given priority placement in a horse race in the event that the race draws more entries than the race track (q.v.) can accommodate; usually consists of horses previously entered in races that were not filled with the minimum number of starters, previous winners, and/or horses bred or foaled in the area.

pregnant mare urine Also known by the acronym PMU; urine collected from pregnant mares standing in production lines on PMU farms (q.v.) from which the estrogen contained in the drug Premarin (q.v.) is extracted; collected from October through March, the period of highest estrogen (q.v.) production in the mare; mares are hooked up around the clock to a harness attached to a funnel that collects the urine from the urethra and carries it down a tube into a one-gallon container; when estrogen levels decrease in the mare's urine prior to birth of a foal (q.v.), around April, the mare is put to pasture; following birth she is reimpregnated while pastured with her foal and, on October 1, returned to the collection line; water intake is often regulated to raise the urine estrogen concentration with higher concentrates more valuable; one mare will produce an average of 100 gallons (455 liters) of salable urine annually; no permits or laws control this industry and it is aggressively contested by animal rights activists; in some European countries, notably The Netherlands, pregnant woman urine is collected by the government and used for this purpose.

Preliminary (1) An American jumping term; a horse at the first level of development as a jumper having won less than $3,000. (2) A British dressage term; the lowest level test

preliminary canter A racing term; the short warm-up canter (q.v.) from the paddock to the gate (q.v.) immediately prior to a horse race.

Premarin An estrogen supplement used to counteract the effects of menopause, osteoporosis (q.v.), and heart ailments in humans; in some countries such as the United States and Canada, the estrogen contained in this drug is extracted from pregnant mare urine (q.v.) from which the name is a contraction; in other countries such as The Netherlands, pregnant women supply the urine from which the estrogen is extracted.

Premium Cream A registry classification of the American Cream (q.v.) having registered stock of any breed on both sides; reproducibility of color is not a requirement.

premolars Deciduous teeth (q.v.) located in the back of the jaw which are adapted for grinding; consist of the first (wolf teeth [q.v.]), second, and third premolars.

preparatory commands Any cue, aid, or notice such as a half-halt (q.v.) given the horse by the rider to alert him to a forthcoming action or transition.

prepotent The breeding power of a stallion or mare as measured by the degree to which inherited characteristics are transmitted to the offspring at a percentage better than the industry average.

prep race A racing term; a workout or race in which a horse is trained or prepared for a future competition.

presentation The appearance of the ho

and/or rider including grooming, riding habit (q.v.), and tack in terms of appropriateness and cleanliness.

press off A cutting term; to use the pressure of the rider's cow-side (q.v.) leg to move the horse away from the cow.

press up A cutting term; to use the pressure of the rider's herd-side (q.v.) leg to move the horse toward the cow being cut.

pressure bandage A wrap used on the lower leg to relieve swelling and provide support to an injured or damaged area; should be applied to both legs of the front or rear pair firmly, yet not too tightly; the injured leg is bandaged to relieve the injury while the sound leg is bandaged to provide support as it will carry more weight until the other leg is healed.

price A British term; the odds quoted by a bookmaker (q.v.) on a particular horse scheduled to compete in a race.

prick (1) *see* QUICK. (2) *see* NICK NO. 1

prick ears Said of the ears of the horse when sharp, pointed, and forward facing.

pricker A hunting term (obs); one who follows hounds on horseback.

pricker pad A bit burr (q.v.) studded with sharp points on the cheek side; is slit from one outside edge to the center and fits around the bit mouthpiece just inside the cheekpiece (q.v.); irritates the corner of the horse's mouth; used to prevent the horse from leaning to, and assist in turning from, that side; generally used on only one side of the bit.

pricket A buck (q.v.) in his second year having straight, unbranched antlers.

primary arthritis Inflammation of a joint resulting from direct trauma such as penetration of a foreign body or a physical blow to the joint.

primary corpus luteum A mass of endocrine cells formed from the ruptured ovarian follicle immediately following release of the unfertilized egg; secretes progesterone.

primitive mark Refers to coat color pattern; any marking on the horse including dark-colored stripes along the spine and over the withers, knees, and hocks; most commonly seen on dun-colored horses; traceable to ancient horse breeds; includes zebra stripes (q.v.), dorsal stripe (q.v.) the cross (q.v.), eel stripe (q.v.), shoulder cross (q.v.), or rib bar (q.v.).

primigravida *see* MAIDEN

Prince of Wales spurs Also known as dropped spur; a spur (q.v.) having a sloping neck and offset shanks, the longer side being worn on the outside of the foot; the neck is worn pointing downward and may be blunt ended, pointed, or fitted with a rowel (q.v.).

Prince Philip Mounted Games *see* PONY CLUB MOUNTED GAMES

prince seat A vaulting term; a position assumed by the vaulter on the horse's back; the vaulter (q.v.) kneels on one knee and places the other foot on the roller (q.v.) with both arms outstretched perpendicular to his sides.

Princess Cart A two-wheeled, cab-fronted, horse-drawn vehicle designed in 1893; had a Governess Cart (q.v.) shaped body which was hung low, commonly between elliptic springs, on a cranked axle; entered from either side of the cab front by steps; driven from a movable transverse seat at the rear; passengers rode on inward-facing side seats.

principal horse *see* CAST HORSE

principal host *see* DEFINITIVE HOST

pritchel A sharply pointed tool used by a farrier (q.v.) to make nail holes in a hot shoe (q.v.).

pritcheling The act of making nail holes in a horseshoe (q.v.).

private auction Any auction (q.v.) restricted to invited participants.

Private Coach *see* DRAG

Private Drag *see* DRAG

Private Omnibus *see* OPERA BUS

private pack A hunting term; a pack of hounds, the expense of which is borne solely by the Master (q.v.).

Prix Caprilli test A dressage term; a test for horses with jumping experience showing Training Level (q.v.) or above in which both flat and jumping exercises are performed; the fence height is a maximum of 2 feet (0.6 m); in Britain, a test of the rider, rather than the horse, and thus not a dressage test (test of the horse's training) as such; formerly very popular in Britain at club level, Prix Caprilli competitions are now quite rare.

Prix des Nations *see* NATIONS CUP

prize money Any sum paid to a competitor as a reward for victory or superiority.

produce (1) The progeny or offspring of a mare; a foal is the produce of a mare and the get (q.v.) of a stallion; may refer to one or more progeny. (2) Horse foodstuff available at a feed store.

producer A racing term; said of a mare who has at least one offspring who has won a race.

produce race A racing term; a flat race for the progeny (q.v.) of selected mares and/or stallions, the entry of which is posted before foaling.

proestrus The two-day period in which the mare becomes increasingly receptive to mating; proceeds estrus (q.v.).

professional One who receives payment for participation in a sport which others engage in as a pastime, e.g. a horse trainer.

professional whipper-in A hunting term; a whipper-in (q.v.) who receives payment for his or her services.

progenitor *see* SIRE

progeny The offspring or descendant of either a mare or stallion; may refer to more than one descendant.

progesterone The female hormone secreted by the corpus luteum (q.v.) of the ovary prior to the implantation of the egg; maintains pregnancy by stopping the estrous cycle (q.v.).

prognathism *see* UNDER-SHOT JAW

progressive color pattern Refers to coat color pattern; a coat pattern that changes as the horse ages, as in Andalusians (q.v.).

prolapse The slipping down of some organ or structure as in displacements of the rectum, uterus, etc., which result in the appearance to the outside of the body.

prolapsed sole *see* DROPPED SOLE

promethazine *see* ACETYLPROMAZINE

prop (1) A racing term; a horse who refuses to break (q.v.) at the start of the race. (2) Said of a horse who suddenly stops by planting his front feet. (3) *see* THE PROP

Prophet Strain A line of horses selected, according to legend, by the Prophet Mohammed as the foundation stock of his horses used for war purposes; the ten horses which established the strain were known as Mohammed's Ten Horses (q.v.).

Prophet's thumb Also known as thumb print of the Prophet; a pronounced dimple or indentation in the shoulder muscles of Arabs (q.v.) and occasionally other breeds; believed to be a sign of good luck as legend has it that the mark was made by the thumb of the Prophet Mohammed.

propping *see* SCOTCHING

proppy Said of the horse; having short action and gait as due to a straight shoulder, lack of flexibility in the knees, and/or straight pasterns.

proprietor A historic coaching term; one who owns his own team and drives his own coach.

proprioception The reception of stimuli produced within the organism enabling the horse, especially when moving over or between obstacles, to know the position of his legs in relation to his body and the object jumped; a natural sense.

proprioceptor Any of the sensory organs i the muscles, tendons, etc. sensitive to t stimuli originating in these tissues by movements of the body, or its parts; functions in proprioception (q.v.).

prop, the Also known as number 1; a vaulting term; the first vaulter (q.v.) in the saddle when performing exercises in pairs and threes; is positioned closest to the vaulting roller (q.v.) and assists other vaulters to mount and/or dismount from the horse; dismounts first, after which, the second vaulter becomes the prop.

prostaglandins A group of hormone-like, fatty-acid substances active in many physiological processes including inflammation (q.v.), reproduction, and the lowering of blood pressure.

prostation Complete physical or mental exhaustion.

protein Any of numerous naturally occurring extremely complex substances that consist of amino-acid residues joined by peptide bonds; contain the elements carbon, hydrogen, nitrogen, oxygen, usually sulfur, and occasionally other elements (phosphorous or iron), and include many essential biological compounds such as enzymes, hormones, or immunoglobulins; responsible for growth, maintenance, and repair of body tissues; unused, excess protein is converted into alternative energy; rations containing 30 percent or more total protein may cause metabolic stress and digestive disturbances.

proteinaceous sweat *see* LATHER

protein bumps Hives (q.v.) triggered by excess systemic protein levels, as found in some feed.

protein supplements Any animal or plant protein source fed a horse to compensate for dietary deficiency; plant proteins are more commonly fed than those from animal sources, and are usually seeds following oil extraction as in soybean meal (q.v.), cottonseed meal (q.v.), peanut meal (q.v.), linseed meal (q.v.), rapeseed meal (q.v.), and sunflower meal (q.v.); animal sources include meat and bone meal (q.v.), fishmeal (q.v.), and milk protein.

rotest *see* OBJECTION

prothrombin A substance formed in the liver with the assistance of vitamin K (q.v.); essential for blood clotting.

protrusion of the nictitating membrane A condition of the eye in which the third eyelid, interior to the true eyelid, protrudes from the eye; may be caused by severe pain associated with eye disease, the presence of a foreign body, tetanus (q.v.), dehydration (q.v.), tumors, etc.

proud flesh Excessive granulated tissue (q.v.); rounded, swollen masses of flesh composed of capillaries and connective tissue cells which grow outward to fill a wound defect often beyond the skin's surface; brought about by the use of excessively strong antiseptics or by continual movement of the injury which retards complete healing; inhibits healing and must be removed; so called because the tissue is swollen, as if by pride.

proven sire Also known as tested sire; any stallion used for breeding purposes, for which the transference of breed characteristics, temperament, color, athletic ability etc. has been, in prior matings, established.

provinces A hunting term; hunt country located anywhere in England, Scotland, or Wales, except in the Midlands or Shires (q.v.).

proximal Nearest the point of attachment or insertion, as the extremity of a bone or limb.

proximal sesamoid bones Also known as proximal sesamoids; two small bones located behind the fetlock joint held against the canon bone and the long pastern (q.v.) by ligaments and involved in relieving pressure from the deep flexor tendon.

proximal sesamoids *see* PROXIMAL SESAMOID BONES

pruritis Itchiness resulting from the systemic release of histamine (q.v.); caused by most parasitic skin diseases.

Przewalski's Horse Also known by the scientific name *Equus ferus przewalski*; one of two subspecies of wild horse found in Eastern Europe and Asia, discovered in 1876 by Russian explorer Przewalski for whom the breed was named; originally ranged throughout the Gobi desert and the steppes of Mongolia; intermediate in character between the equine and asinine groups having calluses on all four limbs as in the horse and a tail only half of which is covered with hair as in the ass; generally has a dun coat with a yellowish tinge on the back, becoming lighter towards the flanks and almost white under the belly, a dark brown, short and erect mane, and no forelock; presumed extinct in the wild since 1968; it has bred well in captivity and a stud book is held at the Prague Zoo, Czechoslovakia; total world count is less than 1,000 animals; being reintroduced into the wild in Mongolia and in China.

psalion A classical Greek cavesson (q.v.) resembling a hackamore (q.v.).

PSGAG *see* POLYSULFATED GLYCOSAMINOGLYCAN

PSL *see* LUSITANO

psoroptes A parasitic mite, one species of which, *Psoroptes ovis* is responsible for psoroptic mange (q.v.) in horses.

Psoroptes ovis A species of mite, infestation of which causes psoroptic mange (q.v.).

psoroptic mange A type of mange caused by infestation of the parasitic mite, *Psoroptes ovis*; two varieties of this type of mange occur in the horse: one in the ear and one on the skin; characterized by lesions that usually start in the dorsal line where the hair is long or in sheltered body areas such as the forelock, mane, root of the tail, under the chin, between the hind legs, and sometimes in the ears; lesions are similar to those resulting from sarcoptic mange (q.v.), but involve larger and thicker crusts on the skin with less severe itching, and the mites may be more easily found in the crusts; these mites are surface dwellers and do not burrow; a quarantinable disease not reported in horses in the United States for many years.

psyllium *see* FLEAWORT

psyllium seed *see* FLEASEED

PtHA *see* PINTO HORSE REGISTRATION OF AMERICAS, INC.

PTR *see* PERFORMANCE THOROUGHBRED REGISTRY

public auction Any open auction (q.v.) for which personal invitation is not required.

public stable *see* STABLE NO. 2

public trainer A racing term; one who trains horses for more than one owner or stable, usually on a *per diem* or flat fee basis.

Puckle noseband *see* KINETON NOSEBAND

pudding A hunting term; a mixture of meal (q.v.) and meat cooked in the kennel (q.v.) and fed to the hounds (q.v.).

puddle The shuffling action of the horse in motion.

puffer *see* SHILL

puffing the glims An obsolete practice; to make an aged horse appear less so by making a small incision in the skin of the hollow above the eye and blowing air through a quill inserted therein to fill the hollow with air.

pughree *see* PUGHRI

pughri Also spelled pughree or incorrectly as purgi; a woven cotton cloth used by Indian men for their turbans and by some polo players as a pughri martingale (q.v.).

pughree martingale *see* PUGHRI MARTINGALE

pughri martingale Also spelled pughree martingale or incorrectly as purgi martingale; a standing martingale (q.v.) used on some polo ponies (q.v.) consisting of a length of colored pughri (q.v.) cloth, such as is used to make turbans in India, tied at one end to the girth and at the other to the underside of the noseband (q.v.).

Puissance Previously known as potenza; a non-timed show jumping competition in which competitors jump a course consisting of 3 to 8 obstacles ranging from 4 feet 6 inches to 5 feet 3 inches (1.4–1.6 m) high in the first round, the height and width being progressively increased in each successive round until only one competitor jumps clear.

pull (1) To thin, shorten, or improve the appearance of the mane or tail by removing individual or groups of hairs by hand or with the aid of a pulling comb, knife, etc. (2) *see* THROW A RACE. (3) *see* PULL UP. (4) To draw blood, e.g. "The vet pulled 3 cc of blood from the horse." (5) Also known as hame draught or bullet; a metal protrusion on the lower part of the hame (q.v.) through the eye of which the hame clip passes before being riveted to the trace tug or shoulder piece

pull a race *see* THROW A RACE

pulled suspensory *see* SUSPENSORY DESMITIS

pulled tail Said of the tail when the hair on the side of the dock (q.v.), from the base to the tip, and any excessive growth on top is pulled by hand to give a tidy and trimmed look.

puller A horse who leans on the bit, thus drawing the reins from the rider's hands; may be difficult to stop.

pulley bit A bit with pulleys for the gag rein (q.v.).

pulling comb Also known as mane drag; a metal-toothed comb (q.v.), frequently attached to a handle, used to trim and thin the mane or tail.

pulling leather Also known as grabbin' the apple; a rodeo term; said of a bronc rider in competition who touches any part of the saddle with his free hand during his eight-second ride.

pulling slack Also known as grabbing slack or jerking slack; a roping term; said of a roper; to take hold of the lariat (q.v.) with the hand after the loop has settled on the target so as to pull the loop tight.

pull in the weights A racing term; said of a horse who runs with a weight advantage, i.e., less weight than other competing horses; in Britain, the term is also used to signify a more favourable distinction in respective weights compared to a previous meeting between the horses concerned.

pull off (1) Also known as pinchers; a pritchel-type farrier's tool with knobs on the ends of the handles which distinguish them from hoof nippers (q.v.) used to remove horseshoes, nail stubs, and improperly driven nails and to turn the clinches (q.v.). (2) *see* QUIT A COW. (3) To remove.

pull off a cow *see* QUIT A COW

pull up Also known as pull; to intentionally slow or stop a horse or horse-drawn vehicle.

pulmonary Of or pertaining to the lungs.

pulse The rhythmic beating or throbbing of the arteries caused by contractions of the heart which force blood to move through the vessels.

pulse magnetic therapy A type of magnetic therapy (q.v.); a non-invasive therapeutic technique used to increase circulation, reduce inflammation, and expedite healing; a series of magnetic signals or pulses, approximately 12 volts or less, are applied to an area to stimulate cells and influence their interaction with ions; all the cells in tissue or bone have a weak, natural, electrical current flowing through them caused by electrically charged ions; treatments commonly take from 20 to 60 minutes.

pulu *see* POLO

pumiced foot *see* DROPPED SOLE

pump handles Also known as plow handles; two curved metal handles attached to the rear body of a horse-drawn coach (q.v.) used as a handhold when entering.

punch (1) *see* BRAND NO. 2. (2) An obsolete term; any English horse having short legs and a barrel body.

Punch Carriage A four-wheeled, horse-drawn carriage drawn by a single horse popular during the 19th century; seated two rear-facing passengers, had a coupé body mounted in reverse protected by a falling hood, and a driving apron; used by passengers adverse to draft and allergic to the odor of horses, as well as doctors, the infirm, and the elderly.

punch holes in the horizon *see* RUN A HOLE THROUGH THE WIND

punching A dressage term; the exaggerated or artificial action of the forelegs; usually applied to the trot.

puncture (1) Known as puncture wound; any cut deeper than it is wide; deceptively dangerous and accounts for roughly 10 percent of all equine injuries; does not drain well and enables bacteria to flourish in an anaerobic (q.v.) environment; deep-seated infections and abscesses often result. (2) The act or action of pricking or perforating as with a pointed instrument or object.

puncture wound *see* PUNCTURE

punter *see* BETTOR

puppy show A hunting term; a competition for young, unentered (q.v.) hounds evaluated on the basis of conformation, gait, and training.

puppy walker A hunting term; one responsible for the care of hound puppies from about ten weeks of age until returned to the kennels for entering (q.v.).

puppy walking *see* WALK NO. 2

purchase That part of the bit above the mouthpiece (q.v.); affects both timing and bit leverage.

Pure Blood Lusitano *see* LUSITANO

pure-bred (1) Relating or pertaining to an animal bred from a strain of generations of pure, unmixed ancestry. (2) A horse from a strain of generations of pure, unmixed ancestry.

pure-bred Arab One of three basic types of Arab (q.v.) resulting from crossing of the three primary sub-breeds of the Assil (q.v.): the Kuhailan (q.v.), the Siglavy (q.v.), and the Muniqi (q.v.).

pure-bred percentage The percentage of pure blood present in a horse who is the progeny (q.v.) of a pure-bred (q.v.) stallion and an unregistered mare or mare of another breed.

Pure Spanish Horse *see* ANDALUSIAN

pure trot *see* TROT

purgative Also known as cathartic; any substance or medicine that brings about a bowel movement.

purge To produce evacuations of the bowel by means of a cathartic (q.v.).

purgi *see* PUGHRI

purgi martingale *see* PUGHRI MARTINGALE

purity A dressage term; correctness of the order and timing of the footfalls of the gait.

purple corn Refers to coat color; a purple roan (q.v.) with corn spots (q.v.).

purple roan Refers to coat color; a mixture of red, white, and black hairs or red hairs with black tips and white hairs, with black more abundant along the top line (q.v.) and around the croup and withers; the head and points will be colored.

purpura hemorragica Also known as petechial fever or petechial hemorrhage; an acute, non-contagious, potentially fatal disease characterized by sudden onset of fever, depression, lower limb edema, skin and mucous membranes hemorrhages and, in some cases, colic (q.v.); thought to be an allergic-hypersensitive reaction to bacterial antigens circulating in the bloodstream; the walls of small blood vessels are damaged allowing blood and plasma to escape into the surrounding tissues.

pur sang Pure-bred (q.v.), as in a horse.

purse A racing term; prize money consisting of nomination and entry fees, and any added money, generally paid to the first five finishers; originally, prize money was contained in a purse hung on a wire across the finish line, a system from which the present name derived.

pus A yellowish-white, more or less viscid inflammation product; consists of liquid plasma in which leukocytes are suspended; of two types: sterile and infected; the latter being of inconsistent texture, contains bacteria, is darker than sterile pus, and often has a strong odor.

push button horse Said of a well-trained horse who is extremely sensitive to a rider's signals and who serves as a good mount (q.v.) for a novice rider.

pushing out A dressage term; said of the horse when his hind legs work too far behind instead of carry him.

pus pocket *see* ABSCESS

puss *see* HARE NO. 2

put a rein on him A Western term; to train a horse to respond to neck reining (q.v.).

put down *see* EUTHANIZE

put him on his head To be bucked off a horse as in, "That horse really put him on his head."

put to (1) Said of a stallion bred (q.v.) to a mare (2) *see* HITCH NO. 2. (3) A hunting term; said of a fox earth (q.v.) closed with a fox inside on the morning of a hunt.

putting to (1) The act of hitching a horse to a vehicle. (2) A hunting term; the process of closing an earth (q.v.).

pyre Refers to foxhound coat color; a lighter tan than the Belvoir tan (q.v.).

pyridoxine Originally known as vitamin B_6; a B-complex vitamin (q.v.) synthesized in the horse's lower intestines; required for metabolism of protein and fat; abundant in whole grains; deficiency is unlikely.

pyramidal disease Also known as buttress foot or extensor process disease; a condition of the foot involving new bone growth in the region of the extensor process of the distal phalanx; may result from fracture of the extensor process caused by excessive pull of the tendon insertion; an advanced form of low ringbone (q.v.); symptoms include pointing (q.v.) with the affected foot, a shortened stride with a tendency to land heavily on the heel, heat, pain, some swelling in the early stages, lameness in all gaits, and secondary arthritis a likely complication; horses such as the Paso Fino (q.v.) with high heels and short toes and horses that move with limbs lifted high in a short and rapid manner appear to be predisposed; prognosis is unfavorable in most cases.

Q

qarajai One of two types of the wild, ruthless and sometimes deadly national sport of Afghanistan known as buzkashi (q.v.); a rudimentary form of mounted rugby or polo played by two teams of 10 players each during two 45-minute halves with a short intermission between the halves; each team has a goal, a circle drawn with stones or lime, in which a decapitated calf carcass, which may weigh as much as 66 to 88 pounds (30–40 kg), is to be deposited; at the start of the game, the carcass is placed between the two goals; riding around a flag located at the far end of a field while carry the carcass earns one point while dropping the calf carcass in the goal earns two.

quad Cockney slang; a horse.

Quadrille An orchestrated ride to music generally performed by teams of four riders or groups of four who execute dressage figures or movements on horseback; derived from the formal dance of the same name which consists of five figures or movements executed by four couples each forming one side of a square.

quadrem Four horses harnessed one in front of the other.

Quadriga A Grecian Chariot (q.v.) pulled by four horses abreast; the two strongest horses were put on either side of the pole, under yokes; the other two horses were put to with ropes on each side.

Quagga Also known by the scientific name *Equus quagga*; an extinct South African mammal closely related to the zebra, but only striped on the head, neck, and shoulders.

qualifier *see* QUALIFYING RACE NOS. 1 AND 2

Qualifying Race (1) Also known as qualifier; a racing term; a horserace for which there is no purse (q.v.) nor betting, used to determine the horse's ability, manners, and eligibility. (2) Also known as qualifier; a British racing term; one of a series of races run with the intention of selecting runners for a final race at a prestigious meeting; usually the first four participants or sometimes all qualify to run in the final.

quality The element of refinement in the appearance of horse breeds and types; generally due to Thoroughbred (q.v.) or Arab (q.v.) influence.

quarantine (1) A process used to isolate foregin horses for a short period to ensure that they are not carrying any diseases; may be at a race track, airport or specially designed facility; horses must be cleared by a veterinarian (Federal veterinarian for American race horses) before being released from quarantine. (2) *see* QUARANTINE BARN NO. 1

quarantine barn (1) Also known as quarantine; any building equipped with stalls in which infected horses are isolated from the general horse population until no longer contagious. (2) A facility equipped to isolate horses for a short period of time following transportation across international borders to ensure they are not carrying disease; requirements vary between countries; frequently located adjacent to an airport, racetrack, or other designated location.

quarry A hunting term; that which is hunted, generally stag, coyote, or fox, or people as in the sport of blood hounding (q.v.).

quarter (1) The portion of the hoof between the toe and the ground-side hoof surface and coronary band (q.v.) on either side. (2) A racing term; a distance of two furlongs (q.v.). (3) To groom a horse quickly.

quarterback *see* NUMBER THREE POSITION

quarter blanket *see* QUARTER SHEET NO. 1

quarter boot A flexible boot that cups the heel bulbs (q.v.) and coronet (q.v.) on the rear-portion of the hoof; may or may not have an open front where it is closed by means of buckles or velcro; worn on the forefeet to protect the quarter of the front heel from the toe of the hind.

quarter clip A V-shaped metal extension of the horseshoe (q.v.) located on the left or right sides, commonly both, between the toe and heel; pressed into the hoof wall to help secure the shoe to the hoof.

quarter crack A fissure on either the medial or lateral sides of the hoof wall, starting at the bearing surface and extending a variable distance up the hoof wall, or originating at the coronary band (q.v.), and extending downward; may occur in either the fore or hind feet; more severe than toe cracks (q.v.) and may involve the sensitive laminae (q.v.); in severe cases, affected horses are usually lame and may hemorrhage following exercise.

Quarter Horse An American horse breed developed in the 17th century by settlers in Virginia and Carolina, USA by crossing Spanish-type mares with imported English Thoroughbred (q.v.) stallions; has massively muscled large, rounded hindquarters, is compact, agile, fast, well-balanced, and possessed of quick reflexes, stands 14.1 to 16 hands, and may have a coat of any solid color although chestnut is most common; has a short-coupled body, a short and wide head, a long neck, and well-defined withers; subsequent breed selection was based on performance in sprint races over ¼ mile (400 m) stretches from which the name derived; the breed registry was established in 1940; bred in three specialized types: racing Quarter Horse consisting of Thoroughbred (q.v.) with some ranch horse blood, the show and halter Quarter Horse of the old bulldog (q.v.) type with more refinement, smaller bones, and longer legs, and the stock-type Quarter Horse; used as a trail mount, cutting horse, hunter, show jumper, polo mount, pleasure horse, and for racing.

quartering The process of quickly grooming a horse; traditionally performed first thing in the morning to ensure the horse looked tidy before exercising.

quarter marks Patterns placed or made, by modifying hair direction on the horse's hindquarters (q.v.) for appearance, as by means of a stencil.

quarter pole A racing term; a colored post located adjacent to the infield rail (q.v.) exactly two furlongs (q.v.) (¼ mile/400 m) from the finish.

quarters *see* HINDQUARTERS

quarters falling out Said of a horse who moves with the forehand in the correct position on the line, but whose quarters have left that line, falling to the outside of the required track.

quarter sheet Also known as exercise sheet, galloping sheet, loin rug, loin sheet, quarter rug, or quarter blanket; a natural fiber, usually wool, or synthetic blanket fitted over the horse's quarters and, occasionally tucked under the rider's legs or the saddle flap, to keep the large muscle groups of the quarter in the riding or carriage horse warm when exercising in cold weather, preparatory to competition, in dress parade, when standing in for any period of time, etc.

quarters in *see* TRAVERS

quarters leading A dressage term; said of the horse whose quarters (q.v.) lead the forehand in the lateral movement when performing a half-pass (q.v.).

quarters not engaged Said of a horse whose hind legs are not sufficiently brought under his body; the horse may be on the forehand and have a hollowed back.

quarters out *see* RENVERS

quarters trailing A dressage term; said of a horse performing a half-pass (q.v.) who has insufficient bend in his body leaving the quarters (q.v.) behind the movement; the horse will not cross his hind legs.

quarter strap (1) That portion of the harness passing over the quarters of a horse which connects to the breeching. (2) *see* BEARING STRAP

quarter rug *see* QUARTER SHEET

quarter white stocking A leg marking; the white extends up to and includes the lower one quarter of the cannon bone.

Quashquai An Iranian horse breed; contributed to the development of the

Plateau Persian (q.v.); stands approximately 15 hands.

queen of saddles *see* SIDE-SADDLE

Queensland itch An Australian term; sweet itch (q.v.).

question *see* ASK A QUESTION

quick (1) Also known as nail, nail prick, nail quick, or prick; to penetrate the sensitive structures of the foot with a horseshoe nail; traces of blood may be apparent on the nail when removed and generally results in lameness; more serious than nail bind (q.v.). (2) *see* SENSITIVE LAMINAE

quick-response diagnostic test *see* STALL-SIDE DIAGNOSTIC TEST

quick-stop A Western training bridle that exerts significant pressure under the horse's jaw; used sparingly to train a horse to stop quickly on his haunches.

quiddor A horse who drops food from its mouth while chewing.

quinela *see* QUINELLA

quinella Also spelled quinela; *see* EXACTA BOX.

quinsy Any abscess in the throat such as strangles (q.v.).

quintain *see* QUINTAINE

quintaine Also spelled quintain; an object to be tilted (q.v.) at, especially a post with a revolving figure, tree trunk, post, pile, or shield, against which to break one's lance.

quirt (1) A small riding crop with a short handle and a braided or plaited lash. (2) To strike with a quirt.

quit *see* QUIT A COW

quit a calf *see* QUIT A COW

quit a cow Also known as quit, pull off, pull off a cow, or quit a calf; a cutting term; to stop working a cow; in NCHA (q.v.) competitions, is permissible without penalty if the cow has obviously stopped, turned away from the cutter, or if it is behind the time line.

quitter One who gives up.

quit the stirrups *see* DROP THE STIRRUPS

quittor Also known as coronary sinus; an ulcer on the hoof; a pus-forming chronic inflammation of the collateral cartilages of the foot in which pus is discharged above the coronary band (q.v.); rare today, although was once quite common in draft horses; results from an injury to the coronet or pastern or puncture to the sole of the foot; symptoms include inflammatory swelling over the area of the lateral cartilage, followed by abscess and ultimately, lameness.

R

rabbit Also known as pacemaker (Brit); a racing term; a fast horse entered in a race with a stablemate who sets a fast pace to suit his stablemate.

rabbit-bitten holly Holly (q.v.) when nibbled and chewed at the base; the base being used for whip handles; considered decorative and is usually not covered with leather as is customary.

rabicano Also known as squaw tail; refers to coat color; a white color pattern occurring in a number of breeds including the Quarter Horse (q.v.), Arab (q.v.), Noriker (q.v.), Brabant (q.v.), and North American Spanish; may consist of a few white hairs on the flanks and at the base of the tail or a pattern of white hair extending out from the flanks and numerous white hairs at the base of the tail; strongly marked horses may be confused with roans (q.v.).

rabid Affected with rabies (q.v.).

rabies An acute fatal viral infection of the central nervous system affecting warm-blooded animals; transmitted from animal to animal by means of a bite from a rabid (q.v.) animal who introduces the virus-bearing saliva; is rarely transmitted by viral contamination of fresh, pre-existing wounds; the incubation period is variable, but is generally 15 to 50 days and in rare cases, as long as six months; death usually occurs within ten days of appearance of the symptoms; the clinical course occurs in three phases: the prodromal, the excitative, and the dumb or paralytic; general symptoms include a slight change in body temperature, an inability to retain saliva may not be noted, a loss of appetite and thirst, solitary behavior, irritation of the urinary tract as evidenced by frequent urination, erection and sexual desire in the male, and a change in behavior which may be indistinguishable from a digestive disorder, injury, a foreign body in the mouth, poisoning, or an early infectious disease; following the early warning or prodromal period of one to three days, horses may show signs of paralysis or become vicious, biting other animals or people at the slightest provocation; in some horses the excitative phase is predominant, in which case the term furious rabies applies (q.v.); in others paralytic rabies (q.v.) may dominate; the pre-exposure vaccine is 96 percent effective; the virus dies quickly in a warm and/or dry environment.

rabies vaccine A modified micro-organism of the rabies (q.v.) virus used for preventive inoculation; is 96 percent effective.

race (1) Also known as horse race or horserace; a contest of speed between horses as in running (with or without jumping), driving, etc., run over a set course where the result is determined by speed. (2) Also known as rache, reach, or rase; a face marking; any long, narrow white marking on the horse's face which runs from the forehead to, or almost to, the muzzle, and which diverges to the near or off side of the face; differs from a stripe (q.v.). (3) A breeding stock of animals.

race card Also known as card or race program; a racing term; the printed program of a race meeting (q.v.) including the name and time of each race and the names of all horses, their owners and trainers, and the weights to be carried.

racecourse (1) *see* TRACK NO. 1. (2) A racing term; the race track including all relevant facilities such as grandstands, paddock, stables, offices, etc. maintained by appointed officials.

racecourse paddock *see* PADDOCK NO. 2

race declared off Also known as declared off; a racing term; any horse race invalidated or canceled by the race stewards; stakes races canceled will generally be rescheduled at a later date, while normal races will not be re-run.

racegoer One who frequents a racetrack.

race de trait Belge *see* BRABANT

racehorse *see* RACE HORSE

race horse Also known as bang tail, racer and spelled racehorse; any horse bred or kept for racing on the flat or over hurdles; normally applies to Thoroughbreds (q.v.).

race horse cross Also know as bridge (Brit); a two-handed grip on the reins sometimes used by the rider; the left rein is crossed over the withers and gripped by the right hand and the right rein crossed over the withers and gripped by the left.

race meeting (1) A racing term; the place where a fixed number of horse races are held. (2) A racing term; the specific period during which a race program is conducted.

Race of Champions Also known by the acronym ROC; the premier United States endurance race (q.v.); competing teams are assembled geographically and consist of 3 to 15 riders per team; at least half of the team members must finish the race; the times of those competitors finishing the race are averaged and the team with the lowest time average wins; to qualify, horses must have completed 5 or more 100-mile (160 km) races with at least 2 top-ten finishes, while qualifying riders must have completed at least one 100-mile race.

race position A racing term; the location of the horse in the field of horses competing in a race.

race program *see* RACE CARD

racer (1) *see* RACE HORSE. (2) A riding boot worn by jockeys when racing on the flat.

race track *see* TRACK NO. 1

racetrack *see* TRACK NO. 1

race-track *see* TRACK NO. 1

race tracker One who frequents a racetrack (q.v.).

raceway A track (q.v.) upon which harness races (q.v.) are conducted.

rache *see* RACE NO. 2

Racing Biga An ancient Roman racing Chariot (q.v.) drawn by a pair of horses harnessed in curricle gear (q.v.); noted for its forward-inclined, bow-shaped front, and wooden wheels which usually had eight spokes each.

racing blinkers A type of blinkers (q.v.); a hood fitted over the horse's head which allows the ears to protrude and has leather cups; restrict the horse's vision to the sides and rear in either or both eyes; fit is very important; in most countries, use or disuse must be approved by the race stewards and the change reported on the official program.

racing breastplate *see* AINTREE BREAST GIRTH

racing cap *see* RACING HELMET

Racing Calendar Also known as sheet calendar; a race industry publication in which upcoming races, advertisements for sales breeding, weights and acceptances for handicaps, forfeit notices and lists, names registered, racing colors, etc. are noted; may be published weekly, monthly, quarterly, etc.

racing colors *see* COLORS

racing form (1) A racing term; an information sheet used by bettors (q.v.) which contains the details of a race horse's performance history. (2) A racing term; the actual performance history of race horses.

racing gallop A regular, balanced, and extended gallop (q.v.) with speeds ranging from 30 to 45 mph (48–72 kmph); faster than a hand gallop (q.v.).

racing girth *see* AINTREE BREAST GIRTH

racing irons Small, lightweight, sturdy, stirrups designed to lend stability to the jockey when mounted; in America are generally custom-made to fit the jockey's feet and only accommodate the toes.

racing helmet Also known as crash skull, racing cap, or generically as helmet (q.v.); protective headgear fitted with anti-concussive pads and a chin strap worn by a jockey and upon which the owner's colors (q.v.) are worn.

racing on the flat *see* FLAT RACING

racing plate *see* RACING SADDLE

racing plates Also known as plate; a type of horseshoe (q.v.) typically used on competing racehorses made of drop forged aluminium with high-carbon steel grabs molded onto the toes; available in many styles in sizes 3 to 7; one-third the weight of steel.

racing saddle Also known as racing plate (Brit) on account of the size; a race horse (q.v.) saddle; where weight is at a premium, especially in flat racing, the saddle may be very light, generally weighing less than 2 pounds (90 g), in jump racing, where higher weights are carried, more substantial saddles are often used so long as the jockey has no difficulty riding at the allotted weight.

racing seat An American racing term; the position assumed by the jockey in the saddle when riding a race horse whether in competition or workout; the leathers (q.v.) are adjusted very short so that the jockey's knee, when seated, is approximately level with the height of the withers; the jockey adopts a balanced, poised position with his seat out of the saddle and his weight over the horse's withers.

racing secretary An American racing term; one responsible for prescribing track conditions and sometimes for assigning weights to handicap race entrants.

racing silks *see* COLORS

racing snaffle *see* DEE-RING SNAFFLE

racing sound A racing term; said of a horse who, although not in perfect health, is able to compete in a horse race.

racing strip *see* TRACK NO. 1

racing trot A maximally extended trot (q.v.) having a longer stride than an extended trot (q.v.), which may be achieved at the expense of, or as a consequence of, the diagonal pair separating, the hind leg grounding (q.v.) first; the head and neck are high and extended; common to racing Standardbreds (q.v.).

rack (1) Also known as broken amble or single foot because only one foot strikes the ground at the time; a smooth, bilateral, four-beat, natural gait in which each foot strikes the ground separately, at equal intervals, and at a high speed; there is no head movement and the entire body drops slightly; a gait midway between a pure trot (q.v.) and a flat pace (q.v.) with the sequence of footfalls similar to, but more distinct than, the slow gait (q.v.); characteristic to the five-gaited American Saddle Horse (q.v.); is very comfortable to ride. (2) To travel at a rack (q.v.) as in a horse. (3) A hunting term; a break in the bush or hedge caused by the repeated passage of deer. (4) The antlers of a deer or stag inclusive of the crown. (5) *see* HAY RACK

rack chains *see* CROSS TIES

racking To put fodder for horses or cattle in a hay rack (q.v.).

racking boots *see* OVER-REACH BOOTS

Racking Horse An American horse breed descended from the Walking Horse (q.v.) and recognized as a breed in 1971; possessed of a unique natural gait, attractive and graceful build, with a long sloping neck, full flanks, good bone, smooth legs, and finely textured hair; stands approximately 15.2 hands and is considered a light horse; coat colors may include black, bay, sorrel, chestnut, brown, and gray; named the official state horse of Alabama in 1975.

Racking Horse Breeders' Association of America Also known by the acronym RHBAA; an American organization established in 1971 to create and maintain the registry for and to protect and perpetuate the Racking Horse (q.v.) breed.

rack up (1) A racing term; said of a jockey who interferes with other horses running in a race so severely that they all slow down. (2) To tie a horse, as to a ring attached to the wall.

racy Said of a horse; to have a body suited for racing.

radial paralysis Also known as dropped elbow; a condition in which the horse stands with the elbow dropped lower than when the knee, elbow, and fetlock joints are flexed; most often caused by fracture of the first rib on the same side of the body affected; the broken ends of the rib lacerate the nerve fibres as they pass the rib or press against them; in other cases, the origin of the paralysis is situated in the nerve-fiber end-plates where they are distributed to the muscles; there is little or no associated pain unless accompanied by rib fracture or some inflammation which causes the paralysis; the horse holds the limb in the position assumed at the commencement of the stride, but the horse cannot advance it in front of the sound limb; the horse cannot bear weight on the limb and the muscles are flaccid and soft; if the horse is made to move, it does so in a series of hops off and onto the sound forelimb.

radiograph An image or picture on film produced by the action of X-rays (q.v.) or rays from other radioactive substances.

radiography The art or process of producing radiographs (q.v.).

rag Also known as rake; a herd of young horses.

ragged hips Said of a horse having prominent hips (q.v.), as in those that are poorly fleshed and/or muscled.

rail (1) Also known as pole; a round wooden bar generally 12 feet (3.6 m) long (although shorter 10 foot [3 m] poles are also used), used to create a jump when horizontally supported in cups between two standards (q.v.), or as a guide to teach a horse to jump, in which case it is known as a ground rail (q.v.). (2) Also known as fence; a racing term; the barrier located on either side of the racing strip between which race horses run when competing or working out; referred to specifically as either the inside rail (q.v.) or outside rail (q.v.).

rail runner A racing term; said of a horse who prefers to run along the inside rail (q.v.).

railway crossing Also known as level crossing; a jumping obstacle consisting of two large winged gates over which a horse is jumped; a red circle is painted in the center of each gate.

rainrot *see* RAIN SCALD

rain scald Also known as rainrot; a painful, infectious skin inflammation caused by the organism *Dermatophilus congolensis* which lives without consequence in the equine coat and gains entry into the skin when it is saturated by prolonged rain; slow-drying, humid conditions enable the organism to multiply, which irritates the hair follicles and skin of afflicted horses; the hair appears matted and tufted and with gentle pulling, will lift off revealing a green-gray pus stuck to the ends; lesions generally follow the water run-off pattern over the horse's back, belly, and lower limbs where the condition is known as scratches (q.v.); without treatment will run its course in one to four weeks; most common in the fall and winter during extended periods of rain; spread mechanically by biting and non-biting flies; prolonged wetting and a dirty coat appear to be predisposing factors.

rake (1) Also known as rake him up; a rodeo term; said of the spurring action of the rider on rough stock (q.v.) in which the rider drags the spur from the shoulders to the flanks through a swinging action, rather than jabbing; bareback and saddle bronc riders are required to spur throughout the duration of their ride, although bull riders are not, yet may score higher when they do. (2) *see* RAG. (3) An agricultural implement with teeth or tines for gathering together hay or leaves, or breaking and smoothing the surface of the ground.

rake him up *see* RAKE NO. 1

Ralli Car Also known as Clothes Basket or incorrectly as Ralli Cart; a small, open, light, two-wheeled, horse-drawn, English passenger car with crosswise seating for two, back-to-back; first introduced in the late 19th century; had side panels which curved outward over the wheels to form splash boards, rearward shaft extremities attached to the bodywork rather than the undercarriage, was hung on sideways semi-elliptical springs, and pulled by a single horse, cob, or large pony; named after the family by whom it was originally designed; built in two- and four-wheel versions; the two-wheel variety seated four back-to-back; suspension methods varied and included two side-springs, Dennett springs, cee-springs, or elliptic springs.

Ralli Cart *see* RALLI CAR

Ralph A hoof-shape pattern; the hoof is generally asymmetric, with the widest part of the hoof located in the rear third.

ram-headed Said of a horse having a convex head profile; commonly used to describe a Barb (q.v.).

ranch Also known as rancho; an established tract of land for raising and grazing livestock, especially in the western USA.

ranch brand *see* BRAND NO. 1

rancher Also known as ranch man; one who owns or is employed on a ranch.

ranchero In the southwestern United States, South America, and Mexico, one who owns, manages, or is employed on a ranch (q.v.).

ranch house The ranch owner's house or the principal building on a ranch (q.v.).

ranch man *see* RANCHER

rancho (1) *see* RANCH. (2) A hut, building, or groups thereof inhabited by ranch and/or farm workers.

randem Also spelled random; three horses hitched in single file, usually to a Dogcart (q.v.).

random *see* RANDEM

range (1) To roam, to walk about freely. (2) To place, as horses and cattle, on grazing land. (3) An expanse of open country used for livestock grazing.

range horse (1) Any horse foaled and raised on the range, having never been handled until brought in from the range to break. (2) *see* COW HORSE

range the quarters Said of the mounted rider, to move the horse's haunches either left or right using leg or seat aids.

rangy Said of a slender and long-limbed horse.

rank A racing term; said of a horse who refuses to submit to a jockey during a race, running in a headstrong manner without respect to pace.

rape Also known as rapeseed; a European herb, *Brassica napus*, of the mustard family grown as a forage crop for sheep and pigs and for its seeds which yield oil.

rapeseed (1) The seed of the rape (q.v.). (2) *see* RAPE

rapeseed meal A high energy protein supplement produced from the residue of the rapeseed (q.v.) after oil extraction; contains 36 percent digestible protein, 2 percent lysine, and a fiber and calcium content double that of soybean meal (q.v.); early varieties contained high levels of goitrogenic factors (q.v.), but new varieties and processing methods have reduced this factor; recently the term canola meal has been used for products from varieties of rapeseed containing less than three milligrams of glucosinotate per gram of seed.

rapping Also known as poling; training practice; to use a rapping pole (q.v.) to encourage a horse to lift his feet when jumping.

rapping pole A training device; a pole (usually wooden) approximately 10 to 12 feet (3–3.6 m) long used as a training aid to encourage the horse to lift his feet higher when jumping an obstacle; the pole is either suspended by the jump standards or held on either end by ground support (q.v.); in either case, the pole is raised as the horse jumps, so that his hind feet hit the pole; encourages the horse to lift his feet higher on subsequent jumps to avoid the pain of striking the pole; may be set with tacks; use is forbidden by some show jumping Associations.

Rarey, John A 19th-century American who demonstrated the technique of horse whispering (q.v.) to calm and train horses worldwide.

rase *see* RACE NO. 2

rasp (1) *see* TOOTH RASP. (2) To scrape or abrade with a rough instrument as in the teeth or the hoof. (3) *see* HOOF RASP

rasper A hunting term; any large, untrimmed

hedge, that when jumped, scratches the horses and riders.

ratcatcher (1) A hunting term; an informal riding outfit worn during cub hunting (q.v.) before the official start of the foxhunting season. (2) A formal long- or short-sleeved riding shirt with a standing banded collar worn by English rather than Western riders; the name and design were adopted for riding in the 18th century from a garment worn by English street urchins in which they collected and carried live rats and dormice to the merchants; the jacket was made of lisle or corduroy, was closed at the wrist and waist, and had a high, banded collar which could be buttoned to prevent the rodents from escaping; worn over a heavy shirt which protected the rat catchers from being bitten; the design and name was adopted for use by the rider because of its warmth and ability to keep out the damp.

rat catcher An antiquated British term; historically, one whose vocation it was to catch mice and rats for sale as food.

rate (1) A cutting term; the action of a horse when he paces his actions with those of a cow; the ability of the horse to stay in the correct cutting position, parallel with the cow being worked. (2) A roping term; the action of the horse as he moves behind the calf, maintaining an even speed with it while the roper swings the lariat (q.v.) and prepares the throw. (3) A barrel racing term; a maneuver in which the horse shortens or adjusts his stride to turn around a barrel. (4) A racing term; to restrain a horse early in a race to save his energy for a push later, as at the finish. (5) A hunting term; to scold a hound.

rated A racing term; said of a horse restrained by the jockey early in a horse race to save his energy for a push later on.

rat tail Said of the horse's tail when sparsely covered with hair.

rat tailed Said of the horse having a tail with sparse hair growth on the dock (q.v.).

rat tails *see* MULE EARS

rattle (1) A racing term; said of a horse who prefers to run on a firm track (q.v.). (2) Also known as rattle a fox; a hunting term; said of the hounds when they press hard on the trail of a fox forcing him to hurry along. (3) A hunting term; the note sounded on the hunt horn at a kill.

rattle a fox *see* RATTLE NO. 2

rattlers Also known as rollers; weights, links of chain, or wooden, rubber or plastic balls strung on a cord or strap which are placed around the fetlock, usually of the forefeet, to encourage the horse to increase action and step higher at the trot.

Rau, Gustav (1880–1954) A famous German hippologist (q.v.).

rawhide The untanned, usually dried skin of cattle; is very tough; used to make some types of rope, bosals (q.v.), saddles, whips, etc. (2) A rope or whip made of rawhide.

ray *see* DORSAL STRIPE

razor backed Said of a horse having a prominent and sharp backbone.

reach (1) *see* RACE NO. 2. (2) *see* PERCH NO. 1. (3) Refers to the horse; forward extension of the forelimbs, hind limbs and neck.

read a cow *see* READ CATTLE

read cattle Also known as read a cow; a cutting term; said of a horse or rider who is able to anticipate the movements of a cow.

Reading Cart A general-purpose, two-wheeled, horse-drawn vehicle of the Dogcart (q.v.) type; the paneled body was railed at the top, the sides extended with a low panel to join the dash to create a ledge to be stepped over when entering the vehicle, was hung on side-springs, and had shafts bolted to the underside of the body; seated four back-to-back.

ready To prepare a horse to participate in an event.

ready-made shoe Also known as cold shoe; a short-heeled machine-made version of a cowboy shoe (q.v.); usually manufactured in a compromise pattern whereby the shoe may be adapted to either the fore or hind feet; has cut and rounded heels and open, graduated nail holes from toe to heel that do not require pritcheling (q.v.); available in sizes 0, 00, 1, 2, 3, 4, and so on; nail holes are punched perpendicular to the shoe instead of corresponding to hoof slope.

reagent Any substance which, by the reaction it produces, may be used in chemical analysis.

rear (1) A vice; said of a horse who rises up onto his hind legs with his forelegs raised off the ground and frequently pulled in close to his chest. (2) A class of accommodation offered on Diligence (q.v.) horse-drawn vehicles operated in Europe during the 19th and 20th centuries; seated two to three, hood-protected rearward-facing passengers over the rear boot (q.v.).

rear boot A receptacle located on the rear portion of a coach or carriage, used to contain luggage.

rear leg *see* HIND LEG

reata *see* LARIAT

reata strap A short strap used to secure a lariat (q.v.) to a Western saddle.

receiving barn An American racing term; a barn in which horses shipped in for a race which do not have a stall at the race track are stabled.

receptivity *see* ESTRUS

recessive Pertaining to or exhibiting a hidden characteristic, as opposed to a dominant characteristic.

recessive gene *see* GENE RECESSIVE

recognized hunt A hunting term; a Hunt (q.v.) having received permanent status from the hunting association governing hunt activity in the area.

recover A hunting term; said of the hounds; to pick up the scent again following a check (q.v.).

recovery The act or power of regaining; said of the horse who regains his normal balance and resumes a forward gait following a jumping error, trip, stumble etc.

recurrent uvetis *see* MOON BLINDNESS

red bay Also known as cherry bay; the most common shade of bay (q.v.); the body is a clear shade of red with little variation in intensity.

red blood cell Also known as erythrocyte; a red corpuscle; a cell that gives the red color to the blood of vertebrates; transport oxygen.

red and green lights A principle of Richard Shrake's program of resistance free training (q.v.); "red lights" indicate resistance; the horse may appear confused, disobedient, panicked, emotionally shut down, or tense; "green lights" are messages from the horse that he is willing and ready to learn; if the horse drops his head, licks or chews, takes a breath, yawns and is otherwise relaxed, he is ready to listen and learn.

redboard (1) A racing term; one who claims to have selected the winning horse in a horse race, but who always does so following the race; a derogatory term. (2) A racing term; the obsolete practice of declaring a race official; to post a red flag or board on the tote board (q.v.).

red corn Also known as strawberry corn; refers to coat color pattern; a red dun (q.v.)

red dun Also known incorrectly as claybank dun (q.v.); refers to coat color; a variety of dun (q.v.); a washed out red or yellow coat color with brown, red, or flaxen points, and, often, primitive marks (q.v.); the lower legs are usually a darker red than the body.

red flag A piece of red cloth of varying size, shape, and design, usually attached at one edge to a staff or cord, and used to mark the right side of a jumping obstacle.

red fox Also known by the scientific name *Vulpes vulpes*; a carnivorous mammal of the dog family, especially of the genus *Vulpes*; has a reddish coat, pointed muzzle, erect ears, and a long bushy tail; noted for its cunning and alertness; originally native to Canada, Alaska, and the northern United States and now found in all but the desert regions of the latter; the primary quarry of foxhounds (q.v.) in the USA.

red hot scent *see* BURNING SCENT

redopp *see* PASSAGE

red ribbon A narrow strip of red silk, satin, or other material; when tied around the tail of a horse, indicates he is a known kicker; may also mark an endurance or cross-country course when tied to bushes or trees.

red roan *see* BAY ROAN

Red Rum Also known as Rummy or King of Aintree; a beautiful big bay who competed in five Grand Nationals in which he won three times and came in second twice; he withdrew on the eve of the sixth Grand National in 1978 due to injury; ran 100 races over fences and hurdles, winning 24.

redworm *see* LARGE STRONGYLE

referee *see* THIRD MAN

refit *see* RESET

refuse A jumping term; said of a horse who declines to attempt to jump an obstacle.

refusal (1) Said of a horse who refused (q.v.) to attempt to jump an obstacle, e.g. "The horse had one refusal on the course." (2) A racing term, said of a horse who fails to break the start in a race.

Regimental Coach A Drag (q.v.) owned by the officers of a military regiment; the corps badge was displayed on the hind boot, door panels, and harness.

regional anesthesia An artificially produced state of insensibility, especially to the sense of pain, to an area of the body.

regional anesthetic Any substance possessing the power to deprive feeling or sensation to a region of the body, as in the lower or upper body.

registered Hunt An American hunting term; a Hunt (q.v.) which meets Association standards, but which has not been granted permanent status; the status is provisional and the Hunt is expected to improve its facilities and performance before being recognized.

Registered Shoeing Smith Also known by the acronym RSS; one of three levels of training certification awarded to practicing farriers in Britain; awarded by the Worshipful Company of Farriers (q.v.) on the basis of written, oral, and practical examinations; now known as Diploma of the Worshipful Company of Farriers (q.v.).

regular Refers to the evenness with which the horse puts each foot on the ground, i.e. the horse must take each step at a regular speed and rhythm and an even length.

regulator Any device used on a harness race horse to prevent side pulling.

reiki An ancient system of hands-on healing believed to have originated in Tibet thousands of years ago in which cosmic energy flows into the attuned practitioner through the crown chakra located at the top of the head, down through the body, expands the auric field, and flows through the practitioner's hands to the recipient; energy is drawn through the practitioner's body in direct proportion to the amount of energy required by the recipient; 15 hand positions corresponding to the chakras, glands, and energy meridians are used to treat everything from minor ailments and accidents to chronic disease by working on physical as well as psychological issues; speeds up and enhances the healing process when used alone or in conjunction with other modalities such as chiropractics, allopathic medicine (including veterinary), TTEAM (q.v.), TTOUCH (q.v.), massage, etc.

rein (1) To direct or maneuver and control a horse by means of the reins (q.v.). (2) One of two reins (q.v.).

rein aid Use of the reins to impart instruction to the horse; includes direct rein (q.v.), neck rein (q.v.), indirect rein (q.v.), etc.

rein back Also known as back or back up; a movement in which the horse steps rearward at an even, two-time gait with the diagonal pairs of feet touching the ground simultaneously; the horse must remain straight in the movement; only two hoof beats are heard.

rein back crooked Said of the rein back (q.v.) movement when the horse's haunches swing to the in- or outside.

rein billet The point of the rein (q.v.) that passes through and around the bit cheekpiece (q.v.) and back to itself where it is buckled or otherwise attached.

reiner One who participates in the sport of reining (q.v.).

rein holder A coaching term; a brass or white metal rail bolted to the top of the dashboard (q.v.) of a horse-drawn vehicle used to support the reins and prevent them from catching beneath the horses' tails.

reining A Western, non-timed competition in which the athletic ability of a ranch-type horse is demonstrated in the confines of a show pen through execution of any of nine patterns; all reining patterns include small circles, large, fast circles, flying lead changes (q.v.), rollbacks (q.v.) over the hocks, 360 degree spins in place to the left and to the right, and the sliding stop (q.v.).

reining horse Any horse trained for reining (q.v.) maneuvers; most commonly a Quarter Horse (q.v.).

reining pattern Any of nine patterns in a reining competition; each pattern includes small circles, large, fast circles, flying lead changes, roll backs over the hocks, 360 degree spins in place to the left and to the right, and the sliding stop.

reining point A cutting term; a one-point penalty given to a rider who picks up his left hand and the reins while working a cow in competition.

rein lame Also known as bridle lame; apparent lameness due to the rider's restricting rein aid and/or too harsh a bit; evidenced by a lack of engagement of the haunches and uneven acceptance of the bit.

rein on him A Western term; said of a horse responsive to neck reining (q.v.).

rein ring Also known as Roger ring or wheeler terret; the rosette on a wheeler or shaft horse's bridle through which the leader's rein passes.

reins (1) Also known as ribbons or lines; straps of rope, leather, or synthetic material attached to the cheekpieces (q.v.) of the bit or to the bridle on one end and held in the rider's or driver's hands on the other; used to guide and control the horse. (2) *see* LONG LINE S

rejoneo The art form of bull fighting from horseback in which the bull is never killed; originated in Portugal.

rejoneador The mounted participant in a rejoneo (q.v.); historically used Lusitano (q.v.) mounts, but in today's modern bull-rings the Andalusian (q.v.) and Lusitano are used almost equally; Thoroughbred (q.v.), Azteca (q.v.), and Quarter Horses (q.v.) are also used.

relaxed (1) Said of the horse's mental state; calm, without anxiety or nervousness. (2) Said of the horse's physical state; a lack of muscular tension (contraction) other than that required for optimal carriage, strength, and range and fluency of movement.

relieved A horseshoe beveled or depressed on the inner half of the web (q.v.) on the hoof-facing surface, except for the heels; prevents the shoe from applying pressure to the hoof sole.

remedy *see* HOMEOPATHIC REMEDY

remount (1) A fresh horse used to replace a tired or lame one, as those formerly used by the pony express (q.v.), cavalry, etc. (2) To mount a horse again.

remouthing The process of correcting or attempting to correct a spoiled mouth (q.v.); to resensitize the horse's mouth to the bit; may involve the use of a more gentle bit and soft hands.

remuda A group of riding horses used on a roundup (q.v.); a relay of mounts.

rental horse Also known as job horse (obs); any horse let for hire or "jobbed" out.

renvers Also known as haunches out, tail to the wall, hindquarters-out, or quarters-out; a dressage movement in which the horse's head, neck, and shoulders follow a straight track about 1 yard (90 cm) off of the wall or line at an overall mean angle of approximately 30 degrees, while the loins and quarters are displaced to the outside, being bent around the rider's outside leg; the horse's head is flexed in the direction of the movement.

renvers half-volte Also known as half-volte reversed; a dressage movement in which the horse moves off the track haunches out (q.v.), scribes one half of a 6-meter circle haunches-out, and returns to the track traveling in the opposite direction.

renvers volte A volte (q.v.) movement performed in dressage; the horse performs a 6-meter circle with the haunches-out (q.v.).

rep A cowboy employed to search for and round up stray cattle from a specific ranch.

repository An auction yard where horses are sold.

re ride A rodeo term; a second ride awarded a bronc or bull rider in the same go-round when either the cowboy or animal is not afforded a fair opportunity to perform, as when the animal fights in the chute and cannot be mounted, if the animal falls, if the animal is impossible for the rider to mount, or if the animal falls or drags the rider off in the chute gate.

resciant *see* BLISTER NO. 2

reserve Also known as upset price; the minimum price a consignor will sell a specific horse for at public auction; the consignor can either register the reserve with the sales company, which will not let the horse be sold unless the price exceeds that amount, or the consignor can bid on the horse himself until the reserve is reached.

reserved (1) A racing term; said of a horse held for a particular race. (2) A racing term; said of a horse held off the pace in a race.

reserve not achieved Also known by the acronym RNA; when the reserve (q.v.) amount a consignor will sell a specific horse for at public auction is not reached.

reset Also known as shift, refit or remove (Brit); said of the farrier (q.v.); to remove a horseshoe from the hoof, trim the hoof, and reattach the same shoe.

resin Any of various solid or semisolid substances exuded from various plants and trees or prepared synthetically; soluble in ether, alcohol, etc., are non-conductors of electricity, and are used in medicines, varnishes and lacquers.

resin back *see* ROSINBACK

resist Said of a horse who attempts to evade any or all the rider's aids (q.v.) as by opening his mouth, crossing his jaw, hanging out his tongue, swinging his hindquarters, tossing his head, etc.

resistance free training A horse training technique developed by Richard Shrake; involves a gentler, kinder way of developing a partnership with the horse using a system based on interpreting the horse's "red and green lights" (q.v.); when the horse is ready and willing to accept training, he will be in a green-light zone; if the horse demonstrates "red lights" of resistance, the trainer should retreat and delay the training until the horse's confidence returns and he demonstrates a willingness and desire to learn; "red lights" may look like confusion, tension, disobedience, panic, or shutting down; dropping the head, licking, chewing, taking a deep breath, or yawning are all "green lights" and indicate the horse is relaxed and interested and that his mind and heart are receptive to the trainer and the lessons.

resisting Said of a horse who resists (q.v.).

respiration The act of breathing; the inhalation and exhalation of air.

respiratory system The system of organs enabling the horse to breath; consists of the nostrils, nasal passages, pharynx, larynx, trachea, and lungs.

rest (1) A metal projection on a suit of armor located four fingers above the waist, upon which a knight or tilter (q.v.) would rest his lance while tilting (q.v.). (2) Cessation or temporary interruption of motion, exertion, or labor.

rest horse *see* SPARE NO. 3

rest shoe *see* PATTEN SHOE

resting leg The leg of the horse not bearing weight when at a halt; the horse may bear weight evenly on all four legs, or alternatively, on three legs, with one leg free of weight.

result chart Also known as chart; a racing term; a chart upon which the numerical results of a given race are posted; include the names of competing horses and riders or drivers, fractional and final times, and odds and payoffs.

retained placenta Afterbirth (q.v.) not expelled within six hours of foaling.

retained sole Also known as false sole; said of the horse's hoof when it does not exfoliate normally; although not a normal condition, provides extra protection for the internal foot structures.

retainer (1) An advance fee paid to a jockey or rider of a competed horse(s) to secure the rights to the rider's services for a predetermined amount of time. (2) One who retains the riding services of a professional.

retina The sensory membrane lining the back surface of the eye's interior; receives the focused image and transmits it to the optic nerve.

retire Also known as put out to pasture or out to pasture; to withdraw a horse from competition and regular work.

retired Also known as out to pasture; said of a horse withdrawn from active life.

reverse field A hunting term; to change the direction traveled in pursuit of a fox.

reverse shoe *see* BACKWARDS SHOE

reverse wedge shoe A horseshoe graduated in thickness from a thick toe to a thin heel; elevates the hoof toe and thus lowers the hoof angle (q.v.).

rhabdomyolosis Breakdown of skeletal muscle; as a consequence, the urine contains myoglobin (q.v.).

rhabdovirus A group of bullet-shaped viruses which includes the rabies virus and that of vesicular stomatitis (q.v.).

RHBAA *see* RACKING HORSE BREEDERS' ASSOCIATION OF AMERICA

Rhenish *see* RHINELAND HEAVY DRAFT

Rhineland *see* RHINELAND HEAVY DRAFT

Rhineland Heavy Draft Also known as Rhenish, Rhineland, or German Coldblood; a coldblood developed in 19th-century Germany (Rhineland, from which the name derived); descended from the Ardennes (q.v.), Ancient Forest Horse (q.v.), and the Flanders Horse (q.v.); stands 16 to 17 hands, weighs around 2,200 pounds (998 kg), is strong, has massive quarters and shoulders, a deep broad back, crested neck, and short, strong legs with heavy feathering; matures early; coat colors include bay chestnut or red roan (q.v.) with flaxen (q.v.) or black mane and tail; used for heavy draft and farm work; the stud book was established in 1876.

rhinopneumonitis *see* EQUINE VIRAL RHINOPNEUMONITIS

rhythm The regularity and evenness of the footfalls and phases of a given gait.

rib Any of 18 (17 in Arabs) pairs of slender, arched bones attached on either side of the horse's vertebral column, which enclose the chest and protect such organs as the heart, lungs, and liver.

rib bar Refers to coat color pattern; a primitive mark (q.v.); dark hair markings appearing over the horse's ribs.

ribbed up Also known as well-ribbed up; said of a horse whose ribs are well arched and incline well backwards, bringing the ends closer to the point of the hip and making the horse short coupled (q.v.).

ribbon Also known as rosette (Brit); a strip of silk, satin, or other material awarded to signify a place winner in a competition; different colors are used to identify the contestants placing in the competition: 1st – blue (red in Britain), 2nd – red (blue in Britain), 3rd – yellow, 4th – white (green in Britain), 5th – pink (or sometimes orange in Britain), 6th – green (usually pink or mauve in Britain), 7th – purple, 8th – brown, champion – blue/red/yellow, and reserve champion red/yellow/white.

ribbons (1) *see* REINS. (2) More than one rein (q.v.).

Rib-Chair Gig An unsprung, two-wheeled, horse-drawn vehicle popular in the 18th century; a semi-circular-shaped seat with a similarly shaped backrest supported on wooden spindles was fixed above the shafts.

riboflavin Also known as vitamin B_2 (obs) and spelled riboflavine; a B-complex vitamin essential for proper energy release and nervous system function; synthesized in the horse's small intestine and found in good quality hay and/or pasture which, together, provide sufficient amounts to meet the daily dietary requirement; highly resistant to destruction by heat and air; deficiency is uncommon, but causes stunted growth, hair loss, etc.

riboflavine *see* RIBOFLAVIN

Ribot One of the 20th century's greatest racehorses, named for 19th century French painter Theodule-Augustin Ribot; foaled in Italy in 1952, ran unbeaten in 16 races over 3 seasons, was sent to stud in England in 1957 and the United States in 1960 and died in 1972 of a twisted gut.

rice bran The outer layer of the rice kernel removed during the rice milling process to produce white rice; fed to horses to facilitate weight gain by increasing energy and calorie intake without increasing bulk; stabilized at high temperatures to prevent spoilage; has a shelf life of up to one year, and a fat content of 18 to 24 percent.

rice hulls The husk, shell, or outer covering of rice grain; used as a bedding (q.v.) material by horsemen; highly absorbent, dust free and attractive, but difficult to store, and in some areas difficult to obtain.

Richmonds *see* LEGGINGS

ridable (1) Capable of being ridden, as a horse. (2) Capable of being ridden through or over, as a wooded area.

ridden out (1) A racing term; said of a horse who wins a race because of the jockey's careful pacing and strategy, who has little energy remaining at the finish. (2) A British racing term; said of a horse pushed out quite strongly at the end of a race who is likely to have little residual energy at the race finish.

ride (1) Also known as horse riding; to sit on the back of a horse and manage him in motion through the use of natural and artificial aids. (2) A hunting term; a wide path or trail in a wooded area.

ride and drive horse *see* COMBINATION HORSE

ride and tie A sport born in the United States in 1971; a very strategic cross-country horse race between teams consisting of two runners and one horse in which the partners alternate turns running and riding a minimum of six times; the first rider rides up the trail a predetermined distance, dismounts, ties the horse to a tree and continues on foot; when the first runner reaches the tied horse, he mounts, and rides to catch his partner running in front of him; this process of riding and tying continues until both riders and the horse have crossed the finish line; races range from 20 to 100 miles (32–160 km) in length and average 10,000 feet (3,048 m) elevation change; top teams averaging a sub-six-minute-mile pace; 90 percent of the competing horses are Arabs (q.v.).

Ride and Tie Association Also known by the acronym RTA; an American organization founded in 1989 to organize and promote the sport of ride and tie (q.v.) in the United States.

ride for a fall Said of a competitor; to intentionally lose a competition or to embark upon an undertaking that seems doomed to fail; originated in horse racing, particularly the steeplechase, in which the rider with the favored mount would deliberately ride in such a way as to disqualify himself by being thrown from the horse.

ride for hire To receive payment, directly or indirectly, for riding in a race or other competition as a professional.

ride hard Said of the rider; to push the horse to his physical limits without riding him into the ground (q.v.).

ride hard to the hounds A hunting term; said of a member of the field; to push one's horse hard, riding close to the hounds.

ride hell for leather *see* HEEL BENT FOR LEATHER

ride in the Master's pocket A hunting term; said of a green rider (q.v.) who, not wishing to fall behind the pack, follows closely on the heels of the Field Master (q.v.).

ride into the ground Said of the rider; to ride a horse to the extent of its physical limits so that it is unable to continue.

ride off A polo term; said of a polo player who rides up upon his opponent from an acute angle and applies pressure of his body, except the elbows, and/or that of his horse against his opponent to move the opponent off the line of the ball (q.v.) and prevent him from striking it; charging at an angle greater than about 45 degrees is not allowed.

ride on a long rein To ride a horse with the reins as long as possible without losing contact with the bit to allow the horse to stretch his neck freely.

ride on a loose rein To ride a horse with the reins so long that there is no contact on the bit.

ride on the lunge A training exercise for a mounted rider; the rider rides a horse lunged (q.v.) in a circle to gain balance, learn leg and seat aids, etc; may be performed hands-free, with or without stirrups.

rider One who rides a horse, mule, or the like.

ride short To ride with short stirrups.

ride to a blue Said of a rider in competition who, on the basis of the performance or ride, wins the blue ribbon or first place.

ride to hounds Also known as riding for hounds; a hunting term; to hunt, or follow the hounds (q.v.) on horseback.

ridgeling *see* RIG

riding coat A dense, wind- and rain-resistant coat made of natural or synthetic fabric including melton wool, lightweight wools, or cotton, worn by a mounted rider; originally long enough to cover and protect the upper leg, is vented in the back to accommodate the cantle (q.v.) of the saddle, and has slanted and flapped pockets for easy hand access and to protect the contents from the weather.

riding crupper *see* SADDLE CRUPPER

riding fee A sum of money paid to a professional to show or compete a horse.

riding for hounds *see* RIDE TO HOUNDS

riding horse Any horse suitable for use as a mount (q.v.).

riding instructor One who teaches others the art of horsemanship (q.v.).

riding mount *see* MOUNT NO. 3

riding out *see* HACK NO. 1

riding pony (1) A type rather than a breed; recently developed in Great Britain by putting small Thoroughbred (q.v.) and Arab (q.v.) stallions to native pony mares including the Welsh (q.v.), Dartmoor (q.v.), and Exmoor (q.v.); all coat colors are permitted; of three size categories: up to 12.2 hands, 12.3 to 13.2 hands, and 13.3 to 14 hands. (2) Any pony (q.v.) ridden for pleasure or competition.

riding school Any facility where people are taught the principles and practices of riding by a trained instructor.

rig (1) Also known as cryptorchid, risling, ridgeling, or original; a male horse with improper, bilateral (double cryptorchid) or unilateral testicular descent; the retained testicle may lie within the inguinal canal, but external to the body wall, or within the abdomen internal to the inguinal canal; will demonstrate stallion-like behavior including attempting to round up mares, attraction to a mare in heat (q.v.), full erection, and occasionally, ejaculation; is infertile, except in the case of a unilateral cryptorchid, who will be fertile from the scrotal testis (q.v.); improper bilateral testicular descent is an inherited genetic feature classified as a partial lethal (q.v.). (2) Slang; any horse-drawn or mechanical vehicle; a truck. (3) A 19th century term; any dilapidated horse-drawn vehicle.

right diagonal The horse's right foreleg and left hind leg move as a pair at the trot.

right lead Said of the horse when the right foreleg and right hind leg lead at the canter (q.v.) or gallop.

right of way A polo term; a governing law in the game of polo which entitles the player having hit the ball to follow the line of that ball from the offside of his pony and to take a further shot; play will flow backward and forward, parallel to an imaginary line of the ball extended ahead of, and behind, the ball.

right price A racing term; the point at which, under any betting system, the odds on a particular horse are sufficiently attractive to encourage bettors (q.v.) to bet.

right rein (1) *see* ON THE RIGHT REIN. (2) The rein(s) attached to the right bit cheek or to the right side of a cavesson (q.v.), halter, etc.

rim fire (1) A rodeo term; to place a burr or other irritating object between the saddle blanket and the back of the horse to make it buck more purposefully. (2) An American cowboy term; said of a cowboy when his rope lodges under his horse's tail, as when roping.

rim shoe Any horseshoe (q.v.) with a long cleat on the outer edge; occasionally used correctively for horses with tendon problems.

ring bit *see* TATTERSAL BIT

ringbone Also known as interphalangeal arthritis; formation of new bone in the area of the first or second phalanx of the pastern; forms slowly and may result from faulty conformation such as too upright pasterns, improper shoeing, repeated concussion through work on hard ground, working a young horse (under three years of age) too hard too quickly, bruises, sprains, strains, injuries to ligaments, tendons, or joints, or may follow trauma, infection, or wire-cut wounds; may or may not result in lameness; more common in the fore than hind feet; produces a characteristic bell-shaped pastern; of two types, high ringbone (q.v.) and low ringbone (q.v.).

ring boots *see* FETLOCK RING BOOT

ringer (1) Also known as ring in; a racing term; a horse entered in a race under a false name to obtain more favorable betting odds. (2) A racing term; to enter a horse, using a false name, in a race below the class in which it normally is competed so virtually ensure a win; a dishonest practice. (3) An Australian term; a station hand on a large property, generally those in the wetter areas of Australia; appears to have originated in the days when cattle ranged on large, unfenced properties and gathering would take many months at a time; at night, one of the men would ride around the herd to keep them from escaping to their previous grazing territory; the act of riding around the herd was always performed in a circle or ring, and thus, the rider was a ringer. (4) Also known as ringing fox; a hunting term; a fox who runs in circles, twisting and doubling back in covert (q.v.), rather than running in a straight line.

ring in *see* RINGER

ringing fox *see* RINGER NO. 4

ringing the bell A coaching term; said of a one who drives with rough hands, jerking the rein(s) left or right to indicate a turn rather than giving a light, steady hand signal.

ringmaster *see* RING STEWARD

rings *see* RUNNING MARTINGALE

ring sour Said of a horse who, because he is ridden continuously in an enclosed area such as a riding ring, becomes disinterested and difficult to work in that environment, i.e., the horse is bored; easily treated by varying the work schedule and location.

ring steward Also known as ringmaster; one responsible for oversight of competitive activity in the riding or show ring or arena including assisting, but not advising, the judge.

Ring, The A racing term; bookmakers, collectively.

ringworm Also known as dermatophytosis; a fungal infection of the skin and hair resulting in hair loss and lesions; the affected area is generally circular in shape; most commonly transmitted by contaminated grooming equipment, saddle blankets, and harnesses.

riot A hunting term; said of the hounds (q.v.) when they hunt quarry (q.v.) other than that selected, e.g. a rabbit instead of a fox.

risen clinch Said of a clinch (q.v.) which rises and pulls away from the hoof wall, an indication that the horseshoe is loosening.

riser *see* CHEEK NO. 4

rising The age of the horse when close to, but less than a specific year, e.g., a horse rising eight will not yet be eight years old.

rising trot *see* POST NO. 4

risling *see* RIG

RNA *see* RESERVE NOT ACHIEVED

roach To cut or shear the mane 1 to 3 inches (2.5–7.5 cm) long leaving a few long wisps of hair at the withers for a hand hold; used on polo ponies to prevent the mallet from entangling in the mane and in breeds such as the cob, to highlight his muscular neck structure.

roach back Also known as hog back or hogged back; said of the horse's spine when convexly curved between the withers and loins; a conformation defect; the back will appear arched.

roach backed Also known as hog-backed; said of a horse having a convexly curved spine between the withers (q.v.) and loins; the opposite of sway backed (q.v.); a conformation defect.

roached mane Also known as pony roach; a mane cut or sheared 1 to 3 inches (2.5–7.5 cm) long and tapered so that it stands upright; the outside hairs of the mane are shorter than the inside hairs; not as short as a clipped or hogged mane (q.v.).

roaching The process by which the horse's mane is sheared or roached (q.v.).

Road Cart An American two-wheeled, horse-drawn, single-passenger vehicle drawn by a single horse or pony; superseded by the modern Racing Sulky (q.v.).

Road Coach A horse-drawn multi-passenger, public transportation vehicle which gained popularity during the last quarter of the 19th century; generally weighed in excess of one ton (1 tonnes), seated 12 outside passengers as well as the guard and coachman, was brightly colored, had small-paned windows, a folding ladder secured under the boot (q.v.), and was strongly built to withstand heavy daily mileage.

road founder Inflammation of the sensitive laminae (q.v.) of the hoof caused by excessive concussion over hard surfaces.

road hack Also known as ordinary hack or pad horse (obs); a horse who, due to gaits and conformation, is ill-suited as a park hack (q.v.), but good for pleasure riding outside of competition.

road hunter A hunting term; a hound particularly proficient at following the line of a fox (q.v.) along a hard, dry road where the scent does not stick well.

roading hounds A hunting term; to exercise hounds down a road rather than through the country.

road puff *see* WINDPUFF

Road Phaeton *see* DOGCART PHAETON

Roadster *see* NORFOLK TROTTER

road studs Low-volume metal heads screwed into the ground-side surface of a horseshoe (q.v.) to increase traction on slippery asphalt or concrete surfaces; have a hardened metal core which is slower wearing than the shoe itself; usually fitted when the horse or pony is shod and can be removed when not required; do not distort foot balance.

Road Wagon A four-wheeled, horse-drawn open wagon suited for carrying merchandise.

roan Refers to coat color; a specific color pattern consisting of a uniform mixture of colored and white body hairs and a colored head and points; a non-progressive seldom dappled color pattern; scarred areas will grow in colored; the coat color changes throughout the year being lightest in the spring and darkest in the winter; further described by the base color of the horse followed by the term roan as in bay roan (q.v.), strawberry roan (q.v.), honey roan (q.v.), purple roan (q.v.), and lilac roan (q.v.).

roarer A horse suffering from laryngeal hemiplegia (q.v.).

roaring *see* LARYNGEAL HEMIPLEGIA

ROC *see* RACE OF CHAMPIONS

Rockalette A small, two-passenger, American Rockaway (q.v.) with a movable top.

Rockaway Also known as American Rockaway, Rockaway Coupé or Station Wagon; an American two-passenger, horse-drawn, vehicle used throughout the 19th century; manufactured in a variety of types and sizes, was usually headed (q.v.), had semi-open sides protected by curtains or roll-down blinds, hung on crosswise springs in the style of an American Buggy (q.v.), and had a driver's seat sheltered by a forward extension of the roof canopy; drawn either by a horse in shafts or a pair in pole gear (q.v.).

Rockaway Coupé A cut-down version of the Rockaway (q.v.).

Rockaway Landau A type of Rockaway (q.v.); a horse-drawn vehicle popular during the late 19th century; combined the best features of the Rockaway and the Landau (q.v.); a half-hood protected the rear seats and a standing top the fore and the driver's seat.

rockered toe shoe *see* ROCKER-TOE SHOE

rocker shoe *see* ROCKER-TOE SHOE

rocker-toe shoe Also known as roller-motion shoe, rockered-toe shoe, rocker shoe, set toe, or set-toe shoe; a horseshoe (q.v.) with thick quarters, beveled or rolled from the center third up onto the toe of the hoof; the hoof surface is left flat; used to treat arthritic conditions of the forelegs, chronic bowed tendons, to speed break-over and/or relieve stress of breaking over the toe, and, in some cases, founder (q.v.).

rocking Also known as rolling; the left-right sideways motion of a horse-drawn coach pulled at the gallop; may lead to over-turning of the vehicle.

rocking canter *see* ROCKING HORSE CANTER

rocking-chair canter Said of the smooth, collected canter of the Tennessee Walking Horse (q.v.); is a high-rolling movement.

rocking horse Also known as hobby horse (Am); a traditionally crafted wooden horse mounted on rockers, which a child rider can move in a to-and-fro motion, somewhat resembling a canter.

rocking horse canter (1) Also known as rocking canter; an American dressage term, a canter in which the neck/forehand moves too much up and down, due to the lack of sufficient ground coverage, lack of sufficient engagement, or to interference by the rider. (2) Applied loosely to signify a relatively comfortable canter.

rock 'n' roll A vaulting term; a freestyle exercise in which the vaulter (q.v.), standing on the horse's back, assists a partner in an aerial forward roll dismount using a wrist grip.

Rocky Mountain canary *see* ASS

rodeo (1) Also known cattle men's carnival (Aus); a public performance of cowboy (q.v.) skills including bronc riding (q.v.), steer wrestling (q.v.), calf roping, etc.; from the Spanish *rodear* meaning to go round. (2) *see* ROUND UP

rodeoin' Slang; to compete in a rodeo (q.v.).

Roger rein *see* REIN RING

rogue Also known as outlaw; a consistently fractious horse who demonstrates a fierce disposition and, frequently, cannot be broken; a renegade.

rogue's badge *see* RACING BLINKERS

rollback Also known as set and turn; a Western term; said of the galloping horse which stops, lifts his forelegs, turns 180 degrees, and gallops back in the same direction from which he came.

rolled toe A horseshoe rounded on the outer edge of the ground surface at the toe while the hoof-side surface of the shoe remains flat.

roller (1) Also known as body roller; a leather or webbing girth (q.v.) or surcingle (q.v.) with pads attached to the underside that fit on either side of the withers, used to prevent pressure and rubbing and to hold a rug or blanket in place. (2) Also known as bit roller, cherry roller, or in Western circles as a cricket; a round, bead-shaped, stainless, blue steel, or copper ball which rotates freely about the mouthpiece or port (q.v.) when played with by the horse's tongue; often several on a bit; encourages salivation and prevents a puller (q.v.) from setting his jaw.

roller bolt Also known as bollard; an upright, metal projection from the end of the splinter bar (q.v.) to which the traces of a pair, or coach wheelers (q.v.) attach.

roller-motion shoe *see* ROCKER-TOE SHOE

roller pad A rectangular piece of felt, wool, cotton, or other material 1 inch (2.5 cm) thick, placed under a roller (q.v.) to provide protection and absorb sweat.

rollers (1) *see* RATTLERS. (2) More than one roller (q.v.). (3) A snorting, rattling sound made by a horse when spooked.

rolling (1) Excessive lateral shoulder movement common to horses with protruding shoulders. (2) *see* ROCKING

Romanic Also known as Romanic style; a riding style inherited from the Roman period; implies a highly collected, agile style of riding based on lightness and dexterity of hand.

Romanic school A riding style based on the Romanic style (q.v.)

Romanic style *see* ROMANIC

Roman nose Also known as Roman profile; said of a horse having a convex profile from poll (q.v.) to muzzle; the nasal bone protrudes when the head is viewed from the side; considered undesirable for aesthetic reasons, and is a definite conformation defect in some breeds such as the Arab (q.v.); mainly associated with coldblood heavy-horse breeds.

Roman profile *see* ROMAN NOSE

romp A racing term; an easy race.

rompre en lice A 16th and 17th-century French term; in competition, to break one's lance in the lice (q.v.), on a pile, revolving figure, tree trunk, or opponent's shield.

roof (1) An accommodation class offered on Diligence (q.v.) horse-drawn vehicles operated in 19th and 20th-century Europe; driver and guard seats were situated above the coupé (q.v.). (2) *see* ROOF SEAT

roof of the mouth *see* PALATE

roof seat Also known as outside seat or roof; any seat located on the roof of a horse-drawn vehicle.

rooster pull A mounted game performed in the United States in the 18th and 19th centuries; a mounted rider traveling at high speed, would lean out of the saddle, reach down and pull loose a rooster previously buried neck-deep in the ground, and complete the competition by racing the other competitors in a circle.

root crop Any vegetable fed to the horse either as a dietary supplement or a treat including carrots, rutabagas, mangels, sugar-beets, and turnips.

roots A hunting term; a field of tuberous plants such as carrots, turnips, potatoes, etc.

rope (1) A thick, long cord of twisted or

braided fibers, as hemp, wire, nylon, or other material. (2) *see* LARIAT. (3) Also known as lasso; to catch, tie, or fasten a horse or other animal using a rope.

rope bag Also known as rope can; a Western roping term; a soft or hard container in which a lariat (q.v.) is packed or stored for traveling.

rope can *see* ROPE BAG

rope horse *see* ROPING HORSE

roper One who catches a horse or other animal using a lariat (q.v.).

rope shoe Also known as fiber shoe; a traction horseshoe now replaced by the St. Croix rim shoe and studs (q.v.); the ground-side surface is grooved and set with a tarred rope; used to prevent the horse from slipping on smooth pavements; special long-headed nails were used.

rope walking Also known as winding, plaiting, lacing, or crossing feet; a gait defect in which the horse moves in such a manner that the hooves are placed in front of each other through a twisting of the striding leg around the supporting leg in a manner similar to a person climbing a rope or plaiting two pieces of rope together; common to horses wide at the base or having broad chests, or in the hind legs of pacers; a severe example of paddling (q.v.); to some extent, may be corrected with shoeing.

roping (1) *see* LUNGE. (2) The act of catching, tying, or fastening as with a rope.

roping dummy Any target a roper (q.v.) uses to practice throwing a loop, including a plastic calf's head.

roping horse Also known as rope horse; any specially trained horse, such as a Quarter Horse (q.v.) or Quarter Horse cross, from which the rider is able to rope cattle and/or horses.

rosadera The parts of a jaquima (q.v.) contacting the lower jaw and shanks.

rose gray Refers to coat color; a mixture of black and white; such horses are born either chestnut or sorrel and never have a true gray appearance or become progressively whiter with age; the most common shade of gray (q.v.).

rosette (1) Also known as boss; a disc, often emblazoned with the owner's monogram, crest, or engraving, attached to the sides of the browband (q.v.) of a harness bridle; depending on the type of team, may be attached to the left, right, or both sides of the bridle (q.v.); designed in many different styles and materials; rosettes with outward protruding terrets, through which the leader's reins pass, were often used with a tandem (q.v.) shaft horse or the wheelers (q.v.) of a unicorn or four-in-hand team (q.v.). (2) A silk or cloth ribbon gathered to resemble a rose; awarded to placed competitors in an equestrian event. (3) On a Western stock saddle, a small leather disc with two slits through which the thongs or saddle strings pass to secure the skirts to the saddletree. (4) *see* RIBBON

rosin (1) A resin (q.v.) formed from the oil of turpentine when distilled from crude turpentine; used by vaulters to provide traction. (2) To rub or cover with rosin.

Rosinante (1) The trusted mount of Don Quixote de la Mancha, the protagonist in Miguel de Cervantes' book of the same title. (2) A horse who has reached the end of his usefulness.

rosinback Also known as resin back; a circus term; a generally wide or flat-backed horse on which one or several vaulters (q.v.) perform; the term derived from the use of rosin (q.v.) applied to the back of the horse, mainly around the quarters, to prevent performers from slipping.

rosinback riding machine A crane-like device used in the circus to train bareback riders; a safety line, suspended from the crane, attaches to a waist belt worn by the rider; in the event of a fall from the horse, the crane and safety line support the rider.

Rostopchin A Russian breed of English Thoroughbred (q.v.) and Arab (q.v.) extraction.

Rottaler A Bavarian warmblood bred in the Rott Valley.

rough country Difficult terrain to ride through, e.g. heavily wooded, steep, rocky, etc.

roughing off Also known as roughing up; the process of preparing a stabled horse for turn out to grass or pasture by reducing and ultimately removing grain from the diet and allowing his natural coat to fill in.

roughing up *see* ROUGHING OFF

rough out Also known as rough-out leather or grain (Brit); the rough side of a tanned hide when worn to the outside, as in chaps and some types of boots.

rough-out leather *see* ROUGH OUT

rough rider (1) Also known as rough stock rider; one who rides rough stock (q.v.) including saddle broncs (q.v.), bareback broncs, and bulls. (2) A British term; one who rides horses during breaking and early training.

rough shod *see* COWBOY SHOD

rough stock A rodeo term; untrained stock, horses, or bulls used in mounted bucking competitions such as saddle bronc, bareback bronc, and bull riding.

rough stock event Any Western riding event in which competitors ride bulls, saddle broncs, or bareback stock.

rough stock rider *see* ROUGH RIDER NO. 1

rough transition *see* TRANSITION ROUGH

Roulette A horse-drawn sedan chair popular in 17th-century France.

rouncy *see* COB

round Also known as go-round or heat; a single effort, round, bout, or trial, especially in competition, the winners of which compete in the final round.

Round-Cornered Wagonette A four-wheeled, horse-drawn carriage similar to the Governess Cart (q.v.); had inward-facing seats reached by a rear door and was hung on elliptic springs above a straight axle.

rounded back Also known as arched back; a dressage term; the horse's back when the hollow between the withers and croup is reduced, the loin more horizontal, the tail swinging, and the back muscles moving freely.

rounding A hunting term; the antiquated process of cutting off the tips of puppy's ears for appearances.

roundness (1) The convexity of the profile of the horse's topline. (2) The circular, as opposed to the linear or flat quality, characterizing the movements or action of the horse's limbs.

round pen *see* BULL PEN

round the world *see* MILL

round turn A cutting term; said of a horse who, when working a cow, walks through the turn rather than planting his hind legs and swinging his forelegs around the planted hind in an arc.

round up Also known as catch up, gather, or rodeo; the driving together of cattle or other animals for inspection, branding, and the like, generally from pasture.

Round-up Wagon *see* CHUCK WAGON

roundworms Also known as nematodes; a class of parasites infecting the horse; most lay eggs, yet some produce living larvae and the life-cycle may be direct or indirect (involving an intermediate host); found in the small intestine: *Strongyloides westeri* (q.v.) and *Parascaris equorum* (q.v.), the cecum and colon: *Strongylus vulgaris* (q.v.), *Strongylus edentatus* (q.v.), and *Strongylus equinus*(q.v.) and the stomach: *Habronema* (q.v.), *Drascheia megastoma* (q.v.), and *Trichostongylus axei* (q.v.).

rount Also known as grizzle or grissel; an early English term; a horse with a roan (q.v.) coat mixed with white or peach.

rouse A hunting term; to drive from cover as in a stag (q.v.).

Roussin One of two sub-breeds of the Breton (q.v.), the other being the Sommier (q.v.); found in southern France and some central parts of Brittany during the Middle

Ages; believed to have descended from the Bidet Breton (q.v.); popular as a saddle horse, especially by military leaders, due to its comfortable, ambling fourth gait and, perhaps, as a food source; was more slender and finer boned than the Sommier.

route Also known as route race or distance of ground; an American racing term; any horse race 1⅛ miles (1.8 km) long or longer, generally around two bends.

router An American racing term; a horse who runs best in races of 1⅛ miles (1.8 km) or longer.

route race *see* ROUTE

rowel (1) The revolving wheel-like attachment of the spur (q.v.) neck; of many varieties including smooth-edged, notched, or having sharp points or projections. (2) A quick goad or prick with a rowelled spur (q.v.)

Royal Canadian Mounted Police Also known as Mounties; the famous mounted police force of Canada; founded in 1873.

Royal College of Veterinary Surgeons The governing body of the veterinary profession in Great Britain and Ireland, organized in 1844.

Royal Horse of Europe *see* ANDALUSIAN

Royal International *see* ROYAL INTERNATIONAL HORSE SHOW

Royal International Horse Show Also known as London International, Royal International, and formerly as the International Horse Show; an international horse show first held in 1907 in London, England and continued there annually except during the years of 1915 to 1919, 1933, and 1940 to 1944; classes are open to hunters, hacks, cobs, and ponies under saddle, Hackneys, and jumpers; granted the prefix of Royal in 1957.

Royal International Horse Show (CHI) Also known as Championnat Hippique International or the acronym CHI; any horse show having competitions open to one or more international riders who participate as individuals authorized by their National Federation, at the invitation of the hosting National Federation, or by personal invitation; no team or individual competitor is ever officially sent to such shows.

Royal International Horse Show (CHIO) Also known as Championnat Hippique International Officiel or by the acronym CHIO; any international horse show which, being authorized by its National Horse Show Federation, and having obtained consent from the FEI (q.v.), is entered into the FEI Calendar; riders are sent to such shows officially by their National Horse Show Federations.

Royal Society for the Prevention of Cruelty to Animals A British organization founded in 1824 to encourage kindness and prevent cruelty to animals.

RSHANA *see* RUSSIAN SPORT HORSE ASSOCIATION OF NORTH AMERICA

RSS *see* REGISTERED SHOEING SMITH

ruano Refers to point color; light flaxen points; sometimes used in combination with other color distinctions for greater color specificity, e.g. chestnut (q.v.) ruano.

rubber band Also known as developer; an elastic band; a resilient cohesive solid made from the sap of certain tropical trees and shrubs used to hold show braids in the mane and tail.

rubber curry comb An oval, round, or square-shaped, hand-held instrument made of rubber and having rows of short rubber teeth or indentations on one side and a loop through which the hand is passed on the other; used to massage the horse, clean dirt and debris from the horse's coat, and to clean grooming brushes.

rubber shoe A horseshoe (q.v.) popular for use on horses employed in slow road work; is clipped, thicker than conventional shoes, and manufactured of rubber with a steel center; fitted cold.

rub-down To rub the horse with a rough towel, usually following exercise, to promote circulation, reduce fatigue, and dry the coat.

rubefacient Any substance applied externally to the horse's body to reduce pain and heal trauma; produces mild to moderate heat and skin redness without a blister (q.v.); normally applied 36 hours post-injury.

rug *see* HORSE BLANKET

rug fillet *see* FILLET STRING

rugged up Said of a horse wearing a horse blanket (q.v.).

ruined Said of a spoiled horse, or one who does not obey the aids; generally due to rider, owner, or trainer error.

rule off *see* SUSPEND NO. 2

rumble The rear-most seat in a horse-drawn vehicle such as a Road Coach (q.v.); built to accommodate two grooms, is supported by iron branches above the hind boot.

Rummy *see* RED RUM

rump *see* CROUP NO. 1

Rum Pony An ancient strain of Highland Pony (q.v.) found on the island of Coll, Scotland; limited numbers remain; is small, sturdy, and generally has a grullo or chestnut coat and a pale mane.

run (1) Also known as running; a hunting term; the period of time when the hounds are actually on the line of the fox (q.v.). (2) A Western term; also known as gallop; a fast, four-beat gait in which each foot strikes the ground separately, the sequence being near hind, off hind, near fore, and off fore or vice versa. (3) A cutting term; the 2½ minute time period allotted to each cutting (q.v.) contestant in a competition during which the cutter attempts to cut and work as many calves as possible from the herd. (4) A racing term; the position a horse takes at the finish line, as in to run fourth. (6) *see* RUN OF THE FOX

Runabout An American four-wheeled, horse-drawn, general-purpose vehicle; accommodated two forward-facing passengers; was hung on a perch undercarriage with two elliptic springs; some were designed with a parasol top.

run a hole through the wind Also known as punch holes in the horizon (Brit); a racing term; said of a very fast horse.

runaway (1) *see* BOLT NO. 2. (2) A race or event decisively or easily won.

runcy *see* COBB

run down (1) A racing term; said of a horse who scrapes the flesh off his heels on the track surface while racing; may be associated with weak pasterns. (2) Weak or tired.

run-down bandage A 3 to 6 inch (7.5–15 cm) wide bandage wrapped around the horse's lower leg and fetlock to provide support and prevent abrasive injury to the fetlocks when they sink groundward during weight-bearing in races or workouts.

run-down boots *see* TENDON BOOTS

run heel A hunting term; said of the hounds (q.v.) when they hit the line of the fox (q.v.) and run it back in the direction from which it came.

run his foil *see* DOUBLE BACK

run in (1) An American racing term; said of a horse who unexpectedly wins a race. (2) A British jumping or steeplechase term; the distance from the last fence or hurdle to the winning post.

run in the money *see* IN THE MONEY

run mute A hunting term; hounds who run after the quarry (q.v.) so fast they are unable to speak (q.v.).

runner (1) A racing term; one who runs to and from the mutuel windows to place bets for those seated in club boxes. (2) A racing term; any horse entered to compete in a horse race. (3) *see* KEEPER

running (1) The act of one who runs. (2) *see* RUNNING DOWNHILL. (3) *see* RUN NO. 2. (4) To compete in a contest. (5) Having a chance to win a contest, e.g. "Secretariat was in the running." (6) *see* HUNTING NO. 1

running a train scent A hunting term; a drag hunt (q.v.) race popular in late 16th and early 17th-century England; the predecessor of drag hunting (q.v.); a drag (q.v.) was laid in a pattern closely simulating the run of the wild fox, hounds were put on the line (q.v.) to run it at racing pace; the horse in the lead at the end of the drag was declared the winner.

running downhill Also known as running; said of a horse when he takes quick, hurried strides with little or no balance or rhythm, very little suspension, and too much weight on the forehand.

running gear *see* CARRIAGE NO. 1

running heel *see* HEEL NO. 3

running iron The predecessor of the modern branding iron (q.v.); a ½ inch (1.27 cm) wide iron rod slightly curved at one end.

running loose (1) A racing term; said of a horse who runs unbacked (q.v.) in a horse race due to the owner's or stable's lack of confidence in his ability. (2) Said of a horse who has lost his rider. (3) A racing term; said of a horse who had been carrying big weights in lower class handicaps and who is now carrying a lower weight in a higher class race, as in "He'll think he's running loose with just that weight on his back."

running martingale Also known as rings, training fork, or training yoke; a Y-shaped, split, auxiliary rein; assists bit action and helps to moderate the horse's head and neck position with rein pressure; a single adjustable strap attached to the girth (q.v.) on one end which passes between the forelegs and divides into two branches at the base of the neck; each branch ends with a ring through which the left and right reins pass.

running out (1) *see* RUN OUT. (2) Said of a horse turned out to grass.

running over a horse *see* RUN THROUGH

running quick mount Also known as flying mount; a method of mounting a horse; to run towards a standing horse, jump with the left foot into the left stirrup, and quickly swing the right leg over the saddle; requires a quiet horse.

running rail *see* INSIDE RAIL

running rank A racing term; said of a horse who refuses to be restrained or rated (q.v.) early in the race to conserve his energies for a push later on.

running reins Two separate leather straps used to control the head position of the horse; differ from draw reins (q.v.) in that they are not held by a rider or driver; adjacently attached on one end to the girth, pass between the horse's legs, and then one rein passes through the left bit ring and the other through the right bit ring; the reins then return to the surcingle (q.v.) or roller (q.v.) where they are attached.

running up light Said of a poorly muscled horse, particularly over the haunches.

running W A contraption used in the movie industry to tumble a horse headfirst to the ground when necessary for stunts; superseded by a toe tapper (q.v.); a cable runs from screws placed between the horseshoe and hoof of both front feet to a ring on a surcingle, where the two cables run into a single cable drawn off the horse at an slight angle and anchored to a stake in the ground; the length of cable attached to the stake determines the distance the horse can travel before the end of the cable is reached and the fall triggered.

running walk A natural, inherited, loose, four-beat gait, intermediate in speed between the walk and the rack (q.v.), in which each foot strikes the ground separately at regular intervals: left fore, right hind, right fore, left hind; the hind hooves may overstep the print of the fore by as much as 24 inches (61 cm) and the speed varies from 9 to 20 mph (14–32 kmph); characterized by a bobbing or nodding of the head, flopping of the ears, and a clicking of the teeth in rhythm with the movement of the legs; the center of balance is somewhat to the rear so that the horse appears to squat and there is no suspension; a faster gait than the flat-foot walk; the middle gait of the Tennessee Walker (q.v.); different from running in the walk, which is an incorrect form of the normal walk characterized by the loss of the true four-beat rhythm and too much weight on the forehand.

run of the fox Also known as run; a

hunting term; the route traveled by a fox (q.v.).

run on heart Said of horse of great pride and stamina; literally, a horse with a larger-than-normal heart which, due to increased blood oxygenation, has extraordinary stamina; the average size of a horse's heart is 8 to 10 pounds (3.63–4.54 kg); extraordinary race horses such as Secretariat (q.v.) and Phar Lap (q.v.), had hearts weighing 20 and 21 pounds (9.072 and 9.53 kgs) pounds, respectively

run out (1) A racing term; said of a horse who finishes out of the money (q.v.). (2) A racing term; said of a horse who prefers to run along the outside rail. (3) Also known as running out; a jumping term; said of a horse who deliberately avoids jumping an obstacle by running to one side or the other of it.

run-out-bit A racing bit designed to give the rider extra leverage on one side; used to prevent the horse from bearing out (q.v.) to the left or right.

runs hot and cold *see* IN-AND-OUTER

run through Also known as running over a horse; a cutting term; said of a cow that tries to run under a horse in an attempt to return to the herd.

run-under heels *see* UNDERRUN HEELS

run up a stirrup iron To slide the stirrup iron (q.v.) to the top of the stirrup leather (q.v.).

run wide A racing term; said of a horse who runs far from the inside rail (q.v.) and therefore covers extra ground.

rupture *see* HERNIA

rushing A dressage term; said of a horse whose movement (q.v.) is too fast and hurried and lacks balance and rhythm.

Russian Cab *see* DROSKY

Russian Droschki *see* DROSKY

Russian Heavy Draft A small Russian heavy-draft breed gradually developed for agricultural work in 1850; descended from local mares put to a variety of heavy draft breeds including Swedish Ardennes (q.v.), Belgian Draft (q.v.), Percheron (q.v.), and Orlov Trotter (q.v.); is strong, hardy, quiet and energetic, and stands 14.1 to 15 hands; may have a chestnut, roan, or bay coat, is well balanced and muscular, has well-sprung ribs, full mane, tail, and forelock, short, lightly feathered legs, and a short, straight back.

Russian Saddle Horse Also known as Orlov-Rostopchin; a horse breed descended from the Orlov Trotter (q.v.) crossed with the Rostopchin, a horse of English Thoroughbred (q.v.) and Arab (q.v.) extraction.

Russian Sport Horse Association of North America Also known by the acronym RSHANA; an American organization formed in 1994 to cultivate a U.S. market for Russian-bred horses and those from other republics of the former Soviet Union; horses eligible for registration include the Russian Saddle horse (q.v.), Orlov Trotter (q.v.), Russian Trakehener, Budyonny (q.v.), Ukrainskaya, Akhal Teké (q.v.), Don (q.v.), Latvian (q.v.), Russian Hannoverian, Tersky (q.v.), and crosses of these native breeds.

Russian Steppe Horse *see* KUSTANAIR

Russian style *see* TROIKA

Russian Trotter *see* ORLOV TROTTER

Rustic Cart A general-purpose version of the horse-drawn, two-wheeled Dogcart (q.v.); had slatted sides and seated four back-to-back.

rut (1) The noise emitted by a stag (q.v.) when desiring to mate. (2) Sexual arousal of deer, stag, and some other animals due to hormone changes, as during the mating season.

rutting season The period during which deer, stag, and other animals experience sexual arousal associated with mating.

rye (1) Also known as rye grass; a hardy annual grass, *Secale cereale*, widely grown for grain and as a cover crop; neither the grass nor grain is a popular feed for horses as the only available rye products for livestock are mill by-products such as rye middlings which are relatively low in fiber, a poor source of vitamins or minerals, and not particularly palatable; has a digestible protein content of 12 to 13 percent; grain mixtures should never contain more than ⅓ rye which should be processed rather than whole; susceptible to the fungus *Claviceps purpuria* which produces the compound ergot (q.v.). (2) The seed of rye.

rye grass *see* RYE

rye grass hay Cut and dried grass hay made from rye (q.v.) following harvest of the grain; is generally low in palatability and contains a fiber content of about 38 percent and an incomplete digestible protein content of around 4 percent.

rye straw Any of several dried rye grasses; highly prized as a stuffing for horse collars.

S

sabino Also known as flecked roan, buttermilk roan, or calico paint; refers to an asymmetrical coat color pattern in which the white patches are variable ranging from distinct, sharp patches to small spots of white on the background color; a pattern of both white patches and flecks which usually cover the belly is common; the head is usually white, the upper lip pigmented, and the legs white, although a dark leg is not uncommon; minimum acceptable markings consist of three or four white stockings (q.v.) and a bald (q.v.) or apron (q.v.) face; predominantly white sabinos will have colored ears, a colored chest patch, and in some cases, a colored patch on the flank and base of the tail; solid white sabinos will have colored ears, but are uncommon.

Sable Island Pony A Canadian pony breed descended from French stock imported from New England during the early 18th century; indigenous to Sable Island located off the coast of Nova Scotia; due to the lack of natural vegetation and harsh climate, evolved into an extremely hardy, frugal pony standing about 14 hands; the coat may be bay, brown, black, gray, or chestnut, has a heavy head, large ears with turned-in tips, a short neck which is broad at the base, short back, full girth, strong legs, and small hoof; lives in small groups consisting of one stallion and six to eight mares; used for riding and light harness.

sabre hocks *see* EXCESSIVE ANGULATION OF THE HOCK JOINTS

sabre-legged *see* SICKLE-HOCKED

sacrum The five sacral bones located below the lumbar vertebrae that fuse by birth and constitute the posterior pelvis.

sack out A breaking technique; to rope a horse, snub (q.v.) him to a post and let him struggle against an unbreakable halter as the handler flaps a burlap sack over his body; the horse ultimately submits out of exhaustion.

sacroiliac desmitis *see* HUNTER'S BUMPS

saddle (1) Also known as hull or wood; a girthed (q.v.), usually padded, covered seat attached to the horse's back by means of a girth, upon which a rider sits; preceded by a girthless cloth placed on the horse's back; treed saddles came into use by the cavalry soldiers of the Roman Empire; of various designs according to the purpose for which it is required. (2) To put a saddle upon a horse. (3) To mount a saddled horse. (4) Also known as pad; a cushion used under harness.

saddle airer Also known as saddle horse, saddle stand, or airer saddle; a wooden or metal, trestle-like stand upon which one or more saddles are placed to be aired when not in use.

saddle back *see* SWAY BACK

saddle backed *see* SWAY BACKED

saddle bags Also known as Spanish cantinas; a pair of covered, connected pouches laid across the back of a horse behind the saddle to which they are attached by saddle strings (q.v.).

saddle bars *see* STIRRUP BARS

saddle blanket Also known as blanket; any square or rectangular wool, cotton, or synthetic covering placed between the back of the horse and the saddle to absorb sweat, provide padding, and prevent galling (q.v.); sometimes confused with a saddle pad (q.v.).

saddle bow The arched front part or bow of a saddle, the top of which is the pommel (q.v.).

saddle bracket *see* SADDLE RACK

Saddlebred *see* AMERICAN SADDLEBRED

saddle bronc Any bronc (q.v.) ridden with a saddle.

saddle bronc riding A standard rodeo event in which a bronc rider (q.v.), using a regulation saddle, rides a bronco (q.v.); the rider is only allowed to use one rein attached to a halter (q.v.), may not touch or hold onto the saddle, the horse, or himself with the free hand, and must remain mounted for at least 10 seconds; the rider is judged on how hard the horse bucks, spurring action, and how well the horse was ridden.

saddle chamber *see* CHANNEL

saddle channel *see* CHANNEL

saddle cloth (1) *see* NUMNAH. (2) *see* NUMBER CLOTH

saddle crupper Also known as riding crupper or crupper (q.v.), riding tack consisting of a back strap attached on one end to the saddle skirt by means of metal dees and, on the other, to the crupper dock (q.v.) which is fitted under and around the base of the horse's tail; used to prevent the saddle from slipping forward onto the withers (q.v.).

saddle dee Any dee-ring (q.v.) when used on a saddle.

saddle fall A movie industry term; a maneuver performed by a stuntperson; to fall from a moving or standing horse on cue.

saddle flap *see* FLAP NO. 1

saddle fork *see* FORK NO. 1

saddle gaits Any of the horse's gaits including lateral gait (q.v.), slow gait (q.v.), and the rack (q.v.).

saddle hood *see* POMMEL

saddle horn Also known as horn; a horn-like prolongation of the pommel (q.v.) of a stock saddle (q.v.); has an enlarged, flat-topped head, is constructed of metal, fiberglass, or wood and covered with leather or rawhide.

Saddle Horse *see* AMERICAN SADDLEBRED

saddle horse (1) A horse suited or trained for riding. (2) *see* SADDLE ARIER

saddle leather Vegetable-tanned leather made of cattle hide used in saddlery.

saddle linen A linen covering sewn over the serge panel for cleanliness and to protect the serge (q.v.) from wear.

saddle marks An acquired mark (q.v.); altered hair or skin pigment due to abrasion or damage to the hair follicles as caused by a poorly fitted saddle or saddle blanket.

saddle pad Also known as pad; a piece of felt, cotton, wool, sheepskin, or synthetic material placed between the saddle and the horse to protect the back of the horse, provide padding, and absorb sweat; may be thin or thick, square, rectangular, or shaped to fit the contour of the saddle.

saddle panel *see* PANEL NO. 3

saddle patch (1) The area of body hair slightly larger than the shape of an English saddle, left after clipping the horse as an alternative to a body clip (q.v.). (2) *see* SADDLE PATCH CLIP

saddle patch clip Also known as saddle patch; to remove the horse's winter coat except for the area beneath the English saddle; an alternative to a full body clip (q.v.).

saddler One who makes, repairs, or deals in saddlery and other furnishings for horses.

saddle rack Also known as saddle bracket; a metal or wooden shelf-like support attached to a wall upon which a saddle rests when not in use.

saddlery (1) Also known as tack; the tack consisting of the bridle, saddle, etc. used on a horse which is to be ridden, not driven. (2) The shop and manufactured products of a saddler (q.v.). (3) The trade or craft of a saddler (q.v.).

saddle seat A riding style designed to showcase gaited breeds such as the American Saddlebred (q.v.) and Tennessee Walker (q.v.).

saddle seat saddle *see* CUTBACK SADDLE

saddle shy Said of a horse possessed of an abnormal fear of a saddle or being saddled.

saddle skirt (1) *see* SKIRT NO. 1. (2) *see* SKIRT NO. 2

saddle soap A mild soap used for cleansing and conditioning leather.

saddle sore (1) A gall (q.v.) or open sore on the horse's back, belly, or haunches at points of pressure from an ill-fitting or ill-adjusted saddle. (2) An irritation or sore on the parts of the rider chafed by the saddle.

saddle stand *see* SADDLE AIRER

saddle strings Narrow strips of leather attached to the front and rear skirts of a stock saddle (q.v.) used to tie objects to the saddle.

saddle tree Also known as tree; a form or frame around which a saddle is built; may be made of wood, metal, or synthetic materials reinforced with steel plates.

Saddle-type Pinto One of four Pinto (q.v.) conformation types developed with specific breed goals and standards in mind; an English horse of predominantly Thoroughbred (q.v.), Saddlebred (q.v.), Hackney (q.v.), or Tennessee Walking Horse (q.v.) breeding and conformation; displays the high head carriage and animated, high action necessary for standard gaited and parade events; may range from a fine, medium-sized animal to a tall, slightly heavier animal suitable for carrying heavy silver tack.

Sado A two-wheeled, horse-drawn taxi used on the island of Java, Indonesia to transport people and goods; generally pulled by a Java (q.v.).

safe Leather lining of some tack such as saddles, girths, etc. that prevents tack fittings such as buckles and bars from rubbing on the horse's hide and thus causing chafing, galling or rubbing against other portions of the tack to cause wear.

safed A horseshoe in which the ground-side surface of the medial branch is beveled; decreases the chance of the shoe being pulled off by the opposite foot, or injury if the horse interferes (q.v.).

safety *see* PENALTY 6

safety chain A heavy-link chain used in case either one or both drag shoes (q.v.) used on a horse-drawn vehicle is/are displaced; one end of the chain is affixed to the front axle alongside the drag shoe chain (q.v.) while the other is attached to a leather-covered hook secured to the fellow (q.v.) and iron tire.

safety stirrup A material fitting connected to the saddle by stirrup leathers (q.v.) used to support the rider's foot when seated in the saddle; designed to enable the rider to remove his foot quickly in the case of an accident or other emergency; available in a number of designs including those that break away from the rider's foot when torque is applied.

sagging back *see* HOLLOW BACK NO. 1

sainfoin Also spelled saintfoin; a European leguminous herb, *Onobrychis viciaefolia,* cultivated as a forage plant; grows best in chalk or limestone soil and is drought resistant.

Saint Christopher The patron saint of all travelers, and thus of horsemen.

saintfoin *see* SAINFOIN

Saint George The patron saint of horsemen.

Saint Hubert The patron saint of huntsmen.

sais (1) *see* SYCE; an Indian groom. (2) An ancient Russian equestrian game played by mounted herdsmen; a duel in which each rider attempts to grab his opponent by the hands or arms and pull him off his horse; participants are divided into weight classes.

Salerno An Italian warmblood native to the Maremma and Salerno; descended from the Neapolitan breed popular in the Middle Ages, crossed with Spanish and Oriental blood; the breeding program was suppressed in 1874 and it wasn't until the beginning of the 20th century that the breed was restored with the systematic introduction of Thoroughbred (q.v.) blood; the modern horse is quiet, balanced, and energetic, stands 16 to 16.2 hands, and may have any solid-color coat, with bay, black, and chestnut occurring most commonly; has a light head, long neck, pronounced and muscular withers, short loins, and a deep girth; historically a popular cavalry mount, now used as an all-purpose riding horse, particularly suited to jumping.

saline Consisting of or containing salt.

saline solution Typically, a 0.9 percent solution of salt in water.

Salisbury boot *see* SALISBURY COACH BOX

Salisbury Coach Box Also known as Salisbury boot; an oval-shaped, leather covered 'box' or container placed on the front beds of a horse-drawn carriage; surmounted by the coachman's seat.

Salisbury gag *see* SALISBURY GAG BIT

Salisbury gag bit Also known as Salisbury gag; a gag bit (q.v.) consisting of a single thin jointed mouthpiece with large loose-ring gags (q.v.) used with a single set of reins; has a thinner mouthpiece than the Balding gag bit (q.v.).

Salisbury, Marchioness Emily Mary (1749–1835) Believed to be the first female Master of Foxhounds (q.v.) having held that position for the Hertfordshire Hunt in Great Britain from 1793 to 1819 at which time she retired on her 70th birthday.

saliva The watery, slightly viscid, acid fluid, produced in and secreted by the salivary glands of the mouth; serves to correct the food pH to neutral or slightly alkaline so that it can be readily absorbed further down the intestinal tract, and to moisten the mouth and food; contains the enzyme ptyalin, which starts the digestive process before the food reaches the stomach; horses may secrete up to 7 or more gallons (31 liters) per day depending on the moisture content of the feed – the larger the portion of hay, chaff, and grain in the ration, the greater amount of saliva produced.

saliva test A chemical analysis of the horse's saliva (q.v.) performed to detect the presence of drugs or other prohibited substances; routinely conducted on those race horses who finish in the money (q.v.).

sallenders A sub-acute or chronic condition of the skin involving an eruption on the front of the hock joint of the hind leg, characterized by scurfy thickening of the skin, watery discharge, and hair loss; may be caused by injury or infection; (obs).

sallengs Fringe on Hungarian harness.

salmonellosis A disease caused by any of a number of rod-shaped bacteria, genus, *Salmonella*: *S. typhimurium*, *S. anatum*, *S. newport*, *S. enteritidis*, or *S. heidelberg*, associated with food poisoning or intestinal inflammations; most commonly occurs sporadically without apparent predisposing causes; infection can occur from the environment via feed or water, by contact with active carriers, or activated in the intestines of carriers by stress as due to transport or surgery; may also occur within two to four days following stress due to worming, overtraining, hot weather, close stocking, yarding, or transport of groups of horses, antibiotic therapy, or food depravation; two clinical forms: *mild* characterized by depression, anorexia, fever, and loose feces which is generally self-limiting and *severe* characterized by sudden onset, severe depression, anorexia, abdominal pain, and explosive, liquid, bloodstained, foul-smelling diarrhea usually containing mucosal elements occurring within 6 to 24 hours; may result in death.

salmon marks Refers to coat color pattern; white hairs on the quarters and back; (obs).

salt *see* SODIUM CHLORIDE

salt block Also known as salt lick; a natural or man-made block or irregularly shaped chunk of sodium chloride (q.v.) upon which horses lick; available in weights from 1 to 50 pounds (450 g–23 kg) or more, mineralized or plain; a dietary supplement.

Salterno A Peruvian-bred Criollo (q.v.); one of three subtypes: the Chola (q.v.), Morochuco (q.v.), and Costeño (q.v.); descended from Spanish stock brought to South America by the Conquistadors in the 16th century.

salt lick (1) A place where animals lick an exposed natural or artificial salt deposit. (2) *see* SALT BLOCK

salute To bow or otherwise show homage or courtesy; to greet or hail, as by means of a nod of the head or tip of the cap, both of which are used to indicate to the judge(s) that a performer/racer is ready to begin an event, give a sign of greeting, request to be excused or, as in racing, to indicate a request to dismount.

salve A soothing ointment applied to wounds or sores.

Sam Chee *see* LEGEND OF THE EIGHT HORSES

Sandalwood An Indonesian pony breed indigenous to the islands of Sumba and Sumbawa; named for the island's principal export of the same name; resembles the Batak (q.v.) due to the common influence of the Arab (q.v.); stands 12 to 13 hands, has a small, well-shaped head, a full forelock, mane, and tail, wide chest, deep girth, and strong, hard legs; the coat may be any color and is generally quite fine; is quiet and energetic, quite fast for its size, and possessed of good endurance; used for bareback (q.v.) racing, riding, packing, light draft, and farm work.

sand colic Digestive distress resulting from the casual and inadvertent consumption of sand while grazing or eating hay rations directly from the ground; precolic symptoms include mild discomfort accompanied by diarrhea; in full colic, sand accumulated in the intestine may harden and form an enterolith (q.v.) which traps intestinal gases and stretches the bowel wall.

sand bath (1) A natural or artificial hollow or depression, generally denuded of vegetation, in which a horse will roll. (2) Said of a horse when he rolls in sand or dirt.

sand crack Also known as crack; a vertical break in the hoof wall beginning at hoof ground level and moving upward following the line of the tubules to the coronary band (q.v.); may occur in any part of the hoof wall, although generally on the front of the hoof where it is called a toe crack (q.v.) or on the side of the hoof where it is known as a quarter crack (q.v.); can result from genetics, dry hooves, injury to the coronet, excessive hoof length, fungal infection, uneven weight-bearing, concussion from work on hard ground, and excessive rasping; although lameness is usually not present, deep sand cracks can result in severe lameness and when unattended may result in false quarter (q.v.) and damage to the laminae (q.v.).

sandshifter *see* PACER

sandy bay Also known as honey bay or mealy bay; refers to coat color; the lightest shade of bay (q.v.); a light red coat that appears yellow.

San Fratello A Sicilian horse bred in the wild; descended from native stock crossed with Spanish Anglo-Arab (q.v.), Anglo-Arab (q.v.), Salerno (q.v.), and, recently, Nonius (q.v.) blood; is strong, powerful, stands 15 to 16 hands, weighs 1,100 to 1,300 pounds (499–590 kg), has a brown, bay, or black coat, a slightly heavy head, sloping croup, wide and deep chest, and prominent withers; used for riding, light draft, and packing.

sanitary ride A racing term; said of a horse who did not give his all in a race, or of a jockey who rode a race so safely as to diminish his chances of winning.

Sarcoptes A parasitic mite with one species, *Sarcoptes scabiei*, and numerous varieties; infestation causes sarcoptic mange (q.v.).

sarcoptic mange Also known as scabies; the most serious form of mange (q.v.); caused by infestation of a parasitic mite, *Sarcoptes scabiei* var. *equi*; spreads quickly because the mites burrow into the epidermis making treatment difficult; the disease commences with patchy hair loss, papule formation, and intense continuous itching; the hair becomes thin and broken, abrasions are present, and the skin is hard and folded; emaciation is progressive and death may result from exhaustion; the disease usually attacks thin-skin areas while areas covered in long hair or the extremities are not usually involved; most severe in spring and declines in summer and fall.

Sardinian Also known as Miniature Sardinian Donkey or Sardinian Donkey; a type of Miniature Mediterranean Donkey (q.v.) native to the Italian island of Sardinia; an ancient donkey breed which lives in the wild at about 2,000 feet (600 m) above sea level where it survives on sparse vegetative growth; females stand 12.1 to 12.2 and males 12.2 to 13 hands; the coat is generally bay, brown, black, or liver chestnut (q.v.); has a square head, heavy jaw, long neck, full mane, tail, and forelock, slightly hollow back, slender legs, and small feet; cow hocks (q.v.) are common; is lively, highly strung, rebellious, frugal, and agile; used for farm work and riding.

Sardinian Anglo-Arab A Sardinian horse breed developed from Arab (q.v.) stallions put to native mares; in the early 16th century, the breed was improved with Andalusian (q.v.) stallions; in the beginning of the 18th century, the breed went into a period of decline, but was revived in the early 20th century with the input of Arab and ultimately, Thoroughbred (q.v.) blood; stands 15.1 to 16 hands plus, has a light, square head, pronounced withers, straight or slightly hollow back, short loins, full tail, broad chest and full girth, thinly cannoned, but strong legs due to bone quality, and a gray, chestnut, or bay coat; is hardy, swift and has good staying power; used for riding and makes a good jumper.

Sardinian Donkey *see* SARDINIAN

satchel A small pouch used to hold the watch carried by a coach guard.

saturation theory A unsubstantiated principle of breeding; it is believed that the offspring of a mare repeatedly put to the same stallion will increasingly resemble the stallion.

saucer fractures Small fissure fractures (q.v.) of the bone caused by stress or fatigue, the result of repetitive loading of the bone; occur more frequently in the United States than Britain, probably due to the different training and racing conditions; almost unique to young Thoroughbred (q.v.) race horses.

Saugor The Indian Army Equitation School formerly located in central India, closed in 1939.

Saumur A town in western France where the School of Mounted Troop Instruction known as the French Cavalry School of Saumur (q.v.) was established in the early 18th century; now the home of the Cadre Noir (q.v.).

sausage boot Also known as doughnut or doughnut boot; a well-stuffed leather or rubber ring with an adjustable strap, placed around the pastern of a horse prone to capped elbow (q.v.).

savage (1) A mean horse, particularly one who attempts to bite another horse or person. (2) Said of a horse; to bite or attempt to bite another horse or person.

savaging A vice; said of a horse; the act of attempting to bite another horse or person.

Savanilla Phaeton A light, horse-drawn carriage or Phaeton (q.v.) widely used throughout Thailand from the 19th century; a semi-open cab hung on sideways elliptical springs in the front and sideways semi-elliptical springs (q.v.) in the rear; drawn by a single horse or large pony in shafts.

save ground A racing term; to cover the shortest distance in a race by hugging the inside rail on the turns and running straight on the stretches (q.v.).

sawdust Bedding (q.v.) consisting of small bits and other particles of wood produced by the operation of a saw; is finer than wood shavings (q.v.), inexpensive, and easy to obtain, but like shavings, is difficult to store; also contains wood chips and splinters and has a high dust factor which makes it unsuitable for horses with allergies or other respiratory ailments; in some cases, combined with shavings to improve absorbency.

sawhorse stance The position assumed by a horse afflicted with tetanus (q.v.); both fore and hind legs are spread and extended forward and rearward, respectively.

scab A crust formed over a wound when healing.

scabies *see* SARCOPTIC MANGE

scale *see* SCALE OF WEIGHTS

scale of weights Also known as scale; a

racing term; an official tabulation of the correct weights for horses of different age groups to carry, for all distance races, and at all times of the year in non-handicap races.

scale weights A racing term; the extra pounds carried by an older horse running against a younger horse in a weight-for-age race (q.v.).

scallywag A worthless horse.

scalping Limb contact when the toe of the forefoot hits the hairline at or above the coronary band (q.v.) on the hind foot of the same side; impact the dorsal face of the pastern or cannon bone is common.

scapula Also known as wing or shoulder bone; the large, triangular, flat bone that lies on the outside of the front of the chest, to which are attached many of the muscles that unite the forelimb to the trunk.

Scarborough Phaeton A four-wheeled, horse-drawn carriage similar in design to a four-wheeled Dogcart (q.v.); had back-to-back passenger seating for four, the body was hung on four elliptic springs.

scarf (1) Also known as Newmarket tie; a long or rectangular piece of white material worn by members of the drag (q.v.) prior to the 20th century; resembled a stock tie (q.v.).

scarf pin *see* STOCK PIN

scarlet coat *see* PINK COAT

scattered white hairs A leg marking; white hairs founds on any part of the legs; may be described as "heavy," "numerous" or "faint".

scenic route *see* OVERLAND

scent The odor of the fox or other quarry (q.v.) emitted from the tail and pad glands; generally left on the ground, thus leaving a trail or line for the hounds (q.v.) to follow; dry, hard ground does not hold a scent well, while vegetation such as grass and shrubs does.

scent hound A hunting dog who uses his nose instead of sight to pursue quarry (q.v.); include stag hounds, buck hounds, foxhounds (q.v.), coon hounds (q.v.), basset hounds (q.v.), beagles (q.v.), and harriers (q.v.).

schalanken Fly fringe (q.v.) on a Hungarian harness.

schaukel Also known as swing or see-saw; a German dressage term; a prescribed sequence of rein-backs (q.v.) interspersed with a few forward steps of walk performed on a straight line with the hooves leaving the ground distinctly and without a halt between steps; the backwards movement is performed in two-time while the forward movement is performed in four-time.

Schleswig Horse *see* SCHLESWIG HEAVY DRAFT

Schleswig Heavy Draft Also known as Schleswig Horse; a coldblood originating in Schleswig-Holstein, Germany in the 19th century from which the name derived; descended from the Jutland (q.v.) to which Yorkshire Coach Horse (q.v.), Thoroughbred (q.v.), Norfolk Punch (q.v.), and more recently Boulonnais (q.v.) and Brenton (q.v.) blood was introduced; stands 15.1 to 16.1 hands and may weigh upwards of 1,700 pounds (771 kg); has a well-proportioned head, small eyes, a short, arched neck, low, broad withers, a strong, short back, short and muscular legs with feathering (q.v.), and large round hooves; the stud book was established in 1891; historically used for drawing Omnibuses (q.v.), farm work, and transportation; due to mechanization its numbers are on the decline, although it is still used for draft.

Schlitz 40-horse hitch Also known as 40-horse hitch or Forty Horse Hitch; a hitch of 40 chestnut Belgian Draft horses (q.v.) with white blazes and light-colored manes and tails débuted in 1972 by the Schlitz Beer Company in the United States; is driven by one man and has an overall length of 135 feet (41 m), including wagon and horses; the driver holds five reins in each hand; the hitch is accompanied by outriders to assist in case of emergency.

school (1) Any prescribed area, in which the horse is exercised, ridden, or trained. (2) Also known as school work; to train or educate a horse, with or without a rider;

involves teaching the horse movements and gaits required for future use or refining those movements and gaits previously taught through specific exercises; schooling techniques differ in some respects for each riding discipline. (3) To warm up a horse prior to competition.

schooled Said of a horse trained, generally at home, to do what is required in competition or races.

school exercises *see* SCHOOL FIGURES

school figures Also known as school exercises, schooling figures, or manège figures; any exercise performed on horseback to improve the balance, rhythm, timing, and use of aids of the rider, the rider's control over the horse, and the flexibility, rhythm, and smoothness of the horse's gaits; include serpentine (q.v.), figure eight (q.v.), changes of rein, transitions, and turns and circles.

school horse (1) Any calm, obedient horse with correct basic training used by a trainer or riding school as a mount (q.v.) for new or inexperienced riders in training. (2) Historically, a horse trained to an ultimate level in dressage.

schooling The act of training or educating a horse.

schooling figures *see* SCHOOL FIGURES

schooling list An American racing term; a list of horses eligible to train at the starting gate (q.v.) before being allowed to race.

schoolmaster An experienced and well-trained horse whose ability generally exceeds that of the rider; is generally better trained than a school horse (q.v. No. 1).

school movements A dressage term; any action, gait, and/or figure performed to strengthen and supple the horse and improve his versatility for riding; include: shoulder-in (q.v.), renvers (q.v.), travers (q.v.), half-pass (q.v.), flying changes (q.v.), pirouettes (q.v.), etc.

School of Mounted Troop Instruction *see* FRENCH CAVALRY SCHOOL AT SAUMUR

School of Saumur *see* FRENCH CAVALRY SCHOOL AT SAUMUR

school rider One trained or specializing in dressage (q.v.).

school riding Riding exercises from the Classical School (q.v.).

schools above the ground *see* AIRS ABOVE THE GROUND

school work *see* SCHOOL NO. 2

Schwarzwald Also known as a Schwarzwalder; a small, agile, cold blood (q.v.) from the upper regions of the Black Forest, Germany.

Schwarzwalder *see* SCHWARZWALD

Schweiken A hardy horse breed indigenous to the former area of East Prussia, now Germany and Poland; contributed to the development of the Trakehner (q.v.).

schwung A dressage term; the condition in which the energy produced by the horse's hind legs is transmitted through a swinging back and manifested in the horse's elastic, whole-body movement.

scintigraphy A lameness diagnostic technique; distribution of intravenously injected radioactive isotopes into the bones and soft tissues of the limbs is evaluated.

scissors A vaulting (q.v.) term; a movement in which the mounted vaulter shifts between forward- and rearward-facing positions; the vaulter (q.v.), starting from a basic seat (q.v.), swings both legs forward and then backward high above the croup of the horse and, when almost in a handstand, he rotates his hips 90 degrees to the inside, continuing the rotation until he straddles the horse facing forward; the vaulter then performs the same movement in the opposite direction, ending the movement in a basic seat, facing forwards; a compulsory movement (q.v.) performed in competitions.

sclera Also known as white of the eye; the dense, fibrous, opaque, white outer coating of the eyeball which is contiguous with the cornea; characteristic of the eye of the Appaloosa (q.v.).

sclerostome *see* LARGE STRONGYLE

scope (1) The athletic ability of the horse. (2) A dressage term; reach and roundness of a movement.

score (1) A rodeo term; the distance the lead calf or steer is given from the chute opening to the score line (q.v.); is usually determined by the arena size, with 8 to 15 feet (3.6–7 m) average. (2) A roping term; to hold the horse in the box (q.v.) to train him not to anticipate the release of the calf. (3) The point aggregate accumulated by an individual or team in competition. (4) A racing term; to win a bet or a race. (5) A harness racing term; a lap of the racetrack's circumference.

scoring (1) A harness racing term; the number of preliminary, warm-up laps taken before beginning the race; generally no more than three score (q.v.) arc permitted. (2) The act of evaluating the ability of a rider or team to ride within the rules of the competition; determined by one or more judges on a point basis. (3) A preliminary warm-up ride prior to the start of competition.

score line A rodeo term; the line that marks the distance of the predetermined head start the steer or calf is given before the roper leaves the box (q.v.); length varies with arena size.

score well A roping term; said of a roping horse who does not anticipate release of the calf from the chute, waiting instead for a signal from the roper.

scorpion A cutting term; an athletic, agile, quick, stylish-moving horse.

scotch collar The housing over the collar (q.v.) of draft show harness, as differentiated from Scottish collar (q.v.).

Scottish collar A heavy and ornately peaked show collar.

scotched Said of a horseshoe in which the outer edge slopes outward from the hoof surface towards the ground; commonly used on draft horses to create a greater support base and the appearance of a larger foot.

scotching Also known as propping; a reining term; said of a horse who bounces in a slide (q.v.) rather than setting his rear feet and walking with the front; hock engagement is restricted.

scrambler A horse who, when trailered and in motion, overreacts to anything touching his sides; he feels as though what is touching him is trying to push him over and he reacts by pushing back, and in some cases falls over.

scraper Also known as sweat scraper or water scraper; any hand-held, thin metal, plastic, or wooden tool used to remove liquid such as sweat or water from a horse's coat and to gently massage the main muscle masses; usually concave in appearance and approximately 6 to 12 inches (15–30 cm) long and 2 inches (5 cm) wide; from *streetle* an ancient Roman tool used to scrape and collect sweat and olive oil from men's bodies for use by the cosmetics industry.

scratch (1) Also known as forfeit; to withdraw a horse from an equestrian event after officially entered. (2) A rodeo term; to spur a horse vigorously in a continuous raking motion from front to back; compulsory in all rodeo events.

scratched Said of a horse formally withdrawn from an event or competition.

scratches Also known as greasy heal, grease heal, greased heel, or cracked heels; dermatophilus (q.v.) infection of the lower limbs, specifically the pastern and fetlock, involving the skin and its glands in the hollow of the heel; caused by the organism *Dermatophilus congolensis* which gains entry into the skin when dirty and/or saturated by prolonged rain; most common in the winter; occurs on the hind legs below the fetlock on horses with marked feather (q.v.) or heavy hair growth, stabled in unhygienic conditions or grazing in pasture subject to flooding; the skin in the affected area becomes moist, sensitive to the touch, thickens, develops grapes (q.v.), and has an offensive odor; is usually accompanied by pus formation; lameness may or may not result; infection is transmittable to man.

scratch sheet A racing term; a daily

publication listing graded handicaps, tips, and scratches at a specific racetrack.

screaming scent *see* BURNING SCENT

screw An inferior, unsound, or worn-out horse; (sl).

screw fixation A procedure in which steel-alloy screws are surgically inserted into a fractured bone to hold it together.

screwworm Larvae (q.v.) of the screw-worm fly (q.v.).

screwworm fly One of many species of blow fly (q.v.); lays 200 to 400 eggs on edges of wounds, cuts, bites, navels of newborns, and other locations on the skin; after 12 to 21 hours, the larvae hatch, crawl into the wound and burrow into the flesh where they feed on wound fluids and live tissue; in 5 to 7 days they exit the wound, drop to the ground, and burrow into the soil; infected wounds characteristically contain a number of screwworm larvae, are usually foul smelling, and contain copious amounts of a reddish-brown fluid.

scrotal hernia Descent of intra-abdominal tissue through the inguinal canal into the scrotum, resulting in an enlarged scrotal sac; may or may not correct itself in foals; in older horses requires immediate surgical attention.

scrotum The sac containing the testes (q.v.) which hangs between the thighs of the male horse.

scrub (1) A low-grade horse. (2) Also known as scrubbing; a racing term; said of the action of the jockey's hands, legs, and whip at the finish of a race; the act of riding a finish in a horse race. (3) Also known as riding hands and heels; a British term; the action of the jockey's hands and feet (heels) at the finish of a race.

scrub bashing Also called scrub dashing; an Australian term; to chase cattle, often semi-wild, through timbered country during round up.

scrubbing *see* SCRUB NO. 2

scrub dashing *see* SCRUB BASHING

scurry A show jumping contest conducted over a course consisting of fences up to, but not exceeding, 4 feet (1.2 m) high; the event is scored on the basis of time and faults with a refusal carrying no penalty; the rider with the fastest time and least number of faults wins.

scut The tail of a hare.

scutch grass *see* BERMUDA GRASS

SDF *see* SYNCHRONOUS DIAPHRAGMATIC FLUTTER

Seabiscuit A rough-hewn, undersized bay Thoroughbred (q.v.) with crooked legs who went on to become one of the world's greatest race horses; during his six-year tenure, he won 33 races and set 13 track records at 8 tracks over 6 distances; he smashed a world record in the shortest of sprints, the ½ mile (0.8 km); set 2 track records under 133 pounds (60 kg) impost and 4 more under 130 pounds (58.4 k); earned a world record $437,730, nearly 60 times his purchase price; an American-bred descendent of Man O'War (q.v.) through Hardtack, was foaled in 1933 and died at the age of 14 in 1947.

sealant *see* HOOF SEALANT

seal brown Refers to coat color; a shade of brown (q.v.) close to black, but distinguishable by brown or yellow areas on the muzzle, eyes, flanks, and inner legs; in coats of dark seal brown, the lighter shades are not visible.

seals The wooden hames (q.v.) of farm-horse harness.

season (1) *see* ESTRUS. (2) A racing term; the period during which racing is conducted on a particular circuit or track. (3) *see* HUNTING SEASON. (4) A hunting term; the number of years a hound (q.v.) has been hunted since being entered (q.v.).

seat (1) The posture of the rider in the saddle, on the horse. (2) The part of the saddle upon which the rider sits; located between the pommel (q.v.) and cantle (q.v.).

seat bones The two prominent points of the rider's pelvis upon which his weight is balanced when riding.

seat box A wooden, lidded box fitted under an inside passenger seat of a horse-drawn vehicle, used for storage.

seating out To slope the inner, hoof-side portion of the horseshoe web away from the hoof to prevent the shoe from applying pressure to the sole.

Seattle Slew Also known informally as Baby Huey or People's Horse; a champion race horse foaled in the United States in 1974; won 14 of 17 starts and the prestigious American Triple Crown (q.v.) in 1977.

seat worm *see* OXYRURIS EQUI

seborrhea A skin disease which may result from the abnormal production of keratin; usually a secondary disease in horses following dermatitis (q.v.) or eczema.

secondary arthritis Inflammation of a joint resulting from poor conformation; predisposes a horse to joint trauma, bone disease, and localization of a systemic joint infection.

second call Also known as secondary call; a racing term; a second mount taken by a jockey in the event that his primary mount is scratched (q.v.).

secondary call *see* SECOND CALL

secondary corpora lutea A mass of endocrine cells formed in follicles other than the ovarian, about one month after conception.

second dam *see* GRAND DAM

second horse A hunting term; an extra mount used by a participant in a hunt when a change of mount is necessary; may be ridden to the change by a pad groom (q.v.).

second-horse man *see* PAD GROOM

second horseman A hunting term; one responsible for riding a fresh hunter to a check.

second incisors *see* LATERAL INCISORS

second leg A racing term; the second half of a double event.

Second Level Roughly equivalent to Elementary Level (Brit. and Aus.); a dressage competition level in which the horse is required to carry more weight on the his hindquarters (q.v.) to demonstrate collection (q.v.), increase thrust and engagement at the medium gaits, perform turns on the haunches (q.v.), rein back, and more difficult lateral work and transitions and he must exhibit further development of straightness, bending, and engagement by executing 10 and 8 meter circles.

second man A second groom (q.v.) employed on a horse-drawn vehicle such as a Drag (q.v.); sat on the nearside (q.v.); was responsible for standing by the leaders when the coach was stationary and applying the drag shoe (q.v.) when necessary.

second pastern *see* SHORT PASTERN

second phalanx *see* SHORT PASTERN

second pommel *see* HUNTING HEAD

second season hound A hunting term; said of a hound hunted for the second year since being entered (q.v.).

second sire *see* GRAND SIRE

second thigh *see* GASKIN

second wind Also known as comes again; said of a horse who, although evidently tired and falling back, finds renewed energy and strength to move forward again or work with enthusiasm.

second whipper-in One of two principal assistants to the huntsman (q.v.); provides the huntsman with an extra set of eyes and is usually positioned at the far end of a covert (q.v.) to view a fox while drawing that covert (q.v.).

Secretariat Also known informally as Big Red; a large, powerful chestnut Thoroughbred (q.v.) with long, straight limbs and three white socks, hailed by some as the greatest race horse of all time and voted the Horse of the Year as a 2-year-old; stood 16.2 hands, had a girth of 6 feet 4 inches (1.93 m) and weighed 1,130 pounds (513 kg); foaled in the United States in 1970 he was raced as a

2- and 3-year-old over most distances: 6 furlongs (q.v.) (1200 m) to 1 mile 5 furlongs (2600 m); in his career of 21 starts, he logged 16 wins including the prestigious American Triple Crown in 1973; was put to stud in 1974; a horse who truly ran on heart (q.v.), he had a heart weight of 20 pounds (9.072 kg); he was put down in 1989 at the age of 19 due to an incurable case of laminitis (q.v.).

section (1) A measurement of land, equally about one square mile. (2) *see* FLAKE

Section A Pony *see* WELSH MOUNTAIN PONY

Section B Pony *see* WELSH PONY

Section C Pony *see* WELSH PONY OF COB TYPE

Section D Pony *see* WELSH COB

sediola A large, round-backed, horse-drawn Gig (q.v.) of the dead-axle type having high wheels and suspended from long, highly flexible shafts; popular in France and Italy during the 18th century.

seed *see* SPERM

seed hay *see* CEREAL GRASS HAY

seedy toe Also known as hollow wall or dystrophia ungulae; generally affects the hoof wall in the toe region, although it may also occur elsewhere on the hoof; a symptom of chronic laminitis (q.v.) characterized by hoof wall separation from the sensitive laminae (q.v.); the outer surface of the hoof wall appears sound, but the inner surface is mealy and there may actually be a cavity due to loss of horn substance; lameness is infrequent, but will accompany the occasional infection and abscessation.

seeling An obsolete term; the growth of white hairs in the horse's eyebrows.

see-saw *see* SCHAUKEL

Sefton Landau *see* CANOE LANDAU

Seglawi *see* SIGLAVY

Selby *see* SELBY CAPE

Selby cape Also known as Selby; a short, loose, double-breasted, sleeved cape made of box cloth (q.v.) worn by coachmen outside the apron in bad weather; designed and popularized by James Selby.

Selby, James (1844–1888) A coachman and proprietor in the coach building firm Cowland & Selby, London, England; most remembered for a coaching match referred to as the Selby Run (q.v.).

Selby Run, The A famous match between James Selby (q.v.) and the clock; he drove his 'Old Times' coach 108 miles from London, England to Brighton and back in 7 hours 50 minutes.

selection on the turf An English term; to select breeding stock on the basis of its performance on the racecourse.

selective breeding area A region or protected area where a breed from another area is isolated to maintain breed purity.

selenium A non-metallic element chemically resembling sulfur and tellurium; identified as an essential mineral in the diet of the horse in 1950, can be administered by injection or added to feed; acts in combination with vitamin E (q.v.) to prevent muscle degeneration and dystrophy as in white muscle disease (q.v.) which is common in foals and less so in mature horses; used as a treatment for azoturia (q.v.) or tying-up syndrome (q.v.); doses up to 2 ppm per day may produce improved performance, reduced respirations, and a better general condition in race horses; a level higher than 2 ppm per day can be toxic; toxicity is most likely to occur in alkaline or desert climates where the levels in forage are extremely high; symptoms of toxicity include loss of vitality, anemia, joint stiffness, rough hair coat, loss of mane and tail, development of hoof rings, deformities, or hoof loss, and death due to respiratory failure; deficiency is a problem in all or part of 42 of 50 states in the United States.

selenium accumulator Any plant containing high levels of selenium (q.v.); emits an unpleasant garlic-sulfur odor which discourages horses from consuming it if other forage (q.v.) is available.

selenium poisoning Consumption of toxic

levels of selenium (q.v.); all species are susceptible; levels as low as 4 to 5 ppm will inhibit growth; three distinct forms: acute selenium poisoning (q.v.); chronic of the blind staggers (q.v.) type and chronic of the alkali-disease (q.v.) type; occurs in animals consuming highly seleniferous plants or grains; occurs in Western Canada, South Africa, Ireland, Australia, Israel, China, the Soviet Union, Mexico, and the United States, most commonly, Colorado, Nebraska, South Dakota, and Wyoming; characterized by a 'garlicky' odor of the horse's breath, diminished visual acuity, poor appetite, weak forelegs, subnormal temperature, hair loss, and paralyzed tongue; no known methods of counteracting toxicity; may result in death.

self-carriage *see* COLLECTION

self-colored Refers to coat color; said of the mane and tail when the same color as the body coat.

sell at halter To sell a horse without a veterinary check (q.v.) and no guarantee other than title.

Selle Français (1) Also known as French Saddle horse; a horse breed descended from the Norman (q.v.) and was influenced by introduction of Arab (q.v.) and Thoroughbred (q.v.) blood; the stud book, a continuation of the Anglo-Norman (q.v.) book, was established in 1950; selected, but not necessarily pure-bred mares, and Thoroughbred, Arab, Anglo-Arab (q.v.), and French Trotter (q.v.) stallions contributed to the present day breed; stands 15.2 to 16.3 hands, has a robust frame, powerful shoulder, strong and long back, deep girth, and a smallish head; the predominant coat color is chestnut, but brown and bay, and rarely roan or gray, occur; used for riding and competitions including show jumping, dressage, eventing, etc. (2) *see* FRENCH SADDLE PONY

selling plater *see* PLATER NO. 2

selling plate race *see* SELLING RACE

selling race Also known as selling plate race; (obs); a claiming race (q.v.) in which the winning horse was auctioned off following the race and all other competing horses were offered for claiming.

Semaituka *see* ZEMAITUKA

semen A thick, white-colored secretion of the testes (q.v.) and the accessory gland of a stallion; contains the spermatozoa (q.v.) for fertilization of the mare's egg; consists of three fractions: watery containing little or no sperm, thin and watery containing the sperm, and gel from the vesicular gland; each ejaculation of semen is estimated to contain 4 to 18 billion sperm.

Semi-Mail Phaeton *see* DEMI-MAIL PHAETON

send A racing term; to enter a horse in a race.

send away A racing term; said of the official starter who opens the starting gate (q.v.) and begins a horse race, thus sending the horses away.

send on A hunting term; to send the hunters (horses) to a meet (q.v.) in advance of their riders.

sensitive frog That portion of the hoof covering part of the plantar cushion (q.v.) and resting beneath the coffin bone (q.v.); composed of very small, short papillae much like those of the perioplic ring (q.v.) of which it should be considered a continuation; nourishes the stratum germinativum (q.v.) that produces the horny frog.

sensitive laminae Also known as quick; the blood-engorged area of the hoof between the hoof wall and coffin bone (q.v.); interlocks with the insensitive laminae (q.v.).

sensitive sole That part of the hoof covering the crescent-shaped bottom of the coffin bone composed of small, short papillae; nourishes the horn-producing layer of cells that produces the horny sole (q.v.).

sensory nerve Any of the whitish fibers extending from the brain and spinal cord and spreading throughout the body to different organs, e.g. the skin which they enervate; when stimulated, trigger sensations including pain, pressure, temperature, etc.

sepsis A poisoned state of the system due to a spread of infection throughout the blood.

septicaemia *see* SEPTICEMIA

septicemia Also spelled septicaemia and known as blood poisoning; the presence of infectious microorganisms and/or their toxins in the bloodstream.

septicemic salmonellosis Salmonellosis (q.v.) typically occurring in foals; illness is acute, depression marked, and fever 105 to 107 °F (40.5–41.5 °C); death occurs within 24 to 48 hours.

sequela The consequence of a disease.

serge A strong cloth, usually made of wool but sometimes other fibers, used in the construction of some English saddles.

serous Resembling serum (q.v.); of a thin, liquid nature; containing or secreting serum.

serous arthritis Inflammation of a joint resulting from trauma and characterized by excessive accumulation of serous (q.v.) fluid in the joint space; the synovial membrane is inflamed, but the bony structures are uninvolved; often seen in poorly conformed horses; onset may be acute, or recur on a chronic basis.

serpentine A dressage movement consisting of a series of like-sized half-circles, curved alternately in different directions, connected by straight lines; the figure thus resembles the winding motion of a serpent; its gymnastic value lies in promoting bend and suppleness on both reins.

serpent tail Said of the horse's tail when the curve of the dock is concave rather than convex.

serum (1) A clear, pale yellow liquid which separates from the clot in coagulation of blood. (2) A fluid obtained from the blood of an animal rendered immune to some disease by inoculation.

serve *see* COVER NO. 1

servant *see* GROOM NO. 2

service *see* COVER NO. 1

serviceably sound Said of a horse who has no defect, ailment, or illness that will impair his value for the intended use.

serviced *see* COVERED

service fee *see* STUD FEE

serving hobbles *see* BREEDING HOBBLES

service in-hand *see* HAND BREEDING

sesamoid bones Also known as sesamoids; three small bones in the horse's lower leg consisting of the proximal sesamoids (q.v.) (medial and lateral) and the distal sesamoid (q.v.) navicular bone; the proximal sesamoids are two small, pyramid-shaped bones located at the back of the fetlock joint which are bound into the suspensory apparatus by strong ligaments and act to form a pulley over which the deep flexor tendon runs; the distal sesamoid is located at the back of the third phalanx (pedal bone) and is covered by a smooth "skin" of fibrocartilage over which the deep flexor tendon runs before inserting into the underside of the pedal bone.

sesamoid boots *see* ANKLE BOOTS

sesamoid fracture A break (q.v.) in one or all of the bones comprising the fetlock joint including the two proximal sesamoids and the distal sesamoid; may consist of small chips or involve all the bones.

sesamoiditis Also known as popped sesamoid; a term loosely applied to several inflammatory conditions involving the sesamoid bones (q.v.) or sesamoidian ligaments; generally a tear of the insertion of some of the ligaments which hold the sesamoids (q.v.) in place as caused by stress placed on the fetlock during fast exercise; symptoms include swelling and varying degrees of lameness; despite a variety of treatments, the prognosis for recovery is poor.

sesamoids *see* SESAMOID BONES

set (1) To attach a horseshoe to the foot, as in, "He set the shoe." (2) Four horseshoes. (3) Also known as set the head; to position the horse's head as with auxiliary reins or devices so that he is on the bit; his head will be bent at the poll and perpendicular to the ground. (4) A racing term; a group of horses exercised together.

set-and-turn *see* ROLLBACK

set back *see* HALF-STRUCK

set down (1) Also known as stand down (Brit); a racing term; to suspend a jockey, horseman, stable hand, or trainer from racing for a specific period of time as for a rule infraction. (2) An American racing term; to shake up (q.v.) a horse and urge him to increase speed or effort in a work-out or race.

set fair Said of a horse when bedded down and settled in for the night; (obs).

set fast *see* TYING-UP SYNDROME

set for the stop A cutting term; the position a cutter (q.v.) assumes in the saddle when cutting; he pushes forward on the horn with his right hand, relaxes into the saddle, and drops his heels into the stirrups; allows the horse to stop and prevents the rider from bouncing in the stirrups or moving forward on the horn during the stop.

set tail Also known as cut and set tail; the horse's tail when intentionally broken and positioned so that it heals in an elevated position, or in which the tendons on the underside have been nicked (q.v.); performed on gaited horses including Saddle-bred (q.v.) and Tennessee Walking horses (q.v.); the horse is left without tail control.

set the head *see* SET NO. 3

settle (1) Also known as settle to service; said of a broodmare who has conceived as a result of mating. (2) *see* SETTLE CATTLE

settle cattle Also known as settle; a cutting term; said of a mounted cutter (q.v.) who quietly calms a contained herd of cattle by moving back and forth in front of them prior to cutting.

settled A cutting term; said of cattle that are familiar enough with a horse and rider not to spook by them, but not so overly familiar as to have lost their curiosity.

set toe *see* ROCKER TOE SHOE

set toe shoe *see* ROCKER TOE SHOE

settle to service *see* SETTLE NO. 1

seven-eighths brothers The male off-spring of a horse and his son, produced by the same dam.

seven-eighths sisters The female offspring of a horse and his daughter, produced by the same dam.

Seven-Spring Gig *see* TILBURY

Seven years for my brother, seven years for me, and seven years for my enemy An ancient description of the Arab horse's range of performance throughout his average life span of 21 years.

Seydlitz, Baron von Friedrich Wilhelm (1721–1773) A famous Russian cavalry general.

sex allowance A racing term; a weight concession given to mares or fillies competing in races against males, except handicap races or where conditions state otherwise; mares and fillies are allowed weight below the scale (q.v.): in America, is usually 3 pounds (1.3 kg) for 2-year-old fillies, 5 pounds (2.3 kg) for fillies and mares 3 years and older prior to September 1, and 3 pounds (1.3 kg) thereafter; other racing nations have similar systems.

shabrack *see* SHABRAQUE

shabraque Also known as housing or shadrack and spelled shabrack; an ornamental cloth or leather covering for the saddle and horse.

shadbelly Also known as cut-away coat or tail coat; a formal black coat cut to waist length in the front and with long, weighted tails behind; the tails may be lined with leather or faux leather; primarily worn by competitors in advanced dressage competitions.

shadowing An obsolete coaching term; said of the guard and coachman when they shared dishonestly acquired short fares from passengers.

shadow roll noseband Also known as sheepskin noseband, anti-shying noseband, anti-shadow noseband, or French noseband; a piece of tack used to restrict a horse's downward vision; particularly used on race horses who shy at real or imaginary objects or on horses raced under lights to prevent them from attempting to jump their own shadows; essentially a cavesson (q.v.) where the noseband is wrapped in wool or sheepskin; fitted further up the face than a normal noseband.

shadrack *see* SHABRAQUE

shaft (1) Also known as till; one of two long, round, wooden poles between which a horse is harnessed and by which he is connected to a vehicle; an extension of the vehicle which may be attached to either the vehicle body or frame. (2) The straight middle portion of a long bone, e.g. femur (q.v.). (3) *see* SHAFT HORSE

shaft horse Also known as shaft, thill, thiller, phill horse, or thill horse; a driving term; the horse to which the shafts (q.v.) are connected in a horse-drawn vehicle.

Shagya Arabian Also known as a Hungarian Arabian or Hungarian Shagya; a relatively rare breed developed after 1816 at Austro-Hungarian military stud farms, primarily in Hungary at Babolna and Radautz; developed for cavalry and carriage purposes, as well as to supply prepotent breeding stallions as improvers for other breeds; the foundation sires were original desert-bred Arab (q.v.) put to Arab-type mares; English Thoroughbreds (q.v.) and Lipizzaners (q.v.) were also used to increase size and improve movement; the name and predominant cream-colored coat derived from an Arab stallion, Shagya, a horse of the Kehil/Siglavi strain, born in Syria in 1830 and imported to the stud in 1836 for restocking purposes; stands 15 to 16 hands and should have a minimum cannon bone circumference of 7 inches (18 cm); the coat is generally gray and rarely black; breeds consistently true to type; is taller, has a bigger frame, longer hip, and possesses better riding horse qualities than a pure-bred Arab and has 17 ribs, 5 lumbar bones, and 16 tail vertebrae in comparison with the 18–6–18 formation of other breeds; used for riding and driving; numbers less than 2,000 worldwide.

shaker foal syndrome *see* BOTULISM

shake up A racing term; said of a jockey, to strike a horse with a whip or use the heels and rein aids in an effort to make him run faster.

Shan *see* BURMESE

Shanderidan A four-wheeled wagon generally harnessed to a pair (q.v.).

Shandry A large, strongly constructed market cart used widely in the Lake District and NW England for business and pleasure during the second half of the 19th century; seated six; hung on sideways semi-elliptical springs.

Shandrydan A two-wheeled sprung cart used in Ireland.

shank (1) That part of the bit below the mouthpiece; gives the rider leverage on the mouthpiece; the shorter the shank, the less control. (2) Also known as metatarsal, metatarsal bone, shannon, or shannon bone; the principal bone of the hind leg located between the hock and the fetlock; the corresponding bone in the foreleg is known as the cannon bone (q.v.). (3) A chain attached to a lead rope (q.v.).

shannon *see* SHANK

shannon bone *see* SHANK

Shan Pony *see* BURMESE

shape cattle A cutting term; to manipulate a herd of cattle so that they move in a specific direction.

shaping A conditioning technique; to reward behavior that comes close to that required, gradually altering or modifying the behavior by reducing the realm of acceptable rewarded behavior.

shaping a cow A cutting term; to separate and move a cow away from the center of the herd to the middle of the arena to begin work.

shaps *see* CHAPS

shavings *see* WOOD SHAVINGS

shay *see* CHAISE

sheared heels Structural breakdown of the hoof between the heel bulbs (q.v.); characterized by a disproportionate use of one heel; the degree of lameness and resulting damage is proportional to the duration and degree of foot imbalance.

she-ass *see* JENNY

sheath The fleshy pocket located in front of the scrotum (q.v.) which contains the genital organ of the male horse and has the anterior end open.

shebang An American-Irish term; an old or worn-out carriage.

shedding coat *see* SHEDDING OUT

shedding out Also known in England as casting coat or shedding coat; said of a horse who loses his coat due to climate or seasonal change; generally occurs twice a year, in the spring and autumn, the exact time of which is contingent on the condition of the horse's nutrition, whether a mare is in foal, and stabling conditions, e.g. at grass, kept in a box stall with or without lights, blanketing, etc.

shed row A racing term; race track barns generally located in the backstretch (q.v.).

sheep knees *see* BACKWARD DEVIATION OF THE CARPAL JOINTS

sheepskin noseband *see* SHADOW ROLL NOSEBAND

sheet *see* SUMMER SHEET

sheet calendar *see* RACING CALENDAR

sheets An American racing term; a handicapping tool which assigns a numerical value to each race run by a horse; enables different horses running at different tracks to be compared objectively.

Shelborne Landau *see* SHELBURNE LANDAU

Shelburne *see* SHELBURNE LANDAU

Shelburne Landau Also known as Shelburne, Square Landau, Angular Landau, and spelled Shelborne Landau; a four-wheeled, heavy, horse-drawn town carriage with a square or angular profile, two doors, and a double folding hood; seated four vis-à-vis; was usually pulled by a pair of horses and coachman driven; designed for the Earl of Shelburne.

shell cordovan *see* CORDOVAN NO. 4

shell harness Any harness decorated with sea shells; popular in Arab countries, Tyrol, and the Netherlands.

shelling *see* KICKING

shelly The hollow center of a newly cut incisor (q.v.).

shelly cordovan *see* CORDOVAN NO. 4

shelly feet Said of the horse's hooves when thinly soled and brittle walled.

shelt A Highland Pony used by deer hunters to carry game (q.v.).

Shetland Pony Also known as Sheltie; the smallest of Great Britain's nine native breeds; indigenous to the Orkney and Shetland Islands, Scotland; believed to have originally migrated from Scandinavia around 8,000 BC; registered stock must not exceed a height of 40 inches (101 cm) at 2 years nor 42 inches (106 cm) at 4 years; it is traditional to measure Shetland height in inches; may have a piebald (q.v.), skewbald (q.v.), brown, chestnut, gray, or black coat with the latter being the foundation color; the coat is smooth in the summer, but thick and wiry in the winter; is hardy, strong, lively, and possessed of a quick, free action; typically has a well-shaped but small head, crested neck, broad chest, short back with heavily muscled loins, considerable depth around the girth, broad quarters, short legs with sharply defined joints, light feathering, and an exceptionally thick mane, forelock, and tail; has extra large nasal cavities that enable the air to warm before entering the lungs; historically used to haul and carry peat and seaweed and for mining; now used for riding and light draft.

Shetland Pony Stud Blood Society A British organization founded in 1891 to encourage the breeding of registered Shetland Ponies (q.v.).

Sheltie *see* SHETLAND PONY

Sheykh Obeyd Arabian A Bedouin Arab descended exclusively in all lines from 66 foundation Arabs; identified as a unique blood group in 1987; is an endangered blood group.

shift *see* RESET

Shifter A single-horse sleigh popular in New England, USA; had shafts directly in front of the runner to enable the horse to use the same track created by a pair horse sleigh.

Shifting Seat Wagon *see* JUMP SEAT WAGON

shill Also known as bonnet (obs), chaunter, puffer (obs), or trotter (obs); one posing as a horse buyer to run up the price of a horse at auction and to decoy onlookers into participating in the bidding, yet who has no intention of buying.

shim A wedge (q.v.) that is thicker at the toe than at the heel, placed between the horseshoe and hoof.

shin *see* CANNON BONE

shin and ankle boot *see* HEEL BOOT

shin bone *see* CANNON BONE

shinbuck *see* BUCKED SHINS

shin sore Said of a horse suffering from bucked shins (q.v.).

shinted *see* COVERED

ship To transport a horse, as by truck, rail, boat, or plane.

Ship-of-the-Plains *see* PRAIRIE SCHOONER

shipping boots Also known as traveling boots; padded, often fleece-lined, boots which provide protection and support to the horse's legs during shipping; extend from just below the knee to well beyond the coronary band while the rear boots extend above the hock.

shipping fever Also known as transit fever; a severe respiratory ailment generally occurring in young animals, predominately cattle, as a result of the stress associated with shipping, castration, winter weather, change of food, etc.; symptoms include fever, loss of appetite, weakness, followed by nasal and eye discharge, distressed breathing, and coughing.

Shire A heavy draft breed descended from the Great Horse (q.v.) with some contributions of Flemish, Friesian (q.v.), and Oriental stock; usually stands 16.1 to 17.3 hands, and in some cases as tall as 19 hands, weighs 1,760 to 2,688 pounds (798–1,219 kg), and may have a bay, brown, black, chestnut or gray coat with white markings – a black coat with white feathering, reminiscent of the foundation sire, is the most popular color; has a small head relative to its body size with a wide forehead and long ears, a long, arched and muscular neck, short back, powerful croup, relatively short legs with heavy, silky feather and is large boned; is docile and good natured; the foundation sire was the Packington Blind Horse (q.v.); the stud book was established in 1878; historically used to pull Carriages or Omnibus (q.v.) and for agricultural purposes, now used for heavy draft and farm work; so called because it was raised in Great Britain's Midland regions of Lincolnshire, Leicestershire, Staffordshire, and Derbyshire.

Shiragazi An Iranian breed; contributed to the development of the Plateau Persian (q.v.).

Shires, The (1) An area in Britain hunted by a group of fashionable packs including the Quorn, Fernie, Belvoir Pytchley, Cottesmore, and Grafton; covers prime grazing land located in the counties of Leicesteshire, Northamptonshire, and Rutland; the country is strongly fenced with cut and laid (q.v.) hedges. (2) An area in England consisting of Leicestershire, Rutland, Warwickshire, Northamptonshire, and parts of Lincolnshire.

shiver To shake involuntarily or tremble as with cold, fear, or excitement.

shock Circulatory collapse characterized by a progressively diminishing circulating blood volume relative to the capacity of the vascular system, leading to acute failure of perfusion of vital organs; of three primary types: (a) cardiac shock (q.v.) caused by damage to the heart pump, (b) hypovolemic shock (q.v.) due to decreased blood volume, or (c) vasculogenic shock (q.v.) in which the blood volume is normal but blood is pooled in dilated peripheral vessels, a condition which may be caused by the presence of endotoxins or trauma; associated conditions include accident trauma, severe diarrhea, massive hemorrhage, colic (q.v.), and acute coliform mastitis; symptoms include lengthened capillary refill time (q.v.), pale mucous membranes, ataxia (q.v.), low pulse pressure, increased/decreased respiratory rate, diminished cardiac output, elevated temperature, and cold, clammy skin.

shock condition Any circumstance leading to a tissue fluid imbalance and the onset of shock (q.v.).

shod Said of a horse who has had horseshoes (q.v.) put on, e.g. "When was the horse last shod?"

shod too close *see* NAIL BIND

shoe (1) Also known as horseshoe or horseshoeing; to fit horseshoes to the horse's hooves. (2) *see* HORSESHOE

shoe board An American racing term; a sign which identifies the type of horseshoes (q.v.) each horse entered to race wears; may be included as a panel on the totalizator board (q.v.).

shoe boil *see* CAPPED ELBOW

shoeful London slang; an imitation or counterfeit product; as a two-wheeled horse-drawn vehicle that was manufactured in an attempt to copied or improve upon the Hansom cab (q.v.).

shoeing block *see* FOOT STOOL

shoeing chaps Leather or canvas leg coverings worn by a farrier (q.v.) to protect the thighs while shoeing a horse; held in place by means of a belt and extend to the knees.

shoeing forge *see* FORGE NO. 2

shoeing hammer *see* DRIVING HAMMER

shoe pad *see* HORSESHOE PAD

shooter A cutting term; a cow that bolts from the herd for no apparent reason and interferes with the cutter's (q.v.) performance.

shooting To hunt for and kill game using a gun; different than hunting (q.v.).

Shooting Break Also known as Body Break; a light, horse-drawn vehicle of the Break (q.v.) type having a Dogcart (q.v.) body which extended forward to a high box seat and a sloping dashboard; had two boots (q.v.): a large one located under the driver's seat and another, smaller, ventilated one, centered under the passenger seats used to carry hunting dogs; popular in the mid-19th century with shooting parties; carried 6 to 8 passengers on crosswise or lengthwise seating, was hung on sideways-elliptical or semi-elliptical springs, and drawn by a single horse in shafts or a pair in pole gear (q.v.).

Shooting Cart A four-wheeled, horse-drawn sporting vehicle; had a high seat over the front axle, a slatted body, forward-facing seats for two passengers and sufficient space beneath the seating for dogs and game; pulled by a pair or team of ponies.

Shooting Phaeton A four-wheeled, horse-drawn vehicle of the Phaeton (q.v.) type popular in the late 18th century; noted for its tray-like body and strong underperch, which made it suitable for driving over rough tracks; had a large boot (q.v.) above the rear axle, an elevated driving seat with room for two, rearward cross seats for passengers seated vis-à-vis, and a half hood which protected the rearward seat; originally hung on whip springs, but later on sideways semi-elliptical springs; usually drawn by a pair of horses in pole gear (q.v.).

shooting your wheelers A coaching term; to move the wheelers (q.v.) into their collars to draw the weight of the load.

short (1) *see* SHORT ON A COW. (2) A racing term; said of a horse who drops out of contention in the homestretch or close to the finish in a race. (3) A racing term; a horse in need of more work or racing to reach winning form. (4) *see* GOING SHORT

short-coupled Also known as close-coupled; said of a short-bodied horse in which the distance between the last rib and the point of the hip (q.v.) is short, i.e. not more than 4 inches (10 cm) wide.

short harnessed Said of the wheel horses when harnessed as close to the carriage and leaders as close to the wheelers as possible; the team thus harnessed is easier to drive and takes up less road room than a team harnessed loosely.

short head *see* NOSE NO. 2

short of a rib *see* SHORT OF RIB

short of blood *see* OUT OF BLOOD

short of bone *see* TIED-IN BELOW THE KNEE

short of rib Also known as short of a rib; said of a horse in which the distance between the last rib and the point of the hip is greater than normal; indicative of a long-backed horse.

short on a cow Also known as short; a cutting term; a horse who, when moving parallel to a cow, is out of position or too far behind it to influence its movements.

short pastern Also known as P2, PII, second pastern, second phalanx, short pastern bone, or coronary bone; the middle of three pastern bones making up the lower part of the horse's leg and foot located between the long pastern (q.v.) and third pastern (q.v.).

short pastern bone *see* SHORT PASTERN

short price A racing term; low odds of return.

short side One of two short ends of a rectangular arena or manège (q.v.).

short tommy A coaching term; a short, stiff, leather thong approximately 3 feet (91 cm) long, used on the wheel horses pulling a coach to encourage their forward movement; frequently used by the passengers.

short-wheel rein A coaching term; to drive a team with the leader's reins normal length while the wheeler's reins terminated in a loop laid over the driver's third and fourth fingers.

shotgun chaps Ankle-length, straight-legged chaps (q.v.) worn to protect the rider's leg from the elements, temperature, or abrasion; close around the leg with zippers or buckles; held on to the body by a belted waistband.

shot on goal A polo term; said of a player who strikes the polo ball in an attempt to make a goal.

shoulder That part of the horse's body to which the forearm (q.v.) is attached.

shoulder atrophy *see* SWEENEY

shoulder bone *see* SCAPULA

shoulder cross Also known as cross or the cross; a primitive marking (q.v.); a dorsal stripe (q.v.) of darker hair starting at the top of the head and running to the end of the tail which is crossed at the withers with another darker line of hair thus forming a cross; may be seen on any coat color, commonly found on donkeys; a dominant trait.

shoulder falling out A dressage term; said of the horse when his outside shoulder falls to the outside of the intended line of a turn or circle; may indicate inherent crookedness in the horse, that the rider has lost control of the horse's forehand, or that the rider is using incorrect aids, especially pulling back on the inside rein.

shoulder hang A vaulting term; an exercise performed by a vaulter (q.v.), in which he hangs inverted, with a straight body, against the horse's shoulder supporting his weight by his arms by which he holds onto the grips of the vaulting roller (q.v.).

shoulder-in A lateral movement in which the horse travels forward while bent uniformly from head to tail away from the direction in which he is traveling; correctly executed, the angle of the horse should be approximately 30 degrees to the track.

shouldering Also known as swallowing; a coaching term; said of the coachman and guard who permit a passenger who has not paid in advance to ride for a short distance, the fare collected being unreported.

shouldering the pole An obsolete

coaching term; said of a wheeler (q.v.) when he pushes the center pole against his partner.

shoulder-out The opposite exercise to shoulder-in (q.v.).

shoulder paralysis *see* SWEENEY

show (1) A racing term; said of a horse finishing in third position. (2) *see* HORSE SHOW. (3) Also known as hack (Aus); to present, exhibit, or compete, as in a horse show (q.v.).

show bet An American racing term; a wager on a horse to finish in the money (q.v.), third place or better; the show pool (q.v.) is split three ways and results in the lowest payoff.

show bridle (1) see DOUBLE BRIDLE. (2) Any bridle maintained and used on horses in competition; may be adorned with silver or other accoutrements.

Show Buggy Also known as Show Ring Buggy; an extremely light, four-wheeled, single seat, horse-drawn vehicle of the American Buggy (q.v.) type; has a full undercut forecarriage, wire-spoked wheels and equal sized bicycle or rubber tires; used for showing trotting horses or ponies such as Hackneys (q.v.); popular from the late 1890s to present.

show circuit A calendar of horse shows within a defined geographical region.

show class Any competition held at a horse show (q.v.) in which participating horses are judged on conformation, condition, action and/or suitability for whatever purpose they are or will be used.

shower *see* CHATTER

shower down on one *see* CHATTER

shower the ground *see* CHATTER

show horse Any horse used, presented, exhibited, or competed in an equestrian event.

show hunter Also known as hunter; any hunter-type horse shown in classes in which the horse is judged on style, gaits, conformation, manner and way of going on the flat and/or over fences.

showing too much daylight *see* ON THE LEG

show jumper Any horse competed in show jumping (q.v.) competitions.

show jumping (1) Also known as lepping or lepping contest; a jumping contest in which the horse and rider jump a series of man-made jumps in an enclosed area, in a predetermined order, and within a set time; may be conducted in indoor or open-air arenas which usually have 10 to 12 jumps, and at least one combination; the start and finish of the course are clearly marked and all jumps are numbered or flagged; originated in Paris, France in 1866; in 1912 it was first introduced as an Olympic sport, and in 1921, standardized regulations were established. (2) One of the phases of a three-day event conducted on the third day of competition; riders navigate a course 750 to 1000 yards (700–900m) in length having 10 to 12 obstacles; penalties are incurred for falls or refusals at the obstacles and for exceeding the time allowed.

Showman's Wagon *see* BURTON WAGON

show pony An American term; any pony (q.v.) presented, exhibited, or competed in equestrian events.

Show Phaeton A horse-drawn vehicle built for show and pulled by a single or pair of light horses; the body was hung on four elliptic springs.

show pool A racing term; a sum of money set aside by the track (tote, in Britain) from wagers placed on horses to show in a specific race; winning show ticket holders are paid from this pool.

Show Ring Buggy *see* SHOW BUGGY

Show Wagon *see* BOX WAGON

show wear A racing term; said of a horse with fetlocks swollen by overwork.

show white of the eye Said of a horse when some part of the white sclera shows between partially closed eye lids.

shredded paper *see* PAPER

shuffle A racing term; a style of riding assumed by most jockeys whereby the hands are pumped and the feet moved in rhythm with the horse's stride.

shuffled back A racing term; said of a horse who loses ground or racing position because of a jam up of horses on the track.

shut off A racing term; said of a jockey who crosses in front of another horse during a race, forcing another jockey to pull back or go around.

shut out A racing term; said of a bettor (q.v.) who arrives at a betting window after wagering for a particular race has closed and is refused the opportunity to bet.

shut the stable door after the horse has bolted *see* LOCK THE STABLE DOOR AFTER THE HORSE IS STOLEN

shy Said of a horse; to start, recoil, or jump sideways in fright or revulsion from something seen, heard, or imagined.

shy feeder Said of a horse or hound with a poor appetite.

Siberian Tiger Horse *see* TIGER HORSE

Sicilian (1) An Anglo-Arab (q.v.) indigenous to Sicily; stands 14.3 to 15.2 hands, has long legs, a short back, prominent withers, small ears, is spirited, and has good stamina; the coat may be dapple gray (q.v.), bay (q.v.), black (q.v.), or chestnut (q.v.); used for riding and light draft. (2) Also known as Miniature Sicilian Donkey and Sicilian Donkey; a Miniature Mediterranean Donkey (q.v.) native to Sicily.

Sicilian Donkey *see* SICILIAN NO. 2

sickle hocks *see* EXCESSIVE ANGULATION OF THE HOCK JOINTS

sickle-hocked Also known as sabre-legged or sickle-legged; said of a horse afflicted with excessive angulation of the hock joints (q.v.).

sickle-legged *see* SICKLE-HOCKED

side boards *see* BOARDS

sidebones Also known as knots; ossification of one or both of the lateral cartilages of the pedal bone; most common in the forefeet of heavy horses, mules, hunters, and jumpers and is rare in Thoroughbreds (q.v.); symptoms include heat and the appearance of hard lumps on the coronet (q.v.) on either side of the heel; may be due to genetics, improper shoeing, repeated concussion of the quarters of the foot causing trauma to the cartilages, traumatic lesions, and poor conformation; lameness may or may not be present depending on the degree of ossification.

Side Car (1) Also known as Irish Car; a shafted, but wheel-less horse- or mule-drawn vehicle similar to a travois (q.v.); consists of two shafts, one attached to either side of the animal's body by means of strapping, the ends of which drag on the ground behind and between which a large box or wicker basket is fitted; rollers or disc-wheels were eventually incorporated to the design; the prototype of all carts (such as the Jaunting Car [q.v.]), wagons, and carriages. (2) JAUNTING CAR

sideclaws Sharp projections on the inside of the bit cheekpieces; historically used on side-pullers; cause sores on the lateral lips and corners of the mouth.

side clip A horseshoe clip (q.v.) on the middle of the quarter (q.v.) on either side of the foot.

side jockey Also known as Western side jockey; the portion of leather on a Western saddle attached to the left and right sides of the saddle seat upon which the rider's thigh rests and which covers the insertion of the fender (q.v.) into the saddle tree.

side line A polo term; one of two, 300 yard long (274 m) sides of a polo field (q.v.) which, in conjunction with the end lines (q.v.), define the playing area of a polo field; previously identified by boards (q.v.), are now marked by chalk; the ball is considered out of bounds and play is stopped if the ball passes outside this line.

sidelines A device used to break or train a horse; two equal lengths of rope used to connect the fore and hind leg pasterns on each side; the lines are shorter than the distance between the horse's fore and hind feet when standing normally, yet long enough to enable the horse to stand; when the horse attempts to strike or kick, he pulls the other leg on the same side from underneath and thus falls over.

sidepass *see* FULL PASS

sidepiece *see* CHEEK

side pull *see* LINDELL

side puller A horse who pulls on the bit harder to one side, i.e. left or right, than the other.

side pulling Said of a horse who pulls against the bit and thus the reins, harder to one side, e.g. left or right, than the other.

side reins Auxiliary reins that may be fixed length, elasticized, or adjustable; attach on one end to the bit rings and to the roller, training surcingle (q.v.), or girth on the other; used especially with young horses on the lunge to encourage bit contact and also to modify head carriage.

side-saddle Also known as queen of saddles; a saddle (q.v.) designed for women which enabled them to ride without sitting astride the horse; use dates back well into the 12th century although it was not formally introduced into England until the early 14th century at which time the saddle was based on the pack saddle design fitted, on the nearside (q.v.), with a foot rest and only one pommel; in 1580, Catherine de Medici, Queen of France, added a second pommel below the first; the saddle was further revolutionized in 1830 by the addition of the leaping head (q.v.); the rider sits with both feet on the near side (q.v.) of the horse with her right leg hooked over the upper of two padded, diagonally placed projections, while her left leg fits under and against the lower one, the leaping head, with the foot resting in the stirrup.

side-saddler One who rides sidesaddle (q.v.).

Side-Seated Platform Wagon A four-wheeled, horse-drawn vehicle used to transport large numbers of passengers; had a 9-foot (3 m) long, fringed-top body and vis-à-vis (q.v.) passenger seating behind the coachman's seat in the front; was hung on two sets of three springs consisting of two side- and one cross-spring.

side step (1) *see* TRAVERSE. (2) *see* TWO-TRACK. (3) *see* FULL PASS

side steps *see* LATERAL WORK

side stick A device historically used on horses prone to biting to enable grooming without danger; a strong, yet narrow stick attached on one end to the bit and on the other to the surcingle (q.v.) that prevents and ultimately conditions the horse against bringing his head around to bite.

sidewheeler *see* PACER

side wheeling The side-to-side roll of a pacer (q.v.) when moving at the pace (q.v.).

sifting A technique used by some horse show judges to evaluate large show classes; the class is divided into smaller, more manageable groups from which the judge(s) selects the top performers; the top performers are then judged together as a single class, the balance of the horses being excused from the ring.

sight The power or faculty of seeing; the sense whereby objects are perceived by the eye.

sight hound A hunting dog who uses his eyes to pursue the quarry (q.v.); include Greyhounds, Whippets, Borzois, and Salukis.

Siglavy Also known as Seglawi; one of three distinct sub-breeds of the Assil (q.v.); characterized by beauty and elegance.

sign Any objective indication of animal disease or ill health; a horse may show signs of illness, pain, etc.

silage A brown colored, wet material produced by the controlled fermentation of high moisture herbage such as grasses and legumes under anaerobic conditions; the production of lactic acid eventually stops the fermentation process; commonly fed to ruminants such as cattle and sheep and less so to horses because of possible unpalatability, toxicity, the likelihood of spoilage, and the need to feed quickly to prevent same; should be introduced to the horse's diet slowly.

silent heat The estrus (q.v.) period during which the mare ovulates, but fails to show behavioral signs of heat (q.v.).

silks *see* COLORS

Silky Sullivan, a A racing term; said of a horse who makes a big run from far back in the field to the finish; named for the horse known as Silky Sullivan, who once made up 41 lengths to win a race.

silver buckskin Refers to coat color; of the color group buckskin (q.v.); creamy yellow coat hair with black points and no primitive marks (q.v.).

silver dapple Refers to coat color; sepia brown coat hair with light dapples (q.v.), which may be somewhat subdued, and flaxen or nearly white points; unique to Shetland Ponies (q.v.) in the United States, but seen in a variety of breeds throughout Europe; may be confused with chestnut (q.v.).

silver dun Refers to coat color; of the color group dun (q.v.); creamy yellow coat hair with primitive marks (q.v.) and black points (q.v.).

silver grullo Refers to coat color; a grullo (q.v.) of the color group dun (q.v.); the lightest of the grullo colors; a cream-colored body with slate blue, instead of black points and head, and blue eyes.

silver ring A racing term; the cheap and secondary betting enclosure at a racetrack (q.v.) where small bookmakers (q.v.) conduct business.

simbu virus A virus caused by a strain of *Shuni virus*; previously isolated in South Africa; transmitted by species of mosquitoes and Culicoides (q.v.); host range amongst vertebrates includes both mammals and birds; is seasonally prevalent and follows a distribution pattern similar to African horse sickness (q.v.); characterized by febrile reactions and other vague clinical signs.

simple change Also known as simple lead change, simple change of leg, or simple change of leg at the canter; a movement in which the cantering horse is brought into the walk and, after three to five strides, resumes the canter (q.v.) on the new lead; in training of the horse precedes the flying change (q.v.).

simple change of leg *see* SIMPLE CHANGE

simple change of leg at the canter *see* SIMPLE CHANGE

simple dismount A compulsory vaulting exercise performed in competitions; from a sitting position, the vaulter (q.v.) swings the outside leg up in a semi-circle, bends forward at the hip, brings the outside leg together with the inside leg behind, and pushes away from the grips to land, feet together.

simple fracture A break of the bone along a single line which does not penetrate the skin.

simple lead change *see* SIMPLE CHANGE

simpler's art *see* HERBALISM

simple whorl A hair pattern; a whorl (q.v.) created by a change in direction of hair flow in which hairs converge from different directions.

simulator A device that emulates the action of the driven horse; used to teach drivers the rein grips used in harness or cart driving without a horse.

simulcast A simultaneous live television transmission of an event, generally a horse race, to other tracks, off-track betting offices, or other locations.

sinew *see* TENDON

singeing The obsolete practice of trimming the horse's mane and tail hair using a gas flame or lamp; now replaced by clippers (q.v.).

single a jump An Irish term; said of the horse; to touch and clear a bank (q.v.) with only one step of each foot.

single bank A jumping obstacle (q.v.); a bank (q.v.) having a ditch on only one side.

single bar *see* LEAD BAR

single break *see* BREAKING CART

single foot *see* RACK

single-gutted *see* HERRING-GUTTED

single-jointed true kimblewick One of five types of kimblewick (q.v.) bit (q.v.); a type of pelham (q.v.) requiring one instead of two reins (q.v.), having a straight, jointed mouthpiece (q.v.), short cheeks (q.v.) with dee-rings running the full length, and a square eye on the upper end of the cheeks.

Single-Shaft Cart *see* BREAKING CART

single tree *see* SWINGLE TREE

sinker A grave case of founder (q.v.) in which laminitis (q.v.) has destroyed so much of the laminae (q.v.) that the pedal bone is no longer supported and begins to sink or descend into the foot.

sinking fox A hunting term; said of a hunted fox (q.v.) who begins to tire after a hard hunt.

sinuous whorl A hair pattern; a whorl (q.v.) created by two opposing sweeps of hair which meet along an irregular curving line.

sire (1) Also known as progenitor; the father or potential father of a horse; a colt is said to be "by" his sire; appears on the top side of the pedigree (q.v.). (2) To beget foals.

sired by *see* BY

sire stake A racing term; a stakes race (q.v.) restricted to the progeny (q.v.) of stallions standing at stud in a given state or province.

sisters Also known as full sisters or own sisters; a relationship of female horses "by" the same sire (q.v.) and "out" of the same dam (q.v.).

'sit fast' A coaching term; a warning given by the coachman to the passengers before moving off.

sitfast A hard and painful swelling on the back; a gall (q.v.).

sit-still An American racing term; said of a jockey who loses a race due to failure to use the whip.

sitting trot Said of the rider; to ride the trot without rising from the saddle to post (q.v.).

sixes The third pair of mules from the front of a wagon in a twenty-mule hitch.

six nail A farrier's term; to fasten a horseshoe (q.v.) to the hoof using six nails; more common than eight nail (q.v.).

Sjees *see* FRIESIAN CHAISE

Sjurpapach A Russian equestrian sport similar to the Argentinean game of pato (q.v.) in which two teams compete to score points by throwing a stuffed, long-haired sheepskin hat through the opponents' ring fixed on top of a high post; the rings are located on opposite ends of a randomly shaped field.

skate A horse of marginal or poor quality.

skeebald *see* SKEWBALD

skeleton The total bony framework which sustains the softer body parts of the horse.

Skeleton Break Also known as Dealer's Break; a horse-drawn vehicle of the Break (q.v.) type; a training and exercising vehicle used by professional horsebreakers, especially during the second half of the 19th century; had an open platform with an elevated box located directly above the fore-wheels; horses, usually one older and more experienced in harness work than the other, were driven in pairs harnessed to pole gear (q.v.); a groom generally stood behind the driver and, when necessary, would jump from the platform to aid the novice horse.

skeleton bridle A harness bridle without blinkers (q.v.).

Skeleton Gig A high, two-wheeled, open, horse-drawn exercising vehicle of the Gig (q.v.) type used with sporting harness; had a curved open stick-back seat suspended by iron stays on two side and one cross-spring; the shafts ran outside the bootless body.

skep Also known as skip; a wicker or plastic basket used in stables for the collection of manure.

skepping out *see* MUCKING OUT

skewbald Also known as skeebald; refers to coat color; a nonblack horse with tobiano (q.v.), overo (q.v.), sabino (q.v.), or splashed (q.v.) asymmetric patterns of white; the lines of separation between the colors are well defined; from the Anglo Saxon *scuwa* meaning shadow which may be related to the Latin *obscurus* meaning dark shadowed, a coat shadowed by another color.

skiboy A competitor in a skijoring (q.v.) event.

skid *see* DRAG SHOE

skid boots Protective leg wraps fitted below the hocks and covering the fetlocks of the hind legs of the horse; used on Western horses to protect the fetlocks when performing a sliding stop.

skid pan *see* DRAG SHOE

skid-shoe *see* DRAG SHOE

skied One of five natural gaits of the Icelandic (q.v.) used to cover short distances at great speed.

skijoring A mounted winter sport in which a rider pulls a skier behind his horse using a long rope attached to the stock saddle (q.v.), on a straight-away or counter-clockwise roughly circular course of around 250 yards (229 m) consisting of 4 wedge-shaped jumps and about 6 knee-high rubber gates around which the skier weaves; the skier wears standard downhill ski gear while Western tack is used on the mostly Quarter Horse (q.v.) mounts, sharp-shod with an alloy of tungsten and brass welded onto their shoes, snowball pads (q.v.) are optional; derived from the Finnish sport of the same name in which competitors ski behind reindeer or dogs.

skim sheet *see* FLY SHEET

skin (1) A racing term; to make a racetrack faster by rolling and hardening the surface. (2) To strip of money or belongings; to fleece. (3) The anatomical boundary and principal organ of communication between the horse and his environment; the largest body organ, constituting 12 to 24 percent of the horse's total bodyweight depending on age; consists of a variety of cellular and tissue components: the epidermis (q.v.), appendageal system (q.v.), derma (q.v.), arrector pili muscles, panniculus carnosus, and panniculus adiposa (a fatty subacute layer).

skip *see* SKEP

skirt (1) Also known as saddle skirt, bastos, wings, and incorrectly flaps; the small flaps on either side of the seat of the English saddle covering the stirrup bars. (2) A hunting term; said of a hound who cuts corners and does not follow the true line when following the scent of the fox. (3) *see* APRON NO. 2. (4) Also known as saddle skirt; the square leather base upon which the Western saddle is built; rests against the horse blanket or pad and is frequently shearling lined.

skirter A hunting term; a hound (q.v.) who runs wide or skirts (q.v.) the pack (q.v.) hoping to be the first to pick up the line of the fox (q.v.) after it has made a sharp turn.

skittish Said of a horse who is easily frightened, shy, or timid.

skiving The process by which the flesh is shaved from a cured hide; to split or cut a hide into layers or slices.

Skogruss *see* GOTLAND

Skogsruss *see* GOTLAND

skunk tail *see* FROSTY

Skyros A pony breed indigenous to the Greek island of Skyros from which the name derived; is the smallest and is believed to be the oldest of the Greek breeds, bearing some resemblance to the Tarpan (q.v.); stands 9.1 to 11 hands and may have a gray, bay, brown, or palomino (q.v.) coat; has a small head, short back, poorly developed croup and chest, and slender legs; cow hocks (q.v.) are common; is quiet and trustworthy; used principally for packing and as a child's mount.

slab fracture A break (q.v.) in the bone in a joint that extends from one articular surface to the other; occurs most commonly in the third carpal bone of the knee.

slab-sided *see* FLAT-SIDED

slack (1) Not drawn tightly, loose, as in a rope or reins. (2) A British term; a depression between hills in a hillside or on the surface of the ground. (3) A British term; a boggy or wet hollow. (4) A Western riding term; in competition, extra or overflow entries that cannot be fitted into the performance period; slack is usually run prior to the scheduled event. (5) A dressage term; said of the reins when lacking contact. (6) Said of the horse's musculature when sagging, lacking muscle tone or springy resilence.

slack in the loins Said of a horse who has weak loins.

slaframine A toxic alkaloid produced by the fungus *Rhizoctonia legumnicola* found in forages such as clover; ingestion causes slaframine toxicosis (q.v.).

slaframine toxicosis Also known as slobber factor; a noninfectious disease affecting both horses and cattle, although horses are particularly susceptible; caused by the ingestion of forages such as clovers, infected with the fungus *Rhizoctonia leguminicola* which produces a toxic alkaloid called slaframine; symptoms include profuse salivation and, in some cases, frequent urination and defecation; is not deadly, and removal of the infected forage results in rapid recovery.

slate grullo *see* GRULLO

slat-sided *see* FLAT-SIDED

SLE *see* SYSTEMIC LUPUS ERYTHEMATOSUS

Sledge *see* SLEIGH

sleeper A racing term; an underrated horse whose performance exceeds expectations.

sleeping sickness *see* EQUINE ENCEPHALOMYELITIS

Sleigh Also known as Sledge; any horse-drawn vehicle having sleds or runners instead of wheels; used to travel snow- or ice-covered terrain.

Slice of an Omnibus *see* BOULNOIS CAB

slicing A barrel racing term; said of a horse who attempts to turn a barrel too soon and either strikes it or turns improperly so that he is out of position for the next barrel.

slick (1) Said of a flat horseshoe. (2) *see* SLICK EAR

slick ear Also known as slick; an unbranded horse.

slicker A long, loose, oilskin or waterproof outer coat; a raincoat.

slide *see* SLIDING STOP

sliding stop Also known as slide; an abrupt stop performed by a galloping horse in which he sets his hind feet, engages his hocks, rounds his back, sits down low on his haunches, walks with his front feet and slides to a stop on his hind feet, tucking them well under his body.

slip (1) *see* TICKET NO. 2. (2) Premature birth or delivery of a foal, too underdeveloped to survive.

Slipe A horse-drawn vehicle; a shaftless version of the Irish Side Car (q.v.) attached to a horse or mule by means of a crude harness and dragged along the ground.

slip head That part of the bridle supporting the bit; positioned behind the horse's ears or that part of a noseband, including the cheeks and headpiece, which fits behind the horse's ears.

slipped Said of a mare who aborts a pregnancy naturally.

slipped shoulder *see* SWEENEY

slipped stifle Also known as dislocated knee or dislocated patella; a condition in which the patella either slides in and out of the trochlear depression in front of the femur (partial dislocation) or becomes fixed above the outer lip of the trochlear surface (complete dislocation), causing all joints of the affected leg to straighten and the limb to be held pointed behind.

slipper (1) *see* DRAG SHOE. (2) *see* TIP SHOE

slipping a point A jumping term; (obs); the point at which the rider begins to adjust the horse's stride for a jump.

slip rein To secure a rein to something, such as a head collar, so that it can be released quickly if necessary.

slip the reins To allow the reins to slide through one's fingers to their maximum length.

slitting the nostrils A practice dating back to ancient Egypt, 1350 BC; practitioners slit the horse's nostrils in belief that it would make him breathe more freely; may have also begun in an effort to compensate for impaired breathing caused by pressure from a drop noseband; still practiced.

Sloan, James Todhunter (1874–1933) An American jockey who popularized the crouched style of flat racing in which the rider is positioned well over the shoulders of the horse, riding with very short leathers (q.v.).

slobber factor *see* SLAFRAMINE TOXICOSIS

sloping shoulder Also known as oblique shoulder; said of the horse's shoulder when the humerus is the desired length and the scapula is long and slanting.

sloppy track A racing term; said of a racing strip (q.v.) covered with puddles, but not yet muddy, the surface remaining hard.

slot (1) A racing term; a post position (q.v.). (2) The track or trail of a deer or other animal.

slough Separation of a dead part from the rest of the living body by natural processes; may be a small part such as a piece of skin.

slow gait (1) Also known as stepping pace, slow gait, or four-beat stepping pace; the slow, four-beat, broken gait performed by five-gaited horses such as the American Saddlebred (q.v.) at a speed less than 10 mph (17 kmph); emphasis is on precision and form; there is a slight break in cadence from the pace, in which the near fore and the near hind feet leave the ground simultaneously, followed with an interruption, by the off fore and off hind; primarily a show gait producing a characteristic sideways swinging motion of the rider; is very comfortable to ride; a collected form of the rack (q.v.). (2) *see* WALK

Slow Heavy *see* STAGE COACH

slow pace *see* SLOW GAIT NO. 1

slow track A racing term; a slightly wet, but not muddy race track.

slug A lazy or slow horse who requires considerable urging to move forward.

Slurazi *see* DARASHOURI

small horse An American term; any pony taller than 51.2 inches (130 cm).

small metacarpal *see* SPLINT BONE

small metacarpal bones *see* SPLINT BONE

Small Station Cab *see* BROUGHAM

small strongyle One of many species of roundworm found in the horse's cecum and colon, specifically *Tridontophorus tenuicollis* (q.v.); many are appreciably smaller than the large strongyle (q.v.), but some may be as large as *Strongylus vulgaris* (q.v.); is much less destructive than large strongyles, feeds superficially on the intestinal mucosa, and has a three-week life cycle; migrates to the small intestine and may remain dormant in nodular enlargements on the wall of the large intestine; in temperate areas may cause acute diarrhea and death in young horses and ponies in the late winter and spring.

smart money (1) A racing term; an insider's bet. (2) An American racing term; those who give inside information or tips on future races.

smithy (1) *see* BLACKSMITH. (2) The building or shop in which a farrier (q.v.) or blacksmith works and keeps his tools.

smoke eye *see* WALL EYE

smoky black Refers to coat color; the body

coat color is a lighter black than the points (q.v.).

smooth *see* BAREFOOT

smooth-mouthed Said of a horse whose teeth have been worn smooth due to use; normally indicates the horse is at least 12 years old.

smooth muscle Any nonstriated, involuntary muscle (q.v.) which operates in such involuntary movements as breathing and digestion, the principal exception being the heart, which consists of involuntary, striated muscle.

smooth rein Any rein made of leather or other material without lacing or plaiting; attached to the bit cheekpieces on one end and held in the rider's hands on the other.

Smudish An ancient horse breed indigenous to the Baltic states, specifically former Lithuania; generally had a dun (q.v.) coat with a light mane and tail, although mouse dun (q.v.) and bay coats also occurred; had a dark dorsal stripe (q.v.), small head, muscular neck, strong forehand, and strong, lean, small-boned legs; stood 13 to 15 hands; a highly regarded horse.

smutty buckskin Also known as dark buckskin; refers to coat color; any horse with a yellow coat into which black hairs are mixed; will have black points (q.v.) and a head of a color similar to the body.

smutty grullo Also known as dark grullo; refers to coat color; a grullo (q.v.) of the color group dun (q.v.); any grullo color where black is mixed into the body color, the points (q.v.) are black, and the head dark.

smutty palomino Also known as sooty palomino; refers to coat color; of the color group palomino (q.v.); a yellow coat and sometimes tail hairs evenly mixed with black; may be as dark as some chestnuts (q.v.).

snaffle *see* SNAFFLE BIT

snaffle bit Also known as snaffle; the simplest and most commonly used of all bits; primarily a straight or jointed mouthpiece with a ring on either end to which one pair of reins is attached; action varies in accordance with the horse's head position and use of auxiliaries such as a martingale (q.v.) noseband; many subtypes characterized by mouthpiece and ring variances; the mouthpiece may be jointed or mullen and the bit rings are either loose (running through a hole in the butt end of the mouthpiece) or fixed as in the eggbutt and most types of cheek snaffles; derived from the Dutch word *snavel* and the German *schnabel*, meaning to mouth or break.

snaffle bridle A bridle (q.v.) used in conjunction with a snaffle bit (q.v.).

Snail of the King's Highway *see* BROAD-WHEELED WAGON

snatch (1) *see* STRINGHALT. (2) Said of the horse; to attempt to jerk the reins from the rider's hands. (3) A dressage term used in reference to one or both hind legs; to pick up the leg jerkily and, sometimes, excessively high; is not stringhalt (q.v.).

snip A face marking (q.v.); an isolated white marking located between, in the region of, or extending into the nostrils, but not extending above the nostrils.

snip lower lip A face marking (q.v.); any marking found on the lower lip.

snorter An excitable horse.

snowball hammer A farrier's tool; a hoof pick (q.v.) and hammer combined into the head of one instrument; used to break up and remove packed snow and ice from the underside of the horse's hooves.

snowball pad A horseshoe pad (q.v.) inserted between the ground-side surface of the hoof and the horseshoe to prevent balling (q.v.).

snowflake Also known as snowflake marking; refers to a coat color pattern; one of six symmetrical coat color patterns of the Appaloosa (q.v.) approved by the Appaloosa Horse Club (q.v.); a solid body color with dominant spotting over the hips; spots may range in size from ⅜ to 1¼ inches (1–3 cm) in diameter, may not appear until the horse is 3 to 5 years old, and can increase with age until the pattern stabilizes, after which time, on some horses, the white spots can disappear; in the advanced pattern, called speckled, the horse appears almost white with small colored spots throughout the coat.

snowflake marking *see* SNOWFLAKE

snub To tie short to restrict head and neck movement, e.g. "He snubbed the colt to the patience post."

soaping *see* LATHER

Sociable *see* SOCIABLE BAROUCHE

Sociable Barouche Also known as Barouch Sociable, Sociable, or Vis-à-Vis; a narrow, horse-drawn, four-wheeled, open pleasure or passenger carriage popular in the late 18th and 19th centuries; had seating for four passengers seated vis-à-vis, and double or two half hoods protecting both the front and rear of the vehicle; drawn by a pair of horses and driven from a high box.

Sociable Landau *see* LANDAU

Société Hippique Percheronne A French organization founded to maintain the Percheron (q.v.) stud book (q.v.), a duty it has performed since 1883.

sock (1) Also known as half cannon; a leg marking (q.v.); white on the horse's foot which extends from the coronet (q.v.) along the pastern to the middle of the cannon bone. (2) *see* HALF-PASTERN

sobre pass A Spanish term; a gait in which the horse canters with his forelegs and trots with his hind legs.

sodium *see* SODIUM CHLORIDE

sodium chloride Also known as common salt, salt, or sodium; a crystalline compound consisting of equal parts sodium and chlorine; important to maintain osmotic pressure, acid-base equilibrium, water metabolism, and to regulate body temperature; is not stored in the body tissues and is therefore required in the daily ration, a mature horse requiring approximately 60 grams of salt per day; the requirement increases in working horses and lactating mares; excess dietary salt is not toxic if sufficient water is available, although insufficient water may cause digestive disturbances, weakness, loss of coordination, paralysis of the hind limbs, and even death.

soft (1) Said of an out-of-condition horse who fatigues easily. (2) A team penning and roping term; said of a cow who has little play and is easily tired.

soft bone *see* CARTILAGE

softening of the bones Said of the mare in the first stage of parturition (q.v.) during which the central joint of the pelvic girdle expands to allow for passage of the foal; concurrently, the muscles drop in over the bones of the hindquarters to protect the foal during birth.

soft mouth The horse's mouth when sensitive to bit or rein action.

soft mouthed (1) Also known as soft-mouthed hound; said of a hound who has a low voice or bark. (2) Said of a horse who requires minimal bit and rein action to achieve the desired response; the opposite of hard mouth (q.v.).

soft-mouthed hound *see* SOFT MOUTHED

soft palate The muscular tissue at the posterior part of the roof of the mouth; in conjunction with the hard palate (q.v.) separates the nasal and oral cavities.

soft palate disease *see* CHOKING UP

soft track A racing term; said of a racing surface which contains a large amount of moisture and into which horses' hooves sink.

Sokolsky A Polish-bred warmblood developed during the 19th century; influenced by the Norfolk Trotter (q.v.), Brabant (q.v.), Belgian Ardennes (q.v.) and the Anglo-Norman (q.v.); stands 15 to 16 hands, has a chestnut, brown, or gray coat, a large head, sturdy frame, short and straight back, short legs, and large, round feet; is patient, hard-working, particularly well suited to heavy draft and farm work; a very economical keeper.

soil To feed a stall-bound horse sufficient quantities and types of feed to fatten him.

solar The bottom aspect of the horse's hoof.

solid blanket Refers to coat color pattern; a symmetrical, solid pattern of white on the haunches of a non-white horse with sharply defined edges; common to many breeds, most notably the Appaloosa (q.v.) and Pony of the Americas (q.v.).

solid color Refers to coat color; a coat consisting of only one color and no black or white markings.

solid horse A racing term; said of a horse who is a contender in a race.

Somali Wild Ass *see* AFRICAN ASS

Somali Wild Donkey *see* AFRICAN ASS

somer *see* PACK HORSE

Sommier Also known as Brittany Pack Horse; one of two sub-breeds of Breton (q.v.) horses, the other being the Roussin (q.v.), found in northern France during the Middle Ages; believed to have descended from the Bidet Breton (q.v.) bred to Oriental stallions and mares; used mainly for farm work and as a pack animal.

son of the desert *see* ARAB

sonogram *see* ULTRASOUND

sooty palomino *see* SMUTTY PALOMINO

sophomore A racing term; a three-year-old horse; so called because he is in his second year.

sore (1) A place on the body where the skin or flesh is bruised, cut, infected, or painful; a wound. (2) Stiff and tender, as from physical exertion.

sore backed Said of a horse who is sore (q.v.) along the top line (q.v.) in the general area of the saddle; generally caused by back strain, lameness in the hind legs, or primary back muscle stiffness due to underlying spinal problems.

sore kidneys Tenderness along the top line (q.v.) in the general area of the saddle; rarely an indicator of true kidney soreness unless other signs of urinary problems are present.

sore knee *see* CARPITIS

soreing To cut the Paso Fino's (q.v.) forehooves intentionally short to make them sore and thus encourage the horse to pick his feet up quickly; an unacceptable practice.

sore shins *see* BUCKED SHINS

sorghum Also known as grain sorghum or milo; a low-growing cereal plant well adapted to semi-arid climates, cultivated for fodder, grain, and juice; has an extensive root system and modest leaf area; varieties include milo, kafir, hergari, feterita; a high-energy, high carbohydrate feed (approximately 75 percent), low fiber, (less than 3 percent), low fat (less than 3 percent), and having a protein content ranging from 8 to 16 percent, but averaging 9 percent in most cases; although a yellow grain, contains less carotene than corn; not a good source of vitamins or minerals; a heavy feed which can result in founder (q.v.) or severe or fatal digestive disturbances such as enterotoxemia if overfed.

Sorraia *see* SORRAIA PONY

Sorraia Pony Also known as Sorraia; an ancient pony breed originating in western Spain in the area bordering the Sorraia river from which the name derived; Spain's only native pony; thought to have descended from the Tarpan (q.v.) and Asiatic Wild Horse (q.v.) which it resembles; stands 12.2 to 13 hands and may have a dun, gray, or palomino coat, with zebra markings (q.v.) on the legs and an eel stripe (q.v.); has a large head, long ears with black tips, a slender and long neck, high withers, poor hindquarters, low-set tail, and long, solid legs; is independent, an easy keeper, frugal, resistant to both heat and cold, and has good endurance (q.v.); historically used for agricultural work and presently for riding and packing; its numbers are on the decline.

sorrel Refers to coat color; a clear light red coat with non-black points; sometimes confused with chestnut (q.v.), the difference between the two colors depending largely on the breed under consideration; variations include sorrel tostado (q.v.), sorrel alazán (q.v.), sorrel ruano (q.v.), and blond sorrel ruano (q.v.).

sorrel alazán Refers to coat color; of the color group sorrel (q.v.); a clear light red coat with a lighter mane and tail than the body, but not near the white of the ruano.

sorrel roan *see* STRAWBERRY ROAN

sorrel ruano Refers to coat color; of the color group sorrel (q.v.); a clear light red coat with a flaxen mane and tail and lower legs lighter than the body; may look similar to a palomino (q.v.).

sorrel tostado

sound Said of a horse free from illness, disease, physical or conformation defect, injury, or blemish that may affect his future performance or ability to work.

sounding board *see* FINO BOARD

sound in the wind Also known as sound of wind; said of a horse free of any respiratory ailment that may impair or restrict performance.

soundness The state or condition of being sound (q.v.).

soundness certificate *see* VETERINARY SOUNDNESS CERTIFICATE

soundness examination *see* VETERINARY INSPECTION

sound of wind *see* SOUND IN THE WIND

soup plate Said of a horse's feet when they are round and disproportionately large for his body size.

sour Also known as stale; an over-trained or over-competed horse who has become lethargic and uninterested in work; to become bored, as in cattle.

sour cattle Also known as stale cattle; a cutting term; said of cattle that have been used for cutting (q.v.) too often and no longer respond well to the horse; inactive cattle.

Southern and Eastern European Gidran One of two types of Gidran Arabian (q.v.); a Hungarian breed developed in 1816; descended from an Arab (q.v.) of the Siglavy strain crossed with Thoroughbred (q.v.) blood; is lighter than the Middle European Gidran (q.v.) and is thus used for all-purpose competition.

Southern Plantation Walking Horse *see* TENNESSEE WALKING HORSE

South German Coldblood *see* NORIKER

Sovereign (1) An ornately finished, four-wheeled, horse-drawn vehicle similar in design to the Clarence (q.v.). (2) The London and Brighton, England, Stage Coach.

Soviet Heavy Draft A heavy-draft breed developed in Russia between 1890 and 1930 by putting native mares to imported Percheron (q.v.) stallions; breed characteristics were firmly established by the 1940s; has a massive build, weighs 1,430 to 1,720 pounds (649–780 kg), stands about 15 hands, has a well-proportioned head with pronounced jaws, relatively short neck, low and broad withers, deep chest, short legs with mild feathering, and a chestnut, roan, or bay coat; is quiet, energetic, strong, and has a sure and easy gait, both at the walk and trot; used for heavy draft and farm work.

sowar A trooper in an Indian cavalry regiment.

sow mouth *see* UNDERSHOT JAW

soybean A protein-rich leguminous plant, *Glycine max*, used for forage (q.v.), and its seeds used as a source of oil, flour, and other foods.

soybean meal A high energy, high protein supplement produced from the residue of the soybean (q.v.) following oil extraction; contains the highest protein level of all grains, varying from 41 to 50 percent, a fat content of 1.5 to 5 percent, is a good source of calcium, provides moderate amounts of riboflavin and thiamin, contains all ten essential amino acids, is highly digestible, low in fiber, and commonly fed to horses.

spa *see* TRIPLE BAR

space loop *see* KEEPER

spade (1) Also known as spade bit; bit with leverage like a curb (q.v.), having a high spoon (q.v.) instead of a port (q.v.); connected to the cheekpieces by copper braces. (2) *see* SPOON

spade bit *see* SPADE NO. 1

span A pair of horses harnessed in a team to pull a vehicle.

Spanish Anglo-Arab *see* HISPANO

Spanish Arab *see* HISPANO

Spanish cantinas *see* SADDLE BAGS

Spanish fly *see* CANTHARIS

Spanish hackamore A bitless bridle consisting of a bosal (q.v.), headstall, and mecate (q.v.); control is effectively maintained by the heel knot (q.v.) behind the bosal, that lies in the chin groove and functions in a way similar to a curb chain.

Spanish Horse *see* ANDALUSIAN

Spanish jumping bit *see* KIMBLEWICK

Spanish Riding School *see* IMPERIAL SPANISH RIDING SCHOOL OF VIENNA

Spanish Riding School of Vienna *see* IMPERIAL SPANISH RIDING SCHOOL OF VIENNA

Spanish School *see* IMPERIAL SPANISH RIDING SCHOOL OF VIENNA

Spanish snaffle *see* KIMBLEWICK

Spanish step *see* PASSAGE

Spanish walk An artificial allure (q.v.); an exaggerated, elevated walk, in which the horse extends his straightened forelegs up and forward to about chest height; the forelegs show much greater activity and extension than the hind legs.

SPAOPD *see* SUMMER PASTURE-ASSOCIATED OBSTRUCTIVE PULMONARY DISEASE

spare (1) A racing term; any horse in partial training who is not working with the main string. (2) A British racing term; an unexpected ride picked up by a jockey, usually to take the place of the booked jockey who has been injured, delayed, etc. (3) Also known as rest horse; an obsolete coaching term; an extra horse kept at a change (q.v.) station along a coach route who replaced a tired, spent, or lame horse in the team pulling the coach.

spasms of the gastrointestinal tract *see* COLIC

spavin Any of certain diseases or conditions of the horse affecting the hock including bog spavin (q.v.), bone spavin (q.v.), blood spavin (q.v.), and occult spavin (q.v.).

spavined Said of a horse suffering from spavin (q.v.).

spavin shoe A horseshoe (q.v.), the toe of which is rolled up to prevent the horse from hitting his toe on the ground; the heels are sloped and left high, approximately 1 inch (2.5 cm), to relieve joint stress; used on spavined (q.v.) horses.

spavin test Also known as hock flexion test; a test performed to determine, but not guarantee, spavin (q.v.), since the fetlock and stifle joints are also flexed; the hind limb is flexed so that the metatarsus is approximately parallel to the ground surface; the leg is held in this position for 1 to 1½ minutes after which the horse is observed for lameness; increased lameness is considered a positive test for spavin.

spay To perform any procedure on a mare or filly, such as surgically removing the ovaries, that renders her incapable of conception.

spayed mare A mare who has had a procedure to render her incapable of conception.

speak Also known as cry; a hunting term; said of a hound (q.v.) when he barks or "gives tongue."

specialized shoe Any horseshoe (q.v.) adapted for a specific breed or type of horse.

specialized shoeing A horseshoeing

procedure for a specific breed or type of horse.

speck in the eye *see* FEATHER IN THE EYE

speckled Refers to a coat color pattern; one of six symmetrical coat patterns of the Appaloosa (q.v.) approved by the Appaloosa Horse Club (q.v.); an advanced version of the snowflake (q.v.) pattern; the coat becomes very light, appearing almost white, with small colored spots throughout; often confused with flea-bitten (q.v.) grays.

spectacles *see* IRISH MARTINGALE

speed and endurance One of three main components of a three-day event (q.v.); a four-phase test conducted on day two consisting of: Phases A and C held over roads and tracks 6 to 12 miles (10–20 km) long, mainly ridden at a trot and slow canter; Phase B, a steeplechase (q.v.) course, roughly 1 to 2.5 miles (1.6–4 km) long with 8 to 12 fences ridden at a gallop; Phase D, a cross-country course, between 3 to 5 miles (5–8 km), with 20 to 32 obstacles ridden at fast canter and gallop; penalties are incurred for falls or refusals at the obstacles and for exceeding the time allowed for each phase.

speed figure A racing term; a handicapping tool used to assign a numerical value to a horse's performance.

speedy-cut (1) A wound or injury to the knee or upper part of the cannon bone caused when the horseshoe of one foot, usually a hind, strikes the inside of the opposite front leg. (2) High scalping (q.v.) common to trotters.

speedy-cutting Any limb interference occurring at a fast gait.

speedy-cutting shoe *see* FEATHER-EDGED SHOE

spelt A type of wheat (q.v.); grain of the genus *Triticum spelta*, grown as a livestock feed in western Asia and southern Europe; has a large fibrous hull, high fiber content, and a digestible energy slightly lower than that of oats (q.v.).

spent grains *see* BREWERS DRIED GRAINS

sperm Also known as seed or spermatozoa; the microscopic fertilizing cell contained in the white, opaque seminal fluid of the male horse, which is produced in the testicles; contains the genetic material of the stallion.

spermatozoa *see* SPERM

spermatozoon More than one sperm (q.v.).

spider *see* SPIDER WEB BANDAGE

spider bandage *see* SPIDER WEB BANDAGE

Spider Phaeton A light, four-wheeled, horse-drawn vehicle of the Phaeton (q.v.) type popular in the 1860s; had a spindle-backed driving seat, a rumble seat for a groom, a skeletal structure mounted on arched irons for improved cut-under, and was hung on sideways-elliptical springs, front and rear; drawn either by a single horse in shafts or a pair in pole gear (q.v.).

spider web bandage Also known as spider; cloth or gauze used to apply pressure to the knee joint area; consists of a sufficient length of muslin to cover 6 to 8 inches (15–20 cm) above and below the knee; is about 16 inches (41 cm) wide; is folded in half and strips 1 inch wide by 5 inch long (2.5 × 12.5 cm) are cut perpendicularly into the folded material; the unstripped portion of the muslin is laid against the front inside portion of the leg while the strips are braided down the outside of the leg; the top left and right strips are tied and knotted around the leg; all subsequent strips are braided down the leg; may be applied over standing bandages (q.v.), dressings, ice packs, etc.

spider wheel Also known as hickory; an American wheel used on horse-drawn vehicles; constructed of elastic wood such as hickory, the spokes were thinner and lighter than those used on English-made wheels.

spiffing The obsolete practice of blowing snuff into the nostril of an unpredictable or cantankerous horse to control it.

spike (1) *see* UNICORN. (2) A hoof shape pattern in which the hoof is generally square, with straight quarters and sharply turned-in heels; the widest part of the hoof located midway between the toe and heels.

spike team *see* UNICORN

spin A Western term; a 360 degree turn in which the horse's forelegs swing, in bounding movements, around the hind legs, while the hind feet remain, more or less, in one place; the radius of the turn is equal to the length of the horse; forehand lightness is essential; similar to the canter pirouette (q.v.).

spinal column *see* VERTEBRAL COLUMN

spinal cord The cord of nervous tissue extending through the spinal canal, and enclosed within the spinal column (q.v.).

Spindle Wagon An American horse-drawn Buggy; had paneled lower sides with spindles above to lighten the appearance.

spine *see* VERTEBRAL COLUMN

spinny A hunting term; a small covert (q.v.).

spiral fracture A crack or break in a bone that turns or spirals around the bone circumference; caused by a sudden torque or twist of the bone; may or may not be comminuted (q.v.) or displaced (q.v.).

spit box A racing term; a barn where horses are brought for post-race drug testing.

Spiti A pony breed indigenous to the Himalayan mountain region of Northern India; the name derived from the Spiti tract in the central Himalayas; principally bred by the Kanyat, a high-caste Hindu tribe, who use it for trade; is tough, sturdy, sure-footed, vigorous, best suited for mountain use, and ill-suited to the warm and humid conditions of the lowlands; stands approximately 12 hands, has a rather heavy neck, sharp ears, strong, short back, short legs, round feet, and a full mane and tail; the coat is usually gray or steel gray; tends to temperamental; used for packing; is smaller, but similar in type and conformation to the Bhutia (q.v.).

spit out the bit *see* SPIT THE BIT

spit the bit (1) Also known as spit out the bit; a racing term; said of an exhausted horse who sucks back, releasing pressure on the bit. (2) A generic racing term; said of an exhausted horse.

spiv (1) Also known as spivvey; a groom (q.v.) lacking full-time employment who is capable and willing to perform odd jobs. (2) A British term; someone untrustworthy and likely to engage in underhanded acts, which may have a dishonest basis.

spivvey *see* SPIV

splashboard Also known as mudguard, splashguard, or fender; a panel on a horse-drawn vehicle which protects the passengers from splashes of water, mud, etc., kicked up from the road by the horse.

splashed *see* SPLASHED WHITE

splashed white Also known as splashed; refers to a coat color pattern; an asymmetrical pattern of white consisting of large, distinctly marked patches, white legs, a predominantly white head, and a mostly white belly; the eyes are commonly blue.

splashguard *see* SPLASHBOARD

splatter A cutting term; the action of a horse when it drops down in front of a cow.

splay footed *see* TOE OUT

splenic fever *see* ANTHRAX

splint Enlargement of the splint bones (q.v.) resulting from a proliferation of fibrous tissue and osteoperostitis; usually occurs in the forelegs of young horses in the early months or years of training on the medial aspect of the forelimbs between the second and third metacarpal bones; associated with hard training, poor conformation, improper hoof care, or malnutrition; characterized by swelling, heat, and lameness which is only observed during splint formation; splint size is usually dependent on the degree of inflammation and the surface area involved; usually assumes an elongated form lying parallel to the small metacarpal bone; of four types: interosseous splint (q.v.), edge splint (q.v.), creeping splint (q.v.), and knee splint (q.v.).

splint bone Also known as small metacarpal, small metacarpal bone (foreleg), or metatarsus bone (hind leg); either of two small bones which lie along the posterior parts of the cannon bone (q.v.) in the horse's fore or hind legs anchoring tissues to the accessory carpal bone at the joint's rear and thereby preventing the knee from collapsing backwards.

splint boots *see* BRUSHING BOOTS

splinter bar *see* SWINGLE TREE

splintree *see* LEAD BAR

split (1) A hunting term; said of a hound pack which separates into two different packs to follow the scents of two different foxes traveling in different directions. (2) A racing term; a fraction of time, e.g. the time it takes a horse to reach the eighth pole instead of run the entire race.

split up behind Also known as split up quarters; a conformation fault; said of a horse with weak gaskins; when viewed from behind, the thighs divide too high, just below the dock (q.v.); typical in cold bloods (q.v.).

split up quarters *see* SPLIT UP BEHIND

spoiled mouth Said of the horse's mouth when no longer sensitive to minimal bit and rein action to achieve the desired response.

spoke (1) A Western roping term; the length of rope between the honda (q.v.) and the roper's hand. (2) A metal or wooden bar, radiating from the nave (q.v.) of the wheel of a horse-drawn vehicle on the inside and set to the fellow (q.v.) on the other, which, in numbers, support the wheel rim.

spoke brush A long, narrow brush with thick, hard bristles used to clean carriage wheels on a horse-drawn vehicle.

sponge (1) A racing term; to insert a piece of sponge or other foreign material into the horse's nostrils to impede his ability to breath, and thus impair his performance. (2) The skeleton or framework of any aquatic animal belonging to the phylum *Porifera*, composed of horny elastic fibers, easily compressible, readily imbibing fluids, and as readily giving them out again upon compression; used for bathing and general cleaning. (3) To cleanse or wipe with a sponge.

spook To cause to stampede; to frighten.

spooky Said a nervous or jumpy horse, who reacts to sounds, movement and changes of light and color.

spoon (1) Also known as spade; a projection from the center of the mouthpiece of a spade bit (q.v.) usually 3 to 4 inches (7.5–10 cm) long and approximately 1½ inches (38 mm) wide near the top, commonly has a center opening to accommodate a cricket (q.v.); prevents the horse from getting his tongue up over the bit. (2) *see* LAME HAND

Sporting Phaeton Also known as Malvern Phaeton; a four-wheeled horse-drawn vehicle of the Dogcart (q.v.) type; had two seats placed back-to-back, was hung on four elliptic springs, and the body had an arch under the front seat to allow a full lock.

sport of kings *see* HORSE RACING

spot (1) A face marking (q.v.); any white mark on the horse's forehead less than 1 inch (25 mm) in diameter, except where the number of white hairs are very few. (2) A jumping term; the most suitable place from which a horse should leave the ground to clear an obstacle with ease and minimum effort; located in front of the obstacle at a distance determined by obstacle height and type as well as the horse's jumping ability.

spot play A racing term; a wager in which the bettor (q.v.) only bets on races and horses he feels are worthwhile risks.

spotted Refers to coat color; the horse's coat when marked with a spotted coat pattern of any color.

spotted blanket One of six symmetrical coat color patterns of the Appaloosa (q.v.) recognized by the Appaloosa Horse Club (q.v.); consists of a solid colored body with white over the hips and having colored spots on the white.

spotted horse (1) Any horse having a spotted coat pattern; known by a variety of names throughout history in Europe and Asia, notably the Danish Knabstruper (q.v.), French Tigre, British Blagdon, Chubbarie (q.v.), or Appaloosa (q.v.). (2) *see* APPALOOSA

spotters Employees of an auctioneer who, acting as intermediaries between the auctioneer and bidders, acknowledge each bid made on a horse and notify the auctioneer of such bids.

spotty scent A hunting term; said of uneven, periodic scent.

sprain (1) Wrenching of a joint, often with simultaneous tearing of a ligament. (2) Inflammation of a tendon, which is generally the result of excessive fiber stretching.

sprained tendon Sprain of the superficial or deep flexor tendon during maximum weight-bearing on the limb; an extremely common condition in both heavy and light draft horse breeds; signs include: inflammation, heat, pain, and swelling; affected horses may walk sound, but when asked to trot show pronounced lameness.

sprain of the suspensory ligament *see* SUSPENSORY DESMITIS

spread (1) The width of a jumping obstacle. (2) Also known as spread fence; any show or cross-country jumping obstacle which has width and, generally, some height; include, but are not limited to, parallel bars (q.v.), hog backs, triple bars (q.v.), oxers (q.v.), walls with rails behind, water ditches, and open water jumps (q.v.). (3) Also known as spreading a plate; a horseshoe (q.v.) that has shifted out of position or becomes loose on the hoof. (4) Also known as plate spread; the distance between the horseshoe (q.v.) heels.

spread fence *see* SPREAD NO. 2

spreading a plate *see* SPREAD NO. 3

spring bar *see* STIRRUP BAR

springing (1) *see* GALLOP. (2) The earliest form of suspension used on horse-drawn vehicles; originally provided by leather thoroughbraces (q.v.); whip spring came into general use about 1700, with cee-springs appearing in 1790 and elliptic springs in 1804.

spring the team A coaching term; to gallop a team.

spring tree A saddle tree (q.v.) with a strip of metal at the waist which gives the tree increased flexibility.

Spring Wagon A four-wheeled, horse-drawn American passenger wagon with at least two rows of crosswise seating; had a long, shallow, box-shaped body mounted on shallow semi-elliptical or platform springs and drawn by a single horse in shafts (q.v.); had a hand brake.

sprint (1) Also known as sprint race; a racing term; a race seven furlongs or less long, generally with no more than one turn. (2) To race, run, or move at a high speed especially at short intervals or over a short distance.

sprinter (1) A racing term; a horse who performs best over short distances, generally 1 mile (1.6 km) or less, and lacks the stamina to compete over long distances. (2) Also known as wild cow; a cutting term; a cow who wants to run parallel to the herd. (3) One of three morphological types of Thoroughbred (q.v.); is tall, has a long back and loins, and is very fast.

sprint race *see* SPRINT NO. 1

spur (1) To encourage action of the horse with the spur (q.v.); from the modern German *sporn*, meaning to kick. (2) Also known as gad; a metal instrument having a rowel (q.v.), or a blunt or sharp point, worn on the boot heel of the rider for decoration or to reinforce the rider's leg aids (q.v.); generally worn in pairs; attached to the boot by a spur strap (q.v.).

spur box Also known as spur rest; a small, square piece of leather attached to and projecting from the boot heel upon which a spur rests.

spurred (1) Said of the rider; wearing spurs

(q.v.). (2) Said of a horse whose action has been encouraged by the rider by means of spurs (q.v.).

spur rest *see* SPUR BOX

spurrier One who makes spurs.

spur shield A square-shaped safe (q.v.) fitted beneath the top of the spur strap (q.v.) to prevent excessive buckle wear.

spur strap A leather or material strap by which the spur (q.v.) is held into place on the rider's boot heel.

squab A small cushion or pillow sometimes kept in horse-drawn vehicles; was hung on strings or buttons and served as a head or shoulder rest.

Square Landau *see* SHELBURNE LANDAU

square oxer A jumping obstacle utilizing two sets of standards and any combination of poles, angles, or spreads, where the rails are even; jumped as a single unit.

square tail *see* BANG TAIL

square toe A square-toed horseshoe; the horseshoe does not follow the natural curve of the hoof toe, and the hoof toe extends over the front of the shoe; commonly used on the hind feet to speed breakover and/or to prevent injury to the foreleg should the horse be prone to overreaching.

square volte A dressage term; a volte (q.v.) in which the horse scribes a square, rather than a circle, making each corner with a quarter turn on the haunches; the size of the square depends on the horse's ability and may be from 6 to 12 meters.

squaw tail *see* RABICANO

squeeze into the cow A cutting term; said of the horse who, in response to leg pressure applied by the rider, drops down on his haunches and draws them under his body; no forward movement of the front end actually occurs.

SSI *see* STANDARD STARTS INDEX

'S' spring *see* WHIP SPRING

stab (1) Said of a horse who strikes the ground with his hind hooves, toes first. (2) To strongly jab or poke, as with a spur (q.v.).

stable (1) A building in which one or more horses are kept. (2) Also known as livery or livery stable; an establishment where privately owned horses belonging to one or more owner(s) are lodged, fed, exercised, and, in some cases trained, for a set fee, or where stable-owned horses are maintained for lease or rent. (3) A collection of horses owned by an individual or group or kept at one location. (4) To maintain a horse in a stable as opposed to keeping it at pasture. (5) *see* STALL NO. 1

stable bandage *see* STANDING BANDAGE

stable blanket Also known as stable rug; a covering worn by horses confined to stalls; generally has a medium-weight outer shell and one to three layers; provides warmth, protection from biting insects and the weather (if turned out for a short spell), and keeps the coat clean; available in a variety of designs, weights, and materials as dictated by the use for which it is intended; held in place by a roller or strapping.

stable boots Also known as calking boots; round, disc-shaped, leather boots strapped onto the ground-side surface of the hoof to protect the other hooves from injury inflicted by the horseshoe heel.

stable colors The colors used to denote a trainer, stable, rider, farm, etc., as for awnings, blankets, show trunks.

stable cough *see* EQUINE INFLUENZA

stable connections Also known as connections; a racing term; those involved with custodianship of a horse running in a race, e.g. the owner, trainer, groom, etc.

stable fly Also known as *Stomoxys calcitrans*; a swarming daytime-feeding fly (q.v.) slightly smaller and grayer than a housefly (q.v.) with needle-sharp mouthparts which inflict painful bites; adults are bloodsuckers which feed only once or twice daily on all warm-blooded animals, usually on the legs; particularly bloodthirsty just prior to weather changes; the primary cause of summer and fall foot stomping in horses; may contribute to the spread of anthrax (q.v.), swamp fever (q.v.), encephalomyelitis (q.v.), and trypanosomes.

stable fork *see* FORK NO. 2

stable hand One employed to work in a stable (q.v.).

stableman One connected with the ownership or operation of a stable (q.v.).

stable management The act of treating, directing, or administrating the activities associated with stabled horses.

Stable Release A document, exchanged for the delivery order, which authorizes removal of a sale horse from the sale grounds or stable.

stable return A racing term; a monthly summary of all race horse activity, e.g. horse transfers in and out of the track, death, etc.

stable rubber Also known as grooming stable rubber; a towel or cloth used to put the final polish (q.v.) on a horse following grooming.

stable rug *see* STABLE BLANKET

stables (1) The first and last work or exercise of the day performed by a horse as in, morning stable; (obs). (2) More than one stable (q.v.).

stable sheet *see* SUMMER SHEET

stable vice Any specific unpleasant or atypical habit, practice, and/or condition a horse may develop as a result of boredom, improper handling, mimicking other horses, etc., e.g. cribbing (q.v.), wind-sucking (q.v.), and weaving (q.v.).

stabling (1) The act of someone who stables horses or other animals. (2) Accommodation for horses or other animals in a stable. (3) Stables collectively.

staccionata A show jumping obstacle similar to a fence (q.v.).

stag (1) A male horse castrated after reaching maturity, the time at which the secondary sex characteristics develop. (2) A gelding (q.v.) more than one year old; (obs). (3) *see* BUCK NO. 3

stage A coaching term; the distance between coaching inns where the horses of Mail and Stage Coaches or postillion (q.v.) driven carriages, were changed; the lengths varied greatly

Stage *see* STAGE COACH

Stage Coach Also known as Stage, slow heavy, old heavy, or American Stage Coach; a four-wheeled, public transportation coach pulled by a team of two, four, or six horses operating between designated stopping places; heavier and slower than the Mail Coach (q.v.); always enclosed, with interior and roof-top passenger seating; luggage was carried on the roof or in the boot (q.v.); driven from an elevated box seat, its footboard supported by brackets; a guard was positioned in the rear; at first unsprung or dead axle, but later hung on braces, elbow, and finally telegraph springs (q.v.).

Stage Wagon (1) *see* BROAD-WHEELED WAGON. (2) *see* LONG WAGON

stag face *see* DISH FACE

staggart *see* BUCK NO. 3

staggers Also known megrim (obs); a disease of horses and cattle attended with sudden, short-term reeling and/or dizziness; may be caused by worm infestation, impaired circulation, poor digestion, etc.

staghound One of a breed of hounds (q.v.) used to hunt stags (q.v.).

stag hunting The sport of mounted following, chasing, or searching for stags (q.v.) behind a pack of hounds (q.v.).

stain *see* FOIL

stained *see* FOILED

stained line *see* FOILED LINE

stainless steel An alloy of steel having a small percentage of chromium and other elements making it highly resistant to rust or corrosion; used among other things, in the construction of bits (q.v.), stirrups (q.v.), and horseshoes (q.v.); when used in a bit mouthpiece (q.v.) has less taste than sweet steel (q.v.) and results in less salivation.

staircase A cross-country obstacle; a series of ascending or descending steps, usually intended to be jumped on bounce strides.

stake (1) A racing term; a commission paid to a winning jockey, trainer, or groom. (2) *see* BET NO. 1. (3) *see* BET NO. 2

stake and bind *see* STAKE AND BOUND

stake and bound Also known as stake and bind; a jumping obstacle; a fence or hedge consisting of thin, vertical stakes interlaced horizontally with supple saplings, or wire, and bound between strong upright poles.

stake money (1) *see* PARIMUTUEL POOL. (2) *see* BET NO. 1

stakes (1) *see* SWEEPSTAKES. (2) A betting term, odds for or against. (3) *see* BET NO. 1

stakes engagements A racing term; the sweepstakes (q.v.) races to which a horse has been nominated.

stakes-placed A racing term; a second or third placing horse competed in a sweepstakes (q.v.).

stakes-producer A racing term; said of a mare who has produced at least one foal who finished first, second, or third in a sweepstakes (q.v.).

stakes race *see* SWEEPSTAKES

stale (1) *see* SOUR. (2) *see* URINATE

stale cattle *see* SOUR CATTLE

stale line Also known as cold, cold line, cold scent, old scent, stale scent, old scent, or pad scent; a hunting term; the quarry's scent (q.v.) when old and difficult to follow; generally does not lead to a quarry (q.v.); is not necessarily a function of scent freshness.

stale scent *see* STALE LINE

stalking-horse A horse behind or alongside which a hunter walks in concealment while pursuing game (q.v.).

stall (1) Also known as box, box stall, stable, or loose box; a 3- or 4-sided compartment in a stable (q.v.) for the accommodation of one horse or a mare and foal; opens on one side and may vary significantly in size, although 6 to 10 feet by 12 to 14 feet (1.8–3 m × 3.6–4.2 m) is common; normally occur in multiples sharing two common walls; include such types as standing stall (q.v.), pipe stall (q.v.), and tie stall (q.v.). (2) To put or keep in a stall or stalls, as animals.

stalled A horse who regularly fails to eat all his food, but appears to perform without problem; (obs).

stall gate A racing term; a starting gate consisting of individual compartments for each horse.

stallion Also known as entire, stud, stud horse, full, full horse, stone horse, stock horse, or bull (Aus); an ungelded male horse 4 years or older capable of or used to reproduce the species; in Thoroughbreds (q.v.), a horse 5 years or older; the term originated in Italy sometime in the 14th century and literally meant one kept in a stall.

stallion breeding report A form listing the stallion's name, registration number, owner, the names of all mares covered during the calendar year, the dates they were covered, their breed and registration numbers, and the name of the mare's owner at the time of service.

stallion cage Also known as stallion support; a truss used to support a strong, athletic, or big stallion during mating.

stallion donkey *see* JACK

stallion groom One whose responsibility it is to care for stallions.

stallion hound A hunting term; a male hound used for breeding purposes.

stallion ring *see* STUD RING

stallion roll A thickly padded stick placed

between the stallion and the mare to prevent over-penetration during mating.

stallion season The period of time during the year when a stallion stands at stud (q.v.).

stallion share A lifetime breeding right to a specific stallion, with one covering allowed per season per share.

stallion station *see* STUD NO. 2

stallion support *see* STALLION CAGE

stalljack A miniature anvil (q.v.) attached to a stand on which farriers shape light horseshoes.

stall-side diagnostic test Also known as a quick-response test, on-site diagnostic test, or on-site evaluation test; any of a number of new biotechnologies developed to provide 1- to 10-minute turnaround time on tests conducted on site rather than in the laboratory; tests exist to detect reproductive concerns (time of a mare's ovulation, pregnancy, prediction of an impending birth, and testing the status of a foal's passive immunity system), a variety of ailments, including influenza (q.v.) and equine infectious anemia (q.v.), and to monitor various body systems such as liver, kidney, muscle, and digestive function; test types include test strips (q.v.) and enzyme-linked immunosorbent assay.

stall walker Also known as boxwalker (Brit); a horse who paces in his stall, consuming energy.

stampede A sudden rush or headlong flight of animals such as horses in fright.

stand (1) *see* STAND AT STUD. (2) A vaulting term; a compulsory exercise performed in vaulting competitions; the vaulter (q.v.), from the basic seat (q.v.) facing forward, swings both legs up and behind his body, bending at the hips, to land softly on both knees on the horse's back; he then jumps into a crouched position and slowly straightens to stand with both arms outstretched to the sides at eye level; in the Kür (q.v.) may be performed facing any direction. (3) A racing term; said of a non-cancelable wager, e.g. "The bet stands."

Standard One of three types of Basque (q.v.) pony, a semi-wild, exceptionally hardy pony indigenous to the Basque region of France, standing 11 to 13 hands.

standard (1) Also called jump stand, jump standard, or upright; a metal, wooden, or plastic stand used in jumping events to support horizontal rails (q.v.) over which a horse jumps; has calibrated holes on the inside into which the cups that support the rail are inserted; the height of the cups, and therefore the jump, is adjustable; each standard consists of a vertical post attached at right angles to a stable base; two standards are required to support each rail(s). (2) A Western term; any barrel, log, or pole used to mark a pattern or course to be navigated by the horse and rider in competition. (3) The uprights at the end of the bolsters that hold the wagon bed in position on a horse-drawn wagon. (4) The back of the seat on a Road Coach (q.v.) or Drag (q.v.).

Standardbred Also known as American Trotter or American Standardbred; an American-bred warmblood descended from the English Thoroughbred (q.v.) stallion, Messenger, a Darley Arabian descendant, imported to the United States in 1788; the foundation sire is Messenger's inbred descendant Hambletonian 10, foaled in 1849; more than 90 percent of the modern breed trace to four of Hambletonian's sons: George Wilkes, Dictator, Happy Medium and Electioneer; early in breed selection, crossed with Morgan (q.v.) and Clay blood; stands 14.1 to 16 hands and generally has a bay, brown, black, or chestnut coat; although body shape varies from horse to horse as it is bred for speed not conformation, the breed is generally a muscular Thoroughbred type with a long back, short legs, and powerful shoulders; has tremendous speed and stamina, displaying great aptitude for harness racing, trotting, and pacing (q.v.); the breed includes both trotters and pacers, the average speed of which is 30 mph (48 kmph); the breed name was first used in 1879 and refers to the speed standard for the mile distance required for entry into the American Trotter Register.

Standardbred racing *see* HARNESS RACING

standard donkey A donkey (q.v.) standing 36 to 48 inches (91–122 cm) tall.

standard event A rodeo term; any of five competitive events recognized by the Rodeo Cowboys Association including bareback riding (q.v.), bull riding (q.v.), calf-roping (q.v.), saddle bronc riding (q.v.), and steer wrestling (q.v.).

standard hunting iron *see* HUNTING IRON

standards More than one standard (q.v.).

standard starts index Also known by the acronym SSI; a racing term; a statistic by which the racing classes of horses are compared based on earnings, with inflation factored out; the average earnings of each crop of foals at the start of the year is calculated and divided into male and female categories; any horse earning the average for his or her sex has a SSI of 1.00, while a horse with a SSI of 2.00 would have earned twice the average.

stand at stud Also known as stand or at stud; said of a stallion available to cover mares for a fee.

stand back A jumping term; said of a horse who initiates the jump to clear an obstacle abnormally far from that obstacle.

standing Said of a stallion standing at stud (q.v.).

standing bandage Also known as stable bandage; a full-size bandage/wrap 4 to 5 inches (10 to 12 cm) wide and 7 to 8 feet (2.1–2.4 m) long made of wool, stockinette, or man-made fiber used to support, protect, and prevent swelling and/or injury to the horse's lower leg during shipping or while stabled.

standing halter *see* STANDING MARTINGALE

standing martingale Also known as standing halter, fast martingale, tiedown martingale, or tiedown; an auxiliary rein or strap used to assist the action of the bit by ensuring that the horse cannot raise his head too high; is attached to both the jaw-side of the noseband and the girth; has a neck strap to keep it in place.

standing over *see* STANDING OVER IN FRONT

standing over in front Also known as standing over; a disease-related or conformation defect in which the entire forelimb from the elbow down is positioned behind the perpendicular and too far under the horse's body when viewed from the side.

standing rein A vaulting term; a short, 3 foot (91 cm) rein (q.v.) sometimes attached to the center of the vaulting roller (q.v.) and always to a trick riding saddle used by the vaulter (q.v.) or trick rider (q.v.) when performing standing moves.

standing stall An 8 to 10 foot (2.4–3 m) long by approximately 5 to 6 feet (1.5–1.8 m) wide enclosure in a barn where a horse is kept at night or when not in use; enables the horse to stand, but not lie down or turn around.

standing under behind Also known as under behind; when viewed from the side, the horse's hind legs attach too far forward under his body.

stands near the ground Said of a deep-bodied horse with short legs.

stand square Said of a horse who stands straight with his weight evenly distributed over all four legs; fore and hind legs are abreast of each other.

Stanhope *see* STANHOPE GIG

Stanhope Gig Also known as Stanhope; a horse-drawn vehicle of the Gig (q.v.) type designed by the Hon. Fitzroy Stanhope in England around 1814; was open, had a stick-back driving seat balanced on two crosswise members above the passenger luggage compartment which was large enough for two seated side-by-side, double side or telegraph springs, iron-reinforced shafts attached to the axles by independent brackets, and 56 inch (1.4 m) wheels.

Stanhope Phaeton A lightweight, horse-drawn gentleman's driving Phaeton (q.v.) popular in the early 19th century; noted for its detachable shafts attached to the axles by span irons; seated four forward-facing passengers, was hooded, had a railed-up rearward seat for a liveried groom, was hung on sideways-elliptical or telegraph springs, and driven to a small horse or pony or a pair.

star (1) A face marking (q.v.); any white mark on the horse's forehead (except where the number of white hairs are very few) that varies from a small white spot to a large irregular area; the position, size, and shape of the star should be specified when describing the horse. (2) An American racing term; credit extended to a horse by the racing secretary if he is excluded from an over-filled race, giving him priority placement in future races. (3) *see* DENTAL STAR

star and stripe A facing marking (q.v.); any white marking on the horse's forehead with a stripe (q.v.) to the nasal peak; the stripe is not necessarily an extension of the star.

Star Appeal A Thoroughbred stallion foaled in 1970 at the German Stud, Röttgen; earned a record sum of DM 1.5 million.

star gazer A horse who holds his head too high.

staring coat Said of the horse's coat when dull and generally unhealthy and the hairs do not lie flat; may indicate malnutrition, parasite infestation, illness, etc.

starling Refers to coat color; a brown or blackish-gray coat intermixed with white; (obs).

star, stripe, and snip A face marking (q.v.); a white marking on the forehead which extends to between or below the nostrils.

start (1) To commence a course or race. (2) The moment and point at which a horse-race begins; (3) To move suddenly and spasmodically; to make a sudden and involuntary motion of the body caused by surprise, pain, or any sudden feeling. (4) *see* START A HORSE

start a horse Also known as start; to begin training a young or previously untrained horse.

starter (1) A racing term; one responsible for ensuring the fair start of a horse race, includes overseeing the loading of horses into and opening the starting gate (q.v.). (2) Also known as runner; a racing term; any horse in the starting gate and under starter's orders at the beginning of the race; may or may not run.

starter race An American racing term; any handicap race (q.v.) restricted to horses which have previously started for a specific claiming price or less at some time during their careers or during a fixed period of time.

starter's list A racing term; a list of horses entered to run in a specific horse race; maintained by the starter (q.v.) at the gate.

starter's orders A racing term; a determination by the official starter that all horses entered to compete in a specific flat race have been loaded into the starting gate (q.v.) and are ready to race; in a jumping race, that all competitors are ready and attentive to the starter's signal to begin the race.

starting fee A racing term; a sum paid, in addition to the nominating fee, to qualify to race.

starting gate Also known as gate or barrier; a flat-racing term; a partitioned mechanical device consisting of stalls with front and back doors used to insure a fair and equal start to a horse race; starters (q.v.) enter by the rear door and are confined until the front doors are opened thus beginning the race; electric gates were first used in the United States in the 1940s; historically, the swing of a flag was first used to initiate a horse race; that was followed by a string held in front of the aligned competitors, barriers without front or back doors, and, in present day, the mechanical gate.

starting order *see* JUMPING ORDER

starting price A racing term; the betting odds on any horse at the beginning of a horse race in which the horse is competing.

starting price bookmaker A professional who accepts wagers, cash or credit, placed by others on horses competing in a race or performance at prices posted at the start of the race or event.

state-bred Said of a horse bred in a particular state in the United States;

eligible to compete in races restricted to state-bred horses.

State Coach Also known as Coronation Coach; an elegant, enclosed horse-drawn vehicle built for formal use by nobility on occasions of state; hung on cee-springs from a perch undercarriage, seated four, had elegantly appointed interiors, glass windows, painted panels, and a rear platform for standing servants; usually drawn by a team of four horses driven from the box and two, postillion-driven leaders.

static exercise A vaulting term; any figure a vaulter holds for three canter strides in a freestyle competition or four in a compulsory test; include the basic seat (q.v.), flare (q.v.), and stand (q.v.).

Station Bus *see* OPERA BUS

Station Wagon *see* DEPOT WAGON

stay apparatus The anatomical structure of the horse which enables it to stand with little muscular effort.

stayer (1) A racing term; a horse who performs best over long distances, lacking the quick early speed required for shorter distances. (2) One of three morphological types of Thoroughbred (q.v.); is smaller and more gathered with good stamina over distances.

stay hooked A cutting term; said of a cutter (q.v.) who continues to work the same cow rather than quit it and cut a different one from the herd.

staying power The ability of a horse to run long distances or, sometimes, resistance to tiredness.

St. Croix rim shoe A traction horseshoe (q.v.) developed in the United States during the 1980s; a steel shoe with a flat hoof-side and a rounded ground-side surface into which a hollow groove is cut along the circumference; the groove fills with dirt when the horse is used, the dirt becoming the traction device.

steadied A racing term; said of a horse taken in hand by his rider; generally necessary when a horse is in confined or tight quarters or inclined to run too freely.

steady A hunting term; said of a hound (q.v.) who is not prone to riot (q.v.), chase farm livestock, or shy at the flurry of hunt (q.v.) activity.

steed A horse, especially a spirited one.

steeplechase Also known as chase or steeplechase race; a form of racing over obstacles, usually on turf; originated in 1752; early forms were run across country over natural terrain, the finishing point being a church, of which the steeple often served as a visual guide during the race; similar cross-country forms still exist, but many steeplechases are now run in circuits over permanent courses; these sometimes include obstacles such as banks, but more usually consist of a mixture of "regulation" brush fences about 4 feet 6 inches (1.3 m) high, "open ditches" with a dry ditch in front of the jump, and "water jumps", which are spreads of water with a small brush fence on the take-off side; differ from hurdle races in that the obstacles are higher and include water hazards.

steeplechase jockey One who rides in steeplechases (q.v.); frequently weighs more than a jockey who races on the flat.

steeplechase meeting The location where a steeplechase (q.v.) is held.

steeplechaser (1) Also known as chaser; a horse raced in steeplechases. (2) One who rides in a steeplechase (q.v.).

steeplechase race *see* STEEPLECHASE

steeplechasers (1) A tall riding boot worn by a steeplechaser (q.v.); has a sturdy leg and generally fitted tops or cuffs. (2) More than one steeplechaser (q.v.).

steer A young castrated bovine, especially one raised for beef.

steer roping A standard rodeo event in which two mounted riders pursue and attempt to rope (q.v.) a steer; one rider ropes the steer's head while the other ropes the heels; when successfully performed the steer is held taut between the two riders by their lariats (q.v.).

steer wrestler Also known as bulldogger or wrestler; one who competes in steer wrestling (q.v.) events.

steer wrestling Also known as bulldogging or wrestling; a timed rodeo event in which a mounted rider gallops up along the side of a moving steer, drops from the back of the moving horse onto the steer, and attempts to throw it to the ground using the head and horns for leverage; the bulldogger (q.v.) locks the right horn into his right elbow and the left horn into the left, and after slowing the forward motion of the steer, twists its head to bring it to the ground; a hazer (q.v.) rides on the far side of the steer wrestler (q.v.) to keep the steer moving in a straight direction; the contestant completing the event in the shortest time is the winner; steers used in this event may weigh in excess of 800 pounds (363 kg) and travel upwards of 35 mph (56 kmph).

step into the cow A cutting term; said of a horse who drops onto his haunches and moves toward the cow at the encouragement of the cutter (q.v.).

step oxer Also known as ascending oxer; a jumping obstacle utilizing two sets of standards and any combination of poles, angles, or spreads in which the front rail is lower; jumped as a single unit.

Steppe Bashkir Also known as Steppe Bashkir Curly; one of two distinct types of Bashkir (q.v.), a centuries-old pony breed originating in Bashkiria, around the southern foothills of the Ural Mountains in Russia; due to the introduction of Ardennais (q.v.) and Trotter blood, is heavier than the Mountain Bashkir (q.v.); is generally used for pulling troikas (q.v.), although it is also used for packing, riding, and to provide meat, milk (in a 7- to 8-month lactation period a mare can yield as much as 350 gallons [1,590 liters] of milk), and clothing; stands 13.1 to 14 hands, has a distinctive thick, curly long winter coat which is spun into cloth, a thick mane, tail, and forelock, a bay, chestnut or palomino coat, a long neck, low withers, elongated and sometimes hollow back, a wide and deep chest, short and strong legs, and small feet for his size; the breed standard quotes a bone measurement of 8 inches (20 cm) below the knee and a heart girth (q.v.) measurement for stallions of 71 inches (1.8 m); is kept outdoors where he can withstand severe winter temperatures; is docile, strong, quiet, and hardy; due to the exceptionally hard hooves, is generally left unshod.

Steppe Bashkir Curly *see* STEPPE BASHKIR

stepper A horse who has a high or showy gait.

stepping pace *see* SLOW GAIT NO. 1

step up A racing term; said of a horse who moves into a higher class to compete against faster competition.

sterile (1) Incapable of or not producing offspring. (2) Free from living germs or microorganisms.

sterility The quality or state of being sterile (q.v.).

sterilize (1) To inhibit or destroy by surgery the reproductive capabilities of the sex organs. (2) To render sterile (q.v.), especially to make free from living organisms.

stern The hind end of a hound (q.v.).

sternum *see* BREAST BONE

Steward Also known as Stipendiary Steward; a racing term; one of three appointed arbiters of racing law who judge the conduct of horses and personnel at each race (q.v.).

Steward's list A racing term; a list of horses ruled out of action due to chronic misbehavior at the gate or for which ownership is an issue; such horses are barred from racing or entry into future competitions until the bad habit(s) or other matters are corrected and verified by the starter; maintained by the track stewards.

stick (1) Also known as goad; to prod as with a spur. (2) A riding crop; a jockey's whip. (3) *see* POLO MALLET. (4) A racing term; to whip a horse.

stick and ball A polo term; to practice polo strokes and movement of the ball down the field using a mallet; an exercise performed by a mounted rider to work hand to eye coordination.

stick and ball race A polo term; a mounted game in which each contestant, assigned a number or color, takes his place at the edge of the polo field opposite the polo ball with the same number or color, and when signaled, races to get his ball to the finish line; the first contestant to place his ball across the finish wins; contestants may utilize acceptable polo moves including the ride off (q.v.) and hooking (q.v.) to improve position.

stick basket Also known as umbrella basket; a 2 to 3 foot (61–91 cm) deep and 10 inch (25 cm) wide basket with flat sides attached to the rear body of a horse-drawn coach (q.v.) in which the coach horn (q.v.), umbrellas, and sticks are carried.

sticker (1) An American term; a outside light, sharp heel calk (q.v.) frequently used on the outside of the hind horseshoes on race horses. (2) *see* CALK

stick horse (1) A racing term; a horse who runs better when the jockey uses the whip. (2) *see* HOBBY HORSE NO. 3

Stick-seat Slat Wagon A four-wheeled, horse-drawn American passenger vehicle; had a forward-facing, stick-back and side seat supported on iron braces, and a slatted floor; the body was hung on Concord springs (q.v.).

sticky (1) A cutting term; said of cattle who bunch closely together and are difficult to separate. (2) Said of a horse uncertain when jumping fences; will generally slow down, half refuse to jump, then jump from a standstill or a slowed trot. (3) Said of a horse who is reluctant to lift his feet off of the ground; earthbound.

stiff (1) Said of the horse moving around a circle or corner without bend or even flexion. (2) *see* THROW A RACE. (3) A racing term; an unfit or outclassed horse. (3) Lacking in suppleness or responsiveness, as in muscles.

stifle Also known as genu or true knee; the equivalent of the patella (kneecap) in man; the joint in the hind leg where the tibia meets the femur.

stifled An American general reference term; said of a horse who has a permanent injury to a hind leg which affects his normal action; may or may not be due to direct injury to the stifle.

stile A jumping obstacle most commonly used in show jumping; based on a traditional foot stile, is essentially a very narrow fence, usually constructed of short poles set between a pair of wings.

still birth (1) The birth of any fetus or offspring which is dead. (2) A fetus or offspring that is dead at birth.

still born Dead at birth.

stimulant Any substance or medication producing a quickly diffused and transient increase of vital energy, activity, and strength in an organism or some part of it such as the circulatory, respiratory, and/or central nervous systems

stint (1) *see* AGISTMENT. (2) The right to pasture one or more horses on common or publicly owned land. (3) SEE COVER NO. 1

stinted *see* COVERED

stipe A racing term; the office of the Stipendiary Steward (q.v.).

Stipendiary Steward *see* STEWARD

stirrup (1) Also known as pedal (Am, sl), stirrup iron, stirrup cup, or iron; a loop, ring, or D-shaped metal, plastic, leather, or other material fitting connected to the saddle by stirrup leathers (q.v.) into which the rider places his foot; used to facilitate mounting, enhance the rider's seat, promote proper body alignment, and facilitate the smooth and moderate delivery of hand, leg, and seat aids; from the English *stige-rap* where *stigan* meant to mount and *rap* meant rope. (2) *see* COSSACK HANG STRAP

stirrup bar Also known as saddle bar or spring bar; one of two metal bars built into the front of the English saddle (q.v.) on either side of the seat beneath the skirt to which the stirrup leathers (q.v.) attach; rest parallel to the seat; the distal end opens as a safety release.

stirrup cup (1) Also known as jumping powder; the pre-hunt drink taken from the saddle, as to give the rider courage to tackle strongly fenced hunt country. (2) Also known as one for the road; the cup of wine or other refreshment offered to the traveler, who having mounted his horse, was in the stirrups and ready to proceed on his journey. (3) *see* STIRRUP NO. 1

stirrup iron *see* STIRRUP NO. 1

stirrup leathers *see* LEATHERS

stirrup lights Small, battery-powered, night-safety lights that attach to the stirrups (q.v.) and, when turned on, emit a red light rearward.

stirrup pad Also known as pad; a rubber, plastic, or brush insert fitted into the portion of the stirrup upon which the foot rests; provides improved grip for the foot in the iron.

stirrups More than one stirrup (q.v.).

stirrup straps *see* LEATHERS

St. Leger The oldest and the last run each season of England's five classic races for three-year-old Thoroughbreds; a 1 mile 6½ furlong (2,917 m) race run every September since 1778; the third leg of the Triple Crown (q.v.).

stock (1) A restraining chute used on many breeding farms to allow palpation, culturing, insemination, suturing, etc. of mares. (2) *see* STOCK TIE. (3) The handle of a whip (q.v.). (4) A line of descent; a family or body of descendants from a common ancestor. (5) *see* BARSTOCK. (6) A large framework used to immobilize a horse and hold the hoof in position for shoeing; commonly used for heavy breed horses or unmanageable smaller ones. (7) *see* LIVESTOCK

stock class An equestrian show class for stock or ranch horses and ponies.

stocked (1) *see* COVERED. (2) Said of a field or natural area when pastured with horses or other stock.

stocked up Said of a horse whose limbs are swollen, as following strenuous exercise.

stocker Any animal such as a young steer kept until matured or fattened before killing.

stock horse (1) Any horse trained to work and herd stock. (2) *see* STALLION

stockinet Also spelled stockinette (Brit); an elastic machine-knitted fabric used for making bandages.

stockinette *see* STOCKINET

stocking A leg marking (q.v.); white extending from the coronet (q.v.) to the top of the cannon bone, but excluding the knee.

stockman One owning or having charge of stock (q.v.), as on a large ranch; specifically a cattleman, sheep man, horseman, etc.

stockmen More than one stockman (q.v.).

stock pin Also known as scarf pin; any pin or broach used for decorative purposes or to hold a stock in place on the rider's neck.

stock saddle Also known as Western saddle or working saddle; a saddle design based on that used by Conquistadors and popularized in the American west; has a large, deep seat bound on the front by two pommels (q.v.) between which projects a saddle horn (q.v.) and on the rear by a cantle (q.v.); the stirrups are supported by wide fenders under which is a full leather, felt- or wool-lined skirt (q.v.).

stock seat The formal term for Western horsemanship.

stock tie Also known as hunt tie, hunting stock, or stock; a long, white neck cloth detachable from the shirt, knotted and held in place with a stock pin (q.v.) worn when hunting, competing, and for formal occasions; originally cut long so that in the event of an accident, could be used as a bandage or sling.

Stock-Type Pinto One of four Pinto (q.v.) conformation types; a Western horse of predominantly Quarter Horse (q.v.) breeding and conformation; may range from small and heavy-muscled to the large and well-developed (modern) type; should display characteristics necessary for all standard Western working events, including well-developed jaws, relatively heavily-muscled shoulders, withers the same height as the croup, deep chest, well-muscled forearms, and broad, well-muscled quarters.

stock up Also known as Monday morning leg, Monday morning complaint, Monday morning evil, filled leg, big leg, humour, humor, or weed (obs); a condition of the horse characterized by generalized swelling of the entire leg or a portion of; caused by excess fluid accumulation in the soft tissues; commonly caused by stabling a horse without exercise following a period of strenuous exercise, especially if the ration is not adjusted during the period of inactivity; also triggered by strain, excessive standing, localized and systemic infection, and a decrease in the protein (q.v.) level in the blood plasma; in most cases, swelling will usually disappear following exercise because the flow of the lymph is increased by the massaging action of the muscles and tendons.

stock whip A short-handled whip (q.v.) with a very long thong (q.v.) used by mounted stockmen when driving cattle or other livestock.

stockyard A yard, especially an enclosure with pens or sheds, connected with a slaughterhouse or market for the temporary keeping of cattle, horses, etc.

stökk One of five naturally occuring gaits of the Icelandic (q.v.); a gallop (q.v.).

Stolkjaere A two-wheeled, horse-drawn vehicle popular in Norway; had two forward-facing passenger seats and a rumble (q.v.) for the driver or groom.

stomach The pouch-like enlargement of the alimentary canal (q.v.) being the primary organ of digestion where food is acted upon to yield nutrients to the body; connects the gullet to the small intestine.

stomach staggers *see* COLIC

stomach worm *see* HABRONEMA

Stomoxys calcitrans *see* STABLE FLY

stomping divots *see* DIVOT STOMPING

stomping earth *see* DIVOT STOMPING

stone (1) *see* ENTEROLITH. (2) A hard concretion of earth or mineral matter such as lime, silica, or clay; a generally moveable mass of such matter. (3) A common measure of weight, the English standard stone being 14 pounds (6.35 kg).

stone bruise Also known as strawberry; an injury to the hoof sole with discoloration resulting from impact with a hard or sharp object as a rock, hard mud ball, ice, etc.

stone cold A racing term; a horse who has exhausted himself physically and cannot run any faster or in some cases further.

stone horse *see* STALLION

stone wall A solid jumping obstacle consisting of faux or real stone blocks; a wall (q.v.).

stoop *see* STOOP TO THE LINE

stooper An American racing term; one who collects mutuel tickets mistakenly discarded at race tracks by other bettors and cashes them.

stoop to the line Also known as stoop; a hunting term; said of a hound (q.v.) who hunts with his nose close to the ground.

stop hound A hunting term; a hound who ceases to pursue the line of a fox (q.v.), sits on his haunches, and speaks (q.v.).

stop hounds A hunting term; to call the hounds off the line of the fox (q.v.) when they run into impassable or forbidden ground; stopped by the huntsman using his voice, a thong, and the aid of the whipper-in (q.v.).

stopped *see* STOPPED OUT

stopped out Also known as stopped; a hunting term; said of the fox den (q.v.) when closed the night before a hunt.

stopper Any substance or medication producing a quickly diffused and transient decrease in vital energy, activity, or strength in an organism or some part of it such as the circulatory, respiratory, and/or central nervous systems.

stopping earth *see* DIVOT STOMPING

stopping out A hunting term; the process of closing a fox den (q.v.) the night before a hunt.

stopping the feet To moisturize the hoof.

stops (1) Metal projections on the shafts of a horse-drawn vehicle which keep the harness of a single horse at the proper place on the shafts; support much of the vehicle weight when descending a hill. (2) Round or rectangular pieces of rubber or leather through which the rein is threaded perpendicularly to prevent the rings of the martingale (q.v.) from sliding forward and catching on the bit rings or shafts. (3) Narrow strips of leather sewn incrementally across the width of English reins from the buckle approximately three quarters of the distance to the bit rings to facilitate the rider's grip on the reins.

straddle An Irish term; a driving saddle.

straddle jump A vaulting term; a move in which the vaulter (q.v.), from a standing position on the horse, leaps into the air with arms and legs straight and stretched away from the sides of his upright body; post jump, the vaulter returns to a standing position on the horse's back.

straight *see* WIN

straight as a string A racing term; said of a horse competing in a race who gives his all.

straightaway Also known as stretch; a racing term; the straight part of the racecourse.

straight bar The mouthpiece of a bit when straight and unbroken.

straight behind Said of the horse who, when viewed from the side, shows very little angle between the tibia and femur; the hock joint and pasterns are correspondingly straight; predisposes a horse to bog spavin (q.v.).

straight bucking *see* JACK-KNIFING

straight forecast *see* EXACTA

straight necked A hunting term; said a fox (q.v.) who runs in a straight line.

straight-necked fox *see* STRAIGHT-NECK FOX

straight-neck fox Also known as straight-necked fox; a hunting term; a fox (q.v.) who runs in a straight line.

straightness Said of a horse; the extent to which a horse moves in a straight line, the hind feet following the track of the forefeet e.g., haunches neither left nor right. (2) Said of the horse; alignment of the body parts appropriate to the task at hand, e.g., not a twisted neck. (3) A dressage term; directness of the line of travel, e.g., not weaving (q.v.).

straight shoulder Also known as upright shoulder; a conformation defect; said of the horse's shoulder when lacking sufficient angulation; may be caused by a too short or too straight scapula; when the line from the point of the shoulder (q.v.) to the withers is relatively straight rather than rearward sloping.

straight snaffle A snaffle bit (q.v.) having a single-piece, straight-bar mouthpiece; often used for stallion or in-hand bridles.

strained tendon *see* BOWED TENDON

straight triactor *see* STRAIGHT TRIFECTA

straight trifecta Also known as straight triple or straight traitor (Can); a betting option in which the bettor (q.v.) selects the first, second, and third placed horses in that order in a specific race.

straight triple *see* STRAIGHT TRIFECTA

strangles Also known as distemper; an acute, infectious, transmissible disease of the lymph glands of the upper respiratory tract or throat caused by bacterium *Streptococcus equi*, especially common in young horses; takes a number of days following initial infection to develop; symptoms include nasal discharge, elevated temperature, and swelling of the lymph glands; so called because if swelling in the lymph glands becomes too severe, breathing may become labored or strangled.

strangulation Occlusion of the blood supply to a loop of bowel as caused by intussusception (q.v.), volvulus (q.v.), torsion (q.v.), and incarceration (q.v.); causes tissue death and consequently toxemia and death.

strap *see* GROOM NO. 1

straps *see* LEATHERS

strappings (1) Ceremonial harness including the saddle and bridle. (2) Also known as grips or patches; leather or synthetic patches sewn onto the inside legs of riding breeches (q.v.) and jodhpurs (q.v.) which extend below and to slightly above the knee; lengthen the life of the breeches and provide additional grip.

stratum germinativum The horn-producing layer of cells that produces the horny sole (q.v.).

straw The stalk or stem of certain species of grain collectively when cut, and after being threshed; used for bedding (q.v.) horse stalls, trailers, etc.; has a nice appearance, relatively wide availability, and is soft, affordable, and pleasantly scented, but lacks absorbency and can be quite moldy and dusty, potentially aggravating or causing respiratory ailments.

strawberry *see* STONE BRUISE

strawberry corn *see* RED CORN

strawberry roan Also known as sorrel roan; refers to coat color; of the color group roan (q.v.); a clear light red coat uniformly mixed with white hairs, a colored head, and colored, nonblack points (q.v.).

strawyard An outdoor area deeply bedded with straw (q.v.) in which horses on rest or recovery are turned out.

streak *see* STRIPE

street car *see* HORSE CAR

Strelets A Russian horse breed descended from native mares put to Anglo-Arab (q.v.), Turkish, Persian, and pure-bred Arab (q.v.) stallions; basically a large Arab; used for riding.

stress fracture A bone fracture (q.v.) resulting from repeated concussion; generally occurs in the front of the cannon bone (q.v.) and tibia where it causes a hard-to-diagnose hind limb lameness.

stretch (1) *see* STRAIGHTAWAY. (2) A harness racing term; the last ⅛ mile (201 m) portion of the racetrack before the finish line. (3) *see* HOMESTRETCH

stretch call A racing term; a call of racehorse splits (q.v.) made at the eighth pole (q.v.), usually one furlong (q.v.) from the finish on the straightaway (q.v.), made for charting purposes.

stretched out A coaching term; said of the horse when standing with the forelegs (q.v.) slightly in front of perpendicular and the hind as far back as possible; a horse standing in this position is unable to move forward or backward until moved into a square stance; thus, the horse would remain stationary until passengers disembarked the vehicle.

stretch runner A racing term; a horse who runs fastest near the race finish.

stretch the top line To encourage the horse to extend his head and neck out and downward to a loose rein.

stretch turn A racing term; the final turn on the racetrack before the homestretch (q.v.).

stride (1) An act of forward motion consisting of a cycle of coordinated movements of all four legs. (2) *see* STRIDE LENGTH

stride length Also known as stride, the distance from where one foot leaves the ground to the spot where the same foot again touches the ground.

strike (1) To scrape or knock one leg with the other. (2) A vice; said of a horse who reaches out quickly with a foreleg to hit a handler or other horses. (3) *see* STRIKE A FOX. (4) Said of a tent-pegger (q.v.) when he hits the tent peg in the mounted sport of tent-pegging (q.v.), but does not successfully lift it from the ground. (5) To make contact with, as a polo mallet (q.v.) with a polo ball.

strike a fox Also known as strike; a hunting term; said of a hound who finds a fox.

strike dog A hunting term; a hound who is adept at locating foxes (q.v.).

strike-off The first step of the canter (q.v.).

strike-off early A dressage term; said of the horse when he takes the first step of the canter (q.v.) before the appropriate arena marker.

strike-off late A dressage term; said of the horse when he takes the first step of the canter after the appropriate arena marker.

striking Said of a horse who strikes (q.v.) due to meanness; a vice.

string (1) The horses owned by one stable or handled by one trainer or packer (q.v.). (2) A racing term; two or more race horses exercised together. (3) *see* PACK STRING

stringhalt Also known as snatch (obs); a condition characterized by the sudden, abnormal, and excessive flexion of one hind leg upward, in some cases as high as the belly; usually seen at the walk or when the horse is turning, backing, or rising from lying down or rolling; diminishes with exercise; thought to be caused by strain or trauma to the hock resulting in scar tissue which restricts the movement of the extensor tendons (q.v.) and results in the jerky movement; is usually harmless and non-degenerative; may be surgically corrected.

string the foot A roping term; said of the roper (q.v.); to place the loop of the pigging string (q.v.) around one of the front feet of a calf in preparation for the tie (q.v.).

strip (1) A face marking (q.v.); a narrow white mark, no wider than the width of the flat nasal bones, which does not extend onto the forehead and is narrower than a stripe (q.v.). (2) *see* TRACK

stripe (1) Also known as streak or flash; a face marking; any long, narrow white marking on the horse's face; which is no wider than the nasal bone and runs in a relatively straight line from the forehead, at eye level, to, or almost to, an imaginary line connecting the top of the nostrils to the muzzle. (2) *see* DORSAL STRIPE

stripe and snip A face marking (q.v.); a narrow white marking extending vertically, from just below the eyes to just below or between the nostrils, which is no wider than the width of the nasal bone.

striped hoof A hoof having vertical stripes of alternating layers of pink and black; it is believed that the pink hoof is soft and the black hoof hard, almost brittle, and that the striped hoof perfectly combines the strong layers between softer pink layers; common in the Appaloosa (q.v.).

striped muscle Any nonstriated muscle, as those controlled by will and which operate in such voluntary movements as kicking and walking; attaches to the bones by tendons and contracts on stimulation to produce bodily motion; a voluntary muscle (q.v.).

strongyl *see* STRONGYLE

strongyle Also spelled strongyl; the singlular of strongyles (q.v.)

strongyles Any of certain roundworms (q.v.) constituting the family Strongylidae, parasitic in horses worldwide; divided into two groups: large strongyles (q.v.) which consist of the *Strongylus* species (*Strongylus edantatus* (q.v.), *Strongylus vulgaris* (q.v.), and *Strongylus equinus* (q.v.), adults of which are ⅔ to 1¾ inches (1.5–4.5 cm) long and a number of different species of small stongyles (q.v.), i.e. *Cylicodontophorus*, *Cylicostephanus*, *Cylicocyclus*, and *Cyathostomum* species, all ⅓ to ⅔ inches (1–1.5 cm) long in the adult stage; both large and small strongyles cause disease in horses; outside of the horse, the life cycle of all strongyles is similar: eggs are passed in the horse's feces, with the greatest number of eggs being passed in the spring and fall months; the larvae migrate from the manure onto the grass where they are ingested by the horse.

strongyloide Also known as threadworm; a parasitic roundworm of the species *Strongyloides westeri* found in the small intestine of foals during the first eight weeks of life; larvae are passed to the foal in the mare's milk; infestation may cause diarrhea and broncho-pneumonia.

Strongyloides westeri Also known as threadworm or equine intestinal threadworm; a hair-like roundworm measuring approximately ⅓ inch (8–9mm) found in the small intestine; pass through both parasitic and free-living stages; in the parasitic phase, female adults lay eggs in the intestines where the eggs develop by parthenogenesis and are passed in the feces; once on the pasture, the eggs hatch and molt within 24 to 48 hours at which point they infect by skin penetration or ingestion; may also be passed in colostrum (q.v.) making nursing one of the most common means of transmission of threadworm infections to young foals; foals with heavy worm burdens suffer from acute diarrhea, weakness, and emaciation while older horses may harbor large burdens without clinical manifestations; natural immunity develops in foals around 6 months of age.

strongylosis Any disease caused by strongyles (q.v.).

Strongylus edentatus A species of large strongyle (q.v.) measuring up to 1¾ inches (45 mm) in length; found in various parts of the horse's body including the liver, peri-renal tissues, flanks, and pancreas; significant infestations may cause peritonitis, bleeding, and anemia; after two to three months they return to the large intestine and become adult worms.

Strongylus equinus A species of large strongyle (q.v.) measuring up to 1⅞ inches (50 mm) in length; produce nodules in the cecum and colon, later migrating to the liver and pancreas.

Strongylus vulgaris A species of large strongyle (q.v.) measuring up to 1 inch (25 mm) in length; migrate extensively in the cranial mesenteric artery and its branches where they may cause parasitic thrombosis and verminous arteritis.

strung out A dressage term; said of the horse when his body is too elongated, lacking good carriage, longitudinal balance and connection.

stub-bred Also known as stub; a hunting term; a fox cub raised above ground rather than in an earth (q.v.).

stub (1) *see* STUB-BRED. (2) A wound on the sole of the hoof; (obs).

stubby A hoof shape pattern in which the hoof is generally rounded, but wider than it is long with the widest part of the hoof located midway between the toe and heel.

stuck A dressage term; said of the horse's foot when it remains too long grounded, thus breaking the rhythm of the gait.

stud (1) *see* STALLION. (2) Also known as stallion station or stud farm; a farm or place where horses are maintained for breeding purposes. (3) Any large establishment of racehorses, hunters, etc. belonging to one owner.

stud billet *see* STUD FASTENING

Stud Book (1) Also known as General Stud Book, The Book, or Weatherbys; a permanent book or registry of breeding records for the English Thoroughbred (q.v.); includes all pure-bred mares and their progeny, the pedigrees of these accepted pure-bred mares, and the sires of their offspring; any horse registered must be traceable to the Darley Arabian (q.v.), the Godolphin Arabian (q.v.), or the Byerley Turk (q.v.) on the male side and to the Royal Mares on the female side; founded in 1793 by the Weatherby family, it is still published by them under control of The Jockey Club (q.v.); all Thoroughbred Stud Books throughout the world are affiliated with this parent stud book. (2) Any permanent book or registry of breeding records for any established horse breed, the requirements for inclusion therein vary by breed.

Stud Book restriction Any rule established by a specific breed society to limit or prevent a horse from being registered in its book of defined parentage.

stud-bred Any horse of a breed whose breed society maintains its own stud book (q.v.).

stud farm *see* STUD NO. 2

stud fastening Also known as French clip, stud billet, billet, and hook fastening; an L-shaped metal stud projecting from the end of a leather strip such as reins, which fits through a small slit, cut length-wise approximately ½ inch (13 mm) from the end of the same strip and which is pulled down against the end of the cut to lock it and create a closed loop.

stud fee Also known as fee, service fee or mating fee; a sum paid to a stallion owner for breeding services whether by natural cover (q.v.) or artificial insemination (q.v.).

stud groom A senior groom at a stud (q.v.).

stud horse *see* STALLION

stud mule An uncastrated male mule (q.v.); usually sterile.

stud record A history of the overall performance of a stallion at stud.

stud ring Also known as stallion ring; a metal, non-corrosive metal, or plastic ring slipped over the head of a horse's penis behind the glands to prevent masturbation, erection, and to discourage ejaculation when not covering a mare.

studs Also known as pegs; metal heads screwed into the ground-side surface of a horseshoe (q.v.) to increase traction on slippery or deep surfaces such as grass, snow, or asphalt; depending on the purpose, may be set into all four shoes as for snow or asphalt surfaces or the front or back only for grass or dirt; a maximum of three screws may be set in each shoe, one on each heel and, more rarely, one on the toe; the farrier drills a tap hole in the shoe and fills it with an Allen screw; when traction is required, the horse owner removes the Allen screw and screws in the appropriate stud; available in a variety of shapes and sizes including pointed, thick, flat, and oblong and may be made of a variety of materials including steel, borium, and tungsten; include road studs (q.v.) and competition studs (q.v.).

stumble To trip when walking.

stumour A horse, especially a race horse, who proves disappointing, generally because he does not exert himself; (sl).

stump sucking *see* CRIBBING

stunt horse Any horse used specifically to perform a daring feat, especially to attract attention, as in a film.

subacute laminitis A broad classification of laminitis (q.v.); inflammation of the laminae (q.v.) characterized by a rapid onset and a brief duration; often there will only be a mild change in the stance of the horse, who may demonstrate an increased sensitivity on the soles of the affected feet; may lead to chronic laminitis (q.v.) if left untreated.

subluxation Incomplete dislocation of a joint in which the normal joint relationship is disturbed, but the articular surfaces are still in contact as in two vertebrae in a motor unit (q.v.).

submit Said of the horse; to be obedient to the rider or handler.

submission A dressage term; compliance, throughness (q.v.) and obedience; the yielding of the horse's will to that of the rider as revealed by his constant attention, willingness, and confidence and well as in the harmony and ease he displays in execution of the movements appropriate to his age and stage of development, including correct bend, acceptance of and obedience to the rider's aids, and the balance appropriate to the task at hand.

Subscriber *see* SUBSCRIPTION COACH

subscription A racing term; the fees paid by the owner of a horse(s) to nominate or maintain eligibility for the horse in a stakes race (q.v.).

Subscription Coach Also known as Subscriber; any public-transportation coach, the service of which was underwritten by fees collected from individuals in exchange for unrestricted vehicle use.

substance The build of a horse; the physical quality of a horse's body as a function of bone width and depth, muscularity, etc.

sucked up *see* TUCKED UP

sucker *see* SUCKLING

sucking lice More than one sucking louse (q.v.).

sucking louse Also known as *Haematopinas asini*; a louse (q.v.); an external, biting and sucking parasite which feasts on the horse's blood; although less than 1⁄10 inch (2 mm) long, is visible to the naked eye as a small, light-gray object; may be detected by inspecting the mane, root of the tail, inside the thighs, or on the underside of the saddle blanket following exercise; not transmitted to people.

suckling Also known as sucker; a foal of either sex, until weaned (q.v.) or, if unweaned, until it is ranked as a yearling (q.v.).

sudadero *see* FENDER

Sudan grass A grass sorghum, *Sorghum vulgare sudanensis*, introduced into the United States from Sudan and grown for hay.

Sudan grass hay A cut and dried grass hay (q.v.) of the Sudan grass (q.v.) type grown throughout the United States in most soil types; best cut at the pre- or early-bloom stage to ensure palatability and nutritional quality; if cut prematurely, may contain large amounts of prussic acid; in newer varieties the threat of prussic acid poisoning is reduced but still an issue; it is therefore advisable to test the prussic acid content prior to feeding; contains a digestible protein content of approximately 5 percent, and 35 percent fiber.

sudden death A polo term; an overtime period played when a match is tied at the end of the sixth chukker (q.v.); continues until the first goal is scored.

Suffolk *see* SUFFOLK PUNCH

Suffolk Punch Also known as Suffolk; the smallest and oldest of the British heavy-draft breeds native to Suffolk, Great Britain; descended from the Great Horse (q.v.) crossed with Norfolk Trotter (q.v.), Norfolk Cob, and English Thoroughbred (q.v.) around 1506; all modern Suffolks can be traced to one stallion, Blakes Farmer, foaled in 1760, who handed his chestnut coat color to all his descendants; a pure breed, is frugal, early maturing, long-lived, possessed of exceptional pulling power, quiet and gentle; stands 15.3 to 16.2 hands, weighs 1,980 to 2,200 pounds (898–998 kg), has a compact, yet large body set on short, powerful, clean legs with little feather (q.v.), which, in this breed, is referred to as 'hair'; the coat color is exclusively chestnut (always spelled chesnut by the Breed Association) which may be one of seven shades ranging from nearly brown to a pale, mealy shade; no white markings are permitted; historically used to draw Omnibuses (q.v.) and brewer's drays and for farming and heavy draft; the modern horse is used for heavy draft.

Suffolk Horse Society A British organization founded in 1878 to maintain the purity of, generate interest in, and maintain the breed registry for the Suffolk Punch (q.v.).

sugar-beet pulp Also known as beet pulp; a by-product of the sugar production process, made by drying the residual beet chips after the sugar extraction; a highly digestible and palatable fiber with a high energy and fiber content; the digestible energy (q.v.) is slightly lower than that of oats (q.v.); a good source of calcium, but is low in phosphorus, selenium, and vitamins A and D; used for supplementing an inadequate hay supply and as a dust-free roughage substitute; available in cubed and shredded forms, both of which must be rehydrated before feeding.

Suicide Gig *see* COCKING CART

Sulfur Also spelled sulphur or sulpur; a metallic element present in the amino acids methionine and cystine as well as in chondroitin sulfate, a constituent of cartilage; as no dietary requirements have been established for the horse, deficiency is not of practical concern, yet over-supplementation can result in death.

sulk A racing term; said of a horse who refuses to run or respond to the urging of the jockey.

Sulkette A horse-drawn exercising Sulky (q.v.) similar in construction to a Racing Sulky (q.v.), but more heavily constructed.

Sulky Also known as Bike or Gig; a modern, very light, two-wheeled, one-horse, single-seated cart for one with a skeleton body used for harness racing; weighs 29 to 37 pounds (13–17 kg), uses bicycle-type wheels and is generally constructed with hardwood shafts, although aluminum and steel may be used; equipped with adjustable foot rests.

Sulky stirrup An adjustable footrest fitted on a Sulky (q.v.).

Sullivan, Con A 19th-century horse whisperer (q.v.).

sulphonamides Antibacterial compounds used both topically and internally for the prevention and treatment of nonspecific infections by controlling multiplication of some bacteria; a common ingredient of wound powders and dressings.

sulphur *see* SULFUR

sulpur *see* SULFUR

Sumba A Indonesian pony breed indigenous to the island of Sumba from which the name derived; similar in appearance to the Chinese (q.v.) and Mongolian (q.v.) ponies which suggests they may have common ancestry; is almost identical to the Sumbawa (q.v.); is very tough, willing, intelligent, and docile, and has good endurance; the coat may be any color although dun (q.v.) with an eel stripe (q.v.) and dark tail, mane, and points is most common; the mane is frequently shaggy and upright; has a slightly heavy head, almond-shaped eyes, a short, broad neck, long back, and short, strong legs; used for lance-throwing, dancing competitions (q.v.), riding, and packing.

Sumbawa An Indonesian pony breed indigenous to the island of Sumbawa from which the name derived; similar in appearance to the Chinese (q.v.) and Mongolian (q.v.) ponies which suggests they may have common ancestry; almost identical to the Sumba (q.v.); is very tough, willing, intelligent, docile, and has good endurance; the coat may be any color although dun (q.v.) with an eel stripe (q.v.) and dark tail, mane, and points is most common; the mane is frequently shaggy and upright; has a slightly heavy head, almond-shaped eyes, a short, broad neck, long back, and short, strong legs; used for lance-throwing, dancing competitions (q.v.), riding, and packing.

summer coat The horse's hair coat during the summer; typically short and smooth.

Summerhays, R.S. (1881–1976) A British hippologist (q.v.) and author of several books about horses.

summering To turn horses out to pasture during the summer months.

summer-pasture-associated obstructive pulmonary disease Also known by the acronym SPAOPD; a chronic allergic airway disease caused by developing hypersensitivity to soil- or grass-borne fungus; allergens cause muscle constriction in the walls of the small airways, swelling of the airways' lining, and excess mucus production, all of which contribute to airway narrowing and increased effort required to breathe; symptoms include difficulty exhaling, flared nostrils, elevated heart and respiratory rates, abnormal respiratory sounds such as crackles and wheezes, and coughing not associated with exercise; affects pastured horses from June through September.

summer sheet Also known as sheet, stable sheet, or paddock sheet; a lightweight, rectangular, linen, cotton, or synthetic, single-layer blanket strapped or buckled onto the horse's body to keep him clean rather than warm and to protect against flies and/or rain.

summer sores *see* CUTANEOUS HABRONEMIASIS

sumpter (1) *see* PACK HORSE. (2) One who jerks (q.v.) a string of pack horses.

sunburn Inflammation of the skin caused by prolonged exposure to the sun's rays; usually appears on the white facial markings where hair is sparse; the skin may appear red and irritated, or blisters may develop.

sun circle *see* SUNFLASH

sunfishing The action of a buckjumper (q.v.) when he twists his body into a crescent while off the ground.

sunflash Also known as sun circle; one of four primary historic patterns of horse brasses (q.v.) used on horse harnesses to ward off the Evil Eye; the pattern of the sun, one of the images of the pagan gods, was struck into brass or other metal and attached to the browband so that it rested on the horse's forehead; so called because it flashes gold in the sun as the horse moves.

sunflash brass A protective metal amulet struck with the pattern of the sun attached to draft horse harness to protect the horse from evil spirits or the evil eye; so called because it flashes as the horse moves; one of four primary historic horse brass (q.v.) patterns.

sunflower meal A high energy, high protein supplement produced from the residue of the sunflower seed following oil extraction; is a good feed supplement for horses, but lacks some essential amino acids and is low in lysine.

sunstroke *see* HEAT STROKE

superfecta A racing term; a betting option where the bettor (q.v.) selects perfectas (q.v.) in two nominated races; may be played straight or boxed (q.v.).

superficial crack Also known as surface crack; any crack in the exterior hoof wall that does not expose sensitive tissues or result in lameness.

superficial digital flexor tendon Also known as superficial flexor tendon; a tendon (q.v.) that runs down the back of the foreleg between the knee and foot, and between the hock and foot in the hind leg (q.v.), splitting below the fetlock, and attaching to PI (q.v.) and PII (q.v.); functions to extend the hock (q.v.) and the foot in the hind leg and to flex the pastern and knee and extend the elbow in the foreleg; injuries most commonly occur in the front legs.

superficial flexor tendon *see* SUPERFICIAL DIGITAL FLEXOR TENDON

superficial laceration An injury penetrating only the upper skin layers; typically the edges of the wound will remain close together; generally results in more bleeding than an abrasion (q.v.).

superficial wound Any injury to the horse's flesh which only damages the upper skin layers; include abrasions (q.v.) and lacerations (q.v.).

superior check ligament A ligament (q.v.) originating above the knee and attaching to the superficial flexor tendon (q.v.) which it supports.

super trifecta A betting option in which the bettor (q.v.) selects the first, second, third and fourth place horses in exact order in a race.

supple (1) Said of a horse who is pliant, flexible, smooth, and limber in movement; has the ability to shift his balance easily and quickly forward, backward, and/or sideways. (2) To make a horse flexible as by stretching, exercise, etc. (3) Said of pliant, smooth leather.

supporting hand The rider's hand holding the rein which applies pressure to the horse's neck when neck reining (q.v.); on the opposite side of the acting hand (q.v.).

supporting rein The rein that aids the direct rein (q.v.) during any movement off a straight line, as in a circle.

supporting limb lameness Lameness that becomes apparent in a limb or limbs other than the limb originally injured; may be a consequence of additional weight or strain placed on the supporting limb(s) as the horse seeks to minimize use of the limb originally injured.

surcingle Also known as overgirth; a 2½ to 4 inch (6–10 cm) wide band of leather or webbing that encircles the horse just behind the forelegs which is used to hold a blanket or pad in place or as a secondary girth to hold a saddle in position and prevent it from slipping.

surefooted Said of a horse, mule, donkey other equine stable on his feet, as over rough ground or trails; mules (q.v.) are renowned for their surefootedness and are thus exceptionally well-suited for mountain or trail travel.

sure thing *see* LOCK NO. 1

surface crack *see* SUPERFICIAL CRACK

surfeit To stuff or gorge as with food.

surgical leg brace Also known as leg brace; a device used to support the horse's leg post trauma or surgery while healing; often constructed with hinged or bolt-on portions using a horseshoe base; size varies according to the extent of support required.

surgical shoe *see* THERAPEUTIC SHOE

surgical mark An adventitial mark (q.v.); permanent white coat hairs resulting from destruction of the pigment cells of underlying skin due to surgery.

surpanakh A game of mounted basketball.

Surrey A light, four-wheeled, horse-drawn passenger vehicle or family carriage drawn either by a single horse or pair of ponies in pole gear (q.v.) developed in Surrey, England from which the name derived; originally seated four on double, forward-facing cross-seats and later up to six; had a rearward folding half-hood, and later, an umbrella, canopy, or extension top; known as a jerky (q.v.) when not fitted with a hood (q.v.).

suspend (1) To debar or cause to withdraw temporarily from privilege, office, or function. (2) Also known as declare off or rule off; a racing term; to bar a horse, jockey, horseman, or stablehand from participation in a race, access to a race track, etc.; usually ordered by the race steward (q.v.).

suspension (1) The act of suspending or the state or period of being suspended, interrupted, or abrogated, as to declare a jockey, horseman, or stable hand ineligible for participation in an event. (2) *see* MOMENT OF SUSPENSION

suspension time A jumping term; the period following take-off during which the horse is in the air over the obstacle.

suspensory desmitis Also known as sprain of the suspensory ligament or pulled suspensory; a sprain of the suspensory ligament (q.v.) anywhere along its length; symptoms may include localized heat and/or enlargement of the medial palmar vein on the inside of the limb, or slight lameness following fast work or long periods of exercise; the most common location of the injury is at the point where the suspensory ligament divides into two branches; if one of the branches of the suspensory ligaments is damaged, injury to the sesamoid bone to which it is attached may also occur; most common in race horses.

suspensory ligament Also known as interosseous tendon; a broad band of elasticized fibrous tissue attached to and behind the cannon bone over the fetlock joint to the pastern bones; supports the fetlock joint, preventing it from sinking to the ground; may be strained or torn.

suspensory ligament strain Injury to the suspensory ligament (q.v.) due to excessive tension, work on rough ground, poor conformation, or incorrect shoeing; generally occurs on or near the lower end of the ligament in the region of the sesamoid bones; symptoms include swelling, pain, and lameness.

suture (1) To unite the lips or edges of a wound or incision by stitching. (2) The material by which a wound or incision is united by stitching.

suturing (1) *see* SUTURE NO. 1. (2) *see* CASLICK'S OPERATION

swag block *see* SWEDGE BLOCK

swaged-side stirrup iron *see* HUNTING IRON

swallows his head Said of a bucking (q.v.) horse when he places his head well between his forelegs.

swallowing *see* SHOULDERING

swallow-tail pad A dressage saddle pad (q.v.); is square cut in the front, providing plenty of protection for the saddle flap (q.v.), and swooped up in a curved line carried a little beyond the "true square" of the pad, terminating in a long point or "swallow tail" just behind the flap, which keeps it out of the way of the whip; used to protect the back of the horse, provide padding, and absorb sweat.

swamp fever *see* EQUINE INFECTIOUS ANEMIA

swan neck (1) Also known as deer neck; a conformation fault in which the upper part of the horse's neck is long and narrow through the throat and concave or lacking muscle development at the base where it joins the forequarters; the head joins the neck in a near vertical line and the gullet appears to stand out in a convex shape as in the throat of a cock; a swan-necked horse may be cock-throttled, but a cock-throttled horse will not necessarily be swan-necked. (2) *see* POLE HOOK

swap horses in the middle of the stream An phrase coined by US President Lincoln when renominated for the Presidency, meaning it is best not to switch political sides in the middle of the Civil War; thus, it is best not to change one's position in the middle of an action.

sway back Also known as hollow back, saddle back, dropped back, dipped back, or bobby back; said of the horse's back when concave between the withers and loin; may be caused by age, faulty conformation, mineral imbalance, or in broodmares, by the weight of foals carried during pregnancy; the opposite of roach back (q.v.).

sway backed Also known as hollow backed, saddle backed, dip backed, drop backed, or bobby backed; said of a horse with a sway back (q.v.).

sweat (1) Also known as perspire; to excrete fluid from the pores of the skin. (2) A treatment used to promote interosmotic passage of fluid from edematous tissue to reduce swelling; consists of the topical application, as to the legs, of either an oil- or water-based mixture of which the most consistent ingredients include menthol and/or thymol and, in some mixtures, capsicum due to its pain-reducing capability; the treated area is normally covered with a wrapping such as plastic to promote heat.

sweat flap Also known as flap or panel; the leather under portion of an English saddle which lies against the horse's body and/or the saddle pad; protects the rider and finer leather of the saddle from the effects of the horse's sweat.

sweating The act or function of producing sweat (q.v.).

sweat scraper *see* SCRAPER

sweat the brass A racing term; to overwork a horse.

swedge block Also known as swag block; a molding tool strapped onto an anvil (q.v.) used to shape barstock (q.v.) which can then be forged into rim shoes, polo plates, and other specialized horseshoes with cross-sections.

swedged shoe Any horseshoe in which the ground-side surface is molded into a traction modifying pattern; will generally have a deep groove running the circumference of the shoe.

Swedish Ardennes A heavy-draft cold-blood developed in 19th-century Sweden by crossing Belgian and French Ardennais (q.v.) horses with the Swedish Horse (q.v.); stands 15 to 16 hands and weighs upwards of 1,500 pounds (680 kg); similar in appearance to the Belgian Ardennes (q.v.); may have a black, bay, chestnut, or brown coat, has a heavy head, short, crested neck, short back, rounded and muscular (often double) croup and short, sturdy legs with light feathering; is docile and quiet but energetic in nature; used for heavy draft and farm work.

Swedish Gotland *see* GOTLAND

Swedish Half-bred *see* SWEDISH WARMBLOOD

Swedish Warmblood Also known as Swedish Half-bred; a warmblood developed in 16th-century Sweden by crossing native mares with high-quality imported Arab (q.v.), Andalusian (q.v.), Friesian (q.v.), Hanoverian (q.v.), Trakehner (q.v.), and Thoroughbred (q.v.) stallions; once used for military purposes, it is a strong, sound riding horse of good temperament; popular as a dressage mount, but is equally suited to jumping, eventing, and driving; stands 16.2 to 17 hands, and may have a coat color of any solid color including bay, brown, chestnut, and gray; has maintained an open stud book since 1812; foals are eligible for registration if sired by an approved Swedish Warmblood stallion and out of a mare approved by one of the recognized European registries (Hanoverian [q.v.], Dutch Warmblood [q.v.], Holsteiner [q.v.], etc.) or out of a Thoroughbred registered by The Jockey Club (q.v.).

Swedish Warmblood Association A Swedish organization founded to preserve the characteristics of the Swedish Warmblood (q.v.) and to maintain the stud book.

sweeney Also known as shoulder atrophy, slipped shoulder, or shoulder paralysis; shoulder-muscle atrophy due to disuse following lesion of the leg or foot that leads to prolonged diminished use of the limb or damage to the suprascapular nerve; polo ponies (q.v.) are commonly affected because of competitive collisions; lameness may be difficult to detect until atrophy; if atrophy persists, may result in a noticeable hollowing on either side of the spine or scapula and shoulder looseness.

swelled heel The heel of the horseshoe when folded up onto the hoof-side surface and leveled; raises the heels of the hoof without creating as much traction as blocked heels (q.v.) or heel calks (q.v.).

sweep (1) A cutting term; the action of a horse when he sits back on his haunches and swings his spread forequarters left to right to track a cow. (2) To win all events or races entered.

sweeps *see* SWEEPSTAKES

sweepstakes Also known as stakes race, stakes, sweeps, or sweepstakes race; a racing term; a horse race in which the entry, nominating, eligibility, starting, or other fees or contributions of three or more owners, are divided amongst the first four place getters in previously agreed percentages of the total; all stakes can qualify a horse for black type (q.v.) in a sale catalogue; a higher class of race than allowance races (q.v.), overnight handicaps, and claiming races (q.v.).

sweepstakes race *see* SWEEPSTAKES

sweet feed Any feed, single grain or mixed, to which molasses has been added to improve flavor.

sweet feed bumps Hives triggered by systemic reaction to sugars or proteins in sweet feed (q.v.).

sweet iron A type of iron used in the mouthpiece (q.v.) of certain types of bits; the iron is intended to rust and, when it does so, it has a sweet taste that enhances salivation.

sweet itch Also known as Culicoides hypersensitivity, Queensland itch (Aus), or Kasen; an annual, widely occurring seasonal skin condition caused by allergic reaction to Culicoides (q.v.), midges, sandflies, punkies, and no-see-ums; the insects swarm only in the warmer months of the year before and at dusk, feeding on the mane, tail, and belly of the horse, causing intense irritation and producing patches of thick, scaly, and sometimes ulcerated skin; immature horses are rarely affected.

sweet spot The place in the saddle where the rider is naturally intended to sit.

swell (1) To grow bulkier; to increase in size or bulk; to protuberate. (2) Also known as front; that portion of the Western saddle (q.v.) in front of the pommel and to the left and right of the saddle horn into which the latter is inserted; the width left-to-right varies considerably by type.

Swell Body Cutter *see* CUTTER

swell fork *see* FORK NO. 2

swine chopped *see* PIG MOUTHED

swing *see* SCHAUKEL

swing bar *see* SWINGLE TREE

swingers *see* FLY TERRETS

swing horse The middle horse in a randem (q.v.).

swinging A dressage term; the active lateral displacement of the shoulders or haunches in a series of flying changes (q.v.).

swinging back A dressage term; said of the horse's trunk muscles when they function with springy tension rather than rigidity or slackness; creates the impression that the horse's back swings and allows the energy produced by the hind legs to be efficiently transmitted forward through the horse.

swinging head A dressage term; said of the horse when his muzzle moves left and right in the trot and canter or in circles (usually in the canter); indicates incomplete acceptance of contact or constraint.

swinging limb lameness Lameness (q.v.) evident when the limb is in motion.

swingle bar *see* SWINGLE TREE

swing leg *see* CARPITIS

swingle tree Also known as bar, whippletree, whipple tree, wiffletree, wiffle-tree, splinter bar, badikins, single tree, swingle bar, or swing bar; the pivoted, horizontal swinging bar located at the front of a horse-drawn vehicle to which the harness traces or chains are fastened and by which a vehicle or implement is drawn.

swing pair Also known as pole-end horses; the middle pair in a six-horse team.

swings *see* SWING TEAM

swing team Also known as swings; the middle pair in a six-horse hitch or the team in front of the wheelers (q.v.) in an eight-horse hitch.

swing up *see* INDIAN STYLE

swipe (1) Racing slang; a groom, stable hand, or exercise boy. (2) *see* GROOM NO. 1

swirl A hair marking; a twist or curl of the hair on the horse's head; may be used for identification purposes.

swishing tail The continuous movement of the horse's tail; a form of resistance.

Swiss Anglo-Norman *see* EINSIEDLER

Swiss Halfbred *see* EINSIEDLER

Swiss Warmblood A Swiss horse breed developed in the 1960s by putting Thoroughbred (q.v.), Swedish and German horses to the Einsiedler (q.v.); stands 15 to 16.3 hands, has a straight back, slightly sloping croup, prominent withers, a slightly convex or straight head, strong, well-jointed legs, and a coat of any solid color with chestnut and bay occurring most commonly; used for riding and driving.

switch tail Also known as broomtail; the horse's tail when pulled to about half its length; the terminal hairs are either pulled or allowed to grow to a natural point.

swooping ends Said of a bucking horse when his hind end and head come together as a result of a very tight longitudinal body bend.

sword case Also known as booge or boodge (a word derived from the Saxon times meaning to bulge out); a case attached or built into a horse-drawn vehicle in which a sword was stored during travel.

sword pencil *see* DAGGER PENCIL

swung round A dressage term; said of the horse having performed a walk or canter pirouette (q.v.) too fast and without control; in the case of the canter pirouette, the strides of the canter may be lost and the horse may swing or pivot on one or both hind feet.

syce Also spelled SAIS; an East Indian groom.

Sydney Galvayne *see* GALVAYNE, SYDNEY

symbolic mange *see* CHORIPTIC MANGE

sympathetic nervous system That section of the autonomic nervous system (q.v.) originating in the thoracic and lumbar regions which stimulates the heart beat, dilates the pupils, contracts the blood vessels, and, in general, functions in opposition to the parasympathetic nervous system (q.v.).

synchronous diaphragmatic flutter Also known as thumps or by the acronym SDF; an abnormal heartbeat caused by the involuntary contraction of the diaphragm in rhythm with the beat of the heart, resulting from electrolyte losses occurring during physical exertion, hypocalcemic tetany, or blister beetle toxosis; symptoms include a noticeable twitch or spasm in the flank area which may cause an audible sound, dehydration, decreased plasma volume, lack of gut motility, an increase in blood pH, and lowered levels of chloride (q.v.), calcium (q.v.), sodium (q.v.), and magnesium; most commonly seen in electrolyte-depleted/exhausted horses.

Syndicat des Eleveurs de Cheval Breton A French breed association established in 1909 to maintain the stud book for both the Heavy Draught Breton (q.v.) and Postier Breton (q.v.); only horses born in the four departments of Brittany, France, and in the Loire-Latalnatique may be registered; registered foals are branded on the left side of the neck with two distinctive marks.

syndicate A partnership arrangement formed for the purpose of buying a horse for race, show, or breeding purposes; investors put up the money and share in the profits and tax benefits.

synovial *see* SYNOVIAL FLUID

synovial fluid Also known as synovia, joint fluid, tendon oil or joint oil; the sticky, transparent lubricating fluid in the joint cavities and tendon sheaths secreted by the synovial membrane (q.v.) which prevents friction and allows smooth joint and tendon action.

synovial joint A moveable joint consisting of articulating bone ends held together by a joint capsule and ligaments and which contains synovial fluid (q.v.).

synovial membrane The lining of the tendon sheaths and joint capsules which secretes synovial fluid necessary for smooth joint action.

synovial sheath The inner lining of a tendon sheath which produces synovial fluid (q.v.).

synovitis Inflammation of the membrane lining a joint; usually accompanied by effusion of fluid within the synovial sac of a joint; associated with various injuries and joint inflammation conditions.

Syrian An ancient pony breed originating in Syria; has similar origins to the Arab (q.v.) from which it is believed to have descended; stands 14.2 to 15.2 hands and has a gray or chestnut coat, is slightly larger than the Arab and has more angular conformation, yet is equally elegant; is long-lived, fast, frugal, energetic, and possessed of good endurance and strength; used for riding.

systemic lupus erythematosus Also known by the acronym SLE; a rare auto-immune disease; symptoms are diverse and depend on the organ systems involved; may include swollen eyelids, facial pain and swelling, visual impairment, photo-sensitivity, whitening of the hair in patches, and scabbing.

T

tabanid Also known as tabanid fly; any of a number of large, dipterous, bloodsucking insects belonging to the family Tabanidae, including horseflies (q.v.).

tabanid fly *see* TABANID

tables (1) The polished surfaces of the front incisor teeth formed by contact with teeth of the lower jaw; table shape is an indicator of age. (2) *see* TABLES 1, 2, AND 4

Tables 1, 2, and 4 Also known as tables; American Horse Show Association (q.v.) rules by which classes for jumpers (q.v.) are judged.

table bank A jumping obstacle consisting of a constructed mound of dirt with, generally, a three-stride platform or flat top and vertical take-off and landing sides.

tack (1) *see* SADDLERY. (2) *see* HARNESS. (3) An American racing term; the weight of a jockey including his gear, e.g., "The jockey tacks 110 pounds."

tack room Any enclosed space where tack, saddlery, and/or accessories are kept.

tact The rhythmic beat of the horse's footfalls in all gaits.

tag (1) A racing term; the claiming price paid for a horse. (2) The tip of the fox's tail. (3) A farrier's term; a hoof shape pattern in which the hoof is somewhat pointed at the toe, straight through the quarters, and turns sharply in at the heels, with the widest part located across the rear one third of the hoof.

tail (1) Also known as horsetail; that part of the horse including the dock (q.v.), tail bones, and tail hair; a direct extension of the spinal column consisting of coccygeal bones numbered 15 to 21. (2) Also known as male tail; the sire line or top line in a pedigree. (3) *see* TAIL SHOT. (4) To follow.

tail bandage Also known as tail wrap; a bandage (q.v.) approximately 2½ to 3 inches (6–7.5 cm) wide made of stockinet (q.v.) or synthetic material wrapped around the tail from the dock to the end of the tail bone to protect it from injury or rubbing while traveling, to improve appearance, and to keep the hairs of a pulled tail in place.

tail board The rear portion of a horse-drawn vehicle; may let down to form a passenger foot rest.

tail bones *see* COCCYGEAL BONES

tail carriage The manner in which the horse carries his tail.

tail coat *see* SHADBELLY

tailer A roping term; one whose responsibility it is to rope the hind legs of a calf; works with a header (q.v.).

tail going round Said of a horse who swishes his tail in a circular motion; believed to be a sign of irritability or exhaustion.

tail guard A soft leather, cloth, or synthetic covering for the top 10 to 12 inches (25–30 cm) of the tail; used to protect the tail hair from rubbing during trailering or while stabled.

tail hound A hunting term; a hound who follows at some distance behind the pack (q.v.), rather than leading, when running a fox (q.v.).

tail notch A cut into the horse's tail hair to facilitate identification when turned out on public land.

tailor seat A vaulting term; a static exercise (q.v.) in which the vaulter (q.v.) sits on the back of the horse with both legs crossed in front of him.

tail rubbing Said of a horse who persistently rubs the tail dock (q.v.); due to many circumstances including boredom, pinworm infestation, external parasite infestation, or other localized skin irritation.

tail set (1) A rigid, crupper-like contraption

used on a nicked (q.v.) tail to lift it sufficiently high to be doubled and tied down; maintaining the horse's tail in an unnatural, high-set position while the horse is stabled and to give it an arch and extremely high carriage when driven or ridden. (2) The set position or carriage of the horse's tail.

tail shot A polo term; a stroke in which the polo player strikes the ball from behind and across the rump of his horse.

tail string *see* FILLET STRING

tail swish Also known as tail switch (Brit); the horse's tail when the hairs are pulled so that the tail terminates in a finished point.

tail switch *see* TAIL SWISH

tail to the wall *see* RENVERS

tail wrap *see* TAIL BANDAGE

take Also known as take out; a racing term; money deducted from each mutuel pool (q.v.) to cover track revenue and state and local taxes.

take a fall (1) *see* THROW A RACE. (2) A hunting term; a fall of both the horse and rider. (3) A racing term; said of the jockey; to fall from the horse.

take back *see* TAKE UP

take down A racing term; to disqualify a horse for an infraction after he has finished in the money (q.v.), at which point his number is removed from the list of early finishers.

take hold Said of the horse who clamps down on the bit and pulls against the rider's or driver's hands through the reins.

taken back *see* TAKEN UP

taken up Also known as taken back; a racing term; said of a horse checked (q.v.) by the jockey to conserve the horse's energy or to avoid trouble on the track.

take off (1) A vaulting term; the moment when the vaulter (q.v.) leaves the ground in preparation to mount the horse. (2) A jumping term; the moment at which a horse leaves the ground in preparation to clear a jump; preceded by the approach (q.v.) and followed by flight (q.v.). (3) *see* BOLT NO. 2

take-off rail *see* GROUND POLE

take-off side The side of any jumping obstacle from which the rider begins his jump; the opposite of the landing side (q.v.).

take off too late A jumping term; said of the horse who takes off too close to an obstacle and is therefore likely to hit it with his forelegs or forefeet.

take off too soon A jumping term; said of the horse who takes off to jump an obstacle too far away from the take-off point appropriate for his stride; the horse will therefore be descending from his jump before fully clearing the obstacle and thus may hit it with his body or hind legs.

take out *see* TAKE

take the bump *see* POST

take up Also known as take back; a racing term; said of a jockey who sharply checks or rates (q.v.) his horse to avoid a collision or other trouble on the track.

take with the hand Said of the rider; to tighten the finger grip on the reins to apply bit pressure on the bars of the horse's mouth.

taking down the purse A racing term; (obs); to award the purse to the winner of a horse race; originally, prize money was contained in a purse hung on a wire strung across the finish line.

tally-ho Also known as tally o; a hunting term; the huntsman's cry to urge on his hounds; indicates a fox has been sighted.

Tally-Ho TALLY-HO BREAK

Tally-Ho Break Also known as Tally-Ho; a horse-drawn, light sporting break popular in the late 19th century with fox hunting and horse-racing groups; supported by high wheels and hung on elliptic and/or semi-elliptic springs; drawn by a single horse in shafts or a pair in pole gear (q.v.).

tally-ho over *see* TALLY OVER

tally o *see* TALLY-HO

tally over Also known as tally-ho over; a hunting term; a cry to the field indicating that a fox has crossed a ride (q.v.) in a wood.

tampering *see* BISHOPING

tandem Two horses, one hitched in front of the other, as to pull a vehicle; the wheeler (q.v.) is placed between the shafts of the vehicle and the leader is out in front.

Tandem Cart A two-wheeled, horse-drawn Dogcart (q.v.) generally used for show purposes driven to a tandem (q.v.); had dummy slatted sides, as dogs were not carried, and a rear groom's seat situated at a slightly lower level than the driving seat.

Tandem Sporting A two-wheeled, tandem-drawn Dogcart (q.v.) or Gig (q.v.) used to transport a saddled, bridled, and harnessed hunter to a hunt; the hunter was driven in the lead at the canter, while the wheeler (q.v.), a harness horse, was driven at the trot; with destination reached, the hunter was unharnessed from the lead and mounted; the vehicle was then drawn back to the stable by the wheeler, driven by a groom.

tandem whip *see* COACHING CROP

Tanghan A subgroup of the Bhotia (q.v.) pony breed which originated in the Himalayan mountains of northern India; stands 13.2 hands, has a gray coat, short neck, shaggy mane, straight shoulder, and short, strong legs; is frugal and has good endurance; used for riding.

tap *see* TAPADERO

tapadero Also known as a tap; one of two hooded leather coverings of the front of a Western stirrup (q.v.); used to protect the rider's foot from brush and weather; available in many styles.

tape (1) *see* ADHESIVE TAPE. (2) To tie or secure with tape. (3) *see* BARRIER

taproot The direct female line of descent traced back to the origin.

taproot mare *see* FOUNDATION MARE

tapeworm Also known as flatworm; a gastrointestinal parasite; of three species in the horse: *Anoplocephala manga* (q.v.), *Anoplocephala perforliata* (q.v.), and *Paranoplocephala mamillana*; vary in length from 8 to 25 cm; found in the cecum, small intestine, and occasionally the stomach where they feed on nutrients consumed by the horse; in light infestations, no signs of disease are present, while in heavy infestations, digestive disturbances, unthriftiness, and anemia (q.v.) may occur.

Tarai A pony breed indigenous to Nepal, standing about 11.2 hands.

Tarbenian A horse breed from Tarbes located at the foot of the Pyrenees mountains between France and Spain; descended from the Iberian Horse (q.v.) improved with Arab (q.v.) stallions imported by Napoleon Bonaparte at the beginning of the 19th century; later English Thoroughbred (q.v.) stallions were put to Tarbenian mares to increase breed height and create the Bigourdan Horse (q.v.); is light boned, stands about 15 hands, is fast, courageous, intelligent, and generally has good conformation.

tare Any of several species of vetch, especially *Vicia sativa*, or any seed of a vetch; a weed pest of grain fields

target a cow A cutting term; said of a cutter (q.v.) who identifies a cow in the herd he wants to work and slowly and deliberately separates it from the herd; the opposite of cut for shape (q.v.).

Tarpan Also known by the scientific name *Equus ferus ferus*; one of two sub-species of ancient wild horse found in eastern Europe and Asia; was about the size of a mule (q.v.) with a tan, Isabella (q.v.), or mouse coat with a whitish surcoat, an arched forehead with the ears set far back, thin neck, narrow, high, and pointed hooves, hock-length tail, and a high croup; the fronts of the fore and hind legs were black from the knees to the hoof; although extinct since the 18th century, two attempts have been made to breed it back; the Turkoman word for wild horse.

tarsal hydrathrosis *see* BOG SPAVIN

tarsus *see* HOCK

tarsus valgus *see* MEDIAL DEVIATION OF THE HOCK JOINTS

tat A native Indian pony.

Tattenham Corner The final bend in the Epsom Derby (q.v.) course; located 4 to 3 furlongs (q.v.) from the finish, this left-hand bend begins at the base of Tattenham Hill and terminates in the straight.

Tattenham Hill Also known as Epsom Hill; the notoriously steep and highest point of the Epsom Derby (q.v.); the course rises 5 furlongs (q.v.) to the top of this hill where the course remains more or less flat for another 2 furlongs before dropping; Tattenham Corner (q.v.) is the bend beginning at the base of this hill.

Tattersall bit Also known as yearling bit, ring bit, or colt bit; a circular bit that attaches to the headstall; the upper half of the circle is placed in the horse's mouth while the lower half fits under the horse's jaw; may or may not have keys (q.v.).

Tattersal check A checked fabric pattern created by intersecting lines of red, blue, and yellow on a white background; the pattern consists of a bold check about 1 inch (2.54 cm) square with smaller checks approximately ¼ inch (.64 cm) square; commonly used for summer sheets (q.v.), driving aprons, men's waistcoats, collar lining, etc.

tattoo (1) The act or practice of marking the skin with indelible patterns, legends, or numbers by making punctures in it and inserting pigments. (2) A mark or marks on the horse's skin made with a sharp instrument and injected indelible dye, used for identification or registration purposes; frequently a series of numbers or a code placed inside the horse's upper or lower lip; a horse cannot be tattooed until it is at least two years old as the immature immune system will recognize the dye as a foreign substance and sweep it to the lymph nodes; required by some stud books for registration purposes, and in the United States for race eligibility; will fade and stretch over time and may be temporarily altered or masked for a period of up to 48 hours by injection of condensed milk into the dyed areas.

tattooer One trained, certified, or registered to tattooing (q.v.) horses.

tattoo mark An adventitial mark (q.v.); permanent white coat hairs resulting from destruction of the pigment cells of underlying skin by the tattoo process.

Tattu A subgroup of the Bhutia (q.v.); a pony breed originating in the Himalayan mountains of northern India; stands 11.2 hands, has a gray coat, short neck, shaggy mane, straight shoulder, and short, strong legs; is frugal and has good endurance; used for mountain packing.

Taxis ditch The most grueling of 31 jumping obstacles in the Grand Pardubice (q.v.), a steeplechase (q.v.) held annually in Czechoslovakia every second Sunday in October since 1874; is 16 feet 5 inches (5 m) wide and fronted by a natural fence 5 feet (1.5 m) high and 5 feet (1.5 m) wide.

TB *see* THOROUGHBRED

TBFV loop *see* TIDAL-BREATHING FLOW-VOLUME LOOP

T-Cart *see* T-CART PHAETON

T-Cart Phaeton Also known as T-Cart; a light, horse-drawn, four-wheel vehicle of the Phaeton (q.v.) type driven to a small horse or large pony; popular in military circles throughout the second half of the 19th century; had a forward driving seat much wider than the groom's rearward seat, which when viewed from above appeared T-shaped.

Tchenarani An Iranian half-breed indigenous to the north; bred since 1700 by crossing Persian Arab (q.v.) stallions with Turkmene (q.v.) mares; stands 14.1 to 15.1 hands, has an athletic, wiry build, sloping croup, powerful hindquarters, and usually has a bay, chestnut, or gray coat; is spirited yet gentle; historically used as a cavalry mount, now used for riding.

TDN *see* TOTAL DIGESTIBLE NUTRIENT SYSTEM

tea A racing term; any illegal chemical administered to a horse to hamper or improve his performance.

team (1) Two or more horses harnessed together to draw a wagon or other vehicle. (2) Generally four or more, although occasionally three, horses harnessed together to draw a wagon or other vehicle. (3) The draft horse(s) together with the harness and the drawn vehicle. (4) A number of riders associated by country, riding style, breed ridden, etc., participating in a joint activity or action as in sides of a competition.

team handicap A polo term; the sum of the goal ratings (q.v.) of all four players on a team; used to equalize playing ability; the side with the lower goal rating total receives the difference between the two team totals as a score at the beginning of the match.

team penning Also known as penning; a relatively young mounted team competition fostered under the auspices of various cattlemen's associations and rooted in traditional ranch work; consists of three skills: cutting (q.v.), reining (q.v.), and sprinting; a trio of three horses and riders proceed into one end of an arena toward a herd of 30 cattle clustered at the opposite end; each cow is identified by a number from zero to nine on its shoulder, and when the first horse and rider reach the start/foul line, a judge calls out a number and the clock begins; the team then attempts to isolate the three cows bearing the specified numbers, cut them from the herd, and drive them down the arena and into an enclosed pen within 2 minutes; when the last cow is confined, one or all the riders raises a hand, thus stopping the clock and ending the competition; generally conducted in three rounds; scored in one of two ways: (a) the team with the lowest cumulative time for all three rounds wins or (b) teams with the lowest times advance to second and third rounds, the one with the lowest third-time round wins; because it is governed by more than one association, the rules may vary between competitions.

team rope To participate in team roping (q.v.).

team roper A mounted horseman, either a header (q.v.) or heeler (q.v.); who participates in team roping (q.v.).

team roping A timed horseback competition; originated on American cattle ranches as a utilitarian event; two riders, a header (q.v.) and heeler (q.v.), pursue a calf; one ropes the head and the other the heels; the clock stops when the calf is securely roped and held tight by ropes from each rider.

team sorting A relatively new sport originating in central California, USA around 1990 as a ranch competition similar to team penning (q.v.); a timed event in which each participating team (consisting of three mounted contestants) attempts to herd 10 calves, numbered 0 to 9, to one end of an arena; the end quarter of the arena is marked with painted posts or flags on either side, between which an imaginary line known as a foul line is drawn; this line serves as a starting line for the timer, a boundary line for the cattle, and should be located 50 to 75 feet (15–23 m) from the corners, depending on the width of the arena; one team at a time rides to the foul line and waits for the announcer to draw and call out a number from 0 to 9; the riders attempt to cut each of the 10 calves in numerical order (starting with the number called by the announcer) away from the herd and drive them across the foul line; the calves must be sorted in proper numerical order and cross the line in that order; "no-time" is called if any calf crosses the foul line out of order or passes across the line and then retreats to the original side; each team has 2 minutes (90 seconds in Southern California, USA) to cut 10 cattle; if more than one team sorts 10 cattle, the team with the fastest time wins; if no team sorts the herd in the allotted time, teams are scored by the number of calves correctly herded across the line within 90 seconds; the next team does not cut until the 10 calves are settled (q.v.).

tease To sexually stimulate the mare with a teaser (q.v.) to determine if she is ready for mating and to encourage her to come into heat (q.v.); generally, a mare will be brought to a fence or padded partition such as a trying board (q.v.) on the other side of which is a stallion (q.v.), ridgeling (q.v.), or gelding; the partition prevents full contact between the horses; if the mare is ready she will adopt the mating posture (q.v.), holding her tail up and to the side.

teaser Also known as teaser stallion; a horse, usually a stallion or a ridgeling (q.v.), used to test the response of a mare prior to mating, or to determine if a mare is in heat (q.v.) and ready to mate at which time the mare will be mated to a selected stallion, generally other than the teaser; use of a teaser prolongs stallion fertility and libido.

teaser stallion *see* TEASER

technical delegate One responsible for insuring that an international horse show or three-day event competition is run according to international FEI (q.v.) rules and that the course is correct; usually from a country other than the host nation.

teeth More than one tooth (q.v.).

Telega A crudely made, four-wheeled, horse-drawn Russian passenger or Stage Coach (q.v.); frequently unsprung or dead axle.

telegraph spring Also known as mail spring or platform spring; an elastic contrivance or body, as a wire of steel coiled spirally, which when compressed, bent, or otherwise forced from its natural shape, has the power of recovering this by virtue of its elasticity; specifically, a combination of four double-elbow springs, two positioned sideways and two crossways, used on such horse-drawn vehicles as the Mail Coach (q.v.), Mail Phaeton (q.v.), Stanhope Gig (q.v.), etc.; so called because the first ones were used on the English Telegraph Coach.

teletheater A racing term; a movie theater in which horse races are simulcast.

teletimer A racing term; an electronic timer that flashes the fractional and final race times of horses running in races on the tote board (q.v.).

teller *see* MUTUEL CLERK

Tellier's rod A contrivance used on horse-drawn carriages to prevent them from overturning in the case of wheel loss; a rod hinged on one end to the vehicle and from which, on the other, hung a rotating rowel suspended inches above the ground; if a wheel were to drop off, or the vehicle became unbalanced for any reason, the rowel would dig into the ground and serve as an ancillary wheel; developed in 1828 by American Jean Tellier.

Tellington-Jones Equine Awareness Method Also known as TTEAM or TTEAM training; a system of integrated training, therapeutic and holistic healing, and overcoming common resistances or tension in the horse's body using a technique of functional integration and body work; developed by Linda Tellington-Jones (q.v.); consists of three sections: the Tellington TTouch (q.v.), ground exercises, and riding with awareness, including tools and exercises to improve equine and rider balance and coordination.

Tellington-Jones, Linda An accomplished horsewoman, educator, trainer, and healer most noted for her technique of holistic body work, ground exercises, and riding with awareness to train, heal, and overcome common resistances in the horse known as the Tellington-Jones Equine Awareness Method (q.v.).

Tellington TTouch Also known as TTouch; a method of training, healing, and overcoming common resistances in the horse developed by American Linda Tellington-Jones (q.v.) in the 1970s; based on the Feldenkrais method of functional integration and body work; a component of TTEAM (q.v.) training.

Tell that to the Horse Marines A phrase of derision said to one guilty of gross exaggeration; (obs).

temperature Body heat; the normal rectal temperature for a horse at rest is approximately 99.1 to 100.5 °F (37.5–38 °C); the temperature of a horse at work may rise by as much as 5 degrees.

tempi changes A dressage term; lead changes performed by the cantering horse at every stride or at specific intervals such as every second, third, or fourth stride.

tempo The measure of speed within the movements of the horse's various gaits; the number of feet or meters covered per minute.

temporary teeth *see* DECIDUOUS TEETH

tenderfoot (1) A 17th century term; a horse with tender feet. (2) An Americanism since the early 19th century; one unused to traveling who became footsore. (3) *see* DUDE

tenderfooted Said of a horse with tender or sore feet.

tendinous windgall *see* TENDINOUS WINDPUFF

tendinous windpuff Also known as tendonous windgall; a soft, fluid-filled enlargement of the digital flexor tendon sheath; usually confined to above the fetlock and does not cause lameness, although must be regarded with suspicion in the presence of lameness; swelling occurs between the suspensory ligament and flexor tendon and should be distinguished from distension of the fetlock joint capsule (articular windpuff [q.v.]); may be caused by intense training followed by a period of rest, excessive exercise on hard surfaces, or the cumulative effects of imbalances produced by poor conformation or improperly trimmed hooves.

tendon Also known as sinew; tough, fibrous, slightly elastic, white cords connecting muscle to bone and supporting the joints; tendons transmit the energy generated by muscular contraction to the bones.

tendon boots Also known as run-down boots; a protective leg covering for the cannon bones of the horse's forelegs; support the tendons in the back of the leg and protect them from injury; may have a closed or open front.

tendon oil *see* SYNOVIAL FLUID

tendonitis Inflammation of the tendon (q.v.) caused by irritation from use or injury.

tenectomy Surgical removal of a portion of a tendon.

ten-minute halt An eventing (q.v.) term; a compulsory 10-minute stop of the horse and rider at the end of Phase C of the Speed and Endurance Phase, during which time the second compulsory veterinary inspection occurs and the horse is cooled down and refreshed.

Tennessee Walker *see* TENNESSEE WALKING HORSE

Tennessee Walking Horse Also known as Plantation Walking Horse, Southern Plantation Walking Horse, Plantation Walker, Tennessee Walker, Walking Horse, Walker, Turn-Row (because of its ability to travel between the rows of crops without damaging them), or Turn-Row Horse; an American horse breed developed in the 19th century in Tennessee from which the name derived; bred for the purposes of riding, driving and light farm work; descended from a cross of Standardbred (q.v.), Thoroughbred (q.v.), Morgan (q.v.), Canadian and Narragansett Pacers (q.v.); the foundation sire, a black stallion of Morgan and Hambletonian ancestry, named Allan, was also the founding sire of the Standardbred; noted for its three natural gaits: the running walk (q.v.), the flat-foot walk (q.v.), and the canter (rocking-chair canter [q.v.]); exhibits an overstriding action which serves as a shock absorber, whereby the hind foot is placed ahead of the track left by the forefoot by as few as 12 and as many as 40 inches (30–102 cm); comfortably travels in the running walk at speeds from 6 to 12 mph (9.7-19.3 kmph); is large-boned, deep and short-coupled, with a square appearance to the barrel, stands 15 to 17 hands, has a steady and reliable temperament; the breed displays a number of coat colors including bay, black, chestnut, brown, roan, palomino, white, or gray; recognized as a breed in 1950; included in the American Saddlebred Registry until the late 1950s as more than 25 percent of the foundation sires were registered American Saddlebreds.

Tennessee Walking Horse Breeders' and Exhibitors Association Also known by the acronym TWHBEA; an organization founded in 1935 in Lewisberg, Tennessee, USA, to collect, record, and preserve the pedigrees of the Tennessee Walking Horse (q.v.), maintain a registry, develop rules and regulations governing all aspects of the breed, and to sponsor promotional programs; the stud book opened in 1947; to qualify for the registry both parents must be registered Tennessee Walkers.

tenosynovitis Inflammation of the membrane lining of a tendon.

tense Also known as worked up; the mental and physical state of the horse when not relaxed, obedient, and/or responsive to the aids of the rider.

tent-pegger One who participates in the mounted sport of tent-pegging (q.v.).

tent-pegging A mounted sport originating in India for military purposes; a mounted rider carrying a 10 to 12 foot (3–3.6 m) long lance, would charge on a galloping horse at the tent of the enemy, place the tip of his lance through an eye in a tent peg and lift it from the ground, thus dropping the tent on those inside; now a competitive sport; the size of the peg varies depending on the expertise of the competitors, with larger pegs used by beginners and progressively smaller pegs used by more advanced riders.

Terek *see* TERSKY

termino The natural foreleg action of the Peruvian Paso (q.v.) when performing the paso (q.v.) gait; the forelegs arc, or dish, to the outside in the forward strides.

terms race *see* CONDITION RACE

terra-à-terra *see* TERRE-A-TERRE

terra terra *see* TERRE-A-TERRE

terre-à-terre Also known as terra terra and spelled terra à terra; a rocking movement of small, controlled, low-to-the-ground forward and sideways bearing advancing prances; often performed against the wall or between pillars (q.v.); a dressage air (q.v.) which served as the foundation for the high airs (q.v.), although it is no longer performed; a very cadenced, elevated canter (q.v.) performed in two-time on two tracks (q.v.) in which the forelegs are raised together, then put down together, followed by the deeply engaged hindquarters in the same motion.

terret One of the round loops or rings on the hames (q.v.), pad, or saddle, through which the driving reins pass.

terrier man Also known as fencing man; a hunting term; one responsible for carrying terriers for the purpose of bolting a fox (q.v.); adjunct responsibilities include repairing hunt jumps and fences damaged during the day's hunting, attending to the hunt terrier, and divot stomping (q.v.).

Tersk *see* TERSKY

Terskij *see* TERSKY

Tersky Also known as Tersk, Terskij, or Terek; a Russian-bred warmblood developed at the Tersk and Stavropol Studs in Northern Caucasus between 1921 and 1950; descended from the old Tersky breed which was founded on the Strelets Arabian selectively crossed with pure and part-bred Arabians (q.v.) which it closely resembles; stands 14.3 to 15.1 hands and always has a gray coat; is good-natured, active, and possessed of good stamina; used for riding, racing, and in the circus; officially recognized as a breed in 1948.

test barn A racing term; an area where blood and urine samples are taken immediately following each horse race to screen for the presence of illegal drugs.

tested sire *see* PROVEN SIRE

testes Also known as balls (sl), nuts (sl) or testicles; more than one testis (q.v.); a typically paired male reproductive gland that produces sperm and that is contained within the scrotum at sexual maturity.

testicles *see* TESTES

testis Also known as gonad; a single reproductive gland in the male which produces sperm and testosterone.

tetanus (1) Also known as lockjaw; an acute infectious disease characterized by tonic voluntary muscle spasms especially of the jaw; caused by the bacillus toxin, *Costridium tetani*, which is usually introduced through a wound such as a puncture (q.v.); found in spores in the soil; estimated to be fatal in 25 to 50 percent of all equine cases, as horses are the most sensitive to it of all mammalian species; the incidence is generally higher in the warmer parts of the continents; the incubation period varies from one to several weeks, but usually averages 10 to 14 days following introduction of the bacteria into an anaerobic (q.v.) wound environment; symptoms include localized stiffness in the wound area, followed by generalized stiffness, increased intensity of the reflexes, excitement of the horse into spasms by sudden movements or noises, an inability to chew (hence the common designation lockjaw), protrusion of the third eyelid, erect ears, stiff tail, stiff walking, difficulty backing and turning, sweating, and due to leg muscle stiffness, a sawhorse stance (q.v.); the temperature usually remains slightly above normal, but may rise to 108 to 110 °F (42–43 °C) toward the end of a fatal attack; may be prevented by active immunization with tetanus toxoid (q.v.), including boosters at annual intervals; if a horse has not been immunized prior to the occurrence of the wound or puncture, tetanus antitoxin (q.v.) administered up to two days following the injury will still provide temporary protection. (2) The specific bacterium that causes tetanus.

tetanus antitoxin Antibodies formed in a host inoculated with tetanus (q.v.) bacteria; injected into a horse to provide temporary protection against tetanus.

tetanus toxoid A tetanus toxin whose toxic property has been eliminated, usually by a chemical agent, but which retains the antigenic (q.v.) qualities that produce immunity on injection into the body by stimulating production of immune antibodies in the blood; provides prolonged protection against tetanus (q.v.).

tether (1) A rope or chain by which a horse is fastened to restrict range to a set radius around the object to which it is tethered. (2) To fasten or restrain by, or as with, a tether.

Tevis Cup *see* TEVIS CUP

Tevis Cup Ride Also known as Tevis Cup or 100-mile Western States Ride; a 100-mile (160 km) endurance race run in the United States from Tahoe City, Nevada to Auburn, California, over the steep Sierra Nevada mountain range; riders climb 9,500 feet (2,896 m) to Squaw Pass and drop into El Dorado Canyon where temperatures can reach 100 °F (37.7 °C); generally covered by the winners in 11 to 12 hours; first held in 1955.

Texas fever *see* EQUINE PIROPLASMOSIS

Texas Racing Commission An eight-member board that governs all horse and Greyhound racing activities in Texas, USA.

The Art of Horsemanship *see* ART OF HORSEMANSHIP, THE

The Book *see* STUD BOOK

the box *see* BOX NO. 1

the brace *see* BRACE NO. 5

the cough *see* EQUINE INFLUENZA

the cross *see* SHOULDER CROSS

The Derby *see* EPSOM DERBY

The Derby Stakes *see* EPSOM DERBY

The Distance *see* DISTANCE, THE

The Downs *see* EPSOM DOWNS

The Elephant *see* ELEPHANT AND CASTLE

The Garden *see* NATIONAL HORSE SHOW

The Grand National *see* GRAND NATIONAL STEEPLECHASE

The Heythrop *see* HEYTHROP HOUNDS

The Maneige Royal *see* MANEIGE ROYAL, THE

The Master *see* MASTER

The Master of the Game *see* MASTER OF THE GAME, THE

The Mounties *see* ROYAL CANADIAN MOUNTED POLICE

The National (1) *see* GRAND NATIONAL STEEPLECHASE. (2) *see* NATIONAL HORSE SHOW

The Oaks *see* EPSOM OAKS

Théodore Géricault *see* GERICAULT, THEODORE

the off *see* OFF NO. 1

the office *see* OFFICE, THE

The Polo Association *see* UNITED STATES POLO ASSOCIATION

the prop *see* PROP, THE

therapeutic riding Riding as used in physiotherapy or psychotherapy.

therapeutic horseshoe *see* THERAPEUTIC SHOE

therapeutic shoe Also known as therapeutic horseshoe, pathological shoe, surgical shoe, or corrective shoe; a horseshoe (q.v.) used in conjunction with veterinary medical treatments to treat or correct conformation defect, disease, or injury of the foot or leg.

therapeutic shoeing Any specialized shoeing technique used to correct or remedy a disease or injury of the foot or leg.

therapeutic ultrasound Use of high frequency sound waves, above the range of the human ear, to break down unwanted tissues and promote healing by stimulating circulation.

thermography A lameness diagnostic technique in which a visual image is produced from infra-red radiation emitted from the skin surface; the infra-red radiation is detected by a proton detector, converted to electrical impulses, and displayed in colors on a television monitor, the different colors corresponding to variances in body temperature with areas of trauma or injury registering an elevated temperature.

thermoregulation The control and/or regulation of the body temperature.

the scale *see* SCALE OF WEIGHTS

Thessalian An ancient Greek pony breed-now extinct.

the taller the port, the tighter the curb A rule of thumb used to estimate the tightness of a curb chain whereby the higher the port (q.v.) sits above the bit (q.v.), the tighter the curb chain should be adjusted.

the tie *see* TIE, THE

the V *see* V, THE

the whip *see* WHIPPER-IN

thiamin Originally known as vitamin B1 and spelled thiamine; a white crystalline compound found in the outer coating of cereal grains, greens, brewer's yeast, peas, beans, liver, etc. and also prepared synthetically; essential for normal metabolism and nerve function; lacking in most horse rations, particularly low-quality hay and is destroyed by heat and cooking; deficiency is detected by blood analysis;, symptoms include loss of appetite, nervousness, reduced fertility, and a lack of coordination.

thiamine *see* THIAMIN

thick wind Said of the horse; to have difficulty breathing.

thief A racing term; a horse who runs worst when his chances appear to be best.

thigh aid The rider's thigh when gently squeezed or pressed into the horse's side to communicate instruction or address the horse's reflexes.

thigh bone *see* FEMUR

thill (1) *see* SHAFT HORSE. (2) *see* SHAFT

thiller *see* SHAFT HORSE

thiller gear *see* FILL GEAR

thill horse *see* SHAFT HORSE

third eyelid *see* NICTITATING MEMBRANE

third incisors *see* CORNER INCISORS

Third Level Similar to Medium Level (Brit and Aus); a dressage competition level in which the horse performs specific test movements and gaits; the horse is required to demonstrate extended, collected, and medium gaits, and show a clear distinction between them; movements are more specialized, demanding increased impulsion, straightness, and acceptance of the bit; new movements include the half-pass (q.v.), single flying changes, and 8-meter circles at the canter.

third man Also known as referee; a polo term; a referee (q.v.) who sits on the sidelines during a polo match and who arbitrates in the event that the two field umpires disagree on a call.

third pastern Also known as os pedis, third phalanx, coffin bone, distal phalanx, distal phalange, pedal bone, or PIII; the largest bone in the horse's foot and the most distal bone in the leg; a hoof- or crescent-shaped bone which, together with the navicular and lower portion of the coronet bone, forms the pedal or foot joint; one of three primary bones which make up the lower part of the horse's leg and hoof.

third phalanx *see* THIRD PASTERN

third sire The paternal great-grandfather of a horse.

this grass This coming spring, as in "The horse will be four years old this grass."; (obs).

thong The long, plaited portion of a whip attached to the crop (q.v.) on one end and to the lash (q.v.) on the other, the length of which varies from 1 to 2 yards (91 180 cm); generally found on lunge (q.v.) and hunting whips.

thoracic Pertaining to the thorax (q.v.).

thoracic cavity *see* CHEST

thoracic inlet The bony, oval opening in the front of the horse's chest through which the windpipe (q.v.), esophagus (q.v.), and major vessels to and from the head pass.

thorax *see* CHEST

thoropin *see* THOROUGHPIN

thorn bit A very severe bit (q.v.) with a spiked mouthpiece still used in some parts of the Orient.

thoroughbrace A strong leather strap, or straps on which the body of a horse-drawn vehicle was sometimes suspended in lieu of shocks or springs.

Thoroughbred Also known as English Thoroughbred, British Thoroughbred, TB, bloodstock, blood horse, blood 'un (obs), Thro-bred, or bred horse (obs); a horse breed developed in the early 18th century; based upon three Arab stallions imported into England: the Byerley Turk (q.v.), the Godolphin Arabian (q.v.), and the Darley Arabian (q.v.); these three stallions, and mares of varietal stock, are the foundation from which all Thoroughbreds trace their descent on the male side; the General Stud Book (q.v.) dates back to 1791 and is kept by The Jockey Club (q.v.); although the breed does not present uniform physical characteristics, it can be generally categorized into three basic physical types: the stayer (q.v.), the sprinter (q.v.), and the middle distancer (q.v.); stands 14.3 to 17 hands, has fine skin, a bay, dark bay, black, chestnut, or gray coat and white face and leg markings; roan and red roan are rarely found; used for riding, racing, and improving other breeds.

Thoroughbred Breeders Association A British organization founded in 1917 to encourage and ensure the cooperation and unity of Thoroughbred (q.v.) breeders in improvement of the Thoroughbred.

Thoroughbred Racing Association Also known by the acronym TRA; a trade association of North American racetrack owners and managers founded in 1942 to maintain the integrity of racing, a database of racing statistics, and to provide racetrack management support.

Thoroughbred Racing Protective Bureau An intelligence network operating in the United States responsible for fighting corruption within racing.

thoroughpin Also spelled thoropin; distention of the tarsal sheath of the deep digital flexor tendon just above the hock (q.v.) characterized by a fluid-filled swelling visible above the point of the hock on either side; caused by trauma or strain to the tendon and is most common in draft and jumping horses although any sudden stop can cause the condition; considered a blemish which rarely affects the horse's performance.

Thracian An ancient Greek pony breed, now extinct.

threadworm *see* STRONGYLOIDES WESTERI

three abreast *see* TRANDEM

three-day event Also known as Concours Complete, Concours Complete d'Equitation, or complete test; a three-phase competition conducted over a period of three days and consisting of dressage (q.v.), show/stadium jumping (q.v.), and speed and endurance (q.v.) phases, the later including steeplechase (Phase B), roads and tracks (Phases A and C), and cross-country (Phase D); the three phases are performed by the same rider/horse team; three compulsory veterinary inspections take place, the first prior to when competition begins, the second following Phase C of the speed and endurance phase, and the third occurring on the third day before the start of the jumping phase; in America, differs from horse trials (q.v.) in that it includes an endurance phase.

three-eighths pole A racing term; a distance marking pole located on the inside rail three furlongs (q.v.) from the finish line.

three feet of tin *see* COACH HORN

three-gaited Said of any horse who performs the three natural gaits of walk, trot, and canter.

three-gaited saddler One of three types of horse show classes for the American Saddlebred (q.v.) in which demonstration of the walk, trot, and canter is required.

three-quarter pole A racing term; a distance marking pole located on the inside rail (q.v.) exactly six furlongs (q.v.) from the finish.

three-quarters brothers A relationship between male horses having the same dam (q.v.) and whose sires (q.v.) had identical sires but different dams.

three-quarters in blood Said of male or female horses having the same dam and whose sires had identical sires but different dams.

three-quarters pastern A leg marking; white covers the lower three-quarters of the pastern.

three-quarters sisters A relationship between female horses having the same dam (q.v.) and whose sires (q.v.) had identical sires but different dams.

three-quarters stocking A leg marking; the white extends up to and includes the lower three-quarters of the cannon bone.

three rein A method of holding the reins when driving a tandem (q.v.); the driver's right hand is placed on the reins in front of the left; the second and third fingers rest on top of the two offside reins, effectively making them one rein.

Three-seat Surrey An American horse-drawn vehicle of the Surrey (q.v.) type; had three identical forward-facing seats placed one behind the other.

three-to-one Also written 3 to 1; one of three methods of holding the reins of a double bridle; three reins are held in the left hand (the two curb reins divided by the ring finger and the left snaffle rein around the little finger) with the right snaffle rein and the whip held in the right hand; the method is only effective if the horse has been properly trained and worked through on the snaffle; the only method accepted at the Spanish Riding School (q.v.).

thrifty A horse who is healthy, alert, and active.

throat (1) The passage that leads from the nose and mouth to the lungs and stomach and includes the esophagus and pharynx; the front part of the neck. (2) The bottom of the inside of a collar (q.v.).

throat band *see* THROAT LATCH

throat lash *see* THROAT LATCH

throat latch Also known as throat lash or throat band; the narrow strap of the bridle which encircles the head from the crown piece under the throat (q.v.) where it buckles; prevents the bridle from slipping over the horse's head.

throat latching A coaching term; a method of restraining a horse inclined to pull; to pass the coupling rein of the puller through his partner's throat latch (q.v.) before buckling it to the puller's bit.

Thro-bred *see* THOROUGHBRED

thrombosis Blocking of a blood vessel by a blood clot; may follow atheroma (q.v.) or some injury to the vessel or the heart during life.

thrombus A fibrous clot of blood which forms in and obstructs a blood vessel.

throughness Also known as durchlässigkeit; a dressage term; the supple, elastic, unblocked, connected state of the horse's musculature which permits an unrestricted flow of energy through the horse, especially from the hindquarters forward; allows the influence of the aids to move freely to all parts of the horse, e.g., the influence of the rein aids on the hind legs.

throw (1) To toss or fling through the air, as a cow to the ground in preparation for branding, the tie (q.v.), horseshoe (q.v.), etc. (2) *see* THROW A RACE

throw a race Also known as throw, take a fall, stiff, pull a race, or pull; a racing term; said of the jockey in competition, to intentionally restrain a horse or use other means to prevent it from winning a race.

throw a shoe Also known as throw; said of a horse who loses a horseshoe by any means other than intentional removal.

throw his tongue *see* GIVE TONGUE

throw-in Also known as bowling; a polo term; the action of the umpire tossing the polo ball into play between the two teams from midfield.

throwing hobbles A set of leather straps attached to the horse's pasterns and used to throw a horse to the ground.

throwing their tongues A hunting term; said of the hounds when they give tongue (q.v.).

thrown (1) Said of a rider bucked or tossed off the back of the horse; an unintentional dismount. (2) Said of the horse when intentionally cast to the ground by his handlers as for medical treatment, etc. (3) Said of a horseshoe which, for any reason other than intentional removal, becomes detached from the hoof.

thrown out A hunting term; said of a member of the field who becomes lost or falls behind when hunting.

throw off Also known as cast (Brit); a hunting term; said of the huntsman (q.v.) when he takes the hounds (q.v.) from the meet to search for a fox (q.v.)

throw tongue *see* GIVE TONGUE

thrush Also known as frush (obs); a yeast infection of the frog resulting in degeneration of frog tissue; caused by standing in wet, dirty conditions for prolonged periods of time and failure to clean the hooves; most common in the hind feet; symptoms include a softening of the hoof horn and a black, thick, foul-smelling discharge; if left untreated may result in lameness.

thrust A hunting term; said of a member of the field when he/she rides hard to the hounds (q.v.).

thruster A hunting term; a member of the field who rides too aggressively and close to the hounds (q.v.) and/or hunt staff (q.v.).

thumb a horse To make a horse buck by digging one's thumb deep into his neck and running it along the neck muscles.

thumb of the Prophet *see* PROPHET'S THUMB

thumps *see* SYNCHRONOUS DIAPHRAGMATIC FLUTTER

thymus *see* THYMUS GLAND

thymus gland Also known as thymus; a ductless gland located in the upper thoracic cavity near the throat; largest early in life and gradually dwindles in size; involved with immunity.

thyroid *see* THYROID GLAND

thyroid gland Also known as thyroid; the two-lobed endocrine gland located in the neck on either side of the larynx that controls the rate at which basic body functions proceed and releases the hormone thyroxin (q.v.).

thyroid stimulating hormone Also known by the acronym TSH, a hormone secreted by the pituitary gland; stimulates the thyroid gland to increase production of thyroxin (q.v.).

thyroxin Also spelled thyroxine; the hormone produced by the thyroid gland (q.v.) which regulates the cellular metabolic rate.

thyroxine *see* THYROXIN

Tibetan A Tibetan pony breed originating in the mountains, thought to have descended from Mongolian (q.v.) and Chinese (q.v.) ponies; related to the Bhutia (q.v.) and Spiti (q.v.) which it closely resembles; stands approximately 12 hands, may have a coat of any color although yellow dun (q.v.) is most common, has a straight profile, broad forehead, full forelock, mane and tail, small ears and eyes, a short, muscular neck, short back, and short, sturdy legs; used for riding, packing, and farm work.

tibia The inner and usually larger of the two bones of the hind limb between the knee and ankle.

tick (1) A jumping term; said of a horse who barely touches, but does not dislodge any portion of the jump. (2) An external, bloodsucking parasite belonging to the order Acarina and family Ixodidae; each species may have one or more favored feeding sites on the host, although in severe infestations other areas of the host body may be utilized; feeds chiefly on the head, neck (including the mane), shoulders, ears, and tail; infestation can cause anemia, unthriftiness, and can result in the transmission of a large variety of diseases including equine encephalitis (q.v.), swamp fever (q.v.), and billary fever (q.v.).

ticket (1) A racing term; a bet (q.v.) placed on a horse, e.g., a combination pari-mutuel ticket. (2) Also known as betting ticket, slip, or card; a slip, usually of paper or cardboard, serving as evidence or token of the holder's title by reason of payment.

tick fever *see* EQUINE PIROPLASMOSIS

tick-tack A British racing term; hand signals by which tick-tack men (q.v.) communicate betting odds to the bookmakers.

tick-tack men A racing term; (Brit); those employed by bookmakers to communicate betting odds, bets laid, and prices quoted by means of hand signals.

tidal-breathing flow-volume loop Also known by the acronym TBFV loop; a breath-by-breath measurement of the changing airflow, volumes, pressures, and frequencies occurring throughout the breath cycle, from inhale to exhale, breath after breath; is usually dumb-bell shaped, showing one airflow peak as the horse inhales and another as he exhales; in horses with heaves (q.v.) there is a peak in airflow, but only when the horse exhales.

tie *see* TIE, THE

tie-back surgery *see* LARYNGOPLASTY

tied-in at the knee Said of a horse whose flexor tendons appear too close to the cannon bone below the knee; a conformation defect which inhibits movement.

tied-in below the knee Also known as short of bone; said of a horse whose legs are much narrower just below the knee than near the fetlock (q.v.); a conformation fault that indicates a horse is light of bone (q.v.).

tied-in knees Said of the horse's knees when the flexor tendons appear to be too close to the cannon bone at a point just below the knee; inhibits free movement; a conformation defect.

tied on A racing term; the reins when knotted and crossed; give the jockey a stronger hold.

tiedown *see* STANDING MARTINGALE

tiedown martingale *see* STANDING MARTINGALE

tie line Also known as high line; a rope or line generally tied between two trees to which the lead ropes of horses are tied; horses stand parallel and, if space is available, alternating one side of the line and the other; used by horsemen to hold horses in the outdoors when a corral or other means is unavailable.

tie man One who regularly ties his lariat (q.v.) to the saddle horn.

tie off A roping term; to tie and secure the feet of a roped calf or steer with a pigging string (q.v.).

tierce *see* TOTALIZATOR

tiercé *see* TRIFECTA

tie stall A partitioned space about 6 by 12 feet (1.8 × 3.6 m), normally occurring in multiples, in which a horse is tied, in some cases using a log head collar (q.v.) when not being used; allows limited movement, although fighting between the horses sharing a common wall may occur.

tie, the Also known as tie; a roping term; to place three of the calf's legs together, wrap a pigging string (q.v.) around them and secure the string with a half-hitch.

tie up (1) To restrain a horse with a halter and rope to a rail or post so he cannot move away. (2) Present tense reference to tying-up syndrome (q.v.).

tiger An obsolete British term; a tiny groom who rode behind a Cabriolet (q.v.) standing on the platform; always immaculately dressed in a yellow and black horizontally striped waistcoat (denoting a member of the outside staff); it was from the tiger-colored waistcoat that the name derived.

Tiger Horse Also known as El Caballo Tigre and Siberian Tiger Horse; an ancient Spanish American breed; originated in the Steppes of Asia, the Don Region of Russia, near the boarder with China; originally used to hunt Siberian tigers and thus the name; is strongly built, moderately sized, standing about 15.1 hands, and has strong legs and feet; is a gaited horse (q.v.) possessed of the Lp color pattern (leopard complex gene) which is also found in the Noriker (q.v.), Knabstrupper (q.v.), Appaloosa (q.v.), Altai, and other such colored breeds; efforts are underway to establish breed characteristics.

tiger stripes *see* ZEBRA STRIPES

tight A racing term; said of a horse ready to race.

tightener (1) A racing term; a race intended to bring a horse to his peak physical fitness level, a level not attainable in morning workouts alone. (2) *see* BRACE

tight on a cow A cutting term; said of a horse who controls a cow in tight confrontation.

Tilbury Also known as Seven-Spring Gig or Tilbury Gig; a light, two-person, two-wheeled horse-drawn vehicle of the Gig (q.v.) type developed by Hon. Fitzroy Stanhope in early 19th-century Britain, and built by Mr. Tilbury for whom it was named; much heavier than the Stanhope Gig (q.v.); hung on seven springs and two braces which made it cumbersome, but comfortable for travel over rough roads; had a spindle-backed driving seat, generally no luggage space, and was entered by means of bucket-shaped shaft steps.

Tilbury Gig *see* TILBURY

Tilbury springs The method of suspending the Tilbury; consisted of seven springs.

Tilbury Tug Also known as French Tilbury Tug; a stout, oval-shaped, metal reinforced leather loop buckled to each side of the short harness backband, used to support and stabilize the shafts; principally used on four-wheeled horse-drawn vehicles.

tilt (1) The fence separating two jousters in the Mediaeval sport of tilting (q.v.). (2) *see* TILITNG. (3) The cloth covering of a cart or wagon.

tilter One who tilts (q.v.).

tilting A mounted knightly sport, military exercise, and exhibition event practiced between AD 476 and the 17th century; jousting whereby two mounted participants would rush at each other, separated by a wall (the tilt) and would strike, by means of a lance, the opponent or the opponent's shield; in some derivations, the tilter would strike at a revolving figure, tree trunk, post, or pile upon which he would break his lance.

tilting head *see* TIPPING HEAD

tilting the head *see* TIPPING HEAD

tilt the quintaine Said of a knight or sportsman who successfully broke his lance against a quintaine (q.v.); performed from AD 476 through the 17th century.

timber (1) A hurdle or other obstacle constructed of wood which is jumped. (2) Growing trees.

timber rider A racing term; a steeplechase jockey; in Britain, more commonly a rider over hurldes.

timber splitter (1) A horse skilled in maneuvering his way through an area of burned timber. (2) A British term; said of a horse; a clumsy jumper, especially of post and rails (q.v.) while hunting, i.e. a horse who tends to break rails.

timber topper A racing term; a horse who runs in jump races; most accurately, a horse who jumps over timber fences.

time allowed Also known as optimum time; the period of time in which a competitor must complete a course (q.v.) or event to avoid time faults (q.v.).

time clock Also known as clock; an automatic electronic device used to measure elapsed time from the start to finish of a competition round or event.

timed event In Western competitions, any event including barrel racing (q.v.), calf roping (q.v.), team roping (q.v.), steer wrestling (q.v.), and steer roping.

time fault Also known as time penalty; a penalty for exceeding the time allowed (q.v.) to complete an event or course.

Timeform A weekly English publication in which all the British race horses are listed with racing form and the relative assessments of their form in pounds.

timekeeper One who monitors the official game or event clock used to regulate the period of play or competition.

time limit The period of time, often twice the time allowed (q.v.), in which a competitor must complete a course to avoid automatic elimination.

time line A line marking the location of the timing beam projected by an electronic timer (q.v.) which starts and stops the time clock.

time out A polo term; a temporary cessation of action in a polo match (q.v.) called by an umpire (q.v.) when a foul is committed, an accident occurs, or at his own discretion, or by a player due to broken tack or injury to himself or his horse; may not be called to replace a broken mallet or change horses.

time penalty *see* TIME FAULT

Timor A pony breed indigenous to the island of Timor, Indonesia; the smallest of the Indonesian breeds standing 9 to 11 hands, usually has a black, bay, or brown coat, a relatively large and heavy head, short ears, flared nostrils, short neck, short back, and strong quarters; has good endurance, is sure-footed, agile, strong, docile, and willing; used for riding, farm work, and light draft; has been exported to Australia where it contributed to the development of the Australian Pony (q.v.).

Timothy (1) *see* TIMOTHY GRASS. (2) *see* TIMOTHY HAY

Timothy grass Also known as Timothy; a perennial European coarse grass, *Phleum pratense*, with dense cylindrical spikes or bristly spikelets, widely grown for hay.

Timothy hay Also known as Timothy; cut and dried coarse grass, *Phleum pratense*, with cylindrical spikes, valuable as fodder; of average nutritional quality; preferred as a feed hay because it is generally free of dust and mold; highest in nutritional content, palatability, and quality in the pre-bloom stage; second and third cuttings tend to have the highest nutritional value with a digestible protein content of approximately 6.6 percent; the fiber content of all cuttings is just above 30 percent; frequently grown in a mixture with legumes such as alfalfa (q.v.) and clover (q.v.).

tip (1) To give private or secret information. (2) Private or secret information, as in the anticipated success of a horse competing in a race or event. (3) *see* TIP SHOE. (4) To strike lightly and sharply; to tap. (5) To give a small present of money for some service. (6) The pointed, tapering, or rounded end or top of something long and slim, as a whip.

Tip Cart Also known as Dump Cart (Am);

any horse-drawn cart that could be tipped backwards to unload the contents.

tipping head Also known as tilting head, tilting the head, or tipping the head; a dressage term; said of a horse who holds his head position left or right of the vertical; an evasion.

tipping the head *see* TIPPING HEAD

tip shoe Also known as tip or slipper; a horseshoe (q.v.) that only covers the bearing surface of the hoof from just in front of the quarters to the toe, or approximately 25 percent of the hoof circumference; provides no protection to the quarters or heels.

tipster A racing term; one legitimately employed to try and "tip" the winners of races.

tits (1) A 19th-century term; a pair of horses. (2) Slang; light and/or little horses.

tittup A canter (q.v.) or easy gallop (q.v.), as of a horse; a prancing movement, a springing.

toad eyes A British term; said of the horse's eyes when prominent with mealy upper and lower lids; typical of the Exmoor Pony (q.v.).

to be at fault *see* AT FAULT

to be at loss *see* AT LOSS

tobiano Refers to coat color pattern; a white base coat with large, asymmetrical patterns of colored, vertically arranged patches typically originating from the head, chest, flank, buttocks, and often including the tail; the color will cover one or both flanks; there is a sharp definition between the white and colored areas and the spots will be regular and distinct as ovals or round patterns that extend down over the neck giving an appearance of a shield; all four legs are generally white, at least below the hocks and knees; the head is usually conservatively patterned with patterns like those of a solid-colored horse – solid or with a blaze (q.v.), star (q.v.), or snip (q.v.); the pattern may range from little spotting to a predominantly white body and colored head; the eyes are generally not blue; results from a dominant gene and requires at least one tobiano parent; the most common Pinto Horse (q.v.) coloring in the United States.

tocopherol *see* VITAMIN E

toe angle *see* HOOF ANGLE

toe calk A calk (q.v.) affixed to the toe of the horseshoe.

toe clip A V-shaped extension of the horseshoe (q.v.) at the toe, pressed into the hoof wall to hold the shoe onto the hoof in those situations or on those hoofs where nails are insufficient.

toe crack A crack in the hoof wall at the toe, starting at the bearing surface and extending a variable distance up the hoof wall, or a crack originating at the coronary band (q.v.) and extending downward; may occur in either the front or hind feet.

toed in *see* PIGEON-TOED

toe flipping *see* FALSE EXTENSION

toe grab Also known as cleat; an extended toe calk; follows the horseshoe contour and is usually sharper than conventional calks; used on race horses to prevent slipping.

toe in *see* PIGEON-TOED

toeing knife A mallet-driven blade used to trim the hoof wall; now largely replaced by hoof nippers (q.v.).

toelt *see* TØLT

toe out Also known as splay footed; when viewed from the front, the toes of the horse's hoof point away from each other; generally a congenital condition; may cause the forelegs to swing in during movement as in winging (q.v.) and results in stress.

toe plate A horseshoe used on race horses having a toe grab (q.v.) in front; used to prevent slipping.

toe tapper A discouraged and outdated method of tumbling a horse headfirst as to perform a movie stunt; so called because the toes of the horse's forefeet are tapped with screws between the horseshoe and hoof to which cables are connected; the cables are drawn to the proximal aspect of the hoofs and up to rings on each side of a surcingle; the two cables merge into a single cable connected to a wooden handle held by the rider.

toe weight A metal weight attached by clips to the front feet of trotters and harness horses to improve action by changing the balance in motion.

to fence *see* FENCE NO. 3

to have whip A harness racing term; a horse possessed of geat speed.

tolt *see* TØLT

tölt *see* TØLT

tølt Also spelled tolt, toelt, or tölt; one of five natural gaits of the Icelandic (q.v.); an extremely smooth, four-beat gait, much like the running walk (q.v.) or rack (q.v.) that allows the rider a virtually bounce-free ride at speeds up to 20 mph (32 kmph).

Tonga An Indian two-wheeled, hooded vehicle originally pulled by two horses and subsequently by one.

tongue (1) The freely moving organ within the horse's mouth with the power to shape itself for different purposes including grazing and drinking. (2) *see* CRY NO. 2

tongue bar shoe A therapeutic horseshoe (q.v.); a combination of heart-bar (q.v.) and egg-bar (q.v.) shoes; the egg-bar, which connects the two heels of the shoe, is squared to give lateral support and the heels are bent down to raise heel angle without putting pressure on the heel wall or rear of the frog; the tongue is welded to the center of the bar to distribute weight over the front third of the frog; used in conjunction with a strong toe clip.

tongue loller A horse who evades bit action and control by putting his tongue over the top, rather than under the bit mouthpiece (q.v.).

tongue out Said of a horse who evades bit action by putting his tongue out of the side of his mouth.

tongue over the bit Said of the horse who evades bit action and control by putting his tongue over the top of the bit rather than underneath.

tongue strap Also known as tongue tie; a leather or cloth band laid over the top of the tongue and connected under the chin by means of a buckle; prevents a race horse from "swallowing his tongue" during a race or other workout, or to prevent the tongue from sliding up over the bit.

tongue swallowing *see* CHOCKING UP

tongue tie *see* TONGUE STRAP

tool (1) *see* DRIVE NO. 6. (2) To decorate, ornament, or carve leather using a stamp or other tools as by hand or machine.

tool budget A leather box attached to the fore-carriage of a horse-drawn vehicle in which tools are stored.

too low *see* ON THE FOREHAND

tooth One of the hard bodies or processes attached in a row to each jaw, serving for the prehension and mastication of food and as a weapon of defense and attack; composed chiefly of dentin surrounding a sensitive pulp and covered on the crown with enamel; of two types: deciduous teeth (q.v.) and permanent teeth (q.v.); tooth wear patterns may be used to determine, with some degree of accuracy, horse's age; tooth infections will generally drain through the nose; specific teeth include the canine teeth (q.v.), incisors (q.v.), molars (q.v.), temporary teeth (q.v.), premolars (q.v.), and wolf teeth (q.v.).

tooth decay *see* CARIES

tooth file (1) *see* FLOAT NO. 1. (2) *see* TOOTH RASP

tooth rasp (1) Also known as rasp or tooth file; a long-handled file having separate, point-like teeth, used to smooth off the rough edges on the horse's molar teeth (q.v.). (2) *see* FLOAT

tooth star *see* DENTAL STAR

top *see* CARRIAGE HOOD

top bar Also known as upper bar, the uppermost slot into which the reins can be buckled on a curb bit. (q.v.).

top boot A tall riding boot with a cuff of a different color than the leg; traditionally and, still formally, worn by members of a Hunt (q.v.); women's boots have a black patent leather cuff and a black leg, while men's have a brown or cordovan (q.v.) cuff and black boot leg; tops are earned and are a symbol of status in each Hunt with the conditions upon which tops are awarded varying from Hunt to Hunt; more an American custom than a British one.

top horse A racing term; the first horse listed in a race program.

top line (1) Also known as back line; the visual line created by the horse's neck, back and croup. (2) On a pedigree (q.v.) chart, the breeding on the sire's side.

top of the ground A hunting or British racing term; said of the footing over which horses travel when so firm that their feet do not sink into it.

top pommel *see* HUNTING HEAD

top rein The cord bearing rein used on Hackneys (q.v.) in show; released from the hook on the pad when the horse comes to a standstill in the lineup and is refastened when the horse moves off.

top rider An accomplished rider; an 'A' rider whether professional or amateur.

top weight *see* HIGH WEIGHT

Tor di Quinto A cavalry school in Rome, Italy opened in 1891 and made famous by Federico Caprilli (q.v.), who was a prime mover in the development of the forward seat (q.v.); closed since World War II.

Toric Also known as Estonian Klepper, Double Klepper, or Torisky; an Estonian-bred warmblood of fairly recent origin; developed in the 19th century by crossing Arab (q.v.), Ardennais (q.v.), Hackney (q.v.), East Friesian (q.v.), Hanoverian (q.v.), Orlov (q.v.), Thoroughbred (q.v.) and Trakehner (q.v.) blood with the Klepper (q.v.); a fast-moving, active, light draft horse with a good temperament; stands 15 to 15.2 hands and may have a bay or chestnut coat; has quite a long neck, a short back, deep and wide chest, and a notably tough hoof; the name derived from the Toric Stud where breeding first began; well suited to draft and farm work.

Torisky *see* TORIC

torsion When one end of a body part is twisted in one direction, while the other end remains motionless, or is twisted in the opposite direction, as in colic (q.v.).

torsion colic Also known as twisted gut or twisted bowel; colic (q.v.) resulting when the intestine twists on itself, blocking passage of feed, may be caused by falls, heavy feed following hard work, etc.; causes intense abdominal cramping.

torso *see* BODY NO. 1

torticollis *see* WRY-NECK

tostado Refers to point color; brown points; sometimes used in conjunction with other color distinctions for greater color specificity, e.g. chestnut tostado.

total digestible nutrient system Also known by the acronym TDN; a method of measuring the feed energy value by rating the different nutrient components of the feed according to digestibility; the assessed feed is given a numerical value which indicates the percentage of the nutrients in the feed used by the horse; the sum of the contents of the digestible protein, digestible crude fiber, digestible nitrogen-free extract, and digestible ether extract (crude fat) multiplied by 2.25; calories are the preferred method of determining energy value.

totalisator *see* TOTALIZATOR

totalisator board *see* TOTALIZATOR BOARD

totalizator Also known as tote or tierce and spelled totalisator; a mechanical apparatus that automatically registers and totals each betting ticket as it is issued on a per race basis in parimutuel wagering (q.v.), keeps a running total of all money bet on each horse in the win, place (q.v.), and show (q.v.) pools, and calculates the betting odds on each horse; the betting odds and number of bets placed on each horse are openly displayed to the public on the totalizator board (q.v.).

totalizator board Also spelled totalisator board and known as board, odd board, or tote board; an electronic board located in the race infield upon which the up-to-the-minute betting odds for each horse, as calculated by the totalizator (q.v.) on a per race basis, are displayed; may also show the amounts wagered in each mutuel pool and changes in equipment and jockeys.

total plasma protein Also known by the acronym TPP; a blood test performed to determine dehydration in the horse; levels of plasma protein increase with dehydration.

tote *see* TOTALIZATOR

tote board *see* TOTALIZATOR BOARD

touched in the wind Said of a horse slightly unsound in the wind (q.v.).

touched up fox *see* DOPED FOX

touch the horn A hunting term; to blow the hunt horn (q.v.).

tournament A series of games or athletic events in which teams or individuals compete against one another.

tout A racing term; one who obtains information on horses for betting purposes and peddles such information or tips and betting systems to the racegoer prior to a race.

tovero Refers to a coat color pattern; a horse showing both overo (q.v.) and tobiano (q.v.) coat patterns.

towel An obsolete coaching term; to flog a coach horse.

Town Coach A heavy, elegantly appointed, horse-drawn vehicle; driven from a box seat covered with a fringed hammer cloth, seated four passengers vis-à-vis (q.v.), and had a rear platform for two footmen; originally hung on cee springs, but later on elliptical and semi-elliptic side springs; drawn by a pair of matching coach horses, usually bays with black tails; is less formal than the State Coach (q.v.).

Town Plate *see* NEWMARKET TOWN PLATE

toxaemia *see* TOXEMIA

toxemia Also spelled toxaemia; the presence of a toxin in the bloodstream; generally results from absorption of bacterial products formed at a localized source of infection.

toxicosis An abnormal or diseased condition produced by action of a toxin or poison.

toxin An unstable organic poison produced in living or dead organisms or their products, e.g. venom.

to you A hunting term; a verbal warning from one rider to other members of the field to indicate the presence of a ditch on the near side of an upcoming fence.

TPP *see* TOTAL PLASMA PROTEIN

TRA *see* THOROUGHBRED RACING ASSOCIATION

trace (1) A path or trail made by passage of animals or people. (2) Either of two straps, chains, or lines of a harness by which the horse is attached to a vehicle to be drawn.

trace bearer *see* BEARING STRAP

trace carrier *see* BEARING STRAP

trace clip To remove the coat hair from a horse in a broad line from the shoulder, belly, haunches (historically, the area where the traces would go), and occasionally from under the neck leaving the legs, back, neck, and head unclipped; a common clip for harness horses.

trace element *see* TRACE MINERAL

trace heel The end of the trace (q.v.) closest to the horse-drawn vehicle.

trace horse The leader of a tandem (q.v.); any horse added to the existing equipage to assist in pulling a vehicle up an incline.

trace mineral Also known as trace element; a chemical element essential to the physiology of a horse in minute quantities.

trachea Also known as windpipe; the tube extending from the larynx to the bronchi which serves as the passage for conveying air to and from the lungs.

trachectomy *see* TRACHEOTOMY

tracheotomy Also known as trachectomy or tubing; to surgically incise the trachea (q.v.) and insert a breathing tube to enable a horse to breath in emergency situations where the trachea is obstructed or swollen.

track (1) Also known as racetrack, race-track, race track, racecourse, course, racing strip, or strip; a racing term; any specific area where horses run during training or racing; is generally grass or dirt footed, fenced, and maintained. (2) The beaten path or trail left by repeated passage of persons, animals, or vehicles. (3) A series of footprints or other marks left by a horse, fox, etc. (4) To leave tracks or footprints, as a fox. (5) To follow the scent or mark of a beast or man. (6) Direction of travel, as in "track right" (q.v.). (7) A dressage term; the path next to the rail in a dressage arena.

track bandage *see* EXERCISE BANDAGE

track bet Also known as on-course bet or on-track bet; a racing term; any wager placed at the race track (q.v.).

track bias A racing term; a racing surface that favors a particular running style or position.

track condition A racing term; the nature of a racing surface, as in fast track (q.v.), muddy track (q.v.), good track (q.v.), sloppy track (q.v.), frozen track (q.v.), hard track (q.v.), firm track (q.v.), soft track (q.v.), or heavy track (q.v.).

tracking (1) A cutting term; said of a horse who follows the movements of a cow from behind. (2) The process or act of following the scent or mark of beast or man.

tracking up A dressage term; said of a horse whose movement is straight and whose hind feet step into the impressions of the forefeet; does not normally occur in the collected gaits, in which the steps are characteristically shortened and elevated.

track left A dressage term; said when the direction of travel consists of all left turns.

track master An American racing term; one responsible for maintaining the condition of the track (q.v.).

track right A dressage term; said when the direction of travel consists of all right turns.

track sour Said of a horse having temporary vitamin B complex deficiency; commonly diagnosed in race horses; symptoms include reduced performance, nervousness, weight loss, and foot shuffling.

traction horseshoe Any horseshoe (q.v.) adapted (as with studs [q.v.], grooving, etc.) to provide traction on slippery surfaces such as ice, pavement, stone, etc.

traditional acupuncture *see* ACUPUNCTURE

tractive power The pulling strength of a horse, approximately 453.51 (1,000 kg) pounds.

Traekehner *see* TRAKEHNER

traffic jam *see* JAM

trail (1) To drag or let drag behind one, especially on the ground. (2) To make a mark (path, track, etc.,) as by treading down; the usual, repeated passage of men or animals. (3) A cutting term; said of a working horse who lags behind the movements of the cow being worked.

trailer (1) To transport cattle, horses, etc. in a conveyance pulled behind a truck. (2) Also known as box, horse-box, or horse trailer; any vehicle attached to, and drawn by, a car, truck, tractor, or van used to haul one or more horses; does not have an engine. (3) An extended outside heel (¼ inch [6.5 mm] or more beyond the heel of the horse's foot) of a hind-hoof horseshoe commonly turned 45 degrees away from the center line of the hoof and the line of travel.

trailing (1) A cutting term; said of a horse in a working position who lags behind the movements of the cow. (2) A dressage term; said of the half-pass (q.v.) or leg-yield (q.v.) when there is a lack of parallelism to any long axis of the arena, e.g., trailing haunches.

trailing foreleg *see* TRAILING LEG

trailing leg Also known as trailing foreleg or non-leading leg; the horse's foreleg which does not lead in the canter.

trail horse A horse trained, bred, or used for cross-country riding either on or off trail.

trail ride To ride a horse outside of the manège or stable on a groomed or blazed path or track through the country.

trail up A racing term; said of a physically fit horse who loses his competitive edge.

trainer (1) Also known as horsebreaker, conditioner, horse tamer, or horse trainer; one who teaches horses to move or perform in a predetermined manner. (2) One responsible for teaching another the art of horsemanship (q.v.).

training barn (1) Also known as barn; a training operation located within a larger facility where all boarders and their horses are trained by a professional horse trainer (q.v.). (2) A boarding facility in which horses must be in training to board there.

training cavesson *see* LUNGEING CAVESSON

training fork *see* RUNNING MARTINGALE

training gallop A racing term; to gallop (q.v.) a horse on stretches of turf or other track surfaces in preparation for running on the racecourse; the stretches may be of varying lengths.

Training Level Similar to Preliminary Level (Brit and Aus); a lower-level dressage competition test; the horse is required to move freely forward in working gaits, maintain a steady rhythm, be physically supple, and accept the bit with relaxation; test movements are simple, requiring gradual transitions and large circles (20 meters).

training plates A type of horseshoe (q.v.) typically used on racehorses in training and some young riding and show horses; made of swedged steel in sizes 3 to 9; available in several widths of light patterns and a heavy pattern.

training roller Also known as breaking roller; a girth (q.v.) or surcingle made of leather or webbing; the strap buckles under the barrel; consists of two pads separated by a space; the pads fit on either side of the withers and prevent pressure and rubbing on the withers; is adjustable on both sides and is fitted with rings to which a crupper (q.v.), side reins (q.v.), and bearing reins may be attached; used in the ground training of a horse.

training track A racing term; a race track used for exercising, rather than competing horses; may be located on the track grounds or offsite.

training yoke *see* RUNNING MARTINGALE

train off *see* OVER TRAIN

Trait du Mulassier *see* MULASSIER

Trait du Nord Also known as Ardennais du Nord; a horse breed originating in northeastern France around the turn of the 20th century; descended from a cross of Ardennais (q.v.), Belgian Draft (q.v.) and Boulonnais (q.v.) blood; is heavily built, incredibly strong for its size, hardy, calm, stands 15.3 to 16.1 hands, and weighs 1,320 to 1,760 pounds (599–798 kg); the coat may be bay, roan, or red roan; has a large head set on a thick neck and a short-coupled, muscular body set on short legs; used for heavy draft and farm work; breed population is on the decline; the stud book was established in 1919.

Trait Mulassier Poitevin *see* MULASSIER

Trait Poitevin *see* MULASSIER

Trakehner Also known as East Prussian Horse and spelled Traekehner; a warmblood indigenous to that part of Prussia which is now Poland; developed at the Lithuanian stud of Trakehnen founded in 1732 by Frederick William I of Prussia to breed horses for military purposes and from which the name derived; breed development was particularly influenced in the 16th century by the native Schweiken infused with Oriental blood, followed by Arab blood in the early 19th century, and thereafter, Thoroughbred (q.v.) blood; made an excellent cavalry remount due to its tremendous stamina and was capable of light farm work; following the German retreat from Poland in 1945, approximately 1,000 registered horses were taken on a three-month trek to West Germany where the stud farms were reconstructed; Trakehners left in East Prussia became known as Masuren (q.v.), which were crossed with the Poznan to create the Wielkopolski (q.v.); stands 16 to 16.2 hands, may have a chestnut, bay, brown, black or rarely gray coat, has pronounced withers, a well-proportioned head, long neck, slightly sloping croup, and deep chest; is intelligent, lively, and kind; used for riding and competition.

trandem Also known as three abreast or Manchester team; three horses driven abreast harnessed with two poles.

transfer dray *see* DRAY

transit fever *see* SHIPPING FEVER

transition A change from one gait or movement to another, or a change from one gait variant to another, e.g. working trot to medium trot.

transition not defined A transition (q.v.) in which there is no distinct change or difference shown between the gaits, e.g., no discernible variation between the working and medium gait.

transition rough A change from one gait to another which is other than smooth, straight, and balanced, as resulting from resistance to the hand.

transom A wood or iron transverse member used to secure the wheel plate or fifth (spare) wheel to the body of a four-wheeled, horse-drawn vehicle.

transom plate An iron reinforcement plate placed above and below the axle-tree bed on a four-wheeled, horse-drawn vehicle.

transtracheal aspirate Also known by the acronym TTA; a procedure performed to remove fluid from the lungs; a needle is inserted into the windpipe through the skin, about halfway down the underside of the neck; moderately flexible, fine-gauge tubing is threaded through the needle and into the airway down towards the lungs, and the needle removed; finally a syringe is used to flush the airway with sterile saline solution, which dilutes and liquefies lung exudate for sampling.

trap Any two-wheeled, horse-drawn cart designed for country driving.

trapper A trotting harness horse.

trappings Ceremonial harness including the saddle, bridle, and all ornamental coverings.

trappy (1) Short and rapid action of the horse; a condition predisposed in horses with upright pasterns and straight shoulders. (2) Also known as trappy country; any rough country having a number of blind or semi-blind jumps or where the jumps have difficult approaches and/or landings.

trappy country *see* TRAPPY NO. 2

trauma A wound or bodily injury produced by violence or shock.

travel in straw Said of stablehands who travel in the vans with the horses during transport.

traveling boots *see* SHIPPING BOOTS

travers Also known as haunches in, hindquarters-in, quarters-in, or head to the wall; a lateral dressage movement performed on two tracks (q.v.) in which the horse's head, neck, and shoulders follow a straight track along the arena wall, his head flexed in the direction of movement, while the hindquarters are displaced to the inside about 1 yard (90 cm) off the wall, the horse being bent around the rider's inside leg; the horse moves parallel to the wall with an overall mean angle in his body of approximately 30 degrees.

traverse Also known as side step; a lateral, two-track movement in which the horse demonstrates imperceptible forward or backward movement and no flexion.

travois Also spelled travoise or travoy; an A-shaped carrying frame consisting of two trailing poles serving as shafts bridged by woven twigs, small planks, or thongs for supporting a load; the apex rested on the back or hindquarters of a dog or horse; widely used by the North American Indians for conveying people and belongings.

travoise *see* TRAVOIS

travoy (1) *see* TRAVOIS. (2) A military stretcher used during World War I; attached at one end to a horse, mule, or pony, while the rear end was supported and steered by a medical orderly on foot.

tread (1) Any wound to the coronet (q.v.) of a driven horse as caused by another horse in the team. (2) A coaching term; the single iron step attached to a horse-drawn vehicle by means of an iron stem; used by the passengers to reach the rear seats.

treadmill A machine consisting of a wide belt which rotates around two moving cylinders upon which the horse is compelled to walk, trot, and/or canter; the speed is adjustable up to 37 mph (60 kmph) and the incline adjustable up to 6 degrees; used by practitioners to conduct orthopedic, cardiovascular, and pulmonary workups on horses.

treats Also referred to as nibbles; any food item given to the horse that is not a normal part of his regular ration; may include apples, carrots, molasses, and sugar; are generally more flavorful than nutritional; may be used as a training aid.

treble (1) A racing term; a bet in which the bettor (q.v.) backs three different horses in three different races; the bet can either be a win or an each way treble. (2) *see* TRIPLE COMBINATION

treble of oxers *see* TRIPLE OXER

tree *see* SADDLE TREE

trencher A square or circular flat piece of wood on which food was formerly served or cut; from the French *trenchier* meaning to cut.

trencher-fed A hunting term; said of hounds who live with and are fed by individual farmers and other Hunt supporters rather than kept in a hunt kennel (q.v.).

triactor *see* TRIFECTA

trial A racing term; a timed preparatory race or workout in which the horse, generally accompanied by two others to create competitive conditions, is asked for speed; generally held near the time of an important race.

Tribus A three-passenger horse-drawn cab introduced in 1840; passengers entered from a door on the nearside rear of the vehicle, which was driven from a seat on the offside of the roof.

tricast A racing term; a betting option in which the bettor (q.v.) attempts to select the first three horses to finish in one race.

Trichonstongylus axei A species of worm inhabiting the duodenum; seldom more than ⅓ inch (8 mm) long; affects both cattle and horses.

tri-color hound Refers to hound coat color; any hound with a mixed black, tan, and white coat.

Tridontophorus tenuicollis A small strongyle (q.v.); has a three-week life cycle and is less destructive than the large strongyles (q.v.); causes diarrhea and constipation; migrates to the small intestine.

trifecta (1) Also known as triple, triactor (Can), or tiercé (Fr); a betting option in which the bettor (q.v.) selects the first, second, and third placed horses in any race; of two types: straight trifecta (q.v.) and trifecta box (q.v.)

trifecta box Also known as box trifecta or boxed trifecta; a racing term; a betting option; a wager in which the bettor selects the first three horses to cross the finish line in any order in a single race.

Triga A Grecian chariot pulled by three horses harnessed abreast.

trim To make free of extraneous or extra matter by or as if by cutting; the process of cleaning up a horse including, but not limited to, pulling the mane and tail, clipping the whiskers, feathers, bridle path, and ears, or removing excess hoof wall.

trimmer A coaching term; one responsible for upholstering the interior of carriages and other horse-drawn vehicles with materials such as silk and lace.

trip (1) Said of a horse who stumbles in one or more strides. (2) A racing term; the course taken by a horse from the start to finish. (3) A British racing term; a race distance as in, "He'll be better suited by this trip."

triple *see* TRIFECTA

triple bar Also known as spa; any single-element jumping obstacle consisting of three rails (q.v.) set up as a ramped slant with the highest pole in the back and lowest in the front.

Triple Buckboard A horse-drawn vehicle of the Buckboard (q.v.) type, having three seats in a row.

triple combination Also known as treble; any show or cross-country jumping obstacle consisting of three consecutive elements (q.v.), with one or two strides between each element, numbered and judged as one; may include any type of fence or any combination of non-jumping strides between the elements.

triple crown A series of three important races.

Triple Crown (1) A program of three classic races for three-year-olds; run in the United States as the American Triple Crown [q.v.], in Canada as the Canadian Triple Crown [q.v.], and in England as the English Triple Crown [q.v.]. (2) *see* AMERICAN TRIPLE CROWN

triple oxer Also known as treble of oxers (Brit); a jumping obstacle; a triple combination (q.v.) consisting of three consecutive oxers (q.v.), each separated by one to two strides

tripler (1) A horse able to perform the Dutch triple (q.v.). (2) A Gaucho term; a horse with a fast rolling gait between a trot and canter.

tri-super A racing term; a betting option in which the bettor (q.v.) selects the top three finishing horses in a race; if the wager wins, the bettor is paid a price from the wagering pool and is allowed to make a second trifecta (q.v.) bet, free, on the race that comprises the second half of the bet; in the second half, the bettor must select the top four finishers.

tristeza *see* EQUINE PIROPLASMOSIS

triticale A grain; a cross between wheat (q.v.) and rye (q.v.) developed in 1969 to combine the quality and uniformity of wheat with the hardiness and disease resistance of rye; the name derived from a contraction of triticum (wheat) and secale (rye); has a high yield and rich protein content; uncommonly fed to horses.

trocha The diagonal trot of the Paso Fino horse (q.v.); an unacceptable gait which most young horses grow out of; the Paso Fino should always travel with a lateral gait

troika Also known as Russian style; a method of harnessing three specially trained horses abreast, in which the two outside horses are bent to the outside by tight side reins and canter or gallop, while the center horse, held in an arched douga (q.v.), works at a fast trot; a Russian word meaning three.

Troika Curricle A large vehicle of the Curricle (q.v.) type drawn by three horses abreast in troika (q.v.); the center horse was put to, between shafts, under a douga (q.v.) while the outside horses were harnessed to outriggers, with swingle trees, and put to outside shafts.

Trojan Horse In classical mythology, a large, hollow horse made of wood used by the Greeks to win the Trojan War; in a plan devised by Odysseus, the Greeks hid soldiers inside the horse, left it outside the gates of Troy, and set sail, apparently for Greece; instead, they anchored their ships just beyond sight of Troy; a man they left behind was instructed to say to the Trojans that the goddess Athena would be pleased if they would bring the horse inside the city and honor it, which they did; that night, the Greek army returned to Troy and were let inside the gates of the walled city by the men who emerged from within the horse; as a result, the Greeks won the war.

tropilla A South American term; 6 to 12 horses owned by a gaucho (q.v.); only the male horses (usually piebald [q.v.]) are ridden; a bell mare (q.v.) is used to hold the herd together.

trot Also known as pure trot; a natural two-beat gait in which the diagonal pair of legs, such as the left fore and right hind, leave the ground simultaneously followed by a moment of suspension where the feet do not touch the ground and then the simultaneous strike of right fore and left hind; this sequence remains unchanged in the collected trot (q.v.), working trot (q.v.), medium, and extended trot (q.v.); only the length of stride and duration of suspension change; the speed of the medium trot is approximately 220 yards (201 m) per minute, although the gait will vary considerably from breed to breed.

trot Englais *see* POST NO. 4

trot level Said of a sound (q.v.) horse who moves at the trot without defect.

trotter (1) Any horse bred and gaited to trot (q.v.), especially in harness racing (q.v.). (2) *see* SHILL

trotting light *see* POST

trotting man's bit *see* DR. BRISTOL BIT

trotting vanner *see* VANNER

trouble line An American racing term; the words included in the eastern edition of the Daily Racing Form (q.v.) which appraise a horse's past-performance efforts or excuse his loss.

TRTA *see* RIDE AND TIE ASSOCIATION

truck (1) A two- or four-wheeled, horse-drawn, heavy freight vehicle popular in the 18th century; headed by a length of canvas stretched over hoops and drawn by teams of two or more; from the Latin *trochus* meaning hoop. (2) A class of mechanized vehicles of various sizes and designs used to transport goods or livestock; may have a separate trailer unit attached.

true canter Also known as galop juste; said of a cantering horse who leads with his foreleg on the side to which he is turning.

true gallop *see* GALLOP

true knee *see* STIFLE

true lethal An inherited lethal (q.v.) condition; any disease or condition genetically transmitted to the foal that results in foal death prior to or shortly after birth.

trueness of gait The lack of medial or lateral deviation from the line of travel as seen in the horse's limbs.

true splint A sprain or tear of the interosseous ligament generally in the forelegs of young horses resulting in an enlargement of the splint bones; the enlargement is most frequently seen 2⅓ to 2¾ inches (6–7 cm) below the carpus (q.v.) on the medial side.

true skin *see* CORIUM

true to type Said of a horse who shows characteristics typical of his breed, e.g. conformation, size, temperament, aptitude, coloring, etc.

trunk (1) *see* BOOT NO. 4. (2) The body apart from the head and limbs.

trying board Any fence or padded partition used to separate a mare from the teaser (q.v.) or stallion (q.v.) to determine if she is ready to be mated or to encourage her to come into heat (q.v.).

TSH *see* THYROID STIMULATING HORMONE

Tschenburti A Russian equestrian sport similar to polo (q.v.) in which two teams of six riders attempt to score by placing the ball into the opponents' goal using sticks similar to long tennis racquets.

Tschiffely, Aimé Felix (1895–1954) The naturalized Argentinian who rode his Criollo (q.v.) horses, Mancha (q.v.) and Gato (q.v.), approximately 10,000 miles (16,000 km) from Buenos Aires, Argentina to Washington DC, USA in a period of 2½ years.

TTA *see* TRANSTRACHEAL ASPIRATE

TTouch *see* TELLINGTON TOUCH

TTEAM *see* TELLINGTON-JONES EQUINE AWARENESS METHOD

TTEAM training *see* TELLINGTON-JONES EQUINE AWARENESS METHOD.

Tubal-cain The son of Lamech and Zillah, traditionally purported to be the first shoeing professional of whom written record exists based upon Genesis 4:22.

Tub Car *see* GOVERNESS CART

Tub Cart *see* GOVERNESS CART

tubed Said of a horse having had a tube inserted into his trachea (q.v.) to facilitate breathing.

tubed horse A horse having had a tracheotomy (q.v.) and in whose trachea (q.v.) a breathing tube still exists.

tubing *see* TRACHEOTOMY

tucked up Also known as sucked up or ganted up; said of a horse whose loins are drawn up tightly behind the ribs as due to illness, overwork, lack of water or bulk in the diet, and/or underfeeding, rather than conformation.

tuck jump A vaulting term; a leap performed by a vaulter (q.v.) on the back of a horse; the vaulter, from a standing position on the horse's back, jumps into the air, bends his knees and brings them into his chest while his body remains upright and the arms straight with the fingers pointing towards the ground; he returns to a standing position on the horse's back.

tudabarai One of two types of the wild, ruthless and sometimes deadly national sport of Afghanistan known as Buskashi (q.v.); a rudimentary and rugged type of polo or mounted rugby sometimes involving more than 1,000 participants competing for control of a decapitated calf carcass; there are no teams, no boundaries, and every man rides only for himself – for money and honor; to score, a chapandanzan (q.v.) must simply grab and break away with the carcass, which may weigh as much as 66 to 88 pounds (30–40 kg), from the middle of the starting circle and carry it in any direction, if only for a second; traditionally held to celebrate marriage, circumcision, or other rite of passage.

tufted whorl A whorl (q.v.); a change in direction of hair flow in which hairs converge from different directions and pile into a tuft or point.

tufter A stag hunting term; an old hound (q.v.) selected by the harbourer (q.v.) and brought to a hunt to start the chase of the stag (q.v.).

tug A stout, oval-shaped, leather loop connected to the harness (q.v.) backband through which the shafts (q.v.) pass when a horse is hitched to a vehicle; prevents the shafts from moving up and down when the vehicle is moving; types include the Tilbury Tug (q.v.) and Open Tug (q.v.).

Tumbler Cart A two-wheeled cart with a watertight body made of iron plates; the body revolved on the axle to facilitate loading and dumping of liquids such as sewage.

tumbleweed *see* HORSE DEVIL

Tumbrel (1) Also spelled Tumbril; a traditional farm cart used throughout Western Europe. (2) Also spelled Tumbril; a low-slung ammunition cart used by many European armies throughout the 18th century; drawn by a single horse in shafts.

Tumbril *see* TUMBREL

tune *see* TUNE-UP

tune-up Also known as tune; to polish the performance of the horse by conducting gymnastics, routines, or exercises prior to a competition.

tunica Any membrane or tissue which lines a body cavity or covers an organ.

tuppy A coaching term of encouragement to the horses, asking them to move forward.

turf (1) A racing term; the sport or business of horse racing. (2) A racing term; the upper stratus of soil bound by grass and plant roots into a thick mat. (3) *see* TURF COURSE

turf course Also known as turf; a racing term; a grass track or course used for horse racing.

turf grass clippings *see* LAWN CLIPPINGS

turfman One interested in or devoted to the sport of horse racing.

turgid Swollen, distended beyond its natural state.

Turinsky A lesser-known native horse breed indigenous to the former Soviet Union.

Turk Also known as Turkish Horse; a Turkish horse breed; a characteristic oriental type, having predominantly Persian and Arab (q.v.) blood.

turkey bit *see* MAMELUKE BIT

turkey curb *see* MAMELUKE BIT

Turkish Horse *see* TURK

Turkmen *see* TURKOMAN

Turkmene *see* TURKOMAN

Turkoman (1) Also known as Turkmen or Turkmene; an Iranian-bred warmblood indigenous to the region of Turkmenistan where it was bred for centuries; survived by the Akhal-Teké (q.v.) and the Iomud (q.v.); has exceptional speed and endurance and is used for flat racing. (2) Any horse bred in the Turkmenistan region of Iran.

turn To change direction.

turnback *see* TURNBACK RIDER

turnback help *see* TURNBACK RIDER

turnback rider Also known as turnback help or turnback; a cutting term; a mounted rider in a cutting horse competition positioned between the performing cutter, time line, and judge(s), responsible for turning the cow being worked back toward the cutter; work in pairs; considered herd help (q.v.).

turn down A horseshoe (q.v.) used on race horses; the heels of the rear shoes are turned down ¾ to 1 inch (19-25 mm) to provide better traction; illegal in many jurisdictions.

turned Also known as turned to the horse; said of a mare whose last mating will not produce a foal.

turned out Said of a horse kept at pasture (q.v.).

turned to the horse *see* TURNED

turn for home A racing term; said of a race horse and his jockey when they round the last turn on the track before striding the home stretch (q.v.) for the wire (q.v.).

turn of foot (1) An American racing term; said of the manner in which a horse runs, a good race horse having a nice turn of foot. (2) A British racing term; said of the horse's ability to accelerate, e.g., "He's got good turn of foot."

turn on center Also known as turn on the center, pirouette on the center, or pirouette sur le centre; a dressage term; a turn (q.v.) in which the horse's forehand moves in one direction while his hindquarters move the other, so that literally he turns around his own center; only ridden out of the walk.

turn on the center *see* TURN ON CENTER

turn on the forehand Also known as pivot; a movement in which the horse pivots around his inside foreleg, cutting an outer concentric circle with the other legs; the pivot leg marks time in the rhythm of the movement; only ridden from the halt, or out of the walk following a brief halt.

turn on the haunches Also known as turn on the quarters, pirouette sur les haunches, or pivot; a movement in which the horse turns around his inner hind leg, which remains on the spot or describes a small circle, cutting a larger outer concentric circle with the other legs; corresponds to the half-pirouette (q.v.) at the canter; taught and executed at the walk.

turn on the quarters *see* TURN ON THE HAUNCHES

turnout (1) To release a horse in a paddock (q.v.) for exercise. (2) The general appearance of either a horse or rider.

turnout blanket Any blanket (q.v.) intended for horses in a pasture or paddock circumstance; are usually very water-resistant and constructed with a tough outer shell to resist tearing and snags; made be lined or unlined.

turnout rug Any protective body covering strapped to the horse to protect him when not stabled from cold, moisture, insects and the light; generally has a waterproof outer layer lined with wool or synthetic material; of sturdier construction than a stable blanket or sheet.

turnpike gate Also known as pike (sl); a location along a coaching route where toll fees were collected.

Turpin, Dick (1706–1739) A British highwayman and common thief, believed to have ridden Black Bess (q.v.) in his famous ride from London to York as recounted in Harrison Ainsworth's novel *Rookwood*.

Turn Row *see* TENNESSEE WALKING HORSE

Turn-Row Horse *see* TENNESSEE WALKING HORSE

turn tail A cutting term; a horse who quit a working cow; results in a 5-point penalty action in competition.

turtle back boot *see* TURTLE BOOT

turtle boot Also known as turtle back boot; the fore-boot (q.v.) located beneath the box seat of some horse-drawn coaches and carriages; detached from the main bodywork.

tushes *see* CANINE TEETH

TWHBEA *see* TENNESSEE WALKING HORSE BREEDERS' ASSOCIATION OF AMERICA

twin One of two young brought forth at birth usually resulting from the fertilization of two eggs; the young will not be identical.

twinning The conception of twins (q.v.).

twin trifecta A racing term; a betting option in which the bettor (q.v.) places a trifecta (q.v.) wager on one race; if that wager wins, the bettor is paid a winning price from the pool (q.v.) and is allowed to make a second trifecta bet, free, on a second race.

twist a horse To break (q.v.) a horse.

twisted bowel *see* TORSION COLIC

twisted gut *see* TORSION COLIC

twisted snaffle A variably sized snaffle bit (q.v.) with a twisted mouthpiece; the tightness of the twist may vary – the thinner the mouthpiece and the greater the number of twists, the more the severe the bit.

twitch A device used to distract the attention of, or restrain, a horse for a specific purpose such as clipping, covering, shoeing, minor operations, administering medication, etc.; of many varieties, the most common of which consists of a loop of rope or other material, fastened to a wooden, plastic, or metal handle, the loop being passed over the upper lip or the base of the ear of the horse, the latter being illegal in Britain; the handle is turned until the rope is sufficiently tight around the lip or ear so that the resulting pain distracts the horse sufficiently to restrain it; causes release of endorphins and concentrates the horse's attention on the discomfort.

two-day event A three-phase eventing (q.v.) competition consisting of dressage, show jumping, and speed and endurance phases, the later including steeplechase, roads and tracks, and cross-country conducted by the same rider and horse over a period of two days; dressage and show jumping phases are generally conducted on the first day while the speed and endurance phase occurs on the second.

two hole position Also known as win hole; a harness racing term; the position immediately behind the leading horse.

two sweats *see* BOTH SIDES OF THE ROAD

2000 Guineas A 1 mile (1.6 km) horse race for 3-year-old colts and fillies run annually since 1809 in Great Britain although eligible fillies more commonly compele in the 1000 Guineas, for which colts are not eligible.

two-time Any gait marked by two hoof beats per stride.

two-track Also known as pass, side step, two-track movement, or appuyer (Fr); any movement where the horse's hind legs travel on a track parallel to, but different than that of the forelegs; in dressage, such movements include shoulder-in (q.v.), shoulder-out (q.v.), half-pass (q.v.), full pass, renvers (q.v.), travers (q.v.), pirouettes (q.v.), and haunches-out (q.v.).

two-tracking Said of a horse performing any two-track (q.v.) movement.

two-track movement *see* TWO-TRACK

two/two A method of holding the reins of a double bridle (q.v.) in which two reins are held in each hand, the curb rein around the little finger and the snaffle between the ring finger and little finger.

two-wheeler (1) *see* HANSOM CAB. (2) Any two-wheeled, horse-drawn vehicle.

two-year old Also known by the acronym T-Y-O or two-year-old horse; a horse having reached the second, but not the third, anniversary of birth.

two-year-old horse *see* TWO-YEAR-OLD

tying up *see* TYING-UP SYNDROME

tying-up disease *see* TYING-UP SYNDROME

tying-up syndrome Also known as tying up, tying-up disease, cording-up, set fast, or incorrectly as equine myoglobinuria (q.v.); thought to be a mild form of azoturia (q.v.) and, therefore, to have similar causes and symptoms, although the metabolic changes responsible may be quite different; a condition affecting the horse's skeletal muscles following prolonged, exhaustive physical activity, appearing to occur primarily as a result of muscle energy depletion; the urine may be dark-colored varying from a red wine to a dark coffee color because of the myoglobin (q.v.) released by breakdown of affected muscle tissue; symptoms include profuse sweating, rapid pulse, a stiff, stilted gait, particularly of the hindquarters, muscle trembling, cramping, spasms of varying degrees, and a disinclination to move; survivors sometimes suffer from lameness and prolonged, or occasionally permanent, muscle atrophy; more common in mares than geldings.

tyger spot Refers to coat color pattern; a spotting variant common to donkeys (q.v.) in which the body is covered with small round color spots; the color pattern resembling that of a leopard Appaloosa (q.v.).

T-Y-O *see* TWO-YEAR-OLD

type (1) *see* BREED TYPE. (2) A horse who serves a particular purpose, but who does not belong to a specific breed, e.g. hunter, cart horse, cob, hack, etc.

U

U bolt Also known as clip; a 'U'-shaped metal fitting used to attach the spring to the axle of a horse-drawn vehicle; the inverted 'U' is secured over the spring and axle by nuts on the threaded end below the axle.

uberstreichen A dressage term; the brief release of rein contact, wherein the rider in one clear motion extends the hand(s) forward along the crest of the horse's neck, then rides for several strides without contact; performed in tests to demonstrate that, even with no rein contact, the horse maintains his carriage, balance, speed, and tempo.

Ukrainian Riding Horse A horse breed developed in the former Soviet Union in the late 1940s by crossing Trakehner (q.v.), Hanoverian (q.v.), and Thoroughbred (q.v.) stallions with local mares or Hungarian-bred Nonius (q.v.), Furioso (q.v.) and Gidran Arabian (q.v.) mares; breed selection continued using only Thoroughbred and Hanoverian stallions; stands approximately 15.1 to 16.1 hands, usually has a chestnut, bay, or black coat, has a long neck, slightly hollowed back, deep chest, and long croup; colts are broken at 18 months at which time they undergo aptitude testing consisting of flat racing, cross-country, show jumping and dressage elements, with top colts in each category going on to serve as breeding stock in state-owned studs; used for competition, light draft, and farm work.

ulcerative lymphangitis *see* EQUINE ULCERATIVE LYMPHANGITIS

ultrasound Also known as sonogram or ultrasonography; high-frequency sound waves, above the range of the human ear, produced by the conversion of high-frequency electrical energy waves to sound waves by a piezoelectric crystal in the head of a machine, are directed into tissue to break down unwanted tissues, promote healing by stimulating circulation (therapeutic ultrasound [q.v.]), and as a diagnostic aid (diagnostic ultrasound [q.v.]).

ultrasonography *see* ULTRASOUND

umbilical hernia Protrusion of the intestine through the incompletely closed umbilical opening shortly after birth; reasonably common in foals and is easily correctable; if the condition appears in horses older than 12 months of age, complications may result.

umbrella basket *see* STICK BASKET

umpire One of two mounted officials who enforces the rules of play in polo (q.v.), polocrosse (q.v.), or other mounted sports; in polo, one umpire is positioned on either end of the field during play; may consult with sideline referees to impose penalties.

unbacked A racing term; a horse competing in a horse race upon whom no bets have been placed.

unbalanced Said of the horse when his weight and/or that of the rider are not equally distributed over each foot/leg; the rider's seat, posture, and/or leg position may contribute.

uncertain fencer A horse who tentatively jumps a fence or who balks (q.v.), half refuses a jump, and then jumps from a standstill or slow trot.

uncouple (1) To detach a horse from the vehicle he is pulling. (2) To unbuckle the coupling reins used in team or pair harness.

under behind *see* STANDING UNDER BEHIND

undercarriage *see* CARRIAGE NO. 1

underlay A racing term; a horse running at odds shorter than seem warranted by his past performances.

under pad Also known as vaulting pad; a saddle pad (q.v.) positioned between the back pad and the vaulting roller (q.v.); is slightly wider than the roller and long enough to encircle the horse; used to distribute the weight of the roller and vaulter (q.v.) evenly on either side of the spine and prevents the formation of girth galls (q.v.).

underpinning The horse's legs and feet.

under reach A gait defect; said of the horse when the toe of the front horseshoe strikes the toe of the hind shoe at the trot.

underrun heels Also known as run-under heels or underslung heels; said of heels of the hoof when the angle is greater than that of the toe; largely due to poor trimming.

under saddle Said of a horse in tack including the saddle, bridle, martingale, etc.

undershot Said of the horse's jaw when the lower jaw protrudes beyond the upper.

undershot jaw Also known as bulldog bite, hog mouth, sow mouth, or prognathism; a congenital malformation of horse's mouth in which the lower jaw protrudes beyond the upper; as a result, the incisors do not meet properly, are therefore not worn down by use, and impair the horse's ability to graze or eat; frequent floating (q.v.) of the incisors is necessary to prevent the intruding teeth from lacerating the soft mouth tissues.

underslung heels *see* UNDERRUN HEELS

under starter's orders A racing term; said of the jockeys and their mounts when ready to race.

under the neck shot *see* NECK SHOT

under weight *see* ADDED WEIGHT

under wraps (1) A racing term; said of a horse whose ability has been kept quiet or concealed by legitimate means. (2) A racing term; said of a horse running under restraint to prevent him from pulling away from the competition by too wide a margin.

unentered A hunting term; a hound who has not completed his first cub hunting (q.v.) season.

uneven A dressage term; said of a horse moving with unequal length of steps.

unharness To remove harness (q.v.) from a horse.

unhitch To separate a horse from the vehicle to which he is attached.

unhooked A cutting term; said of a cutting horse who loses the attention of the cow being worked.

unhorsed *see* UNSEATED

unhulled peanut meal A type of peanut meal (q.v.); the peanut shells are left on the nuts during processing; contains about 60 percent less protein and energy than hulled peanut meal (q.v.).

unicorn Also known as spike team or spike and incorrectly as a pick-axe team (q.v.); a hitch of three horses consisting of two wheelers (q.v.) and one leader; developed to spare a tired horse or to hitch a fresh horse to the front of a tired pair for additional pulling power; commonly used by breweries and other trade operations.

unilateral Pertaining to or affecting only one side.

unilateral cryptorchid Any horse with improper descent of one testicle; a rig (q.v.).

united Said of the action of the horse, generally the canter, when properly coordinated and executed.

United States Combined Training Association Also known by the acronym USCTA; an American organization founded in 1959 to educate horse owners and riders in those principles and practices of horsemanship embodied in the term combined training (q.v.), and founded on the essential relationship between classical dressage and cross-country riding; sponsors and/or facilitates organization of horse trials (q.v.), combined tests (q.v.), two-day events (q.v.), and three-day events (q.v.).

United States Equestrian Team Also known by the acronym USET; an American organization founded to support teams representing the United States in international show jumping, eventing, dressage, and driving competitions.

United States Polo Association Also known by the acronym USPA and previously as The Polo Association; an

American organization founded in 1890 to coordinate polo matches, standardize rules, and establish handicaps for the game in the United States; at the time of its founding, seven clubs were accepted into the association.

United States Team Penning Association Also known by the acronym USTPA; one of three organizations in the United States devoted to the sport of team penning (q.v.); publishes *Team Penning USA*.

unkennel Also known as find; a hunting term; to dislodge a fox from his covert and to get it moving.

unlevel A dressage term; said of a horse who places more weight on one fore foot than the other, one leg comes further forward than the other, and/or he lifts one hock higher than the other; causes the horse to look slightly lame; may be due to the horse being bridle lame (q.v.), having uneven physical development, or unbalanced lateral training.

unmade Said of an unschooled young horse.

Unmol A rare pony breed indigenous to Northern Punjab, India; is strong, elegant, and shapely, having a compact body and long mane.

unnerve *see* NERVE NO. 2

un pas un saut A movement performed in three stages: a short gallop, courbette (q.v.), and a capriole (q.v.).

unpatterned leopard Refers to coat color pattern; a distinct type of leopard spotting in which the coat spots tend to be rounder and do not appear to flow from the flank as on a patterned leopard (q.v.).

unraced A racing term; a horse who has not yet competed in his first race.

unregistered Said of a horse who is not accepted as a specific breed type or who has not been accepted by a specific performance horse organization as qualified to compete in events controlled or sanctioned by that organization.

unsaddle (1) To remove the saddle from a horse. (2) To be unseated (q.v.) from the saddle, as in the rider.

unsaddled *see* UNSEATED

unseated Also known as unsaddled or unhorsed; said of a rider who has been, for any reason, dislodged from the saddle, but not necessarily from the horse.

unsettled *see* FRESH CATTLE

unshod *see* BAREFOOT

unskid A coaching term; to remove the skid (q.v.) from the wheel of a horse-drawn vehicle.

unsound Said of a horse not free of illness, disease, physical or conformation defect, injury, or blemish that affects future performance or ability to work.

unsound in the wind Also known as unsound of wind; said of a horse who is not free from breathing impairment as indicated by whistling (q.v.), roaring (q.v.), broken wind (q.v.), etc.

unsoundness Any condition affecting the horse's ability to perform; may result from injury, accident, disease, conformation defect, unnatural stress caused by use for which he is not trained, poor feed, etc.

unsound of wind *see* UNSOUND IN THE WIND

unsprung Without springs, as in a horse-drawn vehicle.

unsteady halt Said of a horse who comes to a halt, but does not remain motionless; the horse may fidget, shift his legs or head, or move off the line.

unsteady head Said of a horse lacking steadiness of the head and/or head carriage; may result from loss of balance of either the horse or rider or failure of the horse to accept the bit (q.v.).

untried (1) A racing term; a horse not previously raced or tested for speed. (2) A stallion not been previously used for breeding.

unwind (1) A racing term; to gradually withdraw a horse from intense training. (2)

Said of a horse who starts to buck. (3) To make relaxed or less tense.

uphill (1) Also known as built uphill; said of the horse's longitudinal balance when higher in the forehand than the croup (q.v.). (2) Said of the feeling of riding a horse who has some degree of relative elevation of the forehand as a consequence of engaged hindquarters.

upper aids Both hands of the rider when employed to communicate gait, speed, and direction to the horse by acting on, resisting, or yielding on the bit through the reins.

upper bar *see* TOP BAR

upper Benjamin *see* BENJAMIN

upper-cheek snaffle A half-cheek snaffle bit (q.v.); consists of a straight or jointed mouthpiece fitted at either end with fixed rings to which straight- or spoon-shaped (wider and slightly curved toward the horse's jaw at the top) arms are attached above the mouthpiece; the arms prevent the bit from running through the horse's mouth if he runs sideways or refuses to turn; the straight-arm upper-cheek snaffle bit acts on the sides of the mouth, the lips, and the corners of the mouth, while the spoon-cheek provides a small amount of leverage and places more pressure on the jaw; is accepted in the dressage arena.

upper ground Also known as high ground; a 19th-century coaching term; the first part of the road encountered on a coach journey.

upright (1) *see* STANDARD. (2) *see* VERTICAL

upright mane Said of the horse's mane when it falls to both sides of the neck; common in northern pony breeds and cold bloods (q.v.).

upright shoulder *see* STRAIGHT SHOULDER

upset price *see* REVERSE

up to their bit(s) A coaching term; said of the horse(s) pulling a horse-drawn vehicle and moving freely forward.

up-wind In the direction from which the wind is blowing.

urea A colorless, soluble basic nitrogenous compound $CO(NH_2)_2$, the chief solid component of urine and an end product of protein composition produced in the liver; synthesized from carbon and ammonia and is used in animal rations and fertilizer.

urethra A tubular canal through which urine is discharged from the bladder; in males also serves as the sperm duct.

urinate Also known as piss, pee, void, or stale; to eliminate urine from the body by means of the urethra (q.v.).

urine Also known as pee (sl) or piss (sl); the liquid, deep yellow to brown colored kidney secretion, conducted to the bladder by the ureters, and discharged through the urethra (q.v.); a full-grown horse will average 5.5 quarts (6.2 liters) of urine per day.

urine test Chemical analysis of a horse's urine to detect whether illegal substances were administered to alter performance or mask injury.

Urocyon cineroargenteus *see* GRAY FOX

urticaria *see* HIVES

used up Said of an exhausted horse.

USCTA *see* UNITED STATES COMBINED TRAINING ASSOCIATION

USET *see* UNITED STATES EQUESTRIAN TEAM

USPA *see* UNITED STATES POLO ASSOCIATION

USTPA *see* UNITED STATES TEAM PENNING ASSOCIATION

uterine Pertaining to the uterus (q.v.).

uterine body That portion of the uterus (q.v.) which lies between the uterine horns (q.v.) and the cervix.

uterine horn That portion of the uterus (q.v.) which lies between the oviducts (q.v.) and the uterine body (q.v.).

uterine prolapse Inversion of the uterus (q.v.) resulting in partial or complete expulsion from the vulva.

uterus The hollow, muscular organ in the female of a mammal consisting of the cervix, uterine body (q.v.), and uterine horns (q.v.), serving as a protective place for the ovum (q.v.) while it develops into an embryo (q.v.) or fetus.

Utility Cart A two-wheeled, horse-drawn, skeleton cart used for breaking young horses; usually low-slung with the seat positioned near road level; is difficult to overturn.

utility saddle *see* ALL-PURPOSE SADDLE

Uxeter kimblewick One of five types of kimblewick (q.v.) bit; a pelham (q.v.) bit requiring one instead of two reins (q.v.), having a straight, low-ported mouthpiece (q.v.), and short cheeks (q.v.) with flat, double-slotted D rings running the full length, and a square eye on the upper cheek end; the reins may be attached at the mouthpiece or lower down on the cheeks; when the rider's hands are held in a standard position, the bit acts as a snaffle (q.v.), but when the hands are lowered, or when used in conjunction with a martingale (q.v.), the resulting action is similar to that of a curb (q.v.).

V

V *see* V, THE

vaccine A preparation of matter from attenuated organisms administered to produce or artificially increase immunity to a particular disease.

valance A coaching term; a deep strip of patent leather (q.v.) buttoned to the front of the rumble seat of a Drag (q.v.) to prevent drafts when passengers are carried instead of grooms; may also be made of heavy cloth or leather.

valet A racing term; one responsible for a jockey's clothing and tack, and, in some countries, to carry the saddle and equipment to the paddock (q.v.), help the trainer saddle the horse, and meet the rider after the race to carry the saddle and equipment back to the jockeys' room (q.v.).

valeting room A hunting term; a room used by the hunt staff (q.v.) for cleaning and drying hunting clothes and boots following a hunt.

van To transport a horse in a van.

Van A high-sided, two- or four-wheeled, generally headed, horse-drawn vehicle used by trade and businessmen to collect and deliver goods; drawn by a single horse in shafts or, less frequently, by a pair in pole gear (q.v.); frequently pulled by a vanner (q.v.).

vanity brand *see* BRAND NO. 1

vanner Also known as parcel carter or trotting vanner; any horse used to pull a tradesman's van (q.v.); generally a cross between a light horse such as a Thoroughbred (q.v.) and a draft horse.

vaquero *see* BUCKAROO

varmint Hunting slang; a fox.

varnish marks Refers to coat color pattern; a concentration of dark hairs occurring on bony prominences; common to the Appaloosa (q.v.), specifically the roan Appaloosa.

varnish roan Also known as marble; one of six symmetrical Appaloosa (q.v.) coat color patterns recognized by the Appaloosa Horse Club (q.v.); a pattern of white that may vary from a roan (red or blue) blanket to white hairs scattered over the horse's entire body including the head, with colored hairs concentrated over the bony prominences; a progressive pattern (q.v.), with horses generally born sorrel.

vasculogenic shock: Circulatory collapse characterized by a progressively diminishing circulating blood volume relative to the capacity of the vascular system, leading to acute failure of vital organs; blood volume is normal, but blood is pooled in dilated peripheral vessels; may be caused by endotoxins or trauma.

vaulter One who vaults (q.v.).

vaulting Also known as voltige (Fr); an ancient competitive equine sport dating to AD 1500 in southern Scandinavia; gymnastics performed by vaulters (q.v.) on the back of a horse; the horse circles on the left rein at a trot or canter on the end of a 25 to 30 foot (7.6–9 m) lunge line (q.v.); the vaulting circle measures no less than 43.2 feet (13 m); vaulters may compete as individuals, pairs, or as a team; the upper age limit for team members is 18 while there is no age limit for individuals; first included as an Olympic sport at the 1920 Games where individual teams were formed from cavalry regiments; was brought to the United States in the 1960s, and was recognized by the FEI (q.v.) as an international equestrian sport in 1985.

vaulting barrel Also known as barrel or metal horse; 55-gallon (250 liter) drums welded together to which 4 legs and handles are welded; stands 4 feet (1.2 m) high and is covered with padding; used by vaulters (q.v.) to develop a sense of balance and to learn or practice movements; spares the horse from overuse and wear and tear.

vaulting pad *see* UNDER PAD

vaulting roller Also known as vaulting

surcingle; a wide leather band fitted around the horse's girth behind the shoulder; buckled on both sides; has two leather padded handles built onto rigid steel plates on either side of the withers and two, optional, Cossack hang straps (stirrups); the position of the handles may vary both in size and angle to the roller.

vaulting surcingle *see* VAULTING ROLLER

vault on A compulsory vaulting (q.v.) exercise; from a position facing the horse's haunches the vaulter places his left hand on the vaulting roller (q.v.), swings his right leg high above the horse, rotates his hips to a position parallel to the horse's back at a height above the level of the horse's head, and lowers himself onto the back of the horse behind the vaulting roller (q.v.) facing forward.

vealers Any English riding boot made with veal hide, the leather of which is extremely fine and soft.

VEE *see* VENEZUELAN EQUINE ENCEPHALOMYELITIS

vehicle *see* HORSE-DRAWN VEHICLE

vehicle skid *see* DRAG SHOE

venery The act or practice of hunting using hounds; became common to the English language in the early 14th century; an important aspect of social life for the European feudal elite; derived from the Latin *venari*, meaning to hunt.

Venezuelan equine encephalomyelitis Also known by the acronym VEE; one of three alphaviruses associated with equine encephalitis (q.v.); occurs in cycles in the Florida Everglades, the western United States, Mexico, Panama, Central and South America, and some Caribbean islands; transmitted to horses by biting insects, principally mosquitoes and swallow bugs; clinical signs occur about 5 days after infection and most deaths occur 2 to 3 days later; signs include fever, impaired vision, irregular gait, wandering, reduced reflexes, circling, incoordination, yawning, teeth grinding, drowsiness, pendulous lower lip, inability to swallow, photophobia, head-pressing, inability to rise, paralysis, occasional convulsions, and death; those with mild cases recover within a few weeks, but may suffer from residual brain damage; mortality is 50 to 75 percent; a vaccine is available; outbreaks have occurred naturally in north and south America since the early 20th century.

venous bleeding Loss of blood from veins varying from minimal to profuse, depending on the size of the blood vessels involved; the blood is less red than from an artery.

ventral Toward the belly.

ventral hernia Protrusion of the intestine through the weakened abdominal wall; may be caused by kicks from other horses, falls, (in mares) the weight of having carried many foals, etc.

ventricle stripping *see* LARYNGEAL VENTRICULOTOMY

venule Any of the small vessels that collect blood from the capillaries to join and form veins.

verminous arteritis *see* EQUINE VERMINOUS ARTERITIS

verminous aneurysm Thickening of the horse's veins or arteries caused by irritation of some types of immature strongyles (q.v.) that migrate within the intestinal and arterial walls; thickening is permanent and may reduce blood flow; most commonly affects the blood supply to the intestines, and may result in colic (q.v.) and thrombosis (q.v.).

vertebra Any of the bones or segments composing the spinal column; typically of a more or less cylindrical body and an arch with various processes, forming a foramen through which the spinal column passes.

vertebrae More than one vertebra (q.v.).

vertebral Of or pertaining to the vertebra (q.v.).

vertebral column Also known as spine, backbone, or spinal column; the series of small bones or vertebrae (q.v.) forming the axis of the skeleton and protecting the spinal cord.

vertical (1) Also known as upright or vertical jump; a jumping term; any show or cross-country jumping obstacle consisting of a fence built vertical to the ground, with all parts placed one above the other, that is, it has no spread; verticals include, but are not limited to, gates, planks, stiles, straight post and rails; requires the horse to make a steep arc in his effort to jump. (2) Said of the horse's head when perpendicular to the plane of the horizon; upright; a horse's head may be in front of the vertical (q.v.) or behind the vertical (q.v.).

vertical jump *see* VERTICAL NO. 1

vesicant *see* BLISTER NO. 2

vesicle A small, circumscribed elevation of the epidermis containing serous fluid; a blister (q.v.).

vesicular Formed like a vesicle (q.v.).

vesicular exanthema A viral disease of pigs and rarely horses; eradicated from the United States in 1959 and has never been recorded elsewhere; the virus is thought to have been a `land variant' of the San Miguel sea-lion virus, isolated from sea-lions off of the California coast.

vesicular stomatitis A contagious viral disease caused by a rhabdovirus (q.v.) resulting in inflammation, usually blisters, of the mouth, tongue, teats, coronary band (q.v.), and occasionally, other body parts, weight loss, and mild lameness; occurs epidemically in temperate and warmer regions mainly of the Western Hemisphere, especially in the Caribbean, between late spring and early fall; thought to be spread by insect vectors and the movement of animals; the route of infection is unknown, but may be through the skin or respiratory system; affected horses may stop drinking and develop mild lameness; in severe cases may lead to laminitis (q.v.); has an incubation period of 2 to 8 days with complete recovery usually within about two weeks; broken blisters leave painful ulcers that cause the horse to drool or froth at the mouth; similar to foot-and-mouth disease; also affects cattle and pigs and, occasionally, sheep; may be transmitted to man, causing flu-like symptoms such as fever, muscle aches, headache, and malaise.

vestige A degenerate or incompletely developed organ or structure having little or no utility, but which in ancestral forms performed a useful function.

vestigial Said of an organ or structure having little or no utility, but which in ancestral forms performed a useful function, e.g., vestigial toe.

Vestlandhest *see* FJORD

vet *see* VETERINARIAN

vetch Any of the various, usually climbing, leguminous plants of the genus *Vicia*, allied to the bean, some of which are cultivated for fodder for cattle and, rarely, horses.

vet check *see* VETERINARY INSPECTION

vet clean Said of a horse who, when inspected by a veterinarian, is found to be sound (q.v.) and free from contagious disease, structural degeneration, injury or other disorder or condition.

veterinarian Also known as horse doctor, vet, veterinary surgeon, or veterinary medical doctor; one who practices prevention, diagnosis, medical and surgical treatment of animal ailments, and the general study of animals; a practitioner of veterinary medicine (q.v.).

veterinarianitis Excessive use of a hoof knife (q.v.) by a veterinarian; (sl).

veterinary Of or pertaining to the medical or surgical treatment of animals.

veterinary certificate Also known as soundness certificate; a certificate of soundness which documents the veterinarian's evaluation of a horse's physical condition and ability to perform.

veterinary examination *see* VETERINARY INSPECTION

veterinary inspection Also known as vet check, soundness examination, or veterinary examination; to evaluate the physical condition and/or soundness of a horse, identifying illness, disease, physical or conformational defect, injury, or blemish that may affect the horse's present or future performance or ability to work; generally performed on a horse offered for sale or trade and compulsory in endurance riding and eventing.

veterinary medical doctor Also known by the acronym VMD; a veterinarian (q.v.).

veterinary medicine The branch or division of medical science concerned with the prevention, diagnosis, treatment, and general study of animal diseases.

veterinary surgeon *see* VETERINARIAN

vet's list An American racing term; a list of ill or injured horses declared ineligible to run by the track veterinarian.

Vettura A usually four-wheeled, horse-drawn, Italian cab or hired carriage; headed and drawn by a single horse in shafts.

Viatka A pony breed indigenous to the former Soviet Union where it is bred primarily in the Viatka and Obva river basins; descended from the Klepper (q.v.) and Konik (q.v.); stands 13 to 14 hands, may have a bay, gray, roan, mouse dun, palomino, or dun coat (ponies with dun and palomino coats will also have an eel stripe [q.v.]), zebra markings (q.v.) on the legs, and a full, black mane, forelock and tail; has pronounced jaws, flared nostrils, a rather snub profile, a muscular, long neck, long back, wide and deep chest, and solid legs; is sturdy, lively, energetic and quiet; the action of the trot is more vertical than forward and is particularly well suited to travel on snow-covered terrain; a good all-around pony used to draw Troikas (q.v.) and perform light farm work; is an easy keeper; breeding is government controlled.

vice Any specific unpleasant or atypical habit, practice, and/or condition a horse develops and exhibits, as from boredom, mimicry, or improper handling; includes biting (q.v.), balking (q.v.), bolting (q.v.), bucking (q.v.), cribbing (q.v.), halter pulling (q.v.), kicking (q.v.), striking (q.v.), weaving (q.v.), rearing (q.v.), savaging (q.v.), and napping (q.v.).

Viceroy A horse-drawn vehicle; a very lightweight, cut-under, elegant, four-wheeled, air-tired, single-horse vehicle of the Spider Phaeton (q.v.) type designed and built by Mills & Sons; used for some heavy harness classes, and especially for showing Hackney (q.v.), Shetlands (q.v.), and harness show ponies.

Victoria A low, semi-open, horse-drawn carriage with a rearward half-hood, seating two forward-facing passengers side-by-side; hung on four elliptical side springs, but often having double suspension with rearward cee springs; the English version of a Victorian pleasure carriage; popular in the late 19th century and named for Queen Victoria in 1869; frequently used for semi-formal or park driving; driven from a box seat (q.v.) to a single horse in shafts or, less often, to a pair in pole gear (q.v.).

Victoria Gig A horse-drawn, cab-fronted Gig (q.v.); had a hooded body hung low between the wheels on two side springs and one transverse spring; easily entered from a low step.

Victoria Hansom A horse-drawn vehicle of the Hansom Cab (q.v.) type built with a folding hood instead of a solid roof.

Victoria Phaeton A light, elegant, open, horse-drawn vehicle of the Phaeton (q.v.) type adapted for park driving; hung on elliptic springs and had 33 inch (84 cm) diameter rear wheels, and frequently had a rumble seat and a falling hood; drawn by a team of postillion-driven ponies; built in 1828 for Princess Victoria.

Victoria top *see* CLOSED TOP

video endoscope A diagnostic instrument consisting of a flexible tube containing light-conducting fiber bundles which reflect an image into an eyepiece, and a small camera at the tip of the instrument, inserted through a body passage; enables a veterinarian (q.v.) to view and film the interior of a body cavity.

view A hunting term; to see a fox.

viewed A hunting term; said of a fox when seen.

viewed away A hunting term; said of a fox seen leaving a covert (q.v.).

view halloa *see* VIEW HALLOO

view halloo Also known as halloo and spelled view halloa; a hunting term; an utterance by the huntsman (q.v.) when the fox is viewed.

Village Phaeton A four-wheeled, horse-drawn carriage built to carry six passengers: four passengers sat back-to-back on seating placed over the back axle between two elliptic springs, while another seat for two passengers was located just aft of the forecarriage; a high rein rail surmounted the back of the two-passenger seat to carry the reins above the passenger's heads; the vehicle rear resembled that of a Dogcart (q.v.).

viral abortion Expulsion of the fetus before fully developed as due to viral infection.

viral arteritis *see* EQUINE ARTERITIS

vis-à-vis Face-to-face; said of seating arrangements in some horse-drawn vehicles in which the occupants sat facing each other on opposite seats.

Vis-à-Vis *see* SOCIABLE BAROUCHE

visiting fox A hunting term; a dog fox who has left his home territory in search of a vixen (q.v.).

vital force The dynamic energy of an organism which is stimulated by the homeopathic remedy (q.v.).

vitamin One of several organic compounds occurring in minute amounts in natural foods and necessary for proper metabolism; of two groups: fat-soluble vitamins (q.v.) consisting of vitamin A (q.v.), vitamin D (q.v.), vitamin E (q.v.), and vitamin K (q.v.) and water-soluble vitamins (q.v.) consisting of thiamin (q.v.), riboflavin (q.v.), niacin (q.v.), pyridoxine (B_6), pantothenic acid (q.v.), biotin (q.v.), folic acid (q.v.), vitamin B_{12} (q.v.), and vitamin C (q.v.).

vitamin A A fat-soluble, aliphatic alcohol, $C_{20}H_{29}OH$ required for healthy skin, hair, and hooves, proper eye function, reproduction and lactation; derived from carotene in carrots and other vegetable matter such as good quality hay; the horse's exact daily requirement is undetermined, although it has been approximated at 12,500 IU per day for the mature horse weighing about 1,000 pounds (454 kg); supplementation is necessary for pregnant mares and horses in heavy training or under stress; deficiency can cause infertility, fragile bones, night blindness (q.v.), loss of appetite, reduced resistance to infection, respiratory illnesses, elevated spinal fluid pressure, convulsions, rough coat, poor hoof growth, scaly hooves, etc; overdose is uncommon, but may cause bone fragility; as much as a six-month's supply may be stored in the liver; first identified in 1913.

vitamin B_1 *see* THIAMIN

vitamin B_2 *see* RIBOFLAVIN

vitamin B_6 *see* PYRIDOXINE

vitamin B_{12} Also known as cobalamin; a complex, cobalt-containing compound essential to normal blood formation, neural function, and growth; sufficient levels are produced in the cecum and large intestine to meet daily requirements; is not stored in the cells and all excess is excreted in the urine; deficiency can cause anemia, weight loss, reduced performance, and poor coat hair.

vitamin B complex Ten water-soluble vitamins consisting of thiamin (q.v.), niacin (q.v.), riboflavin (q.v.), pyridoxine (q.v.), folacin (q.v.), biotin (q.v.), choline (q.v.), inositol (q.v.), pantothenic acid (q.v.), and vitamin B_{12} (q.v.) which were previously thought to be members of the same group; are present as co-enzymes in virtually all the horse's metabolic processes necessary for utilization of proteins, carbohydrates, and fats; although daily dietary requirements have not been established, it appears sufficient amounts are synthesized in the intestines to prevent deficiency; supplementation is not harmful, and may be helpful in horses with poor appetites, slow growth patterns, in competition, or late gestation; temporary deficiency is known as track sour (q.v.); are sensitive to heat and strong light.

vitamin C Also known as ascorbic acid; a water-soluble vitamin (q.v.) found in plants and especially in fruits and leafy vegetables or made synthetically; necessary for production of certain essential amino acids and building of intracellular material;

synthesized from glucose in the horse's liver and in other tissues in sufficient amounts to meet the dietary requirements; supplementation is thought to improve reproductive performance in both mares and stallions, to decrease the incidence of epistaxis (q.v.) and respiratory diseases, and to calm stressed horses; excess is destroyed in the digestive tract.

vitamin D A fat-soluble vitamin (q.v.) necessary for formation of calcium-binding protein, which aids in the absorption, transportation, and metabolism of calcium and phosphorus; the exact daily dietary requirement of the mature horse is undetermined although requirements will generally be met by grazing or exercising the horse regularly in sunlight and feeding sun-cured hay; hay alone may not supply sufficient levels for horses exposure to limited sunlight; excess is stored in the liver; toxicity due to excess may occur and is characterized by weakness, loss of body weight, calcification of the blood vessels, heart, lungs, and other soft tissues, and bone abnormalities such as enlargement of the head and jaw; deficiency can result in poorly mineralized bones (rickets), swollen joints, stiffness of gait, and reduced serum calcium and phosphorus levels.

vitamin E Also known as tocopherol; the tocopherols collectively; a fat-soluble vitamin (q.v.) associated with muscle development, oxygen transportation in the bloodstream, proper development of red blood cells, and fertility; also works in conjunction with selenium (q.v.) to prevent nutritional muscular dystrophy; if the levels are sufficient, then vitamin A is used more efficiently and less of the latter is required; deficiency can cause white muscle disease (q.v.), anemia, infertility, muscular dystrophy in foals, and may be a factor in azoturia (q.v.); supplementation is shown to improve breeding performance and speed and stamina in performance horses, particularly race horses; is quickly oxidized by air and is therefore lost from feeds during storage.

vitamin H *see* BIOTIN

vitamin K A mostly fat-soluble vitamin (q.v.) which promotes blood clotting and is required for formation of prothrombin in the liver; synthesized by the micro-organisms of the cecum and colon in sufficient quantities to meet the minimum daily dietary requirement of the mature horse; occurs in alfalfa (q.v.); deficiency is rare in horses, but may cause internal hemorrhage.

vitiligo A disease-related skin disorder characterized by loss of hair or skin pigmentation; results in white skin patches and, in some cases, if hair growth returns, white hair.

vixen Also known as bitch fox; a female fox.

Vizir One of Napoleon's grey Arab (q.v.) stallions.

Vladimir Heavy Draft A heavy draft breed developed in the second half of the 19th century in the former state of Vladimir, Soviet Union from which the name derived; descended from crossings of heavy draft breeds including the Ardennais (q.v.), Suffolk Punch (q.v.), Cleveland Bay (q.v.), Clydesdale (q.v.) and Shire (q.v.); in the 1930s a policy of no interbreeding was invoked and introduction of all non-breed blood was eliminated; registered as a breed in 1946 under its present name; breed stock selection is strictly controlled by means of rigorous practical trials; stands 15.1 to 16.1 hands and may have a chestnut, bay, brown, or black coat; white markings are common; has an average head, but heavy jaw line, arched neck, high and long withers, short back, deep chest, and short, powerful, well-feathered legs; is energetic, vigorous and willing; used for heavy draft and farm work.

VMD *see* VETERINARY MEDICAL DOCTOR

vocal folds Membranes in the larynx (q.v.) attached to the arytenoid cartilages (q.v.) which, when vibrated, produce vocalization.

voice *see* CRY NO. 2

voice box *see* LARYNX

void (1) Also known as a void bet; a racing term; any bet declared off (q.v.) and all monies returned to the bettors (q.v.). (2) *see* URINATE

void bet *see* VOID NO. 2

Volante *see* CUBAN CARRIAGE

volar *see* PALMAR

volte A small circle, a High School (q.v.) movement in which the horse scribes a circle, the norm being 6 meters, on one or two tracks (q.v.) with bend from poll to dock; when performed correctly, the horse circumscribes the circle without leaning in; of several varieties including half-volte (q.v.), renvers-volte (q.v.), half-volte and change (q.v.), double volte (q.v.), and square volte (q.v.); from the French word for turn.

voltige *see* VAULTING

voluntary muscle Any nonstriated muscle, such as those controlled by will, which operate in such voluntary movements as kicking and walking; attached to the bones by tendons and contract on stimulation to produce bodily motion.

voluntary withdrawal Said of a rider who makes a unilateral decision not to continue participation in a competitive event and to leave the competition area; will usually nod the head or tip the hat in the direction of the judge(s) to indicate withdrawal; may be due to a problem with the horse, failure to remember or negotiate the course, accumulation of too many faults, injury, etc.

volvulus Intestinal blockage caused by a segment of the bowel twisting on its mesenteric axis.

vomit To eject the contents of the stomach through the mouth; almost impossible for a horse.

von Achenbach, Benno (1861–1936) A German horseman who improved the English style of driving; he made small alterations to harness and carriages and devised an different method of holding the reins, which systematically increased the number of reins a driver could hold; his system of holding the reins gives the driver more control over the single horse, the tandem (q.v.), or the four-in-hand (q.v.) when they perform dressage movements.

von Osten, William A Russian psychologist who developed a theory of equine intelligence in 1900 using a group of stallions known collectively as the Elberfeld Horses (q.v.); he purported to have trained one of the horses, a Russian stallion named Hans Klug (q.v.), to calculate by pawing the ground with his hoof, to read, and differentiate colors, up to the general standard of knowledge of a 14-year-old child; von Osten's studies gained enormous publicity, but in 1904, the German psychologist Oskar Pfungst demonstrated that the stallion answered to unconscious signs from von Osten.

V, the Also known as V; a roping term; the V shape created by bringing and holding together the calf's fore and hind legs in the middle of his body in preparation for the tie (q.v.).

vulpecide To kill foxes (q.v.) as by some means other than using hounds (q.v.).

Vulpes vulpes *see* RED FOX

W

wager *see* BET

waggon *see* WAGON NO. 1

waggoner *see* WAGONER

Waggonette *see* WAGONETTE

Wagon (1) Also known as wain (early English) and spelled waggon (Brit); a four-wheeled, medium-heavy, horse-drawn vehicle originally designed without brakes, suspension, or driving seat; had semi-open or ladder sides and a pivoting fore-carriage connected to the hind-carriage by a reach pole or underperch; later types had box-shaped bodies, hand brakes, and sprung driving seats; derived from the German or Dutch *wagen*, meaning wheeled vehicle. (2) Any lightly built, four-wheeled show vehicle.

wagoner Also spelled waggoner; one who drives a wagon.

Wagonette Also spelled Waggonette; a four-wheeled passenger vehicle drawn by a single horse in shafts or a pair in pole gear (q.v.) first constructed in the 1840s; usually open, entered through the rear via a small door and step iron, fitted with three interior, inward-facing seats, a lever brake which acted on both rear wheels, and a fairly low driving seat; widely used throughout Britain and North America throughout the second half of the 19th century; hung on sideways-elliptic springs in the front and sideways semi-elliptic springs in the rear.

Wagonette Break A large Wagonette (q.v.), having a high box seat and, commonly, a canopy top on fixed standards; seated eight passengers and was drawn by a pair of horses in pole gear (q.v.).

Wagonette Omnibus A Wagonette (q.v.) with a raised coach- or carriage-type driving seat elevated well above the passenger level, generally drawn by a four-in-hand team (q.v.).

Wagonette Phaeton A small, light Wagonette (q.v.) having a double driving seat.

Wagonette Trap A four-wheeled American Phaeton (q.v.) drawn by a single horse in shafts and having a shifting rear seat.

wagon-lock *see* DRAG SHOE

wagon train A group or train of wagons (q.v.) traveling together for a common purpose as for transporting people and supplies.

WAHDS *see* WESTERN AUSTRALIAN HARNESS DRIVING SOCIETY

Wah Lau *see* LEGEND OF THE EIGHT HORSES

wain (1) *see* WAGON NO. 1. (2) Any two-wheeled, horse-drawn farm vehicle or float used in harvesting; frequently spindle-sided and drawn by a single horse in shafts.

wainwright A wagon maker

waist That narrowest point of the seat of a saddle.

wait on your horse A cutting term; said of a rider who waits for his horse to react to a cow.

Waler Also known as Australian Waler; a horse type rather than breed; predominantly Thoroughbred with some Arab (q.v.) and pony blood; the foundation stock for the Australian Stock Horse (q.v.); the name derived from its place of origin in New South Wales, when in the early days of settlement waler was a name given to all newly settled areas of Australia.

walk (1) Also known as ordinary walk, working walk or slow gait; a natural, flat-footed, four-beat gait, executed in four-time in which each foot strikes the ground independently in a regular rhythm, the footfall sequence, with a left lead, will be: near fore, off hind, off fore, and near hind; there is no moment of suspension; the sequence of steps remains unchanged in the ordinary walk, extended walk (q.v.), and collected walk (q.v.); the average speed of a medium walk is approximately 4 mph (6.4 kph). (2) Also known as puppy walking (Brit), at walk or out to walk; a hunting term; the time when hound puppies between the ages of two and seven months of age are sent, usually in couples, to boarding facilities and farms to learn their names and to be trained and socialized.

walkabout disease *see* KIMBERLEY HORSE DISEASE

Walker *see* TENNESSEE WALKING HORSE

Walking Horse *see* TENNESSEE WALKING HORSE

Walking Horse bit A curb bit (q.v.) having shanks, usually S-shaped, approximately 7 to 9 inches (18–23 cm) long.

Walking Horse class Any of a number of competitions held for the Tennessee Walking Horse (q.v.) in the United States.

walking out A hunting term; said of hounds (q.v.) when exercised by a huntsman on foot.

walk on To set the horse into motion at walk by means of aids (q.v.).

walk on a free rein Also known as walk on a loose rein; said of the horse when allowed complete freedom to lower and stretch out his head and neck to walk freely with the reins completely loose and unrestricted by the rider's hands.

walk on a long rein Said of the horse when allowed to walk with the reins long enough to allow a considerable stretching of the head and neck, but still with a light contact retained.

walk on a loose rein *see* WALK ON A FREE REIN

walkover A racing term; a race in which all horses but one have scratched (q.v.); the one remaining horse wins the race and collects the purse by walking or galloping, rather than running, past the winning post; a rare occurrence.

walk ring *see* PADDOCK NO. 2

walk the course To walk on foot the show jumping or cross-country course as set by the course designer, to evaluate the footing and obstacles, determine distance between the jumps, and plan the track between them prior to riding in the competition; neither the rider nor horse may practice on a course prior to competition.

walk-up start A racing term; start of a horse race conducted without a starting gate (q.v.); the horses walk toward the starting line and begin running at the starter's command.

wall (1) An upright show jumping obstacle made of hollow wooden blocks painted and stacked to look like bricks or stone. (2) A cross-country obstacle constructed of brick or stone. (3) *see* HOOF WALL

wall eye Also know as glass eye, smoky eye, watch eye, china eye, blue eye, fish eye, or crockery eye; the eye of the horse lacking iris pigmentation, either partialy or completely; thc eye has a white, blue, or pinkish-white color; is not indicative of blindness.

wall of the hoof *see* HOOF WALL

wallop (1) Slang; to strike hard as with the hand or whip. (2) A quick, rolling, movement; a gallop (q.v.).

wanderer *see* BARKER

wandering (1) Deviation of the horse from the straight line or circumference of a circle which he is supposed to be executing. (2) *see* WALKABOUT DISEASE

wap-John A coachman's term of contempt; (sl); a gentleman's coachman (q.v.).

warble A tumor or small swelling found under the skin on an animal's back, caused by the larvae of a warble fly (q.v.).

warble fly Any of the various flies of the families *Oestridae* and *Hypodermatidae*, the larvae of which cause subdermal swellings in the horse and other animals; lays its eggs on the lower extremities of the horse, when hatched, larvae migrate beneath the skin towards the subdermal tissue of the back where they secrete an enzyme to make a breathing hole through the skin; within four to six weeks the larvae emerge through the holes and drop to the ground.

warbles The plural of warble (q.v.).

war bonnet paint Refers to coat color pattern; the specific arrangement of colored areas on a predominantly white horse in which both ears and/or eyes, the poll, and most of the neck have color, while the body shows little color; some American Indian tribes thought horses so colored were imbued with supernatural powers; it was further believed that the rider of such a horse could not be injured in battle.

Warde, John (b.1752) Also known as Father of Foxhunting; born in 1752 in Britain, he pioneered the modern style of fast foxhunting (q.v.) and invented the telegraph springs (q.v.).

'ware A hunting term; said by the huntsman to the field to advise or caution, e.g. 'ware hound, 'ware hole, 'ware wire.

war horse A horse used in war; a charger.

warmblood Also known as halfblood; in general terms, a cross between coldblood (q.v.) and hotblood (q.v.) breeds; any horse with a mixture of blood occurring in the foundation of the breed or breed stock; pedigree, performance, and conformation are considerations for inclusion in the Stud Book; often used for dressage and jumping.

warmblooded Said of a warmblood (q.v.)

war knot A type of knot tied into the end of the horse's tail hair to keep the tail out of the way when roping, etc. and clean during inclement weather; the custom was developed by the buckaroos (q.v.) from the Lone Region (q.v.) of the United States.

warm out of it Also known as work out of it or work sound; said of a horse who does not move freely and/or soundly until his muscles have warmed up as with exercise.

warm up Any process of gradual activity performed to prepare the horse for strenuous activity or competition.

warrantable A British term; a deer five years or older.

war shield A coat color pattern; pigmented patches on the chest, flanks, and base of the tail on a white body.

wart A small, dry, hard, nonmalignant skin lesion.

washed out Said of a horse suffering from systemic and physical exhaustion resulting from heavy use or stress beyond his condition level; such a horse is generally electrolyte and fluid depleted.

washy (1) A racing term; said of a horse who breaks into a heavy sweat prior to a race. (2) Said of a washed out (q.v.) horse.

waste energy The usable power or energy lost in the urine and other nitrogenous wastes, in the feces, the bacterial fermentation process in the intestines, and in consuming and digesting feed.

watch eye *see* WALL EYE

water (1) To take a horse to, or provide him with, water to drink. (2) *see* WATER JUMP. (3) The liquid which in a more or less impure state constitutes rain, oceans, lakes, and rivers, and which in a pure state is a transparent, odorless, tasteless liquid; a compound of oxygen and hydrogen freezing at 32 °F (0 °C) and boiling at 212 °F (100 °C). (4) A hunting term; a ditch or stream having no fence, but containing water.

water bag *see* AMNIONIC SAC

water brush (1) A grooming tool made of bristles set into a handle, used to wash the coat, mane, and tail of the horse. (2) *see* WATER BUSH

water bush Also known as water brush; a small hedge or row of bushes positioned on the take-off side of a water jump (q.v.) over which a horse jumps; considered part of the jumping obstacle.

water founder A founder (q.v.) condition; inflammation of the sensitive laminae (q.v.) of the hoof caused by rapid intake of a large volume of water, particularly cold, following strenuous exercise.

water hole A hole or hollow in the ground in which water collects

watering hole Also known as watering place; a natural pool or small pond of water used by animals for drinking.

watering place *see* WATERING HOLE

water jump Also known as water; any show, steeplechase or cross-country jumping obstacle consisting of a shallow, water-filled ditch at least 6 inches (15 cm) deep and as big as 16 feet (5 m) wide by 14 feet (4.25 m) in spread; there may be a fence of some type preceding or spanning the water; most commonly there is a small water bush on the take-off side; used to test jumping ability and bravery.

water line The inner, unpigmented, white-colored hoof wall which is sometimes mistaken for the white line (q.v.).

water out A racing term; to water a horse while he cools down following exercise.

water scraper *see* SCRAPER

water soluble vitamin Any vitamin having the property of dissolving in water; is not stored in the body tissues and must be ingested or manufactured in the body to meet the minimum daily requirements; excess amounts are excreted in the urine.

wattle (1) A hunting term; poles interwoven with slender branches, withes, or reeds used in the formation of a hurdle or jumping obstacle. (2) Light poles used for the construction of a wattle.

wax The buildup of dried colostrum (q.v.) on the teats of a pregnant mare prior to foaling.

waxing The slow leakage and drying of colostrum (q.v.) from the teats of a pregnant mare prior to foaling; occurs between 48 and 2 hours before foaling.

way of going The way in which a horse moves.

WBC *see* WHITE BLOOD CELL

WCF *see* WORSHIPFUL COMPANY OF FARRIERS

WCTPA *see* WORLD CHAMPION TEAM PENNING ASSOCIATION

wean To accustom a foal to do without the mare's milk as food; can occur at any time from an age of about 3 months to a year; 6 months is average.

weanling A foal separated from the dam and accustomed to do without her milk as food; the term is applied up to the foal's first birthday, regardless of when weaning actually occurred.

weanling colt A male foal, until one year old, accustomed to taking nourishment otherwise than by nursing from the mare.

weanling filly A female foal, until one year old, accustomed to taking nourishment otherwise than by nursing from the mare.

wear itself well Also known as carry both ends; said of a horse who moves with his head and tail carried high.

Weatherby An English family who maintained and first published the English Thoroughbred Stud Book (q.v.) for the Jockey Club (q.v.).

Weatherbys *see* STUD BOOK

weatings Also known as offals, miller's offal, pollard, or middlings; the particles of the wheat husk finer than bran (q.v.); contain about 6 percent crude fiber and are low in protein and calcium.

weaving (1) A vice; the rhythmic swaying of the horse from side to side in which the horse shifts his weight from one foot to the other while nodding or swinging his head and neck back and forth; usually results from boredom, is most common in stall-bound horses, and is generally corrected when the horse is turned out to pasture. (2) Moving forward on a zigzag or not-straight course.

weaver A horse who weaves.

web (1) The area between the left and right sides of a horseshoe (q.v.). (2) The width of the barstock (q.v.) from which a horseshoe is made.

webfoot *see* MUDDER

web martingale *see* BIB MARTINGALE

wedge A piece of horseshoe-shaped leather, plastic, or rubber, thick at the heels and tapering to the toes, placed between the horseshoe and ground-surface of the hoof to elevate the heel and thus change the hoof angle (q.v.).

wedge-heeled shoe *see* WEDGE SHOE

wedge pad A saddle pad, the thickness of which gradually increases towards the rear portion of the pad; used to level the saddle on the back of the horse; available in a variety of thicknesses.

wedge shoe A horseshoe which graduates in thickness from a thin toe to a thicker heel; elevates the hoof heel and thus changes the hoof angle (q.v.).

wedging *see* BEANING

WEE *see* WESTERN EQUINE ENCEPHALOMYELITIS

weed (1) *see* STOCK UP. (2) A small, underdeveloped horse generally lacking stamina and quality.

Weedon *see* JUMPING CHUTE

Weedon lane *see* JUMPING CHUTE

weedy (1) An American term; said of a horse who consumes too much black sage resulting in malnutrition and incoherence. (2) Said of a long-legged, unimpressive horse.

weigh in A racing term; to weigh the jockey, saddle, and associated gear upon completion of a race or competition; the ending weight of the jockey and gear should equal the weight at weigh in (q.v.); required to ensure that the horse has carried the correct weight during competition.

weighing room *see* JOCKEYS' ROOM

weigh out A racing term; to measure the weight of the jockey, saddle, and associated gear prior to a race or competition; the starting weight of the rider and gear should equal that at weigh out (q.v.); required to ensure that the horse has carried the correct weight during the performance.

weight (1) The amount of heaviness of the horse as measured on a scale or approximated from the heart girth (q.v.). (2) The extra poundage a horse carries; the average horse can carry loads or riders equal to 25 to 30 percent of his weight, with lateral-gaited horses such as the Tennessee Walking Horse (q.v.) often tolerating heavier loads because they keep at least two legs on the ground during each of their gaits and are able to more evenly support the weight. (3) *see* LEAD NO. 3

weight aid The rider's bodyweight when used to communicate to the horse, as by shifting the position of the weight in the saddle.

weight allowance (1) A racing term; a reduction in the amount of weight carried by an apprentice jockey (q.v.) or other jockey due to inexperience or lack of success in riding winners. (2) A racing term; a reduction in the amount of weight carried by a mare or filly when racing against colts and geldings.

weight cloth *see* LEAD PAD

weight for age Also known by the acronym WFA; a racing term; a race condition in which the weight a horse carries depends on his age and is determined according to a scale developed by The Jockey Club (q.v.); the spread of weight carried by horses of different ages depends on the time of year and the distance run, with younger horses carrying less weight than older horses.

weight-for-age race A racing term; any race that is neither a handicap race (q.v.) nor a selling race (q.v.) in which participating horses carry scale weight (q.v.) or weight assigned arbitrarily according to their age, the race distance, and month of the year.

Well-bottom Gig A horse-drawn vehicle of the Gig (q.v.) type; was hung low between elliptic springs on a cranked axle; the driver's and passenger's feet rested in a low box-shaped part of the body in front of and below, the axle.

well let down (1) Said of the horse's hock when long, low, and dropping straight to the ground. (2) Said of the horse's body when cylindrical in shape from the ribs through the flanks; the opposite of tucked-up (q.v.).

well-ribbed up *see* RIBBED UP

well-sprung Said of the horse's ribs when the front ribs are flat and the back ribs are long and well rounded/arched allowing ample room for expansion of the heart and lungs.

well to the ground *see* KNEES AND HOCKS TO THE GROUND

Wells cavesson A lightweight form of lungeing cavesson (q.v.) in which the noseband fastens below the bit in a similar manner to a drop noseband (q.v.); adopted and used by the Spanish Riding School (q.v.)

Welsh *see* WELSH MOUNTAIN PONY

Welsh Cart Horse An ancient Welsh pony breed; developed around the 12th century; was moderately sized and powerful.

Welsh Cob Also known as Section D Pony or generically as native pony (q.v.); an ancient Welsh pony breed developed in the early 11th century by crossing Welsh Mountain Ponies (q.v.) with Spanish- and Barb-type horses to produce the Powrys Cob (q.v.) and the Welsh Cart Horse (q.v.), which in the 18th and 19th centuries were put to Norfolk Roadsters (q.v.) and Yorkshire Coach Horses to create the present breed; has splendid action, a dished face, strong shoulder, compact body, deep, powerful back, and slight, silky feathering (q.v.); stands 14 to 15.2 hands and is the strongest and largest of the Welsh breeds; all coat colors are permitted except piebald (q.v.) and skewbald (q.v.); historically used as a carriage horse, but now also used for competitive driving and riding including, hunting, jumping, eventing, and trekking; famed for its trotting ability; previously shown with both a hogged mane (q.v.) and docked tail (q.v.).

Welsh Mountain *see* WELSH MOUNTAIN PONY

Welsh Mountain Pony Also known as Welsh, Welsh Mountain, Section A Pony (q.v.) or generically as native pony (q.v.); the smallest of the four pure-bred pony and cob breeds native to Wales; descended from Arab (q.v.), Andalusian (q.v.), and Thoroughbred (q.v.) stock crossed with native mares; originally used underground to haul coal, now used for both riding and harness; stands up to 12 hands, generally has a gray coat, although brown, chestnut, and palominos also occur; piebald (q.v.) and skewbald (q.v.) coats are not permitted; has a compact body with great girth depth, powerful loins and hind legs, a dished face, wide and alert eyes, strong hock joints engaged well under the body, and exceptionally hard hooves; is an easy keeper (q.v.), has an easy and elegant flowing action, and is sure-footed; is spirited, intelligent, and has good endurance.

Welsh Pony Also known as Merlin (due to the influence of a small Thoroughbred (q.v.) named Merlin), Section B Pony (q.v.), or generically as native pony (q.v.); one of four ponies and cobs native to Wales; descended from the Welsh Mountain Pony (q.v.), upgraded with Hackney (q.v.), and small Thoroughbred blood; the coat may be of any solid color; piebald (q.v.) or skewbald (q.v.) coats are not accepted; the second smallest of the Welsh breeds, standing 12 to 13.2 hands; characteristics are similar to those of the Welsh Mountain Pony (q.v.), but the action is lower to the ground with less, yet notably straight, knee action; has good girth depth, a full mane and tail, long, well-proportioned limbs, and strong quarters and hocks; is hardy, quiet, and energetic; historically used for shepherding, now used primarily for riding and harness.

Welsh Pony and Cob Society A British organization established in 1901 to encourage the breeding of and to maintain registries for Welsh Cobs and Ponies; the stud book, established in 1902, has four sections: Section A – Welsh Mountain Pony (q.v.) standing under 12 hands, Section B – Welsh Pony standing 12 to 13.2 hands, Section C – Welsh Pony of Cob Type standing 13.2 to 14 hands, and Section D – Welsh Cob standing 14 to 15.2 hands.

Welsh Pony of Cob Type Also known as Section C Pony or farm pony; a Welsh pony breed descended from the Welsh Mountain Pony (q.v.) mares put to smaller Norfolk Trotters (q.v.) and Hackneys (q.v.); a smaller version of the Welsh Cob (q.v.); neared extinction in 1949, although the numbers are now on the increase; the mane and tail are silky and there is a small amount of heel feather (q.v.); has good girth depth, powerful quarters, a laid-back shoulder, straight profile, long neck, slightly pronounced withers, short back, deep chest, and relatively short legs, originally used for sheepherding and general farm work; is now popular for light draft and riding, particularly as a children's or small adult hunter; the coat may be of any solid color.

welter weights An American racing term; 28 pounds (12.7 kg) over the official scale of weights carried by horses competing in a race; used to test the weight-bearing ability of entrants.

western A novel, movie, or play of the western United States, especially relating to Indians, pioneers, and cowboys.

Western bit A bit consisting of two metal cheekpieces and, typically, a ported mouthpiece which brings pressure to bear on the bars of the mouth using leverage instead of direct pressure; the reins are attached to shanks (q.v.); used in conjunction with a curb strap (q.v.) or curb chain (q.v.); has longer shanks and is bigger than a curb bit (q.v.).

Western Australian Harness Driving Society Also known by the acronym WAHDS; established in 1975 to further the interest in driving in Western Australia.

Western equine encephalomyelitis Also known by the acronym WEE; one of three alphaviruses associated with equine encephalitis (q.v.); appears to occur in all of the Americas; wild birds serve as the principal reservoirs of the virus which is transmitted by biting insects, principally mosquitoes; epidemics tend to occur in mid- to late-summer and are more common in pastured than stabled horses; clinical signs occur about 5 days after infection and most deaths occur 2 to 3 days later; signs include fever, impaired vision, irregular gait, wandering, reduced reflexes, circling, incoordination, yawning, teeth grinding, drowsiness, pendulous lower lip, inability to swallow, photophobia, head-pressing, inability to rise, paralysis, occasional convulsions, and death; those with mild cases recover within a few weeks, but may suffer from residual brain damage; mortality is 20 to 50 percent.

Western horse A type of horse rather than a breed, suited to trail, cutting, roping, etc.

Western Isles Highland Pony One of two distinct morphological types of Highland Pony (q.v.) standing 12.2 to 13.2 hands.

Western riding Also known as Western style; a riding technique popularized by the American cowboy, in which a stock saddle (q.v.) and Western-type bridle are used.

Western saddle *see* STOCK SADDLE

Western show classes Competitive events for Western-type horses; of four main divisions: Western Riding Horse, Pleasure Horse, Trail Horse, and Parade Horse.

Western side jockey *see* SIDE JOCKEY

Western stirrup Any stirrup (q.v.) attached to a western saddle by means of a fender (q.v.), available in a variety of shapes and sizes.

Western stirrup leather *see* FENDER NO. 1

Western style *see* WESTERN RIDING

Westfaliches Pferd *see* WESTPHALIAN

Westlands Pony *see* FJORD

West Nile virus A flavirus with widespread distribution throughout Africa, the Mediterranean, and Eurasia; infects numerous vertebrate species including horses; symptoms may include fever, hind-limb paralysis, ataxia (q.v.) tetraplegia, flaccid paralysis of the lower lip, coma, or death; transmitted by infected mosquitoes to humans and other animals; no vaccine is available; preventing exposure to mosquitoes, especially during mosquito feeding times – dusk and dawn – is essential to disease control.

Westphalian Also known as Westfaliches Pferd; a Hanoverian (q.v.) bred in Westphalia, Germany; stands 16 to 17 hands, is quiet, powerful, and athletic, has a solid build and may have a coat of any solid color; used as a competition and riding horse.

wet mare A mare with a nursing foal.

wet work A cutting and reining term; to train, work, or show a horse using cattle.

Weymouth bit A curb bit (q.v.) with straight shanks about 6 inches (15 cm) long; the mouthpiece slides up and down on the shanks within a ½ inch (13 mm) space.

Weymouth bridle *see* DOUBLE BRIDLE

WFA *see* WEIGHT FOR AGE

whangtree A yellow riding cane having closely spaced rings or knots, made from the stem of Chinese or Japanese plants similar to bamboo.

wheal A welt or other raised surface of the skin.

wheat The grain of the widely distributed cereal grass of the genus *Triticum*; most commonly fed as milling by-products, specifically wheat bran (q.v.) or wheatings (q.v.).

wheat bran The outer coating of the wheat grain separated from the flour in milling; contains less digestible energy but more protein, fiber, and phosphorus than whole grain; is highly laxative, contains 1.3 percent phosphorus, 11 to 13 percent digestible protein, and 5 percent fat.

wheat grass hay A cut and dried grass hay made from crested wheat grass; contains high quality roughage with a fiber content of about 34 percent and a digestible protein content of approximately 4.4 percent at first cutting and 3.4 percent for second cut; grows best in moist climates and is best cut before it blooms, after which the nutritional value drops dramatically and the grass becomes tough and fibrous.

wheat middlings The coarser particles of ground wheat mingled with bran; although a good source of niacin and vitamins B_1 and B_2, tends to pack in the stomach and cause digestive disturbances such as colic (q.v.).

wheel (1) A racing term; said of a horse who turns sharply. (2) A racing term; said of a bettor who bets every type of combination (daily-double [q.v.], perfecta [q.v.], or quinella [q.v.]) for a specific horse(s).

wheel back A hunting term; said of a hound (q.v.) who has an upwardly curved spine over the loins; characteristic of Walker field trial hounds.

wheel bar *see* SWINGLE TREE

wheelers The pair of horses in a team of four or more horses who are hitched directly to the vehicle.

wheeler terret *see* REIN RING

wheel hub *see* HUB

wheeling *see* BASEBALL

wheelwright One who makes wheels and puts tires on same.

whelp (1) A hunting term; an unweaned hound puppy. (2) A hunting term; said of a gyp (q.v.) when pregnant. (3) A hunting term; said of a gyp (q.v.) when she gives birth.

whicker *see* NICKER

whiffle-tree *see* SWINGLE TREE

whiffletree *see* SWINGLE TREE

whinny (1) Also known as neigh; the common calling or communication between horses. (2) To neigh in a low and gentle way.

whip (1) Also known as fiddle, horse whip, leather, or absolute ensurer (sl); a hand-held device used as an aid to control, drive, correct, or punish the horse; generally consists of a wood, fiberglass, bone, plastic, metal, or leather rod to which is attached a thong of leather or cord of varying lengths as determined by intended use. (2) *see* WHIPPER-IN. (3) One who handles the whip expertly. (4) One who drives a horse(s). (5) To lash or flagellate with or as with a horsewhip.

whip-across bars Also known as whip-across bar shoe or Canadian bars; a therapeutic horseshoe (q.v.) of the bar shoe (q.v.) type; the outside, trailing heel is turned at right angles toward the inside heel; commonly used on harness horses to keep the shoes from spreading when they become worn.

whip-across bar shoe *see* WHIP-ACROSS BARS

whip collar Also known as collar or collar of the whip; the narrow metal band which separates the leather, bone, or synthetic handpiece from the shaft of a whip (q.v.).

whipcord (1) A hard, twisted cord from which whip lashes are made. (2) A hard, woven, diagonally-ribbed fabric, often used for making riding habits or sportswear.

whip hand Historically, the coachman's hand used to hold the whip when driving; now, the hand used to hold the whip in any equestrian event.

whip-in A hunting term; to keep the hounds in the pack from scattering by use of a whip.

whiplash *see* LASH

whip off A hunting term; to use the whip to redirect the hounds from one line to another.

whipper-in Also known as whip, the whip; a hunting term; the huntsman's principal assistant; traditionally there are two whippers-in: the first whipper-in (q.v.) and the second whipper-in (q.v.); of four levels of proficiency: (a) learning the name and appearance of every hound (q.v.) in the pack, (b) learning the characteristics of each hound, (c) learning the temperament of each hound, and (d) learning the voice of each hound; proficiency in all four levels must be attained before hunting the pack.

whipping To punish a horse with a whip; to flagellate.

whipping up An American dressage term; the repeated active upward evasion of the croup (usually in canter (q.v.) or in piaffe (q.v.) when there is insufficient engagement and forward reach).

whippletree *see* SWINGLE TREE

whipple tree *see* SWINGLE TREE

whip spring Also known as 'S' spring; a suspension spring first used on horse-drawn vehicles around 1700; one end of the spring was attached to the under-carriage platform and the other to the vehicle body.

whirlicote *see* LONG WAGON

whisk *see* DANDY BRUSH

Whiskey A light, one-horse Chaise popular in the late 18th and early 19th centuries; hung on shallow, sideways platform springs, was seldom headed, frequently lacked a dashboard, and seated either one or two passengers; in some cases the bodywork was covered in canework, those vehicles being known as Caned Whiskies (q.v.) while others had panel or half-panel sides; so named because it "whisked" over the ground at great speed

Whiskey-Curricle A large, horse-drawn vehicle of the Whiskey (q.v.) type driven to a pair of horses in curricle gear (q.v.).

whisperers *see* HORSE WHISPERERS

whistling *see* LARYNGEAL HEMIPLEGIA

whistle on the play A polo term; to blow a whistle to indicate a foul has been committed; an indication to stop play

white Refers to coat color; a solid white coat with a few pigmented skin spots; the horse will usually have brown eyes unless the white coat results from extremely marked overos (q.v.), sabinos (q.v.), and blanket patterns, in which case, the horse will have pink skin and blue eyes.

white blanket One of six symmetrical Appaloosa (q.v.) coat color patterns recognized by the Appaloosa Horse Club (q.v.); a solid colored body with white over the hips and an absence of colored spots.

white blood cell Also known as leukocyte, leucocyte, or by the acronym WBC; a colorless blood cell active in the defense against infection and bacteria, and occasionally found in the body tissues.

white brass *see* GERMAN SILVER

white castor A white coaching hat; (sl).

Whitechapel Buggy An American four-wheeled, horse-drawn vehicle; had a forward-facing, stick-sided seat, folding hood, and a large, open boot (q.v.) in the back; was hung on a perch with side-bar springing – these bars ran the vehicle length, outside the body, and were fixed to the ends of two transverse semi-elliptic springs.

Whitechapel Cart An all-purpose, horse-drawn, two-wheeled Dogcart (q.v.) used for country driving; had a high seat and was driven to a tandem (q.v.); a popular shooting vehicle.

white face *see* BALD FACE

white flag A white piece of cloth of varying size, shape and design usually attached at one edge to a staff or cord, and used to mark the left side of a jumping obstacle.

White Horse of the Sea *see* CAMARGUE

white lethal A inherited genetic condition of a foal with a lethal dominant white (q.v.) gene.

white line The ⅛ inch (3 mm) wide, pale yellow-colored margin between the laminae (q.v.) of the hoof wall and the sole; acts as a slightly pliable cementing material between the hoof and sole.

white line disease Any physiological or mechanical damage to the white line (q.v.); may be brought about by bacteria or mechanical disruption of the white line triggered by concussion or poor or incorrect shoeing, i.e. trimming, pressure on the sole by the shoe.

white mark *see* WHITE SPOT

white muscle disease Also known as nutritional muscular dystrophy or by the acronym WMD; a disease occurring in foals up to seven months of age triggered by either vitamin E or selenium (q.v.) deficiency in the pregnant mare, which leads to muscle-cell death in the embryo; symptoms include lethargy and a stilted, stiff gait; when muscle damage is extensive, the foal will generally go down and die unless treatment is administered; so called because of the white striations and patches that occur in the muscles, particularly those of the hind legs and neck.

white muzzle A face marking (q.v.); white hairs covering both lips and extending into the area of the nostrils.

white of the eye *see* SCELERA

white pastern *see* PASTERN NO. 3

white spot (1) Also known as white mark; the smallest of the leg markings (q.v.) consisting of a concentration of white hairs on the foot anywhere but on the heel. (2) A mark on the horse's eye; indicates a past eye injury that may or may not interfere with vision.

whitewash act Said of a coachman (q.v.) unable, but wanting to fold the whip thong on the stick; he holds the team whip, point down, over the side of the coach and stirs the whip and thong in a circle until the thong is wound around the stick.

Whitmore kimblewick One of five types of kimblewick (q.v.); a pelham (q.v.) bit; may be used with one or two reins (q.v.); has a straight, low-ported mouthpiece (q.v.) and short cheeks (q.v.) to which D rings attach; a square eye supplants the upper end of the cheeks and a second curb ring attaches directly below the D ring; when used with a single rein, the bit acts as a snaffle (q.v.), but when the hands are lowered, or when used in conjunction with a martingale (q.v.) or second rein, the resulting action is similar to that of a curb (q.v.).

whoa A verbal command to the horse to stop or stand still, or when repeated softly, to slow down or pay attention.

whole colored Refers to coat color; the coat of the horse, inclusive of the head, body, and limbs, when entirely composed of hairs of one color.

whorl A hair pattern; changes in direction of the lie of the hair; may take various forms, depending on the interface at which two or more flows of hair meet, e.g. simple whorl (q.v.), tufted whorl (q.v.), linear whorl (q.v.), crested whorl (q.v.), feathered whorl (q.v.), and sinuous whorl (q.v.); may be used for identification purposes.

wid A horse unsound in the wind; (obs).

wide behind (1) A dressage term; said of the horse in motion; an evasion of engagement which occurs most commonly in piaffe (q.v.), lengthening of stride in trot, and in the halt; the hind feet are further apart than the fore. (2) A conformation defect; said of the horse when his hind legs attach wider than his fore.

Widner Breaking Cart An American version of the Breaking Cart (q.v.) with balloon-type cycle tires.

Wielkopolski Also known as Polish Warmblood; a recently developed, Polish-bred warmblood descended from the Ponzan and Masuren (q.v.) regional types having Arab (q.v.), Hanoverian (q.v.), Trakehner (q.v.), and Thoroughbred (q.v.) ancestry; matures early, has a free-flowing action, is sturdy, well balanced, and hard-working; stands 15.1 to 16 hands, has a compact body, and a deep chest; any solid-color coat is acceptable; used for riding and driving.

wiggler *see* PACER

wild burro An American term; a feral ass (q.v.) running wild in the western part of the United States; may be registered as a standard donkey (q.v.) with the American Donkey and Mule Society (q.v.) with the origin and breeding identified as wild burro.

wild cow *see* SPRINTER NO. 2

wild game *see* GAME

wild goose chase One of two types of drag hunting sport popular in late 16th- and early 17th-century England; the predecessor of drag hunting (q.v.); the drag (q.v.) was laid and the hounds were put on the line (q.v.) to run it at a racing pace; the horse in the lead at the end of the drag was declared the winner.

wild horse (1) *see* MUSTANG. (2) Any horse living and breeding in a wild, undomesticated state.

Wild Horses of America Registry An American organization established in 1974 to register and campaign for the protection of wild horses and burros in North America; dissolved as a corporation in 1992 and subsumed into the International Society for the Protection of Mustangs and Burros (q.v.).

Wild Huntsman A spectral huntsman who, in European, especially German, folklore, with a phantom host of followers, ran through the woods, fields, and villages during the night, accompanied by shouts of huntsmen and the baying of hounds.

William Barrad *see* BARRAD, WILLIAM

William Cavendish, Duke of Newcastle *see* CAVENDISH, WILLIAM, DUKE OF NEWCASTLE

William Felton *see* FELTON, WILLIAM

William von Osten *see* VON OSTEN, WILLIAM

Wilson snaffle A jointed driving snaffle (q.v.) with tapered arms and two rings on each side; one ring is attached to the mouthpiece while the other, to which the cheekpieces are attached, floats on the mouthpiece; the reins may be connected to the cheek rings for normal and mild action or to the floating rings for more severe action; available in many variations.

win (1) Also known as straight or win only; a racing term; a betting option in which the bettor (q.v.) places a wager on a horse to come in first place. (2) To gain victory through competition.

win and place Also known as straight forecast (Brit); an American racing term; a betting option in which the bettor selects the winner and the second placed horses.

win bet A racing term; a wager on a horse to finish in first place.

win by a nose *see* NOSE NO. 2

wind (1) A horse's capacity for breath. (2) *see* FLATULENCE. (3) *see* WIND A FOX

wind a fox Also known as wind; a hunting term; said of the hounds (q.v.) when they catch the scent (q.v.) of a fox (q.v.) before finding his line (q.v.).

wind broke Also known as windy; said of a horse suffering from laryngeal hemiplegia (q.v.)

windgall *see* WIND PUFF

winding *see* ROPE WALKING

windpipe *see* TRACHEA

windpuff Also known as windgall or road puff; a soft, painless, fluid-filled swelling commonly found near the fetlock joint and occasionally elsewhere on the lower portion of the fore- and hind legs, generally without associated lameness or heat; occur when excessive synovial fluid fills a stretched joint capsule or associated tendon sheath; of two types which often occur together: articular windpuff (q.v.) and tendinous windpuff (q.v.); may be caused by intense training followed by a period of rest, excessive exercise on hard surfaces, and the cumulative effects of imbalances produced by poor conformation or improperly trimmed hooves; must be regarded with suspicion in the presence of lameness; bandaging overnight or massaging the area may temporarily reduce swelling, but reoccurrence is common when established, and treatment difficult.

Windsor Greys Any of the grey carriage horses used in the Royal Mews in Britain; harnessed on ceremonial occasions, for the British Royal Family; bred at the Royal Stud at Windsor, England since 1923 at which time the original stock was received as a gift from Wilhelmina, the former Queen of The Netherlands; Isabellas (q.v.) were used prior to that; frequently kept at Windsor Castle.

wind-sucker A horse who exhibits the habit of wind-sucking (q.v.).

wind-sucking Also known as cribbing or aerophagia; a vice; the aspiration and swallowing of air by the horse through the mouth; the horse arches his neck and inhales air; may be facilitated by the horse biting or setting his teeth against a firm object; an acquired habit; may be controlled to some degree by the use of a cribbing collar (q.v.).

windy *see* WIND BROKE

wing (1) One of a pair of standards (q.v.). (2) *see* SCAPULA

winging *see* DISHING

wings (1) *see* SKIRT NO. 1. (2) Also known as hounds; the two arms which act as strengtheners between the perch and rear axle of a horse-drawn vehicle; joined on either side of the perch at one end and then they spread out, to form two sides of a triangle, and join the axle.

win hole *see* TWO HOLE POSITION

winkers *see* BLINKERS

winker stays *see* BLINKER STAYS

win in a canter A racing term; said of a horse who passes the finish line at an easy pace, well ahead of the rest of the field (q.v.).

winner A person or horse who wins; a victor in a competition.

winner's circle Also known as winner's enclosure; a racing term; the location on the racecourse reserved for the first three placing horses where awards are given and photographs taken.

winner's enclosure *see* WINNER'S CIRCLE

winning post *see* FINISHING POST

win only *see* WIN

winter coat The horse's coat hair during the winter months; typically long, thick, and heavy.

winter horse An Australian term; a horse kept at the home ranch for use during the winter, rather than being turned out on the range.

winter out To leave a horse out to pasture or on the range during the winter rather than stabling him.

wire (1) *see* FINISH LINE. (2) *see* BARBED WIRE

wire cutters A metal, hand-held device used to cut wire, as in barbed wire (q.v.).

Wise We Boys A racing term; a network of reporters and clockers that operated in concert, 24 hours per day, in an attempt to catch and time Seabiscuit (q.v.) training in preparation for his epic race against War Admiral in 1938; his trainer, Tom Smith, was notorious for training Seabiscuit at odd hours throughout the night and early morning to keep the speed and agility of his horse a secret.

wisp An egg-shaped, grooming brush without a handle, made of horse hair, straw, rope, or hay, coiled in the form of a figure eight to make a tight pad; used to massage the horse to stimulate circulation and tone the muscles.

with a strain Said of a well-bred horse who has some common blood (q.v.).

wither pad *see* POMMEL PAD

withers The ridge located at the junction of the base of the horse's neck, his back at the point of the first thoracic vertebra, and the top of the scapula between the shoulders; the highest part of the horse's back.

with foal at foot Said of a mare after birth of a live foal.

WMD *see* WHITE MUSCLE DISEASE

wobbler Any horse afflicted with symptoms including slight swaying of the hindquarters or stumbling, with worsening of the condition until, after 6 to 9 months, he cannot trot without rolling from side to side and falling; the cause is unknown, although thought possibly to result from spinal cord injury; generally seen in yearlings, two- and, occasionally three-year-olds.

wobbler disease *see* ATAXIA

wobbler syndrome *see* ATAXIA

wobbles *see* ATAXIA

wolf *see* WOLFING FEED

wolf teeth Also known as permanent premolars or first premolars; one to four shallow-rooted, rudimentary teeth occasionally present in front of the premolars (q.v.) which have no function in the intake or chewing process; appear in the top of the mouth in front of the first premolars (q.v.) at the age of about six months and occasionally appear in the bottom of the mouth; mythically thought their presence would impair the horse's vision, ultimately causing blindness if not removed; may interfere with bit placement, in which case they are extracted.

wolfing feed Also known as wolf; said of a horse who eats extremely fast.

wood *see* SADDLE

wood chewing *see* CRIBBING NO. 2

woodcock eye *see* COCK EYE

wood shavings Also known as shavings; thin slices of wood used as bedding (q.v.) material in horse stalls, trailers, etc.; are absorbent, soft, unpalatable, fragrant, and carry fewer mold spores than straw (q.v.); can be dusty or treated with chemicals that irritate the horse's skin and are difficult to store; any type of wood shaving may be used except black walnut which has been linked to laminitis (q.v.); sometimes combined with sawdust (q.v.) to improve absorbency.

work (1) To exercise a horse. (2) To compete, as in "When do you work"?

work a line *see* CARRY A LINE

worked up *see* TENSE

work for a dead horse *see* PAY FOR A DEAD HORSE

working A dressage term; a gait variation of trot and canter in which the horse moves in an energetic but calm way, with a stride length between that of the collected and medium variants; the foundation of these gaits, from which the collected, medium and extended variations are developed through training.

working advantage A cutting term; said of the horse when parallel to the cow, his head next to the cow's shoulder, a position from which he is able to influence the cow's actions.

working canter A rocking, three-beat gait between the collected and the medium canter (q.v.); the horse has a slightly shorter stride than at medium canter (q.v.), but is not fully collected; the horse is balanced, on the bit, and moves forward with even and light strides.

working cow A cutting term; a cow that is

trying to return to the herd from which it has been separated; enables the horse to work it.

working cow horse A reining (q.v.) event consisting of two dry work (q.v.) and wet work (q.v.) competitions.

working saddle *see* STOCK SADDLE

working trot A natural two-beat gait between the collected and the medium trots (q.v.); the horse displays a slightly shorter stride than at the medium, but not as short as at the collected trot (q.v.); the hind feet will be placed on the ground more or less in the forefeet marks; the horse is balanced and moves with an even and elastic gait; ridden sitting or rising.

work in the hand To train the horse from the ground; the trainer, standing at the horse's shoulder, controls the frame and movement of the horse using the curb reins held in one hand and a dressage whip (q.v.) held in the other; care must be taken to produce even results on either rein, as unbalanced training may result in a lack of symmetry.

workman Coaching slang; a good coachman (q.v.).

work off Any tie-breaking competition.

work on the long reins To train a horse from the ground using two long reins (q.v.); reins attach to the snaffle bit (q.v.) rings, lungeing cavesson, or hackamore (q.v.) and are used to influence the rhythm, activity, and lateral bend of the horse in all movements; the trainer holds one rein in each hand and a 4½ foot (1.35 m) whip, pointing forwards, in the right; whether the trainer stands behind or to the inside of the horse, the reins will run from the bit along the sides of the horse to the trainer's hands.

work on two tracks *see* LATERAL WORK

workout (1) *see* AIRING. (2) To exercise a horse through various gaits and movements to maintain athletic capability or prepare for competition.

work out of it *see* WARM OUT OF IT

work sound *see* WARM OUT OF IT

work tab An American racing term; a list of morning race workouts identified according to distance and time.

World Champion Team Penning Association Also known by the acronym WCTPA; an American organization founded in 1978 to promote, organize, and regulate the sport of team penning (q.v.).

World Elephant Polo Association Games An invitation-only polo tournament played on elephants; held every December (usually the 8th to 13th) at the Tiger Tops Jungle Lodge in southern Nepal; conceived by Jim Edwards and James Manclark in 1982.

worm *see* LARVA

Woronesh A light-bodied, agile Russian cold blood (q.v.).

worry (1) *see* KILL NO. 2. (2) A hunting term; said of the hounds when they bite or tear at the carcass of the quarry (q.v.) once it is dead.

Worshipful Company of Farriers *see* WORSHIPFUL COMPANY OF FARRIERS OF LONDON

Worshipful Company of Farriers of London Also known as Worshipful Company of Farriers or by the acronym WCF; one of the oldest active guilds in the world being organized and having remained active in Great Britain since AD 1356 to train, conduct exams, and certify farrier members at three levels: Diploma of the Worshipful Company of Farriers (q.v.), Associate of Farriers Company of London (q.v.), and Fellow of the Worshipful Company of Farriers (q.v.).

Wouwermans, Philip (1619–1668) A famous Dutch painter of horses.

wound (1) A cut or rupture in the skin or flesh of a person or animal. (2) To inflict a wound on.

wrangle Also known as wrangling; the act of herding or rounding up horses or other livestock.

wrangler Also known as horse wrangler; a cowboy or herdsman; one who looks after a herd of horses or ponies.

wrestler *see* STEER WRESTLER

wrestling *see* STEER WRESTLING

wring off the nails Said of the farrier when he twists off the nail points protruding from the hoof wall when attaching a horseshoe to the hoof; the nail point is positioned in the fork of the shoeing hammer, and the hammer twisted.

wrong bend A dressage term; failure of the horse to achieve and maintain the correct degree of bend when executing corners, circles, etc.; may result in a loss of balance and rhythm in the movements.

wrong leg not corrected A dressage term; said of the rider who allows the horse to strike-off in the canter on the wrong lead and who fails to correct it.

wrung withers Said of the horse's withers (q.v.) when bruised, but not chafed, by an ill-fitting saddle.

wry-neck Also known as torticollis; a condition of foals; lateral deviation of the head and neck to the right or left side of the body, so pronounced as to ultimately hinder or prevent foaling; the bones of the head and neck are frequently distorted and the ligaments, tendons, and muscles on the inside of the curve shorter than those on the outside.

wry nose A congenital abnormality of the horse's nose in which the nose is askew.

Württemburg A German warmblood developed in the late 16th century by putting native mares to Arab (q.v.) and Suffolk Punch (q.v.) stallions from the Marbach Stud; East Prussian (q.v.) and Norman blood (q.v.) was later introduced, followed by infusions of Oldenburg (q.v.), Nonius (q.v.), Anglo-Norman (q.v.), and Trakehner (q.v.); originally used for farm work in the Württemburg area from which the breed name derived; the stud book was established in 1895; is strong and hardy, cob-like, stands about 16 hands, and may have a bay, brown, black, or chestnut coat; is a good worker and economical feeder; used for riding and driving.

X

X (1) A dressage term; the center point of a dressage arena located midway from each short and long side and through which many movements are performed. (2) A suffix to a horse's registered name; indicates the horse is a pure-bred Anglo-Arab (q.v.).

xanthos The color of all ancient Greek chariot horses; probably chestnut or dun.

Xanthos Also spelled Xanthus; in mythology, one of two immortal horses, the other being Balios (q.v.), that Poseidon gave to Peleus as a wedding present; was the offspring of Zephyrus, the west wind, (or Zeus) and the Harpy Podarge; pulled Achilles' chariot during the Trojan War; was given the power of speech and foretold of Achilles' death.

Xanthus *see* XANTHOS

Xenophon (427/8–354 BC) An Athenian cavalry officer, writer, historian, and horseman; achieved fame for his essays on horsemanship and hunting, most notably, *The Art of Horsemanship*.

xerophthalmia A disease of the eye associated with Vitamin A deficiency; blindness may result.

xeroradiography (1) Radiography (q.v.) that produces an image using X-rays (q.v.). (2) A process in which an electrostatically charged selenium-coated aluminum plate is exposed by an X-ray (q.v.) to produce an image of internal structures; provides greater resolution than X-rays.

xerosis Abnormally dry skin.

X-ray photograph A picture produced by an X-ray (q.v.).

X-ray (1) High-frequency, short-wave electromagnetic rays generated by the impact of high-speed electrons on a metal target; capable of penetrating solid masses, destroying living tissue, and affecting a photographic plate; used in medical diagnosis. (2) To make an image of an area for diagnostic and curative purposes using X-rays.

X-ray therapy Treatment of certain diseases such as cancer, by the use of X-rays.

XX A suffix to the registered name of an English Thoroughbred (q.v.).

xylazine The active ingredient of the sedative "Rompum"; serves also as a muscle relaxant and analgesic; increases blood glucose levels and urine output; side effects may include slowed breathing, lowered blood pressure, and bradycardia (q.v.).

Y

yaboo *see* NAG

yabusame Classical Japanese equitation in which fully armed, mounted Samurai warriors shoot arrows at a target while galloping; now generally performed in Whinto ceremonies.

Yamoote An Arab-type breed; a Plateau Persian (q.v.).

yap Said of a hound; to bark or yelp.

yard of tin *see* COACH HORN

yawn To open the mouth wide usually as an involuntary reaction to fatigue, boredom, or illness as in Kimberley horse disease (q.v.).

yawning Expressing a yawn; a sign of Kimberly horse disease (q.v.)

yearling A foal of either sex between one and two years of age.

yearling bit *see* TATTERSALL BIT

yearling colt A male foal between one and two years of age.

yearling filly A female foal between one and two years of age.

yeld *see* OPEN MARE

yellow body *see* CORPUS LUTEUM

Yellow Bounder *see* POST CHAISE

yellow dun Refers to coat color; yellow coat hair with brown not black points; differences between the shades of yellow are difficult to discern; resemble buckskins (q.v.) and zebra duns except that the points are brown instead of black.

yelp To give a quick, short, shrill cry, as hounds or foxes, as from surprise, pain, or excitement.

yerk (1) Said of the horse; to lash or strike out with the heels. (2) To crack a whip.

yielding A racing term; said of a turf course with a high moisture content but short of being "soft", or "heavy".

yoi A hunting term; a cheer to encourage the hounds, i.e. "Yoi rouse 'im."

yoick *see* YOICKS

yoicks Also known as hoicks, hoick, yoick, or huick; a hunting term; a cry of excitement and encouragement to the hounds.

yoke (1) A wooden frame or bar with loops or bows at either end, fitted around the necks of a pair of oxen, etc., for harnessing them together. (2) A pair of animals harnessed together. (3) The pair of straps used in double harnessing to connect the horse's collar (q.v.) to the tongue of the wagon or carriage. (4) To harness an animal to a plow, etc. (5) *see* BUGLE

Yomud *see* IOMUD

Yorkshire boot A light-duty brushing boot (q.v.) used to protect the fetlock; consists of a triangular piece of felt, heavy, lined cloth, or other material with a long strip of tape stitched horizontally to the boot; the boot is placed on and above the fetlock joint where it is tied in place using the tape; the portion of the boot above the tape is then folded over the tape providing a double-layer of protection to the fetlock.

Yorkshire boarding Vertically arranged boards with a gap between each used in parts of a livestock building; results in improved ventilation and limits condensation, thus reducing the risk or incidence of bronchitis and pneumonia.

Yorkshire Coach Horse An English horse breed developed about 1790; similar in appearance to the Cleveland Bay (q.v.) from which the breed descended when crossed with Thoroughbred (q.v.), Arab (q.v.), Barb (q.v.), and, in the 19th century, Hackney (q.v.) blood; stands about 16.2 hands, has a long body and relatively short legs, deep girth, and a bay or brown coat.

Yorkshire Derby *see* KIPLINGCOTES RACE

Yorkshire gallop A British term; a canter of medium speed.

Yorkshire Packhorse *see* CLEVELAND BAY

Yorkshire Wagon *see* BARREL TOP WAGON

'you can lead a horse to water, but you can't make him drink' A proverb; you can show people the way to do things, but you cannot force them to act accordingly.

young entry A hunting term; a young hound (q.v.) until completing its first formal hunting season.

young prospect Any young horse broken or not, acquired on the basis of his show potential.

Y'sabella *see* PALOMINO

yucca Any of the genus *Yucca* of sometimes arborescent plants of the lily family having long, often rigid fibrous, margined leaves on a woody base; used by ancient cultures including the Roman Empire and several North American Indian tribes as a treatment for arthritis; a desert plant, *Yucca shidigera* is the source of most yucca-based supplements fed to horses; has anti-inflammatory properties; the active ingredient is saponin, a protein with soap-like properties; studies suggest that yucca blocks release of toxins in the intestines that inhibit normal cartilage formation.

Yu Lung *see* LEGEND OF THE EIGHT HORSES

Z

zebra An African mammal of the genus *Equus*, which is related to the horse and ass, and has a whitish body striped with numerous brownish-black or black bands.

zebra dun Refers to coat color; a dun (q.v.) with a yellow coat, black points, a head of a similar color to the body, and primitive marks (q.v.); an ancestral color in the Norwegian Fjord Horse and the Highland Pony (q.v.).

zebra marks *see* ZEBRA STRIPES

zebra stripes Also known as zebra marks, tiger stripes, or leg barring; a primitive mark (q.v.); a color pattern of dark-colored stripes wrapping front to back at the level of the hocks and knees.

zebroid Offspring of a male zebra and a female ass; a hybrid; generally sterile.

Zeeland Horse An ancient Dutch breed originating sometime before the 6th century; had a snub nose, broad and deep chest, muscular loins, wide-set flanks, and good bone and feet.

Zemaituka Also known as Zhmud, Zmudzin, and spelled Semaituka; a Lithuanian pony breed thought to have descended from the Asiatic Wild Horse (q.v.) with recent infusions of Arab (q.v.) blood; stands 13 to 13.1 hands, has a brown, bay, black, mouse dun, dun (q.v.), or palomino (q.v.) coat with an eel stripe (q.v.) and zebra marks common in the duns and palominos, a medium-sized, coarse head, broad forehead, medium neck, low withers, short back, and short, reasonably well-muscled legs; is exceptionally frugal, indifferent to fatigue and cold, and is capable of traveling tremendous distance; used for riding, light draft, and farming.

Zetland Phaeton A horse-drawn vehicle of the Dogcart (q.v.) type; had two back-to-back seats situated high on the body; the seats had iron sides and independent lazy backs; the body had wooden rails at the top below the seats and an arch under which the front wheels turned.

Zhmud *see* ZEMAITUKA

zigzag (1) A jumping obstacle consisting of timbers placed at angles to each other creating a series of alternating Vs. (2) A dressage movement; a line or course of progression characterized by angled changes from one lead to the other.

zigzag half-pass *see* COUNTER HALF-PASS

zinc A metallic element essential in the horse's diet; although no exact dietary requirement has been established, 12 parts per million in the diet is considered sufficient; necessary for several enzyme systems and occurs in epidermal tissues, bone, muscle, blood, and internal organs; deficiency is not common, but can cause depressed appetite, skin lesions, and stunted growth, particularly in foals; can be toxic when consumed in excess.

Zinkeisen, Doris Clare (b 1918) A contemporary English artist specializing in equestrian themes; her style is distinctive using bright, fresh, but not hard coloring.

Zmudzin *see* ZEMAITUKA

zoonosis Any disease communicable from animals to man or vice versa under natural conditions.

zoophobia An abnormal fear of animals.

zygoma The bridge of the bone which runs from the base of the ear to the lower posterior part of the eye-socket; protects the side of the bony eye orbit, forms part of the support of the outside of the joint of the lower jaw and the head, and serves as the attachment for part of the masseter muscle which closes the mouth and is important in the chewing of food.

zygote The mass that results from fertilization of an egg cell by a sperm.